# THE LETTERS AND CHARTERS OF GILBERT FOLIOT

# THE LETTERS AND CHARTERS OF
# GILBERT FOLIOT

## ABBOT OF GLOUCESTER (1139–48)
## BISHOP OF HEREFORD (1148–63)
## AND LONDON (1163–87)

AN EDITION PROJECTED BY THE LATE

### Z.N.BROOKE

*Professor of Mediaeval History, University of Cambridge
and Fellow of Gonville and Caius College*

AND COMPLETED BY

### DOM ADRIAN MOREY

*Monk of Downside Abbey
Headmaster of the Oratory School*

AND

### C.N.L.BROOKE

*Professor of Mediaeval History, University of Liverpool*

CAMBRIDGE
AT THE UNIVERSITY PRESS
1967

PUBLISHED BY
THE SYNDICS OF THE CAMBRIDGE UNIVERSITY PRESS

Bentley House, 200 Euston Road, London, N.W.1
American Branch: 32 East 57th Street, New York, N.Y. 10022

©

CAMBRIDGE UNIVERSITY PRESS

1967

LIBRARY OF CONGRESS CATALOGUE
CARD NUMBER: 66–11623

The publication of this book has been assisted by
generous grants from the Marc Fitch Fund, the Master and
Fellows of Gonville and Caius College, Cambridge, and
the University of Liverpool

*Printed in Great Britain at the University Printing House, Cambridge*
*(Brooke Crutchley, University Printer)*

# CONTENTS

# PLATES

*(between pp. 24 and 25)*

I   *A twelfth-century bishop, possibly Gilbert Foliot* (Kempley, Glos). (Photograph by the Rev. J. E. Gethyn-Jones.)

E. W. Tristram, *English Medieval Wall Painting: the Twelfth Century* (Oxford, 1944), pp. 42–4, 134–6, dates this wall-painting *c.* 1150. The bishop has no halo, so can hardly be intended for a saint. Kempley was in the diocese of Hereford, and had a link with St Guthlac's priory (*Taxatio*, p. 161). Gilbert Foliot is thus a possible candidate. But the date is far from certain, and Mr Gethyn-Jones tells us that there are grounds for an earlier date (possibly *c.* 1120; see his *St Mary's Church, Kempley, and its paintings,* 1 (1961), pp. 13, 65; a fuller study will appear in vol. II).

II   *Hand I: King's College, Cambridge, Muniment Room, no. B 15 (no. 391: see pp. 3–4, 23 ff.)*

III   *Hand I: Oxford Bodleian MS E Musaeo 249, fo. 195 (nos. 474, 355, 266: see pp. 3–4)*

IV   *Oxford, Bodleian MS E Musaeo 249, fo. 200 v (no. 170, opening: see pp. 3 f., 20 f.)*

# PREFACE

Early in 1940 Dom Adrian Morey wrote to Z. N. Brooke to say that he was thinking of undertaking an edition of the letters of Gilbert Foliot. Dr Brooke replied that he had had the same idea—each had conceived it as an effort to refresh his mind in his scanty leisure—and a collaboration was happily arranged. The chief manuscripts were not available until 1945, so that work moved slowly for some years. In 1945–6 serious work on the texts was begun; but in October 1946 the senior editor died. Since then the work has been continued by Dom Adrian Morey and C. N. L. Brooke. Dom Morey has been helped on by two years' freedom from administrative duties in 1950–2; C. N. L. Brooke by some years as a Research Fellow in Gonville and Caius College and by a term's leave of absence in the University of Liverpool. Both have been held back by many other calls on their time and by much other work. Z. N. Brooke and Dom Morey had made some progress with the letters before the former's death, and had begun to collect a list of charters, although it was only some years later that a definite decision was made to include them. The main manuscript of the letters, Bodleian E Musaeo 249, includes a substantial number of charters, and so we had the choice of presenting these alone or adding charters from other sources; since the interest of a considerable number of the letters lies in diocesan administration, and the number of surviving charters of Gilbert Foliot is quite exceptional for a diocesan bishop of this period, there seemed little doubt that the right course was to include all the available charters. For the most part the study of the manuscripts, detailed notes on people and events referred to in the letters and charters, and other notes necessary for an edition are in this book; a fuller commentary on a few especially interesting letters, and a study of Gilbert Foliot and his milieu, are contained in a companion volume, *Gilbert Foliot and His Letters*. We have tried to reduce to the minimum repetition between the volumes, and to include fairly copious cross-references. This has led to some divisions of function: thus notes on most of the people who figure prominently in the letters are contained in the Biographical Index to this volume, but those on men who were members of the chapter of Hereford or St Paul's or clerks in Gilbert Foliot's household are contained in appendix IV of *Gilbert Foliot and His Letters*.

Nearly twenty years have passed since the death of Z. N. Brooke, but his help and inspiration have been in our minds throughout, and his own work and notes were of direct use in many parts of this book; Mrs Brooke lived to know that the book was virtually completed and to give us much encouragement, though it is our special regret that she did not see it in print. Our warm thanks are also due to Professor David Knowles, for constant encouragement and guidance, to Dr Rosalind Brooke for equally constant help and encouragement, to the late Professor W. Holtzmann for generously providing much of the material used in appendix VIII, to Professor and Mrs C. R. Cheney for references to and transcripts of a number of charters, to Dr R. W. Hunt, the custodian of our chief manuscript, for much help, and in particular for reading chapter I of the Introduction and giving us invaluable guidance and advice, and to Dr Eleanor Rathbone for her early and lively interest in the work and for many references.

Professor Brooke thanks his colleagues in the School of History of Liverpool University who have borne patiently with Gilbert Foliot and given him valued help, and particularly Dr D. J. A. Matthew and Dr H. Mayr-Harting for help in pursuit of charters, Miss Vera London for generous help with the proofs, and Dr A. R. Myers for taking the Department off his hands so that a period of continuous work was possible; and also the School's secretaries for their labours in typing the manuscript, and his three sons for help with the index. We are grateful for generous help to all the following: Dr Patricia Barnes, Mr John Cain, Sir Charles Clay, Dr Helen Clover, The Reverend J. and Mrs Collins, Dr J. Conway Davies, Dr G. R. C. Davis, Mr R. H. C. Davis, the Reverend J. C. Dickinson, Miss B. Dodwell, Dr and Mrs C. Duggan, Mademoiselle Marthe Dulong, The Reverend J. E. Gethyn-Jones, Miss Diana Greenway, Dr B. R. Kemp, the late Dom E. Kendall, Professor S. Kuttner, Mr R. E. Latham, Dom Jean Leclercq, Professor G. G. Meersseman, O.P., Dr C. D. Ross, Professor A. Saltman, Professor P. Stein, Mr P. Walne, Professor F. Wormald. In various ways many other friends and colleagues have helped us through the years, and we hope they will forgive us that we cannot here give a full list. But we should like to make particular mention of the Librarians and Archivists and their staffs in the Libraries and Archives from which our material was drawn, from whom we have had many acts of kindness, and who have helped us to obtain the leave of their institutions to print documents preserved in them. We have had kind permission for this from the following: The Prefect of the Vatican Library, The Bodleian Library, Oxford, The Trustees of the British Museum, The Librarian of the National Library of Wales, the Deans and Chapters of Canterbury Cathedral, Gloucester Cathedral, Hereford Cathedral, Christ Church, Oxford, St Paul's Cathedral, Salisbury Cathedral, Wells Cathedral, Westminster Abbey and Worcester Cathedral; the Diocesan Registrar of Hereford; Messieurs the Archivistes of the Archives Départementales, Eure and Maine-et-Loire, the Town Clerk and Museum Committee of Colchester, the Librarians of Shrewsbury Borough Library and the Guildhall Library, London, the County Archivist of Essex, the Master and Fellows of Balliol College, the Warden and Fellows of New College, the President and Fellows of St John's College, Oxford and the Provost and Fellows of King's College, Cambridge, and the Board of Governors of St Bartholomew's Hospital. Transcripts of Crown copyright records in the Public Record Office appear by permission of the Controller of H.M. Stationery Office. We should also like to thank the Librarian and Assistant Librarian to the Dean and Chapter of Exeter and the Direttore of the Biblioteca Universitaria Alessandrina in Rome. Gilbert Foliot himself worked and worshipped in what is now Gloucester Cathedral, in Hereford Cathedral and in Old St Paul's, and it is a special pleasure to record our thanks to the successive Librarians of these three Cathedrals for their generous kindness to us.

We would also like to acknowledge the kind permission of Dr Ernest Blake and the Council of the Royal Historical Society to reproduce nos. 395–7 from Dr Blake's edition of the *Liber Eliensis*, and of the editor of the *English Historical Review* and Messrs Longmans, Green and Co. Ltd to reproduce the substantial extract from our article in that review which forms appendix III.

Our notes to Nos. 334 ff. have benefited from the kind help of Dr B. R. Kemp. A full account of the early endowment of Reading Abbey is given in his Ph.D. thesis (Reading University), completed while this book was in proof.

Downside Abbey, Gonville and Caius College, and Liverpool University have provided the setting for our work, and we are most grateful to those institutions for their support and financial assistance in the preparation of the book and to many colleagues in them for help and encouragement. Dom Morey has to thank the Leverhulme Trustees for a generous research grant, Professor Brooke the Liverpool University Joint Committee on Research for help from its funds.

For the plates we owe thanks to the Reverend J. E. Gethyn-Jones (plate I), King's College, Cambridge (plate II) and the Bodleian Library, Oxford (plates III and IV).

Finally, we are grateful to the Syndics of the Cambridge University Press for undertaking the publication of this book, and to their staff for their help and skill. Its publication has been made possible by generous grants from the Marc Fitch Fund, the Master and Fellows of Gonville and Caius College, the University of Liverpool, and from a friend who wishes to remain anonymous. To all these we offer our warm thanks.

R. A. M.
C. N. L. B.

# LIST OF PRINTED BOOKS AND ARTICLES CITED, WITH ABBREVIATED REFERENCES

A few items referred to only once are omitted; sources, books and articles with significant information about Gilbert Foliot cited in *Gilbert Foliot and His Letters* (*GF*) are included.

*Acta Chichester: The Acta of the Bishops of Chichester, 1075–1207*, ed. H. Mayr-Harting, Canterbury and York Society, 1964.

*Acta Stephani Langton, Cantuariensis archiepiscopi, A.D. 1207–1228*, ed. K. Major, Canterbury and York Society, 1950.

*Adalbertus Samaritanus Praecepta Dictaminum*, ed. F.-J. Schmale, *MGH, Quellen zur Geistesgeschichte des Mittelalters*, III, Weimar, 1961.

Adams, G. B., *Councils and Courts in Anglo-Norman England*, New Haven, 1926.

*Ancient Charters, royal and private, prior to A.D. 1200*, ed. J. H. Round, PRS, x, 1888.

*Anglia Sacra*, ed. H. Wharton, 2 vols., London, 1691.

Ann. Bermondsey, in *Ann. Mon.* III.

Ann. Burton, in *Ann. Mon.* I.

Ann. Dunstable, in *Ann. Mon.* III.

Ann. Margam, in *Ann. Mon.* I.

*Ann. Mon.: Annales Monastici*, ed. H. R. Luard, 5 vols., RS, 1864–9.

Ann. Nevers, in *MGH, Scriptores*, XIII (1881), 88–91.

Ann. Oseney, in *Ann. Mon.* IV.

Ann. Tewkesbury, in *Ann. Mon.* I.

Ann. Waverley, in *Ann. Mon.* II.

Ann. Winchcombe, ed. R. R. Darlington, in *Misc. D. M. Stenton*, pp. 111–37.

Ann. Winchester, in *Ann. Mon.* II.

Ann. Worcester, in *Ann. Mon.* IV.

Anselm, St, *Opera Omnia*, ed. F. S. Schmitt, 6 vols., Edinburgh, 1946–61 (*Epistolae* in vols. III–V).

*Antiquus cartularius ecclesiae Baiocensis*, ed. V. Bourrienne, 2 vols., Société de l'Histoire de Normandie, Paris–Rouen, 1902–3.

*Appendix Concilii Lateranensis* (decretal collection), in Mansi, XXII, 248–454.

Arnulf: *The Letters of Arnulf of Lisieux*, ed. F. Barlow, Camden 3rd series, LXI, 1939.

Arnulf, ed. Giles: *Arnulfi Lexoviensis episcopi Epistolae...*, ed. J. A. Giles, Patres Ecclesiae Anglicanae, London, Oxford, 1844.

Bale, J., *Index Britanniae Scriptorum*, ed. R. L. Poole and M. Bateson, Oxford, 1902.

Bannister, A. T., *A Descriptive Catalogue of the Manuscripts in the Hereford Cathedral Library*, Hereford, 1927.

Barkly, H., 'The earlier house of Berkeley', *Transactions of the Bristol and Gloucestershire Archaeological Society*, VIII (1883–4), 193–223.

Bede, *Hist. Eccl.*: Bede, *Historia ecclesiastica gentis Anglorum*, ed. C. Plummer, 2 vols., Oxford, 1896.

Bernardi, S., *Opera*, I– , ed. J. Leclercq, C. H. Talbot, H. M. Rochais, Rome, 1957– .

Bernard, St, *Ep.*: Letters of St Bernard, cited from *PL*, CLXXXII, 67–662.

*BIHR*: *Bulletin of the Institute of Historical Research*.

Billanovich, G., 'Petrarch and the textual tradition of Livy', *Journal of the Warburg and Courtauld Institutes*, XIV (1951), 137–208.

Bishop, E., *Liturgica Historica*, Oxford, 1918.

Bishop, T. A. M., *Scriptores Regis: facsimiles to identify and illustrate the hands of royal scribes in original charters of Henry I, Stephen, and Henry II*, Oxford, 1961.

Blair, C. H. Hunter, 'A second calendar of Greenwell deeds', *Archaeologia Aeliana*, 4th series, VII (1930), 81–114.

*Book of fees: Liber feodorum. The book of fees commonly called Testa de Nevill*, PRO Texts and Calendars, 2 vols. in 3, 1920–31.

Borst, A., *Die Katharer, Schriften der MGH*, XII, Stuttgart, 1953.

*British Museum, Catalogue of Seals in the Department of Manuscripts in*, ed. W. de G. Birch, I, London, 1887.

—— *Catalogue of Western Manuscripts in the Old Royal and King's Collections*, ed. G. F. Warner and J. P. Gilson, I, London, 1921.

—— *Facsimiles of Royal and other Charters in*, ed. G. F. Warner and H. J. Ellis, I, William I–Richard I, London, 1903.

Brooke, C. N. L., 'The Archbishops of St David's, Llandaff and Caerleon-on-Usk', *SEBC*, pp. 201–42.

—— 'Canons of English Church Councils in the early decretal collections', *Traditio*, XIII (1957), 471–80.

—— 'The Deans of St Paul's, c. 1090–1499', *BIHR*, XXIX (1956), 231–44.

—— 'Episcopal charters for Wix priory', *Misc. D. M. Stenton*, pp. 45–63.

—— 'Gregorian reform in action: clerical marriage in England, 1050–1200', *CHJ*, XII, i (1956), 1–21 (Appendix in *CHJ*, XII, ii (1956), 187–8). Reprinted in *Change in Medieval Society*, ed. S. L. Thrupp, New York, 1964, pp. 49–71.

—— review of Saltman in *Journal of Theological Studies*, New Series, VIII (1957), 187–90.

—— 'St Peter of Gloucester and St Cadoc of Llancarfan', *CS*, pp. 258–322.

—— *The Saxon and Norman Kings*, London, 1963.

Brooke, Z. N., *The English Church and the Papacy from the Conquest to the Reign of John*, Cambridge, 1931.

Brooke, Z. N. and C. N. L., 'Henry II, Duke of Normandy and Aquitaine', *EHR*, LXI (1946), 81–9.

—— 'Hereford Cathedral Dignitaries in the twelfth century', *CHJ*, VIII, i (1944), 1–21; 'Supplement' in *CHJ*, VIII, iii (1946), 179–85.

Caenegem, R. C. van, *Royal Writs in England from the Conquest to Glanvill*, Selden Society, LXXVII, 1959.

*Cal. Charter Rolls: Calendar of the Charter Rolls preserved in the Public Record Office*, 6 vols., PRO Texts and Calendars, 1903–27.

*Capes: Charters and Records of Hereford Cathedral*, ed. W. W. Capes, Cantilupe Society, Hereford, 1908.

*Cart. Bath: Two Chartularies of the Priory of St Peter at Bath*, ed. W. Hunt, Somerset Record Society, 1893.

*Cart. Boarstall: The Boarstall Cartulary*, ed. H. E. Salter and A. H. Cooke, Oxford Historical Society, LXXXVIII, 1930.

*Cart. Brecon:* 'Cartularium Prioratus S. Johannis Evangelistae de Brecon', ed. R. W. Banks, *Archaeologia Cambrensis*, 4th series, XIII (1882), 275–308; XIV (1883), 18–311.

*Cart. Bruton: Two Cartularies of the Augustinian Priory of Bruton and the Cluniac Priory of Montacute...*, Somerset Record Society, 1894.

*Cart. Chertsey: Chertsey (Abbey) Cartularies*, vols. I, II, Surrey Record Society, XII, [1915]–58.

*Cart. Chichester: The Chartulary of the High Church of Chichester*, ed. W. D. Peckham, Sussex Record Society, XLVI, 1946.

*Cart. Clerkenwell: Cartulary of St Mary Clerkenwell*, ed. W. O. Hassall, Camden 3rd series, LXXI, 1949.

*Cart. Colchester: Cartularium monasterii S. Johannis Baptiste de Colecestria*, ed. S. A. Moore, 2 vols., Roxburghe Club, 1897.

*Cart. Colne: Cartularium prioratus de Colne*, ed. J. L. Fisher, Essex Archaeological Society, Occasional Publications, no. 1, 1946.

*Cart. Dunstable: A Digest of the Charters preserved in the Cartulary of the Priory of Dunstable*, ed. G. H. Fowler, Bedfordshire Historical Record Society, X, 1926.

*Cart. Eynsham: Eynsham Cartulary*, ed. H. E. Salter, 2 vols., Oxford Historical Society, XLIX, LI, 1907–8.

*Cart. Gloucester: Historia et cartularium monasterii sancti Petri Gloucestriae*, ed. W. H. Hart, 3 vols., RS, 1863–7.

*Cart. Harrold: Records of Harrold Priory...*, ed. G. H. Fowler, Bedfordshire Historical Record Society, XV, 1935.

*Cart. Huntingdon:* 'The cartulary of the priory of St Mary, Huntingdon', ed. W. M. Noble, *Transactions of the Cambridgeshire and Huntingdonshire Archaeological Society*, IV (1930), 89–280 *passim*.

*Cart. Lewes: The Chartulary of the Priory of St Pancras of Lewes*, ed. L. F. Salzman, 2 vols., Sussex Record Society, XXXVIII, XL, 1933–5 (with additional vol., ed. J. H. Bullock *et al.*, for 'The portions relating to counties other than Sussex', 1943).

*Cart. Missenden: The Cartulary of Missenden Abbey*, ed. J. G. Jenkins, Buckinghamshire Record Society, I– , 1938– .

*Cart. Oseney: Cartulary of Oseney Abbey*, ed. H. E. Salter, 6 vols., Oxford Historical Society, LXXXIX–XCI, XCVII–XCVIII, CI, 1929–36.

*Cart. Ramsey: Cartularium monasterii de Rameseia*, ed. W. H. Hart and P. A. Lyons, 3 vols., RS, 1884–93.

*Cart. Sandford: The Sandford Cartulary*, ed. A. M. Leys, 2 vols., Oxfordshire Record Society, XIX, XXII, 1938–41.

*Cart. Stoneleigh: The Stoneleigh Leger Book*, ed. R. H. Hilton, Publications of the Dugdale Society, XXIV, 1960.

*Cart. Thame: The Thame Cartulary*, ed. H. E. Salter, 2 vols., Oxfordshire Record Society, XXV–XXVI, 1947–8.

*Cart. Trentham:* 'A chartulary of the Augustine priory of Trentham', ed. F. Parker, in *Collections for a History of Staffordshire*, XI, William Salt Archaeological Society, 1890.

*Cart. Wardon: Cartulary of the Abbey of Old Wardon*, ed. G. H. Fowler, Bedfordshire Historical Record Society, XIII, 1930.

*Cart. Winchcombe: Landboc sive Registrum monasterii B.M. Virginis et sancti Cenhelmi de Winchelcumba...*, ed. D. Royce, 2 vols., 1892–3.

*Cart. Winchester: Chartulary of Winchester Cathedral*, ed. A. W. Goodman, Winchester, 1927.

*Cat. Ancient Deeds: A Descriptive Catalogue of Ancient Deeds in the Public Record Office*, 6 vols., PRO Texts and Calendars, 1890–1915.

*CDF: Calendar of Documents preserved in France illustrative of the History of Great Britain and Ireland*, I, A.D. 918–1206, ed. J. H. Round, PRO Texts and Calendars, 1899.

Cheney, C. R., 'Church building in the Middle Ages', *Bulletin of the John Rylands Library*, XXXIV (1951–2), 20–36.

—— *English Bishops' Chanceries, 1100–1250*, Manchester, 1950.

—— *From Becket to Langton: English Church Government, 1170–1213*, Manchester, 1956.

—— 'Magna Carta Beati Thome: another Canterbury forgery', *BIHR*, XXXVI (1963), 1–26.

Cheney, M., 'The Compromise of Avranches of 1172 and the spread of Canon Law in England', *EHR*, LVI (1941), 177–97.

*CHJ: Cambridge Historical Journal*.

*Christina of Markyate, The Life of*, ed. and translated C. H. Talbot, Oxford, 1959.

*Chron. Abingdon: Chronicon monasterii de Abingdon*, ed. J. Stevenson, 2 vols., RS, 1858.

*Chron. Anjou: Chroniques des églises d'Anjou*, ed. P. Marchegay and É. Mabille, Société de l'Histoire de France, Paris, 1869 (and see Halphen).

*Chron. Coggeshall: Radulphi de Coggeshall chronicon Anglicanum...*, ed. J. Stevenson, RS, 1875.

*Chron. Evesham: Chronicon abbatiae de Evesham...*, ed. W. D. Macray, RS, 1863.

*Chron. Ramsey: Chronicon abbatiae Rameseiensis...*, ed. W. D. Macray, RS, 1886.

*Chron. Walden:* 'The Book of the Foundation of Walden Abbey', translated H. Collar, *Essex Review*, XLV (1936), 73–236 *passim*; XLVI (1937), 12–234 *passim*; XLVII (1938), 36–220 *passim*.

*Chrons. of the Reigns of Stephen etc.: Chronicles of the Reigns of Stephen, Henry II, and Richard I*, ed. R. Howlett, 4 vols., RS, 1884–9.

Classen, P., *Gerhoch von Reichersberg*, Wiesbaden, 1960.

Clay, Sir Charles T., 'The early abbots of the Yorkshire Cistercian houses', *Yorkshire Archaeological Journal*, XXXVIII (1952–5), 8–43.

—— 'The early precentors and chancellors of York', *ibid.* XXXVI (1940–3), 116–38.

—— 'The early treasurers of York', *ibid.* XXXV (1940), 7–34.

—— 'Notes on the chronology of the early deans of York', *ibid.* XXXIV (1939), 361–78.

—— 'Notes on the early archdeacons in the Church of York', *ibid.* XXXVI (1944–7), 269–87, 409–34.

—— *York Minster Fasti*, 2 vols., Yorkshire Archaeological Society, Record Series, CXXIII, CXXIV, 1958–9.

*Code: Codex Iustinianus*, see *Corpus Iuris Civilis*.

Colvin, H. M., 'Holme Lacy: an episcopal manor and its tenants in the twelfth and thirteenth centuries', *Medieval Studies presented to Rose Graham*, ed. V. Ruffer and A. J. Taylor, Oxford, 1950, pp. 15–40.

Constable, G., 'The alleged disgrace of John of Salisbury in 1159', *EHR*, LXIX (1954), 67–76.

—— 'The disputed election at Langres in 1138', *Traditio*, XIII (1957), 119–52.

—— *Monastic Tithes from their Origins to the Twelfth Century*, Cambridge, 1964.

Conway Davies: *Episcopal Acts and Cognate Documents relating to Welsh Dioceses, 1066–1272*, ed. J. Conway Davies, I–II, Historical Society of the Church in Wales, 1946–8.

*Corpus Iuris Civilis:* I, *Institutiones*, ed. P. Krueger, *Digesta*, ed. T. Mommsen; II, *Codex Iustinianus*, ed. P. Krueger; III, *Novellae*, ed. R. Schoell and W. Kroll; 16th, 11th, 6th edn, Berlin, 1954.

Cottineau: Cottineau, L. H., *Répertoire topo-bibliographique des abbayes et prieurés*, 2 vols., Mâcon, 1939.

*Councils and Synods*, II: *Councils and Synods, with other documents relating to the English Church*, II, ed. F. M. Powicke and C. R. Cheney, 2 parts, Oxford, 1964.

Courtney, F., *Cardinal Robert Pullen: an English Theologian of the Twelfth Century*, Analecta Gregoriana, LXIV, Rome, 1954.

*CP: The Complete Peerage*, by G.E.C., revised edn by V. Gibbs, H. A. Doubleday, Lord Howard de Walden, G. H. White and R. S. Lea, London, 1910–59.

*CS:* K. Jackson, P. Hunter Blair, B. Colgrave, B. Dickins, J. and H. Taylor, C. Brooke, N. K. Chadwick, *Celt and Saxon: Studies in the early British Border*, Cambridge, 1963.

*Curia Regis Rolls*, PRO Texts and Calendars, I– , 1922– .

Damian, St Peter, *Opusculum XXXI, PL*, CXLV, 529–44.

*Danelaw Charters: Documents illustrative of the Social and Economic History of the Danelaw from various Collections*, ed. F. M. Stenton, British Academy, London, 1920.

Daniel, Walter, *The Life of Ailred of Rievaulx*, ed. and translated F. M. Powicke, NMT, 1950.

David, C. W. (ed.), *De expugnatione Lyxbonensi*, Columbia Records of Civilisation, XXIV, New York, 1936.

Davis: Davis, G. R. C., *Medieval Cartularies of Great Britain: a Short Catalogue*, London, 1958.

Davis, H. W. C., 'Henry of Blois and Brian Fitz-Count', *EHR*, XXV (1910), 297–303.

—— 'Some documents of the anarchy', *Essays in History presented to Reginald Lane Poole*, ed. H. W. C. Davis, Oxford, 1927, pp. 168–89.

Davis, R. H. C., 'The authorship of the "Gesta Stephani"', *EHR*, LXXVII (1962), 209–32.

—— 'The treaty between William earl of Gloucester and Roger earl of Hereford', *Misc. D. M. Stenton*, pp. 139–46.

*Decretum: Decretum Gratiani*, ed. E. Friedberg, *Corpus Iuris Canonici*, I, Leipzig, 1879.

Delisle, *Recueil*: *Recueil des actes de Henri II...concernant les provinces françaises et les affaires de France*, Introduction and 3 vols., ed. L. Delisle and E. Berger, Académie des Inscriptions et Belles-Lettres, Chartes et Diplômes, Paris, 1909–27.

*Devon Fines: Devon Feet of Fines*, 2 vols., ed. O. J. Reichel *et al.*, Devon and Cornwall Record Society Publications, 1912–39.

*Dialogus de Scaccario: The Course of the Exchequer by Richard, son of Nigel...*, ed. and translated C. Johnson, NMT, 1950.

*Diceto: Radulfi de Diceto decani Lundoniensis opera historica...*, ed. W. Stubbs, 2 vols., RS, 1876.

Dickinson: Dickinson, J. C., *The Origins of the Austin Canons and their Introduction into England*, London, 1950.

*Dictionnaire de Droit Canonique*, I– , Paris, 1935– .

*Dictionnaire de théologie catholique*, ed. A. Vacant, É. Mangenot, É. Amann, 15 vols., Paris, 1902–50.

*Digest: Digesta*, see *Corpus Iuris Civilis*.

*DNB: Dictionary of National Biography*, ed. L. Stephen and S. Lee, 66 vols., London, 1885–1901, repr. 22 vols., Oxford, 1921–2.

Dodwell, B., 'Some charters relating to the honour of Bacton', *Misc. D. M. Stenton*, pp. 147–65.

*Draco Normannicus*, in *Chrons. of the Reigns of Stephen etc.*, II.

Dugdale, W., *History of St Paul's Cathedral*, 3 edns, London, 1658, 1714–16, 1818.

Duggan: Duggan, C., *Twelfth-century Decretal Collections and their Importance in English History*, University of London Historical Studies, XII, London, 1963.

Duggan, C., 'The Becket dispute and the criminous clerks', *BIHR*, XXXV (1962), 1–28.

Eadmer, *Historia novorum in Anglia...*, ed. M. Rule, RS, 1884.

Eadmer, *The Life of St Anselm Archbishop of Canterbury*, ed. and translated R. W. Southern, NMT, 1962 (1963).

*Early Cheshire Charters, Facsimiles of,* ed. G. Barraclough, Record Society of Lancashire and Cheshire, 1957.

*Early Scottish Charters,* ed. A. C. Lawrie, Glasgow, 1905.

*EHR: English Historical Review.*

Ellis, A. S., 'On the landholders of Gloucestershire named in Domesday Book', *Transactions of the Bristol and Glos. Archaeological Society,* IV (1879–80), 86–198.

Erdmann, C., *Studien zur Briefliteratur Deutschlands im elften Jahrhundert,* Schriften der MGH, I, Leipzig, 1938, repr. Stuttgart, 1952.

*Extra:* 'Decretalium Gregorii pp. IX compilatio', ed. E. Friedberg, *Corpus Iuris Canonici,* II, Leipzig, 1881.

*EYC: Early Yorkshire Charters,* I–III, ed. W. Farrer, Edinburgh, 1914–16; IV– , ed. Sir Charles T. Clay, Yorkshire Archaeological Society, Record Series, Extra Series, I– , 1935– .

Eyton, *Itinerary:* Eyton, R. W., *Court, Household and Itinerary of King Henry II,* London and Dorchester, 1878.

Eyton, *Salop:* Eyton, R. W., *Antiquities of Shropshire,* 12 vols., London and Shifnal, 1854–60.

*Facsimiles of English Royal Writs to A.D. 1100 presented to Vivian Hunter Galbraith,* ed. T. A. M. Bishop and P. Chaplais, Oxford, 1957.

Farrer, W., *Honors and Knights' Fees,* 3 vols., London, Manchester, 1923–5.

Finberg, H. P. R., *Early Charters of the West Midlands,* Leicester, 1961.

*Flete: Flete's History of Westminster Abbey,* ed. J. Armitage Robinson, Cambridge, 1909.

Florence: Florence of Worcester, *Chronica ex chronicis,* ed. B. Thorpe, 2 vols., English Historical Society, London, 1848–9.

Floyer, J. K. and Hamilton, S. G., *Catalogue of Manuscripts preserved in the Chapter Library of Worcester Cathedral,* Worcestershire Historical Society, 1906.

Foliot, Gilbert, *Expositio in Cantica Canticorum, PL,* CCII, 1147–1304 (and see *GF,* p. 70 n.).

Foreville, R., *L'Église et la royauté en Angleterre sous Henri II...,* Paris, 1943.

Fowler, J., 'Dean Azo of Sarum', *Notes and Queries for Somerset and Dorset,* XXIII (1942), 319–20.

Fox, L., 'The honor and earldom of Leicester: origin and descent, 1066–1399', *EHR,* LIV (1939), 385–402.

Friedberg, E., *Die Canones-sammlungen zwischen Gratian und Bernhard von Pavia,* Leipzig, 1897, repr. Graz, 1958.

Friend, A. C., 'Serlo of Wilton: the early years', *Bulletin Du Cange,* XXIV (1954), 85–110.

G, Giles: *Gilberti ex abbate Glocestriae episcopi primum Herefordiensis deinde Londoniensis epistolae...,* ed. J. A. Giles, 2 vols., Patres Ecclesiae Anglicanae, London, Oxford, 1846.

Gaimar, Geoffrey, *L'Estoire des Engleis,* ed. A. Bell, Anglo-Norman Texts, XIV/XVI, Oxford, 1960.

*Gallia Christiana,* 16 vols., Paris, 1715–1865.

Geoffrey of Monmouth, *Historia Regum Britanniae*, ed. E. Faral, *La légende arthu-rienne*, I, iii, Bibliothèque de l'École des Hautes Études, CCLVII, Paris, 1929.

Gerhoh von Reichersberg: *Opera inedita*, ed. D. and O. van den Eynde and A. Rijmersdael, 2 vols. in 3, Spicilegium Pontificii Athenaei Antoniani, VIII–X, Rome, 1955–6 (other works ed. E. Sackur, in *MGH, Libelli de Lite impera-torum et pontificum...*, III, Hanover, 1897, pp. 131–525).

Gervase: *The Historical Works of Gervase of Canterbury*, ed. W. Stubbs, 2 vols., RS, 1879–80.

*Gesta, Gesta Stephani: Gesta Stephani*, ed. and translated K. R. Potter, NMT, 1955.

*Gesta Henrici II: Gesta regis Henrici secundi Benedicti abbatis...*, ed. W. Stubbs, 2 vols., RS, 1867.

*GF:* A. Morey and C. N. L. Brooke, *Gilbert Foliot and His Letters*, Cambridge Studies in Medieval Life and Thought, New Series, 11, Cambridge, 1965.

Gibbs: *Early Charters of the Cathedral Church of St Paul, London*, ed. M. Gibbs, Camden 3rd series, LVIII, London, 1939.

Giles, J. A., see G.; also *Epistolae Sancti Thomae Cantuariensis...*, ed. J. A. Giles, 2 vols., Patres Ecclesiae Anglicanae, London, Oxford, 1845.

*Giraldi Cambrensis Opera*, ed. J. S. Brewer, J. F. Dimock and G. F. Warner, 8 vols., RS, 1861–91.

Gleason, S. E., *An Ecclesiastical Barony of the Middle Ages: the Bishopric of Bayeux, 1066–1204*, Harvard Hist. Monographs, X, Cambridge, Mass., 1936.

Graham, R., 'Four alien priories in Monmouthshire', *Journal of the British Archaeo-logical Association*, 2nd series, XXXV (1929), 102–21.

—— 'An appeal about 1175 for the building fund of St Paul's Cathedral Church', *ibid.* 3rd series, X (1945–7), 73–6.

Gratian, see *Decretum*.

Greg., Greg. Mag.: Gregory the Great, *Dialogi*, ed. U. Moricca, Fonti per la Storia d'Italia, Rome, 1924; *Registrum epistolarum*, ed. P. Ewald and L. M. Hartmann, 2 vols., *MGH, Epistolae*, I–II, Berlin, 1887–99.

Halphen, L. (ed.), *Recueil d'annales angevines et vendômoises*, Collection de Textes, XXXVII, Paris, 1903.

*Handbook: The Handbook of British Chronology*, 2nd edn, ed. F. M. Powicke and E. B. Fryde, Royal Historical Society Guides and Handbooks, II, London, 1961.

Hardy, T. D., *Descriptive Catalogue of Materials relating to the History of Great Britain and Ireland*, 3 vols. in 4, RS, 1862–71.

Harmer, F. E., *Anglo-Saxon Writs*, Manchester, 1952.

Harris, S., 'The Kalendar of the *Vitae Sanctorum Wallensium*', *Journal of the His-torical Society of the Church in Wales*, III (1953), 3–53.

Haskins, C. H., *Norman Institutions*, Harvard Historical Studies, XXIV, Cambridge, Mass., 1918.

*Hatton's, Sir Christopher, Book of Seals*, ed. L. C. Loyd and D. M. Stenton, Oxford, and Northamptonshire Record Society, XV, 1950.

Heltzel, V. B., *Fair Rosamund: a Study of the Development of a Literary Theme*, Northwestern University Studies in the Humanities, XVI, Evanston, Ill., 1947.

Henry of Huntingdon: *Henrici archidiaconi Huntendunensis Historia Anglorum*, ed. T. Arnold, RS, 1879.

*Hereford Breviary: The Hereford Breviary*, ed. W. H. Frere and L. E. G. Browne, 3 vols., Henry Bradshaw Society, 1904–15.

*Herefs DB: Herefordshire Domesday*, c. *1160–70*, ed. V. H. Galbraith and J. Tait, PRS, 1950.

*HF: Recueil des historiens des Gaules et de la France*, ed. M. Bouquet *et al.*, nouv. édn, ed. L. Delisle, 24 vols, Paris, 1869–1904 (cf. *Obituaires*).

Hildebert, *Epp.*: Hildebert of Lavardin, bishop of Le Mans, archbishop of Tours, *Epistolae*, in *PL*, CLXXI, 135–312.

*Historical Monuments Comm.: Hereford: Royal Commission on the Ancient and Historical Monuments and Constructions of England: An Inventory of the Historical Monuments in Herefordshire*, 3 vols., London, 1931–4.

*HMC: Royal Commission on Historical Manuscripts*, Appendices to Reports, and Calendars, London, 1870– . (*See also Rep.*)

*HMC Wells: HMC, Calendar of the manuscripts of the Dean and Chapter of Wells*, 2 vols., 1907–14.

Holdsworth, C., 'John of Ford and English Cistercian writing, 1167–1214', *Transactions of the Royal Historical Society*, 5th series, XI (1961), 117–36.

Holtzmann, W., 'Beiträge zu den Dekretalensammlungen des zwölften Jahrhunderts', *ZRG, Kan. Abt.* XVI (1927), 37–115 ('Die Collectio Dertusensis', pp. 39–77; 'Die Collectio Aureaevallensis', pp. 77–109).

——— 'Die Collectio Eberbacensis', *ibid.* XVII (1928), 548–55.

——— 'Quellen und Forschungen zur Geschichte Friedrich Barbarossas (Englische Analekten I)', *Neues Archiv der Gesellschaft für ältere deutsche Geschichtskunde*, XLVIII (1930), 384–413.

——— 'Über eine Ausgabe der päpstlichen Dekretalen des 12. Jahrhunderts', *Nachrichten von der Akademie der Wissenschaften in Göttingen*, phil.-hist. Klasse, 1945–8, 15–36.

Howden: *Chronica Rogeri de Houedene*, ed. W. Stubbs, 4 vols., RS, 1868–71.

Howell, M. E., *Regalian Right in Medieval England*, University of London Historical Studies, IX, London, 1962.

Hugh of St Victor, *De sacramentis*, in *PL*, CLXXVI, 173–618.

Hugh the Chantor, *The History of the Church of York*, *1066–1127*, ed. and translated C. Johnson, NMT, 1961.

Hunt, R. W., 'English learning in the late twelfth century', *Transactions of the Royal Historical Society*, 4th series, XIX (1936), 19–42.

Hurry, J. B., *Reading Abbey*, London, 1901.

*Inst.*: Justinian's *Institutiones*, see *Corpus Iuris Civilis*.

*Inventaire sommaire des Archives Départementales antérieures à 1790: Maine-et-Loire, Archives Ecclésiastiques, Série H*, II, ed. M. Sache, Angers, 1926.

Ivo, bishop of Chartres, *Epp.*: *Epistolae*, in *PL*, CLXII, 11–288 (new edn by J. Leclercq, vol. I only so far, Classiques de l'Histoire de France au Moyen Âge, Paris, 1949).

James, M. R., *The Ancient Libraries of Canterbury and Dover*, Cambridge, 1903.

—— 'The Library of the Grey Friars of Hereford', *Collectanea Franciscana*, I, British Society of Franciscan Studies, V, Aberdeen, 1914, pp. 114–23.

Janauschek, L., *Originum Cisterciensium, tomus* I, Vienna, 1877.

JL: *Regesta Pontificum Romanorum* [to 1198], ed. P. Jaffé, rev. G. Wattenbach, S. Loewenfeld, F. Kaltenbrunner, P. Ewald, 2 vols., Leipzig, 1885–8.

John of Avranches, *De officiis ecclesiasticis*, ed. R. Delamare, Bibliothèque Liturgique, XXII, Paris, 1923.

John of Hexham: John of Hexham's continuation to the *Historia Regum* attrib. to Symeon of Durham, in *Symeonis monachi opera omnia*, ed. T. Arnold, RS, II, 1885.

John of Worcester: *The Chronicle of John of Worcester, 1118–1140*, ed. J. R. H. Weaver, Anecdota Oxoniensia, Mediaeval and Modern Series, XIII, Oxford, 1908 (also in Florence of Worcester *q.v.*).

John, E., 'The litigation of an exempt house, St Augustine's, Canterbury, 1182–1237', *Bulletin of the John Rylands Library*, XXXIX (1956–7), 390–415.

JS Epp.: (usually cited by number) *The Letters of John of Salisbury*, I: *The Early Letters*, ed. and translated W. J. Millor and H. E. Butler, revised by C. N. L. Brooke, NMT, 1955; vols. II and III forthcoming.

JS Epp. ed. Giles: *Joannis Saresberiensis...opera omnia*, ed. J. A. Giles, 5 vols., Patres Ecclesiae Anglicanae, London, Oxford, 1848, vols. I, II; also in *PL*, CXCIX.

JS HP (C), (P): John of Salisbury, *Historia Pontificalis*; (C) = ed. and translated M. Chibnall, NMT, 1956, (P) = ed. R. L. Poole, Oxford, 1927.

JS *Policraticus*: John of Salisbury, *Policraticus siue de nugis curialium et uestigiis philosophorum*, ed. C. C. J. Webb, 2 vols., Oxford, 1909.

Juncker, J., 'Die Collectio Berolinensis', *ZRG, Kan. Abt.* XIII (1924), 284–426.

Kantorowicz, H. and Buckland, W. W., *Studies in the Glossators of the Roman Law*, Cambridge, 1938.

Ker: *Medieval Libraries of Great Britain: a List of surviving Books*, ed. N. R. Ker, Royal Historical Society Guides and Handbooks, III, 2nd edn, London, 1964.

KH: Knowles, D., and Hadcock, R. N., *Medieval Religious Houses: England and Wales*, London, 1953.

Knowles, Dom David, 'The case of St William of York', *CHJ*, V, ii (1936), 162–77, 212–14, repr. in *The Historian and Character*, pp. 76–97.

—— 'Essays in Monastic History. IV. The Growth of Exemption', *Downside Review*, L (1932), 201–31, 396–436.

—— *Great Historical Enterprises: Problems in Monastic History*, London, 1963.

—— *The Historian and Character and other Essays*, Cambridge, 1963.

—— *The Monastic Order in England, 940–1216*, 2nd edn (pagination unaltered from 1st edn, 1940), Cambridge, 1963.

Knowles, EC: *The Episcopal Colleagues of Archbishop Thomas Becket*, Cambridge, 1951.

Kuttner, S., 'New Studies on the Roman Law in Gratian's *Decretum*', *Seminar, Annual Extraordinary Number of The Jurist*, XI (1953), 12–50.

—— 'Notes on a projected Corpus of twelfth-century decretal letters', *Traditio*, VI (1948), 345–51, with supplements in later vols. (in *Bulletin of the Institute of Research and Study in Medieval Canon Law*; see e.g. *Traditio*, XVI (1960), 534 ff.).

—— and Rathbone, E., 'Anglo-Norman canonists of the twelfth century', *Traditio*, VII (1949–51), 279–358.

Landon, L., 'The early archdeacons of the Norwich diocese', *Proceedings of the Suffolk Institute of Archaeology and Natural History*, XX (1930), 11–35.

*Lanfranc, The Monastic Constitutions of*, ed. and translated D. Knowles, NMT, 1951.

Långfors, A., 'Histoire de l'abbaye de Fécamp en vers français du XIIIe siècle', *Annales Academiae Scientiarum Fennicae*, ser. B, XXII, i (1928).

Leclercq, J., *Pierre le Vénérable*, S.-Wandrille, 1946.

Lees, B. A. (ed.), *Records of the Templars in England in the Twelfth Century*, Records of the Social and Economic History of England and Wales, IX, British Academy, London, 1935.

Legg, L. G. Wickham (ed.), *English Coronation Records*, London, 1901.

Levison, W., *England and the Continent in the Eighth Century*, Oxford, 1946.

*Liber Eliensis*, ed. E. O. Blake, Camden 3rd series, XCII, 1962.

*Life of King Edward who Rests at Westminster, The*, ed. and translated F. Barlow, NMT, 1962.

*Lincoln Statutes: Lincoln Cathedral Statutes*, ed. H. Bradshaw and C. Wordsworth, 2 parts in 3, Cambridge, 1892–7.

Lindley, E. S., 'Kingswood Abbey, its lands and mills', *Transactions of the Bristol and Glos. Archaeol. Soc.* LXXIII (1954), 115–91; LXXIV (1955), 36–59; LXXV (1956), 73–104.

*Literae Cantuarienses...*, ed. J. B. Sheppard, 3 vols., RS, 1887–9.

Liverani: *Spicilegium Liberianum*, ed. F. Liverani, I, Florence, 1863.

Lloyd: Lloyd, Sir J. E., *A History of Wales from the Earliest Times to the Edwardian Conquest*, 3rd edn, 2 vols., London, 1939.

Lohmann, H.-E., 'Die Collectio Wigorniensis (Collectio Londinensis Regia)', *ZRG, Kan. Abt.* XXII (1933), 36–187.

(London, St Paul's Cathedral) *A History of St Paul's Cathedral and the Men associated with it*, ed. W. R. Matthews and W. M. Atkins, London, 1957.

—— *The Domesday of St Paul's of the Year 1222...*, ed. W. H. Hale, Camden Society, LXIX, 1858 (see also Gibbs, *Rep.*).

Lot, F., *Études critiques sur l'abbaye de Saint-Wandrille*, Bibliothèque de L'École des Hautes Études, CCIV, Paris, 1913.

Loyd, *Origins*: Loyd, L. C., *The Origins of some Anglo-Norman Families*, ed. C. T. Clay and D. C. Douglas, Publications of the Harleian Society, CIII, Leeds, 1951.

Luchaire, A., *Études sur quelques manuscrits de Rome et de Paris*, Bibliothèque de la Faculté des Lettres de l'Université de Paris, VIII (1899).

Lunt, W. E., *Financial Relations of the Papacy with England to 1327*, Mediaeval Academy of America, Publication XXXIII, Cambridge, Mass., 1939.

Lupus: *Epistolae et Vita divi Thomae martyris et archiepiscopi Cantuariensis...*, ed. F. Christianus Lupus, Iprensis, 2 vols., Brussels, 1682.

Lyttelton: Lyttelton, George Lord, *The History of the Life of King Henry the Second: Notes to the Second and Third Books*, London, 1767.

Maccarrone, M., 'Il papa "Vicarius Christi"', *Miscellanea Pio Paschini*, I, Lateranum, Nova Series, XIV, 1–4, Rome, 1948, pp. 427–500.

Maisonneuve, H., *Études sur les origines de l'Inquisition*, L'Église et l'État au moyen âge, ed. G. Le Bras, VII, 2nd edn, Paris, 1960.

Mansi: Mansi, J. D. (ed.), *Sacrorum conciliorum nova et amplissima collectio...*, 53 vols., Florence, Venice, Paris, 1759–1927.

Map, Walter, *De nugis curialium*, ed. M. R. James, Anecdota Oxoniensia, Mediaeval and Modern Series, XIV, Oxford, 1914 (also translated M. R. James, Cymmro-dorion Record Society, IX, London, 1923).

Marchegay, P., 'Les prieurés anglais de Saint-Florent près Saumur...', *Bibliothèque de l'École des Chartes*, XL (1879), 154–94.

Martène, E., and Durand, U., *Thesaurus novus anecdotorum*, III, Paris, 1717.

—— *Veterum scriptorum...amplissima collectio*, 9 vols., Paris, 1724–33.

Matthew, D. J. A., *The Norman Monasteries and their English possessions*, Oxford, 1962.

Mayr-Harting, H., *The Bishops of Chichester, 1075–1207: biographical notes and problems*, The Chichester Papers, XL, Chichester, 1963.

—— 'Henry II and the papacy, 1170–1189', *Journal of Ecclesiastical History*, XVI (1965), 39–53.

—— 'Hilary, bishop of Chichester (1147–69) and Henry II', *EHR*, LXXVIII (1963), 209–24.

MB: *Materials for the History of Thomas Becket, Archbishop of Canterbury...*, ed. J. C. Robertson and J. B. Sheppard, 7 vols., RS, 1875–85.

*MB Epp.: ibid.* vols. V–VII, letters cited by number.

*Memorials of St Edmund's Abbey*, ed. T. Arnold, 3 vols., RS, 1890–6.

*MGH: Monumenta Germaniae Historica* (see also Gerhoh).

*Miracula S. Nectani martyris*, ed. P. Grosjean, S.J., *Analecta Bollandiana*, LXXI (1953), 405–14.

*Misc. D. M. Stenton: A Medieval Miscellany for Doris Mary Stenton*, ed. P. M. Barnes and C. F. Slade, PRS, LXXVI, London, 1962.

*MLWL: Revised Medieval Latin Word-List from British and Irish Sources*, ed. R. E. Latham, London, 1965.

*Mon., Monasticon:* W. Dugdale, *Monasticon Anglicanum*, rev. edn by J. Caley, H. Ellis and B. Bandinel, 6 vols. in 8, London 1817–30, repr. 1846 (*Monasticon* I edn = 1st edn, 3 vols., London, 1655–73).

Montfaucon, B. de, *Bibliotheca bibliothecarum manuscriptorum nova*, 2 vols., Paris, 1739.

Morant: Morant, P., *The History and Antiquities of the County of Essex*, 2 vols., London, 1768, repr. Chelmsford, 1816.

Morant, *Colchester:* Morant, P., *The History and Antiquities of...Colchester*, London, 1768, repr. Chelmsford, 1816.

Morey: Morey, Dom Adrian, *Bartholomew of Exeter, Bishop and Canonist*, Cambridge, 1937.

—— 'Canonist evidence in the case of St William of York', *CHJ*, x, iii (1952), 352–3.

—— and Brooke, C. N. L., 'The Cerne Letters of Gilbert Foliot and the Legation of Imar of Tusculum', *EHR*, LXIII (1948), 523–7.

Mortet, V., *Maurice de Sully, évêque de Paris*, Paris, 1890.

Narducci, E., *Catalogus codicum manuscriptorum praeter orientales qui in Bibliotheca Alexandrina Romae adservantur*, Rome, 1877.

*New Palaeographical Society, Facsimiles of Ancient Manuscripts*, First Series, II, London, 1912.

Newcourt: Newcourt, R., *Repertorium ecclesiasticum parochiale Londinense*, 2 vols., London, 1708–10.

Norman Moore: Moore, Sir Norman, *The History of St Bartholomew's Hospital*, 2 vols., London, 1918.

Nott, J., *Some of the Antiquities of 'Moche Malverne'*, Malvern, 1885.

*Novel.: Novellae*, see *Corpus Iuris Civilis*.

*Obituaires de la province de Sens*, ed. A. Molinier, A. Longnon *et al.*, I– , Recueil des Historiens de la France: *Obituaires*, I– , Paris, 1902– .

Odo of Deuil, *De profectione Ludovici VII in orientem*, ed. V. G. Berry, New York, 1948.

Orderic: *Orderici Vitalis...Historiae Ecclesiasticae Libri Tredecim*, ed. A. Le Prevost and L. Delisle, Société de l'Histoire de France, 5 vols., Paris, 1838–55.

*Osbert de Clare, prior of Westminster, The Letters of*, ed. E. W. Williamson, with an introduction by J. Armitage Robinson, London, 1929.

—— 'La vie de S. Édouard le Confesseur par Osbert de Clare', ed. M. Bloch, *Analecta Bollandiana*, XLI (1923), 5–131.

Ott, I., 'Der Regalienbegriff im 12. Jahrhundert', *ZRG, Kan. Abt.* XXXV (1948), 234–304.

*Oxford Charters: Facsimiles of Early Charters in Oxford Muniment Rooms*, ed. H. E. Salter, Oxford, 1929.

Painter, S., *William Marshall*, Baltimore, 1933.

Perkins, V. R., 'Documents relating to the Cistercian monastery of St Mary, Kingswood', *Transactions of the Bristol and Glos. Archaeological Society*, XXII (1899), 176–256.

Peter of Blois, *Epp.: Epistolae*, in *PL*, CCVII, 1–560.

Peter of Celle, *De panibus*, in *PL*, CCII, 927–1046.

Peter the Lombard, *Sententiae*, in *PL*, CXCII, 519–964.

*Petrus Venerabilis, 1156–1956: Studies and texts commemorating the eighth centenary of his death*, ed. G. Constable and J. Kritzeck, Studia Anselmiana, XL, Rome, 1956.

PL: *Patrologiae cursus completus, series Latina*, ed. J. P. Migne, 221 vols., Paris, 1844–64.

*PN Essex*: P. H. Reaney, *The Place-names of Essex*, English Place-name Society, XII, Cambridge, 1935.

*PN Glos:* A. H. Smith, *The Place-names of Gloucestershire*, 4 parts, Cambridge, 1964–5.

*PN Herts:* J. E. B. Gover, A. Mawer and F. M. Stenton, *The Place-names of Hertfordshire, ibid.* xv, 1938.

*PN Middlesex:* idem, *The Place-names of Middlesex, apart from the city of London, ibid.* xviii, 1942.

*PN Worcs:* A. Mawer and F. M. Stenton, *The Place-names of Worcestershire, ibid.* iv, 1927.

Pollock, F. and Maitland, F. W., *The History of English Law before the time of Edward I*, 2nd edn, 2 vols., Cambridge, 1898.

*Pontifical of Magdalen College, The*, ed. H. A. Wilson, Henry Bradshaw Society, xxxix, 1910.

Poole, A. L., *From Domesday Book to Magna Carta*, Oxford History of England, iii, Oxford, 1951.

Poole, R. L., *Studies in Chronology and History*, ed. A. L. Poole, Oxford, 1934.

Poupardin, R., 'Dix-huit lettres inédites d'Arnoul de Lisieux', *Bibliothèque de l'École des Chartes*, lxiii (1902), 352–73, 769.

Pouzet, P., *L'Anglais Jean dit Bellesmains...*, Lyon, 1927.

*PR: Pipe Roll*, cited by regnal year, ed. in PRS.

PRS: Pipe Roll Society, London, 1884– .

*PUE: Papsturkunden in England*, ed. W. Holtzmann, 3 vols., Abhandlungen der Gesellschaft der Wissenschaften in Göttingen, phil.-hist. Klasse, Berlin, Göttingen, i = neue Folge xxv (1930–1), ii = 3. Folge xiv–xv (1935–6), iii = 3. Folge xxxiii (1952).

Rathbone, E., 'John of Cornwall: A brief biography', *Recherches de théologie ancienne et médiévale*, xvii (1950), 46–60.

(Rawlinson, R.), *The History and Antiquities of the cathedral church of Hereford*, London, 1717.

*Records of Merton Priory, The*, ed. A. C. Heales, London, 1898.

*Recueil d'annales angevines et vendômoises*, ed. L. Halphen, Collection de Textes, xxxvii, Paris, 1903.

*Red Book of the Exchequer, The*, ed. H. Hall, 3 vols., RS, 1896.

*Reg.: Register.*

*Reg. Cantilupe: Registrum Thome de Cantilupo...*, ed. R. G. Griffiths and W. W. Capes, Cantilupe Society and Canterbury and York Society, 1906–7.

*Reg. Caroli Bothe: Registrum Caroli Bothe...*, ed. A. T. Bannister, Cantilupe Society and Canterbury and York Society, 1921.

*Reg. G. Giffard: Register of Bishop Godfrey Giffard...*, ed. J. W. Willis Bund, 2 vols., Worcestershire Historical Society, 1902.

*Reg. Hulme: St Benet of Holme, 1020–1210: the Eleventh and Twelfth Century Sections of...the Register of the Abbey of St Benet of Holme*, ed. J. R. West, 2 vols., Norfolk Record Society, ii–iii, 1932.

*Reg. Lichfield: The Great Register of Lichfield Cathedral known as Magnum registrum album*, ed. H. E. Savage, William Salt Archaeological Society, 1924 (1926).

*Reg. Lincoln: The Registrum antiquissimum of the Cathedral Church of Lincoln*, ed. C. W. Foster and K. Major, I– , Lincoln Record Society, 1931– .

*Reg. Malmesbury: Registrum Malmesburiense*, ed. J. S. Brewer, 2 vols., RS, 1879–80.

*Reg. Regum Scottorum*, I: *Regesta Regum Scottorum*, I: *The Acts of Malcolm IV King of Scots, 1153–1165...*, ed. G. W. S. Barrow, Edinburgh, 1960.

*Reg. Roffense: Registrum Roffense...*, ed. J. Thorpe, London, 1769.

*Reg. St Osmund: Vetus registrum Sarisberiense alias dictum registrum S. Osmundi episcopi...*, ed. W. H. R. Jones, 2 vols., RS, 1883–4.

*Reg. Simonis de Sudbiria: Registrum Simonis de Sudbiria, diocesis Londoniensis...*, ed. R. C. Fowler, C. Jenkins and S. C. Ratcliffe, 2 vols., Canterbury and York Society, 1927–38.

*Reg. Stapledon: The Register of Walter de Stapledon...*, ed. F. C. Hingeston-Randolph, London, 1892.

*Reg. Swinfield: Registrum Ricardi de Swinfield...*, ed. W. W. Capes, Cantilupe Society and Canterbury and York Society, 1909.

*Regesta Regum Anglo-Normannorum*, II, *Registrum Henrici primi*, ed. C. Johnson and H. A. Cronne from the collections of...H. W. C. Davis, Oxford, 1956.

'The Register of Master David': Z. N. Brooke, 'The Register of Master David of London, and the part he played in the Becket crisis', in *Essays in History presented to Reginald Lane Poole*, ed. H. W. C. Davis, Oxford, 1927, pp. 227–45.

*Rep.: HMC, Ninth Report, Appendix*, I: including H. C. Maxwell-Lyte's report on the MSS of the Dean and Chapter of St Paul's.

Richardson, H. G., 'The letters and charters of Eleanor of Aquitaine', *EHR*, LXXIV (1959), 193–213.

Richardson and Sayles: Richardson, H. G., and Sayles, G. O., *The Governance of Mediaeval England from the Conquest to Magna Carta*, Edinburgh, 1963.

Robertson, J. C., *Becket, Archbishop of Canterbury*, London, 1859.

Robinson, J. Armitage, *Somerset Historical Essays*, British Academy, London, 1921.

Robson, C. A., *Maurice of Sully and the Medieval Vernacular Homily*, Oxford, 1952.

Round, J. H., *The Commune of London, and other Studies*, Westminster, 1899.

—— 'The early sheriffs of Norfolk', *EHR*, XXXV (1920), 481–96.

—— 'The families of St John and of Port' *and* 'The Ports of Basing and their priory', *Genealogist*, New Series, XVI (1900), 1–13; XVIII (1902), 137–9.

—— *Geoffrey de Mandeville: a Study of the Anarchy*, London, 1892.

—— 'The origin of the Stewarts and their Chesney connexion', *Genealogist*, New Series, XVIII (1902), 1–16.

—— *Studies in Peerage and Family History*, Westminster, 1901.

Salter, H. E., 'Geoffrey of Monmouth and Oxford', *EHR*, XXXIV (1919), 382–5.

—— 'Two Lincoln documents of 1147', *EHR*, XXXV (1920), 212–14.

Saltman: Saltman, A., *Theobald Archbishop of Canterbury*, University of London Historical Studies, II, London, 1956.

—— 'Two early collections of the Becket correspondence and of other documents', *BIHR*, XXII (1949), 152–7.

*Sarum Charters: Charters and documents illustrating the history of the cathedral, city and diocese of Salisbury, in the twelfth and thirteenth centuries*, ed. W. (H.) R. Jones and W. D. Macray, RS, 1891.

Sauvage, R. N., *L'abbaye de St-Martin de Troarn...*, Mémoires de la Société des Antiquaires de Normandie, XXXIV, Caen, 1911.

Scammell, G. V., *Hugh du Puiset, bishop of Durham*, Cambridge, 1956.

Scholz, B. W., 'The canonization of Edward the Confessor', *Speculum*, XXXVI (1961), 38–60.

Schönsteiner, F. 'Die Collectio Claustroneoburgensis', *Jahrbuch des Stiftes Klosterneuburg*, II (1909), 1–154.

Schramm, P. E., *A History of the English Coronation*, Oxford, 1937.

Scott, J. R., 'Charters of Monks Horton priory', *Archaeologia Cantiana*, X (1876), 269–81.

*SEBC*: Chadwick, N. K., Hughes, K., Brooke, C. and Jackson, K., *Studies in the early British Church*, Cambridge, 1958.

'Sempringham, Charters relating to the priory of', ed. E. M. Poynton, *Genealogist*, New Series, XV (1899), 158–227 *passim*; XVI (1900), 30–228 *passim*; XVII (1901), 29–239 *passim*.

Smalley, B., 'Andrew of St Victor, Abbot of Wigmore: a twelfth-century Hebraist', *Recherches de théologie ancienne et médiévale*, X (1938), 358–73.

—— *The Study of the Bible in the Middle Ages*, 2nd edn, Oxford, 1952.

Southern, R. W., 'The Canterbury forgeries', *EHR*, LXXIII (1958), 193–226.

—— *St Anselm and his Biographer: a Study of Monastic Life and Thought, 1059–c. 1130*, Cambridge, 1963.

*Statuta Capitulorum Generalium Ordinis Cisterciensis, 1116–1786*, ed. J. M. Canivez, 8 vols., Bibliothèque de *la Revue d'Histoire Ecclésiastique*, IX–XIV B, Louvain, 1933–41.

Stubbs, W., *Registrum Sacrum Anglicanum: an attempt to exhibit the course of episcopal succession in England from the records and chronicles of the Church*, 2nd edn, Oxford, 1897.

Swynnerton, C., 'The priory of St Leonard of Stanley, Co. Gloucester, in the light of recent discoveries, documentary and structural', *Archaeologia*, LXXI (1921), 199–226.

Tanner, T., *Notitia monastica...*, London, 1744; ed. J. Nasmith, Cambridge, 1787.

*Taxatio: Taxatio ecclesiastica Angliae et Walliae auctoritate P. Nicholai IV, circa A.D. 1291*, Record Commission, London, 1802.

Thomas of Elmham, *Historia monasterii S. Augustini Cantuariensis*, ed. C. Hardwick, RS, 1858.

Thomas, W., *Antiquitates prioratus Majoris Malverne...*, London, 1725.

Thorne, William, *Chronica de rebus gestis abbatum sancti Augustini Cantuariae*, ed. R. Twysden, *Historiae Anglicanae Scriptores X*, London, 1652, cols. 1753–2202.

Tillmann: Tillmann, H., *Die päpstlichen Legaten in England bis zur Beendigung der Legation Gualas (1218)*, Bonn, 1926.

*TLL: Thesaurus linguae latinae*, ed. auctoritate et consilio Academiarum quinque Germanicarum..., I– , Leipzig, 1900– .

Torigny: *The Chronicle of Robert of Torigny* in *Chrons. of the reigns of Stephen etc.* IV (also ed. Delisle, L., 2 vols., Société de l'Histoire de Normandie, Rouen, 1872–3).

*UGQ: Ungedruckte anglo-normannische Geschichtsquellen*, ed. F. Liebermann, Strassburg, 1879.

Ullmann, W., *The Growth of Papal Government in the Middle Ages*, London, 1955.

—— 'Nos si aliquid incompetenter...', *Ephemerides Iuris Canonici*, IX (1953), 279–87.

Vacarius, *The Liber Pauperum of*, ed. F. de Zulueta, Selden Society, XLIV, 1927.

*Valor: Valor Ecclesiasticus temp. Henr. VIII...*, ed. J. Caley and J. Hunter, 6 vols., Record Commission, 1810–34.

*VCH: Victoria County Histories*, e.g. the following:

*VCH Glos* II: *The Victoria History of the County of Gloucester*, II, ed. W. Page, London, 1907.

*VCH Hants: The Victoria History of the County of Hampshire*, ed. W. Page, 5 vols., Westminster and London, 1900–12.

*VCH Herts: The Victoria History of the County of Hertford*, ed. W. Page, 4 vols., Westminster and London, 1902–14.

*VCH Lincs* II: *The Victoria History of the County of Lincoln*, II, ed. W. Page, London, 1906.

*VCH Wilts: The Victoria History of the County of Wiltshire*, ed. R. B. Pugh and E. Crittall, I– , London, 1953– .

Vetulani, A. 'Gratien et le droit romain', *Revue historique de droit français et étranger*, 4th series, XXIV–XXV (1946–7), 11–48.

—— 'Le Décret de Gratien et les premiers décrétistes à la lumière d'une source nouvelle', *Studia Gratiana*, VII, Bologna, 1959, pp. 275–353.

*VN: The Valuation of Norwich*, ed. W. E. Lunt, Oxford, 1926.

Voss, L., *Heinrich von Blois, Bischof von Winchester, 1129–71*, Historische Studien, CCX, Berlin, 1932.

Walberg, E., *La tradition hagiographique de S. Thomas Becket*, Paris, 1929.

Walker, D., 'Charters of the earldom of Hereford', in *Camden Miscellany*, XXII, Camden 4th series, I, London, 1964, pp. 1–75.

—— 'The "Honours" of the earls of Hereford in the Twelfth Century', *Transactions of the Bristol and Gloucestershire Archaeological Society*, LXXIX (1960–1), 174–211.

—— 'Miles of Gloucester, earl of Hereford', *ibid.* LXXVII (1958–9), 66–84.

Walther, *Initia*: Walther, H., *Initia Carminum ac Versuum Medii Aevi posterioris latinorum*, *Carmina Medii Aevi posterioris latina*, I, Göttingen, 1959.

—— *Proverbia sententiaeque Latinitatis Medii Aevi*, *ibid.* II, Göttingen, 1963.

Westlake, H. F., *Hornchurch Priory: a kalendar of documents in the possession of the Warden and Fellows of New College, Oxford*, London, 1923.

White, G. H., 'The career of Waleran, Count of Meulan and Earl of Worcester', *Transactions of the Royal Historical Society*, 4th series, XVII (1934), 19–48.

—— 'King Stephen's earldoms', *ibid.* XIII (1930), 51–82.

Wilkins: Wilkins, D., *Concilia Magnae Britanniae et Hiberniae...*, 4 vols., London, 1737.

William of Newburgh: *Chrons. of the reigns of Stephen etc.* I, II; also *Guilielmi Neubrigensis Historia sive Chronica Rerum Anglicarum*, ed. T. Hearne, 3 vols., Oxford, 1719 (for the *Historia* of Holy Trinity Priory, Aldgate, printed as an Appendix).

Williams, W. W., *St Bernard of Clairvaux*, Manchester, 1935.

Willis, Browne, *The History of the Mitred Parliamentary Abbeys, etc.*, 2 vols., London, 1718–19.

WMHN: *The Historia Novorum of William of Malmesbury*, ed. and translated K. Potter, NMT, 1955.

Wood, Susan, *English Monasteries and their Patrons in the Thirteenth Century*, Oxford, 1955.

Woodruff, C. E., 'Some early professions of canonical obedience to the see of Canterbury', *Transactions of the St Paul's Ecclesiological Society*, VII (1911–15), 161–76.

*Wulfric of Haselbury, by John, abbot of Ford*, ed. M. Bell, Somerset Record Society, XLVII, 1933.

ZRG, Kan. Abt.: *Zeitschrift der Savigny-Stiftung für Rechtsgeschichte, Kanonistische Abteilung*.

# MANUSCRIPTS CITED BY INITIALS

| | |
|---|---|
| A | Rome, Biblioteca Alessandrina, 120 |
| Ar | BM Arundel 219 |
| B | Bodl. E Musaeo 249 (27835) |
| Bn | Paris, Bibliothèque Nationale, Lat. 5320 |
| C | BM Cotton Claudius B. ii |
| Co | Cambridge, Corpus Christi College, 295 |
| D | Bodl. Douce 287 (21861) |
| Da, Db | BM Cotton Domitian A. x |
| Du | Bodl. Dugdale 11 (6501) |
| E | Cambridge, Trinity College, O. 2. 1 |
| Eh | BM Harleian 3763 |
| Ev | BM Cotton Vespasian B. xxiv |
| F | Ely, Dean and Chapter, MS of *Liber Eliensis* |
| G | BM Cotton Titus A. i |
| Ga, Gb | PRO C150/Cart. Gloucester |
| Gh | BM Harleian 662 |
| Gl | Gloucester Cathedral, Reg. B |
| Gr | London, Guildhall Library, MS 9531, vol. 6, Reg. Gilbert |
| H | Hereford Cathedral Library, P. i. 15 |
| Ha | BM Harleian 215 |
| Hi | Hereford, Dean and Chapter Muniments, no. 2777 |
| Ia | London, Lambeth Palace Library, 136 |
| Ib | Bodl. 937 (3088) |
| Ic | Bodl. Rawlinson Q. f. 8 (27836) |
| Id | Bodl. 509 (2672) |
| Ie | Bodl. Laud Misc. 666 (1051) |
| Ja | Oxford, St John's College, 126 |
| Jb | Oxford, St John's College, 15 |
| K | Hereford Diocesan Registry, Reg. Cantelupe |
| Ka, Kb, Kc, Kd | Cambridge, King's College, Muniments, B17, B18, B19, B15 |
| Kn, Ko | BM Cotton Nero E. vi |
| L | BM Cotton Domitian A. iii |
| Li | Dom Lenoir MS XXIII (see no. 331) |
| M | Cambridge University Library, Ely Diocesan Muniments, Liber M |
| N | BM Egerton 3031 |
| Na | BM Cotton Vespasian E. xxv |
| Nb | BM Harleian 1708 |
| O | Cambridge, Trinity Hall, 24 |
| Ob | Bodl. Laud Misc. 647 (1595) |

| | |
|---|---|
| Pa, Pb | BM Cotton Claudius D. x |
| Pr | PRO E40/14395 |
| Qa, Qb | Hereford Diocesan Registry, Reg. Swinfield |
| R | BM Royal 8 A. xxi |
| Rb | BM Royal 13 A. xiii |
| Rc, Rd | Bodl. Rawlinson B 329 (11668) |
| S | Bodl. Carte 108 (10553) |
| Sa, Sb, Sc | BM Harleian 3697 |
| Sd | Gloucester Cathedral, Seals and Documents, viii, 1 |
| T | BM Harleian 6976 |
| U | BM Cotton Faustina A. iii |
| Va | Vatican Lat. 6024 |
| Vb | Vatican Lat. 1220 |
| W | Westminster Abbey, Domesday Cartulary |
| Wa | Wells Cathedral, Dean and Chapter Muniments, Liber Albus I |
| Wb, Wc | *Ibid.*, Liber Albus II |
| Wd | London, St Paul's Cathedral Library, MS W.D. 1 |
| X, Y, Z | Oxford, Balliol College, 271 |
| Za, Zb | BM Harleian 4015 |

# LIST OF OTHER ABBREVIATIONS

Ann.          Annals
Biog. Index   Biographical Index (to this book, p. 530)
BM            British Museum
Bodl.         The Bodleian Library, Oxford
Cart.         Cartulary (or Chartulary)
Chron.        Chronicle
dep.          dependency
*Ep(p)*.        *Epistola(e)*, letter(s) (citing by number in a printed
                  letter collection)
*MGH*           *Monumenta Germaniae Historica*
NMT           Nelson's Medieval Texts
PRO           Public Record Office
Reg.          Register
RS            Rolls Series
trs.          transcript

# TABLE A

The first number refers to the editions of Giles and Migne; the second to the present edition.

| | | | | | |
|---|---|---|---|---|---|
| 1 | 64 | 45 | 42 | 89 | 349 |
| 2 | 2 | 46 | 58 | 90 | 106 |
| 3 | 22 | 47 | 59 | 91 | 92 |
| 4 | 5 | 48 | 60 | 92 | 53 |
| 5 | 23 | 49 | 11 | 93 | 84 |
| 6 | 24 | 50 | 54 | 94 | 102 |
| 7 | 25 | 51 | 17 | 95 | 99 |
| 8 | 14 | 52 | 63 | 96 | 85 |
| 9 | 6 | 53 | 18 | 97 | 67 |
| 10 | 28 | 54 | 20 | 98 | 34 |
| 11 | 31 | 55 | 73 | 99 | 86 |
| 12 | 7 | 56 | 70 | 100 | 117 |
| 13 | 38 | 57 | 15 | 101 | 118 |
| 14 | 32 | 58 | 29 | 102 | 119 |
| 15 | 39 | 59 | 30 | 103 | 90 |
| 16 | 45 | 60 | 12 | 104 | 97 |
| 17 | 67 | 61 | 71 | 105 | 98 |
| 18 | 34 | 62 | 19 | 106 | 104 |
| 19 | 43 | 63 | 68 | 107 | 89 |
| 20 | 46 | 64 | 13 | 108 | 91 |
| 21 | 44 | 65 | —[1] | 109 | 128 |
| 22 | 65 | 66 | 3 | 110 | 129 |
| 23 | 66 | 67 | 50 | 111 | 130 |
| 24 | 8 | 68 | 72 | 112 | 108 |
| 25 | 36 | 69 | 61 | 113 | 112 |
| 26 | 9 | 70 | —[1] | 114 | 127 |
| 27 | 4 | 71 | 16 | 115 | 125 |
| 28 | 47 | 72 | 62 | 116 | 126 |
| 29 | 10 | 73 | 78 | 117 | 124 |
| 30 | 40 | 74 | 69 | 118 | 120 |
| 31 | 33 | 75 | 74 | 119 | 139 |
| 32 | 49 | 76 | 75 | 120 | 140 |
| 33 | 48 | 77 | 76 | 121 | 123 |
| 34 | 27 | 78 | 77 | 122 | 314 |
| 35 | 21 | 79 | 26 | 123 | —[1] |
| 36 | 37 | 80 | 116 | 124 | 131 |
| 37 | 41 | 81 | 1 | 125 | 321 |
| 38 | 51 | 82 | 82 | 126 | 135 |
| 39 | 56 | 83 | 79 | 127 | 137 |
| 40 | 87 | 84 | 83 | 128 | 132 |
| 41 | 35 | 85 | 114 | 129 | 294 |
| 42 | 57 | 86 | 115 | 130 | 101 |
| 43 | 55 | 87 | 80 | 131 | 94 |
| 44 | 52 | 88 | 81 | 132 | 122 |

| | | | | | |
|---|---|---|---|---|---|
| 133 | 103 | 186 | 326 | 239 | 459 |
| 134 | 88 | 187 | 396 | 240 | 191 |
| 135 | 93 | 188 | 418 | 241 | 217 |
| 136 | 107 | 189 | 472 | 242 | 180 |
| 137 | 109 | 190 | 473 | 243 | 199 |
| 138 | 95 | 191 | 425 | 244 | 234 |
| 139 | 121 | 192 | 377 | 245 | 206 |
| 140 | 100 | 193 | 148 | 246 | 258 |
| 141 | 111 | 194 | 170 | 247 | 208 |
| 142 | 96 | 195 | 198 | 248 | 239 |
| 143 | 105 | 196 | 260 | 249 | 157 |
| 144 | 110 | 197 | 230 and App. VI, 5 | 250 | 158 |
| 145 | 142 | 198 | 262 | 251 | 238 |
| 146 | 141 | 199 | 197 | 252 | 242 |
| 147 | 143 | 200 | 254 | 253 | 243 |
| 148 | 133 | 201 | 249 | 254 | 134 |
| 149 | 146 | 202 | 250 | 255 | 253 |
| 150 | 179 | 203 | 264 | 256 | 187 |
| 151 | 149 | 204 | 257 | 257 | 147 |
| 152 | 251 | 205 | 154 | 258 | 192 |
| 153 | 247 | 206 | 266 | 259 | 355 |
| 154 | 212 | 207 | 256 | 260 | 241 |
| 155 | 218 | 208 | 231 | 261 | 237 |
| 156 | 214 | 209 | 204 | 262 | 205 |
| 157 | 233 | 210 | 375 | 263 | 232 |
| 158 | 221 | 211 | 227 | 264 | 267 |
| 159 | 213 | 212 | 272 | 265 | 152 |
| 160 | 222 | 213 | 176 | 266 | 229 |
| 161 | 150 | 214 | 259 and App. VI, 7 | 267 | 175 |
| 162 | 161 | 215 | 145 | 268 | 201 |
| 163 | 246 | 216 | 188 | 269 | 220 |
| 164 | 162 | 217 | 189 | 270 | 244 |
| 165 | 185 | 218 | 268 | 271 | 177 |
| 166 | 245 | 219 | 252 | 272 | 178 |
| 167 | 193 | 220 | 172 | 273 | 171 |
| 168 | 223 | 221 | 173 | 274 | 169 |
| 169 | 224 | 222 | 113 | 275 | 168 |
| 170 | 225 | 223 | 209 | 276 | 201 |
| 171 | 228 | 224 | 353 | 277 | 203 |
| 172 | 156 | 225 | 452 | 278 | 151 |
| 173 | 183 | 226 | 382 | 279 | 194 |
| 174 | 155 | 227 | 437 | 280 | 196 |
| 175 | 200 | 228 | 428 | 281 | 195 |
| 176 | 160 | 229 | 366 | 282 | 163 |
| 177 | 215 | 230 | 423 | 283 | 190 |
| 178 | 226 | 231 | 350 | 284 | 261 |
| 179 | 219 | 232 | 474 | 285 | 159 |
| 180 | 255 | 233 | 449 | 286 | 174 |
| 181 | 153 | 234 | 413 | 287 | —[1] |
| 182 | 471 | 235 | 390 | 288 | 273 |
| 183 | 418 | 236 | 352 | 289 | App. VI, 1 |
| 184 | 184 | 237 | 386 | 290 | 274 |
| 185 | 383 | 238 | 235 | 291 | 136 |

| | | | | | |
|---|---|---|---|---|---|
| 292 | 230 | 305 | 424 | 323 | 414 |
| 293 | 252 | 306 | 475 | 324 | App. VI, 22 |
| 294 | App. VI, 3–4 | 307 | 476 | 325 | 469 |
| 295 | 275 | 308 | 281 | 326 | 436 |
| 296 | 397 | 309 | 419 | 327 | 363 |
| 297 | 263 | 310 | App. VI, 14 | 328 | App. VI, 23 |
| 298 | 276 | 311 | 282 | 329 | 270 |
| 299 | 265 and App. VI, 5 | 312 | 450 | 330 | 269 |
| 300 | 277 | 313 | 236 | | .............. |
| 301 | 278 | 314 | 448 | 363 | 164 |
| 302 | 279 | 315, 316 | App. VI, 15, 16 | 375 | 186 |
| 303 | App. VI, 7–13 | 317 | 283 | 412 | 144 |
| 304 | 280 | 318–22 | App. VI, 17–21 | 471 | 207 |

[1] Giles nos. 65, 70, 123, 287 (see pp. xxxvii–xxxix, xlix–l nn. 1, 2, 3, 6) are not printed in this edition; Giles nos. 331–520 are not letters of Gilbert Foliot (for many of these, see Table B).

ANALYSIS OF MS BODL. E MUSAEO 249 (B)

The number in the first column is written in B in a nineteenth-century hand (possibly Giles's)—with a few later corrections—and was used in Giles's concordance; it is therefore convenient to retain it, although the numeration has several errors.

| B | | H | | R | | A | | No. in this edition | Date |
|---|---|---|---|---|---|---|---|---|---|
| No. | Folio | No. | Folio | No. | Folio | No. | Folio | | |
| *Hand II (Quire I)* | | | | (SECTION I) | | | | | |
| 1 | 1 | (1) | 147 | (lost) | | — | | 1 | 1140 |
| 2 | 2 | (2) | 147v | (1 | 205v) | (1) | 123 | 2 | 1140 |
| 3 | 2v | (3) | 148 | 2 | 206 | (2) | 123v | 22 | 1143 |
| 4 | 3 | (4) | 148v | 3 | 206 | (3) | 124v | 5 | 1139–48 |
| 5 | 3v | (5) | 149 | 4 | 206v | (4) | 125 | 23 | 1143 |
| 6 | 3v | (6) | 149v | 5 | 206v | (5) | 125 | 24 | 1143 |
| 7 | 4 | (7) | 149v | 6 | 207 | (6) | 125v | 25 | 1143 |
| 8 | 4 | (8) | 149v | 7 | 207 | (7) | 125v | 14 | 1140–8 |
| 9 | 4v | (9) | 150 | — | | (8) | 126 | 6 | 1139–48 |
| 10 | 5v | (10) | 151 | — | | (9) | 127v | 26 | 1143–4 |
| 11 | 7v | (11) | 153 | 8 | 207 | (10) | 130v | 28 | 1144–8 |
| 12 | 8 | — | | 9 | 207v | (11) | 131 | 31 | 1144–5 |
| 13 | 8v | (14) | 153v | 10 | 207v | (12) | 131v | 7 | 1139–48 |
| 14 | 8v | (15) | 154 | 11 | 208 | (13) | 132 | 38 | 1144–5 |
| *(Quire) Ius (in 14)* | | | | | | | | | |
| *(Quire II)* | | | | | | | | | |
| 15 | 9 | (16) | 154 | 12 | 208 | (14) | 132v | 32 | *c.* 1144–5 |
| 16 | 9v | (17) | 154v | 13 | 208 | (15) | 133 | 39 | 1145 |
| 17 | 10 | — | | 14 | 208v | (16) | 133v | 45 | 1145 |
| 18 (also 316) | 10 | — | | 15 | 208v | (17) | 133v | 67 | ?1145–8 |
| 19 (also 317) | 10v | — | | 16 | 209 | (18) | 134 | 34 | 1145 |
| 19* | 10v | — | | 17 | 209 | (19) | 134v | 43 | 1145 |
| 20 | 10v | — | | 18 | 209 | (20) | 134v | 46 | 1145 |
| 21 | 11 | — | | 19 | 209 | (21) | 134v | 44 | 1145 |
| 22 | 11 | — | | 20 | 209 | (22) | 135 | 65 | prob. 1145–8 |
| 23 | 11 | — | | 21 | 209v | (23) | 135 | 66 | prob. 1145–8 |
| 24 | 11v | — | | 22 | 209v | (24) | 135v | 8 | 1139–48 |
| 25 | 12 | — | | 23 | 209v | (25) | 136 | 36 | 1145–7 (?1145) |
| 26 | 12 | — | | 24 | 210 | (26) | 136 | 9 | 1139–48 |
| 27 | 12v | — | | 25 | 210 | (27) | 136v | 4 | prob. 1139–45 |
| 28 | 12v | — | | 26 | 210 | (28) | 137 | 47 | 1145 |

| B | | H | | R | | A | | No. in this edition | Date |
|---|---|---|---|---|---|---|---|---|---|
| No. | Folio | No. | Folio | No. | Folio | No. | Folio | | |
| 29 | 13 | — | | 27 | 210v | (29) | 137v | 10 | 1139–48 |
| 30 | 13 | — | | 28 | 210v | (30) | 137v | 40 | 1145 |
| 31 | 13v | — | | 29 | 210v | (31) | 138 | 33 | 1143–5 |
| 32 | 13v | — | | 30 | 211 | (32) | 138 | 49 | 1145–6 |
| 33 | 14v | (12) | 153 | 31 | 211v | (33) | 139 | 48 | 1145 |
| 34 | 15 | (13) | 153v | 32 | 211v | (34) | 140 | 27 | 1144–6 |
| 35 | 15v | — | | 34 | 212 | (35) | 140v | 37 | 1145–7 (?1145) |
| 36 | 15v | — | | 33 | 212 | (36) | 140v | 21 | 1143–8 |
| 37 | 16 | — | | — | | (37) | 141 | 35 | 1145 |
| 38 | 16 | — | | 35 | 212 | (38) | 141 | 41 | 1145 |
| 39 | 16v | — | | — | | (39) | 141v | 57 | ?1146 |

(Quire) IIus (in 39)

(Quire III)

| B | | H | | R | | A | | No. in this edition | Date |
|---|---|---|---|---|---|---|---|---|---|
| 40 | 17 | — | | 36 | 212v | (40) | 142 | 51 | 1145–6 |
| 41 | 17 | — | | — | | (41) | 142v | 55 | 1146 |
| 42 | 17 | — | | 37 | 212v | (42) | 142v | 56 | 1146 |
| 43 | 17v | — | | — | | (43) | 143 | 52 | 1145–6 |
| 44 | 18 | — | | — | | (44) | 143v | 42 | 1145 |
| 45 | 18 | — | | 40 | 212v | (45) | 144 | 58 | ?1146 |
| 46 | 18v | — | | — | | (46) | 144 | 59 | ?1146 |
| 47 | 18v | — | | — | | (47) | 144 | 60 | ?1146 |
| 48 | 18v | — | | — | | (48) | 144v | 11 | 1139–48 |
| (also 75) | | | | | | | | | |
| 49 | 18v | — | | — | | (49) | 144v | 54 | 1146 |
| 50 | 19 | — | | — | | (50) | 145 | 82 | 1148–53 |
| 51 | 19 | — | | — | | (51) | 145 | 79 | prob. 1148 |
| 52 | 19v | — | | — | | (52) | 145v | 83 | 1148–53 |
| 53 | 19v | — | | — | | (53) | 146 | 114 | 1148–63 |
| 54 | 20 | — | | — | | (54) | 146 | 115 | 1148–63 |
| 55 | 20 | — | | — | | (55) | 146v | 80 | 1148 |
| 56 | 20v | — | | — | | (56) | 147 | 81 | 1148 |
| 57 | 20v | — | | 38 | 212v | (57) | 147 | 87 | prob. 1148–54 |
| 58 | 21 | — | | 39 | 212v | (58) | 147v | 116 | 1148–63 |
| 59 | 21 | — | | — | | (59) | 147v | 349 | c. 1148 |

| B | | A | | No. in this edition | Date |
|---|---|---|---|---|---|
| No. | Folio | No. | Folio | | |
| 60 | 21v | (60) | 148 | 106 | 1153 |
| 61 | 21v | (61) | 148 | 92 | prob. 1148–50 |
| 62 | 22 | (62) | 148v | 17 | 1142–8 |
| 63 | 22 | (63) | 149 | 63 | 1147–8 |
| 64 | 22v | (64) | 149v | 18 | 1142–8 |
| 65 | 23 | (65) | 149v | 20 | c. 1142–8 |
| 66 | 23 | (66) | 150 | 73 | c. 1147–8 |

| B | | A | | No. in this | |
|---|---|---|---|---|---|
| No. | Folio | No. | Folio | edition, etc. | Date |
| 67 | 23v | (67) | 150v | 70 | 1147 |
| 68 | 23v | (68) | 151 | 15 | 1140–8 |
| 69 | 24 | (69) | 151 | 29 | ?1144–8 |
| 70 | 24 | (70) | 151v | 30 | ?1144–8 |
| 71 | 24v | (71) | 151v | 12 | ?1139–48 |
| 72 | 24v | (72) | 152 | 71 | prob. 1147 |
| 73 | 24v | (73) | 152 | 19 | 1142–8 |

(*Quire III*)*us* (*in* 73)

(*Quire IV*)

| B | | A | | No. in this | |
|---|---|---|---|---|---|
| 74 | 25 | (74) | 152 | 53 | 1146 |
| 75 | 25 | (75) | 152v | 11 | 1139–48 |
| (also 48) | | | | | |
| 76 | 25v | (76) | 153 | 68 | ?1146–8 |
| 77 | 25v | (77) | 153 | 13 | 1139–48 |
| 78 | 26 | (78) | 153v | Giles no. 65[1] | 1143 |
| 79 | 26 | (79) | 153v | 3 | 1139–43 |
| 80 | 26v | (80) | 154 | 50 | 1145–6 |
| 81 | 26v | (81) | 154 | 72 | c. 1147–8 |
| 82 | 27 | (82) | 154v | 64 | 1148 |
| 83 | 27 | (83) | 155 | 61 | 1146 |
| 84 | 27v | (84) | 155 | Giles no. 70[2] | prob. 1147–8 |
| 85 | 27v | (85) | 155v | 16 | 1140–8 |
| 86 | 28 | (86) | 155v | 62 | 1147 |
| 87 | 28 | (87) | 156 | 78 | 1148 |
| 88 | 28 | (88) | 156 | 69 | 1147 |
| 89 | 28v | (89) | 156v | 74 | 1148 |
| 90 | 28v | (90) | 156v | 75 | 1148 |
| 91 | 29 | (91) | 157 | 76 | 1148 |
| 92 | 29 | (92) | 157 | 77 | 1148 |
| 93 | 29 | (93) | 157 | 117 | 1148–63 |
| 94 | 29v | (94) | 157v | 118 | 1148–63 |
| 95 | 29v | (95) | 157v | 119 | 1148–63 |
| 96 | 29v | (96) | 158 | 90 | prob. 1149–50 |
| 97 | 30 | (97) | 158 | 97 | 1150–3 |
| 98 | 30 | (98) | 158v | 98 | 1150–3 |
| 99 | 30v | (99) | 159 | 104 | 1153 |
| 100 | 30v | (100) | 159 | 89 | 1149–50 |
| 101 | 31 | (101) | 159v | 91 | c. 1149–50 |
| 102 | 31 | (102) | 159v | 128 | 1155–7 |
| 103 | 32 | (103) | 160v | 129 | 1155–7 |
| 104 | 32v | (104) | 161v | 130 | 1155–7 |

(*Quire*) IIII*us* (*in* 104; *fos.* 27, 30 *single sheets*)

(*Quire V*)

| B | | A | | No. in this | |
|---|---|---|---|---|---|
| 105 | 34 | (105) | 163 | 108 | 1153 |
| 106 | 35v | (106) | 165 | 112 | 1153–61 |
| 107 | 35v | — | | 127 | 1156 |
| (incomplete: half column blank) | | | | | |
| 108 | 36 | — | | 125 | 1154–63 |

| B | | D | No. in this | |
|---|---|---|---|---|
| No. | Folio | No. | edition, etc. | Date |
| 109 | 36 | — | 126 | c. 1160–3 |
| 110 | 36v | — | 124 | 1151–63 |
| 111 | 36v | — | 120 | 1148–63 |
| 112 | 37 | — | 139 | c. 1161–2 |
| 113 | 37 | — | 140 | 1162–3 |
| 114 | 37v | — | 123 | prob. 1148–50 *or* 1162–3 |
| 115 | 37v | — | 314 | 1148–63 |
| 116 | 38 | — | Giles no. 123[3] | 1143 |
| 117 | 38v | — | 321 | 1148–63 |
| 118 | 38v | — | 135 | 1161–2 |
| 119 | 39 | — | 137 | 1162 |
| 120 | 39 | — | 253 | 1163–c. 1180[4] |
| 121 | 39v | — | 172 | 1163–6 |
| 122 | 39v | — | 459 | 1163–c. 1180 |
| 123 | 40 | — | 159 | 1165 |
| 124 | 40v | — | 148 | 1163–4 |

*(Quire V)us (in 124)*

*(Quire VI)*

| | | | | |
|---|---|---|---|---|
| 125 | 41 | — | 353 | 1163–c. 1180 |
| 126 | 41 | — | 146 | 1163 |
| 127 | 41v | — | 160 | 1165 |
| 128 | 42v | — | 262 | 1163–c. 1180 |
| 129 | 42v | — | 179 | 1166–73 |
| 130 | 42v | — | 147 | c. 1163 |
| 131 | 43 | — | 149 | 1163 or shortly after |
| 132 | 43v | — | 251 | prob. 1174–81 |
| 133 | 43v | — | 197 | c. 1168–9 |
| 134 | 44 | — | 145 | 1163 |
| 135 | 44v | — | 255 | prob. 1163–84 |
| 136 | 44v | — | 174 | 1163–6 |
| 137 | 45 | — | 247 | 1163–81 |
| 138 | 45 | — | 195 | 1163–8 |
| 139 | 45v | — | 133 | 1160 |
| 140 | 47 | — | 261 | 1163–c. 1180 |
| 141 | 47 | — | 194 | 1163–8 |

*Hand V*

| | | | | |
|---|---|---|---|---|
| 142 | 47v | — | 141 | 1163 |
| 143 | 48 | 2, 26 | MB Epp. 37 | 1163 |
| 144 | 48v | — | 143 | 1163 |

*(Quire VIus in 144)*

*(Quire VII)*

| | | | | |
|---|---|---|---|---|
| 145 | 49 | — | 142 | 1163 |
| 146 | 49 | 6 | MB Epp. 93 | 1165 |
| 147[5] | 50 | 7 | 155 | 1165 |

| B | | D | No. in this | |
|---|---|---|---|---|
| No. | Folio | No. | edition, etc. | Date |
| 148 | 51 v | 8 | *MB Epp.* 106 | 1165 |
| (7 lines blank) | | | | |

*Hand IIa*

| | | | | |
|---|---|---|---|---|
| 149 | 52 v | 12 | 167 | 1166 |

*Hand IIb*

| | | | | |
|---|---|---|---|---|
| 150 | 53 v | 16 | *MB Epp.* 224 | 1166 |

*Hand I*

| | | | | |
|---|---|---|---|---|
| 151 | 55 | 45 | *MB Epp.* 486 | 1166 |
| 152 | 56 | 31 | 168 | 1166 |
| (a few lines blank) | | | | |

(Quire) *VIIus*

(Quire VIII)
*Hand VI:*

| | | | | |
|---|---|---|---|---|
| 153 | 57 | 10 | *MB Epp.* 198 | 1166 |
| 154 | 57 v | 11 | 166 | 1166 |

*Hand I*

| | | | | |
|---|---|---|---|---|
| 155 | 58 v | 35 | 199 | 1169 |
| 156 | 59 | — | 205 | 1169 |
| 157 | 59 | 24 | *MB Epp.* 342 | 1167 |
| 158 | 60 | 62 | *MB Epp.* 362 | 1167–8 |
| 159 | 60 | — | *MB Epp.* 363 | 1167–8 |
| (a few lines blank) | | | | |
| 160 | 60 v | 25 | 181 | 1167 |
| 160★ | 61 | 37 | 182 | 1167 |
| 161 | 61 v | 38 | 183 | 1167 |
| 161★ | 62 | 44 | *MB Epp.* 400 | 1168 |
| (also 220) | | | | |
| 162 | 62 v | 46 | *MB Epp.* 423 | 1168 |
| (also 220★) | | | (incomplete) | |

(Quire) *VIIIus*

(Quire *VIIIa*)    (SECTION 2)
*Hand VII*

| | | | | |
|---|---|---|---|---|
| 163 | 63 | — | Giles no. 287[6] | — |
| (fos. 65 v–66 v blank) | | | | |

(Quire IX)
*Hand III*

| | | | | |
|---|---|---|---|---|
| 164 | 67 | fo. 43 | *MB*, IV, 201–5[7] | 1163–4 |
| 164★ & ★★ | 68 v | fo. 44 | *MB*, IV, 206–8 | 1164 |
| 164★★★ | 70 | fo. 45 v | *MB*, IV, 209–12 | 1164 |
| 165 | 71 | — | *MGH, Constitutiones*, I, no. 183[8] | 1159 |
| 166 | 71 v | — | *MB Epp.* 100 | 1165 |
| 167 | 72 v | — | *MB Epp.* 98 | 1165 |

| B | | D | No. in this | |
|---|---|---|---|---|
| No. | Folio | No. | edition, etc. | Date |
| 168 | 74 | 19 | 169 | 1166 |
| 169 | 74v | 13 | MB Epp. 74 | 1164 |

(*Quire* IXus in 169)

(*Quire* X)

| | | | | |
|---|---|---|---|---|
| 170 | 75 | 14 | MB Epp. 73 | 1164 |
| 171 | 76 | 23 | MB Epp. 354 | 1167 |
| 172 | 77 | 50 | MB Epp. 489 | 1169 |
| 173 | 77v | 57 | MB Epp. 506 | 1169 |
| 174 | 78 | 58 | MB Epp. 528 | 1169 |
| 175 | 78 | 59 | MB Epp. 518 | 1169 |
| 176 | 79 | — | MB, IV, 213–43[9] | prob. 1169 |

(*Quire*) Xus (*fo.* 82v)

(*Quire* XI)

| | | | | |
|---|---|---|---|---|
| 177 | 89 | 64 | MB Epp. 599[10] | ?1166 |
| 178 | 89 | 64★ | App. VII, no. 5 | 1170 |
| 178★ | 89v | 65 | MB Epp. 515 | 1169 |
| 179 | 89v | 71 | MB Epp. 169 | 1166 |
| 180 | 90 | 72 | MB Epp. 340 | 1167 *or* 1169 |
| 181 | 90 | 73 | MB Epp. 604 | 1169 |
| 182 | 90v | 74 | MB Epp. 686 | 1170 |
| 183 | 90v | 75 | MB Epp. 153 | 1166 |

(*Quire*) XIus (*in* 183)

(*Quire* XII)

| | | | | |
|---|---|---|---|---|
| 184 | 93 | 76 | MB Epp. 690 | 1170 |
| 185 | 93 | 78 | MB Epp. 701 | 1170 |
| 186 | 94 | 79 | MB Epp. 700 | 1170 |
| 187 | 95v | 80 | MB Epp. 723 | 1170 |
| 188 | 97 | 81 | MB Epp. 738[11] | 1171 |
| 189 | 98 | 82 | MB Epp. 741 | 1171 |
| 190 | 98v | 85 | MB Epp. 750 | 1171 |

(*Quire*) XIIus (*in* 190)

(*Quire* XIII)

| | | | | |
|---|---|---|---|---|
| 191 | 99v | 86 | MB Epp. 521 | 1169 |
| 192 | 100 | 89 | MB Epp. 758 | 1171 |
| 193 | 100v | 91 | MB Epp. 763 | 1171 |
| 194 | 101v | — | 212 | 1170 |
| 195 | 102v | — | MB Epp. 734 | 1171 |
| 196 | 103 | — | MB Epp. 736 | 1171 |
| 197 | 103v | — | MB Epp. 743 | 1171 |
| 198 | 104 | — | MB Epp. 729 | 1171 |
| 199 | 104v | — | MB Epp. 529[12] | 1169 |

*Hand* IIIa (fo. 105)

| | | | | |
|---|---|---|---|---|
| 199★ | 105v | — | 214 | 1170 |
| (also 201) | | | | |
| 200 | 106 | — | 218 | 1171 |

| B | | D | No. in this | |
| No. | Folio | No. | edition, etc. | Date |
|---|---|---|---|---|
| *Hand I* | | | | |
| 201 | 106 v | — | 214 | 1170 |
| (also 199*) | | | | |
| (Quire) XIIIus (in 201) | | | | |
| | | | | |
| (Quire XIV) | | | | |
| 202 | 107 | — | 215 | ?1170 |
| | | | | |
| *Hand XI* | | | | |
| 203 | 107 | — | 219 | ?1171–2 |
| 204 | 108 | — | 217 | 1171 |
| 205 | 108 v | — | 229 | 1163–73 |
| | | | JL 13,583 = | |
| 206 | 109 | — | Giles no. 353 | 1171–80 |
| (also 242, 304) | | | | |
| 207 | 109 v | — | Giles no. 513[13] | ?1173 |
| 208 | 109 v | — | 234 | 1175 (*c.* April) |
| (3 lines blank) | | | | |
| | | | | |
| *Hand I* | | | | |
| 209 | 110 | — | Giles no. 517[14] | 1163–*c.* 1180 |
| 210 | 110 v | — | 267 | 1163–*c.* 1180 |
| 211 | 110 v | — | Giles no. 515[14] | 1163–*c.* 1180 |
| 212 | 111 | — | 273 | ? |
| 213 | 111 | — | App. VI, no. 1 | ? |
| 214 | 111 v | — | 239 | *c.* 1177 |
| 214* | 111 v | — | 274 | ? |
| 214** | 111 v | — | App. VI, no. 2 | ? |
| (half column and fos. 112–14 v blank) | | | | |
| (Quire) XIIIIus | | | | |
| | | | | |
| (Quire XV) | | (SECTION 3) | | |
| *Hand VIII* | | | MB Epp. | |
| 215 | 115 | 36 | 257 | 1166 |
| 216 | 115 | 28 | 178 | 1166 |
| 217 | 115 v | 29 | 173 | 1166 |
| 218 | 116 | 15 | 258 | 1166 |
| 219 | 116 v | 42 | 395 | ?1167–8 |
| 220 | 117 v | 44 | 400 | 1168 |
| (also 161*) | | | | |
| 220* | 117 v | 46 | 423 | 1168 |
| (also 162) | | | | |
| | | | | |
| *Hand I* | | | | |
| 221 | 118 | 43 | 81 | 1164–5 |
| | | | | |
| *Hand VIII* | | | | |
| 222 | 118 v | — | 26 | 1163 |
| 223 | 119 | 69 | 659 | 1170 |

| B No. | B Folio | D No. | No. in this edition, etc. | |
|---|---|---|---|---|
| 224 | 119v | 70 | 660 | 1170 |
| 225 | 119v | 68 | 627 | 1170 |

*Hand I*

| | | | | |
|---|---|---|---|---|
| 226 | 120 | 92 | 767 | 1172 |

(*Quire*) X(*Vus*)

| B No. | B Folio | Belverensis[15] | Wigorniensis Altera | JL | Date |
|---|---|---|---|---|---|
| *Hand III (Quire XVI)* | | | | | |
| 227 | 121 | i, 1–8[16] | — | — | 1163 |
| (several lines blank) | | | | | |
| 228 | 122v | i, 9 | 2–3 | 12,254 | 1164 |
| 229 | 123 | i, 10 | 4–5 | 13,162 | 1167–9 |
| 230 | 124 | i, 11 | 10 | 13,873[17] | 1159–81 |
| 231 | 125 | i, 12 | 1 | 12,180 and 13,771 | 1171–2 |
| 232 | 126v | i, 13 | 6 | 13,163 and 14,132 | 1164–79 |
| 233 | 127 | i, 14 | 7 | 12,253 and 14,146 | 1159–74 |
| (also 289, 371) | | | | | |
| 234 | 127v | i, 15 | 8 | 13,982 | *c.* 1173 |
| 235 | 127v | i, 16 | 9 | 13,164 | 1164–79 |
| 236 | 128 | i, 17 | — | 13,930 and 14,228 | 1162–81 |
| 237 | 128 | i, 18 | 12 | 12,293 | 1173–4 |
| (*Quire*) XVI*us* (in 237) | | | | | |
| (*Quire XVII*) | | | | | |
| 238 | 129 | ii, 1[18] | — | 14,267 | 1171–81 |
| 239 | 129 | ii, 2 | — | Giles no. 442 | 1163–77 |
| 240 | 129v | ii, 3 | — | 11,398 | 1168 |
| 241 | 130 | ii, 4 | — | 12,636 | 1173–6 |
| 242 | 130v | ii, 5 | — | 13,583 | 1171–80 |
| 243 | 130v | ii, 6 | — | 14,222 | 1163–81 |
| (also 287) | | | | | |
| 244 | 131 | ii, 7 | — | 14,223 | 1163–81 |
| (also 288) | | | | | |
| *Hand IIc* | | | | | |
| 245 | 131 | ii, 8 | — | 12,201 (*MB Epp.* 784) | 1173 |
| 246 | 131v | ii, 9 | — | 12,203–4 (*MB Epp.* 785) | 1173 |
| *Hand IX* | | | | | |
| 247 | 132 | iii, 1–20[19] | — | — | 1175 (18 May) |
| (247*) | 133v | iii, 21[20] | — | — | |

| No. | B Folio | Belverensis[15] | Wigorniensis Altera | JL | Date |
|---|---|---|---|---|---|
| *Hand I* | | | | | |
| 248 | 133 v | iv, I[21] | — | 13,814 | 1159–81 |
| | | | (= Giles no. 340; *MB Epp.* 64) | | |
| 249 | 134 | iv, 2 | — | 12,448 and 14,314 | 1175 (23 March) |
| 250 | 134 | iv, 3 | — | 13,821 | 1159–81 |
| 251 | 134 | iv, 4 | — | 12,412 | 1161–75 |
| *Hand IXa* | | | | | |
| 252 | 134 v | iv, 5 | — | 11,660 | 1162–70 |
| 253 | 134 v | iv, 6 | — | 13,978 | 1159–81 |
| 254 | 135 | iv, 7 | — | 14,023 | 1159–81 |
| 255 | 135 | iv, 8 | — | 13,829 | 1159–81 |
| 256 | 135 | iv, 9 | — | 13,739 | 1159–81 |
| *Hand I* | | | | (this edition) | |
| 257 | 135 v | — | — | 257 | 1163–*c.* 1180 |

(half column and fos. 136 r–v blank)

(*Quire*) *XVIIus*

| No. | B Folio | D No. | No. in this edition, etc. | Date |
|---|---|---|---|---|
| (*Quire XVIII*) | | (SECTION 4) | | |
| *Hand IV* | | | | |
| 258 | 137 | — | 144 | 1163 |
| 259 | 137 v | — | 186 | 1167–8 |
| 260 | 137 v | — | 132 | 1160 |
| 261 | 138 | — | 206 | 1169 |
| 262 | 138 | — | 258 | 1163–*c.* 1180 |
| (also 280) | | | | |
| 263 | 138 v | — | *MB Epp.* 22 | prob. 1161[22] |
| 264 | 138 v | — | 207 | 1169 |
| 265 | 139 | — | 208 | 1169 |
| 266 | 139 | — | 209 | 1169 |
| 267 | 139 v | — | 131 | 1157–8 (or 1161–3) |
| 268 | 139 v | — | Giles no. 468[23] | 1163–*c.* 1180 |
| 269 | 140 | — | —[24] | ?*c.* 1169–70 |
| 270 | 140 v | — | 237 | 1163–77 |
| 271 | 141 | — | 157 | 1165 |
| 272 | 141 v | — | 294 | 1161–3 |
| 273 | 141 v | — | 187 | 1167–8 |
| 274 | 142 | — | 188 | *c.* 1167–8 |
| 275 | 142 v | — | 151 | 1163–5 (?1163) |
| (also 375) | | | | |
| 276 | 142 v | — | 136 | 1161–2 |
| 277 | 143 | 33 | 260 | 1163–4 or 1174–*c.* 1180 |

| B | | D | No. in this | |
|---|---|---|---|---|
| No. | Folio | No. | edition, etc. | Date |
| 278 (also 387) | 143 | — | 230 | 1163–73 |
| 279 | 143v | — | 231 | 1163–73 |
| 280 (also 262) | 143v | — | 258 (incomplete) | 1163–c. 1180 |
| 281 (also 378) | 143v | — | 252 | 1163–83 |
| 282 (also 380) | 144 | — | 191 | 1168–9 |

*Hand I*

| | | | | |
|---|---|---|---|---|
| 282* | 144 | — | App. VI, nos. 3–4 | — |
| (282**) | 144 | — | Liverani, p. 735[25] | 1170 |
| 283 | 144v | 77 | MB Epp. 698 | 1170 |
| 284 | 144v | — | 275 | ? |

(*Quire*) *XVIIIus*

(*Quire XIX*)
*Hand IVa*

| | | | | |
|---|---|---|---|---|
| 285 | 145 | — | MB Epp. 524 | 1169 |
| 286 (also 356) | 145v | — | 233 | 1163–74 |
| 287 (also 243) | 145v | — | JL 14,222 | 1163–81 |
| 288 (also 244) | 146 | — | JL 14,223 | 1163–81 |
| 289 (also 233, 371) | 146 | — | JL 12,253 and 14,146 (= Giles no. 367) | 1159–74 |
| 290 | 146v | 51 | 201 | 1169 |
| 291 | 147 | — | Giles no. 478[26] | c. 1163 |
| 292 (also 385) | 147 | 47 | 198 | 1169 |
| 293 | 147v | 27 | MB Epp. 34 | 1163–4 |
| 294 | 147v | 4 | MB Epp. 152 | 1166 |
| 295 | 148 | 1 | MB Epp. 199 | 1166 |
| 296 | 148v | — | 375 | 1173–4 |
| 297 | 149v | — | 221 | 1173 |
| 298 | 150 | — | MB Epp. 790 | 1173 |
| 299 (also 445) | 150v | — | 452 | 1173–c. 1180 |
| 300 | 151 | — | 164 | 1172 |
| 301 | 151v | — | 213 | ?1170 |
| 302 | 151v | — | 227 | prob. 1173–4 |
| 303 | 152 | — | 222 | 1173 |

*Hand I*

| | | | | |
|---|---|---|---|---|
| 304 (also 206, 242) (3 lines blank) | 152v | — | JL 13,583 (= Giles no. 353) | 1171–80 |

(*Quire*) *X(IXus)*

| B | | D | No. in this | |
|---|---|---|---|---|
| No. | Folio | No. | edition, etc. | Date |

(Quire XX)  (SECTION 5)
Hand IId

| No. | Folio | D No. | No. in this edition, etc. | Date |
|---|---|---|---|---|
| 305 | 153 | — | 101 | 1153 |
| 306 | 153v | — | 84 | 1148–53 |
| 307 | 153v | — | 94 | 1150 |
| 308 | 154 | — | 102 | 1153 |
| 309 | 154v | — | 122 | ?1148–63 |
| 310 | 155 | — | 103 | 1153 |
| 311 | 155 | — | 99 | 1152 |
| 312 | 155v | — | 88 | prob. 1148–54 |
| 313 | 156 | — | 93 | 1150 |
| 314 | 157 | — | 85 | 1148–53 |
| 315 | 157 | — | 107 | c. 1153 or later |
| 316 (also 18) | 157v | — | 67 | ?1145–8 |
| 317 (also 19) | 157v | — | 34 | 1145 |
| 318 | 158 | — | 109 | 1154 |
| 319 | 158 | — | 95 | 1150 |
| 320 | 159 | — | 121 | 1148–63 |
| 321 | 159 | — | 100 | 1152 |
| 322 | 159 | — | 111 | 1150–61 |
| 323 | 159v | — | 96 | 1150 |
| 324 | 160 | — | 86 | 1148–53 |
| 325 | 160v | — | 105 | 1153 |

(Quire) XXus (in 325)

(Quire XXI)

| No. | Folio | D No. | No. in this edition, etc. | Date |
|---|---|---|---|---|
| 326 | 161 | — | 110 | 1150–9 |
| 327 | 161v | — | 158 | 1165 |
| 328 | 162 | — | 268 | ?1163–c. 1180 |
| 329 | 162 | — | 154 | 1165 |
| 330 | 162v | — | 153 | 1164 |
| 331 | 163v | 9 | 156 | 1165 |

Hand I

| No. | Folio | D No. | No. in this edition, etc. | Date |
|---|---|---|---|---|
| 332 | 163v | — | 471 | 1163–c. 1180 |
| 333 (also 403) | 164 | — | 418 | 1163–c. 1180 |

Hand IId

| No. | Folio | D No. | No. in this edition, etc. | Date |
|---|---|---|---|---|
| 334 | 164 | — | 382 | 1163–73 |
| 335 | 164 | — | 437 | 1163–c. 1180 |
| 336 | 164v | — | 184 | 1167–8 |
| 337 | 164v | — | 232 | 1165–73 |
| 338 | 165 | — | 238 | ?1177 |
| 339 | 165 | — | 264 | 1163–c. 1180 |
| 340 | 165v | — | 176 | ?1165–7 |
| 341 | 165v | — | 397 | 1163–c. 1180 |

| B | | D | No. in this | |
| No. | Folio | No. | edition, etc. | Date |
|---|---|---|---|---|
| 342 (also 334) | 166 | — | 382 | 1163–73 |
| 343 | 166 | — | 196 | 1163–8 |
| 344 | 166v | — | 242 | 1164–79 |
| 345 | 166v | — | 175 | prob. 1165–7 |
| 346 | 167 | — | 150 | prob. c. 1163 |
| 347 | 168 | — | 161 | 1166 |
| 348 | 168v | 3 | MB Epp. 154 | 1166 |

(Quire X(XIus (fo. 168v)

(Quire XXII)

| | | | | |
|---|---|---|---|---|
| 349 | 170 | — | 189 | c. 1167–8 |
| 350 | 170 | 5 | MB Epp. 219 | 1165–7 (?1166) |
| 351 | 171 | — | 243 | 1164–79 |
| 352 | 171v | — | 241 | 1163–79 |
| 353 | 172 | 20 | 177 | 1166–70 (prob. 1167) |
| 353* | 172 | — | 428 | 1163–c. 1180 |
| 354 | 172v | — | 383 | 1163–72 |
| 355 | 173 | — | 256 | 1163–84 |
| 356 (also 286) | 173 | — | 233 | 1163–74 |
| 357 | 173 | 21 | 171 | 1166–7 |
| 358 | 173v | — | 246 | 1163–5 or 1174–81 |
| 359 | 174 | — | 163 | 1166–72 |
| 360 | 174v | — | 162 | 1166 |
| 361 | 175v | 30 | 178 | 1166–73 |
| 362 | 175v | — | 254 | 1164–c. 1180 |

Hand I

| | | | | |
|---|---|---|---|---|
| 363 | 176 | — | 173 | 1163–6 |
| 364 | 176v | — | 263 | 1163–c. 1180 |
| 365 | 176v | — | 276 | ? |

(Quire) XXIIus

(Quire XXIV)          (SECTION 6)
Hand IIIb

| | | | | |
|---|---|---|---|---|
| 366 | 177 | — | 235 | 1175 (prob. c. May) |
| 367 | 178 | — | 185 | 1167–8 |
| 368 | 179v | — | 249 | 1163–81 |
| 369 | 179v | — | 152 | c. 1163 (or 1160) |
| 370 | 180v | — | 134 | 1161 |
| 371 | 181 | — | MB Epp. 20[27] | 1163 |
| 371* (also 233 and 289) | 182 | — | JL 12,253 and 14,146 (= Giles no. 367) | 1159–74 |
| 372 | 182v | — | MB Epp. 702 | 1170 |
| 373 | 183 | — | 326 | c. 1155–c. 1158 |
| 374 | 183v | — | 113 | c. 1153–61 |

# INTRODUCTION

## I. THE MANUSCRIPTS

This book is an attempt to bring together, in a single critical edition, all the letters and charters of Gilbert Foliot, abbot of Gloucester (1139–48), bishop of Hereford (1148–63) and London (1163–87), which we have been able to discover. Most of the charters have been gathered from the usual sources, from collections of originals and from cartularies in the national collections, in local record offices and cathedral muniment rooms; a few have been preserved in the Archives Départementales of France.[1] But a number of the charters, and all but a handful of the letters, are to be found in Bodleian MS E Musaeo 249 (27835), our MS B. This manuscript inevitably forms the chief basis of our edition, and we believe it to have been written, in part at least, in Gilbert Foliot's own scriptorium. It contains both letters and charters, and so is itself one of many factors which decided us to include charters as well as letters; it also illustrates another, namely the difficulty of distinguishing clearly between letters and charters. We do not pretend to have been entirely consistent. A basic distinction has to be made on grounds of form—charters have the formal elements discussed below,[2] and conclude with sealing clauses or the like and witness lists; letters have their own, more informal rules of diplomatic, never have sealing clauses or witness lists,[3] and end with *Valete* or the equivalent. Frequently, however, letters were sent on formal business, and in a few cases we have deliberately included a charter among the letters or a letter among the charters to avoid breaking a group of documents dealing with a single case or theme.[4] It is none the less convenient to keep them (for the most part) separate. The majority of the letters can be arranged (up to a point) chronologically, and have some personal element in them; often a group of letters illustrates a great issue—and groups of letters dealing with the Cerne dispute or with some particular aspect of the quarrel with Thomas Becket must in any case be placed together. We have divided the charters between the three main periods of Gilbert's official career—as abbot, as bishop of Hereford and as bishop of London. Most of them cannot be closely dated within those periods, and are most conveniently arranged by religious houses and the like from whose muniments they come; only so can like be placed with like and any semblance of reason be put into their order.[5]

[1] For a full list of sources, see Index of Manuscripts.
[2] Chapter II.
[3] Except for no. 13, which incorporates the will of Gunni of Stanton.
[4] E.g. no. 153 (a charter among the letters); no. 347 (a letter among the charters).
[5] Religious houses, etc., from whose muniments they came are arranged in alphabetical order, as in the comparable collections by Professor Saltman of Theobald's *acta* and by Dr Mayr-Harting of those of the bishops of Chichester. Several arbitrary decisions have had to be made as to which of two houses to attach an agreement to; and the charters in MS B have been distributed about the collection, where they seemed most reasonably to belong, although all derive from Gilbert's archives.

The manuscripts of the letters fall into two groups: those which emanated from Gilbert Foliot's own *familia* or circle, or derived from collections made in his household; and manuscripts containing the correspondence of the Becket controversy. The latter provide us with texts of only a handful of Gilbert's letters; but they include the most interesting of all his letters, the celebrated attack on Becket, *Multiplicem nobis*,[1] and they form a link with one of the most remarkable and interesting groups of letter collections of the period.

### Bodleian E Musaeo 249 (27835)—B

B is a comparatively small book—now 8 × 5½ in.[2] (written space *c.* 4 × 6½/7½)—of xviii + 207 leaves (fos. i–vi, viii–xviii, 207 paper, fos. vii, 1–206 vellum). It is written in a variety of hands of approximately the third quarter of the twelfth century, with initials and other details in red, green and blue; on fos. 122 v ff. there are marginalia in red. Details of quires and hands, and an analysis of the contents of the MS, are given in table B.

The contents fall into six main groups.

(1) Fos. 1–62 v. 165 letters ranging in date from 1140 to 1169 (or later), the first 142 (to fo. 47 v) in a single book-hand (hand II); other hands then take over, most of the later additions being in a charter-hand which recurs in every section of the book, which we call hand I. It seems likely, however, that these additions came from the same source as some at least of the later letters in this group copied by hand II, since London letters in both hands overlap the collection represented by the Douce MS (D: see p. 14). But this does not mean that all the letters in this section form a homogeneous group. Hand II opens the book with no. 1, 'A te longe positi...'; hand I[3] has added the heading 'Epistole uenerabilis Gilleberti Hereford(ensis) episcopi: epistolam hanc domno Radulfo decano Hereford(ensi) transmisit'. It is strange that hand I should call Gilbert bishop of Hereford in a collection containing London letters. Closer examination of section 1, however, shows that there is a notable break in the chronological sequence *c.* 1153–61: these years are represented by very few letters; none certainly later than 1153[4] occurs before fo. 31; fos. 31–5 v have a small group of the 1150's; on fo. 36 there is half a column blank, and from then on there is only one document (a charter of Gilbert's predecessor as bishop of Hereford attached to Gilbert's own confirmation of it) which can be proved earlier than 1161. Thus the first part of section 1 seems to contain a collection made while Gilbert was bishop of Hereford, and this is confirmed by comparison with MSS R and H (below, p. 13), which also contain some part of the same collection; the rest of section 1 is based on materials also underlying MS D (below, pp. 14 ff.).

(2) Fos. 63–6 form an insertion: a detached quire of vellum of a coarse quality not found elsewhere, containing an anonymous sermon (Giles, no. 287) which may be by Gilbert, but cannot be proved to have any connexion with him, and three blank leaves. Section 2 itself runs from fo. 67 to fo. 111 v (fos. 112–14 v are blank), and, like section 1, consists of a substantial group of documents in a single book-hand, hand III, with additions in two or three

---

[1] See *GF*, pp. 167 ff. and below, pp. 20 f.

[2] The margins of many of the leaves have been cut back by the binder(s), sometimes quite severely. It is in double column except for fos. 63–5, 115–20 v, 122 v–129, 199–200.

[3] This identification is not quite certain.

[4] And only five which could possibly be later than 1153.

hands, mainly in hand I. It opens, like MS D, with an account of the controversy between Henry II and Becket known as the *Summa cause*[1] and Frederick Barbarossa's invitation to Henry II to the council of Pavia (1160) which confirmed Frederick's anti-pope. The group of documents in hand III is very closely related to MS D: see below, p. 15.

(3) Section 3 (fos. 115–36 v) consists mainly of the decretal collection known as the *Collectio Belverensis*, which fills most of two quires (xvi and xvii, fos. 121–36 v); prefixed to it is another quire of papal letters, relating to the Becket controversy and especially to Gilbert's role in it (quire xv, fos. 115–20 v). Quire xv is in hand VIII, with at least one addition in hand I; with the *Belverensis* we return to hand III, the scribe of section 2; as usual, there are additions in other hands, mainly in hand I. The *Belverensis* has been analysed by Dr Duggan[2] and discussed in *GF*, pp. 230–4.[3]

(4) Section 4 consists of two quires (xviii and xix, fos. 137–52 v), written in one or two hands (IV and IV a), with additions at the end of each quire by hand I. The material mostly belongs to the 1160's (1160–*c.* 1173/4); eleven of the items, out of 49, occur elsewhere—an exceptionally high proportion—and one more is repeated within the section. Some items also occur in D, but there is no such relationship with D as occurs in section 2.

(5) Section 5, consisting of three quires (xx–xxii, fos. 153–76 v), is similar in character to section 1: it contains letters by Gilbert alone[4] ranging in date from 1145 to *c.* 1177.[5] It is noteworthy that the only overlap between these letters and section 1 occurs in two letters (nos. 34, 43) which are here disguised by a protocol making them belong to the Hereford instead of the Gloucester period; and also that, with the exception of these two and two other letters wrongly attributed to London instead of to Hereford, the scribe has carefully segregated the letters between Gilbert's two episcopates. There is no other indication of chronological order within this section; and since we know that section 1 was based on an earlier collection, it is clear that section 5 was put together as a supplement of Gilbert Foliot's own letters not in section 1. It is written in hand II d with the usual supplements in hand I.

(6) After quire xxii a quire is missing (see below, p. 4); section 6 (fos. 177–206 v) consists of a miscellany, possibly always intended as a supplement to 1 and 5, but more varied in character, with some overlap with section 4. The first hand in this group, III b, completed his work on fo. 189 with a group of letters related to a group also in D. A few lines were left blank, then hand I took over, completed the quire[6] and added another—the only one which is entirely his work. Most of these letters are Gilbert's, or at least passed under Gilbert's name, since many from this section are charters. As the section advances, the items become more fragmentary and anonymous, and there are a fair number which seem to belong to the world of rough drafts and formularies.[7] On the verso of the final leaf of this quire another hand, not to be found elsewhere, embarked on Gilbert's masterpiece, *Multiplicem*, which he completed in one further quire. As in D, Gilbert's name is prudently suppressed; but in D it takes its place in an approximately chronological framework. Here it is

---

[1] *MB*, IV, 201 ff.

[2] Duggan, pp. 155 ff., cf. pp. 71 ff.

[3] Precision of analysis is made more difficult in this case by the complex interweaving of different hands (see table B).

[4] With the exception of two letters of Becket (*MB Epp.* 154, 219) and possibly one or two letters at the end of the section whose authorship is not quite certain.

[5] Or later: 16 out of the 62 items cannot be dated closely to 1177 or before.

[6] Fos. 193 and 194 are attached to the end of quire xxv. They are in hand I, but it cannot be proved that this was their original position.

[7] See especially the items in Appendix VI, nos. 5–23.

added as an afterthought. Since it was clearly copied from the materials used in section 2 (see pp. 14–15), and begins in a quire on which hand I had already inserted his final gleanings, it seems reasonable to assume that the afterthought was part of the original composition of the book, not a later addition made years afterwards (see pp. 20–1).

Apart from *Multiplicem*, hand I's contribution to section 6 is the conclusion of the book; and indeed he has filled in blank spaces in every section, so that his presence is (after the common links with Gilbert himself) the unifying factor in the collection. It is therefore fortunate that we can identify him as a scribe employed to write at least three of Gilbert's original charters: his hand wrote no. 422 and both surviving originals of no. 391; possibly also no. 466. It is possible that the scribe of any one or two of Gilbert's charters might have been employed for the occasion, or by the beneficiary; but when we find him treating a substantial collection of Gilbert's letters in the way hand I treats MS B, and especially when we find him filling a whole quire at the end with what can reasonably be described as the scourings of the bishop's office, we can be confident that he was a clerk in Gilbert's household. This does not establish that the whole of B was written in the *familia*. No other identifications can be made with any show of probability, and the book-hands, in whole or part, may represent professional scribes employed for this purpose. But there can be no reasonable doubt that with the probable exception of fos. 63–6 the whole book represents collections and materials available in the bishop's household; that the enterprise was supervised and partly executed by his clerks; that the author of hand I, who wrote with authority, reckoned himself the director of the enterprise. It sits on the surface of the document that the office whose files it reproduces was still in being, and we shall see reason presently for dating the completion of the manuscripts some years before Gilbert's death. One may doubt whether hand I would have acted as it did without the bishop's support. How much Gilbert was involved in the composition of the book we cannot tell; but it is reasonable to suppose that he took an interest at least in what seems to have been the preparation of a definitive collection of his letters and of other materials relating to his career.

### The order and later history of B

At the end of most of the quires there is a trace of a number written in the thirteenth century—and perhaps in two or three cases trace of a yet earlier number; but none of these can now be read. These quire numbers show that the manuscript was bound up in the thirteenth century as it is now; but they also show that, unless a mistake was made in numbering the quires, there is one missing, probably between fos. 176 and 177 (quire xxiii); the nature of the material in quires xxii and xxiv makes it impossible to conjecture with any precision what has been lost.

With the exception of fos. 63–6 the manuscript is clearly a unity; apart from the relation which all sections bear to Gilbert Foliot, all other quires either contain some documents written by hand I or have always been attached to quires in which he wrote. We can be clear that what we now have all passed under the eye of the scribe of hand I and (almost certainly) was written in Gilbert's lifetime.

There is, however, a difficulty in supposing that the manuscript retains its original order or the character first conceived for it. The quire numbers show that its present order has a venerable antiquity, and it is possible, even likely, that it was never actually bound in any other order. The continuity of quires i–vii, ix–xiv, xvi–xvii, xx–xxii, xxiv–xxv, xxvi–xxvii is guaranteed by the fact that the breaks all occur in the middle of a letter or other document.[1] Catchwords link quires v–vi, vi–vii, vii–viii. Thus we are left with the following blocks of quires: i–viii, ix–xiv, xv, xvi–xvii, xviii, xix, xx–xxii (xxiii missing), xxiv–xxv, xxvi–xxvii. Nothing so far forbids us from concluding that the book is bound up in its original order. But at the end of quire viii there occurs the catchword *Th'*, which should mean (in view of the nature of the collection) that the next quire opened with a letter of Archbishop Thomas. The only quires so beginning (or opening with any word which could be abbreviated *Th'*) are viii itself and xviii, where the opening *Thomas* has been cancelled and replaced by *Teodbaldus* in another hand. It is, of course, possible that the catchword was an error, or that it referred to a quire now lost; but it is much more likely that quire viii was originally intended to be followed by quire xviii. It is noteworthy that the intervening quires form sections 2 and 3; that section 3 (papal letters and the *Collectio Belverensis*) is the most heterogeneous in the book; and that section 2, closely parallel to MS D, can be shown to have existed as a separate collection before B was compiled (see p. 15). The same is true of the first part of section 1. The evidence, none the less, strongly suggests that the whole book was originally conceived as a supplement to a copy of the earlier collection represented by the nucleus of section 1, and that sections 2 and 3 were not part of the original design.

It is possible that sections 2 and 3 were originally intended to go after quire xix or at the end. But this is hardly probable: the whole book gains in coherence if they are omitted, and there are strong grounds for supposing that the end of the book, like the beginning, is that originally intended. The manuscript opens with the same group of letters as the other manuscripts representing Gilbert's earliest surviving collection (see p. 13); this is clearly the original opening. The manuscript closes with two quires, the first written solely by hand I—the only quire in which he was not content to fill in blank leaves of a quire begun by another scribe[2]— which was completed by the scribe of *Multiplicem*, who added the second quire and left $2\frac{3}{4}$ pages blank at the end. This is the only part of the manuscript in which there is more than one leaf blank, save for the intrusive quire between sections 1 and 2 and the conclusion of section 2. It seems clear that it was the original conclusion of the book.

[1] In a few cases this could, of course, be due to later filling in; but since it is clear that on the whole the various hands did their work at much the same time this does not seriously affect our argument. The catchword linking quires vii and viii is 'Th(omas)': this could be a link to quire xviii, but see below.

[2] This is not, of course, wholly watertight: it is hypothetically possible that here or there is a quire whose final leaves he filled before the early leaves were written on (though such a hypothesis would be more probable if there were signs of the sort of difficulty this operation would make for the scribes of the earlier leaves), and at least one quire is missing.

This would suggest that hand I found the book in loose quires: that he took sections 1, 4–6 and himself filled blank spaces in the quires, finally adding a new quire of his own at the end and leaving it to the scribe of *Multiplicem* to complete the work. There are, however, two reasons for doubting if this is an adequate account of his work. The first is that sections 2 and 3, though very probably intrusive to the original design, also show signs of his work. He treated them, in fact, exactly as he treated the other quires written by his fellow scribes—he filled the blank spaces. We can hardly doubt that sections 2 and 3 were part of the same enterprise as the rest of the book—added, that is, not much later than the rest; and this is confirmed by the fact that they were written on sheets of vellum of the same size as the rest[1] and could be fitted in without great incongruity. Whether the book was bound up in Gilbert's lifetime is impossible to say—possibly the disappearance of quire xxiii suggests that it was not; on the other hand, it is a little difficult to understand how so much survived in such good shape after the death of the bishop and the dispersal of his household if it was not bound, and a quire can easily have been lost in a later rebinding.

B must have been written for Gilbert and we may presume that it remained within his household until his death. It contains several medieval inscriptions: two establish that it was once in the library of Westminster abbey, another that it was presented to Belvoir priory by Prior William of Belvoir.[2] The Westminster inscriptions are earlier in character than those from Belvoir, and probably belong to the mid thirteenth century. Those from Belvoir associate the manuscript with a group of surviving books presented by Prior William of Belvoir to his priory, all of which have very similar inscriptions of the fourteenth century.[3] The prior probably (though not certainly) held office in the mid fourteenth century. B also contains a finely written eighteenth-century inscription, in the hand of Bodley's Librarian of the day, which records that Sir Thomas Cave, of Stanford Hall in Leicestershire,[4] presented the book to the Bodleian; it is dated 1754.

[1]  Though this may have been a standard size for a work of this kind made in or commissioned by Gilbert's office.

[2]  *Westminster*: fo. 67 (top, half cut away) and fo. 206v: 'S.X. Pe. 7 Ed. West.' (cf. Ker, p. 196).
      *Belvoir*: fo. 1 (top): '...de Beluero' (in red, cut away); (foot) 'Hunc (?) librum dedit fr. Willelmus de Beluero prior eiusdem ecclesie Deo et beate Marie de Beluero, quem qui alienauerit uel titulum (?) deleuerit anathema sit. Anima dicti Willelmi et anime omnium fidelium defunctorum requiescant in pace amen'; fo. 89v (foot, in a different hand): 'Hic est liber sancte Marie de Beluero, quem qui alienauerit anathema sit.'
      For other additions, see p. 11 n. There are a few 'Nota' signs in the margin (see p. 11); a number of sixteenth–eighteenth-century interpretations or corrections of words; and two verses (= Walther, *Initia*, nos. 12100, 16256) and the opening of a prayer on fo. 206v. (thirteenth–fourteenth century).

[3]  Ker, p. 230, and below, p. 7 n.

[4]  Unlike his father, who incurred large debts in horse-racing, Sir Thomas Cave (the fifth baronet, 1712–78) had been a fellow commoner of Balliol and was a man of scholarly tastes. He was chairman of the committee which sponsored the publication of Bridge's *Hist. of Northamptonshire* and collected materials which were used in Nichols' *Hist. of Leicestershire*—including the Belvoir material (from Gale MSS, now in Trinity Coll., Cambridge) in Peck's transcript in BM Add. MS 4936, one of a group presented to the BM by Cave (Sir L. Namier

Prior William's gifts of books to his priory included a copy of Aimo of Fleury's *Historia Francorum*, formerly at Winchester, a copy of a set of Notule on the Pentateuch and a copy of William of Malmesbury's *Gesta Pontificum* whose earlier history is unknown, and a copy of an *Ysagoge in Theologiam* formerly at Cerne.[1] Of these, the last is the most interesting to us, since the book is dedicated to Gilbert Foliot and was written in his lifetime. It is possible that this was the dedication copy, and that, like B, it came from his *familia*. But if so, it came by a different route. Thus there emerges the picture of a Benedictine monk with access to the libraries of other Benedictine houses and with an interest in twelfth-century books—and in particular, it seems, in Gilbert Foliot. The reasons for his interest seem to be beyond conjecture.

## The date of MS B

It will be convenient to lay out the range of date of the documents contained in each section, distinguishing the dates[2] of the letters in the main hand of the section (*a*), in other hands apart from hand I (*b*), and in hand I (*c*).

1. (*a*) 142 letters, 1140–*c*. 1168–9 and probably 1174 or later.
   (*b*) 11 letters, 1163–6.
   (*c*) 12 letters, 1166–9.
2. (*a*) *Summa cause* and 34½ letters with the *Causa* between Gilbert and Thomas in their midst, 1163–71 (with a backward glance to 1159).[3]
   (*b*) 8½ letters, 1169–75.
   (*c*) 10 letters, 1170–*c*. 1177.

and J. Brooke, *The House of Commons, 1754–90*, II (London, 1964), p. 200; *Verney Letters of the 18th Century...*, ed. M. M. Lady Verney (London, 1930), esp. II, 215 ff., 234 ff., 263; S. Ayscough, *A catalogue of the MSS preserved in the BM hitherto undescribed...*, I (London, 1782), pp. ix, 62).

[1] Ker, p. 230 (cf. p. 9) lists Cambridge, Trinity Coll. B. 14. 33 (317) (the *Ysagoge*, on which see *GF*, p. 54 n.), Eton Coll. 48 (the Notule), Bodl. 755 (Aimo of Fleury's *Historia Francorum*); to these can be added BM Cotton Claud. A. v, fos. 46 ff. (William of Malmesbury: noted by Ker as a Belvoir book on p. 9, but not on p. 230 among Prior William's), whose inscription is partly illegible but was clearly very similar to those in the others, which are very similar to each other. (We have to thank Dr D. Luscombe and Mr F. P. McGivern for help with these MSS.) Three Priors William of Belvoir are known: William of Huntingdon, *c*. 1270–7 (*VCH Lincs*. II, 206–7; Trinity Coll., Cambridge, MS O. 9. 25, fo. XII; cf. fo. XVIIv); William of Belvoir I, 1319–20, and William of Belvoir II, 1333–*c*. 1366 (*VCH Lincs*. II, 206–7; J. Nichols, *Hist. Leicestershire*, II, i, App. p. 21—from Peck from Gale: see previous note). The *ex libris* inscriptions seem to make it clear that William 'of Belvoir' was distinct from William 'of Huntingdon' (donor of Trinity O. 9. 25), and William of Belvoir seems most probably to be the notable prior who ruled from 1333 to *c*. 1366.

[2] I.e. the approximate earliest and latest dates of letters in each group which can be fairly closely dated. There are a considerable number which cannot be closely dated, though in most groups those which can form a substantial proportion: dates are noted in table B to make this clear; the table also shows the order of hands.

[3] The Emperor Frederick Barbarossa's invitation to the council of Pavia (Giles, no. 510; for English MSS of this cf. W. Holtzmann in *Neues Archiv*, XLVIII (1930), 386–7), quoted at the same point in both B and D. For the *Causa*, see *GF*, p. 163 and n.

3. (a) Canons of council of Tours (1163) and 17 papal decretals, 1163–73/4.
   (b) 18 decretals and bulls, 1163–73, and canons of council of Westminster, 1175.
   (c) 2 bulls, 1164/5, 1172, and 4 decretals, 1175.
4. (a) 25 letters, 1160–9, possibly 1157/8–1174 or later.
   (b) 19 letters, c. 1163–73/4.
   (c) 5 letters, 1170–1 or later.
5. (a) 57 letters, 1145–67/8, probably 1177.
   (c) 5 letters, c. 1163–6.
6. (a) 26 letters, c. 1155–75.
   (b) 1 letter, 1166.
   (c) 63 letters and fragments, 1172–4/5, but mostly undatable.

It is immediately clear that no section can have been copied before the 1170's; and in most cases the dates of the documents give no grounds for supposing that (b) and (c) were added long after (a). Indeed the sections appear remarkably homogeneous in date. The latest documents in four out of the six sections are +1174, 1174/5 or 1175; section 5 produces one probably of 1177 in (a), section 2 one of c. 1177 in (c), its latest stratum. The earliest stratum in section 3 is related to the collection known as *Wigorniensis Altera*, which was composed in or after 1173; the latest documents are of 1175. In the whole manuscript there are approximately 200 documents (out of just over 450) which can be dated with reasonable precision to a particular year. They range from 1140 to 1177, with gaps (at least in precisely dated letters) in 1141–2, 1144, 1149, 1151, 1154–5, 1157–9 and 1176. Although there is a clear purpose behind some of the sections, the selection of material as a whole does not suggest any principle which might lead to later documents being purposely or consistently omitted. A date c. 1175 would be possible for most of the collection; a date c. 1177 acceptable for the whole of it. It is difficult to believe that it was compiled much later than 1177; a date later than c. 1180 seems virtually inconceivable.[1]

### The materials employed in B

Ancient and medieval letter collections were normally put together in one of two ways: either from the author's own copies or drafts, or by collecting such letters as survived from the recipients. In some cases both methods may have been employed, but far and away the commonest basis for a collection was the author's own files. It is clear, in fact, that B derived from earlier collections made by or for the author, and from schedules, copies and drafts in his office. The first half of section 1 derived from an early collection of the 1150's, also represented in MSS R and H. Section 2 represents a collection made in the early 1170's, also represented by MS D. They will be analysed more closely when the other manuscripts have been described. It seems clear that the collection of the 1150's had been added to in the 1160's, though some of the additions may have been made as B was being compiled. But it is noticeable that there are no letters copied both in sections 1 and 2, and very few

---

[1] Though an item here and there might be a later addition: but the place of hand I makes this very improbable (except for fos. 63–6 and, much more doubtfully, *Multiplicem*: see above).

repeated in 1, 2 and 5. Comparison with D will show that a number of the letters in section 1 were probably in the common source of D and section 2, and this strongly suggests that they were omitted from section 2 deliberately because already in section 1: if they were omitted by accident, the absence of overlap between the sections would be a very curious coincidence.[1] Thus it seems very likely that section 5 is a supplement to 1 and 2, and that 2 was itself intended to give the letters, etc., relating to the Becket controversy not already copied in 1. At some stage, perhaps after the book was complete, someone has noted a few cross-references and other memoranda designed to place some of the letters in section 2 in their historical setting.[2]

Section 3 represents Gilbert's files of papal letters and decretals; most of it consists of the *Collectio Belverensis*, and is itself based on a primitive decretal collection very similar to the earliest Worcester collection, *Wigorniensis Altera*, but has been added to in the process of copying.

Section 4 is too miscellaneous for one to say more than that it seems to be based on copies or schedules of letters of the 1160's rather than on an earlier collection.

Section 6 completes the work of hand I, which appears in every section, amplifying and completing. Commonly hand I provides material more or less appropriate to the section he is completing, and some of his additions in section 1 at least seem to come from an earlier collection—the common source of section 2 and D. But a considerable part of his material consisted of drafts or extracts from charters, and his contribution to section 6 is something like a rough formulary. The conclusion of section 6, *Multiplicem*, was evidently added as an afterthought from the common source of section 2 and D.[3]

---

[1] The argument at this point is complicated by the diversity of hands in the later part of section 1 of B (see table B); it could be argued that some of these items were later supplements made *after* section 3 had been compiled.

[2] His notes are on fos. 70 (marginal correction to a section of *Summa cause*, see *MB*, IV, 209 n. 8), 78 ('Seueritatem uestram, Seueritatem domne', referring to nos. 198, 200, B, fos. 147, 187), 78 v ('Placuit excellentie', no. 165, B, fo. 74; 'circa initium Quadrag.', giving the date of Gilbert's appeal in 1169; 'in Ramis Palmarum', the date of Gilbert's excommunication in 1169), 102 r–v, no. 212 ('Placuit excellentie uestre' as above; 'Ad uestram pater audientiam', no. 173, B, fo. 61 v; 'In Norm(annia)', see note to no. 212; 'circa initium xl.' and 'in Ramis Palmarum' as above), 106, no. 218 ('post passionem domni Cant.'), 106 v ('Con(tra) Oportuerat', i.e. an answer to *MB Epp.* 700, B, fo. 94), 107, no. 215 ('Quamuis cure pastorum', i.e. *MB Epp.* 720–1, not in B), 107, no. 219 (see note to letter), 119 v, *MB Epp.* 627 ('Videtur esse illa [...] quam orat sibi [...]ieri quod deceret (?) [...] illi [...] siquidem [...] sequitur illa [Dil]ecte mihi pater', i.e. no. 212), 163 v, no. 156 (see note to letter; includes reference to *MB Epp.* 157, not in B), 172, no. 177 ('Non plene liquet quo tempore uel de qua appellatione hoc dicat'!), 175 v, no. 178 (see note to letter). These notes were evidently written by someone with a fair but not very precise knowledge of the events and correspondence, with access to letters not in B, as we have it, or D, and sufficiently near the events to describe Becket's death as 'passio domni Cant.' rather than 'passio sancti Thome'. The notes range over sections 2, 3 and 5. There seems clearly to be no connexion between them and D.

[3] See pp. 20–1 and textual notes to the letter: the text evidently derives from a version very similar to D, in which the author's name was left blank as in D. A common source seems

The ultimate source in most cases seems to have been drafts of the letters actually sent; and in several cases (as is common in such collections) we seem to have two drafts for the same letter.[1] Most of the time it is impossible to tell precisely how close what we now have was to the letter actually sent. The exceptions are those letters of which copies survive in other manuscripts of the Becket correspondence. For the most part these suggest that the copies we have are reasonably faithful, and that the scribes of MS B did their work with tolerable accuracy. There is one letter of which the text in MS C is very different from that in B (no. 197); this seems to be due to revision before B was copied. In one other case a version common to B and other manuscripts is surprisingly different from one preserved in Master David's dossier (no. 203): the former clearly represents the letter sent to the king, the latter a copy sent to David for his information as ambassador for Gilbert in the Curia. The differences are entirely stylistic, and no doubt due to inadvertence— perhaps the copy was sent to David before final revision of the letter.

No. 197 is one of the few in B which show signs of revision. Comparison of B, R and H shows that nos. 26, 27 and 34 were slightly revised before B was copied; but there is no sign of revision in the other letters common to the three manu-scripts.[2] In most cases we have no check, but there is little reason to suppose that any elaborate process of polishing has taken place with more than a handful of the letters. They can be taken to be faithful copies, on the whole, of what Gilbert intended to send at the time each letter was drafted. The way B is compiled suggests that it was intended as a substantial collection of material to form the basis for a fuller edition of Gilbert's letters. The cancellations[3] and the rough way in which some items are entered suggest that it was meant to be a working copy from which a fair copy would be taken. If this is correct, one might expect to find evidence of revision to the text of the manuscript itself, such as Arnulf of Lisieux gave to Paris Bibl. Nat. Lat. 14763,[4] but there is remarkably little evidence of revision or of

certain. Hand I's additions in sections 1–4 are appropriate enough, though his last entries in section 2 are very miscellaneous, and his additions to 4 are fragments. To 5 he has added two personal letters and a testimonial, not in context. Section 6 opens with two testimonials, then a group of letters of the years 1173–4. Folios 193–4 and quire xxvi contain mainly charters and formulary fragments.

[1] For specific evidence of the use of drafts, see notes to nos. 152, 197, 203, 252; for duplicates, see *GF*, p. 27, and esp. no. 25 and n. 1.

[2] For no. 34, B offers two versions, B1 revised, B2 unrevised. The conclusion of no. 155 raises a curious problem. The Becket MSS agree with B that Gilbert concluded this letter with a reference to Peter's Pence; but the greater part of the last paragraph occurs in B only: D omits the whole of it (and so gives no evidence one way or the other on the state of this part of the letter in Gilbert's archives), and even the faithful Howden abbreviates this section. The most probable explanation is that B here represents Gilbert's draft, the Becket MSS what was actually sent, rather than that B shows the fruit of revision—the passage seems to be essentially something of temporary, ephemeral interest (cf. below, p. 15).

[3] Fos. 105 v–106, no. 214 (not repeated elsewhere), 148 v, no. 375 (the witness list), 179 v, nos. 249, 152 (opening: this may have appeared too much of a draft to be preserved). Two items on fo. 200 (nos. 363, 472, the latter a repetition) are marked 'uacat'.

[4] See F. Barlow, *The Letters of Arnulf of Lisieux*, pp. lxxix ff.

early use.[1] It may well be that the aftermath of Becket's martyrdom disinclined Gilbert to advertise his past; or that his growing blindness prevented him from making detailed revision. We have Walter Map's word for it that Gilbert continued to write after blindness overtook him,[2] and neither explanation is wholly satisfactory. But the manuscript received some use: sections 2 and 3 and 5 were annotated by a student of the controversy, section 5 by someone concerned to use the letters as models. The later medieval marginalia, which are comparatively few, mostly drew attention to a nicely phrased platitude or a pious sentiment; and it is clear that the manuscript had some use (though perhaps not much) as a formulary.

## Subsidiary manuscripts

### (i) Rome, Biblioteca Alessandrina, MS 120—A

This is a mid-thirteenth-century manuscript ($10\frac{1}{4}$ in. $\times$ $6\frac{3}{4}$ in.) containing a miscellany of items, many connected with Thomas Becket,[3] which came to the Alessandrina, along with a number of other manuscripts, from the collection of the nineteenth-century antiquary P. F. de Rossi; its earlier history is unknown. A contains, on fos. 123–65, copies of the same letters as in MS B down to no. 106 (our no. 112, B, fo. 35 v), except the first of all. This omission is strange, since R and H both start or started with the same letter as B, and because in any case it is clear that A is a copy of B. It follows B's order against R and H, and is very close textually to B. It adds a number of errors of its own, and is the work of a comparatively mechanical scribe, who has provided only trivial improvements of obvious slips in B.[4] There are several cases in which errors in A can be best explained by palaeographical tricks in B. Thus in no. 17 A reads *in minimis* for *a minimis*; B has *in* (marked for deletion) *a minimis*; in no. 18 A has *lumen* for *linum*; B has *l*, five indistinct minims, and a mark of abbreviation, which could easily be read as *lum'*; later in the same letter A has *ramenti* for *iuramenti*, where B has *iu|ramenti*; in no. 19 A has

---

[1] The following are the significant marginalia: (i) notes by a student of the controversy, see above, p. 9 n. 2; (ii) rubrics, made by the original scribe, to *Belverensis*, fos. 122 v ff. (i.e. part I only, the section derived from a collection very similar to *Wigorniensis Altera*); (iii) notes by someone interested in letters in section 5 as models (see notes to letters), fos. 154–9 v; (iv) occasional headings and summaries by hand I, fos. 1, 11 v, 135 v, 147 v, 148, 163 v, 189 v; (v) corrections, mostly by the original scribes or hand I (though certainty is often impossible), on fos. 34, 40, 42, 43 v, 47 v, 50–2 v *passim*, 54 v, 74 r and v, 115, 116, 137 (see above p. 5), 147, 166 v, 179–82 *passim*, 184, 203.

[2] See *GF*, p. 72.

[3] They include Grim's Life (?), Herbert of Bosham's *Cathalogus eruditorum*, the Constitutions of Clarendon, Alexander III's bulls of canonization, John of Salisbury's letter describing the murder, etc. For a description see E. Narducci, *Catalogus codicum manuscriptorum praeter orientales qui in Bibliotheca Alexandrina Romae adservantur* (Rome, 1877), pp. 91–3 (we owe our knowledge of this manuscript to the kindness of Dom Jean Leclercq).

[4] Qdam/quedam (no. 15); G./G.G. (in protocol of no. 27); incremetum/incrementum (no. 34, and frequent similar cases; this error not noted in our apparatus); prefanus/profanus (no. 53); a uestram/ad uestram (no. 58); statui/statu (no. 61); purior purior/purior (no. 64); ergo/erga (no. 68); domni domni/domni (no. 75); reliosorum/religiosorum etc. (nos. 78, 349); ampectimur/amplectimur (no. 92); pparasse/preparasse (no. 114).

*prophetis consideranti se* for *profecisse considerant*—a remarkable achievement, until one sees that B has *considerant profecis/se* (marked for transposition); in no. 6 *esset* for *centum, communionem* for *conicerem* and *a uia prudentia* for *a tua prudentia* are all made intelligible by palaeographical weaknesses in B; there are two cases where a difference of word order can be explained by A's failure to note marks for transposition in B; and several cases where omissions in A fit exact lines in B.

A ends at the foot of fo. 165 in the middle of a letter. Fo. 165 v is blank, so that it looks as if the scribe copied no more; but a different hand has added the gnomic sentence: 'hic subsequuntur duo fol' prox' anno Domini MCCCXIIII in oct' sanctorum Petri et Pauli'. A was probably copied half a century before 1314; and it seems likely, therefore, that it was copied from B while B was still at Westminster. A later table of contents in A describes Gilbert as 'S. Bernardo equalis', a sentiment open to doubt.

## (ii) A lost manuscript

Apart from A there is trace of another manuscript, now probably lost, which may also have been a copy of B. In John Bale's *Index Britanniae Scriptorum* there is a note of a copy of Gilbert's letters with the *incipit* 'A te longe positi', which Bale knew 'ex officina eiusdem (i.e. Roberti) Stoughton'.[1] Bale's index was compiled *c.* 1549/50–*c.* 1557, and Stoughton was a printer who is only known to have printed books in the years 1548–51, and may have died in 1553.[2] He evidently possessed a manuscript of Gilbert's letters in his shop under the sign of the bishop's mitre on Ludgate Hill. The books he possessed and the books he printed show him to have had a special interest in Protestant theology, and it may be conjectured that he was interested in Gilbert as an enemy of Thomas Becket. If he ever conceived the idea of printing Gilbert's letters, it seems that he never executed it. His manuscript bore the same *incipit* as B, H and R (before they were mutilated), but not A. But H seems always to have been at Hereford; B was on the border of Leicestershire and Lincolnshire in the later Middle Ages and reappears in Leicestershire in the eighteenth century;[3] and the likelihood (it cannot be put more strongly) is that R was in the west country at the time of the Dissolution. The contiguity of Stoughton's office to St Paul's suggests that his copy may have come from Gilbert's cathedral library, and have belonged to his London days; in which case it may have been a fair copy of B, or the immediate source of section 1 of B. But this line of reasoning is highly conjectural, and Stoughton may in fact, for example, have had possession of R.

[1] John Bale, *Index Britanniae Scriptorum*, ed. R. L. Poole and M. Bateson (Oxford, 1902), p. 90.

[2] E. G. Duff, *A Century of the English Book Trade* (London, 1905), p. 152; A. W. Pollard and G. P. Redgrave, *A Short-title Catalogue of Books Printed in England...1475–1642* (Oxford, 1926), Index, *s.v.* Stoughton; for books in Stoughton's possession, see John Bale, *op. cit.* Index, *s.v.* Stoughton.

[3] Though Cave could have obtained it, e.g., in London; and it may well be that it caught his attention because the manor of Stanford, his home, had once been held by Robert Foliot, probably Gilbert's brother (*HMC, 10th Report*, VI, 106, describing a charter in the Stanford muniments).

## (iii) *Hereford Cathedral Library MS P. i. 15 (H) and BM Royal MS 8 A. xxi (R)*

H and R each contain the opening quire of a collection of Gilbert's letters akin to the first part of section 1 of B. H, fos. 147–54 v ($8\frac{1}{2} \times 6\frac{1}{2}$ in.), is marked quire 1 (with a catchword joining it to the next quire, now lost), and written in a hand of the late twelfth century. It is now part of a manuscript formerly in the library of the Franciscans at Hereford;[1] whether or not this quire also came from their library, it seems highly likely that it has always lived in or near Hereford.

R, fos. 206–12 v ($8 \times 5\frac{1}{2}$ in.), is likewise a fragment, and the first leaf has been cut down almost to a stub. It is written in a small hand of the early–mid thirteenth century, and the quire numbers show that the miscellany of which it now forms part was put together in the thirteenth century. Although it cannot be proved to have been written at or possessed by Gloucester abbey, two items suggest a link with Gloucester,[2] and it is possible that it was collected either at Gloucester or at one of its dependencies. The final item on fo. 212 v is in a different hand, which might suggest that the collection originally intended is complete; but this item (no. 58, opening sentences) is incomplete, and it is hard not to think that a continuation is now missing.

H contains only Gloucester letters; R contains mainly letters from the Gloucester period, but also two written early in Gilbert's time as bishop of Hereford. Although there are divergences between each of them, it is clear that H and R represent the opening of a collection very similar in character to the opening of section 1 of B. Since both H and R are fragments, we cannot be certain how extensive this collection was; but we have already seen in the composition of B reason to think that the earliest identifiable collection was made *c.* 1153. The provenance of H (perhaps too of R) in any case makes it likely that it represented a collection made while Gilbert was still at Hereford.

A comparison of B, H and R shows that each has a number of good readings not in any other. It is clear that they are independent of one another, even though H is so careless that most of its private readings are worthless. But R is comparable in virtue to B, and both act as a very useful check on B, not only for the letters which they contain, but as a general guide to the reliability of B's section 1. In particular they show that some revision, though only a little, had taken place between the 1150's and 1170's. Indications, such as the evidence that a passage in no. 7 stood in the margin of the common source of B, H and R, suggest that a single MS may lie behind all three, on which corrections were made from time to time.

---

[1] Ker, p. 100; M. R. James in *Collectanea Franciscana*, 1 (1914), p. 119. On H see A. T. Bannister, *A descriptive Catalogue of the MSS in the Hereford Cathedral Library* (Hereford, 1927), pp. 111–12.

[2] Section 2 of the manuscript is a florilegium with substantial quotations from the works of Osbert of Gloucester (see *GF*, p. 80 and n. ); and Gilbert's own letters would most naturally come from the area of Gloucester or Hereford. On the manuscript see G. F. Warner and J. P. Gilson, *Cat. of Royal MSS*, 1, 216–18.

## (iv) *Bodl. Douce MS 287 (21,861)—D*

D is written in a single, ill-formed hand of the late twelfth or early thirteenth century. It belonged at one time to Lessness abbey in Kent, which was founded in 1178 by Richard de Lucy in honour of St Thomas of Canterbury.[1] It contains:

1. Fos. 1–36v: William FitzStephen's Description of London (incomplete at the start) and Life of St Thomas.
2. Fos. 37–42v: John of Salisbury's Life of St Thomas.
3. Fos. 43–102v. The *Summa cause inter regem et archiepiscopum* (*MB*, IV, 201 ff.), followed by 94 letters, etc., all but one printed in Robertson's *Materials* (*MB*), and all, with one possible exception,[2] dating from the years 1163–72.

At the end of the manuscript, in the same hand, are extracts from Henry of Huntingdon's *Historia Anglorum*.

Seventeen of the letters are by Gilbert himself (twenty-one including nos. 166–7, 181–2), and of these five occur nowhere else but in D and B; the bulk of the remainder were either addressed to him or concerned with him; the letters which were written after the martyrdom all (or almost all)[3] deal with Gilbert's excommunication and absolution; and the remarkable series of testimonials for Gilbert elicited in 1169 survives in part in both B and D, in part in D alone. Although D opens, like B, section 2, with the *Summa cause*, a tract written very definitely from the archbishop's point of view, it is clear that this collection has some close link with Gilbert Foliot.

Most of the letters in D are also in B; several small groups and one large group of letters are found in the same order in both; the *Summa cause* and its train of satellites (which comprise a small treatise on the events of 1163–4) are found only in B and D. In detail they have much in common. In a number of cases they share bad readings; in comparison with other MSS of Gilbert's letters (where comparison can be made) B and D nearly always hunt together—save that each has its own private errors, and the errors of D are legion.[4] No. 180 breaks off unfinished at the same point in each. Each has a text of *Multiplicem* (no. 170) in which Gilbert's name and title have been omitted from the protocol, but space left for them. It is clear that D derives, at one or two removes, from Gilbert's archives.

B and D each retain good readings absent in the other, and in general B is considerably the more accurate. It is clear that they come from a common source or

---

[1] Gilbert and Richard de Lucy, Henry II's justiciar, must often have met in the royal court, and they were partners in misfortune in the Becket dispute (see esp. no. 170). If the Ralph Brito, a vassal of Richard, of no. 464, was a nephew of Gilbert (see *GF*, p. 33), this formed a further link. There is, however, no indication of an intimate link between Gilbert and Richard or Lessness to explain D's presence in the abbey.

[2] No. 260, possibly 1174 or later.  [3] See previous note.

[4] For this reason only select variants of D are given in our apparatus; but sufficient are given, we think, to establish the independence of the MSS. It should be said that our study of B and D is based on a collation of Gilbert's own letters in them: a full collation of all their texts might lead to some revision of our findings. There are a few cases, noted in the apparatus, in which B and D agree with other manuscripts against each other.

sources, that neither is a copy of the other, and that the text of B represents the source more faithfully than D. In the text of no. 155 B seems to have an earlier, less revised version;[1] and there may well be other cases in which they used individual letters, copies of letters or schedules containing groups of letters—the extreme differences in arrangement suggest that this may have been so. But the common ground, and especially the common faults of the two, establish beyond reasonable doubt that a substantial schedule or group of schedules, perhaps a group of quires or even a book, provided the common source for much of the common material. It is noticeable that D opens with the *Summa cause*, which is also the opening of section 2 of B (apart from the inserted fos. 63–6), in which it is item 164, etc.; and that later on D contains all but three of the items down to B, no. 193 (which is six short of the end of the documents in hand III in B), and that with one exception they are all in B's order. As D progresses, it resembles B, section 2, more and more. Its only other resemblances to B in order, indeed, occur in little groups whose sub-ject-matter or date peremptorily dictated that they go together; and the first two of these, D, nos. 6–8, 13–14, are also grouped in other MSS—though, again, the nature of the letters makes this a fact of no special significance. The character of B, section 2, is quite marked: it contains Becket materials, which Gilbert no doubt had to take pains to collect, opening with the strongly pro-Becket *Summa cause*, but with one exception excludes Gilbert's own letters—of which, as with Mrs Bay-ham Badger, he had the originals and had no need to go searching for copies. It seems clear that D's collection is based on something very similar to B, section 2, into which have been injected a number of other letters, many of them Gilbert's own, relevant to the issues involved. B and D are independent of one another, and so D is clearly not based on B, section 2, itself, but on a common source. B's text of no. 155 might suggest that B was taken off this source before D. But D here seems to represent the text actually sent in 1165, so that it is more probable that they simply derive from different drafts in Gilbert's office. D contains no letter certainly later than 1172, and the author of this collection seems to have made some effort at chronological order in his arrangement of the materials. Both points may suggest that D's collection is earlier than B, though this cannot be established. In its present form, D's rubrics, referring to *St* Thomas, are probably not earlier than 1174. But it is unlikely in any case that D is an immediate copy of the common source(s) of B and D. There are incoherences in the arrangement of the letters in D, there is one repetition, and several letters are only fragments. But the whole manuscript is written in one inexpert hand (which perhaps makes its origin in an episcopal *familia* unlikely), and shows no signs of the difficulties of copying off archive material which beset the authors of B. It is unlikely, moreover, that the man who first compiled the letter collection would have thought of adding the two lives to the dossier, and that for two reasons:

(1) It seems likely, though far from certain, that the collection was made soon after 1172. At that date neither of the lives was written, still less circulated—

[1] See notes to the letter, and p. 10n.

FitzStephen's was composed in 1173–4, John of Salisbury's not earlier than 1173, and probably *c.* 1176.[1]

(2) The contents of the collection suggest that the author was concerned to produce a vindication of Gilbert in moderate terms—in a sort of way it resembles the imaginary disputation between Gilbert and Thomas, apparently composed by Gilbert himself or one of his clerks in 1169.[2] Such a purpose would hardly be served by introducing the two lives, since FitzStephen was hostile to Foliot and John of Salisbury hardly mentioned him.

From another direction we can adduce more cogent evidence not only of an intermediate source for the letter collection, but also of an earlier collection of a character similar to the whole of D. D passed early to Lessness in Kent, if it was not composed there, and ceased to have any influence on the textual development of the correspondence it contained until it was used by Dr Giles in the 1840's. But the material of which it consists does seem to have influenced the transmission of the biographies of St Thomas, and that within a generation of its composition. The text of FitzStephen is preserved in two recensions: the one comparatively pure, the other considerably interpolated.[3] Fragments apart, the pure version is represented by D and by one other manuscript; the interpolated by four manuscripts, of which the most important (though not the original) seems to be Cotton Julius A. xi, fos. 115–52, of the late twelfth or early thirteenth century.[4] The second version is based on three documents: FitzStephen itself, John of Salisbury's Life, and the *Summa cause.* It is remarkable that all three occur in D, and that no two are found together in any other surviving manuscript;[5] furthermore, there is no reason to suppose that the *Summa cause* was widely known outside Gilbert's familia and the circles in which B and D were to be found.[6] On the other hand, the interpolated version of FitzStephen was not directly based on D, since it has good readings not to be found there.[7] It looks very much as if D had a source containing the same material which was also the foundation for the second version of FitzStephen; and the close association of D with the bishop of London and of FitzStephen with the City suggests London as the place of its origin.[8]

[1] See E. Walberg, *La tradition hagiographique de S. Thomas Becket* (Paris, 1929), pp. 58 n. 2, 173 ff.; the date of John's Life will be discussed in *JS Epp.* II.

[2] *MB*, IV, 213–43; see *GF*, p. 163 and n.

[3] This simplifies a complex textual history: see *MB*, III, p. xvi, and see notes to text. Robertson paid no attention to Hereford Cathedral MS O. iv. 14 or Bodl. Laud Lat. 18, which both represent the shorter, interpolated version (and had been noted by T. D. Hardy).

[4] At one time, with H, in the Library of the Franciscans in Hereford (Ker, p. 100; M. R. James in *Collectanea Franciscana*, I, 155). See previous note; the fourth MS is Lambeth 138 (not 168, as Robertson), fos. 205–13 v (incomplete).

[5] Although manuscripts of John of Salisbury's Life are very numerous.

[6] But Dr R. W. Hunt has pointed out to us that it was used in the *Quadrilogus* in Bodl. MS Lyell 5.

[7] This is a very provisional statement, based on Robertson's apparatus.

[8] The process of revision included the omission of some of the passages damaging to Gilbert. The reviser may well have been FitzStephen himself.

## The Register of Master David of London

This is contained in Vatican MS Lat. 6024, fos. 140–54, and it has been analysed and its history told by Z. N. Brooke.[1] It consists mainly of letters to or from David of London, canon of St Paul's and at one time Gilbert's confidant and emissary at the papal Curia. It contains eleven letters certainly or very probably written by Gilbert, and two others, which may be attributed to him, though not confidently.[2] The collection as a whole clearly reflects the personal archives of Master David, and, apart from letters which are not otherwise preserved, a special interest attaches to its text of no. 203, which differs from all other versions of this letter, and seems to represent a draft sent to David at the papal Curia for his information.

## Minor manuscripts

No. 138, to the abbot and convent of St Victor, is known from the Victorine letter-books, and occurs in two seventeenth-century transcripts, one in the Bibliothèque Nationale, the other represented by the *Amplissima collectio* of Martène and Durand (see notes to letter).

No. 269 occurs only in Ja, with the bull of Pope Urban III to which it refers, in the midst of a collection of the letters of Arnulf of Lisieux.[3]

Nos. 270–2, the introductory letters to the Homilies, and to the commentaries on the Pater Noster and the Song of Songs, occur in the unique manuscripts of those works, BM Royal 2 D. xxxii, where Gilbert's Homilies immediately follow Ailred's Sermons on Isaiah, which were dedicated to Gilbert—the book is from Christ Church, Canterbury—Worcester, Dean and Chapter, Q. 48 (at Worcester in the Middle Ages), and BM Royal 2 E. vii (from Rochester).

## The manuscripts of the Becket correspondence

It is a characteristic of the materials for the Becket dispute that letters play a part of special importance among them. This may be due in the first instance to Becket himself, but collecting letters was already a well-formed habit with several of the protagonists before the crisis began. It is almost certain, furthermore, that it was the personal initiative of John of Salisbury which founded the project—quite in the nineteenth-century manner—of raising a massive 'Life and letters of St Thomas' to the memory of his friend, even though its final execution was left to Alan of Tewkesbury.[4] The role of John of Salisbury will be discussed at length in the

---

[1] 'The Register of Master David' in *Essays in History presented to R. L. Poole*, ed. H. W. C. Davis (Oxford, 1927), pp. 227–45. Cf. also R. Poupardin in *Bibl. de l'École des Chartes*, LXIII (1902), 352–73, 769, and Barlow in *Arnulf*, p. lxxiii.

[2] Nos. 133, 155, 198, 200, 202–3, 210–11, 216, 240, 248, and Appendix VII, nos. 2–3.

[3] See Barlow in *Arnulf*, pp. lxvi, lxxxiii ff.; Introd. to *JS Epp.* II (forthcoming).

[4] See Introduction to *JS Epp.* II, where there will be a provisional discussion by Sir Roger Mynors and C. N. L. Brooke of the collections as a whole, with particular reference to John's role in their formation. The early manuscripts of Alan's collection, and some of the earlier collections (group I below), have John's and Alan's Lives attached.

forthcoming introduction to the later collection of John's own letters; fuller elucidation of the relations of all the manuscripts must await a full study of Becket's own letters.[1] We give here a simple list of manuscripts which contain Gilbert's letters, arranged in groups according to the nature of the letter collection in each manuscript. The groups themselves are placed in what we believe to be chronological order;[2] but we cannot here discuss the grounds for this view, nor is it of great moment to an edition of Gilbert Foliot's letters. Four of the manuscripts which contain more than two or three of his letters, Ia, Ib, C and Co, are early and reliable, and their combined witness gives a sure guide to the text of Gilbert's letters as they entered the circles in which these collections were made, and makes it unnecessary to quote the variants of the other manuscripts, with occasional exceptions.

(I) Manuscripts containing Becket's own letters, and a considerable number by other hands in a variety of different orders, none of any great coherence.

Ia—London, Lambeth Palace Library, 136, of the late twelfth century (nos. 155, 166–9, 171, 181, 198, 200–1, 203).

Ib—Oxford, Bodl. 937 (3088), parts II and III, of the early thirteenth century (for part I see below) (as Ia).

Id—Bodl. 509 (2672), of the late twelfth century (nos. 166–7).

Ie—Bodl. Laud Misc. 666 (1051), of the thirteenth century (no. 167).

Ic—Oxford, Bodl. Rawlinson Q. f. 8 (27836), of the late twelfth century, from Ely (nos. 155, 165–7); on this manuscript, see A. Saltman in *BIHR*, XXII (1949), 152–7.

Ha—BM Harleian 215, of the fourteenth century, which is in part a copy of Ic, in part a copy of a manuscript similar to Rb and Va (perhaps of their common source) (no. 165).

(II) Manuscripts containing Becket's own letters and the pope's, with only a small number by anyone else.

Rb—BM Royal 13 A. xiii, of the late twelfth century (nos. 167, 182, 199, 204).

Va—Vatican Lat. 6024, fos. 85v–139v,[3] of the late twelfth or early thirteenth century; additional letters connected with the dispute on fos. 71–85v (nos. 155, 166). This manuscript consists of several independent letter collections, including the Register of Master David (see above).

Jb—Oxford, St John's College, MS 15, of the fifteenth century, which has approximately the same letters as Rb, in the same order, and is probably a copy of Rb.

(III) Alan of Tewkesbury's collection, probably revised from the materials used for I and II *c.* 1176–9. The following manuscripts contain the complete work.

C—BM Cotton Claudius B. ii, of the late twelfth century (a book exceptional for both its fine execution and its accuracy) (as Ia, also 170, 197).

[1] Which is being undertaken by Mrs Anne Duggan.
[2] Of the groups, not of the MSS; on this see *JS Epp.* II.
[3] The order of this part of Va is curious: it seems that the scribe copied a manuscript closely resembling Rb, but leaving a number of letters out, which he subsequently added in order at the end. This is confirmed by the fact that the order in Rb is roughly chronological. None the less, the two manuscripts are independent of one another.

Co—Cambridge, Corpus Christi College, 295, of the early thirteenth century (as Ia, except for no. 166).

Vb—Vatican Lat. 1220, of the fourteenth century, from which the edition by Father Christian Lupus, *Epistolae et Vita divi Thomae*... (2 vols., Brussels, 1682) was derived (as Ia).

The following texts are incomplete or fragmentary:

Ib, part I: parts II and III formed a copy of the earlier collection (see above), to which was later added part I, items in Alan's collection not already copied.

Ar—BM Arundel 219, of the fourteenth century, containing books I–III of Alan, with certain omissions; this is close to (perhaps derived from) Co (nos. 168–9, 181, 198, 200–1, 203).

Bn—Paris, Bibliothèque Nationale, Lat. 5320, of the late twelfth or early thirteenth century (an abbreviated version, breaking off soon after the opening of Book II); perhaps a copy of Co (167–9, 198, 200).

O—Cambridge, Trinity Hall, 24, of the early or mid thirteenth century, a text doubtless originally complete, now breaking off just before the end of Book I (155, 167–9, 171, 198, 200).

(Jb—Oxford, St John's College 15, fos. 252–6v, of the fifteenth century, only a table of contents.)

(Ja—Oxford, St John's College 126, fos. 79–91, of the late twelfth or early thirteenth century: Guy of Southwick's *florilegium*, containing only a few letters, in a highly abbreviated form, and none of Gilbert's.)

Finally, the Life by Roger of Crowland (early thirteenth century) contains a number of letters, apparently abstracted from some text of Alan's collection.[1]

For our purposes Ja and Jb can be ignored; and Vb, O, Ar and Bn are textually worthless. Of the remainder, C, Ia, Ib and Co are excellent manuscripts, and Ic–Ie occasionally useful. It appears that two editions of Alan's collection were made under his eyes; of the first C is a fair copy, and of the second Ib and Co are close copies of the archetype. At an early date—perhaps about 1190—the archetype of the second edition was collated with C, and a conflate text produced from which it would seem that Vb and O were derived. But they are too careless to offer anything of textual value.

### Biographies and chronicles

A small number of letters also occur in the biographies of Becket and the chronicles of Ralph de Diceto and Roger of Howden: thus the ubiquitous *Mandatum uestrum* (no. 155) is in William of Canterbury's Life and in the two chronicles. William's and Ralph's readings are worthless and one cannot pronounce on their source; but Howden, although his text is careless, is of interest because he provides the version otherwise known only from B. Howden has three good readings not in B, but this does not prove that he used B's source, because he undoubtedly had access to other

---

[1] This is preserved in Paris, Bibl. Nat., Lat. 5372 (dated 1411) and (incompletely) in the earlier Bodl. E Musaeo 133 (3512) (not collated for this edition).

manuscripts which contained the letter, and these readings could be the fruit of collation. But whether he used B or its source or a manuscript related to B in some other way, it is highly probable that Howden had access to Gilbert's files.[1]

## Conclusion

Even if Roger of Howden had access to Gilbert's files, it seems unlikely that the compilers of the Becket correspondence collected Gilbert's letters from him. Textually, there is nothing to forbid the hypothesis that Gilbert's letters in these collections derived from the originals received by Becket or from copies collected at the time. It may seem a little strange that Becket should have had access to Gilbert's letters to the king; but Becket or John of Salisbury or Alan of Tewkesbury somehow obtained access to a considerable amount of Henry's correspondence, and it is hardly probable that they obtained these letters by direct application to Henry. It seems most likely that copies of them circulated among the clerks who moved in both circles at the time. If it is unlikely that Henry would be asked after the martyrdom to supply copies of letters which he had sent or received in the heat of the crisis, it is by the same token even more improbable that John or Alan would have approached Gilbert. In the case of *Multiplicem* this seems really inconceivable. *Multiplicem* (no. 170) embarrassed almost everyone who handled it after Becket's death. In B and D the author's name has been suppressed; in manuscripts deriving from Becket's archives, it is known only in C, and was omitted from Alan's revised edition and from all the manuscripts deriving from C. Nor can the text in C come from B or D or their common source.[2]

As has been argued elsewhere, we can be reasonably confident that the copies in B and D go back to a draft or copy preserved by Gilbert in 1166, and that the copy in C goes back to the original received by Becket in 1166. We can observe in the manuscripts the gradual change of Gilbert's attitude towards his masterpiece: first, in 1166, the author parading his rhetorical and dialectical skill, rejoicing in his strength; the Gilbert Foliot of five or six years later, broken by illness and excommunication and baffled by the martyrdom, too doubtful of the letter to confess his authorship, still too attached to it to suppress it altogether; the old man, putting together the final collection of his letters,[3] a convert to the martyr,

---

[1] Roger of Wendover and Matthew Paris were later to quote from nos. 167, 169 and 155 (Paris, *Chron. Maiora*, ed. H. R. Luard, RS, II, 236, 238, 242–4).

[2] See notes to the letter, and especially the variants in the protocol; also *GF*, p. 168. It is clear that C derives from a slightly more polished text, and this is most naturally explained if B and D come from Gilbert's penultimate draft, while C is from the version actually sent to Becket. Yet in other letters there are cases where C contains variants suggesting access to a manuscript with B's or D's readings, or where there is some evidence of agreements between B and/or D and other manuscripts of a surprising kind. They are noted in the apparatus where they occur, but they are too trivial to establish any arguments sufficient to counter what is said above.

[3] Or permitting his clerks to do so (to call B the final collection is perhaps begging the question whether any later collections were made, and then lost, and also that of the precise date of the source of D).

leaving out *Multiplicem*—yet it found its place at the last moment.[1] Why, one cannot tell.

Meanwhile at Canterbury a similar drama was enacted. It seems that John of Salisbury would have nothing of *Multiplicem*;[2] but Alan at first included it. It was, however, and always will be, a stumbling-block to the martyr's closest friends, and it was omitted from the second edition. A later scribe collating C was tempted by it—tempted twice[3]—but refrained; perhaps for the same reason, perhaps daunted by its massive bulk.

This hesitation in no way diminishes the conclusive evidence that it was acknowledged at both Canterbury and London as Gilbert's work. Thus the textual history of *Multiplicem* helps to confirm the other evidence of its authenticity.[4] In general, the most important conclusion from this inquiry into the manuscript materials for the letters of Gilbert Foliot is that B was written in Gilbert's own household; and this may be taken to guarantee the genuineness of all the letters which it attributes to him. This is not to say that he dictated or wrote them all himself,[5] but that he would have acknowledged them as his own.

## II. PREVIOUS EDITIONS

A handful of Gilbert's letters were printed by Father Christian Lupus (or Wolf) in his edition of Alan of Tewkesbury's collection, based on Vb, a 'corpulent little quarto'[6] in two volumes which appeared in Brussels in 1682. In the next century Lord Lyttelton printed *Multiplicem* (no. 170). In spite of these efforts, and in spite of the hints suggested by the presence of a manuscript in a Protestant printer's shop in the reign of Edward VI, and the somewhat later marginalia in MS B, that an edition may from time to time have been projected, most of Gilbert's letters remained unprinted until the appearance of Dr J. A. Giles's edition in 1846.[7] This edition was reprinted in Migne's *Patrologia*, and for the bulk of the correspondence scholars have depended since on Giles and Migne. Giles was a clergyman of the

---

[1] See *GF*, pp. 102–3, 169.

[2] There is no trace of it in Groups I and II of the correspondence.

[3] It occurs twice in the index of Vb, but not in the text. The reason for this seems to be that the attempt to follow the different orders in C and Alan's second edition quite naturally led the scribe of Vb or its archetype to traverse some stretches of ground twice—and so brought him again to *Multiplicem*, which he had omitted the first time.

[4] See *GF*, pp. 167 ff.; Knowles, *EC*, pp. 171–80.

[5] On this, see *GF*, pp. 29 ff., and chapter III below. One presumes that he dictated the majority of those of which he was the author: he refers directly to dictation in no. 165. But in no. 128 he speaks as if he were writing 'manu propria'—one cannot be sure that he meant this literally, but it is possible that he wrote some of his letters with his own hand; possible too, though not likely, that one of the hands in B is his. In no. 107 (under circumstances of special secrecy) he asks his uncle of Lincoln to remember what he learnt at school, 'et propria exarare manu'. Three *acta* not in B may have been issued by Gilbert the Universal (1128–34: nos. 364, 369, 463).

[6] J. C. Robertson, *Becket*, p. 4—possibly referring to the 2 vols. bound as I.

[7] See *DNB* for Giles's career. He died in 1884.

established Church, a schoolmaster, and the editor and translator of a multitude of medieval texts. In none of these activities was he wholly successful. He worked with incredible speed, and it is hardly to be wondered at that the quality of his editions was uneven. It was most severely criticized in Canon Robertson's biography of Becket (1859), in which Giles was taken particularly to task for his arrangement of the letters—especially for placing them 'by the rank of the receivers.... The clergy take precedence, and after the most insignificant of these come emperors, kings and queens, from whom the scale descends by due gradations to the rest of the laity. For this, indeed, a precedent had been given by a late voluminous baronet, who published the letters of his correspondents in their strict heraldic order'— and he went on to show how inconvenient the arrangement is, how difficult to discern the proper order of letters in an edition devoid of notes or index, and concluded by quoting Carlyle: 'editing, as you edit waggon-loads of rubbish, by turning the waggon upside-down.'[1] Robertson did less than justice to Giles, but nemesis has overtaken him, as it overtakes all those who criticize unduly previous workers in the same field. For, having observed the need for a competent and conscientious scholar to do again what Giles had done, and having expressed a hope that a place would be found for such a work in the Rolls Series, he presently found the task allotted to himself. The seven volumes of the Becket *Materials* (completed by Dr J. B. Sheppard) were indeed a splendid achievement. We have not been able to discover any comment by Dr Giles—who outlived Robertson and so may well have seen the first six volumes[2]—on his supplanter. But he could justly have observed that he knew more of manuscripts than Robertson—so far as the correspondence is concerned, it seems that Robertson added none to the list of manuscripts seen and used by Giles—and that the *Materials* have not much more annotation than his own edition. Robertson's apparatus and notes leave much to be desired. But his texts are sounder and better arranged than this would lead us to expect, and for this one may offer three reasons: he was a better Latinist than Giles, he had a thorough and intimate knowledge of the history of the crisis, and he had the sound judgement to rely so far as he could on the work of a better textual critic than himself, the scribe of Cotton Claudius B. ii.

Quite a number of Gilbert's letters are in Robertson's *Materials*, and a small number have been edited or re-edited elsewhere; but the bulk of them have hitherto had to be consulted in Giles or Migne. We hope we have made some improvement on the work of Giles and Robertson, but it would be churlish not to record our respect and gratitude. Giles was a notable pioneer, and Robertson's volumes will remain for many years to come the unreplaced corpus of Becket *Materials*.

[1] *Becket*, pp. 170–2; in Foliot's letters, this order only obtained among those written as bishop of London; for the rest, Giles somewhat disarranged the order in B.

[2] Vol. VI, of 1882, carries a notice of Robertson's recent death; vol. VII appeared in 1885. An eighth volume, to contain an edition by Paul Meyer of the French metrical lives, never appeared.

### III. THE DIPLOMATIC OF THE CHARTERS

The mid and late twelfth century represented an epoch in the development of charter forms emanating from the writing-offices, the 'chanceries', of English bishops.[1] From being scarce, divergent in character and commonly imprecise in language, they became a recognizable type of document, owing much to the influence of the papal chancery, much, too, to the English royal writ; but having a great deal in common among themselves which distinguished them from both their parents. The forms were not, however, stereotyped; on the contrary, dictators or scribes of bishops' charters took a special delight in providing variety within a uniform medium.

Of all this the charters of Gilbert Foliot provide striking illustrations. Let no. 391 serve as an example. We may be unusually confident both of its authenticity and of its being the work of Gilbert's writing-office, because two originals of it survive, both in 'hand I' of Bodl. E Mus. 249 (MS B), the presiding genius of the chief manuscript of Gilbert's letters. It opens 'G. Dei gratia Lundon' episcopus', using the formula normal among episcopal titles at this time. In his letters, Gilbert was commonly 'minister humilis', especially when he addressed a superior; in his charters he was 'Dei gratia' abbot or bishop. In the few surviving charters as abbot, the protocol tends to follow the pattern of a private charter: 'Sciant omnes presentes et absentes quod ego Gilebertus Dei gratia ecclesie Gloucestrensis abbas', runs no. 286; and the practice of placing the title after the address was not uncommon among Gilbert's charters as bishop of Hereford. It was rare, though not unknown, among his charters as bishop of London; and he did not live to see the borrowing of 'divina miseratione' from the cardinals,[2] or the return of the practice of placing the address before the title, normal in episcopal as in private charters before the end of the century. In no. 391 Gilbert addresses 'dilectis sibi in Domino uniuersis sancte matris ecclesie filiis'. This particular formula occurs about a dozen times; general addresses similar in character, though with many characteristic slight variations, over a hundred times. This formula occurs as early as c. 1148 (no. 300), and address and greeting are both identical in no. 343, of 1158–61, save only that 'Herefordensi' is added to qualify, and narrow, the Church addressed. In effect one could say that all the elements of the protocol of no. 391 were in existence in 1148, when Gilbert first became a bishop. None the less, one can discern a definite trend. The order of the protocol, the use of the general formula, and the use of the triple greeting 'salutem, gratiam et benedictionem', all become more common and regular down to the 1170's, when no. 391 and MS B were written; from then to Gilbert's death there is no discernible change. The limitation of the address to one diocese occurs from time to time throughout the period, down to no. 389, issued within a year of

---

[1] As was first fully shown by C. R. Cheney in *English Bishops' Chanceries, 1100–1250* (Manchester, 1950); this chapter owes much to Professor Cheney's book, and much that follows repeats or confirms his findings. See also Sir Frank Stenton, 'Acta episcoporum', *CHJ*, III, i (1929), 1–14; *Acta Stephani Langton*, ed. K. Major, introd.; Saltman, pp. 190 ff.; *Acta Chichester*, ed. H. Mayr-Harting, pp. 25 ff.

[2] But see no. 344.

Gilbert's death. In early days an address to, or including, a named person is not uncommon; this, along with other irregularities—especially the confusion of letter and charter form[1]—steadily declined.

Very much the same trend, and the same formulas of address, can be found in the charters of Archbishop Theobald (1139–61), whose chancery seems to have been the chief seed-bed of episcopal diplomatic in England at this time.[2] Theobald's salutations, however, were usually simpler—'salutem' alone was far the commonest, as was normal in the mid century; in Gilbert's *acta* it comes third, after the triple greeting of no. 391 (easily the most popular, especially in later years) and 'salutem in Domino', but well ahead of the ten or so other alternatives. 'Salutem, gratiam et benedictionem' occurs only once among Theobald's surviving charters, in a document for Wix priory certainly spurious in its present form, and possibly based in part on a lost charter of Gilbert's.[3]

Whether the choice of 'salutem in Domino' and 'salutem, gratiam et benedictionem' was in the first instance made by the bishop himself is impossible to say. There is beyond question a gradual assimilation between his charters and his more formal letters in later years; but this may be due to his losing interest in letter-writing, or it may be due to the freezing effect of the science of *dictamen*.[4] In general, we may be reasonably certain that the influences at work in his writing-office were those of one scriptorium on another, and even if we discern, rather particularly, the influence of Theobald's 'chancery' on Gilbert's, the bishop's part in this may well have been little more than to give his clerks the chance to mingle with those of his admired superior.

The first element in the text of a charter was the pious preamble or arenga, of which Gilbert's *acta* offer about fifty examples. This is the clearest example of an element in the English episcopal charter borrowed from the papal chancery, but once it had been imported the clerks of English bishops delighted to devise variants of a common stock of platitudes. Professor Cheney pointed out that observations on what 'Ad pastoris spectat sollicitudinem' (or 'curam' or 'officium') could be found in charters of Theobald, of Henry of Winchester, of Walter of Rochester and of Jocelin of Salisbury. This in its turn was a variant of 'Ad nostri officii...' or 'Ad nostrum spectat officium...'[5] which one meets in papal bulls, and in the form 'Ad nostri curam spectat officii...' and the like in Gilbert's charters (447, cf. 342) or as 'Ad officii nostri sollicitudinem...' in Theobald's (Saltman, no. 246). In the nature

---

[1] E.g. in the title, the use of 'minister' or 'minister humilis', appropriate to letters, for 'Dei gratia episcopus'.

[2] Cheney, *op. cit.* pp. 52 ff.; Saltman, *loc. cit.*

[3] See Brooke in *Misc. D. M. Stenton*, p. 48 and n.; cf. 49 n.

[4] See *GF*, pp. 9 ff. It is, however, noticeable that the arengas in the charters constantly vary, whereas the formula 'Verborum facile suadet paucitas...' served for no less than five letters (nos. 160, 196, 226–7, 250). This may suggest that the letters were dictated by the aging bishop, whose inspiration was running dry, while the charters were composed by his clerks. But it would be impossible to establish anything like a watertight distinction between his work and theirs.

[5] Cheney, *op. cit.* pp. 72–3; cf. Saltman, p. 199; JL 11,117, 9,413 = *PL*, CC, 332, CLXXX, 1484.

1    A twelfth-century bishop, possibly Gilbert Foliot (Kempley, Glos)

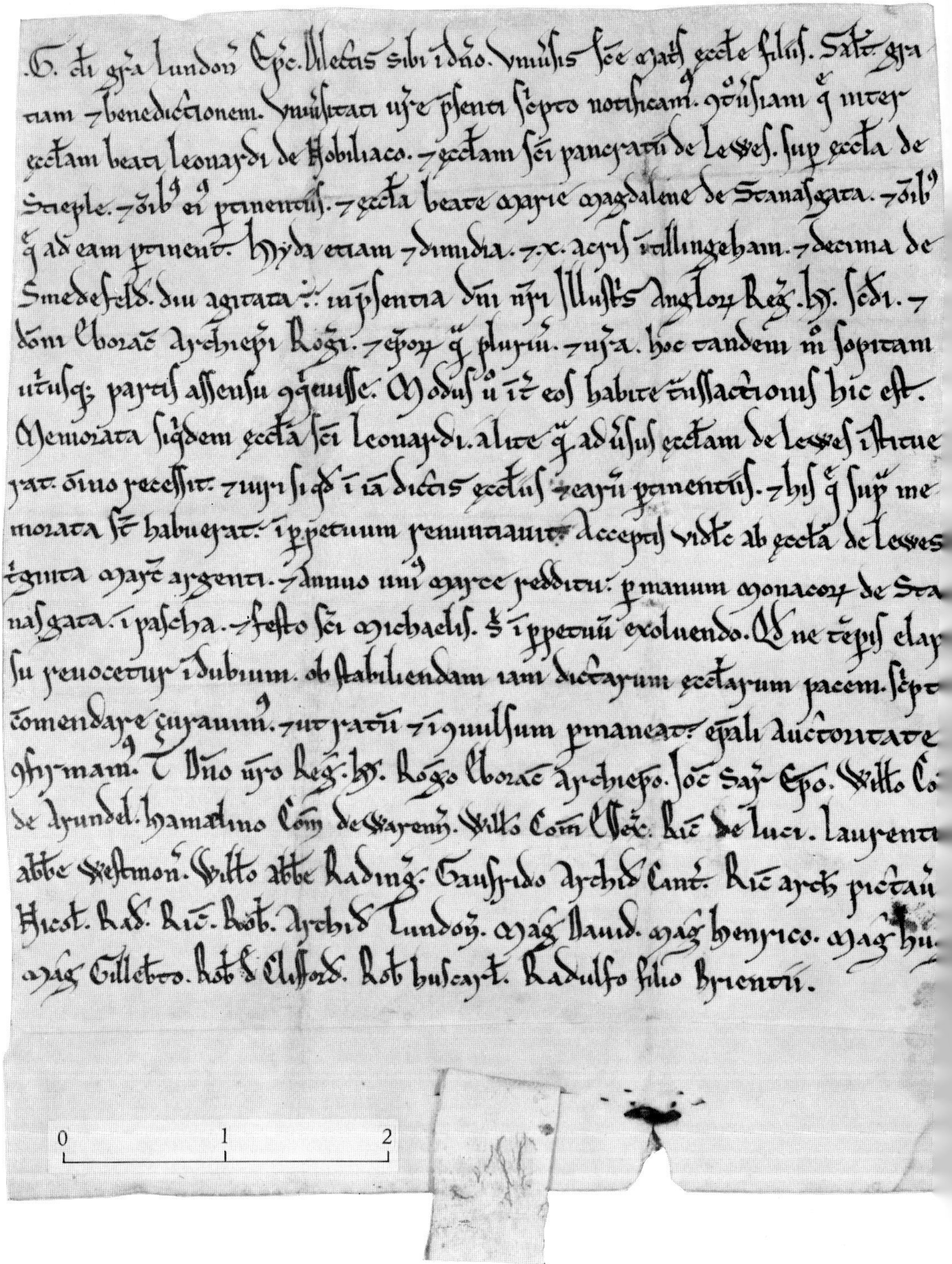

Hand I: Oxford, Bodleian MS E Musaeo 249, fo. 195 (nos. 474, 355, 266: see pp. 2-4)

447

Multiplicem nobis ⁊ diffusam late
materiam perfundendo p̄r̄ ⁊ copiose referen-
do opponentis · ⁊ nos licet sup[er] appellatione
ad d[omi]n[u]m papam p[ro]sequenda sollicitos · tm̄ u[est]re
sublimitati referre · cui q[ui]dem ⁊ nos grauiter urgente necessitate compellimur·
Emissis enim sparsim elogiis · nos de toto
fratrum n[ost]r[o]r[um] collegio · seorsum ponitis ad
conuitia · ut singularit[er] in nos · ⁊ si immen-
sos ignominiosa agerentur ⁊ opprobria · Sobrii
u[er]i sensus ho[m]i[num] · Grauaretur reuerende p[er]so-
ne · Magistru[m] ratione platonis · ⁊ dogmatis
ueritati reuerenter obnoxiu[m] · munus est ad
istam iratam exarsisse tam gr[aui]ter · ⁊ uelut
euocatum ad coleras · innocentia filii pie
p[at]r[is] osculent[er] · no[n] solum non admisisse·
s[ed] ⁊ ip[s]i opinione nota q[ua]dam malicie
e[ss]e sibi minime o[mn]is[ci]us est· eu[m] no[n] id gr[au]ga-
te mirto· respersisse · Vnde c[um] ecclesiam
dei subuiere · fas nefasq[ue] o[con]fundere· (M)on-
rem illu[m] q[ui] ecclesia ⁊ columpna uiuentis di
est non sano capite uelle denice· ad ea
q[ue] u[er]a sunt ambisse· ⁊ q[uo]d ab his opprimen-
dis repulsi fuerint· ob id u[est]ram eccles[ie] ⁊
pace[m] tim̄e p[er]turbasse· (I)n bello d[omi]ni t[er]ga de-
disse· emissis sepius publice denotem̄·
difficile est ut sileam· ut hanc aduersum
nos opinione[m] uel apostemus admittere· ut
in defensa fuit posteritati transmittere· o[con]fessi-
onem inuenire silentio p[er]mittam· luxu-
riaq[ue] malo[rum] radix ⁊ origo cupiditas· s[ecundu]m
ne nos hui[us] suspectos haberi q[ui]b[us] preual-

prava

suadens e facili: nos hinc ip[s]a iuber[e]
necessitas exordiri. Arcaps[s]. Quis
scit hominis occulta ho[m]i[n]is· n[is]i sp[iritu]s ho[m]i[n]is
qui est in ip[s]o· Latent q[ui]dem homines
occulta ho[m]i[n]um· ⁊ abyssu[m] cordiu[m] de-
celo d[omi]n[u]s intuet[ur]· Ip[s]um ignota no[n] t[er]ret
uirt[us]· occulta no[n] fallit· est enim sermo
dei uiuus ⁊ efficax· penetrabilior q[ue] o[mn]i
gladio ancipiti· Hec est illa exarra[n]s
inuisibilis inspectu illi[us]· Ip[s]i ⁊ cordi
ip[s]o loq[ui]t[ur]· Sub ip[s]o examine non
uana aut ficta· s[ed] q[ue] u[er]itate ⁊ scientie subni[x]a su[n]t· ⁊ fidenter ⁊ libere re-
spondem[us]· asserentes utiq[ue] qm̄· ad ea
q[ue] u[est]ra su[n]t ambitionis stimulos nu[m]q[uam]
uel monito sensim· honore[m] hu[n]c nul-
li u[m]q[uam] inuidim[us]· Nulli ad hanc
gr[ati]am munie uel obseq[ui]o gr[ati]a uel
fauore deseruuim[us]· ut ad hui[us] ecclesi-
gia culminis accessu[m] nobis sacre
gr[ati]am q[ui]busq[ue] modis aut administr[ati]-
culis aptarem[us]· Quis hoc p[at]r[e] meli[us]
qm̄ uos q[ui] potu[is]tis liq[ui]di estimare· q[uia]
ip[s]i ecclesie u[est]re t[em]poris archidiaconu[m]·
⁊ d[omi]ni n[ost]ri Reg[is] electu[m] e milib[us] no[n] con-
siliariu[m] solu[m]· s[ed] cor fuisse ⁊ stat[um]
⁊ osiliu[m]· sine quo n[on] q[ui]dem facile·
s[ed] nec erat possibile ad hec o[mn]ino
q[uae]mpiam obtinere progressu[m]· Nobis
itaq[ue] q[uia] ap[u]d uos gr[ati]am collocuim[us]·
Hu[n]c p[ro] nos aut aliu[m]· u[est]ram u[m]q[uam] gr[ati]am
teruim[us] aut obseq[u]is attentauim[us]· ut
ad quod n[on] p[er] uos attingi no[n] pot[er]at·
in id ope u[est]ra subleuarem[us]· hinc
u[est]ram p[at]r[e] iustiti[am] ⁊ meam prudentia[m]·

88

IV   Oxford, Bodleian MS E Musaeo 249, fo. 200 v (no. 170, opening : see pp. 3 f., 20 f.)

of things, this is not a form of literature which lends itself to precise source-criticism. It is sufficiently clear, however, that Gilbert's clerks were under direct papal influence, but were also, and probably more, influenced by their and his English colleagues.[1] Thus it is noticeable that the transition after the arenga is most commonly contrived by 'Inde est quod', also the favourite in Theobald's charters, only rarely by such a common phrase in papal bulls as 'Eapropter'. On the other hand, no. 456, with its arenga 'Eapropter' and general confirmation 'inter que suis hec duximus exprimenda uocabulis...', is so close to the papal pattern as to make direct influence probable; and the use of the tittle abbreviation and of tall ascenders in some originals and one hand in MS B probably also shows that papal models had been studied directly.[2]

The main body of the text was normally introduced by a formula of notification: in early days on the model of private charters—'Nouerit' or 'Sciatis quod'; later on with the common episcopal type of formula, 'Ad uniuersitatis uestre notitiam...' or the like; or, as in no. 391, 'Vniuersitati uestre presenti scripto notificamus...'. No. 391 carries on, as one expects by the 1170's, with a precise statement of the function of the charter—in this case a decision in a legal dispute—and concludes with a corroboration clause in general terms and a substantial witness list. The corroboration clause was rare in Theobald's acta, but coming into general use in the third quarter of the century, and it provided Gilbert's clerks with their chief opportunity to find an infinite variety of ways of saying the same thing. Very few of his charters, even of the Hereford period, lack it; hardly ever do two use precisely the same formula. 'Quod ne temporis elapsu reuocetur in dubium, ob stabiliendam iamdictarum ecclesiarum pacem, scripto commendare curauimus; et ut ratum et inconuulsum permaneat, episcopali autoritate confirmamus', says no. 391. 'Et ut hec donatio firma et inconuulsa in perpetuum maneat, presenti scripto et sigilli mei attestatione ipsam confirmo', ran a confirmation of his early years at Hereford (no. 333). The seal is sometimes mentioned, sometimes omitted; it is quite clear, however, that the writing-office early established a rule or a convention that there should be a corroboration clause and that each charter should have a different one.[3] We know from MS B that a considerable number of copies of charters and drafts of bits and pieces of them were available in Gilbert's office. The success with which exact repetition of the corroboration formula was avoided suggests that these drafts and copies were carefully studied. And the use of this

[1] Examples of papal influence could be multiplied. Cheney, p. 72, quotes the familiar arenga 'Iustis postulantium desideriis...' from no. 236 (which is, however, a letter, but a very formal one).

[2] Though these could have been learned from Theobald's acta: see Cheney, op. cit. p. 53 and plate II. But a glance at the contents of MS B shows how familiar Gilbert's clerks must have been with the appearance of papal bulls.

[3] There are a few exceptions: e.g. nos. 315, 323, 422, 439–40 are very close, and 184 and 350 virtually identical. A few early charters have an anathema also. Indulgences had formulas of their own, not including a corroboration clause. A curious example is no. 418, which seems really to be two indulgences on a single model—a repetition otherwise unparalleled in Gilbert's surviving charters.

formula underlines a basic principle natural in the second half of the twelfth century. The episcopal charter was a kind of sandwich, in which a statement of legal rights and decisions lay between formulas of an unspecific character. The legal rights became increasingly precise and formal in statement; the general formulas gave opportunity for literary exercise of a kind much favoured in the golden age of *dictamen*.[1]

Minor variations need not detain us: in early days they were legion, and a number of the documents printed below were evidently not the work of Gilbert's scribes. Most surviving charters were grants or confirmations or settlements of legal disputes, commonly by Gilbert acting as papal judge-delegate. There are also a certain number of indulgences. These were the kinds of documents which the beneficiaries took pains to preserve. MS B, representing the bishop's archives, also gives us a rare glimpse of types of instrument otherwise almost entirely lost, such as mandates to rural deans, celebrets and the like.[2] Even when the charters came to conform to a pattern, variety of function dictated considerable variety of form.

To each of his charters was originally attached Gilbert's seal. Of this only about ten examples survive in any condition to be recognized, but these are sufficient to make it clear that he used throughout a single pattern of a kind common for the period—vesica-shaped, with the bishop full length, wearing his mitre, lifting his right hand in benediction, holding a pastoral staff in the left, surrounded by an inscription GILEBERTVS DEI GRATIA LVNDONIENSIS (or HEREFORDENSIS) EPISCOPVS.[3] It is quite probable, indeed, that a single matrix served for his episcopate at Hereford, and another for his time at London.

The chief interest of Gilbert's charters lies, however, in their witness lists, whose message has been considered elsewhere. No. 391 provides a cross-section of the men with whom Gilbert worked. It is one of a group of ecclesiastical decisions from the 1170's made in the presence of the king.[4] It was drawn up in the brief interval between Gilbert's absolution and the mission of the legates Albert and Theoduin. It is ironical to find Gilbert in the royal court at this period with his chief partners in the last act of the Becket tragedy, Roger of York and Jocelin of Salisbury, with Richard de Lucy the justiciar, who had enforced Becket's election in 1162 and not long after fallen foul of the archbishop (cf. no. 170, p. 231), and with two leading members of Henry's *curia* soon to be bishops, Becket's disobedient archdeacon Geoffrey Ridel, and Gilbert's cousin Richard of Ilchester. These are

[1] Cf. Cheney, *English Bishops' Chanceries*, pp. 72–3, and on the use of *dictamen* and the cursus, pp. 77 ff. Gilbert's clerks were acquainted at least with cursus rhythms 'but showed no desire to be bound by them', as Professor Cheney has said (p. 81) of English bishops' chanceries at large.

[2] Nos. 264, 280.

[3] The seal survives substantially on nos. 293, 339, 351, 374 (c), 410, 416, 421, 426. In the large majority of cases it was attached *sur double queue* (on a parchment tag put through a slit at the foot of the parchment, which was folded to give greater strength). The seal is or was attached *sur simple queue* to nos. 316 (a letter), 339 (an indulgence) and 422 (a confirmation). For descriptions of the seal, see W. de G. Birch, *Catalogue of Seals in the BM*, I, nos. 1599, 1901.

[4] See H. Mayr-Harting in *Journal of Eccl. History*, XVI (1965), 41 ff.

unusual witnesses, followed by the normal leaders of Gilbert's entourage in unusual strength: his four archdeacons and five of his canons, led by Master David, recently returned from Bologna, not yet at loggerheads with Gilbert.[1] With so many grand witnesses Gilbert's clerks are not named. We may be sure some of them were present, and the handwriting of both originals, which is also that of hand I of MS B, is a precise reminder of their presence, as well as a guarantee of the charter's authenticity.

We have 38 originals of Gilbert's charters, of which four at least were not products of his clerks.[2] Curiously enough, the 34 remaining documents seem to have been written by at least 24 scribes, so that analysis of any one of the scribes' work is difficult. But it is possible to identify the hand of at least six scribes in more than one charter.[3] On the whole, the evidence of these does not suggest that Gilbert's clerks had a substantial freedom of choice in drafting his charters. They played many variations on standard themes, but so far as one can observe they were all taught to play the same sort of variation on the same themes.

None the less, it seems clear that some of the formulas of no. 391 represent the scribe's own choice. This is made likely by the evidence of no. 422, written in the same hand, which also contains the greeting 'salutem, gratiam et benedictionem' and introduces the witness list with the formula 'His testibus'. On the other hand, the greeting is common in other scribes' work, and one original of 391 has 'Testibus' alone. Nos. 393, 410 and 411 are all in one hand; 410–11 have identical protocols, and that of 393 is very similar; all have arengas and introduce the dispositive clauses with 'Inde est quod' and the witness lists with 'His testibus'. Nos. 404 and 432 have identical protocols and 'Testibus his'; 405 and 407 have identical protocols and 'Testibus'. Nos. 421 and 426 have forms of greeting which suggest a scribe used to writing letters rather than charters, and no witness lists; 426, indeed, is in letter form. But 421 is otherwise in charter form; and all these charters have

[1] *GF*, pp. 205–6; cf. no. 240.
[2] No. 289, his profession, was presumably written by one of the archbishop's clerks; no. 332, for Saint-Florent, was probably written by a Monmouth priory scribe (cf. *Facs.... of Charters in the BM*, I, nos. 16, 41), and has little in common with Gilbert's other charters; no. 293 was the work of a group of judges-delegate, and there is no reason to attribute it specially to Gilbert's clerks; no. 400 is an agreement, written in a book-hand, and most probably drawn up by or for the chapter rather than the bishop. It is probable that a number of other charters were not written by his scribes; in particular this may help to explain those confirmations which simply add a sentence or two to another charter (nos. 318–19, 354; cf. no. 332; though this practice was by no means uncommon; Cheney, *English Bishops' Chanceries*, pp. 91–2), and the unusual elements in nos. 420 a–c. No. 420 a is the only *inspeximus* in this collection (see Cheney, *op. cit.* pp. 90 ff.). The figure 38 excludes no. 395, whose 'original' must be a thirteenth-century copy; but counts in the three originals of 374 and the two of 391.
[3] Nos. 393, 410–11 are in one hand; 404, 416, 432 are in another; in addition there are the following pairs: 374 (B and C, possibly the beneficiary's work); 405, 407; 421, 426. As already stated, there are two originals of 391, both in hand I of MS B, which also wrote no. 422 and possibly no. 466. The hands of the following occur only once: 311, 316 (both rather rough book-hands), 339, 351, 374 (A), 376, 381, 394 (this might prove to be the hand of a Lewes scribe), 398, 401, 403, 406, 408–9, 412, 429, 451, 465. To these should be added those listed in note 2.

different corroborative clauses ringing the changes on the same basic theme, as is normal throughout Gilbert's later acts. Furthermore, the protocols, for example, of nos. 405 and 410 (by different scribes) only differ in one word.

It is interesting to observe that of the three originals of no. 374, two are in a single hand, the third in a different hand; yet the formulas are virtually identical. Neither hand can be shown to be from Gilbert's familia, and it is possible that both worked under the direction of a single *dictator*, or one copied the other's draft. Nos. 465–6, however, show us two different scribes settling the same case in different words; since no. 466 is probably (though not certainly) in the same hand as 391, it may well be that Gilbert or one of his leading clerks was dissatisfied with no. 465, and had no. 466 engrossed as an improved version. The two originals of 391 are in the same hand and virtually identical.

These cases suggest interesting reflections, but are an insecure basis for definite conclusions on the methods of Gilbert's writing-office: in general, it is clear that the office devised ruling themes and a stock of formulas, that these were clearly established by the 1170's at latest, but that some measure of choice was permitted to individual clerks. In particular, the protocol and witness list were composed by selection from a stock of formulas; the corroboration clause was normally expected to show a new variation on the standard theme.

By intensive study of the original royal charters of this age, Mr T. A. M. Bishop has been able to identify the hands of a considerable number of royal scribes (though it is very rare for us to know their names). He has also shown that a great number of royal writs and charters were still written by scribes specially hired for the occasion or by beneficiaries, even though these would (by Henry II's time) normally adhere quite faithfully to the formulas of the royal chancery.[1] The great diversity of hands among Gilbert's originals might suggest a similar practice. But it is clear that an episcopal office contained far more clerks than were strictly needed for the work in hand—it was a school for church government as well as an administrative headquarters[2]—and it seems likely that the diversity of hands mainly reflects the number of underemployed clerks who attended in Gilbert's train. A few hands appear often enough for us to feel tolerably secure that they were in regular employment. But our study of Gilbert's diplomatic may have suggested that in his later years there was some direction in his office over and above that provided by his own presence. We have seen how freely hand I organized the completion of MS B; the hand, as it were, speaks with authority. We have seen that it was the hand of one of Gilbert's clerks. If we study Gilbert's witness lists we shall find one name far and away the most common, and that a name which assumes in almost all the later witness lists in which it occurs first place among the clerks—but never passed out of the ranks of the clerks. It is a guess, no more, that hand I and the hand of nos. 391 and 422 belonged to Richard of Salisbury. It is a natural inference from the witness lists that Richard was for a time Gilbert's chief clerk.[3] It would be

---

[1] *Scriptores Regis*, introd., *passim*. We gratefully acknowledge Mr Bishop's help also in the identification of the hands of Gilbert Foliot's charters.

[2] See *GF*, pp. 214 ff.          [3] This is discussed more fully in *GF*, pp. 213–14.

interesting to know if it was more than a coincidence that Gilbert received a leading clerk from the city which gave Archbishop Theobald his most eminent secretary and possibly also gave Roger the Great of Sicily his chancellor.[1]

## IV. THIS EDITION

Our aim is to print the letters and charters, as nearly as possible, as they left the hands of Gilbert Foliot or his clerks and passed into those of the recipients. For charters whose originals survive, the task is straightforward.[2] When the original does not survive, we follow the text and spelling of the earliest or best copy, correcting it where other evidence shows its readings to be unacceptable. The spelling is that of the first manuscript listed unless otherwise stated. The majority of the letters survive in MS B alone. This is based on copies or drafts preserved in Gilbert's office, but it has already been shown that in most cases these probably differed little from the letters actually sent—and the letters of which substantially divergent texts are known or were probably never sent have been noted above, on p. 10. A number of the early letters are also in H and R, which both contain a number of good readings and evidently go back, like B, to copies and drafts in Gilbert's office; the same applies to the letters in D. MS A is a copy of B, and so is ignored except where it helps with a word illegible in B. The letters which found their way into other manuscripts of the Becket correspondence probably came there from the recipients. The consensus of their evidence is therefore a better guide to the state of the letter as it actually passed to the recipient than MS B, and for this reason is usually preferred—though the spelling of B is followed, where B provides a text. *Multiplicem* (no. 170) offers a special problem, since it survives in one Becket MS only; fortunately this is the best of all, MS C, but it is often difficult to know whether its readings are due to changes made by Gilbert himself or by Alan of Tewkesbury's scribe, and in several places C itself offers variants. A final decision in each case, as in all textual matters, depends on the editors' judgement—but the differences in almost every case are of negligible importance.

Variants of H, R, D, Va, C, Co, Ia, Ib, Ic, Id, Ie, Rb are noted where they could conceivably be correct or establish some point of textual history; private errors and minor slips (which are frequent in H and D) are not noted, except in MS B, for which we record every variant save the omission of a mark for 'n' or 'm'. The lists of manuscripts after each letter are comprehensive, save that we omit references to A,

---

[1] John of Salisbury and Robert of Salisbury—or Saleby (or Selby); on Robert see *DNB*. The only English writer known to give him his surname is John of Hexham, ed. Arnold, p. 318. The only MS (Corpus Christi College, Cambridge, MS 139, fo. 145v) reads 'Salesb'ia' (' = *er* abbreviation), corrected (by the original scribe or an early corrector) to 'Salesbia'. (We owe this information to the kindness of Professor C. R. Cheney.) If the latter form has any authority, it points to Saleby (Lincs.: 'Salesbi' in *PR* 1166, according to E. Ekwall, *Concise Oxford Dict. of Place-names, s.v.* Saleby), and it is easy to see how Salisbury could come into a scribe's mind. On the other hand, there is nothing surprising about a great Anglo-Norman administrator emanating from Salisbury in the age of Bishop Roger.

[2] In the descriptions of originals we give the size in inches, and usually ignore modern endorsements.

Ha and Roger of Crowland (see pp. 11 f., 18, 19),[1] and give only the printed reference for letters in William of Canterbury, Howden and Diceto (although the manuscripts have been checked where necessary); we omit references to later chronicles (see p. 20, n. 1). Variants of A, O, Vb, Ar, Bn are not given. Most of the manuscripts, except B, and many of the cartularies from which texts of charters are taken, include rubricated headings. These are only noted if they provide useful information not in the texts; they are quoted in the apparatus of those letters whose protocol has been omitted in the Becket manuscripts, but not where the protocol is given.

The spelling of B has been followed, save in a few cases (recorded in the apparatus) where the spelling is eccentric or confusing. c and t cannot be consistently distinguished in B, and so have been printed throughout this edition according to modern convention. e cedilla (for æ) has been ignored, since it is never used by most of the scribes, even though it was commonly (though not consistently) used by hand I. Where words are usually abbreviated, a number of somewhat arbitrary decisions have had to be taken as to spelling, normally on the basis of a consensus of readings when the words are not abbreviated. We have modernized the punctuation though sometimes following the indications in B and in the original charters.

The letters are in chronological order, save that a few groups have been kept together where it seemed desirable even at the risk of doing some violence to chronology; the charters are arranged in alphabetical order of monastic houses, etc., from whose muniments they come or of churches to which they refer (see p. 1)—though both letters and charters are divided into three sections, one each for the three stages of Gilbert's official career, and a few letters are misplaced owing to an error or change of view discovered or made too late to alter the arrangement.[2] Evidence of date is commonly given in a note at the head of letter or charter; frequently, however, a group of letters is dated in a single note, and a considerable number of dating criteria recur at intervals throughout the collection, and so are noted, once for all, in Appendix 1. References to Canon Law are given to Gratian (see *GF*, p. 241 and n.). In early life, at least, Gilbert must have used other collections; but we do not know which, and it seems more convenient to refer to Friedberg's edition for further references than to give here an elaborate list of possible sources.

The English headings are intended as a rough guide to contents, to help speedy reference, not as a calendar, though they are comparatively full for the charters. They also give opportunity for the identification of place-names (where necessary, references are given to support these in notes). Notes on persons to whom there are frequent or scattered references in the letters are collected in the Biographical Index—except for canons of Hereford or St Paul's or members of Gilbert's household, for whom see *GF*, Appendix IV.

[1] Changes of folio in B are noted in the margin; for this reason only the opening folio of B is noted in the list of manuscripts (full references are given for other manuscripts).

[2] Nos. 420 a–c came to light (through the kindness of Professor C. R. Cheney) after the order had been settled.

# I

# LETTERS OF GILBERT FOLIOT AS ABBOT OF GLOUCESTER
## 1139–1148

## Nos. 1–78

## 1   To Ralph, dean of Hereford

[1140] A letter of consolation for the dean, who has been expelled from Hereford.

Nos. 1 and 2 are adjacent in the manuscripts, and the reference to the expulsion of the dean from Hereford in no. 2 proves that they were inspired by the same events. What these were is stated more clearly in no. 2: fighting in Hereford, and its consequences—'...aporiatur ecclesia, muniuntur castella'. Serious trouble in Hereford is recorded on two occasions in the anarchy, in 1140 and 1143. From Gilbert's own account of the 1143 episode (below, no. 22), there is no hint of violence in the city, and the earlier occasion seems clearly the more appropriate. In 1140 Hereford was besieged by Geoffrey Talbot and Milo of Gloucester, and the graphic account in the *Gesta Stephani*[1] specifically says that the insurgents converted the cathedral into a castle, which seems exactly to fit the implications of the passage in no. 2.

Epistole uenerabilis Gilleberti Herefordensis episcopi: epistolam hanc domno Radulfo decano Hereford(ensi) transmisit.

A te longe positi tuas non de longe contumelias experimur, ipso doloris transuer-berati gladio quo te scimus uulneratum. Directa est manus persequentis in te, sed unum omnibus infixit uulnus quibus te non ficte diligentia caritatis astrinxerat. 5
Exul et profugus[2] ab ecclesia tua et ciuitate expelleris, et tanquam sacra leseris omnia, gladios in te male iuratus miles exacuit—nil tamen habens quod obiciat nisi quod eius audacie in sanctitate et iustitia[3] restitisti. Restitisti quidem et gaudemus, expulsus es et dolemus. Dolemus inquam magis irruentium in te ignominiam quam tue laudis honorem et gloriam. Scimus enim quod uenali illi turbe et in omnem in 10 quam conducitur impietatem promtissime de celis ira reuelatur,[4] sed humilitati tue et patientie gloria in perpetuum reseruatur. Gaude, dilecte mi, gaude et attende. Attende inquam quam pio uoto te bonorum omnium turba prosequitur, dum portas in corpore tuo stigmata Christi Iesu, dum crucem eius baiulas, dum pro iustitia et ecclesie libertate in agone decertas.[5] Non delicatus miles in Domini bella 15

1   G, no. 81; B, fo. 1; H, fo. 147r–v (and R, fo. 205Ar–v, now lost).

1–2 Epistole…transmisit. *In B only. A general heading to the collection—see above, p. 2; this does not mean that the letter was written when Foliot was bishop of Hereford.* Epistole…transmisit *was probably written by hand I (above, p. 2)*     5 infixit B     11 condicitur B

---

[1] Pp. 72–3. On Geoffrey Talbot, see *Gesta*, pp. 38–43, 68; Orderic, v, 110–12; John of Worcester, pp. 49–50; Florence, II, 128; *CP*, IX, 424–6. He held 20 knights' fees in Kent in 1135 (*Red Book of the Exchequer*, I, 195); became a supporter of the empress. He seized Hereford Castle in 1138 and held it against Stephen for nearly five weeks. He was taken prisoner at Bath and exchanged for the bishop. In 1140 he besieged Hereford Castle and died of wounds on 22 August 1140 (John of Worcester, pp. 49f., 58n.). He was a cousin of Gilbert de Lacy and uncle of Cecily, wife of Roger, earl of Hereford (see pedigree in *CP, loc. cit.*).

[2] Cf. Num. xxxv. 32.          [3] Cf. Luc. i. 75.

[4] Cf. Rom. i. 18: 'Reuelatur enim ira Dei de coelo, super omnem impietatem et iniustitiam hominum eorum qui ueritatem Dei in iniustitia detinent.' Gilbert's sentence is not entirely clear; presumably 'in omnem…promtissime' means 'every impiety for which it is hired'.

[5] Cf. Gal. vi. 17; Luc. xiv. 27; II Tim. ii. 5.

uenisti. Pedes nudi, uestis lanea, uexillum crucis in manibus, summi regis exprimunt armaturam. Quod cantauimus hactenus iam uidemus in te illud summi confessoris elogium: 'Ego signo crucis non clipeo protectus aut galea hostium cuneos penetrabo securus.'[1] Hec est framea Christi et baculus peregrinationis eius quo contriuit portas

20 ereas, et uectes ferreos confregit.[2] Tu quoque sapienti consilio cornu crucis inimicos tuos uentilasti,[3] et insurgentes in te multa animi nobilitate contempsisti. Que de te audio letam resonant cuncta uictoriam. Insidiantium laqueos, etsi nudus, expeditus tamen et alacer euasisti. Expulsus quidem es ab ecclesia tua, sed quam gratulabunda occurrit tibi ecclesia sancta mater tua. Hec ab hora uestimenti sui,[4] cui decenter

25 inherebas, te sustollit, totum tibi sinum apperit, te intus colligit, tenet, demulcet, et nutrit. A sponse tue amplexibus ad tempus auelleris, sed matris gremio confoueris. Insultant tamen pessimi quod et domum et urbem egressus es. Es quidem egressus, sed cogita antiquos dies: nunquid Dauid a facie filii fugiens insultantem sibi et dicentem 'egredere uir sanguinum, egredere' cum modestia non sustinuit?[5] Vos,

30 etsi persona dispares, estimo tamen pares in causa. Dominicis utamur exemplis. Nosti quia Dominus a facie Pilati egressus est, in ludibrium sui coronatus spinis, et indutus purpura.[6] Nouissime etiam quasi repurgium quo pollui posset ciuitas, ipse extra portam passus est ultimam passus iniuriam, ne mundus ulterius iniuriam pateretur. Hac nos armari cogitatione oportet, ut ipsum extra castra sequentes

35 improperium ipsius semper in capite nostro portemus.[7] Felix tua egressio, qua sanctorum collegio denominaris. Sed inproperant quod fugisti. Nec fugisti quidem, sed te ad dimicandum acrius pro iustitia reseruasti. Paulus tamen Damasci in sporta ⟨fo. 1v⟩ demissus effugit;[8] nec istud scribens rubore suffunditur sed hoc ipso gloriatur. Nisi enim fugisset, frementem mundi bestiam non confudisset, nec in

40 ipso imperii fastigio uexillum Domini statuisset. Docet nos magister bonus, 'si persecuti uos fuerint in ciuitate una, fugite in alteram'.[9] Fuge ergo, dilecte mi, hoc usus imperio, fuge de Vr Caldeorum[10] in Ierusalem ut habeat in quo pugnet ecclesia, habeat quem reseruet sibi in tempus hostis et belli. Stabis adhuc pro matre filius aduersus eos qui festinant suscitare Leuiatan. Iam nos odore bono respersisti, et tue

45 uirtute constantie bene fraglat ecclesia qui dedignatus es humiliari principi et genu curuare ante Baal.[11] Datur optio confessori ut abiuret quod sancte fecerat uel cedat his que possidebat. Vilescit animo tuo temporale stipendium, et subito factus inops, quanta animi serenitate decantas: 'Ego uero egenus et pauper sum: Deus adiuua me.'[12] Dauitycos ymnos decantauimus et nos, sed que canimus tu legis in te; et

---

1 21 multa animi] magnanimi *corrected to* magna animi B    25 totum *om.* B    29 *om.* uir sanguinum egredere (*by homoioteleuton*) H    30 Domesticis MSS    36 improperarent H 40 fastigio imperio, *corrected and* (?) *transposed* B    44 aduersus…suscitare] in eam fortassis acrius insurgente B (*presumably a revision*)    46 curuare ante B; cruciare H    49 decantamus B

---

[1] Sulpicius Severus, *Vita S. Martini*, i. 4, *PL*, xx, 163.
[2] Cf. Ps. cvi. 16.      [3] Cf. Ps. xliii. 6.
[4] Cf. Ps. cxxxii. 2 (hora = ora).      [5] Cf. Ps. lxxvi. 6; II Reg. xvi. 7.
[6] Cf. Joh. xix. 5.      [7] Cf. Heb. xiii. 11, 13.
[8] Cf. Act. ix. 25; II Cor. xi. 32–3.      [9] Cf. Matt. x. 23.
[10] Cf. Gen. xv. 7.      [11] Cf. Rom. xi. 4.      [12] Ps. lxix. 6.

laudabilia sanctorum que extollimus, sacrum et elucubratum plenius tue tibi 50
uolumen conscientie representat. Percurre psalmos, resonent ab hore tuo illa
Spiritus Sancti plena suauitatis instrumenta; quod pietatis, quod iustitie, quod
fortitudinis in his laudabile decantatur, totum habes in te. Vere beatus philosophus
qui tua ibi bona collocasti, unde ea nec auidi raptoris manus eripiat. Iam dudum in
scolis positi de paupertate spiritus diuersa a diuersis audiuimus. Iam nunc ipsa tibi 55
de propinquo respondeat, utpote que tecum tue domus limen egressa est, te in
itinere comitata, te de regni celorum promissione uberius consolata. Nam quantulum est quod obtractant? Apostolicum illud opponunt: 'omnis anima potestatibus sublimioribus subdita sit', et 'qui potestati resistit, ordinationi Dei resistit'.[1]
Verum quidem hoc est. Sed habet secularis potestas legem qua teneatur, habet 60
statutos terminos intra quos ipsi obediatur—scilicet si legem seruauerit, si mandata
custodierit, si in Deum nulla animi temeritate presumpserit. Quod si in summi regis
iniuriam inpudenter excesserit, non potest eius uti priuilegio cuius iura contempnit.
Iam quod reliquum est circa prudentie et discretionis partes insudant. Aiunt discreti
uiri esse in culpis leuibus non toto zelo ascendi—uerum si profunde peccetur, totus 65
feruor inardescat; ideo leuem principis offensam de muri quadam parte diruta
fuisse mitius uindicandam. Ista pulcre componuntur; sed iuxta Sapientiam, qui
minima contempnit paulatim atterritur.[2] Omitto prosequi quanta sit indurati cordis
audacia, loca sancta non solum uilipendere sed uastare. Festino ad hec que te uirtutis amatorem non solum non accusent sed potenter excusent. Magnum estimo 70
uirtutis indicium nascentia uitiorum germina suffocare. Serpens ubi capud inmiserit
facile totus illabitur. Hec tu considerans ad primos impetus restitisti. Quidni? Nisi
restitisses, iam forsitan ad templi fastigium rabies inchoata asscendisset. Sed
asscendisti ex aduerso, et obiecisti te murum pro muro domus Israel.[3] Licet ex
minimis magna conicere: quid si tibi pro fide, pro sacramentis ecclesie decertare 75
contingat?—ad crucem Petro, Paulo comes ad gladium constanter assisteres. Eat
satelles, stricto pugione tibi funestus ⟨fo. 2⟩ occurrat. Si sacrum atrectauerit corpus,
celo uictor exciperis; si pepercerit, tibi nil minus a gloria. Iugi ergo inter nos bonorum laude donaberis; tu enim tempora nostra uirtutum meritis exornasti, tu nos in
melius exemplo tui reformasti, tu uirile robur et constantiam martirum in tempora 80
tepida reuocasti—percussor enim tibi defuit, non tu uirtuti. Viues ergo clarus gloria
quam meruisti. Viues, inquam, sed felix qui pro iustitia mori decreuisti.

1 50 qui H    52 quod pietatis *om.* H    54 unde ea manus auidi raptoris B *before correction*
(*it is uncertain whether corrected version is* raptoris manus, *as* H, *or* manus raptoris; H *reads* auide)
57 te *om.* B    58 detrectant H    65 ascendi *i.e.* accendi    70 sed potenter excusent *om.* H
76 contingeret B

---

[1] Rom. xiii. 1–2.    [2] Cf. Ecclesi. xix. 1.    [3] Cf. Ezech. xiii. 5.

## 2  To Robert de Bethune, bishop of Hereford[1]

[1140] He gives the bishop news of the expulsion of the dean of Hereford, and of violence and fighting in and around the city, and urges him to action.

Poteram me choibere silentio si non animum meror impulisset. At instantis pondus iniurie me in lamenta ire compellit. Pridie ex quo recessisti a nobis, auditis peiora percepimus: referebat frater Herefordia reuersus carum illum nostrum, quem digne uirum nominem, Herefordensis ecclesie decanum, lacessitum iniuriis, piis
5 bonorum ciuium prosecutum lacrimis urbem exisse. Angariatus in se dispendia rerum tulit e facili; leuiter enim in scelus est protracta impietas. Confracte sunt domus, apothece dirupte, sublata uasa, distracte pecunie, suppellex undique dissipata.[2] Sed quid ista? Nunquid ita ardens illa habendi sitis extincta est? Non hanc huius naturam passionis agnouimus? Verum suo cupiditas plus nouit accendi
10 remedio. Itur in ulteriores iniurias: transitur in uillas, deuenitur in horrea, excutiuntur annone, deportantur stramenta, aporiatur ecclesia, muniuntur castella. Proh 'quanta malignatus est inimicus in sancto!'[3] Prorumpat ecclesie fletus, erumpat eiulatio, treni deducantur in medium, cithara eius conuertatur in luctum et organum in uocem flentium.[4] Sare dominatur Agar; que libera erat facta est ancilla, et filia
15 principis facta est sub tributo.[5] Datur ei pro crispanti crine caluicium, in cilicium stola glorie eius et pectoralis fascia commutatur.[6] In sanctuarium Caldeus ascendit, licenter operatus est malum, gloria Domini deputatur in nichilum. Stant lacrime in maxillis filiorum: quis absterget eas? Desolata est facies filiarum Syon: quis easdem consolabitur?[7] O multum ascendit eorum superbia qui oderunt Syon; et quis erit
20 tandem finis miserie? Que iniuriarum futura satietas? Quis obstabit sceleri? Quo presidente compescetur iniquitas? Nempe capitis interest corpori prouidere, ad ipsum spectat partis cuiusque molestia. Hoc in alto situm est ne fallatur intuitu, sed infima queque uisu liberiore collustret. Forma rotundior, eminens statio, sensus inpressi, dignitatis ecclesiastice magistratum certa quadam ratione depingunt.

25    Te, pater, ista respiciunt, te lenimen sibi lamenta deposcunt. Si tenes baculum quo sustentes, non cesset uirga qua corrigas. Iuxta prophetam: gladius exacutus est, ut splendeat limatus est.[8] Stet in manu percutientis et uindicantis opprobria agminum Dei Israel.[9] Audisti atheum improperantem Domino: et manus tuas ad prelium et digitos ad bellum non aptasti?[10] Nunquid citra necessitatem strenuus ad

---

**2** G, no. 2; B, fo. 2; H, fos. 147v–148; R, fo. 205v (*defective at start*).
1 choibere *sic* B   2 in lamenta *om.* H   2 Pridie MSS   9 suo *om.* B   15 crispante B
19–20 O multum...miserie? H; Sic accsendente superbia quis iam erit miserie? B (*om.* finis)
23 queque *om.* H   24 ministerium B   27 splendat B   28 etheum BH

---

[1] The *pastor insignis* (see end) to whom this letter is addressed can only be the bishop.
[2] Cf. Joel i. 17.                           [3] Ps. lxxiii. 3.
[4] Cf. Job xxx. 31.                          [5] Cf. Gal. iv. 22–31; Lam. i. 1.
[6] Cf. Is. iii. 24; Ecclesi. vi. 32 (and xv. 5).
[7] Cf. Lam. i. 2; ii. 13 (and Apoc. vii. 17 and xxi. 4).
[8] Cf. Ezech. xxi. 9.                        [9] Cf. I Reg. xvii. 45 (and Ezech. vii. 9).
[10] Cf. Ps. cxliii. 1.

belli discrimen inanesces? Absit hoc a tua gloria ne tale sortiatur laus tua dispendium. 30
Consensum reputo cum possis et debeas non ulcisci; et quidem debes, quia pastor
es; potes, quia gladium portas. Portas quidem gladium et omnis armatura fortium[1]
ipsa te munit. Si queris expeditum, succinctus lumbos in area Domini perstitisti;[2]
si loricam desideras, iustitiam induisti ut gigas; si galeam, spem com⟨fo. 2 v⟩munem
prestolaris; si gladium, sermo Dei uiuus et efficax et ipse de ore tuo deuorabit 35
carnes;[3] si clipeum, inpugnantibus te fides orthodoxa furabitur; si calciamenta,
patrum redundamus exemplis.

Procedat ergo miles in castra, prelia Domini bellaturus, procedat et agat cum
fiducia; poterit hostis in lapide de torrente et uertigine funde prosterni.[4] Sed rerum
fortasse dispendia pertimescis ne multiplicatis incommodis coaceruet hostis iniurias. 40
Pius timor sed magna constantia: nam si pro iustitia pauca amiseris sacrificium est
quod fecisti; si cuncta raptor abstulerit holocaustum est quod libasti. Denique nulla
cadit estimatio in uirtutem; hec tanto pretiosior est quanto tibi rerum temporalium
dampno maiore constiterit. Tesaurus absconditus et margarita celestis bono nego-
tiatori iure cesserunt, quia uenditis omnibus illam sibi comparauit.[5] Tibi quoque 45
uirtus adiudicabitur si tibi magno constiterit. Virtus granum sinapis est quo magis
ateritur eo fortius inardescit. Hec puluis pigmentarius est quo magis pilo tunditur
eo efficacior ad salutem. Si prophetam aduertimus: sub umbra quercus, populi et
terebinti non bene timyama accenditur.[6] Vmbra terebinti est totum quo in infimis
delectamur. Sub palpebra diluculi, illucescente sole cum magna dies aspirauerit 50
inclinabitur hec umbra, quia uanitas est. Beatus homo cui fit ipsa uanitas uirtutis
occasio. Ideo iustus ut palma florebit[7] quia stringitur eius appetitus ad infima sed in
superna dilatatur. Ideo iustus Domini ut lampas ascenditur, quia renuens consolari
in infimis aperit os suum et de sursum attrahens spiritum totus in superna illucescit.[8]
Age ergo, pastor insignis, excutienti tibi pallium proice et tunicam.[9] Si tibi uepres 55
tollimus, tu gregem pasces in liliis;[10] ubi etiam uirtuti quam secutus es totus ap-
plaudes.

2 31 reputo *om.* B (reputo *seems necessary:* '*I reckon it as (showing) consent when...*')
33 expendium B    38 ergo *om.* B    39 poterit R *starts here*    39 funde HR; fundi B
40 forte R    46 magno *om.* B    47 eo] magis *added in* B    49 quo infimis B; quod in infimis
H; quo in infimis R    50 illucescente HR; illuscense *corrected to* illuscente B    51 Beatus]
est *added in* B    53 iustus ut B; iustus Deum (*!*) sicut H; iustus Domini ut R    53 ascenditur
*i.e.* accenditur

---

[1] Cf. Cant. iv. 4.
[2] For the whole of this passage, cf. Ephes. vi. 13 ff.
[3] Cf. Heb. iv. 12; Deut. xxxii. 42.    [4] Cf. I Reg. xvii. 40.
[5] Cf. Matt. xiii. 44–6.    [6] Cf. Os. iv. 13.
[7] Cf. Ps. xci. 13.    [8] Cf. Ps. cxviii. 131.
[9] Cf. Matt. v. 40.    [10] Cf. Cant. vi. 2.

### 3  To Simon, bishop of Worcester

[1139–43] On behalf of himself and his monks, he complains of the depredations of William de Beauchamp, and asks leave to excommunicate him.

This letter must be approximately contemporary with Henry of Winchester's letter on the same subject to Bishop Simon.[1] Since Henry was still legate at the time, both letters can be dated before the end of 1143. The incidents complained of by Gilbert may well refer to the period 1139–41 when William de Beauchamp was still on King Stephen's side, while Gilbert was already a declared supporter of the empress.

Patri suo et domno S(imoni) Wigorn(ensi) Dei gratia episcopo frater G(ilebertus) G(loecestrie) dictus abbas et ecclesie sancti Petri conuentus humilis, salutem et obedientiam.

Que sint ea, domne, que a domno Willelmo de Bellocampo iamdiu sustinuimus
5 fratrum nostrorum relatu plenius agnoscetis. Nam ut omittamus que retro sunt, non diu quod xliiii summas bene purgati tritici, que ad usus fratrum nostrorum deferebantur, per eum amisimus et earundem recuperationem usque adhuc spe promisse pacis dolo capti distulimus. Singulis preterea mensibus in procurationem seruientium suorum tres solidos dare iamdiu cogimur, et unoquoque anno ad
10 utramque sementem[2] lx iugera terre sue arare, serere, et illi metere compellimur. Sunt preter ista cotidiana seruitutes ⟨fo. 26v⟩ operum innumere, quibus homines nostros angariare et usque ad extremam miseriam persequi et affligere non cessat; et quo maiori erga eum paciencia sumus, tanto minus seuire in nos et totum quod libet facere formidat. Flagrat ecce recens maleficium eius, et hac ebdomada ad bene
15 inchoanda ieiunia sua[3] domos nostras confregit, annonam excussit et asportauit, et de cetero peiora promittit. Vnde preces sullimitati uestre porrigimus ut hanc eius audaciam compescatis, et nobis iustitiam exibere ulterius non differatis. Voluntate quidem nostra iustitia in eum non differetur ulterius, nisi nobis ablata non promisso sed facto restituerit, et amodo in tota terra beati Petri iniustas exactiones istas
20 abiurauerit. Vocatus ter in ecclesia nostra, hac proxima Dominica licentia uestra excommunicabitur. Valete.

### 4  To Theobald, archbishop of Canterbury

[Probably 1139–45] A letter of recommendation for Gilbert's relative Richard de Belmeis (II, archdeacon of Middlesex, 1138–52, and later—1152–62—bishop of London), who is seeking for confirmation of some benefice(s) which had been granted by the bishop of Chichester (or Chester; if so, a reference to the deanery of St. Alkmund's, Shrewsbury, is likely: cf. Eyton, *Salop*, VIII, 212 ff.).

For the date, cf. Appendix II.

3  G, no. 66; B, fo. 26.
4  G, no. 27; B, fo. 12v; R, fo. 210.

---

[1]  L. Voss, *Heinrich von Blois* (Berlin, 1932), pp. 170–1; on William, see H. W. C. Davis in *Essays in History pres. to R. L. Poole* (Oxford, 1927), pp. 168 ff.
[2]  I.e., presumably, autumn and spring sowing—implying, perhaps, a three-field rotation.
[3]  'This week, to make a good beginning to his fasts': this may mean that Gilbert was writing in the first week of Lent.

Patri suo et domno T(heobaldo) Cant(uariensi) Dei gratia archiepiscopo frater G(ilebertus) Gloecestrie dictus abbas, pie conplendo senarium[1] sabbata sabbatorum feliciter adipisci.

Gratiarum dilecte pater de toto corde non sufficimus actioni, quod uestra nobis munificentia sinum iam pridem beniuole karitatis aperuit; et, ut ipso rerum argu- 5 mento cognoscimus, suorum etiam numero plenius assignauit. Et quidem sic est non quia meruimus nos, sed quoniam sic complacuit uobis ut eo ipso, quo in amicitiarum gratiam admisistis inmeritum, nos ampliori quodam iure semper possideatis in integrum. Habetis enim multiplicis gratie debitorem, quem collata nobis beneficia satis obligant, et penes nos nulla merita commendant. Sed quia 10 preteritorum exhibitio certa nobis est et futurorum expectatio, audemus plurimum et pia semper caritate presumimus ut sullimitati uestre etiam pro cognato nostro et amico karissimo Ricardo de Bealmeis preces ex affectu porrigamus, quatinus eum in ecclesie ipsius beneficia admittatis quam sibi domnus Cicestrensis plena donatione concessit; et ab auctoritate uestra donationis sue astipulationem confirmari precibus 15 etiam porrectis exposcit. Et quidem illum Ricardum nostra uobis plurimum commendaret oratio si non eundem in publicas iamdiu gratulationes susceptum fama omnibus ostendisset, utpote uirum, cui et ad doctrinam scientia et ad hones-tatem mores exuberant, uirum uestro dignum ocupari seruitio, simul et beneficiis ampliari; ut unius elegantia operis et nobis gratiam, uirtuti etiam uestre gloriam 20 inpendatis. Valete.

## 5  To Simon, bishop of Worcester

[1139–48] He describes how the church of St Mary, Slaughter (Glos), has been converted into a castle, and urges the bishop to take action.

Nos. 5–13 cannot be dated more closely than the limits of Gilbert's abbacy.

Patri suo et domno Simoni Wigorn(ensi) Dei gratia episcopo frater Gilebertus ecclesie beati Petri Gloec(estrie) dictus abbas, cum pietate fructus operari iustitie.

Compellit me caritas et debita uobis suadet obedientia, ut quod ad honorem uestrum conseruandum uel aliquatenus ampliandum spectare cognouero, hoc uobis cum oportunum fuerit et presens suggeram et absens scripto commoneam. Instant 5 enim tempora periculosa et dies mali superuenerunt nobis, in quibus manu inimici hominis superseminata zizania messem bonam pene suffocare preualent aut com-primere.[2] Nec tamen gentilitas est in qua sumus sed omni gentilitate peior inhumana

---

4 5 beniuolentie B    8 amicitia, *perhaps for* amicitie B    10 penes merita nulla B    13 R. de Beaumis R    13 eum *om.* B    14 Cestrensis (*perhaps rightly*) B; R *omits* domnus    15 dotionis B; sue *om.* R    16 R. R    17 iam gratulationes diu B    20 gratiam *om.* B    21 Valete *om.* R
5 G, no. 4; B, fo. 3; H, fos. 148 v–149; R, fo. 206 r–v.
1 Dei gratia R; *om.* B; Simoni gratia Wigorn' (*sic*) H; R *agrees with Foliot's normal, though not invariable, practice*    1 G. BR    6 inimici *om.* B

---

[1] I.e. by labouring six days to earn the rest of the eternal Sabbath—*illa Sabbata* of Abelard's hymn; cf. nos. 25, 170 (p. 239).        [2] Cf Matt. xiii. 25, cf. 22.

crudelitas, cui totum quod libet licet, totum uiluit quod honestum est, nil amplec-
10 tens desiderio quod christiane simplicitati et sacris legibus obuiare non constet.
Nempe, ut audita taceamus, uidimus anteacta ebdomada ecclesiam sancte Dei
genitricis apud Slohtres mirabili modo dirutam, tectum eius manu sacrilega
conuulsum, in parietibus eius undequaque edificata propugnacula, inmissos satellites
impietati deseruire promtissimos. Vidimus inquam et doluimus locum sanctuarii
15 sine honore, ecclesiam Dei contaminatam turpiter, et ausu temerario in domicilium
Satane commutatam. Huius etiam occasione malitie quidam illos expugnare adorsi
sunt. Istis itaque in ecclesiam ipsam lapides, tela, faces iacientibus, aliisque resistenti-
bus, non sine sanguinis effusione et multa hominum lesione biduum ibi miserabile
confectum est. Scimus adhuc lupos intra parietes eiusdem ecclesie in ipso ouili
20 Domini latitantes et inde gregem Domini sinplicem et innocuum laniantes, aliter
fugari non posse quam si ⟨fo. 3 v⟩ bonus pastor adueniens eos sonitu bucine et
latratu canum terreat, dissipet, et disperdat. Hortor itaque paternitatem uestram,
consulendo uobis caritate qua debeo, ut cum honestioribus et eruditioribus clericis
uestris locum flagitii festinanter adeatis, et commissam uobis ecclesiam primo
25 purgari deinde redintegrari faciatis. Vel si monitionem uestram manus sacrilega
minus audierit, actores et adiutores sceleris scientibus et uidentibus ipsis gladio
domini feriatis, ut dum in futuro concilio huiuscemodi tractabuntur excessus, honor
sit uobis coram simul discumbentibus opposuisse uos murum pro domo Israel,[1] et
illatas sibi contumelias repulisse uiriliter aut uindicasse. Valete.

## 6  To Robert de Bethune, bishop of Hereford

[1139–48] He expresses his thanks, literally and allegorically, for a present of fish, but
expostulates with the bishop for his refusal to permit a fishpond (? in Hereford).

See *GF*, pp. 20–3.

Patri suo et domno Roberto Herefordensi Dei gratia episcopo, frater Gilebertus
ecclesie beati Petri Gloecestrie dictus abbas, sagenam missam in mare plenam bonis
piscibus ad litus usque pertrahere.[2]

Experta michi totiens tua, dilecte pater, munificentia me et hoc ipso gratie sibi
5 reddit debitorem, quod nuper directis xeniis me pascere simul dignata est et docere.
Perfectum munus estimo quod corpori in refectionem est et anime nichilominus in
saginam. Infelices epule ubi totum corpus absumit et spiritus in nullo reficitur.

---

5 12 dirumpta H; diruptam R    12 sacrilega manu H    13 undique H    14 impietatis R
15 turpiter contaminatam R    19 effectum H    20 nocuum B    21 non posse *om.* B
21 bucine B, *corrected by a modern hand to* buccine (H, R buccine)    26 audierit B; auderit H;
auderet R.
6 G, no. 9; B, fo. 4 v; H, fos. 150–1.
1 Dei gr. Her. H

---

[1] Cf. Luc. xiv. 10; Ezech. xiii. 5. Of the councils of this period, that of March 1143 is the only
one known to have issued canons on this subject; but there may well have been others (see
references in *Handbook*, 2nd ed., London, 1961, p. 549).
[2] Cf. Matt. xiii. 47; Joh. xxi. 11.

Verum me longe aliter epulari tui ratio muneris introspecta persuadet. Misisti michi pisces, sed duos: maiorem unum, minorem alterum, eiusdem generis utrumque bonum. Que omnia interiorem hominem meum tot replent ferculis quot 10 erudiunt documentis. Nam primo omnium quia pisces misisti michi piscatorem illum magnum ad memoriam reuocasti—illum inquam piscatorem quem Dominus uocatum de naui non solum homines piscari uoluit, sed ob promtam fidei confessionem apostolico etiam culmini prerogauit.[1] Suggeris anime mee suis indesinenter illum presentare conspectibus, eo quod me diu iactatum fluctibus hamo sue pisca- 15 tionis extraxerit, et in magna monachorum urbe sanctorum collegio deputauerit.[2] Quod tamen non ita dixerim ac si de conuersione uel conuersatione iam michi securus sim, cum ignoret homo ⟨utrum⟩ amore sit dignus an odio et unicuique omnia in posterum reseruentur.[3] Non enim in sancto loco fuisse sed magis in sanctitate perstitisse laudabile est. Frustra enim currimus si non comprehendimus,[4] 20 et bene inchoata principia consumatio sola remunerat. Vnde et filii Israel post exitum de Egipto et maris transitum quia corde non steterunt, temptati sunt et perierunt. Quem res ista non moueat? Ad nos respicit hec parabola: Egipto enim exire est a cecitatis et ignorantie tenebris in lucem fidei peruenire; maris transitus est uirtute baptismatis a uetustate peccati in nouitatem gratie respirare; in deserto 25 perire est post acceptam notitiam ueritatis et gratie, peccatorum seruituti subcumbere et in his uitam finire.[5] Non enim qui egreditur delicias statim accipit repromissas. Nam Iordanis ille famosissimus uirga Domini percussus in se diuisus est; et que a sinistris erant aque impetu suo in mare perlate sunt; que uero a dextris, in unum collecte sese sursum extulerunt.[6] Virga Domini est totum quo percutimur. 30 Quidam enim corpore alii spiritu fatigantur; sed filiis dextere omnia cohoperantur in bonum.[7] Qui siue aduersa de manu Domini suscipiant seu prospera a gratiarum actione non recedunt, sed sursum leuantes cor in celum principale mentis extollunt. Qui uero a sinistris sunt hii ad tempus credunt sed tempore temptationis recedunt.[8] Qui uirge leuem non ferentes ictum cito perlabuntur et effluunt, admixtique salsugini 35 uertigine miserabili demerguntur et pereunt. Vnde michi de corporali sanctorum collegio gloriari non permittitur, nisi studia sanctorum caritas in me sollicita consideret et imitetur. Istud michi pio suggeris ipse consilio dum pisces michi dirigis extractos de profundo sed mortuos; docens prudentissime ut caueam ne de profundo seculi extractus opus mortis incurram. Nam longe aliter sue piscationis opus 40 noster piscator excercet: in peccato mortuos piscari nouit ad uitam, unde qui extractus moritur intra sagene ipsius ambitum non tenetur. ⟨fo. 5⟩ Quod uero duos misisti, magnum unum, paruum alterum, sua michi significatione iocundum est, et

**6** 15 illum *om.* B   16 sanctorum H; suorum B (*cf. below*)   18 utrum *nos* (*cf. Eccles. loc. cit.*); BH *omit*

---

[1] Cf. Matt. xvi. 16–19.
[2] This is no doubt a reference to the abbey of St Peter of Cluny—though Gloucester was also dedicated to St Peter.
[3] Cf. Eccles. ix. 1–2.          [4] Cf. I Cor. ix. 24.
[5] Cf. *Glossa ordinaria* on Ex. xiv. 15–17, etc.; Rom. vi. 4–6.
[6] Cf. Jos. iii. 13, 16; Ex. vii. 20.          [7] Cf. Rom. viii. 28.          [8] Cf. Luc. viii. 13.

ipsa mittentis intentione iocundius. Principis apostolorum labores michi misticos
45 representas. Ipsum bis piscationi dedisse operam euangelica lectione cognoscimus:
in prima ob multitudinem copiosam, rete scissum est; in secunda plenum magnis
piscibus ad litus usque pertractum.[1] Prima piscatio omnium uocatio est; secunda,
electorum in uitam introductio. Vnde primo recte rete rumpitur quia a gratia in
quam uocati sunt plurimi elabuntur, et culpis exigentibus in eternum reprobantur.
50 Secundo rete non rumpitur, quia Dominus electos suos ad uitam omnes pertrahet
et non est qui aliquem de manu eius eripiat. Efficaci me ammonitione instruis, et
informas ne uelut rupta sagena piscis elapsus uage peream, sed magnis illis piscibus
centum quinquaginta tribus uite qualitate conformis ad electorum formam uitam
moresque componam. Quod si tui sensus archanum altius intelligerem, fortasse
55 conicerem dono piscium michi pisces euangelicos ad mentem reduci; torporemque
meum ad lectionis studium artius amplectendum occasione hac a tua prudentia non
mediocriter instigari. Illi namque panes unde populi saturantur et inplentur cophini
legis libri quinque sunt; et duo pisces prophetie et psalmi.[2] Nam uitam degunt dum
profundum pisces inhabitant. Quod si extrahuntur ad lucem morientes extinguntur
60 a lumine. Sic ante Saluatoris aduentum tenebrosa aqua in nubibus aeris[3] obscura erat
doctrina in prophetis. In profundo hoc suo modo prophetia uiuebat, dum quod
uenturum erat preloquendo promittebat. Sed iam promissione completa, et orbem
Christo irradiante plenius, prophetia in lucem extracta et quodamodo extincta est,
cum promissorum completa ueritas amplius promissione non egeat. Vnde Dominus,
65 lex, et prophete usque Iohannem.[4] Sic michi nectis inuolucra et me undequaque
spiritualiter excerceri desideras, dum hinc obscuritate prophetica ad lectionem me
pertrahis, illinc ipsa psalmorum suauitate tamquam alterius piscis oblectamento ad
orationem me laudemque compellis.

Iam restat quod intelligam cur pisces quos misisti generis eiusdem esse decreuisti.
70 Vnitatem michi pacemque commendas.[5] Binarius enim in bono est, sed et ipse in
malo repperitur; binarii bonum est dilectio Dei et proximi, bonum ipsius est quod
ad predicandum discipuli missi sunt bini et bini;[6] nam caritas ad minus inter duos
est. Habet idem sua infortunia; inmunda enim animalia in archam missi sunt bina
et bina.[7] Nam quia primus defluit ab unitate binarius, totum, quo pax scinditur aut
75 dissipatur concordia, merito illi assignatur. Vnde persuades michi illum sequi qui
in sancto est, qui inhabitare facit unius moris in domo;[8] ne distrahar iracundia uel
inflammer odio, sed pace ad omnes et caritate seruata, uarietates et scismata studeam
declinare, et unius generis pisces, fratres uidelicet unius obseruantie caritatis et fidei,
in domo Domini congregare. Sub eodem intellectu Moysi a Domino dictum est:

---

**6** 51 est *om.* B    58, 67 spalmi, spalmorum B    60 aqua *om.* B    62 pmittebat B    62 iam *om.* B
65 usque] ad *added*; et *om.* H (*Vulg.* Lex et prophete usque ad Iohannem)    69 quod] ut H
70 et *om.* B    72 duos] binos *added in* H    77 scimata B

---

[1] Cf. Luc. v. 6; Joh. xxi. 11.
[2] Cf. Matt. xiv. 17–20 and *Glossa ordinaria* on Matt. xiv. 17, etc.; Mc. vi. 42–3.
[3] Cf. Ps. xvii. 12.            [4] Cf. Luc. xvi. 16.
[5] Cf. Eph. iv. 3.             [6] Cf. Luc. x. 1.
[7] Cf. Gen. vii. 2.            [8] Cf. Ps. lxvii. 6–7.

'altare michi facies de lapidibus non sectis, quos ferrum non tetigit'.[1] Lapides secti 80
sunt qui, licet politi scientia, a fratrum tamen societate diuiduntur scismate uel
discordia; ex quibus altare Domino non construitur, quia de uita eorum gratum
Domino nil offertur. Ex lapidibus uero non sectis altare Domino construitur, quia
ex his qui per fidem in unitate solidantur Christi corpus adimpletur.[2] Quod uero
utrumque bonum dixerim, tale est. Pisces mundi sunt qui squamas habent et 85
pennulas.[3] Squame sibi coniuncte sunt, corpus undique contegentes. ⟨fo. 5v⟩
Vnde et uirtutes significant, que omnes sibi in radice caritatis coniuncte interiorem
hominem polimita quadam et talari ueste tegunt, muniunt, et exornant.[4] Pennule
contemplationis alta significant; his enim pisces de profundo eleuantur et super
aquas quosdam quasi saltus faciunt, licet item naturali pondere ad easdem relabantur. 90
Quid his pennulis nisi conatus anime designatur?—quibus quandoque in summum
illud bonum et inuisibile lumen erigitur et de interna illa dulcedine aliquid gustare
nititur, licet ipsa corporali sarcina cui alligata est retardetur. 'Corpus enim quod
corrumpitur aggrauat animam et deprimit terrena inhabitatio sensum multa
cogitantem.'[5] Hec michi de tui ratione muneris ad tempus occurrunt; que, cum 95
optato conspectu perfruemur et alloquio, plenius ipse edocebis de cetero, si placet
aduertas.

Mandasti michi per tui muneris latorem nuntium ne torquerer inuidia, ne
tabescendo deficerem, ne de concessa tibi felicitate et copia talium et tantorum
piscium arida mea siccitas angeretur. Verbo mones ne inuideam, sed facto ad 100
\*inuidiam trahis. Quid mirum si marcescer inuidia, cui uicini diuitis extensa late
potentia stangni iacentis opusculum interdicit? Inuidiam iubes tollere: faciendi
stangni concessa licentia, hanc ipse poteris extirpare.[6] Experimentum erit amici
non modicum, sed diu torqueri non permiseris cuius opem morbi a te dependere
cognoscis. Valete. 105

**6** 89 de] uel ex H   91 designantur H   93 redardetur B   101 \*uidiam B   102 interdicitis H
103 stagna H

---

[1] A conflation of Ex. xx. 24–5; Deut. xxvii. 5 (and Jos. viii. 31).
[2] Cf. Eph. iv. 12–13.
[3] Cf. Levit. xi. 9–11; Deut. xiv. 9–10.       [4] Cf. Eph. iii. 16–17; Gen. xxxvii. 23.
[5] Sap. ix. 15 (and for 'inuidia…tabescendo' below, ll. 99 f., cf. Sap. vi. 25).
[6] This seems to imply that Gilbert wished to build a fishpond, which the bishop had forbidden;
if this is a correct interpretation, it is a likely conjecture that the fishpond was connected with
the priory of St Guthlac in Hereford, in which case the letter must be later than St Guthlac's
foundation in 1143. There may be an echo in the previous sentence of Horace, *Carm.* II, 15,
1 ff. (cf. *GF*, p. 22 and n.); 'torqueri' in the next sentence is perhaps an echo of Horace,
*Ep.* I, 2, 37: 'inuidia…torquebere'; and 'opem morbi' presumably means 'cure of (my)
sickness' as, approximately, in Ovid, *Met.* VII, 572.

## 7 To Hamo, abbot of Bordesley

[1139–48] As requested, he has written something for Hamo: possibly the preface to a collection of sermons.[1]

Caro suo dilectori Hamoni Bordesleie abbati, frater G(ilebertus) Gloecestrie dictus abbas, regem magnum quem diligit in decore suo conspicere.[2]

Memor tue dilectionis et benigne petitionis, qua me aliquid scribere uel dictare postulasti, tandem pareo; et si quid datur otii libenter id ipsum studio tue benigni-
5 tatis inpendo. Nam cum tibi auditum fuerit me, pro credite michi dispensationis officio,[3] uerbum exortationis aliquotiens habuisse cum fratribus, cepisti et ipse presens exortari ut, si quid michi Dominus de Spiritu suo in scripturis reuelasset, munificentie non ingratus stilo illud exciperem; et quod gratis acceperam, aliquorum edificationi profuturum gratis ipse publicarem. Afirmas enim multifor-
10 mem gratiam sinplicis uerbi Dei uariis tractandam esse doctrine scematibus, non uno tantum modo piis mentibus intimandam. Verum sicut ipsos corporum sensus, per quos ad intelligentiam nobis uia est, diuersos inter se uariosque natura constituit, sic uerbum Dei uariis tractandum esse doctrine scematibus, et nunc annuntiatione, nunc scripture subministratione ad pia corda traiciendum, donec formetur
15 Christus in nobis et simus omnes docibiles Dei.[4] Annectis insuper eorum, que in ecclesia uelut declamationis modo pronuntiantur, uelud cum sonitu deperire memoriam, nisi scripture uelud quodam retinaculo teneantur; et sic, internuntio uisu, redintegrande memorie legentium animis ingerantur. Quantum replicas illud sapientis elogium; 'aurum melius dispersum rutilat quam signatum; nichil a
20 uilibus thophis gemme differunt nisi publicentur'.[5] Sententia quoque distributa suscipit incrementum; et auarum dedignata possessorem, nisi publicetur, elabitur. Postremo, ne quod habeat excusatio diuerticulum, desidiam nostram uehementer illa Domini uoce perterres: 'serue nequam, quare non posuisti pecuniam meam ad mensam?'[6] Multa quidem sic colligis ut torporem excutias, repellas ignauiam, et

---

7 G, no. 12; B, fo. 8v; H, fos. 153v–154; R, fos. 207v–208.
1–2 Caro...conspicere om. H; frater G....conspicere om. R (⟨c⟩aro B)    1 Dilectori
Hamoni R; dilecto B    4 et si] sed B    7 de suo spiritu in scripturis suis H    10–11 uerbi
Dei...intimandam B; uariis...scematibus om. H; R places sed uariis...scematibus after
intimandam (it is possible that uariis...scematibus was an afterthought, and it clearly stood in the
margin in the archetype; stylistically, B's text seems the best)    11 corporis B    12 nobis uia] nobis
ipsis una H    16 uelut] H adds quodam    18 ingerantur B; inquerantur R; ingenerantur H
20 thophis om. R (leaving a space)

---

[1] It seems clear that Hamo had been present at one of Gilbert's conferences with his monks, and asked him to set on paper ('write or dictate') some biblical expositions; since one of the points Hamo had made is that it was fitting for sermons to be written down, it seems likely that what he had asked for, and Gilbert had supplied, was a collection of sermons on a biblical theme, in the tradition of St Bernard's—such, indeed, as Gilbert's own Homilies (see no. 270).

[2] Cf. Is. xxxiii. 17.    [3] Cf. I Cor. ix. 17.
[4] Cf. Gal. iv. 19; Joh. vi. 45.    [5] Hildebert, Ep. I, I (cf. GF, pp. 57–9).
[6] Luc. xix. 22–3.

44

me uix ausum hactenus prodire in publicum de latibulo silentii in lucem eloquentie 25
trahas. Imperiosa me caritate perurges. Vndequaque inuoluis me, ut non sit quid
respondeam, nisi me uel non posse quod exigis, uel amico nolle prestare quod
possim. Horum quodcumque dixerim eo animo es ut aut doli me arguas aut
iniurie: utrumque uereor, et dum aurea me karitatis compede uinctum tenes, facio
quod captis hodie mos est dum de pretio requiruntur et timent; totum spondent 30
quod exactor uult. Sic ego ne caritatis dampna sustineam, ne minus in Christo
diligar, negare tibi nil audeo. Verum ea que tutis tantum auribus hucusque com-
miseram iam nunc examini tuo oculisque introspicienda committo. Scio quanta
amplecteris gratia quicquid est illud quod offero, et quod duo minuta[1] que amicus
dat magni faciet apud te, quod eadem non ex habundanti sed ex modico dat.      35

## 8   To Simon, bishop of Worcester

[1139–48] He complains that a rural dean named Algod has been oppressing some of his
clerks, in particular forbidding Bernard of Colne from performing the offices of his order;
and he requests the bishop, if he cannot hear the case himself, to have it settled by the
archdeacon.

Patri suo et domno S(imoni) Wig(ornensi) Dei gratia episcopo frater G(ilebertus)
Glocestrie dictus abbas salutem.

   Vobis sepe scribere et beniuolentiam uestram frequenter interpellare negotia nos
multiplicata compellunt.[2] Vnde enim inquietationibus nostris speramus et exspecta-
mus solacia, ibi sepe plangimus et nostra manifestamus incommoda. Quidam 5
ministrorum uestrorum sicut a multis audiuimus in commisso sibi officio ministrans
pessime, Algodus scilicet decanus, clericos nostros odiose persequi et affligere ex
credita sibi dispensatione[3] non desistit. Qui quanto celebriores et sacratiores cernit
iminere festiuitates, quasi nocendi nactus oportunitatem, ecclesias nostras interdicit
et clericos nostros in suis ordinibus ministrare deffendit. Vnde uestram rogamus pia 10
semper presumptione dulcedinem ut clericum nostrum Bernardum de Colna in
ordine suo diebus istis ministrare concedatis; et statuto sibi die, si uos ad hoc uacare
non *poteritis, totum quod in illum ille e contrario dictus Algodus iaculari poterit
coram archidiacono uestro terminari iubeatis. Nos enim illius suspectum habemus
iudicium cuius manifestum scimus odium; et si uestre placeret discretioni, clericos 15
nostros talem iudicare oporteret quem uite commendaret ⟨fo. 12⟩ honestas; qui ex
arce pudicitie iudicaret incestuosos, non ex stratu mollitie Domini sacerdotes
offenderet. Valete.

**7** 26 me inuoluis R    29 uinctum] ligatum H    32 audeo] quod ualeo *added in* B
**8** G, no. 24; B, fo. 11v; R, fo. 209v.
4 multiplica B    6 sibi *om.* B    7 odisse B    10–11 semper pia B (*omits* rogamus)    11 B.R
12 istis] is B    13 *potestis B    17 pudicitie] prudentie R

---

[1] Cf. Mc. xii. 42.
[2] Cf. no. 21.                        [3] Cf. I Cor. ix. 17.

## 9   To Simon, bishop of Worcester

[1139–48] He asks for the case against Wimund his clerk to be postponed until his return.[1]

The interpretation of this obscure letter seems to be as follows. Wimund, a clerk of Gloucester abbey (i.e. presumably serving one of the abbey's churches) had received a lady into his house as surety for her husband's debt. He made all due efforts to have her ransomed, but she died before this was accomplished, and Wimund was accused by the bishop, presumably of illicit relations with the lady, and instructed to obtain compurgation by the oath of seven colleagues. Gilbert regards this as severe, partly on the technical ground that the judge should not also be the accuser unless the offence is notorious.[2] The circumstance, and Gilbert's plea, both seem very extraordinary; but it seems possible that the lady's husband had been taken prisoner during the anarchy, and that her (or Wimund's?) brother's plea that the lady be a 'hostage' for her husband may have been part of a scheme to ransom him; that is to say, it may have had a humane aspect. But this is not made clear in the letter.

Patri suo et domno S(imoni) Wigorn(ensi) Dei gratia episcopo frater G(ilebertus) Gloecestrie dictus abbas, obedientiam debitam et quam potest caritatem.

Directis litteris preces uestre sullimitati poreximus, ut causam, que in Wimundum clericum nostrum intendebatur, usque ad reditum nostrum ex sola gratia differretis.
5 Hoc tamen altiori prouidentia aliter actum est et est ei purgatio obiecti criminis per manum septimam adiudicata. Vnde uestram ex amore presumendo rogamus beniuolentiam, ut sententiam hanc ea qua potestis misericordia temperetis et qua debetis ratione leuigetis. Scitis enim in causis etiam secularibus quantum caueri soleat, ne qui iudex est, sese acusatorem exhibeat, nisi forte cessante acusatore ad
10 hoc ipsum publica alicuius infamatio compellat. Quod si iudici quandoque contigerit in hoc ipso non iam accusator sed fame publice prolocutor existit nec iudicis sibi tollit officium, persequenti fame uocis inpendendo suffragium. Sed in causa hac aliter res est. Scimus enim quid uicini clament, quid in ore multorum populus atestetur. Femina enim illa de qua Wimundus arguitur, non ipso cogente uel
15 suadente sed fratre ipsius Aelwino presbitero perurgente, in obsidem pro marito suo concessa atque directa est. Cumque illo mitteretur opem illi debitam Wimundus non subtraxit, sed prout suppetebat facultas benigne contulit. Post etiam fratrem suum maritum scilicet eiusdem usque ad inimicitias persecutus est, ut *eiusdem redemptioni effectiue operam daret. Quid ergo si mulier illa morte preuenta est?
20 Nunquid luet qui non meruit? Sed quis unquam innocens periit? Vel ecclesie iudicio recti quando deleti sunt? Si clericus beati Petri predicte mulieri cum in obsidem mitteretur sua dando subuenit, si maritum eius de ipsa redimenda commonuit, si idem fratri eius Elwino suggessit, quid aliud iudicabitur nisi quod animam

9 G, no. 26; B, fo. 12; R, fo. 210.
2 quam *om.* B   4 differetis B   8 etiam *om.* B   11 iudiciis B   13 enim *om.* B   13 in *om.* R   15 Eilwino R   18 *eisdem B   21 iudicio *om.* B   23 eidem...Eilwino R

---

[1] There seems no clue as to which journey of Gilbert's is referred to.
[2] Cf. *Digest*, 48, 2, 8 and 12; *Decretum*, C. 2, q. 1, c. 18; for *crimina manifesta*, cf. *Decretum*, C. 2, q. 1, cc. 15–16, 21 and *dictum post* c. 20; *MB*, IV, 213–14.

suam magna ex parte liberauit? Vestram itaque ⟨fo. 12v⟩ supplicando rogamus beatitudinem, ut in presenti negotio oculi uestri uideant equitatem,[1] et eum qui a 25 nemine accusatur, quem infamia nulla persequitur, qua soliti estis gratia suscipiatis, et uestre fulgore presentie exhilaratum remittatis. Valete.

## 10 To Osbern, a monk[2]

[1139–48] He sends encouragement to a subordinate, evidently in charge of a lonely cell in Wales: the Welsh may be bad neighbours, but the English are worse.

Frater G(ilebertus) Gloecestrie dictus abbas dilecto filio suo Osberno, non trepidare ubi non est timor.[3]

Moneo te fili karissime edificare et plantare et terram tuam eo uomere quo tu scis exercere diligenter et excolere. Satis hactenus spinas et tribulos germinauit tibi;[4] sed, sicut bene cepisti, si labori bono et excercitio instanter incubueris, scio, scio quod 5 fructu bono non fraudabit te Dominus. Volo ut uasa omnia domus tue salua et munda custodias, et ipsam domum tuam qua poteris suppellectile munda et honesta munias et exornes. Laudo etiam te seras portarum tuarum confortare, domum tuam uallo bono et muro inexpugnabili circumdare,[5] ne scilicet gens illa que, sicut tu dicis, hirsuta fronte et toruis occulis respicit, irrumpat in eam et omnes labores tuos et 10 sudores impetu uno diripiat. Nolo uasa transmigrationis sint apud te, nec quod in aliquo pretendas transmigrationis habitum, sed stabilitatis in terra uestra quam dedit uobis Dominus Deus et mansionis diuturne propositum.[6] Dices uero amicis nostris Gualensibus nos de hoc quod audierunt nichil penitus illis inconsultis acturos. Videmus enim gentem nostram timorem Domini et reuerentiam sanctuarii 15 paruipendere, et illos audimus Deum et loca sancta et personas consecratas Domino diligenter honorare. Propter hec omnia durum est nobis illis, qui fere non curant nos, magis inseri et ab his qui nos uenerantur auelli. Vale, et noueris nos malle stationarium uel progressionarium te esse quam retrogradum.[7]

**9** 25 uestri] tui B (*so Vulg.*)   27 Valete *om.* R
**10** G, no. 29; B, fo. 13; R, fo. 210v.
1 pater B   4 tibi *om.* R   6 Dominus *om.* B   7 ipam B   12, 13 *?* nostra/? nobis

---

[1] Cf. Ps. xvi. 2.
[2] Presumably Osbern was in charge of one of Gloucester's Welsh dependencies, Cardigan or Ewenny, or, less probably, of Ewyas, in Herefordshire, on the border. Ewenny was founded only in 1141, its prior in 1145 was John, and it was in one of the parts of Wales fairly securely in Norman hands at this time; whereas Cardigan, from 1136, lay surrounded by Welsh forces, while the Norman power was only represented by the garrison in Cardigan castle (Lloyd, II, 472 ff.). Cardigan is therefore the more likely. It is possible that Osbern was the scholar-monk Osbern of Gloucester (see *GF*, p. 80 n.), but the name was not uncommon.
[3] Cf. Ps. xiii. 5.                    [4] Cf. Gen. iii. 18.
[5] Cf. Ps. cxlvii. 12–13; antiphon for second nocturn at Matins on Sundays in November.
[6] Cf. Jer. xlvi. 19; Deut. i. 25.
[7] The meaning is plain, though the words seem to be partly of Gilbert's coining. The metaphor is perhaps from the stars: 'retrogradus' was normally used of stars (e.g. Pliny, *Nat. Hist.* II, 15, 77), and 'stationalis' also (*op. cit.* II, 12, 60); 'progressionarius' is not otherwise known.

## 11  To Simon, bishop of Worcester

[1139–48] He asks the bishop to deal leniently with Ralph of Worcester.

Patri suo et domno S(imoni) Wigorn(ensi) Dei gratia episcopo, frater G(ilebertus) G(loecestrie) dictus abbas, salutem et si quem potest ex caritate famulatum.

Rogat nos Rad(ulfus) de Wirecestria ut apud sullimitatem uestram pro ipso interueniamus. Sed in re ista petere nil audemus nisi quod honori uestro et saluti
5 eius utile iudicamus. Scimus enim non dimitti peccatum nisi restituatur ablatum. Sed hoc in his uerum est, quibus facultas suppetit qua possint ablata restitui. Que si forte defuerit, licet quod ablatum est ⟨B2, fo. 25v⟩ ex impossibilitate non redditur, tamen cordi contrito et humiliato uenia non negatur.[1] Vnde si hunc corde penitentem uestra aduerterit discretio, debet quidem ad ipsum absoluendum prudens
10 admitti dispensatio, ut quod minus est in ablati restitutione habundet in seueritate penitentie. Ideo quantum licet uestre supplicamus beniuolentie ut memor illius— 'calamum quassatum non conteres et linum fumigans non extingues'—accepta securitate non redeundi ad uomitum, et iniuncta simul penitentia eum in spiritu lenitatis reuocetis, et erroneam ouem, si fieri potest, ad caulas Domini pio humero
15 reportetis.[2] Valete.

## 12  To a friend, unnamed

[?1139–48] He congratulates his friend, who is evidently a bishop, on living up to his profession.

The style of the letter and its position in the manuscript make it virtually certain that it was written by Gilbert; its place strongly suggests that it was written when he was abbot of Gloucester. This cannot be proved, but it is confirmed by the way he talks of the episcopal office, which seems to suggest that he himself was not yet a bishop.[3]

Letatus sum in his que dicta sunt michi,[4] que nuper de te fama diuulgante cognoui. Audio presulem digna presule cogitasse et illicite presumtioni sanctitatis animo restitisse. Est aliquando profecta sententia ut sub tributum Christi sponsa redigatur. Sed in te cura pastoralis euigilat, ut quod animo presumptum est nequaquam opere
5 compleatur. Arguis, obsecras, increpas et defendis, et quos fomento non preuales precisionis ferro curare non pertimescis—pectus sane commendabile quod mansuetis exibet gratiam et contumacibus disciplinam.[5] Cum manna uirgam in sanc-

---

**11** G, no. 49; B, fos. 18v (B1) and 25 (B2) (*spelling as* B1).

1 B2 *places* Wigorn' *after* episcopo (*contrary to Foliot's normal practice*)  6 qua B1 quo B2
7 inpossibitate B2  8–9 penitentem si hunc B1 (*omits* corde)  11 Ideo B1 Vnde B2
12 conteras B2  12 limum B1
**12** G, no. 60; B, fo. 24v.

---

[1] Cf. Ps. l. 19.
[2] Cf. Is. xlii. 3; Prov. xxvi. 11; Gal. vi. 1; Luc. xv. 5.
[3] It is interesting to compare Gilbert's view of the episcopal office in this letter with the story told of him by John of Salisbury, *GF*, pp. 94–5.
[4] Cf. Ps. cxxi. 1.   [5] Cf. II Tim. iv. 2; *Regula S. Benedicti*, c. 28.

tuario diuina reponit auctoritas,[1] sic plenitudinem pastoris erudiens ut et de pectore gratiarum bonis exibeat totum quod dulce est, et contumaciam reprimat diciplina. Gratulor equidem te pastoralem regulam perspicaciter attendisse et quod exequen- 10 dum noueras ut decebat episcopum non minus fortiter quam prudenter adimplesse.[2] Sane in ipso uirtutis opere tota michi uirtus elucescit. Est namque prudentia nosse quid deceat, iustitia cuique exibere quod oporteat, fortitudo hominem non timere quia caro est, et in uirtute spiritus totum audere quod sanctum est; temperantie est non ex ira quippiam uel commote uoluntatis inpulsu fuisse gestum, sed solo 15 uirtutis amore ad summi regis ulciscendas iniurias igne spiritus incanduisse. Ages ergo cum fiducia. Vale.

## 13 To Robert de Bethune, bishop of Hereford

[1139–48] He is unable to attend the bishop's synod; and so he asks for action against Welsh raiders from Archenfield,[3] and for confirmation of the will of Gunni of Stanton, clerk.

Patri suo et domino R(oberto) Dei gratia Here(fordensi) episcopo frater G(ilebertus) G(loecestrie) dictus abbas, die cotidie bene prosperari in gratiam.

Ad sinodum quam, dilecte pater, celebratis iter ipse arripueram; sed domni Wigornensis littere nos ipsum hac die lune Gloecestrie prestolari obedientie et caritatis imperio compulerunt. Ideo quod ad presens non possumus, dilecte nobis 5 sanctitati uestre scripto supplicamus, ut de Walensibus de Herchenefeld, Idel et Chenedin et eorum complicibus, nobis iustitiam exibeatis. Ipsi enim in nos inmeritos suas ulciscuntur iniurias; et cum eis in nullo nocuerim, plusquam sexaginta marcarum dampnum nobis intulerunt, et totum ⟨quod⟩ in Brantonia[4] diu laborauimus, uno impetu et incursu abstulerunt. Speramus quod dampna nostra et in- 10 commoda tanquam pensabitis, et quod opem quam nulli iuste petenti subtrahitis, filiorum iuste postulationi non negabitis.

Notum preterea sanctitati uestre facimus quia clericus uester Gunni de Stantuna in nouissimis agens, a uobis ut patre et pastore anime sue sanctarum orationum uestrarum suffragium expetit, ut uestro interuentu ⟨fo. 26⟩ communitus, iamiam exiturus 15 Domini misericordiam possit securius expectare. Rerum uero suarum dispositio hec est, quam in conscriptorum testium presentia ipse subscripsit. Quantum annone in domo sua est, hoc seruientibus suis et his quibus aliquo debito obligatus est concedit. Reliquorum omnium ⟨partem⟩ tertiam uobis legauit, et ecclesie nostre in qua habitum monasticum suscepit duas reliquas consignauit. Huius extreme 20

**13** G, no. 64; B, fo. 25v.
9 quod *Giles; om.* B    10 impeto B

---

[1] Cf. Heb. ix. 4.
[2] A general reference to Gregory the Great's *Reg. Pastoralis.*
[3] Archenfield in west Herefordshire was the old Welsh kingdom of Erging and still bore its Welsh character. The Welsh leaders Ithel (Idel) and 'Chenedin' (this form is probably corrupt) cannot now be identified.
[4] Brampton Abbotts (Herefs).

uoluntatis sue testes hi sunt: Nicholaus sacerdos,[1] Grimpater, Walterus. Et quia nichil magis debetur humanitati quam quod extreme uoluntatis liber sit stilus et licitum quod ultra non redit arbitrium, suppliciter petit ut quod a se pietatis intuitu actum est, auctoritate uestra stabiliatis; uel si uobis aliter uisum fuerit, uoluntati
25 uestre sua non preiudicet. Valete.

### 14 To Uhtred, bishop of Llandaff

[1140–8] He asks the bishop to take action against a wandering monk who has occupied the church of Chepstow (Monmouthshire: 'Strigueil'; very likely Chepstow priory, dep. of Cormeilles).
    Nos. 14–16 bear the dates of Bishop Uhtred (1140–8).

Patri suo et domno Vthredo Landauensi Dei gratia episcopo, frater Gilebertus ecclesie beati Petri Gloecestrie dictus abbas, apto rationis moderamine sibi credita dispensare.[2]
5    Dilectioni uestre rogatus litteras mitto quas misisse debueram non rogatus. Nequit uestram latere prudentiam quin pax domus Dei sit ordinata imperandi obediendique concordia cohabitantium; et quin eadem recte amministretur cum maiorum pio prudentique consilio filiorum paret humilis et promta deuotio. Quod si prelatorum iustis imperiis subditorum obedire contempnit audacia, non est
10 dubium quin in prelatorum omnium redundet iniuriam quod in unius contemptum fuerit ignominiose commissum. Vestram ideo rogamus beniuolentiam consulendo etiam caritate qua debemus, ut erranti oui pastoris exibeatis officium; et fratrem illum inordinate ambulantem, qui ecclesiam de Strigueil contra abbatis sui et totius ecclesie sue uoluntatem ocupare presumsit, ad pacem et obedientiam reuocetis; et
15 ne totus intereat, ipsum tamquam ouem de ore leonis ereptam pastorali humero ad caulas gregis reportetis.[3] Periculosum namque est aliquem ecclesie communicare beneficiis, nedum sacramentis, qui aduersus eos quibus obedire oportet contumax inuenitur aut rebellis. Monita salutis mansuete sustinebit humilitas; uel, si pertinax extiterit, uirgam uigilantem adhibeat karitas; ut et inobedientia ⟨fo. 4v⟩ con-
20 pescatur et zelo uestro qualiter rebellionem remunerari oporteat omnibus intimetur. Valete.

**14** G, no. 8; B, fo. 4; H, fos. 149v–150; R, fo. 207.
1 V. R; B *om.* Dei gratia    12 Stringueil R    16 nedum R; necdum H (?) B

---

[1] Giles read 'sacrista', and so Nicholas has sometimes been taken for a monk and sacrist of Gloucester abbey, and even identified with the later bishop of Llandaff. As Gunni had been clothed in the monastic habit, the witnesses may have been monks, but Nicholas was more probably a secular associate of Gunni.
[2] Cf. no. 40.                         [3] Cf. Luc. xv. 5 (and no. 11).

## 15 To Uhtred, bishop of Llandaff

[1140–8] He answers and accepts an admonition from the bishop.

The occasion of this letter is unknown; but the reference to 'Radulfo clerico nostro' links it with no. 16.

Patri suo et domno V(thredo) Land(auensi) Dei gratia episcopo, G(ilebertus) dictus abbas G(loecestrie), Deo iure meritorum complacere. ⟨fo. 24⟩

Gratum munus estimo quod me, dilecte pater, litterarum commonitorio prouocas ad uirtutem. Nichil est enim quod pater filio uel utilius suadere uel intimare possit honestius. Nam sola est uirtus que Domino uirtutum dignum 5 prestat obsequium, et totum exosa quod preterit, affectare presumit eterna. Virtus est que animos eueit, et totum fugiens quo turbamur in infimis locum sibi querit et inuenit in supernis. Species eius amabilis est et concupiscibilis forma, que, ut ait sapiens, si corporalibus ad plenum intuenda daretur oculis omnium in se appetitus excitaret non modicos.[1] Gratias itaque paterne diligentie refero, que mentem meam 10 ad eam quam commendo uirtutem non mediocriter incitauit. Nam quod mee commissa sollicitudini tractare me diligenter edoces et hortaris, ad prudentie me fines applicas et ea que in omni officio pernecessaria est plenitudine me discretionis informas. Vnde si dilecte michi beniuolentie tue frater quem in partes illas direxi reuerentie minus inpendit, offensam profecto geminauit in me quod non solum 15 offendit episcopum sed et domnum immo et patrem experimentis quamplurimis amicissimum. Precor itaque ut correctum suscipias et amonitum, et hanc nobis donando iniuriam uestram nobis cumulare beneficia et gratia super gratiam[2] addita coronare non desistas. Partem uero tibi quam iuste repetis in integrum reddi precepi et precipio, et quedam tibi mandanda secretius usque ad aduentum Radulfi 20 clerici nostri ad presens ommitto. Valete.

## 16 To Uhtred, bishop of Llandaff

[1140–8] He tells the bishop that he has raised no unjust claim against Tewkesbury abbey for Ralph his clerk, and that the abbot of Tewkesbury has surrendered tithe which Ralph[3] claimed for the church of Llancarfan,[4] in exchange for a pension.

Patri suo et domno V(thredo) Land(auensi) Dei gratia episcopo, frater G(ilebertus) G(loecestrie) dictus abbas salutem.

Quoniam habitio[5] mandato comparatur, dilecte nobis excellentie uestre presenti scripto notificamus, quod sicut nullam Radulfo clerico nostro aduersus Tehesb(eriam)

15 G, no. 57; B, fo. 23 v.
20 qdam B    20 mandanda *or* mandata B
16 G, no. 71; B, fo. 27 v.

---

[1] We have not traced this quotation.        [2] Cf. Eccli. xxvi. 19.        [3] Cf. no. 15.
[4] On the important church of St Cadoc of Llancarfan, see *SEBC*, p. 223 and n.; *CS*, pp. 276–7, 283 ff., esp. 309 ff. See also nos. 70–1.
[5] Possession, presumably.

₅ hactenus calumniam iniuste mouere mandauimus, ita nec si in iniustitia sua pertinax inuenitur, id quantum nostra interest aliquatenus ratum habemus. Nam cum precepta iuris hec sint, honeste uiuere, alterum non ledere, ius suum cuique tribuere,¹ sicut ea que nostri iuris sunt nobis illesa manere uolumus, sic que competunt aliis nullam nostra opera lesionem aut detrimentum sustinere desideramus.

₁₀ Paternitatis itaque uestre notitiam latere nolo, quod domnus abbas de Thechesberia decimam de terra R. Foliot michi uolens satisfacere pro tribus solidis uno anno dimisit, decimam dico quam predictus R(adulfus) reclamabat iuris esse ecclesie de Lancarwan. Prudentie itaque uestre palam uolo esse hoc modo ad illum eiusdem decime inuestituram deuolutam esse. Quapropter karitatem uestram diligenter et

₁₅ obnixe precor ne occasione mei uel predicti R. prefatum abbatem super hoc in aliquo grauetis uel grauari per⟨fo. 28⟩mittatis. Alienum contra iustitiam et patrum decreta omnino nolo, quia non debeo, affectare aut possidere. Valete.

### 17  To Jocelin de Bohun, bishop of Salisbury

[1142–8] A petition for kindlier treatment for one A(d)elardus, and particularly to allow him to present to the church of Finchampstead (Berks.).

Nos. 17–19 are addressed to Jocelin, who became bishop of Salisbury in 1142. Nos. 17 and 18 are a doublet (see no. 25). They reveal a lenient attitude to lay patronage—anyway in this instance; why Gilbert was concerned in A(d)elardus' affairs, we do not know.

Patri suo et domno I(ocelino) Sar(esberiensi) episcopo, frater G(ilebertus) G(loecestrie) dictus abbas, miseris non plus irasci quam satis est.

Stilus humilis est et summissa materies exorare pro iam mortuo, ut ipso agente satis et patre tandem miserante quoquomodo reuocetur ad uitam. Gladio spiritus, quod est uerbum Dei,² precidisti Ælardum iamdiu a uita quod utinam non meruisset,
₅ aut si meruit, spiritum apud uos utinam condigne satisfaciens inuenisset. Quod actum quia nondum est, pulsamus ad hostium non amici solum, sed et patris et domni, si quomodo tandem aperiatur nobis et audiatur clamor noster in intimis, ubi in cubili conscientie bone amicus idem et domnus cum pueris suis qui sunt purificati iam animi delectatione optimi requiescit.³ Speramus enim quod in
₁₀ necessitate recurrenti ad uos nec pro pane lapidem, quod est repulsa durissima, nec pro pisce serpentem que laboriosa est et in dolo protractio, nec pro ouo scorpionis nouissima porrigetis.⁴ Dignum est e manu pontificis alia longe donatiua splendescere. Quorundam gloria est, sed non apud Deum,⁵ miserorum plus letari casu quam de reditu gloriari. Longe monet aliter qui redeunti in amplexus occurrit.⁶ Rogamus
₁₅ itaque, dilectissime in Domino, ut iniuriarum paulisper immemor ad se redeat ille

**16** 16 permittetis B.
**17** G, no. 51; B, fo. 22.
3 materias B (? materia *before correction*)    10 purifati B    10 delectatur B    12 pice B
(s *added by modern hand*)    12–13 *sic; perhaps for* scorpionem nouissime

¹ Justinian, *Inst.* I, 1, 3.
² Cf. Eph. vi. 17.                                    ³ Cf. Luc. xi. 5–8.
⁴ Cf. Luc. v. 5–12 (for the whole passage).    ⁵ Cf. Rom. iv. 2.
⁶ Cf. Luc. xv. 20.

uester in nullo unquam degener sanguis, et se tum demum uictum estimet cum sibi iam supplicatur a uictis. 'Quem persequeris, rex Israel, quem persequeris? Canem mortuum et pulicem unum.'[1] Si de libertate ecclesie que sancta sunt in corde uestro disponitis, si fratres et coepiscopos uestros in ecclesiis de manu laicorum eruendis, 20 ut nec eis personas presentare liceat, omnes anteire proponitis; totum hoc quidem laudabile est ut religio semper collocetur in summo, sed queso non tam aspere requiri a minimis quod nondum atemptatur in summis. Scitis equidem quam sit periculosa desperatio. Quid si inmoderate persequentem Asahelem lancea Abner exceperit? Videte ne de manu uestra sanguis utriusque requiratur.[2] Consuetudinis 25 ususque longeui non uilis est auctoritas,[3] et ubi non peccatur in Deum tollerabile est ut radicibus suis antiquitas inconcussa permaneat. Si nobis indulgetis quid omnes coepiscopos uestros suis omnibus indulgere notissimum est, quis umquam obsecro reprehendet? Scio apud quem michi sermo est, apud patrem et domnum, cui innata bonitas animi totum quod laudabile est persuadet. Aelardum quacumque 30 inuoluatis amaritudine; dum sibi tantum personam presentare liceat in ecclesia de Finchehamestude, uestris per omnia mandatis obediat et acquiescat. Valete.

## 18 To Jocelin de Bohun, bishop of Salisbury

[1142–8] A petition similar to no. 17.

Patri suo et domno I(ocelino) Sar(esberiensi) Dei gratia episcopo frater G(ilebertus) G(loecestrie) dictus abbas, salutem et seruitium.

Vrget me inportuna Aelardi lamentantis improbitas, ut quod forte negandum esset temeritati negari nequeat improbitati.[4] Vnde preces sullimitati uestre solita confidentia porrigo, ut quam in Adelardum intendisti uel iam dedisti sententiam, 5 ea qua filios consolari oportet sobrietate leuigetis, ut nec quassatam confringatis arundinem nec linum fumigans extinguatis.[5] De rebus presbiteri quas iuste petitis, si quid minime restitutum est, plenius sub iuramenti taxatione restituet. Si in dignitatem uestram quoquomodo presumptum est misericordie uestre condigne satisfaciet. Vnum tamen rogamus humiliter ut quod nulli parochiano uestro 10 hactenus negare consueuistis, ipsi in ecclesia de Vinchamstude concedatis, ut personam uobis presentet idoneam quam in prefata ecclesia ministrare permittatis. Iustum tamen foret sicut donationem ecclesiarum, ita et presentationem per- sonarum laicorum non esse; sed quod in regno isto nondum in consuetudinem inductum est, a minimis inchoari non oportet nec a minoribus exigi quod a 15 maioribus nequeat extorqueri. Si igitur antiquitatem suis aliquatenus uultis conuelli radicibus, inchoandum erit a capite, ut inde in barbam descendens unguentum

17 24 despatio B  27 pmaneat B  31 sib B  31 liceat] que added in B  32 uris B
18 G, no. 53; B, fo. 22 v.

---

[1] Cf. I Reg. xxiv. 15. 'uester sanguis' perhaps implies that Jocelin and Adelardus were related.
[2] Cf. II Reg. ii. 26, 19–23; Ezech. iii. 18.    [3] Cf. Code, 8, 52 (53), 2 (cf. GF, pp. 240–1).
[4] Cf. Luc. xi. 8.
[5] Cf. Matt. xii. 20 (also Isa. xlii. 20; Regula S. Benedicti, c. 64).

Domini horam etiam uestimenti attingat,[1] et sic totum corpus ecclesie tanto melius quanto diffusius sue flagrantie suauitate perfundat. Petitioni mee assensum dari non
20 alia fiducia deprecor, nisi ut quia semper audistis inmeritum, audiatis adhuc et non ingratum. Valete.

### 19 To Jocelin de Bohun, bishop of Salisbury

[1142–8] An appeal for justice (apparently for a just judgement) on behalf of himself and his community.

Patri suo et domno I(ocelino) Salesber(iensi) Dei gratia episcopo, frater G(ilebertus) dictus abbas G(loecestrie) et humilis ecclesie beati Petri conuentus, id modicum quod sunt et deuotionis obsequia si qua possunt.

Ad uos, dilecte domne, iamdiu nostra querela perlata est, cui si nondum subuenit
5 pietas, a uestra tamen beniuolentia nostra non desperat humilitas. Vnde angariati et afflicti plurimum ad uos iterato recurrimus, nostris opem ferri poscentes incommodis et iuuamen detrimentis. Nam quia uobis conquesti sumus solito magis affligimur, et quia nos de conquestione ⟨fo. 25⟩ nostra nichil aut parum profecisse considerant, ipsa impunitate sua armati nos uelud expositos arbitrantur, et sibi
10 cuncta licere in nos uelud a uobis quadam data licentia gloriantur. Vnde rogamus humiliter ego (quod quidem parum est) et omnes fratres nostri (quod equidem magnum est) ut nostras si placet non paruipendatis iniurias, sed nobis exibendo iustitiam, uestrum, ut dignum est, ministerium honoretis, et nos, si quid possumus, gratie debitores habeatis. Valete.

### 20 To William de Chesney

[c. 1142–8] A diplomatic answer, accompanied by fifteen silver marks, to a harsh demand from his uncle, followed by a reminder of the brevity of life.

The circumstances suggest that William was already at the height of his power, and so point to a date later than 1142 (see *Cart. Eynsham*, I, 415 ff.).

G(ilebertus) Dei gratia abbas Gloecestrie Willelmo de Cheisneia salutem.

Gratias tibi ago de omnibus bonis que michi fecisti, bene sperantes de te ut semper de bonis in meliora procedas. Nam si dure ad presens respondisti michi, necessitatem que te urget culpare possum, sed te culpare non possum. Scio quod
5 amicus amico, nepoti auunculus libenter parceret si necessitas instans hoc permitteret. Et quidem hoc bonum esset michi sed multo melius tibi. Nam si tu nos in temporalibus adiuuas, nos tibi spiritualia nostra non negamus. Si⟨c⟩ omni die apud

---

**19** G, no. 62; B, fo. 24v.
9 armati] uel ni B (*interlined; i.e.* animati, *perhaps the true reading, but* expositos *suggests that he is following out a military metaphor*)
**20** G, no. 54; B, fo. 23.

---

[1] Cf. Ps. cxxxii. 2.

nos omnes, ibi tui memoria agitur ubi Patri Filius immolatur.¹ Sed hoc fortasse quid sit ignoras uel si bene nosti non curas, nec permittit instans necessitas ut multum inter amicos et alios discernas. Ideo quindecim marcas argenti tibi mittimus, 10 rogantes ut sicut eas bona uoluntate mittimus, ita et eas bona uoluntate suscipias; ne si nimis spiras ad censum, illorum qui pro te su⟨pplica⟩nt ad Dominum erga te minuas affectum. Memento quod uita tua fumus exiguus est et tota tua gloria puluis et uermis. Hodie es et cras non eris, uel si cras eris, nescis si eris post cras; et si exieris de corpore, de gloria tua nichil tecum portabis.² Castella tua stabunt hic et habebit 15 ea qui nullas tibi gratias aget, et in labore tuo forsitan gloriabitur extraneus. Solummodo peccata tua te sequentur, et nondum tibi uidetur quod satis peccator sis, sed tunc uelles quod hic minus peccasses. Ea die cum miser respexeris et ululatum uiduarum et pauperum gemitum et orphanorum planctum, querelas ecclesiarum super te uideris, quis tibi sensus erit? Ad quem respicies? Quis omnium sanctorum 20 est quem non offenderis? Quis pauperum Dei circa te est quem non leseris? Nisi dum potes tibi prouideris, tam uehementer coram Deo accusabunt te opera tua ut nec in hac uita te diu possit tolerare iustitia eius nec in futura aliquatenus misereri. De propinquo te monuit Dominus: caros tuos de medio tulit; uirga eius iam nunc est extensa in te. Aperiat ipse cor tuum et infundat ei gratiam suam, ut ante tuum 25 diem nouissimum bonum opus germinet ex te, in quo possit Dominus saluare te. Vale.

## 21 To Warin, prior of St Guthlac's, Hereford

[1143–8] He reassures the prior of his affection (*caritas*).

St Guthlac's was founded as a dependency of Gloucester in 1143.³

Frater G(ilebertus) Gloecestrie dictus abbas, dilectis suis dilectoribus Guar(ino) priori et fratribus qui cum eo sunt Herefordie, bonum bene consummare principium.

Libentius uos ipse uisitassem quam ad uos litteras nuntiosue dirigerem; sed quia prepediunt negotia multiplicata quod uellem,⁴ litteras interim nostras uice colloquii habeatis, ut pensetis ex his quid de nostra erga uos caritate estimare debeatis. Non 5 est credendum omni spiritui; quidam enim spiritus ex Deo non sunt.⁵ Vnde, si caritatis nostre sinceritatem impius homo superseminatis zizaniis offuscare conatur, discretio nobis spirituum necessaria est; ut non circumferamur omni uento doctrine uel facile adquiescamus errori, sed probantes semper potiora solidemus in Christo caritatem, in quem anchora nostre spei proiecta est. Frustra namque credimus et 10

**20** 12 su't B
**21** G, no. 35; B, fo. 15v; R, fo. 212.
1 Frater] Pater B (*in a group beginning* Pat(ri)); Gloecestrie…abbas *om.* R  1 Guar(ino)]
G. R  6 ex Deo spiritus B  7 nostre] uestre MSS  10 spei] fixa est uel *added in* B (*which is clumsy, and reads like a marginal suggestion or emendation which has become part of the text*)

---

¹ Presumably this means that William was remembered in the Memento of the living in the conventual mass.  ² Cf. I Mach. ii. 62–3; I Tim. vi. 7.
³ See *GF*, pp. 84 n., 85–6; *CS*, pp. 264 n., 280.
⁴ Cf. no. 8.  ⁵ Cf. I Joh. iv. 1.

speramus ⟨fo. 16⟩ nisi inuicem diligamus.[1] Attendamus illud apostoli: caritas nunquam excidit,[2] uerbum breue sed fecunda sententia. Hic plane conuincitur, nos aut in Christo non dilexisse, aut leuiter a caritate non excidisse. Non enim in Christo diligit qui facile permouetur ad odium.

## 22 To Henry of Blois, bishop of Winchester and papal legate

[1143, before November] The bishop of Hereford has laid an interdict on the earl, and city of Hereford, and the sentence has been extended to Gloucester's churches in the diocese of Worcester by the bishop of Worcester: Gilbert asks the legate to temper the bishop's severity and explains the state of the case to him.

Milo of Gloucester was created earl of Hereford by the empress on 25 July 1141, and died on 24 December 1143. Earlier in 1143 he had attempted to raise a tax from the churches on his domain, and so was involved in a dispute with the bishop.[3] A comparison of this letter with nos. 1 and 2 makes it very probable that it is this dispute, not the outbreak of violence in 1140, to which Gilbert is referring; nor was Milo earl in 1140. The bishop retired to the priory of Shobdon (later Wigmore):[4] it was presumably from there that he laid the city of Hereford under interdict.

The letter cannot be later than November 1143, when Henry of Blois relinquished the legateship.

Patri suo et domno H(enrico) Winton(iensi) Dei gratia episcopo et sancte sedis apostolice legato frater G(ilebertus) ecclesie beati Petri Gloecestrie dictus abbas, totius obedientie et caritatis obsequium.

    Quoniam discretioni uestre in Christo amabilis pater sollicitudo ecclesiarum Dei
5 laudabili circumspectione commissa est, ideo super his que inter domnum Here-fordensem et domnum Milonem eiusdem ciuitatis comitem acta sunt quedam que ad nos spectant uestre diligentie designamus. Dissensionis itaque inter eos multis emergentibus causis res eo tandem perducta est ut domnus Herefordensis comiti ipsi suisque, toti etiam ciuitati Herefordie diuina interdiceret sacramenta. Vnde
10 comes non minus pietate quam necessitate compulsus tam nobis quam multis aliis astantibus sese ipsi presentans ecclesie, primum data in manu canonicorum spon-sione, postmodum textu super altare posito, se die asignata in presentia episcopi et ecclesie ipsius affuturum et quicquid ecclesiastica iuri⟨s⟩dicione decretum foret inpleturum sub ecclesie testimonio repromisit. Statuto die utroque presente res in
15 medium deducta est et aliquorum petitione, domni etiam episcopi assensu, in diem

21 12 coniungitur R    13 excedisse B
22 G, no. 3; B, fo. 2v; H, fo. 148r–v; R, fo. 206.
13 iuridicione B; iuriditione HR

---

[1] Cf. Matt. xiii. 35–9; I Cor. xii. 10; Eph. iv. 14; Phil. i. 10; Heb. vi. 18–19; I Joh. iv. 7, 12.
[2] I Cor. xiii. 8.
[3] Cf. *Gesta Stephani*, pp. 104–6 (which takes the bishop's side). On Milo, Gilbert's relative and patron, see *GF*, pp. 35–7; Biog. Index, *s.v.* Hereford; cf. also no. 24.
[4] *Monasticon*, VI, 345.

alterum est dilata, sic tamen ut si rem item differri imperialium officiorum[1] necessitas ulla compelleret, id ante contestate actionis diem denuntiaretur alterutro. Prepediente necessitate quesiuit comes inducias actioni; uerum id domnus ⟨fo. 3 r⟩ episcopus non ex condicto actum esse reputans, seueritati nichil detrahens sententiam promulgauit; cumque litteris ab auctoritate uestra susceptis domnum Wigornen- 20 sem in ecclesias Gloecestrie eandem ferre sentenciam instanti summonitione compelleret, comes tum per directos litterarum suarum apices tum per honestas et idoneas personas sese plenarie satisfactioni offerens, secundum placitum domni Wigornensis locum sibi et tempus exequende et implende iustitie postulauit addici. Et ne tergiuersationis aut duplicitatis cuiuspiam haberetur suspectus, domnum 25 abbatem Teochesberie, priorem etiam Lantoniensem[2] et me eiusdem promissionis inplende fideiussores asignauit. Verum tam eius humilitate quam nostra omnium fideiussione parui habita, sententia nichilominus in nos data est. Vnde cum apud nos uiuis interdicantur monasteria mortuis sepultura, diuina quoque intermittantur officia, multipliciter ligamur in pena qui non tenemur in culpa, uestre igitur 30 intererit diligentie rem si nimis agrauata est ex animi modestia temperare, cum iuxta papam Stephanum pulsationes huiusmodi ultra prouincie terminos nequa- quam progredi sed intra prouinciam audiri et a comprouincialibus terminari oporteat, nisi forte (quod hic minime actum est) ad sedem apostolicam fuerit appellatum.[3] Vestram etiam nequit latere prudentiam tunc multum fore detrahen- 35 dum seueritati cum subuersiones ecclesiarum et strages imminent populorum, sicut eidem uehementer est incumbendum cum sic correpti simplices fiunt meliores non cum exasperati mali redduntur nequiores. Valeat et imperpetuum illibata conseruetur uestra sublimitas.

### 23  To Pope Celestine II

[*c.* December 1143] He rejoices in the Pope's accession and commends Nigel bishop of Ely to him.

Celestine II was elected Pope on 26 September 1143 and died on 8 March 1144. Since the news of his election seems to have arrived in England in November, this letter must belong to the turn of 1143 and 1144, perhaps *c.* December 1143. This date is made more precise by the reference to the bishop of Ely.

At the Council of London, which opened on 10 November 1143, the papal legate, Henry of Winchester, ordered the bishops of Ely and Chester to Rome.[4] Bishop Nigel's precise

---

**22** 16 differri item B     26 me] uestre sanctitatis utinam seruum *added in* H     28 nichilo- minus sententia R     29 monasteria *sic MSS*, *? for* sacramenta     30 in pena *om.* B     30 igitur] ergo B
**23** G, no. 5; B, fo. 3 v; H, fo. 149; R, fo. 206 v.

---

[1] This presumably means 'the affairs of the empress'; this slightly oblique reference is a re- minder that Henry of Winchester, though politically committed to his brother once again, was still legate for the whole English church.
[2] Roger, abbot of Tewkesbury, and William, Bishop Robert of Hereford's successor as prior of Llanthony.
[3] *Decretum*, C. 3, q. 6, c. 4.          [4] Ann. Waverley, *Ann. Mon.* II, 229.

movements are uncertain,[1] but he clearly went to Rome early in 1144, and with the support of Archbishop Theobald he secured redress from Celestine's successor, Lucius II, in May 1144. No doubt he collected his dossier of testimonials, of which this is one, shortly after the council of November 1143.

Patri suo et domno summo Dei gratia pontifici Celestino, frater Gilebertus ecclesie beati Petri Gloecestrie dictus abbas, totum quod obedientie et obsequii ualet humilis et promta deuotio.

Fidelis Dominus in omnibus uerbis suis,[2] qui, quod ecclesie repromisit, incessanter
5 operari non desinit; ipse, ad stabiliendam fidem et confirmandam spem, promisit se usque ad consumationem seculi[3] ecclesie non deesse, et iuxta uerbum suum nobiscum manens in secula, sanctus in opere et promisso uerax indubitata fide cognoscitur. Nuper animos omnium nostrum nubilosa caligo confuderat, et ad decessum domni et patris nostri honorande memorie Innocentii fugerat dilectus a nobis super
10 montes Bethel et ad supernorum colles aromatum aliquandiu declinauerat.[4] Sed dum uos in ipso apostolatus culmine eiusdem loco suscipimus, ipsam in uobis dilecti presentiam reamplectimur, et cum omni gratiarum actione et tota animorum alacritate ueneramur. Obscuratum nobis fuerat aurum et immutatus color optimus, sed ecce magis rutilat festiuus ornatus ecclesie, totum nobis conuertens in gaudium
15 et letitiam et solempnitatem preclaram.[5] Noctem mundo fecerat sol conuersus in tenebras[6] sed reasumpta claritate totum quod tenebratum erat radio gratissime lucis illuminat. Herebant lacrime in maxillis nostris,[7] et intra precordia dolor estuabat inclusus, dum in ipso rerum culmine ad tantum casum dissensionis scisma pio timebamus pauore contingere. Sed subitum infortunium subita et secunda fortuna
20 secuta est; et sicut unus Deus, una fides, unum baptisma,[8] sic unus pastor in terris totam moderatur ecclesiam qui cuncta sibi caritate compaginans omnes ecclesie partes una facit pietate gaudere. Vestre igitur cure et prouidentie nos et nostra committimus; et quantum pia presumit deuotio etiam pro domno et amico nostro Nigello Heliensi episcopo serenitati uestre supplicamus, ut ea qua filios amplecti
25 caritate non desistitis ipsum suscipiatis, et necessitatibus eius pie subueniendo ceteros filios uestros artiori uobis caritatis uinculo astringatis. In eternum conseruetur incolumis uestra sullimitas, in Christo dilecte pater.

23 1 summo BR; *om.* H    4 ecclesie] sue *added in* H    6 usque *om.* B    7 et] in *added in* B
11 ipsam *om.* B    14 gaudium] gladium B    16 erat] fuerat B    18 cisma B    20 sic] sicut B
23 etiam *om.* R    24 N. B (Helieneni R)    25 desistis B    26 artiori H, arciori R; acriori B

---

[1] The *Liber Eliensis* makes him visit the empress at Wareham, then return to Ely, between the council and his visit to Rome; if this is correct, the visit to the empress would be a likely occasion for collecting a testimonial from one of her supporters. But Dr E. O. Blake has suggested that the visit to Wareham in fact took place earlier in 1143 (*Liber Eliensis*, p. 435). Nigel was accused of alienating the lands of his see and inciting rebellion. The latter charge—due to Nigel's temporary adherence to the empress—no doubt partly explains Gilbert's interest in his case.

[2] Cf. Ps. cxliv. 13.    [3] Cf. Matt. xxviii. 20.

[4] Cf. Cant. v. 17; viii. 14, etc.; *reamplectimur* in the next sentence may be of Gilbert's coining.

[5] Cf. Lam. iv. 1; Ps. l. 10.    [6] Cf. Act. ii. 20.

[7] Cf. Lam. i. 2.    [8] Cf. Eph. iv. 5–6.

## 24  To Theobald, archbishop of Canterbury

[*c.* December 1143] The archbishop is bound on a journey whose object is to restore the ancient dignity of his church: Gilbert excuses himself from accompanying him, since he is engaged in defending the property of his church against the earl of Hereford.

The phrase 'libertatem dignitatis antique' is most naturally taken as a reference to Theobald's primacy, which he successfully recovered in May 1145. If so, the journey in question must be that undertaken by Theobald at the turn of 1143 and 1144 (see Appendix II). In no. 48, written in the second half of 1145, the primacy is undoubtedly referred to as 'dignitas pristina'; and the date 1143 receives some confirmation from the fact that Theobald is not addressed as primate. Finally, Gilbert here refuses categorically to accompany Theobald, whereas in 1146–7 and 1148 he went with the archbishop.

Patri suo et domno Theobaldo Cantuariensi Dei gratia archiepiscopo, frater Gilebertus ecclesie beati Petri Gloecestrie dictus abbas, totum quod pacis, quod gratie, quod salutis.

Gratias ago beniuolentie uestre, in Christo dilecte pater, que me dignata est et filium nominare et amicum reputare, et ut fierem suscepti comes itineris michi 5 uoluit etiam in expensis prouidere. ⟨fo. 4⟩ Gratulor equidem si uenit tempus, et a Domino oportunitas data est, qua possit ecclesia uestra de manu suffocantis eripi, et quocunque modo, quocunque labore, in libertatem dignitatis antique restitui. Nouit inspector cordium Deus quam promtus forem huic exequendo negotio, nisi ecclesie cui alligatus sum timerem undique emergenti periculo; sed nouerit 10 sanctitas uestra equidem usque ad diem hanc non irruit uehementius tempestas in nos. Hodie contra comitem Herefordie, cuius sitis in omne quod habemus excanduit, causam multo sudore distringimus: et ipsum, quem si absentes essemus nostre sperabamus ecclesie protectorem, presentes experimur infestissimum hostem. Episcopalia iam contra ipsum arma acuimus, et contra ipsum et omnes suos uelud 15 in procinctu astamus. Aliorum infestantium nos non est numerus contra quos hinc ferrum tenentes, hinc lapidem, pugnamus, et uix proficimus. Habebit itaque excusatum hac uice me filium uestrum paterna benignitas, quem uobis ad presens neccessitas subtrait, non uoluntas. Erunt omni die lacrime mee in maxillis meis[1] donec reditum uestrum et successus audiam, et redeunti patri letus occurram. 20 Interim oratione prosequar domnum meum; cui, si absens ero corpore, in omni negotio presens spiritu et affectu mentis astabo. Valete.

**24** G, no. 6; B, fo. 3 v; H, fo. 149 v; R, fos. 206 v–207.
1 T. B; Theobaldo H; Teodbaldo R    6 in expensis etiam B    10 undequaque B    15 acuimus] conciuimus B    20 successum R

---

[1] Cf. Lam. i. 2.

## 25 To Theobald, archbishop of Canterbury

[*c.* December 1143] He excuses himself from accompanying the archbishop on a journey (probably the same as in no. 24).

This letter does not specify the occasion of Theobald's journey; but as in no. 24 the fact that Gilbert refuses to accompany him and the absence of the primatial title in the address suggest 1143 rather than any of Theobald's later journeys. This is confirmed by the mention of Christmas: the archbishop certainly left about the turn of the year in 1143–4; apparently earlier in 1146 (cf. no. 56); and certainly in March in 1148.

If 24 and 25 are correctly dated, they repeat one another; nor are they the only repetitions in the collection—cf. nos. 17–18, 36–7. Presumably one or other is a draft, not actually sent.[1]

Patri suo et domno Thebaldo Cant(uariensi) Dei gratia archiepiscopo, frater Gilebertus ecclesie beati Petri Gloecestrie dictus abbas, pie complendo senarium sabbata sabbatorum feliciter adipisci.[2]

Habui, dilecte pater, a uestra sublimitate commonitorium ut ante diem Natalis 5 Domini me uestro presentarem conspectui, paratus suscepto a uobis itineri et labori. Et eo quidem erga uos animo sum ea caritate deuinctus, ut propter uos leue reputem totum quod minari potest—difficultas itineris aut uexatio corporis uel urgens auctoritas obuie potestatis. Sed sunt preter hec instantia mea cotidiana innumera,[3] que me uinculis non solum ligatum tenent, sed etiam uelud immobilem reddunt; 10 quibus explicandis cum nullo modo sufficiam, arduum michi est ut ad presens maiora attemptare presumam. Valete.

## 26 To Brian FitzCount

[1143–4] He congratulates Brian on a manifesto in favour of the claims of the Empress Matilda, and himself expounds the case in her favour and the dispute at the Lateran Council of 1139.

On this letter, see *GF*, chapter vii. This letter and an account in the *Historia Pontificalis*[4] are the only evidence for the empress's appeal to Rome in 1139; and the letter is the most elaborate contemporary statement of her case. It refers to Pope Celestine II, and so can certainly be dated between November 1143 and the Spring of 1144 (cf. above, no. 23). Brian's manifesto is evidently not identical with his letter to Henry of Winchester, which survives,[5] and was probably written *c.* September 1142.[6]

Domno et amico suo karissimo Brientio filio comitis, frater G(ilebertus) ecclesie beati Petri Gloecestrie dictus abbas, bene currendo fructu non priuari iustitie.

---

**25** G, no. 7; B, fo. 4; H, fo. 149v; R, fo. 207.
1 Thebaldo H; T. BR    11 temptare B; atemtare H; attemptare R
**26** G. no. 79; B, fo. 5v; H, fos. 151–3.
1 Briennio H

---

[1] Such duplicates occur in other collections of this time: cf. John of Salisbury, *Epp.* I, nos. 25–6.
[2] Cf. no. 4.                    [3] Cf. II Cor. xi. 28.
[4] *HP* (P), pp. 85 ff., cf. Poole's commentary, pp. 107 ff.; (C), pp. 83 ff.; and for the possibility that John's account refers to a different occasion, *GF*, p. 105 n.
[5] Ed. with commentary by H. W. C. Davis, *EHR*, xxv (1910), 297–303.        [6] *GF*, p. 107.

Quosdam pertrahit in stuporem quod cum litteras non didisceris, librum nichilominus edidisti. Verum scias id michi non fuisse miraculo, cum quod artis tibi negabat industria, uehementiam amoris in te et per te dictasse cognouerim. Amor 5 enim non accipit ex impossibilitate solacium, uel ex difficultate remedium. Semper enim operatur magna si est; uel si operari renuit, amor non est. Hinc est quod, cum litteras non didiceris, in campum tamen litterarum non mediocriter inpegisti. Hereat animo tuo diui regis Henrici honore digna memoria, cuius dies bonos et aurea quondam secula, patre gens orbata deplorat, et rubigo presentis etatis 10 frequenti sed tristi recordatione commemorat. Non est tibi elapsum a memoria quod te promouit a puero, quod iuuenem educauit, et donatum militie cingulo, donis et honoribus ampliauit.[1] Verum hinc est quod te sui memorem fecit, et recenti memoria uiuit apud te; quoniam obisse sibi totius Anglie facies admodum desolata, crebra miseriarum inundatione recognoscit. Ab illo non degenerans amor 15 tuus propagatur in stirpem regiam unicam eius filiam et regni ipsius heredem; cuius causam non solus armis, sed sicut audiuimus, et iam uidimus, eloquii uenustate simul et ueritate sustines et defendis. Totum namque breui complecteris argumento, quod hactenus ueritatis ignaros in fauorem sue partis alliciat, et iamdiu ueritatis conscios uel confirmet, si amici sunt, uel obtundat ut reuerberet 20 inimicos.

Ipsam tamen de qua tibi sermo est, in nullius commendes iniuriam. Ea que regis Henrici fuerunt, unice eius filie et legitimo matrimonio procreate asseris iure deberi. Videtur ad id quod asseris iuris cuiusque regula coaptari: est enim diuinum ius, est naturale, est et humanum.[2] Ex iure diuino Dominum in Euangelio audiuimus, 25 dicente sibi matre sua, 'Fili, quid fecisti nobis sic?' respondit ei Dominus: 'quid est quod me querebatis? ⟨fo. 6⟩ nesciebatis quia in his que patris mei sunt oportet me esse?'[3] Magnus est Dominus ad comparationem ancille, et magna eterna hereditas temporali comparata et transitorie. Sic tamen loquitur Dominus ac si neminem dubitare oporteat, quin ea que patris sunt naturali eius filio iure debeantur. Sed qui 30 nullam pretermittit occasionem (si sibi oblata est) quin tua dicta remordeat, non filium sed filiam de qua agimus esse contendet; et que filio magis competunt, non debere filie regalia sceptra addici. Quid contra istud lex diuina respondeat, audiamus. In libro Numeri, capitulo ultimo, inuenies quod a comite Gloec(estrie) sepe commemorasse audiuimus: Salphaat homo erat Iudeus de tribu Manasse; huic filie 35

**26** 3 ptrahit B   5 cognoueram H   9 Heret H   10 quondam *om.* H   11 stristi B   11 a *om.* B   15 cognoscit H   20 conscisos B   20 ut] et H   22 commendas H   25 audimus H   27 querebatis...quia B, *Vulg.*; querebasti...quod H   28 eterna H; est celestis B   31 est H; fuerint B   34–5 inuenies...audiuimus] super hoc aliquid inuenies B (H *reads...* commemorasti...; B *is evidently the fruit of revision*; cf. *GF*, pp. 116–17)

[1] Henry I gave him the honour of Wallingford, with the heiress of the honour, Matilda of Wallingford.

[2] No immediate source for Gilbert's division can be offered: his definition of natural law is based on Ulpian rather than on the more commonly used text of Isidore (quoted e.g. by Gratian): see *GF*, p. 64.

[3] Luc. ii. 48–9.

tantum erant et nullus filius.[1] Visum est quibusdam illas ob sexus inbecillitatem non debere in bona patris admitti. De hoc requisitus Dominus legem promulgauit, ut filiabus Salphaat totum cederet in integrum quod fuerat ab earum patre possessum. Eant qui uolunt, ponant in celum os suum,[2] astris si placet machinentur insidias.
40 Nobis fixum erit quod eterna lege sanccitum est. Si uero ius naturale percurras, cause huic non mediocre firmamentum et robur[3] inuenies. Ius enim naturale est quod natura non tantum nos sed et omnia animalia docuit, secundum quod singula, iuxta genus suum, amorem sibi quendam conciliant, fetus propagant, propagatos diligunt et conseruant.[4] Si te ex tenore huius iuris interrogem quid rebus huiusmodi
45 sit natura propinquius, recte respondeas, id esse quibusque natura propinquius ad quod ea naturalis plus trahit affectus. Sed uolo dicas manifestius quid illud est. Scio quod hoc audiam a te: singulorum ad id magis affectus trahitur quod ex eisdem quodam uelut carnis et sanguinis participio procreatur. Attende igitur, ut uel homines a natura secernas, uel idem in his esse debere naturali iure concedas.
50 A patre et matre prima est in filium filiamue progressio. Nepotem statue uel quemlibet alterum in sanguinis linea gradum; iam languet amor et tepescit affectus, et sanguis ipse cursu quodammodo longiore deferbuit. Est ergo in filium et filiam eque feruentior amor, affectus promtior, et natura coniunctior. Sed dices hec omnia, que de naturali iure adduximus, ad interioris habitus qualitatem, non ad
55 possessionis spectare successionem. Non ita est: quem enim reputas natura proximum, restat ut ab eo quod possidetur minus estimes alienum. Vide quid te natura perdoceat. Tractus maris et sinus litorum pisces inhabitant, in quibus eos naturalis partus effuderit, in quibus educati sunt, saltus fere non desinunt. Siluas auicule, in quibus concreate sunt, suis replent organulis; et natura in singulis non solum
60 intime trahicit qualitatis affectum, sed ipsi successiue sue soboli, exteriora que possidet, quo potest iure, largitur. Vide naturam, ne expellas a te; prudenter eius adquiesce iudicio. Regis Henrici condignam sobolem, unicam eius filiam, legibus editam et educatam, regis ipsius heredem inconcussa ratione pronuntia. Hoc diuinum, hoc ius naturale suadet, hoc iuris humani sanxio protestatur. Nam ius
65 humanum partim ciuile, partim ius gentium appellatur. Ciuile est quod obseruandum sibi ciuitas unaqueque constituit. Ius gentium est quod non ciuitas una sed unaqueque gens sibi censuit obseruandum.[5] Sed et ciuili et iure gentium caute

---

**26** 36 illas] B *omits, and adds* eas *after* debere   38 in *om.* B   42 et *om.* B   46–7 manifestius ...id] *sic* H; manifestius singulorum ad id B   48 participatio B   52–3 eque et filiam H 54 adduximus] diximus B   58 educate BH   59 implent B

---

[1] Num. xxxvi. The reference to this as a favourite passage of the earl of Gloucester, the empress's half-brother and chief supporter, is an interesting sidelight on the arguments in the case, and also on the earl, who was noted for his intellectual interests and as a patron of scholars. (The passage was omitted in Giles's edition, because not in B: see *GF*, p. 116 n.)

[2] Cf. Ps. lxxii. 9.

[3] A traditional legal phrase going back to Cicero, *Mur.* xxvIII, 58. Cf. Lanfranc, *Ep.* 5 (ed. Giles): 'quasi robur totiusque cause firmamentum' (of the papal letters supporting Canterbury's primacy); and *GF*, p. 117 n.

[4] Cf. Justinian, *Inst.* I, 2, pr.; and *Digest*, I, I, I, 3 (Ulpian).

[5] Cf. *Inst.* I, 2, 2; *Dig.* I, I, I.

decretum est, ne liceat cuiquam patrifamilias filium filiamue legitimo procreatam matrimonio (nisi certis intercurrentibus causis) abdicare. Cause uero huiusmodi sunt: ut si quis patri manum iniecerit, uel eius mortem indiciis manifestis optauerit 70 uel beneficiis ingratus exstiterit, et cause huiusmodi; ⟨fo. 6 v⟩ quibus interuenientibus culpis lex etiam liberos abdicare permittit.[1] Sed nichil horum in presenti causa repperies. Illa enim, cuius causam tam sollicita cura perstringis, quando patri rebellis exstitit? Quando ingrata beneficiis? Audiuimus eam ad patris consilium temtasse maria, transcendisse alpes,[2] ignotas adisse regiones, nupsisse ibidem ad 75 patris imperium, et in ipso rerum fastigio et imperii culmine honeste sancteque tam diu perstitisse, donec post uiri decessum non necessitate urgente uel impetu feminee uoluntatis leuiter inpellente, sed patre qui miserat reuocante, ad ipsum reuersa est. Et licet in ipso culmine rerum, ut dictum est, perstitisset, ut regina Romani orbis et diceretur et esset, nequaquam supercilio elata est; sed ad omnem patris nutum 80 ipsius subdita uoluntati, eius item consilio secundis potita nuptiis, uiro nubens forti sicut audimus et strenuo, Andegauiensium, Cenomannensium, Turonensium domno, Normannorum etiam iam nunc triumphatori serenissimo.[3] In his omnibus que dicta sunt, non inuenies cur exheredari uel abdicari a patre debuerit; nec quidem abdicata *est, sed pio prudentique consilio potius est in totius Anglie, et 85 Normannie, dominationem episcoporum omnium et totius regni huius nobilium iuramento firmata. Eorum namque qui statuto consilio propriis, ut dicitur, consueuerant appellari nominibus,[4] nemo plane relictus est qui non ei consilium de optinendo et tuendo post regis obitum regno Anglie et ducatu Normannie sub iuramenti religione promitteret. O tempora digna taceri! Reminisci pudet com- 90 munis opprobrii. Nonne quod opprobrio duxerim—id quemque iurasse quod oportuit, sed ab eo quod sancte iuratum est cito leuiterque recessisse? Quis infatuauit Angliam? Miserum dico capud, quisquis ille est, in quem tot redundant periuria, homicidia, incendia, flagitia, desolationes, et scandala. Quando sibi securus erit qui contaminauit regnum, polluit sacerdotium, et non solum presenti 95

**26** 71 et que huiusmodi sunt B    75 transcendere B    81 subdita subdita B    82 audiuimus B 82 Andegauensium, Cenomanensium, Thuronensium H    83 triumphatori] B adds ut audiuimus 84 nec] ne B    85 *est om. B    87 statuo BH (corrected in B by modern hand)    91 Non H; Non corrected to nonne (?) in B

[1] Cf. Novels, 115, 3.
[2] It is not clear whether this means 'mountains' or 'Alps'; more probably the latter, the more normal use, since Matilda did cross the Alps with her first husband for her imperial coronation in 1117—they were in Italy 1116–18.
[3] Geoffrey of Anjou, the empress's second husband, completed the conquest of Normandy in the years 1141–4; most of Normandy was his by the end of 1143. What Gilbert says about Matilda's obedience to her father seems justified, although she was sometimes clearly unwilling to submit to his demands, and she and her husband were estranged from Henry when he died.
[4] Those who were called to counsel 'propriis...nominibus' were evidently the higher barons; this seems to imply that the summons to a council, like the military summons, was already at this date sent individually to the leading tenants-in-chief, collectively (presumably through the sheriffs) to lesser men (cf. G. B. Adams, Councils and courts in Anglo-Norman England, New Haven, 1926, p. 8 n.).

etati sed future posteritati graue inflixit opprobrium? Vere hereditas ad quam festinatur in principio, in fine benedictione carebit.

Quis iam Anglie clades enumeret? Vetus habet istoria quod, Alexandro mortuo, pueri eius inposuerunt sibi diademata et regnare ceperunt unusquisque in loco suo,
100 et multiplicata sunt mala in terris.[1] Sic sic multiplicata sunt et hodie. In aures amici deploro quod sentio: tot reges patimur quot municipiis angustamur. In luto seruimus et latere, et solam libertatis seruamus umbram,[2] iam nichil agendo libere, sed seruis qui increuerunt hodie, tamquam uoluntarie obsequendo. Nam 'leuius fit patientia quod corrigere non est fas'.[3] Et quis erit finis miserie? Dicam quod sentio:
105 dum stabit abominatio, deesse non poterit desolatio. In Deum grauiter offensum est, et contra insensatos pro ipso pugnat orbis terrarum.[4] Reuocetur ad iustitiam status; bona principia laudabilis exitus prosequetur. Inter cetera que dixisti, laudabiliter et hoc positum est: non ex toto in perniciem uadit qui de medio male uie reuertitur. Reuersus quidem es, ⟨fo. 7⟩ nec reuersus solum, sed conuersus. Audisti
110 peccasse multitudinem, et ad horam impetum multitudinis es secutus. Ore magis peccasti quam corde; et quicquid ore promitteres, fidem corde seruabas. Filii etiam Israel quandoque commixti sunt inter gentes, et didicerunt opera eorum, et seruierunt scultilibus eorum.[5] Tu quoque, in pronum currente multitudine, non ad primos inpetus restitisti, nec contra torrentem brachia inutiliter uaneque iactasti.[6]
115 Nactus oportunitatem, quod corde fouebas apud te, illud opere demonstrasti; sed qui te emulo liuore persequitur, geminati periurii calumpniam fortassis opponet. Semel peierasse malum est, iterasse periurium multo peius; magis igitur bis quam semel periuros a iustitia recessisse. Quod si cum rege stetisses? Semel quidem peierasses, periurium tamen non iterasses. Ideoque melius fecisses? Ne te siliqua
120 uana perterreat: fidelitatem uni, fidelitatem promisisti et alteri; primo cui debebas, postmodum cui non debebas. Primo non peierasses, nisi secundo aberrasses. Ab illo errore declinasti, et sic omnia sanasti. Hos euasisti laqueos, sed alios fortassis incurres. Tibi regis obiectatur electio pariter et consecratio, ut te iure repellat ecclesia cuius instituta despicis et sacramenta contempnis. Sed numquid ad iniustitiam te
125 sacramenta perducent? Sacra suos operentur effectus; sanctificent nos potius quam a proposito sanctitatis auertant. Nos potius mundatos peccato iustificent, quam crimine irretitos, manibus ligatis et pedibus, in inferna demergant. Male de sacramento presumitur si per ipsum non laxatur culpa, sed reatus augetur. Nostro quidem arbitrio nichil in his est quo te iuste premat ecclesia, si causam tamen hanc
130 iudex equilibris examinet; nisi si forte rubore suffunditur, quod ei uiam qua ire oporteat, quasi preuius ostendisti.

**26** 96 hereditas] benedictio H   101 municipiis H; nuptiis B   102 seruamus H (seruaueris, Lucan); *om.* B   104 quid B (cf. no. 2)   111 promitteris H (*? for* promiseris)   111 etiam *om.* B   113 currente multitudine B; currentem multi diem (*!*) H; *? read* corruente (cf. II Para. vii. 3)   121 illo H; hoc B   123 pariter et consecratio *om.* B   124 iusticiam B   129 iudicio *with* arbitrio *interlined* B

---

[1] Cf. I Mach. i. 8–10.   [2] Cf. Ex. i. 14; Lucan, *Phars.* III, 146.
[3] Horace, *Car.* I, 24, 19–20: 'sed leuius fit patientia | quicquid corrigere est nefas'.
[4] Cf. Sap. v. 21.   [5] Cf. Ps. cv. 35–6.   [6] Cf. Juvenal, *Sat.* IV, 89–90.

Volo tamen attendas quid in partem hanc audierim uehementius iaculatum. Non diu est quod audisti dominum papam Innocentium conuocasse ecclesiam, et Rome conuentum celebrem habuisse. Magno illi conuentui cum domno et patre nostro domno abbate Cluniacense, interfui et ego Cluniacensium minimus.[1] Ibi causa hec 135 in medium deducta est, et aliquamdiu uentilata. Stabat ab inperatrice domnus Andegauensis episcopus;[2] qui cum causam eius diligenti percurrisset oratione, contra ipsum quasi sub uoce preconia in communi audientia declammatum est. Et quia domnus Andegauensis duo inducebat precipue, ius scilicet hereditarium et factum imperatrici iuramentum, contra hec duo in hec uerba responsum est. 140 'Oportet in causis omnibus, que multiplici iure nituntur, hoc considerare precipue —quod sit ius principale in causa, quo causa ipsa principaliter innititur; quod uero secundarium sit et ab ipso principali*iure dependens. Sublato enim iure principali necessario tollitur et secundarium.[3] In hac igitur causa principale est quod domnus Andegauensis de hereditate inducit, et ab hoc totum illud dependet quod de 145 iuramento subiungitur. Imperatrici namque sicut heredi iuramentum factum fuisse pronuntiat. Totum igitur quod de iuramento inducitur, exinaniri necesse est si de ipso hereditario iure non constiterit. Ipsum uero sic infringitur: imperatricem de qua loquitur non de legitimo matrimonio ortam denuntiamus. Deuiauit a legitimo tramite Henricus rex, et quam non licebat sibi iunxit matrimonio, unde istius sunt 150 natalitia propagata: quare illam patri in heredem non debere succedere, et leges et sacra denuntiant.' Hoc in communi audientia multorum uociferatione declamatum est, ⟨fo. 7v⟩ et nichil omnino ab altera parte responsum. Rogo michi in parte ista respondeas; interim dicam ipse quod sentio.

Maiores natu, personas religiosas et sanctas, sepius de re ista conueni. Audio 155 illius matrimonii copulam sancto Anselmo archiepiscopo ministrante celebratam. Ipsum enim non aliter quam sanctum audeam appellare, nam cum frater quidam dubitaret utrum sanctus appellari debuisset, ei diuinitus hec facta est reuelatio.[4] Dum oraret, et ab oratione in mentis raperetur excessum, liber ei in manibus datus est; cuius, dum primas reuolueret paginas, nichil scriptum nisi 'sanctus Anselmus' 160 inuenit. Et cum cetera queque percurreret, nichil repperit nisi 'sanctus Anselmus'.

---

26 132 parte hac B 135 Duniacense interfui/Duniacensium B; Duiniacence inter filium (!)/ Cluniacensium (?) H 139 Andegauensis] episcopus *added in* H 143*iure *om.* B 148 sicut confringitur H 151 leges et *om.* B 153 in] de H 156 matmonii B 159 manus H

---

[1] The Second Lateran Council, April 1139, to which Gilbert tells us he went in the company of his abbot, Peter the Venerable (see *GF*, p. 105 n.). John of Salisbury tells us that the leading advocates of the empress and Stephen were Ulger, bishop of Angers, and Arnulf, archdeacon of Séez, later bishop of Lisieux, with the bishop of Chester and Lupellus, clerk to the former archbishop of Canterbury, as official royal representatives.

[2] Ulger had been archdeacon of Angers (he occurs in 1119); he was bishop 1125–48 (*Chron. Anjou*, pp. 36, 146, 190–1; *HF*, XII, 480 n.). On him see JS *HP* (C), pp. 83–5, (P), pp. 85–8; Diceto, I, 252 ff.

[3] Cf. *Digest*, 50, 17, 129; 50, 17, 178 (but *secundarium* is apparently not used in this sense in the *Corpus Iuris Civilis*, though the word occurs in *Code*, 8, 2, 3, 1).

[4] This story is told, in a somewhat different form, by Eadmer, *Vita S. Anselmi*, ed. R. W. Southern (NMT), pp. 167–8.

Vnde certum est non placere diuinitati ipsum aliter appellari quam sanctum. Certum est perfectam huic non defuisse caritatem que foras mittit timorem.[1] Mirabile namque de ipso testimonium a sanctis audiuimus: manus ante sibi precidi 165 permisisset, quam eas ad opus illicitum extendisset. Longe sit igitur ab intellectu bonorum, abradatur a cordibus omnium, ut a sapientissimo rege et summe sanctitatis episcopo quicquam nisi legitime et sancte fuisse credatur admissum. Nec Romanas unquam amplius aures pulset tale ludibrium, quod omnium bonorum attestatione constat esse mendosum. Verum de ipsa matre imperatricis sancto 170 quorundam relatu cognouimus, ipsam a cunabulis ipsis in dignitatem regiam ostenso diuinitus oraculo presignatam. Nam dum ipsam regina Matildis, regis Willelmi sponsa, de sacro fonte leuaret, puellula ipsa iniecta manu uelamentum quod capiti regine supererat apprehendit, suumque capud inuoluit. Quod quidam, quorum nunc etiam uita superstes est, altius attendentes, signum quod preostensum 175 est exponentes, dignitatem regiam in quam postmodum sublimata est, manifeste sunt prelocuti.

In longum se extendit epistola, eo quod materiam magnam attigimus, etsi non plene explicuimus. Et tu per uerba que per militem tuum mandasti michi excitasti me; et cum currere cepissem, augebat michi stimulos ipsa tui memoria, ut ab 180 opusculo quod michi tui presentabat memoriam uix auelli potuerim, sed me fere in tedium lectoris extenderim. Vnum in fine teneas, ut memor sis finis, et in ecclesiam Dei et pauperes eius caritatem beniuole mentis excerceas: memor esto matris tue que diripitur, et conculcatur ab omnibus; et quos in diebus angustie sue deberet filios experiri karissimos, hostes repperit infestissimos. Nec aduersus eam 185 tuus inde zelus accendatur, si in causa presenti non ea qua oportuit libertate uocis usa est, cum eam presidentis auctoritas non solum inpedierit, sed quasi ligatam uinculis in hoc ipso uelut immobilem fecerit. Sed iam nunc Deo propitio, et fauente parti huic domno papa Celestino, uincula soluentur, que muta fuere loquentur. Vale. Et biduo saltem ores pro me, quia biduo michi aliquantulum est intermissa 190 oratio ut litteras dictarem ad te.


## 27  To Simon, bishop of Worcester

[1144–6] He pleads for action against Henry and Ralph of Caldy (?).[2]

The adventures of Henry and Ralph ended in disaster in 1146, after a career of crime which is described in the *Gesta Stephani*.[3] This dates the letter to 1146 or a year or two earlier. The part played by Theobald suggests that this letter was written after Henry of Blois had ceased to be legate and leader of the English Church. This is perhaps confirmed by the

**26** 168 aures pulset amplius B   169 constet H   172 puella B   179 michi *om.* H   179 ipa B
181 extendi H   188 dnͦo B   188 uicla B   189 aliquantulum *om.* B
**27** G, no. 34; B, fo. 15; H, fo. 153 v (defective at end); R, fos. 211 v–212.

[1] Cf. I Joh. iv. 18.
[2] Spelt Calderi in BR, Chaldri in H, Caldret in *Gesta* (Caldoet of the old edition is evidently a mistake); presumably from a place-name in Flanders, though Gilbert's scribes seem to have spelt it with some name like Caldy (Ches.) in mind.   [3] Pp. 124–5.

length of time ('anno…integro') Gilbert had been waiting for a meeting of bishops—councils were common while Henry was legate (four or five are recorded in 1143 alone), whereas there is no evidence of any between 1143 and 1151. But it is hardly likely that there were no councils, or at least no meetings of bishops, in this period; and it may be conjectured that the long delay here envisaged was due to a prolonged absence of the archbishop (or some other crisis in his affairs) such as took place between the end of 1143 and the summer of 1144. On any ground a date *c.* 1145 seems likely for this letter.

Patri suo et domno S(imoni) Wigor(nensi) Dei gratia episcopo, frater G(ilebertus) Gloecestrie dictus abbas, bella Domini cum fiducia preliari.[1]

Quod palam est et multorum diuulgatum notitie testibus aut argumentis euincere citra necessitatem est.[2] Vnde si promptum seruiendi uobis habuimus animum, argumentis non approbo de quo nullum aut fere nullum dubitare non dubito. 5 Equidem, si uobis in magnis seruire nequiuimus, sedulam tamen dedimus operam ut in minimis saltem in subsidiaria uobiscum actione staremus. Ideo nostra, si placet, merebatur humilitas et in uos hucusque continuata caritas, ut uices nostras, quas aduersus Henricum et Radulfum de Calderi sullimitati uestre commiseramus, prudentia uestra aliquanto fuisset diligentius executa. Scitis enim et multorum 10 constat testimonio domnum archiepiscopum uobis palam prohibuisse ne quis illorum absolueretur nisi nobis ecclesiastica satisfactio exhiberetur. At illos ad satisfaciendum nobis nullo adhuc commonitorio induxistis, nichilominus tamen absoluistis. Palam est et luce clarius quid consequatur expositis. Dicam, salua pace uestra et gratia, dicam quia hoc ipso nec domno archiepiscopo obedientiam nec 15 nobis quam sperabamus amicitiam, nec ordini uestro uel officio honorem exibuistis aut reuerentiam. Equidem molles iste et remisse facilesque nimis misericordie auctoritatem uestram in opprobrium, et commissam uobis iustitiam deducunt in nichilum. Anno quidem expectauimus integro ut in episcoporum conuentu malefactores nostros anatematis uinculo teneremus. Sed quam facile labor noster 20 euanuit! Inflauit buccas domnus Henricus et sonuere tube. Ad unum spiritus inflati sonum, quid dicam? Expauit episcopus, pro pudor, ad eius minas expauescere, cuius dedignandus erat et gladius. Iam totiens lesi ad quem de iustitia nobis exhibenda recurramus? Numquid nobis facile est circuire prouincias, domnum archiepiscopum sollicitare, conuocare concilium et a multis expetere quod unius 25 item possit gratia uno quodam fauore remittere? Equidem ⟨fo. 15v⟩ post susceptum onus hoc, in quo laboro sustinens, nil michi molestius accidit, nil amarius. Pudet enim me simul et penitet quod cucurri in incertum, pugnaui sed quasi aerem uerberans,[3] et post dampna simul et labores insultant michi inimici mei et iam prorsus effrenati tutam nacti peccandi licentiam ad tenserias[4] item faciendas 30

27 1–2 frater…Gloec(estrie) H; Gloecestrie *om.* B; frater I. *sic, omits* dictus abbas R 5 aut fere nullum *om.* B 9 contra B 9 H. et R. R 9 Chaldri H 10 exequta B 12 ipsorum H 12 illum BH 13 adhuc nullo B 14 consequitur B 14–15 Dicam…gratia *om.* H (*by homoioteleuton*) 20 quam *om.* B 21 H. BR 22 dicam?] H *ends here* 23–4 exibenda curramus R; exhibendam recurram B 24 nobis] michi B 26 uno *nos*; uano BR

---

[1] Cf. I Reg. xviii. 17.  [2] Cf. no. 9, n. 2.
[3] Cf. I Cor. ix. 26.  [4] Cf. Council of London (1151), c. 1, in Saltman, p. 547.

imperiosa uoce nos prouocant. Hec itaque uestre duximus communicanda notitie ut qualitercumque res hactenus acta sit, uestro si fieri potest reformetis consilio, ut et uobis honor augeatur et cause nostre si non ad plenum in aliquo saltem prouideatur.

## 28 To R., prior and the monks of Great Malvern

[1144-8] He asks them to reconsider their refusal to institute a relative and household clerk of his to the church of (or their share in the church of) Eastleach (Glos).

The manor of Eastleach was granted to Gloucester abbey by Walter son of Richard in 1144 in exchange for Glasbury; but Gloucester retained the church of Glasbury, while Malvern priory was to retain the church of Eastleach.[1] This letter reflects the situation in which Malvern had the right of presentation, but Gloucester an interest in Eastleach church; and it may possibly belong to the period in or about 1144 when the rights of the two churches had not been clearly separated.

Domno R. priori et fratribus qui cum eo sunt Maluernie, frater Gilebertus ecclesie beati Petri Gloecestrie dictus abbas, amantium se non penitus obliuisci.

Confisus de beniuolentia non quam merueram sed quam sperabam de uobis, quendam propinquum et familiarem nostrum direxi ad uos, preces cum humilitate
5 porrigens, ut quod in ecclesia de Estleche habebatis, ei de uobis habendum beniuola caritate concederetis: facta tamen super sacramenta fidelitate non fraudandi uos ab eo ⟨fo. 8⟩ comodo non quod modo habebatis, sed quod de ecclesia ipsa in tempore tranquille pacis habueratis. Vos tamen rem altius inspicientes et beneficium, quod diu inter manus dantis hesit, ingratum esse non curantes, amicum qui etsi magna
10 rogaret ex merito caritatis audiri debuerat in modico non audistis, sed dilato consilio quos ad uos miseram ad nos uacuos remisistis. Egre fero non quod infectum est quod rogabam, sed quod de amicis minus solito sperare conpellor. Rogabam equidem cum fiducia, quod amantium me petitioni non negarem; rogabam unde certe rogari debueram; rogabam, ne comodum ecclesie uestre eo ipso displiceret, si per
15 nos illud in parte aliqua ministrari contingeret.[2] Et quia magna repulsa est cum negatur amico quod modicum est, rem uobis ante occulos pono; ut ex ipsa iudicetis quantum est quod rogauerim, et quam modicum quod negastis. Cum uobis de ecclesia illa partem, que uos contingit, ad plenum persoluero, ministro altaris

27 31-4 Hec itaque...prouideatur] *so* R; ...duximus uestre...ut qualiter potest reformetur consilio, ut et uobis honor augeatur et nobis salus prouideatur B (B's *version seems clearly to be the fruit of revision*)
28 G, no. 10; B, fo. 7v; H, fo. 153; R, fo. 207r-v.
1 Ricardo H    14 ipse *before correction* B    15 continget R    18 ad plenum *om.* B

---

[1] No. 284; cf. *CS*, p. 282.
[2] This seems to be an involved way of reminding the monks of Malvern that Gloucester still had rights in the church: 'I asked—lest the advantage (or profit) of your church dissatisfy you, precisely if it (the profit or the arrangement) should happen in any degree (or particular) to be administered by us.' The implication seems to be that some of the profits of the church came from, or *via*, Gloucester, and could be withheld.

ministerii sui mercedem adimpleuero, episcopali auctoritati de his que sunt penes
illam respondero, emolumentum quod his omnibus superesse contigerit uix tanti 20
est ut de hoc amicus ab amantibus se repulsam pati debuerit. Vnde, si consilium
uestrum mutari placeret in melius, haberetis me de re modica gratie magne debitorem, et clerico illi cui rem hactenus concessistis uel ad uotum satisfacerem uel
aduersus eum uos in omni audientia ad plenum excusabiles redderem. Rogo michi
per presentium latorem literas uestre uoluntatis indices remittatis. Valete.      25

## 29   To Henry of Blois, bishop of Winchester

[?1144–8] On behalf of Roger Foliot, domestic knight of Brian (FitzCount), who has been
imprisoned by the bishop's men at Merdon Castle (in Hursley, Hants).[1]

Nos. 29 and 30 both deal with the case of Roger Foliot,[2] and must be contemporary.
No. 29 does not give the bishop the title legate: if the omission means that he had lost the
title when the letter was written, it must be later than November 1143, and almost certainly
later than the travels on which he was engaged between that time and some date in the
middle of 1144.

Patri suo et domno H(enrico) Wint(oniensi) Dei gratia episcopo frater G(ilebertus)
ecclesie beati Petri Gloecestrie dictus abbas, pie miserando misericordiam promereri.
   Conpellit me karitas serenitatem uestram, in Christo dilecte pater, humiliter
implorare, ut quendam militem nomine Rogerum Foliot, quem homines uestri
apud Merendune incarceratum tenent, gratia uestra et petitione nostra ad redemp- 5
tionem mitti iubeatis. Qua in re sullimitati uestre presumendo deuotus supplico ut
fucos et superflua uerba Willelmi de Cheisnei non admittatis, nec secundum uoluntatem eius illum grauari permittatis, nec uerbis eum odientium de ipso fidem
habeatis. Nouerit enim sanctitas uestra quod pater eius nunquam nisi dimidiam
hidam terre habuit, ipse prorsus nichil nisi quod usu militie adquisiuit. Ad dona- 10
tiuum enim domno Brientio seruiuit actenus, et iam nunc equos et arma amittendo
totum quod habebat semel et simul perdidit. In pauperem itaque rogamus ut
respiciant oculi uestri et uinctum de carcere educendo, ab eo qui soluit compeditos
gratiam optineatis,[3] et me si quid possum gratie debitorem habeatis. Valete.

**28** 19 auctoritate B    22 habetis B
**29** G, no. 58; B, fo. 24.

---

[1] One of the castles fortified by Henry of Blois himself: Ann. Winchester, *Ann. Mon.* II, 51;
   *VCH Hants*, III, 418 (the site awaits proper investigation).
[2] See *GF*, p. 42. His lord, Brian, was presumably Brian FitzCount.
[3] Cf. Ps. x. 5; cxlv. 7.

## 30   To Geoffrey (III), prior of Winchester[1]

[? 1144–8] He acknowledges the prior's aid to his relative Roger Foliot, and asks the prior to intercede with the bishop of Winchester for Roger's release.

Cf. no. 29.

G(ilebertus) Dei gratia abbas Gloecestrie uenerabili domno suo et amico karissimo Gaufrido priori Vintonie, salutem et dilectionem.

Gratias beniuolentie uestre habeo referre multimodas quia parenti nostro Rogero Foliot benigne subuenistis, et in necessitatibus suis sibi beniuole prouidistis. Sed quia
5 inter amicos preteritorum bonorum exibitio certa est et futurorum expectatio, rogamus ut non tepescat karitas uestra, quatinus hoc a uobis deseruiat humilitas nostra. Rogamus itaque ut apud domnum Vintoniensem pro ipso interueniatis, quatinus eum de carcere educi fa⟨ fo. 24 v ⟩ciat et ad redemptionem mitti precipiat. Ignominiose enim tenetur in carcere et iam extrema aflictus est egestate. Vnde
10 precor obnixe ut presenti negotio intendatis, quatinus si quid possumus nos gratie debitores habeatis. Valete.

## 31   To Pope Lucius II

[1144–5] Trouble has broken out at Salisbury, and Gilbert writes in behalf of the new bishop, Jocelin (1142–84),[2] and Canon Roger de Meisi, who is visiting the Pope in support of a case against the dean, Azo.

Nothing further is known of these troubles (but see no. 48). The letter suggests a dispute between bishop and dean which had divided the chapter: it also suggests trouble with external enemies—possibly an echo of fighting near Salisbury in 1143.[3] Lucius II was Pope from March 1144 to February 1145.

Patri suo et domino summo Dei gratia pontifici Lucio, frater G(ilebertus) ecclesie beati Petri Gloecestrie dictus abbas, pacis et salutis incrementa.

Quantis miseriarum sit concussa turbinibus Salesberiensis ecclesia serenitatem uestram, dilecte pater, estimo non latere, cuius sollicitudinis interest ecclesiarum
5 omnium non solum detrimentis compati, sed etiam comodis prouidere. Hec iam diu proprio uiduata rectore, dum fluctuaret in incertum tum peruersorum homi-num incursione tum suorum circa patris electionem non unanimi uoluntate, ad desolationem ultimam peruenisset si non ei Dominus dignum sibi famulum,

**30** G, no. 59; B, fo. 24.
7 donum B
**31** G, no. 11; B, fo. 8; R, fo. 207v.
3 turbinibus sit concussa B     5 etiam] et R     7 uoluntatem R

---

[1] His predecessor, Robert, occurs in 1130 (*PR 31 Henry I*, p. 38); Robert has commonly been identified with the bishop of Bath (see Biog. Index, *s.v.* Bath), but there seems to be no evidence of this. Geoffrey occurs 1139–53 and 1142–7 (*Cart. Winchester*, pp. 4, 6). His succes-sor, William, was dead by 1165 (*ibid.* p. 35).
[2] On his election see Saltman, pp. 97–8; Knowles, *EC*, p. 7 n.
[3] *Gesta Stephani*, pp. 97–8 (Wilton).

electum ut speramus antistitem uite commendabilis et gratie, domnum Iocelinum condignum sanctitatis uestre filium in patrem pastoremque prerogasset. Hunc, 10 quantum humillimi non dicam filii sed serui presumit deuotio, sublimitati uestre commendari preoptamus, quem dignum commendatione cognouimus; utpote qui, ante uocationem suam, studiis honestatis incessanter incubuit, et iam sibi non sumens honorem sed uocatus ut speramus a Domino, episcopalem cathedram merito uite laudabilis honorare non desistit. Hic irruentes in ecclesiam suam impetus 15 uiriliter sustinet aut repellit, et in quibus sibi forte non sufficit, a beniuolentia uestra manum sibi auxilii consiliique porrigi humilitas nostra pie presumendo desiderat et exposcit. Eius etiam canonicum magistrum Rogerium de Meisi, uirum uita moribusque commendabilem, sanctitati uestre commendamus. Et quoniam ipsum aduersus domnum Azonem Saresberiensem decanum presens negotium 20 suscepisse cognoscimus, beatitudini uestre de hoc ipso supplicamus ut eundem causa iustitie et ueritatis sustentetis, et Saresberiensis ecclesie honori et utilitati paterna gratia prouideatis. Valeat sullimitas uestra in Christo dilecte pater.

## 32 To Jocelin de Bohun, bishop of Salisbury

[c. 1144–5] He describes the depredations of John of Marlborough (John the Marshal) and Walter de Picquigny, and requests the bishop to proceed against them.

The outside limits are Jocelin's accession in 1142 and Walter de Picquigny's imprisonment in 1145. Walter was certainly active in 1145 and John in 1144,[1] and so the likely date for the events of this letter is 1144 or 1145. John succeeded to the office of marshal c. 1130 and died in 1165; he was the father of the famous William Marshal.[2] He was a supporter of the empress in the years following 1141.

Patri suo et domno Iocelino Saresberiensi Dei gratia episcopo G(ilebertus) suus ecclesie beati Petri Gloecestrie dictus abbas, cum gaudio et exultatione fructus reportare iustitie.

Communi, dilecte pater, lamentatione in aures sanctitatis uestre nostra deploramus incomoda, deprecantes humiliter ut malefactores nostros uestra uel reuocet 5 admonitio uel choerceat disciplina. Iohannes enim de Merleberga et Galterus de Pincheni nos, humiles amicos uestros, infestare non desinunt et solacia peregrinationis nostre uiolenta manu diripere et in prauitatis usus expendere non erubescunt.

31 9 Gocelinum R (om. domnum)    12 quem] quantum R, and B before correction
18 R. R    20 domnum om. B    21 suppicamus B    21 eundem] in added in R
32 G, no. 14; B, fo. 9; H, fo. 154r–v; R, fo. 208.
1 Salesberiensi H (I. Saresberiensi R)    6 enim om. R    7 Pinchenni HR (Gualterus H, Walterius R)

---

[1] Cf. *Gesta Stephani*, pp. 111, 118 (for Walter's name cf. Loyd, *Origins*, p. 78). Walter was released c. 1147, but was shortly after killed (*op. cit.* pp. 140–1); this provides an alternative date; but the circumstances of 1144–5 are much more probable. Walter's activity c. 1147 was evidently brief and very local, and there is no indication that he was working in alliance with John of Marlborough.

[2] *CP*, x, Appendix G, pp. 93–5; S. Painter, *William Marshall*, pp. 1 ff.

Patienter quidem pondus diei et estus hucusque portauimus,[1] sperantes tandem
10 malignorum hominum rabiem uel posse expleri uel eosdem ad legitimos tramites
salubri cuiuscumque persuasione conuerti. Sed quia, iuxta Sapientiam, quem Deus
despexerit homo corrigere non potest,[2] rogamus ea qua de uobis bene speramus
fiducia ut quos reuocare ammonitio sancta non ualet, de manu uestra uirga pastoralis humiliet. Nouerit enim sanctitas uestra predictos illos duos in nummis et
15 nummorum pretiis nobis plusquam ducentas marcas abstulisse, et possessiones
nostras que circa eos sunt pene ad nichilum redegisse. Optamus itaque uos illius
roborari spiritu qui dixit: 'confidite, ego ui⟨ fo. 9 v ⟩ci mundum'; qui inimicos
suos omnes ponet scabellum pedum suorum, per quem in interitu malignorum
ridebimus et subsannabimus, cum eis quod merentur acciderit.[3] Illius gladium non
20 frustra portatis, sed ut allophilos non solum cum sem⟨in⟩e Gad in stiua aratri sed etiam
cum Aoth in ore gladii feriatis.[4] Non ebetetur in manu uestra gladius eius qui, iuxta
prophetam, exacutus est, ut splendeat limatus *est.[5] Vobis undique uirtutis occurrit
occasio. Refrigescit karitas,[6] crebrescunt scandala. Ad uos, tanquam ultores scele-
rum, undique clamat ecclesia. Exeratur itaque, rogamus, sermo Dei ille uiuus
25 et efficax pertingens usque ad diuisionem anime ac spiritus compagum quoque *et
medullarum; ut in conuiuio illo magno gloria sit uobis coram simul discumbentibus
opposuisse uos murum pro domo Israel, et eius iniurias uel repulisse uiriliter aut
uindicasse.[7] Valete.

### 33  To Theobald, archbishop of Canterbury

[1143–5] He asks the archbishop to give the bishop of Worcester leave to absolve William
Cumin.

William Cumin, chancellor of the king of the Scots and archdeacon of Worcester, was
deprived of all his benefices by the legatine council of London in March 1143 and excommunicated by the Pope,[8] on account of an attempt which he had made to occupy the bishopric
of Durham by force. By 1146 Cumin was in favour with the archbishop, since he witnessed
a charter in that year among his clerks.[9] This letter can thus be dated c. 1143–5; and the
terminus ad quem is confirmed by the absence of primatial style in the address, which suggests
a date before c. June 1145 (see Appendix ii).

Patri suo et domno T(heobaldo) Cant(uariensi) Dei gratia archiepiscopo frater
G(ilebertus) Glocestrie dictus abbas totum quod potest humilis et promta deuotio.

**32** 16 ad nichilum pene H    20 stiue R    21 Ahot H    22 *est] stet in manu percucientis
et uindicantis opprobria agminum Dei Israel *added in* H (*repeated from a very similar context in
no. 2, at p. 36, n. 9*). *There is a c over* limatus *in* R, *possibly referring to a lost marginal note*
23 crebescunt B    25 *et B; *om.* H; ac R (*so Vulg.*)    28 Valete *om.* H
**33** G, no. 31; B, fo. 13 v; R, fos. 210v–211.

[1] Cf. Matt. xx. 12.                       [2] Cf. Eccl. vii. 14.
[3] Joh. xvi. 33; Ps. cix. 1, etc.; Prov. i. 26.    [4] Cf. Ps. lv. 1; Eccli. xxviii. 22.
[5] Cf. Ezech. xxi. 9–10.                  [6] Cf. Matt. xxiv. 12.
[7] Cf. Heb. iv. 12; Luc xiv. 10; Ezech. xiii. 5.
[8] John of Hexham, p. 314. See Biog. Index, *s.v.* Worcester.
[9] Saltman, p. 538.

Humilitatem karitas non repellit. Vnde quia Willelmum Cumin humiliatum uidimus audere cepimus ut apud sullimitatem uestram pro illo interpellemus. Qui si ab unitate recessit ecclesie ipso qui temptat instigante ad eandem iam redit ipso 5 qui uiuificat Spiritu Sancto reuocante. Vnde ad tronum misericordie uestre pia tamen presumptione pulsamus, ut si eum testimonio magnarum et religiosarum personarum de ea in quam inpeierat culpa satisfecisse cognoscitis a communione suspensum teneri non permittatis. Domnus enim Wigornensis nisi per uos in communionem non recipit quem auctoritate uestra a communione priuauit. 10 Rogamus itaque uestri animi moderationem ut quem de Vr Caldeorum ad Ierusalem suspirasse gaudetis intrare uolenti portas eius obser⟨ar⟩i non sinatis ne cui etiam calciamenta stolam pariter et anulum indulsit pietas celestis ipsum nudatum turpiter ad siliquas remittatis.[1] Valete.

### 34   To Pope Eugenius III

[1145] He asks that Master Godfrey be confirmed in the archdeaconry of Worcester, to which he has been appointed to succeed the deposed William Cumin.

Cumin was deprived in March 1143 (cf. no. 33); a full year elapsed before his deprivation was considered sufficiently definitive for his successor to be appointed. Godfrey was appointed, then, in 1144; and this letter cannot be many months later than his appointment. Since Eugenius III became Pope in February 1145, it can safely be assigned to that year.

In later years Cumin was fully pardoned and won the patronage of archbishop Theobald and King Henry II; he was even restored to his archdeaconry.[2] There was evidently some ground for the bishop of Worcester's caution in filling his place in 1143–4.

Patri suo et domno summo pontifici E(ugenio) frater G(ilebertus) Gloecestrie dictus abbas, eterne uite gloriam feliciter adipisci.

Necessitati, dilecte pater in Domino, reluctari non possumus quin caritati, que nobis de fraternis cordibus potenter inperat, obediamus. Hec est que nos magis delitescere cupientes producit in medium ut ad audientiam uestram, cui ad presens 5 asistere non ualemus, ueritatis uerba mittamus. Hinc est quod uiro illustri et honesto scripturarum etiam tam diuinarum quam secularium adprime erudito, magistro scilicet Godefrido, negare nequiuimus quin sullimitati uestre que de eius negotio uidimus et audiuimus[3] testaremur. Willelmo itaque Cumin multis exigentibus causis uinculis anatematis irretito, cum iam plus anno integro sub eodem 10 uinculo perstitisset, cumque eum omni ecclesiastico beneficio generalis concilii iurisdictio spoliasset, domnus Wigornensis consilio religiosorum uirorum predictum

---

33 8 inpeierat *i.e.* impegerat (*so* R)   12 suspirare B   12 obseri MSS; B *om.* eius
14 Valete *om.* R
34 G, no. 18,98; B, fo. 10v (B1), 157v (B2); R, fo. 209 (*spelling as* B1; *note in top margin of* B2: Attestatio ueritatis de processu negotii ad domnum papam).
1 Domno et patri suo B2   1–2 Gloecestrie...abbas] Hereford' ecclesie minister B2   2 feliciter *om.* B1   3 ea caritate B2   4 magnis B1   6 uitatis B1; saltem *added in* B2   8 negare] deesse B2   9 Gillelmo B1   11–12 iurisdictio B2; iuriditio B1; iuridicio R

---

[1] Cf. Gen. xi. 31; Luc. xv. 16, 22.   [2] See Biog. Index, *s.v.* Worcester.   [3] Cf. I Joh. i. 1.

Godefridum archidiaconatu suo inuestiuit ecclesieque sue archidiaconum religiosa ⟨B 2, fo. 158⟩ deuotione constituit. Scimus eum in eodem officio religiose perstitisse, 15 et que ad curam eius spectabant prudenter et discrete ministrasse. Scimus etiam ipsum eidem ecclesie, si uobis placet, necessarium, et in eo non solum istud immo et multo amplius—saluum esse beneficium. Decernat in hoc consideratio uestra ut semper habeat incrementum gloria uestra, concipiantque bonam spem qui recurrunt ad uos, optinendi consilium pariter et auxilium in his unde recurrunt ad uos. 20 In longitudinem dierum uos protegat omnipotens Dominus, in Christo dilecte pater.

### 35   To Pope Eugenius III

[1145] He asks for assistance for Abbot Peter[1] and the monks of Malmesbury, whose church has become the site of a castle and a theatre of war; and suggests that the Pope send a legate.

Fighting in Malmesbury is recorded at two periods in the anarchy: in 1139 and again in 1144–5.[2] Since Eugenius was only elected in February 1145, this letter cannot refer to the first occasion. In 1144 Malmesbury was attacked by William of Dover and Robert earl of Gloucester, and blockaded by the erection of three castles; the fighting culminated in the capture and imprisonment of Walter de Picquigny, the castellan of the town, in 1145 (see no. 32). 1145 is thus the probable date of this letter: presumably not early in the year, since the suggestion at the end of the letter seems to imply that the legate Imar was no longer in the country.

Patri suo et domno summo Dei gratia pontifici E(ugenio) frater G(ilebertus) Gloecestrie dictus abbas, obedientiam humilem et debiti famulatus obsequium.

   Cum suspiret, dilecte pater, ad uos ecclesiarum totius Anglie facies admodum desolata, una tamen est Malmesberiensis ecclesia cui, nisi cito subuentum fuerit, nil 5 iam sibi solacii superest nisi quod est in aduersis pessimum, felicem aliquandiu exstitisse. Nam sicut ouicula lupi faucibus deprehensa quo euadat non inuenit, sic ipsa castelli quod in eius fundo simul et atrio situm est[3] angustata menibus et habitatoribus afflicta, totum fere quod facultatis terrene prodidit et quod religionis aput se fouebat et ordinis euanuisse penitus ingemiscit. Vix est quod eius calamitati 10 iam possit adici, cuius et locus in extremam desolationem datus est et filii in dispersionem. Vbi enim a sancti patris Aldelmi tempore laus Dei resonabat, illic hodie

34 13 inuestitum B 2    13 archidiaconem B 2    16 ipsum] episcopum R    16 si uobis placet] fore B 2    16 immo et] et mmo (sic: istud om.) B 2    17 detur (sic, followed by a space) B 2 17 uestra om. B 2    21 pater] Amen added in B 2 (om. in Christo)
35 G, no. 41; B, fo. 16.
9 calimitati (corrected by a modern hand) B

---

[1] Peter Moraunt, monk of Cluny, prior of La Charité-sur-Loire, and superior of St-Urban, near Joinville, was abbot of Malmesbury from April 1141 until his death on 5 February in or about 1158: see A. Watkin in *VCH Wilts.* III, 217, 230.
[2] *WMHN*, pp. 27, 36; *Gesta Stephani*, pp. 113–14, 118.
[3] Cf. *WMHN*, p. 25 (of the castle built at Malmesbury by Roger, bishop of Salisbury): 'in ipso cemeterio, ab ecclesia principali uix iactu lapidis'.

armata satellitum turba et in omnem in quam conducitur impietatem promtissima cohors militum debachatur. Restat igitur dilecto fratri nostro et eiusdem ecclesie abbati domno Petro uestri pietate consilii ecclesiam suam aut ab infestationibus iam dictis erui, aut ad ipsam penitus non reuerti. Si iuxta prophete uocem gladius 15 Domini exacutus est, ut splendeat limatus est, stet optamus in manu percutientis et uindicantis opprobria agminum Dei Israel.[1] Nil equidem misericordius uestra nobis posset caritas exhibere quam in partes nostras quempiam dirigere qui ea que Dei et uestra sunt zelo sciret congruo pertractare. Conseruet incolumitatem uestram in longa tempora qui non dormitat custos Israel, in Christo dilecte pater.[2]　　　　20

## 36　To Pope Eugenius III

[1145–7, ?1145] On behalf of the bishop of Lincoln.

Nos. 36 and 37 were both written on behalf of the bishop of Lincoln, and although there is no close verbal link between them, it is probable that, like nos. 17–18 and 24–5, they form a doublet, both written on the same occasion—the one a draft, the other the letter actually sent. Eugenius was elected in 1145; and in the years 1145–8 Alexander is recorded to have made two visits to Rome, in 1145 and 1147.[3] He received bulls from Eugenius in February 1146,[4] after the first visit; and in any case would have been less in need of a testimonial on his second visit than on his first. On these grounds we are inclined to date both letters to 1145. But it is not impossible that one or other of them belongs to 1147.

Patri suo et domno summo Dei gratia pontifici E(ugenio) frater G(ilebertus) Gloecestrie dictus abbas, unam quam petit a Domino feliciter optinere.[5]

Quod missis litteris maiestatem uestram, dilecte pater, interpellare presumimus, hinc persuadet caritas, hinc humilitas expauescit. Plus tamen eligimus apud patrem de pietate corripi, quam apud domnos et fratres nostros dilectissimos de spreta 5 caritate dampnari. Ideo sullimitati uestre preces humiles supplicantis affectu porrigimus, ut uenientem ad uos domnum Lincolniensem episcopum, qua decet bonitatem uestram gratia suscipiatis, et in suis eum postulationibus iustis audiatis. Cui enim et ad doctrinam scientia et ad honestatem mores exuberant, dignum est apud patrem totum quod gratie, quod pietatis est, experiri. Optamus ut erga eum 10 uox illa Domini conualescat: eum qui uenit ad me non eiciam foras;[6] ut qui currit post gratiam, comprehendat et gratiam; et qui festinat ad patrem, patrem se gaudeat inuenisse. Accendentur uirtutis amore quam plurimi, cum honestatem condigne munerari uiderint apud uos, et uirtuti suam nec minui nec deesse mercedem. Conseruet uos longa in tempora qui non dormit custos Israel.[7]　　　　15

35　14 aut] et B
36　G, no. 25; B, fo. 12; R, fo. 209v–210.
7 Lincolniesem B; Lincolnensem R　　13 uirtutes R　　15 in longa tempora R

[1] Ezech. xxi. 9 ff; I Reg. xvii. 45.　　　　[2] Cf. Ps. cxx. 4 (and nos. 36, 47).
[3] Henry of Huntingdon, *Historia*, ed. T. Arnold, RS, pp. 278, 280.
[4] *PUE*, II, nos. 48–9.
[5] Cf. Ps. xxvi. 4: Vnam petii a Domino, hanc requiram, ut inhabitem in domo Domini omnibus diebus uitae meae....
[6] Cf. Joh. vi. 37.　　　　[7] Cf. Ps. cxx. 4 (and no. 35).

### 37  To Pope Eugenius III

[1145–7, ?1145] As no. 36.

Patri suo et domno summo Dei gratia pontifici Eugenio, frater G(ilebertus) Gloecestrie dictus abbas, in decore uirtutum delicias regibus ministrare.

Cum in singulorum commoda uestre se, dilecte pater, diligentia karitatis excerceat, fortasse minus in sui admiratione suspenditur; et que ad innumeros bene5 ficiorum inmensitate diffunditur, intra proprii iudicii terminos arcta humilitatis regula cohibetur. Quanto tamen gratiarum imbre mentem uestram diuinitatis unda perfuderit, hinc datur intelligi, quod in uehemens sui desiderium non paucos de ultimis terre finibus uirtutis uestre fragrantia sanctique nominis suaue redolens opinio iam pertraxit. Scimus enim multos multa animi alacritate festinare ad uos, 10 ut iam dicant singuli, clament uniuersi: 'Trahe nos; post te curremus in odore unguentorum tuorum.'[1] Inter quos domnum Alexandrum Lincol(niensem) episcopum tanta decet a maiestate uestra ueneratione suscipi quanta scimus eum ad uos caritate perduci; perhibent enim eius uite testimonium bonum familiares eius, uiri probate religionis et gratie, qui cum eo quo familiarius conuersantur tanto magis de 15 eiusdem honestate gloriantur in Domino. Scimus quoque Dominum flagello tribulationis ipsum iam diu aliquatenus attigisse, ut si quid in eo fuit scorie, iam ad purum excoctum sit;[2] et si quid in excessu mediocri uaga regni Anglie aliquandiu permisit licentia, iam penes eum euacuatum sit, et perfecte reprobatum. Hoc quia uerum credimus precipuo ueritatis amico denuntiamus, ut non pigeat uos filium 20 uestrum in gratia suscipere cui dignum est honorem et gratiam exhibere. Valeat sullimitas uestra, in Christo dilecte pater.

### 38  To Jocelin de Bohun, bishop of Salisbury

[1144–5] He expresses his consent to the election of the new abbot of Cerne, and asks for the bishop's confirmation.

For letters 38–41, 46, 49–57, 62–4, and the case of Cerne abbey, see Appendix III.

Patri suo et domno Iocelino Saresberiensi Dei gratia episcopo G(ilebertus) suus ecclesie beati Petri Gloecestrie dictus abbas, die cotidie prosperari in gratiam.

Rogati sepius ut super negotio fratrum Cerneleie uestre sullimitati scriberemus ⟨fo. 9⟩ id hucusque distulimus, attendentes non eatenus processisse negocium ut 5 super hoc uobis scribere duceremus oportunum. Nam qui eidem incubabat ecclesie, multa licet accusatione pulsatus, pendula tamen quadam expectatione aliquatenus herebat, et pastoralem quam susceperat curam nondum ea qua oportebat solenni-

---

**37** G, no. 36; B, fo. 15v; R, fo. 212.
1 Ew'o R   11 ungentorum B   11 quos om. R   11 A. R   16 in eo om. B   18 sit] est R
18 probatum R
**38** G, no. 13; B, fo. 8v; H, fo. 154; R, fo. 208.
1 I. Saresberiensi BR; Iocelino Salesberiensi H   2 cotidie] H adds bene   3 Cernelie HR

---

[1] Cant. i. 3.                    [2] Cf. Is. i. 25.

tate refutauerat. Sed iam nunc, ut audiuimus, ipsi celebrastis exequias, et securi ad radicem arboris infructuose iam posita eandem, quia inutiliter stabat, laudabili, ut fama est, seueritate succidistis.[1] Vnde quia fructuose iam arbori locum preparastis, 10 rogamus—*rogamus inquam et optamus ut quod uobis digne reputatur ad iustitiam laudabili consumatione perducatur ad gloriam. Fratres quidem Cernelie uenientes ad nos secum etiam sub ecclesie sue sigillo litteras afferentes, communi, ut aiunt, omnium fratrum electione unum e fratribus nostris sibi in patrem pastoremque dari petierunt et dimitti; et ipsum quidem quem eligunt honore dignum 15 speramus et gratia, utpote uirum cui et ad doctrinam scientia et ad honestatem mores exuberant, regendis animabus rebusque tuendis idoneum: quem nisi laudabilem crederemus, uobis utique commendare nollemus. Sed de re ista nichil nisi ex uestre uoluntatis arbitrio statuentes, rogamus si placet uestrum nobis aperiri consilium: si petitioni huic uos prebere uelitis assensum, iussioni enim uestre 20 uoluntas nostra deseruiet. Quod si honorificentiam ecclesie nostre hac ipsa electione quodammodo prelibatam uestra stabi⟨fo. 9v⟩liret auctoritas, nos in immensum gratie debitores et ad uestre deseruiendum uoluntati per omnia promtiores haberetis. Vobis spiritum optamus adesse consilii,[2] qui uos dirigat opusque uestrum placita sibi moderatione disponat. Valete. 25

## 39  To Bernard, abbot of Cerne

[Early 1145] He comforts the abbot in his difficulties, and promises to inform the papal legate that the bishop (of Salisbury) is withholding the abbatial blessing.

Dilecto fratri suo filioque karissimo Bernardo Cernelie Dei gratia abbati frater G(ilebertus) Gloecestrie dictus abbas, uiriliter agere et confortari in Domino.[3]

Viri boni est non extolli prosperis nec incomodis frangi. Hoc quidem ipse nosti, hanc ipse tibi formam induisti. Vide ergo ne propter alicuius minas uel propter instantem et urgentem inopiam cito terrearis, aut de tuo sensu mouearis. Si procella 5 aliqua aduersum te surrexerit, flante Sancto Spiritu cito statuetur in auram et silebunt fluctus eius.[4] Si premit inopia in timore pio semper obedies Domino et ipse non derelinquet sperantes in se.[5] Memento quam simpliciter ambulaueris,[6] memento quod non cupiditati, sed soli obedientie et ueritati tua uela commiseris. Habe coram occulis quod, cui militas, obedientiam pre omni acceptat holocausto.[7] Ambula 10 simpliciter et ibis confidenter. Clamabimus omnes ad Dominum et ipse aperiet

---

**38** 8 refutabat R    8 audimus H    10 fructuosos R    11 *rogamus om. B    15 et ipsum quidem R; ipsum quidem H; ipsum om. B    19 ex uestre uoluntatis] So HR; uoluntatis uestre ex corr. to ex uoluntatis uestre B
**39** G, no. 15; B, fo. 9v; H, fo. 154v; R, fo. 208r–v (incomplete at end).
1 Bernardo H; B. BR    3 est] decet R    8–9 simpliciter…memento quod om. H (memento quam/memento quod)    10 acceptat pre omni B

---

[1] Cf. Matt. iii. 10; Luc. iii. 9.
[3] Cf. Ps. xxvi. 14; etc.
[5] Cf. Ps. ix. 11 (and cxliv. 15, 20).
[7] Cf. I Reg. xv. 22.

[2] Cf. Is. xi. 2.
[4] Cf. Ps. cvi. 29.
[6] Cf. Ps. xvii. 31; Prov. xxviii. 18; etc.

manum suam et implebit uos benedictione.[1] Non inuenis in domo tua uel intus consilium uel extra possessionem. Domus tua penes te est, in ipsa habes unctionem spiritus que docebit te de omnibus.[2] Habes et filium karissimum Iocelinum quem
15 quia timet Dominum sano credimus habundare consilio. Domnum Hugonem dirigimus ad te qui tibi diligenter obediet et deuoto famulatu assistet. Si quem uel quos de nostris plus uolueris, his ipsis equos quos placuerit de tuis siue iuuenes siue senes mittes ad nos, et de nostris inpetrabis quos uoles. Nostros uestitos mittemus, nudos et pannosos tuos cooperante Domino uestiemus. De libris nostris accipies
20 ipse quos uoles. Negotia tua nostra reputabimus. Aduersa sustinere potes sed solus habere non potes. Vnum sumus et semper erimus in Domino et seruiemus ei humero uno. Cetera si desint solacia unum tamen deesse non poterit: domus tua quocunque labore uel consilio proficere de die in diem potest sed in deterius ire non potest. Malum, tamquam in summo est, quo procedat non inuenit; bonum tuum
25 cotidianos poterit habere profectus; benedictio tua si differtur non aufertur. Nosti quod abbatem episcopi non facit benedictio sed fratrum communis electio.[3] Sarcinam hanc in hum⟨ fo. 10 ⟩meros beati principis apostolorum Petri inponemus, facies nostra confundi non poterit.[4] Minister apostolorum et nuntius ipse direxit te; nuntiabimus illi quod audimus de te, de quo per omnia speramus optime ne planta-
30 tionem primam quam in hoc regno plantauit dextera eius, cuiuscunque labore uel industria in ignominiam sui patiatur euellere. Vale et diuitie si affluant noli cor aponere; si paupertas exusserit obedi et patientiam habe. Nosti illud sapientis: 'suas habet paupertas sancta diuitias.'[5] Honesta etiam res est leta paupertas, et eadem non est paupertas si est leta.

### 40  To Jocelin de Bohun, bishop of Salisbury

[1145, before 10 June] He presses the bishop to give Bernard (abbot of Cerne) his abbatial blessing, offering himself to meet the bishop's request for payment, and threatens an appeal to the Pope if the blessing is further postponed.

Patri suo et domno Ioc(elino) Sar(esberiensi) Dei gratia episcopo frater G(ilebertus) Gloucestrie dictus abbas, apto rationis moderamine sibi credita dispensare.[6]
    Sciat uestra sanctitas, in Christo dilecte pater, nos fratri nostro Bernardo per-suadere non posse ut sub aliqua cuiuscunque pecunie reddende condicione bene-
5 dictionem suam uel a uobis uel aliunde suscipiat. Hoc enim licet malum fortasse non sit, menti tamen simplici scrupulum generat, ⟨fo. 13 v⟩ ut aliquid a puritate minus

**39** 12–13 consilium uel intus H   13 posses/ssionem B   13 in ipsa unctio est B (unctionem habetis *in Vulg.*)   17 equis MSS   18–20 Nostros…uoles *om.* R (quos uoles/quos uoles) 21 potes *end of* H (non potes *catchword of next quire*)   25 prouectus R   26 bedictio B; bendictio R   31 nolite B   32 obedi *om.* B   33 leta est R
**40** G, no. 30; B, fo. 13; R, fo. 210v.
1 I. R   5–6 malum non si fortasse non sit R

---

[1] Cf. Ps. cxliv. 16.
[2] Cf. I Joh. ii. 20; Joh. xiv. 26.
[3] Cf. *Decretum*, C. 18, q. 2, cc. 2–4.
[4] Cf. III Reg. ii. 20.
[5] Cf. II Cor. viii. 2 (?).
[6] Cf. no. 14.

suus sibi habere uideatur introitus. Vnde uestre supplicamus beniuolentie ut animi uestri seueritatem paulisper deflectatis ad nos; et, his pecunie repetende condicionibus omissis, paululum post datam simpliciter benedictionem quicquid exigendum iudicabitis exigatis. Ego enim erga sanctitatem uestram me uinculo fideiussoris ad 10 plenum obligo, quod post ipsam benedictionem quicquid de his omnibus sibi adiudicabit ecclesia obediens et humilis et deuotus implebit. Si post ista benedictionem eius uoluntas uestra distulerit, nil restat aliud nisi ut, in commissa sibi domo, uoluntatem domni pape sedulus prestolator exspectet. Valete.

### 41  To Imar, cardinal bishop of Tusculum and papal legate

[1145, before 10 June] He tells Cardinal Imar of the bishop of Salisbury's failure to bless the abbot of Cerne, presses for a further mandate to the bishop, and apologizes for not having visited the cardinal.

Patri suo et domno I(maro) sancte sedis apostolice Dei gratia legato frater G(ilebertus) G(loecestrie) dictus abbas, salutem et de toto corde dilectionem.

Litteras dignationis uestre, dilecte pater, domno Saresb(eriensi) direximus, ut quem statuistis abbatem Cerneleie loco eidem episcopali confirmaret benedictione. Quod ipse (quo animo uel qua industria nescimus) hucusque differens, in ipsum, 5 sicut a multis audiuimus, post dicessum uestrum uexationes et argumenta multiplicat. Quod utinam absit a uestra gloria ne tale sortiatur laus uestra dispendium, ut plantatio uestra sic euellatur et uestrarum opus manuum in ignominiam uestri deleatur. Quapropter honori uestro supplicamus et glorie, ut directis iussionis uestre litteris domnum Sar(esberiensem) commoneatis ut ultra illum quem ei 10 statuetis diem benedictionem eius non differat; et quod, si uere religionis amator est, animo grato uoluntate promtissima iam fecisse debuerat, uestra saltem auctoritate iam secundo commonitus ulterius explere non differat. Rogamus ut in opere uestro non confundatur facies uestra, sed incrementum semper habeat gloria uestra; ut 'sciant omnes quia manus tua hec, et tu domine fecisti eam'.[1] Valeat domnus meus 15 et pater dilectissimus. Sicut precepistis iamdudum uenissem ad uos nisi de die ⟨fo. 16v⟩ in diem inter nos iterate calumpnie me non impeditum solummodo sed et compeditum grauissime detinuissent.

40 8 repetende R; petende B (*Foliot evidently had the classical* pecunie repetunde—*extortion— in mind;* B *repeats* pet- *from the previous word*)   12 istam R   13 uestra *om.* R
41 G, no. 37; B, fo. 16; R, fo. 212r–v.
2 Gloecestrie...abbas *om.* R   4 Cernelie R   6 audiuimus *corrected to* audimus R   7 ne] non (?) B   9 uisionis (?) R   10 ultra *om.* B   14 confundetur B (*Vulg.* confundentur)   15 eum B   17 diem inter *om.* R

[1] Cf. Ps. xxxiii. 6 (also III Reg. ii. 20 and p. 78, n. 4); Ps. cviii. 27.

## 42   To Uhtred, bishop of Llandaff

[Early 1145] He asks the bishop to withdraw his suit against the monks (of Ewenny priory) for the body of the sister of Maurice (of London, lord of Ogmore and Kidwelly), since Gloucester and its dependencies are defended in such matters by a papal privilege.

Nos. 42–5 deal with the case between Ewenny Priory (a dependency of Gloucester) and the bishop of Llandaff over the body of Matilda of London which was due to be heard before the legate Imar on the First Sunday after Pentecost, 10 June 1145 (nos. 43, 45; for the year, cf. Appendix III and *EHR*, LXIII (1948), 526–7). No. 45 contains the appeal, and must be shortly before that date; no. 43, recommending the appeal for 10 June if the bishop does not acquiesce, must be slightly earlier. Nos. 42 and 43 appear to be contemporary with one another: verbal similarity seems to establish that 42 is the letter to the bishop mentioned in 43. No. 44, in which Gilbert appears to be excusing himself to the bishop for making the appeal, is presumably somewhat later than 42–3, but still before 10 June.

No. 45 seems to show that the church of St Michael, Ewenny, was given to Gloucester by William of London, father of Maurice and Matilda, in the time of Bishop Urban of Llandaff (1107–34); but it only became a priory in 1141.[1]

Patri suo et domno Vctredo, Landa(uensi) Dei gratia episcopo, frater G(ilebertus) ecclesie beati Petri G(loecestrie) dictus abbas, salutem et debitam patri caritatem.

Rogamus beniuolentiam uestram et expertam nobis totiens animi uestri moderationem ut causam hanc, quam aduersus fratres nostros de corpore sororis domni
5 Mauritii iam mouistis, sic deducatis ut nec caritatem minuatis in nos, nec priuilegio domni pape contraire temptetis. Habetur enim priuilegium quod uobis oportuno etiam tempore presentabimus, quo nobis apostolica concedit auctoritas ut quorumcunque liberorum hominum corpora qui extrema se uoluntate locis nostris in sepulturam concesserint absque alicuius preiudicio apostolica auctoritate sepelienda
10 suscipiamus.[2] Rogamus itaque dilectionem uestram ne occasionem queratis aduersus nos quominus seruiamus uobis, et ab ea quam hactenus erga uos habuimus caritate deferueamus. Parati enim sumus uobis omni loco et tempore tanquam domno deseruire, dum uestre tamen thronum iustitie apostolice uiderimus auctoritati obedire. Valete.

42 G, no. 45; B, fo. 18.
9 sepilienda B   12 caritatem B

---

[1]  *Cart. Gloucester*, I, 75–6; cf. *CS*, p. 266 and n. On Ewenny priory, and the London family, see J. Conway Davies in *Nat. Library of Wales Journal*, III (1943–4), 107–37; Lloyd, II, 430 and n., 470, 593.
[2]  This privilege seems to have disappeared; so wide a burial privilege seems, indeed, distinctly improbable.

### 43  To John, prior of Ewenny

[Early 1145] He tells the prior to deliver no. 42[1] to the bishop of Llandaff. If the bishop persists in his case, the prior is to resist him, since Gloucester and its dependencies are protected in burial cases by papal privilege. If he persists, the prior is to appeal to the legate for the First Sunday after Pentecost.

G(ilebertus) Dei gratia abbas Gloecestrie dilecto filio suo Iohanni priori sancti Michaelis salutem.

Litteras uobis directas domno Landauensi deferetis. Si uos audierit gratias illi; si uero perstiterit in proposito, apostolica ipsi auctoritate resistetis. Apostolicum enim priuilegium habemus pre manibus ut liberos quosque, qui se locis nostris 5 sepulture dederint, libere suscipiamus. Quod si super hoc perstiterit et uos interdicto tenuerit, audientiam domni legati adhibitis testibus appellabitis, et ei huius actionis diem ad *Domine in tua misericordia*[2] nominabitis. Valete.

### 44  To Uhtred, bishop of Llandaff

[Early 1145] He apologizes to the bishop for insisting on his right (supported by papal privilege) to the body in dispute.

Patri suo et domno ⟨Uctredo⟩ Land(auensi) Dei gratia episcopo frater G(ilebertus) Gloecestrie dictus abbas, salutem et debitam reuerentiam.

Cure et labori uestro quem ut res nostre apud uos crescerent inpendistis gratias agimus; et nos hoc ipso uobis obnoxios gratieque debitores exhibemus. Iniuriam uobis ullam uel a nobis uel a nostris fratribus inferri nec uolumus nec probamus. 5 Corpus quod repetitis apostolicam minuendo auctoritatem de ecclesia in quam allatum est sibique extrema uoluntate concessum expelli iubere non presumimus. Vnde rogamus dari nobis, si placet, hanc ueniam, simulque solite munificentie dono superinpendi gratiam ut nobis mortuorum cadauera que nobis ex ratione competunt non negetis, et a nobis nostrisque omnibus honorem quem possumus obse- 10 quiumque debiti famulatus optineatis. Valete.

44 G, no. 19; B, fo. 10 v (following no. 34, without break); R, fo. 209.
4 ipsi *om.* B
44 G, no. 21; B, fo. 11; R, fo. 209.
4 et *om.* R    10–11 obsequmque B

---

[1] The reference to the papal privilege and the bishop of Llandaff seems to make the identification clear. Prior John is only known from these letters. His predecessor, Robert, was prior 1141–4 (BM Cotton MS Vesp. A. v, fo. 199); his successor, Bertram, occurs 1148–66 (*Nat. Library of Wales Journal*, III, 129).

[2] Introit for the First Sunday after Pentecost.

## 45  To Imar, cardinal bishop of Ostia and papal legate

[May–June 1145] He supports the appeal of the prior of Ewenny against the bishop of Llandaff in the case of the body of Matilda of London, and explains its foundation.

Patri suo et domno I(maro) sancte sedis apostolice Dei gratia legato frater G(ilebertus) Gloecestrie dictus abbas, debitam patri karitatem et obedientiam.

Instanti pater necessitate compellimur ut de qua multum confidimus uestre nobis munificentie auxilium requiramus. Causa inter domnum Landauensem episcopum
5 et fratrem nostrum Iohannem priorem ecclesie sancti Micaelis in ipsa Landauensi diocesi constitute nuper exorta est de corpore cuiusdam domne Matildis, scilicet de Lundoniis, que in nouissimis agens presente uiro suo parentibusque simul astantibus sacerdote etiam cuius erat parochiana id ipsum suadente et requirente, sese in manu predicti prioris loco nostro humandam extrema uoluntate concessit. Tempore enim
10 predecessoris istius, domni scilicet Vrbani episcopi, in ipsa ecclesie nostre dedicatione, pater istius et mater, hec etiam ipsa et eorum tota progenies, se ibidem loco nostro nullo reclamante in ipsa episcopi presentia concesserunt. Suscepta et non multo post defuncta et in ecclesiam nostram immo *et suam allata est. Inde in nos plus iusto domni Landauensis ira succensuit et de ecclesia nostra corpus efferri et in
15 suam etiam a nostris deferri precepit. Iussioni huic prior apostolicam obtendit auctoritatem, que ecclesiis nostris fratrum suorum et sororum humanda corpora signata priuilegii ratione concedit. Vnde, quasi profanum aliquod prior ipse nominasset, statim a communione suspensus est et ecclesie nostre interdicte. In quo prior se grauari sentiens, ad *Domine in tua misericordia* ad uestram appellauit audien-
20 tiam. Sub hoc uestre supplicamus beniuolentie ut ecclesiis nostris diuina concedatis officia, quia prefixo die uestre, uita comite, assistemus presentie, sententie quam uestra decernat iurisdicio promtis animis parituri. Valeat domnus meus dilectissimus.

## 46  To Bernard, abbot of Cerne

[Probably 3–10 June 1145] He comforts the abbot and tells him that he is visiting the legate from whom he hopes for a solution to their business (the abbot's benediction).

Cf. above, nos. 38–41.

Dilecto fratri suo filioque karissimo B(ernardo) Cerneleie Dei gratia abbati frater G(ilebertus) Gloecestrie dictus abbas, salutem mentisque constantiam.

Singulis que nobis inscriptione litterarum mandastis respondere ad tempus omittimus, quia negotii nostri finem qualem disposuerit Dominus, cito nobis
5 iminere cognoscimus. De ipso tamen largitore bonorum Domino meliora semper

45 G, no. 16; B, fo. 10; R, fo. 208 v.
2 Gloecestrie *om.* B      3 quo R      6 M. R      7 Londoniis R      8 suadente] uolente R
8 manus B      11 eidem R      12 nullo *om.* B      13 *et *om.* B      14–15 et in...deferri *om.* B
(efferri...deferri)      17 profanum quasi B      21 prefixa R      21–2 quam...iuridicio B; quam
decernet uestra iuriditio R
46 G, no. 20; B, fo. 10 v; R, fo. 209
1 suo *om.* B      1 Cernelie R      2 Gloecestrie *om.* R      3 inscr. littarum B; litterarum inscriptione R

expectamus, ut qui bona contulit nobis *bona multiplicet; et gratiam qua preuenit nos, subsequenti etiam cumulare non desinat. Ipse ue nostrum si quod in presenti est conuertet in gaudium:¹et si liuenti oculo in aliquo perstrinxit nos exitum letitia con⟨fo. 11⟩sum⟨m⟩abit. De cetero noueritis me, uita comite et sospitate, hac proxima uentura dominica Winton(iam) ad domnum legatum esse uenturum. 10 Quo uobis mandamus mandandoque pariter iniungimus, ut nobis occurrere nulla omnino occasione pretermittatis. Valete.

## 47  To Theobald, archbishop of Canterbury

[Second half of 1145] The bishop of Worcester has been summoned to the archbishop's court: Gilbert explains the bishop's troubles with the monks of Worcester and his deposition of the prior (David).

The prior's deposition took place in 1145.² Since the archbishop is addressed as primate, it may presumably be dated later than the end of June 1145 (see Appendix II).

Patri suo et domno T(heobaldo) Dei gratia Cant(uariensi) archiepiscopo et totius Anglie primati frater G(ilebertus) Gloecestrie dictus abbas, in regione luminis optato ad uotum perfrui desiderio.

Placuit sullimitati uestre dilecte pater in Domino domnum et patrem nostrum domnum Wigornensem, responsurum quibusdam que sibi obiecta sunt, ad audien- 5 tiam uestram euocare. Nec minus illi complacet iussioni et uoluntati uestre deuote in omnibus obedire. Vnde in omni timore Domini³ et cordis humilitate uenit ad iudicem; spe tamen bona et tota caritatis plenitudine festinat ad patrem. Nec est quod in iudicio patris formidet filius cum intus apud patrem sit qui pro ipso pulset et exoret affectus. Ne tamen in cause presentis inspectione uester caliget oculus, 10 quod nobis inde notum est discretioni uestre notificamus. De statu Wigornensis ecclesie uos hoc ipsi decreuistis ut ob redintegrandam tam episcopi quam ecclesie sue dignitatem prior ipse qui fuerat ad tempus restitueretur, et infra prescriptum diem substituto altero ecclesie ipsius necessitudini consuleretur. Cumque a uobis ad ecclesiam suam domnus episcopus uestre pariturus uoluntati remearet, quidam e 15 fratribus ecclesie sue uestre dispensationis ignari, restitutionem prioris sui moleste plusquam oportuit sustinentes, res ipsius ecclesie statim ut fama est distrahere ceperunt; et male ut clamat populus impletis marsupiis abcesserunt. Quod quale sit satis ipsi iudicabitis: res ⟨fo. 13⟩ enim ecclesie sibi commissas infami uenditione distrahere malum fuit; a facie patris in nullo persequentis sed consilium a uobis utile 20 reportantis fugam repentinam arripere, multo peius; quod uero a uobis decretum fuerat, nec una dignari auditione multo pessimum. Quod uero captos se con- queruntur, et dum ad uos pro ecclesie sue utilitate festinarent male in itinere

46  6 *dona R  8 est *om.* B  10 dominica uenturum R (esse uenturum *om.*)
47  G, no. 28; B, fo, 12 v; R, fo. 210 r–v.  9 patris *om.* B  9–10 pulsat et exorat R

¹ Cf. Esther xiii. 17.
² Ann. Tewkesbury, *Ann. Mon.* I, 46; cf. Saltman, p. 86. David was prior 1143–5 (Biog. Index).  ³ Cf. I Pet. ii. 18.

6 2

detentos, omnes fere testantur apud nos domnum episcopum hoc et cum fieret
25 ignorasse, et factum ex quo resciuit paterna caritate pertractasse. Credendum etiam
plus estimo episcopo uni et ueraci quam irate monachorum turbe et contumaci, qui
etsi eosdem ab inordinato reuocasset uel detinuisset itinere, in hoc culpa uel nulla
uel permodica extitisset. De hoc tamen euocatos audietis. De cetero scimus domnum
episcopum priorem suum a prioratu amouisse, sed ob tumultuantium inquietu-
30 dinem fratrum nondum quenquam substituisse. Quod ideo diuinitus actum estimo,
ut uos suppremam operi bono manum imponatis et filie uestre idoneum prouidendo pastorem ad uoluntatem uestram et eius utilitatem consulatis. Vestris monitis
Wigornensis adquiescet ecclesia quibus domnum episcopum iuxta placitum uestrum
pariturum non ambigimus. Conseruet incolumitatem uestram in longa tempora
35 qui non dormitat custos Israel.[1]

## 48 To Cardinal Robert Pullen, chancellor of the Holy See

[Second half of 1145] He congratulates Pullen on his promotion, thanks him for his share in
restoring to Canterbury its ancient dignity, and asks his assistance for Master Ernald and
other clerks from Salisbury.[2]

Robert Pullen went to Rome as cardinal late in 1144, and was promoted chancellor in
January 1145; he died in the second half of 1146.[3] The mention of Canterbury must refer to
the grant to Theobald of the primacy in May 1145 (known in England in June at earliest).
Since that was presumably a recent event, and Pullen's promotion not long distant, we can
safely date this letter to the second half of 1145.

Magistro suo karissimo domnoque meritis honorando Rodberto, sancte sedis
apostolice cancellario, frater G(ilebertus) Gloecestrie dictus abbas, reuerentiam
debitam et de corde toto dilectionem.

   Exultauit cor meum dilecte pater in Domino, et spirituali sum iocunditate
5 perfusus, quia de celo respexit Dominus[4] et uestre memor humilitatis gratiam
donauit pro gratia, et a uobis digne seruatam hactenus honestatem morum et
elegantiam condigna munificentie sue gloria munerauit. Inuitatus ad nuptias locum
elegeratis optinere nouissimum, sed in uobis bene patri complacuit ut ewangelicum
illud tandem ipse personaret 'amice ascende superius', gloriamque uobis pariter et
10 honorem pre discumbentibus aliis exhiberet.[5] Mirabar equidem et rem tacitus
attendebam cui Dominus noua sua pariter et uetera reseruasset,[6] quid congesta
totius honestatis insignia sic in unum cumulasset. Et licet innumeris uite uestre
decor et doctrine suauitas illuceret, et in sui imitationem mirabiles multorum

**47** 25 ex quo] est eum R   29–30 fratrum inquietudinem R   34 ambigimur R
**48** G, no. 33; B, fo. 14v; H, fo. 153r–v; R, fo. 211v.
1 R. R   3 toto *om.* B   4 in Domino *repeated before* dilecte R   5 et uestre] uestreque
H (*Vulg.* et…et gratiam pro gratia)   6 morem B   7 gloria] gratia B   10 quidem B
11 attendebam uel considerabam H   13 illucesceret H

[1] Cf. Ps. cxx. 4 (and no. 35).
[3] On Pullen, see *GF*, pp. 53–5.
[5] Cf. Luc. xiv. 8–10.
[2] Cf. no. 31.
[4] Cf. I Reg. ii. 1; Ps. xxxii. 13.
[6] Cf. Cant. vii. 13.

appetitus accenderet, maius tamen aliquid animo sompniabam lucemque tantam
etsi non sub modio reconditam,[1] ab eminentiore tamen quodam loco fulgoris sui 15
beneficia prestituram ecclesie, spe quadam certa concipiebam. Teneo quod uole-
bam, uideo quod sperabam ut iam magna predicem opera Domini exquisita in
omnes uoluntates eius.[2]

De quo magna sperare potui, magna uidere iam merui, et quem dilexisse iustitiam et odio habuisse iniquitatem[3] non dubito in consilio iustorum et congrega- 20
tione secundum a beato summoque pontifice totius equitatis iura dictare totus
applaudo. Hinc est quod gratiarum non sufficimus ⟨fo. 15⟩ actioni, quod patrem
nostrum domnum Cant(uariensem) exhilarastis, quod ecclesiam eius in dignitatem
pristinam reformastis ut que mutila facie incedebat, hinc archiepiscopatus gloria,
illinc soliti primatus honore iam plena luce refulgeat. Et quia diuinitus actum est ut 25
de fonte iustitie ipsa uestra promotione procederet et pietas in nos, rogamus beniuo-
lam et benignam nobis semper gratiam uestram et pro Domini Iesu reuerentia
suppliciter exoramus ut magistro Ernaldo manum misericordie porrigatis et uestre
fretum pietatis auxilio letum ad propria remittatis. Scitis quam indecens sit et im-
portunum clericum bonum in publicas iamdiu gratulationes susceptum iam nunc 30
emendicatis elaborare suffragiis, et diebus uite sue nouissimis insolita preter morem
inedia pregrauari. Confido de domno meo magistroque carissimo ut cordis sui
locum misericordie semper aperiat et tam huic quam ceteris Saresberiensis ecclesie
clericis, iam instante necessitate et uehementer urgente tempestate subueniat.
Conseruet omnipotens Dominus magistrum et domnum meum in tempora longa 35
ecclesie sue profuturum.

### 49   To R., prior, and the monks of Cerne

[1145–6] He admonishes them at length to show obedience to their abbot, and warns against
an appeal to Canterbury and Rome, of which he has heard a rumour.

Nos. 49–57 and 62–4 continue the case of Bernard abbot of Cerne: cf. above, nos. 38–41,
46.

Dilectis in Christo fratribus R. priori ceterisque Cerneleie fratribus frater G(ilebertus) Gloecestrie dictus abbas, militando prudenter assequi gratie donatiuum.

Mouet nos aliquamdiu erga nos et iamdiu erga domum nostram a uobis habita et
exibita karitas; ut quod nondum presentia corporali potuimus, missis saltem litteris

**48** 17 magna predicem RH; predicem magna B (*Vulg.* magna opera...)   17 exquisita *om.*
H (*in Vulg.*)   20 et iniquitatem odisse non dubito et H   22–3 patrem nostrum domnum
H; nostrum *om.* B; domnum *om.* R   25 illinc soliti R; hinc B; illinc solliciti H   26 processerit
(et *om.*) H   26–7 beniuolentiam B   28 Hernaldo H; Aernaldo R   35 Deus B   35 Dominus
magistrum meum et domnum in H   35 longa tempora H
**49** G, no. 32; B, fo. 13 v; R, fo. 211 r–v.
1 Cerneleie R (fratribus *om.*; *an erasure in* R); et ceteris Cerneleie fratribus B   3 ? monet B
3 ? uos MSS

---

[1] Cf. Mc. iv. 21–2, etc.          [2] Ps. cx. 2.          [3] Cf. Ps. xliv. 8.

5 uos ultra uisitare non differamus. Gratias igitur per omnia uestre referentes sanctitati nos uobis in omni gratia spirituali profitemur obnoxios, qui et de nobis iamdiu
bene sperare cepistis; et, quod in donis summum est et precipuum, nos profectus
uestri et incrementi spiritualis in Domino participes esse uoluistis. Nam quanta
karitatis plenitudine beniuolentiam uestram superextendatis in nos,[1] hinc datur
10 intelligi quod, cum toto orbe terrarum ecclesia Dei clara meritorum laude titulisque
gloriosis longe lateque resplendeat, uestre tamen complacuit sollicitudini ut ecclesie
nostre uos artiori quodam dilectionis uinculo iungeretis, et de ipsa uobis patrem
pastoremque eligeretis. Quod quidem non ita scribimus tanquam de infula uel
cathedra loci uestri, uel in nobis uel in nostris gloriantes, sed gratam habentes per
15 omnia unitatem spiritus que inter nos mediante quodam uinculo caritatis et pacis
firmo et indissolubili constituitur.[2] Nam cum de iminenti uobis negotio recurreretis
ad nos, equidem uobis caritate non ficta[3] ⟨fo. 14⟩ subuenimus; et de corpore nostro
uobis non tanquam saucium aliquod uel putridum membrum abiciendo proiecimus
sed corporis nostri partem sane meliorem et commodiorem, licet in dispendium
20 nostri, plena tamen uobis pietate concessimus. Nam si quod sanctum est, quod
honestum, quod doctrine sane, quod bone fame, quanto speramus amore concu-
piscitis, habetis procul dubio, habetis in patris adeptione unde et Domino gratiarum
referatis actiones, et nobis sitis in inmensum gratie debitores. Habetis nempe uirum
cui ad doctrinam scientia, ad honestatem mores exuberant. Habetis in cuius uita et
25 moribus uobis plene uirtus illucescet. Habetis cui humiliter obediendo, quod
arripuistis iter uirtutum, uirtutis assequendo premium gloriose consu⟨m⟩mabitis.
Sed sunt in uobis fortassis aliqui quos in appetitum sui nondum plene uirtus allexit;
immo sunt ut tristis audio qui uirtutis opus quanto laboriosius est tanto odiosius
aspernantur. Sunt etiam qui ab eo quem in patrem elegistis et assumpsistis inpu-
30 denter auersi iam retrorsum abierunt;[4] nec iam uocem eius audientes, sed alienum
nescio quem sequentes, non solum ipsi non obediunt sed et ipsum nefariis, ut fama
est, ausibus eradicare et explantare moliuntur. Numquid sic nostra debuit remunerari benignitas? Numquid hoc nostra meruit promta uobis deseruire uoluntas? 
Audite karissimi et quod ex caritate loquimur aure caritatis aduertite. Timeo, timeo
35 ne forte uos urgeat ueniens ex alto sententia. Scitis enim quod iuxta merita subditorum disponitur et uita rectorum; et sicut cum sancto sanctus est Dominus, ita
etiam peruersis merito peruersus inuenitur.[5] Bonis equidem pie disponit, et qui
suspirant ad uitam his patrem prestat et pastorem quo ducantur et pertrahantur ad
uitam. Pharaoni iamdudum Israelite seruierant, et ciuitates illi de latere et luto
40 construxerant; sed ex quo cepit eis seruitus Egiptiaca displicere, clamauerunt ad
Dominum et iter trium dierum Moise ducente profecti sunt: uolentibus ad uitam

---

**49** 5 uestre per omnia R    14–15 per omnia habentes R    15 et pacis *om.* B (pacis *is in Vulg.*)
16 recurretis B    18 uel] et B    37 merito *om.* B    38 suspirat B    40 eis *om.* B    40 dis-
picere B

---

[1] Cf. II Cor. x. 14.                    [2] Cf. Eph. iv. 3.
[3] Cf. II Cor. vi. 6.                    [4] Cf. Joh. xviii. 6.
[5] Cf. Eccli. x. 2; Ps. xvii. 26–7, and II Reg. xxii. 26–7.

ingredi merito preesse conceditur per quem pateat ingressus ad uitam.[1] Secure pronuntio: si filiis Israel Pharaonis adhuc opera placuissent nec clamassent ad Dominum, nec saluatorem adhuc habuissent. Iustitie regula est ut qui iustus est iustificetur adhuc; et qui in sordibus est sordescat adhuc.[2] Si qui ceci sunt *et ut a 45 ceco ducantur expostulant sententia celi est ut pariter in foueam cadant.[3] Nec quidem hec dicimus de maiori et meliori parte uestri diffidentes, sed mirantes equidem et indignantes quod illos, qui uos conturbant, inter uos dominari et principari permittitis. Audio illum non dico carnalem sed carnem[4] Aelardum demigrasse Cantuariam, Romam inde forsitan profecturum. Sed quid si Romam 50 uenerit? Sentiet axis onus et ad tantum pondus curia forsitan inclinabitur. Vetus ista querela est et inter carnem et spiritum ab ipsis ecclesie cunabulis uehementer agitata. Iamdiu est quod caro concupiscit aduersus spiritum et spiritus aduersus carnem. Nos uero ambulabimus aduersus carnem et carnis opera recidemus. Audiat, aduertat carnis opera, et faciem suam domnus Aelardus intelligat. Nam 55 opera carnis hec sunt: fornicatio, immunditia, impudicitia, luxuria, et que huius-modi sunt.[5] Qui sectatur huiusmodi nulla sibi erit cum nostro commilitone com-munio. ⟨fo. 14v⟩ Nec tamen hec dicimus tanquam fratrem uestrum persequentes in aliquo, uel de ipso talia suspicantes: persequimur uitia non personam. Aspera dicimus, optantes ipsi meliora. Vano seducitur fortassis intuitu: Romam estimat 60 uelut arundinem omni posse spiritu agitari.[6] Rome scimus ueritatem obscurari posse, nunquam tamen, si fuerit agnita, reprobari. Tronus ille iustitie est; equitatem sedes illa diudicat.[7] Nec est causa ista que in lucem uenire erubescat. Nichil in aure diximus quod super tecta predicari nolimus. In innocentia ingressi sumus et sperantes in Domino non infirmabimur.[8] Rogamus itaque dilectissimi ut unani- 65 mitati studeatis et paci; et patrem uestrum per omnia sicut decet filios honorantes, illi quam oportet reuerentiam et nobis quam sperabamus caritatem non tantum labiis sed corde potius exhibeatis. Habetis unum quem si corde suscipitis et hono-ratis, in uno illo nos omnes integre possidebitis; quod si faciem ab illo auertitis, quo spiritus impetu ducamini nulli dubium relinquetis. Filio nostro fratrique karissimo 70 nequaquam deesse poterimus sed uestros cum illo incursus toto anisu sustinere temptabimus. Aduersa nempe sustinere poterit sed solus habere non poterit. Sed auertat hoc Dominus ut societatis nostre iocunda principia exitus habeant tam

---

**49** 42 per] propter R   44 adhuc saluatorem R   45 Si] sic R   45 *et om. R 46 celi (uel ci *interlined*) est ut (*expunged*) ut B   49, 55 Adelardum/Adelardus R   51–2 Vetus est hec querela B   53 est quod caro om. B   56 sunt hec B (*Vulg.* que sunt)   58 hec om. B 63 iudicat R (*Vulg.* iudicabit)   63 Nec causa ista est R   69 quo] quo quo B

---

[1] Cf. Ex. i. 14, etc., and xv, esp. 22.   [2] Cf. Apoc. xxxii. 11.
[3] Cf. Luc. vi. 39.
[4] The point of this heavy pun is not entirely clear, but it seems from what follows that Aelardus was a mountain of flesh; 'Sentiet axis onus' (Cf. Lucan, 1, 57), and, in introducing the famous passage from Galatians, Gilbert says, 'let Aelardus hear and take heed of the works of the flesh, and let him understand his appearance'; a play on 'Aelardum'/'lardum' is not impossible. In the previous sentence there is an echo of Mc. x. 42.   [5] Cf. Gal. v. 19–21.
[6] This seems to be a conflation of Matt. xi. 7; I Joh. iv. 1; and Eph. iv. 14.
[7] Cf. Ps. ix. 8–9.   [8] Cf. Ps. xxv. 1.

amarissimos, et ipse qui est initium et finis principia nostra iocundo fine concludat.¹
75 Valete. Et si uestra nos dignos amicitia creditis nos quoque amicos uestros et per omnia beniuolos estimate.

### 50 To Jocelin de Bohun, bishop of Salisbury

[1145–6] The ex-abbot of Cerne has returned: Gilbert asks the bishop to excommunicate him and his accomplices in the community, and forwards a letter from the archbishop on the subject; he threatens an appeal to the Pope.

Patri suo et domno I(ocelino) Sar(esberiensi) Dei gratia episcopo, frater G(ilebertus) G(loecestrie) dictus abbas, in meditatione cordis et oris eloquio Domino complacere.²

Quoniam scripsistis bene, rogamus ut faciatis et bene, et opem quam nobis uerbo promittitis opere compleatis. Incubus ille Cernelie quod alieni iuris est audacter 5 ocupat; qui inde uiolenter excussus est ad aliena limina solo iustitie defectu mendicat. Ad uestre igitur sanctitatis genua prouoluti suppliciter exoramus, ut tam nostris fatigationibus quam extremis ecclesie desolationibus caritas uestra compatiatur et subueniat, et aduersus contumacem, inobedientem et rebellem non suspecte nobis iustitie uestre zelus incandescat. Non est uobis aduersus postulationes nostras 10 excusatio. Potestis enim quod petimus et debetis; anatematis itaque sententiam in ipsum et eius complices qui manifeste³ digni sunt proferatis, et animas nostras ne diutius suspensas teneatis. Litteras domni archiepiscopi uobis mittimus; cui, nisi plene obedieritis iam solus unus superest quem pro iustitie defectu requiramus. Valete.

### 51 To Theobald, archbishop of Canterbury

[1145–6] He complains that the bishop of Salisbury has failed to act on the letter referred to in no. 50, asks the archbishop to excommunicate the ex-abbot of Cerne (William Scotus) himself, to stir the earl of Gloucester to action against him, and to issue another mandate to the bishop of Salisbury.

Patri suo et domno Cant(uariensi) Dei gratia archiepiscopo et totius Anglie primati T(heobaldo) frater G(ilebertus) G(loecestrie) dictus abbas, salutis gaudium et obedientie famulatum.

Adhuc etiam domne incubus ille Cern(eleie) quod sui iuris non est, audacter 5 ocupat; et qui inde expulsus est, ad aliena limina pro defectu iustitie mendicat.⁴ Domnus uero Sar(esberiensis) expulsi abbatis inopie et extreme ipsius ecclesie desolationi fortasse compatitur, sed nec abbati inopi nec ecclesie iam ruenti aliqua eius miseratione subuenitur. Mandati uestri litteras deuote suscipit, uestro tamen

50 G, no. 67; B, fo. 26v.
51 G, no. 38; B, fo. 17; R, fo. 212v.
4 etiam domne] domne et B    8 uestro *om.* B

---

¹ Cf. Apoc. i. 8; xxi. 6.                    ² Cf. Ps. xviii. 15.
³ Cf. p. 46, n. 2                            ⁴ Cf. no. 50.

obedire mandato alta nescio qua consideratione omittit. Iustitiam itaque, quam alias non inuenimus, a uestra iam paternitate requirimus: ut Scotum illum inobe- 10 dientem, uobis manifeste contumacem et improbum, si placet, excomunicetis; et ecclesiam ipsam quamdiu ei incubuerit interdicatis. Quod si deinceps comiti Gloec(estrie) de eiciendo excommunicato uestro preceperitis, scimus quod uobis obedire non differet, uerum domno Sar(esberiensi) obedientie formam sine mora obediendo prescribet. Valete.                                                                15

## 52   To Theobald, archbishop of Canterbury

[1145–6] A messenger taking the archbishop's letter to the earl of Gloucester has been attacked by the party of William Scotus, ex-abbot of Cerne: Gilbert asks the archbishop for sterner measures to enlist the assistance of the earl and his son and the bishop of Salisbury.

Patri suo et domno Cant(uariensi) Dei gratia archiepiscopo et totius Anglie primati T(heobaldo), frater G(ilebertus) G(loecestrie) dictus abbas.

    Sustinuimus domne pacem et non uenit, quesiuimus bona et ecce turbatio.[1] Frater Iohannes Cern(eleie) monacus mandati uestri litteras ad comitem Gloec(es-trie) deferebat, sicut ipsi nostis, non continentes nisi quod ad pacem et utilitatem 5 eiusdem pertinebat ecclesie. Cum itaque Cern(eleia) egressus litteras ipsas deferens festinaret ad comitem, quidam filiorum Willelmi Scotti, illius quondam abbatis Cern(eleie), cum quibusdam aliis paratis ipsi occurrens insidiis, deiectum equo grauissimis afflixit uerberibus ipsoque semiuiuo relicto se ad speluncam latronum Cern(eleiam) receptauit.[2] Nec quidem illis in partibus cuiquam dubitare permittitur 10 quin pater Scotus filio Scotto huius operis incitamentum occasio et materies exstiterit. Vnde et hec manifesta sunt iamiam ad iudicium precedentia.[3] Preterea iamiam dictus Willelmus, uestro plane rebellis imperio, ecclesiasticam per omnia respuens disciplinam Cern(eleie) monasterio adhuc incubat, et in ipso sibi totius plenitudinem potestatis usurpat. Cumque toto orbe Britannico lateque patentibus 15 insulis occidentis, ecclesia Dei uestro se parere glorietur imperio,[4] una tantum est Cern(eleie) ecclesia, que contra uos calcaneum leuans presumptiue exclamat: 'que nobis pars cum Dauid uel que hereditas in filio Ysay?'[5] Filii alieni hii sunt inueterati pessime semper claudicantes a semitis bonis. Hii filii Belial quem sibi uolunt abbatem constituunt, constitutum cum uolunt eiciunt, eiectum reuocant cum uolunt 20 et obediunt tantum cui uolunt; cumque ut iumenta pessima in suo iamdiu stercore

**51** 10 Scottum R   12 ei *om.* R
**52** G, no. 44; B, fo. 17v.

---

[1] Cf. Jer. xiv. 19: 'expectauimus pacem, et non est bonum: et tempus curationis, et ecce turbatio.' 'Sustinuimus' is odd—it is more naturally associated with 'persecutionem' (as in I Cor. iv. 12); perhaps Gilbert had in mind some such usage as Ps. xxiv. 3, 5 ('sustinent te'— i.e. God), or the word may echo something in the archbishop's letter.
[2] Cf. Luc. x. 30; Jer. vii. 11.                          [3] Cf. I Tim. v. 24, and p. 46, n. 2.
[4] A high-flown reference to Theobald's primacy: cf. Appendix II.
[5] II Reg. xx. 1 (also for 'filii Belial' below); cf. Joh. xiii. 18; and, for the next sentence, Ps. xvii. 46.

computruerint, nec solum incontinentie sed et omnis turpitudinis fetorem ex se diu
et habundanter emiserint, non fuit iustus qui respiceret, uel qui ipsos uie reuocando
eorundem animas ad lucrum reportare intenderet. Virgam igitur in manu uestram
25 propheticam, uirgam scilicet uigilantem uideamus[1] et locum illum spurcitiarum et
criminum ⟨fo. 18⟩ quem non incorrectum solum sed et neglectum penitus ob-
soleuisse cognouimus, ad honorem Dei et uestrum, ad decorem domus Dei et
totius ordinis monastici reuerentiam purgari, de Vr Caldeorum eripi,[2] et in faciem
condignam religioni restitui et reparari gaudeamus. Forma uero reparationis, si
30 placet, hec est. Si in predicti sceleris patratores et consocios sententiam condignam
dederis, et illam domno Sar⟨esberiensi⟩ denuntiaueritis; si comiti Gloec⟨estrie⟩ ex
obedientia iniunxeritis, ut predictum Scotum amoueat, et si uobis placet, cure et
custodie nostre committat; si Rob⟨erto⟩ de Arundel, et Rogero filio eius, et Roberto
de Nicole[3] sub anathemate preceperitis ne Scotti ipsius stultitiam amplius foueant,
35 nec terras Cern⟨eleie⟩ ocupando Bernardum uestrum inpediant; si Willelmum
filium comitis de hoc ipso commoueritis; si benedictionem uestram scripto publico
adiutoribus Bernardi abbatis concesseritis, et malefactores eius sententia maledicti
terrueritis; si zelum etiam domni Sar⟨esberiensis⟩ exuscitaueritis ut aduersus
huiuscemodi incandescat et reprimendo contumaces in domni Bernardi auxilio non
40 tepescat: unctio uero sancta edocet uos de omnibus.[4]

### 53   To Pope Eugenius III

[Summer 1146] He explains the case of Bernard abbot of Cerne, and supports his appeal.

Patri suo et domno summo pontifici E⟨ugenio⟩ G⟨ilebertus⟩ ⟨Gloecestrie dictus
abbas⟩, salutis gaudium et debitum obedientie famulatum.

Quoniam dilecte pater amici ueritatis esse cupimus, ideo quod de causa domni
Bernardi Cerneliensis abbatis ipsi presentes uidimus et audiuimus[5] in presentia
5 uestra cum fiducia contestamur. Vidimus enim ipsum Cernelie priorem quam-
pluresque eiusdem ecclesie personas ad pedes domni Hiemari Tusculani episcopi eo
tempore apud nos legati, prostratos et prouolutos, humiliter postulare, ut eis
predictum Bernardum Gloec⟨estrie⟩ ecclesie tunc priorem, in abbatem concederet, et ipsum concedendo tam eorum quam totius conuentus sui petitioni satis-
10 faceret. Scimus etiam domnum Himarum ad eorum postulationem[6] predicto fratri

**52** 22 computrauerint B      36 commoueritis *sic, perhaps for* commonueritis (*as Giles*)
**53** G, no. 92; B, fo. 25.
1–2 Herefordensis ecclesie minister B

---

[1] Cf. Jer. i. 11.                           [2] Cf. Ps. xxv. 8; Gen. xi. 31.
[3] Robert of Arundel may be the former patron of Powerstock church, referred to in no. 421;
see esp. Round, *Geoffrey de Mandeville*, p. 93 and n. Robert of Lincoln may have been the son
of Alfred of Lincoln; he was castellan of Wareham in 1138 (*Cart. Montacute*, nos. 9, 118–19,
124, 164 and p. 249; *Wulfric of Haselbury*, pp. 154–5; Henry of Huntingdon, p. 261).
[4] Cf. I Joh. ii. 27.                        [5] Cf. I Joh. i. 1–3.
[6] The use of this word may imply some defect in Bernard's election, which had to be put right
by the papal legate; but it is far from certain that it would only be used in this sense at this
date.

Bernardo renuenti licet et inuito, ea qua preerat auctoritate iniunxisse ut honus Cerneliensis ecclesie regende susciperet, eique per omnia (prout competeret abbati) prouideret. Scimus nichilominus conuentum Cernelie eum gratuito solemni processione suscepisse et domnum Saresberiensem eorundem postea petitione episcopali benedictione ipsum in abbatem confirmasse. Quem quia tam uita quam doctrina multa dignum commendatione cognouimus, pro ipso preces sublimitati uestre porrigimus, ut eum in suis iustis postulationibus audiatis, et Cerneleienses monachos aduersus eum iniuste et inprobe contumaces, apostolica auctoritate reprimatis. Domus enim illa Cernelie est, cui ut publica fama est honestas sola iamdiu displicuit, nichil quod non religioni contrarium foret, et ordini, potuit complacere. Quorum emendande potius quam in presentia uestra commemorande dissolutioni quia predictus frater Bernardus quo potuit uigore restitit, eorundem uiolentia quasi profanus expulsus est et ab eorum communione sequestratus. Non nobis itaque domne non nobis sed nomini uestro gloriam donetis,[1] ⟨si⟩ improborum audaciam reprimendo, culpam similem in aliis compescatis, bonosque condigne munerando, uirtutis studium in compluribus augeatis. Sibi uos in longa tempora conseruet incolumem omnipotens Dominus, in Christo dilecte pater.

## 54   To Robert de Bethune, bishop of Hereford

[Summer 1146] He asks the bishop to write to the Pope in support of the appeal of Bernard abbot of Cerne.

Patri suo et domno Roberto, Herefor⟨densi⟩ gratia Dei episcopo, frater G⟨ilebertus⟩ G⟨loecestrie⟩ dictus abbas, salutis gaudium et obedientie famulatum.

Instanti necessitate compellimur, ut de negotio quod uobis pre manibus est, a domnis et amicis nostris ad domnum papam subsidii litteras expetamus. Rogamus itaque be⟨fo. 19⟩niuolentiam uestram ea qua de uobis caritate confidimus, ut nobis litteras uestras ad domnum papam concedatis, quibus fratri nostro Bernardo abbati Cern⟨eleie⟩ testimonium quale uel de ipso forsitan audistis uel a religiosis fratribus audire potuistis prebeatis. Quem enim tam doctrina quam uita dignum commendatione cognouimus, ab amicis ueritatis in ipsa sponsi presentia commendari cum fiducia postulamus; et quoniam ipsi⟨us⟩ aduersus aliquot fratres Cern⟨elienses⟩ causa est, rogamus ut et de electione ipsius et expulsione et de ipsa Cern⟨eliensis⟩ ecclesie dissolutione, quod in ore omnium est, et quod ipsi uerum esse et cause nostre prodesse cognoueritis adiciatis. A domno et amico magna exposcimus, cui in magnis etiam et arduis obedire et obsequi non recusamus. Vos Deo diuque ualere optamus, in Christo dilecte pater.

**53** 23 prefanus B    24 si] ut B
**54** G, no. 50; B, fo. 18 v.

---

[1] Cf. Ps. cxiii (2), 1.

## 55   To Jocelin de Bohun, bishop of Salisbury

[Summer 1146] He asks the bishop to have the church of Symondsbury restored to Bernard abbot of Cerne, the refractory monks removed in accordance with the archbishop's mandate and order restored in the abbey in accordance with the papal mandate, so that the *status quo* is restored while the abbot prosecutes the appeal to the Pope. He also forwards a letter from the archbishop written before the appeal.[1]

Patri suo et domno Ioc(elino) Sar(esberiensi) Dei gratia episcopo frater G(ilebertus) G(loecestrie) dictus abbas, seipsum.

Hoc est, dilecte pater, quod crebris litteris intendebam, ut de negotio quod inter nos est, michi nec onus augeretur, nec uobis honor aut reuerentia debita ulla ex
5 parte minueretur. Sed quoniam quod uerebar accidit et appellationis iam inter-currit auctoritas, precor ut de his que spectant ad uos negotium ipsum (si uobis placet) expediatis, et nos de remittenda appellatione apud domnum archiepiscopum quod poterimus exequemur. Requirit domnus Bernardus sibi cuncta restitui, que post denuntiatum uobis iter suum ad domnum papam amisit. Postulat ecclesiam de
10 Simundesberga sibi reddi, et monachos illos per quos sibi hec est orta contentio secundum mandatum domni archiepiscopi ad claustra regularia transmitti et in ecclesia Cern(eleie), consilio et auxilio uestro, religionem monachis condignam iuxta mandatum domni pape reformari. Super his nobis uelle uestrum rescribatis et in his que nobis benigne conceditis nos humiles et obedientes et adiutores habebitis.
15 Valeat sanctitas uestra. Litteras domni archiepiscopi que uobis ad presens mittuntur ante appellationem factam datas esse noueritis.

## 56   To Theobald, archbishop of Canterbury

[Summer 1146] He asks for news and for instructions: he will join the archbishop, but asks for the latter's journey to be postponed until Michaelmas. He informs the archbishop of the abbot of Cerne's appeal, and asks for protection for him and for the *status quo* in the affairs of the abbey while he prosecutes the appeal. He recommends that it be put under the care of Aelelm, archdeacon (of Dorset).[2]

Patri suo et domno Cant(uariensi) Dei gratia archiepiscopo et totius Anglie primati T(heobaldo), frater G(ilebertus) G(loecestrie) dictus abbas, salutis et gaudii plenitudinem.

Quia fortis est ut mors dilectio,[3] sicut uni preiudicare non possumus sic alteri
5 reluctari non ualemus. Hinc est, dilecte domne, quod id quod uultis me quoque

---

55 G, no. 43; B, fo. 17.
5 minuetur B   11 regulaia B
56 G, no. 39; B, fo. 17; R, fo. 212v.
5 relucta R

---

[1] And therefore presumably, in Gilbert's eyes, still effective—part of the *status quo* before the appeal.
[2] Aelelm or Adelelm was archdeacon by *c.* 1130 and held office until after *c.* 1160 (*JS Epp.* I, 131 n.). See no. 81 n.        [3] Cf. Cant. viii. 6.

uelle necesse est. Set quia redeuntes a ⟨B, fo. 17v⟩ uobis quidam michi sic, alii uero sic, locuntur, precor ut michi litteras uestre uoluntatis indices per hunc fratrem nostrum mittatis, et quod de me uestro sederit arbitrio ea qua preestis et potestis potestate iniungatis. Eo enim erga uos animo sum, ea uobis caritate deuinctus, ut in quo sanctitati uestre me obedire cognouero et placere, totum leue reputem quod 10 michi minari potest uel difficultas itineris uel urgens auctoritas obuie potestatis. De cetero frater Bernardus, abbas Cern(eleie), ad sedem apostolicam appellauit. Cum ergo sua omnia in protectione domni pape esse oporteat, a suis tamen persecutoribus non minus nunc quam ante diripiuntur. Vnde rogat per me, et de hoc precor uestra sit exorata paternitas ut ecclesiam suam in protectione domni pape et 15 uestra suscipiatis, et ipsam domno Aelelmo archidiacono custodiendam committatis; ut et huic ad domnum papam adeundum secundum quod se res habet necessaria conferat, et si quem in loco ipso Domino deseruire cognouerit, ipsi cura diligenti prouideat. Itineris uestri diem, si placet, michi notificetis; quem, si usque ad festum sancti Michaelis differri placeret, eos qui uobiscum ituri sunt fortasse magis paratos 20 haberetis. Valete.

## 57   To John of Canterbury

[? Summer 1146] Gilbert has appealed to the Pope; he thanks John for his offers of assistance, and indicates that he can handle the case himself. He concludes with a humorous discussion about a Seneca belonging to him and other matters.

This letter fits the circumstances of the Cerne appeal, the only one in this period which Gilbert is known to have prosecuted in person (as he indicates in this letter he is prepared to do), and the quotation from Psalm cxiii may be an echo of no. 53. In addition, it is likely that John of Canterbury was not active before the second half of Gilbert's abbacy. On these grounds we attach the letter to those which announced the appeal in the summer of 1146 (nos. 53–6). On John of Canterbury see *JS Epp.* I, xxvii–xxviii and n.; *GF*, pp. 203 ff., 286.

Sedulo maiestatis apostolice defensori domno Iohanni de Cant(uaria) frater G(ilebertus) G(loecestrie) dictus abbas, sales[1] si placet suos intra fines modestie modo laudabili cohibere.

Quod imitatus apostolum paternarum traditionum ceteris contribulibus tuis amplius et perfectius emulator existis, letus audio,[2] zelusque tuus bonus ut in- 5 crementa semper excipiat ampla caritate desidero. Veruntamen si qua penes nos acta uel dicta sunt que ad domnum papam usquequaque pertineant, nolo te frater commoueri super hoc, nolo tui sabbati pacem delicatam[3] aliquatenus exinde

**56** 6 quidam] qui R    9 potestate *So MSS;* B pietate *before correction (perhaps rightly:* pietate *is the less obvious word, but seems better;* pot... *could have come by attraction to* potestis)    10 et placere cognouero R    12 B. R    16 A. R    17 se *om.* R    19 quem/quem R    20 uobis B
**57** G, no. 42; B, fo. 16v.

---

[1] There seems to be a play on words here: 'sales' replaces the usual 'salutem'; both words seem to be echoed in 'uel saltem' at the end of the letter. The meaning of this would be clear only if John's letter survived.
[2] Cf. Phil. iii. 4 ff. (and for 'contribulibus' I Thes. ii. 14).         [3] Cf. Is. lviii. 13.

perturbari. Ad domnum namque papam appellauimus et ad eius nomen tota nobis
10 controuersia conquieuit. Nomen pacis in commune protulimus et ad eius flagran-
tiam nobis pacifica sunt uniuersa. Ne tamen nomen gratiarum in nostrum tantum
commodum et in ipsius iniuriam assumpsisse uideamur, nuntii nostri iam in hoc
ipso sunt ut domno pape litteris nostris intimemus quid a nobis actum sit et ad
ipsum quatenus appellatum. Apellationis itaque uinculum, quod ipsi nexuimus,
15 non ipsi sicut estimas presumendo soluere sed domno pape presentare curauimus,
ut de manu nostra suscipiat unde nos trahat, si uoluerit; uel, si eius sederit arbitrio,
nos remittat. Nobis ipsi etenim si iusserit assistere gloriosum, et si permiserit ab
agendo quiescere tutum erit. Non nobis itaque non nobis sed nomini suo dabit
gloriam,[1] et dis⟨ponet im⟩perio (?) suo quod uolet, cui obediemus in omne quod
20 uolet. Cum ergo zelum plane tuum approbem, in hoc tamen discretissimo nostri
seculi uiro minime conformaris, quod tibi rumor uagus auctoritas est et certam
reputas ex opinione sola scientiam. Si qua infirmamur in parte, te karissime infirma
terre nostre exploraturum minime estimabam. Sed eius gladius fortasse hic est qui
non pacem mittere uenit sed gladium.[2]
25 De cetero, quod annectis redundare in curiam, me magistro W. Senecam meum
bis negasse, benigne consulo ut in quibus audacter prouocas, prouideas et prudenter.
Qua enim facie me bis negasse contendis, quod diutino labore conscriptum domno
et amico poscenti ipse iamiam defero uel transmitto? Vides ergo, Iohannes, quos in
uanum conatus dederis, amicum quam sine causa prouocaueris, quem si foro loro
30 iniusto pertraxeris, quomodo non michi in meis fatigationibus et expensis con-
dempnaberis qui innocuum ad dampna requiris? Neue ergo liquasse culicem et
camelum deglutisse uidearis,[3] mee queso si qua forte est negligentie paulisper
oblitus ad magna te conuertas. Refrigescit enim karitas et habundant scandala[4] et
late circa regionem Iordanis oriuntur germina, que falce apostolica recidere iudici
35 proueniret ad gloriam, impetenti ad coronam. In his ⟨fo. 17⟩ queso te excerceas, in his
ingenium ocupes tuum, et quibus exosa lux est, beneficia lucis impertire. In talibus
enim tibi poterit gratia collocari, nec fortasse deerit in cuius possis nomine bap-
tizari. Ages ergo ut is cui nec Iouis cerebrum nec Maiugene[5] petasum deesse cognoscimus. Nos domni pape uoluntatem donante Deo audiemus in breui, ipsoque
40 uel iubente aderimus uel remittente gratias exoluemus. Optamus te ualere tibi et
amicis (dum tibi bene est) uel saltem parcere.

**57** 13 intimemur B    19 disperio B

---

[1] Cf. Ps. cxiii (2), 1.          [2] Cf. Matt. x. 34.
[3] Cf. Matt. xxiii. 24.          [4] Cf. Matt. xxiv. 12.
[5] Mercury's cap (Mercury was Maia's son—Maiugenes is a common periphrasis for Mercury
in Martianus Capella): this phrase occurs in Odo's dedicatory letter of his *Ysagoge in theologiam*
to Gilbert Foliot (see *GF*, pp. 53–4).

## 58  To Theobald, archbishop of Canterbury

[? Summer–autumn 1146] The bishop of Llandaff's excuse for not attending his case with the monks of Goldcliff is genuine—he is really sick; and so he asks for a postponement until the archbishop's return.

Nos. 58–60 form a series, all dealing with the dispute between the bishop of Llandaff and Goldcliff priory (Monmouthshire, a dependency of Bec), which had evidently been referred to the archbishop's court by appeal. The case was held up by the expected departure of the archbishop: in no. 58 Gilbert tells him that the bishop's delays have a reasonable basis, and that he wishes the case to be postponed until the archbishop's return; in no. 59 Gilbert forwards a letter from the archbishop accepting this proposal; and in no. 60 he tells the prior and monks of Goldcliff that the postponement ordered by the archbishop has been accepted by the bishop.[1]

Theobald went abroad (so far as we know) only three times in the period 1139–48: at the turn of 1143 and 1144, returning about the middle of 1144; late 1146 or later, returning in the summer of 1147; March 1148, returning in the autumn. According to no. 60 the archbishop must have expected to return from the journey in question some time about Epiphany. In fact he did not apparently return from any of the three journeys in late December or early January; but he might plausibly have expected to do so from one, and only one, of the three— that of 1146. Neither of the other two seems at all to fit the date; there were no public preparations (so far as we know) for the journey to Rheims in 1148; and the title primate in no. 58 argues against a date before 1145.

We conclude that 58–60 were written, in that order (which is also the order of MS B), in the weeks leading up to the archbishop's departure some time about or soon after Michaelmas 1146.

Patri suo et domno Cant(uariensi) Dei gratia archiepiscopo et totius Anglie primati T(heobaldo), frater G(ilebertus) G(loecestrie) dictus abbas, pie uelle que Dei sunt et actu semper implere.

Sullimitati uestre, domne, pro amicis supplicare compellimur qui nec pro nobis audiri digni satis inuenimur. Plus tamen eligimus apud patrem de pietate corripi 5 quam apud fratres de spreta caritate dampnari. Ad uestram uocatus audientiam domnus Landauensis multiplicibus se causis excusat—hinc difficultatem itineris, inde suspectas aduersantium insidias, et pre ceteris, sui corporis infirma pretendens. Inde uero nuper redeuntes fratres nostri, de quorum fide et ueritate non ambigimus, de ipsius infirmitate contestantur. De lecto itaque egritudinis sue, tum etiam per 10 nos, supplicando postulat ut cause presentis actio usque ad uestrum reditum differatur, sic tamen ut res ipsa que in controuersia est a fratribus de Goldcliue interim inconcusse possideatur. Qua in re si nec maiestatem uestram minui, nec fratrum uestrorum iustitiam impediri uideritis, petitioni huic annuendo nos sicut

58 G, no. 46; B, fo. 18; R, fo. 212v (*a fragment*, pie uelle...spreta caritate, *added in a different hand*).
6 A B

---

[1] The bishop's letter referred to in no. 60 could have been written somewhat earlier, and be that referred to in no. 58. On Goldcliff, see R. Graham in *Journal of the Brit. Archaeol. Assoc.*, 2nd series, XXXV (1929), 102–21, esp. 104 f.

15 in ceteris omnibus sic et in hoc ipso per omnia gratie debitores efficeretis. ⟨fo. 18 v⟩
Glorificetur in uobis Deus, uestrique corona meriti semper augeatur, in Domino
Iesu Christo dilecte pater.

### 59   To Uhtred, bishop of Llandaff

[? Summer–autumn 1146] He is forwarding to the bishop a mandate from the archbishop to
suspend the bishop's case with the monks of Goldcliff until the archbishop's return.

Patri suo et domino V(ctredo) Land(auensi) Dei gratia episcopo, frater G(ilebertus)
G(loecestrie) dictus abbas, salutem et dilectionem.

De uestra erga nos benignitate certo rerum argumento non dubitamus: si
gratiam meritis non equamus, tamen in quo possumus uobis obsequi parati sumus.
5 Litteras itaque domni archiepiscopi uobis mittimus, ut attendatis ex his quid uobis
factu opus sit, et quod agendum uideritis, prudenti cura adimpleatis. Opportet
enim, sicut scripsistis, ut possessionem, de qua contenditis, monachis de Gold(cliue)
usque ad reditum domni archiepiscopi inconcusse dimittatis, eisque pacem interim
de cetero obseruetis. Sicque faciendo et iudicem poteritis habere propitium, et cum
10 ad causam accingi opportuerit, melius poterit reformari negotium. Valete.

### 60   To the prior and monks of Goldcliff

[? Summer–autumn 1146] The archbishop has suspended their case against the bishop of
Llandaff until the Octave of Epiphany or his return thereafter.

Frater G(ilebertus) G(loecestrie) dictus abbas, dilectis in Christo fratribus domno
priori de Gold(cliue) ceterisque fratribus, salutem et dilectionem.

Paci uestre et quieti sollicite prouidens domnus archiepiscopus uobis istud per me
denuntiat, ut prosequende cause, quam aduersus domnum Land(auensem) habetis,
5 hac uice operam non detis. Placuit enim serenitati eius ut actio ipsa usque ad octabas
Epiphanie, uel ad reditum eius deinceps differatur—sic tamen ut possessio que in
controuersia est a uobis interim inconcusse possideatur. Domnus enim Land(auensis) sicut scripto suo testatur, hoc idem annuit et uobis interim pacem se per omnia
seruaturum compromittit. Valete, et paterne circa uos gratias reddentes affectioni
10 eius per omnia consiliis adquiescite.

### 61   To Theobald, archbishop of Canterbury

[Probably late 1146] He is preparing to accompany the archbishop, and asks the archbishop
to instruct the bishops of Worcester and Hereford to protect his church in his absence.

If Gilbert's intention of accompanying the archbishop took effect, this letter must belong
to the second half of 1146 (cf. no. 56, etc.) or early 1148 (cf. no. 74, etc.). The second journey

59 G, no. 47; B, fo. 18 v.
1 Vn' B    3 ? dubii B
60 G, no. 48; B, fo. 18 v.
61 G, no. 69; B, fo. 27.

was secret: whereas in this case Gilbert is making public preparations for departure, and Bishop Simon's public letter of protection (G, no. 65) was probably the fruit of the present letter. This makes the earlier date highly probable; and Gilbert's expectation that the bishop of Hereford would protect his church in his absence—whereas the bishop of Hereford preceded the archbishop to Rheims in 1148—strongly confirms the earlier date.

Patri suo et domno Cant(uariensi) Dei gratia archiepiscopo et totius Anglie primati T(heobaldo) frater G(ilebertus) G(loecestrie) dictus abbas, delicias regibus in pane pinguissimo ministrare.[1]

Officiosum michi, domne, munus ⟨fo. 27v⟩ existimo, totum quod anime mee memoriam uestri representat aut suggerit. Vnde presentium hunc latorem trans- 5 misimus ad uos, ut per eum directis literis nos de statu uestro simul et uoluntate certificetis. Nostra enim huiusmodi sunt. Infestant nos quamplurimi et non solum nostram sed et omnes circa nos ecclesias multiplicatis angariis inquietant. Quos si percutimus in gladio aurem Malchi, Domino manum extendente, cito sanari con- siderant[2] et ab hoc inperterriti peccant. Vnde uestre nobis litere ad domnum 10 Wigornensem et ad domnum Herefordensem necessarie sunt ut ecclesie nostre protectioni inuigilent, et quo nos abesse contigerit eo sibi consilii manum et auxilii propensius inpendant. Nos uero itineri accincti sumus, et ad iussionem uestram Domino annuente parati aderimus. Aduersantur nobis quamplurima, sed amor offendicula prorsus ignorat. Valeat in longa tempora uestra sullimitas, in Christo 15 dilecte pater.

## 62  To Robert Warelwast, bishop of Exeter

[Spring 1147] The bishop had been appointed one of the papal judges delegate in the Cerne case, and Gilbert urges him to be present at the hearing at Bath on the Sunday after Ascension Day (1 June 1147).

Nos. 62–4 are a continuation of the letters dealing with the affair of Cerne abbey, for which see nos. 38–41, 46, 49–57 and Appendix III.

Patri suo et domno R(oberto) Exoni(ensi) Dei gratia episcopo frater G(ilebertus) G(loecestrie) dictus abbas, salutis gaudium et obedientie famulatum.

Quanta, domne, debetur apostolice maiestati reuerentia, que etiam mandatis eius obedientia, uestra satis nouit discretio cuius non minus ad doctrinam scientia quam ad honestatem et omnem gratiam mores exuberant. Preces itaque serenitati uestre 5 porrigimus ne uos Cerneliensium disuasio possit auertere, quo uos minus domno pape contingat obedire. Adest dies actioni cause domni Bernardi abbatis et monacorum Cerneliensium constituta, dies scilicet dominica post Ascensionem

61 6 de statui nos B
62 G, no. 72; B, fo. 28.
4 cuius Giles; cui B

---

[1] Cf. Gen. xlix. 20.
[2] Cf. Joh. xviii. 10; Luc. xxii. 49–51. 'Angariis' in the previous sentence probably means 'forced services' (originally 'forced journeys'—see TLL, II, 44).

Domini, quo ceteri omnes Batonie aderunt quibus una uobiscum eiusdem est cause
10 cognitio a domno papa delegata. Vnde si uos abesse contigerit, dabitur predictis
monachis occasio subterfugiendi iudicium, si aliquem abesse uiderint iudicum
asignatorum. Quod quidem nobis non solum laboris esset continuatio sed etiam
iteratio, et choaceruata grauaminum multiplicatio. Prouideat itaque si placet uestra
discretio, ne absentia uestra tam cause nostre sit detrimentum quam fatigationibus
15 nostris prebeat incrementum. Vno enim aduentu uestro domno pape obedietis, et
nos humiles amicos uestros amplioris uobis gratie debitores statuetis. Valete.

### 63   To the Empress Matilda

[1147–8] He answers a charge made by Nivard,[1] the brother of St Bernard of Clairvaux, and
explains that the action taken against the Cerne monks was based on the judgement of papal
judges delegate and on a papal mandate.

Venerabili et illustri domne M(atildi) inperatrici regis Henrici filie, frater G(ilebertus) G(loecestrie) dictus abbas, in decore ⟨fo. 22 v⟩ uirtutum summo regi complacere.

   Super his que uestra michi mandauit excellentia meum si placet responsum
5 equanimiter audiatis. De religione domni Niuardi, fratris dilectissimi patris nostri
domni abbatis Clareuall(ensis), ita michi certus sum, quod si ea que inter nos et
Cernelienses acta sunt plenius agnouisset, non solum michi querelam non mouisset
sed que dictante equitate et domno papa statuente gesta sunt, firma manere uoluisset et uobis tenenda suasisset. Cernelienses enim monachi domnum papam adeuntes,
10 cause, quam aduersus abbatem suum intendebant, sibi iudices in Anglia statui
petierunt, et ad hoc episcopos quattuor inpetrauerunt. Ad hos itaque litteras domni
pape afferentes, iuxta earundem litterarum tenorem, die constituta solenniter
auditi sunt, et per omnia deficientes iudicio publico condempnati. Preterea non
solum sacerdotio priuati sunt, sed etiam infames in perpetuum iudicati et custodie
15 claustrorum regularium et scripto et precepto domni pape mancipati. Cum itaque
quosdam eorum domni pape auctoritate suscepimus, ipsos nisi eadem auctoritate
remittere nec possumus nec debemus. Non turbetur ergo uestra serenitas si apostolico mandato obedimus, a cuius uoluntate resilire instar sacrilegii iudicamus. In his
uero que possumus et debemus mandatis uestris acquiescere parati sumus, uerum in
20 quo ecclesie auctoritas offenditur, plena nobis excusatio est si quod non debemus
exigimur. Valeat in perpetuum sullimitas uestra.

**63** G, no. 52; B, fo. 22.

---

[1] St Bernard's youngest brother. He became a novice at Cîteaux and a monk of Clairvaux
between 1115 and 1119; novice-master at Vaucelles in 1132, prior of Buzay in 1135. C. 1147
he was involved in the foundation of Soleuvre, later the abbey of Val-Richer. He last occurs,
in Bernard's company, in 1150 (E. Vacandard, *Vie de S. Bernard*, 4th ed., Paris, 1910, I, 8,
84–5; II, 400 and n.; W. Williams, *St Bernard of Clairvaux*, Manchester, 1935, pp. 29, 46, 51,
80 f., 83 f.).

## 64 To Bernard, abbot of Cerne

[February–March 1148] He comforts the abbot, urges him to ask the Pope at the forth-coming council (Rheims, March–April 1148) to release him from his office, and then to return to Gloucester. Gilbert will be going (to Rheims) himself.

Karissimo fratri suo B(ernardo) Cerneleiensi Dei gratia abbati frater G(ilebertus) G(loecestrie) dictus abbas, consolationis et consilii spiritu semper refoueri.

Fortunam uestram plangitis et deploratis incommoda, que et ipsi pari mestitia plangeremus, nisi bonis omnia chooperari in bonum ipso Domini spiritu doceremur.[1] Sed quia certum nobis est quoniam his qui ex proposito uocantur ad uitam [ . . . ], ideo 5 in omnibus que de manu Domini accipimus gaudemus et gratias agimus, attendentes in his que prospera sunt bonitatem, in aduersis disciplinam, in utrisque scientiam, quoniam flagellat Dominus omnem filium quem recipit et bonus pater si in uirga uisitat iniquitates, in ira tamen misericordias non continebit.[2] Vnde si inter incudem et malleum gemuistis hactenus, gemitus iste uobis erit pro cantu cum tanquam uas 10 mundum in omnem uoluntatem opificis summi formatum auro purior quod per ignem probatur post crebras Domini concussiones enitescetis,[3] et fortitudinis et constantie et laboris, et tolerantie premia ab ipso cui obedistis reportabitis. Quia uero conuersa est hereditas uestra ad alienos et mentiti sunt uobis filii alieni inuete-rati dierum malorum, claudicantes semper a semitis bonis, abeuntes retro post 15 Sathanam, eligentes magis in uobis Christum persequi quam sequi per uos, utile non arbitror ulterius solo sterili mandare semina, porcis spargere margaritas, fetorem sentire de proximo perditorum.[4] Exiens itaque de Egipto in proxime futuro concilio absolutionem a domno papa postulabitis, et dante Domino, im-petrabitis, incontaminata uita, fama in omnibus permanente illesa, spiritu a 20 Domino ⟨ad⟩ seruiendum promtissimo, qui eduxit quasi lumen iustitiam uestram et iudicium uestrum deducet tanquam meridiem, cui notas fecisti uias uestras et sperastis in eo et ipse faciet.[5] Ipse dante Domino adero et coadiutor existam: unum tamen obsecro ut nec corde nec corpore discedatis a nobis, sed sit nobis una bono-rum communio, caritas una, indiuidua uite societas, ut ubi uite bone tirocinia 25 transegistis, perfectionis ornamenta reponatis, et iam pene omnem expertus for-tunam mundum et que sua sunt contempnatis, et ipsum de sullimi iam ipso altior irrideatis. Valete. De itinere certior—uere tamen iturus—uobis certiora mandabo.

**64** G, no. 1; B, fo. 27.
5 uitam [ . . . ] *Some words seem to be missing, including the verb following* quoniam (qm̄) 11 purior purior B 17 arbritror B

---

[1] Cf. Rom. viii. 28.
[2] Cf. Heb. xii. 6; Ps. lxxxviii. 33 and lxxvi. 10.
[3] Cf. Eccli. ii. 5.
[4] Cf. Lam. v. 2; Ps. xvii. 46; Matt. vii. 6.     [5] Cf. Ps. xxxvi. 6; cii. 7; xxxvi. 5.

## 65   To Theobald, archbishop of Canterbury

[Probably 1145–8] He excuses himself from attending a meeting (perhaps a council)[1] in London: a Welsh raid on his properties across the Severn forces him to attend a meeting of Welsh princes in Glamorgan.

Nos. 65 and 66 were presumably written after Theobald was granted the primacy (see Appendix II).

Patri suo et domno Cantuariensi Dei gratia archiepiscopo et totius Anglie primati T(heobaldo) frater G(ilebertus) Gloecestrie dictus abbas, humilem ex caritate non ficta[2] obedientiam.

Rogamus beniuolentiam uestram, in Christo dilecte pater, ut excusationem quam
5 ad presens ex necessitate pretendimus ipsi suscipiatis, et de mandato uestro si quid minus agimus paterna hoc nobis caritate remittatis. Absit enim ut quid audeam in presentia uestra confingere, qui summum michi solamen estimem, una uobiscum dies huius incolatus indiuidua uite coniunctione transigere. Sed his qui circa nos sunt satis superque notum est quomodo nuper irruerint Gualenses in nos, et quod
10 trans Sabrinam fluuium potissimum habebamus, totum fere usque in ipsas Gualie profunditates abegerint. Vnde necesse est michi hac ipsa Dominica qua Lond(onie) conuenietis, colloquio regum Gualensium interesse in Glamorgan uel plusquam trescentarum marcarum dampnum irrecuperatorie sustinere. Quia ergo in tota terra cordis uestri ad plenum dominatur caritas, dabitis filio exoranti hanc ueniam
15 ut paterna licentia ad presens urgenti et instanti plurimum ecclesie nostre necessitati deseruiam. Valeat domnus et pater meus dilectissimus.

## 66   To Theobald, archbishop of Canterbury

[Probably 1145–8] He describes how, on the archbishop's instructions, he himself, in company with the bishop of Hereford, the dean of St Paul's, the archdeacon of Oxford, and others, had heard the suit between the abbot of Reading and the monks of St-Denis (near Paris)[3] about parochial rights in Stanton Harcourt and Northmoor (Oxfordshire). The third hearing was brought to a close by the prior of Reading appealing to the Pope.

The final judgement of the archbishop by which the case was settled has been printed by Sir Frank Stenton in *CHJ*, III, 3–4 (1929), and again by Prof. Saltman, *Theobald*, pp. 433–4. St-Denis was permitted to build its chapel, in return for a payment in recognition of the rights of Stanton as mother church. There is no hint in Theobald's settlement of papal inter-vention,[4] and it seems possible that the appeal to Rome was dropped.

**65** G, no. 22; B, fo. 11; R, fo. 209.
5 ex *om.* R   9 irruerunt B   9–10 Gwalenses, Gwallie R   12 Gualensium *om.* B
**66** G, no. 23; Saltman, pp. 434–5; B, fo. 11; R, fo. 209v.

---

[1] No council in this period is recorded, but it is unlikely that none met in the whole period between 1143 and 1151. For Welsh affairs in these years, see Lloyd, II, 500 ff.   [2] Cf. II Cor. vi. 6.
[3] Taynton (Oxon) was held by Deerhurst Priory, a cell of St-Denis (*VN*, p. 605). Roderick was probably prior of Deerhurst (cf. *Monasticon*, II, 73).
[4] It seems to imply, indeed, that the case came to Theobald on appeal to his court. He gives judgement at Canterbury with the assistance and co-operation of five bishops named 'et multis aliis abbatibus et clericis...'.

The archbishop's settlement is addressed to A(lexander) bishop of Lincoln, who died on (or about) 20 February 1148, which gives a *terminus ad quem* for this letter. In it, as here, the archbishop is 'totius Anglie primas'.

Patri suo et domno Cantuariensi Dei gratia archiepiscopo et totius Anglie primati T(heobaldo) frater G(ilebertus) Gloecestrie dictus abbas, obedientiam humilem et de toto corde dilectionem.

Ad agendum quod inperastis quam plures amici nostri iam semel et iterum tertioque conuenimus, ut causam domni abbatis Rading(ensis) et fratrum eius 5 aduersus domnum Rodericum ceterosque beati Dionisii monacos plenius audiendo discuteremus. Causa itaque deducta in medium ad hunc finem usque perducta est. Conquerebantur Radingenses ecclesiam suam de Stantona parrochia de la Mora, que terra quedam est beati Dionisii, iniuste spoliatam fuisse. Asserebant enim predictam ecclesiam de Stantona in terra ⟨fo. 11 v⟩ illa de Mora, parrochialia iura tam 10 in spiritualibus quam in temporalibus continue et quiete triginta et eo amplius annis habuisse.[1] Huius rei testes producebant in medium quamplures monachos, sacerdotes, et clericos multos, honestos etiam laicos non paucos, probationi predicte possessionis, si eis adiudicaretur, paratissimos. Postulabant itaque Radingenses probationem suam suscipi seque in possessionem induci. Sed domnus Redericus et 15 qui cum eo stabant e contrario perorabant; aiebant enim super hac re Radingensium nec debere probationem suscipi nec ipsos oportere possessione predicta aliquatenus inuestiri. Hanc parrochiam in integrum de iure beati Dionisii esse dicebant et ad ecclesiam suam de Tentona non noua quadam usurpatione sed antiqua et longi temporis prescriptione pertinere. Constanter asserebant ecclesiam suam de Tantona 20 a prima fundatione sua plusquam sexaginta annis predictam possessionem continue et quiete possedisse; se etiam adhuc in ipsa actionis die eadem possessione inuestitos in ipsa tanquam in sua consistere. Asertionis etiam sue testes producebant domnum abbatem de Egnesham[2] et conuentus eius partem non modicam, aliosque sacerdotes, clericos, et quamplures laicos probationi iam dicte promptissimos. Quoniam igitur 25 in causis huiusmodi melior est affirmantis et possidentis quam solummodo repetentis conditio,[3] probationem possessionis sue postulabat domnus Rodericus suscipi, seque deinceps inconcussum si iustum foret dimitti. Cum itaque de singulis cum domno Hereford(ensi), decano Lond(oniensi), archidiacono Oxenefor(die) ceterisque aliis uiris qui conuenerant decerneremus, nulla data sententia prior 30 Rading(ensis) se ab archidiacono Oxenefor(die) et abbate de Egnesham, nescimus in quo, grauari conquerens, audientiam domni pape appellans iniuncte nobis finem imposuit sollicitudini. Vnde ne uestram que penes nos acta sunt possint latere prudentiam, uobis ista transcripsimus; quem munitum per omnia et esse semper incolumem preoptamus. Valete. 35

**66** 6 Rericum B    9 terram B    11 temporalibus] corporalibus B    14 itaque *om.* B 19, 20 Teintona R    25 iam dicte *om.* R    27 Redericus B    29, 31 Oxonie, Oxon' R 31 Egenesham R

[1] For the *longi temporis praescriptio* (see below) see *Decretum*, C. 16, q. 3, cc. 15–17; *JS Epp.* 132 n.
[2] Eynsham (Oxon).        [3] Cf. *Digest*, 50, 17, 154.

## 67 To Pope Eugenius III

[? 1145–8] He commends Master Roger of Pont l'Évêque, who is appealing to the Pope.

This letter cannot be earlier than 1145, when Eugenius became Pope. But one of the versions makes Gilbert bishop of Hereford, which would suggest a date between 1148 and 1153, when the Pope died. It is just possible that the letter was written *c.* 1148 and not used by Roger until later. But it is more likely that the heading preferred in the text is correct, and that the letter was written in or before 1148. In 1148 Roger became archdeacon of Canterbury, and it is probable that if he was already archdeacon his office would be here referred to (he is simply called a clerk of the archbishop); furthermore, in both places this letter accompanies no. 34, which also has the alternative title, and which certainly belongs to the period of Gilbert's abbacy at Gloucester.

Patri suo et domno summo Dei gratia pontifici E(ugenio) frater G(ilebertus) Gloecestrie dictus abbas, obedientiam et debitam patri caritatem.

Id modicum dilecte pater quod sumus amicorum nostrorum karitati negare non possumus, et communis pietas exigit ut alter alterius onera portantes[1] opem nobis
5 uicariam consilii simul et auxilii impendamus. Vnde licet apud maiestatem uestram nulla nos merita commendent, nec penes uos gratiam nobis ullam seruitia non inpensa locauerint, ex caritate tamen audemus ut, qui nec pro nobis digni audiri sumus, ad paternam misericordiam pro alio interpellaturi pie presumendo irrumpamus. Clericus enim dilecti filii uestri domni Cantuariensis archiepiscopi, magister
10 Rogerus de Ponte Episcopi, uestrum adit urgente necessitate presidium, ut ad tuenda ea que canonice possidet a uestra imploret serenitate patrocinium. Rogamus itaque ad ⟨B 1, fo. 10 v⟩ genua sanctitatis uestre corde prostrati, ut de fonte iustitie procedat et pietas, et eum quem apud apostolicam maiestatem commendari dignum credimus tam uita quam scientia suscipiatis in gratia et in iustis postula-
15 tionibus suis clementer exauditum remittatis. Sullimitatem uestram diu sibi suisque incolumem conseruet excelsa maiestas.

## 68 To Jocelin de Bohun, bishop of Salisbury

[? 1146–8] He is shortly going to visit the archbishop; he hopes for a chance to see the bishop of Salisbury on the way, preferably at Abingdon or Reading.

This letter cannot be earlier than 1142, the year of Jocelin's accession. If 'iter meum ad

---

**67** G, nos. 17, 97; B, fo. 10 (B1), fo. 157v (B2); R, fo. 208v (*spelling as* B1; *note in top margin of* B2: intercessorie ad domnum papam pro clerico ad curiam properante).
1 E(ugenio) *om.* B1; Dei gratia *om.* B2  1–2 frater...abbas frater G. Hereford' ecclesie minister B2  4 et...exigit *om.* B2  5 uestram maiestatem B2  6 merita] nostra *added* (*inserted*) B2  6 nobis *om.* B1  8 simus R  8 interpellari (*om.* pie) B2  10 R. R  10 adit *om.* B2  10 presidium] remedium (ut *om.*) B2  14 dignum...scientia] tam uita quam scientia dignum credimus B2  15 exauditum clementer B2  16 conseruet incolumem B2  16 maiestas] Amen *added in* B2
**68** G, no. 63; B, fo. 25v.

---

[1] Cf. Gal. vi. 2.

domnum archiepiscopum' refers to one of the occasions when he accompanied the archbishop across the channel, the letter must belong to 1146 or 1148.[1]

Patri suo et domino I(ocelino) S(aresberiensi) Dei gratia episcopo frater G(ilebertus) ecclesie beati Petri dictus abbas, penitenti ueniam non negare.

Iustus in exordio sermonis sui accusator est sui.[2] Quia ergo iustitie conformari desidero meipsum inprimis arguo. Quantum enim fuit in me maiestatem uestram et honorem meum in parte minui cum occurrenti michi humilitati uestre et 5 mansuetudini amplexu gratissimo et corde humillimo non occurri. Cur tamen supersederim? Si uestro michi daretur frui alloquio, ipse dicendo quam scribendo melius intimarem. Si que ergo pristine karitatis erga nos supersunt usquequaque reliquie, si iuxta mandatum Domini penitenti pectus episcopale non clauditur, precor ut in proximo cum iter meum ad domnum archiepiscopum dirigetur uestri 10 michi colloquii facultas non negetur. Quia uero locum diemque colloquii uobis statuendo nuper excessi, presumtiue reus non id amplius ago sed uestre totum uoluntati committo. Quid super hoc uestro sedeat arbitrio parce memor irarum si placet michi rescribatis. Triduum uero antequam uos ad locum destinatum uenire oporteat nuntium item meum habebitis. Quod si Abendune uel Redingis locum 15 dederitis meo plurimum labori parcetis. Valete.

## 69  To Robert de Bethune, bishop of Hereford

[*c.* May 1147] He gives the bishop the greetings of Pope and Curia and asks for stern action against the Lord Baderon (evidently of Monmouth)[3] and his wife.

Gilbert is known to have been to the papal Curia twice in his time as abbot: in 1146–7—he and Archbishop Theobald were with the Pope in May 1147—and in March 1148, at the Council of Rheims: see Appendix II. But on the latter occasion Robert de Bethune was also present; so this letter was presumably written from the Curia, or soon after Gilbert's departure from it, in 1147.

Patri suo et domno R(oberto) He(refordensi) Dei gratia episcopo frater G(ilebertus) G(loecestrie) dictus abbas, salutem et obedientiam.

Salutationem domni pape, totius etiam curie congratulationem, quorundam etiam suorum soliloquia, libenter uobis seorsum posita conquestione nuntiaremus, sed nos ad presens ad queri⟨fo. 28 v⟩moniam iniuriarum compellit atrocitas, ut 5 postquam multa sustinuimus seram saltem querelam apud iustitiam uestram deponamus. Seuit in nos domini Badoronis et uxoris eius plus iusto seuera potentia,

---

68  8 erga] ergo B
69  G, no. 74; B, fo. 28.

---

[1] 'Iter meum' suggests a personal visit to the archbishop, not attendance at a council.
[2] Cf. Prov. xviii. 17.
[3] The name is sufficiently rare for the identification to be confidently made. Cf. nos. 152, 302, 338, for evidence of better relations in later years between Gilbert and Baderon. Baderon of Monmouth's wife was a daughter of Gilbert FitzRichard de Clare, a great marcher lord, and the dispute may have arisen out of a disagreement on proprietary rights.

et cum eos nulla ex parte leserimus confractionibus et uerberibus, hominum etiam nostrorum incarcerationibus, rerumque direptionibus quod non rapuimus multi-
10 plici seruitute exoluere conpellimur. Cum itaque manifesta sunt hec iamiamque ad iudicium precedentia,[1] rogamus si placet ut nobis iustitiam super his exhibeatis, ipsamque exibendo a peccato ipsos, nos ab incomodo, defendatis. Valete.

## 70   To Uhtred, Bishop of Llandaff

[Second half of 1147] He protests that he has done nothing to the bishop's dishonour—quite the contrary, as the archbishop of Canterbury and the Pope and his entourage will witness. He asks the bishop to settle the case on tithes between Gloucester and Leofric[2] in a suitable way.

Nos. 70 and 71 both refer to the same dispute about tithes, presumably tithes pertaining to Llancarfan: no. 71 seems to be a more urgent reminder of the burden of 70. The reference to Pope and archbishop clearly refers to one of the occasions when Gilbert accompanied Theobald to the Curia; since Uhtred had died and been succeeded by Bishop Nicholas before the Council of Rheims met, the reference must be to the visit of c. May 1147, and these letters date from the second half of 1147. C. January 1148 is not impossible for no. 71.

Patri suo et domno V(ctredo) Land(auensi) Dei gratia episcopo frater G(ilebertus) G(loecestrie) dictus abbas, quoniam dies mali sunt uirtutem in infirmitate perficere.[3]

Testis michi pater dilecte ueritas est, et que michi non mentitur de me conscientia, quam puro corde et karitate non ficta[4] uos a prima uestri cognitione dilexerim, et
5 honori uestro simul et commodo sicubi quicquam potui sollicita circumspectione coadiutor semper et cooperator extiterim. Quod licet ad uos forte non peruenerit attamen istos non latuit, domnum scilicet Cantuariensem, domnum etiam papam et qui de latere eius sunt, in quorum presentia cum ipse adessem si de uobis aliquid sinistrum quandoque uentilatum est me et reclammante et aliqua uehementia
10 resistente non solum suppressum resedit sed uelut quedam mendacii nubes prorsus euanuit. Vt uerum fatear equidem si non uobis in multo seruiuimus attamen consciliauimus uobis potentum animos et bona que de uobis speramus nequaquam reticendo sed palam edicendo uos in ipsorum gratiam nec modicam nec quidem contempnendam induximus. Karitas enim nunquam excidit[5] et ipsa enim cum
15 perfecta est prossus nescit occasum. Hec uero est que facile nobis persuadet bene de uobis sperare per omnia et in quibus nobis iurisditio uestra necessaria est equitatem et iustitiam quadam confidentia postulare. Preces itaque sullimitati uestre porrigimus ut nostra de uobis non fraudetur spes et ut litem contestaturam super decimis

70 G, no. 56; B, fo. 23 v.
7 attm' B    15 prossus *i.e.* prorsus    18 litt'e (*as for* littere) contestantura B

---

[1] Cf. I Tim. v. 24, and pp. 46 n. 2, 89 n. 3.
[2] Leoric or Leofric, the 'monk' of Llancarfan: he probably bore the same name as Lifris, 'Master' of St Cadoc of Llancarfan, who wrote the first *Life of St Cadoc c.* 1100; he may even have been the same man, but was more probably a younger relation. See *CS*, pp. 287–9.
[3] Cf. Eph. v. 16; II Cor. xii. 9 (and also a reference to the bishop's illness; cf. no. 58).
[4] Cf. II Cor. vi. 6.                    [5] Cf. I Cor. xiii. 8.

quas a domno Leourico iuste requirimus ea diligentia terminetis ne nobis in ecclesie nostre detrimento turpi quadam mutilatione grauamen inferatur et ut uobis 20 tanquam patri et domno non solum a me sed a toto etiam nostro collegio gratiarum actio et debiti honoris exibitio referatur. Iudicium equilibre non recusamus. Ne tamen offendantur qui amici sunt rem magis honesta transactione finiri uellemus.[1] Valete semper in Christo Domino, dilecte pater.

## 71 To Uhtred, bishop of Llandaff

[Probably second half of 1147] A stiff reminder that the case against Leofric is still not settled (cf. no. 70).

Patri suo et domno H(uctredo) Land(auensi) Dei gratia episcopo frater G(ilebertus) G(loecestrie) dictus abbas, salutem.

Inportunus effectus sum sed uos me coegistis; petiui sed non accepi; pulsaui sed nondum aperuistis michi. Spero tamen quod pulsanti amico paterno tandem affectu aperietis nec panem petenti lapidem uel piscem aut ouum postulanti serpentem 5 porrigetis aut scorpionem.[2] Pacem a filio pacis et patre et domno et multis rerum experimentis amico postulamus. Leta michi dies non erit qua contra uos in iudicio sistere urgente etiam necessitate compellar. Agat ergo pontifex digna pontifice et si quid inter filios suos litis aut controuersie motum est ad pacis statum redigat uniuersa. Decimas a domno Leorico repetimus quibus inuestita fuit eclesia nostra et 10 absque iudicio spoliata. Iactura grauis est amittere que iustitia repetit manifesta. Cetera iuxta quod dixit uobis domnus Iocelinus[3] beneplacito uestro committemus. Vigilet hec cura circa patris et pastoris affectum ut a filiis condigno merito et gratiam reportet et seruitium. Valete.

## 72 To Bernard, abbot of Clairvaux

[c. 1147–8] He testifies, from what is common knowledge, to the formal steps leading up to the foundation of Kingswood Abbey. See Appendix IV.

The events Gilbert describes appear to lie well in the past:[4] since in fact they took place in 1139, the letter presumably belongs to the later years of his abbacy. Gilbert must be answering an inquiry from St Bernard; and it may be that the abbot of Gloucester was an obvious person to consult in such a case. But it is highly likely that Bernard and Gilbert met each other at the papal Curia in Paris in 1147 (cf. no. 70), and certain that both were present at Rheims in March 1148 (and cf. no. 75); and an acquaintance struck up on either occasion

71 G, no. 61; B, fo. 24v.
3 peti'i B
72 G, no. 68; B, fo. 26v.

---

[1] The implications of this sentence are not clear: it appears to mean that Gilbert would prefer a negotiated arrangement to a formal judgement, which seems surprising in the context.
[2] Cf. Matt. vii. 8–10 and Luc. xi. 10–12.   [3] Perhaps the same as in no. 39.
[4] During the years 1141–3 Milo of Gloucester would probably be called earl of Hereford; by the late 1140's it would be more natural to revert to his earlier style, correct for 1139.

would account satisfactorily for Bernard's inquiring from Gilbert, a Benedictine and an ex-Cluniac, rather than from one of the local Cistercians.

Adiutori Domini fidelissimo Bernardo Clareuall(ensi) abbati, frater G(ilebertus) G(loecestrie) dictus abbas, orationum utinam uestrarum participem me fieri.

Dignum est apud filios lucis si quid forte noctis interuenit ut plenius illuscescente claritate non solum dispareat sed etiam potius euanescat. Vnde quod apud nos nulli 5 fere dubium est serenitati uestre significamus ne forte in his que nouimus ueritatem in presentia uestra obscurari permittamus. Scimus enim Willelmum quondam abbatem Tinternie locum de Chingesuude quem nondum quisquam monachorum inhabitauerat ab eiusdem loci aduocato Willelmo ⟨de⟩ Berchelai assensu presidentium potestatum, imperatricis uidelicet et Milonis de Gloec(estria), nullo reclam- 10 mante suscepisse, edificasse, et de ipsa domo Tinternie conuentum in loco ipso instaurasse et iam statuto conuentu abbatem de eadem domo sua, Tomam uidelicet Tinterneie priorem, prefecisse. Deinde processu temporis predictus abbas Willelmus Tinternie, adhibito sibi karissimo fratre nostro Hamone abbate Bordesleie, ⟨fo. 27⟩ predictum etiam Thomam domno Wigornensi presentauit et ut in abbatem 15 benediceretur obtinuit; et ipsi deinceps ut filio, domui etiam de Chingeswde tanquam unice filie, prouidit in pluribus et subuenit. Cum itaque iuri suo renuntiare cuique liberum sit uideat Tinternensis ecclesia si iuri suo renuntiauit, si quod obtinebat abiecit, et a se quod susceperat alienauit. 'Etatem habet: loquatur ipsa de se.'[1] Nos quod apud nos celebre est et in ore ut dicam omnium uobis manifestare curauimus. 20 Incolumitatem uestram sibi in longa tempora profuturam conseruet omnipotens Dominus, in Christo dilecte pater.

## 73  To Abbot Edward and the monks of Reading

[c. 1147–8] He has heard that Serlo of Arundel is attempting to make an arrangement with Reading Abbey by which he will grant the church of Berkeley (Glos) to the abbey for a consideration. Some of what he claims to possess is not his to give: the churches of Cam and Arlingham are Gloucester's, and their clerk Reginald has a prebend in Berkeley in no way subject to Serlo.

The fate of the collegiate church of Berkeley (formerly a convent of nuns) is one of the strangest stories of the anarchy. It may be that several lay proprietors had acquired a right to different members of the group of churches subject to Berkeley—the Berkeley 'Hernesse';[2] or simply that a number of men made capital out of the confusion of the anarchy. The effect in either case was the dismemberment of the group of churches, and a series of disputes between their new owners. Among the ultimate beneficiaries were the abbeys of Gloucester, Bristol and Reading, and Reading seems to have had the largest slice of the cake. One of Reading's benefactors was Queen Adela, widow of Henry I, whose charter of donation can be dated

73 G, no. 55; B, fo. 23.

---

[1] Joh. ix. 21.
[2] Or district. This story is discussed in CS, pp. 280–2, on which the following is based; the account there given needs some correction, as has been shown by Dr B. Kemp of the University of Reading, who very kindly made his findings available to us.

1147–50. Her donation was a confirmation of a grant made by one Master Serlo, evidently the Serlo of Arundel of this letter; and this circumstance, and the fact that she was lady of the honour of Arundel, strongly suggest that Serlo was her protégé. Thus Serlo can be identified with Master Serlo, the queen's clerk, who occurs in 1136 and 1147;[1] and this letter can be dated, with the queen's charter, *c.* 1147–8.

Patri suo karissimo E(dwardo) Radingensi Dei gratia abbati omnibusque Radingensis ecclesie filiis frater G(ilebertus) G(loecestrie) dictus abbas et hi quorum ipse ministerio deputatus est, salutem et dilectionem.

Peruenit ad nos karissimi magistrum Serlonem de Arundel crebra uos prece sollicitare ut de ecclesia de Berchalaie contractum aliquem cum eo ineatis et quedam 5 que inter uos nominata sunt sibi concedendo predictam ecclesiam amodo habeatis. Asserit etiam (ut audimus) se quedam possidere que non possidet et ostensione quarundam cartarum quas pretendit uos in credulitatem eorum que affirmat inducit. Vnde uestram premonemus dilectionem ut sic dictis eius adquiescatis ne inconsiderata quadam commutatione dampnum quod facile reformari nequeat 10 incurratis. Certum enim habeatis nos ecclesia de Camme et ecclesia de Herlingeham et omnibus que ad eam pertinent apostolica auctoritate inuestitos esse et uos nec ⟨fo. 23 v⟩ commutatione aliqua nec ullo domni Serlonis dono uel cuiuscumque assensu aliquid in eis nisi cum summa nostri iniuria uendicare aliquatenus posse. Preterea et illud noueritis clericum nostrum Reginaldum in ecclesia de Berchelaie 15 prebendam unam habere et Serloni in nullo subiectum esse. Vnde si de ecclesia in qua iste parem Serloni personatum habet ipso non solum nolente immo et reclamante commutationem feceritis, uestrum magis libitum quam quicquam iuri congruum facietis; nam que publici iuris sunt nullius numerantur in bonis nec contractus unius transferre potest in re communi dominium. Vos nequaquam latere uolumus 20 predictum Reginaldum anno preterito cum eum Serlo de his que uobis modo uendicat fatigaret ad domnum papam appellasse et seipsum statuto die presentasse et cum domnus Serlo non apparuerit, inuestitum suis cum gratia domni pape ad propria remeasse. Vt uero quod summum est non taceam certum uobis esse non dubito quod ecclesiam optinere contractus illicitus est. Vnde preces sedulo discre- 25 tioni uestre porrigimus ut in re ista sic omnia moderetis ut nec religioni uestre notam inferatis nec habitam hactenus inter nos karitatem emolumento facili minuatis. Valete.

**73** 19 iuri B    23 non] nec B (*some words after* nec *may be missing*)    26 moderitis B

---

[1] Master Serlo of Arundel is probably to be identified with Master Serlo, chaplain to Queen Adela, who occurs in 1136 and 1147 (A. C. Friend in *Bulletin Du Cange*, XXIV (1954), 89; *Cart. Chichester*, no. 95; *Acta Chichester*, no. 55). Friend tentatively suggested that Master Serlo might be Serlo of Wilton, the poet; the present letter, in which he is called Serlo of Arundel, makes this identification unlikely.

## 74 To Hywarth(?) sacrist, Master John and the whole chapter of St Davids

[April–May 1148] The case between Gloucester and the monks of Sherborne (?) about the church of St Ishmael[1] has been suspended by the death of the bishop of St Davids:[2] he asks for it to stay in suspense until a new bishop has been appointed.

Nos. 74–8 were written in the aftermath of the Council of Rheims. The main session of the council opened on 21 March; the Pope finally left Rheims *c.* 19 April. After the council Theobald returned to England, but was forced into exile again, still accompanied by Gilbert (cf. no. 78). Nos. 74 and 75 were both written in England: 'we have returned swiftly by God's good help' (75); 'we are wearied by our journey, recently completed' (74). They can be dated *c.* April–May 1148.

Three pieces of business arising from the Council of Rheims claimed Gilbert's immediate attention: the case with the monks of Sherborne, which had been suspended by the death of the bishop of St Davids; the long-standing suit between his abbey and the archbishop of York, which had been postponed by the advice of the abbot of Clairvaux (St Bernard) and at the Pope's wish until the new archbishop, Henry Murdac, was allowed to take over his see (75); and the suspension of the bishops who had failed to answer the Pope's summons to the council (75–6). In no. 75 Gilbert gives his uncle Robert de Chesney a list of the bishops, all of whom (save the bishop of Winchester) could expect a speedy release from the archbishop. In no. 76 he writes to one of them, the bishop of Bath, giving the same message, and asking him to pass it on to the bishop of Exeter. No. 76 was evidently written about the same time as 75.

Frater G(ilebertus) G(loecestrie) Dei gratia dictus abbas amicis suis Hieuardo sacriste ecclesie sancti Dauid et magistro Iohanni et toti capitulo, salutem et dilectionem.

Speramus uestram non latere prudentiam quod mandatum mandatoris mor⟨t⟩e

**74** G, no. 75; B, fo. 28 v.
1 Hienardo B

---

[1] The Church of St Ishmael, Penallt, near Kidwelly, Carmarthenshire, was given to Gloucester by Maurice of London as part of the endowment of Ewenny priory. (*Cart. Gloucester*, I, 76; J. Conway Davies in *Nat. Library of Wales Journal*, III (1943–4), 109–10, 136, 129). The church appears in two of Maurice's charters, one before, one after 1148; but the original of the second (see facsimile, art. cit., facing p. 109) seems to be written in a very late twelfth-century hand, and one other charter of Maurice's aroused Dr Conway Davies's suspicions (p. 110). It is possible, therefore, that some of the early Ewenny charters are forgeries; but St Ishmael's church only plays a small part in the series, and the forgery must be later than the dispute discussed in this letter.

The rival house is given in the manuscript as *Ferneleia*, which suggests Monkton Farleigh (Wilts), a Cluniac priory dependent on Lewes. But there is no evidence that the latter held any property in the neighbourhood of Kidwelly (cf. *Monasticon*, v, 24–32), whereas Sherborne abbey (Dorset) is known to have had a claim on St Ishmael's, as part of the endowment of Kidwelly priory: it was granted by Richard, son of William, before 1148 and later confirmed by Pope Alexander III (*Monasticon*, IV, 65). It therefore seems likely that *Ferneleia* is an error for Sherborne, unless the identification of the church of St Ishmael in the Ewenny and Kidwelly documents is itself an error.

[2] Bishop Bernard probably died on 22 April 1148 (*SEBC*, p. 218 n.).

finitur. Vnde si mandatum aliquod a domno et patre uestro bone memorie episcopo 5
Bernardo super causa que de ecclesia sancti Ismaelis inter nos et monacos de Ferneleia uentilatur constat illud re adhuc manente integra episcopi eiusdem decessu
expirasse. Nos itaque cum uos adeundi super hoc nulla cogat necessitas monet
tamen uoluntas et suadet amicitia uestrum super eadem causa iudicium si uobis
tantum iniunctum est aut ad uestrum spectat officium non declinare. Set quia 10
confecto nuper fatigati sumus itinere et negotiis domni pape non solum magnis
immo et multis ocupamur rogamus ut ob ipsius reuerentiam nos et nostra in
presenti pace esse permittatis et presentem actionem usque ad episcopi in ecclesia
uestra sustitutionem differatis. Valete, et amicum iusta postulantem audire non
omitt⟨it⟩e.                                                                                  15

## 75   To Robert de Chesney, archdeacon of Leicester [1]

[April–May 1148] He discusses various matters (arising from the Council of Rheims); the
postponement of his case against the archbishop of York; the suspension of several bishops by
the Pope, especially the bishop of Winchester; the granting of full power for the affairs of
the see of Lincoln to the archbishop of Canterbury;[2] and the repudiation of three abbots (as
candidates for the see of Lincoln).

Rodberto Lincolniensi archidiacono karissimo suo, suus G⟨ilebertus⟩ ueram et
ualituram in tempora prosperitatem.

Actio cause nostre usque ad aduentum domni Eboracensis in Angliam consilio
domni Clareualensis et domni pape uoluntate dilata est. Omnibus itaque in integritate manentibus sani pariter et alacres Domino per omnia bene iuuante rediuimus, 5
domno Eboracensi post quadragesimum ab aduentu suo diem si sibi placuerit in
presentia et curia domni regis S⟨tephani⟩ responsuri. Dunelmensis, Wigornensis,
Bathoniensis, Exoniensis, et precipue Wintoniensis ab omni officio episcopali
suspensi sunt, gratiam fortassis in posterum per bonos nuntios habituri. Domnus
Cantuariensis et alii quamplures episcopi et nos omnes pro domno Wintoniensi 10

---

**74** 15 omitte B
**75** G, no. 76; B, fo. 28 v.

---

[1] The intimate tone makes the archdeacon of Leicester, Gilbert's uncle, much more likely
than Robert, archdeacon of Lincoln.

[2] This no doubt refers to the vacancy in the see: Bishop Alexander died in February; Robert de
Chesney himself succeeded in December (see no. 80 and note). Henry of Blois and his brother
the king evidently tried to place a nephew or protégé at Lincoln. Henry de Sully, monk of
Cluny and abbot of Fécamp, 1140–87, was their nephew; Hugh, monk of Tiron and abbot
of St Benet's Hulme, from before 1146 until c. 1150 (later abbot of Chertsey and Lagny-sur-
Marne), was their nephew, an illegitimate son of Count Theobald; Gervase, abbot of
Westminster, was the king's illegitimate son. On Henry, see *Gallia Christiana*, XI, 209;
Orderic, V, 123 and note; John of Worcester, p. 61; Torigny, p. 139; also ed. Delisle, II, 149,
193; *HF*, XIII, 254, 289, 76; XVIII, 358; his obit is recorded on 10 January in the obituary of
St Benigne, Dijon, Montfaucon, *Bibliotheca bibliothecarum*, II, 1160. For Hugh, see *Reg. Hulme*,
II, 193 ff.; *Cart. Chertsey*, II, p. x. For Gervase, see Biog. Index, *s.v.* Westminster. On the
suspension of the bishops and their release (except for Winchester) by Archbishop Theobald,
see JS *HP* (C), pp. 10–11, 78 ff., (P), pp. 11–12, 80 ff.

supplicantes in nullo prorsus auditi sumus; sed quod nos minus potuimus comes Theobaldus instantia nuntiorum episcopi sperat obtinere. Domnus papa super his que ad ecclesiam uestram spectant domno Wintoniensi in nullo penitus adquiescens plenitudinem potestatis in consulendo ecclesie uestre domno Cantuar⟨iensi⟩ con-
15 cessit, ut in omnibus que ad id spectant domno Cantuariensi tanquam domno pape obediatis. Litteras domni pape super his Robertus Foliot ante dicessum nostrum iam inpetratas uobis allaturus est. Agatis itaque cum fiducia. Quod enim domno Wintoniensi super hac re magis placuerit hoc domno pape per omnia ⟨fo. 29⟩ displicebit. Fiscamensem, Hulmensem, de Westmustier illum depulsat domnus
20 papa, iam nunc multa cum indignatione et seueritate reprobauit. Valete.

## 76 To Robert, bishop of Bath

[April–May 1148] The archbishop of Canterbury has been empowered by the Pope to release the bishops from their suspension (see no. 75); Gilbert asks him to inform the bishop of Exeter.

Venerabili domno fratrique karissimo Rodberto Bathoniensi Dei gratia episcopo frater G(ilebertus) G(loecestrie) dictus abbas salutem.

   Preueniente nos in multis gratia uestra iuste se uobis offerunt et presentant seruitia nostra. Si quid enim sumus aut scimus aut possumus hoc honori uestro esse
5 et scire et posse desideramus. Promto igitur ac libenti animo notificamus uobis quod commodo uestro et honori profuturum speramus. A domno papa domno Cantuariensi creditum est et commissum ut iuxta quod inter eos dispensatum est non solum abbates sed et episcopos terre istius possit ab ea qua tenentur apostolica sententia relaxare. In quo uobis a Domino prouisum esse confidimus, ne maris et
10 montium et exterarum regionum discrimina experiri oporteat, cui remedium oportunum in ipso domni archiepiscopi aduentu Domino sic disponente accelerat. Dilectioni uestre suggerente caritate istud notificandum duximus, ut sic et uobis iuxta hoc prouideatis et id si placet domno Exoniensi domno et amico nostro karissimo nuntietis. Valete, et me uestros precor inter amicos habete et reputate.

## 77 To the canons of Hereford

[April–September 1148] Acting as vicar of the diocese of Hereford, and on the authority of Pope and archbishop, Gilbert instructs the chapter to publish an interdict throughout the diocese, on account of the offences of the earl of Hereford.

   The bishop of Hereford, Robert de Bethune, went to Rheims, fell sick and died there on 16 April. The affairs of the diocese were put into Gilbert's hands by Pope and archbishop; and some time between 16 April and his own consecration to the see on 5 September Gilbert wrote this letter to the chapter.

G(ilebertus) G(loecestrie) dictus abbas et Herefordensis ecclesie mandato domni pape uicarius, dilectis fratribus suis omnibus Herefordensis ecclesie canonicis, salutem et dilectionem.

75 16 domni domni pape B    19 Hulmensem. illum de Westmustier illum B
76 G, no. 77; B, fo. 29.
77 G, no. 78; B, fo. 29.

Quoniam dilectissimi comitem Herefordie semel et iterum, tertioque commoni- tum, ab errore uie sue pessime reuocare non possumus, hoc solum nobis restat ut 5 ipsius audaciam ecclesiastica iustitia compescamus. Vnde uobis, auctoritate domni pape et domni Cantuariensis iniungimus ut statim ex quo litteras nostras susce- peritis, a diuinis officiis, excepto baptismo et confessione et uiatico, cessetis, et quia lugente matre filias gaudere non oportet, mandamus uobis ut sententiam eandem in tota parochia uestra denuntietis et firmiter teneri faciatis. Valete.    10

## 78   To Pope Eugenius III

[c. August 1148] He describes how he and the archbishop of Canterbury witnessed the election of Hugh archdeacon of Arras as bishop of that see; commends the elect to the Pope; and asks him to give the elect the reward he has deserved.

Some time about May or June 1148 Archbishop Theobald was forced to return to the continent; he was accompanied, once again, by Gilbert. This letter shows that they were in Arras in July, and must have been written soon after—certainly before Gilbert's own con- secration on 5 September.

Alvisus, bishop of Arras, had gone on the Second Crusade with Louis VII, and died at Philippopolis on 6 September 1147.[1] We gather from Gilbert's letter that Master Hugh, archdeacon of Arras, was elected to succeed him in or shortly before July 1148. Thierry, count of Flanders, wrote to Abbot Suger, the celebrated French royal minister, to arrange for the confirmation of Hugh's election. But it would appear that an appeal was made to the Pope immediately before or immediately after the election took place. In October or November 1148 Pope Eugenius III wrote to the bishops of Auxerre and Soissons to quash the election if made after the appeal.[2] What lay behind the dispute is unknown, but it would appear that the appeal, on whatever ground, was upheld, since Hugh's election must ulti- mately have been quashed. It was the appeal, no doubt, which occasioned Gilbert's letter.

The dispute seems to have lingered on for two or three years: it was not until 1151 that Godescalc, abbot of Mont-Saint-Martin, was elected and consecrated to the see of Arras.

Patri suo et domno summo pontifici E(ugenio) frater G(ilebertus) dictus abbas, dies utinam bonos et in longum beata tempora.

Sullimitati uestre, dilecte pater, rem notam facimus quam ecclesie necessitati profuturam, iuuante Domino, uestra in hoc fauente gratia confidimus. Nam cum filio uestro domino et patre nostro karissimo domno Cantuariensi diebus exilii sui 5 commorantes utpote sedem certam aut locum proprium non habentes, sed nego- tiorum necessitate de loco ad locum demigrantes, Attrebatum Iulio mense perueni- mus. Vbi desiderio mirabili totius fere cleri et populi concordia uota repperimus in electione dilecti fratris nostri Hugonis, ipsius Attrabatensis ecclesie archidiaconi. Quem ab ineunte etate tota fere uita nostra cognitum, primo conuersationis 10

**78** G, no. 73; B, fo. 28.

---

[1] Odo of Deuil, *De profectione Ludovici VII in orientem*, ed. V. G. Berry (New York, 1948), pp. 44–6.

[2] *HF*, xv, 519, 452 (= JL 9306); on Godescalc and his succession see *HF*, xiii, 275, 332, 471, 506. It looks as if a part of the chapter of Arras may have appealed *ad cautelam*, as in the Langres election a few years earlier: see *GF*, p. 166 n.

honeste discipulum, post nota satis auctoritate magistrum in publicas gratulationes susceptum, ad ultimum ecclesie Attrabatensis archidiaconum illesam bone opinionis famam continuasse scimus et scripto presenti secure testificamur, in quod multorum religiosorum testimonia concordare non ambigimus. Vnde quantum audet apud
15 maiestatem uestram caram nobis et semper honorandam paruitas nostra presumere, rogamus ut quem in humilitate sua respexit Dominus, uos ea qua uobis omnes anteire datum est benignitate respiciatis, et data uobis auctoritate a Domino uirtutem in ipso remuneretis, eatenus ut unius exemplo in religionis amorem cultumque uirtutis quamplurimos accendatis. Inexpugnabili muro suo circumcingat uos
20 Dominus, et armis sue potentie protegat semper, in ipso dilecte pater. Valete.

**78** 14 reliosorum B

# II

# LETTERS OF GILBERT FOLIOT AS BISHOP OF HEREFORD
## 1148–1163

Nos. 79–143

## 79 To Theobald, archbishop of Canterbury

[Probably late 1148] The archbishop is suffering persecution: Gilbert asks for news and offers asylum.

Archbishop Theobald was twice persecuted by King Stephen, in 1148 and 1152.[1] The implication of the letter is that Gilbert's neighbourhood would be a refuge from Theobald's persecutors, which suggests that the Angevin power was still in being.[2] This and the fact that Theobald is addressed as primate but not legate (see Appendix II) suggest 1148 rather than 1152.

'Expectans expectaui iamdiu domnum meum...desiderans uidere uos et alloqui.' Evidently a personal visit from the archbishop was in prospect, or anyway possible. In fact Theobald visited Worcester early in 1149: he and Gilbert were witnesses to a charter there on 26 January.[3] It was apparently no more than a transitory visit. But it seems likely that when this letter was written (late 1148) a plan had been arranged for Theobald to settle in the Angevin lands in the west on his return from exile. The plan (if it existed) would help to explain Stephen's speedy reconciliation with Theobald c. October 1148.

Patri suo et domno Cant(uariensi) Dei gratia archiepiscopo et totius Anglie primati T(heobaldo), suus G(ilebertus) Herefordensis ecclesie minister, in tribulatione non deficere.

Expectans expectaui iamdiu domnum meum sperans a uestra sullimitate nuntium aliquem delegari qui michi prospera uel aduersa nuntiando uel de aduersis tristem 5 redderet uel de letis exilararet. Nam si ea caritatis est plenitudo ut cum fratre quolibet infirmante infirmari uel cum quis scandalizatur uri oporteat, cum patrem nostrum et domnum, immo nostrum in Christo caput, concuti, fatigari, turbari cernimus, quid iam restat nisi non tantum infirmari aut uri, uerum intus intimi flamma zeli medullitus concremari? Si itaque nondum surrexit Dominus ut uentis 10 imperet et mari, si procella uestra nondum in auram statuta est, summo ut michi uidetur opere necessarium ⟨fo. 19v⟩ est ut sacrum pectus uestrum omnis armatura fortium muniat et hostis quanto insurgit acrior eo uos acriorem et Sancti Spiritus igne feruentiorem inueniat. Non enim nouum est aut insolitum Egyptios Israel Caldeos Ierusalem infestare. Ait Christus in Apostolo: 'Omnes qui uolunt pie in 15 Christo uiuere persecutionem patientur.'[4] Sed per eundem ipse loquitur: 'Quod leue est aut momentaneum tribulationis nostre supra modum eterne glorie pondus operatur in nobis.'[5] Persecutionem patienti propter iustitiam non leue aliquid sed regnum celorum repromittitur. Amictitur Helyas pallio dum persequentium

**79** G, no. 83; B, fo. 19.

---

[1] Saltman, pp. 25 ff., 37; JS *Epp.* I, p. xv, n. 2; see *GF*, pp. 89 ff. These were the only two occasions, in Stephen's later years, when Theobald was forced into exile.

[2] The empress left in 1148, and Stephen's power was gradually reasserted. He was never, however, in complete control of the country—some of the earls and barons were 'never my men' (so the treaty of 1153, Delisle–Berger, I, 63; cited A. L. Poole, *From Domesday Book to Magna Carta* (Oxford, 1951), p. 150).

[3] Saltman, p. 546 (it is just possible that the dating clause means 1150, not 1149).

[4] II Tim. iii. 12.                    [5] II Cor. iv. 17.

20 declinat rabiem et stans in spelunce hostio gloriam Domini speculatur.[1] Vobis quoque corona glorie repromittitur, quam reddet uobis in illa die iustus iudex. Inpatiens mei factus sum desiderans uidere uos et alloqui, uel aliquid audire a uobis quo de his que circa uos sunt certior efficerer. Parati sunt principes nostri, presto sunt et ecclesie nostre uos (si sic opus est) non solum suscipere sed et in amplexus 25 uobis gratanter occurrere et de suis quicquid potuerint ministrare. Nollem tamen hoc sed si necesse est beniuolos et ad omnia paratos habebitis. Obsecro dilecte pater michi litteras uestras non negari et in aliquo uoluntatem uestram et statum et consilium aperiri. Valere uos optamus in Domino et ipsi per omnia complacere.

## 80   To Pope Eugenius III

[Late December 1148] After referring to the part the Pope had played in his promotion, Gilbert asks for assistance in reclaiming property alienated by his predecessor in the see, and announces that Robert archdeacon of (Leicester) has been elected bishop of Lincoln, and received the archbishop's consent.

Alexander bishop of Lincoln died on 20 February 1148, and in December the chapter eventually chose Gilbert's uncle Robert de Chesney, archdeacon of Leicester, to succeed him. It is evident that his election led to a dispute between the chapter and the higher powers—the bishop of Winchester, perhaps supported by his brother the king. Hence the interest of the Pope in the affair. We learn from no. 75 that the bishop of Winchester had been attempting to place another of his nephews or protégés—the abbot of Fécamp (Henry de Sully), of Hulme (Hugh of Blois) or of Westminster (Gervase of Blois). The Pope condemned these suggestions, and gave Theobald full authority to settle the affair.[2] The formal election took place at Westminster in the presence of the king and queen and eight bishops; on the following Saturday the bishops elect of Lincoln and St Davids were ordained priests at Canterbury by the archbishop; on the next day (Sunday, 19 December) they were consecrated bishops.[3]

The two letters 80 and 81 are written in very similar terms, and clearly refer to the same stage in the transaction. They must have been written very soon after 19 December.[4] Since they are in fact duplicates,[5] it is doubtful if both were sent. Possibly 80 was the first draft, from which the business of the Lincoln election was abstracted to form a separate letter.

Patri suo et domno summo pontifici Eugenio G(ilebertus) H(erefordensis) ecclesie minister, pedibus sanctis conculcato Satan triumphare semper in Domino.

Sicut domno meo placuit ita factum est et ad iussionem uestram michi manus est consecrationis imposita et Her(efordensis) ecclesie cura commissa. ⟨fo. 20v⟩ Inde 5 est quod attentius spectant oculi nostri ad uos, a uestra sullimitate sperantes et exspectantes auxilium unde habuimus honoris et ordinis incrementum. Clamat et conqueritur ecclesia nostra predecessorem nostrum bone memorie domnum Robertum episcopum quatuor prebendas suas ad ecclesiam Lantonie transtulisse, et

80 G, no. 87; B, fo. 20.

[1] Cf. III Reg. xix. 9 ff., esp. 14.                    [2] Cf. Saltman, p. 106.
[3] Profession roll, *Trans. St Paul's Ecclesiological Soc.* VII (1911–15), 169; Hunt., p. 281; Gervase, I, 138; cf. Diceto, I, 258; Saltman, pp. 106–7.
[4] 81 was written wholly, and 80 partly, to enlist papal support and confirmation for the new bishop.                    [5] See *GF*, p. 27.

pre nimietate amoris quo erga Lanton(iam) ut ipsos ampliaret tenebatur, proprios
clericos eisdem quatuor prebendis spoliasse.[1] Vnde serenitati uestre supplicamus 10
humiliter si maiestatem uestram predicti Lanton(ienses) adierint, ne uestra auctoritate
eis firmetur quod clerici nostri sibi fuisse iniuste ablatum conquerentur. Duo etiam
castella ecclesie nostre idem predecessor noster nobilissimis uiris comiti de Mellent
et Hugoni de Mortemer magno ecclesie ipsius incommodo et detrimento concessit.[2]
Que quia male distracta sunt, et quantum ad nos quasi ad desperationem alienata 15
sunt, uestra petimus auctoritate reuocentur.

Quod uero ad Lincoln(iensem) ecclesiam spectat utpote quod audiuimus et
uidimus[3] secure loquimur et testificamur. Eiusdem enim ecclesie clerus et populus
religiosarum episcopatus personarum unanimi consensu, nullo prorsus contradicente, domnum Robertum eiusdem ecclesie archidiaconum sibi in episcopum 20
elegerunt, et electionem domno Cantuariensi presentantes propter multas et
necessarias causas optinuerunt. Quod uestro petimus cumulari examine quatinus ei
manum gratie porrigendo ipsum in quo positus est stabiliatis, et de cetero fidelem
filium, et ad omnem patris sui uoluntatem promtissimum habeatis. Illesa nobis et
inoffensa maiestas uestra seruetur in secula, in Christo dilecte pater. 25

## 81  To Pope Eugenius III

[Late December 1148] He describes the election and consecration of Robert archdeacon of
Leicester as bishop of Lincoln, and commends the person of the new bishop.

Patri suo et domno summo pontifici E(ugenio) G(ilebertus) H(erefordensis)
ecclesie minister, deuotum et debitum totius obedientie famulatum.

Quia caritati dilecte pater plurimum expedit obedire ideo petitioni Lincoln(iensis) ecclesie negare non possumus, quin ea que de negotio eius ipsi presentes uidimus
et audiuimus[4] sullimitati uestre notificemus. Cum enim Lund(onie) cum patre 5
nostro domno Cantuar(iensi) et fratribus et coepiscopis nostris quamplurimis
essemus, uidimus decanum et cantorem et archidiac(onos),[5] omnes etiam ipsius

---

**80**  12 ablata B    22 cumalari (*corrected by modern hand*) B    23 stabilitatis B
**81** G, no. 88; B, fo. 20v.

---

[1] Bishop Robert had been canon and prior of Llanthony: the assistance he gave to the priory is
described in his life by William of Wycombe, *Anglia Sacra*, II, 312–13 (four prebends, the
church of Frome, and the village and church of Prestbury, during his lifetime).

[2] Waleran count of Meulan, twin brother of Robert earl of Leicester (see Biog. Index), count
of Meulan, 1118–66, also earl of Worcester from 1138 (on him see G. H. White, in *Trans.
Royal Hist. Soc.* 4th series, XVII (1934), 19–48, also *ibid.* XIII (1930), 51 ff.); and Hugh de
Mortimer, son of Ralph de Mortimer, the Domesday tenant-in-chief; Hugh succeeded his
father after 1104 and died *c.* 1148–50 (*CP*, IX, 267–9).

[3] Cf. I Joh. i. 1–3.          [4] Cf. *ibid.*

[5] Adelelm, dean *c.* 1142–*c.* 1165; Roger D'Ameri, precentor, 1147/8–1160/1; and presumably
a group of archdeacons of the Lincoln diocese (unless one should read *archidiaconum*). Adelelm
may well be the same as the royal treasurer of that name (probably from 1133, occurs 1137)
(Richardson and Sayles, pp. 220–1; Dean Adelelm and A(d)elelm archdeacon of Dorset—
see no. 56—were clearly distinct, and the identification with the dean seems the more probable;
the treasurer is known to have had links with Lincoln, although a royal treasurer in the 1130's

Linc(olniensis) ecclesie canonicos, cum religiosarum personarum eiusdem episcopatus non modica multitudine, omnes in hoc instantissime perseuerare ut liceret eis
10 consilio domni Cantuar(iensis) Robertum archidiaconum Leicest(rie) in patrem et
episcopum sibi eligere. Cumque domnus Cantuar(iensis) in ipsum omnium con-
currere uota conspiceret, nolens predictam ecclesiam turbari amplius aut magis
atteri, petitioni eorum episcoporum consilio assensum prebuit et predictum
archidiaconum ingenti postulantium gratia et fauore episcopum consecrauit. Cuius
15 et doctrine et uite et intus et foris testimonium bonum est, et in officio quo ministrauit hactenus conspicua gratia. Vnde uestram, reuerende pater, precamur benignitatem, ut quod ei sola suffragante iustitia debetur, id nostre paruitatis precibus
facilius et benignius assequatur. Valeat sanctitas uestra in Christo dilecte pater.

## 82   To Henry Murdac, archbishop of York

[1148–53] On behalf of Gilbert, precentor of Hereford and canon of York.

The archbishop died on 14 October 1153.

Patri suo et domno H(enrico) Eborac(ensi) Dei gratia archiepiscopo frater G(ilebertus) Herefordie dictus episcopus, sincere diligentis affectum et gratanter obsequentis
officium.

Caritas quandoque presumtuosa est et quod alteri facile rogata concederet hoc
5 apud dominum et amicum impetrare non desperat. De ipsa itaque que intra cordis
uestri dominatur caritate plurimum confidentes preces sullimitati uestre porrigimus,
ut communi amico et canonico uestro Gilb(erto) ecclesie nostre precentori uos
benignum et misericordem exibeatis, et si quid aduersum uos ab aliquo suorum
ipso ignorante et nolente commissum est, in clericum uestrum et in quantum potest
10 amicum commissi culpam non refundatis. Ipse enim et uos et diligentes uos diligit,
et si quis suorum aduersatur uobis aut extollitur contra uos hunc, quicumque ipse
est, et abdicare et eliminare paratus est. Si itaque sibi non sua sed alterius culpa
ablata restitueretis, iustitie non excederetis fines, et tam comitem Herefor(densem)
quam nos, qui pro illo pariter excellentie uestre supplicamus, uobis amplioris gratie
15 debitores efficeretis. More nichilominus ipsius ambo rogamus ueniam ut in hoc
aculeos seueritatis uestre non sentiat, in quo uoluntatis sue non difficultas solum
uerum impossibilitas preiudicat. Adiuuante Domino et itineris sibi securitatem
prouidente in proximo ueniet ad uos, per omnia uobis tanquam patri et domno
libentissime pariturus. Valete et ab amicorum uestrorum petitione faciem nolite
20 auertere, et ne sepe pro amico rogare oporteat, diem aduentui eius Natale Domini
constituite.

**82** G, no. 82; B, fo. 19.    13 ? excideretis B

might very well have links with both Lincoln and Salisbury). Adelelm succeeded Philip de
Harcourt, who became bishop of Bayeux in 1142 (cf. *Monasticon*, VI (ii), 820); Adelelm died
on 24 February in some year later than 1163, but not later than 1166 (*Giraldi Cambrensis Opera*,
VII, 155; *Reg. Lincoln*, I, no. 255, III, no. 939; *Cart. Oseney*, VI, 147). On the precentor, see
*EHR*, XXXV (1920), 212–14; *Reg. Lincoln*, VII, 203 n.

## 83 To Pope Eugenius III

[1148–53] He asks for a papal privilege to confirm the union of the churches of St Guthlac and St Peter in Hereford to form a monastic house dependent on Gloucester.[1]

Nos. 83–6 are all addressed to Pope Eugenius III who died on 8 July 1153.

Patri suo et domno summo Dei gratia pontifici Eug(enio) G(ilebertus) Herefordensis ecclesie minister, obedientiam humilem et debitam patri karitatem.

Cum paruitati nostre, dilecte pater, ecclesia Dei aliqua sui portione Domino sic operante commissa sit, eiusdem prouidere et inuigilare commodis ipsa nobis a Domino credita dispensatio compellit. Quoniam uero que statuuntur a nobis nisi 5 apostolica auctoritate fulciantur minus firma sunt sublimitati uestre preces humili deuotione porrigimus ut quod ad honorem Dei et cultum eius ampliandum de ecclesia sancti Guthlaci de Herefordia a nobis actum est, hoc auctoritas uestra corroboret suoque priuilegio confirmet. Ecclesiam enim illam de manu laica multo tandem labore eruimus et quia in eadem minus officiose Domino seruiebatur, ipsam 10 dilecto filio nostro Hamelino, abbati Gloec(estrie) et ecclesie sancti Petri, cui idem preesse dinoscitur, assensu clericorum eiusdem ecclesie, capitulo etiam nostro id consentiente et uolente, concessimus, et tam ipsam quam ecclesiam sancti Petri de Herefordia, diu ante a predictis monacis habitam, in corpus unum adunare curauimus et conuentum monachorum ibidem deuote ministrantium Domino iamiam 15 instaurauimus. Quod quia Domino credimus placere, audemus serenitati uestre supplicare ut quod a nobis intentione recta actum est soloque pietatis intuitu, hoc serenitas uestra stabiliat et ecclesie sancti Petri de Gloec(estria) in perpetuum confirmet. Glorificetur Deus in uobis uestrique corona meriti semper augeatur in Domino, in Christo dilecte pater. 20

## 84 To Pope Eugenius III

[1148–53] On behalf of Lewes Priory (Sussex), which is not only a community of monks, but a refuge for great numbers of the poor, of pilgrims, sailors and the infirm.[2]

Patri suo et domno sanctissimo pape Eug(enio) frater G(ilebertus) Herefordensis ecclesie minister, pie salutantis affectum et humiliter obsequentis officium.

Sublimitati uestre dilecte pater pro Leuuensi ecclesia eo confidentius supplicamus

83 G, no. 84; B, fo. 19 v.
8, 14 Herefor B
84 G, no. 93; B, fo. 153 v.
1 Ēg. B

---

[1] The union of these two churches to form a priory dependent on Gloucester took place while Gilbert was abbot of Gloucester, in 1143 (see *GF*, p. 84 n.; *CS*, pp. 264 n., 280. Gregory of Caerwent (cf. *GF*, p. 36 n.) gives the date 1144). The wording is odd, and it is just possible that this is a letter of Bishop Robert de Bethune, with the bishop's initial and abbot's name altered in error. Cf. Giles, no. 123, and below, no. 321.

[2] There seems no indication of what occasioned this letter, which is a conventional testimonial. Lewes was the leading Cluniac priory in England, and would naturally turn to Gilbert, the ex-Cluniac, when in trouble.

quo totum quod pium est, quod honestum, uestre conplacere serenitati non am-
5 bigimus. Predicta siquidem ecclesia inter ecclesias Anglie tam firma ordinis obseruantia quam perfecte caritatis operibus in tantum irradiat ut occidentis nostri
tenebras luce quadam honeste conuersationis et cultu defecate religionis expellat.
Hec mater pauperum mestorumque solatium preclara meritorum gratia eam se
omnibus exhibet, ut in publicas iamdudum gratulationes suscepta quasi speculum
10 quoddam in ultimis terre finibus et singulare sanctitatis exemplar niteat. Vnde
preces excellentie uestre affectuose porrigimus ut iustas eius postulationes paterna
mansuetudine audiatis, ipsamque in his in quibus predecessorum uestrorum tempore
fundata feliciter et aucta est nequaquam minui permittatis. Quod eo faciet circumspectio uestra securius quia quod ecclesie uni indulgebitis id non solum monacorum
15 magno cuidam et probabili collegio, sed et inmense pauperum, peregrinantium,
naufragorum, debiliumque multitudini erogabitis, ut si quid in hoc facto decre-
torum iuri derogatum fuerit id apud summum iudicem karitas Christi membris
latissime subministrans potenter excuset. Valeat domnus meus et pater in Christo
karissimus.

## 85   To Pope Eugenius III

[1148–53] On behalf of Reading abbey, attacked by both sides in the civil war and lying on
the boundary between them.

If this letter is taken to mean that Reading was suffering from an attack at the time of
writing, the siege and relief of Wallingford in 1152–3 or the renewed civil war of the latter
year would seem the most probable occasion for it.

Patri suo et domno summo pontifici E(ugenio) frater G(ilebertus) Herefordensis
ecclesie minister pie salutantis affectum et humiliter obsequentis officium.

A tribulatione malorum et dolore ad uestram pater serenitatem ecclesia Radingensis confugit, inde sibi sperans expectansque remedium ubi lesi quique sibi
5 gloriantur non deesse solacium. Hec in ipso diuisarum regni nostri partium limite
constituta utriusque in alterum iamdiu sustinuit impetus, et ab ipsis bellorum initiis
per eius fines exstitit utriusque in alterum transitus et regressus. Vnde tam inscendiis
quam cede suorum debilitata, direptione rerum tam mobilium quam immobilium
imminuta, cum iam multa in medicos nil agentes erogauerit ad uestri fimbriam
10 uestimenti properat et decurrit, sperans inde remedia unde uirtus exit que curat
aliena.[1] Vnde preces sullimitati uestre humili deuotione porrigimus quatinus deuote
filie erigendo lapsa, solidando confracta subueniatis et suggerente pietate iustitiaque
in uobis semper efficaciter agente amissa restitui faciatis, ut que decedente fundatore
suo[2] sibi mortua sunt feliciter in rebus agente patre sibi placide reuiuiscant. Valeat
15 domnus meus et pater in Christo karissimus.

85 G, no. 96; B, fo. 157 (*in top margin:* Deprecatorie ad domnum papam pro ecclesia desolata).
1 Fratri, *corrected to* Patri B    7 transsitus B    14 mortua] *A symbol in* B *here, perhaps referring
to the margin, now cut away*    14 reuiuiuiscant B

---

[1] Cf. Luc. viii. 43–6.                       [2] King Henry I.

## 86 To Pope Eugenius III

[1148–53] On behalf of the son of a rural dean of the diocese, who had been instituted to his father's living, and on that account deprived and excommunicated: he has now done penance and merits absolution.[1]

Patri suo et domno summo pontifici E(ugenio) G(ilebertus) H(erefordensis) ecclesie minister, debitum dilectionis et obedientie famulatum.

Clericum hunc latorem presentium, dilecte pater, ad sublimitatem uestram scripto titulo cause sue transmisimus, ut qui Satane iaculis pene confossus strauit ad uitam solacio gratie uestre reducatur. Hic quendam decanum nostrum sacerdotem 5 honestum in agendis et sustinendis ecclesie negotiis per omnia strenuum scientie antique[. . .]merito ⟨fo. 160v⟩ in publicas iam gratulationes susceptus, non aliis eius meritis nisi quod ecclesiam quandam que patris istius exstiterat dono bone memorie predecessoris nostri domni R(oberti) episcopi susceperat, et in ipsa ministrabat, ob hanc causam excomunicatus publice post longam afflictionem et inediam absolui 10 meruit, iuramento in hunc modum prestito, quod uita comite necessario casu non obsistente, sublimitatem uestram sub prescripta sibi lege penitentie adhibit iussioni uestre quecumque fuerit ob culpe ueniam pariturus. Qua in re iuxta datam uobis a Domino sapientiam et gratiam peccatori prouidebitis et ut culpa condigne puniatur, et qui de triumpho lapsus est antiquus hostis minime glorietur. Sublimitas uestra in 15 longa tempora conseruetur illesa et incolumis.

## 87 To Robert de Chesney, bishop of Lincoln

[Probably 1148–54] He asks Robert to intercede with the king for the abbot of Gloucester, who has fallen into disfavour; and also asks for a lenient judgement on an unnamed knight.

Hamelin was elected abbot of Gloucester in succession to Gilbert in 1148. In this letter Gilbert approaches the king through the bishop of Lincoln, which strongly suggests that the king was Stephen, not Henry II, since Gilbert was a consistent Angevin, whereas Robert de Chesney (consecrated 19 December 1148) was one of Stephen's episcopal supporters. Hence the date—but it is possible that the trouble arose over Hamelin's election and that the letter should be dated c. 1149.

86 G, no. 99; B, fo. 160.
7 antique *or* anteque. *There is clearly something missing in this passage; and a sign over* antique *indicates that there was probably once a note in the margin (now lost) supplying the missing words. The missing words evidently completed the encomium of the dean and stated that he was father to the clerk who is the subject of the letter (cf.* patris istius) 7 susceptum (*by attraction to* decanum/strenuum *as a result of the lacuna*) B 9 ipso B 12 prescpta B 12 adhibit *i.e.* adibit 15 lampsus B
87 G, no. 40; B, fo. 20v; R, fo. 212v.

[1] Among rural deans and below, the neglect of celibacy and the custom of inheritance were still not uncommon (cf. *CHJ*, XII (1956), 6–7). Inheritance was condemned in many councils of the period (cf. London, 1102, c. 8; Westminster, 1125, c. 5; Westminster, 1138, c. 6; Westminster, 1175, c. 1 (*ad fin.*) (Wilkins, I, 382, 408, 415, 477); and for the church at large, Toulouse, 1119, c. 8, Rheims, 1119, c. 4 (Mansi, XXI, 227, 236)). The subject of this letter would also doubtless have needed dispensation to be ordained at all; but this is not mentioned here. Cf. no. 248.

Venerabili domno fratrique karissimo Roberto Dei gratia Lincol(niensi) episcopo G(ilebertus) Herefordensis ecclesie minister, gaudia pacis et salutis.

Pro anima michi res est et sunt oculi mei ad uos ut impleatis in necessitate ⟨B, fo. 21⟩ hac desiderium meum. Regis ira aduersus abbatem Gloec(estrie) et
5 ipsius ecclesiam maliuolorum consilio uehementer incanduit et nisi uoluntati eius abbas ipse infra breue spatium obtemperauerit terras ecclesie ipsius omnes que in sua potestate sunt rex sibi sumere et ecclesie ipsi alienare comminatur. Vnde quanta de uobis speramus confidentia preces beniuolentie uestre porrigimus ut opponatis uos murum pro domo Israel,[1] et regis iram mittigando, abbatem et ecclesiam ipsam
10 reconciliare domno regi et negotium istud iuxta possibilitatem ecclesie terminare studeatis. In hoc positi estis a Domino ut per uos bene prouideat his qui infra sunt et quod per se aut per Her(efordensem) nequit per Lincolniensem obtineat Gloec(estrensis). Ad plene explicandum affectum nostrum multa foret opus litterarum prolixitate; sed stilum duo comprimunt quia sapiens docetur paucis[2] et amico
15 suadetur ex facili. Sit uobis a dextris Dominus ut in hoc et in omnibus gratiam uobis comparari studeatis. Miles iste militauit aliquandiu non Deo sed Satane.[3] Seruiuit enim excommunicatis uestris mense integro postquam ipsos excommunicatos esse cognouerat. Nolentes itaque excommunicatum uestrum absoluere nisi per uos, rogamus ut quod in eum iustitia dictauerit misericorditer prece nostra
20 temperetur.

## 88   To William (?), earl of Gloucester

[Probably 1148–54] He congratulates the earl on not being corrupted by the world in which he lives, and petitions him on behalf of Winchcombe abbey (Glos).

The manuscript makes Gilbert address Earl Robert, who died in 1147. Either we should read 'Willelmo' (1147–83), or Gilbert was abbot of Gloucester when the letter was written. It is clearly addressed to a young man ('hominem…etate iuuenem') which seems decisive for the former solution. The letter reads as if William had not been earl long; it was certainly written while he was still a 'iuuenis'; and the circumstances suggest that it was written in Stephen's reign.

G(ilebertus) Dei gratia Herefordensis episcopus ⟨Willelmo⟩ Gloec(estrie) illustri comiti, pacis et iustitie comitatum.

Inter meriti uestri laudabiles titulos id, dilecte comes, speciali quadam lampade pure lucis irradiat quod in locis uestre potestatis ecclesiam Dei benigne fouetis ac
5 protegitis et pacem seruientium Deo non uili rubiginosi eris conductus pretio sed

**87** 2 ecclesie *om.* R    5 ipsius *om.* R    15 ex] e R    16 comparare B    16 aliquid diu B
18 uestrum *om.* B    19 rogantis R    19 misecorditer B *and* R *before correction.*
**88** G, no. 134; B, fo. 155v (*in top margin*: Laus et comonitorium ad principem eo deuotum).
1 Willelmo] Roberto B (*see above*)

[1] Cf. Ezech. xiii. 5.
[2] Cf. the Roman proverb, 'Dictum sapienti sat est' (Terence, *Phormio*, iii, 3, l. 541); cf. no. 135.
[3] We cannot tell who this was; the rest of the letter suggests that the reference was left intentionally obscure.

liberalitate mentis purissima conseruatis. Quia uero 'datum optimum et omne donum perfectum desursum est descendens a patre luminum'[1] hoc procul dubio beneficium non uobis de terra deorsum sed de celo sursum collatum est quod unus inter regni huius potentes et nobiles sapientia, moribus, honestate prefulgetis et ipsi auctori uite uestre condignos ut audimus fructus eundo semper in melius ubertim 10 exhibetis. Hoc quia thesauri celestis est donum eo conseruandum est diligentius et obsignandum. Equidem michi gratulor et congaudeo Dominum Iesum sub bisso et purpura[2] sibi apud uos domicilium inuenisse et hominem licet etate iuuenem, sensu tamen maturum inter regni huius male corruptos principes absque uitii corruptela incessisse et paci potius et sapientie quam ludibriis iuuenilibus sollicitam operam 15 laudabiliter inpendisse. Hoc est, dilecte comes, quod uobis apud Deum gratia collocat, quod uobis religiosarum mentium uota ⟨fo. 156⟩ conciliat, quod uobis Deo famulantium non orationes solum sed etiam soliloquia sancta communicat. Optamus itaque ut qui bene currere incepistis cursum optime consummetis, et ab inspectore cordium et largitore gratiarum totiens sibi et ecclesie sue exhibite 20 reuerentie condigna premia in illa die reportetis. De cetero supplicat uobis per nos paupercula Winchelcumbensis ecclesia ut apud edituum[3] uestrum, Petrum de Saltemareis, per uos gratiam inueniat et paci eius apud ipsum pietas uestra prouideat. Quam si exaudieritis tam ipsos obnoxios seruitio quam nos gratie debitores efficietis. Valete.                                                                              25

## 89 To Theobald, archbishop of Canterbury

[1149–50] He describes the state of the community of Evesham (during an election to the abbacy); since the rival party are appealing to Rome, they must send representatives, and the archbishop must solicit testimonials to the effect that a majority (both in numbers and wisdom)[4] of the community support the election of William.

The William of this letter was William of Andeville, prior of Dover and formerly monk of Christ Church, Canterbury, who was elected to succeed—and in the event did succeed—Gilbert's uncle Reginald Foliot, who had died on 25 August 1149.[5]

No. 89 is the only surviving evidence known for the dispute, unless no. 90 refers to a later stage of the same case. It was presumably written within a few months of August 1149.

Patri suo et domno Cant(uariensi) archiepiscopo T(heobaldo) frater G(ilebertus) Herefordensis ecclesie minister, salutem et obedientiam.

88 17 con/conciliat B
89 G, no. 107; B, fo. 30v.

---

[1] Jac. i. 17.                                    [2] Cf. Prov. xxxi. 22; Luc. xvi. 19.
[3] Originally a sacristan or temple-keeper. No doubt here (perhaps ironically) a household official or steward (edituus regius is recorded c. 1178 as 'palace-keeper', MLWL).
[4] The medieval Church was very reluctant to accept the principle that an election might be determined by a purely numerical majority; it clung to the notion of 'maior uel sanior pars'—larger or wiser part. It was not until 1179 that a numerical majority was established as the rule even for the election of a pope (and then it was to be a two-thirds majority of the cardinals). Cf. p. 176 n. 4.
[5] Chron. Evesham, p. 99 n.; BM Harl. MS 3763, fo. 172; cf. Gervase, I, 141.

Ex quo litteras uestras suscepimus fructus nostri laboris hic est. Rogerum sub-
priorem uirum bonum, domnum Dauid, G., R. et eorum complices in partem
5 nostram conuertimus. Nicholaite[1] uero sicut ab initio sic uobis aduersantur adhuc,
et que itineri suo necessaria sunt hec adquirere et preparare modis omnibus molliun-
tur. Vnde nisi ⟨fo. 31⟩ uobis uidetur aliud consilium fore estimo ut domnus
Ricardus prior et domnus Sanson iter ad domnum papam quam citius arripiant.
Indignum est enim illos tanquam conscientia bona se curie presentare, nostros autem
10 qui uiam Domini gradiuntur in ueritate tanquam male conscios delitescere.
Vnde opus est ut litteras communes prelatis ecclesiarum et conuentibus qui in
partibus nostris sunt dirigatis ut iuxta conscientiam suam literis suis ad domnum
papam testentur in re ista, pars illa conuentus Eueshamensis que in electione domni
Willelmi est quam longe et numero amplior et merito purissimo sanior habeatur.
15 Cetera uero que negotio necessaria sunt uobis domnus Reginaldus aperiet, qui ad
presentiam uestram et ad uidendam electi sui faciem, toto festinat desiderio. Valete.

### 90  To Godfrey, archdeacon of Worcester

[1148–60, probably 1149–50] He asks him to restrain the bishop of Worcester, who—so he
hears—has been persecuting the monks of Evesham even after they had appealed to the Pope.

It is possible that the appeal referred to is the same as the appeal over the election of 1149–50
(see no. 89). In that case the letter must be before the death of Bishop Simon in March 1150,
which was followed by a vacancy of nearly a year.

In any case, the bishop must either be Simon (died 1150), John (1151–7) or Alfred (1158–
60).

It is perhaps more probable that the appeal and the bishop's persecution arose out of the
old dispute over Evesham's exemption, which had been discussed in Simon's lifetime,
probably at the Lateran Council of 1139.[2] If so, the most likely occasion for the bishop to
revive the dispute was undoubtedly the election of a new abbot, and this would also point to
1149–50 as the date.

Gilebertus Dei gratia episcopus Herefordensis caro suo magistro G(odefrido)
archidiacono Wig(ornensi) salutem.

Scitis, karissime, scitis quod pacifici in prerogatiuam filiorum Dei adoptati sunt.[3]
Vnde proximorum paci eo diligentius attendendum est quo maius est quod ex hac
5 opera a Domino speramus et expectamus. Rogamus igitur ut hac spe beniuolentia

---

**89** 5 Nichoalite B    13 Eueshanensis B
**90** G, no. 103; B, fo. 29v.
1 Dilebertus B

---

[1] The 'Nicolaitans' were normally clerics who repudiated celibacy, named after Nicholas the
deacon of Antioch, who gave them his name, just as Simon Magus gave his name to Simoniacs
—but by a confusion (see *CHJ*, XII (1956), 3 n.). Gilbert can hardly mean Nicolaitans in the
usual sense. It seems likely that the leader, or the candidate, of the opposite party among the
monks was called Nicholas, and so the group were called *Nicholaite* as a term of abuse.
[2] On this dispute, see Knowles, in *Downside Review*, L (1932), 396 ff., esp. p. 398.
[3] Cf. Matt. v. 9.

uestra facilem se nobis prestet et exorabilem ut domnum Wigor(nensem) a persecutione fratrum nostrorum monachorum scilicet ⟨de⟩ Evesham reuocetis et paci inter ipsos reformande operam impendatis. Ad quod si uos preces nostre non inpellerent reuerentia tamen domni pape iamdiu traxisse et compulisse debuerat. Ad ipsum namque appellatione facta pacem omnem et securitatem appelatoribus 10 obseruari iustum esset. Audiuimus tamen a multis domnum Wigorn(ensem) predictos fratres postquam ad domnum papam appellauerunt non solum suis ordinibus suspendisse, sed ad hoc operam dare ut eos de monasterio suo eiciat et ne domnum papam adire possint custodia carcerali chohibeat. Quod si fecerit de graui in domnum papam offensa excusari non poterit. Igitur domni pape reuerentia, 15 caritas etiam domno Wigorn(ensi) debita, preces quoque nostre uos moueant, ut aut paci huic reformande studeatis, aut his qui in archidiaconatu uestro ad nomen domni pape confugiunt consilium uestrum et auxilium non negetis, nec eos manu quacumque laica extrai et affligi aut ⟨fo. 30⟩ que eorum sunt distrai permittatis. Vobis hec ex caritate scribimus ne consentientem cum agente par reatus inuoluat. 20 Consensus enim est non resistere cum possis aut debeas. Qua in re manifesta conclusio uobis aut consensum ingerit aut monachis defensionem. Valete.

## 91 To Theobald, archbishop of Canterbury

[c. 1149–50] William, prior of Ste-Barbe-en-Auge, is intervening in the Stanley case and himself claiming rights against the church of Gloucester: Gilbert states the foundation of Gloucester's right to the church of Stanley St Leonard.

A small house of Augustinian canons was established in the church of St Leonard at Stanley (Glos) in the 1120's by Roger of Berkeley II.[1] In 1146, under somewhat peculiar circumstances, it was transferred to Gloucester and became a cell of Gloucester monks.[2] Its own rights and status seem to have been tied up with the problem of the Berkeley prebends (see above, no. 73); and this may have given the prior of Ste-Barbe the cue to try and save it for the Augustinians. In the early months of 1150 Archbishop Theobald issued a confirmation to Stanley,[3] in which no mention was made either of Gloucester or of Ste-Barbe. This may have been intended to guarantee the integrity of Stanley's properties as a preliminary to settling the tangled issue of Gloucester, Ste-Barbe and the inheritance of the Berkeley prebends. If so, this letter, written at the outset of the case with Stanley, must precede the charter, though probably not by a long time. It was probably written before Theobald became legate (i.e. before March 1150), and certainly before 1153, when the prior of Ste-Barbe died.

William d'Évreux, first prior of the Augustinian house of Ste-Barbe-en-Auge (1128–53),

90 7 ⟨de⟩ om. B (possibly Eveshamenses was intended)
91 G, no. 108; B, fo. 31.

---

[1] Cf. C. Swynnerton, *Archaeologia*, LXXI (1921), 199 ff.

[2] Cf. *CS*, pp. 280–2; *Cart. Gloucester*, I, 113. The grant was made by Roger of Berkeley IV, and there is no reason to doubt his or Gloucester's *bona fides*. But Roger's right to the greater part of his estates was perhaps already in question, and he subsequently lost Berkeley itself and its appurtenances to Robert FitzHarding. Stanley itself seems not to have been affected, but some of its possessions were.

[3] Saltman, pp. 476–7 (probably 1150, because Theobald is legate).

was a frequent visitor to England from at least 1148.[1] He had established small groups of canons on his manors of Beckford and (?) Cold Ashton in Gloucestershire, and had frequent occasion to defend them against the depredations of unruly neighbours during the anarchy.[2] His original claim to Stanley may well have been made on the occasion of his visit in 1146, when he came fortified with papal approval and support for the recovery of his English lands. The portrait of William which emerges from the somewhat confused narrative of the Ste-Barbe chronicle seems to reveal him as a devoted religious, but at the same time an exceedingly active and litigious administrator and a stickler for the rights of his house. Whatever the nature of his claim to Stanley, it seems to have been somewhat remote.

Patri suo et domno C(antuariensi) Dei gratia archiepiscopo T(heobaldo) G(ilebertus) e(cclesie) Herefordensis ⟨minister⟩, dilectionis et obedientie famulatum.

Quorundam, domne, relatu agnouimus W(illelmum) priorem sancte Bar(bare) in causa de Stanleia suas quodammodo partes interponere et ius sibi in ecclesia sancti
5 Leonardi contra ecclesiam Gloec(estrie) uendicare. Quod quam legitime faciat hinc potestis si placet aduertere. Predicta quippe ecclesia petitione domni Sar(e)ber(iensis) et eorum quos ibidem secum habebat, Walteri scilicet et Rogeri atque Henrici,[3] de manu domni Wigornensis a nobis suscepta, domnus prior ilico aduersus nos apud domnum Wigorn(ensem) querelam deposuit, et nos de predicta ecclesia
10 responsuros in ius uocari fecit. Cumque iam statuto die in presentia iam dicti episcopi foret inter nos aliquandiu actio uentilata et idem episcopus in sepe dicta ecclesia priori nichil se unquam concessisse assereret, domnus prior aduersus nos die certo audientiam uestram appellauit; cumque appellationem prosecuti uestro nos presentaremus conspectui, auditis omnibus que de ecclesia sancti Leonardi prior
15 contra nos allegauerat responsioni nos optulimus iudicium in nullo recusantes. Ipse uero nos preueniens ante omnem responsum nostrum in audientia uestra liti renuntiauit in totum, seque in predicta ecclesia nil uendicaturus ulterius sub multorum testimonio proclamauit. Vnde uestra discernat equitas cum liti de predicta ecclesia mote sponte renuntiauerit, si ipsam item instaurare satis desiderat.
20 Nos enim que uera nouimus testificamur et ea oportuno loco et tempore probare parati sumus. Valete.

---

[1] See *Chronique de Sainte-Barbe-en-Auge*, ed. R. N. Sauvage, *Mémoires de l'Académie de Caen* (1906), *passim*, esp. pp. 29 and n., 29 ff. He died on 13 January 1153 (*ibid.* p. 48 and n.).

[2] *Chronique*, pp. 25, 29 ff.

[3] It is possible that Bishop Jocelin's three associates were three of his four archdeacons: Roger of Ramsbury (brother of Dean Azo) and Henry were archdeacons of Wiltshire and Salisbury in this period; Walter is unknown, but we do not know who was archdeacon of Berkshire in 1146 (Roger occurs before 1139, *Reg. St Osmund*, I, 232, cf. 351, 337, 343, 349, *Sarum Charters*, p. 19; and as late as 1157, *Cart. Gloucester*, II, 106. Henry occurs in 1149 and 1155, *Sarum Charters*, pp. 16, 19. The last document can be dated 1155 because Dean Robert became bishop of Exeter in that year and a case could not have been settled 'ex precepto' of Henry II earlier). We do not know why the bishop of Salisbury was involved; possibly because of the interests of Reading abbey.

## 92 To Theobald, archbishop of Canterbury

[Probably 1148–March 1150] On behalf of the bishop of Llandaff, who has aroused the archbishop's indignation, but is now duly penitent.

For the problem of the archbishop's title and its bearing on the date of this letter, cf. Appendix II.[1]

Patri suo et domno T(heobaldo) Cant(uariensi) Dei gratia archiepiscopo G(ilebertus) Herefordensis ecclesie minister post iram misericordie reminisci.

Si aduersus domnum Landauensem aliquantulum mota est tranquillitas uestra, tanto sublimitati uestre humilius supplicandum est quanto aduersus predictum episcopum iustiore causa motam esse cognoscimus. Sufficiebat enim ad subleuan- 5 dam causam suam contra aduersarium suum appellatio etsi uobis per omnia debitam obseruasset reuerentiam. Quod si minus factum est improbitati procul dubio Landauensium clericorum non ipsius episcopi malitie aut ingratitudini imputandum est. Opus enim manuum uestrarum ipse est et plantatio uestra, quem si iusta forte causa conteritis opus quidem manuum uestrarum conteretis et quem plantauit 10 dextera uestra euelletis. Absit hoc a uestra gloria, nec tale sortiatur laus uestra dispendium[2] ut quem semel inter amicos asscripsistis ab aditu gratie uestre eliminatum tam facile proscribatis. Venit quidem ad uos in humilitate et mansuetudine nil sapiens altum aduersum uos, sed quicquid actum sit a uobis tantum totum quod bonum domnum, quod pium patrem decet, expetens et exspectans. Absit autem ut 15 dies mentis uestre sic conuertatur in tenebras[3] ut ira in uobis aut gratie preiudicet aut naturam euacuet, quin in paterno pectore sit intus apud uos qui pro filio pulset, et exoret, et exaudiatur afectus. Si quid igitur apud uos nostra potest supplicatio, si quod tristes dicimus a corde uestro propter inanem causam non prossus excidimus, episcopum uestrum suscipiatis in gratia et paci et honori eius prouideatis, ne patrem 20 alibi querere compellatur, sed totum quod pium est, quod modestum se apud uos reperisse glorietur. Ad pedes uestros ⟨fo. 22⟩ in prece hac corde prosternimur quos supplicando libentius ipsi manibus amplectimur. Prouideat itaque si placet uestra discretio, ne nobis postulata negando, preces nostras amodo muto claudatis silentio. Bene ualere uos optamus in longa tempora, in Christo dilecte pater. 25

## 93 To Ralph of Worcester

[c. April–May 1150] Ralph of Worcester has a case against the earl of Hereford, who had infringed sanctuary by capturing some of Ralph's knights in Evesham abbey. Gilbert explains that he has no jurisdiction in the case, because the late bishop of Worcester had appointed his archdeacon to be vicar in the vacancy of the see, and also because the earl has appealed to a

92 G, no. 91; B, fo. 21v.
2 misericordia B (cf. Ps. xxiv. 6: reminiscere...misericordiarum...) 23 ampectimur B
93 G, no. 135; B, fo. 156 (in top margin: excusatorie iudicis ordinarii, quod subtracta sibi iurisdictione cognoscere de causa non possit).

---

[1] The issue here is not known, but the letter may well refer to the same dispute as no. 121.
[2] Cf. no. 102.　　　　　[3] Cf. Job iii. 4 (and Joel ii. 31).

higher court, that of the papal legate (i.e. Archbishop Theobald). He supports his point with elaborate citations from Roman law.

Letters 93–6 deal with two cases in which the earl of Hereford was alleged to have committed sacrilege, by invading a church and by breaking sanctuary—three cases, including the reference to Leominster in no. 96. From 96 we learn that the outrage at Evesham (no. 93) preceded the attack on Gilbert de Lacy's knights (nos. 94–6).

The anarchy must be the context of these events, and so the outside limits of date are 1148–54.[1] When the attack on Evesham took place, Gilbert was expecting to be vicar of the diocese of Worcester. This dates the event to the vacancy between the death of Bishop Simon on 20 March 1150 and the consecration of John of Pagham on 4 March 1151. In fact it may be dated very shortly after Bishop Simon's death, since the administration of the diocese was still unsettled when the outrage occurred. No. 93 must have been written in spring or summer, 1150.

The attack on Gilbert de Lacy's knights took place on one of the Ember Days after Pentecost. If the outrage at Evesham took place in March–April 1150, the Ember Days of 1150 are a possible occasion for the later event—or any later year down to 1154. It is unlikely that Gilbert would have acted on a royal mandate in the summer of 1153, when the young Duke Henry was in control of the west country. No. 94 was written at a time when it was thought that the archbishop might be forced to leave the country (cf. no. 79). This suggests a date in the period 1148–52, when his relations with Stephen were strained, first by his journey to Rheims, and later following his refusal to crown Stephen's son Eustace against the papal prohibition; it does not suit the circumstances of 1153–4. In 1152 Theobald actually went into exile—but he had probably left the country well before Pentecost.[2] This evidence suggests, though it does not absolutely prove, that letters 94–6 belong to 1150 or 1151.

There is, however, a striking coincidence between the two cases which strongly suggests that both took place in the same year. In both cases the earl of Hereford appealed to the archbishop; and in both cases the appeal was for the morrow of St Lawrence (nos. 93, 94). This can hardly be due to chance, and it seems safe to date the attack on the Lacy knights to the same year as the Evesham incident (i.e. 7, 9 or 10 June 1150), and both appeals to 11 August 1150 (10 August was the only feast of St Lawrence regularly celebrated at this time). Letters 94–5 thus belong to c. June–July 1150; 96, which seems to be an amplification of 94 for the appeal court, may be slightly later—c. July–August (and see p. 133 n. 2).

G(ilebertus) Dei gratia Herefordensis episcopus karissimo amico suo R(adulfo) de Wirecest(ria) salutem.

Quod laboranti fame mee amicali condoletis affectu multimoda gratiarum actione remunero solamen infortunio reputans eam quam in uobis experior amicitie
5 ueritatem. Verumtamen uos eum esse cupio qui dolenda doleat non dolenda equanimiter ferat. Vno namque raptantur errore quamplurimi ut nisi uoluntati sue quecumque fuerit pareatur sibi iustitiam fieri nullatenus arbitrarentur. Hi michi si detrahant, si famam meam quecumque est liuidis latratibus mordendo dilanient,[3] equanimiter fero et dum mecum ratio faciat, dum iuris forma concordet, omnes hos
10 uelut e quadam rationis et intelligentie superioris arce despicio. Non enim quam multis displiceam sed qualibus attendo. Vos quoque difficilem habere uolo aurem

**93** 8 dethrahant B

---

[1] In any case the earl of Hereford died in 1155, having become a monk earlier in the year.
[2] See Saltman, pp. 37–8.　　　　　[3] Cf. no. 103 n. 1.

ad crimina:[1] ad penitendum properat cito qui iudicat. Si minus quam oportuerit egi, si excessi, ipsi iudicate, ipsi queso decernite. Cum peruenit ad me comitem Hereford(ie) milites uestros in ecclesia Eueshamensi cepisse, sperabam me Wigornensis ecclesie uicarium et nostrum super hec spectari et exspectari debere iudicium. 15 Inde est quod diem partibus statui, ipse quoque in medio, ut sperabam, cogniturus et iudicaturus resedi. Meis ibidem e manibus iudiciaria potestas sublata est et Wigorn(ensis) archidiaconus plenitudinem potestatis huius adeo ad se pertinere protestatus est, ut inter ipsum et domnum Cantuariensem nullum omnino medium admitteret, omnesque personas que conuenerant coniurando et contestando a me 20 prorsus auerteret. Sic domnum Wigorn(ensem) in suo dicessu statuisse, sic plena auctoritate sancxisse multorum testimonio affirmabat. Quid michi inter hec? Me sibi in iudicandis ecclesie causis inferiori quodam gradu inferiorem submittere episcopalis dignitas non ferebat; pari uero aut superiori consistere commissa sibi potestas et gloria non sinebat. Dampnum uestrum et militum uestrorum, R(adulfe), 25 aduertitis sed si michi predictus archidiaconus in faciem conspuit illud plane negligitis. Iam iudicate, iam decernite quid michi agendum supererat. Nunquid in ipsa ecclesia iudicandi que nec me iudicem agnoscebat, nec michi suas causas iudi-⟨fo. 156v⟩candas committebat? Culpa quippe est inmisceri negotio ad se non pertinenti. Sed hic fortassis obicies: 'Quicquid archidiaconus ille proclamaret, 30 Wigorn(ensis) tamen ecclesie uicarius eras, et si quid inordinate ab ipso etiam pronuntiatum fuerat, in ipso uindicare et punire debueras.' Bella michi, R(adulfe), moues. Plane tibi illud respondeo: 'Non est michi tibia tanti. Onus michi non honorem estimo alienis implicari negotiis. Obsequium michi prestitit, qui me huic cure subduxit. Agant magna sua quibus commissa sunt, michi pauca mea sufficient; 35 felices illos sua sequantur preconia, michi semper animo sedeat, aut nullis aut ueris laudibus delectari. Age ergo et me lacerantium dentibus iam si placet eripias, et qui mali nil merui, detrahentium uerbis suffocari non permittas. Habent tui quem sequantur, a quo suas exposcant iniurias, qui uigore iustitie peccata puniat, lapsa reparet, amissa restauret, quem suis exstollant preconiis si bene fecerit; sin autem 40 male hec et inueniet.'

Volo tamen ut quod actum est intelligas. Dies comiti Hereford(ie) a domno archidiacono statuta est, et auditis allegationibus partium sententia dicta est. Sententie comes paruit et a iudice absolutus dicessit. Quid tibi iudicium illud contulerit satis nosti. Ego unum scio quia litteris domni legati quas misisti in comitis 45 presentia perlectis, comes statim ad ipsum legatum appellauit, se nimium grauari asserens eo quod causa super qua iudicio Wigor(nensis) archidiaconi et ecclesie stetit per omnia paruit, denuo aduersus eum instauratur et rediuiua suscitatur. Habet pre manibus quod scriptum est: inpetrata rescripta non placet admitti si decise semel cause fuerint iudiciali sententia quam prouocatio nulla suspendit, sed 50 eos qui talia scripta meruerint etiam a limine iudiciorum expelli.[2] Sed iam item

---

**93** 19 donnum B    25 potestas et gloria *Giles*; potestatis et glorie B    30 pclamaret B

---

[1] A Roman proverb (cf. Publilius Syrus, *Sententiae*, l. 133; Walther, *Proverbia*, no. 5691).
[2] Cf. *Code*, 1, 21, 1–2.

inflammaberis et nisi post factam appellationem in comitem quem iudex uester absoluerit interdicti aut anathematis sententiam tulero, me [ . . . ], me iustitie ecclesiastice contemptorem, me tuorum causam dampnorum, non tuo quidem sed tuorum
55 iudicio reputabis. Quod si feceris, patientiam michi, molestiam tibi necessariam estimo. Verumtamen inter molestie fines, te laudabiliter queso contineas. Siquidem militari me crederem usquequaque negotio quia te in huiusmodi satis expertum non ambigo, consilium in hoc tuum omni iocunditate conplecterer. Tu quoque quia in campum litterarum et causarum ecclesiasticarum non mediocriter inpegisti, amici
60 queso consilium ne despicias. Nam quia in rebus huiusmodi meam ut ita dicam etatem consumpsi, michi aliqua saltem magisterium hoc iure quo⟨d⟩dam uideor uendicare. Scriptum noueris karissime: 'nouum quod postulas non est quod etsi rescripti mei auctoritas intercesserit, prouocandi ⟨fo. 157⟩ tamen facultas non denegetur'.[1] Hinc quidem patet post susceptas domni legati literas, me comitem ab
65 appellatione prohibere non potuisse. Item loco post illum proximo scriptum noueris: 'appellatione interposita, licet ab iudice repudiata sit, in preiudicium deliberationis nichil fieri debere, et in eo statu omnia esse quo tempore pronuntiationis fuerunt sepissime constitutum est'.[2] Vnde manifeste cognoscitur post appellationem factam, michi quicquam circa statum appellantis aut interdicto aut
70 anathemate innouare non licuisse. Sed id fortasse a sententia non ab executione sententie appellanti non attribuisse. Sed scriptum noueris, quia 'iudicati executio suspendi solet, si falsis allegationibus circumuentam esse religionem iudicantis is contra quem iudicatum constat esse promiserit'.[3] Quod quia comes die proximo post festum beati Laurentii se facturum asserit, nos ut a nostra ad presens iurisdic-
75 tione elapsum inconcussum dimittimus, et ipsum una cum litteris nostris ordinem rei geste continentibus domno legato iuxta legum et canonum auctoritatem committimus. Vale.

## 94   To Theobald, archbishop of Canterbury

[*c.* June–July 1150] He asks for news of the archbishop and his projected crossing, and requests him to consider the case between the earl of Hereford and Gilbert de Lacy:[4] Gilbert de Lacy had accused the earl of (breaking sanctuary by) capturing a knight of his, Richard

93  53 *A space left in B, presumably for another item in the indictment of Foliot, to balance* me...
contemptorem, me...causam dampnorum   59 ca'ur' B   64 lit'eras B   72 circūmuentam B
94 G, no. 131; B, fo. 153 v.

---

[1] *Code*, 7, 62, 2.                         [2] *Code*, 7, 62, 3.
[3] *Code*, 7, 58, 4 (*allegationibus* seems to come from a similar context in *Code*, 5, 71, 5).
[4] For the earl's enmity with Gilbert de Lacy, see his charters of alliance with the earl of Gloucester (ed. R. H. C. Davis in *Misc. Stenton*, pp. 144–5) and with William de Braose (*CHJ*, VIII (1946), 185). In the latter he commits himself not to make peace or truce with Gilbert de Lacy after 1 August without William's consent. It seems likely that the treaty preceded the outrage described in these letters; if so 1 August can only refer to 1149, which must be the date of the treaty. Gilbert de Lacy was the fourth baron, son of Emma de Lacy, daughter of Walter the first baron (on him see no. 96 and n.; H. M. Colvin in *Essays...presented to Rose Graham*, pp. 15 ff.; Eyton, *Salop*, v, 240, 248 ff.; *DNB*, *s.v.* Lacy, Hugh de).

Brito,[1] in a cemetery; Gilbert Foliot had ordered the earl to allow Richard to attend the hearing, and the earl had suspended the case by appealing to the archbishop. Furthermore, the earl communicates with William de Beauchamp, who is under the archbishop's ban: Gilbert asks for stern measures.

Patri suo et domno T(heobaldo) Cantuariensi Dei gratia archiepiscopo Anglorum primati et sancte sedis apostolice ⟨fo. 154⟩ legato, frater G(ilebertus) Herefordensis ecclesie minister, salutem et obedientiam.

Scire que circa uos sunt et ad posse nostrum uobis in omnibus obedire cupientes, ad uos presentium latorem dirigimus, ut de transfretatione uestra, de mora etiam 5 citra uel trans mare rescripto uestro certum aliquid intelligamus. Adiuuante namque Domino non in incertum curremus[2] cum de uobis certa nouerimus.

De cetero rogamus si placet, ut causam que inter comitem Herefordie et G(ilebertum) de Laci uertitur, breuiter aduertatis. Conquestus est nobis G(ilebertus) de Laci comitem Herefordie quendam militem suum Ricardum scilicet Britonem in quo- 10 dam cimiterio cepisse. Cuius rei probationem miles de carcere quo tenebatur directis ad nos nuntiis offerebat, supplicans officio nostro liberam sibi sui facultatem ad tempus concedi, ut pro se stare posset in iure et si qua in sui liberationem haberet, hec allegare. Quod equitati concordare iudicantes hec comiti ex sententia iniunxi- mus, ut statuto die predicto militi sui copiam concederet, quatinus et in iure ut 15 dictum est stare et pro se agere posset, cautione tamen interposita, ut nisi eum ecclesia liberaret, item comiti se redderet. Comes uero se grauari asserens diem proximam post festum beati Laurentii statuens, ad uestram audientiam appellauit. Quia uero inhumanum uidetur predictum militem appellatione in longinqua protrahi, et tamen in carcere et uinculis detineri, preces super hoc sublimitati 20 uestre porrigimus ut comiti iniungatis, ut predictum militem coram uobis statuta die exhibeat, omni tamen securitate interposita, nisi eum sententia uestra liberauerit, in sua uincula reuertendi. Hoc enim equm arbitramur et bonum, et uestra ad quam appellatus est auctoritate dignissimum, et non solum in hoc honori uestro, sed et paci nostre quamplurimum prouidebitis. 25

Vnum enim superest quod aduertere consultissimam prudentiam uestram obnixe deposcimus: comes Herefordie excommunicato uestro Willelmo de Bellocampo per omnia communicat. Qua in re summe necessarium est ut districto tam ipsum quam nos mandato urgeatis, ut aut eius communione et societate abstineat, aut ipsum par anathematis sententia inuoluat. Vilescet enim anathematis auctoritas, 30 nisi et communicantes excommunicatis corrumpat digna seueritas. Vnde si uestrum circa hec zelum excerceri placuerit nisi a predictis cessauerit, excommunicatum eum publice denuntiari oportebit. Valeat domnus meus karissimus.

---

[1] There is a curious discrepancy between this letter and nos. 95–6, which refer to more than one knight (four in 96). Richard Brito may be the same as the tenant of Hugh de Lacy who occurs in 1166 (*Red Book of the Exchequer*, I, 283).

[2] Cf. I Cor. ix. 26.

## 95  To Gilbert de Lacy

[c. June–July 1150] The case which he had been trying on a mandate from the king had passed by appeal out of his competence to the archbishop's court. He explains the circumstances to Gilbert de Lacy, advises him that R(ichard) Brito's squires and the captured knights[1] should go to the archbishop's court. His own case against Gilbert de Lacy he is not resigning, but he will not press it for the moment.[2]

G(ilebertus) Dei gratia Herefordensis episcopus domno Gileberto de Laci, agendo bene commoda salutis optinere.

Mandauit michi domnus meus rex ut canonicam uobis iustitiam facerem de comite Hereford(ie), qui milites uestros in ecclesia et cimiterio captos dicitur ad
5 redemptionem conpellere. Qua in re sciatis quod in quantum saluo ordine meo potero preceptioni regie libenter parebo. Sed iuxta statuta legum, iuxta auctoritatem sacrorum canonum michi in re ista nichil amplius licet facere, quam quod ante susceptas litteras constat a me factum esse. Diem enim cause huic statui, partium altercationem ⟨audiui⟩, super auditis ⟨fo. 158v⟩ iudicaui, et quia neminem ab
10 apellatione prohibere possum aut potui, appellationem comitis aduersus rem iudicatam audiui. Facta appellatione, hoc iustum est, hoc canonicum, ut nulla audacia me amplius de causa hac intromittam, nisi ut litteras totam ⟨cause⟩ seriem continentes ad iudicem, ad quem appellatum est, per partem utramque transmittam. Has uero litteras que etiam apostoli[3] uocantur, post appellationem statim tam comiti
15 quam militibus uestris optuli, quas quia non suscepistis, in ipsa appellationis die minus forsitan obtinebitis. Vltra hoc non michi de hoc licet ⟨maius(?)⟩ quam minimo clerico episcopatus mei. Testor autem ipsam ueritatem que Deus est, quod nisi me comes per appellationem interpositam impedisset, nec amore, nec odio, nec ulla omnino gratia sententia in eum dilata fuisset. Quod uero contra appellationem
20 nichil possim, si michi non creditis, ipsum ecce canonem audiatis: 'Si quis spreta iudicis auctoritate ad quem appellatum est, rem a se etiam legitime iudicatam nichilominus exequendo inpleuerit, ipsa qua fulgebat iudiciaria potestate se eximit.'[4] Item alibi scriptum est: 'Appellatione interposita licet et ab iudice repudiata in preiudicium deliberationis nichil fieri debere et in eo statu omnia esse quo tempore
25 pronuntiationis fuerunt sepissime constitutum est. Vnde manifeste cognoscitur post appellationem factam etc.'[5] Si enim oues aut boues aut cetera huiusmodi amittimus, dante Domino recuperare poterimus; quod si per inscientiam, fatuita-

95 G, no. 138; B, fo. 158.
9 audiui Giles; space left here in B    12 ⟨cause⟩] cere B, with a symbol indicating a marginal note now lost; possibly the exemplar read c'e (for cause), which was read as cere. The same corruption could have been caused by attraction to seriem (Giles has fere)

---

[1] See p. 131 n. 1.
[2] This may possibly refer to a dispute over the two knights' fees held by Gilbert of the bishop, which were certainly the occasion of disagreement in the next decade (H. M. Colvin, in Essays...presented to Rose Graham, pp. 15 ff., esp. pp. 17 ff.).
[3] See GF, p. 65 n.    [4] Not identified.
[5] Code, 7, 62, 3 (cf. no. 93).

tem aut contumacem inobedientiam ab episcopatu et ordine semel deiecti fuerimus, qui alium nobis det non facile inueniemus. Vnde nobis melius in huiusmodi rebus quantamcumque iacturam pati, quam circa ordinem periclitari. Quod si meum uobis 30 placeret audire consilium, non occasionem quereretis aduersum me, quia ego Deo gratias ad omnem fortunam et prosperam et aduersam paratus sum, et quanto minus habeo, minus certe timebo, et adiuuante Domino plus potero.

Si litteras quas supradixi acciperetis a me, et diem statutum exspectaretis, et armigeros R(icardi) Britonis et milites captos ad archiepiscopum mitteretis, quia 35 iuuante Domino ipsum ibi facta probatione liberare poteritis, et qui ex parte mea aderunt, ad hoc utique non nocebunt. De hoc quod mandat michi rex ut ad memoriam reducam de duobus bobus quid in eius presentia actum sit, bene utique in memoria habeo. Quia causam quam habebam aduersum uos ipso etiam postulante non remisi, sed archiepiscopo se postea intromittente in bonum respectum posui. 40 De hoc mandato archiepiscopi hoc respondebo, quod si appelationem ad se factam cognouisset, nichil utique de re ista precepisset. Hoc itaque est ipsi obedire: rei ipsius seriem, ⟨si(?)⟩ aliquid innouetur, ipsi in omnibus aperire quicquid in nos dixeritis. Vos tamen ualere optamus.

## 96   To Theobald, archbishop of Canterbury

[c. July–August 1150] He reports the progress of the case between four[1] knights of Robert[2] de Lacy and the earl of Hereford, which had been suspended by appeal to the archbishop. The knights complained that they had been captured in a cemetery. This was the third recent scandal of the kind perpetrated by the earl—there had already been sacrilege at Evesham and a similar outrage at Leominster.[3]

Patri suo et domno T(heobaldo) Dei gratia Cant(uariensi) archiepiscopo Anglorum primati et sancte sedis apostolice legato frater G(ilebertus) Herefordensis ecclesie minister, salutem et obedientiam.

Causam pater actam apud nos, et facta ad uos appellatione suspensam, sublimitati uestre notifico. Quatuor milites Rodberti de Laci aduersus comitem Hereford(ie) 5 hoc apud nos in querelam deduxerunt, quod ipse comes eos in cimiterio quodam ad quod eius timore confugerunt uiolenter captos ad redemptionem compulerit, supplicantes officio nostro sibi ablata restitui, seque ut ab ostio euulsos ecclesie de

---

**95** 29 Vnde] *Possibly* uidetur *is missing; but the sentence stands without it*
**96** G, no. 142; B, fo. 159v (*in top margin*: relatio iudicis ordinarii ad iudicem superiorem de processu cause—*the last four words added by modern hand*).
4 suspensa B    8 uestro B

---

[1] See p. 131 n. 1.
[2] The change of name is puzzling: it may be due to later revision, or a slip, or indicate that some time had elapsed between 94–5 and 96. Robert de Lacy was Gilbert's son and heir, and he appears to have held his father's land for a short time after his father's retirement to the Order of Templars c. 1158; apparently he had himself died and been succeeded by his brother Hugh before his father actually died a few years later (Colvin, *art. cit.* pp. 18–19).
[3] See no. 93 for the outrage at Evesham; that at Leominster seems otherwise unrecorded.

manu comitis liberari. Comes uero se eos extra cimiterium cepisse, et ob hoc ad
10 redemptionem legitime conpulisse respondebat, ut sibi in insidiis positos, excommunicationi etiam qua pacis ⟨sacrorum⟩ dierum uiolatores tenentur obnoxios quia
pace non seruata ecclesie ipsa sancti Pentecostes ebdomada, sub sacro quattuor
temporum ieiunio nocte,[1] ad quandam domum eius capiendam uenerant, et in
opere suo comprehensi tunc ⟨in⟩ manus ipsius inciderant. Preterea, quo dictis eius
15 fidem certius haberemus, comes se testium idoneorum assertionem probaturum
quod dictum est adiciebat. Hanc quoque probationem quod eos extra cimiterium,
scilicet in maleficio quod sibi moliebantur cepisset, sponte semel et sepius offerebat.
Scientes utique de manifestis et ocultis aliter atque aliter iudicandum, tam clericos
quam laicos eiusdem loci adiurantes, nil potuimus repperire uestigii quo nobis
20 elucesceret. Congruebat namque tempus misterio, et sub noctis conticinio fuerat
opus perpetratum. Attendentes etiam quia agenti incumbit probatio, et quod is qui
agit probationes afferre debeat, quibus id probet quod intendit, ⟨fo. 160⟩ et ob hoc
a militibus scicitantes quam eius quam intendebant in comitem probationem afferant,
nichil aliud inuenimus, nisi quod tres eorum mutuis uolentes uti testimoniis, singuli
25 duos eiusdem litis consortes testes in sue intentionis assertionem producebant; de
quarto nichil adicientes, nisi quod eum non in cimiterio sed per cimiterium duci
conspexerant. Cumque super hoc testimonio fuisset aliquamdiu disputatum, ipsum
tandem minus conueniens reputauimus, tum propter suspectam mutui beneficii
uicissitudinem; tum quia unusquisque in causa hac aduersus comitem actorem se
30 pariter exibebat et testem; et quia frequenter inpunita foret ex lege malitia, si
d⟨eprehensi⟩ in flagitio honesta de se comminiscentibus mutuis in hunc modum
testimoniis uti concederetur. His itaque circa probationem deficientibus nobisque
eorum probationem nil certum indagare ualentibus, comiti probationem quam in
iure obtulerat adiudicauimus, ut sic finem controuersie poneremus. Hec sententia
35 est quam tulimus cuius executioni priusquam lata foret, se comes obtulit. Postquam
lata est, ad audientiam uestram post octo ⟨dies⟩ appellauit. Hanc itaque iuxta datam
uobis sapientiam aut corrigetis si placuerit, aut si de iure quoquomodo stare potest
roborabitis. Noster enim potest oculus caligasse; at tamen sorde corrupti uel gratia
nichil iudicauimus, sed in eundem modum multa a patribus iudicata non ambigimus,
40 ut actore circa probationem uacillante, reo iuramentum uel ob purgationem uel
causam aliquam nociuam detulerint, sicque iurgiis ⟨finem⟩ imposuerunt. Scriptum
tamen nouimus: 'Actore non probante reus etsi nichil prestiterit obtineat.'[2] Inde
quoque prosequimur, quia si reus nichil prestans obtinet, multo magis multorum
probationem prestans obtinebit. Iudex quoque ratione motus, reo sepius defert
45 iuramentum; nos quoque et ad hec commouit hec ratio: flagrabat adhuc sacrilegium

---

**96** 11 sanctarum (sic) Giles; omitted, leaving a space, in B    11 quia] qui B    14 ⟨in⟩ Giles;
om. B    24 mutuis Giles; mitius B    31 deprehensi nos; d and a space B. The exact word (or
words) missing is uncertain, but this seems as likely as any    36 nostram B    36 dies Giles;
om. B    41 finem Giles; om. B

---

[1] See note to no. 93.
[2] Code, 2, 1, 4 (a more probable source than Bulgarus, as suggested in JS Epp. 1, 126 n.). Cf.
Decretum, C. 6, q. 5, passim; GF, p. 62.

a comite in ecclesia Eueshamensi perpetratum. Crescebat et scandalum apud Leonismonasterium ob similem comitis excessum. Quorundam etiam qui capiendis ipsis una cum comite affuerunt, secreta confessione querimoniam militum ueritate niti cognouimus. Quibus omnibus moti, comitem probatione iamdicta honeraui- mus, qui militum probationem aduersus eum, si ipsa forma iuris admitteret, 50 libentius suscepissemus. Valeat domnus meus et pater in ⟨Christo⟩ karissimus.

## 97 To Robert Warelwast, bishop of Exeter

[1150–3] Hugh of Cotes,[1] a canon, has appealed to the Pope and brought back a letter telling the legate to proceed with his case—and his complaint is that he has been violently ejected from the church of Stanley (St Leonard) by Gilbert. The latter asks the bishop to supply him with an account of Hugh's career in his diocese—if he had entered a stricter observance, that would show that he had renounced all former possessions—and of his reputation.

Nos. 97 and 98 must lie between the appointment of Theobald as legate (early 1150) and the death of Eugenius III (July 1153) (cf. no. 98).

Domno suo dilecto fratrique karissimo R(oberto) Exonie(nsi) Dei gratia episcopo frater G(ilebertus) Herefordensis ecclesie minister, salutem et dilectionem.

Vbi multa est confidentia multa est et sepe presumptio. Inde est quod amabili et amande nobis semper benignitati uestre preces multa securitate porrigimus ut nobis in quibusdam que ad uos spectant in ea que nobis ad presens orta est necessitate 5 subueniatis. Impleuit iamdiu querelis aures omnium canonicus quidam Hugo de Cotes asserens se a nobis ecclesia de Stanleia uiolenter eiectum et rebus suis iniuste spoliatum. In plenam etiam nostri suggillationem ad domnum papam querelam eandem pertulit, et ad domnum legatum litteras huius rei cognoscende reportauit. Quia uero uestram non latet prudentiam qualiter predictus Hugo in partibus uestris 10 aliquandiu conuersatus sit, cuiusmodi etiam religioni addictus, rogamus ut litteras nobis huius rei indices concedatis, et nos uobis in omnibus amplioris gratie debitores efficiatis. Quem artioris obseruantie gratia si se constat inclusisse, constat etiam his que ante possederat renuntiasse. Quod quia de ipso audiuimus ab amico ueritatis testimonium expectamus. Et quia ad multorum correctionem religionis amatoribus 15 inhonesta frequenter honestissime proferuntur, si quid uulgo notum est quod aduersarii nostri faciem confundat, petimus ut et hoc litteris ipsis elucescat. Valete.

**96** 46 Euessah'ensi B (*cf. no.* 93)　50 probatione B　51 Christo *Giles; om.* B
**97** G, no. 104; B, fo. 30.
12 nobis] uobis B

---

[1] Hugh evidently charged Gilbert with ejecting him from Stanley in connexion with the process by which Stanley was converted from a house of canons regular to a dependency of Gloucester (see no. 91). He probably came from Coates in Gloucestershire; but possibly from one of the other places named Coate, Coates and Cotes.

## 98   Robert Warelwast, bishop of Exeter, to Pope Eugenius III

[1150–3] In answer to a request from Gilbert and the monks of Gloucester, he is sending to the archbishop and to the Pope an account of the adventures of Hugh of Cotes. An ex-canon regular and hermit, Hugh had tried to re-establish himself as a hermit or canon, and even pretended to have authority from Rome; but was confounded in his last assertion by a clerk who was living in the Curia with Robert (Pullen), late papal chancellor, at the time when Hugh claimed to have visited it.[1]

Reuerentissimo et sanctissimo domno et patri E(ugenio) summo pontifici R(obertus) Dei gratia Exon(iensis) humilis episcopus et sanctitatis uestre seruus, salutem et debitam cum omni deuotione obedientiam.

Rogatu uenerabilis fratris nostri et amici G(ileberti) Hereford(ensis) episcopi et
5 monachorum Gloec(estrie) et maxime pro ueritate manifestanda scripsimus domno Cantuar(iensi) archiepiscopo, apostolice sedis legato, ueritatem quam scimus de Hugone de Cotes et eandem uobis eorundem rogatu ueraciter scribimus. Relicto, ut audiuimus, canonicorum regularium ordine, ut pro certo sciuimus apud nos inclusus factus, non qualiter uellemus apud nos conuersatus est. Vt enim de ceteris
10 taceamus, de incontinentia etiam apud uulgus infamatus est, et non inmerito ut credimus. Clericus namque iuxta cuius ecclesiam cellam habebat, ut asserit, deprehendit cum eo in cella sua mulierculam, que per fenestram celle ad eum introierat, et quia non erat alius introitus uel exitus, per eandem exiuit; quam cum super introitus sui causa conueniret nichil conueniens, nichil honestum respondere
15 potuit. Hac igitur eius inhonestate et infamia, licet ad hoc magne honestatis et bone fame uiri multum studuerint, nunquam ad plenum sedata, multotiens uolebat a cella sua exire, et secundo hoc etiam religionis proposito relicto, monachalem ordinem se uelle simulat subire. Et certe licet honestorum et religiosorum uirorum honesta et religiosa uiolentia diu detentus, tandem absque conscientia et licentia
20 nostra, non paruam ut audiuimus ⟨fo. 30 v⟩ pecuniam secum asportans exiuit, et tamen nec monachicum habitum assumpsit, nec ad claustrum canonicorum, unde exierat, rediit. Sed post multam uagationem ad nos rediens petiit ut in parrochia nostra et in alia hereditate posset sub heremite nescio uel canonici specie habitare, quod nos nullatenus sine uestra uel legati uestri auctoritate, tum propter eius in-
25 constantiam, tum propter infamiam pristinam permisimus. Quod cum intellexisset predictus Hugo, post multum temporis ad nos rediens dixit se presentiam uestram uisitasse, uite sue seriem totam et ueritatem uobis reuelasse, et sic auctoritate uestra cum hac postulatione et proposito ad nos redisse: sed de hoc procul dubio mentitus fuisse probatus est, utpote qui nec litteras uestras sibi testes ostendere potuit, nec
30 aliquo uero uel ueri simili argumento, quod uos uidisset uel quo tempore dicebat uisitasset, probare. Conuicit enim eum quidam clericus noster qui eo tempore quo se dicebat uos uisitasse, cum domno Roberto bone memorie cancellario uestra in

98 G, no. 105; B, fo. 30.
15 Hac *Giles;* hanc B    23 nescio] ? *an understood.*

---

[1] I.e. in 1145–6: Eugenius ('se dicebat *uos* uisitasse') became Pope in 1145; Pullen died in 1146.

curia morabatur. Hec pauca de multis que honestius tacenda uidentur uobis scripsimus, ne uerbis eius persuasibilibus (quibus habundat) uel falsa religionis specie quam pretendit, uos decipiat. Valeat sanctitas uestra. 35

## 99 To Pope Eugenius III

[c. Spring 1152] On behalf of the church of London in its troubles. Gilbert in particular recommends the person of the bishop elect, Richard de Belmeis, archdeacon of Middlesex, and hopes that his election will be upheld.

The six letters 99–103 and 109 are all connected with the election of Richard de Belmeis as bishop of London in succession to Robert de Sigillo, who had died on 29 September 1150. In January 1152, after a long vacancy, Eugenius III ordered the election of a religious within two or three months, later permitting the choice of a secular canon.[1] The chapter elected Richard de Belmeis, canon of St Paul's and archdeacon of Middlesex, but the choice was at first opposed by the king.[2] In no. 99 Gilbert informs the Pope of Richard's election; the letter presupposes intervention by the papacy and refers obliquely to royal displeasure. In 100, addressed to Archdeacon William and Master Henry, the election has taken place but the royal assent has so far been withheld. No. 100 seems to presuppose papal consent, and so probably follows a favourable answer to 99. Richard was consecrated bishop on 28 September 1152 at Canterbury, and we have to fit the arrival of Eugenius's first letter, the election, further negotiations with the Curia (no. 99) and further negotiations with the king between January and September. We may thus date the election and no. 99 to the spring of 1152 and no. 100 to the late spring or summer.

The remaining four letters deal with Richard's early difficulties with the Pope. On his election the bishop had bestowed his own archdeaconry on Ralph de Diceto,[3] but unfortunately the Pope had appointed John of Canterbury to the same post. John appealed to the Pope, and Gilbert wrote to Richard to condole with him (letter 101, which can be dated to the opening months of 1153 by its reference to the duke of Normandy).[4] Richard had been summoned to the Curia, and Gilbert excuses himself from accompanying him, but promises to write to the Pope on Richard's behalf, a promise which bore fruit in no. 102. No. 103, also to Richard concerning his proposed visit to the Curia, seems to be an answer to a further request for advice: we therefore prefer the sequence of letters given below, although it is not impossible that 103 is earlier than 101.

It appears that the case was delayed by Eugenius III's death on 8 July 1153, and eventually settled by Anastasius IV at the turn of 1153 and 1154. In December 1153 Hugh du Puiset surrendered the treasurership of York on his consecration at Rome to the see of Durham.[5]

---

**99** G, no. 95; B, fo. 155.

[1] JS *HP* (P), pp. 90–1, (C), pp. 88–9. For an account of this affair, see Stubbs, introd. to Diceto, I, pp. xxiv ff. (which dates Bishop Robert's death, wrongly, to 1151); cf. Diceto, I, 295, Gervase, I, 148.
[2] JS, *loc. cit.*, indicates that the king demanded the payment of £500 'exemplo monachorum sancti Augustini', and that the election followed the payment 'non sine nota symonie'. The latter may be gossip; but the date of the St Augustine's election (probably late summer 1151: Thorne, *Chron.* pp. 1810–11; cf. Gervase, I, 147–8) fits the reconstruction given above.
[3] Diceto, I, pp. xxvi ff.; cf. JS *Ep.* 5 n. [4] See notes to no. 104.
[5] Sir Charles Clay in *Yorks Archaeological Journal*, xxxv (1940), 16; G. V. Scammell, *Hugh du Puiset*, pp. 12 ff., esp. 16.

William FitzHerbert was there at the same time engaged in recovering the archbishopric of York, and it is reasonable to presume that the archbishop on his restoration allowed John to be made treasurer of York; and that John accepted this highly desirable office as compensation for resigning his claim to the archdeaconry of Middlesex.[1] It is certain that John's appointment took place about this time, and reconciliation with the bishop of London presumably followed hard upon it.[2]

Patri suo et domno summo pontifici E(ugenio) frater G(ilebertus) Herefordensis ecclesie minister, deuotum et debitum obedientie famulatum.

Cum debitorem uniuersis diuina uos pater munificentia constituerit commune debitum hi propensius exigunt qui uestre se per omnia tuitioni alacriori et ampliori
5 deuotione sumittunt. Vnde plurimum honori uestro conducit et glorie, ut Lundoniensi ecclesie ea qua ad presens tempestate concutitur manum auxilii porrigatis, et causam quam multo sudore perstringit benignitate consilii subleuando, ipsam allidi scopulis aut fluctibus obrui non sinatis. Que cum in Anglorum ecclesia multa meritorum et dignitatum luce prefulgeat, ad presens tamen eggregie laudis titulo
10 hoc ipso nobilitata est quod post patris et pastoris sui decessum inter minas principum ipsosque frementium gladios, Deum contemplata non hominem, immobilis inperterritaque constiterit, et se periculis audacter obiciens honorem Dei et libertatem ecclesie in aliquo minui dedignata, patrem sibi et pastorem idoneum consensu unanimi non minus sancte quam prudenter elegerit ⟨fo. 155 v⟩. Quod cum
15 ipsa eligentium fortitudo mentiumque constantia dignum laude constituat, persona que electa est gratia cumulat et honore, ut totum sit fauore dignissimum, et quod ob honorem et libertatem ecclesie fortiter actum est, et quod in eiusmodi persona laudabili circumspectione prouisum. Nota namque secure scribimus et que scimus loquimur cum fiducia. Lundoniensem[3] archidiaconum R(icardum) de Bealmeis
20 quantum in humanis occulis est uita honestum, laudabilem scientia, liberalitas amabilem, et ab ipsa reddit origine stirps generosa clarissimum. Quem cum ad sui regimen diligenter et uocet et exspectet ecclesia, si quod absit iste repellitur, iniuriam hanc lesa uirtus erubescet et querela dicentium 'sine causa iustificaui cor meum, et laui inter innocentes manus meas'[4] non modicum sumet incrementum.
25 Agat itaque apostolica sublimitas, agat pater; unde sibi Anglorum congratuletur et applaudat ecclesia, fine bono bonum consummet initium. Honor et honore dignissimum, ut in presenti sibi laus, in futuro reponatur et premium; 'et sciant quia manus tua hec, et tu domine fecisti eam'.[5] In longum uestra conseruetur incolumitas, in Christo dilecte pater.

**99** 24 innucentes (? *corrected*) B

---

[1] John had certainly been appointed treasurer before the next archbishop of York, Roger, was consecrated in October 1154—he witnesses as such with Roger as archbishop elect (Saltman, p. 405).
[2] See no. 109.
[3] In fact, of Middlesex; to give an archdeacon the title of his diocese rather than his archdeaconry was normal in the twelfth century.
[4] Ps. lxxii. 13.                    [5] Cf. Ps. cviii. 27.

## 100  To William de Belmeis, archdeacon of London, and Master Henry[1]

[Spring–summer 1152] The election has been canonically celebrated; the Pope and almost everyone else is on their side; and so Gilbert tells them not to despair if the king's assent is still being withheld.

G(ilebertus) Dei gratia Herefordensis episcopus dilectis suis Willelmo Lundon(iensi) archidiacono et magistro Henrico salutem.

Iuxta illud Salomonis, multi assistunt coram faciem principum sed omnium sententia ex Deo procedit. In eius manu corda sunt regum, et ipse ea cum uult ad omne quod disponit inflectit.[2] Inde est quod si negotio quod uiriliter assumsistis 5 suum domnus rex nondum prebet assensum, non tamen desperandum uel a proposito [. . .] resiliendum est, cum sit facillimum Deo cor eius et animum ad id quod sibi placitum fuerit inclinare. Quod in negotio summum est iam conplestis; obsecro ne circa minima deficiatis. Canonice celebrata electio defectu uestro *ne deficiat, que cito plenum robur habitura est si ipsi nequaquam defeceritis. Quo enim 10 uobis maior uel apud Deum gratia, uel apud homines gloria, causam Dei postpositis omnibus uiriliter inchoasse, eo habundantior secutura est confusio si (quod absit) fortitudinis spiritu destituti ab eo quod uobis domni pape et omnium fere conciliat corda recens⟨u⟩eritis. Confortetur itaque cor uestrum,[3] in Domino karissimi, et iuxta uias quas uobis aperiet Dominus, quod cepistis explete, et de 15 nobis in quantum facere possumus in negotio amici confidite. Valete.

## 101  To Richard de Belmeis II, bishop of London

[Early 1153] He comforts the bishop, who has been summoned to the papal Curia to answer the appeal against him. Gilbert offers him advice, but he cannot accompany him since he is prevented by the arrival of the duke of Normandy (the future Henry II).

Venerabili domino fratrique karissimo R(icardo) Lundoniensi Dei gratia episcopo frater G(ilebertus) Herefordensis ecclesie minister, salutem et dilectionem.

Scriptum nosti karissime, 'iusto quicquid acciderit id ipsum minime perturbare'.[4] Illud enim apostoli cordis oculis intuetur: 'bonis in bonum cuncta chooperari'.[5] Vnde prospera si affluant prophete concinit dicens: 'Cantabo Domino qui bona 5

---

100 G, no. 140; B, fo. 159 (*in top margin*: exhortatio ut in opere bono et bene incepto laudabiliter quis (?) perseue[ret]).
7 [. . .] en...B (*space for short word*)   9 *ne] *ins.* B   14 karissime B
101 G, no. 130; B, fo. 153.

---

[1] Canon of St Paul's, probably Master of the Schools (*GF*, pp. 275, 281). Gilbert addresses William and Henry as representatives of the chapter.
[2] Prov. xxix. 26: Multi requirunt faciem principis: et iudicium a Domino egreditur singulorum; and xxi. 1: . . .ita cor regis in manu Domini: quocumque uoluerit, inclinabit illud.
[3] Cf. Ps. xxvi. 14; xxx. 25.
[4] Prov. xii. 21: Non contristabit iustum quicquid ei acciderit.
[5] Rom. viii. 28: . . .diligentibus Deum omnia cooperantur in bonum.

tribuit michi.'[1] Aduersa si obuient, illud cordis labiis modulatur: 'obumbrasti capud meum in die belli.'[2] Hec karissime dum mecum reputo, in te nullius impetum fortune perhorresco, que leta si uenerit, mansuete suscipitur, aduersa si proruat haut timetur. Huiusmodi michi de te facile persuadent mentis tue constantia, et uiarum
10 tuarum iamdiu nota perfectio. Que si quam firme speramus radicem suam solo mentis tue inserunt, te quidem non in luto aquarum multarum uento agitatam harundinem, sed in uirtutum Libano cedrum firme radicatam temptationis flatus inueniet.[3] Nec quidem ista profero quasi aduersum aliquid in te michi tue tenor epistole nuntiauerit. Nuntiat quidem aduersum te appellatum, et iam facte dona-
15 tionis tue celebrationem solempnem ad domnum papam interposita appellatione suspensam. In hoc uero quid aduertitur nisi quod animi tui tepor aut torpor excitatur aut excutitur? Nam qui hominem iuxta cor tuum inueneras,[4] te in melius gratia promouente ipsum quidem debueras, non tantum melius dico, sed et in te alterum promouisse. Iam fere sera in fundo parsimonia est,[5] nisi quod expedit
20 equidem et necesse est ut et corporis fatigatione aliquantula torporem redimas tuum, et quod retro minus actum est exerente se et seipsam strenue excercente animi uirtute perficias. Qua in re non est quod triste reputem. Ad tempus enim a regni huius tempestate semotus, donante Domino quietum carpes iter et placidum, et uirtutum fultus aminiculis, summi pontificis faciem uidebis intrepidus et senato-
25 rum[6] curie utique gratiosus assistes. Nec te moueat aduersarii tui in publicas iamdiu gratulationes suscepta facies. Inde enim spem concipio, unde desperationem forsan aliquis comminatur. Nam si bene morigeratus et litteratus iuuenis inter deos audiri meruit et placere, quid non minus ornato moribus aut munito litteris episcopo subtrahet gratiam, quin et ipse quidem ordine longe sublimior, fortunaque poten-
30 tior inter bonos sibi possit gratiam collocare? Fauorabilis enim reus non de lucro captando sed de dampno euitando contendis. Quod ante susceptas domni pape litteras in personam omnium testimonio idoneam procuratoris beneficio contulisti, ratum manere desideras. Noui templum illud iustitie, pectus scilicet apostolicum, unde ad omnes emanat equitas, modeste omnia ⟨fo. 153 v⟩ dispensare. Qui potuit
35 alteri quod tui iuris est non negare inpensa sibi reuerentia debita non magni quidem estimabit, tibi quod tuum est restituere. Honesta et utilia tibi prouidentur a Domino, et quod in contumeliam aduersarii tibi machinatur improbitas, commutabit in gloriam bonorum oratione propitiata diuinitas.

Me uero ad presens adeo ducis Normannorum oppressit aduentus, ut ad iter
40 istud facultas non suppetat, etsi uoluntas illud omnino suadeat. Ibis ergo sine me anime dimidium mee, et qualitate sui quam preferent suspensum ad te animum

**101** 32 personam omnium *Giles;* persona oī/nium B

---

[1] Ps. xii. 6.    [2] Ps. cxxxix. 8.
[3] Cf. Hab. iii. 15; Matt. xi. 7; Eccli. xxiv. 16–17.
[4] Cf. Act. xiii. 22.
[5] A Roman proverb: 'it is too late to spare when all is spent' (Seneca, *Epp.* I, I, 5).
[6] This description of pope and cardinals was first made (so far as is known) by Peter Damian (*PL*, cxlv, 540; cf. W. Ullmann, *The Growth of Papal Government* (London, 1955), p. 320 and n.).

uela que reportabis afficient. Quia uero post episcopatum domino pape et curie in nullo seruiui, illis uerba mittere formidaui. Quid enim aut in quem modum scribam nescio et presentie uestre scriptum meum modicum conferre non ignoro. Itineri autem tuo in eo quod mandasti, et in eo quod internus amor suadet amplius, 45 iocundissime prouidebo. Interim autem si honesta se obtulit transactio, ipsi stari rogo simul et consulo. Valeat dilectus meus.

### 102    To Pope Eugenius III

[Early 1153] On behalf of the bishop of London, who has not wittingly disobeyed the Pope's mandate to give John (of Canterbury) the archdeaconry (of Middlesex); but in fact had already granted it to Master Ralph de Diceto before he knew the Pope's will.

Patri suo et domno summo pontifici Eug(enio) frater G(ilebertus) Herefordensis ecclesie minister, humilem obedientie famulatum.

Scimus, pater in Christo karissime, scimus quod apostolice non obedire iussioni apostatare est, et instar uere sacrilegii uestre contraire uoluntati. Absit hoc a fideli, absit a catholico, absit potissimum a filio beneficiis a munificentia ⟨fo. 154 v⟩ 5 uestra exhibitis obligato multipliciter et obnoxio. Lundoniensis nimirum episcopus adeo manuum uestrarum opus est et creatio, ut ei recte in faciem possit obici, 'tu quid habes nisi quod a domno papa accepisti?' Nam qualiter illum contra uota et coniurationes principum uirtus apostolica sublimauerit, nullus apud nos qui ignoret, nemo fere qui nesciat. Inde est ut apud serenitatem uestram pro ipso illa 10 recte competere uideatur allegatio 'operi manuum tuarum porriges dexteram'.[1] Quid enim uas etsi formatum optime, quid acturum est si illud in uirga ferrea decreuerit suus auctor elidere?[2] Absit hoc a uestra gloria; nec tale sortiatur laus uestra dispendium,[3] ut quem semel intra fines gratie suscepistis ab ipsius aditu eliminetis inmeritum, aut innoxium excludatis. Archidiaconatum enim quem 15 liberalitate laudabili domno Iohanni Cantuariensi donandum mandastis, ante concessum alteri fuisse uestram credimus ignorare prudentiam. In cuius rei testimonio domnum Lincolniensem a uero nec in modico deuiare confidentissime dicimus; ipsum uero Lundoniensem nec totius episcopatus sui iacturam perpetuam periurio uelle redimere, scimus equidem et constanter asserimus. Ipse quidem 20 Lincolniensis testatur et iurare paratus est domnum Lundoniensem antequam uoluntatem uestram aut scripto aut aliquo referente cognouerit predictum archidiaconatum magistro Radulfo Discetensi cui et ad doctrinam scientia et ad honestatem mores exuberant, concessisse. Est equidem in omni gratiarum amplectendum actione quod honestatem et scientiam in Iohanne remunerare decernitis. Sed hoc 25 apostolico culmini factu leue est ita ut episcopum quem singulari preuenistis gratia non offendatis. Preces in hoc porrigimus, in hoc paterne karitati supplicamus, ut

102 G, no. 94; B, fo. 154 (*in bottom margin:* excusatorie pro amico).
23 Diotecensi B (*the normal spellings of Ralph's name are* de Diceto, de Disceto, *and* de Disci; B's reading is clearly a corruption of the form in the text)    25 remunere B

---

[1] Job. xiv. 15.          [2] Cf. Ps. ii. 9, etc.          [3] Cf. no. 92.

intus apud patrem sit qui pro filio et episcopo pulset et eatenus exoret affectus, ne plus fortasse diligens minus admittatur et ad obsequendum longe promtior minus
30 exaudiatur. Valeat domnus meus et pater in Christo karissimus.

### 103   To Richard de Belmeis, bishop of London

[Early 1153] A letter of comfort to the bishop, who is embroiled with the Pope, and is preparing a journey (to the papal Curia).

Venerabili domno fratrique karissimo R(icardo) Lundoniensi Dei gratia episcopo frater G(ilebertus) Herefordensis ecclesie minister, salutem et dilectionem.

De negotio uestro michi non ad presens aliquid occurrit, nisi ut si honesta se obtulerit transactio stetur illi. Sin autem, propositum iter arripiatis, et aduersantes
5 uobis in Campo Martio iuuante Domino cornu iustitie uentiletis. Liuidorum latratuum Scillas[1] undique erumpentes audimus; omnes aura Sancti Spiritus flante prospere enauigabitis. Si necessitas expetat bonum est in stuporem etiam et miraculum domno pape seruire, quam in certamine cepto subcumbere. Dura dicimus— cum longe meliora speremus—quia et dura scripsit domnus papa, que tamen
10 omnia presentibus et pulsantibus uobis apostolica mansuetudine temperanda pro certo credimus. Valete. 'State in fide, uiriliter agite, et Deus pacis conterat omne Sathan sub pedibus uestris uelociter; amen.'[2] Monachum nostrum ad uos mittimus, ut status uestri certitudinem recipiamus.

### 104   To Henry, duke of Normandy

[Early 1153] He explains why he has not visited the duke, as instructed, to do what he 'had promised in the person of the abbot of Bordesley'.[3] He tells the duke to ignore his detractors.

Letters 101, 104–6 are linked together by their references to Henry duke of Normandy, the future Henry II. He is specifically given the title duke in three of the four letters (106 is the exception); and since it is virtually certain that he was not duke when he visited the country in 1149, they must belong to his last stay in the country before he became king, i.e. to 1153 or early 1154.[4] No. 101 must in any case belong to the later visit, since it relates to circumstances certainly relating to 1152 or 1153.[5] In 101 the duke is just about to arrive or has just

103 G, no. 133; B, fo. 155 (*in top margin*: consolatorie ad hominem in tribulatione positum).
3 alid' B
104 G, no. 106; B, fo. 30v.

---

[1] Cf. Sidonius Apollinaris, *Epistolae*, I, I.
[2] This Pauline postscript is compounded from the final chapters of I Cor. (xvi. 13, 24) and Romans (xvi. 20, 27).
[3] Abbot Hamo of Bordesley was a friend of Gilbert (cf. nos. 7, 72). This may refer to the business of the foundation of Stoneleigh abbey (Warwicks), a daughter house of Bordesley. Stoneleigh owed its origin to a group of hermits in Cannock Chase, who converted themselves into a community of Cistercian monks affiliated to Bordesley in or shortly before 1153, and obtained charters from Duke Henry in that year (*Cart. Stoneleigh*, pp. xii ff., esp. pp. xv, 12–13). They moved to Stoneleigh in 1155.
[4] Cf. *EHR*, LXI (1946), 81–6; A. L. Poole in *Gesta Stephani*, pp. xxiii ff.
[5] I.e. the troubles of the new bishop of London: cf. notes to no. 99.

done so ('Me. . .ad presens adeo ducis Normannorum oppressit aduentus'). Nos. 105 and 106 are both addressed to Robert de Chesney. In the former Gilbert complains that he is ill; he has been summoned by Henry and cannot delay beyond the first Sunday of Lent; in 106 we have the same theme, but a delay has been granted until Palm Sunday and a further delay has been requested. It is reasonable to suppose that both letters refer to the same summons, and belong to the early months of Henry's invasion in 1153. The first Sunday in Lent was 8 March in 1153, and Palm Sunday 12 April; we may therefore date 105 February–March and 106 March–April.

No. 104 provides a more complex problem, arising from its address: 'Regie nobilitatis et indolis, ut audiuimus, egregie, H. comitis Andegauensis filio, Normannorum duci, et regni Anglorum pro magna portione domno.' As it stands the style does not agree with any of those which Henry is known to have used himself. From 1149/50 until his father's death in September 1151 he styled himself simply 'dux Normannorum et comitis Andegauorum filius'. In an article published in 1946,[1] the late Professor Z. N. Brooke and C. N. L. Brooke dated the letter 1149 and emended 'duci' to 'ducis'. This evades the difficulty of making Gilbert call him 'son of the count of Anjou' when his father was dead and he already count himself; but it raises other difficulties even more serious. The order 'comitis Andegauensis filio, Normannorum ducis' is strange, even when applied to Count Geoffrey, even if we suppose further corruption in the text. The opening of the address suits 1149; the close ('regni Anglorum pro magna portione domno') is far more suitable to 1153; there is no evidence that Henry went further west than Devizes in 1149, whereas in 1153 he spent some time in the west so that a visit to Hereford, or the expectation of it, seems entirely natural in that year. In 104 Gilbert is evidently in difficulties with Henry; this fits the tone of nos. 101, 105–6 so well as to be decisive evidence in favour of the later date. If the address of 104 still seems inept, it is certainly far less so than if we assume the earlier date.

It is curious to find so staunch an Angevin out of favour in 1153. It may be that he was not yet forgiven for doing homage to Stephen in 1148, or the trouble may reflect local politics in Hereford—perhaps Gilbert's relations with the earl.[2]

Regie nobilitatis et indolis, ut audiuimus, egregie, H(enrico) comitis Andegauensis filio, Normannorum duci, et regni Anglorum pro magna portione domno, G(ilebertus) Dei gratia Herefordensis episcopus, salutem et seruitium.

Placuit uobis litteris commonere me ut cito uenirem ad uos facturus id quod in manu domni abbatis Bord(esleie) promiseram. Vt promissa complerem quam 5 citius potui promtus accurri, et quia processeratis ulterius, Hereford(ie) reditum uestrum biduo expectaui. Auctoritate uero obedientie me non solum uocante et monente sed urgente et trahente ad aliud, diutius expectare non potui. Precor itaque si placet ut me hac uice excusatum habeatis, et absentiam meam equanimiter sustinendo hac uice, me uobis gratie debitorem efficiatis. Si qui uero sunt emuli aut 10 maliuoli mei qui ob mei odium uos in iniuriam Dei et ecclesie detrimentum sugges-tione maligna trahant, bonum est uobis timorem Dei consiliis malignantium opponere, et illud sapientis elogium memoriter retinere: 'Beatus uir qui non abiit

---

[1] *EHR*, LXI, 81–4.
[2] Who was a leading supporter of Duke Henry in 1153–4 (cf. A. L. Poole, in *Gesta*, pp. xxvi ff.), and whose relations with Bishop Gilbert may not have recovered from the incidents described in nos. 93–6.

in consilio impiorum.'[1] Omnium enim sententia ex Deo procedit, quem si in
15 initiis non bonis offenderis, exitus uestri cum honore esse non poterunt. Det uobis
intellectum et modestiam Dominus, ut et pro uobis orent ecclesie, et dominationem
uestram in longum expetant plebes subiecte. Valete.

## 105 To Robert de Chesney, bishop of Lincoln

[February–March 1153] It is five months since he saw the bishop, and he asks for news. For
himself he is sick and in trouble: the duke of Normandy has summoned him, and he cannot
put the summons off beyond the first Sunday in Lent. He asks the bishop to take one Gilbert
Foliot into his service.[2]

Venerabili domno fratrique karissimo R(oberto) Lincolniensi episcopo G(ilebertus)
H(erefordensis) ecclesie minister, gaudia pacis et salutis.

Ieiunantes et abstemi⟨i⟩ conspectu uestro karissime pariter et alloquio quinque
iam mensium interuallo caruimus. Vnde si bene ualetis aut secus est, significari
5 nobis petimus, ut aut gaudium communicetur ex prosperis, aut si res aliter est
alterutro quoad possumus humerum supponamus aduersis. Leta quippe nobis dies
ceterisque serenior illuscescit qua uobis successisse cognoscimus. Aduersa uero que
nuntiat caligine nos obducit et inuoluit amaritudine.[3] Prestetur igitur animo
desideranti solacium et referatur ad nos cartula de statu et incolumitate uestra,
10 reportans utinam uerbum bonum, de nobis uero nisi qualia sunt nuntiare non
possumus. Capitis infirmitate continua laboramus, commonitorium habentes a
Domino, ut aduertamus non esse perpetuum quod interna pulsantis manu iamiam
constat esse commotum. De cetero magno frequentique commonemur inperio duci
Normannorum assistere, et sibi placitis obtemperare. Quod si hucusque distulimus,
15 incolumi tamen statu ultra dominicam *Inuocauit me* amplius declinare non
possumus. Assistemus igitur imperanti et quod rerum experimento nouerimus
uobis significare non tardabimus.

De cetero quia semel cepi loquar ad domnum meum, ncc queso indignemini si
loquar. Gilebertus Foliot summam gerit animi deuotionem, ut uestro sese mancipet
20 omnino seruitio, et in uestro famulatu expendat, que nunc inani consumit otio.
Vnde supplicat adhibita multorum prece preces pro ipso porrigi, ut ipsum suscipiatis et in uestris eum obsequiis suis expensis excerceatis, ut si ipsum idoneum et
iuxta cor uestrum inueneritis, uestris omnino connumeretis. Quod ipsi licet honori
foret uobis tamen esse nollemus honeri. Vbi namque ⟨fo. 161⟩ multe diuitie sunt,
25 sunt et multi qui eas comedunt. Vnde et ipsum circa uos suis uellemus militare
stipendiis, ut emolumentum hoc de labore percipiat uestri dominium et notitiam,
et si uobis eum complacuisse nouerimus, a uobis impetrandi maiora fiduciam
habeamus. Valete.

**105** G, no. 143; B, fo. 160v.
7 cognouimus *before correction* B    27 a uobis...habeamus] maiora a uobis impetrandi fiduciam *before correction* B

---

[1] Ps. i. 1.    [2] See below, no. 107.    [3] Cf. Job iii. 5.

## 106  To Robert de Chesney, bishop of Lincoln

[March–April 1153] A letter on private business, on the *Digest*, which Ambrose (cf. no. 317 and *GF*, pp. 66, 288–9) is glossing, and on Gilbert's relations with the Lord Henry (the duke of Normandy):[1] his cases have been held over until Palm Sunday, and he has asked for a further extension.

Domno suo fratrique karissimo R(oberto) Lin(colniensi) Dei gratia episcopo G(ilebertus) Herefordensis ecclesie minister, hec gustare et sapere que parauit in dulcedine sua pauperi Deus.[2]

Si bene ualetis[3] sic est ut uolumus et nostrum inde gaudium ad perfectum adducitur et ad omnem letitiam cumulatur. Digestam corrigi et glosari precipitis, et ecce 5 Ambrosius uester laborare non desinit in tritura.[4] Cetera que mandastis dante Domino non differentur. Causarum nostrarum cum potestatibus nostris fata adhuc ambigua sunt, et que sunt in pendulo quam cito stabiliri ceperint, ilico currente cartula cognoscetis. Vsque ad diem Palmarum nobis a domno Henrico concesse sunt, sed eas prorogari ulterius misso nuntio—nondumque reuerso—postulamus. 10 Experiemur in his finem quem concesserit Dominus, de ipso sperantes bona nobis tribui, qui reprobat cogitationes populorum et dissipat consilia principum.[5] Optamus uos in Domino ualere et in ipso de die in diem renouari[6] et proficere in Domino, karissime.

## 107  To Robert de Chesney, bishop of Lincoln

[*c.* 1153 or later] He regrets that the bishop could not get to Prestbury (Glos)[7] to meet him, and urges the bishop to assist G(ilbert) Foliot in the case about his benefice. He asks the bishop to send him a confidential letter in his own hand.[8]

In 105 Gilbert had recommended Gilbert Foliot to the bishop; from this letter it seems clear (on the reasonable assumption that the G. of this letter and the Gilbert of 105 are identical) that he had passed into the bishop's service. The way in which Bishop Gilbert petitions Robert de Chesney suggests that their kinsman's entry into Robert's service was recent; and the account of the attempted meeting at Prestbury would fit the troubled period of civil war in 1153–4.

**106** G, no. 90; B, fo. 21v.
7 Cause nostre B; *the plural seems dictated by* concesse…eas *below, unless a word has fallen out of the next sentence*
**107** G, no. 136; B, fo. 157 (*in top margin*: deprecatorie ad diocesanum pro clerico in causam tracto).

---

[1] Presumably—one cannot imagine any other 'Lord Henry' of this period who could have treated a bishop in this way; at the same time Gilbert would not have referred to a king by this title, which was, however, that used (among others) for heirs to the throne.
[2] Cf. Ps. lxvii. 11.    [3] Cf. no. 105.
[4] For Gilbert's knowledge of the *Digest*, see *GF*, p. 64.
[5] Cf. Ps. xxxii. 10.    [6] Cf. II Cor. iv. 16.
[7] Or Cheshire, but Prestbury in Cheshire seems very far north for them to meet; Prestbury (Glos) is about 40 miles south-east of Hereford.
[8] The meaning of this is not entirely clear—as was evidently intended.

Venerabili domno fratrique karissimo R(oberto) Lincolniensi Dei gratia episcopo frater G(ilebertus) Herefordensis ecclesie minister salutem.

Spe fruende uisionis et allocutionis optate currentes Presteberiam iam ueneramus. Suspendit desiderium nostrum fatalis aduersitas, et uos alia trahente necessitate, 5 allisus ad eam nostri cursus impetus contra uotum et uelle nostrum cohibetur. Scribimus autem uobis in amoris experimentum immo omnium amicitiarum gratiam, quatinus cognatum nostrum et amicum G(ilebertum) Foliot in causa que super ecclesia sua aduersus eum instituitur sustentetis, et uestro et uestrorum consilio eatenus ⟨fo. 157 v⟩ sustentari faciatis, quatinus absentiam nostram uestra illi 10 presentia suppleat, et an quicquam possimus apud uos inpensa sibi benignitate et gratia recognoscat. Ad pedes uestros quos ipsi manibus libentius amplecteremur, quia hoc ad presens non possumus, deprecatorias has supplicando deponimus, habituri de exauditione gloriam, aut de repulsa confusionem non modicam. De cetero si nobis secretum aliquod scriptorum non communicandum consilio 15 intimare placuerit, antiquorum reminisci studiorum et scolam uel ad momentum repetere, et propria exarare manu non tedeat, ad quod sensus nostri tenuitas re alii non communicata respondeat. Valete.

### 108   To Brother William de Hinet'[1]

[*c.* August–September 1153] A letter of consolation, and a lament and panegyric, on the death of (St Bernard) the abbot of Clairvaux.

Bernard died on 20 August 1153, and the opening of this letter implies that the shock of the news was very recent. The letter is full of echoes of the Song of Songs—appropriate to a panegyric on Bernard.

Gillebertus Dei gratia Herefordensis episcopus dilecto fratri Willelmo de Hinet', consecrata Domino tirocinia beato perseuerantie fine concludere.

Auditis que circa te sunt exultaui totus in Domino,[2] illi gratiarum referens actionem qui meritum omne preueniens, gratiarum suis dona benigne distribuit. 5 Audita tamen mutatione tam subita paulisper obstupui, quousque reuersus ad cor illud pre oculis habui, quod uelociter currit sermo Domini quo uult,[3] et ipsius dextera potenter inmutat quem uult. Hic ad te sermo factus est, hec te dextera apprehendit; hic tibi sermo consilium, hec manus auxilium ministrauit; hic uelle bonum formauit in te, hec ad effectum operis ipsum uelle perduxit. Hic sermo cor 10 tuum tangens celitus et illuminans quod in spiritu consilii conceperas, potenter in spiritu fortitudinis[4] roborauit. Hic in tenebris latenti tibi uiam qua progrederis ostendit, hec te per iter quo ostendat tibi salutare Dei iam deduxit. Intueri michi

---

**107** 5 imp. curs. nostri *before correction* B    8 su$\overset{a}{p}$ B
**108** G, no. 112; B, fo. 34.

---

[1] Unidentified, but evidently a friend of Gilbert who had recently become a Cistercian (probably a monk at Clairvaux).
[2] Cf. Hildebert, *Ep.* I, 4 (*PL,* CLXXI, 146).          [3] Cf. Ps. cxlvii. 15.
[4] Cf. Is. xi. 2.

uideor illum superni scribe calamum, cordis tui tabulas exarantem et uocationem qua sponsus et sponsa dicunt 'ueni',[1] eisdem fortiter imprimentem, quam (ut audio) non tu frater tepide, non segniter aduertisti, sed dilecti pulsantis ad hostium, 15 uocem prudenter audiens et intelligens, ut hostii tui pessulum ipsi statim aperires, ilico surrexisti dicens: 'uox dilecti pulsantis'.[2] Vsus consilio sane laudabili, qui auctori uite domicilium non solum in te sed et teipsum preparasti, experiris illud in te quod apostolo de supernis innotuit: 'durum est tibi contra stimulum calcitrare'.[3] Nam quidam uite stimulus est et quidam mortis. 'Et mortis quidem stimulus 20 peccatum est.'[4] Nam ut pecus urgetur stimulo ut irrumpat et impingat quo uult ipse qui stimulat, sic peccatum quem pungit urget et impingit indubitanter ad mortem. 'Stipendia namque peccati mors.'[5] Longe mentem aliter stimulus amoris exagitat. Vite namque stimulus est et amantem fortiter urget ad uitam. Contra quem calcitrare tam durum est quam caritati reluctari difficile. 'Nam fortis est ut 25 mors dilectio.'[6] Separat a carne mors, a mundo diuidit, sic et amor sanctus etsi longe nobilius a mundo tamen et a carne sequestrat. Illo trahit unde est: non a mundo est, non a carne, 'non ex sanguinibus, neque ex uoluntate carnis, neque ex uoluntate uiri, sed ex Deo natus est'.[7] Ad ipsum trahit; ipse finis amoris est. De quo Dauid: 'omnis consummationis uidi finem'.[8] In hunc finem tendit amor, nec est uagus 30 amor ille qui sanctus est. Habet pre se quem diligit, illud corde dicens, illud ore decantans: 'oculi mei semper ad Dominum'.[9] In hunc oculum defixisti, in ipso tibi complacuit cui speramus etiam complacuisse in te. Hunc per uiam arctam et arduam secutus es, et amoris te trahente funiculo non ad dexteram uel ad sinistram declinasti.[10] Non respexisti ad pros⟨fo. 34 v⟩pera et aduersa formidare dedignatus es. 35 Crucifixum crucem eius baiulando prosequeris, crucem exprimis habitu, crucem mente pertractas. Hec sursum caput eleuans iam celis imperat, inferna deorsum premit, ipsius afixi manibus totam mundi latitudinem hinc et inde complectens; his manibus apprehensus es nunc portans inproperium Domini Iesu,[11] ut sis quandoque particeps et corone. Ipsius stigmata portabis[12] ad modicum et in tua clauos eius carne 40 defiges. Vestis horrida, cibus inparatior, lectisternia dura, labor manuum, discipline grauitas, iuge silentium, ipsos qui te pungant in te clauos exprimunt saluatoris. Habes et instar lancee que lateri eius infixa est, ipsum karitatis aculeum qui tuo semper pectori iuge uulnus infligat. In hunc modum uulnerat qui karitatem format in nobis, ille spiritus unus et summus. Hoc languebat uulnere que dicebat: 'fulcite 45 me floribus, stipate me malis, quia amore langueo'.[13] O uulnus bonum et languor suauissimus quem mors illa comitatur de qua scriptum est: 'pretiosa mors sanctorum in conspectu Domini'.[14] Attolle iam non solum mentis oculos sed et corporis. Vinea Domini iam saltus omnes ocupat, impleuit deserta, et sanctorum pugna cum

---

19 stim calcit, *with symbol for marginal note, now lost (the Alessandrina MS reads* stimulum calcitrare, *as Vulg.*)  35 rexpexisti B

---

[1] Cf. Apoc. xxii. 17.  [2] This sentence has several echoes of Cant. v. 1–2.
[3] Act. ix. 5.  [4] I Cor. xv. 56.  [5] Rom. vi. 23.
[6] Cant. viii. 6.  [7] Joh. i. 13.  [8] Ps. cxviii. 96.
[9] Ps. xxiv. 15.  [10] Cf. Num. xxii. 26, etc.  [11] Cf. Heb. xiii. 13.
[12] Cf. Gal. vi. 17.  [13] Cant. ii. 5.  [14] Ps. cxv. 15.

50 spinis est. Ponunt praua in directa, et aspera in uias planas,[1] et quod intus agunt
spiritu, corporis excercitio foris insinuant. Intus enim uitiorum sentes extirpant,
annosa peccati robora karitatis igne conflagrant. Tumoris alta deiciunt, terram
desertam inaquosam et inuiam, uirtutum reddunt copiis habundantem, peccato
mortui simul et mundo, ut se Christo sanctificent preter ipsum omnia contemp-
55 nentes. Mors ista sanctorum est, quam esse propheta memorat in conspectu Domini
pretiosam. Nam quid Christo carius, quid in nobis ipsi pretiosius, quam ut ipsum
imitando mortem morte superemus? Et que tanta mors anime est quam uitiorum
feda congeries? Hac uero morte qua mundo morimur, hec ipsa uincitur et enecatur,
iuxta illud prophete: 'persequar inimicos meos et comprehendam illos, et non
60 conuertar donec deficiant. Confringam illos nec poterunt stare: cadent subtus pedes
meos.'[2] Primis parentibus dictum est: 'morte moriemini'.[3] Mors enim peccati uere
mortis eterne ministra est. Obedientie uero filiis apostolus ait: 'mortui estis, et uita
uestra cum Christo abscondita est'.[4] Vere beata mors que uite illius que cum
Christo est causa simul est et ministra. Hanc tibi mortem uulnus amoris ingerit, ut
65 de iure tibi quod dictum est uendicare iam possis: 'fulcite me floribus, stipate me
malis, quia amore langueo'.[5] Quid enim floribus nisi sanctorum recens conuersio,
quid malis nisi eorundem in uirtute iam solidata consummatio intelligitur? Odor
quippe bonus et futuri fructus in flore spes est, hunc odorem spirat ecclesie sanctorum conuersio, in quibus in uirum perfectum iam formatis fructus uite producitur
70 et maturatur. His igitur iam languens anima fulciri postulat, stipari desiderat, ut
exemplis sanctorum sibi propositis in sue conuersionis initio beate ferueat et
prouectu proficiat, et in exitu fortiter inardescat. Vnde michi flores unde mala
quibus te karissime fulciam, tue quibus anime in Domino Jesu iam languenti
satisfaciam? Sed a me quid exigas que penes te sunt, que liberis iam palam con-
75 spectibus intueris? Cisterciensis ecclesia per orbem late effloruit, que flores mundi
⟨fo. 35⟩ gratissimos undequaque decerpens, ipsos transtulit in se et in quosdam
paradisi flores celesti quadam mutatione transformauit. Ipsos mente conspicias ut
nouellas oliuarum in ipsius mense circuitu pululantes.[6] In ipsorum optime curres
odorem qui uelut adolescentule quarum non est numerus in odorem sponsi currere
80 non desistunt.[7] Quod si poma post flores exigis, ipsa quoque est que celesti sponso
quadam prerogatiua decantat: 'omnia poma noua et uetera dilecte me reseruaui
tibi'.[8] In ipsa grex tonsarum est qui deposito peccati uellere, de penitentie lauacro
nouiter ascenderunt.[9] In ipsa grex fetarum est que in pascuis Bethel iam commorate
diutius uirtutum lanis decentissime uestiuntur. In ipsa et oues emerite que post
85 sobolem numerosam iamiam parere desinentes, ad caulas illas supernorum ciuium
boni pastoris humero transferri desiderant.

O quis ego sum qui pastorem illum sanctum ouemque fecundissimam Clareual-
l(ensem) abbatem clarissimum digne commemorem? Quis michi stilus aut que

**108** 67 ian B    75 Cistrescensis *corrected* B

---

[1] Cf. Is. xl. 4.    [2] Ps. xvii. 38–9.    [3] Gen. ii. 17.
[4] Col. iii. 3.    [5] Cant. ii. 5.    [6] Cf. Ps. cxxvii. 3.
[7] Cf. Cant. i. 2–3.    [8] Cant. vii. 13.    [9] Cf. Cant. iv. 2.

facundia, ut uirtutis eius uel in modico culmen attingam? Vir scientia clarus, sanctitate notissimus, sine fuco sanctissimus, scriptor insignis, predicator egregius, 90 ordinis speculum, ecclesie dilatatio, sui temporis sol, nebule dissipatio, abiectus sibi, mundo Christoque karissimus, sacerdos magnus qui diebus suis Deo placens et iustus inuentus, iracundie tempore in ipso mirabiliter operante Domino Iesu dissidentium factus est reconciliatio. Vir squaloribus horridus, cuius consumptis carnibus, ossibus undique cutis adhesit, cuius nec uenter crapulam, nec os delicias 95 preterquam spirituales sapiebat. Quem cum corporalis intuebatur oculus, mundo despicabilis habebatur; cum spiritualis attendebat, nostri temporis hominem longe uirtutum meritis anteibat. Quis eius labores digne referat? Sociatam sibi Thamar nunquam repulit,[1] sed eius amara toto uite curriculo protrahens, intus uirtutum delicias, foris spinas portabat. Doctus agricola plantabat undique fortiter, affluenter 100 rigabat, et plantationibus eius innumeris habundanter Dominus incrementa prestabat. Vnde non tibi Paulos frater, non Antonios, non Hilariones, non Arsenios,[2] non antiquarum arborum paradisi uetustos fructus in tui recreationem spiritus anteponam. Hic ecce presens est cuius recens auctoritas, quem oculis ipse conspicere quemque docentem (ut arbitror) audire meruisti. A nobis equidem ad superna 105 translatus est, et est aput Dominum merces illius. Porro nomen eius uiuet in secula, et eius ab ecclesia memoria non recedet. Hoc paradisi lignum prudenter his diebus a Domino in oculis ecclesie plantatum est, ut uirtutum gradus quisquis attemptare uoluerit, exemplares in illo uirtutes quas imitetur omnes inueniat. Tu quoque qui malis stipari postulas, hinc tibi quot uoles ipse decerpas. Hoc tamen scribens non 110 statim attemptare summa suadeo. Nemo repente fit optimus. Pecunia seruatur optime que paulatim collecta manu reponitur. Suis incrementis et gradibus uirtus unaqueque perficitur. Ipse etiam uirtutum chorus in mente bene disposita certa ratione distinguitur. Vt edificium spirituale prudenter erigas, prima tibi iaciatur humilitas, et mentis ei benignitas adhibeatur. ⟨fo. 35 v⟩ His adhereat obedientia 115 quam suo patientia uigore corroboret. Has omnes perseuerantia sancta discipline cibo reficiat.[3] Sic in uirum perfectum dispositus, in lata karitatis regna perucnies. Que cum letus intraueris, uirum statim mutatus in alterum, noua omnia nouus ipse in te miraberis. Deinceps in uia Domini nil durum tibi reputabis aut asperum,[4] totum quod horret caro tua tibi spiritus in uirtute dulcescet. Hinc uirtutum pasceris 120 in liliis donec eternitatis aspiret dies,[5] quo Dominum Iesum quem mente secutus es, feliciter apprehendas. In quo uale memor mei karissime.

**108** 96 in/intuebatur B    105 ? arbritror B    113 in bene mente B *corrected to* mente in bene [*sic*]    120 dulces/cescet B

---

[1] Cf. Gen. xxxviii. 15, etc.
[2] Names of noted fathers of the desert: Paul, Anthony and Hilarion are the subjects of the first three lives in the *Vitae Patrum* (PL, LXXIII); for Arsenius see coll. 762–4, 953–5, etc.
[3] Cf. *Regula S. Benedicti*, c. 7.
[4] *Ibid.* c. 58.
[5] Cf. Cant. iv. 5–6.

## 109   To Richard de Belmeis, bishop of London

[Summer 1154] Peace has been restored with John (of Canterbury); but Gilbert regrets that a new dispute has arisen, with Henry. The assistance of the bishop of Lincoln must be invoked; Gilbert suggests a meeting at Oxford on the Wednesday after the Feast of the Assumption,[1] but excuses himself from the journey the bishop had proposed.

Peace with John of Canterbury dates this letter to 1154. Trouble over the archdeaconry of Middlesex was followed by trouble over the archdeaconry of Colchester; and it is probable that the Henry of this letter is to be identified with the Henry of London of John of Salisbury, *Ep.* 5—a settlement by Archbishop Theobald, presumably acting as papal judge delegate,[2] of a dispute over the archdeaconry of Colchester, and the churches of Fulham and Stepney.

The journey mentioned in this letter probably indicates another projected visit to the Holy See by Richard de Belmeis: once again, the bishop is preparing to go to Rome; once again Gilbert refuses to accompany him; and, as before, the bishop of Lincoln, their senior relative on the bench, is to be called in to assist. Gilbert suggests a meeting on 18 August, and so this letter may be dated to the summer of 1154.

Venerabili domno fratrique karissimo R(icardo) Lundoniensi Dei gratia episcopo frater G(ilebertus) Herefordensis ecclesie minister salutem.

Paci uestre congratulor que cum Iohanne reformata est. Opto autem ut que nuper exorta sunt discreta alicuius interueniente prudentia pacificentur. Contristor autem
5 et totus consternor animo quod talia aduersum uos permisistis erumpere, que omnia suffocasse mediocris quidem—dum tamen prouida—circumspectio potuisset. Nam licet falsa sint que dicuntur, que tamen iactantur in uulgus, malam oratione fabulam per multorum aures disseminant. Estimo uero necessariam domni Lincolniensis industriam, ut ipse quocumque poterit modo Henricum ad se euocet et
10 negotio incumbat eatenus, ut que motus iracundia protulit, conuersus ad cor[3] deserat et a proposita intentione simul et appellatione discedat. Quod equidem optinere sapienti non erit difficile, qui lapidem nouerit omnem mouere. Dicere namque leue est, sed episcopum aut honestum clericum in huiusmodi conuincere eius certe uiribus inpossibile.[4] Formidandum sibi equidem ne pena quam in alterum
15 intentat in semetipsum obruat et inuoluat. Quicquid tamen egerit uobis domnum papam adire necesse est, quod multo honestius faceretis, oblitteratis que obiecta sunt confessione penitentis. De cetero uobis ad colloquium occurrere apud Oxe⟨ne⟩ford(iam) ⟨die⟩ Mercurii proxima post Assumptionem Beate Virginis paratus sum—sed ad iter quod exigitis, omnino certe imparatus. Nam etsi in pace
20 sunt que possideo, ipsi tamen conseruande necessariam meam omnino presentiam

109 G, no. 137; B, fo. 158.
7 tamen *nos*; tam B    7-8 oratio-|fabulam *? over erasure* B

---

[1] I.e., if the year was 1154, 18 August (not 19 August, as *JS Epp*, I, no. 5 n.).
[2] Since he invokes papal authority at the end of the letter; but this may be solely in virtue of his office of legate. In any event the case passed to Theobald on appeal from the bishop.
[3] Cf. Ps. lxxxiv. 9, etc.
[4] The meaning of this passage is not entirely clear.

intelligo. Quam etsi me absente non turbari contingeret, residuum tamen locuste apud nos brucus adeo comedit, ut post brucum quod comedat eruca iam non inueniat.[1] Valete, et colloquio nostro (si fuerit) domnum Lincolniensem uocate.

## 110  To Walter Durdent, bishop of Chester

[1150–9] The bishop has consulted him on a legal problem. With copious quotations from Roman law Gilbert attempts to answer the question: if the papal legate (i.e. Archbishop Theobald) has issued a mandate that he submit to judgement in the case between himself and the monk Ingenulf[2] without right of appeal (*remota appellatione*), is an appeal possible under any circumstances?

Theobald probably became legate in 1150 (or late 1149); Bishop Walter died in 1159. See *GF*, pp. 238–9.

Venerabili domino fratrique karissimo W(altero) Cestrensi Dei gratia episcopo frater G(ilebertus) Herefordensis ecclesie minister, salutem et dilectionem.

Queritis an appellationi locus sit, cum mandatum domni legati susceperitis ut Ingenulfo monacho, remota appellatione, respondeatis. Qui forsitan Ingenulfus causam que uertitur inter uos domino pape non adeo diligenter exposuit, ut quod a 5 uobis in ipsum actum est, apostolica gestum auctoritate declararet. Vnde si palliata humilitate et innoscentia simulata iudicem ad pietatem commouendo rescriptum impetrauit, quod uestram non solum grauet sed puniat obedientiam prescriptione mendaciorum opposita, intentionem si placuerit elidetis. Vestram enim non latet prudentiam quod super hoc in primo codicis in hunc modum continetur; 'pre- 10 scriptione mendaciorum opposita, si non in iuris narratione mendacium reperiatur, si non in facti, si non in tacendi fraude pro tenore ueritatis, non deprecantis affirma- tione datum iudicem cognoscere et sententiam ferre oportet'.[3] Vnde et consequenter adicitur, 'puniri iudicis uniuersos iubemus, qui uetuerint precum argui falsitatem', et ilico: 'et si non cognitio sed executio mandatur de ueritate precum inquiri 15 oportet, ut si fraus interuenit de omni negotio cognoscatur'.[4] Quarto quoque loco subiungitur: 'et si legibus quid consentaneum mendax precator attulerit, careat penitus inpetratis et seueritati subiaceat iudicantis.'[5] Litteras itaque domni pape sepius audiri et diligenter inspici bonum est, ut si quid ex his aduerteritis unde precum falsitatem arguere possitis, arguende falsitati insistatis, et per leges iam 20 propositas iudicem secundum uos pronuntiare conpellatis. Quod si ad appella- tionem confugere necessitas extrema decreuerit, super hoc aliud non occurrit, nisi quod in septimo codicis inuenimus, quia 'et in maioribus et in minoribus negotiis omnibus quique lege excipiuntur appellandi facultas est'.[6] Vnde et in eodem codicis Alexander Augustus: 'nouum quod postulas non est, quod etsi rescripti mei 25

110 G, no. 144; B, fo. 161.

---

[1] Cf. Joel i. 4: 'Residuum erucae comedit locusta, et residuum locustae comedit bruchus, et residuum bruchi comedit rubigo.'
[2] Conceivably the Ingenulf was also first abbot of Buildwas (Eyton, *Salop*, VI, 321).
[3] *Code*, 1, 22, 2.    [4] *Code*, 1, 22, 3–4.    [5] *Code*, 1, 22, 5.    [6] *Code*, 7, 62, 20.

auctoritas intercesserit, prouocandi tamen facultas nec denegetur'.[1] Nos tamen nec os ponentes in celum[2] nec scriptum domni pape iudicare presumentes, non quid ⟨fo. 161 v⟩ de iure agendum sit ad presens, sed quod in huiusmodi casu ageremus exposuimus. Leges certe promulgate sunt quorum et in quibus casibus appella-
30 tiones recipi non oporteat. Quarum nos cum nulla tangeret aut notaret, ad ipsum utique appellaremus, quem omni suscipiende appellationi que lege non excipitur, debitorem utique non ambigimus. Valeat, et in spiritu consilii uideat quod agendum est domnus meus in Christo karissimus.

### III To Theobald, archbishop of Canterbury

[1150–61] Gilbert had delayed the case between the monks of Combermere (Cheshire, Cistercian) and Herbert of Helgot's Castle (Holdgate, Salop) about Church Preen (Salop) till the return of the abbot of Combermere; but when the abbot returned the case also proved to involve the prior and monks of Much Wenlock (Salop, Cluniac), and the prior demanded a delay on the technical ground that he had not been cited or named in the dispute. This led the abbot of Combermere to appeal.[3]

Archbishop Theobald probably became legate early in 1150 and died in 1161.[4] It is evident from this letter that monks from Wenlock had already been settled at Preen; in the long run it remained a small Cluniac house, dependent on Wenlock. Preen had been held by Helgot, Herbert's grandfather, in 1086. Richard de Belmeis, who was probably Herbert's tenant, seems to have given it to Wenlock.[5]

Patri suo et domno T(heobaldo) Cant(uariensi) Dei gratia archiepiscopo et Anglorum primati et sedis apostolice legato frater G(ilebertus) Herefordensis ecclesie minister, salutem et obedientiam.

Mandastis nobis ob querelam abbatis et monacorum Combremar', quatinus
5 Herebertum de castello Halgod conueniremus, et ut predictis monacis locum qui dicitur Prena restitueret, et omnia in eodem loco sibi ablata redderet commonere-mus. Quod cum perlatum fuisset ad nos monacis mandati latoribus persuasimus ne litem hanc absente abbate suo ⟨fo. 159 v⟩ inchoarent, et exspectato de transmarinis partibus eius reditu, actionem ipso presente instituerent. Ipsis itaque huic con-
10 silio adquiescentibus rem ipsorum consensu distulimus. Nuper uero cum apud Ledel(eiam)[6] ob quedam negotia sederemus, ⟨abbas Com⟩bremar(ensis), de

III G, no. 141; B, fo. 159 (*in bottom margin*: relatio iudicis ordinarii ad iudicem superiorem de processu cause). 4 qrelam B 11 d'obremarum B (*omitting* abbas), *with symbol for marginal note of which only* [...] em' *survives. It seems certain from what follows that Combermere was represented at the trial by its abbot*

---

[1] *Code*, 7, 62, 2.      [2] Cf. Ps. lxxii. 9 (and no. 128).
[3] The prior of Wenlock was either Reginald (occ. *c.* 1138–9 and after 1151; Eyton, *Salop*, I, 207; *Cart. Oseney*, v, 31) or Humbald (Eyton, *Salop*, IV, 42–3; *MB*, I, 338). The abbot of Combermere was either William the first abbot (1133–46 or later; *Monasticon*, v, 628; G. Barraclough, *Early Cheshire Charters*, p. 1) or Geoffrey (occ. –1155, Eyton, *Salop*, VIII, 217 = *Monasticon*, VI, 263; cf. Barraclough, *op. cit.* p. 3, who dates the document *c.* 1149–50, but so early a date cannot be established).
[4] See *GF*, p. 92 n.      [5] KH, p. 96; see Eyton, *Salop*, VI, 221; see *ibid.* IV, 54–7 for Herbert.
[6] Perhaps Ludlow or Lydley Heys (Salop).

cuius reditu nichil ante noueramus, interfuit. Qui cum ibidem aduersus priorem de Weneloc conquestus fuisset quod prior ipse monacos suos de loco qui Prena dicitur [. . .], et non solum ipsorum pecora sed et calices et libros et uestimenta, totamque domus eorum subpellectilem abstulisset, prior dilatoriam opponens exceptionem, 15 sibi litem hanc nequaquam editam neque se super hoc ad responsionem citatum fuisse, respondit. Cumque omnium sententia consentiente decerneretur equum iurique consentaneum utrique parti diem statui, remque sufficienter auditam iudicio terminari, abbas conquerens non ilico sibi que petebat restitui, ad appellationem conuolauit. Si quid igitur in sic data sententia corrigendum noueritis, ipsi 20 iuxta datam uobis sapientiam corrigetis, uestroque parituris mandato, quod libuerit iniungetis. Valeat domnus meus et pater in Christo karissimus.

## 112   To Pope A(nastasius, Adrian or Alexander)

[1153–61] On behalf of Nicholas, who has been deprived of his archdeaconry.

Only two archdeacons named Nicholas are recorded in the provinces of Canterbury and York in this period: one was archdeacon of Brecon (dioc. St Davids), the other of London (see *GF*, pp. 271–2). Comparison with John of Salisbury, *Ep.* 86, which is in very similar terms,[1] shows that this letter was written on behalf of the archdeacon of Brecon, deposed by his bishop in favour of his recently dispossessed predecessor Archdeacon Jordan. In the event Jordan retained the archdeaconry, to be finally deposed and replaced by Gerald of Wales in 1175.

The Pope addressed could be Anastasius IV (1153–4), Adrian IV (1154–9), or Alexander III (1159–81, but not formally recognized in England before *c.* November 1160); John of Salisbury's letter can be dated 1153–61, and this must be contemporary with it.

Patri suo et domno summo pontifici A. frater G(ilebertus) Herefordensis ecclesie minister, debitum caritatis et obedientie famulatum.

Quo fratrum corda pius amor connectat uinculo, nemo uobis pater altius inspicit, penes quem uirtutum magistra karitas principatum nobiliter optinens, uirtutem condigne remunerante Domino, uos totius Israel currum aurigamque 5 constituit.[2] Hac nobis plurimum inperante, dilecto fratri nostro presentium latori Nicolao compatimur, et lugenti collacrimantes pro ipso sullimitati uestre etsi nulla spe meriti, benignitatis tamen apostolice confisi gratia supplicamus. Absens enim innoxius et ignorans archidiaconatu quem et iuste possidebat et ministrabat sobrie, nulla iuris aut ordinis obseruatione spoliatus est. Qua de re cum suum iam frequen- 10 ter episcopum multorum etiam interuentu conuenerit, nil inueniens solacii, nil omnino remedii, ad oppressorum confugit speciale subsidium ubi facit Dominus iudicium inopi, et afflicte causam uidue intra sui penetral conclauis admittit. Quem

---

**III** 14 *A space left in* B   16 scitatum B   17 consentiente *Giles;* con *and a space in* B
**112** G, no. 113; B, fo. 35 v.

---

[1] 'Porro *lator presentium Nicholaus . . . archidiaconatu, quem* canonice habebat, contra omnem reuerentiam *iuris absens spoliatus est. . . .*' See note *ad loc.* for the two archdeacons.
[2] Cf. IV Reg. ii. 12.

cum id exigente iustitia et agente misericordia, clementer exaudieritis, multos ⟨ad⟩
15 id desiderii et orationis ad Dominum inflammabitis, ut in longa tempora feliciter
disponatis et iudicetis Israel qui causas eius non ex personarum acceptione sed
equitate summa dicernitis. Valeat domnus meus et pater in Christo karissimus.

## 113   To Richard, bishop of London

[c. 1153–61] The bishop of London has passed judgement in a dispute between one Roger (?)
and the monks (of Prittlewell),[1] while ignoring the claims of Richard of Ambli, who was in
possession of the property (a church) in dispute. In spite of a papal mandate to execute the
judgement, the bishop must stay the case and explain the circumstances to the Pope.

The heading in the manuscript is corrupt: it makes one bishop of London address another !
Giles emended the first to R(obert de Chesney) bishop of Lincoln; but comparison with
John of Salisbury's letters 73–5 proves that the letter belongs to c. 1153–61 and was written
to the bishop of London while Gilbert was bishop of Hereford (cf. line 2 ⟨Herefordensis⟩).
The action was collusive: 'Roger' (or Ralph or Robert, as he is variously called in the chief
MS of John of Salisbury's letters) sued the monks behind Richard de Ambli's back in order
to undermine Richard's right to possession of the church of Wakering (Essex)—and in the
first round the conspirators deceived the bishop of London into giving judgement. In the
event the case was referred by the Pope to Archbishop Theobald, but went back to Rome on
appeal from the original plaintiff (Roger or Ralph or Robert), and we hear no more of it.

Venerabili domno fratrique karissimo R(icardo) Lund(oniensi) Dei gratia episcopo
frater G(ilebertus) ⟨Herefordensis⟩ ecclesie minister salutem.

Vobis loquimur sicut et nobis, nec uolunt alii secreta committi. Super causa quam
nobis intimare curastis, ad presens illud in primis occurrit, quod certam promul-
5 gastis super re incerta sententiam; et cum de facto non constaret, pronuntiare tamen
sic curastis ac si de facto constiterit. Nam cum actioni uestre aduersarium pariat
ipsa possessio, non ante sententiam solum, sed in ipso litis ingressu, oportebat
constare qui possideret, a quo petitor ipse quod sui dicebat iuris esse repeteret.[2]
Nunc uero Ricardo de Ambli in possessione posito, et per negotii gestorem rem
10 sui iuris esse protestante, non inter petitorem et ipsum in possessione positum, sed
magis alios extra possessionem constitutos, non quidem cognitum, sed iudicatum
est. Vobis enim notionem ferre non ualuit monachorum de se, uel archidiaconi
uestri uel decani super altero, nulla exhibita probatione confessio. Vnde palam est,
Ricardo de Ambli sententia sic lata, quid officiat cum aliis, res inter alios iudicata

113 G, no. 222; B, fo. 183 v.
2 ⟨Herefordensis⟩] Lund' B (*certainly an error—see above; possibly taken from the addressee, but
the preceding letter in B, no. 326, contains the same mistake*)   6 nostre B   8 constaret B
14 quid] ? *for* quicquid

---

[1] *JS Epp.* I, no. 75 mentions the prior of Prittlewell (Essex, Cluniac) as one of the parties, and
the church of Wakering (Essex) as the subject of the controversy (see note *ad loc.*).
[2] It was a principle of Canon law to establish possession before the question of right could be
investigated. The procedure derived from Roman law, and was also applied in English
secular law (see note to no. 175). Had possession been established at the outset of this case, its
collusive nature would have been disclosed.

non noceat.[1] Aduertat itaque prudentia uestra quid domno pape scripseritis, cui ut 15 literarum ipsius tenor exprimit, causam inter Rogerum et Ricardum uentilatam et iudicio terminatam esse scripsistis. Quod si sic actum est, sicut factum ipsum, sic inprobamus et scriptum. Si uero non, sed ut frequenter humanus caligat oculus, negotium secus quam gestum aut scriptum est domnus papa concepit, uidetur nobis illorum admittenda exceptio, qui precis oblate et suggeste rei arguunt falsitatem. 20 Hec enim non quecumque falsitas est, sed que totam perimit cause substantiam— que ipsi possessionem adimit, qui nunquam citatus est; ⟨fo. 184⟩ aduersus quem nec actitatum in iure, nec unquam pronuntiatum est; inter quem et Rogerum latam sententiam qui confirmat, cum hec nulla sit, nullam confirmare uidetur. Mandatum uero domni pape si difertis, non omittitis, nec frustratoria dilatio illa habenda est, que 25 ueritate simul et ratione subnixa est. Erit itaque (si placet) domno pape rescribendum, et ipsius mandatum qua causa quantaque ratione distuleritis aperiendum. Quod cum ex suggestis pendeat, ipsis derogata fide differendum esse nullus ignorat. Pauperi uero extraordinarie et in alterius iniuriam subuenire, non equum ducimus, cum super hoc diuina lex habeat, 'non misereberis pauperis in iudicio' et iudicem calamitosis 30 illacrimari non debere, Iustinianus ipse decernat.[2] Valete, et saniorem preferre sententiam non omittite.

### 114 To Josce de Dinant

[1148–63] He commends Josce (castellan of Ludlow)[3] and sympathizes regarding an attempt against him; but firmly insists that he must restore the church of Stanton[4] and its goods before the diocesan synod. The pledge he has taken from R. de Furcis in ecclesiastical property is null and void.

Letters 114–22 cannot be dated more closely than the limits of Gilbert's episcopate at Hereford.

Gileb(ertus) Dei gratia Herefordensis episcopus amico suo I(ozoni) de Dinan, salutem et dilectionem.

Audi, karissime, que tibi mando et monitis meis (si ex Deo sunt) adquiescere non despicias. Habes a multis testimonium bonum[5] quod Deum et ecclesiam eius hactenus in magna ⟨fo. 20⟩ reuerentia habuisti, et clericos et alios quosque religiosi 5 ordinis uiros diligentius honorasti. Pauperes etiam qui tuo famulatui obnoxii sunt non oppressisti, sed magis affectu paterno fouisti, et illesos seruasti. Hanc tuam iustitiam et animi bonitatem respexit Deus, et nunc aliquantulum misertus tui in futuro amplius miserebitur. Audio a multis aliquos conspirasse aduersus te, et te

---

**113** 18 freqnter B
**114** G, no. 85; B, fo. 19v.

---

[1] Cf. *Digest*, 48, 2, 7, 2; below, no. 246; *GF*, p. 239.
[2] Cf. *Digest*, 1, 18, 19, 1 (we have not identified the quotation).
[3] Josce was made castellan of Ludlow by Stephen, but rebelled against him in 1139 and remained an Angevin thereafter. He survived into Henry II's reign, and died a monk at Gloucester (Eyton, *Salop*, v, 243–8; cf. *Cart. Gloucester*, I, 95).
[4] Presumably one of the Stantons in Salop.      [5] Cf. I Tim. iii. 7.

10 nesciente et absente in detrimentum tui pessima quedam preparasse. Eorum autem consilium (ut dicitur) dissipauit Dominus[1] et denudauit, et te, qui illum illesum in membris suis seruasti, ipse quoque illesum seruauit. Hoc, karissime, tibi non attribuas, sed magis illi gratiarum referas actionem. Si itaque ad ecclesiam eius et bona ecclesiastica in Stantune manum male extendisti, auctoritate ipsius et ab ipso
15 nobis iniuncto officio te moneo ut ante sinodum cuncta ecclesie ipsi in nullo imminuta restituas, ne ab ea quam predixi gratia graui separatione cadas. Scias enim pro certo, et hoc ultimum firmiter teneas, quod res ecclesiastice cuiuscumque fideiussione nisi presente et fauente episcopo alicui mortalium obligari non possunt. Plegium quod in ecclesiasticis de R. ⟨de⟩ Furcis me nesciente cepisti, tibi non
20 tenetur, sed omni auctoritate liberum esse decernitur. Obedientem te nostris monitis conseruet omnipotens Deus.

## 115    To Robert of Burnham

[1148–63] He urges Robert against withdrawing from the arrangement made between them about the church of Wraysbury (Bucks), and so defrauding Gloucester of its pension from the church.[2]

Gilebertus Dei gratia episcopus Herefordensis amico suo Ro(berto) de Burnaham, salutem et dilectionem.

Quanto erga uos karitate ampliori affecti sumus tanto uobis et fame uestre consultius—quantum spectat ad nos—prouidere, ipsa quam prediximus karitate
5 suggerente commonemur. Verbis oris uestri multorumque relatu didicimus, uos a transactione inter nos habita super ecclesia de Wiredesberia resilire uelle, et ecclesiam de Gloec(estria) super sibi promisso celebriter a uobis annuo censu uelle defrudare. Qua in re moneo ut rerum exitus attendatis, ne forte si aliter fuerit, malefactum penitencia consequatur. Causa enim hec etsi principaliter non spectat
10 ad nos, spectat tamen secundario. Primum in causis locum actor optinet, secundarium testis.[3] Si ergo testis in causa hac productus fuero ecclesie cui tota plenitu-

114 10 pparasse B    16 immimuta B
115 G, no. 86; B, fo. 20.
8 defrudare B corrected to defraudare by modern (?) hand

---

[1] Cf. Job v. 13.

[2] The arrangement between Gloucester abbey and Robert is described in *Cart. Gloucester*, II, 170; Robert was granted Wraysbury church for a pension to Gloucester; also Langley and Laverstock. Master Robert seems to have been a protégé of Robert de Chesney bishop of Lincoln, and canon of Lincoln; after the death of David, brother of Bishop Alexander, on 20 January 1177 (*Giraldi Cambrensis Opera*, VII, 154; *PR 23 Henry II*, p. 156), he became archdeacon of Buckingham; he last occurs *c.* 1189, and he had been succeeded by 1197 (*c.* 1195) (*EYC*, VI, no. 49; *Reg. Lincoln*, II, nos. 323, 339; *Cart. Thame*, II, 105; BM Royal MS 11. B. ix, fo. 26v; *Cart. Eynsham*, I, 99; etc.; *Danelaw Charters*, pp. 213–14; *Cart. Oseney*, V, 326–7, 144; *Lincoln Statutes*, III, 793 (prob. 1189); *Reg. Lincoln*, III, no. 977). Walter Map describes him as 'uir...magnificus multarumque literarum' and describes an account he had from Robert of Arnold of Brescia (*De nugis*, I, 24).

[3] I.e., Gilbert's status is that of witness to the transaction, not plaintiff: as former abbot of Gloucester he is, however, intimately concerned.

dine caritatis astrictus sum in testimonio ueritatis deesse non potero. Astiterunt et nobis in transactione eadem uiri religiosi quamplurimi, qui si quid negare ceperitis in lucem acta producent. Retractetis itaque si placet consilium uestrum, et quod fide interueniente sub multorum presentia pepigistis, fideliter obserueiter; ne si forte 15 aberrare ceperitis multorum conuictus testimonio non solum ecclesiastici beneficii sed ordinis uestri periculum incurratis. Attendens illud sapientis, 'Melior est amici increpatio quam oscula blandientis inimici',[1] amico dura proposui quem ab eo quod sibi inutile et inhonestum reuocare curaui. Valete, et in omni emolumento temporali honestatem preponite.                                                        20

## 116   To Nigel, bishop of Ely

[1148–63] On behalf of Master Robert de Clare:[2] Gilbert asks the bishop to ensure to him full rights in the church he possesses in the bishop's jurisdiction.

Venerabili domno fratrique karissimo Nig(ello) Elien(si) Dei gratia episcopo, frater G(ilebertus) Herefordensis ecclesie minister, sic currere ut comprehendat.[3]

   Virtus et scientia, quanto rarior eo preciosior est, quantoque scientie et uirtuti paucos admodum operam dare cernimus eo studiosos earundem ampliori reuerentia dignos estimare debemus. Inde est quod magistrum Robertum de Clare, cuius et 5 honestas uite et scientie claritas iamdiu uobis innotuit, beniuolentie uestre commendamus attentius, si quid possumus apud uos, rogantes ut ecclesiam quam sub tuitione uestra possidet uestro sibi illesam imperturbatamque patrocinio conseruetis. Nam si placet elidetis e facili totum quod obiciunt qui de possessione eadem iamdiu cum illo transegerunt. Nam sicut rei iudicate sic et transactioni standum 10 esse certissimum est. Apud iudicem non presumo docentis officium, uerum exprimo postulantis affectum. Pro amico postulo, sed si apud amicum, fatear si optinere meruero. Valete.

## 117   To Elias de Say

[1148–63] Elias (a layman) has presumed to try a priest and dean of Gilbert's diocese in his court: that is for the bishop alone to do, and if Elias has a just plea against Walter,[4] Gilbert will give him full justice.

   Elias was lord of Clun (Salop).[5]

**116** G, no. 80; B, fo. 21; R, fo. 212v.
1 N. R    3 quantosque (s *added*) R    5 R. R    13 Valete *om*. R
**117** G, no. 100; B, fo. 29.

---

[1] This seems to be based on Prov. xxvii. 5–6: 'Melior est manifesta correptio, quam amor absconditus. Meliora sunt uulnera diligentis, quam fraudulenta oscula odientis.'
[2] Master Robert de Clare occurs as canon of Hereford 1163–7 (*GF*, p. 270).
[3] Cf. I Cor. ix. 24.
[4] Evidently the name of the priest and dean, perhaps also the Walter of no. 118; the two cases may possibly be connected. The letters are adjacent in B.
[5] *CP*, x, Appendix J, p. 113; Eyton, *Salop*, xi, 228 (for the Say family see *CP*, xi, 464 ff.).

Gilebertus Dei gratia Herefordensis episcopus amico suo Helie de Sai salutem.

Nosti karissime quam constanter amorem michi et ecclesie que circa uos est et honorem et pacem promisisti, quod utinam sic seruasses ut nec querimonia de te perferretur ad nos nec a nobis tibi quicquam nisi pacificum et amicabile scribi 5 oportuisset. Multum quidem de multis mirarer, sed de te multo amplius miror quod sacerdotem nostrum et decanum ad iudicium curie tue trahas, et hanc tibi potestatem contra ecclesiam uendices quam multo sudore et labore reges et in- peratores aduersus eam usque hodie optinere nequiuerunt. Vnde uobis mandamus karissime ut sinas iudicari a nobis clericos nostros, et hunc precipue et alios nequa- 10 quam iudicare presummas, sed iuxta ordinem sibi concessum ipsos Domino in pace seruire permittas. Si nos minus audieris quamcunque poterimus sententiam in te et tua etiam nolentes dare non tardabimus. Quod si quid aduersus domnum Walterum habes plenariam de ipso iustitiam offerimus. Valere te et benefaciendo Domino placere optamus.

### 118  To an official of the diocese, presumably an archdeacon[1]

[1148–63] Walter the bishop's clerk had some money in his possession belonging to Hugh of Clun, which he paid over for a debt owed by Hugh to Gilbert Anglicus (a knight); Hugh, how- ever, denied the debt, and so Walter repaid him. If Hugh's assertion is correct, then Gilbert must be compelled to repay Walter; if false, then the case between Hugh and Walter must be reserved for the bishop.

The letter is somewhat gnomic, but the interpretation given above seems the only one which fits the facts laid out in it. In the manuscript it lacks a heading or protocol; but since it nestles among the Hereford letters, and since Hugh of Clun was certainly a clerk in the diocese of Hereford, there is no reason to doubt that it was written by Gilbert as bishop of Hereford.

Conqueritur Galterus clericus noster duplex dampnum se incurrisse, nam nomine Hug(onis) de Cluna Gilb(erto) Angl(ico) pecuniam quam ab Hug(one) ipsi deberi putabat reddidit, et cum Hugo se predicto Gilb(erto) nichil debuisse asserat, item cum Hug(one) data pecunia transegit. Vobis itaque mandando precor ut tribus his 5 statuto die euocatis, Galterum pecuniam redditam (que tamen, ut asserit, Gilberto debebatur) repetentem ad plenum audiatis, et Hug(onem) de Cluna de re ista ueritatem testari ex parte nostra commoneatis, sique predictum militem indebitum recepisse a Galtero constiterit, ipsi quantum accepit restituere compellatur. Quod si miles pecuniam hanc Hugonem sibi debuisse probauerit, causam inter Hug(onem) 10 et Galterum nobis reseruabitis.

**117** 6 sacerdotum B
**118** G, no. 101; B, fo. 29v.
1 Nonqueritur B (*rubricator's error*)

[1] 'nobis reseruabitis' suggests that the recipient presides over a court inferior to the bishop's, i.e. an archdeacon's.

## 119 To Philip of Sarnesfield[1]

[1148–63] Judgement has been given in the abbot of Reading's court that Philip is to swear with twelve oath-helpers that he and his predecessors never paid a pension of five shillings to the church of Leominster. Gilbert recalls a judgement on the issue made by his predecessor Bishop Robert, and insists that he discuss the matter with Philip before Philip takes the oath.

The letter lacks heading or author's title; but it was certainly written by a bishop of Hereford who had a predecessor called Robert (more probably Robert de Bethune than Robert of Lorraine); and in view of this and of its place in the manuscript, it may be taken as reasonably certain that it was written by Gilbert as bishop of Hereford.

Amico suo et parrochiano Philippo de Sarnef(eld) salutem.

Audio in curia domni abbatis Rading(ensis) tibi legem adiudicatam esse ut manu duodecima iures te nunquam uel predecessores tuos de terra de Sarnefeld ecclesie de Lumin' quinque solidos quos a te querit reddidisse. Certa autem recordatione sancte ecclesie recognosco causam hanc in presentia bone memorie domni Roberti 5 episcopi, et agitatam fuisse et ipsius consilio definitam. Vnde quia in lege hac facienda quedam tue et tuorum saluti contraria michi uideor intelligere, mandamus tibi et super Christianitatem tuam precipimus, ne iuramentum hoc aut ipse facias aut aliquem tuorum facere permittas quousque nobiscum locutus fueris, et super hac ipsa re consilium plenius habueris. Supplico enim domno abbati per litteras 10 meas ne propter expectationem hanc cause tue aliquod detrimentum incurras. Vale.

## 120 To Amice, countess of Leicester

[1148–63] The countess is ill, was perhaps at death's door, but is now better: Gilbert comforts her, tells her to listen to her spiritual advisers, and engage in works of charity.

G(ilebertus) Dei gratia Hereford(ensis) episcopus dilecte sibi et diligende semper in Domino A(micie) Leerc(estrie) uenerabili comitisse, salutem que nunc est et quam speramus in Domino.

Audito karissima eo quem de te fama circumquaque plangit euentu, confestim corde concussus sum, et menti mee si quid iocunditatis aut hilaritatis insederat, hoc 5 ad diri casus auditum anxius repente dolor extinxit. Audimus enim te lecto doloris decubuisse grauiter, et uiam pene carnis ingressam in te totum, quod homini minari potest mors carnis, propemodum excepisse. Sed quem regis lacrime, dum prope mors pulsaret, ut annos sibi ter quinos adderet, ad miserendum inflexerunt,[2] ipse sanctorum pulsatus lacrimis, multorum motus singultibus, te ipsum mente et 10 spiritu desiderantem, te in beatam patriam affectione tota tendentem, tuis et letus

119 G, no. 102; B, fo. 29v.
4 Lumin' sic, for Leoministria, or some such form; the link with Reading suggests this identification (cf. nos. 340 ff.)
120 G, no. 118; B, fo. 36v.

[1] The place was doubtless Sarnesfield (Herefs). For Philip, see Herefs. DB, p. 86.
[2] Cf. IV Reg. xx. 1–6.

audio benigne restituit, et uelut in exitu constitutam ad nos clementissime reuo-
cauit. Flores ut estimo patrie celestis odorare iam ceperas, et pregustata fortasse
gaudia tibi iam differri conquerendo deploras. Patienter obsecro dilectissima sustine
15 Dominum, qui quod differt non aufert, ⟨fo. 37⟩ quod suspendit ad tempus postmodum cumulatum reddit in gloria. Non est in paradiso qui ad profectum sui
bonorum indigere possit exemplis. Vbi non est perfectio opus esse constat exemplo.
Exemplo tui multos profecisse cognoscimus qui te subtracta de medio ne in incertum currant habent unde gratias agant, te uirtutis exemplar retinent quod pre
20 oculis habendo uirtuti sese conformare intendant. Age ergo dilectissima et quam
magno Dei munere restitutam suscepimus, curam adhibe ne per tui incuriam
amittamus. Patres emeritos habes circa te tibi fideliter assistentes, te eadem qua
seipsos karitate amplectentes. Horum obsecro pare monitis, adquiesce consiliis,
defectu nimio caro tua uiribus euacuata est, utpote que cum morte luctata nisi opem
25 ferente Domino non euasisset. Te uero uirtutem semper zelare non ambigo, unde
et de his que nunc instant ieiuniis[1] pertimesco. Obsecro ne quod scribo exorreas,
salubribus interim monitis adquiescas, defectam queso carnem carnis esu sustentes,
et modicum quo reficies in suis Domino pauperibus largiter reconpenses. Fratres
qui circa te sunt in hoc mecum sentire estimo, quatinus usque ad *Isti sunt dies*,[2]
30 debilia membra tua uitamque uelud supremis in labiis constitutam carnis sustentari
patiaris edulio, et uictu et uestitu tredecim interim fratribus erogato, tu tibi a defectu
prouideas, ipsorumque necessitati benigna caritate subuenias. Vale dilectissima et
exauditu pio amici mentem supplicantis exhilara.

### 121    To David FitzGerald, bishop of St Davids

[1148–63] He is trying to make peace between the bishops of St Davids and Llandaff,[3] and
suggests a meeting of the three of them, preferably at Hereford: he has written in the same
terms to the bishop of Llandaff.

G(ilebertus) Dei gratia Herefordensis episcopus uenerabili fratri et amico Dauid
Meneuensi episcopo, salutem et dilectionem.

  Quam iocundum, quam sit utile pacis et concordie bonum facile dinoscitur, si ex
contentione et discordia quanta dampna proueniant diligentius attendamus. Nam

121 G, no. 139; B, fo. 159 (*in top margin:* consilium alicui de pace inter discordantes refor-
manda(?)).
4 dilegentius *partly corr.* B

---

[1] The letter was evidently written about the beginning of Lent—see next note.
[2] The introit for Passion Sunday.
[3] This no doubt refers to a revival of the old dispute between the two sees on diocesan
  boundaries, which started when Urban bishop of Llandaff (1107–34) established his diocese
  (Conway Davies, I, 147–90, esp. p. 180; Brooke, in *SEBC*, ch. IV). The case had been
  effectively settled in Urban's time, and there is no reason to suppose that Bishop Nicholas
  (1148–83) made any headway.
    It is possible that no. 92 is connected with this case, in which event this letter is likely to
  belong to the early years of Gilbert's and Nicholas's episcopates. The reference to 'bella' also
  suggests this.

si motus uarios, et que nos premunt undique bella attendimus, patet liquido quam 5
sit periculosum ecclesie honus super honus assumere, et preter extera que premunt
intestina sibi prelia commouere. Inde est quod si placet uobis consiliis nostris
adquiescere, solicite daremus operam inter uos et domnum Landauensem pacis
modum aliquem inuenire. Quod quia facile non est nisi in locum simul tres conueniremus, precamur locum nobis designari, quo conuenientibus nobis possit inter nos 10
de uestra pace tractari. Quod si ad hoc Herefordiam delegeritis, die quacumque ad
hoc statuetis aderimus, nec apud domnum Landauensem cessabunt preces nostre,
quousque et ipsum adesse faciamus. Nouerit autem dilectio uestra nos in eundem
hunc modum domno Landauensi scripsisse et placitum utriusque uestrum et
rescriptum exspectare. Valete.                                                                    15

## 122   To a bishop

[? 1148–63] The author congratulates his fellow bishop on the successful issue of his business
at the papal Curia and safe return; and asks him to confirm the grants of churches which have
been made to one of his own clerks, Peter, by Peter's lord, Roger de Mand(? eville).[1]

The letter was evidently written by one bishop to another (cf. 'dilecte frater in Domino...
liberalitatem...in ecclesiis...auctoritate uestra...stabiliatis'). The style suggests that the
author is Gilbert,[2] and its place in the manuscript suggests that Gilbert was writing as bishop
of Hereford. But a date after 1163 is not impossible.

Pie salutantis affectum et sincere diligentis oficium.

Incolumitati uestre dilecte frater in Domino, quam quorundam relatu cognouimus, affectu pleno congratulamur; et uos apostolorum limina uisitasse, summoque
pontifici et curie sancte gratiose astitisse, et bene consummatis negotiis domum
reuocasse feliciter animi applausu intimo gaudemus. Vnde cum rogatu quorundam 5
scribendi uobis se prestaret occasio, uobis animi affectionem nostri significare
dignum duximus, quatinus si quid erga nos uestre complacuerit karitati, non supplicatione utatur aut preces porrigat, sed in amici partes se potenter extendens, suo
potius utatur inperio quam aliquatenus ⟨fo. 155⟩ precis oblate blandiatur officio.
Hinc quoque spem inpetrandi concipimus, si benignitati uestre nostrum aut amici 10
nostri desiderium exponamus. Est autem apud uos quidam familiaris noster, Petrus
uidelicet clericus Rog(eri) de Mand', quem tuitioni uestre et patrocinio deuotio
nostra commendat, supplicans ut liberalitatem quam in eum domnus suus in
ecclesiis quibusdam conferre disposuit, auctoritate uestra quantum permittet ratio
stabiliatis, quatinus ipsum seruitio semper obnoxium, et nos gratie debitores 15
habeatis. Valete.

**122** G, no. 132; B, fo. 154 v (*in top margin*: congratulatorie ad amicum de tribulatione ereptum).
1 scincere B     4 donum B

---

[1] Probably Roger de Mandeville, who held land in Wilts and Devon, as well as in the Cotentin
(Loyd, *Origins*, pp. 57–8). If so, the bishop was probably Salisbury or Exeter. But in MS B the
letter is in a group with three others relating to the bishop of London.

[2] It follows the usual lines of Gilbert's petitions, especially in the final sentence (cf. nos. 19, 29,
30, 88, 123).

## 123   To T., archbishop of Canterbury

[Probably 1148–50 or 1162–3] On behalf of a canon of Hereford: Gilbert asks for justice to be done to him in the archbishop's court.

The archbishop may be either Theobald or Thomas: if the former, it most probably belongs to the period before he became papal legate.[1]

Patri suo et domno T. Cant(uariensi) Dei gratia archiepiscopo frater G(ilebertus) Herefordensis ecclesie minister, sic utinam pugnare ut uincat.

Latorem hunc domne presentium familiarem nostrum, ecclesie nostre canonicum, suis quidem commendabilem meritis dilecte nobis in Domino sublimitati uestre
5 commendamus attentius, preces affectuose porrigentes quatinus amore Dei et petitione nostra causam eius quantum nititur iustitia foueatis, nec aduersariorum suorum calliditate ius suum opprimi, aut in uestra deperire presentia permittatis. Quod aduersantes ei multa licet nube falsitatis inuoluant, de uestra speramus equitate iudicii ut cito coram uobis falsitas euanescat, ad uestri lucem examinis
10 iniquitatis tenebre facile dissipentur. Illum optamus igitur in uobis spiritum conualescere, qui dudum in propheta sanguinem saluauit innoxium,[2] ut cum clericum nostrum ab his que aduersus eum malitiose conficta sunt, in spiritu discretionis eripueritis, nos gratie debitores ipsumque seruitio semper obnoxium habeatis. Valere uos optamus in Christo pater karissime.

## 124   To Matthew, archdeacon of Gloucester[3]

[1151–63] He asks him to restore W. of Pedwardine (?),[4] whom he has suspended, a sentence promulgated by the dean.

This letter shows Gilbert intervening in the affairs of the diocese of Worcester, which suggests that the see of Worcester was vacant. Vacancies occurred in 1150–1 (but see above, no. 93), 1157–8 and 1160–4; on the last occasion Gilbert certainly acted as vicar (see *GF*, p. 227). The outside limits are Matthew's entry to the office of archdeacon (not before 1151) and Gilbert's translation.

G(ilebertus) Dei gratia Herefordensis episcopus amico suo Matheo archidiacono Gloecestrie salutem.

Veniens ad nos iamdiu hic lator presentium W. de Pedewre conquestus est uos eum iusta nequaquam interueniente causa suspendisse, et decanum uestrum senten-
5 tiam quam in eum dederat auctoritate uestra promulgasse. Nunc uero ad nos iterato recurrens, se aliter quam se res habet opinatum fuisse fatetur, et quicquid

---

**123** G, no. 121; B, fo. 37v.
10 optamus *inserted in* B
**124** G, no. 117; B, fo. 36v.

[1] Or 1159–60: see Appendix II.          [2] Cf. Dan. xiii. 62.

[3] His predecessor, Richard, occurs 1151–7, Matthew first in 1158–60; he died in 1177 (PRO C115/A1, vi, 42, 68, i, 102; Ann. Tewkesbury and Worcester, *Ann. Mon.* I, 52, IV, 384).

[4] Pedwardine (Herefs) seems the likely identification, though one would expect 'Pedewr*de*' (as in Domesday Book).

decanus uester in eum precipitanter egerit, ipsum hoc absque uestra conscientia fecisse profitetur. Vnde quantum aures uestras uelut ignarus facti tunc repleuit querimoniis, tantum etiam equitatem uestram nunc extollit preconiis. Vnde cum error facti nulli ad damnum esse debeat preces benignitati uestre porrigimus, 10 quatinus beniuolum beniuole suscipiatis, et pristina sibi restituta gratia modicum quod intercessit delicti prece nostra remittatis. Valete.

## 125  To King Henry II

[1154–63] He expounds the blessings of the king's reign and petitions him on behalf of the eldest son of Ralph of Worcester.

The tone of the letter perhaps suggests that it was written not long after Henry II's accession in 1154.

⟨D⟩omno serenissimo et precellentissimo principi[1] illustri Anglorum regi H(enrico), frater G(ilebertus) Herefordensis ecclesie minister, pedibus sanctis conculcato Sathan in Christo triumphare feliciter.

Te, domne dilectissime, ob id diuina bonitas multorum pretulit regimini populorum, ut multis per te subueniat et his quibus prees dono multiplici per te gratie 5 sue munus inpendat. Quod quidem in gente nostra impletum nouimus, cui te sic domnum geris, ut et patrem exhibeas, elatos sic reprimis ut mansuetos et humiles mansuete disponere, regere et suscitare non dimittas. Te ecclesie protectorem, pupilli patrem, uidue consolatorem, et omnes iniuriam passi propitium iudicem ipsis rerum experiuntur indiciis. Et cum omnes alta pace gaudeamus, per te arua 10 solummodo dudum herbis floribusque depicta, se in omnem iam frugum exuberantiam excerceri, nocte dieque ligonibus aratrisque sauciari secure tuo sub imperio conqueri posse uidentur. A Domino in te caput regni et a te in omnes eius oras, oleum gratie diffusum exuberat;[2] quod ad genua sublimitatis tue corde prostratus expostulo, ut et latori presentium nuper orphano, uestri quondam fidelis Radulfi 15 de Wirecestre filio primogenito munus apud te gratie miserantis optineat. Incolumem te et potentem in longa tempora maiestas diuina conseruet, in Christo domne dilectissime.

## 126  To Baldric de Sigillo, archdeacon of Leicester

[c. 1160–3] Gilbert, acting as papal judge delegate, had summoned clerks of Baldric's to plead and act as witnesses in some suit: he asks Baldric to pardon them for being absent from his synod.

**125** G, no. 115; B, fo. 36.
**126** G, no. 116; B, fo. 36.

---

[1] Cf. Pope Honorius I to King Edwin: 'Domino excellentissimo et praecellentissimo filio Aeduino regi Anglorum' (Bede, *Hist. Eccl.* II, 17; the same formula occurs in the spurious Canterbury privilege of Boniface IV, Eadmer, *Hist. Novorum*, ed. M. Rule, RS, p. 261). Honorius's closing sentence also opens 'Incolumem...'.
[2] Cf. no. 170, p. 236.

Baldric probably became archdeacon *c.* 1160–1[1]. He had previously been chaplain or clerk to King Stephen (hence 'de Sigillo') and canon of Lincoln.[2]

G(ilebertus) Dei gratia Herefordensis episcopus uenerabili fratri et amico suo karissimo B(aldrico) Leecest(rie) archidiacono, bene prosperari semper in Domino. ⟨fo. 36v⟩

Quid in nobis obedientia sibi uendicet prudentiam uestram karissime ad plenum
5 scire non ambigimus, quem in castris obedientie laudabiliter agere, Deo deuotis obsequiis militare bone uestre opinionis ad nos pertingentis odore cognouimus. Inde est quod dilecte nobis in Domino fraternitati uestre preces affectuose porrigimus, quatinus clericis uestris quos ad agendum et testificandum apostolica auctoritate citauimus, quod synodum quam celebrastis minime interfuerint remittatis, et
10 amico pulsanti ueniam hanc apostolice etiam auctoritatis intuitu concedatis. Nam quia qui occasionem dampni dat, dampnum quoque dare uidetur, si ob culpam hanc in eorum dampnum zelus uester incanduerit, si absentie sue mul⟨c⟩tam exegerit, nobis id poterit imputari, qui delegata nobis potestate non plene forsitan utentes, eorum cautius inuigilare debuimus inpunitati. Valere uos optamus in
15 Domino.

## 127 To Pope Adrian IV

[1156] The case between Osbert, archdeacon of (Richmond),[3] and the clerk Symphorian has gone to the Pope on appeal: Gilbert asks him not to accept the accusation that Osbert had poisoned William archbishop (of York) too easily, and to give him a fair hearing (incomplete).

Archdeacon Osbert, a nephew of Thurstan, a former archbishop of York, was accused of having poisoned his archbishop, William FitzHerbert, on 8 June 1154. After King Stephen's death, the case was taken into the ecclesiastical courts, and a bench presided over by Archbishop Theobald gave judgement that Osbert was to establish his innocence by compurgation. Against this decision Osbert appealed, and his appeal elicited a statement of the case from the archbishop (John of Salisbury, *Ep.* 16), which can be dated to 1156.[4] This is the letter referred to by Gilbert,[5] and so Gilbert's letter may be dated to the same year. Osbert subsequently claimed to have been acquitted by Adrian IV, but he was certainly relieved of his archdeaconry, and retired to be a layman and the holder of knights' fees.

Patri suo et domno pontifici A(driano) frater G(ilebertus) Herefordensis ecclesie minister, debitum humilitatis et obedientie famulatum.

**127** G, no. 114; B, fo. 35v.

---

[1] See *Reg. Lincoln*, VII, 204 n.; cf. II, no. 613, dated after 19 November 1160, *ibid.* VII, 203 n. Baldric seems to have been alive in or after 1185 (*Genealogist*, n.s., XVII, 33), but to have been succeeded by 1192 (*Cart. Boarstall*, p. 7). He had a son, Master Gerard (*Danelaw Charters*, p. 241; *Reg. Lincoln*, VII, no. 1975).    [2] T. A. M. Bishop, *Scriptores Regis*, p. 24 n. 1.
[3] He is given the title of the diocese, York, in the letter, as was normal at the time; he was almost certainly archdeacon of Richmond. On this case and on Osbert see D. Knowles, *CHJ*, V, 175 f. (1936), reprinted in *Historian and Character*, pp. 92 ff.; Morey, *CHJ*, X, 352–3 (1952); Sir Charles Clay, *Yorks. Arch. Journal*, XXXVI (1944–7), 277–9; *JS Epp.* I, 261–2.
[4] *JS Epp.* I, 261–2, cf. 257 and G. Constable, *EHR*, LXIX (1954), 67 ff.
[5] Gilbert follows it quite closely, though his account of the case is briefer.

Cum spectat ad iudicem singulorum causas diligenter attendere, specialius tamen attendende sunt que in filiorum innocentiam sub annotatione criminis intenduntur. Funeste namque uoces et clammose precludende sunt his, qui uitam innocentium 5 persequentes et famam, quorum non probant culpam, hos tamen inuidiosa malitia trahere moliuntur ad penam. Cause quidem eius que inter Osbertum Eborac⟨en-sem⟩ archidiaconum et S⟨ymphorianum⟩ clericum uertit⟨ur⟩ initium prosecutio et finis appellatione ille suspensus est, quem ex literis legati uestri domni Cant⟨uarien-sis⟩ archiepiscopi plena potest ueritatis luce sullimitas uestra cognoscere. Has quidem 10 et diligenter inspeximus, et omnes cause ipsius articulos in eum processisse modum quo litteris designantur eisdem plane testificamur. Si enim predictum archidiaco-num super morte Willelmo archiepiscopo ueneno (ut dicebat) illata et quibusdam criminibus aliis impeteret, in ipsum uinculum inscriptionis arripere et coram iudice eccle⟨fo. 36⟩siastico agere recusabat; cumque in tanta multitudine parentum et 15 amicorum archiepiscopi defuncti solus ipse staret, et nullis fulta testimoniis uerba funderet, laminam candentis ferri in predictum archidiaconum eo tutius offerebat quo ecclesia Dei probationem huiusmodi nullatenus admissuram attendebat. Ipsumque ad regis audientiam eo confidentius prouocabat quoad iudicium hoc apud cunctum iudicem de iure celebrare non posse a⟨d⟩uertebat. Cumque iudicis 20 animum in eo non oporteat uersus quemquam moueri quod non potest ostendi, pro iam dicto archidiacono preces sullimitati uestre porrigimus, ne apud uos incurrat iram quem et multa liberalitas [ . . . ]

### 128 To Roger of Pont l'Évêque, archbishop of York

[1155–7] Gilbert defends his behaviour to the archbishop: if the progress of the case has led to hard words, let this letter be a 'palinode'; and he invites the archbishop to greet a friend on his return, while he is yet 'afar off' (see *GF*, pp. 124 ff.).

Letters 128–30 are part of a correspondence between Gilbert and the archbishop of York about a case in which they were both involved. No. 128 seems to open the exchanges; no. 129 (which refers to Gilbert's 'palinode' and in other ways shows itself to be an answer to 128)[1] is the archbishop's reply; and no. 130 is clearly Gilbert's response to 129.

**127** 8 uertit B (*this sentence may well be corrupt*)    14 impetens B    23 B *breaks off at this point, leaving half a column blank*
**128** G, no. 109; B, fo. 31.

---

[1] Gilbert develops the theme of how he has spared Roger: '. . .multa. . .tacuimus'; he then hints at what he has 'suppressed', 'cum de litteris corruptis ageretur, poterant in hoc articulo multa. . .obici, et per rethoricam auxesim. . .amplificari' and he goes on to disavow a plea of 'precum falsitatem'. 'Hec friuola sunt et his similia, in quibus uobis pepercimus.' Finally, at the end of the letter, there is an echo of the Parable of the Prodigal Son.
  These themes are taken up by Roger. 'Occurrit ille epistole uestre locus ubi dicitis, leuiora . . . allegata grauioribus deductis. Que etiam. . .friuola nominastis. Sed. . .Nonne in medium deducta est accusatio falsi? Nunquid uobis durius. . .uideretur si precum falsitas argueretur?' Later in the letter he quotes the phrase 'auxesim. . .quam rethoricam dicitis', and he ends the letter by playfully expanding the theme of the prodigal's return.
  In no. 130 Gilbert takes up three points in particular from Roger: his image of the

The lawsuit which was their occasion was evidently no trivial matter: it involved a journey to Rome (for Roger), meetings at Worcester and Bridgenorth (nos. 129, 130) and an appeal to the Pope, who delegated the case to the bishops of Lincoln and Ely. It is reasonably certain that the case must be the old-established dispute between the archbishop of York and the abbey of Gloucester about a group of manors which each claimed, and which was finally settled on 13 December 1157.[1] Gilbert would have been involved as a former abbot of Gloucester, at one time actively engaged—so it seems[2]—in the defence of these properties. The letters must be dated some months at least after Archbishop Roger's consecration in October 1154,[3] but before the final settlement in 1157.

Patri suo et domno R(ogero) Dei gratia Ebor(acensi) archiepiscopo frater G(ilebertus) Herefordensis ecclesie minister, salutem et seruitium.

Si nos admitteret solite iam dilectionis archanum secreta signo clauderemus,[4] nec ad patrem directa multorum occulis intuenda committeremus. Sed quia nos
5 exclusos nouimus ideo non iam intus positas sed foris uix herentes litteras mittimus, ut ueniam postulent et suo gratiam domno si quomodo possint apud uos redintegrando concilient. Quod tamen trementi cartule factu facile non speramus, ad quam nec manum porrigi, nec uestros facile conuerti occulos posse estimamus. Vnde si nos designatio iusta repulerit, uolumus saltem alios non latere quod querimus, quia
10 uestram non ferentes ultra iracundiam ueniam excessui postulamus. Nam si quid in uos diximus hoc ipsum palinodiam[5] in nos manu propria con⟨fo. 31 v⟩scribendo recantamus, et si uestrum uel modicum mouimus animum, ipso culpam fatemur ore quominus caute prorumpendo id nullo uestro exigente merito in domnum offendimus et amicum. Cum caritate quidem stetimus in ecclesie causa quam
15 fouemus et si ferrum de manubrio[6] nobis id considerate moderantibus elapsum est, quid superest consilii nisi ut ad magnum illum Eliseum cum penitentia et lamento recurramus? Magna spes est ut penitentem preco penitentie non repellat et ingemiscentem altius ipse gemituum predicator non abiciat. Poteramus equidem debitum karitati pensum prudenter et honeste persoluere, et in disceptatione
20 ecclesiastica iuxta iuris formam etiam Domino non in hoc indignante resistere. Sed quid ad nos extendere digitum, brachia contorquere in uos, et tanquam alicuius essemus momenti, ore misero non solum spumantia uerba sed et tumida iactitare? Quo nobis ea die pudor, honestas, ecclesiastica disciplina et ipsa bone mentis affectanda sobrietas abierunt. Quam male statim in momento omnia nobis elapsa

---

turtle-dove (which Gilbert comments on at length); his reference to their meeting at Worcester; and once again, the 'auxesim...rethoricam'. The internal evidence thus leaves little doubt of the order of the letters, which is also that of the MS.

[1] *Cart. Gloucester*, II, 105–7; cf. *JS Epp.* 42; *CS*, pp. 271–2. The judges delegate in 1157 were the bishops of Bath, Salisbury and Exeter, so this probably belongs to a somewhat earlier phase of the dispute, but later than 1151, when the bishops of Chichester and Lincoln were delegates (Gloucester Cathedral, Reg. B, pp. 476–7: Eugenius III at Ferentino, 11 May, i.e. 1151).      [2] See *GF*, chap. VIII and *CS*, pp. 271 ff.

[3] To allow time for the visit to the Pope and the meeting at Worcester at least (no. 129).

[4] I.e., under such conditions he would have sent letters *close*.

[5] A recantation: cf. Macrobius, *Sat.* VII, 5, 4.

[6] Cf. Greg. *Dialogi*, II, 6 (ed. U. Moricca, p. 89).

sunt ut nudati bonis intrinsecus statim efficeremur dignissimi ut a gratia caderemus. 25
Sed qui cadit nunquid non adicit ut resurgat? Nos an sic undique premit iniquitas,
ut nobis ad gratiam ullus sit aditus? An si modestia nobis excidit misericordia quoque uobis elapsa est. Et si precincti fune in peccati legem abducimur, zona illa aurea
uobis a mamillis auulsa est.[1] Absit ut qui sibi cotidie remitti supplicat supplicanti
conseruo debitum non remittat,[2] et abstersa pater iracundie nebula si in serenitatem 30
solitam mens sese uestra reciperet, accessum nobis ad ueniam utique non obseraret.
Nam quantulum est quod deliquimus nisi quia summi quelibet offensa culminis
magna quidem habenda est? Verbum uerbo subiunximus, et ut in disceptatione
mos est simile simili coaptauimus. Nam cum dixissetis quia nobis eo usque peper-
ceratis, respondimus quia multa habebamus in quibus sullimitati uestre pepercera- 35
mus et nos. Quia uerborum infausta clausula, nunquid incompositos uite nostre
mores aut animi quod absit uitia cinica rabie mordendo, perstrinximus—absit ut in
mentem uestram hec surrepat opinio, ut suspicione huiusmodi confundatis innoxium. Testor inaccessibilem illam lucem que bonorum occulta mentium penetrat
et illustrat, illam quoque communem spem quam sanctorum est amplexa deuotio 40
nos uerbis illis nil aliud intellexisse, nisi quod multa ad corpus cause spectantia ob
reuerentiam uestri tacuimus, et penes nos compressa tenuimus. Nam cum de litteris
corruptis ageretur,[3] poterant in hoc articulo multa durius obici, et per rethoricam
auxesim ut satis ipsi nostis amplificari. Cumque eisdem litteris et ius et spoliatio
innueretur, non in celum os nostrum posuimus,[4] ut precum falsitatem uel in modico 45
arguere presumeremus. Cum iuris habeat formula ut etsi sacrum oraculum huiusmodi precator attulerit, careat penitus impetratis.[5] Hec friuola sunt et his similia in
quibus uobis pepercimus, ad que mentis occulum dum tumide loquebamur habuimus. Nam si ad tempus urgente karitate ⟨fo. 32⟩ stulti facti sumus ob fratres[6]—sed
non insani tamen—ut probra diceremus in uos, quem pre ceteris huc usque dilexi- 50
mus quemque laudum titulis in multorum inuidiam frequenter extulimus, de
nostris pater occultis nulli rectius quam nobis fidem habebitis, nam quis nouit
occulta hominis nisi spiritus hominis qui est in ipso? Ecce coram Deo quod non
mentior. Nil amaritudinis habuimus intus aduersum uos, nisi quod interprete
presente scripto confessi sumus. Vnde et acerbius quam ipsa res expetat nosmetipsos 55
acusauimus, eo quod indignationem uestram in nos quantulamcumque etiam
molestissime sustinemus. Opinabitur quispiam ex animo non dici quod dicimus, sed
ut uestrum demulcendo animum facte in nos appellationis onus aliquatenus euite-
mus. Non hic noster est occulus si Christi sumus: ipsius uicario confidenter
astabimus.[7] Suo currant fata curriculo, prouisos sibi queque sortiantur euentus. 60

---

[1] Cf. Apoc. i. 13.  
[2] Cf. Matt. xviii. 28 ff.  
[3] Cf. GF, p. 124.  
[4] Cf. Ps. lxxii. 9; cf. no. 110.  
[5] Cf. Code, 1, 23, 7 (also cited in no. 248).  
[6] I.e. the monks of Gloucester (a distant echo in this passage of Rom. i. 22 and I Cor. iv. 10).  
[7] I.e.: our glances were turned to the Pope. This is the period when the phrase 'uicarius Christi' was beginning to be used commonly (and in the end exclusively) of the Pope: cf. St Bernard, *De consideratione*, II, 8, IV, 7 (*PL*, CLXXXII, 752, 788), and for other references M. Maccarrone, in *Misc. Pio Paschini* (Rome, 1948), I, 429–45; W. Ullmann, *The Growth of Papal Government* (London, 1955), p. 428.

Elapse potius amicitie dampna plangimus, quam imminentia timeamus. Valete, et moueat uos utinam spiritus ille pietatis ut amico reuertenti etiam dum longe est in amplexum occurratis.[1]

## 129   Roger of Pont l'Évêque, archbishop of York, to Gilbert Foliot

[1155–7] The archbishop thanks Gilbert for his 'palinode' (no. 128) and expounds his own point of view in the dispute. But he accepts Gilbert's apology and will make it up—and feast with the prodigal on his return!

Venerabili fratri et utinam amico G(ileberto) Dei gratia Herefordensi episcopo R(ogerus) Ebor(acensis) Dei gratia archiepiscopus salutem.

Susceptam de manu dilecti filii H. quam dicitis palinodiam uestram priusquam alicui ipsius copia fieret diligenter inspexi, ueritus in primis ne uiue uocis uestre (ut 5 salua pace uestra dixerim) ardorem, missi litterarum apices exprimerent. Resedissent utique apud nos et in manibus nostris illud deperisset archanum et uaga in publicum exeundi negaretur licentia, ne geminata iniuria omnem reconciliationis uiam excluderet. Fateor quidem me his que uobis calor animi ministrauit, aliquatenus commotum, non tamen ut aut in me fraterne cissura facta sit caritatis aut sol 10 iustitie super iracundie mee affectionem obscuratus.[2] Habeo enim ex pristina consuetudine ut cor ita et labia maxime erga amicum circumcisa, que artiori lege conclusit singulare exemplar patientie Christus, ex quo lubricos animi mei motus per gratiam suam cingulo sacerdotali uoluit astringi. Non enim michi a pectore excidere potest quod sacerdotali ex lege datum est in mandatis—ut cum turturis 15 uel huiusmodi caput ad pennulas reflectat[3]—et quod in descriptione templi mensarum labia intrinsecus reflexa dicuntur per circuitum,[4] quoniam uerbi seminator diuini ex omni parte circumspectus ad cor debet reuocare sermonem, audire que dicit, operari que predicat, ne si intenderit arcum et sagittis sacre scripture uitia percusserit auditorum, conuertatur in die belli et auertatur adiutorium gladii eius 20 nec auxilietur ei in bello. Miror ualde nec satis admirari possum, unde sanctitas uestra tante me simplicitatis esse crediderit, ut quia uoces meas michi reddidistis, putetis offensum. Quibus in uerbis teste Deo et conscientia mea nullam me tunc arbitratus sum sed neque nunc opinor accepisse iniuriam, presertim cum huiusmodi ad iram mitigandam et conciliandam amicorum gratiam proferri soleant. Si uero 25 sub eorum ambiguitate meam in aliquo grauari crederem opinionem, piaculari me subicerem flagitio qui tantum amicum ⟨fo. 32 v⟩ prior ad hanc prouocassem contumeliam. Grauius aliquid extra causam dictum est cuius tanta est et fuit admixtione persone ad quam spectare uidetur acerbitas, ut contra ceterarum iniuriarum naturam dissimulatione minime potuerit aboleri. Sed de his pauca; nam quantumlibet in 30 parte ista oratio succincta odiosa nobis quam periculosa. Ideoque ad priora redeamus.

**129** G, no. 110; B, fo. 32.
9 cissura *sic, for* scissura      14 turturem B

---

[1] Cf. Luc. xv. 20.
[3] Cf. Levit. v. 7–8.
[2] Cf. Mal. iv. 2; Eph. iv. 26.
[4] Cf. I Para. xxviii. 11–12, 16.

Occurrit ille epistole uestre locus ubi dicitis, leuiora ad gratiam nostri allegata grauioribus deductis, que etiam tam uere quam eleganter friuola nominastis. Sed secus se habere facies negotii facile declarabit. Nonne in medium deducta est accusatio falsi? Nunquid uobis durius actum fuisse uideretur si precum falsitas argueretur? Vtinam omnia proposuissetis: facile iudicibus uiolente spoliationis non solum 35 testibus uerum argumentis et instrumentis quibus habundamus fides facta fuisset. Hec et his similia allegare que causa nostri suppressistis, ad officium spectant aduocati, cuius est agere quod causa desiderat ut tamen temperet ab iniuria. Et uos quidem uel duriora dicere absque aduerse partis iniuria potuissetis, nisi uos a cause huius patrocinio leges pariter et canones excluderent. Scitis enim quam diligenter 40 huius negotii secreta non solum antequam iter ad domnum papam arripuissem, uerum post reditum meum Wigornie aperuerim. Facta uobis est litterarum copia, quas super hoc negotio a sede apostolica impetraueram. De his que super transactione posueram nichil omnino uobis est absconditum. Qua in re manum ad iura porrigere non audeo ne forte grauius amicum ledam quam ipse lesus fuerim. Et 45 michi satius est quedam cum detrimento cause tacere, quam uerecundie dicere. Nam quod ad auxesim spectat quam rethoricam dicitis, que potius oratorum est, certum est quia ei nullus ad causam istam patebat accessus, cum ipsa uidelicet in ultimis dumtaxat et questione comprobata locum elegerit. Ideo si interposita fuisset, non tam in nostram quam iuris redundaret iniuriam. Sed quid plura? 50 Numquid epistola uestra tot sacre scripture uallata presidiis, tot grauibus onerata sententiis, tanto rethorice exornationis decorata fulgore, in uanum laborasse et inanis ad domnum suum redire poterit? Absit. Sed ueniam petenti uenia dabitur: si tamen cum uestri copiam Deus dederit, animus uester ab oratione non discrepet. Ecce iam in occursum uestrum uetus festinat amicus. Iam in domo patris mei 55 auditur simphonia et chorus, exultant famuli, occiditur uitulus saginatus, stola uobis paratur et anulus.[1] Expedit ergo ut utrique uitulum in hostio tabernaculi pro peccato pariter immolemus, quatinus aqua sanctuarii lotis pedibus, ueste competenti iterum induti, epulemur simul et exultemus, ne glorientur de nobis fratres qui discordias seminant et exultant in rebus pessimis,[2] sed confundantur et pereant cum 60 his qui perdere cuncta festinant. Valete.

## 130   To Roger of Pont l'Évêque, archbishop of York

[1155–7] He answers the archbishop point by point, but rejoices in their reconciliation (a reply to no. 129).

Patri suo et domno R(ogero) Dei gratia Ebor(acensi) archiepiscopo frater G(ilebertus) Herefordensis ecclesie minister, salutem et seruitium.

Spirat delectabiliter ⟨fo. 33⟩ ortus aromatum et fraglantia⟨m⟩ suauem dat odorum multorum in unum sibi iuncta suauitas. Tale pater quiddam uestra michi

---

**129** 42 Wigorn' B (*cf. no.* 130, *at l.* 58)
**130** G, no. III; B, fo. 32v.
3 fraglantia B *corrected to* fragrantia *by modern hand*

---

[1] Cf. Luc. xv. 20–7.          [2] Cf. Levit. iv. 3–4; viii *passim*; Prov. vi. 19; ii. 14.

5 pagina contulit, quam sepe iam lectam dum repeto orto plane quodam michi uideor
inesse deliciarum. Hinc enim fauorabilis illa uenustas eloquii, inde sententiarum
michi spirat alta profunditas, ut dum delectat pariter et edificat alligatum nexu gemino
totum rapiat in se suum pagina iam dicta lectorem. Ad patrem uerba transmiseram et
placidam mentis uestre tranquillitatem me (quam parum libet) attemptasse mestus
10 ac sollicitus deplanxeram. Sed ecce planctum michi conuertisti in gaudium,[1] et
beate me deliquisse confiteor qui in peccati uicissitudinem non penam quam suspicari poteram sed munus reporto quod desperabam. Munus enim michi grande
reputo, descendentis de monte Moysi faciem uel a longe contemplari, et claritatem
uultus eius, quam infirmus uix capit oculus, obiecti saltem uelaminis quibusdam
15 quasi rarescentibus filis aliquatenus intueri.[2] Transmissa namque nube et caligine, in
ipso mentis uertice qui sacer uere mons est, cum ipsa luce quam sancte mentes
inhabitant, soliloquia sancta tractastis, ubi de fonte lucis hauriens multa in paginam
que nos docendo corrigerent et occidentis nostri tenebras gratiosa sui plenitudine
luminis illustrarent. Hinc habitum michi bene circa uos disposite mentis ostenditis,
20 ut in uirtutis appetitum mentem meam uel coram posito uirtutis speculo prouocetis.
Sic sua sancti bona frequenter intimant, non ut sese laudibus efferant, sed ut aliis in
se quod salubriter imitentur ostendant. Hinc ad mentem michi cordis illa circa uos
simulque labiorum circuncisio sancta proponitur, ut intus apud me de cetero quid
uel cui uel quando dicendum sit, apto rationis moderamine dispensetur, et internus
25 ille calor animi sic erumpat in medium, ut igne illo foris uox ardeat, quem uenit
Dominus in terram mittere, non quem studet a Gehenna semper hostis inflammare.[3]
Purgata sunt prophete labia ad desuper allati carbonis attactum,[4] et oris mei poterunt purgari superflua ad patris et domni pie commonentis exemplum. Patientie
uero quid memorem quam michi sancte proponitis ut hanc michi presentando mee
30 me possessorem anime uel de cetero faciatis? Que nimirum anima dum rationi rebellis est, dum repugnat spiritui, dum lesa remurmurat et in ultionem sese stimulat et
inflammat, nondum quidem possidetur. Ad Christum uero conuersa et in melius
commutata cum ipsius exemplo suas remittit iniurias aduersa iam iocunde sustinet,
iamiam loris alligata patientie ab omni inordinate uoluntatis impetu cohibetur, et
35 subiecta rationis imperio, pleno iam dominio possidetur, attestante ueritate que ait:
'in patientia uestra possidebitis animas uestras'.[5] Persuadet idem michi turtur ille
⟨fo. 33 v⟩ misticus,[6] non abruptum habens in sacrificia sed retortum capud ad
pennulas, hoc michi clamans, hoc predicans ut si quid horum que turtur ipse
figuraliter exprimit in me Domino sacrificem, non inanem gloriam sectando uel
40 gratiam, a uero Christi corpore quod est ecclesia fuco me quodam simulationis
abrumpam, sed principale mentis quod interioris hominis uere caput est, ad ueras
uirtutum pennulas et ad illas quibus uolatur in celum duas alas karitatis sincera
ueritate retorqueam. Nec minus illa me mensa celestis letificat, que dum labia
reflectit in se (sicut sancte scribitis) diuine doctorem legis erudit, ut in his que docet
45 et loquitur consideratione semper sedula recurrat ad se, ne uerbo uita dissentiat, ne

---

[1] Cf. Ps. xxix. 12.   [2] Cf. Ex. xxxiv. 29 ff.
[3] Cf. Jac. iii. 6.   [4] Cf. Is. vi. 6–7.
[5] Luc. xxi. 19.   [6] Cf. Levit. v. 7–8 (and no. 129).

uerbo quos edificat subuertat exemplo, iuxta quod in laude bonorum scriptum est:
'sagitta Ionathe nunquam abiit retrorsum, et gladius Saulis nunquam reuersus est
inanis'.[1] Verbum quippe Dei et gladius et sagitta est: gladius, quia percutit, et eo
sagitta quod pungit. Qui nimirum gladius inanis reuertitur cum prolatus sermo
nec uitia resecat, nec ad frugem uirtutis erigit audientem. At Ionathan qui 'dans 50
columbam' uel 'donum columbe' dicitur,[2] sagitta reflexa non percutit, quia
spiritualis quisque doctor qui a Christo dona gratie percipit, et hec eadem fideliter
ministrare non omittit, reflectit labium prudenter in se, dum sapienter et sancte
uiuit. Hec michi de pagine uestre collecta sunt gremio dum per eam quasi uite
quedam pascua qua possum mentis excercitatione discurro. Quibus nimirum 55
oblectamentis si quid forte coheret asperum, id gratum habeo uelud eius admixtione totum michi sit quasi quodam sale conditum. Vt ab huius me cause patrocinio
repellatis, annectitis quod eiusdem secreta michi sunt per uos Wigornie reuelata.
Sed ut pace uestra dixerim, si mecum secreta quandoque gratia contulistis solum
quid uobis de transactione placuerit, et quas a domno papa litteras acceperitis, 60
ostendistis, et ipsas quidem litteras non multo post episcoporum commissas manibus
omnium indifferenter communicari notitie uidi pariter et intellexi. Quid enim
Brugie[3] quasi triuiatim diuulgabatur, nisi domnum Lincolniensem et Eliensem hoc
accepisse in mandatis, ut causam uestram audirent et appellatione remota dirime-
rent? Vnde uero cause uestre fundetur intentio, quibus nitatur amminiculis, probata 65
sit testium uestrorum an inprobabilis opinio, sufficiens necne numerus eorundem,
possessionis uestre facilis an implicita probatio, et omnino quod obesse uel prodesse
cause quacumque ex parte potuerit, nec michi in minimo patefactum est. Asser-
tionibus itaque partium cum merita pandantur causarum michi de secreto huius
cause quid recte ualet obici, cui nunquam horum nichil contigit aperiri? De cetero 70
sicut orationem qua declamat orator rethoricam dicimus, locos etiam et colores
rethoricos, unde illud: 'Non est rethoricus quem facit ira color',[4] sic et eam quam
suggillatis auxesim licet oratorum sit, rethoricam nichilominus conuenienter
assero, eo quod hanc rethor edocet cum orator eadem quod oportet amplificet.
Que cum questione probata ⟨fo. 34⟩ locum habeat, potuit in hac questione com- 75
petenter interseri, ex quo cepit oculata fide de litterarum deductarum in medio
corruptione non ambigi. Sed quid ista? An ad Ciceronis me dogmata transfero, et
ad salutata iamdudum et uelud antiqua michi studia notabili quadam mentis
leuitate respicio? Absint ista hinc. In patris et domni suspiro gratiam: ob michi
reconciliandam cartule continuaui iam cartulam, etsi plena dignitate currenti minus 80
digne responderim cum ciatum phiala propinanti porrexerim.

**130** 56 choeret B    58 Wigornia *before correction*    59 solum *Giles;* solis B (*possibly by attraction to* contulistis/uobis, *but there may be something missing*)    73 anxesim B    81 ciatum]
*i.e.* cyathum

---

[1] Cf. II Reg. i. 22.
[2] Cf. Jerome, *Liber de nom. hebraic.*, PL, XXIII, 855.
[3] Probably Bridgenorth (Salop).        [4] Evidently a quotation, not identified.

### 131  To Pope Adrian IV (or Alexander III)

[1157–8 (or 1161–3)] On behalf of Simon, canon of Lichfield, who had been robbed of the fruits of a part of his prebend,[1] while it was in dispute between him and the prior of Coventry. Gilbert expounds some of the ramifications of his case.

The Pope addressed must be Anastasius IV (1153–4), Adrian IV (1154–9) or Alexander III (1159–81).[2] The outside limits of date are therefore 1153–63.

The appeal with which this letter is concerned had evidently been recently made; it had been made, furthermore, when the bishops of Chester and Hereford had met at Worcester to settle 'the affairs of the church'. This seems to imply a vacancy in the see of Worcester, such as occurred in 1157–8 and 1160–4. There was no bishop of Chester between December 1159 and c. 18 April 1161[3]—the date of Archbishop Theobald's death. If the reference to Theobald be taken to mean that he was alive,[4] it may be dated 1157–8; if not, 1161–3 is a possible alternative.

**131**  G, no. 124; B, fo. 139v.

---

[1] The vicissitudes of the diocese of Chester, Coventry or Lichfield in the eleventh and twelfth centuries involved complex arrangements with the properties of the bishopric and its two or three cathedrals. The cathedral was at Lichfield until the 1070's, then at Chester until 1102, then at Coventry. Lichfield was not, however, ignored; and its chapter was extensively reorganized by Bishop Roger de Clinton (1129–48). According to Thomas Chesterfield, he founded a number of prebends, including one in the church of Honiton (Worcs) (*Anglia Sacra*, I, 434). Chesterfield is a late source; but the truth of what he says is confirmed by a bull of Pope Innocent II, confirming an arrangement between Coventry, Lichfield and the bishop made at the instigation of Cardinal Alberic and the English church (evidently at the council of London of December 1138, cf. Wilkins, I, 414 ff.; the bull is abstracted in *Reg. Lichfield*, no. 454). Innocent gives an almost identical list of places, confirms land in them to Coventry priory, notes that prebends for Lichfield had been founded out of their churches and tithes, and states that these shall now be held by the bishop, to dispose of as he will. None of these places supported a prebend in Lichfield cathedral after this (cf. the list in *Taxatio* (Record Comm., 1802), p. 243 (1291)). Gilbert's reference to the arrangement between Chester and Coventry may be a slip (by him or by his scribe) for Lichfield and Coventry;—or if the MS is correct in reading 'ecclesiam' it may mean 'between the bishop of Chester and the church of Coventry'—and no doubt refers to this papal decision of 1139. Eugenius is likewise probably a mistake for Innocent II: Eugenius III confirmed the arrangements (*Reg. Lichfield*, no. 262), but without the specific details contained in Innocent's bull.

It is clear that Simon's prebend of Honiton was suppressed in the long run, and it may be that it had already been suppressed before the date of this letter. But it was normal in such cases to leave the sitting holder in possession until he died, and it is likely—if Simon's plea that he had held the prebend before the arrangement was correct—that he had been left in possession by the bishop. Ultimately the church of Honiton was subject to Coventry priory (cf. *Taxatio*, p. 219).

[2] Unless there is an error in the protocol.

[3] The death of Walter Durdent and the consecration of Richard Peche. A few days indeed elapsed between Richard's consecration and Theobald's death, but hardly sufficient to affect the argument.

[4] One would expect some indication to balance the 'dudum' of the bishop of Chester if Theobald were dead (note also that Pope Eugenius was 'sancte memorie'). The prior of Coventry at this time was Laurence, occ. before 1144 to 1176 (*Reg. Lichfield*, no. 455; Morey, p. 139—cf. *PUE*, I, no. 141).

Patri suo et domno summo pontifici A. frater G(ilebertus) Herefordensis ecclesie minister, apostolice sublimitati debitam reuerentiam et karitatem.

Quod beatitudini uestre super causa pauperis et honesti clerici, presentium scilicet latoris, Symonis Lichesfeldensis canonici scribimus, hec, domne, causa est quod illatam sibi iniuriam in credite uobis dispensationis culmen redundantem 5 utique cum molestia sustinemus. Qui cum aduersus priorem Couintr(ensem) et fratres eius eum a parte quadam prebende sue—ecclesia scilicet de Hunitun'— expellere nitentes, ad audientiam uestram appellasset, postea cum dompnus Cestrensis et ego ob ecclesie negotia Wigorn(iam) conuenissemus, appellationem suam presentibus nobis innouauit, et in sui rerumque suarum protectionem et 10 patrocinium priorem ipsum presentem ad sublimitatem uestram ad *Letare Ierusalem*[1] appellauit. Cui cum ob uestre celsitudinis eminentiam in tuto iam omnia esse oporteret, manus tamen sacrilega prorupit in audaciam, ut ipsius decimas et presentis fructus anni multo sibi labore collectos intra cimiterii septa inuaderet, et hinc ablatos asportaret. Quod siue sciente siue nesciente priore actum sit, ab eius 15 tamen hominibus perpetratum esse non ambigimus. Vnde zelum nostrum temperare non possumus, quin sanctitati uestre super hac corrigenda temeritate supplicemus, ut iniuriam suam ob corrigendos alios manus apostolica iuste puniat et misericorditer egeno laboranti subueniat. Carthas enim dompni Rogeri dudum Cestrensis episcopi[2] et dilecti patris nostri dompni Cantuar(iensis) Teodbaldi 20 inspeximus, quibus ecclesiam hanc in prebendam sibi collatam fuisse, ante transactionem inter Cestrensem et Couentr(ensem) ecclesiam[3] per manum sancte memorie pape Eugenii initam, pro certo cognouimus. Valeat in domino sanctitas uestra, dilecte pater.

### 132   To Robert de Chesney, bishop of Lincoln

[Probably spring–summer 1160] He has received a letter from Robert: he rejoices in the good news that peace is on the way and that Robert is safe and well, and looks forward to his return.

This letter was evidently written from England in answer to a letter from Robert de Chesney from France, describing his own affairs and impending return, and the negotiations leading to the conclusion of peace between Henry II and Louis VII.[4] Within the period 1154–63 peace was made between them twice: in 1156 and 1160 (in May, and formally renewed in October). The former occasion, which was really peace between Henry and his brother Geoffrey (cf. John of Salisbury, *Ep.* 13) seems hardly apposite. 1160 fits the circumstances perfectly; and there are possible verbal links between this letter and those of the

---

**131** 22 ecclesiam *sic*, *? for* ecclesias (*see p. 172 n. 1*), *or perhaps add* domnum *before* Cestrensem.
**132** G, no. 128; B, fo. 137v.

---

[1] The Introit for the Fourth Sunday in Lent.
[2] Roger de Clinton, 1129–48.
[3] See p. 172 n. 1.
[4] This is clearly the significance of the phrase 'dissidentes...regum animos'. It is stated specifically later on that the English king is one of these, and it may therefore be presumed that the French king was the other.

archbishop and John of Salisbury dealing with the same events and with the papal schism,[1] and still closer links with Gilbert's no. 133, written in November or December 1160. But the exact point in 1160 is not clear. John of Salisbury's letter 128 (*c.* September 1160) refers to some business connected with the diocese (or bishop) of Lincoln which Becket had recently helped to clear up, and which may have been the occasion of the bishop of Lincoln's visit to the royal curia in Normandy.[2] The circumstances suggest a date in the spring or summer for Gilbert's letter.

Venerabili domno fratrique karissimo R(oberto) Lincolniensi Dei gratia episcopo frater G(ilebertus) Herefordensis ecclesie minister, Christum portando in se ambulare sapienter et sobrie.

Susceptis litteris quibus diligentia nos uestra letificare dignata est, solito gratior
5 et consueto serenior ilico nobis dies illuxit. Auditis enim rerum euentibus, et perplexa quadam ingenii subtilitate, pace iam sublata de medio, nec fracta cito ⟨fo. 138⟩ redintegrari, nec dissidentes admodum regum animos facile sibi conciliari posse sperauimus. Sed qui uentis imperat et mari, procellam cito in auram statuit,[3] et que turbata sunt ad pacis bonum statim ut uult amota nube discordie, imperiosa qua
10 preest potestate conuertit. Vnde cum pax nostra a domni nostri regis pace dependeat spes ipsa pacis quam annuntiatione iam bona concepimus, ecclesie pariter et regno Anglie preparatorium quoddam gaudii iuuante Domino ⟨et⟩ exultationis inducit. Quod uero speciale est ad nos, sospitatis uestre quam directa declarat epistola, intimis congratulamur affectibus ob conseruatam uobis incolumitatem illi
15 gratias referentes qui cum suis benigne graditur, et iter et actus ipsorum angelo comitante prosequitur.[4] Ad uestrum uero iam suspensi tenemur reditum, quia cupienti animo nunquam satis festinat, moram ipsam cum molestia sustinentes, et ut optatos occurramus in amplexus aduentus uestri nuntium de die in diem sperantes pariter et expectantes. Valeat dominus meus et frater in Christo karissimus.

**132** 5 *A space is left in* B *after* rerum    12 quoddam gaudii B *followed by a space, perhaps for another word to balance* preparatorium, *in which case the inserted* et *may be unnecessary*    18 occuramus B    18 de dieiem in diem B (*partly corrected: originally written correctly two lines before, and cancelled because premature*)

---

[1] Here glanced at in the reference to 'ecclesie...Anglie'. The phrase 'spes pacis' is used in a context which suggests a similar situation in *JS Epp.* 1, no. 128 (*c.* Sept. 1160), and the metaphor of the stilling of the storm is a theme running through several of John of Salisbury's letters of this period. See *JS Epp.* 1, Appendix v, for the events of 1160.

[2] *JS Epp.* 1, no. 128, p. 223, refers to what the king had done 'Lincolnien'' and 'Eborac''; these are translated 'in respect of the sees of Lincoln and York', but the meaning is far from plain, and the bishops themselves may be referred to.

[3] Cf. Matt. viii. 26; Luc. viii. 25.          [4] Cf. Tob. v. 21.

### 133   To Pope Alexander III

[November–December 1160] He rejoices that the English and French churches have accepted Alexander, and so ended the papal schism in those countries. He also asks the Pope to permit Laurence abbot of Westminster to translate the body of King Edward (the Confessor), and pleads for the canonization of King Edward.

The special interest of this letter lies in its suggestion that a two-thirds majority should make a man pope: see p. 176 n. 4.

The circumstances described in the first half of this letter—the papal schism of 1159, the imperial council of Pavia (February 1160), the letter of Arnulf of Lisieux (May–July 1160),[1] and the recognition of Alexander III by Henry II and Louis VII (c. November 1160)[2]—prove that this letter was written in or after, but not long after, November 1160. It formed part of a dossier carried by Laurence abbot of Westminster in support of his demand for the canonization of Edward the Confessor.[3] Since the bull of canonization was issued from Anagni on 7 February 1161, Laurence's mission cannot have set out later than December 1160. For the papal schism, see notes to JS Epp. 1, no. 124 and Appendix V.

Patri suo et domno summo pontifici ⟨fo. 46⟩ A(lexandro) frater G(ilebertus) Herefordensis ecclesie minister, deuotum et debitum karitatis et obedientie famulatum.

Qui nube tristitie nuper obducti, matre nostra sancta Romana ecclesia graui scismatis errore concussa, altius ingemiscendo doluimus, luce ueritatis bonorum 5 cordibus illuscescente tota gaudii plenitudine in Christo, dilecte pater, exultauimus, cum munere diuino procella nobis in auram statuta est,[4] et post noctem dies nobis tam profecto grata quam serena resplenduit. Mouebat quidem multos illud celebratum Papie quod dicebant concilium, cuius actionem quidam ab ecclesia nomine peregrinus et re, oratione quidem in audientium gratiam quibusdam quasi uerbo- 10 rum phaleris adumbrata plurimum et ornata conscripsit. Que cum perlata fuissent ad nos et ecclesia presente perlecta que mente sinistra[5] dictata sunt, quibusdam quorum erat in leuam[5] occulus utique placuerunt. Alii uero bestiam que a nequam spiritu nefande conceperat euomentem, alta quadam et in Christo nobili mente

---

**133** G, no. 148; MB Epp. 11; B, fo. 45 v; Va, fo. 150 v (incomplete: omits protocol and most of the first section of the letter (ll. 8–50), but gives the heading Dompno pape Herefordensis episcopus). 4 sancta Romana ecclesia om. B      5 ingemendo Va      8 Mouebat...tradidimus (l. 50) om. Va      9 quidem B

---

[1] Ed. Barlow, no. 28.

[2] JS Epp. 1, 263 and n. (for the chronology, see also Barlow, EHR, LI (1936), 264–8). John comments on the council of Pavia in his Ep. 124.

[3] See Z. N. Brooke, 'Register of Master David', pp. 232, 235–6; B. W. Scholz, Speculum, XXXVI (1961), 38–60, esp. 49 ff.; F. Barlow, Life of Edward the Confessor, Appendix D. The text in Master David's register owes its survival to its place among the canonization dossier.

[4] Cf. p. 174 n. 1. For the edict of the Council of Pavia, see MGH, Constitutiones, 1, no. 190. Gilbert ascribes its authorship to Archbishop Peregrinus of Aquileia, one of its leading supporters, whose name occurs first among the archbishops who issued it.

[5] 'Sinistra/leuam' mean both left-handed and wicked (cf. JS Epp. 1, 193 n.)—the letter was, as it were, both written left-handedly and read so by those naturally wicked enough to accept it.

15 contempserunt, habentes pre manibus sacros uestri nominis apices, quos ad uniuersalem ecclesiam sancte dictauit et direxit auctoritas[1] et huic uelud columpne in loco caliginoso lucenti et plenum ueritatis testimonium intra se continenti firmiter innitentes, conuentum illum sacrilegum uere sinagogam Satane reputantes, et hinc uelud a Pilati pretorio—in quo misere clamatum est: 'Non hunc sed Barrabam;
20 tolle, tolle, crucifige eum; sanguis eius super nos et filios nostros'[2]—mente promtissima declinantes totum, quod ab his profane statutum est, sane mentis iudicio reprobandum per omnia censuerunt. Lumini uero quasi lumen accessit, cum sacram uestram prammaticam episcoporum, presbiterorum, diaconorum cardinalium sancte prosecuta est et prouide plena ueritatis epistola, hoc mundo clamans, hoc
25 uociferans: ad quos apostolica spectat electio, hos quidem omnes apostolatui uestro communi uoto assensu unanimi sincera karitatis integritate per omnia consensisse, et sue deuotionis obsequium in hoc Christo pia fidelitate prestitisse. Nam si de numero pontificum unus exiuit, eius in hoc reminisci oportuit, quo de numero apostolorum exeunte ueritas in hunc modum testificata est, 'nunc clarificatus est
30 filius hominis',[3] et nunc clarificabitur. Duobus etiam fratribus in partem alteram sentientibus nunquid ad hoc totam inclinari oportuit ecclesie plenitudinem cum id clamet auctoritas, ut paucorum absentia siue necessaria siue fortuita quod a maiore parte ordinis statutum est salubriter non debilitet? Et item 'due partes ordinis in urbe posite, totius ordinis instar exhibent'; ⟨B, fo. 46v⟩ et alibi: 'quod maioris
35 partis assensus probauerit, solempnis hoc firmet auctoritas'.[4] Si quid uero tantorum luminum preclaris potuit superaddi fulgoribus, id fidelis uestri domni Lixouiensis episcopi, plena suauitatis gratia et prudentie, ad plenum cumulauit epistola. In qua dum ipsius fidei puritas et obedientie uirtus omnibus in comune residentibus patenter emicuit, micantes in rebus dubiis multorum animos ne de cetero uelut
40 arundo uento agitata[5] mouerentur, quasi coram posito uirtutis speculo, et tanquam Domini spiritu per eum plenius exortante perfectissime solidauit. Nouissime uero consummans omnia sacra legatorum uestrorum attestatio beato fine cuncta compleuit, adeo ut ecclesia sancta quod in aure prius audierat, super tecta secure iam predicet,[6] et apostolatum uestrum piissimus rex noster humili deuotione suscipiat

133 36 superandi B    39 cetetero B

---

[1] Alexander's letters are JL 10584 ff.; cf. *JS Epp.* I, no. 124, nn. 1, 22.
[2] Joh. xviii. 40; xix. 15; Matt. xxvii. 25.                          [3] Joh. xiii. 31.
[4] *Code*, 10, 32, 45; 10, 65, 5, 2. The use of these texts (originally referring to municipal courts) is of exceptional interest, since there seems to be no evidence of their use in this sort of context so early as this; knowledge of this book of the Code had indeed been unusual before this time. The papal election decree of 1059, on which all elections down to 1179 were supposed to be based, did not in fact prescribe a numerical majority nor confine the election strictly to the cardinals. This is the first known occasion on which an authority suggesting a two-thirds majority—or any strict majority principle—among the cardinals as the basis for a papal election is known to have been cited: perhaps on the basis of this authority, perhaps because Alexander did himself receive such a vote (see *JS Epp.* I, no. 124, n. 13), this was the criterion established in the election decree of 1179, which is still in force—though much has been added to it. (On the two-thirds majority, see O. Gierke, *Das deutsche Genossenschaftsrecht*, III (Berlin, 1881), pp. 321 f., 392, 470.)          [5] Cf. Matt. xi. 7.          [6] Cf. Matt. x. 27.

et Anglorum uobis et Gallicana simul ecclesia non in oculto iam loquens sed in 45
omnibus suis finibus iam patenter obediat. Vos itaque, pater in Christo karissime,
in patrem et pastorem animarum nostrarum suscipimus; uocem uestram audiuimus
et agnoscimus; alienum non sequimur, sed qui Christi tunicam que nec in passione
scissa est misere consciderunt, Satane in carnis interitum in spiritus sancti uirtute
tradidimus.[1]                                                                            50

Diuinitus itaque collato uobis honori, pater, ut Anglorum plenius applaudat
ecclesia, in uno deuotissime in beatis his auspiciis uestris postulat exaudiri, ut beati
regis Edwardi corpus liceat fidelissimo filio uestro Westmon⟨asteriensi⟩ abbati
Laurentio prout eius expetit sanctitas honorare, et a terra leuatum et condigna theca
repositum in publicas totius populi gratulationes in ecclesia sublimare, quam a 55
fundamentis erectam constituit et amplissime dotatam, omnibus que ad decorem
domus Dei sunt in honorem Dei et beati Petri nobilitatam beatissime consum-
mauit. Hoc quidem corpus, ut ab his quibus fides ut credimus habenda est frequenter audiuimus, a xxxv annis usque nunc integrum incorruptumque cum
uisitaretur inuentum est, et qui licet in coniugio positus animi tamen summa uirtute 60
toto uite sue curriculo ut predicatur ab omnibus uirgo permansit, post mortem
etiam beata sui corporis incorruptione donatus est. Hunc prophetie spiritum
habuisse ⟨Va, fo. 151⟩ et in carne degentem futura Domino reuelante predixisse
constanter affirmant, mitem et misericordem et mansuetum super omnes et beato
Petro tam deuotum fuisse commemorant, ut diem ⟨fo. 47⟩ qua ipsius ecclesie 65
nichil contulerat, se prorsus amisisse deploraret. Eius adhuc leges apud nos iudicia
temperant, et regni sui pauperes usque hodie in multis illesos prouida ipsius circumspectione conseruant. Honorem uero qui sanctis exhibetur, quia Domino
placere non ambigimus, in hoc communi uoto serenitati uestre supplicamus, ut
regnum Anglie apostolice semper sublimitati deuotissimum honoretis, et fidelem 70
populum, regi suo, quem ob multa que epistolaris breuitatis non capit angustia uere
sanctum existimant, debitum sanctis honorem et reuerentiam exhibere concedatis.
Conseruet uos incolumem in longa tempora diuina uirtus, in Christo dilecte pater.

## 134 To the prior and convent of La Charité-sur-Loire

[Early 1161] The prior of Bermondsey has been elected abbot of Evesham in an ecclesiastical
council[2] at Canterbury, and the election has the royal approval and has been confirmed by
the archbishop of Canterbury. Gilbert asks the community of La Charité (the mother house
of Bermondsey) to release the prior of Bermondsey from their obedience.

**133** 46 omibus B  51 Diuinitus] Celitus Va  52 in/his *om.* Va  54 L. Va  54 techa B
56 construxit Va (constituit *over erasure* B)  56 decorem] honorem Va  57 nobilitatem Va
58 ut credimus fides Va  59 xxxv] centum iam B (Va's *reading is supported by other letters
in the dossier*)  61 permansit] B *adds et*  62 corporis *om.* Va  62 prophete B  64 et/et *om.* Va
71 regem suum B  71 breuitatis *om.* B  72 concedatis] Va *ends here*
**134** G, no. 254; B, fo. 180v.

---

[1] Cf. I Cor. v. 5.
[2] This council is otherwise unrecorded; it was no doubt held at Canterbury because the archbishop was in his final illness.

The prior of Bermondsey (Adam) was elected abbot of Evesham early in 1161 (see Biog. Index). According to the Bermondsey Annals the translation actually took place on 16 April.[1] The consent requested in this letter must have preceded that event, and it is also clear that Gilbert's letter was written before the archbishop's death on 18 April. The prior of La Charité was apparently Rainald.[2]

Gilbert seems to be acting as vicar of the diocese of Worcester in the vacancy of the see (see below, nos. 135-7).

G(ilebertus) Dei gratia ⟨Herefordensis⟩[3] episcopus uenerabili fratri et amico priori Karitatis et toti conuentui, salutem et sincere dilectionis affectum.

Quanta fratres in Christo dilectissimi karitatis plenitudine uos et uestram domum amplectamur, nec uerba explicant nec operis argumenta declarant. Si quid tamen
5 uestrum est apud nos a nostra id solicitudine non reputamus alienum—leta uestra lete suscipimus. Si quid quod absit secus accidit, non id uobis tantum incumbit quod et nos non aliena mentis afflictione pariter sustinemus. Vestre si quid uel eorum in quibus uos promoueri certum est promotionis oportunitas, si quando nobis occurrit, non eam negligere, non eam nos otiose preterire permittit illa proculdubio
10 qua uobis astringimur deuotio karitatis. Vnde cum conuentu fratrum et coepiscoporum nostrorum ⟨fo. 181⟩ necnon et aliorum religiosorum uirorum qui ad expedienda negotia ecclesiastica Cantuarie conuenerant de electione abbatis Eueshamie tractaretur, nostro quidem consilio licet alii quamplures aliorsum tenderent ad hoc tandem omnium inclinata est uoluntas, ut specialem filium
15 ecclesie uestre priorem Bermundesheye illi quorum erat electio eligerent, alii uero quorum in hoc expectabatur assensus unanimiter assentirent. De quo licet morum merita et honesta eius apud nos conuersatio sancte et laudabiliter enuntiarent, in hoc non parum gauisi sumus nobis tam fauorabiliter fuisse aplausum, quod de uestre scola discipline prodeuntem tanti nominis discipulum pastoralis magisterio
20 culminis dignum diceremus. Iam uota nostra concurrunt: quod nos probamus domnus noster rex Anglie approbat, domnus Cantuariensis idem sua auctoritate confirmat. Iam ad uos omnium nostrum spectat intentio, ut supremam manum adhibeatis—huius enim operis consummatio a uestra dependet sententia. Inde est quod dilecte nobis fraternitati uestre pro desolata iamdiu ecclesia Eueshamis que
25 suum expetit et expectat electum preces affectuose porrigimus quatinus sue electioni uestrum prebentes assensum quem sibi elegit pastorem concedatis et quod ad honorem Dei et sancte utilitatem ecclesie pia deuotione inchoauimus benigno fauore mancipetis effectui. Valete.

**134** 1 ⟨Herefordensis⟩] Londonien' B (*see n.* 3)　19 discipulum] discipulii B　24 Euesh'amis B (*possibly for* Eueshamensis)

---

[1] *Ann. Mon.* III, 441. The Bermondsey Annals have a bad reputation, but are probably to be relied on at this date.
[2] According to the *Gallia Christiana*, Rainald occurs in 1154 and 1161, Humbald in 1162 (XII, 406); Rainald died on 13 November (*Obit. Sens*, I, i, 468)—if these dates are correct, in 1161. But the *Gallia Christiana* is unreliable for information of this kind.
[3] The MS makes Gilbert bishop of London. But the letter clearly refers to the Evesham election of 1161, and Abbot Adam outlived Gilbert Foliot, so that no election took place at Evesham while he was bishop of London.

### 135 To the monks of Tewkesbury Abbey

[1161–2] He urges the monks not to give up, in any degree, their right of free election, granted and confirmed by papal authority.

Letters 135–7 all deal with an election at Tewkesbury, and the only possible occasion for this election was between the death of Abbot Roger in 1161[1] and the accession of Fromund in 1162 (see Biog. Index). Gilbert describes himself as vicar of the diocese of Worcester in no. 136 and this fits the vacancy after Bishop Alfred's death in 1160 (see GF, p. 227).

It is clear from 136–7 that there was a dispute between the monks and the advocate of the abbey—apparently the earl of Gloucester[2]—over the election, and it is impossible to decide at what moment Gilbert's pleas to the monks to stand by their liberty (135) and to the earl demanding a free election (136) were written. His letter to the earl of Leicester, Henry II's justiciar (137),[3] clearly belongs to the closing stages—when the election had been made and its validity was being tested by the archbishop and the royal curia. The Annals of Tewkesbury date Fromund's succession to 1162,[4] and it is reasonably certain that the archbishop of Canterbury of no. 137 is Thomas Becket (consecrated 3 June 1162), not Theobald (died 18 April 1161).

⟨G⟨ilebertus⟩⟩ Dei gratia Herefordensis ecclesie minister dilectis sibi in Domino fratribus Theochesber⟨ie⟩ Domino famulatum exhibentibus salutem.

Sapiens docetur e facili[5] et qui doctrinis af⟨fo. 39⟩fluunt, hos satis est succincta breuitate commoneri. Si libertati uestre quam circa patris electionem apostolica uobis concedit et confirmat auctoritas in magnum (quod absit) ecclesie uestre preiudicium 5 sponte renuntiatis, iudicium utique iustum est, ut ea de cetero careatis, et quod ex arbitrio suscepistis iugum illud diu sustineatis. Quod quia uobis captiosum imo summe periculosum est, mandamus uobis et fraterna caritate consulimus, quatinus libertati uestre conseruande unanimiter intendatis, ne si ob cuiuscumque fauorem aliud fortasse feceritis, ecclesie uestre detrimentum, cum id iam emendare non 10 poteritis, sera et infructuosa penitentia lugeatis. Valeat karitas uestra dilectissimi.

### 136 To William, earl of Gloucester (?)[6]

[1161–2] Acting as vicar of the diocese of Worcester, Gilbert warns the earl not to infringe the right of Tewkesbury Abbey to hold a free election—a right based on papal authority and recognized by the earl's father and grandfather.

135 G, no. 126; B, fo. 38 v.
10 non] hec *corrected* B
136 G, no. 291; B, fo. 142 v.

[1] It is just possible, though very unlikely, that there was another vacancy between 1157 and 1161 (see Biog. Index).
[2] See n. 6, below.
[3] The earl was acting as regent in the king's absence in the period 1158–63 (Eyton, *Itinerary*, pp. 43, 56, 58). He was also probably a personal friend of Gilbert: cf. no. 120.
[4] *Ann. Mon.* I, 49.     [5] Cf. p. 122 n. 2.
[6] This letter was clearly addressed to the lay patron of Tewkesbury abbey ('ecclesiam uestram'). Tewkesbury was founded (or re-founded) by Robert FitzHamon, and the patronage passed, with the hand of his daughter and heiress, to Robert earl of Gloucester and so, by this date,

Dum uices agimus Wigorn(ensis) ecclesie, dum honus eius etsi inuiti sustinemus, utique Domino delinquimus nisi parrochianos eius et filios super his que ad salutem sibi sunt, cum id expetit ratio, commoneamus. Inde est quod celsitudinem uestram diligenter obsecramus et commonemus in Domino quatinus ecclesiam uestram de
5 Theochesber(ia), que pro salute uestra et uestrorum manus omni die leuat ad Dominum, libere sibi patrem et pastorem eligere permittatis, et libertatem quam sibi apostolica confirmat auctoritas, quamque et aui uestri et patris ⟨fo. 143⟩ uestri benigna hucusque sibi conserauit pietas, nullatenus impediatis. Hoc enim uobis tam periculosum est et uestre saluti contrarium. Ex eorum namque priuilegiis intellexi-
10 mus quod omnes qui libertatem hanc ui aut metu aut machinatione quacumque impedierint, apostolica ligat auctoritas durissime, et eos Sathane in interitum carnis traditos[1] a corpore et a sanguine Domini nostri Iesu Christi nisi condigne peniteant prorsus reddit alienos. Quod ne umquam deuoluatur in uos, rogamus et monemus et uera utique caritate consulimus, quatinus ⟨ne⟩ offensam habeat, iram declinando,
15 Deo que Dei sunt reddatis[2] et que diuina sunt diuinitus amministrari permittatis; ut cum debitam Deo reuerentiam et in hoc et in aliis exhibueritis, ipse uos et in temporalis uite huius cursu conseruet, et post huius elapsum uite una cum suis debita obedientie et pietati mercede remuneret.

## 137   To Robert, earl of Leicester

[1162, after 3 June] He has received a mandate from the earl about the affairs of the monks of Tewkesbury. He would already have given them a hand, on the day when he was ordered by the archbishop of Canterbury to visit the house and investigate the election, but he was not admitted. He will, however, give the monks his support. He approves the person of the elect, and if he is present when the matter is decided, he will assist in his promotion, 'salua pace prelatorum'.[3]

Venerabili domno et amico in Christo karissimo comiti R(oberto) Legr(ecestrie) frater G(ilebertus) Herefordensis ecclesie minister, salutem et gratiam et a manu patris excelsi benedictionem perpetuam.

In iis karissime que mea potest sedulitas adimplere, debetis non uti prece sed
5 iussione. Est enim uobis eritque aput me semper iubendi plena auctoritas, michi uero nec deest nec unquam deerit promta uobis obsequendi uoluntas. Vestras nimirum preces pariter et precepta sic ratio distribuit, ornat honestas, modestia semper comes moderatur, ut uolentibus quod honestum est, ea recusare sit difficilli-

**136** 10 machnatione B
**137** G, no. 127; B, fo. 39.

to Earl William. It is therefore to be presumed that the recipient was Earl William, and this explains the reference to his father (Earl Robert) and grandfather (Robert FitzHamon, probably, rather than King Henry I) (*Monasticon*, ɪɪ, 60 f.; for Tewkesbury's relations with its later patrons, see Susan Wood, *English Mons. and their Patrons in the Thirteenth Century* (Oxford, 1955), Index, *s.v.* Tewkesbury).
[1] Cf. I Cor. v. 5.                [2] Cf. Matt. xxii. 21; etc.
[3] I.e., so long as his superiors (or the bishops) are agreed.

mum. In eo siquidem negotio super quo mandatum sublimitatis uestre nuper accepi, in negotio uidelicet fratrum de Theochesber⟨ia⟩, promtius quidem et longe 10 expeditius illis consilio pariter et auxilio profuissem, si die quo me urgens mandatum domni Cant⟨uariensis⟩ et iniuncte uis obedientie illuc uenire, et de facta electione inquirere coegit, saltem michi uel uerbo comunicassent, a quibus non admissus non potui inuitis beneficium prestare, quod nunc quidem pro amore Dei et pro reuerentia mandati uestri, non negabo uel ingratis. Honestatem namque 15 electe persone approbo et commendo, et si me cum negotium ipsum tractabitur interesse contigerit, de ipsius promotione ad honorem et utilitatem fratrum et monasterii de Theoche⟨s⟩ber⟨ia⟩, quantum potero, salua pace prelatorum, uestra prece commonitus, operam dabo. Valete.

### 138  To Ernisius, abbot, and the canons of St-Victor, Paris

[1161–3] He asks the abbot to provide a superior for the community of Wigmore (Salop).

Wigmore abbey was a daughter house of St-Victor, and the vacancy was occasioned by the interregnum following the withdrawal of the distinguished scholar, Andrew of St-Victor, from Wigmore. As a result of this letter he was reinstated.[1] Ernisius became abbot of St-Victor in 1161 or 1162.[2]

G⟨ilebertus⟩ Dei gratia Herefordensis episcopus dilectis sibi in Domino E⟨rnisio⟩ sancti Victoris abbati cureque sue commissis fratribus, salutem, gratiam et benedictionem.

Nos uobis ad presens scribere uestreque benignitati preces affectuose porrigere caritas de cordibus fratrum uestrorum imperiosa compellit. Plorans enim plorauit 5 in nocte doloris sui iam diu Wigomorensis ecclesia, nec poterunt herentes maxillis eius lacryme[3] nisi per uos reprimi leuiter aut exsiccari. Optans itaque post amissi damna pastoris patrem sibi de more substitui, recurrit ad pascua unde pastorem primo suscepit, unde primo canonice institutionis rudimenta, Domino sic disponente, sortita est. Vnde cum supplici supplicamus, preces fraternitati uestre cum 10 rogante porrigimus, quatenus ecclesie quam plantauit dextra uestra pastorem idoneum prouideatis, et qualem sibi noueritis expedire de collegio uestro concedatis, ut ipsos iugis obedientie et nos, si quid possumus, gratie et seruitii debitores habeatis. Valere uos optamus in Domino, dilectissimi.

**137** 14 quidem] B *adds* deceret, *cancelled*
**138** E. Martène and U. Durand, *Veterum Scriptorum...amplissima collectio*, VI (Paris, 1729), col. 240, from a MS now lost (cf. A. Luchaire, *Études sur quelques manuscrits de Rome et de Paris* (Paris, 1899), pp. 41, 101) (M); Paris, Bibl. Nationale, Lat. 14615, fo. 290v (seventeenth century transcript) (P); spelling as P.
6 Wigorniensis M   6 ? poterun P   12 prouidentes M   14 optamus] oportet M

---

[1] Cf. B. Smalley in *Recherches de théologie ancienne et médiévale*, X (1938), 367 and n. 34, who was the first to show that the letter referred to Wigmore, and not to Worcester (as in M). See also her *Study of the Bible in the Middle Ages*, 2nd ed. pp. 112–85.
[2] Abbot 1161/2–1172, when he was deposed: see Luchaire, *op. cit.* pp. 45 ff.; F. Bonnard, *Hist. de l'abbaye royale...de S.-Victor de Paris*, I (Paris, n.d.), 210–45.
[3] Lam. i. 2.

### 139 To King Henry II

[*c.* 1161–2] The chancellor[1] has asked Gilbert to take over the affairs of the diocese of London, and to divide its revenues between the bishop and his household and the king: Gilbert begs to be excused from this dangerous assignment.

At the end of his life, after an episcopate troubled by lawsuits and debt (cf. above, nos. 99–103, 109), Richard de Belmeis fell a victim to paralysis, and his affairs had to be managed by his friends and subordinates (cf. no. 140). This letter presumably belongs to the closing months of his life (in the 'extrema...egritudine' referred to in no. 140). He died on 4 May 1162.

Domno suo pre cunctis sibi karissimo illustri Anglorum regi H(enrico) frater G(ilebertus) Herefordensis ecclesie minister, omni die ad Dominum deuote mentis obsequium.

Obsecro ne irascatur domnus meus si clementie sue paucis supplicauerit humilis
5 amicus eius. Sollicitat me domnus cancellarius ut curam Lundon(iensis) episcopatus suscipiam, et ex parte reddituum episcopatus episcopum ipsum et domum eius exhibeam, reliquum uero domno meo regi prout sibi spiritus Dei suggesserit erogandum conseruem. Quod quia periculosum michi est et in multum anime mee dispendium, ad pedes sublimitatis uestre corde prostratus expostulo, quatinus huic
10 oneri me eximat uestra sublimitas, et curam hanc alii cui placuerit administrandam committat. Confido de misericordia Domini ut ad petitionem meam cor domni mei regis inclinet, et me pia exauditione uestra letificet, ut michi redditus Deo deuotius intendam, et ipsum pro salute uestra tanto purius, quanto expeditius, totis anime mee uiribus interpellem. Muro suo inexpugnabili circumcingat uos Dominus
15 et armis potentie sue protegat uos semper, domne in Christo dilectissime.[2]

### 140 To Thomas Becket, archbishop of Canterbury

[June 1162–3] On the advice of Gilbert and the bishop of Lincoln,[3] the late bishop of London, Richard (de Belmeis II) had entrusted his affairs in his last illness to Dean Hugh and Nicholas archdeacon of London. Gilbert asks the archbishop to protect the dean against the late bishop's creditors.

The bishop died on 4 May 1162, and the archbishop addressed (T. in the manuscript) must therefore be Thomas Becket, who was consecrated on 3 June in the same year.

Patri suo et domno T(home) Cant(uariensi) Dei gratia archiepiscopo frater G(ilebertus) Hereford(ensis) minister, ex affectu amoris intimi fidele munus obsequii.

**139** G, no. 119; *MB Epp.* 10; B, fo. 37.
**140** G, no. 120; *MB Epp.* 15; B, fo. 37.

---

[1] Thomas Becket. Becket himself was said to be farming three vacant bishoprics in 1160 (*JS Epp.* I, no. 128, p. 223: a letter addressed to Becket). The present letter may imply that Gilbert's translation to London was already in prospect.

[2] Cf. no. 247; based on the first Antiphon for the Magnificat, 1st Vespers, Sundays in November (cf. *Hereford Breviary*, I, 458).

[3] Bishop Richard's relations on the episcopal bench. Cf. no. 109.

Quod ad presens dilecte nobis et diligende semper in Domino sublimitati uestre scribimus hec causa est, ut uirum uenerabilem Hug(onem) Lundon(iensem) decanum, dampno iminente, quoad possumus eximamus, ne forte occasione damni 5 data, sibi etiam hoc ipso dampnum dedisse uideamur. ⟨fo. 37 v⟩ Dilectus quidem noster bone memorie Ricardus Lund(oniensis) dudum episcopus, cum extrema laboraret egritudine et omnes quos promouerat quosque sibi beneficiis obligauerat rerum suarum amministrationem suscipere ob plures quas pretendebant causas pertimescerent, domnus Lincoll(niensis) et nos cum eius uisitandi gratia aduenisse- 10 mus, in hoc consilium dedimus ne domum suam ulterius incerto statu fluctuare permitteret, sed suarum rerum administrationem et curam iam dicto decano et Nicholao archidiacono, ipsos ad hoc ui obedientie compellendo committeret. Qui nimirum onus attendentes negotii, mandatum hoc multa supplicatione declinassent, nisi tandem in hoc domni Lincol(niensis) nostrisque precibus et monitis adquieuis- 15 sent. Vnde quia pactum contractus cuiusque naturam auget et minuit, factoque cuilibet sue dant formam circumstantie, sublimitati uestre preces affectuose por- rigimus, quatinus actionem quam iam dicti episcopi creditores aduersus iam dictum decanum occasione procurationis huius instituunt, quousque uobis ualeamus assistere differatis, ut qualiter et quo pacto procurationem hanc susceperit relatione 20 nostra simul et testimonio cognoscatis. Ipsum enim onus debitorum episcopi in se nequaquam suscepisse, nec amministrationem hanc aliter subisse noueritis, nisi ut rerum curam ageret, ipsumque et domum suam fideliter exhiberet. Et si quid ex redditibus ipsius et obuentionibus annuis reliquum foret, hoc ubi necessitas debiti plus urgeret, non prout creditor uellet sed ut res esset exsolueret. Quod ob id 25 sanctitati uestre notificare curauimus, ne clericum uestrum quod non rapuit ex- soluere compellatis, nec ipsum pietatis officium iniustis solutionibus aliquatenus affligi permittendo, reliquos filios uestros a patrum suorum de cetero, quod absit, obsequiis absterreatis. Valere uos optamus, in Christo pater karissime.

## 141  Pope Alexander III to Gilbert Foliot

[19 March 1163] The Pope has learnt from King Henry, Archbishop Thomas and R(alph?) archdeacon of (Middlesex)[1] that the king is anxious for Gilbert to be translated to the see of London. Granted that the church of London has postulated the translation unanimously, the Pope approves it, instructs Gilbert to accept it, and grants the necessary dispensation.

Letters 141–3 form a series dealing with Gilbert's translation to London. Richard de

**140** 23 exhiberent B    28 a patr' suode (corrected to ? suorumde or suide) de cetero B
**141** G, no. 146; MB Epp. 18; JL 10,837; B, fo. 47 v (see Diceto, I, 309 = JL 10,838, for a similar bull to the Chapter of St Paul's).

[1]  Or Richard Rufus, archdeacon of Essex (before 1127–1167), who was senior among the archdeacons in appointment and a brother of the former bishop, Richard de Belmeis. But it is more probable that Ralph de Diceto, as the younger man, would represent the chapter at the curia in Paris; and he is known to have been in Paris about this time studying (Arnulf of Lisieux, Ep. 26, of ?March 1160). He was in England some time in 1162 (Gibbs, no. 192); but this could well have been during a break in his period of study at Paris.

Belmeis died in May 1162, and Gilbert's formal election took place on 6 March 1163.[1] The papal mandate for the translation was issued at Paris on 19 March (no. 141), and nos. 142–3 were written soon after its arrival in England—i.e. late March or April 1163; Gilbert was enthroned on 28 April.[1]

Alexander episcopus seruus seruorum Dei uenerabili fratri G(ileberto) Hereford(ensi) episcopo, salutem et apostolicam benedictionem.

 Ex litteris karissimi in Christo filii nostri H(enrici) illustris Anglorum regis et uenerabilis fratris nostri T(home) Cantuariensis archiepiscopi, atque ex relatione
5 dilecti filii nostri R. Lundon(iensis) archidiaconi, accepimus quod idem rex desiderat plurimum et requirit, ut tu ad London(iensem) ecclesiam transferaris, ut in eadem ecclesia curam geras et sollicitudinem pastoralem; hac utique causa et necessitate nobis ab eodem rege proposita, quod Lundon(ie) ciuitas regalis sedes sit et ipse rex diuturniorem ibidem consueuerit et longiorem moram habere, et ibi
10 frequentes baronum ac procerum de toto regno soleant esse conuentus. Quanto autem predicta regia ciuitas inter alias regni ciuitates magis est nobilis et famo-
⟨fo. 48⟩sa, tanto ecclesiam ipsam ab honestiori et tam in diuino quam in humano iure prudentiori prefatus rex regi desiderat et postulat gubernari. Nam cum ipse consilium tibi de anime sue salute commiserit, te cum sibi necesse est desiderat
15 habere presentem. Vnde nos ei tanquam karissimo filio nostro per omnia et in omnibus in quibus secundum Deum possumus deseruire uolentes, et relligionem, honestatem, et litteraturam tuam diligentius attendentes, uoto et proposito ipsius regis in hac parte, si tamen Lundon(iensis) ecclesia hoc unanimiter postulauerit, duximus annuendum, fraternitati tue per apostolica scripta mandantes quatinus
20 iuxta commonitionem predicti fratris nostri archiepiscopi, ad suscipiendam curam et regimen ipsius ecclesie omni occasione et excusatione postposita confidenter accedas, ei tam in spiritualibus quam in temporalibus utiliter auxiliante Domino prouisurus. Licet nanque illius te nouerimus relligionis et honestatis existere, ut libentius ministrares in minimis, quam famosis et magnis ecclesiis premineres, non
25 dubites tamen onus assumere quod ex diuine dispensationis arbitrio noscitur prouenire. Cum enim translationes personarum de una ad aliam ecclesiam absque euidenti et manifesta causa fieri sacrorum canonum inhibeant sanctiones, nos certas necessitates et causas a principe nobis propositas, et ipsius principis uotum et desiderium attendentes, translationem ipsam concedimus, inspectis quidem utilitati-
30 bus quas per studium tuum prefate Lundon(iensi) ecclesie confidimus ex diuina gratia prouenturas. Dat' Paris(iis) xiiii kalendas Aprilis.

## 142 Thomas Becket, archbishop of Canterbury, to Gilbert Foliot

[Late March or April 1163] Acting on a papal mandate, the archbishop instructs Gilbert to accept the translation to London, unanimously postulated by the clergy of the diocese in the presence of king and archbishop.

**142** G, no. 145; B, fo. 49.

---

[1] Diceto, I, 309. No. 143 is dated at Windsor: Henry was there on 31 March (Eyton, *Itinerary*, p. 61).

Tomas Dei gratia Cant(uariensis) ecclesie humilis minister uenerabili fratri G(ileberto) eadem gratia Hereford(ensi) episcopo salutem.

Quam sit nobilis et famosa pre ceteris regni huius ciuitatibus ciuitas London(ie) nulli nostrum incognitum est, in qua uidelicet ob publica regni negotia et domni regis conuersatio et procerum regni soleat frequentior esse conuentus. Inde est quod 5 ecclesia London(iensis) suo iamdudum orbata pastore, talem sibi desiderat episcopum subrogari, qui ciuitatis ipsius excellentie honeste uite merito, litterarum scientia, rerum quoque prudentia secularium adequetur. Magna itaque super hoc deliberatione habita, conuenerunt in hoc unanimis cleri postulatio, uoluntas domni regis et nostra, ordinatio quoque apostolica, ut ob communem regni utilitatem et 10 ecclesie necessitatem, ad ecclesie Lond(oniensis) regimen transferri, et in ea curam et sollicitudinem pastoralem gerere debeatis. Suscepto igitur in hoc domni pape mandato ipsius uobis auctoritate iniungimus, quatinus postulationi London(iensis) ecclesie, que de uestra ad eam translatione in presentia domni regis et nostra unanimi totius cleri assensu celebrata est, assensum prebere non differatis, et ad eius 15 regimen tanto deuotius et maturius accedatis, quanto ipsa tante persone consilio et gubernatione dinoscitur indigere. Ad hoc fraternitatem uestram commonemus attentius, ut ad quod trahit uos obedientie necessitas, nostre quoque delectionis contemplatio affectuosius inuitet, ut quem nobis sincere dilectionis coniungit affectus, loci quoque uicinia ad nostras et ecclesie Dei necessitates commodius ualeat 20 exibere. Valete.

### 143    King Henry II to Gilbert Foliot

[Late March or April 1163] The king values Gilbert's spiritual counsel and advice on affairs of state, and so wishes to have him near at hand. He therefore urges him to accept the petition of the church of London in accordance with the papal mandate.

H(enricus) rex Angl⟨orum⟩ et dux Norm(annorum) et Aquit(anorum) et comes And(egauorum) G(ileberto) Dei gratia Hereford(ensi) episcopo salutem.

Mentis uestre tantis institute uirtutibus soliditas, simul et honesti corporis integritas indemnis uestram michi commendauit commendabilemque reddidit excellentiam, nec michi solum uerum omnibus ad quos uestri nominis fama 5 peruenit; michi tamen pre ceteris experimento fides facta est, cui sepius anime salubre consilium a cordis uestri procedens examine datum est. De persone etiam proprie dignitate, de regni statu, de gerendis in regno negotiis, sepius et sepius sanum et efficax adhibuistis consilium. Hinc itaque uestram corporis et mentis uicinitatem assiduam, si possibilitas admitteret, desiderans et michi et heredibus meis 10 et regno meo, tam honoris quam utilitatis conseruationi et augmento profuturam considerans, obnixe deprecor quatinus Lond(oniensis) ecclesie petitionem in uestram collatam personam, secundum domni pape mandatum, executioni mandare non differatis, michi in hoc plurimum obsecuturi et eo amplius fauorem meum et

142 18 uestre B
143 G, no. 147; B, fo. 48 v.
1 Anglie B

15 amoris augmentum, si erga uos augeri possit, et omnium baronum meorum con-
secuturi. Ibi quippe cum negatur assiduitas, quatenus licet, iterata sepius mentem
meam simul et corpus uestra fouebit uisitatio. Ibi quotiens in regno meo de magnis
aliquid agendum occurrit, concilia celebranda sunt et consilia sumenda; eo barones
pro negotiis suis consilio fulciendis confluunt. Vt igitur latius uestre bonitatis et
20 uirtutis immense diffundatur et pateat magnitudo, non inmerito ⟨fo. 49⟩ uobis ut
London(iensis) ecclesie sollicitudinem et curam pastoralem suscipiatis domnus papa
mandare curauit, ecclesie illi tali indigenti pastore satisfaciens, michi et heredibus
meis et regno meo non mediocriter prouidens. Festinantiam ergo uestram nullum
retardet negotium, nulla prepediat occasio, uerum omnis procul amoueatur dilatio,
25 ut citius mandatum domni pape et nostra omnium uoluntas cum uestri et honoris
et utilitatis expediatur incremento. Teste T(oma) archiepiscopo, apud Windle-
sor(am).

# III

## LETTERS OF GILBERT FOLIOT AS
## BISHOP OF LONDON
### 1163–1187

### Nos. 144–272

## 144   Thomas Becket, archbishop of Canterbury, to Gilbert Foliot

[April 1163] Thomas outlines to Gilbert the motives which led him to promote Gilbert's translation to London. He had hoped to be present at Gilbert's arrival in London, but cannot: his archdeacon and the bishop of Rochester—if he can be present—will act on his behalf.

This letter was evidently written immediately after the translation, and before Gilbert had been enthroned: it is no doubt his enthronement which Becket is apologizing for not attending in person. Since Gilbert's translation was accepted by the Pope on 19 March, and he was enthroned on 28 April, this letter can safely be dated to April 1163.[1]

Thomas Dei gratia Cantuariensis ecclesie minister humilis uenerabili fratri Gileberto quondam Dei gratia Herefordiensi, nunc uero eadem gratia Lundoniensi episcopo, salutem.

Noli grauiter ferre, dilecte in Domino frater, quod tibi maius honus imposuimus, quod te ad maioris ecclesie curam uocauimus, confidentes id diuina miseratione 5 salubriter fuisse prouisum. Hoc mores tui, hoc nota religio, hoc sapientia data de super, hoc opus bonum quod in Herefordiensi ecclesia operatus es, promeruerunt ut dicatur tibi: 'Amice, ascende superius; super pauca fuisti fidelis, merito supra multa constitueris.'[2] Non homini rudi et inexperto nauigationis sicut ex humilitate scribis[3] nauim Petri commisimus, uerum illi qui iamdiu exercitatus in flumine, 10 amodo debet eandem in alto gubernare. Lucerna accensa, que quasi sub modio abscondebatur, iam super candelabrum posita est, ut longe lateque luceat in domo Domini.[4] Cant(uariensi) ecclesie que in regno Anglorum est sicut caput in corpore Londoniensis familiarius adheret pre ceteris, ad quam te Deo auctore transtulimus, ut e uicino matris tue Cant(uariensis) ecclesie, cui debes omne quod potes, nobiscum 15 possis onera sustinere. Preterea cum domnus papa tibi spiritualiter curam anime domni nostri regis commiserit, ubi te sedere magis decet quam in regia urbe quo crebrius propter negotia publica ueniens, frequenter tuis instruatur colloquiis et consiliis solidetur? Venire ergo ne formides quo uirtus tua te uocat, quo Dominus precipit, de ope nostra et auxilio quanta debetur amico et coadiutori consolationem 20 percepturus. Credimus siquidem hanc esse mutationem dextere excelsi, eamque a diuine dispositionis fonte emanare, non modo ut ecclesia Cant(uariensis) in negotiis suis fortius tanto nitatur auxilio, uerum etiam ut imperfectum nostrum quod in multis uidemus tua beatitudine suppleatur. Vtinam si fieri posset priori die Dominico Lond(oniam) uenisses, ut tuum aduentum digno susciperemus honore 25 ubi tunc presentes aderimus; nunc autem quoniam negotia nostra illinc nos auulsere, archidiacono nostro uices nostras commisimus, adiuncto etiam illi domno Roffensi si presens adesse poterit. Valeat in Christo fraternitas tua, dilectissime frater.

**144** G, no. 412; *MB Epp.* 19; B, fo. 137.
1 Thomas *corrected to* Teodbaldus *(by another hand: cf. above, p. 5)* B

---

[1] See *GF*, pp. 99, 247–8 on these dates and this letter.
[2] Cf. Luc. xiv. 10; xix. 17.
[3] Gilbert's letter, here referred to, is lost.       [4] Cf. Matt. v. 15; etc.

### 145 To the bishops elect of Hereford and Worcester

[March–December 1163] There is a dispute between Robert and Henry about the church of Whitbourne (Herefs):[1] on Henry's behalf Gilbert describes how on a previous occasion he had upheld Walter of Bromyard's case (see *GF*, p. 270) against Robert, and on Walter's death he had instituted Roger, and on Roger's resignation Henry.

There were bishops elect of both the sees only twice in Gilbert's time at London, in 1163 and in 1186. It is most unlikely that MS B was still in the making in 1186; and in any case the letter describes events in Gilbert's episcopate at Hereford which are seemingly not long past. 1163, then, must be the date. The bishop of Worcester, Roger, was elected in March 1163 and consecrated in August 1164; Robert de Melun was elected to Hereford after Gilbert's translation in March and consecrated on 22 December 1163.

Sibi dilectis electis domno Hereford(ensi) et Wigorn(ensi) frater G(ilebertus) Lundoniensis ecclesie minister, salutis gaudium et si quem potest in Domino karitas officiosa famulatum.

Vestram scimus non latere prudentiam quod facti sepius ignorantia iuris ignoran-
5 tiam parit, et frequenter in controuersiis cum minus apparet quid actum sit, quid etiam sit statuendum non instructus iudex minus plene intelligit. Inde est quod de causa que inter Robertum et Henricum ad presens uertitur, presenti uobis scripto notificamus quod uidimus, quod audiuimus,[2] immo quod ipsi formam legum secuti et canonum multis nobis assidentibus et iudicauimus et iudicatum executioni
10 legitime mandare curauimus. Defuncto namque Ricardo, qui in ecclesia de Wite-berne multo iam tempore ministrauerat, nos ipsum usque ad diem decessionis sue personatum ipsius ecclesie habuisse, suoque in ea nomine ministrasse existimantes, a Roberto fraude tacendi quod nouerat circumuenti, multaque precum eius instantia tandem moti, ecclesiam iamdictam ipsi concessimus, ipsumque ea etsi
15 iuris alieni conscientiam habentem (hoc quidem ignorantes) inuestiuimus. Quo agnito Walterus de Bromiard Herefordensis ecclesie canonicus presentiam nostram adiens, ecclesiam iamdictam sui iuris esse ipsamque sibi a predecessore nostro bone memorie Roberto episcopo canonice concessam fuisse asseruit, postulans sibi ad id probandum diem constitui et Robertum super hoc in ius euocari. Statuto itaque die
20 duobus ⟨fo. 44 v⟩ Lidebirie conuocatis capitulis Walterus presente Roberto eccle-siam de Witeburne ut iam dictum est sibi de iure competere asseruit, et ipsam a Richewardo in manu domni Roberti episcopi refutatam in se canonice ab eodem episcopo collatam fuisse, sufficienti idoneorum testium copia, iuramentis super hoc corporaliter exhibitis, plenissime comprobauit. Vnde ecclesiam eandem Roberto
25 abiudicatam, iam dicto Waltero ex sententia restituimus, et post ipsius decessum ipsam alii cuidam clerico nostro Rogero concessimus, quam ab eo postmodum

---

**145** G, no. 215; B, fo. 44.
10 Ricardo *sic, ? for* Richewardo (*see below*)    16 Hefordens(is) B    16 uestram B    26 uestro B

---

[1] This seems the only reasonable identification, and it seems clear that the church was in the diocese of Hereford; why the bishop of Worcester was concerned is not clear—the litigant Robert may have been a protégé of his.

[2] Cf. I Joh. i. 1.

refutatam, latori presentium Henrico omni uacantem persona et possessore donauimus. Quorum quis in iure potior habendus sit decernetis e facili qui iure celebrato an qui donatione nititur ex sententia retractata. Valere uos optamus in Domino, fratres in Christo karissimi.                                                                    30

## 146   To Pope Alexander III

[*c*. October 1163] He outlines the case for the primacy of Canterbury over York, and pleads that the traditional dignity be respected, and in particular that the archbishop of York be not permitted to carry his cross in the southern province.

Signs of trouble between archbishop and king began to be revealed comparatively soon after Becket's consecration. One undercurrent which reveals how things were going was the revival of the primacy dispute between Canterbury and York (see *GF*, p. 154 and n.). In July 1162 Alexander III, by an act of inadvertence, accepted Archbishop Roger's request to be allowed to carry his cross throughout England and to crown the English kings.[1] The dispute which followed led to frayed tempers, and increased the king's exasperation—partly, no doubt, because it led to an appeal to the Pope. According to the *Draco Normannicus* the dispute flared up at the Council of Tours in May 1163, and it was apparently one of the chief concerns of the Council of Westminster in October.[2] Thomas must have written his complaint against Roger for carrying his cross in the province of Canterbury shortly after the council (*MB Epp.* 27), and to this Gilbert's letter was evidently a companion. Thomas made an appeal for the following October; but the Pope wrote from Sens in January 1164 smoothing the affair over (*MB Epp.* 41, 43; cf. nos. 36, 42). None the less, the dispute lingered on, bearing bitter fruit at Northampton in November 1164, and leading ultimately to the final explosion over the coronation of the young king in 1170.

Patri suo et domno summo pontifici A(lexandro) frater G(ilebertus) Lundoniensis ecclesie minister, debitum apostolice reuerentie karitatis et obedientie famulatum.

Vt hostium cardine, sic sancte sedis apostolice moderamine sacro omnes quidem eclesie Domino sic disponente et eclesie sue ⟨fo. 41 v⟩ sancte pie per omnia prouidente reguntur. Que cum iudicialis equitatem censure omnibus exhibeat, ius suum 5 unicuique[3] sancte et intemerate conseruat. Sic iras mitigat, sic fomitem reprimit iurgiorum, sic caritatem solidat, et per omnes ecclesie partes pacem si forte inimico homine superseminante zizania[4] in aliquo turbata est sancta summeque laudabili circumspectione reformat. Inde est quod dilecte nobis et diligende semper in Domino sanctitati uestre tota mente totoque hominis interioris affectu preces 10 supplicando porrigimus, quatinus erga illam sancte Romane ecclesie specialem et deuotissimam filiam, Cant(uariensem) uidelicet ecclesiam, sereni cordis et beniuole mentis oculos habeatis, et qui ius suum cuique[3] defenditis ob beati Gregorii et

---

**145** 29 celebrata B
**146** G, no. 149; *MB Epp.* 28; B, fo. 41.

---

[1] *MB Epp.* 13. On this whole question see A. Heslin (Mrs Duggan) in *Studies in Eccl. History*, II (London, 1965).
[2] *Draco*, ed. R. Howlett, *Chrons. of the reigns of Stephen*, etc., RS, II, 744 ff.; *Summa Cause*, MB, IV, 201–5.
[3] Cf. *Inst.* I, I, 3.                                        [4] Cf. Matt. xiii. 25, 28.

sancti fundatoris eius Augustini merita ipsam uestri, quod absit, apostolatus tem-
15 pore nec opprimi, nec iniustis oppressionibus ab antiqua dignitatum suarum luce
obscurari permittatis. Nam si paternis est fides habenda traditionibus, ut a sancta
Romana ecclesia Cantuariensis fide illuminata est, sic est Eboracensis per Cantuariensem ad fidem procul dubio conuersa. Est enim ex historiis notissimum beati
Augustini successorem Laurentium ad hoc Paulinum direxisse, ipsiusque ministerio
20 ciuitatem Eborac(um) ab infidelitatis tenebris eruisse,[1] et in ipsam primatus
dignitatem et gloriam hoc ipso digne promeruisse. Quem quidem primatus
honorem multis predecessorum uestrorum temporibus ecclesia Cantuar(iensis)
obtinuit et in Eboracensem ecclesiam modis pluribus factisque memoria dignis
exercuit. Vnde sublimitati uestre Cant(uariensis) ecclesie tota supplicat plenitudo
25 ne filiam aduersus matrem suam leuare calcaneum[2] et in eius paritatem efficaciter
asspirare permittatis, neue insigne gestande crucis—quod soli Cantuariensi concessum esse testatur antiquitas—in scandalum (quod absit) ecclesie Anglorum et
stuporem regni, Eboracensis ille in aliena ulterius prouincia circumferat auctoritate
apostolica prouideatis. Si enim bene meritos beneficiis ampliare dignum est,
30 Cantuari(ensis) proculdubio ecclesie non solum antiqua conuenit priuilegia conseruare, uerum etiam nouis eam semper dignitatibus insignire consequens est, que
nimirum sedi semper apostolice se in quibus potuit obnoxiam deuotissime recognouit.

### 147   To Stephen, abbot of Cluny

[c. 1163] He congratulates the abbot and his community on his promotion, and asks him to
accept the resignation of Thomas, prior of Lenton (Notts), and replace him by Robert de
Broi.

Shortly before his withdrawal in 1163, Stephen's predecessor Abbot Hugh had written to
Gilbert congratulating him on his translation to London.[3] At the end of his letter he made a
reference to the Cluniac house of Lenton. Gilbert's letter must follow closely on Hugh's,
both because it congratulates his successor, who became established as abbot in 1163, and
because it also refers to the affairs of Lenton. Stephen's reply to this letter is also preserved
(Giles, no. 478). He humbly thanks Gilbert for his felicitations, and mentions at the close his
acceptance of Gilbert's request on behalf of Robert de Broi.

Venerabili domno patrique karissimo Stef(ano) Cluniac(ensi) Dei gratia abbati
frater G(ilebertus) Lundoniensis ecclesie minister ⟨fo. 43⟩ salutis gaudium et si
quem potest apud se karitas officiosa famulatum.

**146** 20 *? for* ipsum   24 execuit B, *corrected in modern hand*
**147** G, no. 257; B, fo. 42v.

---

[1] Paulinus was in fact consecrated and despatched by Laurentius's successor, Justus, according
to Bede, *Hist. Eccl.* II, 9.                    [2] Cf. Joh. xiii. 18.
[3] *MB Epp.* 20; cf. *GF*, p. 3. Hugh was deposed in 1161 for his part in the papal schism, but
apparently did not leave until 1163; in that year Stephen first occurs (*HF*, XII, 453, cf. 328,
440; XII, 315; XII, 332). See also Biog. Index. This letter and *MB Epp.* 20 are the only known
evidence about the two priors of Lenton.

Exultaui karissime totus in Domino[1] et spirituali iocunditate perfusus sum, audiens matrem nostram Cluniac(ensem) ecclesiam tandem respirasse in te, et in 5 patrem et domnum te sibi quam prouide tam ut spero salubriter et feliciter elegisse. Te enim custode commisso tibi gregi papula uite deesse non poterunt, qui pectus tuum Domino in quandam ut sic dicam scripturarum sanctarum apotecam, et aromaticam uirtutum cellulam a puero fere consecrasti. Non eiulabit clamans terra tua post te, que doctrine fluentis affluenter irrigabitur, et ut uirtutum frugi plene 10 respondeat, in te propositum uirtutum exemplis incessanter ad ea que sancta et summa sunt prouocabitur. Beatum collegium cuius id uirtutum debebatur meritis ut a tribulatione malorum et dolore tanti patris respiraret solatio, et procellam quam iamdiu sustinuerat in auram sibi uerteret boni patrisfamilias circumspecta sollici-tudo.[2] Fateor in Christo, karissime, fateor datum michi celitus conspectum tuum et 15 alloquium michi non mediocre incitamentum exstitisse uirtutis, ut ex hoc beatos estimem, qui tibi semper assistunt, qui te comitantur assidue,[3] quibus hoc uirtutis speculum quo semper in meliora proficiant habere concessum est. Annuntiant de homine ut scriptura commemorat uultus eius, incessus et habitus, que tui attendentes in te in uirum facile poterunt transformari perfectum.[4] Que quidem menti mee etsi 20 ad momentum inspecta tamen altius insederunt, adeo ut tui quandoque contem-platione in nouum quendam hominem[5] transiens meipsum michi uidear quodam-modo transilisse. Inde est quod totis ulnis karitatis amplector absentem, quem presentem uidere et deuotis et debitis uenerari obsequiis intime concupisco.

Quia uero presumptuosum quandoque karitas efficit postulationem hanc finis 25 epistole continebit, quatinus fratrem nostrum domnum Thomam priorem Lentone super absolutione sua pro qua plurimum instat clementer exaudiatis, et substituto sibi fratre nostro Rob(erto) de Broi ipsum seruitii et me amplioris si fieri potest gratie tue debitorem sanctitati constituatis. Valeat domnus meus et pater in Christo karissimus.

30

## 148  To Thomas Becket, archbishop of Canterbury

[1163–4] Thomas had given sentence between Hubert a clerk of St Paul's and Baldric clerk, although Hubert had pleaded an exception to prevent judgement. Gilbert supports Hubert's plea, both because the exception was valid, and because Hubert had appealed to the Pope before judgement was delivered.

From May 1162 until at least October 1163, and probably right down to his exile in November 1164, Becket was able to carry out his normal duties as archbishop of Canterbury. The following is the only surviving letter from Gilbert as bishop of London written to Thomas on a matter of routine administration.

**147** 6 feliciter B    28–9 me *after* gratie *before correction* B
**148** G, no. 193; *MB Epp.* 40; B, fo. 40v.

---

[1] Cf. Ps. xxxiv. 9.
[2] Cf. Ps. cvi. 39, 29.
[3] Cf. II Para. ix. 7.
[4] Cf. Eccl. xix. 26–7; Eph. iv. 13.
[5] Cf. Eph. iv. 24.

Patri suo et domno T(home) Cant(uariensi) Dei gratia archiepiscopo frater G(ilebertus) Londoniensis ecclesie minister, apto rationis moderamine semper sibi credita dispensare.

Docet nos magister bonus petere; docet et querere; et ut aperiatur nobis docet ad 5 ostium cordis eius cui supplicatur, non oportune solum sed inportune pulsare.[1] Hoc auctore petimus et pulsamus quatinus apud excellentiam uestram nobis si placet ad gratiam pandatur aditus, et ad id quod iustum est non negetur accessus. Clamat post uos clericus beati Pauli Hubertus, asserens iustam aduersus Baldricum clericum sibi competere exceptionem, ut ad soluendum ⟨solidos (?)⟩ uiginti que ab eo 10 postulat Baldricus, ipse de iure compelli non debeat; unde sibi audientiam preberi supplicat ut Baldricum ab intentione hac sacra legum et canonum auctoritate repellat. Quod quia iuri consentaneum credimus, preces precibus anteuertentes supplicamus, quatinus in re ista quod equm est decernatis et in clericum beati Pauli non imperium ad presens in ligando, sed equitatem potius in iudicando excerceatis. 15 Cum enim liti se offerat ut inpetentis se intentionem potenter elidat, uel si circa hoc defecerit, non id solum quod petitur sed in expensis etiam si iustum fuerit con-dempnationem subeat, sibi diem statui ipsumque in hoc audiri oportere quis ignorat? Nam quod obicitur—acta agi non debere, et esse uarii et inconstantis hominis contra sua pacta uenire, que etiam sententia uel amicabili conuentione 20 finita sunt in litem reuocanda non esse—quale quidem sit, uestra plene nouit autoritas. Non enim quod actum est illud agitur, sed ex transsactione uiginti de nouo petens exceptione repellitur, ex cuius probatione noua in illum lis inchoatur. Quid enim si debitum hoc uel iam soluit Hub(ertus) ⟨fo. 41⟩ uel remisit forte Baldricus uel de non petendo pepigit, uel extra naturam contractus huius (cum sit 25 iuris stricti transactio) auctoritatem si ad euincendum agereetur se prestiturum repromisit? Horum quodcumque probetur, Hubertus plane non tenetur. Huius itaque residui petitionem cum, ut sibi confidit Hubertus, plane repellat exceptio intimo sublimitati uestre supplicamus affectu quatinus sententiam qua clericum nostrum teneri precipitis, amore iustitie nostraque prece relaxetis, et causam que 30 inter clericos de nouo constituitur suo inter eos marte currere permittatis. Quod si nostra non meretur supplicatio, optinuisse tamen debuerat ad domnum papam et ante sententiam sub certo testium numero facta appellatio. Non enim hec causa est quam appellatione remota apostolica terminare iussit auctoritas. Nam in qua aliud intenditur et aliud respondetur, et sententia prorsus alia desideratur, alia procul 35 dubio dinoscitur esse causa. Agat itaque si placet uestra modestia ut relaxatione hac amicum uestrum humilem exaudiatis, et honorem debitum et firme ut estimo promissum domno pape exhibeatis, et ius Baldrici (si quod habet) etsi in tempus dilatum recte in nullo tamen minuatis, et sic a tramite legitimo in nullius offensam uel in modico recedendo uniuersa iocundo fine compleatis. Valete.

**148** 9 ⟨solidos (?)⟩ *or* denarios? *cf. l. 21*    12 anuertentes (anūtētes) B    17 hec (h') B    32 certa B 35 ?agit B

---

[1] Cf. Matt. vii. 7 ff.; Luc. ii. 9 ff.

### 149  To Pope Alexander III

[1163 or shortly after] The case between Master Matthew, chancellor of (Queen Eleanor),[1] and R(obert) prior of Monmouth about the church of Llangarren (Herefs), delegated by the Pope to Gilbert, has been suspended once more by an appeal from Master Matthew to the Pope.

This letter provides the latest known date for both the disputants, and the case itself was evidently an old one, surviving from the time of Pope Adrian IV. Master Matthew, further-more, was a person of some standing, and it would be surprising if he had lived long after 1163 and yet left us no trace of his existence. On all these grounds, it seems safe to assign this letter to the earliest years of Gilbert's episcopate.

Patri suo et domno summo pontifici A(lexandro) frater G(ilebertus) Lundoniensis ecclesie minister, debitum dilectionis et obedientie famulatum.

Cum ex uestri domine forma mandati magistro Matheo illustris Anglorum reg⟨ine⟩ cancellario diem aduersus R(obertum) priorem Monem(utensem) super ecclesia de Langaran statuissemus, ipse eodem die in presentia nostra aduersus 5 iamdictum priorem experiens, ecclesiam iamdictam cum adiacente sibi parochia iniuste sibi ab ipso detineri conquestus est, asserens eandem ecclesiam cum tota sua parrochia ⟨fo. 43 v⟩ ad ius ecclesie sue de Langaran pertinere, ipsamque ecclesiam de Langaran hanc de qua agitur multo tempore possedisse, nec eam aliquatenus iudicio sed sola Monem(utensis) ecclesie uiolentia amisisse. Quod cum coram 10 positis testibus probare paratus esset, prior ilico exceptionem sibi peremtoriam obiciens respondit se super eadem ecclesia in nostra iamdudum presentia cum aduersus eum magister Matheus intenderet, ad audientiam apostolicam appellasse, seque ad sedem ipsam apostolicam instructum uenisse; ubi cum magistri Mathei diu prestolatus fuisset aduentum, nec ipso nec pro se aliquo comparante apostolico 15 tandem iudicio hanc ipsam ut asserit ecclesiam de Langaran ad ius Monem(utensis) ecclesie pertinere, instrumentis et testium iuramentis sufficienter ostendit, et super hac lite uictoriam bone memorie domni pape Adriani sententia reportauit. In cuius probationis sue et secundum eum late sentente testimonium, priuilegium eiusdem domni pape Adriani ostendit, hanc ipsam probationem testificans et ecclesiam de 20 Lanruat' ecclesie Monem(utensi) confirmans. Magister uero Matheus aduersum se absentem et indefensum sententiam latam fuisse audiens, priorem hoc falsa sugges-tione ⟨obtinuisse⟩ asseruit. Quod ut in uestra probet presentia, ad audientiam uestram ad festum Omnium Sanctorum appellauit. Valeat domnus meus et pater in Christo karissimus.                                                                          25

---

**149** G, no. 151; B, fo. 43.

4 reg' (*cf. n. 1 below*) B     9 agitur *sic, perhaps for* agebatur     17 testium et B     21 Lanruat']
*presumably for* Langaran     23 obtinuisse *Giles; om.* B

---

[1] The manuscript reading *reg'* would suggest *regis*; but Matthew was certainly the queen's chancellor, not the king's; on him see H. G. Richardson in *EHR*, LXXIV (1959), 193 ff.; see no. 333 for Prior Robert; and for the early history of Monmouth priory and the mother house of St-Florent, Saumur, see S. Harris in *Journ. Hist. Soc. of the Church in Wales*, III (1953), 6 ff.; also below, no. 152; *CDF*, nos. 1145, 1148.

### 150   To Pope Alexander III

[1163–9, probably *c.* 1163] He describes the case between Richard and Walter about the church of Harlington (Middlesex), which had been suspended by Richard appealing to the Pope. Richard claimed that the church had been assigned to him in a judgement given by the bishop of Chichester acting as judge delegate of Adrian IV (1154–9), and that he had been instituted to the church in the first instance by Bishop Richard senior (Richard de Belmeis I, 1108–27). Walter's plea was that he had been instituted by Bishop Robert (de Sigillo, 1141–50), and that the judgement in Richard's favour had been made between Richard and Walter's proctor Adam when Walter was in France studying.

Like no. 149, this is an old cause revived, and the antiquity of the case, and of at least one of the disputants,[1] proves that it belongs to the opening years of Gilbert's pontificate. The bishop of Chichester who had made the judgement in the 1150's was clearly still alive when this letter was written. Bishop Hilary died in 1169, which must be the latest possible date for the letter.

Patri suo et domno summo pontifici A(lexandro) frater G(ilebertus) Lundoniensis ecclesie minister, debitum caritatis et obedientie famulatum.

Conquestus est apud nos, domne, presentium lator Ricardus se ecclesia de Hardintuna iniuste spoliari et eam a Waltero clerico iniuste sibi detineri, asserens se
5 ut iamdictam recuperaret ecclesiam iamdudum bone memorie domnum papam Adrianum adisse, et ad uenerabilem fratrem nostrum domnum Cicestrensem episcopum mandatum retulisse ut super eadem causa cognosceret et ipsam fine debito terminaret. Iam dicto itaque episcopo suas in hoc partes interponente, iuxta asertionem Ricardi, Adam ⟨fo. 167v⟩ clericus iam dicte ecclesie eo tempore
10 detentor cum eo in hunc modum composuit, ut uiginti solidos annuatim nomine ipsius ecclesie sibi solueret, et hos soluendo ecclesiam ipsam uite sue tempore retineret. Ipso uero postmodum in hac solutione cessante, Ricardus se domnum papam item adisse et iamdictam ecclesiam sibi ab eo adiudicatam fuisse, seque sententie huius executionem ad domnum Cicestrensem detulisse, et iamdictum
15 Adam secum denuo in hunc modum transegisse asseruit, ut quinquaginta solidos annuatim sibi redderet, hacque solutione ecclesiam retineret. Innitens itaque auctoritati apostolice qua sibi ecclesia iamdicta adiudicata est, cum eius nomine iam nec uiginti nec quinquaginta nec aliquid omnino sibi soluatur, petebat ecclesiam sibi restitui et apostolice sententie reuerentiam debitam exhiberi. Walterus uero res
20 inter alios actas et iudicatas aliis nec obesse nec prodesse debere asserens, se iamdictam ecclesiam canonice adeptum, seque a predecessore nostro bone memorie Roberto episcopo ante litis memorate tempora in ea personam constitutum fuisse respondit. Cumque postmodum in Gall(ia) studiorum causa demoraretur, si inter Ricardum et Adam rei sue procuratorem ipso absente et ignorante super ecclesia sua
25 lis actitata et transactio interposita est, ipsam absenti sibi et ignoranti preiudicium

---

**150** G, no. 161; B, fo. 167.

[1] Even if Richard's plea was false, he must have been of an age to make it plausible. If true, he should have been a priest, i.e. aged 23, by 1127; although this would not necessarily make him older than Gilbert himself, he would be a *senex* by twelfth-century standards in the 1160's.

afferre non posse notissimi iuris esse asseruit.[1] Qui reuersus a studiis et in propria ueniens, ecclesiam quam legitime nactus est iure suo possedit nec pactiones Ade super re sua ipso ignorante initas, aut ratas habuit aut ratas habere disponit. Volentes uero ius Ricardi si quod erat plenius intelligere, quis eum in iamdicta ecclesia personam constituerit diligenter inquisiuimus. Ipse uero predecessorem nostrum 30 domnum Ricardum seniorem ecclesiam hanc sibi concessisse respondens, scriptis aut testibus aut aliis quibuscumque amminiculis asertioni huic fidem facere, nec tunc quidem potuit nec de cetero se facturum repromisit. Inquisitus uero an hoc probare sufficeret, Adam scilicet tempore quo cum ipso transegit ecclesiam ipsam suo nomine possedisse, aut Walterum quod inter ipsos gestum fuerat ratum postmodum 35 habuisse, horum etiam probatione omnino se carere respondit. Vnde cum causam eius ueritate niti non liqueret, reuerentiam tamen debitam domni pape litteris exhibentes, W(alterum) ab eius petitione non absoluimus, sed rem ⟨fo. 168⟩ in diem alterum quo sibi Ricardus prouidere posset uberius differendam estimauimus. Ricardus uero denuo penes nos experiri renuens rem distulit, ad sanctitatem uestram 40 ad festum sancti Egidii appellauit. Valere uos optamus in Domino, pater in Christo karissime.

## 151    To Malcolm IV, king of Scotland

[1163–5, ? 1163] He asks the king to enfeoff Elias, Gilbert's closest relation (*proximo cognato nostro*), with his inheritance, which—so he understands—he lost through his fidelity to Malcolm's father.

For this letter, see *GF*, pp. 38 ff. King Malcolm died in 1165; Elias Foliot may have approached him in July 1163, when Malcolm visited Woodstock[2]—his last visit to England, so far as is known.

Domno suo karissimo illustri regi Scotie M(alcolumo) frater G(ilebertus) Lun-doniensis ecclesie minister, per quem reges regnant diu regnare feliciter.

Sublimitati uestre, karissime domne, hac confidentia scribimus quia uos sincero cordis affectu diligimus, et in omnibus haberemus acceptum si gratum uobis in aliquo prestaremus obsequium. Speramus etiam ipsa manu Spiritus Sancti planta- 5 tam esse in corde uestro radicem equitatis et iudicii iusti, et ideo in causis subditorum uestrorum mentem uestram posse bonorum precibus ad id quod iustum est facile in-clinari. Scriptum enim est, 'beati qui custodiunt iudicium et faciunt iustitiam in omni tempore'; et Sapientia ait, 'tolle rubiginem de argento et exibit uas purissimum;

**151** G, no. 278; *Regesta Regum Scottorum*, I, no. 320; B, fos. 142v (B1) *and* 184 (B2) (*spelling as* B2).
1–2 Domno...minister B2; Illustri regi Sco'. G, B1    4 cordis *om.* B1    7 posse...iustum est] ad id quod iustum est posse bonorum precibus B1; ad id qui... *cancelled,* posse bonorum precibus ad id quod iustum est B2. *It looks as if* B1 *represents a draft, subsequently amended, and* B2 *shows both draft and correction*

[1] Cf. no. 113.
[2] Eyton, *Itinerary*, p. 63; *Reg. Regum Scottorum*, I, 19.

10 tolle iniustitiam de corde regis et iustitia firmabitur tronus eius.'[1] Inde est quod
regie nobilitati uestre pro presentium latore Helia proximo cognato nostro
preces affectuose porrigimus quatinus amore Dei et petitione nostra eius seruitium
accipiatis et de hereditate sua ipsum exaudiatis, et nos et multos nobiscum gratie
uobis et seruitii debitores efficiatis. Si gratiam in oculis uestris inuenerit ad seruitium
15 uestrum multos adiutores inueniet, quorum sibi quisque de suo libenter subueniet.
Istud uero postulare nequaquam presumeremus, si patrem eius perfide se aut
maligne aduersum uos et patres uestros habuisse cog⟨B 2, fo. 184 v⟩nosceremus; sed
ipsum pro fidelitate patris uestri exhereditatum audiuimus, et speramus de misericordia uestra ne quem patri uestro fideliter ad posse suum seruisse cognoscitis, eius
20 unquam canos cum merore ad inferos deducatis.[2] Valeat domnus meus karissimus,
et cor eius spiritus Dei repleat atque possideat.

### 152 To Froger, abbot of St-Florent, Saumur

[c. 1163 (or 1160)] He congratulates Froger on his election as abbot, and tries to enlist his
favour for Baderon of Monmouth, and to obtain permission for brother Robert de Castro
Nouo to return to St-Florent.

Abbot Froger was elected on 2 June 1160 and died in 1173.[3] Gilbert's interest in Monmouth priory, a cell of St-Florent, of which Baderon was advocate, and of which it seems
likely that Robert was a monk,[4] must date from his time as bishop of Hereford; and it is not
impossible that the heading of the letter is wrong—its text is certainly very corrupt, and it
stands next to a letter written from Hereford in which Gilbert's title is wrongly given as
'Londoniensis episcopus' (no. 134).

The state of the text is far from satisfactory, and the letter itself often far from clear. Gilbert
seems to say that he is appealing on behalf of three men, but only two are mentioned. The
incomplete sentence on p. 200 (see note to line 41) may have been originally intended to
introduce the problem of the third man; and the correction of Robert de Castro Nouo's name
(see note to line 27) may also be due to a change of plan in the scope of the letter. This in-
consistency and the state of the text suggest that the scribe was copying off an incomplete
draft.

For an interpretation of this letter, see *GF*, pp. 15–18.

G(ilebertus) Dei gratia Londoniensis episcopus uenerabili domno fratrique karissimo F(rogero) Salmurensi eadem gratia abbati, salutem et sincere karitatis affectum.

Vestra frater karissime multa animi benignitate salutamus auspicia, optantes

151 10 tolle] B 2 *omits:* aufer *added in margin by a different hand* (*Vulg. reads for* tolle…tolle aufer
…aufer) 11 pro *om.* B 1 11 Helia…nostro *om.* B 1 12 quatinus] pro *added* B 1 14 uobis
*om.* B 1 15 subueniat B 2 17 aduersus B 1 20 cum merore *om.* B 1
152 G, no. 265; B, fo. 179 v (*crossed out in B to the end of fo.* 179v).
1 B *before* G(ilebertus) *adds* Venerabili domno fratrique karissimo F., *cancelled*

---

[1] Ps. cv. 3; Prov. xxv. 4–5.
[2] Cf. Gen. xlii. 38, presumably implying that Elias was not a young man.
[3] *Recueil d'Annales Angevines et Vendômoises*, ed. L. Halphen (Paris, 1903), p. 123; *Chron.
Anjou*, pp. 192–3.
[4] Perhaps even prior: see no. 149 and Biog. Index.

laudabile illud uestre promotionis initium felici semper cursu dirigi, et Domino manum misericorditer apponente beato tandem fine compleri. Gratulamur equi- 5 dem et plena mentis iocunditate perfundimur atendentes manum Domini multa gloria deducentem uos et a bonis ad meliora continuo pertrahentem. Hec enim est que uos a mundi huius auulsit illecebris, que uos per gradus uirtutum deducens, sobrie ab humili quem elegeratis loco suis utens uerbis quibus humiles ut superius ascendant affari consueuit,[1] ad pastorale tandem iam culmen multa bonorum 10 coniuentia et unanimi fratrum uestrorum ut audimus electione sublimauit. In quo preuenienti gratie gratias redimus, subsequenti preces porrigimus, ut in sublimi positus in domo Domini, tanquam uirtutis speculum eluceatis et uirtutis iter[2] hoc oneste conuersando uirtutis amatoribus—ut dux ad uitam uere preuius—ostendatis. Agit hoc ille qui suos quo leuat ⟨fo. 180⟩ altius dignitate, eo firmat et fundat 15 solidius humilitate et ad perfectum adducit ea que per ipsius spiritum ad omnes diffunditur karitate.[3] Liberet in hunc modum fraternitati uestre plura suggerere, sed confisi de ea que uos intus ad plenum edocet unctione,[4] illi uela uestra com-mittimus quem suos ad portum perducere enauigata mundi huius tempestate, suaui Sancti Spiritus aura sinus mentium feliciter implente, certa ueritate cog- 20 nouimus.

Ad illum stilum uertimus pro quo uobis ad presens scribendi necessitatem sus-cepimus. Tria in petitione proponimus, in quibus a serenitate uestra exaudiri, toto mentis affectu, tota anime pulsantis instantia postulamus—tres pro tribus ad presens quasi legatione fungimur. Hi sunt dilectus filius noster Baderun de Munemue 25 ecclesie uestre benefactor et amicus noster in Christo karissimus, Rodbertus de Castro nouo amicus uester humilis et deuotus. Luget enim Baderun pristina parentum suorum et sua postmodum erga ecclesiam uestram beneficia in irritum adeo deuocari, ut a corde non solum quasi mortuus occiderit, sed et iram uestram nullis suis ut sperat meritis unde totus turbatur incurrerit. Si quid uult, uos illud 30 nolle conqueritur; si quid postulat uos auertere faciem erubescit. Mallet cum domo uestra amicitias non inisse, quam multis acquisitas meritis taliter amisisse. Vnde si quid est quod serenitatem uestram aduersus ipsum obnubilet, donari nobis hanc ueniam et nubilum hoc flante Sancti Spiritus aura prorsus euacuari postulamus et in plenam gratiam magnum uestre domus amicum suscipi et blandis et honestis 35 responsionibus foueri postulamus, mandamus atque precipimus. Expedit enim ecclesie uestre non quemque ab eius alienari gratia cuius liberalitas eidem ampla contulerit beneficia.

Priorem uestrum uirtutum meritis in publicis iamdiu ⟨gratula⟩tion⟨ibus⟩ domus uestra ad nos non intercedente dilatione remittit, rogans et nobis ut amico de quo 40 per omnia bene [. . .] ⟨fo. 180v⟩ Hinc ad fratrem karissimum Rodbertum de Castro

**152** 12 porrmus B   15 Agi *? corr.* B   25 Munemue]*? add* et: *a space in* B *and* et *in the margin* 26–7 de Castro nouo] de Casteillim arco *corrected* B   32 amississise *corrected to* amisise B 33 quod] quid *?* B   35 et blandis et] non *added, then crossed out* B   39 iam diut-/ione B 41 *Some words seem to be missing* (cf. no. 4 l. 17, 48 l. 30, *etc.*)

[1] Cf. Luc. xiv. 10.    [2] Cf. Ps. xlix. 23.
[3] Cf. Rom. v. 5.    [4] Cf. I Joh. ii. 27.

nouo nostre cursus orationis illabitur; cuius dum reminiscimur animo in diuersa distrahimur. Nam si amicus est, eius a nobis elongari presentiam tantopere cur optamus? Sed amicum magis absentem uiuere quam presentem mori optandum
45 est. Sub arthofilace, sub artho, sub axe boreali cuncta sibi infesta sunt. Aer frigidus, estiue glacies, aqua iniqua taliter et coctione potabilis febri, qua fatigatur assidue, plenam prestant causam atque materiam. Inde est quod dilecte nobis benignitati uestre preces porigimus ut eum quasi postliminio reuersum[1] cum gratia suscipiatis et ne iugo pressus obedientie tristius ingemiscendo deficiat uobis commanentem
50 suis stellis et ⟨unde⟩ originem pius hausit aere frui permittatis. Confidenter in amici castra migrauimus, etsi multa tamen ut credimus in offensam uestri postulantes, in quibus nos exaudiens gratia uestra non antiqua solum familiaritate sed et beneficio recenti nostra sibi secure uendicabit seruitia. Incolumitatem uestram et succensus[2] conseruet Dominus.

## 153 To all the faithful

[October 1164] Gilbert gives judgement for John in his case against the abbot of Grestain[3] over the church of West Firle (Sussex), and against the abbot and the priest Henry over the chapel of Charlston (Sussex).[4]

We learn from no. 154 that on the Wednesday after delivering this judgement Gilbert was due at Dover, together with the bishop of Chichester, to set out on embassy to the Pope on instructions from the king. This can only refer to the embassy to Sens in November 1164— the aftermath of the Council of Northampton and Becket's flight from England.[5] According to William FitzStephen, Becket and the royal envoys both crossed on the same day, 2 November.[6] The 2 November was a Monday, and this makes it probable that the day of assembly in Dover was Wednesday 28 October. This judgement must have been delivered in the second half of October 1164.

No. 154 must have been written somewhat later, when Hilary had returned and had time to take stock of what had occurred in his diocese since his departure. The envoys reported to Henry II at Marlborough on Christmas Eve,[7] so that a date early in 1165 seems probable for this letter.

152 46 estue B    46 iniqua taliter] iniq̃? talit B; inutilis *Giles*    50 stellius et originem piis hausit B; *for the meaning of this passage, see GF, pp. 17–18*
153 G, no. 181; B, fo. 162v.

---

[1] Cf. *Digest*, 49, 15, 5.                    [2] I.e. *successus*, presumably.
[3] Herbert, formerly monk of Grestain, abbot ?1139–79 (Torigny, p. 280 and n. (1179), and ed. Delisle, II, 202; *Gallia Christiana*, XI, 843, gives Herbert's predecessor's death as 4 July 1139, his election as Sept. 1139, his death as 15 Jan. 1179, but without references).
[4] For this case, see Arnulf, *Epp.* 45–6 and notes. West Firle was subsequently given to Chichester cathedral as a prebend by the abbot of Grestain (1197–1204, *Cart. Chichester*, no. 194, cf. no. 277).
[5] Cf. *GF*, p. 100 (an additional reference for Gilbert's activity at Northampton and Sens, not noted in *GF* or Knowles, *EC*, is in *The Chronicles of Ralph Niger*, ed. R. Anstruther (London, Caxton Soc., 1851), p. 170, cf. pp. 171–2).
[6] *MB*, III, 70; for the date of Becket's crossing, see also Gervase, I, 189, Bosham, *MB*, III, 324–5; etc.                    [7] *MB*, III, 75.

Dilectis sibi in Domino uniuersis sancte matris ecclesie filiis ad quos litere iste peruenerint frater G(ilebertus) Lundoniensis ecclesie minister, salutem in Christo.

Per apostolica scripta in mandatis accepimus quatinus abbate de Grestene et latore presentium Iohanne in nostra conuocatis presentia, quicquid Iohanni post appellationem ad sedem apostolicam aduersus abbatem factam per ipsum uidelicet 5 abbatem siue per suos ablatum aut subtractum comperiremus, sibi omni occasione et excusatione postposita omnique remedio appellationis sublato cum integritate restitui, et eidem de dampnis et iniuriis illatis congruam faceremus satisfa⟨c⟩tionem exhiberi; restitutione autem facta et satisfactione exhibita, causam que inter eos super capella de Cherlecheston' uertebatur, cessante nichilominus appellatione 10 decideremus. Quam nos quidem formam sequentes quia de appellatione Iohannis utpote coram nobis publice ⟨fo. 163⟩ facta plenam habebamus certamque notitiam, de illata sibi postmodum a monachis de Gresten' uiolentia, de eiectione eius a domo sua, de dampnis per inuasionem datis, per legitimam idoneorum testium asertionem, fide ueri diligenter et districte inquisita, ecclesiam ipsam de Ferles cum omni 15 integritate et pertinentiis suis omnibus memorato Iohanni restitui debere, de fratrum consilio et motu animi nostri—apostolica in hoc freti auctoritate— pronuntiauimus; et de illatis sibi dampnis sub nostra taxatione iuratis, abbatem illi in summam decem et octo marcarum argenti condempnauimus. De cetero in causa quam sepedictus Iohannes super capella de Cherlechestun' diutius intentarat 20 aduersus Henricum presbiterum et memoratum abbatem de Gresten', quem sibi idem Henricus in causa illa laudauerat auctorem, iuxta continentiam rescripti, hoc tenore processum est. Petebat siquidem Iohannes capellam illam nomine matris ecclesie sue de Ferles sibi restitui, utpote intra parrochiales eiusdem ut dicebat terminos ecclesie fundatam et ab ipsa sui fundatione filiali sibi subiectione obnoxiam. 25 Allegabat ad hec quod cum personatum et inuestituram matris ecclesie de Ferles per manum Cicestr(ensis) episcopi presentatione abbatis de Gresten'—sicut idem episcopus tam uiua uoce quam scripto nobis insinuauit—olim reciperet, ipsam quoque capellam una cum maiore ecclesia habendam recepit, eamque tamdiu plene et pacifice possedit donec mota sibi ab Henrico controuersia, monacus quidam de 30 Gresten' qui tunc in Anglia uices agebat abbatis inita cum Henrico transactione, capellam illi cedere eamque ipso reclamante et auctoritate domni pape ne id fieret inhibente, contra iustitiam et iuris ordinem alienare presumpsit. Abbas uero quem sibi Henricus acciuerat capellam illam ad matricem quidem ecclesiam de Ferles pertinere, Iohannemque ipsam diutius possedisse, publice et in iure confessus est. 35 Hoc tamen illi in preiudicium petitionis sue in modum exceptionis obiecit quod transactioni cum Henrico habite interfuit, eamque suo assensu conprobauit. Cum autem super hoc articulo controuersia plurimum uerteretur, abbate tandem in probatione adhibiti consensus penitus ⟨fo. 163 v⟩ deficiente, testes facte reclama- tionis quos Iohannes produxit diligenter examinatos et concordes inuentos utpote 40 fide dignos admisimus, sicque ex eorum assertione et confessione partis aduerse sepedicto Iohanni prefate capelle plenam restitutionem adiudicauimus, estimatisque dampnis medii temporis et sub nostra taxatione probatis, Henricum illi in summam

**153** 26 Feres B    39 de/deficiente B

duodecim marcarum argenti per sententiam condempnauimus. Que quia de com-
45 missione domni pape nostro sunt officio celebrata, ne in dubium de cetero aut in
irritum queat reuocari, uniuersitati uestre notificare et ea qua fungimur auctoritate
confirmare curauimus. His testibus: H(ugone) decano sancti Pauli, Nicholao
archidiacono Lund(oniensi), magistro W.

### 154   To Hilary, bishop of Chichester

[Probably early 1165] He explains that he had instructed the rural dean of Beeding (Sussex)
to execute his judgement as papal judge delegate in the case of John and the abbot of Grestain
so as to save John from unnecessary delays: the bishop and Gilbert himself were both bound
on embassy to the Pope when the judgement was given.

Venerabili domno fratrique karissimo Hil(ario) Cicestrensi Dei gratia episcopo frater
G(ilebertus) Lundoniensis ecclesie minister, salutem et sincere dilectionis affectum.
   Quod in causa Iohannis cognitoris partes sustinuimus obedientia fuit; quod pro
eo aduersus abbatem ⟨fo. 162v⟩ de Gresten' pronuntiauimus iuris et legum
5 obseruantia fuit; quod citra conscientiam uestram per officialem uestrum decanum
uidelicet de Beddi⟨n⟩g' sententiam executioni mandauerim temporis proculdubio
necessitas effecit. Eramus enim nos sicut et uos ex mandato domni regis procincti
ad peregrinandum, proxima quarta feria post latam sententiam apud Duur' ex
condicto conuenturi, et inde ad domnum papam quam citius profecturi. Vnde ne
10 protracta in longum negotia occasione profectionis uestre in dispendium pauperis
clerici differentur ulterius, decano uestro qui in ipso tunc temporis oportunus
aduenit, nos cum multa quidem confidentia dilectionis uestre auctoritate sedis
apostolice huius rei executionem iniunximus. In quo si mansuetudo uestra aduersum
eum aliquatenus exasperata est, hanc nobis pro reuerentia domini pape ueniam dari
15 ipsumque in gradum et gratiam pristinam restitui quanta possumus deuotione
supplicamus, ne in nostram quod absit confusionem destitutus, de uestra quod absit
beniuolentia nos minus solito sperare conpellat. Peteremus adhuc instantius et
preces precibus accumularemus attentius, nisi quia quoddam quasi diffidentis animi
indicium hoc est, et de fraterna karitate minus presumentis. Valete.

### 155   To Pope Alexander III

[Late July–August 1165] He gives an account of how he and the bishop of Hereford had
obeyed the Pope's mandate, waited on the king on the borders of Wales,[1] and taken him to
task for his treatment of the Church and the archbishop (with certain specific points noted).

154 G, no. 205; B, fo. 162.
1 Cistres' B     4 Geresten, *with an R over the G (cf. no.* 153) B     7 procinctu (*possibly for* in
procinctu) B
155 G, no. 174; *MB Epp.* 108 (*extract in* 168); Lupus, 1, 58–62 (i, 38); B, fo. 50; D, fos. 50 v–
51 v; Va, fo. 74 r–v; Ia, pp. 122–5; Ib, fos. 272 v–274 v; Ic, fos. 13 v–15 v; C, fos. 39(38)–40 v
(39 v); Co, fos. 18 v–19 v; Vb, fos. 76 v–77 v; O, *not foliated*, no. 39. *Also in* William of Canter-

---

[1] Possibly at Shrewsbury, where Henry had a conference with some bishops, obscurely referred
to in *MB Epp.* 103.

Gilbert describes how Henry was humble in the face of correction, and the answers he gave to specific questions about his attitude to appeals, his relations with the emperor and his treatment of the archbishop of Canterbury. Gilbert gives the Pope a warning of the consequences of provoking the king too severely—he may lose the allegiance of the English church. In conclusion, he explains that he is doing what he can—with royal assistance—to collect Peter's Pence.

On 8 June 1165, when Becket had been in exile seven months, Alexander III wrote from Clermont to Gilbert ordering him and the bishop of Hereford to urge Henry II to desist from his policies and be reconciled to the archbishop. He also asked Gilbert to collect the Peter's Pence due from England, and to send the Pope an equivalent sum in anticipation before 1 August.[1] No. 155 gives an account of the interview with the king, and from this and its reference to Peter's Pence, it is clear that it is an answer to the Pope's letter. The interview took place in the approaches to Wales, where Henry was campaigning in July–August 1165,[2] and since the Pope was able to reply to Gilbert's letter from the south of France on 22 August,[3] no. 155 must have been written in late July or very early August.

The Pope's second letter urged Gilbert to further efforts with the king, and asked him to collect Peter's Pence as speedily as possible and hand it over to the abbot of St Bertin.[4] Later in the same year Gilbert wrote again (no. 156) to say that he had collected the money, except for the sum due from the bishop of Exeter, and handed it over to the abbot.[5]

Patri suo et domno summo pontifici Alexandro frater Gilebertus Lundoniensis ecclesie minister, debitum sincere caritatis et humilis obedientie famulatum.

Mandatum uestrum, pater in Christo karissime, debita ueneratione suscipientes, ilico filium uestrum domnumque nostrum karissimum illustrem Anglorum regem etsi in ipsis iam Gualie finibus agentem exercitum adiuimus et adiuncto nobis 5 uenerabili fratre nostro Roberto Herefordensi episcopo iuxta uestri formam mandati diligenter et intente conuenimus. Cui singula que uestris nobis expressa sunt litteris ante oculos ponentes, ipsum obsecrando et quantum regiam decebat maiestatem arguendo constanter et instanter hortati sumus, ut de propositis sibi satisfaceret, etsi a rationis tramite deuiauerat, ad uiam ueritatis et iustitie redire, 10

bury, *MB*, I, 58–9 (*extract*); Howden, I, 244–8 (Ho); Diceto, I, 331–2 (Di) (*variants of* VbODi William of Canterbury *not normally given*) (*headings*: IaIbCCoVbO: Alexandro pape Gillebertus (C; G. *ceteri*) Londoniensis episcopus; Gil' episcopi ad Alex. papam Va; *etc.*). *For the text of this letter see above, pp. 10 n., 15*
1 frater *om.* IaIbIc (A. B). Va *om. the protocol*   1 Gilebertus C; G. *ceteri*   5 Gualie BD; Guallie C; Wallie, IaCo; Walie IbIc   6 R. BVa   7 impressa *with* uel ex- *ins.* C; impressa Va

[1] *MB Epp.* 93 (JL 11,205) dated at Clermont, 8 June; during the period when such a letter could have been written, Alexander was only at Clermont in May–June 1165 (cf. Robertson's note: several manuscripts read 'Iulii', but this is impossible).
[2] Eyton, *Itinerary*, pp. 82–3; on this campaign, cf. Lloyd, I, 496 ff.
[3] *MB Epp.* 106; JL 11,237.
[4] This was apparently the traditional arrangement at this time; see *JS Epp.* I, 19 n. 2; W. E. Lunt, *Financial relations of the Papacy with England to 1327*, pp. 3–84, esp. p. 52.
[5] This seems to attach no. 156 to this occasion although it is possible that Gilbert continued the traditional practice of paying the abbot for a year or two longer; but the reference to the Canterbury archives suggests that no. 156 refers to Gilbert's first essay in collecting the tax. Cf. *MB Epp.* 157, which cannot, however, be dated except by reference to this letter. For later practice, see nos. 177–9.

uestra per nos reuocatus admonitione non tardaret, a patre pie commonitus a prauis
actibus omnino desisteret, et Dominum puro corde diligeret, et matrem suam
⟨fo. 50v⟩ sanctam Romanam ecclesiam solita ueneratione respiceret, nec eam
uisitare uolentes inhiberet, appellationes ad eam factas non impediret, et patrem
15 nostrum domnum Cantuariensem benigne reuocans et reducens, in beati Petri et
uestra reuerentia firmus immobilisque persisteret, et pietatis intendens operibus
ecclesias et ecclesiasticas personas tam regni quam terre sue, *nec grauaret per se nec
per alium grauari permitteret, sed ipsas diligens regia protectione conseruaret, ut
ille per quem reges regnant[1] temporale sibi regnum conseruaret in terris et eternum
20 largiretur in celis; alioquin nisi monitis salutaribus acquiesceret, sanctitas uestra que
hucusque patienter sustinuit ulterius in patientia sustinere non posset. Ad hec
adiecimus timendum sibi fore ne si errata non corrigeret iram cito omnipotentis Dei
incurreret, ut nec regnum eius diu stare, nec suos prosperari permitteret, sed qui
humilem exaltauerat[2] iamiam exaltatum ab ipso regni culmine durius allidendo
25 deiceret. Ipse uero correptionem uestram multa gratiarum actione suscipiens, multa
animi temperantia multaque modestia consequenter respondit ad singula; in primis
asserens mentem suam a uobis se nullatenus auertisse, nec id unquam propositi
mente concepisse, quin dum paternam sibi gratiam exhibueritis uos ut patrem
diligat, et sanctam Romanam ecclesiam ut matrem ueneretur et foueat, et sacris
30 iussionibus uestris—salua sibi sua regnique sui dignitate—humiliter optemperet et
obediat. Quod si uos iam aliquamdiu solita reuerentia non respexit, hanc huius rei
causam asserit quod cum uobis in necessitate toto corde, tota mente, totis uiribus
astiterit, sibi postmodum per nuntios in necessitate recurrenti ad uos digne pro
meritis sanctitas uestra non respondit, sed in omni fere petitione sua se repulsam
35 sustinuisse conqueritur et erubescit. De paterna tamen confisus gratia que filium
cum uolet exaudiet, uultus sperans et expectans letiores in beati Petri et uestra ut
dictum est fidelitate immobili constantia perseuerat. Inde est quod sanctitatem
uestram uisitare uolentem nullum prorsus impediet, sed nec hactenus ut asserit
impediuit. In appellationibus ex antiqua regni sui institutione id sibi uendicat
40 honoris et oneris, ut ob ciuilem causam nullus clericorum regni sui eiusdem regni
fines exeat, nisi an ipsius auctoritate et mandato ius suum optinere queat prius
experiendo cognoscat.[3] Quod si nec sic optinuerit ad excellentiam uestram, ipso in

**155** 11 pio B    12 et Dominum IaIbIcC; Deum BDVaCoHo    17 *nec] ne IbIc    22 Dei
omnipotentis BDVaCoHo    25 nostram C    27 unquam BDVaHoDi; iniqua CCoIa; ?
iniquam IbIc    28 paternam…exhibueritis BIaIbIcCHo; uos sibi patrem rebus ipsis cognouerit
VaDiD (*reading* agnouerit); paternam…exhib. *with* uos…cognouerit *added* Co    36–7 in
beati…fidelitate] in beati Petri fidelitate et uestra sicut dictum est D; sicut dictum est in
fidelitate beati Petri et uestra VaCo    39 constitutione IaIbIc; institutione *with* uel con- *ins.* C

---

[1] Cf. Prov. viii. 15.    [2] Cf. Luc. i. 52.

[3] Cf. Const. Clarendon (*MB Epp.* 45), cc. 4, 8, claiming that royal licence was necessary for any
archbishop, bishop or *persona regni* going abroad, and that no appeal could go beyond the
archbishop's court without royal licence (the interpretation of H. G. Richardson and G. O.
Sayles, *Governance of England*, pp. 306–7, that clause 8 only referred to cases initiated in the
archdeacons' courts, seems forced and unacceptable). It is interesting that Henry II is here

nullo reclamante, cum uolet quilibet appellabit. In quo si iuri uel honori uestro
preiudicatur in aliquo, id se totius ecclesie regni sui consi⟨fo. 51⟩lio correcturum in
proximo iuuante Domino pollicetur. Imperatorem illum etsi scismaticum nouerit, 45
a uobis tamen excommunicatum esse usque hodie non resciuit. Quod si denuntia-
tione uestra rescierit, si fedus illicitum cum ipso aut alio quolibet iniit, et hoc
ecclesie regni sui iudicio simul et consilio se correcturum promittit. Patrem nostrum
domnum Cantuariensem suo se regno nequaquam expulisse asserit. Vnde sicut
abscessit ultroneus, sic ad ecclesiam suam cum sibi sederit animo plena pace reuerti 50
sibi liberum erit; dum tamen in satisfaciendo sibi super his unde conqueritur, regias
sibi et in quas ipse iuratus est uelit dignitates integre conseruari. Si qua uero ecclesia
uel ecclesiastica persona ab ipso uel a suis se grauatam ostenderit satisfactioni plene
totius ecclesie iudicio paratus erit.

Hec a domno nostro rege in responsis accepimus, qui utinam ad omnem uolun- 55
tatem uestram uberius aliquid accepissemus. Eadem uero sullimitati uestre notifi-
canda duximus, ut ex ipsius responsis aduertat uestra discretio quo negotium hoc
fine concludat. Causam namque suam domnus rex plurimum sibi iustificare uidetur, cum in omnibus que dicta sunt ecclesie regni sui consilio simul et iudicio se
pariturum, et patris nostri domni Cantuar⟨iensis⟩ reditum iuxta quod dictum est se 60
nullatenus impediturum pollicetur. Vnde uestre supplicandum estimauimus
excellentie, quatinus illud pre oculis habentes, 'calamum quassatum non conteres et
linum fumigans non extingues',[1] zelum illum sanctum qui ad ulciscendam omnem
que ecclesie Dei irrogatur iniuriam, laudabiliter igne diuini spiritus accensus est, si
placet ad tempus intra fines modestie cohibeatis, ne uel interdicti sententiam uel 65
ultimum illud precisionis elogium proferendo ecclesias innumeras subuerti misere
doleatis, et tam regem ipsum quam innumeros cum eo populos a uestra quod absit
obedientia irreuocabiliter auertatis. Bonum est membrum capiti coherere uel
saucium quam a corpore sequestrari iam precisum. Redeunt ad sanitatem saucia sed
corpori uix coalescunt iam precisa. Adducit desperationem precisio; restituit 70
sanitatem uulneri sepe medicantis operatio. Quid enim si sermo uester nondum plene
capit aut capitur? Nunquid diuina desperanda est gratia quin cito cum uolet et
capiat et capiatur?[2] Nunquid ⟨fo. 51v⟩ adbreuiata est manus Domini ut saluare

155 47 aut] VaCo *add* cum (*space in* C)    49 se suo VaC(*corrected*)Co (*the next four sentences
in wrong order in* Co, *but marginal corrections make clear that the scribe was copying a text
in right order*)    50 pace] sua *added in* BDHo    51 tamen BDVaCoHo; tantum IaIbIcC
52 conseruare C    53 grauatum IaIbIc    55 nostro *om.* B    57 discr. uestra VaCoC (C *corrected*)
58 conducat Ia; condudat Ib    58 domnus *om.* B    61 estimamus *with* uel estimauimus *ins.* C
(existimamus William of Canterbury)    62–3 conteret/extinguet BHo (*so Vulg.*)    65 modestia (*corrected*) Ia; modestia Ib    66 innumeras] uel uniuersas *added in* C; inmensas IaIb    69 se-
questrari] proici BHo    69–70 sed corpori uix] uix corpori BHo    70–1 restituit...operatio]
cum sanet uulnus sepissime caute medicantis operatio, unde bonum est si placet (Ho: si placet
bonum est) ut sanando uulneri si quod est ad presens operam detis quam ecclesie Dei partem
nobilissimam precidendo, que turbata sunt hoc ipso longe supra quam possit exprimi perturbetis
BHo    70 restituit] reducit Va    72 cito cum uolet] tempore accepto BHo (cf. II Cor. vi. 2)

reported as prepared to confine his stand on custom to appeals *ob ciuilem causam* in which
clerks were involved.        [1] Cf. Is. xlii. 3.                [2] Cf. Joh. viii. 37.

nequeat, aut auris eius aggrauata ut non exaudiat?[1] Currens ille sermo Domini[2]
75 uelociter statim cum uult immutat omnia et dat sanctorum precibus insperata.
Sanguis regius tum se demum permittit uinci cum uicerit. Nec uerecundatur cedere
cum superauerit. Mansuetudine tolerandus est, monitis et patientia superandus.
Quid enim si iacturam quandam temporalium inuehit, exhibita ad tempus patientia?
Non enim est dubium seueritati detrahendum fore, cum strages imminet populo-
80 rum,[3] et cum tempestas ingruit in mare, debere multa proici, ut ad portum ualeat
nauis salua perduci. Insipienter attamen in caritate non ficta[4] sic loquimur, si hic rei
finis exiterit ut amissis suis domnus Cantuariensis exilium iuge sustineat, et uestris
quod absit mandatis ulterius Anglia non obediat, fuisset satius patienter in tempus
sustinuisse, quam tanto zelo seueritati deseruisse. Quid enim si plures e nobis ab
85 obedientia uestra persecutio separare non poterit? Non deerit tamen qui genu
curuet ante Baal,[5] et de manu ydoli pallium Cantuarie non habito religionis aut
iustitie delectu suscipiat. Nec deerunt qui sedes nostras occupantes et cathedras
insidentes ipsi tota deuotione mentis obediant. Iam multi premasticant ad talia,
optantes ut ueniant scandala, et directa ponantur in praua.[6] Vnde non propria pater
90 plangimus aut ploramus incommoda sed nisi his malis occurreritis, fedam ecclesie
Dei subuersionem imminere cernentes pertimescimus, ne citius ob uite tedium
optemus periisse diem, qua ad spectacula huiusmodi nati sumus.[7]

De cetero super censu beati Petri nemo nobis in regno uel de modico respondisset,
nisi domnus rex mandatum super hoc in commune dedisset. Eius uero mandato
95 statuto antiquitus termino colligetur, et sanctitati uestre per manum nostram
iuuante Domino transmittetur. [Quem si designato uobis die non misimus, ut nos
excusatos habeat gratia uestra supplicando postulamus. Testis enim Deus est quod
summam hanc nec in proprio habuimus nec mutuo inuenire potuimus. Trahit enim
ad se cuncta domni regis exercitus, et agentem in expeditionem domnum suum
100 comitantur fere omnia que in regno sunt aut sequuntur. Conseruet incolumitatem
uestram in longa tempora omnipotens Dominus in Christo dilecte pater.]

155 74 Domini *om.* VaBDHo William of Canterbury    75 statim] potenter BHo; *om.* Va
75 precibus] etiam *added in* BHo    76 tum (tunc *with* uel tum *ins.* C) se demum permittit]
tum scit demum BHo; tum…Nec *om.* D    76 uerecundatur] erubescit BHo    77 tolerandus]
leniendus BHo    78–81 inuehit…perduci] infert, uel exibita uel in tempus exhibenda adhuc
etiam patientia? Nunquid non seueritati detrahendum est cum strages imminet populorum?
Nunquid non in mare multa iactanda sunt, cum iam spondet interitum confusio tetra maris et
fluctuum? BHo    78 ad] uel in *ins.* C; in IaIbIc    81 sic *om.* BHo    83 in] ad, uel in *ins.* C
84 seueritati deseruisse] seueritatis partibus institisse BHo    86–7 aut…suscipiat BDVaCCoHo;
suscipiat delectu (-m? Ic) aut iustitie IaIbIc    90 plangimus aut] aut paucorum C, *with* al' uel
*and the reading of text ins. in margin;* aut priuate Va    90 his nisi BHo (D nisi his malis occurretis)
92 perisse BDVaHo    92 sumus] fuimus D 93 DVa *omit* De cetero *to the end;* De cetero…aut
sequuntur *om.* Ho; IaIbIcCCo *end at* transmittetur    94 dedisset] edidisset B    96–100 Quem
si…aut sequuntur *in* B *only*    100–1 Conseruet…pater *in* BHo *only*

---

[1] Cf. Is. lix. 1.    [2] Cf. Ps. cxlvii. 15.
[3] Cf. *Decretum*, C. 23, q. 4, c. 24.    [4] Cf. II Cor. vi. 6.
[5] Cf. Rom. xi. 4 (and for *ydoli*, JS *Epp.* 124, n. 22, on the schism of 1159, and St Bernard,
*Epp.* 124, 139 on the schism of 1130).
[6] Cf. Matt. xviii. 7, Is. xl. 4 (and Luc. iii. 5).    [7] Cf. Job iii. 3.

## 156 To Pope Alexander III

[Late 1165] He has collected Peter's Pence in accordance with the records in the Canterbury archives, and forwarded the sum due of £200—with the exception of £9. 5s., the bishop of Exeter's contribution, still outstanding—to the abbot of St Bertin, in accordance with the Pope's mandate.

Patri suo et domino summo pontifici A(lexandro) frater G(ilebertus) Londonie(n-sis) ecclesie minister, debitum et deuotum totius obedientie famulatum.

In colligendo denarium beati Petri quantam potuimus sollicitudinem et diligen-tiam adhibere curauimus, dilectique in Christo fratres nostri et coepiscopi quorum episcopatus condicioni huic constat esse obnoxios, a nobis iuxta tenorem et con- 5 tinentiam scriptorum que in scriniis Cantuar(iensis) ecclesie studiose requisita reperimus, uestra sub hoc auctoritate commoniti, debitam penitus omnes quidem agnouerunt et exsoluerunt quantitatem, excepto uenerabili fratre nostro et coepis-copo domno Exoniensi, qui nimirum summam sue diocesis ascriptam minime recognoscens, quia minus quam de ratione scripti exigeretur obtulit, totum quod 10 obtulerat insolutum reportauit, sicque licet sepe et sepe commonitus hucusque tamen penitus a solutione cessauit. Vniuersam uero summam reliquam ducentas uidelicet libras exceptis ix libris et v solidis que a predicto fratre solui debuerant, abbati sancti Bertini iuxta mandatum uestrum per fratrem ab ipso transmissum ad nos et per quendam fidelem nostrum destinare curauimus. De cetero quid super hac 15 portione reliqua que soluenda superest fieri oporteat, uestra cum uoluerit sanctitas prouidebit. Nos enim intra fines iussionis uestre nostrum chohibentes officium, nec minus offerentem admittimus, nec soluere cessantem ulla coercione ferimus. Valeat sanctitas uestra.

## 157 To Roger, bishop of Worcester

[Probably late 1165] The bishop has consulted Gilbert about some heretical weavers[1] who have been caught in the diocese of Worcester. He advises the bishop to place them in solitary confinement and treat them with moderate severity—including lashes—until a gathering of the clergy can settle what is to be done about them.

England was remarkably little affected by the Cathar movement: this is one of the few

**156** G, no. 172; *MB Epp.* 110; B, fo. 163 v; D, fo. 52 (*in bottom margin of* B: concordit illi, ubi dicit domnus papa quod Exon(iensis) ei mandauit quod primus uel intra primos denarium beati Petri soluit: Sepe nobis a pluribus—*i.e. Alexander III's letter, MB Epp.* 157 (*not in* B)). 1-2 Londonie *or* Londonie' (*for* Londoniensis) B; Lund' D 2 deuotum et debitum B 8 cognouerunt D 9 dōnno B 15 et *om.* D
**157** G, no. 249; B, fo. 141.

[1] Evidently a group of Cathars, presumably from the Low Countries; *textores* was one of the labels attached to the Cathars in this period. They rarely appeared in England; on this incur-sion, and on Gilbert's letters, see *GF*, pp. 241 ff.; see also A. Borst, *Die Katharer* (Stuttgart, 1953), p. 94 and n.; Walter Daniel, *Life of Ailred of Rievaulx*, ed. F. M. Powicke (NMT), pp. ci–cii; F. Pollock and F. W. Maitland, *Hist. of English Law* (2nd ed., Cambridge, 1898), II, 547 f.; Maisonneuve, pp. 114-15.

incursions of which there is evidence. This group apparently entered the country about 1160 and was condemned at a council summoned by the king at or shortly after Christmas 1165. At about the time of the council, St Ailred of Rievaulx referred to them in his *De anima*: 'nuptiis detrahunt et sacramentum altaris exsufflant, carnis negant resurrectionem et baptismatis uirtutem euacuant'.[1]

Gilbert anticipates the meeting of a council, but such a council has not yet been summoned. Presumably, then, the letter was written a few months before Christmas 1165, and certainly not earlier than Bishop Roger's consecration in August 1164.

Nos. 157 and 158 appear to be a doublet, and it is unlikely that both of them were sent.

Venerabili fratri et amico karissimo R(ogero) Wigornensi Dei gratia episcopo frater G(ilebertus) Lundoniensis ecclesie minister, salutem cum intimo dilectionis affectu.

Ad tuam frater karissime consultationem in caritate respondeo quod michi 5 karitas super hoc requisita respondet, deprehensos a te et in tua comprehensos parrochia textores de quibusdam ut asseris fidei nostre articulis male sentientes, quos non tantum nuda blasphemie protestatio uerum etiam constans assertio et propositi pertinacia hereticos esse demonstrat; sub arcta consulo cautaque custodia detineri donec aliquo locorum ob ecclesie necessitatem aut negotium regni celeber 10 fiat sacerdotum ceterorumque fidelium conuentus, ubi inuocata Spiritus Sancti gratia de communi negotio communis exeratur sententia que quid super hoc agi oporteat et secure et sincere possit diffinire. Illis uero interim seorsum constitutis ne mutuis se possint in malum obfirmare colloquiis, bonos uiros et graues, uiros probate fidei, diuine legis et litterarum peritos eorum cure conuenit et custodie 15 deputari, qui eos uisitent in uerbo predicationis sancte, monitis emolliant, minis et metu penarum exterreant, flagris interdum et flagellis cum moderata seueritate coherceant, et ad ecclesie unitatem omnimodis prout caritas suggeret reuocare procurent.[2] Hec namque et huiusmodi ecclesiastice correctionis medicamenta, que nobis exempla sanctorum proponunt, cum de salute agitur subiectorum in caritate 20 nos conuenit experiri qui in populo patris nomen et pastoris officium obtinemus ne uel perniciem aut periculum fraterne salutis aliquid umquam preprepere statuamus. Sepe enim quos uerba non ⟨fo. 141 v⟩ mouent uerbera promouent, et quod metus pene non efficit ipsa penarum experientia nonnunquam extorquet; bona est necessitas que uel a malis prohibet uel ad meliora compellit. Vtrumque per Dei 25 gratiam hac nobis uia sperandum est, si nec penitendi illis tempus adimitur, nec ulla relinquitur facultas malignandi. Vtinam uotis tuis sanctorum succurratur consilio, quos altius imbuit, quos ampliori gratia spiritus infundit. Vale.

**157** 5 respondeat B, *corrected*    21 umquam] B *adds* iniquam, *cancelled*    26 sanctiori (?) B, *corrected to* sanctiorumi—*evidently the two i's were meant to be deleted:* sanctorum *perhaps became* sanctiori *by attraction to* ampliori. *But* sanctiorum *is not impossible*

---

[1] Quoted by Powicke, *op. cit.* p. ci. For the date of the council, see Ann. Tewkesbury *s.a.* 1166, *Ann. Mon.* I, 49; Diceto, I, 318 (*s.a.* 1166); cf. Eyton, *Itinerary*, p. 88 and n.

[2] Cf. *Decretum*, C. 23, q. 5, c. 1 (and no. 158).

## 158  To Roger, bishop of Worcester

[Probably late 1165] The bishop has consulted Gilbert about some heretical weavers (see no. 157) who have lately appeared in the diocese of Worcester. He advises the bishop to place them in solitary confinement, and to reserve the question of their further punishment to a gathering of the bishops. He discusses the rival theories about the treatment of heretics.

Venerabili domno fratrique karissimo R(ogero) Wigorn(ensi) Dei gratia episcopo frater G(ilebertus) Lundoniensis ecclesie minister, salutem et affectus intimi dilectionem.

Moris solet esse prudentum, etiam in non dubiis efflagitare consilium. Quod et uestra discretio prudenter obseruans, a nobis sciscitari uoluit quid super his textori- 5 bus sentiamus, qui uestram nuper ingressi diocesim telis aranee quas misere texuerant ipsam operire moliti sunt et inuoluere, et nisi Sanctus per uos eis Spiritus restitisset, nequiter superseminatis zizaniis infatuare,[1] qui corde conceptas hereses in uulgus spargendo predicant et in iure conuenti et commoniti easdem attrita fronte[2] defendere non formidant; quorum sermo ne canceris in modum nimis serpat[3] et 10 errore simili quamplures inuoluat, ipsos arcta consulimus custodia choiberi et ne pietas desit officio, per honestiores et prudentiores clericos uestros uisitari sepius, et ut ad penitentiam et ecclesie unitatem reuocent animos et corda commutent diligentius amoneri. Est sermo Dei uiuus et efficax,[4] qui per idoneum ministratorem cito uertit impium et suscitat ilico peccatorem. Quia uero corrumpunt mores bonos 15 colloquia praua[5] seorsum constituatis singulos, ne si inuicem sibi misceant uerba animentur in pertinacia et respuant consilia sana. Quod si nec uexatio sancta nec pie exhibita commonitio dederit intellectum auditui, questionem hanc ultimam de pena an scilicet plectendi sint, quaue pena plectendi, quo etiam iudicante uel eos ad penam tradente puniendi sint, communi fratrum nostrorum et coepiscoporum 20 conuentu⟨i⟩ consulimus reseruari. Grandis enim hec questio est, et a sanctis patribus et ecclesie doctoribus non mediocriter agitata, quibusdam ecclesie mansuetudinem et clementiam predicantibus—iuxta quod dictum est: 'lex clementie in lingua eius'; et illud Domini: 'nec ego te condempnabo'[6]—aliis ne multi pereant in talium penam sancti proculdubio zeli pietate feruentibus. Hii filium freneticum uinculis 25 arctandum sicque custodiendum commemorant; alii quod in religionem diuinam committitur in omnium ⟨fo. 162⟩ ferri iniuriam protestantes, in crimen hoc publicum legem Iuliam maiestatis intentant; alii exemplis iudicantes huiusmodi cremandos iudicant; alii seueritatem hanc beati Augustini sententia temperant, qui Donatistas non interfici sed flagellis et suppliciis exorat emendari. Vnde quia 30 scriptum est quod 'ad penitendum properat cito qui iudicat'[7] questionem hanc

158 G, no. 250; B, fo. 161 v.

---

[1] Cf. Is. lix. 5; Matt. xiii. 25.  [2] Cf. Ezech. iii. 7.  [3] Cf. II Tim. ii. 17.
[4] Cf. Heb. iv. 12.  [5] Cf. I Cor. xv. 33.  [6] Prov. xxxi. 26; Joh. viii. 11.
[7] For the Roman law of heresy see *Code*, I, 5, 4 *passim*; the *Lex Iulia* was cited by Placentinus; see Maisonneuve, pp. 29 ff., esp. 34, 62–3; on precedents for burning heretics, *ibid.* pp. 96 ff. (based, in fact, on the traditional punishment for witchcraft; cf. *GF*, p. 242 and reference); for Augustine ,Gratian, *Decretum*, C. 23, q. 5, c. 1.

communi fratrum nostrorum conuentu⟨i⟩ reseruari consulimus, ut sicut est in regno hoc donante Deo ecclesia una, sic sit et in talibus eadem omnium sententia et actio non diuisa. Sententie non preiudicamus saniori, qui uos semper cupimus
35 potiora[1] sectari. Valere uos optamus in Domino, frater in Christo karissime.

### 159  To Hugh Bigod, earl of Norfolk

[Late 1165] The canons of Pentney refuse to accept any price in exchange for the vill of Pentney; since the Pope has insisted that the earl restore the vill to them (or have an interdict laid on his properties),[2] Gilbert strongly urges him to put the canons in possession.

The celebrated case of the earl of Norfolk and the canons of Pentney occupied the attention of king, Pope and the bishops of Norwich and London on and off for at least five years. The first act, with which the following three letters are concerned, opened with the earl's attempt to eject the canons and the canons' appeal to the Pope, and closed with the first excommunication of the earl. Some time in 1165 Alexander III addressed a mandate to Gilbert ordering restitution within forty days or an interdict on the earl's property. Difficulties arose with the king,[3] and the earl complained that the canons had obtained the papal mandate by misrepresentation. According to Gilbert (no. 161), the earl agreed to put the canons in possession, and then pursue the case.[4] He pursued it before the king at Oxford, and he attempted to wring a concession out of the prior, which was thwarted by the refusal of his fellow canons to accept it. And so the earl appealed to Rome.

On 7 July 1166 the Pope wrote to Becket announcing the earl's excommunication; he also wrote to Henry II, and Becket to the canons of Pentney, in the same sense.[5] The undercurrent which led to this is obscure, but it is clear that it followed hard upon the events described in Gilbert's letters, and thus that the council at Oxford was that which met at the turn of 1165 and 1166 (see above, p. 208 and n.). Letter 159 urges the earl to comply with the Pope's mandate; no. 160 tells a friendly cardinal that 159 has been written, and that Gilbert is in trouble with the king; no. 161 states that the earl has complied, and describes the council at Oxford. They must thus have been written in that order, in fairly swift succession, culminating in no. 161, c. January 1166.

G(ilebertus) Dei gratia Lundoniensis episcopus uenerabili domno et amico karissimo H(ugoni) comiti Norfolc', salutem et dilectionem.

Responsum canonicorum de Panteneia, nuntio ad nos redeunte et literas capituli sui sigillo inpressas afferente, suscepimus quo uos certificari postulant, quod nec
5 pecuniam, nec terram, nec quicquam aliud a uobis accepturi sunt ut uobis Pantaleiam concedant et ab ea quam aduersus uos intendunt petitione recedant. Exilium subire et aduersa ut asserunt queque perpeti magis eligunt, quam locum Domino

---

**159** G, no. 285; *MB Epp.* 481; B, fo. 40.
4 inpressis B

---

[1] Cf. Phil. i. 10.
[2] The sentence demanded by the Pope is explicitly stated in no. 160.
[3] See *GF*, pp. 184–5 n., 237; R. Foreville, *L'Église et la royauté en Angleterre sous Henri II*, pp. 206–7; Knowles, *EC*, pp. 127–8.
[4] It is doubtful if the earl actually put the canons in possession: see note to no. 161.
[5] *MB Epp.* 484–6; 484 = JL 11,285 (which is dated Lateran, *nonis Iulii*; Alexander III only dated letters from the Lateran in July during the Becket dispute in 1166).

consecratum et diuinis usibus apostolica totiens auctoritate confirmatum cuiquam cedere, et ab ecclesia alienare consentiant. Inde est quod a nobis instanter exigunt ut effectui mandatum domni pape mancipemus, et quod nobis iniunctum est super eis 10 exhibenda iustitia ulterius non differamus. Inde est quod familiarem uestrum et amicum dompnum Stephanum canonicum sancte Osyde ad uos destinare curaui- mus, ut quod nolumus scripto committere per ipsum uobis aperiamus. Scitis quidem necessitatem hanc nobis incumbere, ut aut sententiam proferamus in uos aut causam qua prepedimur domno pape denuntiemus. Quod cum exstiterit in 15 proximo futurum est, ut quod a nobis ad presens omissum est ab ipso proculdubio compleatur, et sententia quam ad presens forte differimus, tanto periculosius in uos, ⟨fo. 40v⟩ quanto a iudice longe sanctiore longeque sublimiore proferatur. Vnde quia rerum exitus prudens metitur, magis quidem ob comodum uestrum quam ob uitandum periculum nostrum discretioni uestre supplicamus, quatinus non tantum 20 cum his qui terrena sapiunt[1] sed cum uiris sapientibus Deumque timentibus con- silium super hoc habeatis, et illum per quem uiuitis, per quem spiritum trahitis, per quem bona multa possidetis, qui uos inter aduersa seruauit, aduersus hostes pro- texit, qui spiritum uestrum cum uolet auferet,[2] qui omnia opera uestra in iudicium deducet, coram occulis habeatis. Hodie estis et cras fortasse non eritis; et inferni 25 miseria sicut et celi gloria sine fine mansura est. Illa quippe die qua hinc erunt acusantia peccata, inde terrens iustitia, foris ardens mundus, intus urens conscientia, subtus patens horridum chaos inferni, desuper iratus iudex, parum proculdubio cuique uidebitur quod Domino dum hic uiuitur exhibetur. Tangat itaque cor uestrum spiritus Dei ut in presenti negotio bonorum sic consiliis adquiescatis, ne 30 sententiam quod absit apostolicam in uos experiendo, confusionem longe quam ad presens estimetis grauiorem sentiatis. Sapere et intelligere et nouissima prouidere uos optamus karissime.

## 160 To Cardinal William of Pavia

[c. December 1165] He has received the Pope's mandate to order Hugh, earl of Norfolk, to restore the vill of Pentney to the canons of Pentney or lay an interdict on the earl's properties. As a result he is in grave difficulties with the king.[3] He has strongly urged the earl to comply, but the earl objects that the mandate was obtained by a false plea. Gilbert asserts that the earl would obey a sentence from judges delegate, if the Pope would appoint them.

Venerabili domno et amico W(illelmo) Papiensi sancte Romane ecclesie cardinali sibi karissimo frater G(ilebertus) Lundoniensis ecclesie minister, salutem et debiti munus obsequii.

**160** G, no. 176; *MB Epp.* 482; B, fo. 41v.
3 obsequium *before correction to* obsequiii (*sic*) B

---

[1] Cf. Phil. iii. 19.          [2] Cf. Ps. ciii. 29.
[3] That this was no form of words is shown by the articles commonly attributed to 1169, which we assign to 1166, which put the bishops of London and Norwich 'in misericordia regis' for laying an interdict on Earl Hugh's lands and publishing the Pope's excommunication of him without licence. See p. xlix n.

       14-2

Verborum facile suadet paucitas, cum ad exaudiendum prona est ipsius ad quem
5 scribitur amica benignitas.¹ Quod quia de uestra sinceritate confidimus, paucis
negotium in quo nobis a beniuolentia uestra subueniri petimus aperimus. Mandatum domni pape suscepimus quatinus Hugonem comitem de Norfol⟨cia⟩ districte
conueniremus, et nisi canonicis de Panteneia uillam ipsam de Panteneia et cetera
que sibi ablata queruntur ammonitus restitueret, ipsum et totam terram ⟨fo. 42⟩
10 suam interdicto subiceremus, et nisi uel sic infra quadraginta dies resipisceret eum
excommunicationis innodare sententia non differremus. In hoc uero nobis regia se
grauiter opponit auctoritas, asserens ad summam regni sui spectare dignitatem, ut,
dum cuique aduersus comitem uel baronem suum super terris aut feudis querelam
habenti plenam paratus fuerit exhibere iustitiam, ipsum nec archiepiscopus nec
15 aliquis regni sui episcopus aut interdicto premat aut excommunicationi subiciat.
Hanc predecessores suos assensu Romanorum pontificum usque nunc optinuisse
affirmat, et nos omnes regni sui episcopos id sibi iuramento firmasse commemorat,²
exigens ut antiquitati stemus et regni sui priuilegia nequaquam sibi minuentes, ab
hiis que sibi a nobis sub iurisiurandi religione sunt promissa non recedamus. Vnde
20 graui nobis interminatione interdicitur quod auctoritate precipitur. Sic nobis in
arto res est ut nisi suum temperet apostolica mansuetudo mandatum, subire nobis
necesse sit aut hinc inobedientie quod absit periculum, aut apud domnum regem
periurii et non obseruate fidelitatis opprobrium. Mallem episcopus non fuisse quam
horum alterutrum incurrisse. Gladius uterque grauis est; quorum unus animam,
25 alter corpus occidit: ille quidem grauior, attamen iste grauis. Et domno meo
karissimo domno pape que utilitas futura est in sanguine meo, si descendero in
corruptionem³ hanc ut aut periurus reputer, aut inobediens quod semper absit
existam? Si domno meo non paruero, mors michi est,⁴ et si paruero solum superest
ut emigrem a regno cuius leges non suscipio, a cuius regis fidelitate recedo. Si causa
30 quidem esset eiusmodi pro qua dignum foret penam subire mortis aut exilii,
gauderem utique in proscriptione mea uel morte obsequium me Domino gratum
exhibere. Sed nunquid sex fratrum in Panteneia miserrime et absque omni et
regule et ordinis obseruatione uictitantium causa tanti est, ut ob sibi restituenda
pauca agri iugera inter summum pontificem et sibi quondam amicum et adhuc
35 dante Deo futurum amicissimum domnum nostrum regem Anglie questionem
oporteat super suarum eminentia dignitatum agitari—presertim cum in expedito
sit in causa hac ius suum unicuique reddere,⁵ et que turbata sunt ad pacem et
debitum iustitie finem pacifice reuocare? Si domno regi permissum fuerit, causam
hanc episcoporum et aliorum uirorum prudentum consiliis ilico terminabit. Si
40 causam domnus papa iudicibus delegauerit, ipsorum stare sententie comes Hugo
non recusabit. Ipsum quippe districte conuenimus, intentando sibi sententiam
domni pape litteris designatam. Quas cum audisset precum statim arguit falsitatem,
asserens se Panteneiam iamdictis canonicis nunquam concessisse, nec scriptum quod

**160** 32 nunquam *corrected by another hand* B

---

¹ Cf. nos. 196, 226–7, 258.                                        ² I.e. at the Council of Clarendon in 1164.
³ Cf. Ps. xxix. 10.                          ⁴ Cf. Dan. xiii. 22.                          ⁵ Cf. *Inst.* 1, 1, 3.

super hoc eius nomine preferunt et ostendunt ipsis tradidisse aut ut conficeretur assensum prebuisse. Vnde cum falsi arguit instrumentum quo nituntur, attendat 45 prudentia uestra ⟨fo. 42 v⟩ si adeo in expedito res est, ut conuictione non egeat, nec in iudicium deduci debeat, cum etsi non cause conuictio sed executio sententie mandetur, de precum tamen ueritate inquiri oporteat.

## 161  To Pope Alexander III

[c. January 1166] The Pope's mandate that Earl Hugh restore the vill of Pentney to the canons of Pentney has been received; but the earl claimed that the canons had obtained it on a false plea.[1] The case was later discussed in the king's presence at Oxford, and the prior agreed to surrender Pentney in exchange for another vill; but this was repudiated by the community. As a result the earl has appealed to the Pope, naming Ascension Day for his term.

Patri suo et domno summo pontifici A(lexandro) frater G(ilebertus) Lundoniensis ecclesie minister, deuotum caritatis et obedientie famulatum.

Perlato pater ad nos mandato uestro super comite Hugone et Willelmo de Vaus[2] debitaque ueneratione suscepto, comes Hugo nuntiis ilico directis ad nos anxie conquestus est fratres de Panteneia in lesionem suam uestram circumuenisse 5 excellentiam, et falsa suggestione hanc que ad presens in eum lata est sententiam obtinuisse. Negotium uero quod inter canonicos et ipsum uertitur asserit eo quem consequenter ostendimus ordine processisse. Villam de Panteneia de feudo comitis Hugonis esse penes nos fere nullus ignorat; quam se canonicis de Panten(eia) nunquam dedisse, numquam scripto confirmasse iurat et modis omnibus asseuerat. 10 Annis uero iam duobus emensis fatetur se Willelmum de Vaus, qui uillam iam-dictam suo ascribebat patrimonio et iure sibi competere dicebat hereditario, quemque et patrem suum iamdicti canonici possessionis quam in uilla ipsa habent auctores laudant, solempni curia conuocata in ius uocasse, et uillam hanc aduersus eum, utpote patri suo nunquam donatam, numquam hereditario iure concessam, 15 coram omnibus sollenniter euicisse, seque post euictionem hanc curie sue iudicio ad uillam ipsam manus extendisse, ipsamque ut suam sceu sperabat sibi aliquandiu possedisse. Predicti uero fratres super hac necessitate recurrentes ad uos, mandatum ad nos pertulerunt ut predictum comitem districte conueniremus, et nisi auctori-tate uestra per nos ammonitus eis uillam iamdictam et omnia ablata in integrum 20 restitueret, terram eius totam sub interdicto ponere, et nisi uel sic satisfaceret, ex-

---

160  46, 47 conuitione/conuitio *corrected by modern hand* B
161  G, no. 162; *MB Epp.* 483; B, fo. 168.
17  *i.e.* ceu

---

[1]  Gilbert says that the vill has been restored: 'uilla ipsa canonicis reddita est'. But if this were really so, the later papal sentence against the earl would be unintelligible. There seems to be some prevarication here, and it may be that the earl made (or perhaps even merely promised) temporary restitution. The earl's case in Rome would have been much stronger if he had made restitution, and it may well be that Gilbert convinced him of this at the council of Oxford, but that the earl subsequently changed his mind.
[2]  William de Vaus was probably the William de Wall' who held thirty knights' fees of the earl in 1166 (*Red Book of the Exchequer*, ed. H. Hall, RS, I, 395). Robert de Vaux held five at the same time.

communicationis in eum ferre sententiam non differemus. Nobis itaque mandatum uestrum multo labore complentibus, domno nostro rege manum efficaciter apponente, uilla ipsa canonicis reddita est, et quecumque sibi ablata fuerant eis
25 iuxta iuramentum et probationem suorum per nos integerrime restituta sunt. Vestre si quid aliter excellentie suggestum est, sic processisse negotium uenerabilis fratris nostri domni Norwicensis episcopi aliarumque eiusdem diocesis ⟨fo. 168 v⟩ personarum testimoniis poteritis euidenter agnoscere. Deinde processu temporis cum ad domnum nostrum regem Oxeneford(ie) conuenissemus quia super uilla
30 hac quam sibi comes Hugo uendicat, lis diu protracta est et in longum sunt protelata certamina, in ipsa domni regis presentia super hoc tractatum est ut canonici rem ipsam litigiosam comiti cederent et aliam ipso donante susciperent, in qua cum pace degerent et in pace Domino deseruirent. Qua in re etsi prior domus ipsius assensum daret, rege tamen sic consulente, prouisum est nil ulterius fieri, negotium
35 effectu non compleri, quousque totius conuentus Panteneie super hoc sciretur uoluntas et communiter haberetur assensus. Conuentu uero non approbante uerum improbante negotium non ultra processum est, nec eis quicquam per domnum nostrum regem, aut comitem, aut quenquam suorum commutatum est, aut ablatum, aut aliquatenus ut asserunt imminutum. Verum quod ad possessiones in
40 eo sibi statu permanent uniuersa, quo uestrorum exstabant tempore predecessorum, cum ipsorum auctoritate inter ipsos et Willelmmum de Vaus lis diu protracta sopita est et finita controuersia. Comes itaque primum per nuntios deinde per se, precum arguens falsitatem, ad uestram appellauit audientiam ostensurus ut asserit se nec possessiones eorum ausu (ut dicunt) temerario occupasse, nec locum suum aut
45 uillam aut quicquam quod eorum sit commutatione que non processit optinuisse, nec datam in se sententiam quam multa humilitate sustinet et patientia promeruisse. Porro appellationi sue terminum diem Ascensionis Dominice constituit, et quia siue cognitio *siue cause mandetur executio, precum semper conuenit argui falsitatem, has appellationis sue testes a nobis litteras impetrauit. Qua in re ne per igno-
50 rantiam facti pars aduersa caperetur sepedictis fratribus de Panten(eia) et formam et causam facte appellationis per litteras et per nuntios fideles denuntiare curauimus. Valere uos optamus in Domino, pater in Christo karissime.

## 162  To Pope Alexander III

[*c.* 9 May 1166] The relatives of Earl Aubrey are attempting to have his marriage annulled on the ground that his wife was previously married[1] to his brother Geoffrey; Gilbert describes this case, which was suspended by the countess appealing to the Pope for the Fourth Sunday in Lent.

**161** 36 baberetur B    48 *siue *Robertson*; sue B    50 capetur B
**162** G, no. 164; B, fo. 174 v.

---

[1] Or at least had entered a liaison with Geoffrey by betrothal which might make a binding marriage and would more certainly bar a marriage between Agnes and Geoffrey's brother. Geoffrey de Vere was lord of Clun, owing to his marriage to Isabel, daughter of Elias de Say (see no. 117); he was sheriff of Suffolk in Stephen's reign and of Shropshire 1167–70 (*CP*, x, App. J, p. 113).

Agnes, daughter of Henry of Essex, was born *c.* 1151–2; in 1162–3 she became the third wife of Aubrey de Vere, first earl of Oxford.[1] Within a year he tried to repudiate her, ostensibly on the ground given in this letter, in fact no doubt because her father had been disgraced and his estates forfeited. It took two or three years for the dispute to develop into the lawsuit here described. The appeal of the countess, by a strange chance, can be very exactly dated. A document dated 1166 in the cartulary of Holy Trinity, Aldgate, describes a quite unconnected case, also in Gilbert's presence, and concludes: 'hoc factum est septimo idus Maii apud Westmon(asterium), in capella infirmorum die illo quo placitum fuit inter comitem Albericum et uxorem eius, quando appellauit apud papam'.[2] The appeal, then, was made on 9 May 1166, and the letter must have been written very shortly afterwards.

The case was slow to mature. In 1172 the Pope finally ordered Aubrey to take his wife back; Aubrey concurred, and they lived together, so far as we know, until his death in 1194. Gilbert's letter 163 could have been written at any stage after the original appeal.

⟨P⟩atri suo et domno summo pontifici A(lexandro) frater G(ilebertus) Lundoniensis ecclesie minister, debitum caritatis et obedientie famulatum.

Ad uestram pater iustum est referri notitiam, que facta ad uos appellatione suspensa uestre sublimitatis expetunt in sui decisione sententiam. Vnde uestre notificamus excellentie nos ob instantem querelam parentum comitis Alberici, diem 5 constituisse et tam comitem ipsum quam comitissam uxorem eius in presentiam nostram euocasse, ut que inter ipsos uertuntur audiremus et fide ueri plenius habita mediante iustitia decideremus. Partibus itaque coram positis, ⟨fo. 175⟩ parentes comitis proposuerunt copulam comitis et comitisse nequaquam fore legitimam, eo quod priusquam comes illam duxisset uxorem, frater ipsius comitis Galfridus 10 scilicet de Ver super ea in uxorem ducenda cum patre ipsius comitisse fide interposita pepigisset. Asserebant etiam eatenus processisse negotium ut pater comitisse ipsam, cum trium iam esset annorum, predicto Gaufrido utpote futuram suam tradiderit, et Gaufridus eam fratri suo comiti Alberico sibi custodiendam comiserit; et cum iam sex complesset annos, susceptam de manu comitis in domum propriam 15 duxerit sibique uenerationem omnem tanquam future uxori sue tam per se quam per suos in omnibus excepta thori communione usque ad annum duodecimum iam fere completum exhibuerit. His igitur inter patrem comitisse et Gaufridum fratrem comitis interposita fide firmatis, asserebant Gaufridi et comitisse firmata fuisse sponsalia, et que fratris sponsa fuerat alteri postmodum fratri legitime non nupsisse. 20 Adiciebant etiam contractum hunc ipso comitisse consensu fuisse firmatum, cum ad etatem iamdictam peruenerit et toto hoc annorum curriculo numquam his que agebantur uel momento contradixerit. Comitissa uero que a patre suo gesta sunt cum trium tantum esset annorum, etate nondum admittente consensum, se penitus ignorasse respondit. Etsi pater suus cum Gaufrido contraxerit ut dictum est, id se 25 nec tunc scisse nec postmodum approbasse nec his que inter eos gesta sunt assensum umquam prebuisse constanter asseruit. Vnde cum in contrahendis sponsalibus eorum

---

**162** 21 *? for* ipsius    25 contraxit B

---

[1] See *CP*, x, 205 ff., where there is a full discussion of the case. They had at least four, probably five, children (*CP*, x, Appendix, pp. 116–17).
[2] Glasgow University Library, Hunterian MS U. 2. 6 (215), fo. 172.

requirendus sit consensus de quorum futuris nuptiis agitur,[1] ipsa Gaufridi sponsam se nunquam fuisse ait que nunquam de coniugali copula cum eo subeunda a
30 quoquam requisita est, nec in hoc umquam animi uoluntate consensit. Si itaque a patre suo Gaufrido tradita, de manu Gaufridi a comite suscepta, si postmodum a comite Gaufrido reddita et ab ipso in domum propriam ducta est, et ibidem annis aliquot conuersata, in his omnibus necessitati paruit: cum Gaufrido nunquam in coniugale uinculum aut opere aut uoluntate consensit. Quod ut manifestis declararet
35 indiciis adiecit se cum iam aliquantulum excreuisset patri suo litteras direxisse, et se connubio Gaufridi nunquam prebituram assensum euidenter ostendisse. Parentes uero comitis patriampotestatem ostendentes in sobolem, obiecerunt ⟨fo. 175 v⟩ patrem posse filie maritum eligere, quem nisi uel degenerem uel indignum elegerit ipsam eius uoluntati dissentire non posse.[2] Partibus itaque sic experientibus alterutro
40 cum iam tertio sedissemus, comitissa conquesta est aduocatos suos ob metum comitis et suorum cause sue patrocinium suum quo minus tute eo minus diligenter exhibere. In quo se grauari asserens, ad *Letare Ierusalem* ad uestram appellauit audientiam, et rem continentes, ut gesta est, has a nobis litteras impetrauit. Valere uos optamus in Domino, pater in Christo karissime.

## 163   To Aubrey de Vere, earl of Oxford

[1166–72] He has heard that the earl keeps his wife in close custody. Gilbert reminds the earl that while the case between them, which has gone to the Pope on appeal, is pending, she is still his wife, and urges him to treat her with greater gentleness.

⟨G⟩ilebertus Dei gratia Lundoniensis episcopus uenerabili uiro comiti Albrico, salutem, gratiam et benedictionem.

Peruenit ad audientiam nostram quod occasione controuersie que inter uos et comitissam aliquandiu uentilata est, et ad sedem apostolicam tandem per appella-
5 tionem suspensa, eam districte supra modum teneatis inclusam, ut nec causam instruere nec parti sue defensorem possit ullatenus procurare sed nec ecclesiam frequentare nec in publicum ut dicitur prodire permittitur, ut non iam custodie deputata sed carceri potius dampnata uideatur. Cubilis quoque corporisque et colloquii uestri omnis sibi iam olim copia negata dicitur, ut quos ecclesie coniunxit
10 auctoritas, uestra quodammodo disiunxisse uideatur uoluntas. Que si uera sunt ut accepimus, quam citius uobis emendanda denuntiamus. Alioquin ualde uobis timendum est ne prouocetis iram et indignationem Dei aduersus uos, que quanto serius aduenit tanto seuerius affligit. Recolite quanta reuerentia dignum sit sacra-

---

**162** 43 ualete B
**163** G, no. 282; B, fo. 174.
8 carcere B    11 Alioquin] B *adds* uobis, *cancelled*

---

[1] Cf. *Decretum*, C. 30, q. 2, c. 1.
[2] On the Canon Law of *desponsatio impuberum* see J. Dauvillier, *Le mariage dans le droit classique de l'Église* (Paris, 1933), pp. 43 ff.; on *patria potestas*, in English law, see Pollock and Maitland, *History of English Law*, II, 436 ff., and the case of Christina of Markyate, in her *Life*, ed. C. H. Talbot.

mentum coniugii quod Dominus ab origine mundi primum introduxit et sua
benedictione confirmauit, quod et ipse in ⟨fo. 174v⟩ Cana Galilee sua corporali 15
sanctificauit presentia,[1] quod et apud omnes gentes tam fideles quam infideles cum
summa ueneratione mandatur obseruandum. Certum est enim et per hystorias
simul et exempla notissimum, quod preuaricatores sacramenti huius non solum
ultime reseruantur ultioni, ut a terra uiuentium que est paradisus Dei proscribantur,
sed et in hac quoque terra morientium in se aut in sua successione frequenter 20
exheredantur ut hereditas eorum transferatur ad exteros et in labores suos introean
alieni.[2] Proinde episcopali uobis auctoritate mandamus orantes et exhortantes in
Domino et consulentes in caritate, et in remissionem uobis iniungentes delictorum,
quatinus propter Deum et propter reuerentiam legis Christiane modestius et mitius
agatis cum uxore uestra, que est pars corporis uestri, amotoque predicte distric- 25
tionis excessu, ipsam sibi ad debitam libertatem et uos ipsi ad societatem et solacium
(sicut decet) sponsum sponse benigne restituatis, ne sine iudicio ecclesie maritali
priuetur contubernio, quod sibi teste ecclesia sub solemni fide sponsaliorum promisistis. In quo si nobis non creditis, apostolo credite qui ait, 'uiri diligite uxores
uestras, sicut et Christus ecclesiam', et iterum 'alligatus es uxori? noli querere 30
solutionem'.[3] Caritas cogit nos et necessitas officii hcc et huiusmodi uestre suggerere
dilectioni. Vnde quia spes nobis est de uobis in Domino, quod nostris sicut debetis
sic et uelitis in his que ad Deum sunt[4] consiliis acquiescere, consilium uobis damus
in caritate, ut legem et condicionem coniugatorum cui subiecistis uos legitime et
sine simulatione obseruare studeatis, ne incidatis in manus iudicis qui non irridetur[5] 35
cuius non potestis iudicium declinare, reus preuaricationis legis sue, quod auertat
omnipotens Dominus. Amen.

### 164  Pope Alexander III to Gilbert Foliot

[30 January 1172] The dispute between Earl Aubrey and A(gnes) his wife has come to the
Pope by appeal from the countess: the Pope gives judgement that the earl is to take his wife
back, and to treat her with due respect, to treat her as his wife *in mensa* and *in thoro*; he is to
do this within twenty days, or an interdict shall be laid on his lands by Gilbert and he himself
excommunicated.

Alexander III was only at Tusculum (Frascati) in late January in 1171, 1172, 1179 and 1181;
even the two former years are surprisingly late, considering that the appeal had first been made
in 1166, but such a delay would not be unparalleled, and the times were difficult. 1179 or 1181
is certainly too late.[6] It is impossible to believe that the Pope would have addressed such a
mandate when Gilbert was excommunicate, and if, as seems likely, he had already heard of
Becket's murder by 30 January 1171, he had other things to think about than solving the
Veres' matrimonial tangles. The letter was probably written in 1172.

**163** 18 sacramti B
**164** G, no. 363; JL 14,254; B, fo. 151.

---

[1] Cf. Joh. ii.  [2] Cf. Joh. iv. 38  [3] Eph. v. 25; I Cor. vii. 27.
[4] Cf. Heb. v. i.  [5] Cf. Gal. vi. 7.
[6] The papal sentence took effect, and the couple's first child seems to have been born *c.* 1172 or
not much later (so *Handbook*, 2nd ed., p. 443; for his early career, *CP*, x, 208).

Alexander episcopus seruus seruorum Dei uenerabili fratri Gileberto Lundoniensi episcopo, salutem et apostolicam benedictionem.

Nobilis mulier A⟨gnes⟩ uxor comitis Alberici lacrimabilem ad nos querelam transmisit, et id ipsum ex commeantium relatione persepe audiuimus, quod cum
5 inter illam et eundem uirum suum super eorum matrimonio controuersia mota fuisset, et iamdicta mulier tuo se conspectui presentasset, licet te sepius inde requisisset, nullum ei dare uoluisti consilium, nec aliquis ei in causa sua patrocinium occasione illa impendit. Vnde cum sola in tuo consistorio quolibet destituta suffragio sisteretur, apostolice sedis audientiam apellauit, demum uero ad castrum quoddam
10 deducta, in turrem dicitur retrusa fuisse, ubi usque in hodiernum diem ab hominum consortio remota penitus custoditur. Quoniam igitur si quis esses, quod officium gereres, recta consideratione pensaris, talia de assensu tuo—aut etiam te sustinente— nullatenus perpetrarentur quorum ad nos prius pena quam culpa deberet perferri. Per apostolica itaque tibi scripta precipiendo mandamus, et in uirtute obedientie
15 iniungimus, quatinus memoratum comitem diligentia pontificali adhibita, infra uiginti dies post harum susceptionem studiose commoneas et inducas, ut prefatam uxorem suam debita cum ueneratione suscipiat, participationem in mensa, com- munionem in thoro, non differat exhibere. Quod si hec omnia infra terminum prescriptum ⟨fo. 151 v⟩ exequi forte contempserit, totam terram eius dilatione et
20 appellatione sullata subicias interdicto, personam quoque illius, si nec sic resipuerit, uinculo excommunicationis astringas, et eum ab omnibus sicut excommunicatum publice uitari denuntians, ad quecumque loca deuenerit, quamdiu ibidem presens fuerit, nisi in curia regis commoretur, omnia diuina officia preter baptisma paruulo- rum et penitentias morientium, auctoritate nostra prohibeas celebrari. Vniuersis
25 etiam episcopis per Angliam constitutis ex parte nostra districte indicas, ut eum per parrochias suas sicut excommunicatum nuntient ab omnibus euitandum, et ipsi eundem prorsus euitent. Dat' Tusculani iii kalendas Februarii.

## 165  To Nigel, bishop of Ely

[Probably *c.* late June 1166] The appeal against the archbishop of Canterbury must be swiftly notified to the Pope, and so he asks the bishop to seal the letter which he[1] has dictated, so that the appeal, already notified to the archbishop, may be sent to the Pope with the support of their two selves and the bishop of Norwich.

On 24 April 1166 Alexander III wrote to Thomas and to the English clergy announcing the appointment of Thomas as legate for England, excepting the bishopric of York.[2] Armed

**164** 10 ubi *Giles*; nisi B (*spelt out in B, doubtless* ů *in exemplar*)
**165** *Not in* G; Ic, fo. 25v; Ha, fo. 10v (*variants of Ha not noted*).

---

[1] This confirms John of Salisbury's view that Gilbert was the author of nos. 166–7 (no. 167 is the letter here referred to); see *GF*, p. 31.
[2] *MB Epp.* 172–3; JL 11,270–1 (there can be no doubt that *MB Epp.* 173 is rightly dated 24 April and the date on 172, Anagni, 9 October, is an error, presumably derived from one of *MB Epp.* 710–12 of 1170, or the like). The dating clause of *MB Epp.* 173 could belong to 1166 or 1167, but there is no doubt that Becket became legate in 1166 (cf. *MB*, III, 397; *MB Epp.* 252).

with this increased authority, the archbishop proceeded to Vézelay, and on Whit Sunday (12 June) he pronounced his first great series of excommunications.[1] At the same time, or shortly after, he suspended Jocelin of Salisbury for his share in the promotion of John of Oxford to the deanery of Salisbury.[2] On 30 June Gilbert received Thomas's letter (MB Epp. 239) enclosing the bull of legation; a few days later he wrote to Henry (no. 168) describing the event, and asking that the ground should be cleared for the English bishops to appeal in force against Becket's proceedings.

Already on or about 24 June the English bishops had issued their counter to the Vézelay censures: they appealed to the Pope for the following Ascension Day (nos. 166–7 and MB Epp. 206–7).[3] The bishops' letter to Thomas (no. 167) was immediately suspected to be Gilbert's work, and he was undoubtedly one of the prime movers in the appeal. Additional evidence of his authorship is given in the notes to no. 166; and evidence of his special interest in this appeal is given in no. 165, written to gather support for it. The receipt of no. 167 stimulated Thomas and his followers to great literary activity, and four replies survive. MB Epp. 221–2 were apparently literary exercises by Herbert of Bosham and Lombardus, but 223 (to the English bishops) and 224 (to Gilbert) were undoubtedly sent. Urged on by John of Salisbury (cf. MB Epp. 231), the archbishop reserved his choicest thunder, and his most closely reasoned defence of his actions, for the bishop of London. It was this letter (MB Epp. 224) which called forth Gilbert's tremendous rejoinder, no. 170.

Venerabili domno fratrique karissimo N(igello) Eliensi Dei gratia episcopo frater G(ilebertus) Londoniensis ecclesie minister, bene prosperari in Domino.

Appellationem quam causam nostram aduersus domni Cantuariensis grauamina releuare curauimus, domno pape significare celerius expedit in commune. Vnde litteris quas ad eum dictauimus quasque uobis mittimus, sigillum uestrum apponi 5 de communi fratrum consilio postulamus, ut qui appellationem ipsam domno Cant(uariensi) aliorum fratrum nostrorum sigillis notificauimus, eandem domno pape, uestro et domni Norwicensis et nostro etiam testimonio, declaremus. Valere uos optamus in Domino, frater in Christo karissime.

## 166  The English bishops and clergy to Pope Alexander III

[c. 24 June 1166] They defend the king and complain of the archbishop's actions, especially the excommunications (at Vézelay) and the suspension of the bishop of Salisbury: they have appealed, naming Ascension Day as term.

That Gilbert was the effective author of nos. 166–7, so strongly suspected by John of Salisbury (GF, p. 31), seems to be in effect confessed in no. 165.[4]

166 G, no. 437; MB Epp. 204; Lupus, I, 206–9 (i, 128); B, fo. 57v; D, fos. 53–4; Ia, pp. 125–8; Ib, fos. 274v–276v; Ic, fos. 23–25v; Id, fos. 103–104v; C, fos. 100 (99)–101 (100); Vb, fos. 109v–110. Also in Howden, I, 266–9 (variants of Vb Howden not given).

---

[1] See especially MB Epp. 194 (cf. J. C. Robertson, Becket, London, 1859, p. 347).
[2] MB Epp. 199; the suspension is referred to in MB Epp. 209 of early July 1166 (certainly before 6 July, which it mentions as a future date).
[3] Cf. GF, pp. 162 ff.; MB Epp. 209, p. 421, gives the date when the appeal was made.
[4] See p. 218 n. 1. Gilbert's authorship receives some confirmation from the style and tone of the letter, and in particular the links in argument with nos. 155, 170.

Patri suo et domno summo pontifici Alexandro prouincie Cantuariensis episcopi et persone per eorundem dioceses locis pluribus constitute, domno patrique debitum caritatis et obedientie famulatum.

Vestram pater meminisse credimus excellentiam, uos deuotum filium uestrum
5 domnumque nostrum karissimum illustrem Anglorum regem per uenerabiles fratres nostros Lundoniensem et Herefordensem episcopos, directis iamdudum litteris conuenisse, et de corrigendis quibusdam que sanctitati uestre in ipsius regno corrigenda uidebantur, paterna gratia commonuisse. Qui mandatum uestrum debita ueneratione suscipiens[1] ut satis notum est, ad uestra quidem monita non iratus in-
10 tumuit, non elatus obedire contempsit, uerum agens gratias paterne correptioni ecclesie se statim submisit examini, asserens de singulis que iuxta uestri formam mandati ⟨fo. 58⟩ sibi diligenter expressa sunt, ecclesie regni sui pariturum iudicio, et que corrigenda decerneret ipsius se consilio laudabili quidem et in principe digne commendabili deuotione correcturum. Ab hoc uero non recedit proposito, non
15 mente reuocat a promisso. Sit qui sedeat, qui cognoscat et iudicet; diuini reuerentia timoris, non maiestatem preferens, sed ut filius obediens iudicio sistere legitimeque parere sententie, seque legibus alligatum principem, presto est in omnibus exhibere. Vnde nec interdicto, nec minis nec maledictionum aculeis ad satisfactionem urgere necesse est diuinarum se legum examini sponte subdentem. Eius enim opera
20 nequaquam luci se subtrahunt, nec occultari tenebris ulla ratione deposcunt. Rex namque fide Christianissimus, in copula castimonie coniugalis honestissimus,[2] pacis et iustitie conseruator et dilatator incomparabiliter strenuus, hoc uotis agit totisque in hoc feruet desideriis ut de regno suo tollantur scandala, cum spurcitiis suis eliminentur peccata, pax totum obtineat atque iustitia, et alta securitate et
25 quiete placida sub ipso gaudeant et refloreant uniuersa. Qui cum pacem regni sui enormi insolentium quorundam clericorum excessu, non mediocriter aliquando turbari cognosceret, clero debitam exhibens reuerentiam, eorundem excessus ad ecclesie iudices retulit episcopos, ut gladio gladius subueniret, et pacem quam regebat et fouebat in populo spiritualis potestas fundaret et solidaret in clero. Qua
30 in re partis utriusque zelus enituit: episcoporum in hoc stante iudicio ut homicidium, et si quid huiusmodi est, exauctoratione sola puniretur in clerico; rege uero existimante penam hanc non condigne respondere flagitio, nec stabiliende paci bene prospici, si lector aut acolitus quemquam perimat ut sola iamdicti ordinis amissione tutus existat. Clero itaque statuto celitus ordini deferente, domno uero rege
35 peccatum iusto, ceu sperat, odio persequente et pacem altius radicare intendente, sancta quedam oborta est contentio quam excusat, ut credimus, apud Dominum

**166** 1 Cantuerensis B   10 non] nec C   11 sumpsit B   15 mentem IbIc   15 iudicet;] B adds ipse   18 urgere BId; urgeri IaIbIcC   20 ulla] aliqua BDId (*the agreements of Id and B(D) in this letter are noteworthy*)   23 totisque] hoc uotis agit totisque IaIbIcId(om. que); hoc uotis agat totus D; totis B   25 placita B   29 in clero] uinculo B   31 eiusmodi BIcId   31 exauctoritate Id   31 clero DId   33, 34 perimad/existad B   36 est oborta BDId   36 Dominum] C adds (in margin) sancta et

[1] The opening words of no. 155, here referred to.
[2] For this and what follows, see no. 170 (esp. pp. 241 ff.).

simplex utriusque partis intentio. Hinc non dominationis ambitu, non opprimende ecclesiastice libertatis intuitu, sed solidande pacis affectu eo progressum est ut regni sui consuetudines et dignitates, regibus ante se in regno Anglie a personis ecclesiasticis obseruatas, et pacifice et reuerenter exhibitas, domnus noster rex deduci uellet in 40 medium, et ne super his contentiosus funis traheretur in posterum, notitie publice delegari. Adiuratis itaque per fidem et per eam que in Deum spes est maioribus natu episcopis, aliisque regni maioribus, retroacti temporis insinuato statu dignitates requisite, palam prolate sunt, et summorum in regno uirorum testimoniis propalate. Hec est domni nostri regis in ecclesiam Dei toto orbe declamata crudelitas, hec ab 45 eo persecutio, hec operum eius peruersorum rumusculis undique diuulgata malignitas. In his tamen omnibus si quid sue periculosum anime, si quid ignominiosum ecclesie continetur, id uestra monitus atque motus auctoritate ob reuerentiam Christi, ob ecclesie sancte quam sibi matrem profitetur honorificentiam, ob anime sue remedium, ecclesie regni sui consilio se correcturum, deuotione sanctissima 50 iamdiu pollicitus est et constantissime pollicetur. Et quidem pacis optatum finem nostra, pater, ut speramus, obtinuisset ⟨fo. 58 v⟩ iam postulatio, si non iras iam sopitas, et fere prorsus extinctas, patris nostri domni Cantuariensis de nouo suscitasset exacerbatio. Verum is de cuius patientia pacem, de cuius modestia redintegrationem hucusque gratie sperabamus, ipsum quem monitis emollire, quem 55 meritis et mansuetudine superare debuerat, per tristes et terribiles litteras[1] deuotionem patris aut pontificis patientiam minime redolentes, cum in pacis perturbatores excercitum nuper ageret, dure satis et irreuerenter aggressus est, in ipsum excommunicationis sententiam, in regnum eius interdicti penam acerrime comminando. Cuius si sic remuneratur humilitas, quid in contumacem statuetur? Si sic 60 estimatur obediendi prompta deuotio, in obstinatam peruersitatem quonam modo uindicabitur? Minis quoque grauibus superaddita sunt grauiora.[2] Quosdam namque fideles et familiares domni nostri regis, primarios regni proceres regiis specialiter assistentes secretis, in quorum manu consilia regis et regni negotia diriguntur, non citatos, non defensos, non ut aiunt culpe sibi conscios, non conuictos aut confessos, 65 excommunicationis innodauit sententia et excommunicatos publice denuntiauit.

**166** 53 prorsus BIaIbIcId; prorsus iam D; iam (*ins. margin*) prorsus C    61 quomodo DId

---

[1] *MB Epp.* 152–4, Becket's famous letters of exhortation to the king, belong to this period, but they contain no specific reference to the threat to excommunicate Henry and lay an interdict on England. Either this was in fact conveyed by messenger or the letter referred to seems to be lost. These precise punishments were referred to by Becket about this time in *MB Epp.* 184 to Nicholas of Mont St Jacques; and John of Salisbury (*MB Epp.* 194) tells us that Henry was warned as part of the Vézelay censures. In no. 167 we are told that Becket was said to have omitted any salutation from his 'comminatorium'. This could refer to *MB Epp.* 154, which is normally without protocol, but in MS B (fo. 168 v) opens 'Henrico regi Angl' Thomas Cantuariensis Dei gratia minister humilis sine sal''; 'sine sal'' seems more likely to be a gloss than what actually appeared on the letter, which may well have been intended as a speech for the archbishop to deliver before the king if he could gain an audience, rather than a letter in the normal sense.

[2] What follows refers to the sentences passed by the archbishop at Vézelay on 12 June 1166 (see *MB Epp.* 194–203).

Adiecit etiam ut uenerabilem fratrem nostrum domnum Saresbiriensem episcopum, absentem et indefensum, non confessum aut conuictum, sacerdotali prius et episcopali suspenderet officio, quam suspensionis eius causa comprouincialium aut
70 aliquorum etiam fuisset arbitrio comprobata. Si hic itaque iudiciorum ordo circa regem, circa regnum tam prepostere, ne dicamus inordinate, processerit, quidnam consequi posse putabimus? Dies enim mali sunt[1] et occasionem habentes malignandi quamplurimam, nisi ut tenor pacis et gratie quo regnum et sacerdotium usque modo coherent abrumpatur, et nos cum commisso nobis clero in dispersionem
75 abeamus exilii, aut a uestra quod absit fidelitate recedentes ad scismatis malum in abissum iniquitatis et inobedientie prouoluamur? Compendiosissima quippe uia hec est ad omne religionis dispendium, ad cleri pariter populique subuersionem et interitum. Vnde ne apostolatus uestri tempore tam misere subuertatur ecclesia, ne domnus noster rex et seruientes ei populi a uestra quod absit auertantur obedientia,
80 ne totum quod priuatorum consilio machinatur possit in nos domni Cantuariensis iracundia, aduersus eum et ipsius mandata, domno nostro regi aut regno eius, nobis aut commissis nobis ecclesiis grauamen aliquod inportantia, ad sublimitatem uestram uoce et scripto appellauimus, et appellationi terminum diem Ascensionis Dominice designauimus, eligentes apud uos in omne quod sanctitati uestre placuerit
85 humiliari, quam ad sublimes animi ipsius motus, nostris non id exigentibus meritis, de die in diem tediosissime pregrauari. Conseruet incolumitatem uestram, ecclesie sue in longa tempora profuturam omnipotens Dominus, in Christo dilecte pater.

## 167 The English bishops and clergy to Archbishop Thomas Becket

[c. 24 June 1166] They complain of the archbishop's actions, argue that he ought to be grateful to the king, whom they defend; they object in particular to the suspension of the bishop of Salisbury, and announce their appeal (as in no. 166).

Evidently written at the same time as no. 166.[2]

Venerabili patri et domno Thome Dei gratia Cantuariensi archiepiscopo, suffraganei eiusdem ecclesie episcopi et persone per eorundem dioceses locis uariis constitute, debitam subiectionem et obedientiam.

166 69 suspenderet BDIcId; suspend' Ib; suspendit CCo    72–3 malignangdi B    73 quo] quam IaIb qua Ic    74 choerent B    78–9 ne...obedientia om. D
167 G, no. 436; MB Epp. 205; Lupus, I, 188–92 (i, 126); B, fo. 52v; D, fos. 54–5v; Va, fos. 76–7; Rb, fos. 2v–4; Jb, fos. 182–3; Ia, pp. 26–9; Ib, fos. 193–195v; Ic, fos. 29v–32 and 88–90 (Icc); Id, fos. 52v–54v; Ie, fos. 34v–38v (incomplete); C, fos. 82v (81v)–84 (83); Co, fos. 44v–45v; Vb, fos. 105–6; O, unfoliated, no. 127; Bn, fos. 170–1; Cambridge, Corpus Christi College 123 (Herbert of Bosham's letters), fos. 16–18; Edward Grim, MB, II, 408–9 (abbreviated); Diceto, I, 321–3; Howden, I, 262–5. Variants of JbVbOBn Herbert Grim Diceto and Howden normally ignored.
1 Cant. Dei gratia BRbIbIcc; Va om. the protocol    2–3 constitute] Rb adds salutem et (uariis in B was pluribus, corrected)

---

[1] Cf. Eph. v. 16.
[2] And for the bishops of London and Hereford's admonition to Henry II, Becket's 'comminatorium' and the Vézelay censures, pp. 220–1 nn.

Que uestro pater in longinqua discessu inopinata rei ipsius nouitate turbata sunt, uestra sperabamus humilitate et prudentia in pacis pristine serenitatem cooperante 5 gratia reuocari. Erat quidem nobis solacio, quod post discessum uestrum ad omnes ilico fama diuulgante peruenit, uos scilicet in transmarinis agentem nil altum sapere,[1] uos in domnum nostrum regem aut regnum eius nulla machinatione insurgere sed sponte susceptum paupertatis onus cum modestia sustinere: lectioni et orationi insistere, preteritorumque iacturam temporum ieiuniis, uigiliis, lacrimisque 10 redimere,[2] et spiritualibus occupatum studiis ad perfectum beatis uirtutum incrementis ascendere. Ad pacis bona reformanda uos studiis huiusmodi gaudebamus insistere, ex quibus spes erat uos in cor domni nostri regis hanc posse gratiam desuper euocare, ut uobis iram regia pietate remitteret, et illatas in discessu et ex discessu uestro iniurias ad cor de cetero non reuocaret. Erat amicis uestris et 15 beniuolis ad ipsum aliquis, dum hec de uobis audirentur, accessus, et ob conciliandam uobis gratiam suplicantes benigne quandoque sustinuit. Iam uero quorundam relatione didicimus, quod ad memoriam anxie reuocamus, uos scilicet in eum comminatorium emisisse, quo salutationem omittitis, quo non ad optentum gratie consilium precesue porrigitis, quo non amicum quid sentitis aut scribitis, sed 20 intentatis minis interdictum aut precisionis elogium in eum iam dicendum fore multa seueritate proponitis. Quod si quam dure dictum est, tam fuerit seuere completum, que turbata sunt non iam speramus ad pacem redigi, sed in perhenne quoddam odium et inexorabile pertimescimus inflammari. Rerum uero finem prudentia sancta considerat, dans operam sollicite ut quod prudenter inchoat, 25 bono quoque fine concludat. Aduertat itaque si placet discretio uestra quo tendat, an conatibus huiusmodi finem queat optinere quem optat. Nos quidem his ausis a spe magna cecidimus, et qui pacis optinende spem quandoque concepimus, ab ipsis iam spei liminibus graui quadam desperatione repellimur, et dum uelut extracto gladio pugna conseritur, pro uobis supplicandi locus utique non inuenitur. Vnde 30 patri scribimus ex caritate consilium, ne labores laboribus, iniurias superaddat iniuriis, sed omissis minis patientie et humilitati inseruiat, causam suam diuine clementie, Dominique sui gratie misericordi committat, et sic agendo carbones ignis in multorum capita coaceruet et congerat.[3] Accenderetur hoc modo caritas, et quod mine non poterant inspirante Domino bonorumque suadente consilio sola 35 fortasse pietas optineret. Bonum erat de paupertate uoluntaria gloriose laudari quam de beneficii ingratitudine ab omnibus in commune notari.

Insedit alte cunctorum mentibus, quam benignus uobis domnus rex noster exstiterit, in quam uos gloriam ab exili prouexerit et in familiarem gratiam tam lata uos mente susceperit, ut dominationis sue loca que a boreali occeano Pireneum 40

---

167 6 gratia] CVa *add* Dei (Diuina coop. gra. Ic; Dei coop. gra. Herbert; Dei gratia Va) 6 consolatio C; solacium Id 11 beatitudinis CCoVa 14 in/ex] ex/in CCoIaVa1 6 dum hec] ut IccIdIe 19 emittitis *with* uel omittatis *ins.* C; omittatis Rb 20 quo *with* uel qua *ins.* C 20 quid] aut humile *ins.* B 34 Accendetur IbIccIcIdIe; accenderetur CVa *with* uel accendetur *ins.* C; accendatur D 36 optineret BIaIdIe; optinebit DIc; optinet Ib; optinet *corrected* Icc; poterit optinere CCo (Rb *illegible*) 38 noster rex Va (*and* C, *before correction*)

---

[1] Cf. Rom. xi. 20; xii. 16.  [2] Cf. Eph. v. 16.  [3] Cf. Rom. xii. 20.

usque por⟨fo. 53⟩recta sunt, adeo potestati uestre cuncta subiecerit, ut in his solum
hos beatos reputaret opinio, qui in uestris poterant oculis complacere. Et ne uestram
gloriam mobilitas posset mundana concutere, uos in his que Dei sunt uoluit im-
mobiliter radicare, et dissuadente matre sua, regno reclamante, ecclesia Dei quoad
45 licuit suspirante et ingemiscente, uos in eam qua preestis dignitatem modis omnibus
studuit sublimare, sperans se de cetero regnare feliciter et ope uestra et consilio
summa securitate gaudere. Si ergo securim accipit unde securitatem sperabat, que
de uobis erit in cunctorum ore narratio? Que retributionis hactenus inaudite
rememoratio? Parcatis ergo si placet fame uestre, parcatis et glorie: et humilitate
50 domnum, filiumque uestrum caritate uincere studeatis. Ad quod si nostra uos
monita mouere nequeunt, debet saltem summi pontificis sancteque Romane
ecclesie dilectio et fidelitas inclinare. Vobis enim suaderi debet e facili ne quid
attemptare uelitis, quod laboranti iamdiu matri uestre labores augeat, quoue
multorum inobedientiam deploranti in eorum qui obediunt amissione dolor
55 accrescat. Quid enim si uestra, quod absit, exacerbatione et opera domnus noster,
quem largiente Domino populi sequuntur et regna, a domno papa recesserit,
ipsumque sibi fortassis aduersum uos solacia denegantem sequi de cetero declinauerit: ipsum namque in hoc que supplicationes, que dona, quot quantaue
promissa sollicitant? In petra tamen firmus hucusque perstitit, et totum quod
60 mundus offerre potest uictor alta mente calcauit. Vnum nobis timori est, ut quem
oblate diuitie et totum quod in hominum gloria pretiosum est flectere nequiuerunt,
animi sui ualeat indignatio sola subuertere. Quod si per uos acciderit, in trenos totus
ire poteritis, et lacrimarum fontem oculis uestris de cetero negare nulla quidem
ratione poteritis. Reuocetis itaque si placet sublimitatis uestre consilium, domno
65 quidem pape, sancteque Romane ecclesie, uobisque si placet aduertere modis
omnibus, si processerit, obfuturum. Sed qui penes uos alta sapiunt uos hac forte uia
progredi non permittunt. Hortantur experiri quis sitis, in domnum nostrum regem,
et omnia que sua sunt, potestatem exercere qua preestis. Que nimirum potestas
peccanti timenda est, satisfacere nolenti formidanda. Domnum uero regem non
70 quidem nunquam peccasse dicimus, sed semper Domino paratum satisfacere confidenter dicimus et predicamus. Rex a Domino constitutus paci prouidet per omnia
subiectorum, et ut hanc conseruet ecclesiis et commissis sibi populis, dignitates
regibus ante se debitas et exibitas sibi uult et exigit exhiberi. In quo si inter ipsum et
uos aliqua est oborta contentio, a summo super hoc pontifice paterna gratia per
75 uenerabiles fratres nostros Londoniensem et Herefordensem episcopos conuentus
et commonitus, non in celum os suum posuit,[1] sed de omnibus in quibus uel
ecclesia uel ecclesiastica quecumque persona se grauatam ostenderet, se non
alienum querere sed ecclesie regni sui pariturum iudicio humiliter et mansuete

---

**167** 42 oculis poterant IaCoRb   43 uos *om.* IccIdIe   45 dignitatem *om.* IbIccIe   49 rememoratio BDVaIaIbIcIccIe (cf. Ps. xxxvii. 1; lxix. 1); remuneratio CCoIdRb   50–1 monita
uos IbRb (monita nostra mouere uos Va)   64 sublimitati BVaIbIcIccRb   70 nunquam
BDIaIcRbVa; nunquam *with* uel non *ins.* CCo; non IbIccIdIe   74 aborta CoId; orbata Ie;
oborta *before* est Ib

---

[1] Cf. Ps. lxxii. 9.

respondit. Quod quidem et factis implere paratus est. Et dulce reputat obsequium, cum monetur ut corrigat, si quid offenderit in Dominum. Nec solum satisfacere, 80 sed etiam si ius exigat in hoc satisdare paratus est. Igitur et satisdare satisque facere uolentem, ecclesie se iudicio in his que sunt ecclesie nec in modico subtrahentem, colla Christi iugo subdentem, quo iure, qua lege, quoue canone aut inter⟨fo. 53 v⟩- dicto grauabitis aut securi quod absit euangelica precidetis?[1] Non impetu quidem ferri, sed iudicio prudenter regi laudabile est. Vnde nostrum omnium una est in 85 commune petitio, ne consilio precipiti mactare pergatis et perdere sed commissis ouibus ut uitam, ut pacem, ut securitatem habeant, paterna studeatis gratia prouidere.

Mouet quidem omnes nos quod in fratrem nostrum domnum Saresbiriensem episcopum, et decanum eiusdem, prepostere, ut quidam existimant, nuper actum audiuimus: in quos suspensionis aut damnationis penam ante motam de culpa 90 controuersiam, calorem ut uidetur iracundie, plusquam iustitie secutus tramitem intorsistis. Ordo iudiciorum nouus hic est, hucusque legibus et canonibus, ut sperabamus, incognitus: damnare primum, et de culpa postremo cognoscere. Quem ne in domnum nostrum regem et regnum eius, ne in nos et commissas nobis ecclesias et parrochias, in domni pape damnum, sancteque Romane ecclesie dedecus 95 et detrimentum, uestreque confusionis augmentum non modicum, exercere temptetis et extendere, remedium uobis appellationis opponimus. Et qui contra metum grauaminum in facie ecclesie uiua iamdudum uoce ad domnum papam appellauimus, iterato iam nunc ad ipsum scripto etiam appellamus, et appellationi terminum diem Ascensionis Dominice designamus, quanta quidem possumus deuotione 100 supplicantes, ut inito salubriori consilio, uestris ac nostris laboribus, expensisque parcatis, causamque uestram in hoc, ut remedium habere queat, ponere studeatis. Valere uos optamus in Domino, pater.

## 168 To King Henry II

[July 1166] He describes the arrival of Becket's letters of legation and an injunction to restore the benefices of the archbishop's clerks and to exact Peter's Pence (cf. no. 155) from the English bishops. He asks the king to allow him to fulfil the injunctions, and asks him to instruct the English bishops (if they find the archbishop's letters prejudicial to the custom of the kingdom) to appeal to the Pope.

167 80 cum monetur *om.* IbIccIdIe    80 offendit B; offendat IbIccIdIe    80 Dominum] Deum RbVa    81 etiam] et DIbIcIeRbVa    81 satisque fac.] et satisfacere CoDIaVa; satisfacereque Ic    88 quidem] *with* uel quoque *ins.* C; quippe Ic    89 eius BCoIaIcRbVa    89 estimant CoIaIbIcIccIdIeRbVa    93 speramus BDIcRbVaCo    99 etiam *om.* DIaRbVa

168 G, no. 275; *MB Epp.* 208; Lupus, I, 218–19 (i, 131); B, fo. 56; D, fos. 76 v–77; Ia, p. 278; Ib, fo. 428 r–v; C, fo. 82 (81) r–v; Co, fo. 52 r–v; Vb, fo. 112 v; O, *not foliated*, no. 131; Ar, fos. 106 v–107; Bn, fo. 175 v (*variants of* ArBnOVb *not noted*) (*headings:* IaIbCCoVbO Henrico (H. IaIbO) regi Anglie Gillebertus (CVb; G. *ceteri*) Londoniensis episcopus; *in lower margin of* C: hec secundum librum emendatiorem scripta fuit inferius post epistolam Multa quidem scribenda,
(a)
j cxxxiij—*i.e. MB Epp.* 252).

---

[1] Cf. Matt. iii. 10; Luc. iii. 9.

Domno suo karissimo illustri Anglorum regi H(enrico) frater G(ilebertus) Lundoniensis ecclesie minister, salutem et seipsum.

Tanta nos, domne, mandati moles ad presens opprimit, tanta se nobis auctoritas opponit, ut consilium pariter et auxilium ⟨fo. 56v⟩ a uobis expetere summa com-
5 pellamur necessitate. Nam quod auctoritas apostolica precipit, hoc apellatio non suspendit, nec aduersus eius mandatum ullum potest esse remedium, cum quod precipitur implere necesse sit, aut inobedientie reatum incurrere. Die namque beati Pauli cum Lundoniis ad altare consisteremus, literas domni pape de manu cuiusdam nobis penitus ignoti suscepimus, quibus legatio in totam Angliam excepto Ebora-
10 censi episcopatu domno Cantuariensi conceditur, et apostolica auctoritate confirmatur. Omnibus etiam nobis regni ipsius episcopis eadem auctoritate iniungitur quatinus ei tanquam apostolice sedis legato humiliter obediamus, et ad eius uocationem absque contradictione conueniamus, et super his que ad nostrum spectant officium ei plene respondeamus, et que statuerit firmiter obseruanda suscipiamus.
15 Adicitur etiam ut omnes, qui beneficia clericorum archiepiscopi in eorum absentia mandato uestro perceperunt, ad plenam eorum infra duos menses restitutionem anathematis sententia omni apellatione remota compellamus. Denarium etiam beati Petri a fratribus et coepiscopis nostris precipimur exigere, et nuntiis destinatis ad nos integre consignare. Literas etiam legationis iamdicte et literas archiepiscopi
20 quas ad plures transmittit episcopos, ipsis aut mittere aut presentare precipimur, si in nostri status et ordinis integritate ulterius perseuerare curamus. Ad pedes itaque sublimitatis uestre corde prostrati deposcimus, ne ob magna negotia que cura regia suministrat, respicere desinatis in nos, sed ne in summam nostri ignominiam ex toto redigamur in nichilum, pietate regia prouideatis. Quod quidem bene facietis, si
25 mandatis apostolicis pace uestra obedire concesseritis, et reddito denario beati Petri, et clericis que sua sunt in misericordia uestra restitutis, episcopis omnibus mandaueritis, ut si in litteris archiepiscopi aduersus regni consuetudinem grauamen aliquod intellexerint, ad domnum papam statim uel ad legatos qui diriguntur ad nos confidenter apellent. Sic enim opus misericordie perficietis, et nos ab inobedientie
30 reatu conseruabitis, et cause uestre ne in aliquo detrimentum accipiat, comuni omnium apellatione prouidebitis. Doceat uos Dominus facere uoluntatem suam, et eam subleuare moneat quam ad presens experimur angustiam. Valeat domnus meus in Christo carissimus.

**168** 1–2 Domno...seipsum *in* BD *only* 4–5 compellamur BD; compellimur *corrected to* compellamur C; compellimur Co; compellamur *corrected to* compellemur Ia; compellemur *corrected to* compellamur Ib 8 Lundoniis Ib; Lundon' B; Lond' D; Londoniis IaCCo (*in margin of* O: [...] conuersione sancti Pauli [...] anno [...] exilii) 11 auctorite B 13 conueniamus] aliqua ueniamus BD 17 sententia *omitted in* D 21 curamus BDCCo; curauimus *corrected to* curamus Ia; curauimus Ib 24 si] BD *add* nos 25 uestra] ad presens *add* BD; *om. ceteri* 29 enim *om.* BD (*in margin of* O, *near* legatos: W. et Oth.) 30 (?) nostre IbCCo

## 169 To King Henry II

[Late 1166]The king had entrusted the churches of the archbishop's clerks in the diocese of London and in Kent to Gilbert's care. He has now received a mandate from the archbishop to restore the churches within forty days; Gilbert has appealed against the mandate, but none the less asks to be relieved of the charge and of the money he has collected from the churches. He also asks for more lenient treatment towards and the restoration (? release) of William the chaplain[1] and other clerks.

Shortly after Becket's flight in 1164, the churches of his clerks were confiscated by royal order; those in the diocese of London and in Kent were put into Gilbert's hands. It was probably early in 1166[2] that the pope wrote *MB Epp.* 164–5 threatening censures if restitution was not made to Becket and his clerks; in *MB Epp.* 166 Becket forwarded these letters to Gilbert. Soon after, on 7 April (or 3 May)[3] the Pope wrote direct to Gilbert, demanding restitution within two months and forbidding appeal. Late in 1166, in *MB Epp.* 223 (p. 496; cf. p. 219), Becket once again demanded restitution, this time shortening the term to forty days. This was evidently the mandate referred to in no. 169; and a date late in 1166 also fits the reference to William the chaplain. It was stated in November 1166 that Gilbert had paid the revenues into the exchequer.[4]

Domno suo dilectissimo illustri Angl(orum) regi H(enrico) frater G(ilebertus) Lundoniensis ecclesie minister, salutem que nunc est et quam speramus a Domino.

Placuit excellentie uestre quod ecclesie clericorum archiepiscopi que in episcopatu Lund(oniensi) siue in Cantia consistunt, sub nostra essent custodia constitute. Quod quia pietatis affectu uobis intelleximus inspiratum, ne per manus scilicet laicas 5 dispensarentur res ecclesiastice, oblationes scilicet fidelium, elemosine pauperum et decimationes populorum, aliter quam fas est, tractarentur; nos cum multa et mera

**169** G, no. 274; *MB Epp.* 167; Lupus, I, 185–6 (i, 123); B, fo. 74; D, fo. 71 r–v; Ia, pp. 278–9; Ib, fos. 440v–441; C, fos. 82v (81v)–83 (82); Co, fo. 44r–v; Vb, fos. 104v–105; O, *not foliated*, no. 124; Bn, fo. 169v; Ar, fos. 94–5 (*variants of* VbOBn *and* Ar *not normally noted*) (*headings*: IaIbCCoVb Henrico (H. Ia) regi Anglie Gillebertus (CVb; *G. ceteri*) Londoniensis episcopus; O G. Lond' episcopus H. regi Angl').
1–2 Domno...Domino *in* BD *only* (Anglor' D)   4 custodite BD   6 pauperum elemosine BD

---

[1] He had been imprisoned by Alan de Neville somewhere in the diocese of Salisbury, on a royal mandate, in 1165 or 1166; see *MB*, III, 78, 413 f.; *MB Epp.* 88, 235, 246, 248, 252 (the last four late 1166): Diceto, I, 332 (Alan's excommunication, *s.a.* 1168). This was one of Becket's urgent grievances in late 1166.

[2] I.e. a few months before *MB Epp.* 178, which was evidently the next step in the campaign for the restoration of the churches. An earlier date—e.g. late 1165—is not impossible, but most of the other references to William the chaplain belong to the end of 1166.

[3] *MB Epp.* 178. If Robertson's apparatus is to be trusted, 7 April is better supported by manuscript evidence. Alexander dated letters from the Lateran in May 1166 and May 1167; but *MB Epp.* 254 shows that Gilbert had given up the money he had acquired from the churches before early November 1166.

[4] *MB Epp.* 254. For the date cf. Eyton, *Itinerary*, p. 101; it must have been written shortly before 18 November 1166, when Henry II was expected at Tours. It refers to a report of the deaths of Earl Geoffrey (of Essex, 21 October) and Robert bishop of Lincoln—who, however, seems to have died on or about 27 December 1166 (see Biog. Index). Cf. *MB*, III, 82: 'ecclesiarum...curam...circa anni finem regi resignauit'.

(Deus scit) caritate libenter onus illud suscepimus, ut et uos a peccato in parte hac mundum et immunem seruaremus, et clericos nichilominus si quando debita
10 humilitate uestram recuperarent gratiam, indempnes pariter conseruaremus. Archiepiscopus autem, qui quasi sedens in insidiis[1] aduersus meam specialiter personam occasiones querit, inde michi nocere nititur, unde aliis prodesse studebam. Qui directis litteris michi nuper iniunxit in ui obedientie et in uirtute Spiritus Sancti, ut quicquid ex eisdem recepissem ecclesiis, infra quadraginta dies post
15 litterarum susceptionem, sibi suisque clericis restituere non omitterem. Ego uero, inuocata Spiritus Sancti gratia, obiectoque appellationis remedio, mandatum quo meam iniuste uolebat grauare innocentiam, usque ad audientiam domni pape suspendi, suspensumque declinaui ad tempus, certus quidem quod hec et grauiora his supra dorsum meum fabricantur ab eo, et ab assistentibus illi. Hinc est quod
20 uestre sullimitati supplico in ea fiducia qua me semper audire consueuistis, ut custodiam predictarum ecclesiarum alii cui honeste prouideritis committatis, et me si placet hoc onere eximatis, ut alia que michi parantur onera fortius sustinere et promtius possim explicare in Domino. Pecuniam quoque quam exinde recepi et consignaui, ad summam centum octo libras et quatuordecim solidos et sex denarios,
25 peto si placet liceat michi cum gratia et permissione uestra in tuto deponere penes quamcumque personam ecclesiasticam, eamque—licet ingratis hiis quorum gratia fit—adhuc consignatam saluamque conseruare, donec Dominus indicauerit ad quem debeat exitum res ista deuenire.

Superest adhuc aliud in quo tota uobis nobiscum supplicat Anglorum ecclesia, et
30 illi precipue qui salutem uestram et honorem uestrum maxime diligunt et amplectuntur. Durius enim quam uestre expediat magnificentie agitur apud nos cum illis, *quos Dominus domesticos suos esse constituit, quos in priuatam asciscit familiam, quos mense sue dispensatores ordinauit, cum sacerdotibus uidelicet, qui in regno Anglie nec laica fruuntur libertate, nec iudiciis tractantur ecclesiasticis. In quo si
35 omnes tacent, ego non tacebo; si omnes desperant, sed non ⟨fo. 74 v⟩ ego. Absens igitur corpore, sed spiritu presens, oro et obsecro uos per salutem uestram et propter salutem uestram, ut Willelmum quondam capellanum archiepiscopi et quamplures clericos per Angliam, quos nec confessos nec conuictos uestri prius presumunt quam iudicent punire ministri ecclesie Dei cuius sunt obsequiis deputati,
40 restitui iubeatis. Valete.

**169**   13,14 iniunxit/Sancti] B *has* b *and* a *over these words as if for transposition*   15 clericis *om.* Ib; restituere clericis D; restituere clericis *marked for transposition* B   16 appellationis] C (*in margin*) prima epistola proxima (*i.e.* no. 198—? *for* no. 167, *three later*); O (*in margin*) Mittimus uobis litteras Vniuersis oppressis (*MB Epp.* 178). Ante appellationem episcoporum ut uidetur (?) 18 declinari D *and* (*before correction*) B   23 expedire BD   24 libras/solidos/denarios] C *adds* (*interlin.*) uel -rum/uel -rum/uel -orum   26 eamque—] et *added in* BD   28 exitum *inserted in* B; debeat *om.* D   29 tota *om.* D   32 *quos] quod ? *corrected* B   32 ascisscit *corrected to* asciuit B; assciuit O; ascistit *ceteri*   34 Anglorum C   36 spiritu presens] non spiritu D (presens *ins. in* B)   36-7 IaIbCo *omit* et propter salutem uestram; *omitted, but inserted in margin* C   38-9 prius...ministri IaIbCCo; prius punire presumunt (*marginal addition*) quam iudicare ministri B; prius punire quam iudicent ministri D

---

[1] Cf. Ps. ix (2). 8.

## 170  To Thomas Becket, archbishop of Canterbury

[Late 1166] He answers the archbishop's charges in circumstantial detail, by denouncing the archbishop's past life and present actions.

On this, Gilbert's most celebrated letter, *Multiplicem nobis*, see *GF*, pp. 166–87.

Venerabili domno et patri in Christo Thome Cantuariensi archiepiscopo Gillebertus Londoniensis ecclesie minister, salutem.

Multiplicem nobis et diffusam late materiam profunde, pater, et copiose rescribendo proponitis, et nos, licet super appellatione ad domnum papam prosequenda sollicitos, uestre tamen sublimitati rescribere graui quidem et nos grauiter urgente 5 necessitate compellitis. Emissis enim sparsim elogiis, nos de toto fratrum nostrorum collegio, seorsum ponitis ad conuitia,[1] ut singulariter in nos etsi inmeritos ignominiosa congeratis et probra. Sobrii sensus hominem, grauitatis reuerende personam, magistrum ratione prelationis et dogmatis ueritati reuerenter obnoxium, mirum est ad uerba ueritatis exarsisse tam grauiter, et uelut euocatum ad coleras, innocentiam 10 filii pie patri consulentem, non solum non admisisse, sed et ipsius opinionem nota quadam malitie cuius sibi minime conscius est, eius non id exigente merito, respersisse. Vnde cum *ecclesiam* Dei sub*uertere, fas nefasque confundere*, montem illum qui ecclesia et columpna Dei uiuentis est non sano capite uelle deicere, ad ea que uestra sunt ambisse, et quod ab his optinendis repulsi fuerimus, ob id uestram 15 ecclesieque Dei pacem temere perturbasse, in bello Domini terga dedisse, emissis scriptis publice denotemur,[2] difficile est ut sileamus, ut hanc aduersum nos opinionem uel a presentibus admitti, uel indefensam future posteritati transmitti, confessionem innuente silentio permittamus.

Cum sit itaque malorum radix et origo cupiditas,[3] ne nos huius suspectos habeant 20 quibus praua suadentur e facili, nos hinc ipsa iubet necessitas exordiri. Ait apostolus: 'Quis scit hominum occulta hominis, nisi spiritus hominis qui est in ipso?'[4] Latent quidem homines occulta hominum, et abyssum cordium de celo Dominus intuetur. Ipsum ignota non transeunt, occulta non fallunt. 'Est enim sermo Dei uiuus et efficax, penetrabiliorque omni gladio ancipiti. Nec est ulla creatura inuisibilis in 25 conspectu illius.'[5] Ipsi et coram ipso loquimur; sub ipsius examine non uana aut ficta, set que ueritate conscientie subnixa sunt, confidenter et libere respondemus

**170** G, no. 194; *MB Epp.* 225; Lyttelton, pp. 185–99; B, fo. 200 v; D, fos. 65–71; C, fos. 93 (92)–100 (99) (*headings*: Thome Cant' archiepiscopo Gillebertus Londoniensis episcopus. cxxvi. C; G. Lund' episcopus. Th. Cantuar' archiepiscopo D); *noted in index of* Vb, *at bk i, nos. cix, cxxix, but omitted from text—see above, pp. 3–4, 20–1; Plate IV.*
1–2 Venerabili...salutem C; Venerabili patri et domno T. Cantuar' archiepiscopo B; Venerabili patri et domno Thom' archiepiscopo Cant' D (*space left in* B *and* D *as if for author's title and greeting*)   5 tamen uestre B   8 Sobrii] BD *add* uero   14 uiuentis Dei B   21 ipsa *om.* C
26 illius] uel eius *ins.* C

[1] *MB Epp.* 224.
[2] For these charges, see *MB Epp.* 223–4 *passim*. The words in italics echo *MB Epp.* 224, p. 512: 'ad omne fas nefasque confundendum, statum sancte ecclesie...uelle euertere'.
[3] Cf. I Tim. vi. 10.   [4] I Cor. ii. 11.   [5] Heb. iv. 12–13.

asserentes utique quoniam ad ea que uestra sunt ambitionis stimulos nunquam uel momento sensimus, honorem hunc nulli umquam inuidimus.[1] Nulli ad hanc
30 gratiam munere uel obsequio, gratia uel fauore deseruiuimus, ut ad huius fastigia culminis accessum nobis sacrilegum quibuscumque modis aut amminiculis aptaremus. Quis hoc melius, pater, quam uos, quis poterit liquidius estimare, quem ipsius ecclesie tunc temporis archidiaconum, et domni nostri regis electum e milibus non consiliarium solummodo, set cor fuisse constat et consilium, sine quo
35 non quidem facile, set nec erat possibile ad hec omnino quempiam obtinere progressum? Nobis itaque quam apud uos gratiam collocauimus? Num per nos aut per alium uestram unquam gratiam xeniis aut obsequiis attentauimus, ut ad quod nisi per uos attingi non poterat, in id ope uestra subleuaremur? Hinc uestram, pater, iustum est metiri prudentiam, ⟨fo. 201⟩ quales nos aliis exhibuerimus, qui nec
40 uestre celsitudini quam rerum summa sequebatur ad turpe supplicare compendium, nec aliqua fauoris gratia unquam, uel in modico blandiri curauimus. Rem hoc fine concludimus, hoc nobis onus ipsi confidenter inponimus, ut sit nobis illa die repositum, si nos huius culpe conscios in aliquo reprehendit cor nostrum. Non nostram itaque, pater, non nostram in uestra promotione repulsam planximus: illo
45 quidem die non nostra querere, sed que Domini nostri Iesu Christi, non nobis sed eius nomini in omnibus gloriam exhiberi, toto cordis affectu desiderauimus.[2] Attendentes rem secus fieri, condoluimus. Cernentes ius ecclesie subuerti, fas nefasque confundi, montis illius magni quem dicitis[3] deorsum cacumen inflecti, sponsam Christi libertate pristina—sibi semper usque tunc obseruata reuerenter et
50 exhibita—inuerecunde priuari, altis utique in Domino suspiriis ingemuimus, et dolorum quos nunc experimur assidue prelibationes et presagia certa quadam diuini spiritus insinuatione multi quidem in ecclesia Dei presensimus. Oportebat equidem eius tunc meminisse quod scriptum est: 'difficile est ut bono peragantur exitu, que malis fuerint inchoata principiis'.[4] Ad ipsa quidem si recurramus initia,
55 quis toto orbe nostro, quis ignorat, quis tam resupinus ut nesciat uos certa licitatione proposita cancellariam illam dignitatem multis marcharum milibus obtinuisse, et aure huius impulsu in portum Cantuariensis ecclesie illapsum, ad eius sic tandem regimen accessisse? Quam pie, quam sancte, quam canonice, quo uite merito id exigente, multis quidem notum est, et stilo quodam doloris intimi bonorum est
60 cordibus exaratum.

Diem suum clauserat ille bonus et bone memorie pater noster Thedbaldus ecclesie Cantuariensis dudum archiepiscopus, et uos qui cordis oculos in casum hunc peruigiles minime claudebatis, confestim a Normannia celeres in Angliam reditus

170 32 pater melius BD    37 per *om.* BD    47 ecclesie ius BDC    57 ecclesie Cantuariensis BD    61 Thedbaldus B; Theodbaldus C; Tedbaldus D    62 Canturiensis B

---

[1] For this charge, see *MB Epp.* 224, p. 517; cf. *GF*, pp. 149–51.
[2] Cf. Phil. ii. 21; Ps. cxiii (2). 1.
[3] *MB Epp.* 224, p. 512, and above.
[4] Not identified. On the charge that Becket paid for the chancellorship see *GF*, p. 171 and n.; Knowles, *Historian and Character*, p. 106 and n.

habuistis.[1] Ex interuallo directus est a domni nostri regis latere uir magnus et sapiens moderator regni Ricardus de Luci, quem laqueis anathematis innodatum hodie 65 digne sic merito honorastis. Regis hic ad omnes habebat imperium, ut Cantuarienses monachi et ecclesie ipsius episcopi suffraganei uos expeterent, uos eligerent, uos in patrem et pastorem, negotium nulla deliberationum mora protrahentes assumerent; alioquin iram regiam non utique declinarent, uerum se regis hostes et suorum procul dubio ipsis rerum argumentis agnoscerent. Quod loquimur, experto nouimus, 70 attendentes ecclesiam Dei suffocari grauiter, ob quod in eius libertatem quodammodo proclamauimus, uerbum ilico proscriptionis audiuimus, et exilio crudeliter addicti sumus[2]—nec solum persona nostra, sed et domus patris mei et coniuncta nobis affinitas, et cognatio tota; hoc quidem calice et aliis propinatum est. Scriptum uero est: 'Leo rugiet, quis non timebit?' Et illud: 'Vt rugitus leonis, sic terror regis.'[3] Quod 75 tante uoluntatis ⟨fo. 201 v⟩ impetu precipiebat rex, quod effectu compleri tanto nuntio perurgebat, in quod cordis oculos uos omnes iniecisse nouerant, in quod omnes uestri minis et terroribus, promissis et blanditiis uigilanter instabant, quis negaret? Torrenti huic uoluntati et precepti regii, quis resisteret? Stabat regni gladius in manu uestra, si in quem toruos oculos habebatis, terribilis in hunc et 80 inportabilis ire quodam uelut igne choruscans. Ille quidem gladius, quem in sancte matris ecclesie uiscera uestra manus paulo ante inmerserat, cum ad traiciendum in Tolosam exercitum tot ipsam marcarum milibus aporiastis.[4] Qui ne limatus denuo per uos aptaretur ad uulnera, iussis obtemperauit ecclesia, et declinando que metuit, simulauit se uelle quod noluit. O quam longe erant omnium corda bonorum ab 85 hoc ipso; quam dissidentia uota! Motu tamen est et inpressione completum, quod interminatione dirissima fuerat imperatum. Sic in ouile ouium, non utique per ostium sed ascendens aliunde introistis,[5] et hoc pater introitu, libertatem ecclesie tot sibi temporum conseruatam curriculis ademistis; que si eius uita est ut scribitis, ipsam utique exanimem reddidistis. Deus bone, quis horror illa die, quis omnes 90

**170** 67 ct] ut BD    68 pertrahentes BD    70 experti B    71 attendentes] BD *add* enim
80 habebatis oculos BD    82 manus paulo ante C (*partly over an erasure*); paulo ante
manus BD    89 uita eius B

[1] Herbert of Bosham (*MB*, III, 180–1) ascribes this visit, doubtless correctly, to a political purpose of Henry II's, though he prefaces it with an exchange between Henry and Becket on the king's intention that the latter should become archbishop. Gilbert seems to have begun that process of foreshortening which affects all later sources—in fact a full year ('Ex interuallo' seems hardly adequate to this) separated Theobald's death from Thomas Becket's election (see *GF*, p. 150). On Richard de Lucy, chief justiciar, see Delisle, *Recueil*, Introd., pp. 434–6; he founded Lessness abbey (former owner of MS D) and died there in 1179.

[2] This confirms other evidence that Gilbert opposed the election, though we need not take his emotive language on the price of opposition too precisely (see *GF*, p. 149, and, on the phrase 'domus patris mei', p. 40 n.).

[3] Amos iii. 8; Prov. xx. 2.

[4] On Thomas's share in the war of Toulouse in 1159, see esp. *MB*, III, 33 f., 175 f., and III, 53 f. for financial transactions connected with the campaign. Gilbert is working on the principle here of laying everything at court to Thomas's credit or discredit, and he may exaggerate Thomas's personal responsibility in the affair.    [5] Cf. Joh. x. 1 ff.

horror inuasit, cum pronosticum illud de more conspectum et circumastantium oculis est oblatum: illud inquam pronosticum, quod in futuri casus indicium ewangelista Matheo quasi uaticinante prolatum est. Ait enim Dominus ficulnee non habenti fructum: 'Nunquam ex te fructus nascatur in sempiternum'; et
95 arefacta est continuo.[1] Oportuisset igitur illa die non recta mandanti principi respondisse, quod oportet *Deo obedire magis quam hominibus*.[2] Illo utinam die corda nostra plene *timor eius* occupasset, *qui potest animam in gehennam* perdere, et non solum *corpus occidere*.[3] Quod quia secus actum est, parit nobis enormitas hec erubescentiam, erubescentia confusionem, confusio penitentiam, que condignam
100 inferet opem ferente Domino satisfactionem, adeo ut in maxillis nostris iuges lacrime perseuerent donec conuertat Dominus captiuitatem Syon,[4] et consoletur merentes in Ierusalem, et clementie reducat oculos in desolatos Ierusalem. Interim, ut quod actum est currente stilo prosequamur, sublimationis uestre quis fructus extiterit, audiamus.
105 A pio rege nostro suscepto regni gubernaculo, ad illum usque diem ecclesia quidem sancta alta pace floruerat, excepto quod, ut diximus, ad instaurandum in Tolosam exercitum manus uestras nimis in se graues agnouerat; de cetero sub bono principe cuncta gaudebant, iocundissime letabantur uniuersa. Regnum sacerdotio deuotum sancte prestabat obsequium, et sacerdotio firmissime fulciebatur ad
110 bonum omne regis imperium. Exercebantur in ecclesia gladii duo, deuoto Domino Iesu famulantes obsequio. Nec sibi stabant ex aduerso, nec tendentes in contraria, repugnabant alterutro. Vnus erat populus, et ut scriptum est unius labii,[5] studens peccata persequi, gaudens uitia fortiter ⟨fo. 202⟩ eradicari. Hec regni fuit et ecclesie pax: alterna sic gratia fouebantur, et unanimi uoluntate iungebantur. In uestra uero
115 promotione gratiarum sperabamus et expectabamus augmenta, et ecce peccatis exigentibus ilico turbata sunt uniuersa. Virtus est peccato cum exurgit occurrere, mentisque sinistros fetus ad petram que Christus est statim cum nascuntur allidere. Oportebat itaque uestram prouidisse prudentiam, ne dissensiones inter regnum et uos paululum in inmensum excrescerent, ne de scintilla tenui in multorum perniciem
120 tantus ignis exsurgeret. Actum secus est, et ob causas quas enumerare longum est, dissensiones adaucte sunt, inflammata est ira, et odium fortiter obfirmatum. Hec causa fuit; hinc emersit occasio, cur ad requirendas dignitates regias et in commune commemorandas, suum domnus noster rex animum applicauerit et consilium: quarum obseruatio cum a uobis et a suffraganeis ecclesie uestre exigeretur episcopis,
125 eo quod in quibusdam earum ecclesie Dei uidebatur libertas opprimi, assensum

**170** 93–4 fructum non habenti ficulnee BD     96 ob. op. Deo BD (*and Vulg.*)     107 nimis in se C; in se iam nimis BD     111 Nec C; Non BD     112–13 studentes peccata persequi, gaudentes (gaudens *corrected*) B; studentes peccatum persequi, gaudens D     113 et ecclesie fuit B     115–16 exigentibus ecce peccatis BD     119 paululum] BD *add* exsurgentes     120 exsurgeret] uel au(geret) *ins.* C     124 nobis B

[1] Matt. xxi. 19. This seems the only record of the prognostic taken at Becket's election (which is hardly surprising, if it is correctly reported).
[2] Cf. Act. v. 29; *MB Epp.* 223, p. 491, from which the words in italics are repeated.
[3] Cf. Lam. i. 2; Ps. cxxv. 1.     [4] Cf. Matt. x. 28.     [5] Cf. Gen. xi. 1.

dare recusauimus, preterquam his que saluo honore Dei et ordine nostro poterant obseruari. Exigebat instanter domnus noster rex obseruationes earum absolute sibi a nobis repromitti, sed quod libertati repugnabat ecclesie et domni pape fidelitati, a nobis nequaquam potuit obtineri. Ob causam hanc coacti sunt cetus, et conuocata concilia.  130

Quid meminisse opus est que sunt acta Lund(onie)?[1] que denuo Oxenefordie? Que gesta sunt Clarendone[2] ad memoriam reuocemus; ubi continuato triduo id solum actum est, ut obseruandarum regni consuetudinum et dignitatum a nobis fieret absoluta promissio. Ibi quippe uobiscum stetimus, quem in Domini Spiritu *stare fortiter* estimabamus. Stetimus quidem immobiles; stetimus imperterriti. 135 Stetimus in fortunarum dispendium, in cruciatum corporum, in subeundum exilium—subeundum quoque si sic Dominus permisisset et gladium. Quis umquam, pater, filios in sua plus habuit confessione concordes? Quis unquam plus unanimes? Inclusi eramus omnes conclaui uno. Die uero tertio, cum iam regni principes et omnes quidem nobiles in summas coleras exarsissent, facto quidem fremitu et 140 strepitu conclaue quo sedebamus ingressi, reiectis palliis exertisque brachiis, nos taliter allocuti sunt. 'Attendite qui regni statuta contempnitis, qui regis iussa non suscipitis. Non nostre sunt manus iste quas cernitis, non nostra brachia, non hec demum corpora nostra: uerum domni nostri regis hec sunt; ad omnem eius nutum, ad omnem eius ulciscendam iniuriam, ad omnem eius uoluntatem, quecunque 145 fuerit, iam nunc applicari promptissima. Ipsius mandatum quodcunque fuerit, ex sola nobis erit eius uoluntate iustissimum. Reuocate consilium, inclinate animos ad preceptum, ut declinetis dum fas est quod iam non poterit euitare periculum.' Quid ad hec? Quis fugit? Quis terga uertit? Quis animo fractus est? Vestra nobis exprobratur epistola quod *in die belli conuersi* sumus; quod *ex aduerso* non *ascend*imus; 150 quod nos *murum pro domo* Domini non *oppo*suimus. *Iudicet* Dominus *inter* nos:[3] ipse iudicet ob quem stetimus, ob quem ad minas principum flecti nequiuimus; iudicet ipse quis fugerit, quis in bello desertor extiterit. Stetit procul dubio uir nobilis et spiritus in Domino constantissimi Wintoniensis Henricus; stetit Eliensis Nigellus; stetit Lincoll(iensis) Robertus; Cicestrensis ⟨fo. 202 v⟩ Hylarius, Sares- 155 bir(iensis) Iocelinus, Exon(iensis) Bartholomeus, Cestrensis Ricardus, Wigorn(iensis) Rogerus, Herefordensis Robertus, Lundoniensis Gillebertus. His omnibus

---

**170** 129 causam hanc *marked for transposition* B    131 Londoniis C    132 Clarendone gesta sunt BD (Clarend' D; Clarendonie C)    147 erit eius uoluntate] *so* BD, *and* C *but marked to be read* uoluntate eius erit    147 inclinetis BD    155 Robertus] BD *add* stetit (Hylarius Cicestr' D)

---

[1] Gilbert refers in passing to the Council of Westminster ('London') in Oct. 1163, at which there was the first outburst of serious trouble; then the meeting at Oxford (prob. December 1163) between the king, Becket, the abbot of L'Aumône (see p. 511) and Robert of Melun, bishop elect of Hereford. Gilbert confirms Herbert of Bosham's evidence that it took place at Oxford, against Guernes and Roger of Pontigny who place it at Woodstock (see Eyton, *Itinerary*, p. 66; Robertson, *Becket*, p. 96 and n.; and, on Westminster, Knowles, *EC*, pp. 56 ff.).

[2] On Gilbert's account of the Council of Clarendon see *GF*, pp. 171–2; and for this passage cf. *MB Epp.* 223, pp. 493–4.

[3] Cf. *MB Epp.* 223, pp. 491, 493–4 (and Ezech. xiii. 5; Gen. xxxi. 49).

percussor defuit, non hii uirtuti; hii quoque temporalia reputantes ut stercora, pro Christo et ecclesia exposuerunt se et sua. Dicatur itaque quod uerum est; fiat sub
160 sole quod presentibus nobis et cernentibus actum est. Terga dedit dux militie: ipse campi ductor aufugit, a fratrum suorum collegio simul et consilio domnus Cantuariensis abscessit; et tractatu seorsum habito, ex interuallo reuersus ad nos, in hec uerba prorupit: 'Est Domini mei uoluntas ut peierem; et ad presens subeo et incurro periurium, ut potero penitentiam acturus in posterum.' Auditis his, ob-
165 stupuimus, et mutuis herendo conspectibus, ad lapsum hunc a summo, ut estimabamus, uirtutis et constantie, suspirantes ingemuimus. Non est *apud* Dominum *est et non*,[1] nec eius sperabamus sic moueri posse discipulum. Languente capite languent cito cetera menbra, et ipsius infirmitas ad cetera statim menbra dilabitur. Ipse quod exigebatur annuens, et dignitates regias et antiquas regni consuetudines,
170 antiquorum memoria in commune propositas, et scripto commendatas, de cetero se domno nostro regi fideliter obseruaturum in uerbo ueritatis absolute promittens, in ui nobis iniunxit obedientie sponsione simili nos obligare.

Sopita est hoc fine contentio: sacerdotio sic est pax conciliata cum regno. Descendit Israel in Egyptum, unde cum multa gloria legitur postmodum ascen-
175 disse. Nobis quoque spes magna resederat, quod domnus noster rex ad tempus ira motus exegerat, sedato ipsius animo, ad Dei gloriam et ipsius honorem in bonum denuo esse reformandum. Inuidit paci tenere pacis ille turbator pristinus; et qui procellis enauigatis sperabamus tenere iam portum, aquilonis ecce flatibus compellimur in profundum. Recens erat illa in uerbo ueritatis regi facta promissio, uos
180 nisi ab eo impetrata licentia non discessurum a regno. Scriptum est, 'uerba sacerdotis comitem semper habeant ueritatem'; illud quoque, 'Quod quis dicit, ueritati debet, et quod promittit, fidei'.[2] Emensis tamen diebus paucis, uentis uela commisistis, et egressum a regno, rem rege penitus ignorante, procurastis. Quo audito, nemo rege plus stupuit; nemo plus doluit. Stupuit—non esse completum quod
185 fuerat a pontifice quasi iuramento promissum. Doluit—in se graue sciens scandalum suscitari, et illesam hactenus opinionem suam ex fuga hac apud gentes et regna grauissime lacessiri. Quid enim ueritatis ignari, quod poterant ex his aliud suspicari, quam regem regie pietatis inmemorem in tiranni rabiem exarsisse, et odio Christi ministrum eius a regno suo et dominationis sue finibus expulisse? Mallet in carne
190 sua manu uestra uulnus grauissimum excepisse, quam hoc fame sue dispendium toto orbe Christiano per uos et uestros incurrisse. Quid plura? Aquilone uela perflante

170 158 non hii uirtuti *om*. C    158 queque B    163 erupit B    163 periurem B    166 constantie] uiro *ins. in* C (*but sense better without it*)    172 iniunxit obedientie D; adiunxit obedientie B; obedientie precepit C (precepit *ins., presumably to complete the sense*)    177 esse reformandum C (denuo esse *over erasure*); reformandi BD    182 promittitur BD    182 Emensis C, *with* uel r *over the* n

---

[1] Cf. *MB Epp.* 224, p. 513; II Cor. i. 18.
[2] Two unidentified quotations; the former quoted by Becket in *MB Epp.* 223, p. 498. For Becket's attempt to visit the Pope after Clarendon, see Robertson, *Becket*, p. 106. The fact of Becket's attempt is confirmed by several of the biographers, who note the king's wrath— it is improbable that Gilbert is right in saying that Henry received Becket 'benigne'.

completa fuisset iam nauigatio, nisi flatu meliore ceptis auster obstitisset, quo flante prospere, nauis ad litus unde cepit nauigare perducta est. In manus itaque regis cum uos rei deduxisset euentus, numquid iram secutus aut potentiam in uos aut excessit opere, aut est quicquam locutus aspere? Absit: at benigne susceptum et ueneratione 195 qua decuit honoratum remisit ad propria, et uos in regno manere, commissam uobis ecclesiam regere, animi uestri dilectionem et dulcedinem sibi rebus ipsis ostendere, humiliter et benigne supplicando commonuit. Vix Auster detonuerat, et iam Circius fulminabat. Motus animorum uix utrimque resederant, et ecce de nouo emersit unde feruentius ebullirent. Perlatum est ad uos mandatum regium, ut 200 cuidam regni nobilium super predio quod a uestra uendica⟨fo. 203⟩bat ecclesia, quod iustum foret exhiberetis.¹ Qui post statutos dies ad regem reuersus, asseruit se penes uos iustitiam assequi nequiuisse, et se id ipsum iuxta regni statuta coram uobis suo congruoque testium iuramento comprobasse. Quo regem prosequente diutius, et super exhibenda sibi iustitia cotidie supplicante, domni nostri regis ad uos 205 est emissa citatio, ut statuto die se uestra sublimitas sibi exhiberet, ut quod ipso mandante non egerat, eo cognoscente litemque iudicio dirimente compleret. Non est a uobis hec admissa citatio, uerum uos in hoc sibi minime pariturum declarauit a uobis ad ipsum delegata responsio. Arbitratus hoc ipso domnus rex iuri suo detrahi grauiter et potestati, ecclesiam regni iussit ad concilium Norhamtoniam 210 conuocari.²

Conuenit populus ut uir unus, et assidentibus sibi quorum id dignitati congruebat et ordini, quod dictum est super exspreto mandato suo, in querelam aduersus uos usus qua decuit modestia et uenustate proposuit. Porro quod intendit, fratrum uestrorum non expectato uel expetito consilio, uestra incontinenti confessio con- 215 firmauit, adiciens uos ob id non paruisse mandato, quod Iohannes ille qui regis ad uos mandatum pertulerat, in uestra presentia non euangelio sed troario quodam proposito iurauisset.³ Est itaque dictum in commune, causam non eam esse, ob quam mandatum regium oportuisset omisisse, regnique fore consuetudinem in offensis huiusmodi, multa pecuniaria suam rem taxante misericordia placari regem. 220 Paruit regie sublimitas uestra sentencie, ad plenum cauens super iudicati solutione. Vestram tamen non latebat prudentiam decretum illud apostolicum, quod in hunc modum expressum est, 'Nullus episcopus neque pro ciuili nec pro criminali causa, apud quemuis iudicem siue ciuilem siue militarem producatur uel exhibeatur'; et illud, 'Clericus apud secularem iudicem si pulsatus fuerit, non respondeat, aut 225

170 200 emersit *om.* BD (*in* C *over erasure*)    204 prosequente C; persequente BD    206 sibi sublimitas BD    213 aduersum BD    218 causam] BD *add* hanc    220 sua BD    221 regie *om.* BD

---

¹ On the case of John the Marshal, see Knowles, *EC*, pp. 68 ff.
² On the Council of Northampton, see Knowles, *EC*, pp. 66 ff., 163 ff.
³ I.e. was attempting to evade guilt of perjury by a trick. We cannot be sure whether this extraordinary story is true; but it is likely that Gilbert is right in saying that the archbishop refused the summons without any more obvious excuse (such as illness, alleged by William of Canterbury and Grim, against FitzStephen: on this problem see Knowles, *EC*, pp. 69–70 n.).

proponat?' et illud Gelasii pape ad Elpidium episcopum, 'Quo ausu, qua temeritate rescribis ad Rauennam te parare proficisci, cum canones euidenter precipiant nullum omnino pontificum nisi nobis ante uisis aut consultis, ad comitatum debere contendere?'[1] Sed hec altiori forte scientia et spiritu clariore discernitis, et quia
230 regem unctio diuina sanctificat[2] ungitur ei manus in sanctitatem operum, brachiorum nexus in castitatem complexuum, pectus in cordis munditiam, scapule in laborum pro Christo tolerantiam; crismate capud infunditur ut secundum Christum (a quo crisma dictum est) et eius nomine consecratum, apto semper moderamine studeat sibi credita dispensare—ipsum a ceteris secernitis, et iudicem non
235 secularem tantummodo sed et ecclesiasticum reputatis. Ad quod roborandum id fortasse proponitis, quod imperiali iudicio papa Leo quartus emendare uoluit, si quid in subditos iniuste commisit, Ludouico Augusto sic scribens: 'Nos, si incompetenter aliquid egimus, et in subditis iuste legis tramitem non conseruauimus, uestro aut missorum uestrorum cuncta uolumus emendari iudicio, ut eorum legitti-
240 mo cuncta terminentur examine, ne sit in posterum quod indiscretum ualeat permanere.'[3] Si uobis mens ista est, discretioni uestre quamplurium in hoc consentit opinio, ut ob sacramenti reuerentiam regem estiment non omnes, sed, quas distingunt, ecclesie et personarum ecclesie causas oportere discutere, et regie iuriditionis examine terminare. Habet enim ecclesia quedam diuino tantum iure,
245 quedam ut testantur humano. Gradus ecclesiasticos, ordines sacros et dignitates hiis choerentes et potestates, diuino tantum iure sortitur. Vnde si baptizat aut consecrat, soluit aut ligat, predicat et informat, hec tantum spiritualia sunt, collata desuper ab homine in hominem, non hominis dono, sed diuino intus operante spiritu propagata. Hunc sibi nemo sumit honorem, sed qui uocatur a Deo tanquam Aaron; affectaue-
250 runt hec Chore, Dathan et Abiron a Domino non uocati, et inaudita morte perierunt.[4] Inmiscentes se sacrificiis Geroboham et Ozias, alter manus aridi⟨fo. 203 v⟩tate, alter lepra percussi sunt.[5] Est igitur in his omnibus sacerdos quilibet ut pater, ut pastor, omni rege superior: rex ut filius, ut discipulus, longe inferior estimatur. Si itaque rex delinquat in Deum, imitando Theodosium, conciliari studeat opera sacer-
255 dotum.[6] Si sacerdotes se accusent alterutro, hec suo rex non usurpet iudicio; sed ne patrum uerenda conspiciat, incedens retrorsum queque huiusmodi pallio laudis

**170** 230 regum, *with* personas *ins.* B    230 unguitur ei *corrected to* ungitur ei C; unguntur ei *corrected to* unguntur enim B; unguitur ei D    235 solummodo BD    237 Ludewico C; Ludeuico *corrected* B    241 quamplurimum B    247 collata C; collocata B *corrected*; collocata D    250 morta B    253 rege] uel grege *ins.* C    254 Deum] Dominum BD    256 queque C; quemque D; *om.* B, *with* causam *ins.*

[1] *Decretum*, C. 11, q. 1, cc. 8, 17 = 47; C. 23, q. 8, c. 26.
[2] On this account of royal anointing, see *GF*, pp. 176–7; and cf. Becket's reference to it in *MB Epp.* 154, p. 280.
[3] *Decretum*, C. 2, q. 7, c. 41; cf. *GF*, p. 174 n.
[4] Cf. Num. xvi; xxvi. 9–11.
[5] Cf. III Reg. xiii. 4; II Para. xxvi. 19. These are conventional examples for this kind of argument; no precise source has been found for Gilbert's discussion at this point.
[6] Referring to the famous story of the Emperor Theodosius accepting rebuke from St Ambrose (cf. Ambrose, *Ep.* I, 51, *PL*, XVI, 1209 ff., esp. 1213–14; Cassiodorus, *Hist. tripartita*, IX, 30).

operiat.[1] Sunt et ecclesie corporalia quedam diuino tantum iure possessa. In his decime numerantur, oblationes et primitie, que segregando sibi sanctificauit Dominus, et in usus sibi ministrantium eterna lege sanciuit. Que quia diuino tantum iure percipit, ad cognoscendum super his potestas se regia non extendit. Humano 260 uero iure multa possidet, que sola sibi sunt hominum donatione concessa, non id precipiente Domino uel legem super hoc statuente, ut iam non leuitica solum portione sit limitata, uerum donis eximiis et possessionibus ampliata. Transtulerunt ad eam ampla sua patrimonia reges, transtulerunt electi principes, ut iam sit etiam corporaliter impletum, quod de filiis ecclesie dudum est, propheta uaticinante, 265 predictum, 'Fortitudinem gentium comedetis, et in gloria eorum superbietis'; et illud, 'Vt det illis hereditatem gentium'; item Ysaias, 'Dilata tentorium tuum, longos fac funiculos tuos; ad dextram et ad leuam dilataberis'.[2]

Vetus quidem habet historia in opus illud tabernaculi antiquum illum populum ea deuotione contulisse donaria, ut compulsi artifices dicerent Moysi: 'Plus offert 270 populus quam necesse est.'[3] Quorum quantacunque deuotio, filiis tamen gratie non equatur; quibus sepenumero satis non est donare singula, nisi supererogent uniuersa. Est uero cuique liberum, cum transfert donando quod suum est, donationi condicionem quam uelit annectere, quam tamen nec legibus nec bonis constet moribus obuiare. Hanc itaque donationi regum condicionem annexam estimant, hoc 275 consuetudine tot temporum obtinente curriculis affirmant, ut regibus ecclesie militaria et annexa prediis alia quedam persoluant obsequia, et possessiones ipsas a regibus, persone sue principalis hominio et fidelitate presente euangelio promissa, ⟨donatas (?)⟩ recognoscant.[4] Sic igitur ecclesie geminata potestas est, ut hinc regi celesti seruiat, hinc terreno principi quod ad eos spectat exhibeat; eiusque ministros 280 efficit potestas hinc a Deo collata pontifices, hinc a rege suscepta comites aut barones. Potestas hec est, qua magnum in palatio obtinet ecclesia principatum, cum in omnibus regni iudiciis, preterquam si de uite periculo tractetur aut sanguine, locum habeat ipsa precipuum. Hec regi nos obligat, ut affirmant, ut ab ipso citati debeamus assistere, et singulorum causas uniuersi discutere et iudicare. Nam qui in 285 his que ad Deum sunt gradu quodam distinguimur, ut superiores quidam, inferiores alii reputemur et simus, nos in hoc pares estimant, ut si de fundis ad ecclesiam liberalitate regia deuolutis, inter nos aut in nos fuerit oborta contentio, apud regem que spectant ad singulos uniuersorum definiat pronuntiatio. Nec mirum si patrem

---

**170** 263 limitata sit BD    272 non satis BD    274 quam tamen] quantum C (*prob. misreading* quātn̄)    274 constat C    281 aut] uel et *ins.* C    288 aborta BD    289 diffiniat BD

---

[1] Cf. Gen. ix. 23; Is. lxi. 3. On the discussion which follows of the distinction of temporalities and spiritualities among the Church's possessions, see *GF*, pp. 177–8, where it is suggested that Gilbert is taking up the threads of a conventional argument based on current practice rather than specifically following Gerhoh of Reichersberg (as has been supposed).

[2] Is. lxi. 6; Ps. cx. 7; Is. liv. 2–3.

[3] Ex. xxxvi. 1–5.

[4] I.e. a frank acceptance of the concession made by Paschal II to Henry I (see R. W. Southern, *St Anselm and his Biographer*, pp. 178–9); the next sentence draws the distinction between bishops as bishops and bishops as earls and barons made by Lanfranc: see *GF*, p. 177 and n.

290 teneat a filio lata sententia, cum ipsum qui est filius patris sui domnum fore conuin-
cat ratio manifesta, et cum hominio fidelitas reuerenter exhibita.

Cum sit igitur a Deo gemina potestas, hinc sacerdotalis, hinc regia, utramque
secundum quid preesse alteri, et ab altera secundum quid posse iudicari patrum
auctoritate confirmant; ut sit regum et presulum uicissitudo hec qua se uicissim
295 iudicant et iudicantur a se forte quoddam caritatis uinculum, reuerentie debitum, et
utrique necessitudo quedam conseruande pacis ad alterum. Hec et his altiora considerans, regem quasi precellentem, prout monet apostolus,[1] honorastis, et eius
parendo sententie recte iudicem agnouistis, sibique seruando quod suum est, ipsum
in hiis que ad Deum sunt, uestre parere sublimitati prudenter et prouide monuistis.
300 Omni humane creature propter Deum sancta se summittit humilitas, et quo se
deicit inferius, eo iuxta uerbum Domini meretur altius et gloriosius exaltari. Atque
in his utinam humilitatis finibus res ipsa tota resedisset, et cum a uobis quedam
debita reposceret domnus noster rex, cum de summa pecunie quam in manu uestra
ex caducis quibusdam excreuisse memorabat, quod ius dictaret id sibi solum peteret
305 exhiberi, ad declinandum regalis curie iudicium tunc se ⟨fo. 204⟩ uester minime
zelus erexisset. Nam quid poterat inferre periculi danda super hac petitione sententia? Ad regimen ecclesie uos a curia transferri uoluit, et ab ipsius nexibus hoc ipso
uos, ut plures opinantur, absoluit. Quod si ad debita minime referendum est, ut
euectus loco sic absoluatur a debito, poterat negotium per exceptionem in rem
310 uersum plurimum expediri, et si quid compoto nequiuisset includi, irate magis
repetenti sua quam auide de reliquo poterat satis dari, et ciuilis hec causa absque hoc
rerum turbine pace poterat honestissima terminari.[2] Sed inauditum dicitis, ut in
regis curia *Cantuariensis* umquam compelleretur ad talia; et id dixeritis in*audi*tum,
officialem curie repentino transitu ad illam sic ecclesiam umquam hactenus ascen-
315 disse, ut hodie quis curiam, cras dispensaret ecclesiam, ab auibus et canibus ceterisque
curie iocundis usibus, cito quis astaret altaribus, et episcopis totius regni spiritualia
ministraret et sacerdotibus. Vsus igitur in diuersa tendente consilio, domum regiam
crucem gestans in manibus introistis,[3] et execrande cuiusdam malitie suspectum
regem omnibus ilico reddidistis; at eius innocentiam summis efferendam preconiis
320 patientia declarauit. Illationem crucis aduersum se etsi moleste tulerit, fines tamen
regie modestie non excessit. Non ira motus efferbuit, non uerbo malignatus aut
opere; causam quam sua repetens intenderat, fine studuit iustitie debito terminare.
At declinando iudicium ad domnum papam appellastis, et sicut in ingressu sic in
egressu uestro, summam regis mansuetudinem et tolerantiam uobis obseruate pacis
325 indiciis agnouistis. Nam ut in Absalonem prodeunte exercitu paterna pietas

170 290–1 cum...manifesta *om.* C (cum/et cum)    292 potestas gemina BD    302–3 debita
quedam BD    303 uestra] BD *add* uelut    305 tunc] utinam BD    314 hactenus] sic *added in* C

[1] Cf. I Pet. ii. 17.
[2] On the question of the archbishop's debts, see Knowles, *EC*, pp. 69 ff. The next sentence
echoes *MB Epp.* 223, p. 494.
[3] See Knowles, *EC*, pp. 77–8 and nn. Gilbert now jumps from the early stages of the Council of
Northampton (8–9 Oct. 1164) to its concluding phase (13 Oct.: see *EC*, pp. 163 ff.), the final
day which started with Becket entering the castle holding his cross and ended with his flight.

exclamauit, 'Seruate michi puerum Absalon',[1] sic eius mandato uoce statim preconaria cunctis innotuit, ut si quis uobis aut e uestris cuiquam molestus existeret, ultore gladio deperiret. Addidistis ad hec, et tanquam uite uestre uel sanguini machinaretur insidias, fuga nocte inita, mutato habitu, post latitationem aliquantulam a regno clam transmeastis, et nemine persequente, nullo uos expellente, extra 330 dominationis sue loca in regno uobis altero ad tempus sedem elegistis. Inde nauem disponitis gubernare, quam in fluctibus et tempestate subducto remige reliquistis; hinc nos uestra iubet auctoritas et hortatur, ut conuertamur ad uos et salui simus,[2] ut uestris inherendo uestigiis pro Christo mortem subeamus, et pro liberanda ipsius ecclesia animas ponere non metuamus. Et utique, si attendamus quanta nobis 335 promittantur in celis, debeant animo uilescere quecunque possidentur in terris. Nam nec lingua dicere, nec intellectus capere ualet, illa superne ciuitatis quanta sint gaudia—angelorum choris interesse, cum beatissimis spiritibus glorie conditoris assistere, presentem Dei uultum cernere, nullo metu mortis affici, incorruptionis sue munere perpetuo gloriari. Passiones huius temporis minime condigne sunt ad 340 futuram gloriam que reuelabitur in sanctis; et quod modo leue est et momentaneum tribulationis, supra omnem modum eterne glorie pondus operabitur in electis.[3] Hec nostris iamdiu sensibus insederunt; nostra iamdiu studia hec post se promissa traxerunt. Caput utinam quod michi scapulis insidet lictoris gladius proiecisset in medium, dum tantum legittimo Deoque placito certamine decertassem. At martirem 345 non pena facit, sed causa.[4] Dura sancte perpeti gloria est: improbe pertinaciter ignominia. Pro Christo subire gladium consummata laus est et uictoria: hunc in se temere prouocare, late patens insania. Et si uestra, pater, non solum dicta, uerum facta pensemus, in mortem nec temere nec leuiter inpingemus. Nam genu Clarendonie curuando, fugam Norhamtone ineundo, mutato ad tempus habitu delites- 350 cendo, a regni finibus clam emigrando, quid actum est? Quid hec agendo procurastis, nisi quod mortem quam nemo dignabatur inferre tam sollicite declinastis? Nos igitur ad mortem qua fronte, pater, inuitastis, quam uos et formidasse et fugisse, indiciis tam manifestis toti mundo luce clarius ostendistis? Que uos suadet caritas, nobis onus imponere quod abiecistis? Gladius nobis imminet quem fugistis, 355 in quem funda iacire non dimicare cominus elegistis. Ad similem forte fugam nos inuitastis; at nobis mare clausum est, et post discessum uestrum naues nobis sunt omnes et portus inibiti. Insule terrarum claustra regum fortissima sunt, unde uix euadere uel se quis ualeat expedire. Si nobis pugnandum est, de proximo contendemus. Si cum rege pugna conseritur, unde percutiemus gladio, nos ibi gladius 360

---

**170** 327 enotuit B    332 gubernare disponitis BD (*the text is a cursus velox*)    333 et hortatur auctoritas BD (a. e. h. *corrected*) (*the text is a cursus velox*)    340 gloriari] letari B    345 tamen C 348 dicta solum BD    349 leuiter C, *with* uel n (*i.e.* leniter) *ins.*    349–50 Clarendone C, B (*corrected*); Clarendon' D    353 fronte] mente B    356 iacere *MSS*    356–7 nos forte fugam BD; quam uos *added in* B *after* inuitastis, *then cancelled*    359 euadere] eundum B (euad'e *read as* eunde', *then corrected*)    359 ualet C

---

[1] II Reg. xviii. 5.    [2] Cf. Is. xlv. 22.
[3] Cf. Rom. viii. 18; II Cor. iv. 17.
[4] A patristic commonplace.

repercutientis inueniet; unde uulnus ⟨fo. 204 v⟩ infligemus, uulnera declinare nequibimus.[1] Et annui uestri redditus, nunquid uobis tanti sunt ut fratrum uestrorum sanguine uobis hos uelitis acquiri? At Iuda reportante pecuniam, hanc Iudei respuerunt, quam sanguinis esse pretium agnouerunt.[2] Sed aliam nobis causam 365 fortasse proponitis.

Paululum itaque diuertamus, ut mortis nobis suadende causam plenius attendamus. Gratias Domino, nulla penes nos est de fide contentio, de sacramentis nulla, nulla de moribus. Viget recta fides in principe, uiget in prelatis, uiget in subditis. Omnes fidei articulos regni huius ecclesia sane complectitur. A summi pontificis 370 obedientia presentis scismatis insania nemo diuiditur.[3] Ecclesie sacramenta uenerantur omnes et excolunt. Suscipiunt in se et aliis pie sancteque communicant. Quod ad mores, in multis quidem offendimus omnes; errorem tamen suum nullus predicat aut defendit, uerum penitentie remedio sperat posse dilui quod admittit. Tota igitur in regem est et de rege contentio, ob quasdam consuetudines suis predecessoribus 375 obseruatas, ut asserit, et exhibitas, quas sibi uult et expetit obseruari.[4] Super hoc a uestra sublimitate commonitus, non desistit a proposito, non renuntiat iis que firmauit antiquitas et longa regni consuetudo. Hec est causa cur ad arma decurritis, et in sanctum caput et nobile gladium librare contenditis. In quo refert plurimum quod has ipse non statuit, sed ut tota regni testatur antiquitas, sic eas repperit 380 institutas. Nam difficilius euellitur quod altius radicatur; heret planta tenacius que suas in altum iamdiu radices inmiserit. Quam si quis transferre desiderat, non uiribus euellenda est, ne protinus exarescat. Circumfodienda est prius, et humus est eicienda, denudanda radix undique, ut sic prudens expleat diligentia quod uis commode non expleret incompetenter adhibita. A bonis exempla sumenda sunt, et 385 cum tractantur huiusmodi, ipsorum sunt opera diligentius attendenda. Predecessor uester[5] ille pater Augustinus multa a regno hoc exstirpauit enormia, et ipsum regem fide illuminans prauas ab eo consuetudines non quidem paucas eliminauit, non maledictis equidem, sed benedicendo potius et predicando, exhortando salubriter, et potentum animos ad bonum fortiter inclinando. Cremensis ille Iohannes diebus 390 nostris in partes has a sancta Romana ecclesia directus, regni consuetudines in

170 377 causa est BD 379 non ipse B 381 immiserat C 382 prius est et est humus BD 386 uester] BD *add* maximus 386 regem *om.* BD 389 et] BD *add* sic 390 directus ecclesia BD

---

[1] Cf. *MB Epp.* 223, pp. 493, 501–2; *GF*, p. 172.

[2] Cf. Matt. xxvii. 3 ff. (and *MB Epp.* 224, p. 516, where Thomas repudiates the role of Judas).

[3] Cf. *GF*, p. 184 and n. It is noteworthy that here Gilbert pours scorn on the idea of the English Church abandoning Alexander III (probably with reason), whereas, in nos. 166, 181, he seems to have led the English bishops in warning the Pope that it was a serious possibility.

[4] On Gilbert's attitude to the Constitutions of Clarendon, see *GF*, pp. 184–5 and nn.; also nos. 155, 166–7.

[5] In BD Augustine is called 'maximus'; the omission of the word in C may possibly suggest that when revising his letter before sending it Gilbert remembered his idea of raising the pretensions of the see of London against the successors of Augustine (*GF*, pp. 151 ff.). One cannot identify the immediate source of Gilbert's reference to Augustine, but it is based at first or second hand on Gregory the Great's *Responsa* to him (Bede, *Hist. Eccl.* I, 27).

quibus iam senuerat inmutauit.[1] Quod non maledictis aut minis, sed doctrina sana
et exhortationibus sanctis obtinuit, benedicendo seminauit, de benedictionibus et
messem fecit. Hii si ad arma decurrissent, nichil aut parum profecissent. A pio
Francorum rege, optata diu prole sibi iam concessa diuinitus, nuper illi regno multa
sunt remissa grauamina, que firmauerat antiquitas hactenus inconuulsa; hec sug- 395
gerente ut audiuimus ecclesia et monente, non in electum principem minas im-
petente, sublata sunt. Que denique quanteue dignitates, libertates, immunitates,
possessiones ecclesie Dei a piis regibus orbe toto, pietate sola non maledicti necessitate collata sint, quis ualeat explicare? Vtique tempus id uolentem explere deficiet,
hec namque regum est laude digna nobilitas. Ab ipsis supplex obtinet quod erectus 400
in minas nullis umquam conatibus obtineret. Ipsis nummi pretium tam reputatur
uile, quam exiguum. Quod sibi ui surripere quisquis uiolenter intenderet, magnos
in re modica rei sue defensores spe cito frustratus agnosceret. Hec itaque non
feruore nouitio,[2] sed maturo fuerant attendenda consilio. Erant fratrum uestrorum
et aliorum plurium in his exquirenda consilia, attendenda patrum prudentium 405
opera, cum incommodis ecclesie pensanda commoda, et hec tum demum danda
forte sententia, cum iam foret spes nulla superesse remedia. Que profecto cum
datur, iuxta sacrorum formam canonum attendendum est in quem detur, cur detur,
quomodo detur, an expediat ecclesie quod detur, et obfuturum sibi si non detur.
Is uero quem impetitis, ut nota uobis referamus, numquid non ipse est quem 410
dulcissima pignora, nobilissima coniunx et honesta, subiecta sibi regna quam
plurima, amicorum cetus et suis obsequentium nutibus tot populorum agmina,
mundi queque pretiosa, uix detinent, uix blandiendo persuadent quin spretis
omnibus post crucem suam portantem Dominum Iesum nudus exeat, et paupertatem contemplando quam subiit, id facto studeat implere quod docuit ipse 415
di⟨fo. 205⟩cens, 'Qui non baiulat crucem suam et uenit post me, non est me dignus.'[3]
Hec mentis eius obstinatio est, hec maledictis opprimenda crudelitas, hec in
ecclesiam Dei toto orbe declamata malignitas.[4] In hunc si maledicta congesseritis,
partem sui nobilissimam suis ledi iaculis ecclesia recte condolebit: ipso namque
uulnerato, lesam se non filiorum paucitas, sed populorum ampla numerositas 420
ingemiscet. In hoc uero sacra sic docet auctoritas, 'In eiusmodi causis ubi per

---

**170**   396 in *om*. BD     396 minas] *sic MSS, perhaps for* minis     399 explicare C (*from preceding sentence*)     402 surripere *om*. C     406 tum] tunc B     407 non foret spes ulla BD     410 im-
petistis B     410 reseramus BD     411 subiect(ur)a B

---

[1] For the legation of John of Crema in 1125 see Wilkins, I, 406 ff. (and notes to Council of
Westminster, 1125, in *Councils and Synods*, I, forthcoming); Tillmann, pp. 27 ff.

[2] Cf. *Regula S. Benedicti*, c. I.

[3] Cf. Luc. xiv. 27; Matt. x. 38. Neither Henry the happy family man nor Henry the ardent
crusader is easy to accept. But the former was probably not so absurd in 1166 as later: see *GF*,
p. 173 n. See *ibid*. for the idea of a Crusade, of which there is no precise evidence so early as
this. But *HF*, xvi, 66 (letter of Reginald of St-Valéry to Louis VII) may show that it had
been mooted (? in 1163); and later in 1166 Nicholas of Mont-S.-Jacques reported to Becket
that Richard de Lucy was said to have taken the cross (*MB Epp.* 254). And cf. *JS Epp.* (ed.
Giles), no. 287 (1169).

[4] Cf. *MB Epp.* 224, p. 517.

graues dissensionum scissuras non huius aut illius est hominis periculum, sed populorum strages iacent, detrahendum est aliquid seueritati, ut maioribus malis sanandis karitas sincera subueniat'; et iterum, 'Non potest esse salubris a multis

425 correctio, nisi cum ille corripitur, qui non habet sociam multitudinem'.[1] Medico namque quis asscribit industrie, ut uulnus unum sanet, aliud longe maius, longe periculosius infligere? Discretioni quis attribuat, ob quedam que poterunt et leuius et expeditius obtineri, ecclesiam sic deserere, in principem exurgere, et ecclesie totius regni concussa pace, animarum in subditis corporumque pericula non curare?

430 Agris cessit Ambrosius, ecclesiam deserere non approbauit.[2] Nam quid a bono principe uestra, pater, prudentia poterat non sperare, quem diuino compunctum spiritu in Christum adeo nouerat hanelare? Ille consuetudines temporalis commodi nil prorsus sibi conferentes quanti sibi sunt, cui ipsa mundi gloria quantamcumque se offerat iam tota fere uiluit, et a cordis sui desiderio tam procul est, ut Domino

435 loquens sepius dicat quod scriptum est: 'Insigne mei capitis odi, Domine tu scis.'[3] Numquid non hic fouendus erat, et in ipso nidificanti columbe sancte[4] dimittendus, donec plene formatus in ipso Christus occulta eius in lucem traheret, produceret, et libertates ecclesie non tantum has de quibus agitur, sed et longe propensiores ipse quasi manu propria distribueret? In his quidem quod scimus loquimur, quod

440 nouimus id confidenter asserimus. Consuetudines in quas plus candescitis, domnus noster rex iam pridem penitus exspreuisset, si non hoc propositum duo grauiter impedissent: unum, quod sibi timet esse dedecori a patribus ad se deuoluto regno diebus suis subtrahi quicquam uel inminui; alterum, si quid remittat ob Dominum, erubescit ut hoc sibi ui reputetur extortum. Primum tamen illud iam sanctitatis

445 pede calcauerat, et ipsum in hoc Dei timor, innata bonitas, domni pape sancta monitio, multorumque in hoc supplicatio continuata perduxerant, ut ob eius reuerentiam per quem ultra omnes suos patres longe magnificatus est, ecclesiam Dei conuocare et regni consuetudines que grauamen sibi noscerentur inferre, multa deuotione spiritus immutare uellet ultroneus et corrigere. Et si penes uos

450 cepta perseuerasset humilitas, ecclesiam Dei in regno hoc exhilarasset iam diffusa late iocunditas; nam finem in quem tenditis euicerat iam supplicatio, cum male totum impediuit a uobis orta recens turbatio. Nam cum suis nondum Britannia titulis accessisset, et leuaret in eum usque tunc indomita gens illa calcaneum, cum produceret in turbatores pacis excercitum, terribiles in illum litteras,[5] deuotionem

455 patris, modestiam pontificis minime redolentes emisistis, et quod summi pontificis

---

**170** 426 asscribat BD    427 infligat C    427 potuerint *corrected to* poterint B; poterant D    430 Agris] Augustinus C    433–4 se cumque *MSS, marked in* C *for transposition*    435 sepius] BD *add* id    435 odi,] BD *add* o    440 excandescitis BD    441 pridem] quidem BD    446 produxerant C    447 suos omnes patres B; omnes patres suos D    450 hoc *om.* C    452 recens orta BD

---

[1] *Decretum*, D. 50, c. 25; C. 23, q. 5, c. 32 (cf. *Causa, MB*, IV, 220–1).
[2] Ambrose, *Ep.* I, 20, 8 (*PL*, XVI, 1038–9).
[3] Cf. Esther xiv. 16 (see Robertson *ad loc.*).
[4] Cf. nos. 194–5.
[5] Henry II was preparing for a campaign in Brittany when he received Becket's 'terribiles… litteras' (the phrase is repeated from no. 166); for the campaign, cf. Eyton, *Itinerary*, pp. 94–5.

ammonitio, multorumque elaborauerat supplex et intenta deuotio, spirando minas ilico sustulistis, et tam regem quam regnum in scandalum cunctis retroactis fere grauius inpulistis.

Auertat Deus finem quem negotio sic procedente metuimus, qui ne nostris erumpat temporibus, ob honorem Dei et sancte ecclesie reuerentiam, ob uestrum si 460 placet commodum, ob pacis commune bonum, ob minuenda scandala, et que turbata sunt ad pacem, iuuante Domino, reuocanda, ad Domnum papam appel-lauimus, ut uestri cursus impetum uos in regem prone rapientis et regnum ad tempus saltem cohibeamus. Qua in re bonum est ut intra fines modestie uester se uelit zelus cohibere, ne ut regum iura subuertere, debitam quoque sic domno pape 465 reuerentiam, appellationes ad ipsum interpositas non admittendo nimis e sublimi studeat exinanire. Quod si placet aduertere, ad Zacheum non diuertisse Dominum, nisi cum de siccomoro iam descendisset,[1] descenderetis forsitan, et quem minis exasperastis, uerbis alloquendo pacificis ⟨fo. 205 v⟩ mitigare studeretis, non solum ⟨non⟩ exigendo, sed et satisfactionem humilem etsi forte iniuriam passus, offerendo. 470 Puerum apostolis proposuit exemplo Dominus,[2] qui Iesus non irascitur, iniurie cito non meminit, nec quicquam malitiose moliens, sibi magna non affectat, sibi totum hoc innocentis uite remedio uiteque iocunditate plenissima recompensat. Singulare itaque uirtutis exemplar ipse est, qui se crucifigentes absoluit, qui lata caritate persequentes et odientes amari precipit, et si peccet frater in nos, ueniam non solum 475 septies, sed et septuagies septies imperat impertiri.[3] Ista quid non posset humilitas apud domnum nostrum regem, quid non obtineret uiarum ista perfectio? Callis iste rectus est,[4] ad pacem recte perducens; quem, pater, cum intraueritis, pacem ilico apprehendetis, et dispersis tristitie nebulis, cuncta pace, gaudio cuncta reple-bitis, et a rege piissimo domnoque nostro karissimo, non solum que ad presens 480 petitis, sed et longe maiora his, Domini spiritu cor eius accendente et in amorem suum semper dilatante, feliciter obtinere poteritis.

### 171   To King Henry II

[Late 1166 or 1167] The bishop of Salisbury has been suspended and is threatened with ex-communication: Gilbert asks the king to assist him to appeal and otherwise frustrate the archbishop's efforts until the arrival of the legates.

**170** 456 multorum BD     456 suspirando C (? *from* sustulistis)     460 ecclesie sancte BD 465 debitam quoque sic D; quoque debitam (*marked for transposition*) sic C; sic quoque debitam (q. d. s. *before correction*) B     467 placet aduertere C; placeret aduertere B; placeret auertere D 469 aliquando C     470 ⟨non⟩ *om. MSS* (*added by modern hand in* B)     472 moliens…sibi] moliens si (bi *ins. in* B) magna non affectat, sibi BD; molitur dum magna (? *over erasure*) non affectat, sibi C, *with* al' moliens si magna non affectat *ins.*     474 itaque *added in* C *in margin*; *om.* BD

**171** G, no. 273; *MB Epp.* 236; Lupus, I, 162–3 (i, 106); B, fo. 173; D, fos. 71 v–72; Ia, pp. 282–3; Ib, fo. 441 r–v; C, fo. 76 (75) r–v; Co, fo. 40 v; Vb, fo. 99 v; O, no. 106 (*variants of* Vb *and* O *not given*) (*headings:* Ia, Idem H. regi Anglie; Ib, Idem eidem; CCoVbO Henrico (? H. O) regi Anglie Gillebertus (C; G. *ceteri*) Londoniensis episcopus).

---

[1] Cf. Luc. xix. 2 ff.     [2] ? Mc. ix. 35, misremembered.
[3] Cf. Matt. xviii. 21–2.     [4] Cf. Is. xxvi. 7.

In two letters written in the second half of 1166, Becket complained of the imprisonment of William the chaplain; and he wrote to the bishop of Salisbury, already under sentence of suspension, threatening graver punishment and laying an interdict on the diocese until William was released.[1] This was presumably the occasion for no. 171, in which Gilbert asks the king for aid for Bishop Jocelin, and refers to the expected arrival of legates. In December 1166 Alexander III, in response to an embassy from Henry, announced the sending of a commission, and in March 1167 William of Pavia and Otto actually set out.[2] Gilbert's letter must have been written late in 1166 or early in 1167.

Domno suo karissimo illustri Anglorum regi Henrico frater G(ilebertus) Lundoniensis ecclesie minister, pie salutantis affectum et fideliter obsequentis of⟨fo. 173 v⟩ficium.

Venerabilem fratrem nostrum domnum Saresbir(iensem) episcopum uestre, 5 domne, sullimitati digni duximus commendandum, quem uobis utique fidelem nouimus et caritate non ficta[3] uestros per omnia desiderare successus indubitanter agnouimus. Vnde maiestati regie, honori proculdubio cedet et glorie ut in ipsum clementer respiciatis et regie pietatis oculos in ipsum attentius habeatis. Fidelem quippe clericum uestrum transmittit ad uos, ut quam pie domnus Cantuariensis 10 sit circa ipsum sollicitus et uerbis eius et scriptis que pre manibus habet agnoscatis. Onus siquidem suspensionis ad presens sustinet et iam citatus, iuste siue iniuste excommunicationis sententiam ut ex scriptis perpendimus, et ex retroactis manifeste conicimus, nisi per uos in proximo non euadet. Quam si contigerit in ipsum dari, erit utique sibi dedecori et omnibus regni uestri personis 15 concussioni pariter et timori. Quem si uestra benignitas euocaret ad se, iter acceleraret ad uos et iminens hoc periculum ope uestra fretus optime iuuante Domino declinaret. Vnde cum petente petimus, cum supplicante supplicamus, quatinus suspiranti in hoc fideli uestro accessum ad uos ad presens si placet concedatis, et ipsum conatus eius qui uobis aduersatur in omnibus et appellationibus et modis 20 aliis quos reuelabit Dominus usque ad legatorum uestrorum aduentum elidere permittatis. Hoc siquidem uobis honori, securitati uero nobis omnibus futurum credimus, qui uices nostras in protectionem uestram fratri nostro fidelissimo committere sane poterimus, ut amoueat abundans cautela si quid in regnum uestrum male machinari uoluerit potestas quod absit indiscreta. Valere uos optamus 25 in Domino diuque regnare feliciter in Christo dilectissime.

**171** 1–3 Domno...officium] *in* BD *only* 9 transmisit Co (*in margin of* O: postquam suspensus est Sal' episcopus [ ] concessione decanatus) 18 uestri C 19 ipsum] et *added* (*ins.*) C 21 quidem BD (*in margin of* O *near* legatorum: [Wi]l' et Oth') 22 uestram] ?nostram BD; uestram *ceteri* 25 diuque...dilectissime] *so* BD; *ins. in* margin C; *om.* IaIbCo

---

[1] *MB Epp.* 235; see notes to no. 169.
[2] *MB Epp.* 257–8 (JL 11,299, 11,302), 334; Tillmann, pp. 57 ff.
[3] Cf. II Cor. vi. 6.

## 172 To Robert de Chesney, bishop of Lincoln

[1163–6] He asks that the gift of the church of Dunton by Master Roger of Dunton—whom he commends to the bishop—be confirmed to the nuns of Haliwell (Shoreditch, London, Augustinian).[1]

The death of the bishop of Lincoln on 27 December 1166 provides a *terminus ad quem* for nos. 172–3.

Venerabili domno fratrique karissimo Ro(berto) Lincol(niensi) episcopo frater G(ilebertus) Lundoniensis ecclesie minister, in senecta uberi[2] pie Christo famulari.

Que sint opes loci qui dicitur Haliwelle diuulgante fama notum forsitan habuistis. Angustus quidem locus est et exiguus, adeo ut trium agri iugerum spatio totus plene limittetur. Locum hunc inhabitant uiginti sorores uelate et consecrate 5 Domino diuinis iugiter insistentes laudibus, et Domino regulariter obsequentes. Temporalem his uictum et uestitum ministrat ecclesia de Dunt(ona), ipsis a presentium latore magistro Rogero pie collata et misericorditer a gratia uestra confirmata. Hac deducta locus quem predicte sorores inhabitant ipsis quidem ad sepulcrum, ad uictum uero nullo modo sufficiet. Mentem itaque uestram moueat 10 precor illa calamitas, in quam iamdicte sorores proculdubio casure sunt si iudicii seueritate quod absit iamdicta ecclesia fuerint destitute. Interponat itaque se pastoralis illa clementia que usque in diem hanc collato beneficio Domini pauit et uestiuit ancillas, ne totum ipsis quod sub celo possident abiudicando, ipsas desolatas reddat et omni penitus auxilio et consilio destitutas. Canonice si placet eis indutie 15 concedantur, dilationes eis legitime non negentur, prouideatur aduocati suffragium, ut pectus in uobis sentiant quantum permiserit equitas paupertati sue compatiens et religionis amicum. Si cause id exegerit arcta necessitas, transsigatur potius quam ouili Domini uellus ad cutem usque iudiciali sententia detrahatur. Latorem presentium magistrum R(ogerum) de Dunton' fraternitati uestre commendamus atentius, quem 20 iamdicte sorores in presenti causa sub testimonio nostro procuratorem sibi constituunt, eo quod uehiculum quo subuehantur ad uos inopia prepediente non inueniunt. Valere uos optamus in Domino, frater in Christo karissime.

## 173 To Robert de Chesney, bishop of Lincoln

[1163–6] The elder son of R. Brito (Gilbert's brother-in-law)[3] has been granted the heiress of William Gulafre and his barony by the king; Gilbert appeals to the bishop to ordain and

172 G, no. 220; B, fo. 39 v.
173 G, no. 221; B, fo. 176.

---

[1] The request was presumably answered, since the church appears among the nuns' properties in the confirmation of Richard I (*Monasticon*, IV, 393). No documents for Haliwell are known to survive earlier than this confirmation.
[2] Cf. Ps. xci. 15.
[3] This can be deduced from the fact that R. was Gilbert's *affinis*, and yet his son was Gilbert's nephew and Robert's great-nephew: see *GF*, p. 33. He may be the Ralph of no. 464.

provide for the younger son, destined for the Church. The petition is supported by R. d'Ameri.[1]

[V]enerabili domno fratrique carissimo R(oberto) Lincoll(iensi) Dei gratia episcopo frater G(ilebertus) Lundoniensis ecclesie minister, salutem quam sibi.

Amicus et affinis noster R. Brito talem se exhibet et tam strenuum in quibus potest negotiis, ut in illis necessitatibus que suam transcendunt facultatem suorum
5 uideatur amicorum auxilio non indignus. Qui largiente Domino in cuius manu corda sunt regum,[2] tantam in conspectu regis gratiam obtinuit quod idem domnus noster rex baroniam Willelmi Gulafre que in sua⟨m⟩ reciderat manum cum filia et herede eiusdem Willelmi primogenito filio suo dotalem concessit, filiam quoque suam honorifice maritare, nobilique marito et grandi maritagio regia liberalitate
10 nobilitare curauit. Qua in re et regis non inmerito laudatur munificentia et patris nichilominus diligentia comprobatur, quia qui bene meretur et qui bene remunerat uterque laudandus est. Superest adhuc filius alter, quem litteris erudire, quem Deo dedere, quem ecclesiastico ordini mancipare destinauit. Ad cuius promotionem quia paterna non possunt nec debent obsequia suffragari, una post Deum spe specialiter
15 ad nos duos suspensus est, quod curam eius habere, ipsique propter Deum prouidere debeamus. Ob hanc igitur causam mea ad uos legatione fungitur, ut gratiam quam non desperat ex se, mea tamen promtius apud uos obtineat intercessione. Pater itaque pro filio, ego pro nepote, ambo pro uestro uobis abnepote suplicamus, ut que paterna deuotio diuinis deputauit obsequiis, uestre si placet ecclesie titulis
20 ascribatis, et in hereditatem sanctam et in ecclesiasticam familiam prestatione presentis seu futuri promissione beneficii adsciscatis, ut sollicitudo patris que tota resedit in filio, re ipsa uel spe saltem ⟨fo. 176 v⟩ exhilarata respiret. Qua in re si mea uobis improba uidetur et onerosa petitio, scitote quia uobis fratrique uestro domno Willelmo de Caineto[3] id potius imputare debetis. Ego namque Britanniam
25 nesciebam, Britones non noueram, R. Britonis neque notitia neque nomen ad me peruenerat, quando uos duo illum michi commendastis ad gratiam, multaque diligentia in amicitiam et affinitatem gentis nostre induxistis, eaque michi necessitudine confederastis, ut non iam improbitas estimari debeat sed officii magis necessitas pro ipso et cum ipso uestre supplicare dilectioni. Preter hec autem et super hec
30 multam michi suggerit audaciam orandi et exorandi fiduciam domnus R. de Almari qui in hoc ipso ut dicitur negotio suas ad uos partes audacter interponit, et more curialium imperiose cuncta disponit. Non enim eam possum apud uos causam

---

**173** 4 qui B

[1] This was presumably Richard d'Ameri, precentor of Lincoln 1160/1–1173 or later, and (concurrently) archdeacon of Stow (Barlow in *Arnulf*, p. 64 n.; *Reg. Lincoln*, VII, 203 n., 204 and n., *Curia Regis Rolls*, VII, 39; etc.). He was still archdeacon in 1188, but may have resigned the precentorship before that date. His successor as archdeacon occurs before 1192 (*Reg. Lincoln*, III, no. 1096). This letter shows that he was a *curialis*, which no doubt explains why he was made farmer of the see with Richard of Ilchester after Robert de Chesney's death (*PR 13 Henry II*, pp. 57–8 to *PR 19 Henry II*, p. 134).
[2] Cf. Prov. xxi. 1.
[3] On Robert's brother William de Chesney, see Biog. Index and *GF*, pp. 33–4.

desperare, quam hinc maiestas curie inde mea et aliorum humilitas amicorum apud uestram nititur beniuolentiam in tam honesto desiderio perorare. Valete.

## 174   To Reginald of St-Valéry

[1163–7] He urges Reginald to deal charitably with the canons of Osney (near Oxford), and entreats him, as an old crusader who has confounded God's enemies in Asia,[1] not to confound his humble servants in England.

Reginald of St-Valéry died on 3 or 4 September 1166/7. He held land in the neighbourhood of Osney; and his name was enrolled in the necrology of the abbey, which suggests that he responded to this letter and became a benefactor—as his successors certainly were.[2]

G(ilebertus) Dei gratia Lundonie⟨nsis⟩ episcopus amico suo karissimo R(ainaldo) de sancto Walerico, uirtute meriti promissam bonis gloriam feliciter adipisci.

Tua karissime munificentia, tua liberalitas in me adeo iam multis innotuit ut in negotiis que habent ad te se sperent aliqui meis posse precibus apud te—si pro se porrigantur—adiuuari. Vnde quos in Christo diligo, de quorum bona in Domino 5 conuersatione non ambigo, tue confidentius karitati commendo, affectuose supplicans quatinus ob beatam illam spem qua in Deum tendimus, qua bene sperando post Christum currimus, ⟨fo. 45⟩ humilibus fratribus de Oseneio misericordie tandem sinum aperias, et eorum compatiendo doloribus ipsorum fatigationibus finem pietatis inponas. Memorare karissime quanti sit meriti loca sancta construere, 10 mansionem Domino qua usque in aduentum suum sine fine laudetur, honoretur et adoretur edificare, considera quantum sit bona spiritualia non solum non inpedire, sed ut in Dei gloriam exuberent his oportunitatem et causam de tuis etiam exhibere? Memento karissime quod bella Domini strenue gesseris, quod tuis etiam stipendiis pro ipso militaueris, quod infideles et incredulos teipsum opponendo et uelut in 15 holocaustum offerendo repuleris, et qui rebelles Domino confudisti in Asia, eius seruos humiles obsecro ne confundas in Anglia. Sed ut bene consummes omnia cum capite Domino caudam etiam hostie offeras, ut cum bono tue satisfactionis initio finem etiam laudabilem addideris, a magna manu Domini cuncta que seruis eius pro ipso inpenderis, in illa die centies multiplicata recipias. Opto ut ualeas, et pro 20 quibus supplico tui apud Dominum memores pie miserando constituas. Vale.

**174** G, no. 286; B, fo. 44 v.

---

[1] It is possible that he went on the second Crusade. It is certain that he knew Louis VII personally and was interested in Jerusalem (*HF*, XVI, 66). But according to a note of the Marquis d'Albon, which no contemporary evidence has been found to support, he was in the Holy Land *c.* June 1157–60 (see B. A. Lees in *Records of the Templars in England in the Twelfth Century*, pp. 190 n., 204–5 n.).

[2] *Cart. Oseney*, I, p. xxiv; II, 432–3, 463. He was the heir (presumably son or grandson) of Bernard of St-Valéry, and occurs from 1130 to his death on 3 or 4 Sept. 1166/7 (see below, p. 512 n. 1. Osney obit., *Cart. Oseney*, I, p. xxiv, gives 3 Sept.; Rouen obit., *HF*, XXIII, 366, gives 4 Sept. It seems that the obit. of Le Tréport, *ibid.* p. 452, which gives 5 Aug. for Reginald and his wife, must be set aside, or attributed to another man). On him see Delisle, *Recueil*, Introd. pp. 421–2: Delisle's error in making him live beyond 1175 was corrected by Haskins, *Norman Institutions*, pp. 325–6.

### 175  To King Henry II

[Probably 1165–7] He complains that the bishop of Hereford, since the king's crossing, has disseised the four serjeants enfeoffed by Gilbert when he was bishop of Hereford on assarts at Malvern granted by the king. He asks the king to order William Folet[1] and the other serjeants to be put in possession until the case can be settled on the king's return.

Henry II confirmed the assarts at Malvern in (or soon after) April 1158.[2] It seems clear that the bishop of Hereford was Gilbert's immediate successor, Robert de Melun (1163–7): his successor, Robert Foliot, was not appointed until 1173, and was a close friend as well as a relative of Gilbert. The letter was written while the king was abroad, i.e. in March–May 1165 or between March 1166 and the death of Robert de Melun on 27 February 1167.

It would be interesting to know whether the letter was written before or after the promulgation of the assize of novel disseisin (1166); but Gilbert's demand gives no hint of the procedure, and the principle was certainly much older than the assize.[3]

No. 176, a protest to the bishop of Hereford, suggests a similar situation—perhaps the same—and may be approximately contemporary.

Domno suo karissimo illustri Anglorum regi H(enrico) frater G(ilebertus) Lundoniensis ecclesie minister, salutem que nunc est et quam ⟨fo. 167⟩ speramus a Domino.

5 Vestra nos domne fouente presentia omnis a nobis alte conquieuit iniuria; in abscessu uero uestro pacis nostre detrimentum illatis ⟨iniuriis (?)⟩ ilico experituri sumus. Nouit enim excellentia uestra quod cum Hereford(ensi) adhuc deseruiremus ecclesie essarta quedam Maluernie ad coronam uestram pertinentia nobis munificentia regia et liberalitate sola concessistis. Illa uero quattuor seruientibus nostris qui in ipsius ecclesie negotiis nobiscum fideliter aliquamdiu laborauerant, tenui quidem
10 seruitii sui remuneratione donauimus et uestrum in hoc assensum et confirmationem a gratia uestra impetrauimus. Venerabilis uero frater noster domnus Hereford(ensis) episcopus post uestrum statim transitum ipsos eisdem possessiunculis expulit et requisitus super hoc nec carte uestre reuerentia nec prece nostra motus in aliqua in omnibus sese nobis inexorabilem exhibuit. Inde est quod ad nota presidia clementie
15 uestre recurrentes, humili supplicamus affectu quatinus collata nobis tot bona hac etiam si placet gratia cumuletis. Willelmum Folet, in quem modicam donationem contulimus, etiam dictos seruientes nostros his quibus post transitum uestrum absque audientia et iudicio spoliati sunt, usque ad reditum uestrum resaisiri precipiatis, et cum in regnum uestrum gratia uos diuina reduxerit, que a nobis gesta sunt
20 presentibus nobis audiatis, et que corrigenda uideritis regia prout placuerit equitate corrigatis. Summa quam restitui petimus non decem plene marcarum est, cum sit

**175** G, no. 267; B, fo. 166v.
11 Bereford' (?) B

---

[1] See *GF*, pp. 225, 292.
[2] Capes, p. 19; *CHJ*, VIII, i (1944), 20.
[3] Cf. R. C. Van Caenegem, *Royal Writs in England from the Conquest to Glanvill*, pp. 261 ff.; cf. G. D. G. Hall in *EHR*, LXXVI (1961), 317–18; on the obscurity of its form in 1166, H. G. Richardson and G. O. Sayles, *The Governance of Mediaeval England*, pp. 197–8.

tamen eius ecclesie—donatione quidem uestra nostroque labore tempore quo in ea ministrauimus—centum plene marcarum redditu melior facta conditio. Incolumitatem uestram conseruet in longa tempora Deus, in Christo dilecte domne.

## 176 To Robert de Melun, bishop of Hereford

[? 1165–7] He thanks the bishop and his clerks for the elegance of their refusal, and demands a hearing for the dispossessed, whose treatment has been contrary to canon and civil and customary law.

For a possible interpretation of this letter, cf. no. 175.

Venerabili fratri R(oberto) Hereford(ensi) Dei gratia episcopo frater G(ilebertus) Lundoniensis ecclesie minister salutem.

Si uerba postulauimus satisfactum est, si rem non adeo. Verum quod tam honorifice, quod tam eleganti repulsa uota nostra reprobastis uobis et notariis uestris quantas debemus gratias referimus, ipsas annuente Domino cum res erit 5 gratiarum actiones relaturi. Quod autem preces nostras quas pro deiectorum nostrorum restitutione uestre porreximus fraternitati, iuxta intelligentiam uestram nequaquam admittendas scribitis, ne in ecclesiam Dei et sacros canones grauiter quod absit comittatis, non satis ammirari sufficimus. Cum prima hec sint tam diuini quam humani iuris elementa, nulli permissum esse sibi ius dicere, ui pulsos ad 10 omnem causam debere restitui, predonibus etiam uiolentisque possessoribus aduersus ueros domnos per interdictum subueniri et multa in hunc modum que leges affirmant, confirmant decreta et optima utrorumque interpres consuetudo commendat,[1] que licet in nostram fortasse dissimulentur iniuriam, uestram tamen prudentiam scimus non ignorare. Nunc uero quia nichil quod amico possitis 15 concedere nobis ut uestra conclusit oratio uultis ullatenus negare, quod nec inimico negandum est, diem uidelicet, locum et audientiam deiectis nostris petimus exhiberi.

## 177 To King Henry II

[1166–70, probably summer–autumn 1167] He has received a papal mandate to collect Peter's Pence, and asks the king to instruct his justices accordingly; he also asks for the king's will and counsel about the appeal to the Pope, whose term is approaching.

Nos. 177–9, like nos. 155–6 and 169, deal with the collection of Peter's Pence. Gilbert was asked to act by the Pope in the absence of the archbishop either as dean of the province, or because, as bishop of London and in favour with the king, he was the most likely person to make an effective collector. Peter's Pence, then, fell to Gilbert's lot when there was no

---

**175** 24 longa tempora] l. tē. (sic) B
**176** G, no. 213; B, fo. 165 v.
6 grarum B
**177** G, no. 271; MB Epp. 107; B, fo. 172 (at foot of fo.: non plene liquet quo tempore uel de qua appellatione hoc dicat); D, fo. 71 v.

---

[1] Cf. Digest, I, 3, 37.

archbishop available, i.e. in the period 1165–73.[1] Nos. 177–9 all refer to the method by which the money is to be transferred to the Pope—by *nuntii* in 177, by *nuntii* in Normandy in 179, by Flemish merchants in 178. The three letters could all belong to one year,[2] although it cannot be proved that they do. They cannot date from 1165, when the money was paid to the abbot of St-Bertin (no. 156). Thus the outside limits for all three are 1166–73. If the references to the bishoprics of Lincoln and Ely in no. 178 are taken to mean that the sees were vacant, the date could be narrowed to 1169–73; if the reference to Rome in the same letter means that the Pope had actually been there at the time, the letter must belong to 1166 or 1167. Neither piece of evidence seems cogent.

The only letter which can be more closely dated is no. 177, which refers to the imminence of the term of some appeal. This is puzzling, because although Gilbert and his associates appealed many times, none of these appeals ever reached a term, being suspended in one way or another by counter-moves from Pope or archbishop. The most likely occasion is November 1167, when the English bishops presented their case before the legates at Argentan. We know from no. 180 that Gilbert regarded this as the presentation of his appeal, and the repetition of the proverb 'minus enim iacula feriunt [ledant *Gilbert*] que preuidentur', though obvious enough in such a context, provides a further link between 177 and 180. On the whole, the summer or autumn of 1167 seems the likely date for 177,[3] perhaps also for 178; 179 may refer to a different occasion altogether.

Domno suo karissimo illustri Anglorum regi H(enrico) frater G(ilebertus) Lundoniensis ecclesie minister, pedibus sanctis conculcato Satan in Christo triumphare feliciter.[4]

Mandatum domni pape, domne, nuper accepimus, quo nobis iniungitur ut
5 censum beati Petri a fratribus et coepiscopis nostris suscipiamus et per nuntios quos direxit ad nos ipsi cito transmittamus. Quod quia de uestra totum pendet misericordia nec potest effectu compleri nisi per uos, uestre id notificamus excellentie ut uestris si placet iustitiis super hoc scribatis, et quod uestre uoluntati placuerit, id fieri precipiatis. Optamus autem ut cor uestrum diuinitas sancta possideat, et actus
10 uestros omnes sic disponat et dirigat, ut nec in Deum offendatis, nec aduersum uos aut regnum uestrum domno pape, quem uos plurimum dilexisse nouimus, iustam querele causam et materiam prebeatis. De cetero dies instat quem appellationi ad domnum papam facte prefiximus, de qua prosequenda necesse est nobis ut uoluntatem uestram et consilium amodo certius agnoscamus. Nam cum minus ledant
15 iacula que preuidentur,[5] timendum nobis est ne si ad momentum temporis omnia

**177** 8 hoc *om.* D    11 uos *om.* D

---

[1] He collected it in some, though not necessarily all, of these years.
[2] In no. 178 the *nuntii*, Flemish merchants, are 'apud nos'; in no. 179 he envisages a meeting with the *nuntii* at Rouen about 1 October. If the three letters refer to the same year, no. 178 could have been written from Normandy after Gilbert's meeting with the *nuntii*—and both could belong to autumn–winter 1167, one of the periods when Gilbert is known to have visited Normandy (see no. 191 n.). If the reference to Rome in no. 178 means that Alexander was himself in Rome, the date would be November 1165 to July 1167.
[3] The reference to the appeal makes a date later than 1170 unacceptable.
[4] Cf. Rom. xvi. 20; II Cor. ii. 14 (and no. 193).
[5] Cf. St Gregory, *Homiliae in Euangelia*, II, 35, 1 (*PL*, LXXVI, 1259); below, no. 180; *JS Epp.* 27 and n.

reseruentur, singula quo prescita minus et minus pretractata fuerint, eo minus comode quam res exigat expediantur. Inscribat cordi uestro digitus Dei quid fieri expediat, et uos manus eius ubique protegat atque custodiat, domine in Christo dilectissime.

## 178   To King Henry II

[1166–73, ? summer–autumn 1167] He has collected Peter's Pence except for £42 from the diocese of Lincoln and 100s. from the diocese of Ely. He had kept the Pope's messengers, Flemish merchants who had made a loan of 300 marks at Rome on expectation of Peter's Pence, for some time, waiting for permission from the king to pay it—but without result. He urges the king again to pay the Pope what is his.

Domino suo karissimo illustri Anglorum regi H(enrico) frater G(ilebertus) Lundoniensis ecclesie minister, salutem et fidele semper obsequium.

Censum domne beati Petri suscepimus, exceptis xl duabus libris quas de Lin-coll(iensi) episcopatu et c solidos quos de Eliensi episcopatu nondum habuimus. Nuntios uero domni pape octo scilicet mercatores Flandrie, qui sibi ccc marchas 5 argenti Rome mutuo prestiterunt, sperantes se summam eandem de manu miseri-cordie uestre suscepturos, apud nos iamdiu detinuimus, sperantes a sublimitate uestra uerbum aliquod audire, per decanum de Waltham,[1] quod et domnum papam et nuntios eius posset exhylarare. Quod quia nondum actum est ipsos ulterius detinere non possumus, sed quod remittuntur inanes posse cause uestre 10 plurimum obesse pertimescimus. Qua in re discretio uestra prouidebit utiliter quid expediat, quid honorem uestrum deceat, quid anime uestre saluti proficiat.[2] Fideles uero uestri qui penes nos sunt qui uices uestras per omnia prosperari desiderant, uellent uestrum in re ista mutari consilium, ut domno pape reddendo suum ipsum ad negotia uestra non aduersarium sed per omnia beniuolum haberetis 15 et obnoxium. Illuminet Dominus uultum suum super uos,[3] et uestra semper negotia bono fine concludat in Christo domne dilectissime.

## 179   To Pope Alexander III

[1166–73] He has not yet finished collecting Peter's Pence, but writes to ask for instructions on how to deliver it: he suggests that the Pope's messengers meet his own at Rouen about 1 October.

Patri suo et domno summo pontifici A(lexandro) frater G(ilebertus) Lundoniensis ecclesie minister, deuotum et debitum caritatis et obedientie famulatum.

**177**  17 res *om.* D
**178**  G, no. 272; *MB Epp.* III; B, fo. 175 v (*at foot of fo.*: uidetur eo tempore, cum preceptum esset denarii beati Petri non reddantur ulterius apostolico); D, fo. 76 r–v.
7 detenuimus BD    10 reuertuntur D    13 uestri uero D
**179**  G, no. 150; *MB Epp.* 109; B, fo. 42 v.

---

[1]  Guy Rufus, who resigned in 1177 (*Gesta Henrici II*, I, 134).
[2]  Cf. St Bernard, *De consideratione*, III, 4 (15).          [3]  Cf. Ps. lxvi. 2.

Iniunctam nobis de colligendo censu beati Petri sollicitudinem quanta possumus acceleramus diligentia, quem licet nondum plene collectam habeamus, qua tamen
5 uia collectum transuehere quaue cautela saluum transmittere ualeamus, anxia nobiscum disquisitione inuestigamus. In quo quia nostra nobis non plene succurrunt consilia, uestram super hoc sublimitatem duximus consulendam. Non enim nobis tutum est per ignotos populos et regna incognita iamdictam deferre pecuniam, nisi quatenus reuerentia pacis et protectionis domni nostri regis Anglorum noscitur
10 dilatari. Non nostros in hoc—teste conscientia loquimur—labores causamur aut expensas, sed ipsa rerum pericula formidamus. Inde est quod uestre supplicamus sanctitati, ut uestri si placet nuntii circiter kalendas Octobris nostris apud Roto-magum nuntiis occurrant, qui aut delatam per nos illuc pecuniam ad uos usque cum ea qua prouidebitis securitate perferendam suscipiant, aut curam ipsam alicui
15 fidelium uestrorum—prout uestra decernet auctoritas—exequendam iniungant.

### 180   To William de Turba, bishop of Norwich

[*c.* November 1167] In view of the archbishop of Canterbury's activities, (the bishops)[1] have long since appealed to the Pope, and by presenting this appeal to the appointed judges (they hope to avert) the storm...

This letter is only a fragment, and its full meaning cannot be recovered. But Gilbert seems to be urging the bishop to assist in prosecuting an appeal which is nearing its term, and the 'iudices' can only refer to the legates William and Otto, whose coming was announced in December 1166, and before whom the bishops stated their case and renewed their appeal at Argentan in November 1167.[2] November 1167 was the nearest that the bishops got, in fact, to prosecuting any of their various appeals (cf. *GF*, pp. 162–3); it is likely that this letter was written as part of Gilbert's preparations for the meeting at Argentan.

Venerabili domno fratrique karissimo W(illelmo) Norwic(ensi) Dei gratia episcopo frater G(ilebertus) Lundoniensis ecclesie minister, salutem et debitum fraterne caritatis obsequium.

Scitis karissime iacula que preuidentur obesse minus,[3] et quod tempore longe
5 melius sit occurrere, quam uulneratam causam de querendo remedio iam nimis sero deliberare. Vnde considerantes patrem nostrum Cantuar(iensem) ad maledic-tionem promtissimum, et potestatem quam in edificationem—et non destruc-tionem[4]—ecclesie suscepisse debuerat, in domnum nostrum regem et regnum eius, in nos et commissas nobis ecclesias, contra formam sacrorum canonum exercere
10 paratum, ad apostolicam iamdiu audientiam appellauimus, et ad datos nobis iudices appellationem hanc prosequendo, tempestatem hanc qua concuti metuebamus, amministrante gratiam Domino, usque...

180 G, no. 242; *MB Epp.* 346; B, fo. 186v; D, fo. 80 (*both texts are incomplete and end at the same point; in D the letter has been crossed out*).

[1] This is clearly a reference to the appeal of nos. 166–7.
[2] See *MB Epp.* 331–2, 339.     [3] See p. 250 n. 5.          [4] Cf. II Cor. x. 8.

## 181 The English Church to Pope Alexander III

[November 1167] The meeting with the legates (at Argentan, November 1167) has failed to produce peace, since they were not, to the king's intense anger, commissioned to settle the case, and the archbishop of Canterbury is very eager to excommunicate the king and lay his kingdom under interdict: the writers have therefore appealed against his sentences and mandates, naming 11 November next (1168) as term.

On the chronology of the appeals, which establishes that this letter and no. 182 belong to November 1167, see *GF*, pp. 162 ff. There is no doubt that Gilbert was the prime mover in this appeal, though there is not so much evidence of his authorship of nos. 181–2 as of 166–7.

Patri suo et domno summo pontifici A(lexandro) Anglicana ecclesia, deuotum et debitum caritatis et obedientie famulatum.

Sublimitati uestre, pater reuerende, gratias affectuose referimus quod ad petitionem filii uestri deuotissimi domnique nostri dilectissimi, illustris Anglorum regis, filios uestros carissimos summeque uobis in ea que ad presens est tempestate 5 necessarios, ad ipsum curastis in longinqua transmittere, affectuque paterno eorundem laboribus nostris parcere et grauaminibus nostra pie grauamina subleuare. Habentes itaque mittenti gratias, missos honore debito totaque cordium alacritate suscepimus, sperantes eorum aduentu finem malis diu iam protractis imponi, et que turbata sunt apud nos in pacis pristine serenitatem cooperante sibi gratia 10 reformari. Inde est quod eis tanquam iudicibus ad hoc a sanctitate uestra directis nostram una cum domno nostro rege presentiam reuerenter exhibuimus, optantes pariter et expectantes omnia que inter domnum nostrum regem et domnum Cantuariensem, queque inter ipsum uertuntur et nos, in eorum presentia palam fieri, et iuxta uestri formam mandati diffinitiua eorum sententia plenissime ter- 15 minari. Ipsis in modum hunc reuerentiam iudiciarie potestati debitam exhibentes astitimus—et ecce sinistro confusi nuntio, a prius concepta spe gaudii in desperationis foueam lapsi, audita satis nequiuimus ammirari. Audito enim et ipsa legatorum uestrorum confessione recognito eos ad iudicandam causam hanc, ob quam uenerant, potestatem omnimodo non habere, et quod a sanctitate uestra domno nostro 20 regi concessum scriptoque firmatum fuerat, id non tenere, domnus noster rex ultra quam dici possit ira totus incanduit, in tantum quidem ut ad solitam erga uos animi mansuetudinem uix eum nostra etiam in comune supplicatio reuocare potuerit. Totum itaque quod in aduentu legatorum uestrorum conceperamus gaudii cepit ilico tristitie nubilo superduci. Ad iram hanc fortius inflammandam incentiua 25 prebebant ipsa nobilium regni colloquia, id domno regi sepius inculcantia, sibi regnoque suo nulla iam aduersus domnum Cantuariensem superesse subsidia, cum apellatio regni dudum ad uos facta iam expirauerit, et ei legatorum uestrorum in nullo cura subuenerit. Hinc apud regni principes tanta est exorta turbatio, ut nisi

**181** G, no. 438; *MB Epp.* 344; Lupus, II, 362–4 (ii, 33); B, fo. 60v; D, fos. 74–5; Ia, pp. 144–6; Ib, fos. 289v–291; C, fos. 164 (163)–165 (164); Co, fos. 84v–85; Vb, fos. 145 v–46; Ar, fos. 192v–194 (*variants of* VbAr *not given*).
6 curatis CoIb; curatis *corrected to* curastis Ia     8 mitenti B     10 sibi *om.* BCoIa     11 eis *om.* IaIb     13 expetentes B     23 reuocare potuerit CIa; reuocare potuit COIb; reuocare iam possit D; reuocari iam possit B     28 ad uos dudum BD

30 iuxta datam uobis sapientiam pericula iam nunc erumpentia prouidendo preclu-
seritis, Christi uestem scindi miserrime de proximo doleatis. Totis enim studiis
domnus in hoc Cantuariensis insudat ut domnum nostrum regem anathemate,
regnum eius interdicti pena constringat. Potestatem quam in edificationem et non
destructionem ecclesie suscepisse oportuerat, sic exercet in subditos ut omnes in
35 regis odium et totius regni nobilium temptet inducere, et eorum substantiis direp-
tionem, ceruicibus gladium aut corporibus exilium intente studeat procurare.
Crebris litteris graues eis mandatorum imponit sarcinas, quas presens ipse non
digito mouere uoluit, nedum humeris ⟨fo. 61⟩ sustinere. Ad mortem nos inuitat et
sanguinis effusionem, cum ipse mortem quam nemo sibi dignabatur aut minabatur
40 inferre summo studio declinauerit, et suum sanguinem illibatum conseruando, eius
adhuc nec guttam effundi uoluerit. Pro Christo quippe mori gloriosum est. In
mortem et imprudenter irrumpere Christo scimus non placere. Libertatem predicat
eclesie quam se Cantuariensi ecclesie uiribus intrudendo sibi constat ademisse.
Regni consuetudines frequenter improperat, quas longe aliter quam se res habeat
45 suis scriptis uestre celsitudini manifestat. De cetero sanctorum canonum auctoritatem erga nos non obseruat, cum appellantes ad uos post appellationem excom-
municat, alios sine citatione omni aut commonitione suspendat; notoria que nec
nota nec ueritate subnixa sunt asserat; et in hunc modum plurima qua preest
potestate confundat. Ad hec quadraginta marcarum milia uel amplius, ut sui
50 asserunt, bone sue fidei commissa domno nostro regi soiuere uel quod iustum est
exhibere detrectat. Et regi suo negat et domno, quod nec ethnico denegare debuerat
aut publicano. Vnde ne ligent nos iamdicta grauamina, ne taciturnitate nostra et
indiscreta quadam conniuentia permittamus id fieri, unde domnum nostrum regem
et regnum eius, ipsum etiam et sequentes populos a uestra contingat obedientia
55 prorsus auerti, aduersus suspectas nobis domni Cantuariensis sententias, aduersus
mandata eius omnia, domno nostro regi et regno eius, personis nostris, et commissis
nobis ecclesiis et parrochiis grauamen aliquod importantia, uestro nos per omnia
committentes consilio et protectioni subdentes, ad audientiam uestram apellauimus,
et apellationi terminum diem transitus beati Martini constituimus. Valere uos
60 optamus, in Christo dilecte pater.

## 182   The English Church to Archishop Thomas Becket

[November 1167] They had appealed last year and submitted their case to the legates; since
no judgement has been pronounced, they renew their appeal (as in no. 181).

Venerabili patri et domno T(home) Cant(uariensi) archiepiscopo, Anglicana
ecclesia, debitam caritatem.

   Vestram scimus non latere prudentiam nos anno iam preterito ad domnum
papam appellasse, et directis ad uos literis id ipsum uobis significasse. Appellationis

181 32 Cant. in hoc C    32 desudat CCo    34 subditis *with* uel -os *ins.* C    42 mortem]
C *adds* uero    44 res se habeat DCo    49 milia marcarum C    51 enhnico B    59–60 Valere... pater *om.* IaIbCCo; B *adds* i(n) D(omino) *after* optamus
182 G, no. 441; MB Epp. 345; B, fo. 61; D, fos. 79r–v; Rb, fo. 107r–v; Jb, *unfoliated (variants
ignored)* 3 iam anno B

huius causas, si dissimulare non uultis, scitis esse iustissimas. Nullum enim ex- 5
communicari iustum est iuri se offerentem, se et causam suam diuinis per omnia
legibus submittentem. Vos tamen in domnum nostrum regem a summo pontifice
cause sue iudices petentem pariter et exspectantem excommunicationis ferre
sententiam et in regnum eius interdicti penam statuere, seueritate si placet
attendere non recte quidem moderata proposuistis. Quo nimirum modo si pro- 10
cessisset negotium, domno nostro pape sancteque Romane ecclesie magnum ex hoc
non ambigimus iamiam prouenisse dispendium. Vnde ne facto uestro uestem
Christi scindi, inconsutilem eius ⟨fo. 61 v⟩ tunicam male dissui taciturnitate nostra
et indiscreta quadam conniuentia sineremus, ad domnum papam appellauimus, et
debitam sibi fidelitatem ad ipsum apellando conseruauimus. Appellationis huius 15
dilata siquidem prosecutio non fuisset, nisi pietatis occulos in nos apostolica clementia reduxisset. Qui nobis et uobis affectu paterno compatiens laboribus nostris et
expensis, ut scribens ipse testatur,[1] misericorditer parcens, uiros sapientes et
honestos, peritos iuris et equitate probatissimos de latere suo transmisit ad nos, ut
causam hanc plene cognoscerent et ipsam suscepta potestatis plenitudine terminando, 20
finem laboribus iamdiu protractis imponerent. Literas in hoc domni pape suscepimus, quibus nobis apostolica auctoritate iniungitur ut eis assistere, appellationis
nostre causas apud eos exponere, eorum parere sentencie et reuerentiam iudiciarie
potestati debitam in omnibus exhibere non ommittamus. Ipsis itaque nostram una
cum domno nostro rege presentiam exhibere curauimus, optantes pariter et 25
expetentes omnia que inter domnum nostrum regem uertuntur et uos, simul et ea
que nos contingunt sub sole fieri et iuxta apostolici formam mandati diffinitiua
eorum sententia terminari. Constat itaque non subterfugisse iudicium quos ad
iudicium subeundum suis se constat iudicibus optulisse. Data uero opera procurasse,
ne qui ob pacem uenerant pacis fungerentur officio, quid est aliud nisi turbationem 30
ecclesie protelasse et eius spiritui qui ait 'Habete sal in uobis et pacem habete inter
uos'[2] animositate fortasse nimia restitisse? Ad iudices ex mandato properauimus, et
ecce qui nos audiant non habemus. Vnde ne apprehendant nos mala apellationis
remedio actenus euitata, ne potestatem quam in edificationem ecclesie et non
destructionem suscepisse debueratis, minus canonice exerceatis in nos, uestram 35
attendentes prudentiam statuta patrum non obseruare, si quid habetis in subditos
defensionis eis locum et tempus non concedere, suspendere statim nec citare,
reputare notoria que nec nota sunt nec subnixa ueritate, mandatis uestris in discrimen eorum quibus scribitis sarcinas graues imponere, contra suspectas nobis
sententias uestras, aduersus mandata uestra omnia domno nostro regi et regno 40
eius, nobis etiam et commissis nobis ecclesiis et parrochiis grauamen aliquod
importantia, ad eum cuius declinari nequid examen, domnum scilicet papam
apellamus et appellationi terminum diem obitus beati Martini constituimus.[3]

**182** 13 cindi B   15 conseruauimus Rb; conseruauerimus BD   32 fortasse Rb; forte BD
32–3 Ad...habemus *om.* D

---

[1] *MB Epp.* 257, to the English bishops, announcing the legation of William of Pavia and Otto
(1 Dec. 1166).
[2] Mc. ix. 49.     [3] This repeats the conclusion of no. 181 almost verbatim.

### 183 To Pope Alexander III

[November–December 1167] His appeal against the archbishop of Canterbury has not been dealt with by the legates in Normandy, and he is therefore compelled to renew it, setting the new term of St Martin's Day (11 November).

Patri suo et domno summo pontifici A⟨lexandro⟩ frater G⟨ilebertus⟩ Lundoniensis ecclesie minister, seipsum et si quid potest obedientie et humilitatis obsequium.

Ad uestram pater audientiam iamdiu ob mandata patris nostri domni Cantuar-⟨iensis⟩ michi grauamen non modicum inferentia appellaui, et audito legatorum
5 uestrorum in Normanniam aduentu, ipsis festinanter occur⟨fo. 62⟩ri, paratus in eorum presentia appellationis ad uos facte causas ostendere et eorum sententie in omnibus humiliter obedire. Quibus in causa hac suas minime partes interponentibus ob euitanda pericula que imminebant, ad uestram denuo sanctitatem appellare, multa proculdubio necessitate compulsus sum. Quia uero ad iter hoc arripiendum
10 ad uos me in Angliam remeare et itineri necessaria prouidere, ipsa propositi necessitas exigebat, non occasione dilationis querende, sed legitime prouisionis intuitu appellationi terminum diem transsitus beati Martini constitui. Vnde si pietatis occulos bonitas in me diuina reduxerit, et iter ad uos peruium michi clementer indulserit, statuto die uita comite Dominoque iuuante sanctitati uestre
15 astabo, que michi obicientur auditurus, uestreque per omnia sententie uel consilio deuotissime pariturus. Testis enim michi est inspector conscientie Deus me in his omnibus que apud nos acta sunt, nec adulationi, nec elationi, nec ambitioni uel in modico deseruisse, sed uestre sancteque Romane ecclesie fidelitati, et totius Angli-cane ecclesie utilitati, iuxsta modicum quod sum et sapio fideliter prospexisse. Hinc
20 enim patrem habens, hinc domnum, inter duos gladios positus—hinc in materialem timens impingere, hinc spiritualem formidans—sola uestri nominis protectus auctoritate, uix hereo, et finem quem his cladibus Dominus daturus est multo iam uite tedio affectus exspecto. Affectioni itaque qua filiis suis et compati et con-descendere pietas apostolica consueuit, deuotissime suplico ne appellationem ad uos
25 honesta causa et iustissima interpositam irritam habeatis, ne capud meum quod iniusto odio pater meus domnus Cant⟨uariensis⟩ dire persequitur ei penitus ex-ponatis, sed causam quam perstringimus ut postulat equitas ipse uel audiatis, uel si hoc difficultas non permittat itineris legatis uestris qui penes nos sunt cognoscendam et terminandam committatis. Quedam nuntio meo sanctitati uestre secretius inti-
30 manda commisi, quibus si misericorditer prebueritis assensum ad nutum uestrum meum hoc condigne remunerabit obsequium. Valere uos optamus in Domino, pater in Christo karissime.

183 G, no. 173; *MB Epp.* 569; B, fo. 61 v; D, fo. 79 v–80.
10 itinere BD    16 Testis est michi enim inspector D (*om.* conscientie)

## 184 To all the faithful

[1167–8] The decision of Gilbert as papal judge delegate in the case between Robert (?)[1] abbot of Ivry and Herlewin clerk of Docking (Norfolk)[2] on the tithes of Docking, in favour of the abbot.

No. 184 gives the decision of the bishops of London and Winchester in the case; no. 185 Gilbert's explanation to the Pope of why they proceeded to judgement in spite of the objection raised; and no. 186 the Pope's confirmation of their judgement. No. 186 is dated at Benevento on 8 November. Alexander was there in 1167, 1168 and 1169; but it is unlikely that Gilbert would have acted in this way in 1169,[3] when he was under Becket's ban, so that the process seems probably to belong to 1167 or 1168.

G(ilebertus) Dei gratia Lundoniensis episcopus dilectis sibi in Domino uniuersis sancte matris ecclesie filiis ad quos littere iste peruenerint, salutem in Christo.

Cum uenerabilis frater noster Robertus abbas de ⟨Ib⟩reio et Herlewinus clericus de Doching' pro causa que inter eos super decimis de Doching' uertebatur in presentia domni Winton(iensis) et nostra—quibus ex mandato domni pape eiusdem 5 cause cognitio delegata fuit—ambo pariter essent constituti, nos ex allegationibus et rationibus memorati abbatis liquido cognoscentes ⟨decimationes iamdictas⟩ ad ius ecclesie sue de Doching' pertinere, easdem abbati et per eum ecclesie sue de motu animi nostri et de communi fratrum nostrorum consilio in perpetuum adiudicauimus, ipsumque et ecclesiam suam a petitione Herlewini qui easdem uendicans 10 decimationes in probatione penitus defecit, per sententiam absoluimus. Quod quia in dubium nolumus aut in irritum de cetero posse reuocari, presenti scripto uniuersitati uestre id notificare et ea qua fungimur auctoritate confirmare curauimus.

## 185 To Pope Alexander III

[1167–8] He explains the decision in the case between Herlewin clerk and the abbot of Ivry (see no. 184), and Herlewin's objection on the ground that the case had been protracted beyond the permitted term.

Patri suo et domno summo pontifici A(lexandro) frater G(ilebertus) Lundoniensis ecclesie minister, ad omne patris imperium humilis obedientie famulatum.

**184** G, no. 184; B, fo. 164v.
3 ⟨Ib⟩reio] *So Giles;* reio B *preceded by a space: cf.* no. 185   7 B *omits, leaving a space for about two or three words; some phrase of this kind is missing, and the noun could be either* decimas (*used above*) *or* decimationes (*used below*). *For the text, cf.* no. 185*:* decimationes...iure plenissimo pertinere *and* decimationes iamdictas (*bis*). *Giles suggests* [predictas decimas]   11 per] p B
**185** G, no. 165; B, fo. 178.

---

[1] Probably for Roger, as in no. 186. The *Gallia Christiana* reckons that there were two Rogers (one occurring 1168, 1172, the other in 1185), but knows of no Robert. We have not been able to check any of these details. The Lire obituary has a Roger, abbot of Ivry, formerly monk of Lire, under 11 Dec. (*HF*, XXIII, 475).
[2] *VN*, p. 406, shows that Ivry had rights in churches in the neighbourhood of Docking.
[3] But cf. no. 209.

Sublimitatis uestre mandata debita domne ueneratione suscipimus, et exequendis his operam quam possumus et diligentiam reuerenter adhibemus. Que si quando
5 non statim ad ipsa conquerentium uota peragimus, non ideo negligenter aut tepide que nobis sunt iniuncta prosequimur, cum res cito decidere aliqua proculdubio iuris aut facti necessitate prepediamur. Vnde si causam Herlewini clerici aduersus uirum uenerabilem abbatem de Ybreio aliquantula ⟨fo. 178 v⟩ mora protraximus, id cause extitit ut sub indulta mora uerbis et ambagibus inuoluta ueritas erueretur et
10 lis in longum protracta fine tandem legitimo sopiretur. Eo uero processit inquisitio ut statutis diebus pluribus et partibus in se inuicem experientibus, domno Wintoniensi et nobis et instrumentis et testibus liquido claresceret decimationes ipsas quas modis omnibus extorquere nititur Herlewinus, ad ecclesiam de Docchinges quam iamdicto abbati uestra iamdiu adiudicauit auctoritas iure plenissimo pertinere, et easdem
15 Herlewino nullo prorsus iure competere. Factum enim quo nititur Herlewinus hoc est. Tempore belli cum in Anglorum regno licebat fere totum cuique quod poterat, ecclesiam iamdictam clericus quidam Willelmus nomine adeptus est. Hunc Herlewinus ob quod ecclesiam ipsam patruus suus quidam uidelicet sacerdos ante possederat infestans plurimum, in hoc tandem induxit, ut decimationes ecclesie sua
20 solum auctoritate annuo sibi censu tenendas concederet, ut Herlewinus uel sic ab eius infestatione conquiesceret. Qui nimirum Willelmus non multo post ad frugem melioris uite se transferens, ecclesiam cum omnibus ad ipsam pertinentibus in manu domni Norwic(ensis) refutauit, ut eam ipse disponeret et personam iam uacanti prouideret. Ecclesia sic uacante Willelmus de Ibreio fundi ipsius domnus abbatem
25 de Ybreio domno Norwic(ensi) presentans, id suplicando obtinuit ut eum in ecclesia ipsa personam constitueret, eamque cum omnibus ad ipsam pertinentibus monasterio suo pia et in perpetuum ualitura donatione concederet. Herlewinus uero ex pacto cum Willelmo inito—nulli, nunquam episcopali auctoritate firmato —abbatem ad prestandas sibi decimationes iamdictas teneri estimans ipsas petere
30 non desistit, quas tamen sibi competere nulla ratione iuris ostendit. Ipso itaque in his ius suum nullum penitus ostendente, et cum has sibi episcopali auctoritate fuisse concessas quandoque diceret in huius etiam rei probatione prorsus deficiente abbatem ab eius petitione absoluimus, et domno Norwic(ensi) ut decima⟨fo. 179⟩tiones iamdictas sibi restitueret, et eius de cetero paci prouideret apostolica auctoritate
35 iniuncximus. Quod totum Herlewinus euacuare moliens falso uestre suggessit excellentie nos cause quam infra duo menses terminandam suscepimus, non nisi post undecim ebdomadas diem constituisse et nos a uestri forma mandati taliter recessisse. Qua in re quod actum est aperimus, ut si in iure errauimus, edocti per uos in obscuritatibus huiusmodi de cetero cautius ambulemus. Mandatum quidem
40 causam intra duos menses terminandi suscepimus, et infra eundem terminum cause diem constituendo Lundonie die ipso dominus Winton(iensis) et ego conuenimus. Domnus uero Winton(iensis) cum ipsum in curiam regis urgentissima eodem die causa pertraheret, atendens mandate sibi iuridicionis diem cedere, seque ob temporis angustias negotio uacare non posse, erga Herlewinum haberi se uoluit
45 excusatum. Herlewino uero instante plurimum et in hoc abbate prebente consen-

**185** 4 reuerentur B   5 tepede B   8 abbem B   9 ambagimus B   19 tanden B

sum, ultra prefixsum nobis terminum diem constituimus et eo quo dictum est causam fine decidimus. Diu tamen super hoc disceptatum est, asserentibus quibusdam id non licere, et hec ea lege probantibus qua dictum est: 'cum non eo die quo preses prouincie precepit iudex ab eo datus pronuntiauerit, sed ductis diebus alieniore tempore sententiam dederit, preses ex integro rem cognoscet.'[1] Aliis uero 50 asserentibus a similibus ad similia iudicem procedere, et ius dicere sic debere de iudice dato ad certam summam illud inducebant: 'Iudex qui usque ad certam summam iudicare uisus est, etiam de re maiore iudicare potest si inter litigatores hoc conuenerit';[2] quod ad simile pertrahentes inferebant, ad certum tempus iudicem datum si partes consentiant ulteriore quoque tempore posse cognoscere—hoc 55 ipsum lege de arbitro comprobantes, qui licet de proferendo die cautum non sit, compromissi diem proferre potest si partes eam sententiam ferre consentiant.[3] Mandatum itaque uestrum in modum hunc interpretantes et quod ob fauorem alicuius indultum est in eius lesionem re⟨fo. 179 v⟩torqueri non debere existimantes, iuxta quod apud nos in mandatis huiusmodi consueuit ecclesia, in negotio dicto iam 60 modo processimus, id precipue secuti quod in libro Digestorum expressum taliter inuenimus: 'si iudex ad tempus datus et omnes litigatores consenserint, nisi specialiter principali iussione prorogatio fuerit inhibita, possunt tempora intra que iussus est litem dirimere prorogari.'[4] Valete uos.

## 186   Alexander III to Abbot Roger and the monks of Ivry

[8 November 1167 or 1168] The Pope gives judgement in the case between the monks of Ivry and Herlewin on the tithes of Docking, in favour of Ivry.

A⟨lexander⟩ episcopus seruus seruorum Dei, dilectis filiis Rogero abbati et fratribus monasterii de Ibreio, salutem et apostolicam benedictionem.

Venerabiles fratres nostri Henricus Winton⟨iensis⟩ et Gilebertus Lundoniensis episcopi, transmissis nobis litteris intimarunt quod cum eis causam que inter uos et Herl⟨ewinum⟩ clericum super decimis de Doching', quas sibi idem Herlewinus 5 concessas fuisse dicebat, diutius uertebatur, commisissemus apellatione remota fine debito terminandam, ipsi auditis rationibus hinc inde et plenius intellectis, quoniam prefatus Herlewi⟨nus⟩ in probatione defecit, prescriptas uobis et ecclesie uestre decimas adiudicarunt, et tam uos quam eandem ecclesiam ab impetitione ipsius super his perpetuo absoluerunt, sicut ex litteris sententie sue quas nos ipsi inspexi- 10 mus manifeste comparet. Vnde cum tam tu, fili abas, quam idem Herl⟨ewinus⟩ in nostra essetis propter hoc presentia constituti, et Herl⟨ewinus⟩ prelibati episcopi Lundoniensis tantum litteras nobis offerens se sicut eedem continebant appellasse proponeret, et sententiam quam non infra terminum mandati nostri lata fuit rescindi instantius postularet, nos attendentes quod ea memoratis episcopis fuit 15 appellatione remota ipso consentiente et petente commissa, considerantes etiam

---

**185** 63 speciliter B    64 iusus B    64 Val'e uos B, *perhaps for* Valere uos optamus
**186** G, no. 375; JL 11,446; B, fo. 137v.

---

[1] *Code*, 7, 64, 6.    [2] Cf. *Digest*, 50, 1, 28.
[3] Cf. *Digest*, 4, 8, 16, 1; 4, 8, 14.    [4] *Digest*, 5, 1, 2, 2.

quod sicut idem episcopi suis nobis litteris intimarunt de assensu illius terminum produxerunt, sententiam prescriptam duximus ratam habendam, et uos a predicti Herl(ewini)—de communi fratrum nostrorum consilio—impetitione absoluimus,
20 et ei perpetuum super hoc silentium imponentes, pretaxatas uobis decimas et per uos ecclesie prelibate auctoritate apostolica confirmamus, et presentis scripti patrocinio communimus, statuentes ut nulli omnino hominum liceat hanc paginam nostre confirmationis et diffinitionis infringere, uel ei aliquatenus contraire. Si quis autem hoc attemptare presumpserit, indignationem omnipotentis Dei et beatorum
25 Petri et Pauli apostolorum eius se nouerit incursurum. Dat' Beneuenti, vi idus Nouembris.

## 187  To Abbot Andrew and the chapter of Cirencester Abbey

[Late 1167–8] He requests them to release Master Osbern, prior of Cirencester, who has been elected prior of Holy Trinity, Aldgate.

For the date of this election and the obscurity as to whether Osbern became prior, see Biog. Index. Gilbert is writing as ordinary of Holy Trinity, Aldgate.

G(ilebertus) Dei gratia Lundoniensis episcopus uenerabili fratri et amico karissimo A(ndree) abati Cirecestrie totique eiusdem ecclesie capitulo, salutem, gratiam et benedictionem. ⟨fo. 142⟩
Ex iniuncto nobis officio ecclesie Dei, quam ipsius permissu aliqua sui portione
5 regendam suscepimus, ad eius honorem cui desponsata est debita sollicitudine prouidere compellimur. Vnde quia uestre conuersationis opinio ipsa meriti sanctitate ad omnes longe lateque diffusa est, insedit ecclesie sancte Trinitatis Lund(onie) Domino ut credimus id inspirante et ecclesia cui presidemus afferente consilium, ut priorem ecclesie uestre magistrum uidelicet Osb(ern)um, cui ad
10 doctrinam scientia et ad honestatem mores exuberant, sibi in priorem unanimiter eligerent ipsumque sibi in patrem et pastorem concedi concorditer omnes exopta- rent. Quia uero iuuanda sunt et promouenda semper honesta consilia, dilecte nobis in Domino beniuolentie uestre affectuose preces porrigimus quatinus iamdictorum fratrum desideriis effectu respondeatis, et ipsum ad honorem Dei et ecclesie uestre
15 ab obedientia uestra regulariter absolutum, et Lundoniensi ecclesie de cetero obediturum, predictis fratribus ad domus sue curam suscipiendam et ag⟨e⟩ndam non interueniente dilatione, que periculum infert sepe negotiis, prompte et libere concedatis, ut totam Lundoniensis ecclesie plenitudinem obsequiis amodo uestris obnoxiam habeatis. Valere uos in Domino optamus, karissimi.

## 188  To Dean Geoffrey and the chapter of Hereford Cathedral

[c. 1167–8] He asks them to allow R(ichard Foliot) archdeacon of Colchester and canon of Hereford to receive his portion from their church while he is absent studying in the schools.

Letters 188–92 are concerned with three canons of St Paul's who were students at Bologna,

187 G, no. 256; B, fo. 141 v.
2 Ci/restrie B    8 ass'entiente B (assentiente consilium *seems incorrect*)
188 G, no. 216; B, fo. 142.

Master David of London and two of Gilbert's nephews, Richard Foliot archdeacon of Colchester and Robert Banastre archdeacon of Essex. They are closely linked with a group of letters written by Master David.[1]

In a letter written early in 1170, the Pope asserts that Master David had been three years or more in the schools (i.e. at Bologna).[2] This suggests that he arrived in Bologna in 1166 or early in 1167. The arrival of Gilbert's two nephews, for which letters 188–9 are a preparation, and which is referred to in one of David's letters,[3] can thus be dated *c.* 1167–8—certainly not later, since Richard Foliot left Bologna again late in 1168 or early in 1169.[4] Thus nos. 188–9 belong to *c.* 1167–8, no. 191, in which Gilbert summons Richard to return, to 1168 or very early in 1169; and no. 190, which belongs to David's early years at Bologna, and seems to come between the two pairs of letters, can be dated *c.* 1168.[5]

G(ilebertus) Dei gratia L(undoniensis) episcopus dilectis sibi in Domino G(alfrido) Hereford(ensi) decano totique capitulo, salutem et sincere dilectionis affectum.

Vsu celebre est ut a quibus repulsa non metuitur, et de quorum karitate fides habetur certior, his cum indubitata obtinendi que cupimus fiducia preces uberius offeramus. Cum itaque preteritorum exhibitio in postulandis nos tutiores efficiat, 5 cum uniuersis singulos affectuose rogamus, quatinus certa negotia R(icardi) Colec(estrensis) ⟨archidiaconi⟩ et canonici uestri diuine pietatis et nostre petitionis intuitu misericorditer agatis, ut dum in scolis moratur portionis que eum contingit non sentiat dispendium. Pium est enim his subuenire quos amor scientie facit exules; nec certe trahendum est ad consequentiam si quid in piis causis fiat extra ordinem. 10 Gratius ut nostis fieri solet accipienti postulatum dum offertur, quam cum ab inuito iudicii calculus emunit, et utinam necessitatem faciendi uoluntas antecedat, et cohercionem mera liberalitas preueniat. Scitis etenim quid nobis datum sit in mandatis, quod exsequi supersedimus, laboribus uestris et expensis parcere cupientes,

**188** 7 ⟨archidiaconi⟩ Ad fidem B (*preceded by a space. There is little doubt that the man in question must be Richard archdeacon of Colchester*) 10 impiis B 12 emungit B

---

[1] See Z. N. Brooke, 'The Register of Master David...', *Essays in History presented to R. L. Poole*, ed. H. W. C. Davis, pp. 227–45. The letters in question here are nos. 1, 2, 5, 7, 8, 12, 72 in the list on pp. 230–3—they will be referred to below by these numbers; they are printed in Liverani, pp. 622–4, 626–8, 610, 618–19, 618, 603–4, 544 (also JL 11,718).

[2] 'Register of Master David', no. 72 (JL 11,718; cf. Z. N. Brooke, *art. cit.* pp. 237 ff.). *Ibid.* no. 2, David, writing possibly to Gilbert, complains that he has been two years and a half under usury in Bologna (this may be an answer to no. 190 below); in no. 12, he had been one and a half years under usury. These letters were presumably written *c.* 1169 and *c.* 1168.

[3] *Ibid.* no. 5, evidently written at the same time as no. 1; they seem to belong shortly before no. 12 (*c.* 1168) from the description of Master David's affairs in them. No. 12 refers to one 'Ruffus' as David's companion on his journey to Bologna; this could be Richard Rufus, canon of St Paul's (see *GF*, p. 287).

[4] See no. 202; even if this refers to Robert Banastre, it is clear that Richard Foliot had already returned (see nos. 191–2).

[5] Evidently David had been some time in Bologna, since Gilbert suggests a visit to England. David's belief that Gilbert was angry with him seems to connect it with 'Register of Master David', nos. 1 (probably addressed to Gilbert; no. 190 may be an answer to it), 5, both written about the time of the archdeacon's arrival. No. 190 thus probably belongs a few months after the latter's arrival in Bologna.

15 sub spe certissima ⟨fo. 142v⟩ id expectantes ut uoto et necessitati iamdicti Ricardi, magis uoluntate quam sententia satisfiat quod adhuc futurum speramus, preces precibus adiungentes quatinus apud uos nostras sibi profuisse preces res ipsa declaret, et ipsum seruitii, nos gratiarum debitores habeatis.

### 189  To Dean Geoffrey and the chapter of Hereford Cathedral

[c. 1167–8] He asks leave for his nephew R(ichard Foliot or Robert Banastre),[1] canon of Hereford, to be abroad for study without losing any of the benefits of his prebend.

[ . . . ]G(alfrido) decano et toti capitulo Hereford(ensi) ecclesie, salutem in Domino.

Magna quadam securitate beniuolentiam uestram et gratiam semper uendicamus, ideoque cum nostra seu nostrorum necessitas efflagitat amicorum confidenter ad uos ingredimur, cum omni spe impetrandi quicquid amico potest et debet amico-
5 rum caritas indulgere. R. siquidem nepos noster uesterque canonicus de proposito suo et consilio nostro per Dei gratiam studiorum causa nuper transfretaturus est. Proinde dilecte nobis et diligende semper in Domino uniuersitati uestre preces obnixe porrigimus, quatinus intuitu tam fauorabilis propositi nostreque si placet petitionis interuentu, unam hanc nobis licentiam indulgeatis, sine diminutione
10 beneficiorum prebende sue, suamque interim absentiam cum sui si placet indemnitate excusatam habeatis, ut et ipsum uestris deuotiorem obsequiis et nos uobis pro ipso amplioris gratie debitores efficiatis. Bene ualeant singuli; bene ualeant et uniuersi.

### 190  To Master David

[c. 1168] He denies the report that he is angry with David and suggests that he pay a visit to England.

Gill(ebertus) Dei gratia Lundoniensis episcopus dilecto suo magistro Dauid, salutem et optatos ad uota successus.

Inspectis litteris a tua michi diligentia directis, palam datur aduertere te et commotionis et ire fomitem inter nos aliquo discordiam seminante concepisse. Quem
5 quicumque ille est de cetero minus audias, nec eius comentis, obsecro, fidem ulterius adhibeas. Amicorum namque sepe confundit animos lingua tertia digna confundi, quam ire et odiorum incentiua portantem a nobis obsecro non admitti. Nil enim de te sinistrum concipio, nil intus aduersum te corde foueo, sed admissum semel in gratiam michi et gratie et beniuolentie uicissitudinem obseruare deposco. De cetero
10 quia sales uestros habunde iamdiu lambit Italia, bonum est ut eosdem amodo—cum tamen libuerit—experiatur et Anglia. Vale karissime.

**189** G, no. 217; B, fo. 170.
**190** G, no. 283; B, fo. 186.
10 lamsit B

---

[1] There is no other evidence that Robert Banastre was a canon of Hereford; if he was not, this must be a duplicate of 188.

### 191 To Richard Foliot, archdeacon of Colchester

[1168–9] He summons him, if he thinks Bologna injurious to his health, to return and pass on his debts to R(obert Banastre), whom he can clear on his return. Gilbert is at present in Normandy.[1]

Gil(ebertus) Dei gratia Lundoniensis episcopus dilecto suo R(icardo) archidiacono Colec(estrie), salutem, gratiam et benedictionem.

Directas a te michi litteras multa gaudii alacritate suscepi, inspectas tamen paululum egra proculdubio mente percurri. Leta michi nuntianda sperabam, et ecce grauem ingerunt michi nuntiata tristitiam. Doleo super iuuene nobilissimo qui 5 premature fati munus impleuit. Casum circa te simile metuens quem morbus ut audio modis iam pluribus attemptauit. Vnde tibi mando mandansque precipio quatinus occasione postposita, si statum Bononie tibi suspectum tueque aduersum ualitudini uel in modico senseris, ad saluandam animam tuam ocius exeas et fugias, et tuum ad nos reditum maturare non obmittas. R(obertum) uero archidiaconum 10 in quibus te impeditum noueris obliges, et ad nos cito ueniens ipsum expedire et debitis exonerare festines. Me uero noueris in Normannia adhuc moram facere, et tuum ad me reditum prestolari pariter et optare. Vale karissime.

### 192 To Robert Banastre, archdeacon of Essex

[1168–9] Robert has been long at Bologna, and Gilbert urges him to work hard and show a profit. Archdeacon Richard has been summoned for his health's sake.

This seems to indicate that no. 191 took effect, and Richard returned.

Gil(ebertus) Dei gratia Lundoniensis episcopus dilecto suo Roberto archidiacono Essex(ie), salutem, gratiam et benedictionem.

Attendas queso karissime in quam longinqua migraueris, quantum etiam laborem quantumque tedium solo litterarum amore subieris, et des operam sollicite ut laboris tanti condignos fructus ad nos quandoque ualeas cooperante gratia 5 reportare. Non effluant tibi dies dum potes et etas permittit idonea; disce quod postmodum doceas, et in sinum mentis collige quod exigente necessitate suo queas tempore pluribus erogare. Nichil est quod idonee tuam possit industriam excusare,

**191** G, no. 258; B, fos. 144 (B1) *and* 186 (B2) (*spelling as* B2).
1–2 Gilebertus...benedictionem *om.* B1   4 pculdubia B1   5 michi ingerunt B1   7 iam pluribus modis B1   10 nos] ad *added* B1   10 archidiaconum *om.* B1   13 me reditum] mare dictum B1   13 Vale karissime *om.* B1
**192** G, no. 240; B, fo. 185v.
2 salutem et B (*contrary to Foliot's otherwise invariable practice*)   3 etiam *Giles*; enim (enĩ) B

---

[1] Gilbert was in France in November 1167 (Eyton, *Itinerary*, pp. 110–11) and again in July–August and November 1169 (see notes to nos. 198, 206, 210). The former occasion seems too early, the latter too late for this letter. No. 193 seems to suggest that he was in Normandy some time in 1168, and no. 210 shows that he was in France at the turn of 1168–9 to be present at the meeting with the legates at Montmirail in January 1169. He was back in England in February when he made one of his appeals (see note to no. 198).

corpus tibi donante Domino sanum est et incolume, etas habilis, facultas suppetens,
10 locus habundans mercibus quas optasti, magistrorum copia, sociorum grata
frequentia. Assit amor studii et mentis applicatio uoluntaria, de die poteris in diem
proficere et longe teipso effectus melior tuis iocundissime laboribus arridere.
Attende quid sit moram fecisse Bononie, et ea quibus iamdicta ciuitas insignis effecta
est turpiter ignorare. Hec altera iam Carihatsepher quod est 'ciuitas litterarum'
15 digne meruit appellari,[1] que summi subtilitate ingenii hebetem tot temporibus
mundum exacuit, legum thesauros aperuit et abdita sapientie summi tandem uigore
studii in lucem potentissime protraxit. Hinc te litterarum quod absit inscium sensus
inopem reuerti, karissime, deprecor erubescas, ne quod cunctis fere cessit ad gloriam,
in ⟨fo. 186⟩ opprobrium tibi cedat et ignominiam. Ricardum archidiaconum reuoco,
20 quem si diutius moram fecerit de medio subtrahi pertimesco. Te eius honera[2]
sustinere necesse est, que statim cum uenerit iuuante Domino leuigabimus. Valere
te et omnimodis proficere desideramus karissime.

### 193   To Pope Alexander III

[1168] He asks the Pope to assist the abbey of Fécamp to recover from a disastrous fire.

The fire was no doubt that referred to by Robert of Torigny under 1168.[3] It is perhaps
likely that Gilbert was in Normandy when this was written: cf. no. 192.[4] Presumably
Gilbert was joining a petition for an indulgence to help the building fund.

Patri suo et domno summo pontifici A(lexandro) frater G(ilebertus) Lundoniensis
ecclesie minister, pedibus sanctis conculcato Satan in Christo triumphare feliciter.[5]
Cum ad uestram, pater in Christo dilecte, sullimitatem omnium sic disponente
Domino spectet ecclesiarum sollicitudo,[6] ad eas tamen oculos misericordie reducere
5 benignius equum est, quos amplior commendat caritas et ad omnes obsequii deuoti
propensior in caritate benignitas. Quod quia in Fiscamensi ecclesia diu uiguisse
ipsa rerum edocet experientia, ad sanctitatem uestram cui sancta placere studia luce
clarius enitescit, in ea qua laborat ad presens necessitate recurrit cum fiducia, inde
prouenturum sibi sperans auxilium unde quique referunt optatum, misericordia
10 sibi laudabiliter compatiente remedium. Que nimirum hoste generis humani
fidelium semper inuidente successibus casuali nuper incendio concremata ad hoc
misere perducta est, ut que nobilissimi dudum fuerat conuentus habitaculum,
pauperum, peregrinorum, et hospitali gratia indigentium quorumcumque refugium
iam non habeat ubi caput reclinet, ubi diuina celebret, ubi conseruet ordinem,
15 aduentantium ubi releuet necessitatem. Vnde cum supplicante petimus, cum
exorante sublimitati uestre preces affectuose porrigimus, ut sibi litterarum uestrarum subueniat indulta pie benignitas, ut quod machinante maligno dirissime

---

**193** G, no. 167; B, fo. 185.

[1] Cf. Jos. xv. 15.         [2] Presumably a reference to Richard's debts: cf. no. 192.
[3] P. 234; cf. the thireenth-century poem ed. A. Långfors in *Annales Academiae Scientiarum Fennicae*, series B, XXII, i (1927–8), 56, 230–1.
[4] But Torigny places the fire early in the year, perhaps *c.* January.
[5] Cf. no. 177.         [6] Cf. II Cor. xi. 28 and no. 223.

conflagratum est, in eius ignominiam Christique perhennem gloriam uestra reformet auctoritas, ut ope uestra dissipatus ordo conualeat, ⟨fo. 185v⟩ caritas antiqua refloreat, et statuto uobis memoriali quodam eterno pre oculis semper 20 habeat conuentus ille fratrum unde sanctitati uestre gratias indesinenter exoluat. Conseruet incolumitatem uestram Dominus, in Christo dilecte pater.

## 194 To Robert II, earl of Leicester

[1163–8] He commends Earl Robert's way of life and charity to the poor.

Letters 194–5 seem to have been sent together: the repetition of 'spero columbam sanctam ...iam nidificasse in te' (194) as 'nidificauit in te columba...' in no. 195, addressed to the countess, seems to establish the point. The countess must be Amice, wife of Earl Robert II (cf. no. 120), and so the earl was Robert II, not his son Robert III. Robert II died in 1168.

Venerabili domno et amico suo karissimo Roberto comiti Legerc(estrie) frater G(ilebertus) Londoniensis ecclesie minister, consecrata Domino tirocinia beate perseuerantie fine concludere.

Cum sit uitiis et diuitiis admodum grata societas gratulor et michi totus applaudo carissime diuitias in te quadam singulari gratia deseruire uirtuti. Audisti diuitem 5 illum purpura et bisso uestitum, epulantem cotidie splendide, miserabiliter ad inferna deductum, ubi cum flammis anxius estuaret, in lingue sue refrigerium nec aque guttam ualuit impetrare.[1] Audisti et in ewangelio diuitem cuius uberes fructus ager attulit, dicentem intra se: 'destruam horrea mea et maiora faciam et illuc congregabo omnia que nata sunt michi bona et dicam anime mee, "Anima, habes 10 multa bona posita in annos plurimos: requiesce, comede, bibe et epulare".' Cui diuinitus dictum est: 'Stulte, hac nocte animam tuam repetent a te. Que autem parasti, cuius erunt?'[2] Et si mentis occulos in mundi plenitudinem Dei spiritu lucem ministrante circumquaque reducimus, diuitibus huius mundi mundum habundare cognoscimus, quibus sue diuitie fomento uitiorum sunt non incremento 15 uirtutum, cum ⟨fo. 47v⟩ magis possideantur ab his quam eas quadam animi sancti nobilitate possideant. Diuites huiusmodi, ait Dominus, non facile regnum Dei adepturos, et camelum per foramen acus intrare posse facilius quam ipsos in regnum celorum[3]—tremenda uox, et diuitibus huiusmodi exhorrenda. Gratulor et totus michi applaudo, carissime, quod istorum abhorres semitas, horum iamdiu uestigia 20 declinasti; gaudeo te tua cogitare nouissima et illud psalmiste mentis occulis intueri: 'Dormierunt sompnum suum et nichil inuenerunt omnes uiri diuitiarum in manibus suis.'[4] Qui sibi credita si fideliter erogassent euigilantes illa die a sompno mortis suis hec in manibus inuenissent. Diuina uoce dictum est: 'Non apparebis uacuus ante conspectum Domini Dei tui.'[5] Totum quod ecclesie Dei, quod Christi 25

**194** G, no. 279; B, fo. 47.
6 splendie B    8 gugtam B

---

[1] Cf. Luc. xvi. 19 ff.
[2] Luc. xii. 16 ff.
[3] Cf. Mc. x. 23–5; Matt. xix. 23–4.
[4] Ps. lxxv. 6.
[5] Eccli. xxxv. 6; cf. Ex. xxiii. 15; xxxiv. 20; Deut. xvi. 16.

pauperibus ad presens erogas, illa die paratum inuenies; et quod modo larga miseratione distribuis, illa die Domino cum fiducia presentabis. Beati multi sunt et sapientes; hos tamen tantum beatos iudico, hos solummodo sapientes qui mansura semper bona crebra meditatione considerant, in his mentem ocupant, his inuigilant,
30 et hec ⟨ut⟩ queant apprehendere tota animi ratione pertractant. Credo karissime Patri complacuisse in te; spero columbam sanctam que super Dominum in Iordane apparuit[1] iam nidificasse in te. Curre post spiritum qui trahit te, qui suis intus bonis ornabit te et amore Christi perfecto ditabit te; cuius amor uerus si tangit te, si rapit te, si absorbet te, leuabit te iuxta prophetam super te, quia super altitudinem
35 extollet te.[2] Scribendi tibi nactus occasionem uix me coibeo, karissime.

### 195 To Amice, countess of Leicester

[1163–8] He regrets the circumstances of his present life, in which he is surrounded by secular cares, and so cannot visit the countess.[3] Cf. no. 120.

G(ilebertus) Dei gratia Londoniensis ecclesie minister A(micie) uenerabili comitisse Legrec(estrie), quod petit accipere, quo tendit pie tandem completo cursu pertingere.

Dilectioni tue dilectissima rogatus litteras mitto, quas quidem misisse debueram non rogatus. Quod si omisi iam aliquamdiu, hec causa exstitit quod de die in diem
5 meum ad te nuntium ipse preire et preuenire existimabam. Et quia spes dubio uultu nos semper protrahit in cras, et quod non feci 'cras' ait 'efficiam', sperabam me finem dare negotiis et sopitis aliquamdiu causis et curis omissis, ocius transmea-
⟨fo. 45v⟩re ad te et optate michi allocutionis tue iocunde solacio recreari. Sed opportunitatem quo plus appeto, minus inuenio, et quibusdam amputatis capitibus
10 cum mundi bestiam extinxisse me reputo, ad capita multipliciter renascentia[4] toto ilico perhorresco. Curarum siquidem nullus est finis, et mundus in dies parturit, unde miseras affligat animas et a pie proposito intentionis auertat. O michi quid memorem soliloquia sancta que cum sponso suo anima quondam mea dum eam claustri silentia tegerent et tenerent, in spiritum eleuata permiscebat? Dum secu-
15 larium nescia in montem quodammodo cum Moyse concendebat, subtus se nubem relinquebat et nebulam,[5] et mundo posthabito in ignem illum quem Deus inhabitat nil nisi illum appetens tota tendebat. Vnde cum ipsam sua reuocasset infirmitas, non abscedens longe, non foras exiens, ad ipsos pedes Domini mente residebat attentius, et annos suos preteritos in amaritudine recogitans, excessus pristinos ipsis suarum
20 lacrimarum fluentis abluebat. Nunc me rei familiaris hinc cura distrahit, hinc causarum secularium pondus inuoluit. Nunc timor opprimit, nunc protrahit spes,

---

**194** 30 ⟨ut⟩ *ins. by modern hand in* B   34 pphetam B
**195** G, no. 281; B, fo. 45.
15 cumoyse B

---

[1] Cf. Is. lxii. 4; Matt. iii. 16, etc.   [2] Cf. Is. lviii. 14 (?).
[3] Gilbert's account of his secular distractions follows in a general way similar passages in Gregory the Great (see esp. *Registrum*, I, 5; V, 53a; IX, 227). But the verbal parallels are not close, and the use of the Canticle, characteristic of Gilbert and his age, is foreign to Gregory.
[4] Like the Hydra.   [5] Cf. Ex. xxiv. 15–18.

nunc leuant prospera, nunc aduersa deiciunt, ut quantis miseriarum cumulis misera subiciatur humanitas, ipsis pene rerum argumentis experiar. Quid tibi ergo dilectissima meus poterit dictare iam spiritus, que puritatem mentis inhabitas et spiritui tuo delicato nichil in refectionem nisi delicias spirituales appetis et exoptas? Nidificauit 25 in te columba illa que super Christum in Iordane uolitans ipsum cum omni gratiarum plenitudine semper inhabitat. Et de hac quidem plenitudine quantum ipse tribuit accepisti, et eius dona quanto gustas uberius tanto et uberius ministrari tibi auida spiritualium mente desideras. Intueri michi uideor tuam illam animam in sui feruore spiritus, hoc declamantem et cantantem: 'Fulcite me floribus, stipate me 30 malis, quia amore langueo.'[1] Vnde michi flores karissima quos tuo subministrem spiritui, ut ardens plus accendatur et tendens in superna auidius illuc rapiatur. Hii flores paradisi sunt, quos tibi sancte communicant, qui[2] nescientes et respuentes que mundi sunt sacrate quodammodo paradisum mentis inhabitant. Quos tua queso prece michi conciles, ut sub curarum gementem pondere ipsorum me apud 35 Dominum interuentu subleues et sustentes. Id enim modicum quod habeo tibi ab amicitiarum nostrarum exordiis in Domino communicare, nec destiti nec omitto. Valere te in Christo opto karissima.

## 196   To Robert II, earl of Leicester

[1163–8 (? 1165–8)] He complains of a summons from the earl to Baldwin canon of St Paul's to appear before him in a case between the canon and one of his tenants. The case—a trivial one anyway—pertains to the bishop's court, and Gilbert is returning the summons, whose authenticity he doubts.[3]

The earl addressed was doubtless Robert II, who was royal justiciar and died in April 1168. Possibly he was to preside at the court at Oxford in the king's absence. Henry II was in France for two periods between 1163 and April 1168, in March–May 1165, and from March 1166 onwards: on both occasions Earl Robert acted as regent.[4]

Venerabili domno et amico karissimo R(oberto) comiti Legr(ecestrie) frater G(ilebertus) Lundoniensis ecclesie minister, salutem que nunc est et quam speramus a Domino.

Verborum facile suadet paucitas cum ad exaudiendum prompta est ipsius ad quem scribitur amica benignitas.[5] De uobis itaque per omnia sperantes optime, 5 caritate sic exhortante confidimus ut unde recurrimus ad uos, in hoc repulsam minime sentiamus. A sublimitate uestra ad quendam canonicum nostrum et amicum Baldewinum nomine littere uestre citationis emisse sunt, ut apud Oxeneford(iam) in conuentu proximo presentem se uobis exhibeat et cuidam homini suo et fere rustico, de non obseruata pactione quadam inter ipsos ut asserit cyrographo 10 confirmata respondeat. Res exhilis est, causa permodica: dimidia uirgata terre est de

**195** 33 que] qui B
**196** G, no. 280; B, fo. 166.

---

[1] Cant. ii. 5.   [2] Presumably the *patres* or *fratres* of no. 120.
[3] Very likely a diplomatic suggestion offering the earl a way out without loss of face.
[4] *CP*, VII, 529.   [5] Cf. no. 160 n.

qua agitur, duodecim nummorum census qui annuatim exsoluitur. Vnde si inter clericum beati Pauli et ipsius hominem super fundo ecclesie sue pertinenti lis aliqua aborta est spectat ad nos si placet audire quod gestum est, et conquerenti iustitiam in
15 ⟨fo. 166v⟩ omnibus exhibere. Qui cum partes nostras despiciat et ad sublimitatem uestram nos transiliendo prosiliat, petimus beato Paulo et nobis si placet hanc reuerentiam exhiberi ut de conseruanda ecclesie Dei dignitate sua mentem uestram et animum ad nos remissus, per uos etiam quod iustum fuerit plene res⟨pon⟩surus, intelligat. Ad uos litteras citationis uestre remittimus, eo quod in his notariorum
20 uestrorum stilum minime recognoscimus. Valere uos optamus in Domino, et sua Cesari sic reddere ut que Dei sunt reddatis et Deo.[1]

### 197 To Richard of Ilchester, archdeacon of Poitiers, and other royal justices

[c. 1168–9] He makes a diplomatic request that two clerks arrested by the royal justices be handed over to the church courts.[2]

In the period 1162–73 Richard of Ilchester (see Biog. Index) must frequently have acted as royal justice, both at the exchequer and on eyre. But Richard was also in frequent attendance on Henry II, at his court in England and Normandy, and on embassies to Pope and emperor. He was certainly the leading figure in the eyre of 1168,[3] and this seems the most likely date for Gilbert's appeal to him and to his fellow justices. It is possible that the eyre continued into 1169.[4]

There are two versions of this letter; that in MS B may be a draft or a revised version: more probably a draft (cf. GF, p. 29).

*Version 1 (MS C)*

Gillebertus Dei gratia Lundoniensis episcopus cognato et amico suo karissimo Ricardo Pictauensi archidiacono ceterisque domni regis iustitiis, fructus operando iustitie mercedem iustitie reportare.

Regium dilectissimi gladium circumfertis quem, quia in uindictam malorum,
5 laudem uero bonorum consecratus est, sic opto de manu uestra experiantur et mali, ne quod absit eo puniantur et boni, sic eo putrida recidantur, ne membra que sana sunt et morbo carentia saucientur. Audistis piaculare flagitium, filios Belial clerici nil male meriti noctu domum irrupisse, ipsique plagis impositis eo semiuiuo relicto disparuisse.[5] Hos in proxime celebrata synodo in sue carnis interitum tradidimus
10 Sathane,[6] ut diuina id agente iustitia pene sentiant exactorem, quem admiserunt

---

**196** 18 res...urus, B, *corrected in margin; but the correction has been cut away, so that only* [  ] surus *remains. It is possible that the word order in this sentence should be emended*
**197** *Both versions: MB Epp.* 433; *version 1:* C, fo. 266 (265) (*in margin:* hec non fuit inter ordinatos—*see introd. to JS Epp.* II, *forthcoming*); *version 2:* G, no. 199; B, fo. 43 v.

---

[1] Cf. Matt. xxii. 21; Mc. xii. 17; Luc. xx. 25.
[2] See *GF*, p. 184 and n.; cf. also the discussion of this issue in H. G. Richardson and G. O. Sayles, *The Governance of England*, ch. XVI.
[3] Eyton, *Itinerary*, p. 117.
[4] *Ibid.* p. 130.
[5] Cf. Luc. x. 30.
[6] Cf. I Cor. v. 5.

intra se sceleris ante suggestorem. Horum quosdam ut fama est comprehendistis, quos iuris laqueis innodatos ad penam meritam legitimos in nullo tramites exce‑ dentes reposuistis. Laudo uos, et commissam uobis sollicitudinem laudabiliter exercere totus applaudo; quorum ne uel in modico decoloretur amministratio, rogans supplico quatinus diaconum illum et acolitum quos ob causam hanc nec 15 conuictos nec confessos includi fecistis, michi ob reuerentiam Domini Iesu—cuius sunt signati caractere, cuius similitudinem gestant corone—si quid aduersus eos habet accusator, ecclesiastica cohercendos iurisdictione restituatis, ne cum multa bene gesseritis, in hoc solo aduersus ordinem ecclesiasticum manum grauiter extendendo, uestre notam glorie inferatis. Valete karissimi, et in menbris sanctis incarcerato 20 Domino Iesu, carcerem quem clausistis aperite, carceremque nouissimum suis paratum contemptoribus expauescite.

## Version 2 (MS B)

G(ilebertus) Dei gratia Lundoniensis episcopus cognato et amico suo karissimo R(icardo) Pictaui(ensi) archidiacono ceterisque domni regis iusticiis, fructus operando iustitie mercedem iusti reportare.     25

Regium dilectissimi gladium circumfertis ad tempus, quem quia in uindictam malorum laudemque bonarum consecratus est, sic opto de manu uestra experiantur mali, ne quod absit eo puniantur et boni, sic putrida recidantur, ne membra que sana sunt morboque carentia plagis et cruciatibus attententur. Audistis piaculare flagitium honestum scilicet ⟨fo. 44⟩ clericum ad malorum insidias non uulneratum 30 solummodo sed et plagis inpositis relictum misere semiuiuum.[1] Cuius quidem perpetratores sceleris in proxime celebrata sinodo Satane tradidimus in sue carnis interitum,[2] ut quem instigatorem admiserunt, commissi sceleris urgente Domino sentiant et experiantur ultorem. Ex his quosdam ut audio apprehendistis eosque iuris laqueis ut potestatis iudiciarie seueritas expetit innodantes legitimos in nullo 35 tramites excessistis. Laudo uos et commissam uobis sollicitudinem laudabiliter excercere totus applaudo. Quorum ne uel in modico decoloretur amministratio rogans supplico quatinus diaconum illum et acolitum quos ob causam hanc includi fecistis ob reuerentiam Domini Iesu cuius sunt signati caractere, cuius similitudinem gestant corone, michi si quid aduersus eos habet accusator ecclesiastica coercendos 40 iuriditione restituatis, ne si Dominum Iesum in membris suis inclusum carcere audaci quod absit securitate detinueritis, ipsum uobis in illa die ianuam uite claudere diuina id exigente iustitia compellatis. Valere uos optamus in Domino karissimi.

**197** 11 sceleris] oculis C, *corrected*     33 celeris B

---

[1] Cf. Luc. x. 30.     [2] Cf. I Cor. v. 5.

## 198   To Archbishop Thomas Becket

[March 1169] He announces an appeal to the Pope by himself and the bishop of Salisbury, made about the beginning of Lent, against the severity of the archbishop's actions, and names the Octave of the Purification of the Blessed Virgin (9 February) as term.

On Palm Sunday, 13 April 1169, Becket at Clairvaux solemnly pronounced the excommunication of the bishops of London and Salisbury and others for the crimes of disobedience and contempt.[1] Some weeks before, about the beginning of Lent, the bishop of London, receiving news of what was in the wind, made his usual counter-appeal for the following 9 February.[2] Ash Wednesday fell on 5 March in 1169, so that 198–9, written shortly after the appeal, must be dated to middle or late March: if the statement in MB Epp. 518 is exact, the appeal was actually made on 18 March.

It was apparently on first hearing the news of the excommunication (though possibly a month or two later) that Gilbert wrote no. 200 to the Pope and no. 201 to Henry II; at about the same time he collected a dossier of testimonials.[3] Soon after (and before the end of May) he wrote no. 202 to Master David, asking him to represent him at the Curia.[4] Meanwhile he was preparing to circumvent the sentence. At a meeting at Westminster in May he made his claim to exemption from the jurisdiction of Canterbury.[5] But on Ascension Day (29 May) the letter of excommunication was dramatically delivered on the high altar of St Paul's cathedral, and Gilbert could ignore it no longer. He summoned a meeting of the London clergy two days later, at which the dean, archdeacon and others appealed on his behalf (MB Epp. 508). He also wrote to the king asking for permission to go overseas (no. 203, referred to in no. 204); and prepared for a wider assembly of ecclesiastics to meet on 7 June, writing to Robert Foliot asking him to attend (no. 204).[6] He respected the excommunication and set to work to prosecute his appeal.

Later in June or early in July Gilbert crossed to Normandy to await Henry II's return from Gascony and the nuncios who were expected from the Pope. In July–August Henry II came north to Angers and Argentan;[7] and it was apparently early in July that Gilbert exchanged letters with Bishop Jocelin on the return of his prodigal son—clearly Reginald FitzJocelin, who had been on embassy to the Curia, and brought back the joyful tidings that Alexander III wished to spare Jocelin.[8] These letters (nos. 206–8) anticipate the king's movements, and refer

---

[1] Diceto, I, 333; MB, III, 87–90; cf. MB Epp. 479–80, 488–90; etc.

[2] Nos. 198–203 (nos. 200–2 supply the date of the appeal).

[3] MB Epp. 518–29. It cannot be proved that all these were written in 1169; but some contain indications (e.g. a reference to the date of appeal or excommunication) which point definitely to that year, and most of them form a group in the manuscripts—though some are among letters of 1170 in D; it is probable that most, if not all, should be dated 1169.

[4] In no. 202 he seems to be treating the excommunication as null, and to have no intention of visiting the Pope in person; this suggests that it was written before 29 May (see below).

[5] See GF, pp. 151 ff.          [6] MB Epp. 510 seems to be Robert's reply.

[7] Eyton, Itinerary, p. 123.

[8] During the period 1163–9 (i.e. before the bishop of Chichester's death) Reginald went twice to Rome on the business of his father and the king, in 1167–8 (MB Epp. 339, 395–6) and in 1168–9 (MB Epp. 476, 515, 530). The movements of the king in 1169 fit better than in 1168; and whereas Reginald failed to raise Jocelin's suspension in 1168, in 1169 Reginald returned ahead of the papal legates (to whom Jocelin may refer) bearing the news that the Pope wished to spare the bishop of Salisbury; this would explain the implication of these letters that Reginald brought good news with him.

to the bishop of Chichester, who died on or about 13 July. Shortly afterwards Gilbert returned to England, and set out for the continent again at the beginning of October,[1] intending to go to Rome if the mission of the nuncios Gratian and Vivian proved ineffective. He was present at the meeting at Montmartre on 18 November,[2] and was held up further by the prospect of another meeting on 13 January at Tours, although the term of his appeal was 9 February. These facts are recounted in his letter to Master David, no. 210, which can be dated *c.* December 1169 (between 18 November and 13 January). He then went south, avoiding Burgundy owing to the suspicion of danger, and then by way of Montpellier and St-Gilles across the Alps to Milan. At Milan he received news that the archbishop of Rouen and the bishop of Exeter had been commissioned to absolve him.[3] Summoning Master David to assist him in the proceedings at Rouen (no. 211), he turned north once again, and at Rouen on Easter Day 1170 (5 April) he was absolved.[4]

Venerabili patri et domno T(home) Cantuar(iensi) archiepiscopo frater G(ile-bertus) Londoniensis ⟨B2, fo. 187v⟩ ecclesie minister, apto rationis moderamine sibi credita dispensare.

    Seueritatem uestram pater domnus Saresberiensis et ego, aliique fratres nostri ex retroactis et agnitis non inmerito suspectam habentes pertimuimus, ne in domnum 5 nostrum regem Anglie aut *in regnum eius, ne in nos Cantuariensis ecclesie suffra-ganeos episcopos, aut commissas nobis ecclesias, maledicti aut interdicti sententiam ferendam esse decerneretis, et nos indefensos—iuri tamen semper stare promtissimos —iamdicte pene nexibus inuolueretis. Quod ne uobis omnino foret liberum, ad clementiam domni pape iuxta Quadragesime initium appellauimus, et appella- 10 tioni diem octabas Purificationis beate Marie constituentes, hoc uobis scripto presenti significare curauimus, ut ⟨B1, fo. 147v⟩ si quid habetis in nos quod iudicio persequi libeat, in eius tunc presentia iuuante Domino respondeamus, et eius per omnia sententie humiliter et deuotissime pareamus. Auertat iram suam Dominus, ne quod proponitis optato fine concludatis. 15

**198** G, no. 195; *MB Epp.* 474; Lupus, I, 187 (i, 124); Liverani, pp. 643–4; B, fos. 147 (B1) *and* 187 (B2); D, fo. 83 r–v; Va, fo. 146v; Ia, p. 281; Ib, fo. 442v; C, fo. 83 (82); Co, fo. 44v; Vb, fo. 105; O, *not foliated*, no. 125; Bn, fo. 170; Ar, fo. 95 (*variants of* BnAr *not noted*) (*headings:* IaIb Domno Cant' G. Lund' episcopus; CCoVbO Thome Cantuariensi archiepiscopo Gillebertus (C; G. *ceteri*) Londoniensis episcopus) (*spelling as* B1).
1–3 Venerabili…dispensare *only in* BDVa    4 domnus…nostri *om.* Va    6, 8 *in/semper *om.* B1 Va    9 foret omnino BD    13 persequi BDVaIbC (*and* VbO); prosequi IaCo

---

[1] 'Octobri mense', no. 210; about Michaelmas, Diceto, I, 335.

[2] For the date, *MB Epp.* 607, etc.; Diceto, I, 335–7.

[3] Diceto, I, 337–8. Some of the sources substitute the bishop of Nevers for Exeter: FitzStephen (*MB*, III, 92), Diceto, the major manuscripts of *MB Epp.* 655 (IbCCo; Vb, by a common slip, has Lisieux), and some of 656, 658 (656: IbD; 658: IaIb) have Exeter; some manuscripts of 656, 658 have Nevers (656: IaCCoVb; 658: CoVbC over erasure). Since Ib is consistently for Exeter, and the other manuscripts all contradict themselves, the manuscript testimony is on the whole in favour of Exeter. To substitute Nevers for Exeter was a natural mistake at this point, since the Pope was addressing a number of letters to Rouen and Nevers, his new com-missioners for making peace between Henry II and Becket (and cf. no. 217); no reason of equal plausibility can be found for an emendation in the other direction. It seems likely that the mistake first arose in the heading of *MB Epp.* 656, and gradually spread.

[4] Diceto, I, 338; *MB Epp.* 658. Gilbert was reinstated on 1 May (Diceto, I, 351).

## 199  To Jocelin de Bohun, bishop of Salisbury

[March 1169] The archbishop of Canterbury has summoned them both to France, and threatens excommunication if they do not obey; Gilbert has already appealed to the Holy See, and is sending a messenger to inform the archbishop; he invites Jocelin to do likewise.

It is not explicitly stated here that Jocelin has already appealed; probably he had.

Venerabili domno et fratri karissimo Ioc(elino) Sar(esberiensi) Dei gratia episcopo frater G(ilebertus) Lundoniensis ecclesie minister salutem.

Domnus Cantuar(iensis) cum aduersus rempublicam regni huius ⟨fo. 59⟩ machinetur quanta potest, precipue tamen nos duos sicut dicitur seorsum ponit ad 5 sagittam,[1] in quos primos effundat impetus et potestatem exerceat in malo, quam non me beneficio memini uel sensisse. Ille namque ut dicitur emissis de nouo uocationibus nos duos in Galliis ex nomine uocauit, comminans et protestans publice se in nos excommunicationis latum ire sententiam, si non in Galliis sue quam citius assistamus presentie. In quo quia me pregrauari sentio, aduersus hoc ad 10 sedem apostolicam publice iam apellaui, quod et per literas et per nuntium, unum uidelicet ex clericis meis proxima die Veneris iuuante Domino profecturum, domno Cant(uariensi) denuntiare disposui. Super quo uestram quoque dilectionem certificare curaui, ut si eisdem placet uti consiliis, aliquis clericorum uestrorum missus a latere uestro simul iter arripiat, ut mutuis uti consiliis et societate mutua 15 possint consolari. Si quid certius accepistis super hac re, significate nobis si placet apud Lundon(iam) ubi moram facere disposui a sexta feria presentis ebdomade usque ad quartam feriam septimane sequentis. Valete.

## 200  To Pope Alexander III

[c. April 1169] He had appealed against the attacks of the archbishop of Canterbury about the beginning of Lent, naming as term the Octave of the Purification; if the archbishop has now launched a sentence against him, he begs the Pope to hold it null and void. The English bishops are so placed that it is impossible for them to obey the mandates of both king and archbishop.

**199** G, no. 243; *MB Epp.* 477; B, fo. 58 v; D, fos. 78 v–79; Rb, fo. 107 (*incomplete*); Jb, *unfoliated* (*incomplete: variants of* Jb *not noted*).
1 fratrique B    3 huius] mala *added in* B    4 quanta Rb; quanta quanta B; quanti D
5 effundit/exercet D    6 sensisse] Rb *and* Jb *end here*    6–7 emisso de nouo uocatione D, *corrected to* uocationibus    8 se...latum ire BD *for classical* latum iri    15 si placet *om.* D
**200** G, no. 175; *MB Epp.* 475; Lupus, I, 187–8 (i, 125); B, fo. 187; D, fos. 83 v–84; Va, fo. 146 v; Ia, pp. 281–2; Ib, fo. 443 r–v; C, fo. 83 (82) v; Co, fo. 44 v; Vb, fo. 105; O, *not foliated*, no. 126; Bn, fo. 170; Ar, fos. 95–6 (*variants of* VbOBn *and* Ar *not normally noted*) (*headings*: IaIb: Idem Alexandro pape; CCoVb: Alexandro pape Gillebertus (G. Co) Londoniensis episcopus).

[1] Cf. Lam. iii. 12.

Patri suo et domno summo pontifici Alex(andro) frater Gilebertus Lundoniensis ecclesie minister, humilem ad omne quod ualet mea paruitas obedientiam.

Seueritatem, domne, patris nostri domni Cantuar(iensis) archiepiscopi ex quibusdam auditis et agnitis recte suspectam habens, ne indebite pene me nexibus artaret et laqueis, ad uestram circa initium Quadragesime appellaui clementiam, et 5 appellationi diem octauas Purificationis beate Marie constitui, ut iram qua me iniuste persequitur uestra declinarem protectione, et nexus quibus inmeritum parabat inuoluere, usque ad diem cognitioni cause in presentia uestra constitutum, obiectu sacri nominis aliquatenus euitarem. Vnde dilecte mi in Domino sanctitati uestre pater, toto prostratus spiritu supplico, ne indultum oppressis omnibus 10 commune remedium michi si placet subtrahatis; ne me tamquam reprobum a uestri protectione tutaminis abiciatis; sed facta ad uos appellatione suscepta, si qua postmodum est in me lata sententia ipsam ut iustum est aut habeatis irritam aut teneatis suspensam, ut in die qua iuuante Domino sullimitati uestre paratus sum assistere, iuxta quod merui statuatis in me, et uel conuictum abiciatis uel innocen- 15 tem si sic uisum fuerit absoluatis. Nam culpa mea si qua est hec utique, quod mandatorum pondere, que utique aut declinare necesse michi fuerat aut cum defectu et omni miseria suscipere, me grauatum sentiens ad apostolicam ausus sum audientiam appellare, ut uestro me per omnia consilio committerem et consultis uobis, aut a regno discederem aut alleuiato mandatorum onere in commissa michi 20 ecclesia residerem. Nam ut breui complectar quod uerum est, dum inter domnum regem et domnum Cantuar(iensem) res in hunc modum uertitur impossibile est me aut alium regni ipsius episcopum unius mandatum suscipere et alterius iram importabilem declinare. Agat itaque si placet paterna pietas ut si in me nec confessum, nec conuictum, nec citatum, *nec ullo modo conuentum, post appellationem 25 etiam ad sublimitatem uestram interpositam ulla est prepropere uel preposter lata sententia hanc uiribus ut iustum est euacuetis.[1] Et si uestram ex sanctitate remittatis, iniuriam saltem beati Petri et sancte sedis eius ad animum reuocetis, et me ad omne quod iusseritis obsequium utique promptissimum inuenietis. Conseruet uos incolumem in longa tempora Dominus, in Christo dilectissime pater. 30

**200** 1–2 Patri...obedientiam *in* BDVa *only*   1 A.B   2 omne...mea] *So* Va; omnem quod(?) mea ualet B; omnem quo mea ualet D   3 domni *om.* Va   9 michi (m̄) BVa   10 omnibus] in *added in* BDVa   14 in *om.* BVa; O *margin*: de illa sententia quam be[...] in die Ascencionis   14 sum paratus BVa   16 utique] est *added in* BVa   19 committerem consilio Va   20 a] *Only in* BDVaIb (?)   23 ipsius regni Va   23 mandatum IaIbCCo; mandata BDVa   25 *nec] ?non B   26 preposter] postere B; Va *adds* in me *before* preposter   27 remittitis Va   30 dilecte Va

---

[1] Cf. *Decretum*, C. 24, q. 3, c. 6 (cited in *Causa, MB*, IV, 219).

## 201  To King Henry II

[*c.* April–May 1169] The archbishop of Canterbury has attempted to wield the spiritual sword against Gilbert, but Gilbert has anticipated it by an appeal to the Pope, which, since it was made at the beginning of Lent, makes null the sentence launched on Palm Sunday (13 April).

This letter may possibly be a draft of no. 203.

Domno suo karissimo illustri Anglorum regi H(enrico) frater G(ilebertus) Londoniensis ecclesie minister, salutem et debitum deuote fidelitatis obsequium.

Vestram domne credimus non latere excellentiam qualiter in me et quosdam alios fideles uestros manum suam domnus Cantuar(iensis) aggrauauerit, et quoad
5 potuit gladium in nos spiritualem in iuris publici lesionem dextera iniquitatis extorsit. Canon namque potissimus hic est, ut nemo prepropere uel prepostere—id est non commonitus neque conuictus—iudicetur nec episcopus omnino quemquam excommunicet donec causa probetur super qua reus impetitur.[1] Vnde cum a iure exorbitauerit de Domino confidimus ut in nos uibrando gladium aerem potius
10 uerberauerit, quam *aut corpore aut anima spirituale nobis uulnus inflixerit.[2] Ictus enim eius ad domnum papam appellando preuenimus, et in initio Quadragesime facta appellatio sententiam die Palmarum latam plene uiribus euacuauit. Sixtus enim papa sic constituit: 'Quotiens episcopus se a suo metropolitano putauerit pregrauari, uel eum suspectum habuerit, mox Romanam ⟨fo. 147⟩ apellet sedem,
15 a qua dum se audiri poposcerit, nullus eum excommunicet antequam causa summi pontificis auctoritate finiatur. Quod si aliter presumptum fuerit, nichil erit, sed uiribus omnino carebit.'[3]

## 202  To Master David

[*c.* April–May 1169] He has heard of David's devotion from his nephew,[4] and asks him to assist in the prosecution of his appeal, made about the beginning of Lent for the Octave of the Purification, against the archbishop's sentence promulgated on Palm Sunday. David is to represent him with the Pope, and to give Gilbert an opportunity to ease the Pope's debts, since he cannot send him presents.

**201** G, nos. 268 *and* 276; *MB Epp.* 503; Lupus, II, 542 (iii, 42); B, fo. 146v; D, fo. 83v; Ia, pp. 281 (Ia 1), 322 (Ia 2); Ib, fo. 443; C, fo. 235v (234v); Co, fo. 133; Vb, fo. 184v; Ar, fos. 312v–313 (*readings of* VbAr *usually ignored*) (*headings:* IaIb: Idem H. regi Anglie; Ia 2CCoVb: Henrico regi Anglorum (Anglie CoVb) Gillebertus (G. Co) Lundoniensis episcopus).
1–2 Domno...obsequium *in* BD *only*    3 excellentiam non latere BD    6 extorsit IaIbCoVb; extorsit C *with* uel in- *added;* intorserit B; intorsit D    6 notissimus B    10 *aut] Ia 2C (*ins.*) *add in*    11 in BDIa 2Co; *om.* Ia 1IbC    13 constituit] statuit B
**202** Liverani, p. 644; *MB Epp.* 513; Va, fo. 145.

---

[1] Cf. *Decretum*, C. 24, q. 3, c. 6 (cf. no. 200).
[2] Cf. I Cor. ix. 26; *Decretum*, C. 2, q. 1, c. 11.
[3] *Decretum*, C. 2, q. 6, c. 16: Felix—Sixtus has been taken in error from c. 15. This, and textual details, clearly indicate that Gilbert was using Gratian here. The same error occurs in no. 203, and the *Causa* (*MB*, IV, 218); cf. *GF*, p. 165 n.
[4] Presumably Richard Foliot; or possibly Robert Banastre (see nos. 188–92).

G(ilebertus) Dei gratia Londoniensis episcopus dilecto filio suo magistro D(avid), salutem, gratiam et benedi⟨c⟩tionem.

Affectum uestrum erga me, karissime, nepote meo R. referente cognoui, et audita quasi certa suscipiens, uobis ut amico karissimo meum, si id tamen libet suscipere, in summa committo necessitate negotium. Sic enim de facto contigit, ut 5 domnus in me Cantuar(iensis) manum aggrauauerit, et in me nec citatum, quod nouerim, nec commonitum, die Palmarum sententiam excommunicationis emiserit. Ego uero seueritatem hanc ante presentiens, ad audientiam apostolicam in initio fere quadragesime appellaui, et appellationi diem octauas Purificationis beate Marie constitui. Latam uero post appellationem sententiam nullam reputans, in ordine 10 meo ministrare non destiti. Vnde michi summe necessarium est, ut onus hoc suscipiatis, et appellationem meam domno pape presentetis, et modis omnibus optinere studeatis, ut appellationem meam admittat et indultum oppressis omnibus in commune remedium michi nequaquam subtrahat; sed in presentia sua, auditis his que proponuntur aduersum me, iuxta quod sue uisum fuerit equitati in me 15 statuendo decernat. Quia uero ad ipsum xenia ob casus uarios mittere nequaquam possum, aliquem creditorum suorum transmittat ad me, per quem mea sibi seruitia copiose, iuxta quod ipse dictauerit exhibeam; uel si ibi creditores inueneritis, ibidem pecunia accipiatur, et tam ipsi quam curie secundum quod uobis uisum fuerit seruiatur.                                                                                    20

## 203   To King Henry II

[Early June 1169] He is sending a confidential messenger to the king, Master Henry;[1] and he asks the king to support his appeal to the Pope.

The first version of this letter (from the register of Master David) presumably represents a copy of the letter sent to Master David in 1169; the second version is either the version actually sent to the king or a later revision (see p. 276 n. 1, which suggests that version 1 is the earlier; it omits 'transfretandi licentiam. . . .' Cf. GF, p. 185 n., where for 204 read 203).

*Version 1 (MS Va)*

Domno suo karissimo illustri Anglorum regi H(enrico) frater Gilebertus Londoniensis ecclesie minister, salutem et debitum deuote fidelitatis obsequium.

Mittimus ad uos, domne, familiarem clericum nostrum magistrum Henr(icum) utique fidelem uestrum, quanto possumus affectu supplicantes, ut ipsum in petitionibus nostris benigne si placet audiatis, et illatam uobis et nobis iniuriam reuo- 5 cantes ad animum in summa nobis necessitate regia si placet clementia subueniatis.

203 *Both versions*: MB Epp. 504; *version 1*: Liverani, p. 643; Va, fo. 146v; *version 2*: G, no. 277; Lupus, II, 545–6 (iii, 46); B, fo. 187v; D, fos. 84v–85; Ia, p. 283; Ib, fos. 443v–444; C, fos. 236v (235v)–237 (236); Co, fo. 134; Vb, fo. 185r–v; Ar, fos. 314v–315 (*variants of* VbAr *not noted*) (*headings*: CCoVb: Henrico (H. Co) regi Anglorum (Angl' Co; Anglie Vb) Gillebertus (C; G. *ceteri*) Lundoniensis episcopus; IaIb: Idem H. regi Anglie).

---

[1] Very likely Henry of Northampton, the only *Master* Henry known among Gilbert's clerks (see GF, p. 289); in 1167–8 he acted as an envoy of Henry II (MB Epp. 339 (p. 273), 395).

Quod quidem bene facietis si domno pape pro nobis affectuose scripseritis, ut appellationem quam ad ipsum fecimus, ut iuris dictat equitas, admittat, et latam in nos post appellationem sententiam ea qua potest et debet equitate suspendat, donec
10 causam nostram audiat et cuique digna meritis compensando diffiniat. Ad cardinales etiam amicos uestros litteras si placet exposcimus, ut ad hoc domnum papam inflectant, et super admittenda appellatione nostra indultum oppressis omnibus in commune beneficium prece uestra nobis optineant. Sixtus enim papa sic statuit: 'Quotiens episcopus se a suo metropolitano putauerit pregrauari, uel
15 eum suspectum habuerit, mox Romanam apellet sedem a qua dum se audiri poposcerit, nullus eum excommunicet antequam causa summi pontificis auctoritate finiatur. Quod si aliter presumptum fuerit, nichil erit, sed uiribus omnino carebit.'[1] Cumque itaque concordet iuri quod petimus, amicis uestris et beniuolis id domne non negetis, quod a summo pontifice facile si uestrum in hoc affectum
20 senserit impetrabitis. Conseruet incolumitatem uestram Dominus, in Christo domne dilectissime. Nuntio uero nostro cetera dicenda committimus. Gregorius magnus: 'priuilegium meretur amittere, qui concessa sibi abutitur potestate'.[2]

*Version 2*

Domno suo karissimo illustri Anglorum regi H(enrico) frater G(ilebertus) Lundoniensis ecclesie minister, salutem et debitum deuote fidelitatis obsequium.
25 Mittimus ad uos, domne, familiarem clericum nostrum H(enricum) utique fidelem uestrum, quanto possumus affectu supplicantes, ut ipsum in petitionibus nostris benigne si placet audiatis, et nobis in necessitate nostra regia clementia subueniatis. Quod bene quidem facietis si domno pape pro nobis aliquantulum affectuose scripseritis, ut appellationem quam ad ipsum fecimus, ut iuris dictat
30 equitas, admittat, et post appellationem in nos latam sententiam ea qua potest et debet equitate suspendat, donec causam nostram audiat et digna meritis cuique retribuat. Ad cardinales etiam amicos uestros litteras si placet exposcimus, ut ad hoc domnum papam inflectant, et super admittenda appellatione nostra indultum omnibus oppressis beneficium prece uestra nobis optineant. Sixtus enim papa sic
35 statuit: 'Quotiens episcopus se a suo metropolitano senserit pregrauari, uel eum suspectum habuerit, mox Romanam appellet sedem, a qua dum se audiri poposcerit, nullus eum excommunicet antequam causa summi pontificis finiatur auctoritate. Quod si aliter presumptum fuerit, nil erit, sed uiribus omnino carebit.'[1] De cetero quia crebra allocutione frui uestra summopere nobis necesse est et consilio,
40 excellentie uestre deuotissime supplicamus, ut nobis transfretandi licentiam con-

---

**203** 23–4 Domno...obsequium *in* BD *only*   25 nostrum] BD *add* magistrum   27 in] BD *add* summa   34 oppressis omnibus BD   36–7 mox...poposcerit *om* B.   37–8 auctoritate finiatur BD, *Gratian, version 1 and* no. 201   39 crebro B   39 frui uestra summopere] uestra frui summe B; uestra frui summa D

---

[1] See no. 201 n. 3. Version 1 is verbally identical here; a free rendering of Gratian's text. Version 2 departs very slightly from no. 201 (and so further from Gratian).
[2] *Decretum*, C. 11, q. 3, c. 63 (the attribution to Gregory is an error of Gratian's). This reads like a gloss.

cedatis, et in partibus transmarinis nuntios quos ad domnum papam mittimus nos expectare permittatis. Conseruet incolumitatem uestram in longa tempora omnipotens Dominus.

## 204 To Robert Foliot, archdeacon of Oxford

[Early June 1169] He expounds his circumstances, and explains that he has asked the king for licence to go to the Pope and make his defence. He asks R(obert) to be present at a gathering of bishops in London on the Saturday before Pentecost (7 June).

Gillebertus Dei gratia Lundoniensis episcopus karissimo suo R(oberto) Oxeneford(ensi) archidiacono, multiplicem ex accepta consolatione gratiarum actionem.

Multis curarum oppresus oneribus quid amico rescribam promtum non habeo, nisi propheticum illud solummodo, quod cum sepe decantauerim nunc in amaritudine positus experiri compellor ut dicam, 'tota die uerecundia mea contra me est, et 5 confusio faciei mee cooperuit me'.¹ Spectaculum factus sum mundo et hominibus, quia fortiter afflixit me inimicus; manus Domini tetigit me, que me multum eleuans tandem grauiter allisit me.² Ad miseriarum acceditur cumulum, quod in promptu non est unde queat expeti uel sperari remedium. Mare michi clausum est, et portus omnes circumquaque prohibiti. Inter amicos et notos commorari mors michi est;³ 10 ab his elongari penitus impossibile. Vnde nuntium ad domnum regem quanta potui festinatione transmisi, ut impetrata transfretandi licentia, domnum papam adeam et penes eum causam meam uel defendam si possibile est uel inflicto uulneri si sic est ab eo medicamenta requiram. Vestrum uero plurimum exopto colloquium, obsecrans ut sabbato Pentecostes uestri copiam Lundon(ie) habeam, ut quid michi 15 in conuentu illo expediat, uestro fratrumque meorum consilio instructus intelligam. Valere uos exopto, karissime.

## 205 To William, abbot of Reading

[c. June 1169] He thanks the abbot for help in his plight: he has appealed against the archbishop of Canterbury's snares, and invoked the Pope's authority against the archbishop's.

This seems to refer to Gilbert's first excommunication;⁴ and is probably to be associated with William's commendation of Gilbert to the Pope (MB Epp. 524), in which the Palm Sunday excommunication is specifically mentioned.

⟨Gilebertus⟩ Dei gratia Lundoniensis episcopus uenerabili fratri et amico W(illelmo) eadem gratia abbati Rading(ensi), salutem et dilectionem.

**204** G, no. 209; *MB Epp.* 509; B, fo. 189; D, fo. 85; Rb, fo. 107 v; Jb, *unfoliated (variants of* Jb *not noted).*
1 karissimo suo *om.* D    8 accedit Rb
**205** G, no. 262; B, fo. 59.

---

¹ Ps. xliii. 16.
² Cf. I Cor. iv. 9; Ps. xli. 10; Job xix. 21; Ps. ci. 11.      ³ Cf. Dan. xiii. 22.
⁴ Gilbert is only explicit that he has engaged in an appeal, but the reference to the archbishop makes it clear both that this was one of his appeals *ad cautelam* and that he is faced with a *personal* threat from Becket; this points clearly to the situation in 1169.

Gratias ago beniuolentie uestre que non solum michi prospicere et meis non desistit utilitatibus excubare, uerum super his que maligne fabricantur aduersum me 5 fraterna me caritate premonere curauit et premunire. Remedium uero quod aduersus extraordinaria quelibet grauamina unicum omnibus sacri suggerunt canones, aduersus emissas iam ut dicitur uocationes, aduersus propositas domni Cant(uariensis) insidias, appellationis subsidium publice iam proposui. Et ne quid circa personam meam aut possessionem meam, ne quid circa ordinem aut honorem 10 meum preiudicii fiat, inuocata auctoritate sedis apostolice me communire curaui, de diuina quidem gratia et de clementia sancte Romane ecclesie penitus confidens quod si quid super hec enormiter in nos actum fuerit, illi potius ad confusionem quam nobis ad penam redundabit. Valete.

## 206  To Jocelin de Bohun, bishop of Salisbury

[c. early July 1169] Like the woman in the gospel who found her coin, they must rejoice in the safe return of those they sent afar. Now they must prepare to meet the king, at Argentan, he suggests, so that they can await him there or go on further as the king instructs them. Jocelin is to consult the bishop of Chichester.

Nos. 206–8 clearly form a series. They all refer to the return of messengers, more specifically in 207–8 to the return of Jocelin's 'prodigal son' Reginald. In 206 Gilbert suggests a move to Argentan, and asks for the bishop of Chichester's opinion; in 207 Jocelin repudiates this advice and suggests that he wait at Le Mans—this is also the bishop of Chichester's opinion; in 208 Gilbert observes that since Jocelin is killing the fatted calf at Le Mans, he will celebrate the *Cerealia*[1] at Séez, while they await the royal summons. For the date of these letters, see note to no. 198.

Venerabili domno fratrique karissimo I(ocelino) Sa(resberiensi) Dei gratia episcopo frater Gilebertus Lundoniensis ⟨ecclesie minister⟩ salutem.

Letatur euangelica mulier que dragmam reperit quam amisit.[2] Nobis quoque gaudendum est quia quos in longinqua direximus, et quasi perdidimus, liuidorum 5 latratuum Scillis[3] tandem enauigatis sanos et incolumes et prospera nuntiantes, Domino cuncta pie disponente, recepimus. Vnde michi uidetur rem fore consilii ut ad locum quem assignauit domnus rex scilicet Argentom rem mora minime protrahente concurramus, ut ibi domni regis aut prestolemur aduentum, aut si nos ad se uenire iusserit, expeditiorem habeamus hinc ad ulteriora progressum. Hoc 10 domno Cicestrensi communicabitis, qui si quid aliter senserit hoc michi si placet recurrente cursore ne panem comedat otiosus signare uelitis.[4] Valere uos opto in Domino karissime.

**206** G, no. 245; *MB Epp.* 336; B, fo. 138.
2 ec. min. *om.* B    9 habeamus] qui si quid aliter sens *added in* B, *cancelled* (*see below*)

---

[1] This cannot, however, mean that the event will take place in April.
[2] Cf. Luc. xv. 8–10.
[3] Cf. Sidonius Apollinaris, *Epp.* I, 1 (and no. 103).
[4] Cf. Prov. xxxi. 27.

## 207 Jocelin de Bohun, bishop of Salisbury, to Gilbert Foliot

[c. early July 1169] Like the father in the Gospel, he rejoices in his son's return and is killing the fatted calf. He proposes to wait for the king's instructions at Le Mans, since the king may summon them to Angers; and if they go to Argentan, they may be reduced from wine to beer—and the bishop of Chichester is of the same opinion (the answer to no. 206).

Venerabili domno patrique karissimo G(ileberto) Lundoniensi Dei gratia episcopo, Ioc(elinus) Sar(esberiensis) ecclesie humilis minister, salutem et modicum munus, seipsum.

Exultat pater euangelicus cui restitutus est filius in longinqua profectus; exultaui- mus Dei gratia et nos reuerso filio euangelico, qui perierat et inuentus est.[1] Occurri- 5 mus ei ⟨fo. 139⟩ in tympano et choro usque ad Osteilli.[2] Occidimus ei uitulum saginatum et altilia preparauimus, quibus utinam et uestram reficerentur ieiunia. Prospera nobis nuntiant Dei gratia nuntii nostri ad domnum nostrum regem properantes, quorum in reditu uel mandato et nostra pendet expectatio, et domni nostri regis responsio, quid nos agere disposuerit. Proinde Cenomannis eligimus 10 moram facere donec nos mandatum regium alias trahat, quod forte Andegauis erit, cum ciuitas illa a uia qua reuersurus est domnus rex non longe distet. Si uero de- scenderemus Argentonium, et longior forsan nobis uia restaret, et pincerna pro uino merascissimo quo habundamus turbatioris substantie ceruisam, generosis inuisam, etiam parcius propinaret. Hoc etiam est domni Cicestrensis consilium, qui 15 minus consiliosum ducit certum pro incerto domicilium mutare, et Bacho Libero ancillam festuce filiam maritare.[3] Valeat karissima nobis uestra dilectio.

## 208 To Jocelin de Bohun, bishop of Salisbury

[c. early July 1169] Jocelin has fulfilled the parable and killed the fatted calf; since he is cele- brating his Bacchanal orgies (cf. no. 207) at Le Mans, he is to summon Gilbert from his *Cerealia* at Séez when he receives the royal mandate (an answer to no. 207).

Venerabili domno fratrique karissimo I(ocelino) Sar(esberiensi) Dei gratia episcopo frater G(ilebertus) Londoniensis ecclesie minister, munus quod penes se maximum reputat, seipsum.

Euangelicum ut audio paradigma complestis, et saginato uitulo occisis altilibus reuerso filio gaudia debita celebrastis.[4] Superest ut cum stola prima calciamenta sibi 5 prouideatis et anulum, ne quid ex euangelio deesse sibi sentiat ad perfectum. De cetero quia Cenomannis Orgia celebrare disponitis, cum mandatum uobis regium insonuerit, me si placet a Sagio a Cerealibus euocetis. Valere uos optamus in Domino karissime.

207 G, no. 471; *MB Epp.* 337; B, fo. 138 v.
208 G, no. 247; *MB Epp.* 338; B, fo. 139.

---

[1] Cf. Luc. xv. 20 ff.
[2] Cf. Ps. cl. 4; Act. xxviii. 15.
[3] Using the traditional pun on *Liber* (Bacchus) and *liber* (free).
[4] See no. 207 (also Matt. xxii. 4).

### 209  To Robert, archdeacon of Lincoln

[*c.* July–August 1169] A peremptory summons to the archdeacon to appear at Windsor on 22 August for the settlement of the case between him and the priest R. before Gilbert as judge delegate. If he repudiates Gilbert's jurisdiction on the ground of the archbishop of Canterbury's illegal sentence against Gilbert, he must prove his *exceptio* in the proper way.

The letter evidently belongs to the time of Gilbert's first excommunication, and so the summons must be for late August 1169. Gilbert was in Normandy in July, then returned to England, crossing again in early October (see note to no. 198).

G(ilebertus) Dei gratia Lundoniensis episcopus R(oberto) Lincolnensi archidiacono salutem.

Diem tibi ad causam que inter te et R. sacerdotem uertitur apostolica auctoritate constituimus ad quem ob purgandam domno pape sancteque Romane ecclesie a te
5 ut dicitur illatam iniuriam nec uenisti, nec responsalem mittere procurasti. Diem igitur alterum et hunc peremptorium constituimus, mandantes et apostolica auctoritate tibi iniungentes ut nisi iamdictum R. sacerdotem a sententia interdicti prorsus absolutum susceperis et ei obuolutiones[1] ecclesie sue dum appellationem suam ad domnum papam prosequeretur subtractas plene reddi feceris, ⟨fo. 139v⟩
10 tuam nobis presentiam xi kalendas Septembris apud Windeleshores exhibeas, ut mandato domni pape super memorata causa prout ius dictabit obedias. Quia uero excipienti incumbit id probare quod excipit, si pronuntiationem illam quam contra statuta canonum aduersum me in domni pape et sancte Romane ecclesie iniuriam dompnus Cantuar(iensis) instituit, me tenere et ligare et ab apostolici
15 executione mandati repellere et prepedire intendis, cum exceptionem hanc in iure probaueris, nostrum tunc recte iudicium declinabis. Vale.

### 210  To Master David

[*c.* December 1169] He thanks David for his letter, and asks him to present his case again to the Pope, to announce Gilbert's arrival, and if he is late for the term of his appeal—the Octave of the Purification (9 February 1170)—to explain the circumstances and urge the Pope not to confirm the archbishop's sentence. He recounts the meeting between the archbishop, Count Theobald and the kings of England and France (18 November 1169) and explains that he has to wait for a further conference between the kings at Tours on St Hilary's day (13 January 1170).

G(ilebertus) Dei gratia Lundoniensis episcopus dilecto filio et amico suo karissimo magistro D(auid), salutem, gratiam et benedictionem.

Que uestra michi nuntiauit epistola multa gratiarum actione suscepi, iam nunc obsecrans et preces in hoc obnixe porrigens, ut quod michi littera significatum est

---

209 G, no. 223; B, fo. 139.
9 subtractas prosequeretur B
210 Liverani, pp. 642–3; *MB Epp.* 621; Va, fo. 146.

---

[1] A curious word: the 'wrappings', evidently meaning the worldly trappings, appurtenances, i.e. revenues.

opere complere uelitis, et uestre mentis affectum erga me eius quod postulo 5
declaretis effectu. Probatio namque dilectionis exhibitio operis est, et operatur
amor magna si est; si uero operari renuit, amor non est. In amoris igitur experimentum et remunerationis condigne premium postulo, ut meum ad presens onus
pro parte suscipiatis, et meum ad domnum papam aduentum tam ipsi quam curie
significetis, ex parte tam nostra quam uestra supplicando, et sollicitudinem quantam 10
poteritis adhibendo, ne latam in me a domno Cant(uariensi) sententiam (quam
nullam esse, iuuante Domino et ipso semper recte iudicante, constabit) sua roboret
auctoritate, nec ratam habere uelit, si die appellationi prefixo—a Purificatione
scilicet beate Virginis octauo—me nondum ad curiam peruenisse contigerit. Nam
cum Octobri mense transfretauerim, et ad domnum regem ueniens querende paci 15
domni Cant(uariensis) operam diligenter impenderim, inspirante Domino rex
adeo pietate motus est, ut, remota ambage et obscuritate uerborum, que in colloquio quod cum ipso Gratianus habuerat uniuersa turbauerat, pacem archiepiscopo
suisque concederet, ipsumque sua suscipere et cum honore Dei et libertate ecclesie
possidere, nulla regalium consuetudinum habita mentione, permitteret. Que cum 20
domno Cant(uariensi), presente Francorum rege comiteque Teobaldo ceterisque
qui conuenerant, primo complacuissent, postmodum, eo quod sibi domnus rex
negabat osculum, repudiata sunt. Speramus uero quod tunc minus actum est, in
colloquio quod inter reges die beati Hilarii Turonis futurum est, Domino iuuante,
complendum est. Hec me causa detinet, ista remoratur occasio, ut cum ceteris 25
querende paci pie studentibus operam dem; ut in longum protracta dissensio fine
tandem terminetur optato. Quod si ad uota processerit, ad domnum papam
uisitandum me pertrahet iamdiu super hoc concepta uoluntas. Re secus accidente,
compellet adesse necessitas. Agatis itaque, karissime, quod presentis articuli est,
summo supplicando et suadendo pontifici, ne his qui sermonibus odii circumdede- 30
runt me fidem habeat;[1] ne latam in iniuriam beati Petri sententiam ipse confirmando
suscipiat; ne ordinem euangelicum, oris ipsius dominici constitutione consecratum,
humane presumptionis immutatione, ut ita dicam, prophanari permittat; presertim
dicente Domino, 'Non est seruus maior domno suo, nec apostolus maior eo qui
misit illum'.[2] Michi, si quidem quicquid circumquaque minentur plurimi, suaderi 35
non potest, apostolica auctoritate quamlibet modicum Christi corporis menbrum,
nedum episcopum orthodoxum, non commonitum, non regulariter citatum,
inauditum, indefensum, et in nullo contumacem aut notorii criminis reprehensione
obnoxium, ab ipsius Christi corpore fuisse precisum. Agetis ita, karissime, confidenter, et interuentu strenuo rem in suspenso tenebitis, quousque meam, iuuante 40
Domino, innocentiam presente me sub sole constituatis.

**210** 27 optate *corrected* (?) Va    39 karissime] Va *adds* prudenter, *cancelled*

---

[1] Cf. Ps. cviii. 3.    [2] Joh. xiii. 16.

### 211 To Master David

[*c.* February 1170] Warned by the royal messengers, through Archdeacon Nicholas, and by David, he escaped the dangers of his journey and arrived safely at Milan (*ad sanctum Ambrosium*). He asks David to await his return at Rouen, there to assist him in his case before the papal judges delegate.

G(ilebertus) Dei gratia Londoniensis episcopus dilecto suo magistro D(auid), salutem et sincere dilectionis affectum.

Ad sugestionem nuntiorum domni regis per dilectum nostrum Nicholaum archidiaconum nobis factam, et ad commonitionem et consilium tuum, latentes
5 insidias, uiarum discrimina, et anceps uite periculum, maturato reditu uitauimus, licet cum multa difficultate, per montium incommeabiles semitas quiete et prospere ad sanctum Ambrosium deuenerimus. Et quoniam necessario presentiam tuam coram iudicibus a domno papa delegatis negotii nostri summa desiderat, quas possumus preces tibi affectuose porrigimus, quatenus ob nostrum prouectum et
10 liberationem aduentum nostrum Rothomagi sustineas, et nos cum omni celeritate illuc properabimus.

### 212 To Pope Alexander III

[? mid 1170] He thanks the Pope for comfort and absolution, complains of the slanders against him—that he has fomented discord, subverted the Church, stirred up litigation, and so forth—and outlines the events of his excommunication, appeals and absolution. Finally, he excuses himself for not having visited the Pope.

The period from Gilbert's first absolution to the murder of Thomas is covered by a small group of letters which are hard to date with exactitude, and do not strictly form a series.

The archbishop was scandalized by Gilbert's absolution, and agitation against him started up almost at once, coming to a head after his participation in the coronation of the young king in June (cf. *MB Epp.* 661 ff.). Nos. 212 and 213 seem to belong to this intermediate period, before the papal censure, or at least before its publication. No. 212 refers to his previous absolution, and so must belong to this year; the lugubrious terms of 213 suggest the same period rather than earlier, but the reference to Alexander III's enemies may possibly imply that Gilbert had been accused of fomenting schism or encouraging Henry II to join the emperor, which would perhaps suggest an earlier date (cf. *MB Epp.* 213–14, 222–3 (p. 503); *GF*, p. 184 n.).

In September the Pope, aware at last of the facts of the coronation, excommunicated Gilbert and Jocelin and suspended the archbishop of York (*MB Epp.* 699–700). The letters of excommunication were forwarded to Gilbert by Becket the day before the archbishop embarked (*MB Epp.* 723–4, pp. 403, 410; *MB*, III, 471–2; IV, 68, 123, etc.), about the end of November. Gilbert and the others received the news as they were waiting to cross to Normandy (*MB*, III, 117, 471–2, etc.; *Diceto*, I, 340–1). Shortly before this (probably *c.* November), when the rumour of papal censure had reached him but not the actual letter, Gilbert wrote no. 214 to the Pope. Two short letters to cardinals (215–16) seem to have been

211 Liverani, p. 644; *MB Epp.* 657; Va, fo. 145.
212 G, no. 154; *MB Epp.* 677; B, fo. 101 v.

written soon after, but before the archbishop's murder. No. 216 refers to a papal censure, which suggests 1170 rather than 1169; and the same seems to be implied in no. 215.[1] The catastrophe of 29 December altered the whole complexion of affairs and carried Gilbert to the nadir of his fortunes.

Patri suo et domno summo pontifici Alexandro frater G(ilebertus) Lundoniensis ecclesie minister, totum quod in se potest humilis et ad obediendum prompta deuotio.

Dilecte michi pater et diligende semper in Domino sanctitati uestre gratiarum refero totis anime mee uiribus actiones, quod apostolica michi uiscera clementer 5 aperiens, et in necessitate summa anxietati mee pie compatiens oculos in me misericordie reduxistis, et cui mortis iniuste nectebat laqueos aduersantis michi potestatis austeritas in uitam me respirare paterna tandem caritate uoluistis—in ira si qua fuit memor misericordie, totum tamen quod oportuit iustitie reseruans et discipline. Quod profecto beneficium eo michi gratius longeque reputatur acceptabilius quod 10 non ad preces regias, non ad multorum in id porrecta suffragia, non ad opum oblata pondera seu promissa, sed de fonte caritatis lucidissimo, pectore scilicet apostolico, in filium pietate progressa, non meis meritis exhibitum, sed omne preueniente meritum sola totum gratia misericorditer indultum est. Vnde quod obsequii possum pater et quod honoris, uestre circa me munificentie fateor in 15 omnibus obligatum, adeo ut me uelle quod uolueritis, totum subire quod iniunxeritis compellat pariter et suadeat non solum sedis cui presidetis auctoritas, sed ex inpensi etiam magnitudine beneficii innata siquidem et iamdiu super hoc concepta uoluntas. Suis itaque circa me sibique placitis uestra sanctitas utetur imperiis, in omnibus que mee possibilitati responderunt patri filius, domno seruus obediet, nec 20 durum reputando nec asperum quod apostolice circa me nouero mansuetudini complacere. Sciat enim domnus meus et certum teneat, me a tempestatis huius qua iamdiu quassamur initio id semper uoluntatis, id habuisse propositi, ut uobis occasione quacumque assisterem, et uobis coram positus anxietatem mei cordis exponerem, ut a sublimitate uestra impetrata clementer eius cui astringor officii 25 absolutione, ab his quibus obruor ⟨fo. 102⟩ fluctibus saltem nudus euaderem, et cum multorum nequeam saluti saltem mee aliquatenus prouiderem. Omnes enim ab Anglie finibus ad uos usque decurrentes, ut quibusdam non certe placeant, me seminarium discordie, subuersorem ecclesie, incentiuum malorum, fomitem litis et odiorum omnium sinistre denuntiant, et que nec uera sunt, nec unquam iuuante 30 Domino probari poterunt sanctis uestris auribus aduersum me quorundam promissis

212 21 mansuetudine B  24 anxietatis B  28 certe *sic* B  29 subuersio/rem B  29 innocentiuum B

---

[1] The obscure reference to a Welshman seems only intelligible if Gilbert had been denounced at the Curia by a Welsh clerk of Becket's—? Alexander Walensis, later archdeacon of Bangor, on whom see Herbert of Bosham, *MB*, III, 528 (and note in JS *Epp.* II). *MB Epp.* 359 shows him acting as envoy in 1167–8; *MB Epp.* 610, 635 show him as envoy to the Curia at the turn of 1169 and 1170, and perhaps a little later. This seems to imply that the censure came from the Pope, and not, as in 1169, from the archbishop. There is also a sentence which implies that the Pope had already once absolved Gilbert: 'onus quo premebar...summouistis'.

et precibus instillare non omittunt. Et ecce pater morior, cum nil horum fecerim, cum horum in nullo conscius sim. Dantur in me sententie nec confessum, nec conuictum, sed nec quidem commonitum. Formatur et confingitur notorium, et ut
35 grassanti nichil desit inuidie, quod nulli notum est audacter asserunt esse notissimum. De manu mea sanguis quem non effudi requiritur, et iniustissime, que non rapui cogor exsoluere. Que nimirum omnia in me recasura metuens, omnem preueniendo sententiam apostolicam iamdudum appellaui presentiam, ei super hiis optans assistere quem in iure certum est non errare.[1] Quam nimirum appellationem si
40 minime prosecutus sum, hec causa extitit quod legatis ad domnum nostrum regem a latere uestro directis eis omnium que inter domnum Cant(uariensem) uertebantur et nos, cognitionem pariter et diffinitionem commisistis, litteris destinatis ad nos, ut nos eis presentes exhiberemus et quod auditis partibus statuerent, in nos firmiter obseruaremus. Quibus rem minime prosequentibus, cum ob imminentis metum
45 periculi in eorum denuo presentia una cum fratribus nostris appellauerim, huius etiam appellationis prosecutio nobis a uestra gratia domni regis interuentu remissa est. Testantur hoc littere que penes nos sunt apostolico signo communite.[2] Cum uero iudicem moueri non oporteat si cum de grauamine suspectus est ad superiorem prouocetur, offensus tamen domnus Cant(uariensis) eo quod ad uestram appel-
50 lauerim audientiam, meum caput impetere, me non seruato ordine proposuit excommunicando suffocare. Cuius rei prescius, sententiam preueniens ad uestram item appellaui clementiam, eius examen expetens qui merita causarum recte ponderans suum unicuique ius[3] equa ratione conseruat. Quod enim legitur ne in una eademque causa tertio appelletur, non eo spectat ut quotiens episcopus se a
55 metropolitano suo grauandum putauerit libere non appellet, sed eo potius ut a sententia a tribus gradatim iudicibus post appellationem approbata qui uinctus est appellare non debeat.[4] Quod quidem non solem facibus adiuuando dicimus, sed ut hiis qui de crebra nos appellatione redarguunt uel paucis respondeamus. Ad culmen igitur apostolicum sic appellaui sperans id subsidio futurum michi, ne ante diem
60 appellationi prefixum meus posset status ab eo contra quem appellatum est aliquatenus interuerti. Sedis enim apostolice soliditas ⟨fo. 102 v⟩ illa est, de qua mari dictum est: 'huc usque uenies et hic confringes tumentes fluctus tuos'.[5] Ad quam appellando allisa iudicis cuiusque sententia iam lata suspenditur, si fuerit preappellatum lata postmodum uiribus omnino caret, ut tam re quam nomine prorsus nulla
65 reputetur habenda magis irrita quam aliqua extrinsecus sollempnitate irritanda. Quia tamen populus iuris apices et canonum occulta non percipit lata in me postmodum post appellationem sententia, a doctis de humilitate culpari quam diuina

212 37 metuens] Placuit excellentie uestre B (*in margin*) (*see p. 9 n.*)   45 appellauerim] Ad uestram pater audientiam B (*in margin*)   46 interuentu] in Norm(annia) B (*in margin*)   52 clementiam] circa initium quadragesime B (*in margin*)   56 uictus B   67 sententia] in ramis palmarum B (*in margin*)

---

[1] Cf. *Decretum*, C. 24, q. 1, c. 9.       [2] *MB Epp.* 400.
[3] Cf. *Inst.* 1, 1, 3.
[4] Cf. *Code* 7, 70, 1, cited *Decretum*, C. 2, q. 6, *dictum post* c. 39; *ibid.* c. 16 (see no. 201 n. 3).
[5] Job xxxviii. 11.

celebrando de ausu quasi sacrilego a multitudine reprehendi ⟨preferens (?)⟩, me sic habens, sic in omnibus exhibens ac si me teneret sententia, quam ab ipso sue pronuntiationis initio apostolica sublimitas elidebat ad quam premissa appellatio 70 sententiam ne quid posset omnino potentissime reprimebat. Qui nimirum articulus cum possit in partem hanc patrum auctoritate suffragante plurimum disputari, inspectis tamen litteris quibus me uestra caritas instruere et consolari dignata est, altercationem respui, et iuxta uestri formam consilii absolutione suscepta presente euangelio me uobis in id quod uestra michi sanctitas dederit in mandatis obligaui, 75 uestro per omnia pariturus imperio pro possibilitate non recessurus a promisso. Temperet obsecro acritas paterna mandatum, quousque meum in iure deprehenderit actore aliquo et idoneo teste peccatum. Si meritis gratiam referri distuli, estiuus calor, difficultas itineris, depredationis metus et carceris id fecere differri. Si progressus in itinere ad uos usque non processi, exploratorum insidiis impeditus sum, 80 et a nuntiis domni regis a uestra sublimitate reuersis sub multa interminatione reuocatus. Obsecro per misericordiam Iesu Christi Domini nostri ut pater iram filio de corde remittat, et in sua protectione susceptum, totum de cetero ad omne posse meum et suum uelle possideat. Conseruet incolumitatem uestram Dominus, in Christo dilecte pater. 85

## 213 To Pope Alexander III

[? mid 1170 (1169–70)] He has always been faithful to the Pope, and cannot understand the cause of his present disfavour.

Patri suo et domino summo pontifici A(lexandro) frater G(ilebertus) Lundoniensis ecclesie minister, debitum caritatis et obedientie famulatum.

Qua confidentia, qua facie domino meo patrique carissimo pro alio supplicaturus assistam, cum ad conciliandam michi penes uos gratiam ipse potissimum aduocato, ut fama late diuulgat, indigeam? Non enim est mediator idoneus, quem constat in 5 eius oculis displicere, quem sese medium constituendo placatum quis debuit exhibere. Attamen in Christo dilectissime pater dum me ipsum considero, dum totum me michi non parcendo discutio, utique non inuenio, michi nullatenus occurrit animo me commisisse quippiam ob quod a facie uestra proici et a sacratissimo uestre benignitatis aditu me iustum sit eliminari. Vestris enim obsequiis me 10 paratum semper exhibui, nec a fidelitate uestra ulla unquam potero uarietate casus auelli. Qui uos oderunt, illos pater odio habui,[1] et ut in libertate spiritus aliquid audeam uestro resistentes honori constanter aliquando repuli pariter et confudi certus.

**212** 79 fac'ere B (sic before correction)
**213** G, no. 159; B, fo. 151 v.
9 B places ob quod before me commisisse

[1] Cf. Ps. cxxxviii. 21.

### 214 To Pope Alexander III

[Probably *c*. November 1170] After his absolution he had hoped to have peace and quiet for the short remainder of his days; but his misfortunes have increased—notably because of the rumour that the Pope has condemned him. His old age prevents him visiting the Pope.[1]

Patri suo et domno summo pontifici A(lexandro) frater G(ilebertus) Lundoniensis ecclesie minister, salutem et debitum honoris et obedientie famulatum.

Benignitati uestre pater michi iam frequenter exhibite corde prouolutus et corpore gratias humillime refero, quod onus a me quo premebar anxie preualente 5 tandem gratia summouistis, et a mestitie me tenebris in quandam optate spe sere-nitatem ⟨B 1, fo. 106⟩ intus apud patrem pulsante pro filio pietatis affectu miseri-corditer induxistis. Vnde soluto uinculo quo tenebar, nil pater est quod optem amplius, quod desiderantius affectem, quam sanctitati uestre presens assistere, pre-sentem me totum uobis exponere, et hanc dierum meorum paucitatem reliquam a 10 tumultibus et turbinibus abstractam, uestri moderamine consilii totam Domino mancipare. Vnde meis grauiter accrescit infortuniis, quicquid obstaculo michi quo minus optata peragam et labores meos diutinos et diu continuata tedia optato tandem fine concludam. Hinc michi dolor insidet et meum undequaque spiritum inuoluit anxietas, dum ex causis plurimis emergunt plurima que me auocant a proposito et 15 non occasione quadam sed necessitate multiplici retrahunt ab incepto. Et quidem in causis illa prima est et precipua quod exiuit in aures omnium iamdiu a celsitudine uestra in me latam sententiam, cum collata michi pro parte gratia uix adhuc paucis innotuerit. Hinc omnium qui uias obsident, qui calles directos ad uos ut formice circumquaque discurrentes obambulant, furor accensus est ut nec Deum uerentes 20 nec homines impune sibi in me cuncta licere iudicent, obsequium Domino prestare se reputent[2] si michi iniectis manibus dampnis me pariter et contumeliis afficiant, et carcerali mancipatum custodie, hominem a summo condempnatum et reprobatum pontifice, ad exactam usque stipis ultime redemptionem exquisita penarum adhibi-tione compellant. Stratas omnes hic aduersus me iam rumor impleuit. Hac trans-25 siturus ille est quem manus apostolica cunctis exposuit, quem ut Egiptium spoliare,[3] suffocare, modis omnibus affligere bonus odor sacrificii Deo et apud ecclesiam con-summata laus est. Aptate manus, adhibete custodiam, ne sub larua aut quoquomodo subornatus euadat. Lundonie uobis opes in ianuis ecce sunt. Inopes uos de cetero negligentia sola constituet. Hic pater aduersum me murus erectus est, hec undique 30 difficultas obiecta quam etsi iuuante Domino transcendere quoquomodo contin-geret, etas tamen ultima que a pluribus me iam annis excepit, impedimento michi

---

214 G, no. 156; *MB Epp.* 562; B, fos. 105 v (*a fragment, cancelled:* B 1) *and* 106 v (B 2) (*spelling as* B 2).

2 famulatum] B 2 *in margin* con(tra) Oportueras (*i.e. MB Epp.* 700, B, fo. 94)    11 grauiter] ${}^{a}_{g}$ B 1; ${}^{a}_{g}$|uiter B 2    12 peragam] B 1 *ends here*    20 prestare *Giles*; pr'are B 2

---

[1] On the meaning of 'etas...ultima' see *GF*, p. 34.
[2] Cf. Joh. xvi. 2.
[3] Cf. Ex. iii. 22.

est ne aut iter istud arripere aut in paribus sibi uiribus laborem hunc aut possim aut audeam aliquatenus attemptare. ⟨fo. 107⟩ Hec michi iam tot inuexit incomoda quot enumerare longum est et que magis supprimere quam scripto propalare compellit erubescentia.

35

## 215   To Cardinal William of Pavia

[? *c.* December 1170] He asks the cardinal for help—he has been condemned and excommunicated unheard, on the evidence, so he is told, of a single Welshman (see note to no. 212).

Venerabili domno et amico karissimo Willelmo Papiensi sacrosancte Romane ecclesie cardinali presbitero frater G(ilebertus) Lundoniensis ecclesie minister, salutem que nunc est et quam speramus a Domino.

Nostis domne quod et orbi satis innotuit, quid animaduersionis iamdiu, quid pene, quoque id modo pertulerim, qui priusquam michi culpe modus innotesceret 5 enormitates pene grauioris excepi. Ad unius quidem ut audio Walensis uocem licet preclare dignitatis honore non fulgeat, non citatus, non commonitus, nec notorii quidem criminis reprehensioni obnoxius, condempnationis sinistrum reportaui calculum, et a sacerdote nec inspecta lepra mea nec cognita extra tamen ecclesie castra proiectus sum.[1] Sed quia nec in celum os[2] ponere fas est et maiorum acta 10 discutere sacrilegii constat instar optinere, ad medentis opem tutius est confugere quam in querele uocem imprudenter erumpere. Assueti uero moris est cum quem sua ledit conditio ut ad eum recurrat potius, cuius promtiorem sibi fore gratiam arbitratur afflictus. Confidens itaque de uestre dilectionis excellentia, cuius sinceritatem et fidem rerum certior edocuit experientia, instante necessitatis articulo a 15 uobis opem postulo, ut prelibata michi per uos gratia uestro ad perfectum studio deducatur, et quod ad mei executionem officii michi deesse cognoscitis, uestra michi sollicitudine iuuante Domino restituatur. Dat postulandi fiduciam quod manum michi iam gratie porrexisti et onus quo premebar anxie pie precis instantia summouisti, et exemptus a confusionis ignominia ut intra castra collocer ecclesie 20 prudenter optinuisti. Vnde uobis ad gratiarum actiones eo magis deuotus obligor quod proprie uoluntatis instinctu absentis amici negotia commodissime procurastis. Mouit uos in hunc pietatis affectum innata bonitas, nullisque meis meritis preuenta gratia—sed quod non merui mereri desidero, et non meruisse penitet nimisque sero uoluisse quod primis atemptatum fuisse studiis oportuisset. Agat itaque si placet et 25 peragat id gratia quod suum est et quem mereri iam cepit totum sibi reddat obnoxium, et restitutum me michi tam sibi quam suis in solidum de cetero pleno iure possideat. Valere uos optamus in Domino.

**215** G, no. 177; B, fo. 107.
3 Domino] Quamuis cure pastorum B (*in margin: i.e. MB Epp.* 720–1, *not in* B)    12 cum]
*presumably* eo *or the like understood; just possibly for* eius    18 restuatur B

---

[1] Cf. Lev. xiii. 2–3; Num. x. 12, 15.    [2] Cf. Ps. lxxii. 9.

### 216 Apparently addressed to a cardinal[1]

[? *c.* December 1170] Because Gilbert is under the papal ban, he does not give the recipient's name; but he asks his help both in obtaining his absolution and in freeing him from the power of the archbishop of Canterbury for the short remainder of his days. He asks his friend to confer with Master David.

There is no heading in the manuscript, but the letter was evidently written by someone who fell under papal ban on account of Becket's displeasure in 1169–70, and the style and mention of David point to Gilbert.

Quod amici mei domnique karissimi nomen supprimo, quod obsequium grate michi salutationis omitto, hec causa est quod apostolica seueritate proiectus foras et extra castra positus,[2] ad eos qui intus sunt nec accedere, nec communis audeo salutationis uerbum uel commissum scedule communicare. Cui tamen salutatio non 5 conceditur, que miseris sola superest saltem supplicatio non negatur. Descendenti namque de monte Domino leprosus occurrit, qui non salutando sed adorando potius et affectuose supplicando, quod postulabat optinuit.[3] Foris itaque consistens, et una cum decem illis ad amicum a longe uocem eleuans,[4] intima cordis anxietate supplico, ut in oborta michi ad presens necessitate manum michi consilii et auxilii 10 porrigatis, ut quem rerum experientia amicum nondum agnouistis, amicum de cetero, non affectu solum sed et operis efficacia, plene possideatis. Duo quidem sunt que postulo, que modis omnibus optinere desidero: unum, a sententia que me premit absolui; alterum, paucis quos adhuc forte uisurus sum annis a potestate domni Cant(uariensis), que me premit et perimit, emancipari. Conferet de his 15 uobiscum magister Dauid, quem deprecor ut instruatis, et in his que erga domnum papam uel curiam dicenda fuerint uel agenda dirigatis, et me, ut dictum est, totum de cetero possideatis.

### 217 To Bernard, bishop of Nevers

[June–July 1171] The absolution of Gilbert and the bishop of Salisbury had been committed to the bishop of Nevers and the abbot of Pontigny, who, they had been told by the bishop of Évreux, had returned to France. But when they had set off to visit the bishop, they received at Le Mans a papal letter entrusting the absolution to the bishops of Nevers and Beauvais. They have written to Beauvais, and ask Nevers to wait at Sens two or three days longer than he had intended so as to receive the reply from Beauvais.

**216** Liverani, pp. 641–2; *MB Epp.* 512; Va, fo. 146.
**217** G, no. 241; *MB Epp.* 761; B, fo. 108.

---

[1] Presumably to a cardinal, since a *domnus* in the Curia, but not the Pope. William of Pavia (cf. no. 215) and John of Naples (no. 219) are possible candidates. Among the testimonials for Master David in his Register are letters to Gilbert from these two cardinals, and also from Cardinal John of Anagni.

[2] Cf. Num. xii. 10, 15 (and no. 215: Miriam the leper, hence the transition of thought to *leprosus* below).

[3] Cf. Matt. viii. 1 ff.  [4] Cf. Luc. xvii. 12 ff., esp. 15–16.

After a long delay, Alexander III eventually wrote to the archbishop of Bourges and the bishop of Nevers to arrange for the absolution of the bishops of London and Salisbury on 24 April 1171 (*MB Epp.* 753; JL 11,889): the ceremony was performed early in August at Chaumont near Gisors by the bishops of Nevers and Beauvais and the abbot of Pontigny.[1] Gilbert's letter to the bishop of Nevers must have been written in June or July. But he was still suspended from office; and in no. 218 he seems to be acknowledging his absolution and pleading for complete restitution (*c.* August 1171). There was a further delay; but on 28 February 1172 the archbishop of Rouen and the bishop of Amiens were appointed to take his purgation and then to reinstate him (*MB Epp.* 767; JL 12,143). This was duly accomplished at Aumâle on 1 May 1172.[2]

B(ernardo) Dei gratia Niuernensi episcopo frater G(ilebertus) Lundoniensis ecclesie minister, si non expressum scedula conceptum tamen corde pie salutationis affectum.

Ex relatione dilecti fratris Ebroicensis episcopi acceperamus ego et domnus Saresberiensis episcopus abbatem Pontiniacensem in Galliam remeasse. Cupientes itaque in nobis adimpleri negotium de absolutione nostra uobis et predicto abbati a 5 domno papa commissum, cum festinatione ad uos labores aripueramus itineris, iamiamque Cenomann(iam) propinquantes festini, nostri a domno papa reditu reuocati sumus, afferentis eius rescriptum continens uobis et domno Beluacensi episcopo sollicitudinem absolutionis nostre esse iniunctam. Quia igitur persone uobis adiuncte mutatio uestrum inmutari poscebat consilium, incontinenti nuntios 10 nostros ad predictum episcopum direximus domni pape rescriptum ei deferentes, et diem et locum nobis designatum a uobis intimantes. Sed quoniam casus fortuitu qui prouideri nequeunt diligentissimis etiam sepius aduersantur, incerti ubi aut qualiter se habens predictus inueniatur episcopus, beniuolentie uestre cui in multis tenemur obnoxii preces affectuose porrigimus, ut duorum uel trium dierum spatio 15 ultra quam in proposito habuistis Senon(ibus) nuntios nostros expectetis, reportaturos uobis predicti episcopi responsum—si ⟨fo. 108 v⟩ mora tamen aduentus eorum id fieri postulauerit. Omnem enim daturi sumus operam ut moram hanc preueniamus et statuto nobis die et loco uobis iuuante Domino occurramus.

## 218  To Pope Alexander III

[*c.* August 1171] He describes his suffering under papal displeasure; the Pope has given him some hope, and he begs him not to let him end his days in misery.

⟨P⟩atri suo et domno summo pontifici A(lexandro) frater G(ilebertus) Lundoniensis ecclesie minister, debitum omnimodo subiectionis et obedientie famulatum.

Ad uestram pater indignationem exhausta fletibus, et erumpna corporis mei iamdiu uirtus elanguit et obnoxia queque sensibus officiis indeuota suis innata

---

217  1 B(ernardo)] P. B    9 absolutinis B    17 si / si B
218  G, no. 155; *MB Epp.* 762; B, fo. 106.
2 o'imo de B    2 famulatum] post passionem domni Cant' B (*in margin: see p. 9n.*).

---

[1] Diceto, I, 347. For Nevers, see Biog. Index; Beauvais was Bartholomew de Mont-Cornet, formerly archdeacon of Rheims, bishop 1162–75 (*HF*, XII, 275; XIII, 277, 707; XIV, 8; Torigny, p. 212, cf. 271).    [2] Diceto, I, 351.

5 doloris intimi pene fecit inmensitas. Ad uestram enim auersionem factus ilico sum plebis abiectio, notis meis obprobrium[1] et amicis plena confusionis occasio. Et nisi pia clementis medici cura languentis uulneri uel in modico lanuginem obduxisset, in salutis desperate cicatricem mora profusior ulcera patientis indurasset. Nunc autem pater cum ex his que paterna filio indulsit pietas aliquam michi liceat 10 sperare salutem, reuiuiscit spiritus meus, exultat anima et pro mansuetudine benignius exibita ad gratiarum actiones mens tota resurgit, et ad sanctitatis uestre prouoluta pedes, totis suplicare uiribus totis hanelat exorare desideriis, ut post mordentia austeritatis uina, pie lenitatis oleum meis infundatur ulceribus,[2] et paterne correptionis asperitas materne tandem circa me pietatis uberibus excipiatur. 15 Intus iam apud patrem sit qui pro filio pulset et exoret affectus, ut punitum iam satis suscipiatis in gratiam et correctum grauiter uestris deuotum firmiter obsequiis habeatis. Intra castra reuocatum pietas paterna promoueat et prelibatam michi gratiam ad perfectum manus apostolica iusta tandem miseratione perducat, ne in luctu et miseria dies meos transigere, et me dierum meorum paucitatem que 20 superest in amaritudine finire compellat. Conseruet incolumitatem uestram Dominus ecclesie sue multis profuturam temporibus, in Christo dilecte pater.

### 219   To Cardinal John of Naples

[? 1171–2] He thanks the cardinal for his kindness to himself and his clerks: he would have set out on the suggested visit to the Pope, but peace between king and Pope seemed more hopeful, and he was afraid to do anything which might appear to be in contempt of the papal legates. His age and illness make it unlikely that the visit will ever be accomplished.

This letter of thanks to Cardinal John of Naples for aid to Gilbert and his clerks at the Curia might refer to any of Gilbert's appeals to the Pope from 1164 to his final restitution in May 1172; the legates referred to could be William and Otto, or any from then until Albert and Theoduin.[3] But the absence of any reference to Thomas Becket and the fact that peace between king and Pope, and not king and archbishop, is in prospect suggest that it was written after Becket's murder, and that the legates are Albert and Theoduin. They were first commissioned in March 1171, although they did not begin active operations until 1172;[4] and it seems likely that this letter belongs to the second half of 1171 or early 1172.

Venerabili domno fratrique karissimo Iohanni Nepolitano sacrosancte Romane ecclesie cardinali presbitero frater G(ilebertus) Lundoniensis ecclesie minister, uotiuis cum salute frui successibus.

In oficiis gratius inpensa suscipimus ⟨fo. 107v⟩ que non extorsit necessitas sed 5 sola gratie sincerioris procurrauit affectio. Approbati quidem moris est, ut his artius teneamur obnoxii, qui meram exercentes liberalitatem ultronea in nos conferunt beneficia, quam quos ad id ipsum precedentis meriti prouocauit amministratio.

**219** G, no. 179; *MB Epp.* 511; B, fo. 107 (*at foot of* fo. 107: uidetur sc(riptum) post mortem domni Cant', cum uenissent Alb(ertus) et Teo(duinus)).

---

[1] Cf. Ps. xxi. 7.           [2] Cf. Luc. x. 34.
[3] See Tillmann, pp. 56 ff., for papal missions in this period.
[4] See Tillmann, pp. 68 ff.

Vnde nos obsequio uestro id fortius obligat, quod preuenistis nos in benedictionibus,[1] et certis rerum experimentis fructum uestre dilectionis ante sensimus quam
affectionis uicarie uobis innotesceret argumentum. Quod inpendistis est gratuitum, 10
quod diligendo rependimus dispar habet meritum. Illius fauorem simplex auget
liberalitas, huius remissiorem gratiam preuenta facit meritis et beneficiis excita
uoluntas. Hec nos omnia ad uberiores inuitant gratiarum actiones quas ut uota
gerimus utinam opere compleamus, personam siquidem nostram et facultates uobis
offerimus, cum Deus oportunitatem dederit, effectu uerba probaturi. Super solici- 15
tudine uestra negotiis nostris exibita et honore clericis nostris inpenso, pro gratiarum
actione nos uobis et ipsos deuouemus, suplicantes attentius ut quod ex parte prospere
gestum est ad perfectum uestre discretionis industria pertrahatur. Iuxta uestri uero
formam consilii iter ad uos arripere temptassemus, nisi pacis inter domnum papam
et regem spes iam uberior appareret et certiora deuotionis eius argumenta claresce- 20
rent. Preterea et id duximus metuendum, ne legati nostri discessum nostrum in
eorum contemptum et iniuriam fieri aliquatenus estimarent et in cause nostre
desperationem fugam interpretarentur. Vnde nostris uisum est non expedire ut eis
inconsultis aliquo diuertamus, cum propter nos ut dicitur eos a latere suo domnus
papa transmiserit. Terret nos quoque difficultas itineris et que peregrinantibus 25
inminent pericula nos in re ista plurimum uacillare compellunt. Conceptum tamen
desiderium curam omnem timoris excluderet, si laborem hunc quoquomodo mei
corporis infirmitas sustinere sufficeret. Nil enim est quod op⟨fo. 108⟩tem amplius,
quod desiderantius affectem, quam domno pape presens assistere ipsoque et curia
sancta presente michi detrahentes et falsa suggerentes aduersum me in eius qui 30
ueritas est uirtute refellere. Quod effectui mancipare crebro sperantes, semper tamen
necessitatis alicuius obiectu substitimus, nunc uero senectuti sociata compellit infirmitas ut licet optemus iudicem, ipsi tamen assistere necessitate multiplici despere-
mus. Vnde uestram instantius exoramus sollicitudinem, ut ope uestra et opera
plenam nobis gratiam domnus papa inpertiat, et prelibatum beneficium ad per- 35
fectum nobis apostolica tandem mansuetudine et miseratione perducat. Nuntio
uero nostro quedam uobis intimanda commisimus, quem precor attentius audiatis
et fidem his que proposuerit habeatis. Valere uos in Domino optamus, karissime.

## 220  To King Henry II

[May 1173] He writes, rather tardily, to describe the discussions about the election of the
archbishop of Canterbury, because the monks of Canterbury have been accusing him of
wishing to be archbishop himself. He combats the charge, saying that none of his previous
appointments (which he lists) was the fruit of ambition; and he describes how the monks
themselves prevented the election of any of the three candidates discussed—the bishop of

---

**219**  28 infirmitas] inbecillitas infirmitas, *corrected to* infirmita B. *Neither makes any sense, and as a
second s before* sustinere *has also been erased, the erasure at the end of* infirmitas *may be an error. It
seems probable that* infirmitas *was intended to replace* inbecillitas, *especially as the verb is singular, but*
inbecillitas et infirmitas *is not impossible*
**220**  G, no. 269; *MB Epp.* 792; B, fo. 190v.

---

[1]  Cf. Ps. xx. 4.

Bayeux, the abbot of Bec and the abbot of Cerisy[1]—by their contumacy. He recommends that some arrangement be made between monks and bishops—e.g. that the prior and one of the bishops should have first voice jointly in announcing the election—and asks the king to lay down what procedure is to be followed.

Negotiations for the elections to the vacant archbishopric and other vacant sees started in earnest in the second half of 1172, but without immediate result. Late in 1172 or early in 1173 the legates Albert and Theoduin sent a mandate from Normandy for free elections to take place in the English bishoprics then vacant.[2] The vacant sees were those of Canterbury, Bath, Chichester, Ely, Hereford, Lincoln and Winchester. Serious discussions began in February; and at a council held in London at the end of April,[3] candidates were elected to all the bishoprics (except perhaps Bath, for which this seems to have taken place somewhat earlier).[4] There was the customary dispute over the election to Canterbury between the bishops of the province and the monks of Canterbury.[5] The dispute was finally settled by the election of Richard, prior of Dover, on 3 June.[6] In no. 220 Gilbert describes an attempt to elect to Canterbury and the difficulties which arose. The discussions must have been spread over several months from the suggestion of the bishop of Bayeux late in 1172, through the election of the abbot of Bec in February and his withdrawal early in April, to the attempt to elect the abbot of Cerisy, evidently at the council in late April; and the letter was written some time later ('tardaui...Nunc autem scribo uel sero'), but before the final election on 3 June.

The letter opens with a sharp reference to his detraction by the monks of Canterbury. But it closes with a suggestion that Henry go at least half-way to meeting the monks' wishes. This is accompanied by a hint that Henry turn back ('reuocetis') from his Norman candidates to an Englishman, or at least someone living in England. One is inclined to suspect that Gilbert had already come to an understanding with Odo prior of Canterbury, and had his eye on a candidate; and Gervase (I, 244) tells us that in the comparatively brief interval between the fruitless council in late April and the election of Richard, prior of Dover, early in June, Richard himself and another monk went to ascertain the king's wishes. The king refused to disclose his views, but sent them secretly; Odo was allowed at least the show of a free election, and Richard was elected. It seems likely that all this was an elaborate face-saving device: the election was free, but Henry was allowed to state his wishes.[7] This view of the case can stand,

---

[1] Roger, abbot of Bec, 1149–79, and Martin, abbot of Cerisy, c. 1167–1185/90 (Torigny, pp. 158, 233, 286–7; Delisle, *Recueil*, II, no. DCCLVI; *Gallia Christiana*, XI, Instr., col. 90).

[2] Tillmann, pp. 71–2; *MB Epp.* 789–90; cf. Diceto, I, 366–7; Gervase, I, 239 ff.

[3] Gervase, I, 243 (cf. Diceto, I, 368). That the election to Chichester took place not long after Easter (8 April) is clear from the Pipe Roll of 1172–3 (*PR 19 Henry II*, pp. 29–30), which shows it as vacant for half the year before the election; but the same is said of Canterbury (p. 90). The bishopric of Bath paid exactly half the annual render to the king (*op. cit.* p. 105, *PR 18 Henry II*, p. 128). No accounts were rendered for the year 1172–3 from the other sees.

[4] *MB Epp.* 790 (cf. 791).

[5] Gervase, I, 244; Gilbert's letter shows that the dispute had started earlier than Gervase indicates. Bishops and monks, at one stage, agreed to the election of Roger de Bailleul, abbot of Bec, but he refused and was released from his election on 5 April (Gervase, I, 241–2). The crucial issue was who should announce the election (cf. H. Mayr-Harting, *Journ. of Eccl. History*, XVI (1965), 50–2).

[6] Gervase, I, 244: cf. pp. 240–2 for what follows (according to Canterbury annals in *UGQ*, p. 6, the election took place on 15 June; and Torigny, p. 256, gives the abbot of Bec's *election* as 4 April. Gervase's account makes better sense).

[7] See H. Mayr-Harting, *art. cit.* p. 50.

whether the choice of Richard was in any sense really Henry's, or the fruit of an agreement between Canterbury and London. If the latter, then Gilbert's letter is in the tradition of those written by John of Salisbury for Theobald at the end of his life in which Henry II was asked to resolve the papal schism (so far as it affected England—see especially JS *Epp.* 125), but was tactfully told which pope he must choose.

Although the elections were conducted in a canonical manner, it is clear that royal influence was far from negligible. It is also clear that the king had his way in the choice of several of the bishops, as can be seen from the following list of the elect. (Robert Foliot had been among the circle of Becket's *eruditi*, his clerks, but had not shared his exile.[1])

*Canterbury:* Richard, prior of Dover.
*Bath:* Reginald FitzJocelin, royal clerk and archdeacon of Wiltshire.
*Chichester:* John of Greenford, dean of Chichester.
*Ely:* Geoffrey Ridel, royal clerk and archdeacon of Canterbury.
*Hereford:* Robert Foliot, archdeacon of Oxford.
*Lincoln:* Geoffrey, son of Henry II and archdeacon of Lincoln.
*Winchester:* Richard of Ilchester, royal clerk and archdeacon of Poitiers.

The consecration of the archbishop elect was fixed for 10 June, a week after his election, but it was prevented by the intervention of the young king, Henry 'III', who took exception to the elections—in particular because his consent had not been given.[2] The incident is described in no. 221, written shortly after 10 June. The result was an appeal to the Pope and the postponement of the consecration of all the other bishops. Between then and the settlement of the case in 1174 Gilbert wrote to the Pope on behalf of the elect of Ely (no. 225), Hereford (no. 224), and Winchester (no. 223): he also wrote to Cardinal William of Pavia in support of the bishop elect of Winchester (no. 226). No. 222, for the elect of Bath, refers to the legates' permission for an election, and does not indicate any later difficulty, so it very likely belongs to spring 1173. Similar letters on behalf of some of the elect were sent by Arnulf of Lisieux, Bartholomew of Exeter, John of Salisbury, and the prior and monks of Christ Church, Canterbury.[3]

The dispute over the election of Richard to Canterbury was settled by the Pope early in 1174. His election was confirmed and he was consecrated by the Pope in person at Anagni on 7 April 1174; he was shortly afterwards given the pallium and made primate and legate.[4] Richard left Italy in May and returned to England. On 23 June he consecrated Reginald FitzJocelin to Bath; and on 6 October all the other bishops except Geoffrey elect of Lincoln. Shortly after 6 October Gilbert wrote no. 228 to Alexander III, pleading for the consecration of Geoffrey, which did not take place.

Domno regi domnus Lundoniensis, salutem et amoris intimam de ipsis cordis sui medullis affectionem.

Vestre domne celsitudini scribere tardaui, quia que de ecclesiis regni uestri gesta sunt uobis priusquam possem scribere per nuntios iustitie uestre manifestata fuisse cognoui. Nunc autem scribo uel sero, et ob Dei misericordiam supplex obsecro, ne 5 michi detrahentibus acquiescatis, ne monachis Cant(uarie) in hiis que maligna ⟨fo. 191⟩ locuntur aduersum me fidem aliquatenus habeatis. Aiunt enim me ad

[1] *MB*, III, 524.    [2] Gervase, I, 245.
[3] Arnulf, *Epp.* 92, 94–6, 98; John of Salisbury, ed. Giles, *Epp.* 311–21.
[4] Gervase, I, 247; *Gesta Henrici II*, I, 69–70 (quoting the contemporary letter of Reginald elect of Bath); Diceto, I, 389–90.

archiepiscopatum Cant(uariensem) ambire, et ob hoc electiones quas de aliis faciunt modis omnibus impedire. Nouit ipse qui ueritas est nullum horum uerum
10 esse. In promotione mea prima Cluniaci prior quidam sum constitutus in ordine, dehinc prior Abbatisuille; hinc abbas Gloec(estrie), post episcopus Hereford(ensis), hinc translatus Lundon(iam). Confidenter assero quod ad nullum horum ambiui, quorum tamen unumquodque permittente Deo consequenter optinui. In secretis itaque cordis mei dico Domino Deo meo, quia sufficit michi gratia sua; dico et
15 uobis domno meo karissimo quia sufficit michi in hiis indulta a uobis benignissime gratia uestra. Auertat a me Dominus hanc cupiditatem; auertat a uobis omnipotens assensum in hoc prebendi omnimodo uoluntatem. Si uero electiones suas aliquatenus impediui, hinc potestis aduertere. Primo de domno Baioc(ensi) actum est.[1] Quod episcopis regni uestri licet graue uideretur, omnes tamen opem ferente
20 Domino ad hoc induxi ut in ipsum assentirent, ipsumque suscipere parati essent. Soli monachi respuerunt quod uos precipue uelle cognouerunt. De Beccense postmodum actum est. Quod licet grauissimum omnibus regni episcopis uideretur, multa tamen instantia et industria optinui ut in ipsum assentiendo sue preiudicarent uoluntati. Ad ultimum ad abbatem de Cereseio decursum est. Quod licet et
25 episcopis et omnibus terre uestre abbatibus omnibusque regni uestri personis non solum graue uideretur uerum et indignissimum, ego tamen ne pax ecclesie turbaretur, nec quam desiderabatis electio ulterius differretur—etsi cum multa ira et indignatione omnium—tandem tamen optinui, ut si monachi Cantuar(ie) in electionis pronuntiatione episcopis regni uestri uel modicam exhibere uoluissent
30 reuerentiam, in ipsum acquiescerent, et ne uester aduersus eos turbaretur animus rem hoc fine terminare permitterent. Verum hii sibi omnia usurpantes et episcopos omnes a consilio et electione et electionis pronuntiatione seuerius excludentes, quod cum aliquantula modestia agentes tunc optinere potuerunt, nimia utentes obstinacia ulterius differri compulerunt. Qua in re si placet honori uestro consulite, diligenter
35 attendentes quid uobis magis expediat: an monachis totum ascribere qui uobis nec hominio tenentur astricti nec fidelitate, aut in eligenda maxima persona regni uestri reuerentiam aliquam episcopis attribuere, qui uobis aut hominio aut fidelitate obligati honorem uestrum in Deo conseruare duplici necessitate tenentur obnoxii. Bonum est itaque si placet ut rigorem monachorum quem tot[iens] de humilitate
40 uestra concipiunt ea qua scitis mode[stia] et sapientia temperetis, et ad aliquam si placet regni[2] uestri personam ipsorum consilium reuocetis, et saluo iure utriusque partis in posterum de prima uoce in electione habenda (cum de eo agi fuerit

**220** 39, 40 tot[iens]/mode[stia] *The margin in B is cut away with the loss of a few letters*

---

[1] The king's attempt to have Henry de Beaumont, bishop of Bayeux, elected seems to have taken place late in 1172 (Gervase, I, 240).

[2] I.e., apparently, to an Englishman, or ecclesiastic holding office in England—and not to a Norman like those previously suggested. This seems implicit in the word 'reuocetis', and for the use of *regnum* to distinguish England from Henry's other dominions, cf. 'episcopis regni uestri', etc., earlier in this letter (the word is used four times). But it is possible that the word was somewhat ambiguous, and could be used as a cover for retreat if such should prove to be necessary.

oportunum) electionem ipsam per priorem et aliquem episcoporum simul aut alio quocumque modo quod Deus uobis et consilio uestro reuelauerit pronuntiari faciatis, ut per sapientiam uestram pacificato statu ecclesie, nebulam que ex dissen- 45 sione hac regno uestro adhuc impendet gratiam prestante Domino prorsus euacuetis.

## 221 To Pope Alexander III

[After 10 June 1173] He describes how, after leave for free elections to vacant sees had been given by the Pope through the legates Albert and Theoduin, Richard prior (of Dover) was duly elected archbishop of Canterbury. But when the bishops of the province were gathered on 10 June for the consecration, they were interrupted by messengers from the young king, appealing against the elections which had been made. Out of deference to the Pope, the consecration has been postponed.

Patri suo et domno summo pontifici A(lexandro) frater G(ilebertus) Lundoniensis ecclesie minister, uere dilectionis affectum et humilis obedientie famulatum.

Lux domne post tenebras gratius illuscescit, et post meroris nubilum restituta letitia mens quam dolor afflixerat iocundius hilarescit. Sic Anglicana pater ecclesia que suis destituta pastoribus longo iam tractu temporis luctum continuauit et 5 lacrimas, ubi uestra sollicitudine quam filiorum commodis studiose semper impenditis per directos a latere uestro uiros uenerabiles Al(bertum) et Th(eoduinum) sedis apostolice sancte legatos in eligendis pastoribus et prelatis gloriam libertatis optinuit, quanto eam dolor grauius afflixerat tanto uberiori perfusa gaudio intus in spiritu habundantius exultauit. Datus ei fuerat iuxta prophetam pro zona funiculus, 10 pro crispanti crine caluitium, et pro fascia pectorali iuge cilicium.[1] Que omnia Domino potenter uirtutem operante per uos sibi iam longe proiecta sunt et electionum sibi concessa libertate, iam quasi uestibus induta glorie sponso suo et regi quam gloriose tam et confidenter assistit, hac usa libertate quam Domino gratiam ministrante per uos assecuta est. Sancta Cantuariensis ecclesia illa sancte Romane 15 ecclesie filia spiritualis et deuotissima, conuocatis episcopis suis suffraganeis et ceteris ipsius prouinthie personis in eligendo sibi patrem et archiepiscopum sanctorum statutis canonum diligenter obseruatis, cum apud se inueniret idoneum ad sui regimen accersire noluit alienum. Habens igitur pre oculis quod scriptum est: 'habeat unusquisque fructum sue militie in ecclesia in qua suam per omnia transegit 20 etatem; in aliena minime stipendia alter obrepat, nec alii debitam alter sibi audeat uendicare mercedem',[2] iuxta illud prophete dicentis, 'pro patribus tuis nati sunt tibi filii',[3] filium quem nutrierat, quem regularis obseruantie sacris iamdiu imbuerat institutis, Ricardum priorem, eiusdem ecclesie monachum, uirtutum meritis commendabilem Deo ut credimus et hominibus acceptabilem, utpote cui ad doctrinam 25 scientia et ad honestatem mores exuberant ⟨fo. 150⟩ totius conuentus sui et episcoporum, ceterarumque personarum in hoc concurrentibus uotis, in patrem

---

221 G, no. 158; B, fo. 149v.
18 statutis *Giles*; statuta B

---

[1] Cf. Is. iii. 24.     [2] *Decretum*, D. 61, c. 13.     [3] Ps. xliv. 17.

sibi et archiepiscopum celebrata sollemniter electione suscepi·, psumque ad hoc in
sublime rapiens, Deo laudes et gloriam cum multa gratiarum actione populique
30 totius applausu gratanter exsoluit. Ad cuius consecrationem sequenti Dominica
post octabas Pentecostes cum suffraganei conuenissent ep scopi, nuntiosque suos et
ratihabitionis litteras qui ex necessitate aberant destinasse t, ex insperato littere sub
nomine regis iunioris concepte in medium prolate et porrecte sunt, apellationem
continentes aduersus electiones que in regno suo nequaquam celebrarentur assensu.
35 Cui cum patre superstite nichil a quoquam debeatur in regno nisi salua patris sui
fidelitate, licetque littere porrecte multis ex causis quas enumerare longum est
suspecte nobis uiderentur, maiestati tamen uestre debita cum ueneratione deferentes,
et honorem uestrum integre cupientes seruare, a consecratione abstinuimus et rem
uestre delegandam notitie, omnes in commune decreuimus. Vnde sanctitati uestre
40 omnes in commune preces affectuose porrigimus, ne cytharam nostram in luctum
et organum in uocem flentium conuertatis, sed operi manuum uestrarum benigne
dexteram porrigatis—ut sciant omnes, domine, quia manus tua hec et tu domine
fecisti eam,[1] et totam Cantuar(iensis) ecclesie plenitudinem uobis uberiorem
obligetis ad gratiam.

## 222   To Pope Alexander III

[Spring or summer 1173] He rejoices that the legates have given leave for the vacant sees to
be filled, and asks the Pope to confirm the election of Reginald archdeacon of (Wiltshire,
dioc. of) Salisbury as bishop of Bath.

Patri suo et domino summo pontifici A(lexandro) frater G(ilebertus) Lundoniensis
ecclesie minister, sincere et uere dilectionis affectum et humilis obedientie famulatum.

In exsoluendis pater sanctitati uestre gratiarum actionibus nostra plane succumbit
humilitas, eo quod ecclesia Dei multis apud nos retro temporibus iugo seruitutis
5 oppressa omnique recuperande libertatis spe uacua, uestra tandem sollicitudine
quam commissi uobis gregis utilitati uigilanter inpenditis, suis restituta natalibus
statum eius Domino commutante in melius desiderata plurimum libertate iam
nunc ex insperato donata est. Legatorum enim quos ad ecclesie perquirenda
remedia in partes nostras circumspectione laudabili uestra direxit auctoritas hoc
10 tandem cura prudenter et potenter optinuit, ut in regno Anglie suis iamdiu uiduate
pastoribus ecclesie ad sui regimen idoneas eligendi personas liberam in omnibus
habeant facultatem. Inde est quod apud nos quamplures ecclesie suis gratulantur
electis de uestra confidentes misericordia, ut hii quos concorditer elegerunt dono
uestre gratie promoti in melius consecrationis etiam munus ualeant optinere. Inter
15 has ⟨fo. 152v⟩ Bathon(iensis) ecclesia in uenerabilem fratrem nostrum Raginaldum
Saresbirensem archidiaconum sua uota porrexit, ipsum concorditer expetens et
nullo reclamante aut contradictionem in aliquo mouente sollempniter eligens, eique

222 G, no. 160; B, fo. 152.
6 gregis *Giles*; exegis B    10 causa *corrected to* cura B    14 promereri *corrected to* promoti B

---

[1] Cf. Job xxx. 31; xiv. 15; Ps. cviii. 27.

sui curam et regimen tota animi uoluntate committens. Quem apud sanctitatem uestram laudum commendare titulis ideo supersedendum credimus, quod eius litteraturam, mores et industriam et in agendis ecclesie negotiis efficaciam ipsis 20 rerum ut credimus agnouistis indiciis, utpote quem uestra donatum gratia et apud nos ex uestra magnificatum notitia, in id gratie culmen erexistis ut que ipsum elegit ecclesia non modicam ex hoc ipso speret apud sanctitatem uestram gratiam collocari. Quem quia iuuante Domino in domo Domini cooperatorem bonum futurum credimus fraterna karitate mouente et in hoc audaciam prestante petimus, ut operi 25 manuum uestrarum benigne porrigatis dexteram[1] et consecrationem eius accelerando, uobis ipsum et propter ipsum plurimos arctius obligetis ad gratiam.

### 223  To Pope Alexander III

[1173–4] The see of Winchester has long been vacant, and virtually vacant still longer, since the late bishop was incapable of administration at the end of his life; Gilbert asks that the elect be speedily consecrated.

Patri suo et domno summo pontifici A(lexandro) frater G(ilebertus) Lundoniensis ecclesie minister, totum quod ex se ualet humilis et ad obediendum promta deuotio.

Suspirat pater ad uos Winton(iensis) ecclesia et quia spectat ad uos ecclesiarum omnium sollicitudo[2] sua coram uobis anxie deplorat incomoda. Orbata patre 5 aliunde iamdiu sibi emendicauit suffragia, et de longinquis finibus euocauit episcopos, ut commissis sibi populis statuta celitus amministrarent sacramenta. Hec etiam uiuente patre suo, patre iamdiu caruit quem ab amministrandis hiis quibus et fundatur et erigitur et ad perfectum adducitur ecclesia Dei, ipsa sui corporis imbecillitas multo quidem tempore prepediuit. Que suis iam finem gaudebat 10 prouenisse suspiriis, et in electo suo quem uotis omnibus exoptauerat, et in patrem sibi pastoremque nullo penitus contradicente uel reclamante sollempniter elegerat, multa animi iocunditate respirabat. Audiens uero sua uota differri et electi sui consecrationem in longum protrahi nubilo iam nunc meroris obducitur, et quia spes que differtur affligit animam,[3] amicos suos undequaque sollicitat et uicinos, ut 15 sua uobis uota proferant, sanctitati uestre preces cum supplicante porrigant, ut eius si placet anxietati condescendere uelitis et compati et in negotio hoc ob multiplicem ecclesie necessitatem, si qua ualet ⟨fo. 190⟩ admitti dispensatio, suum concedatis electum cuius et honestas et conuersationis integritas digne commendabilis est absque dilatione consecrari. Est lignum uite desiderium ueniens;[4] unde si preces in 20 causa hac sublimitati uestre supplicantium admiseritis Wintoniensi ecclesie non in modico subuenietis et omnes nos in omnem quam possumus gratiam uobis pater obligatos habebitis. Conseruet uos in longa tempora D(eus), in Christo dilecte pater.

**222** 27 abligetis B
**223** G, no. 168; B, fo. 189v.

[1] Cf. Job xiv. 15 (and no. 221).
[2] Cf. II Cor. xi. 28 (and no. 193).
[3] Cf. Prov. xiii. 12.
[4] Cf. *ibid.*

### 224 To Pope Alexander III

[1173–4] He commends the elect of Hereford, Robert archdeacon of Oxford, to the Pope, and asks that he may be speedily consecrated.

Domno pape domnus Lundoniensis pro Hereford(ensi) electo.

Herefordensem pater ecclesiam gratum Domino prestitisse speramus obsequium, que eligendi patris sibi libertate concessa—ut communis habet opinio—ad sui regimen pastorem elegit idoneum, uirum ut commune probat arbitrium Deo et
5 hominibus acceptum. Quantis enim uirtutum insignibus Hereford(ensis) electus effulgeat, fama loquitur, probat opinio, una in ore omnium testatur assertio, qui Robertum Oxen(efordie) archidiaconum omnes etatis sue gradus adeo innocenter et honeste percurrisse denuntiant, ut ei uel in modico nunquam fama detraxerit, ⟨fo. 190v⟩ conuersationem eius sinister rumor nullatenus obfuscare potuerit, aut
10 prauitatis eloquio denigrare. Hunc pater in Christo carissime sanctitati uestre commendamus ad gratiam, preces affectuose porrigentes ut decurrentis ad uos Hereford(ensis) ecclesie petitionem quam iustam uere credimus admittatis, et ut eius consecretur electus paterna si placet gratia prouideatis ne si repulsam sustinuerit, lesa uirtus erubescat et alios in appetitum sui et cultum de cetero minus
15 accendat.

### 225 To Pope Alexander III

[1173–4] He asks the Pope to confirm the election of Geoffrey archdeacon of Canterbury to the bishopric of Ely and to speed his consecration.

Domno pape domnus Lundoniensis.

Sanctitati uestre scribere et fratrum nostrorum id exigente necessitate preces affectuose porrigere caritas nos pater imperiosa compellit. Huius enim lege constringimur, eos ut nos ipsos diligere et negotia sua nostra reputando quod in
5 necessitate simili nobis exhiberi uellemus, ipsis procul dubio non negare. Venerabilem itaque fratrem nostrum Gaufridum ecclesie Cant(uariensis) archidiaconum, uirum prudentem testificamur et strenuum, prouidum in consilio, discretum et ornatum eloquio, agendis ecclesie negotiis et ipsius necessitatibus subleuandis et sustinendis aptissimum. Cui cum ad doctrinam scientia et ad honestatem ut
10 credimus mores exuberent, ipsum sibi Eliensis ecclesia per manum nostram susceptis legatorum uestrorum litteris, quibus de eligendo sibi episcopo auctoritate apostolica commonebatur, in patrem et pastorem expetiit, ipsum concordi omnium uoto, nullo reclamante aut contradictionem in aliquo mouente ad Eliensis episcopatus regimen, coniuentiam in hoc prestante principe, facta celebriter electione suscepit.
15 Quem quia ecclesie ipsi ad quam uocatus est opem et gratiam prestante Domino in multis credimus profuturum, et omnem uobis et sancte Romane ecclesie deuotionem in quibuscumque poterit exhibiturum, apud sanctitatem uestram cum ecclesia

224 G, no. 169; B, fo. 190.
225 G, no. 170; B, fo. 190v.
12 expetiit,] huiusmodi ipsius ecclesie [. . .]nes (?) *erased in* B

pulsante pulsamus, cum postulante preces affectuose porrigimus, ut quod actum est ea qua preestis et potestis auctoritate roboratis, et negotio huic manum supremam imponendo, et ipsius consecrationem paterna pietate maturando, et eum et com- 20 missam sibi ecclesiam uobis in omnem gratiarum actionem et caritatis plenitudinem arcius obligetis, ut ecclesie per uos in regno Anglie nuper indulta libertas in suis coalescat initiis et gratiam augente Domino fortiter ipso tractu temporis conualescat.

## 226  To Cardinal William of Pavia

[c. summer 1174] The see of Winchester has been vacant for close on three years;[1] Gilbert asks the cardinal to hasten the consecration of the elect, who is related to Gilbert.

The old bishop died in August 1171; three years would take one to August 1174—the new bishop was consecrated in October.

Domno Willelmo Pap(iensi) pro Winton(ensi) electo, seipsum et si quid potest deuote mentis obsequium.

Suadet e facili uerborum paucitas cum ad exaudiendum prona est ipsius ad quem scribitur amica benignitas.[2] Vnde quia de uestra in nos beniuolentia non nostris quidem meritis, sed uestra solum gratia nobis clementer indulta et potenter 5 exhibita plene confidimus, sublimitati uestre preces affectuose porrigimus, quatinus negotium amici nostri et cognati karissimi domni Winton(ensis) electi sustinendo foueatis, et quia uos et consilio magnum et interuentu strenuum non ambigimus, ut eius maturetur consecratio data uobis a Domino sapientia et industria procuretis. A sapiente dispensatio solet admitti. Postulat ecclesie multiplicata necessitas sibi 10 tandem subueniri; sacramenta si prosunt, si in his animarum salus ulla consistit, detrimentum est non modicum et periculum tot populis ea subtrahi, tot ea requirentibus ob pontificum penuriam uel sero uel nullatenus amministrari. Winton(ensis) ecclesia sub ueste lugubri et habitu uiduali tria iam fere lustra percurrit, episcopalem benedictionem, absolutionem, manus impositionem, clericorum in ordine promo- 15 tionem, crismatis apud se innouationem, ecclesiarum consecrationem, et cetera uite spirituali necessaria, hiis diu carendo, iam fere dedidicit. Silet uerbum Dei, medium tenent cuncta silentium,[3] et multis modis quos enumerare longum est lucra depereunt animarum. Hiis ope uestra periculis subueniri deposcimus, ut electo Winton(ensi) consecrato per uos, in Domino cum ipsa eius ecclesia gaudeamus et 20 exhibitum nobis honorem et beneficium alta semper in posterum memoria teneamus. Valere uos optamus in Domino.

226 G, no. 178; B, fo. 190.

---

[1] If, as seems almost certain, 'tria iam fere lustra' is meant to signify 'nearly three years'; lustrum should be a period of four to five years, but this would make no sense in the context. Henry of Blois died 8 Aug. 1171; he had apparently been ill for some time, but he had not been either ill or absent for as much as ten or a dozen years—indeed the most normal meaning, fifteen years, would take one to about the time when Henry finally returned from his wanderings. In any case, Gilbert seems to be referring strictly to the vacancy in the see.

[2] Cf. p. 212 n. 1 (and no. 227).

[3] Cf. Introit for Sunday within Octave of Christmas: 'Dum medium silentium tenerent omnia.'

### 227　To Robert Foliot (?), bishop elect of Hereford

[Probably 1173–4] He asks him to confirm the rights of the church of Ledbury (Hereford-shire) as Gilbert and his predecessors had done, 'for the sake of the episcopal see which it held long since and out of reverence for the holy bishops whose bodies lie there'.[1]

Robert Foliot was bishop elect from April 1173 to 6 October 1174, and it is probably he who is addressed; but it is not impossible that the letter was written to Robert de Melun in the second half of 1163.

Gilebertus gratia Dei Lundoniensis episcopus uenerabili fratri domnoque karissimo R(oberto) Hereford(ensi) ecclesie eadem gratia ⟨fo. 152⟩ electo, salutem et optatos in Domino semper ad uota successus.

Verborum facile suadet paucitas cum ad exaudiendum prona est ipsius ad quem
5 scribitur amica benignitas.[2] Inde est quod dilecte nobis in Domino beniuolentie uestre preces affectuose porrigimus ut ecclesiam de Lideberi amore Dei nostreque petitionis intuitu, ob sedem episcopalem quam iamdiu optinuit et ob sanctorum episcoporum reuerentiam quorum ibidem corpora requiescunt, tam in capite quam in capellis ad eam pertinentibus in ea conseruetis integritate, qua tam nostro
10 quam decessorum nostrorum tempore stabilita fuisse dinoscitur, ut cum nostras in hoc preces exaudieritis, Deum inde uobis propitium et nos uobis amplioris gratie debitores habeatis.

### 228　To Pope Alexander III

[c. October 1174] The vacant sees are now filled and the new archbishop of Canterbury has consecrated his colleagues: only Lincoln remains, and Gilbert pleads with the Pope to confirm the election of their maligned archdeacon.

In this letter Gilbert makes the remarkable assertion that trust is to be placed in those who have known Geoffrey (Henry II's illegitimate son) from his earliest years up to his present age 'of thirty, as they assert'. In this ambiguous way Gilbert hints that Geoffrey was more or less of canonical age, which he certainly was not. The year of his birth is unknown, but it is doubtful if he was much over twenty in 1174; since his father was at this time only forty-one, he must have been well under thirty. It is not easy to think of a way of emending the passage to save Gilbert's credit; and it is hard to believe that he was really misinformed.[3]

**227** G, no. 211; B, fo. 151 v.
**228** G, no. 171; B, fo. 191 v.

---

[1] This seems to be the only early evidence of the tradition that Ledbury (Herefs, or possibly Lydbury North, Salop) was once an episcopal see. As the early history of the see of the Magonsætan is utterly obscure, it is quite possible that the bishop's headquarters were originally at Ledbury, presumably the centre of the district of *Lydas* referred to in a seventh-century charter (ed. H. P. R. Finberg, *Early Charters of the West Midlands*, Leicester, 1961, p. 202; cf. pp. 207 ff.).

[2] Cf. p. 212 n. 1 (and no. 226).

[3] Walter Map, *De nugis*, v, 6, says that he was born about the beginning of Henry's reign, and wrongly fathered on the king. Map is never reliable, and most of what he says on this point is gossip about an enemy. It is, however, most unlikely that Geoffrey was a mere boy in 1174;

Patri suo et domno summo pontifici A(lexandro) frater G(ilebertus) Lundoniensis ecclesie minister, pie salutantis affectum et deuote subiectionis obsequium.

Anglicana pater ecclesia in omnem gratiarum actionem sanctitati uestre se fatetur obnoxiam, eo, pater, quod presentatas sublimitati uestre fratrum nostrorum electiones placide suscepistis, et easdem patris nostri domni Cantuar(iensis) officio 5 confirmari et electos ipsos eius manu consecrari pia et paterna gratia concessistis. Qua in re iuges lacrimas quas a multis diutinus iam dolor extorserat pietatis apostolice manus extersit et ecclesiam regni in statum dignitatis pristine sullimiter erexit et potentissime reformauit. Per uos enim gratiam ministrante Domino sancta sedes Cantuarie uacuata dudum et diu uacua suum iam in se recognoscit antistitem, 10 et Wintonie clerus cum populo—electi sui sibi consecratione concessa—uoti sui plenissime conpos gratulatur et exultat in Domino; ecclesie uero Bathoniensis, Herefordensis, Cicestrensis, Eliensis, suis in his quos elegerant dono uestro gratie iam potite desideriis in gratiarum actionem diem celebrant sollempnitatis insignem. Sola domne superest Lincolniensis ecclesia, que cum in ecclesiis aliis undique laudes 15 resonent, undequaque pulsentur tympana glorie, gemitum pro cantu habet, et spiritum meroris trahens tota lamentis afficitur.[1] Audiuntur in domo patris undique simphonia et chorus, sed hec foris stans non ingreditur et repulsam passa semel ad patrem ingredi pertimescit.[2] Caritatis tamen affluentiam considerans, que de fonte pectoris apostolici indesinenter emanans ciuitatem Dei circumquaque letificat et 20 euangelicum ⟨fo. 192⟩ illud ad mentem reuocans—omnis qui petit accipit et qui querit inuenit, et pulsanti aperietur[3]—spem concipit ut meroris sui nubilum serenitatis uestre candor euacuet et in electi sui susceptione pariter et promotione preces filie deuotissime supplicantis pius pater exaudiat. Scit tamen apud uos supra dorsum eius quosdam fabricasse plurima, et odii sermonibus eius innocentiam 25 circumdedisse[4] et in hoc eatenus preualuisse ut ab eo clementie uestre facies ut dicitur aliquantulum auersa sit et a pluribus in eum sinistra iam sit concepta suspicio. Set si placet aduertere super eius conuersatione et uita his potissimum fides habenda est quibus a primis annis innotuit, sub quorum oculis ut certissime testificantur innocenter excreuit et ad annum tricesimum ut asserunt iam perductus, primam 30 etatis sue uigiliam sub multorum testimonio et honeste et innocenter compleuit, de quo spem bonam Lincolliensis ecclesia deuota filia uestra concipiens, et ipsius prudentiam in eo quem administrauit archidiaconatu contemplans et approbans, sperans quod eius promotio multis ex causis quas enumerare longum est sibi plurimum profutura sit, ipsum in patrem elegit concorditer, et ut hoc eius desiderium 35 a uestra sibi gratia compleatur instanter exposcit. Spem igitur habentes in Domino

**228** 13 El. Cic. *marked for transposition* B     19 tamen] attendens *added, cancelled* B     29 testi/ tantur B (*? for* testantur)

---

and there is no evidence that Henry was unfaithful to Eleanor before the 1170's (see *GF*, p. 173 n.). It may be conjectured that Geoffrey was the product of a casual liaison shortly before Henry's marriage, or, if his mother was English, perhaps during Henry's first long stay in England as an adult in 1153–4.

[1] Cf. Is. lxi. 3.          [2] Cf. Luc. xv. 25.
[3] Cf. Luc. xi. 10.          [4] Cf. Ps. cxxviii. 3; cviii. 3.

quod eius et honestas et prudentia ad honorem Dei et ecclesie de die in diem habitura
sit incrementum, ipsumque in subleuandis ecclesie necessitatibus cooperatorem fore
strenuum, preces sanctitati uestre cum ecclesia supplicante porrigimus, ut ei manum
40 gratie porrigatis, et sibi concedendo quod postulat, Anglorum ecclesie quod adhuc
deest gaudii suppleatis, et omnes nos ex hoc sublimitati uestre gratie debitores
efficiatis. Conseruet incolumitatem uestram Dominus, in Christo dilecte pater.

### 229   To Laurence, abbot of Westminster

[1163–73] A dispute has arisen between the abbot and the cathedral, the former claiming that
his church of St Margaret[1] is exempt from synodal dues: Gilbert denies the claim and orders
the abbot to pay the synodals to R. the archdeacon.[2]

Abbot Laurence died in 1173. The references to *discessus* and *depressio*, and especially to
'paucitatem...dierum' (cf. no. 214) may suggest 1170, but they are all vague; the first may
refer to departure from London and the last to the end of the world.

G(ilebertus) Dei gratia Lundoniensis episcopus uenerabili fratri et amico L(aurentio)
Westmon(asterii) eadem Dei gratia abbati et dilecto sibi in Domino eiusdem
ecclesie conuentui, bene semper sapere et intelligere ac nouissima prouidere.[3]
Quorundam fratres relatione didici quod priusquam maiori communicetur
5 audientie ad uestram per me referri notitiam tam utile quam humile reputaui. Inter
ecclesiam beati Pauli et uos noue litis est ut dicitur accensa scintillula, que si non
extincta citius in flammas eruperit, in partis utriusque dispendium sese proculdubio
dilatabit. Solent enim cause modice dissensionis grauissime fomitem ministrare, que
nisi in ipsis reprimantur initiis, studio partium tractuque temporis adeo sepius
10 inualescunt, ut post sumptus plurimos et labores inmensos admodum sit difficile
diffidentes sibi diu partes in pacis pristine serenitatem aliquatenus reuocare. Vnde
quia rerum metiri solet exitus inspectio prudens, dilectam michi in Domino
fraternitatem uestram porrecta prece conuenio paterna quoque karitate consilium
do ne aduersus matrem et fratres occasionem queratis discordie, ne a sue matris
15 amplexibus filiam studeatis auellere, sed solitam debitamque sibi reuerentiam
exibendo, paucitatem hanc dierum nobiscum uelitis in pace et karitatis unitate
transigere, sancta quadam animi nobilitate dedignantes ob questum modicum et
ignobilem a bono pacis quod inter commissas nobis ecclesias perseuerauit hactenus
inconsiderata quadam animi presumptione resilire. Ecclesiam quippe sancte
20 Margarete super qua recens hec est orta dissentio, a primis suis fundamentis usque
ad dies hos episcopis Lundoniensibus et eorum archidiaconis sine contradictione et

---

**229** G, no. 266; B, fo. 108 v.

[1] Although Westminster had rights in other churches dedicated to St Margaret in the neighbourhood, this letter seems clearly to refer to St Margaret's, Westminster, for whose parish
the monks claimed exemption. They finally won their case from Archbishop Stephen
Langton in 1222 (J. Armitage Robinson, *Flete's History of Westminster Abbey*, Cambridge,
1909, pp. 61–3, cf. p. 18).

[2] Presumably the archdeacon of Middlesex, Ralph de Diceto.

[3] Cf. Deut. xxxii. 29.

reclamatione fuisse subiectam consonum totius undique uicinie testimonium clamat, et hanc meo quoque tempore R. archidiacono debitum et consuetum cathedraticum exoluisse in illis fere partibus nullus ⟨fo. 109⟩ ignorat. Si itaque matri uestre annuos duodecim ⟨solidos⟩(?) subtraxeritis in modico graue sibi dedecus 25 inferetis et emolumentum communi mense certe permodicum in summa modica conferetis. Vtilibus igitur acquiescendo monitis meum sustinete si placet hac uice consilium, ut appellationibus hinc inde remissis, laxatis si que date sunt in quem-cumque sententiis, memoratos iam nummos archidiacono solui permittatis, et in eo statu quo in discessu meo fuerant stare cuncta permittatis, nec ob leue compendium 30 a matris uestre gratia recedendo dulce reputetis et sapidum quod in eius iniuriam uestra sibi fuerit usurpatione detentum. Sic inter nos gratiam conciliare poteritis, sic ad obsequium me uestrum promptum et paratum habebitis, sic ob depressionem meam uos ad ecclesie michi commisse depressionem minime prosiluisse ipsa uestri operis euidentia luce clarius ostendetis. Sufficit diei malitia sua;[1] satis oneratus sum 35 ea que me premit iniuria. Si dolori dolorem, iniurie iniuriam addideritis, uos meo parum compati infortunio nulli dubium relinquetis. In quantum possumus nobis ⟨dedecus emere?⟩ non possumus, et si ceptis stare contenditis, omnes nos et nostros ad propulsandam pro uiribus iniuriam fortiter exacuetis. Valere uos et nobis in tribulatione parcere desideramus karissimi.                                                    40

## 230   To Geoffrey, archdeacon of Canterbury

[1163–73] He asks the archdeacon to use his influence with the king on behalf of Gilbert's relative by marriage Roger of Durnford (Wilts), whose inheritance the abbot of West-minster is trying to deny him, although it was confirmed by his predecessor and the whole convent and by the empress (Matilda).

The archdeacon was elected to the bishopric of Ely in 1173 (above, p. 293).

Gill(ebertus) Dei gratia Lundoniensis episcopus uenera⟨B2, fo. 188⟩bili fratri et amico karissimo G(alfrido) eadem gratia Cantuar(iensi) archidiacono, salutem et sincere dilectionis affectum.

Talentum uobis karissime commissum est quod augere et in multorum com-moditates expendere discretioni uestre necessarium est, ut cum istud multorum 5 subueniendo necessitatibus adauxeritis, mercedem in centuplum a Domino in illa die reportetis.[2] Talentum hoc domni nostri regis est uobis a Domino conces-⟨B1, fo. 143v⟩sa familiaritas, quam si quis auro comparet pretiosior est, et recte quantacunque pecunia longe carior estimatur. Talentum hoc ut fideliter erogetis opus est, ut ipsum de subleuanda oppressorum miseria frequenter et sollicite com- 10 moneatis et in hoc non oportuna solum sed et inportuna, si id pietas exigat,

---

229 25 ⟨solidos⟩ *om.* B; ? denarios     38 decem B; *emendation is essential, but that in the text is not entirely satisfactory*
230 G, nos. 197, 292; *MB Epp.* 393; B, fos. 143 (B1) *and* 187v (B2) (*spelling as* B2); B1 *runs from* Talentum uobis *to* huiusmodi cumuletur *only.*
5 illud B1     7 hoc] i(d est) *added* B1

---

[1] Matt. vi. 34.                          [2] Cf. Matt. xxv. 15 ff.; xix. 29.

instantia perseueretis,[1] ut et ipsi meritum apud Dominum collocetur, et apud Deum et homines gratia uobis non modica ex studiis huiusmodi cumuletur. Hec ideo prelibauimus quia lator presentium Rog(erus) de Dernefo⟨r⟩d' ea nobis affinitate 15 coniunctus est ut ei deesse nequeamus, quin apud hos de quorum gratia nos et caritate confidimus, ipsius id exigente necessitate supplicemus. In hunc uero domnus abbas Westmonasterii manus in tantum aggrauat ut ab hereditate que sibi predecessoris sui et totius capituli carta confirmata est et insuper domne imperatricis matris domni nostri regis carta roborata, seuere nimis extirpare intendat. Vnde beniuolentie 20 uestre preces quanta possumus affectione porrigimus quatinus huius seruitium suscipiatis, et ut domnus noster rex matris sue donationem sibi ea quam ipse laudabitis seruitii taxatione moderata confirmet optineatis, ut et ipsum seruitii semper obnoxium et me ad placitum uestrum et seruitii et gratie debitorem habeatis. Valere uos optamus in Domino karissime.

### 231  To Robert Foliot, archdeacon of Oxford

[1163–73] He urges the archdeacon to adhere to his arrangement with Master Adam de Longavilla, and retain the church he holds from Adam in his own hand, so that he has no difficulty in recovering possession when Robert is promoted, or enters religion, or dies.

In the event, Robert was promoted, in 1173 (above, p. 293).

G(ilebertus) Dei gratia Londoniensis episcopus R(oberto) Oxenford(ie) archidiacono, salutis gaudium et quem nature gratia superaddit affectum.

Multorum prece commonitus beniuolentie uestre preces offero ne a pactis que inter uos et magistrum Adam de Longauilla firmata sunt quocumque suadente uos 5 aliquatenus aut interpellante recedatis, sed ecclesiam quam eius nomine annua ut asserit pensione tenetis, ipse in manu uestra habeatis, ne si per uos alius in illam irrepserit, post uestram Domino donante promotionem aut ad humillioris uite studia inspirante Domino translationem, aut diem forte quem nullus euadet extremum, ipsum rem suam nancisci denuo suis ut fieri assolet implicata difficultas 10 inpediat. Quia uero quod equum est uos libenter obseruare non ambigo, preces una cum obtinendi fiducia porrigo quatinus quod eratis me non supplicante facturus, oblatis a me precibus effectu compleatis alacrius. Valere uos in Domino optamus.

### 232  To William, abbot of Reading

[1165–73] He had heard rumours of the perils of the abbot's voyage, and is delighted to hear that he is safe. He looks forward to seeing him, but must await his arrival in London, and asks the abbot to let him know if he can visit him at Fulham (Middlesex).

William was abbot 1165–73; for his relations with Gilbert, cf. no. 205 and n.

**230** 12 Deum *omitted* B 1    13 cumuletur] B 1 *ends here*
**231** G, no. 208; B, fo. 143 v.
4 firmata *Giles*; finiata (finita *is also possible*) B    6 alius] alit' B (? aliquis)    8 tnslationem B
10 inueniat *corrected* B
**232** G, no. 263; B, fo. 164 v.

---

[1] Cf. II Tim. iv. 2.

G(ilebertus) Dei gratia Lundoniensis episcopus uenerabili fratri et amico Willelmo eadem gratia abbati Rading(ensi), salutem ⟨fo. 165⟩ et sincere dilectionis affectum.

Suscepimus litteras dilectionis uestre que nos tanto uerius gaudio perfuderunt quanto de statu et salute uestra nostre certius sollicitudini responderunt. Prodiga namque uerborum fama, que uestrum ad nos nuntium preuolarat, de profectione 5 uestra, de statione in litore, de procella, de periculis multa uarie inconstanterque nuntiabat. Vnde pessimus in dubiis augur timor anxie distrahebat nos scientes quidem et expertos totiens, quod nauigatio sepe periculosa est, semper autem incerta. Nunc autem accepto nuntio salutis et incolumitatis uestre, pro uobis diuine gratie gratias referimus que uos in tantis periculis periclitari non permisit. Vestrum 10 autem colloquium sumopere desideramus, sed ante diem aduentus uobis occurrere nos ad aliud trahente necessitate non ualemus. Tunc uero Lundoniis esse disponimus et si usque Fuleham procedere fuerit oportunum et placitum, nobis id recurrente nuntio quam citius significari postulamus. Valere uos optamus in Domino carissime.

### 233 To Pope Alexander III

[1163–74] On behalf of the elderly bishop of Norwich.

The bishop is clearly William de Turba, previously monk and prior of Norwich, who died at a ripe age on 16 January 1174.

Patri suo et domno summo pontifici A(lexandro) frater G(ilebertus) Londoniensis ecclesie minister, humilem et debitum caritatis et obedientie famulatum.

Venerabilis et karissimi fratris nostri domni Norewic(ensis) episcopi preclara ab ineunte etate usque in senectutem bonam id ad plenum exigunt merita, ut quos delectat honestas uite, quibus religio cordi est ipsum digne comendare et apud 5 sanctitatem uestram cum supplicante debeant affectione promptissima supplicare. Notum quippe satis est ipsum ab ipsis fere cunabulis per omnes etatum gradus[1] honeste conuersatum in ecclesia Dei ad senectam iam nunc uberem peruenisse, ipsumque in ecclesia cui presidet et in episcopatu quem disponit in publicas adeo gratulationes susceptum esse, ut quod sibi inpenderitis honoris et gratie id tota 10 ipsius ecclesie plenitudo cum summa gratiarum susceptura sit actione. Cum sit itaque patris in bonis filiis delectari, apostolice supplicamus clementie quatinus in necessitate presenti, de qua per directos nuntios recurrit ad uos, oculos in ipsum misericordie habeatis et eos qui sibi aduersantur inique apostolica seueritate reprimendo, ipsum diem suum cum pace claudere et a uobis ad patrem omnium 15 cum pace uelitis emigrare. Alioquin lesam se uirtus erubescet, et iustitiam supergressa iniquitas in multorum preualebit perniciem, et que nunc alta pace sopita sunt horum exemplo facta securior utique perturbabit. Valete uos.

**233** G, no. 157; *MB Epp.* 347; B, fos. 145 v (B 1) *and* 173 (B 2).
1, 3 Lundon'/Norwic' B 2    2 ecclesie *om.* B 2    5 delctat B 1    8 Dei] ut dicitur (ut *inserted*) B 1    12 filii B 2

---

[1] Cf. *GF*, p. 34 and n.

### 234 To Jocelin de Bohun, bishop of Salisbury

[*c.* April 1175] Richard, archbishop of Canterbury, primate and legate, plans to hold a council on the Fourth Sunday after Easter: Gilbert summons the bishop, his abbots, archdeacons, priors and conventual deans to be in London on that day.

The only council known to have been held by Archbishop Richard in the neighbourhood of *Cantate Domino* Sunday was the Council of Westminster of 1175, whose formal session was actually held on 18 May, a week later than the day of summons given here (*Cantate Domino* fell on 11 May in 1175).[1] The letter was evidently written by Gilbert as dean of the province of Canterbury (see *GF*, pp. 227–9).

(Gilebertus) Dei gratia Lundoniensis episcopus uenerabili fratri I(ocelino) Sar(es-beriensi) eadem gratia episcopo, salutem que nunc est et quam speramus a Domino.

Quoniam in ecclesia regni huius uitia pullulant, et in uinea Domini sarmenta succrescunt, consultioris falce iudicii succidenda uisum est patri nostro Ricardo
5 Cant(uariensi) Dei gratia archiepiscopo, totius Anglie primati et sedis apostolice legato, secundum antiquam patrum consuetudinem, fratres et coepiscopos suos et alios ecclesiarum prelatos ⟨fo. 110⟩ ad concilium conuocare, ut que corrigenda fuerint communicati censura consilii, uel omnino damnentur uel in melius Domino gratiam ministrante reformentur. Quia uero ad sollicitudinem nostram pertinere
10 dinoscitur fratres et coepiscopos nostros ad concilium conuocare, ab ipso ut id faciamus in mandatis accepimus. Inde est quod fraternitati uestre ipsius auctoritate mandamus et in ui obedientie iniungimus, ut Dominica qua cantatur *Cantate Domino canticum nouum*, ob causam memoratam assessuri sibi Lundonie sitis et medio tempore cum omni cautela et diligentia excessus quibus diocesis uestra laborat
15 inquiratis, ut in medium deducti correctioni subiaceant et censure. Ipsius etiam uobis auctoritate iniungimus, ut diocesis uestre abbatibus, archidiaconis, prioribus, et decanis locorum conuentualium uerbum hoc notificetis, et eos ut designato loco et tempore in concilio domno legato presentiam exhibeant ipsius auctoritate citetis. Valete.

### 235 To the people of the diocese of London

[Probably *c.* May 1175] He appeals, on behalf of St Paul himself, for funds for the cathedral fabric; and offers an indulgence and other spiritual benefits to those who join the confraternity of the cathedral's benefactors.

An appeal for funds for St Paul's was issued at the Council of Westminster in May 1175 by the bishop of Winchester.[2] Gilbert's own appeal was no doubt sent out about the same time.

234 G, no. 244; B, fo. 109 v.
235 G, no. 238; B, fo. 177.

---

[1] Cf. *Handbook*, 2nd ed. p. 550; Wilkins, I, 476; and the notes to the forthcoming revised ed. in *Councils and Synods*, I.

[2] See R. Graham in *Journ. Brit. Arch. Assoc.*, 3rd ser. x (1945–7), 73–6. It is doubtful whether it was the nave as a whole or the three western bays which were built in Gilbert's time; on the whole, Hollar's drawing of the nave (for Dugdale's *Hist. of St Paul's Cathedral*, reproduced by

Cf. the fraternity of the clergy of the archdeaconry of London, whose origin was referred to Gilbert's time in a later manuscript (see *Councils and Synods*, II, i, 327 n.).

G(ilebertus) Dei gratia Londoniensis episcopus dilectis sibi in Domino uniuersis ecclesie beati Pauli apostoli parrochianis et filiis, clericis et laicis, salutem, gratiam et benedictionem.

Scribentes caritati uestre dilectissimi uobis ad memoriam beatum ilico Paulum apostolum hac mente reducimus, ut ob Domini nostri Iesu Christi et eius apostoli 5 reuerentiam et gratiam, ad ipsius ecclesiam respiciatis, et eius necessitati que satis omnibus innotuit prout uobis Dominus inspirauerit benigna deuotione subueniatis. Que a multo iam tempore fundata, et uestris elemosinis magna iam sui parte constructa, tot sumptus exigit et haurit expensas, quod quia per nos sumministrare non possumus nisi ferat opem uestra benignitas de cetero prouidere recusando despera- 10 bimus. Quia uero quod inutiliter conatur unitas, hoc sepius efficaciter adimplet uniuersitas, si uos adiutores habuerimus spem bonam concipimus ut in diebus uestris diu protractum opus, Domino per uos manum misericorditer apponente, completum uideatis. Agatis itaque et patrono uestro et aduocato optimo, beato uidelicet Paulo, deuotum prestetis obsequium ut ei domum construendo in terris 15 beatam eius interuentu mansionem obtineatis in celis. Id queso pre oculis habeatis, quod patronus uester et apostolus Paulus plus omnibus apostolis laborauit, qui ut mundum infidelitatis purgaret errore, semel ob Christum lapidatus est, quinquies flagellatus, ter uirgis cesus, et post innumera pericula que terra marique sustinuit, Rome tandem pro Christo gloriosam sustinens passionem, gladio consummatus est.[1] 20 Hoc uobis patrono gaudendum est ⟨et⟩ sub tanto gratulandum aduocato, qui licet ecclesias orbe toto plantauerit, fide mundum illuminauerit, sedes sibi tamen episcopalis nusquam ut audiuimus in terris posita est preterquam hic inter uos, ubi in ipsius uenerationem et sempiternam memoriam fundata est ecclesia et episcopali dignitate Domino uobis hoc misericorditer et specialiter preuidente sublimata. 25 Habetis itaque beatum Paulum apostolum episcopum animarum uestrarum,[2] qui de manu Domini id specialiter suscepit officii ut in carne uiuentes uos oratione sua sancta muniat et defendat et cum exuti carne fueritis, uos perducat ad thronum patris. Vtar ad uos ipsius uerbis. Ait enim: 'nolite errare, Deus ⟨fo. 177v⟩ non irridetur. Que enim seminauerit homo hec et metet'.[3] Audite magistrum uestrum, 30 audite sanum et suscipite consilium. Seminare nunc potestis, quod in eterna uita suscipiatis. Nunc hyemps est, tempus sementis iaciende nunc est, hora uobis oculos extrema si clauserit, non iam seminandi tempus erit. Cum ianuam post se clauserit sponsus fatuarum iam uirginum clamor inanis erit.[4] Audiamus igitur episcopum nostrum sic exhortantem: 'Ergo dum tempus habemus operemur bonum ad 35

**235** 3 benedictoem B    14 aduocato] uestro *added, cancelled* B    15 uidelic B    30 uestrum,] sic ex *added, cancelled* B

---

Miss Graham) suggests that the design belongs to the time of Richard de Belmeis I (1108–27). On fraternities of this kind, see G. G. Meersseman in *Zeitschrift für Schweiz. Kirchengeschichte*, XLVI (1952), 1–42, 81–112; C. R. Cheney in *Bull. John Rylands Lib.* XXXIV (1951–2), 33 f.
[1] Cf. I Cor. xv. 10; II Cor. xi. 24–6.    [2] Cf. I Pet. ii. 25.
[3] Gal. vi. 7–8.    [4] Cf. Matt. xxv. 10–12.

omnes.'[1] Misericordie tempus quod nunc est, iniustitie tempus inpingit. Qui misericordiam in presenti non exhibet, a Domino iustitiam tunc expectet.[2] Ad uos itaque recurrentes, karissimi, uestrum attendatis initium, consideretis cursum, prospiciatis et exitum. Materni uos uteri primo conclusit angustia, postmodum
40 nudos[3] et in hunc mundum nichil preter peccatum inferentes excepit hec uita arta, sepulchri deinceps coartabit mansio, ad ultimum suscipiet proculdubio aut inferni quod absit latitudo ⟨aut celi altitudo⟩. Indicibilis est homini in hac uita tam inferni deorsum miseria quam que sursum est in celis beata gloria; supra linguam est quod electis et reprobis utrimque paratum est. Agat ergo discretio uestra, karissimi, ut
45 iuxta quod monet episcopus uester et apostolus Paulus, uiam declinetis inferni et iuste et sancte uiuendo pertingatis ad gaudia celi. Monet uos per nos episcopus uester ut corporum uestrorum uasa munda et honesta custodiatis, ne sanctum a uobis spiritum qui hec sibi in templum uendicat iuuendo turpiter abigatis.[4] Misericordie partibus insistatis, ne his quod absit omissis a Domino iudicium sine
50 misericordia in uerbo nimis aspero die illa sentiatis.[5] Ad ecclesiam beati Pauli patris et episcopi uestri pietatis oculos habeatis, et ei et annua et ultima in fine uestro beneficia singuli conferentes ipsum uobis artissime beneficiis prestitis obligetis, ut protectioni uestre et saluti inuigilet, et pauca que nunc datis in tempore a summo largitore Domino Iesu uobis in centuplum restitui impetret in eternitate.
55 Omnibus uero qui ecclesie beati Pauli apostoli edificande et conseruande ⟨fo. 178⟩ de suo quicquam annuatim et in fine suo contulerint, si septem uel amplius annorum penitentia onerati sunt, nos de misericordia saluatoris Iesu Christi et ipsius beati apostoli confidentes annis singulis quadraginta sibi dies relaxamus et intra parietes ecclesie diuinis interesse concedimus, excepto quod una quadragesima in singulis
60 septem annis foris sint, et sic ieiunia compleant. Quia uero in missarum celebratione sancta nobis summa saluatio est, totius sinodi nostre consensu et firma et certa promissione statuimus, ut pro omnibus qui fraternitatem hanc susceperint et seruauerint ab uno quoque sacerdote totius episcopatus beati Pauli triginta misse cantentur, pro his qui adhuc in carne sunt quindecim et pro his quindecim qui
65 decesserunt. In ipsa etiam ecclesia beati Pauli singulis septimanis missas duas, unam pro uiuis alteram pro fratribus iam defunctis celebrari totius capituli nostri consensu statuimus; adicientes etiam ut si quis fratrum ecclesie beati Pauli ut exigentibus peccatis sepe contingit morte preuentus in eum casum inciderit pro quo defunctis in locis sacris sepultura negari solet nichilominus tamen tanquam frater et adiutor
70 ecclesie beati Pauli suscipiatur in loco sacro sepeliatur. Ne uero liberalitatem uestram et gratuitam hanc donationem uobis in necessitatem quandoque redigendam suspicetis, omnes a quicquam dandi necessitate et consuetudine presenti scripto absoluimus, ne quid huiusmodi a uobis quasi debitum exigatur, sed gratuito prestitum a Domino uobis in illa die in centuplum retribuatur. Amen.

**235** 40 arta *corrected to* arct. *by modern hand* B    42 aut celi altitudo *added in modern hand in* B; *evidently something of the kind is needed*    52 artissime *corrected to* arct. *by modern hand* B 57–8 apostoli beati apostoli B    59 qdragesima B

[1] Gal. vi. 10.          [2] Cf. Jac. ii. 13.          [3] Cf. Job i. 21.
[4] Cf. I Cor. vi. 19.      [5] Cf. Jac. ii. 13.

## 236 To the prior and canons of St Bartholomew's priory, Smithfield

[1163–76] He supports the petition of the canons of Dunstable (Beds) that T(homas) canon (of St Bartholomew's) be released to become their prior.

If the petition was granted, T. must be Thomas, prior of Dunstable, who had been canon and sacrist of St Bartholomew's before his election to Dunstable. He was certainly prior by 1176, and the community addressed in this letter must be St Bartholomew's.[1] The letter was evidently written by a bishop, presumably by St Bartholomew's ordinary; this and the style of it confirm Gilbert's authorship. The reference to the church, but not the bishop, of Lincoln may suggest that Lincoln was vacant, as it was from late December 1166 until the election of Geoffrey in 1173 (no bishop was consecrated till 1186).

Salutem et honoris debiti reuerentiam.

Iustis postulantium desideriis assensum prebere iustum est quotiens petentium uota a rationis tramite non discordant. Religiosam itaque fratrum de Dunestapl' attendentes affectionem, circa personam dilecti filii nostri canonicique uestri domni T(ome), cuius mores honestatem redolent et prudentia uirtutem sapit, 5 benignum eorum petitioni assensum prebuimus, ipsumque ab ea qua nobis teneba- tur obedientia absolutum in ministerium ad quod a Domino concordi fratrum electione uocatus est liberum concedimus, ut ecclesie Lincol(niensi) de cetero pareat, et eius mandatis et monitis ut iustum fuerit acquiescat. Vnde ne a uestro quod absit capite recedatis, ne in communem etiam legem fraterne caritatis 10 grauiter offendatis, mandamus uobis et consulimus et que nobis a Domino com- missa est episcopali auctoritate iniungimus, ut quod a nobis actum est ratum habeatis, ipsumque ab ea qua uobis tenet obedientia absolutum pie postulantibus concedatis, ut a Domino gratiam et debita carita[tis pre]mia percipiatis.

## 237 To Matthew, archdeacon of Gloucester

[1163–77] The archdeacon had posed a problem about a woman accused of adultery: whether she was to be put on oath in accordance with the judgement passed on her, or to the ordeal of red-hot metal, as she had promised—under threat—to her husband. The oath, Gilbert says, is sufficient in a case of *suspected* adultery, and a promise extorted by force or fear is void (cf. GF, p. 241).

The archdeacon died in 1177 (p. 162 n.).

[...] Matheo Gloec(estrie) archidiacono salutem.

Hec questio est quam formatis cui ut respondeatur exigitis: an mulierem de qua agitur ad iuramentum ut sibi iudicatum est debeatis admittere, an laminam can- dentis ferri subeat prout uiro sibi mortem minitante spopondit, oporteat uos de iure permittere. Et casus quidem uarii frequenter emergunt, et mulier in opere 5

---

**236** G, no. 313; B, fo. 197.
14 [tis pre] *The margin of B is cut away at this point, with the loss of a few letters*
**237** G, no. 261; B, fo. 140v.

---

[1] *Wulfric of Haselbury*, pp. 134, 173; *EYC*, II, no. 774.

quandoque deprehenditur, non deprehensa quoque quandoque suspecta tamen rea postulatur. Deprehensam lex Moysi lapidabat; suspectam lex zelotipie examinabat.[1] Aquas enim amarissimas in quas sacerdos maledicta congesserat suspecta mulier hauriebat, que quidem innocentem non ledebant et ream sceleris ilico dirumpebant.

10 Adulterum et adulteram lex principum puniebat,[2] et miseris mortalibus quorum in lubrico status est pena multipliciter imminebat. Gratias Domino Iesu qui cuncta nouando mutauit in melius, et aquis Maram lignum crucis ammiscendo dura legis et amara temperauit, hic deprehensam et ream sceleris adductam ad se liberauit et duros legis lapides in lapides illos commutauit.[3] De quibus dictum est: 'quoniam

15 placuerunt seruis tuis lapides eius'.[4] Nostri namque lapides hii sunt: increpatio, correptio, peccatoris ad lacrimas, ad gemitus, ad confessionem et satisfactionem multimodam prouocatio. Quibus bene lapi⟨fo. 141⟩datur adultera cum peccato moritur, et illo intus uiuificante qui ait: 'Nec ego te condempnabo; uade, et amplius noli peccare.'[5] A morte anime quam incurrerat in nouitatem uite suscitatur.

20 Quo nimirum modo cum uxorem suam uir bonus lapidari conspicit, debet ipse morienti commori, lugenti conlacrimari, largiri sua ut ad manum penitens habeat quo peccatum redimendo necessitatem patienti subueniat, ut duo non tantum in carne una, sed et in uno spiritu inueniantur.[6] Quod si suspecta solum est, ut suspicio perimatur, ut pax uiro concilietur, taxatum iuramentum sufficiet, cum omnis

25 controuersie finem iuramentum Paulus esse commemorat.[7] Nam si quid coacta spopondit absit ut hoc iudex ecclesiasticus admittat, quod seculi iudices reprobare non ignorat. Nam quod ui metusue causa factum uel dictum est ratum non habet, et iuxta Papam Alexandrum si quid ab aliquo per uim, per metum aut fraudem extortum est, ad nullum eius preiudicium uel nocumentum ualet.[8] Valete.

### 238   To Roger, bishop of Worcester

[? 1177] He asks the bishop to fulfil his promise to William of Northolt.

William of Northolt was clerk to Richard archbishop of Canterbury and canon of St Paul's: in 1177 he became archdeacon of Gloucester in the diocese of Worcester, and it is natural to suppose that it was the archdeaconry which had been promised to him by the bishop of Worcester. The outside limits are 1164–79, the dates of Bishop Roger.

Venerabili fratri et amico Rogero Wigorn⟨ensi⟩ Dei gratia episcopo frater Gilebertus Lundoniensis ecclesie minister, salutem et affectus intimi dilectionem.

Dilectus filius noster lator presentium Willelmus de Northal quadam magna se asserit spe suspensum ad uos quam de promissione uestre liberalitatis et gratie dudum 5 concepit. Verbum namque nec irritum debet nec uacuum reputare quod uestra sibi

---

**238** G, no. 251; B, fo. 165.
5 cconcepit B

---

[1] Cf. Lev. xx. 10; Deut. xxii. 22 ff.; Joh. viii. 5; Num. v. 14 ff.
[2] For the Roman law of adultery, see *Code*, 9, 9, *passim*.
[3] Cf. Ex. xv. 23–5; Joh. viii. 3 ff.     [4] Ps. ci. 15.
[5] Joh. viii. 11.     [6] Cf. Matt. xix. 5; Eph. iv. 4.
[7] Cf. Heb. vi. 16.     [8] *Decretum*, C. 15, q. 6, c. 1.

constat sponsione firmatum. Proinde nos cum ipso et pro ipso uestre supplicamus beniuolentie quatinus propositam promissamque beneficentiam data uobis a Domino oportunitate et sui contemplatione et nostra si placet promptius petitione, ea benignitate compleatis in illo ut et uoto eius et ueritati uestre satisfaciatis, scientes quia quod dicimus ueritati debemus, quod promittimus fidei. Valete.           10

### 239  To Roger (?), bishop of Worcester

[*c.* 1177] He commends brother W(alter), who has been elected prior of (Great) Malvern (Worcs).

Walter was elected in or very soon after 1177.[1] He appears to have been instituted clandestinely by the abbot of Westminster, and to have been suspended by Bishop Roger on that account. Walter was not officially instituted by the bishop of Worcester until 1190.[2] Gilbert's belief that the bishop has already admitted the prior to favour must therefore be erroneous; and it seems likely that the letter was extracted by the monks of Westminster before Roger's attitude had hardened and he had suspended Walter. The letter cannot be later than August 1179, when Roger died, unless it was really addressed to one of his successors.

Dominus Lundoniensis domino Wigorn(ensi), in gratiarum plenitudine uirtutum Domino complacere.

De naturali bonitatis uestre presumens priuilegio quotiens opus est et id fieri res exigit, confidenter ad uestram decurro beniuolentiam, et repulse nescius munus statim gratie ad uotum michi respondentis excipio. Quod quia sepenumero ipsis 5 iam rerum argumentis expertus sum in consuete michi gratie limina confidenter irrumpo, postulans ut fratrem W(alterum) cui ad doctrinam scientia et ad honestatem mores exuberant, quemque ut audio in gratiam iam admisistis et electione fratrum Malu(ernie) priorem constituistis, amore Dei meeque petitionis intuitu de caro cariorem habeatis, ipsumque prout honori uestro congruit et eius expedit 10 humilitati protegendo et honorando et ipsum et me pluresque nobiscum amplioris ex hoc et gratie et seruitii debitores habeatis. Diu ualeat et in Domino perseueret incolumis uestra benignitas dilectissime.

238  10 Valete.] *Added by a different hand in* B
239  G, no. 248; B, fo. 111v (*in margin:* pro priore Maluernie).

---

[1] When his predecessor, Roger Malebranche, became abbot of Burton (see Biog. Index).
[2] Great Malvern was a dependency of Westminster, and the abbot of Westminster disputed with the bishop of Worcester for jurisdiction over the prior. Walter himself confessed that he had not been officially instituted till 1191 in a document printed from the register of Godfrey Giffard in W. Thomas, *Antiquitates prioratus Maioris Malverne . . .* (London, 1725), appendix, *Chart. Orig.*, pp. 96–7; abstract in *Reg. G. Giffard*, II, 198 (also in Worcester Cathedral, Reg. A4, fos. xlv–xli). Walter was still prior in 1193 and 1204 (Thomas, Appendix, p. 97; Westminster Abbey Domesday, fos. 574v–576) and was probably the W. who had been deprived before 1224 (*Acta Stephani Langton*, ed. K. Major, Cant. and York Soc., 1950, pp. 160 ff. The William who occurs 1184–6, Westminster Domesday, fo. 574v, is evidently a mistake for Walter). Thomas was appointed prior in 1216–18 (*Reg. G. Giffard*, II, 178); we may therefore date Walter's tenure *c.* 1177–*c.* 1216.

## 240 To Roger, bishop of Worcester

[Probably July–August 1179] He urges the bishop by their long friendship, to assist him against Master D(avid), once a member of his household, now in Bishop Roger's, who has cast covetous eyes on the highest dignity of Gilbert's church ('in precipuam ecclesie nostre dignitatem'). David is preparing to go to the Pope, and is on his way to collect commendatory letters from the bishops of Worcester and Hereford. His journey was a secret, and so Gilbert is late in writing; and if the bishop has already given David a letter, he begs him to take it away again.

David was still in Gilbert's household at least down to 1171, at which date there was no bishop of Hereford. The outside limits of date must therefore be Robert Foliot's election to Hereford in 1173 and Bishop Roger's death in August 1179. Stubbs interpreted the *precipua dignitas* as the deanery of St Paul's, and it is hard to know what else it could mean (see *GF*, p. 205). Hugh de Marigny last occurs as dean on 2 December 1178 (no. 410), and Ralph de Diceto succeeded him some time in 1180. If this letter implies that the deanery was vacant, as seems probable, Hugh must have died on 27 June 1179, since his obit was on 27 June. In that case, the letter was written in July or August 1179. The ground of David's claim is obscure. See *GF*, pp. 205–6.

Venerabili domno suo fratrique karissimo R(ogero) Wigorn(ensi) Dei gratia episcopo frater G(ilebertus) Londoniensis ⟨ecclesie minister⟩ salutem.

Quantam, in Christo karissime, de beneuolentia uestra amicitiarum spem iam diu percepimus, non facile paucis explicamus. Equidem uos ab ineunte etate usque
5 in diem hanc continua caritate dileximus et profectibus uestris et laudabilibus in Christo successibus tota animi iocunditate semper exultantes applausimus. Quia ergo uos ad hoc iam diuina prouexit clementia, ut in eodem regno pari nos cura ecclesie sue prefecerit et honore, debemus ipsius adimplendo legem alter alterius onera portare,[1] et de fraternis cordibus uicissim nobis imperante caritate, si qua
10 grauant, his simul humeros utrimque supponere et hec confidenter in Domini spiritu sustinere. Huic siquidem nos amicitiarum legi subicimus, et fraternitatem uestram, ut sua nobis confidenter iniungat obsequia preueniendo et obsequium iam nunc exigendo prouocamus. Ne uero diu uos suspendat oratio, quod anxia mente proferimus, quod tristi manu scedule uix committimus, quia sic fieri res expostulat,
15 aperimus. Arma sumit aduersum nos familiaris uester et quondam domesticus noster, magister ille D(auid), et quem laudum titulis extulimus, quem beneficiis honorauimus, quem sperabamus amicissimum, non solum experimur ingratum sed etiam infestissimum. Hic cupide mentis iniecit oculos in precipuam ecclesie nostre dignitatem, et ut eam nobis inuitis optineat, ad domnum papam iter parat, ut eius
20 auctoritate nos ledat, et ipsum circumueniendo quod nostri iuris est, non uiolenter solum sed impudenter extorqueat. In procinctu positus hac de causa festinat ad uos, ut a uobis et a domno Hereford(ensi) commendaticias accipiat, et porrectis pro ipso precibus nos auctoritate et ope uestra expeditius et efficacius non solum offendat sed opprimat. Inde est quod, dilecte nobis in Domino, beneuolentie uestre preces

240 Liverani, p. 641; Va, fo. 146.

[1] Cf. Gal. vi. 2.

affectuose porrigimus, ne insurgenti in nos arma subministretis, nec impugnantem 25
nos aut litteris aut adminiculis aliis in dampna nostra sustentetis. Quod si magnum
in oculis suis hominem ab hoc proposito reuocaretis, labori nos exemptos et oneri
gratie uobis debitores efficeretis. Nam quod corpore, quod animo, quod sensu
ualemus aut censu, totum exhaurire malumus quam hosti licet tanto succumbere.
Quod si litteras (quod absit) iam dedistis, quoniam in dampnum et detrimentum 30
nostrum sunt elicite, rediberi, si placet, eas faciatis, ea qua preestis et potestis
auctoritate. Nam si uobis sero scripsimus, hec causa est, quod iter suum ad uos nobis
penitus occultauit. Nam amicum sceleri uelle nesciri;[1] et qui uias suas occulit,
conscientiam perdit. Aget in Christo karissime, aget exauditio precum, ut nos
promptos habeatis in omne quod poterimus exhibere seruitium. Valete.          35

## 241   To Hamelin, abbot of Gloucester

[1163–79] He tells the abbot with sorrow of the death of Master Walter, asks for his and the
community's prayers on Walter's account, and commends to him Wigod, Walter's only
surviving brother.

Abbot Hamelin died in 1179. Master Walter may have been Walter of Hartpury (Glos),
who was probably clerk to Gilbert and canon of St Paul's early in his episcopate at London
(see *GF*, p. 287).

⟨G⟩ilebertus Dei gratia Lundoniensis episcopus uenerabili fratri et amico suo
karissimo H(amelino) eadem gratia abbati Gloecest(rie), salutem et debitum fraterne
caritatis obsequium.

Decessum cari nostri magistri Walteri sine lacrimis ad memoriam non reuocamus. Habemus in eius occasu quod comuniter doleamus, qui comuniter clericum et 5
amicum fidelissimum, manum in nos aggrauante Domino[2] in ipso flore gratissime
sue iuuentu⟨fo. 172⟩tis amisimus. Que uero bona cum ipso nobis sublata sint, quot
sancta subtracta solacia experiri quidem possumus, paucis explicare non ualemus.
Ipsi uestra quesumus et fratrum nostrorum sancta suffragetur oratio quatinus sub-
latum nobis suorum uelit Dominus admitti collegio. Ipse uero in extremis agens 10
superstitem fratrem suum unicum presentium hunc latorem Wigodum per nos
uestre comendare beniuolentie suplicauit. Vnde dilecte nobis in Domino benignitati uestre preces affectuose porrigimus quatinus amore Dei nostreque petitionis
obtentu et amici in extrema uoluntate supplicantis intuitu, ipsum in protectione
uestra suscipiatis, nec status sui condicionem in aliquo aggrauari permittatis. Sed 15
quod ad presens incurrit dampnum uestre sibi supleat misericordie et caritatis
augmentum. Valere uos optamus in Domino karissime.

**241** G, no. 260; B, fo. 171 v.

---

[1] This seems to mean 'the wish to be unknown is a friend to crime', but we have failed to trace
a literary source for it.
[2] Cf. I Reg. v. 6.

### 242 To Roger, bishop of Worcester

[1164–79] The bishop has asked Gilbert to give testimony about what and how much of the benefice said to have been granted to Master From'[1] by the prior and canons of Studley (Warwickshire, Aug.) was assigned to him in Gilbert's presence. Gilbert cannot exactly remember, but he wishes From' well, and hopes that the failure of his witness will not tell against him.

The dates of nos. 242–3 are those of Roger bishop of Worcester.

Venerabili fratri et amico R(ogero) Wigorn(ensi) Dei gratia episcopo frater G(ilebertus) Lundoniensis ecclesie minister, salutem et dilectionem.

Gratum habemus quod magister From' eam apud uos gratiam inuenit, qua ex scripto uestro sed ex sua certius relatione cognouimus. Desideratis enim sicut eodem
5 asseritur scripto per nos instrui de beneficio quod prior et canonici de Stodleg' in eum contulisse dicuntur, quid illi scilicet et quantum in nostra fuerit assignatum presentia. Desideramus et nos suam in omnibus iustitiam pro hominibus habundare[2] instrumentis ne qua possit unquam falsitate subuerti. Verum nos tantus circumstrepit negotiorum tumultus ut uix nostra possimus curare negotia, nedum aliena
10 que et loco et tempore tam remota existunt ad eam quam exigitis distinctionem recolligere. At si testes non desunt quibus plusquam testimoniis credi oportet, si prior et canonici de quorum facto agitur beneficium non reuocant, si cetera cause necessaria domi succurrunt et suffragantur ut quid nostra requiritur attestatio, ut quid ad superuacua sudatur? Rogamus igitur ne sit scrupulosa aduersus eum con-
15 scientia uestra eo quod nostrum non reportat testimonium, quia si forte factum tenemus non tamen ipsas facti circumstancias quas scripture forma requireret ad memoriam reuocamus. De cetero dictum nostrum dilectioni uestre commendamus ut quem sui merito in notitiam admisistis et gratiam nostra si placet petitione commendatum habeatis, et sua illi iura per uestram integre iustitiam conseruetis, ut
20 et ipsum uestris exinde deuotum obsequiis et nos uobis pro ipso amplioris gratie debitores efficiatis. Valete.

### 243 To Roger, bishop of Worcester

[1164–79] He complains bitterly about the letter which the bishop sent concerning the chapel of St Michael, which was delivered by the 'liar' who is acting for Roger. The appeal against Gilbert was for the First Sunday after Easter, but Roger has shortened the term to the First Sunday in Lent; Gilbert extends the term to Ascension Day. He takes Roger to task for his use of the legal term *apostoli*,[3] and for demanding the reform of the chapel—at a time

242 G, no. 252; B, fo. 166v.
1 Wiorn' B
243 G, no. 253; B, fo. 171.

---

[1] Possibly short for Fromund. Gilbert was doubtless concerned in the transaction when vicar of the diocese of Worcester, 1160–4.      [2] Cf. Matt. v. 20.
[3] Letters from the judge of the lower court to the judge of the appeal court explaining the case: cf. no. 95; *GF*, p. 65 n.; *Dict. de Droit Canonique*, 1 (ed. R. Naz, Paris, 1935), coll. 692 ff.

when the bishop is provoking the 'liar' in charge to appeal against his jurisdiction. The diocese of London, and Gilbert himself, appeal to Roger not to let this man come between them.

⟨V⟩enerabili fratri R(ogero) Wigorn(ensi) Dei gratia episcopo frater G(ilebertus) Lundoniensis ecclesie minister salutem.

Insperatas quidem et plenas ingratitudine gratias uestre michi littere retulerunt quas super capella sancti Michaelis per manus inprobissimi portitoris nouissime suscepi. Quid namque merui ut aduersus me uestra debeat fraternitas excandesce- 5 re, ut in meam personam uestra prorumpat appellatio ut ad lites prouocer et ad labores? Nunquid has michi refertis gratias, quia me partes uestras benigne sustinuisse meministis? ⟨fo. 171 v⟩ Nunquid mediatoris nostri immo mentitoris uestri id de me persuadere potuit oratio ut aut uestri quod iuris est occupem aut occupanti uelim quod absit ullatenus assentire? Non est sanctum de moribus amici tam cito 10 perperam sentire. Vester ille missus et procurator cause quam uestram dicitis aduersus me et aduersus ecclesiam meam pariter appellauit. Vos autem eandem ut scribitis et scripto asseritis appellationem prosecuturi indultam nobis ab ipso prius appellatore dilationem usque ad *Quasimodo* uestra reuocatis auctoritate, et ad *Inuocauit me* appellationi terminum coartatis. Quod quia in grauamen et preiudicium 15 partis nostre redundat petimus si placet desistatis; sin autem persistitis, ne teneat illa coartatio appellationis ut uerbo prius ita etiam nunc scripto appellauimus diem Ascensionis nostre constituentes terminum appellationis. Apostolos quoque postulatis a me. Que est ista rerum confusio? Iudicem agnoscitis a quo petitis apostolos sed aduersarium eligitis in quem libellos editis appellationis. Nosse autem 20 debuerat prudentia uestra neminem sibi in testamento neque in apostolis, neque in publicis instrumentis scribere debere; nemo enim sibi iudex aut testis, aut puplica potest sibi esse persona.[1] Petitis etiam ut pro debito officii mei memorate capelle statum reformem; in quo me prius instrui necesse est an iudicis officium in eo debeam exercere negotio, quod iam per appellationem a mea penitus est iurisdictione 25 exemptum—presertim cum me super hoc tanquam aduersarium prouocatis quem nichilominus ut iudicem interpellatis. Denique supplicat uobis Lundoniensis ecclesia, supplicamus et nos pariter ut non tanti sit apud uos mentientis improbitas ut scissuram inter nos fraterna caritas patiatur. Certum namque teneatis quod sicut non possumus nec uolumus uestro in aliquo iuri derogare; in quo si nostro non 30 creditis testimonio, ueritati credite que certius inquisita uobis attestabitur. Si uero contentiosum funem trahere necesse est, dicimus quod olim Hannibal dixisse legitur. 'O Scipio', inquit Hannibal, 'pacem peto. Ex quo si insolescis utrinque ferrum, utrinque corpora humana erunt.'[2] Valere uos optamus in Domino frater karissime. 35

**243** 22 instrumtis B    33 O Scipio *nos*; suscipio B

---

[1] Cf. *Decretum*, C. 4, q. 4, c. 1; *MB*, IV, 230 (*Causa*).
[2] Livy, xxx, 28–9, 30, 20: 'utrinque ferrum utrinque corpora' is a sound reading only known to the editors of the Oxford Text Livy (1953) from Paris Bibl. Nat. Lat. 5731 and Petrarch's corrections in BM Harl. MS 2493 (cf. G. Billanovich in *Journ. Warburg and Courtauld Institutes*,

### 244 To King Henry II

[1163–80] He asks for justice for Ralph de Diceto, Henry's clerk and Gilbert's archdeacon. Ralph de Diceto, archdeacon of Middlesex, became dean of St Paul's in 1180.

Domno regi dominus Lundoniensis. Salutem et deuotum debite fidelitatis obsequium.

Vestra domne dignos speramus gratia, quos in ecclesia Dei et literatura commendat et uita. Inde est quod apud excellentiam uestram clericum uestrum ecclesie
5 beati Pauli archidiaconum, Radulfum de Diceto, eo securius commendamus quod ei et scientiam ad doctrinam et ad honestatem mores exuberare iam diu experientia rerum certa cognouimus. Accedit ad hec amor integer et affectionis eius erga uos plena deuotio, ut uos ulnis caritatis corde complectens, honori uestro glorieque congratulans, felices uobis in Domino successus semper exoptet, et sibi commissos
10 ut a summo rege uobis id impetrent cum se prestat oportunitas indesinenter ammoneat. Quem in oborta sibi necessitate recurrentem ad uos nilque nisi quod iuri debetur et equitati postulantem, cordis intimo supplicamus affectu quatinus ob Dei reuerentiam nostreque petitionis et honestatis eius, et exhibite uobis et semper exhibende fidelitatis intuitu, clementer exaudiatis, et ut prebende sue[1] portio quam
15 sibi et apostolica et regia uestra concedit et confirmat auctoritas ipsi in integrum restituatur, iuxta datam uobis a Domino sapientiam tam iuste quam misericorditer efficiatis.

### 245 To Pope Alexander III

[Probably 1163–c. 1179] He describes the case between Henry, canon of St Paul's and rector of Stepney, and William of Pontefract[2] about a chapel which William had built in the parish of Stepney. William had appealed to the Pope.

If, as seems probable, Canon Henry was the same as Henry, master of the schools,[3] he was dead by 1180 and the letter is probably some years earlier, since he is not given the title of master of the schools; in any case Pope Alexander died in 1181.

---

**244** G, no. 270; B, fo. 191v.
8 complectentes B
**245** G, no. 166; B, fo. 184v.

---

XIV (1951), 137–208). Most manuscripts read 'utrinque corpora'—as e.g. Thomas Becket's copy, now Trinity Coll. Cambridge MS R. 4. 4, fo. 229. Gilbert may have taken the passage from a *florilegium*, since it is the only evidence of his knowledge of Livy. It is not in any other known source. Livy was a rare book; but Cluny is known to have had two copies of the third decade (A. Wilmart in *Rev. Mabillon*, XI (1921), 94, 115).

[1] It is not known what prebend Ralph held before he became dean (see *GF*, pp. 278, 286–7).
[2] See *GF*, p. 292.
[3] As he was probably the Henry of London who was claiming Stepney church *c.* 1154, and succeeded in winning the succession to it at that time (see *JS Epp.* I, 7–8) it seems very probable that he was the long-lived Henry son of Archdeacon Hugh, prebendary of Hoxton (*GF*, p. 281) who seems to have been master of the schools *c.* 1160–79. The alternative, Henry of Northampton (also a schoolman), is less likely to have been referred to as 'Henry' without a surname, and there is no evidence that he ever had an interest in Stepney.

Patri suo et domno summo pontifici A(lexandro) frater G(ilebertus) Lundoniensis ecclesie minister, totum quod obedientie et obsequii ualet humilis et promta deuotio.

Ad uestram pater iustum est referri notitiam que facta ad uos appellatione suspensa uestre sublimitatis expetunt in sui decisione sententiam. Cum igitur assertione partium merita pandantur causarum, causam inter dilectum filium et 5 canonicum nostrum Henricum et Willelmum de Pontefracto agitatam apud nos, et facta ad uos appellatione suspensam, sublimitati uestre directis his apicibus aperimus. Conquerebatur Henricus dum studiis scolaribus occupatus abesset iam dictum Willelmum intra fines parrochie sue de Stubeheia capellam erexisse, ibique in iniuriam et dispendium ipsius matris ecclesie diuina celebrari fecisse, et ipsius 10 occasione capelle, ipsi matri ecclesie decimationes et alias obuentiones ecclesiasticas iniuste diu subtraxisse. Capellam itaque in parrochia sua clam se constructam dirui, et rem in statum pristinum redigi, et sibi iniuste subtracta officio nostro restitui proposita ad hoc et rationum et auctoritatum multiplici copia postulabat. Willelmus uero nouum opus infitians capellam ipsam in fundo suo antiquitus extitisse, ipsam- 15 que se iure suo ad presens innouasse, seque in ea in nulius iniuriam aut dispendium diuina communicasse respondit; adiciens se decimationes terre sue iuxta pacta inter suos et Henrici predecessores inita et firmata, matrici ecclesie persoluisse et annuatim earum nomine quattuor solidos ut comprehensum fuerat pacto reddidisse, et cum ad euacuandum pactum hoc ad domnum Cantuar(iensem) aliquando appella- 20 tum fuisset, se ab intentione contra pactum proposita sententialiter absolutum exstitisse. Que cum taliter allegaret Willelmus nulla tamen instrumentorum aut testium assertione roborabat. Henricus ⟨fo. 185⟩ uero coram domno archiepiscopo de decimis tantum illius anni quo causa tunc agebatur absolutorium fuisse iudicium asserebat, adiciens se hanc etiam sententiam ad uestram audientiam appellatione 25 interposita suspendisse, uestramque sublimitatem domno Winton(iensi) totius cause cognitionem delegasse, se tamen causam hanc aliis prepeditum negotiis prosecutum non fuisse. Instante itaque Henrico et in iam dictis decimis ecclesie sue ius numerosa testium copia declarante, se etiam easdem percepisse uiua uoce testium ostendente, et ea que possederat sibi restitui postulante Willelmus nostre 30 declinans iuridicionis examen, ad uestre sublimitatis audientiam appellauit, et appellationi diem festum Omnium Sanctorum constituit. Valere uos optamus in Domino, pater in Christo karissime.

## 246   To Pope Alexander III

[1163–5 or 1174–81] Gilbert describes the events leading up to an appeal by Baldwin archdeacon (of Sudbury, dioc. Norwich)[1] against the monks of Saint-Wulmer (Samer-aux-Bois, Pas-de-Calais)[2] about some tithes which had been previously adjudged to the monks by the bishop of Chichester[3] acting as papal judge delegate.

**245** 32 ualete B
**246** G, no. 163; B, fo. 173 v.

---

[1] Before 1143 to after 1168 (he had been succeeded by 1192) (*JS Epp.* 1, 82 n.; Landon, pp. 13–14, 19–23).        [2] A Benedictine abbey near Boulogne: see Cottineau, II, cols. 2945–6.
[3] Either Hilary (1147–69) or John of Greenford (1174–80).

Alexander III died in 1181, which gives the later limit for nos. 246–8. Between 1164 and 1174 there was no archbishop of Canterbury in England save in December 1170; since the earlier case had actually been tried in the archbishop's court—at least a year before this letter was written—it cannot be dated to any year between *c*. 1165 and 1174.

⟨P⟩atri suo et domno summo pontifici A⟨lexandro⟩ frater G⟨ilebertus⟩ Lundoniensis ecclesie minister, salutem et humilis obedientie deuotionem.

Ad uos pater referri conuenit que ad sublimitatem uestram penes nos appellatio facta suspendit. Monachis itaque sancti Wlmari decimationes quasdam a milite
5 quodam parrochiano nostro qui Baldewino Norwic⟨ensi⟩ archidiacono affinitate coniunctus est in presentia nostra repetentibus, idem miles iam dictum archidiaconum earundem decimationum tandem laudauit auctorem. Abbate uero sancti Wlmari et ipso archidiacono statuto die in presentia nostra super eisdem decimationibus aduersum se experientibus, archidiaconus ipse ad patrem nostrum domnum
10 Cant⟨uariensem⟩ appellauit; quibus in ipsius presentia constitutis, abbas a domno Cant⟨uariensi⟩ ad audientiam uestram rem appellando sus⟨fo. 174⟩pendit. Prosequentes apellationem monachi a sullimitate uestra litteras ad domnum Cicestrensem retulerunt ut super causa cognosceret litemque cognoscendo dirimeret. Euocatis ad ipsum partibus, ut ex ipsius literis accepimus, res hunc finem sortita est: decima-
15 tiones iam dicte monachis adiudicate sunt et easdem sepedictus miles abiurauit. Directe sunt ad nos litere domni Cicestrensis testificantes hoc, et auctoritate uestra iniungentes ut iam dictos monachos in corporalem earundem decimationum possessionem induceremus. Sic monachi possessionem nacti sunt. Emenso anno cum iam messes colligerentur, seruientes suos direxit archidiaconus ut iam dictas
20 decimationes susciperent et eius nomine aptarent et in tuto reponerent. Quibus pars altera incontinenti resistens adiudicatas sibi auctoritate uestra decimationes asportari minime passa est, uerum uim inferre uolentes repulit, suumque sibi detinuit. Querelam ad nos referens super hoc domnus archidiaconus, cum statuto die earumdem decimationum restitutionem sibi fieri tanquam uim passus exigeret,
25 auctoritas rei iudicate sibi obiecta est. Qui rem inter alios iudicatam, aliis obesse non debere asserens,[1] se iudicio domni Cicestrensis nequaquam interfuisse, ideoque sententiam ab eo obesse sibi non debere respondit. Aliis possessioni sibi auctoritate nostra adiudicate innitentibus, ipsamque conuelli non debere asserentibus, archidiaconus se grauari conquerens ad uestram appellauit audientiam, et has appella-
30 tionis sue testes literas impetrauit. Valere uos optamus in Domino pater in Christo dilecte.

**246** 5 parrachiano B

---

[1] See p. 155 n. 1.

## 247 To Pope Alexander III

[1163–81] The Pope had asked him for a carpet, which he is sending—an imported carpet, because they are not made locally.[1]

Patri suo et domno summo pontifici A(lexandro) frater G(ilebertus) Londoniensis ecclesie minister, debitum dilectionis et obedientie famulatum.

Etsi rem grandem dixisset michi domnus meus per omnia quidem obedire debueram, quanto magis cum sibi a me tapetum pedum humile substratorium mitti mandauerit. Mitto itaque super quo scripsit, non tamen quale descripsit uestra 5 sublimitas, optans ut munus exiguum mittentis affectus amplificet et si deest forme rotunditas, id que penes nos est penuria artificis tale quid in hunc modum aptare-⟨tur⟩ scientis excuset. Non enim conduntur apud nos tapeta, sed a transmarinis partibus aduehuntur. Quibus in tota ciuitate nostra diligenti scrutinio perspectis quod melius inuenire potui dilecte michi in Domino sanctitati uestre transmittere, 10 multa mentis alacritate curaui. Muro suo inexpugnabili circumcingat uos Dominus, et armis sue potentie protegat semper in Christo dilecte pater.[2]

## 248 To Pope Alexander III

[1163–81] He describes the case between John the clerk and William de Lanual' on the church of Walkern (Herts), delegated to Gilbert by the Pope, but cut short by a further appeal by John.

The archdeacon of Huntingdon referred to below was Henry, the historian. Walkern was in the deanery of Baldock, archdeaconry of Huntingdon (*VN*, p. 293).

Reuerentissimo patri et domno suo karissimo A(lexandro) summo Dei gratia pontifici frater Gil(ebertus) Londoniensis ecclesie minister, salutem et debitum sincere dilectionis et humilis obedientie famulatum.

Mandatum, pater, a uestra sanctitate suscepimus, ut de causa que inter I(ohannem) clericum et Guillelmum de Lanual' super ecclesia de Walcr(ia) uertitur, ueritatem 5 diligenter inquireremus, et si constaret nobis I(ohannem) predicta ecclesia uiolenter et absque ordine iudiciario spoliatum fuisse, eam sibi omni contradictione et

**247** G, no. 153; B, fo. 45.
7–8 aptare⟨tur⟩] penuria *again understood?—but more may be missing*
**248** Liverani, pp. 639–40; Va, fo. 148.

[1] This is interesting evidence that carpets were not made in England in the twelfth century; they were presumably imported, like hangings, mainly from Flanders. The word *tapetum* (etc.) could mean either carpet or hanging, and it is usually impossible to determine its meaning in twelfth-century inventories, though it seems likely that carpets were uncommon in England at this time. But there are already specific references to their liturgical use in Lanfranc's monastic constitutions (ed. D. Knowles, NMT, 1951, pp. 23, 40, 58, 66–7, 70; cf. also the *Pontifical of Magdalen College, Oxford* (also from Canterbury), ed. H. A. Wilson, Henry Bradshaw Soc., 1910, pp. 59, 89).

[2] Cf. the First Antiphon for the Magnificat, 1st Vespers, Sundays in November (cf. *Hereford Breviary*, I, 458).

appellatione remota, cum omnibus inde ablatis auctoritate uestra restitui faceremus
et in pace dimitti. Ad hoc itaque statuto die, partibus euocatis, I(ohannes) se in iam
10 dicta ecclesia, presentatione Hamonis de sancto Claro, qui ad hoc duos e suis cum
signatis suo nomine litteris destinauerat, per manum H(enrici) archidiaconi
Huntedon' personam canonice institutum fuisse asseruit, seque ex tunc ipsam
ecclesiam de Walcr(ia) continue possedisse, donec per Guillelmum de Lamval' et
homines suos ab ecclesia ipsa et fundo ad ipsam pertinente uiolenter, ut asserebat,
15 eiectus est. Horum omnium testes producebat in medium sacerdotes quamplures et
clericos presentationis et institutionis iam dicte, possessionis etiam sue et illate sibi
uiolentie testimonium perhibentes; prolatis etiam in id ipsum astruebat instrumentis, cartam proferens Hamonis, a quo fuerat archidiacono presentatus, cartam
etiam archidiaconi per quem fuerat institutus. Presentes aderant clerici duo, quorum
20 unus in partibus illis decanus erat, alter ante ipsum decanus extiterat. Hii se in carta
archidiaconi testes annotatos fuisse audientes, prosilientes in medium fidem instrumenti non parum uacillare fecerunt, tactis euangeliis iurare parati se presentationem
iam dictam nunquam uidisse aut scisse, nec institutioni I(ohannis), ut carta testa-
batur, interfuisse. I(ohannes) uero uiuas testium uoces sibi sufficere asserens, eorum
25 testimonia postulabat admitti, et iuxta uestri formam mandati sibi et ecclesiam et
cetera, que fuerant ablata, restitui. Guillelmus uero de Lanual' sicut instrumentis sic
et testibus I(ohannis) fidem non habendam esse respondit, asserens Radulfum patrem
I(ohannis) personatum ecclesie de Walcr' de manu Roberti Bloet dudum Lincolniensis episcopi suscepisse, ipsumque in ea toto uite sue curriculo usque ad ipsum
30 obitus sui diem ut personam ministrasse, nec ullum omnino consistere, qui ipsum
in uita sua aut suscepte cure renuntiasse, aut personatum ecclesie susceptum in manu
episcopi aut alicuius officialium suorum refutasse, cognouerit. Assistebant ei testes
quamplurimi, uiri probate opinionis sacerdotes et laici, qui patrem I(ohannis) in
ecclesia memorata usque in ipsum obitus sui diem perseuerasse, et ut personam
35 officium in ea sacerdotale per se aut suos suo nomine adimplesse, firmiter asserebant.
Causabatur etiam Willelmus I(ohannem) in impetratione rescripti uestri in fraude
tacendi deliquisse plurimum, cum se filium sacerdotis dissimulans patri suo in
ecclesia, in qua ministrauerat succedere et auctoritate uestra in ipsam irrepere
contra sacros canones et decretales epistolas,[1] que pre manibus aput multos haben-
40 tur, attemptauerit. Rescriptum itaque uestrum fraude protestans elicitum Iohanni
prodesse non oportere asseruit, cum hec forma sit iuris, ut etsi sacrum oraculum
huiusmodi precator afferat, carere debeat impetratis.[2] I(ohannes) uero hec inquisi-
tioni nostre commissa non fuisse respondens, mandato uestro innitens et insistens
plurimum, probationes suas suscipi et iuxta uestri formam mandati ablata sibi
45 restitui, multa quidem instantia postulabat. Cuius quidem examinatis testibus, cum
in causa procedere disponeremus, Guillelmus ad exceptionem peremptoriam
conuolans obiecit, I(ohannem) in causa hac audiri nullatenus oportere, cum iura-

---

[1] Cf. *Decretum*, C. 8, q. 1, c. 7 (2nd Lateran Council, c. 16); D. 56, c. 1; etc.; and especially
*Council of Westminster*, 1175, c. 1 (Wilkins, I, 477), repeating a decretal of Alexander III.
Cf. no. 86 and n. 1.
[2] See no. 128.

mento coram multis corporaliter et sponte prestito firmauerit, se nunquam in uita sua Guillelmo controuersiam de iam dicta ecclesia moturum, nec contra eius uoluntatem in eiusdem ecclesie petitione quicquam decetero machinaturum. 50 Procedebant quamplures id testificantes se prece I(ohannis) ad hoc Walcrie con- uenisse, ut in eorum se presentia I(ohannes) in hoc, quod dictum est, obligaret, et ecclesiam iam dictam, proprium sequens animum, ipsis presentibus abiuraret. Quam nimirum abiurationem cum iuramento probare parati essent, I(ohannes) se quorundam, qui aduersus eum testificabantur, machinatione in castrum 55 Walcrie inductum, et ibidem ilico per homines Guillelmi compedibus astrictum fuisse, sicque ui mortisque metu compulsum, fidelitatem Guillelmo de corpore suo et omnibus que iuste possidebat sub iuramenti religione promisisse confessus est, asserens tamen ipsam de qua agitur ecclesiam se nullatenus abiurasse. Cumque iuramenti in hanc formam prestiti testes produceret, et nos partis utriusque testes 60 applicare uellemus examini, Iohannes se per nos grauari conquerens, eo quod ante restitutionem suam aliquam sibi exceptionem, etsi peremptoriam, obici permiserimus, ad audientiam uestram appellationem instituit, et actioni diem octabas beati Iohannis Baptiste constituit. Nos uero ex incidenti questione appella- tum fuisse attendentes, appellationi ipsi deferendum esse censuimus, et res gestas 65 aput nos ipso quo geste sunt ordine sanctitati uestre presenti scripto notificare curauimus. Valeat sullimitas uestra in Christo, dilecte pater.

### 249 To Roger of Pont Él'vêque, archbishop of York

[1163–81] He thanks him for his letter, and rejoices in his safe return. If the archbishop will come on the Sunday after Candlemas (Gilbert will meet him on the following day) (?)... (incomplete).

Nos. 249–50 are addressed to Archbishop Roger, who died in 1181.

Venerabili domno et amico karissimo R(ogero) Dei gratia Eborac(ensi) archi- episcopo frater G(ilebertus) Londoniensis ecclesie minister salutem.

Literas dilectionis uestre leti suscepimus que nos tanto uerius gaudio refecerunt quanto certius de statu uestro, de prospero reditu, de aduentu ad partes nostras, et nostris ad uotum desideriis responderunt. Vobis itaque ne nostra longius uota 5 remoremur dante Domino occurremus, ut proxima die Dominica post Purifica- tionem beate Marie gloriose uenientes constituti, in crastino uestro si placet[...]

### 250 To Roger of Pont Él'vêque, archbishop of York

[1163–81] He asks the archbishop to treat his relative W. Foliot, who is clerk to the arch- bishop, with more indulgence.

Venerabili domno patrique karissimo R(ogero) E(boracensi) Dei gratia archi- episcopo frater G(ilebertus) L(ondoniensis) ecclesie minister, apta queque saluti et si quid ipsi possumus honoris et seruitii.

**249** G, no. 201; B, fo. 179v (*incomplete and cancelled in* B).
**250** G, no. 202; B, fo. 194v.

Verborum facile suadet paucitas cum ad exaudiendum prona est ipsius ad quem
5 scribitur amica benignitas. Vnde quia de uestra in nos beniuolentia fiduciam iamdiu
multarum ipsa rerum exhibitione concepimus, ex preteritis futura conicientes de
uestra ad omnes modestia per omnia bene sperantes, preces excellentie uestre quanta
scimus et possumus affectione porrigimus ut clericum uestrum et cognatum nostrum
W. Foliot quem minus benigno iamdiu perstrinxistis oculo clementius respiciatis et
10 in solitam si placet gratiam admittatis. Satis est si placet quod immeritum afflixistis
iamdiu, et patienter omnia sustinentem humiliastis. Excessum eius nullum fortassis
aut certe modicum seuere corripuistis, et in omnibus his filium sapienter erudistis.
Vnde cum iam uulneri uinum habundanter infuderitis, obsecramus ut oleum de
cetero admittatis[1] ut clerico uestro subtracta sibi plene restituendo et ipsum et nos et
15 nostra si placet ad libitum habeatis. Valete.

### 251  To Pope Alexander III

[Probably 1174–81] The case between Godfrey de Lucy archdeacon of Derby[2] and Thomas
the clerk, delegated to Gilbert, had been suspended because Thomas produced a later mandate
delegating the case to the bishop of Winchester. Gilbert asks for instructions.

The letter cannot be later than 1181, when Alexander III died, and the bishop of Winchester was probably Richard of Ilchester, consecrated in 1174. His predecessor, Henry of
Blois, died on 8 August 1171, apparently after a long illness (cf. above, no. 223). Godfrey de
Lucy was not yet archdeacon at the end of 1170,[3] so that it is most improbable that Henry
was the judge delegate of this letter.

Patri suo et domno summo pontifici A(lexandro) frater G(ilebertus) Lundoniensis
ecclesie minister, deuotum karitatis et obedientie famulatum.
Cum instaret apud nos Godefridus de Luci archidiaconus Derbi ut super quibusdam decimis ad suam (ut asserit) prebendam pertinentibus aduersus Thomam
5 clericum iuxta uestri formam mandati iustitiam consequeretur, Thomas ilico
nostrum intendit declinare iudicium, ostendens post directas ad nos litteras uestras
aliud a sublimitate uestra ad domnum Winton(iensem) emanasse mandatum, ut
causam nobis ante delegatam ipse euocatis partibus et audiret et terminaret. Cum
itaque literas uestras super hoc ipse pre manibus haberet et ostenderet, nos negotium
10 ipsum suspensum tenere curauimus, donec nobis per uos plenius elucescat, quem
nostrum liti finem dare oportet. Valeat domnus meus et pater in Christo karissimus.

**250** 4–5 *The arenga is heavily abbreviated in* B ; *for the formula, see no.* 160, p. 212, n. 1, *etc.*
**251** G, no. 152; B, fo. 43 v.

---

[1] Cf. Luc. x. 34.
[2] Also canon of St Paul's and prebendary of Eald Street (*GF*, pp. 279 f.); this was very likely
the prebend to which Godfrey asserted that the disputed tithes pertained.
[3] Giles, no. 345 (to be dated 1170) shows William de Lega still archdeacon in 1170; he was dean
of Lichfield by 1173 (*HMC, 14th Rept.* Appendix VIII, 168), and had presumably been
succeeded by Godfrey, although this letter is the earliest known evidence of Godfrey's tenure.

## 252 To Nicholas, bishop of Llandaff

[1163–83] He excuses himself in a friendly way from the meeting which the bishop had suggested, and asks on behalf of William son of R. that B. his clerk be ordained priest.

Bishop Nicholas died in 1183.

Venerabili domno fratrique karissimo Nic(holao) Landau(ensi) episcopo frater G(ilebertus) Lundoniensis ecclesie minister, salutem et debitum fraterne caritatis obsequium.

Esse me sanum et incolumem noueris, tuumque affectuose desiderare colloquium ut percipiam ex amici presentia quod affectat plurimum anima mea solacium. 5 Quod quia uariis rerum impeditur euentibus quod corporalis alterutro nobis absentia subtrahit, id queso caritas illa suppleat que nescit absentiam, queque ipsum quem diligit sibi semper in spiritu nouit exibere presentem. De cetero Willelmi filii R. prece pulsatus, beniuolentie uestre preces offerre compellor quatinus B. clericum ipsius ad dia⟨B1, fo. 144⟩conatus ordinem promotum iamdiu ad sacer- 10 dotium promouere uelis. Quod amore Dei meeque petitionis intuitu complendo, et ipsum orationis obnoxium, meque tibi gratie ut in omnibus debitorem exibebis. Valeas in Christo karissime.

## 253 To A., abbot of Cirencester

[1163–c. 1180] On behalf of A., a renegade canon who now wishes to join a hospital.[1]

The abbot of Cirencester may be Andrew (died 1176) or Adam (1177–c. 1183).

G(ilebertus) Dei gratia Lundoniensis episcopus uenerabili fratri et amico in Christo karissimo A. Cirecestrie eadem gratia abbati et toti eiusdem loci conuentui, salutem et sinceram in Domino dilectionem.

Presentium lator frater A. iamdudum recessit a uobis spiritu fortasse non bono instigante. Reuertitur autem nunc, sancto ut speramus spiritu reuocante; pulsat ad 5 hostium misericordie uestre et in subsidium miserabilis et meticulose cause quam agit nostra ad uos fungitur aduocatione, ut gratiam quam diffidit ex se nostro queat interuentu promtius optinere. Difficultatem ordinis uestri iamdiu expertus exhorruit, et se tanto honeri et tam arctis obseruantiis inparem esse agnouit. Iccirco pulsat et postulat, et ut pro ipso pariter suplicemus lacrimis nos inuitat et ad hoc inclinat 10 uberrimis, ut ⟨fo. 39v⟩ cum licentia uestra in obedientia fratrum hospitalis inmunis

252 G, nos. 219, 293; B, fos. 143v (B1) and 185v (B2) (spelling as B2; B1 seems to be a copy of an incomplete draft).
1–3 Venerabili...obsequium om. B1    4 noueris et incolumem B1    6 quia om. B1    6 impeditur] perpenditur B1    8 presenti B2    9 uestre] in.b. sic B1    10 clericum ipsius om. B1
11 meeque...intuitu] et petitionis mee B1 (followed by a space)    12 debitorem om. B1
12 exibebis] B1 ends here
253 G, no. 255; B, fo. 39.

[1] 'fratres hospitalis' presumably means the community running a hospital; but this may refer to the Knights Hospitallers.

possit et absolutus de cetero ministrare. Hoc ipsi fratres hospitalis amplius expetunt et exoptant, qui nimirum iam dictum fratrem uestre licet professioni inequalem, suis tamen usibus utilem iam olim experti sunt. In quo et nos quoque si ultra locus
15 est uobis supplicamus, ut de fratris infirmitate compassionem habentes etsi non sit sublime quod petimus pium tamen pro fratre desiderium nostrum exaudiatis, et datis dimissoriis iis quibus expedit, liberum et absolutum assignetis, ne cum nostra quod absit omnium repulsa simplicitatem ipsius malo desperationis confundatis. Valete.

### 254  To Rotrou, archbishop of Rouen

[1165–c. 1180] He asks that the benefice of St-Aignan[1] be restored to Master Ranulf son of Erchemer,[2] and Roger the vicar either removed or compelled to stand by his contract with Master Ranulf.

Archbishop Rotrou succeeded in 1165; Ranulf was dead by 1182.

⟨V⟩enerabili domno patrique karissimo R(otrodo) Rothomagensi Dei gratia archiepiscopo frater G(ilebertus) Lundoniensis ecclesie minister, salutem et sincere dilectionis affectum.

Gratiarum Domino tota mentis alacritate referimus actiones quod in uobis
5 congesta uirtutum bona produxit in medium, et uos altiori superpositum candelabro in totius edificationem ecclesie solito uoluit eminentius elucere. Nos uero ueterem sed nullatenus inueteratam uobis amicitiam seruare uolentes de beniuolentia uestra confidimus, ut qui de collata uobis gratia congaude⟨fo. 176⟩mus amplioris etiam gratie apud uos locum optineamus. Inde est quod dilecte nobis in Domino bonitati
10 uestre preces affectuose porrigimus, quatinus dilecto nostro magistro Rannulfo filio Erchem(eri) beneficium ecclesie sancti Aniani quod sibi predecessor uester sub nostro et multorum testimonio tanquam eiusdem ecclesie persone restituit saluum fore concedatis et uicarium et fraudatorem suum Rogerium, aut a uicaria ipsa si iustum fuerit amoueatis, aut firmatis fide interposita pactis stare compellatis. Aget
15 oblate precis exauditio ut et magistrum Rannulfum obnoxium seruitio, et nos amplioris gratie debitores habeatis. Valere uos optamus in Domino, pater in Christo karissime.

### 255  To the Cardinal Deacon J.[3]

[1163–c. 1180] He asks his friend the cardinal to aid the monks of Saffron Walden (Essex) in their appeal; the bishop of Exeter's letter will explain the injustice they suffer.

**254** G, no. 200; B, fo. 175v.
9 benitati *corrected by modern hand* B (*? for* benignitati)    11 Aniani *or* Amani B
**255** G, no. 180; B, fo. 44v.

---

[1] Perhaps Saint-Aignan-sur-Ry (Seine-Maritime): cf. *Dict. géographique et administratif de la France*, VI (Paris, 1902), col. 4029.    [2] Canon of Hereford: *GF*, p. 269.
[3] The only cardinal *deacon* in this period with the initial I. known to have corresponded with Gilbert was Jacinctus or Hyacinth, the future Pope Celestine III (see Z. N. Brooke, in *Essays . . . presented to R. L. Poole*, p. 233).

Venerabili domno et amico karissimo I. sancte Romane ecclesie cardinali diacono, frater G(ilebertus) Lundoniensis ecclesie minister, affectum pium et si quem potest karitas officiosa famulatum.

Amantium se mutuo sibi corda loquntur et affectione quadam insolubili mentes amicorum—etsi locali distent spatio—potenter tamen intus operante uirtute firme 5 sibi connexe sunt. Presentem enim exhibet amor sibi quem diligit, et unitum sibi quodammodo karitas abesse non sinit. Hinc est quod non obstantibus locis ut presentes sibi in necessitate subueniunt et Christi legem adimplendo sua uicissim onera sustinere non omittunt.[1] Hac suggerente karitate, karissime, et de uestra nobis beniuolentia plurimum suadente dilecte nobis in Domino preces sullimitati 10 uestre porrigimus, quatinus presentium latoris et fratrum eius monachorum de Waleden' causam diligenter attendatis, et ipsis amore Dei nostraque prece (prout eorum expedire uideritis) necessitati prouideatis. Quanta enim opprimantur iniustitia ex literis dilecti fratris nostri domni Exon(iensis) intelligetis, et iuxta datam a Domino uobis sapientiam oppressis pie subueniendo, remuneratorem ut 15 speramus Dominum et nos gratie et seruitii debitores habebitis. Valete.

## 256  To Bartholomew, bishop of Exeter

[1163–*c.* 1180] On behalf of the bearer, who has business with the bishop. Bartholomew died in 1184.

⟨V⟩enerabili domno fratrique karissimo B(artholomeo) Exon(iensi) Dei gratia episcopo frater G(ilebertus) Lundoniensis ecclesie minister, salutem et debitum fraterne caritatis obsequium.

Amicis nostris et beniuolis negare non possumus, quin apud hos de quorum in nos caritate confidimus ipsorum uel suorum id exigente necessitate supplicemus. 5 Vnde quia presentium lator amicorum nostrorum familiaris et amicus est, dilecte nobis in Domino beniuolentie uestre preces benigne porrigimus quatinus ipsius negotium quod penes uos est quantum permittit equitas promoueatis, et eius prouidendo indemnitati ipsum uobis obnoxium seruitio et nos gratie debitores efficiatis. Valere uos optamus in Domino, frater in Christo karissime.                    10

## 257  To the bishop of Chester (?)

[1163–*c.* 1180] He asks the bishop to institute his relative R., who he hears has been presented to the church of *Idelesham*.

If the address is correct in the manuscript, the bishop of Chester-Coventry may be Richard Peche (1161–82) or just possibly Gerard la Pucelle (1183–4): there was no bishop between 1184 and Gilbert's death.[2] But *Idelesham* cannot be identified, and we suspect that it is an error for Ikelesham, i.e. Icklesham in Sussex, and the bishop addressed is the bishop of Chichester (i.e. *Cestr'* for *Cicestr'*, a very common error).

256 G, no. 207; B, fo. 173.
257 G, no. 204; B, fo. 135v.

---

[1] Cf. Gal. vi. 2.      [2] Hugh de Nonant was elected in 1185, but not consecrated until 1188.

Domnus Lundoniensis domno Cestr(ensi), salutis gaudium et cum omni hilaritate promte deuotionis obsequium.

Quod nobis domne reddit natura coniunctos non sinit a nobis ratio caritatis esse disiunctos.¹ Vnde est ut eorum negotiis—quantum cum Deo et iustitia possumus—
5 nos conueniat intendere, et quo nostra diligentia ad optatum perduci debeant effectum modis omnibus laborare. Quoniam igitur sepius experimento uestri gratia didicimus quid apud beniuolentiam uestram in nostris et nostrorum negotiis efficere possimus, certa quodammodo spes nobis promittitur ex preterito quod innata uobis liberalitas refrigescere nesciat in futuro. Deuotissimas itaque preces nostras,
10 carissime frater et domne, affectu quo solebatis si placet accipite, et in R. cognato nostro qui sanctitati uestre sicut audiuimus ad ecclesiam de Idelesham presentatus est ipsam sibi conferendo non remorate munus institutionis quod petimus adimplete. Nostis namque quante soleant in talibus occasiones ex mora reperiri que presuli plerumque auctoritatem instituendi adimant, et ne instituendus beneficio quod sibi
15 iuste conferri potuisset gaudeat iniqua quorundam calliditate prepediant. Diuina ergo misericordia uiscera pietatis uestre commoueat, et que nobis est ad uos dilectio simul et deuotio in cumulum caritatis accedat, quatinus prefatum R. in prescripto negotio dignemini promouere et ob indultam sibi gratiam tam nos quam ceteros amicos suos uestris uelitis obsequiis artius obligare. Valere uos optamus, in Domino
20 carissime.

### 258 To Jocelin de Bohun, bishop of Salisbury

[1163–c. 1180] He asks the bishop not to tax the benefice of twenty shillings which he has granted to Gilbert's nephew in the church of Chilton;² the latter has made an arrangement with his clerk, W., by which W. pays the twenty shillings and also all the other dues from the church.

Bishop Jocelin died in 1184.

Venerabili domno fratrique karissimo I(ocelino) Sar(esberiensi) Dei gratia episcopo frater G(ilebertus) Lundoniensis ecclesie minister, salutem et debitam Domino dilectionem.

Suadet e facili uerborum paucitas³ cum ad exaudiendum prona est ipsius ad quem
5 scribitur amica benignitas, quam quia de uestra gratia spem plene concipimus, dilecte nobis in Domino beniuolentie uestre preces af⟨B 1, fo. 138 v⟩fectuose

---

257 1 Cestr(ensi)] *added in margin* B    9 itaque] B *adds* literas, *cancelled*
258 G, no. 246; B, fos. 138 (B 1) *and* 143 v (B 2).
1–2 Venerabili...minister] I. Salesb'e e. G. d. g. L. e. B 2    2 debitam] B 2 *adds* in

---

¹ Cf. no. 266.
² Of the two Chiltons in the diocese of Salisbury, Chilton (Berks) and Chilton Foliat (Wilts), the latter took its name from a relative of Gilbert who held it (see *GF*, pp. 42, 45), and is no doubt the place referred to here. Gilbert's protégé Ralph of Chilton might be the absentee rector of this letter, but there is no clear evidence that he was related to Gilbert (see *GF*, pp. 45, 286). The reference to the yearling lamb seems to mean that Gilbert's nephew had only been instituted one year.    ³ Cf. p. 212 n. 1.

porrigimus ut uiginti solidorum beneficium quod nepoti meo in ecclesia de Chiltuna concessistis, integrum ipsi manere uelitis, ne si rei modice quippiam detraxeritis, rem ipsam mutilatam quoddammodo suo indignam donatore reddatis. Vestram uero uolumus celsitudinem non latere nepoti meo et ipsius clerico W. 10 pacto rem firmante sic conuenisse, ut W. sibi annuos uiginti ⟨solidos⟩ soluat et ipsius ecclesie onera omnia que uestra uel archidiaconi uestri imponet modestia in se suscipiendo sustineat. Vnde preces iterato porrigimus ut si iuxta quod moris uellus oui detraxeritis agno adhuc anniculo, quousque lanis uestiatur uberius, gratia miserante parcatis. Valere uos optamus in Domino, frater in Christo karissime. 15

## 259   To Robert, bishop of Hereford

[1163–c. 1180] He supports the plan of Ralph of Ledbury, the bishop's clerk, to resign his prebend at Hereford and for it to be given to Henry, Gilbert's nephew.[1]

The bishop of Hereford may be Robert de Melun (1163–7) or Robert Foliot (1174–86); more probably perhaps the latter, in view of the family arrangement proposed.

Domnus Lundoniensis domno Hereford(ensi), salutem et debitum uere dilectionis affectum.

Vereor ad amicum molestus precator accedere et ab eo quicquam unde uel in modico moueatur exigere. Verum cum digne commendabilem illam uestre mentis attendo modestiam, spem mente concipio ut benigne sustineatis amicum etsi magna 5 petentem, uos tamen ad petitiones eiusmodi sibi offerendas et cum Dominus oportunitatem dederit ab ipso hilariter exaudiendas ipsa precis audacia prouocantem. Quorundam relatione didici Radulfum de Lideberi clericum uestrum id habere mentis et propositi ut prebendam quam habet in ecclesia de Hereford(ia) in manu uestra resignare desideret, si spem tamen habuerit ut eam in Henricum nepo- 10 tem meum conferre beniuolentie uestre placuerit. Hoc itaque est quod postulo, quod in affectionis experimentum et caritatis augmentum nobis exhiberi desidero. Quod si uobis in aliquo molestum intellexero, ab ipsa prorsus postulatione recedo. Valeat domnus et amicus in Christo carissimus.

## 260   To the bishops of the province of Canterbury

[1166–70 or 1174–c. 1180] The archbishop of Canterbury has learnt that those on their way to the papal Curia have been molested; the archbishop enjoins all the bishops to prohibit any molestation and denounce offenders.

Gilbert is evidently acting as dean of the province, on behalf of an archbishop who is also papal legate (apostolica auctoritate—unless this refers to the Pope). It would read most naturally

**258** 7 porrigimus] B2 ends here, with Supra est quod restat   11 ⟨solidos⟩] sol(mark of abbreviation deleted)uat B1
**259** G, no. 214; B, fo. 192.
7 hilacriter (possibly for alacriter) B
**260** G, no. 196; MB Epp. 147; B, fo. 143; D, fo. 78 r–v.

---

[1] Presumably Henry Banastre, treasurer of London, who is known to have been a canon of Hereford (GF, pp. 270, 275).

as a routine circular letter of the time of Archbishop Richard (i.e. after 1174); but it could also be one of Gilbert's efforts to be correct in his behaviour during the Becket dispute, and belong to the years following the grant of the legation to Becket (1166–70). On the whole its place among the letters of the dispute in MS D favours the latter view.

Gileb(ertus) Dei gratia Lundoniensis episcopus uniuersis ecclesie Cant(uariensis) suffraganeis, salutem et debitum fraterne karitatis obsequium.

Peruenit ad patrem nostrum dompnum Cantu(ariensem) archiepiscopum eos quos necessitas pro compendio penitentie, uel cause remedio aut uisitationis debito 5 compellit ad domnum papam iter arripere in regno hoc ab itinere suo prepediri, spoliari, tractari atrocius, et a transfretatione prohiberi, uel ab his qui occasiones querunt ut faciant mala, uel coacti illicita de prepediendis clericis uel penitentibus prestiterunt sacramenta. Vnde nobis omnibus apostolica auctoritate in uirtute obedientie et in periculo ordinis nostri iniungit quatinus hoc de cetero fieri inhibea-10 mus, et in eos qui in clericos uiolentas manus iniciunt, qui appellantes uel penitentes ad domnum papam, uel ad ipsum tendentes uel ab ipso redeuntes impediunt, publice excomunicatos denuntiemus et per episcopatus nostros denuntiari faciamus, tam facientes hoc quam hoc facere compellentes. Quod quia nobis districte iniungitur, mandare uobis et denuntiare curauimus, ut mandantis imperio prout 15 iustum est pareamus. Valere uos optamus in Domino.

## 261  To William de Malpalu

[1163–c. 1180] He thanks William for the aid he has given to Gilbert's brother and nephew.

William was a Norman justice and appears to have lived in or near Rouen.[1] The circumstances of this letter are quite obscure, but this indication fits the hint in the letter that the return of Gilbert's relations involved a substantial journey.

None of nos. 261–7 can be dated more closely than the limits of Gilbert's pontificate and the manuscript.

G(ilebertus) Dei gratia Lundoniensis ecclesie minister amico suo karissimo Willelmo de Mala palude salutem et sinceram dilectionem.

Cum me uobis in multis obliget benigna iamdiu seruitiorum exhibitio, hoc tamen in consummatam amicitiam me precipue uobis reddit obnoxium, quod 5 fratri meo et nepoti in necessitate sua subuenistis, et eis consilium et auxilium prout res exigebat inpendistis. Precor autem ut si item urgente necessitate recurrerint ad uos, non ipsis sed michi et ipsis propter me de uestro quod opus fuerit tradatis, ut me seruitii et gratie debitorem habeatis. Ilico uero cum ad nos reuersi fuerint nuntium nostrum habebitis, et si quid erga nos uolueritis per ipsos nobis manda-10 bitis et optinebitis. Valeat amicus meus karissimus.

260  1 Gileb' D; G. B    5 apire corrected B    7 ut D; ne B
261  G, no. 284; B, fo. 47.

----

[1] He occurs ?c. 1160, 1172, 1186 (Haskins, Norman Institutions, p. 326 and n.; Delisle, Recueil, Introd. pp. 490–1. Also in J. F. Pommeraye, Hist. de l'abbaye de S.-Amand de Rouen, Rouen, 1662, p. 84).

### 262 To Maurice, bishop of Paris

[1163–*c.* 1180] He writes about the payment of debts incurred by William de Beaum'
(? Belmeis)[1] to certain citizens of Paris...(incomplete).

Venerabili domno fratrique in Christo karissimo M(auricio) P(arisiensi) Dei gratia
episcopo frater G(ilebertus) Lundoniensis ecclesie minister, salutem et sincere
dilectionis affectum.

Notum sit caritati uestre quod nos secuti fidem mandati uestri simul et auctoritatem scripti uestri auctentici, quod uestro penes nos residet sigillo insignitum, 5
burgensibus Paris(iensibus) pro quibus nobis scripsistis, creditoribus uidelicet
Willelmi de Beaum', quanta potuimus et debuimus diligentia ad indempnitatem
prospeximus. Porro in presentia missorum uestrorum per idoneos et sufficientes
fideiussores pro Willelmo cautum est quod ad instantem festiuitatem sancti
Laurentii octo marce argenti predictis creditoribus in solutum reddentur; infra 10
quindecim uero dies post sequentem sancti Michaelis festiuitatem, item octo marce.
Consequenter autem infra quindecim dies post proximum Pascha, quod residuum
fuerit usque ad summam sexaginta quatuor libras Paris(ienses) et decem solidos
persoluetur. Quod quia pro inopia creditoris promptius expediri non poterat[...]

### 263 To a friend

[1163–*c.* 1180] His friend has sniffed the riches of Sicily and set off abroad in search of wealth.
Gilbert admonishes him on the vanity of riches, and urges him to a speedy return.

G(ilebertus) Dei gratia Lundoniensis episcopus[...]

Audio te Siculas frater olfecisse diuitias fuluique metalli nuper afflatum aura, in
externas non iam animo solum sed et corpore tendere nationes. Qua in re quis sis
quamue turpiter ambias euidenter ostendis, qui fractus animo uel pertesus inedie
diuitias tibi ipso uel anime tue dispendio misere comparare disponis. Fortunam 5
Crassi legisti, qui bibendo quod sitiit ignominiosa morte male satur occubuit.[2] Tu
quoque non ditescere sed statim diues esse desiderans, mauis in mortem diues

---

262 G, no. 198; B, fo. 42 v.
14 [...] *Two lines left blank in B: the text is evidently incomplete*
263 G, no. 297; B, fo. 176 v.
1 [...] *A space left in B* (? *erasure*)

---

[1] As the creditors are from Paris, the recipient of the letter is evidently the bishop of Paris (the
initials M.P. in the manuscript fit this) and the debtor was very likely a clerk or canon who
had studied there. On William de Belmeis, see *GF*, p. 286. Maurice de Sully, formerly canon
and archdeacon of Paris, was bishop from 1160 to his death on 11 Sept. 1196 (V. Mortet,
*Maurice de Sully* (Paris, 1890); C. A. Robson, *Maurice of Sully and the Medieval Vernacular
Homily* (Oxford, 1952); *Obituaires...Sens*, I, i, 176, etc., establishing 11 Sept. against I, ii, 799
(8 Sept.) and I, i, 630 (20 Sept.)).

[2] According e.g. to Florus (*Epitome*, I, 46 (III, 11)), the severed head of Crassus was fed with
gold by the Parthian king after his death. Gilbert's version, which has it that he was poisoned
by drinking gold, was also known to John of Salisbury (see *Policraticus*, III, 11, ed. C. C. J.
Webb, I, 206), but its source is unknown.

inpingere, quam momento temporis quod desideras id non esse. Vnde ne in mortem insalutatus exeas, nolenti iam salutem uerbum tibi salutationis emisi, si quo tandem
10 modo resipiscas, si memor affectionum, si memor patrie, si parentum, si societatis et gratie occuli cecutientis obtalmiam manu tandem discretionis abstergeas, et desperationis foueam, in quam ignauia te pertrahente corruisti, tam prudenter quam fortiter exiens, de bono Iesu qui dat omnibus affluenter et non inproperat nichil ⟨h⟩esitans, cum magna spei certitudine ad nos reditum maturare contendas.

## 264   To I. (or J.), dean of Ongar (Essex)

[1163–c. 1180] He is to suspend any of the priests or deacons of his deanery who are living with concubines (cf. GF, p. 221).

Gilebertus Dei gratia Lundoniensis episcopus I. decano de Ang' salutem.

Audiuimus et pro certo accepimus quod quidam sacerdotes siue diaconi de decanatu uestro, spreta penitus et abiecta ammonitione nostra, interdicta sibi fe⟨fo. 165 v⟩minarum consortia nequaquam deuitant, sed assueta concubinarum
5 suarum contubernia tam impudenter adhuc etiam quam irreuerenter fouent et frequentant. Vnde ne patientia nostra, quam tanto sunt abusi tempore, trahatur ad consensum per presentia uobis scripta in ui obedientie precipiendo mandamus quatinus omnes predicti ordinis personas in uestro decanatu constitutas que tam infami societate et familiaritate tam illicita irretite noscuntur, et adhuc illaqueate,
10 auctoritate Dei et nostra a sacerdotali et a leuitico suspendatis officio, et tamdiu suspensos teneatis donec condigna satisfactione restitutionis gratiam a nobis optinuerint. Valete.

## 265   To the Pope

[1163–c. 1180] On behalf of the canons of Holy Trinity, Aldgate, who are appealing (to the Pope).

The letter carries no heading, but it is rational to suppose that a letter preserved in B written on behalf of one of the leading monastic houses of London was written by Gilbert as bishop of London. The style, especially of the preamble, supports this. It is also clear that the appeal is to the Pope, not to the archbishop.

Quos honestas uite commendat ad gratiam et piis meritis iamdiu declarata religio, hiis apud serenitatem uestram et conuersationis honeste testimonium perhibere iustum est, et ut in iustis petitionibus suis a uestra gratia clementer exaudiantur deuote porrectis precibus exorare. Ecclesia siquidem sancte Trinitatis que a bone
5 memorie Mathilde dudum Anglie regina Lund⟨onie⟩ edificata est et honesto canonicorum regularium conuentu nobiliter instituta, ab ipsa sua fundatione usque

**263** 11 obtalimam B   11 abstergas B
**264** G, no. 203; B, fo. 165.
1 Angy B
**265** G, no. 299 (with a fragment attached, see p. 517); B, fo. 189 v (in margin: ⟨pro⟩ ecclesia sancte Trinitatis).

nunc et plenitudine caritatis et suscepti a se ordinis obseruantia late claruit, et odoris boni suauitatem emittendo ex se, ceteris sui ordinis ecclesiis uelud speculum quoddam et defecate religionis exemplar emicuit. Que cum ad presens in oborta sibi necessitate interposita apellatione confugerit ad uos, cum postulante petimus, cum sup- 10 plicante postulamus ut directum ad sanctitatem uestram eius nuntium benigne suscipiatis et ne possessionis sue, qua multorum necessitati subuenit, detrimentum sustineat, quantum permiserit iustitia paterna si placet gratia prouideatis.

## 266  To Hugh du Puiset, bishop of Durham

[1163–c. 1180] On behalf of W. and H. (who are evidently in the bishop of Durham's service).

Venerabili domno fratrique karissimo H(ugoni) Dunelmensi Dei gratia episcopo frater G(ilebertus) L(ondoniensis) ecclesie minister, salutem et sincere caritatis affectum.

Vsu celeberrimum esse solet, ut quotiens honesta deposcit occasio ⟨fo. 195 v⟩ cum optinendi fiducia his de quorum dilectione spes nobis est uberior affectuosas 5 preces porrigamus. Cum itaque amicis nostris et his precipue quos nature nobis unit ratio,[1] in suis negotiis deesse nec debemus nec possumus, de strenuitate uestra magis quam de merito confidentes, uestram attentius exoramus benignitatem quatinus quod in prouectu uestrorum scilicet W. et H. laudabiliter cepistis feliciori fine consumetis, ut apud uos preces nostras sibi profuisse sentiant et nos gratiarum 10 debitores, ipsos autem seruitii habeatis. Valete.

## 267  To the abbot of Rievaulx

[1163–c. 1180] The sons of Bricthmer of Tanton (Yorks, N.R. ?)[2] complain that a large sum due to their father, a benefactor to the abbey, has not been paid; and only the reverence in which the abbey is held has prevented the king intervening. Gilbert urges the abbot to pay or establish legally that he does not owe the debt.

Probably not early, since the tone of the letter does not suggest close friendship, such as Gilbert had with Abbot Ailred (died 1166).

Dominus Lundoniensis abbati Rieuall(ensi).

Quanto uestra domusque uestre fama predicatur hilarior, tanto magis uobis obseruandum est ut quod communis habet opinio nullius fratrum uestrorum consilio denigretur aut facto. Conqueruntur plurimum filii Bricthmeri de Tantuna dudum fratris et benefactoris uestri, quod summam magnam pecunie patri suo 5

---

266 G, no. 206; B, fo. 195. *See Plate III.*
267 G, no. 264; B, fo. 110v.

---

[1] Cf. no. 257.
[2] Or Taunton (Somerset). Tanton seems much more likely for a benefactor of Rievaulx, but the twelfth/thirteenth-century form was normally Tamet-; Tanton(a) is only doubtfully vouched for in the early thirteenth century (A. H. Smith, *PN North Riding of Yorks*, p. 170).

debitam sibi super hoc iam sepe requisiti reddere contradicitis, nec patris sui meritis iuxta quod uestram deceret religionem opere respondetis. Qui super hoc a domno rege iamdiu litteras ad uos expetissent nisi ob uestram domusque uestre reuerentiam nostra eos sollicitudo retardasset. Vnde beneuolentie uestre preces aff(ectuose)
10 porrigimus, quatinus amore iustitie nostreque petitionis intuitu eis aut quod postulant iuste soluatis, aut si repetunt indebitum, hoc in iure declarare moleste ne feratis.

### 268   To a bishop

[? 1163–c. 1180] He describes the complaint of a lady in his diocese named Matilda that her husband James son of Lebrand, of the bishop's nation, now living in his diocese at *Grennig'* (unidentified), had deserted her; and asks the bishop to restore James to his wife.

According to the manuscript, Vtreh' is the name of the recipient's diocese—a blank is left for the initial of his name (see note to line 1). Giles supposed that Vtreh' was, none the less, the bishop's name, and addressed the letter to Uhtred, bishop of Llandaff (1140–8), in whose time Gilbert was not even a diocesan, let alone bishop of London.

The address is probably corrupt.

Venerabili domno fratrique in Christo karissimo Vtreh' Dei gratia episcopo frater G(ilebertus) Lundoniensis ecclesie minister, salutem in Domino.

Veniens ad nos quedam parrochiana nostra Mathild(is) nomine lacrimabili nobis sepe conquestione monstrauit, quod quidam Iacobus nomine, Lebrandi filius,
5 uester natione et nunc conuersatione parrochianus, qui eam sollempni ut asserit matrimonio et cum sacerdotali benedictione in suam accepit et duxit uxorem, ipsam postmodum absque iudicio et conscientia ecclesie per totum iam septennium desertam, et contra fidem thori et legem Christi tam nefarie quam ireuerenter, altera superducta uirili prorsus destitutam solatio dereliquerit. Super quo ut uera
10 uobis scribere, et certa secure significare possemus, per archidiaconum, per sacerdotem ipsius ministrum et auctorem matrimonii, per laicos etiam quamplures graues et honestos uiros, fide ueri districte et diligenter inquisita, uerum esse manifeste deprehendimus quod nobis memorata Math(ildis) de contractis cum Iacobo nuptiis plus lacrimis quam uerbis sepenumero persuaserat. Vnde quia
15 predictus I(acobus) in iurisdictione uestra et in uestro ut dicitur territorio apud Grennig' commoratur, fraternitati uestre preces affectuose porrigimus, supplicantes et obsecrantes in Domino quatinus illum ob reuerentiam Dei canonica seueritate corripiatis, et ut uxori debitum prouideat et prestet subsidium, ecclesiastice districtione iustitie compellatis, ut sciat eundem esse tam uobis quam nobis zelum
20 legis Christi, et sentiat utrimque aduersus preuaricatores eius non deesse ultores. Valete.

268 G, no. 218; B, fo. 162.
1 Vtreh'] .V. (? A) (*erased*) Vtreh' *sic* B   4 ?⟨...⟩lebrandi   19 distctione B

## 269  To the bishops of the Province of Canterbury

[Early 1186] A covering letter to the bull of Pope Urban III announcing his election.

The bull (JL 15,518 or 15,519; G, no. 381; *PUE*, III, no. 375)[1] was sent *c*. 12 January 1186, and presumably reached England in February or early March. It was addressed to the archbishop of Canterbury and his suffragans, and Gilbert is doubtless circulating it in virtue of his office as dean of the province.

Venerabilibus fratribus et amicis in Christo karissimis sancte Cant(uariensis) ecclesie suffraganeis G(ilebertus) Dei gratia Lundoniensis ecclesie minister, salutem in Domino.

Exemplum litterarum domni et patris nostri Vrbani pape, quas transmittente nobis domno Cant(uariensi) nuper recepimus, fraternitati uestre ex officii nostri 5 debito ⟨dirigere (?)⟩ duximus, ut eius continentia diligentius inspecta, uos de cetero non lateat quo pastore diuina prouisio Romanam de nouo instituerit ecclesiam, et in quantum eiusdem pastoris gratia uenerabilis patris nostri Cant(uariensis) archiepiscopi auxerit dignitatem.

## 270  To a friend, not named

[1163–87] The preface to Gilbert's *Homilies* (see *GF*, p. 70 and n.).

The letter bears no address, and only the title shows that he was bishop of London when he wrote the work, although it is not impossible that this is an anachronism. The greeting 'frater' suggests a bishop or an abbot, probably an abbot, since the recipient was certainly a monk. In the one surviving manuscript the work immediately follows Ailred of Rievaulx's sermons on Isaiah,[2] which were dedicated to Gilbert, and it is not impossible that Ailred was the recipient.

Habes frater quod optasti, quod pulsanti iam diutius caritas ultra negare non potuit. Intus enim positus auocatos ab his que foris sunt sensus meos, ne quibusdam forte distraherentur illecebris, cum intra mentis cubile clauso quidem hostio, quiete placida confouerem, te subito pulsantem foris et aliquid postulantem aduerti. Petebas autem aliquem de scriptura sacra comodari tibi panem,[3] quem amico qui 5

269 G, no. 330; Ja, fo. 42 (Epistola Gilleberti London' episcopi ad suffraganeos Cant' ecclesie de electione Urbani pape).
5 nobis] *or* uobis ?
270 G, no. 329; BM Royal MS 2 D. xxxii, fo. 138 v (Tractatus Gileberti Londoniensis episcopi). *The homilies finish on* fo. 168 v.

---

[1] The text of this bull in Ja is incomplete at the conclusion; it may originally have gone on to grant Baldwin the legateship, as is indicated by the concluding sentence of Gilbert's letter. Alternatively, Gilbert may have been circulating two bulls, this and JL 15,520, in which Baldwin's legation is announced; but 'eius continentia' seems to imply that only one bull was enclosed. See Holtzmann's note in *PUE loc. cit.*

[2] See *GF*, p. 70. Both tracts are written in the same hand, and there is no break between them— Ailred's ends and Gilbert's begins half-way down fo. 138 v.

[3] Cf. Peter of Celle's *De Panibus* (*PL*, CCII, coll. 927 ff.), and John of Salisbury's letter (I, no. 33) thanking him for its dedication to him.

de uia uenerat ad te, auocato scilicet ab exterioribus animo tuo, hospitali gratia in
refectionem condigne apponeres. Qua in re si uere supplicantis agebas affectu,
potius quid porrigerem attendere, quam mee circa te liberalitati legem constituere
debuisti. Nunc uero non que sunt uires mee considerans, tuo potius arbitrio quid
10 tibi dari uolueris elegisti. In illud enim quod in beatorum apostolorum Petri et
Pauli decantatur octauis—'Isti sunt due oliue et candelabra lucentia ante Dominum'[1]
—tractatum tibi aliquem ad gratiam, beatis uero apostolis ad laudem explicari
postulasti, pro libito assignans materiam et explicans dicendi formam. Nam et hoc
in prece complexus es, ne tuam scolarium more propositionem sub breuitate
15 constringerem, sed tanquam in domum meam sapientia declinauerit, iuxta illud,
'sapiens in uerbis producit seipsum', et illud, 'labia sapientis ornant scientiam',[2]
quod proposueras aucto⟨fo. 139⟩ritatibus cingerem, et id uerbis et sententiis
dilatando, non in expositionem solummodo, sed in tractatum extenderem. In quo
animi insolentiam tui recte quis redargueret, si non omnia caritas excusaret? Sed
20 amoris indubitanter experimentum reputo, quod tuum michi desiderium confidenter exponis. Sitque tibi caritatis indicium, quod cum in terra mentis mee fames
uerbi preualeat, panis tamen id modicum quod est penes me, tibi communicare non
omitto. Et fuerat fortasse melius michi pacem comparasse silentio, quam scribendo
quippiam multorum me iudicio submisisse. Sed tu te michi monachum exhibe, et
25 orando discrimen amoue, in quod me iamdiu continuate precis instantia pertraxisti.

## 271  To Walter Foliot, formerly archdeacon of Shropshire

[c. 1178–87] The preface to the *Commentary on the Pater Noster*.

Walter was archdeacon of Shropshire (dioc. Hereford) from c. 1150 to c. 1178; since
Walter is 'dudum archidiaconus' he must have resigned his archdeaconry, and this fits the
statement that Gilbert is an old man going blind; we know that he was going blind at least
by 1181–2 (see *GF*, pp. 71 f., 103 f.).

⟨G⟩il⟨ebertus⟩ Dei gratia Londoniensis ecclesie minister dilecto suo Waltero
Herefordensi dudum archidiacono, id quod petit assequi, et his que uoce Domini
bonis promissa sunt non priuari.

Sacra uestre petitionis me compellit instantia, ut orationis dominice uerba uobis
5 aperiam et ea quibus omnes nos orare precipit, quo intellectu concipienda sint et
qua mentis intentione Domino presentanda transcribam. Que nimirum petitio si
michi iam transactis annorum curriculis pluribus oblata fuisset, potuisset facilius
excipi, et quod mandatis expeditius et securius expediri. Nunc uero se michi
senectus ingerit, uisus deserit, minoratur sensus et mentem caligo occupat, et cetera
10 queque que a studiosis optantur, me michi solum fere relictum destituunt et in
ueteri domicilio mansionem sibi facere dedignantur. Solum michi solacio est amoris

---

**271** Worcester Cathedral Library, MS Q. 48, fo. 60 v.

[1] Apoc. xi. 4; 2nd Antiphon, Vespers, for Octave of Sts Peter and Paul (cf. *Hereford Breviary*,
II, 235).
[2] Cf. Eccli. xx. 13; Prov. xv. 7.

uestri honesta integritas et spes optinendi a Deo quod postulatis: oratio sancta uestra, que apud ipsum pulset precibus ut a quo petens accipit et per quem querens inuenit et qui pulsanti apperit,[1] nobis que de eo digna sint dici aperiat, et que saluti uestre sint utilia me uobis scribente depromat.                                                    15

## 272  To Robert Foliot, bishop of Hereford

[1174–86] The preface to the *Commentary on the Song of Songs* (see *GF*, p. 70 and n.).

It is natural to suppose that the bishop to whom Gilbert dedicated this work was Robert Foliot (1174–86) rather than Robert de Melun (1164–7).

Domno et amico suo karissimo Roberto Dei gratia Herefordensi episcopo frater Gillebertus Lundoniensis ecclesie minister, humil(iter) in his exerceri que Dei sunt, et in eisdem fine beatissimo consummari.

Ne tue domne iussionis uana michi aut uilis uideretur auctoritas, tibi ilico direxi librum quem postulasti: librum siquidem quem in Cantica canticorum iuuante 5 Domino nuper edidi, quem nulli hominum ante te scribendum inspiciendumue commisi. Non enim hic ad laudem preconiiue gratia a me conscriptus est, sed ut quod Domino docente didici, id tenerem memoriter; et hec non secundum Iudeos aspernanda uiliter, sed hec intimo sensu legenda humiliter, et eodem quo dicta sunt spiritu intelligenda demonstrarem. Qui cum a te fuerit atentione plurima ab initio 10 ad finem usque perlectus, multa eum animi alacritate suscepisti, et me meum in hoc studium applicasse, laude ut audio plurima commendasti. Cui ut nichil ad perfectionem deesset, prologum a me aptari postulasti, ut sic operis completio digna foret cui gratiarum redderetur exhibitio. Scriptum quippe est, 'fortis est ut mors dilectio';[2] nam ut mortale nichil est quod nexum queat mortis elidere, sic possibile nil est quod 15 non possit instantia dilectionis optinere. Hec exinaniuit Dominum, humanis illum nexibus alligauit; hec post crucem et sepulcrum ad sedes illum perduxit infimas, ut eos hinc eriperet qui uenturum hunc crediderant et diligenter expectabant. Hec quos ire filios[3] dictante iustitia perfecerat, in libertatem gratie misericordia iudicium temperante reformat. Meum mutat ista consilium, ut operi apponam prologum, 20 quod sine prologo explanandum suscepi. Auctor enim operis extitit Salomon, qui scriptores est imitatus antiquos, qui non prologum premittendo lectores suos attentos faciant, sed ipsis rem de qua acturi sunt demonstrando, eorum excitent attentionem, et eorum studia ad agnitionem eorum que sunt dicta conuertant. Vnde illud Moysi, 'In principio creauit Deus celum et terram; terra autem erat 25 inanis et uacua'—et illud Exodi—'Hec sunt nomina filiorum Israel qui ingressi sunt in Egiptum cum Iacob.'[4] Sic totum percurrens Pentateucum, Iudicum et Regum

272 G, no. 212; *PL*, CCII, 1147–50; BM MS Royal 2 E. vii (see *GF*, p. 70 n.), fo. 4 (*no heading: at foot of fo. in later hand:* Gilebertus super Cantica canticorum).

13 aptari] *A correction inserted:* uel co(aptari)    21–2 quod...prologum *om. MS, added in the margin*

---

[1] Cf. Matt. vii. 8; Luc. xi. 10.                    [2] Cant. viii. 6.
[3] Cf. Eph. ii. 3 ff.                                [4] Gen. i. 1–2; Ex. i. 1.

librosque alios sine prologo scriptos inuenies, quibus si prologi adiecti sunt, illos longo post tempore post aduentum Saluatoris adiectos esse cognoueris. Hos imitans
30 Solomon ab ipsa statim re de qua est acturus incipit, sciens rem ipsam de qua agitur ⟨fo. 4v⟩ utilitatem manifestam habere in se qua alliciat, uel rationem euidentem qua concupita despiciat, uel inspectiones theolog⟨ic⟩as quibus hec a mente reiciat, et soli illi qui horum conditor et creator est adhereat. Tres itaque libros efficit, quos non prologus exornat aut dilatat, Parabolarum unum, Ecclesiasten alterum,
35 Sirasirim hunc tertium. Allicit in Parabolis ad hec possidenda per que presens uita munitur, ut necessitati proprie succurratur, in quibus opus est proximo subueniatur, et indigenti prout necessitas expetit tribuatur. In Ecclesiaste uero monet ne his animus implicetur, nec amor his que transitoria sunt inclinetur, sed hec tamquam uana diiudicet, et que sunt his altiora decernat et apetat. Vnde Sirasirim quod
40 Cantica canticorum appellatur consequenter apponens, in quo cuncta preteruolens diuine maiestati assistit, hunc ut sponsum amplectens, huic totum quod amoris esse potest ex affectu representans; animam igitur uel ecclesiam sic amoris igne succensam non hec uisibilia querentem, sed ad inuisibilia toto cordis affectu, tota mentis intentione suspirantem, sic inducit quasi querentem Deum nondum tamen appre-
45 hendentem et ut apprehensum teneat hec dicentem: 'osculetur me osculo oris sui',[1] de quo quod sequitur sic dicimus, 'que est ista tam inclita etc.'

**272** 31–2 alliciant/despiciant MS (*the construction is not clear, but the transition from plural to singular—to reiciat/adhereat—is awkward, and the subject of* alliciat *seems naturally to be* res, *even though Solomon himself or the reader would be more appropriate for the subject of the other three verbs*) 32 theologas MS 37 et] MS adds unum, *cancelled* 45–6 osculetur...etc. *added in MS.*]

---

[1] Cant. i. 1. The words which follow 'que est...' are the opening words of Gilbert's commentary (*PL*, CCII, 1149).

# IV

## LETTERS OF UNCERTAIN DATE AND AUTHORSHIP*

### Nos. 273–83

---

* The content and style of these letters make it likely enough that all were issued in Gilbert's name; in no case is there decisive proof.

**273**

Petition, apparently to a fellow bishop, to receive H., now prepared to accept the penance enjoined on him of entering an abbey.

[ . . . ] Post iram misericordie reminisci.

Veniens ad nos presentium lator H. lacrimabili nobis planctu monstrauit se mentis uestre tranquillitatem offensa graui perturbasse, et iracundie calore motum se uobis non solum uerbo restitisse, uerum et calcaneum aduersum uos irreuerenter erexisse. Vnde tactus dolore cordis intrinsecus disciplinam regularem quam ipsum 5 decreueritis subire paratus est et uobis humili deuotione satisfacere, et de cetero uobis ut patri karissimo in omnibus obedire. Quia uero dignos penitentie fructus offerentem nunquam repellit Dominus, sed est angelis Dei gaudium super peccatore penitentiam agente, et singulare uirtutis exemplar dans penitenti et reuertenti filio in amplexus occurrit et osculum,[1] rogamus ut ob eius reuerentiam nostreque 10 petitionis intuitu quem repulistis auersum, conuersum suscipiatis, et quia perierat mundus nisi iram finisset misericordia, iram ei remittendo hoc abbati literis uestris significetis qui ut quorundam testimonio didicimus, eum si uobis reconciliatum nouerit fratrum colegio aggregabit.

**274**

To someone who has refused a petition.[2]

[ . . . ] Hospitium in se Domino laudabiliter exhibere.

Beniuolentie uestre frater carissime gratias affectuose referimus, quod petitionem nostram, quocumque processerit tramite, benigne tamen exaudire uoluistis. Nos tamen nostram perscrutantes undequaque conscientiam in nobis aduersum uos nichil penitus odii, nil amaritudinis aut simulationis aut uersute duplicitatis (Deo 5 teste) repperimus. Sed simpliciter ambulantes, quod uobis, quod domui uestre honestum sperabamus et utile, nulla mentis elatione, nullo prelationis fastigio aut exactione aliqua, sed fraterna solum caritate postulare curauimus. Equidem fratrem uestrum R. dileximus et in negotiis uestris que sedule gessit apud nos sustinuimus, atendentes quod eius opera Dominus benigne dirigeret. Hoc ipso gauisi sumus. 10 Quod si faciem uestram altiore fortasse consilio a nostra petitione auerteritis, nos quia caritas alligari non potest ipsum quocumque eum traxerit obedientia,[3] amore saltem prosequemur.

**273** G, no. 288; B, fo. 111.
5 ipse (?) B
**274** G, no. 290; B, fo. 111v.

---

[1] Cf. Luc. xv. 10, 20.
[2] The first sentence says that the recipient has *wished* to accept the petition; the last implies that he has refused it. 'nullo prelationis fastigio' suggests that the author is a bishop; 'fratrem uestrum R.' that the recipient may be a monastic superior.
[3] Cf. *Regula S. Benedicti*, c. 68.

**275**

A request to someone to fulfil what he has promised.

Cum hactenus apud clementiam uestram facilem uotorum nostrorum optinuerimus effectum, euidenter conicimus ex preteritis, quid sperare debeamus de futuris. Hinc est quia de benignitate uestra simul et dilectione confisi, liberalitati uestre deuotissime supplicamus, quatinus pro amore Dei et nostre si placet precis intuitu, opere
5 complere uelitis quod ore promisistis. Exultat siquidem spiritus noster in Deo salutari nostro quia respexit et uisitauit uos oriens ex alto.[1] Cui gratias ago quod zelum penitentie inspirare uobis sua dignata est clementia. Inpulsus eratis machinatione diaboli ut caderetis, et per Spiritum Sanctum suscepit uos dextera Domini.

**276**

Asking a colleague (?) to collate Archdeacon R.[2] to the church of St John, resigned to him by Lambert the clerk.

Pro literatis et honestis uiris atentius interuenire et eorum comodis diligenter intendere, sacerdotalis officii cura nos admonet et debitum exigit caritatis. Inde est quod dilectionem uestram de qua plurimum confidimus, cum omni sedulitate rogamus, quatinus R. archidiacono iamdudum clerico et amico nostro ecclesiam
5 sancti Iohannis quam sibi a Lamberto cessam esse accepimus concedatis, et inde uobis eum clericum deuotum et fidelem nostrarum precum interuentu constituere procuretis, ut de uestre dilectionis effectu cum ampliori presumtione de cetero possimus confidere, et eam exinde debeamus ex meritis commendare. Quicquid enim humanitatis et gratie, nostre presertim petitionis optentu, ei a uobis impensum
10 fore nouerimus, non aliter quam nobis impensum gratum habebimus et acceptum. Valete.

**277**

Encouragement, perhaps addressed to a *causidicus*.[3]

Salutem et debitum cum omni deuotione famulatum.
    Dilectio dilectissime et honoris exhibitio, quam a multis retro annis michi impendere non destitit excellentia uestra, eam in uos affectionem meam pro-

275 G, no. 295; B, fo. 144v.
276 G, no. 298; B, fo. 176v.
10 habeamus B *before correction*
277 G, no. 300; B, fo. 194.
3 meam] nostram B, *not cancelled, but with* meam *written above it*

---

[1] Cf. Luc. i. 47–8 (and 68: Magnificat and Benedictus).
[2] This does not provide us with sufficient indication to identify any of the persons concerned: presumably this is a letter from Gilbert to a fellow bishop.
[3] It reads as if addressed to a *causidicus* (see *GF*, pp. 66–7) who has served Gilbert in the past, and is now working for an abbot (possibly Master David).

meruerunt, ut quecumque ⟨fo. 194v⟩ uestro seu uestrorum comodo aut honori credimus expedire, omni studio et conamine tanquam propria negotia merito 5 debeam procurare. Inde siquidem est quod si domnus abbas sollicitudinem uestram circa negotium hoc affectuosam compererit, nec uolet, ut credo, nec audebit uestre contraire uoluntati. Eo etiam studiosius huic negotio insistere debebitis, quod alii istius exemplis incitati, libentius se uestris consiliis committent, qui istum uiderint in ius suum uestro iuuamine esse promotum. Valete.                    10

## 278

A request for patronage (?) for a connexion[1] and member of the author's household.

Quo penes uestram dilectissime celsitudinem nostra fere nulla sunt merita, eo beneficium gratius estimabitur quod munificentia uestra solis inclinata precibus exhibebit. Lator hic presentium affinis et familiaris noster tuitioni uestre per nos commendari desiderat, sperans sibi successum optinere si uobis obsequentium eum numero uelitis ascribere. Et eum uero multa et animi liberalitas et literarum copia 5 comendat ad gratiam, ut quod alio petente cupit assequi, in id sit ipse propter se dignus admitti. Quem cum prece nostra iuueritis opemque sibi in necessitate contuleritis, et ipsum seruitio obnoxium, et nos uobis amplioris gratie debitores efficietis.

## 279

A request to help R. who has business (apparently) in the royal court.

Si de uestra in nos beniuolentia confidimus, nostra non id exigunt erga uos merita, sed operatur sola uestra liberalitas et gratia. Vos tamen id pro certo nosse uolumus quod seruitio uestro animo promtissimo parati sumus. Idem uero de gratia uestra sperantes, affectuose rogamus ut negotium amici nostri presentium latoris R. diligenter audiatis, et illud per seruitium suum apud domnum regem promouendo, 5 nos et seruitii et gratie debitores habeatis. Valete.

## 280

Letters dimissory for A., a deacon, who wishes to stay in another diocese and country where he has been studying.

Lator presentium A. honeste apud nos conuersatus a nobis susceptus est in clerum, et ad diaconatus gradum canonice promotus. Quem quidem literarum studia ad uestram usque prouinciam secutum, uestre ut asserit mores gentis et amicitia sancta eatenus deuinxerunt, ut natale solum tanta cupiat compensare dulcedine et ibidem

---

277 4 quecumque] B *adds* honori, *cancelled*   4 comidis B, *perhaps for* comodis (*if so, read* uestris)
278 G, no. 301; B, fo. 194v.
4 optime B
279 G, no. 302; B, fo. 194v.
280 G, no. 304; B, fo. 195v.

---

[1] Presumably a relative by marriage (*affinis*).

5 nostra cum licentia conuersando uite consummare curricula. Illius ergo uotis et precibus tandem acquiescentes ad sublimitatem uestram cum huius scripti testimonio eum transmittimus, rogantes quatinus ob amorem Dei et reuerentiam suscepti ordinis ipsum benigne recipiatis, et in ordine suo apud uos ministrare permittatis, et si uite honestas meruerit ad ulteriora uelitis promouere, quem liberum et a nostra 10 de cetero subiectione absolutum uestre si placet obedientie deseruire permittimus. Valete.

## 281

On behalf of R., the bearer.

Vir honeste eruditionis et illibate opinionis lator presentium R. nostris apud beniuolentiam uestram se postulat precibus adiuuari. Cui cum in petitione probabili deesse nec possumus nec debemus, liberalitatem uestram exoratam habere desideramus, pro eo et cum eo rogantes quatinus pietatis intuitu et precum nostrarum 5 interuentu eum in petitione sua exaudiatis, et negotium eius quod penes uos est caritatiue promoueatis, ut ipsum uobis obnoxium seruitio et nos gratie debitores constituatis.

## 282

Acknowledgement of a letter from a distant friend.[1]

Gratum michi pater karissime munus existimo, quotiens directis a sanctitate uestra literis, que circa uos sunt statu perseuerare incolumi recognosco. Exultat siquidem spiritus meus et diem sibi festum agit homo meus ille interior, cum amicum meum domnumque carissimum sanum et incolumem et in cunctis agentem prospere, 5 litteris aut nuntio de uobis leta referente intelligo. Agit hoc illa caritas in uirtutibus optinens principatum que amicorum mentes insolubili sibi lege confederans, locali distantes spatio, unit spiritu, affectione coniungit et absentes sibi presentes asidue potenter intus operante uirtute constituit. Hec a memorie mee pagina deleri non poterit, hanc nulla rerum uicissitudo perturbabit, quin uestris maneam et deuotus 10 obsequiis et promtus obedire mandatis. Valete.

## 283

To a monastic superior, asking him to readmit the bearer, who had followed his late father, Simon, into a stricter order.[2]

Lator hic presentium, zelum ut fatetur habens aliquando sine scientia, patrem quondam suum Simonem secutus, a cetu uestro quod modo lacrimabiliter deplorat

281 G, no. 308; B, fo. 196.
282 G, no. 311; B, fo. 196v.
283 G, no. 317; B, fo. 197v.

---

[1] This is in style characteristic of Gilbert's early letters, and is evidently addressed to someone who is or has been his superior—possibly to Archbishop Theobald.
[2] 'zelum...habens' suggests this rather than apostasy.

minus considerate discessit. Qui modo compunctus et conuersus ad cor,[1] rerum
edoctus experientia quam graue sit a fratrum unitate seiungi, pulsat et suspirat ad
uos, supplicans et totis anime uiribus expetens, ut misericordie sibi ianuas aperiatis 5
et ipsum utpote de cetero prudentius et perfectius obediturum intra numerum
uestrum admittatis. Vnde quia reuertenti nunquam sinum claudit ecclesia, magis
super uno gaudens conuerso ad penitentiam quam super multis qui penitentia non
indigent, cum pulsante pulsamus,[2] cum supplicante preces effundimus, quatinus
amore Dei fraterneque caritatis intuitu iram si qua aduersus eum concepta est, de 10
corde sibi remittatis et petitionem tam eius quam nostram si absque lesione ordinis
uestri fieri potest et sine scandalo, clementer exaudiatis. Valete.

---

[1] Cf. Ps. lxxxiv. 9.  [2] Cf. Luc. xv. 17; xi. 9–10; etc.

# V

# CHARTERS OF GILBERT FOLIOT AS ABBOT OF GLOUCESTER
## 1139–1148

### Nos. 284–8

**284**

[1144] Agreement between the abbot and monks and Walter son of Richard son of Pons,[1] in the presence of Roger earl of Hereford, by which the abbot, with his chapter's consent, grants his manor of Glasbury (Herefs) to Walter, to be held of Roger de Tosny; and Walter, with the consent of his brother Richard, grants his land of Eastleach (Martin, Glos) with all its appurtenances to the abbey, to be held of the abbey's patron, Roger earl of Hereford; with the condition that Glasbury church with all its appurtenances shall remain in possession of the abbot and monks, and the church of Eastleach in possession of the prior and monks of (Great) Malvern, to whom it had been granted by Walter some time before. The agreement was confirmed by Earl Roger, and Walter pledged himself to obtain Roger de Tosny's confirmation; both sides made Earl Roger their surety.

See above, nos. 28, 288.

Notum sit omnibus tam presentibus quam futuris quod anno mcxliiii ab incarnatione Domini et Salvatoris nostri Iesu Christi, inter domnum Gilebertum abbatem et monachos Glouc(estrie) et Walterum filium Ricardi filii Pontii, in presentia domni Rogeri comitis Hereford(ie) et proborum hominum eius, hec est facta conuentio.

Abbas ipse consensu totius capituli sui, concessit Waltero et heredibus suis in 5 perpetuum habendum manerium suum Glasburiam et tenendum de Rogero de Thoeni. Et Walterus, assensu Ricardi fratris sui, concessit ecclesie beati Petri Glouc(estrie) terram suam de Estlecche cum omnibus appendiciis suis, habendam in perpetuum et tenendam de Rogero comite Hereford(ie) ipsius ecclesie beati Petri aduocato; hac tamen conditione, ut ecclesia Glasbur(ie) cum terris et decimis et 10 omnibus ad eam pertinentibus in manu et possessione abbatis et monachorum Glouc(estrie) sicut hactenus ita et semper permaneat, et ecclesia de Estlecche in manu et possessione prioris et monachorum de Maluerna, quibus ex dono predecessorum Walteri iamdiu assignata est, illibata et inconuulsa consistat. Hanc commutationem inter eos factam concessit domnus Rogerus comes Hereford(ie), 15 et Walterus pepigit abbati et monachis quod hanc ipsam conuentionem faceret concedere Rogerum de Thoeni et carta sua firmare absque omni abbatis uel monachorum grauamine uel pecunie uel laboris impensa. Et ut ista conuentio inter eos firma consisteret, uterque alteri dompnum Rogerum comitem Hereford(ie) istius conuentionis tenende fideiussorem ⟨Gb, fo. 205⟩ concessit et ipse se in istud 20 plegium misit. Hiis testibus.

**284** PRO Chancery Records, C 150, Cart. Gloucester, fos. 75 v (Ga) *and* 204 v (Gb) (clearly derived from different originals). *Printed: Cart. Gloucester*, I, 311; II, 246–7.
1–2 anno...Christi Ga; anno Domini mcxliiii Gb    2 Gilbertum Gb    4 eius *om.* Gb
6–7 suum...Thoeni Ga; suum de Glasbur(ia) Gb    8–10 habendam...aduocato Ga; in escambium Gb    10 de Glasbur(ia) Gb    13 de Maluerna Ga; Maluernie Gb    14–18 est illibate...
impensa Ga; illibata est et inconuulsa permaneat Gb    18 ista] hec Gb

---

[1] I.e. Walter de Clifford, ancestor of the house of Clifford: see A. S. Ellis in *Trans. Bristol and Gloucs. Arch. Soc.* IV (1879–80), 165–6; *Ancient Charters*, ed. J. H. Round (PRS), p. 24 and note; *DNB*; Lloyd, II, 477–8 n., 506–7, cf. 438.

## 285

[1139–48] Grant by the abbot and convent to Hugh and Robert his son and Ralph son of Ralph of the whole land of the monk Leoric,[1] their predecessor, at Pennon and Llancarfan (Glam), with all its appurtenances; to be held for the same service as Leoric held it. Hugh, Robert and Ralph have done fealty to the donors, have granted firm peace to them and confirmed it on oath.

Gloucester abbey acquired the ancient Welsh monastery of Llancarfan between 1093 and 1104, but did not entirely dislodge the hereditary 'monks' of the *clas*. A *modus vivendi* was established by a series of arrangements between the old tenants and the new, of which this was apparently one (see *GF*, p. 142; Conway Davies, II, 506 ff., esp. 517 ff.).

Sciant presentes et futuri quod ego G(ilebertus) abbas Glouc(estrie) totusque conuentus eiusdem concessimus Hugoni et Roberto filio eius et Radulfo filio Radulfi, apud Penn(un) et Lancaruan totam terram Leorici monachi antecessoris eorum, cum pratis et ceteris eidem terre pertinentibus; tenendam de nobis pro
5 eodem seruitio quod idem Leoricus et antecessores eius domnis suis ex ea fecerunt; hac conditione, quod prefatus H(ugo) et Robertus et Radulfus fidelitatem uite et menbrorum atque terreni honoris michi G(ileberto) et ecclesie nostre et monachis nostris, a die illa usque in sempiternum fecerunt, pacem firmam omnibus nostris dederunt, sacramento confirmauerunt, apud Glouc(estriam). Hiis testibus [...].

## 286

[1139–48] Grant, with the convent's consent, to the sacrists[2] for the lighting of the high altar of the abbey church, of the church of St Mary before the abbey gate (de Lode), with the other churches subject to it—St Giles, Maisemore, St Lawrence, Barnwood and St Leonard, Upton (i.e. Upton St Leonard's, Glos)—with all their appurtenances.

The practice of subdividing the revenues of an abbey for specific purposes and assigning their administration to leading obedientiaries was very common in the larger Benedictine houses in the mid-twelfth century and later.

Sciant omnes presentes et absentes quod ego Gilebertus Dei gratia ecclesie Gloucestrensis abbas, cum communi consilio et consensu et etiam rogatu totius conuentus mei, concessi ecclesiam sancte Marie que ⟨est⟩ ante portam monasterii, cum aliis ecclesiis sibi subiectis, scilicet ecclesiam sancti Egidii de Maismora, ecclesiam sancti
5 Laurencii de Bernewoda, ecclesiam sancti Leonardi de Uptona, ad luminare altaris sancti Petri apostoli imperpetuum, in manus secretariorum cum omnibus pertinen-

285 PRO Chancery Records, C 150, Cart. Gloucester, fo. 162 (no. 652). *Printed: Cart. Gloucester,* II, 138.
286 Gloucester Cathedral, Dean and Chapter, Reg. B, p. 56.

---

[1] The name appears to be a version of 'Leofric'; but it may be an Anglo-Norman scribe's attempt at some Welsh name. The 'monk' may have been Lifris (= Leofric) of Llancarfan, son of Bishop Herewald and author of the *Life of St Cadoc* (see *CS*, pp. 287 ff.; above, no. 70).
[2] I.e. the sacrist and his successors. For the churches cf. *Taxatio*, p. 224; *PN Glos*. II, 161, 170–1, 286.

tiis suis retinendas atque habendas. Hoc autem pro amore Dei et eiusdem sancti Petri apostoli et pro salute anime mee totiusque conuentus mei feci, cunctis successoribus meis mandans et implorans quatinus ab eis ratum omnino habeatur in nomine Domini nostri Iesu Christi. Amen.     10

## 287

[1139–48] Grant, with the convent's consent, to the sacrists for the lighting of the high altar of the abbey church, of the vill of Rodley (Glos)[1] with two sheaves (i.e. two-thirds) of the tithe of the abbot's demesne in *Portfeld'* (now Portlands Nab in Newnham), in *Cundel* (?) and in Bollow, with the mill and fishing-rights in the Severn and all their tithes, with the wood of *Sudruge* (now Sutridge in Longhope, Glos) with its assarts and their tithes and revenues.

Sciant omnes presentes et absentes quod ego Gilebertus Dei gratia ecclesie Gloucestrensis abbas, cum communi consilio et consensu totius conuentus mei, concessi uillam de Rudela ad luminare altaris sancti Petri apostoli imperpetuum, in manus secretariorum, cum duabus garbis decime dominici nostri in Portfeld' et in Cundel (?) et in Bol', cum molendino et piscariis in Sabrina et omnibus decimis eorum, 5 cum bosco de Sudruge et cum assartis et decimis eorum et cum omnibus exitibus suis retinendam atque habendam. Hoc autem pro amore Dei et eiusdem sancti Petri apostoli feci, cunctis successoribus meis mandans et implorans quatinus ab eis ratum habeatur, in nomine Domini nostri Iesu Christi. Amen.

## 288

[1139–48] Grant with the convent's consent to the precentor, for buying parchment and ink, for increasing the library, and for the monks' needs (?), of the church of St Keneder, Glasbury (Herefs),[2] with its tithes, and the tithes of the demesnes of *Talgart* and of Brecon, as the monks had them—that is, tithes of corn, of game, of freshwater eels;[3] also five shillings and a pig which the sons of Sexil render annually for their land, and the tithe which the monks used to have from the demesne of Rerdric, and two shillings which Roger de Baskerville used to give the monks annually for a piece of land.

Notum sit tam presentibus quam futuris quod ego G(ilebertus) abbas Glouc(estrie) concessi cantori Glouc(estrie) ecclesiam sancti Chenedri de Glasbiria cum omnibus decimis ad eam pertinentibus, et decimam de dominio de Talgart et decimam de

---

**287** Gloucester Cathedral, Dean and Chapter, Reg. B, p. 56.
4 duabis MS
**288** Gloucester Cathedral, Dean and Chapter, Reg. B, p. 500.

---

[1] In Westbury on Severn. For the place-names see *PN Glos.* III, 193, 200–1, 203 (identifying the sacrist's holding in 'Rodele' in *Taxatio*, p. 171b, with Rodley rather than Ruddle).
[2] Cf. no. 284. St Keneder, Glasbury, and the tithe of Brecon had been granted to Gloucester by Bernard of Neufmarché in Abbot Serlo's time (in 1088, according to *Cart. Gloucester*, I, 80, cf. 314, 122; cf. K. Hughes in *SEBC*, p. 191).
[3] Literally, 'from the killing of eels of the lake (or mere)'.

dominio de Brechenio sicut ⟨p. 501⟩ eam monachi Glouc(estrie) soliti sunt habere—
5 hoc est de bladio, de uenatione, de occisione de anguillis de mara, et quinque solidos
et porcum quos filii Sexil debent dare pro terra sua singulis annis, et decimam quam
solent habere de dominio Rerdric, et duos solidos quos Rogerus de Bascheuilla
solebat dare monachis singulis annis pro quadam terra; et omnia hec consilio et
petitione conuentus concessi et inconcusse firmaui in capitulo, ut cantor illa habeat
10 imperpetuum, ad emendum percamenum et incaustum, ad augendum armarium
et ad opus claustrensium.

**288** 4 *? Corrected to* Brecheneo

# VI

# CHARTERS OF GILBERT FOLIOT AS BISHOP OF HEREFORD
## 1148–1163

### Nos. 289–349

**289**

[5 September 1148] Profession to Archbishop Theobald

Ego Gilebertus Herefordensis ecclesie electus, et a te reuerende pater T(eobalde) sancte Cant(uariensis) ecclesie archiepiscope et totius Britannie primas antistes consecrandus, tibi et omnibus successoribus tuis tibi canonice succedentibus debitam et canonicam obedientiam et subiectionem me exhibiturum fore profiteor.

**290**

[1148–54 (?)] Description and confirmation of the making of four cemeteries free of secular dues, at the request of Nicholas of Maund (?) and the prior and monks of Brecon, and revision of rights and endowments of the mother church of St Mary of Bodenham (Herefs) in whose parish they lay. The chapel of Maund may be served three days a week, those at *Ruberh* and *Ferna*[1] twice. Those who have right of sanctuary in the cemetery of Broadfield (Herefs) are to attend service either at the mother church or at the chapel of Maund[2] not far away. They are to attend service at the mother church on certain specified days and pay dues as of old. Nicholas of Maund has granted one fardel (measure of land) to the church, half at Maund, half at Risbury, and one half of his possessions at Maund—and the whole of them after the death of his brother Robert, clerk, or his entry into religion; also one third of his whole substance at the time of his death, and rights of common in his pasture in both Maund and Risbury; Nicholas pledged faith to this grant in (Gilbert's) hand in the presence of Ralph, prior of Brecon, and the parishioners of Bodenham. The others with burial rights in the cemetery of Maund gave two acres from each fardel. Robert de St-Aubin, who holds *Rueberch* in the parish of Bodenham, gave the whole tithe of *Rueberch* and half a fardel there, with a coppice, meadow, rights of common in the pasture and one holding. Henry de *Ferna* gave half a fardel with a holding and rights of common pasture; the men of Broadfield one fardel and common pasture.

*Cogente guerra* perhaps suggests a date before 1154; it seems to have been the circumstances of the anarchy which led Gilbert to consecrate cemeteries as sanctuaries elsewhere. But in places near the Welsh border, *guerra* might flare up at any time.

**289** *Original:* Canterbury Cathedral, Chapter Archives, Chartae Antiquae C 115 (24) (6 in. × 2 in.). *On the dorse (in a different hand):* MCXLVIII dominice incarnationis anno, Theob' Cant' archiepiscopus et totius Anglie primas sacrauit Gilebertum Herefordensem episcopum in transmarinis partibus, non' Septembris apud sanctum Audomarum, asistentibus et cooperantibus duobus episcopis, Tidrico Ambianensi et Nicholao Camberacensi. Ea enim tempestate idem archiepiscopus propter fidelitatem sancte Romane ecclesie exulabat. *Copies* (of profession) in *ibid.* C 117 (prof. roll) and BM Cotton MS Cleop. E. i, fos. 36v–37 (old 35v–36). *Listed* by C. E. Woodruff, *Trans. St Paul's Ecclesiological Soc.* VII (1911–15), 168 (prints dorse in full).

**290** BM Harl. MS 6976, fos. 15–16 (T) (Hutton's transcript, seventeenth century, from lost Cart. Brecon, fo. 53; cf. Davis, nos. 69–70); Bodl. MS Carte 108, fo. 266 (eighteenth-century transcript of Brecon charters) (S: defective at the start). The first sentence is quoted by Tanner, Bodl. MS Tanner 342, fo. 171v from a reg. Brecon, presumably that noted in his *Notitia Monastica,* ed. J. Nasmith (Cambridge, 1787), fo. Oooo (Brecknockshire, no. 1) as 'penes Gulielmum Brewster M. D. Herefordiae'. Text as T; select variants of S.

---

[1] ? The Vern in Bodenham.      [2] Cf. *Herefs. D.B.* p. 105.

Sciant presentes et posteri quod ego Gilebertus episcopus Herefordensis cogente guerra quatuor cimiteria feci in parochia ecclesie sancte Marie de Bodeham propter refugium, rogatu Nicholai ⟨de Machna et (?)⟩ prioris et conuentus Brecon'. Vt igitur matris ecclesie sit salua dignitas, nec capelle cimiteriorum maius ab ea 5 requirant seruitium quam coram me et clericis meis diffinitum et determinatum fuit [ . . . ] Ex prioris de Brecch(onia) cuius est ecclesia de Bodeham et parochianorum consensu hoc presenti scripto et seruitium et donationes parochianorum episcopali auctoritate confirmo. Capella de Machna tribus diebus in ebdomada deseruiatur; capella uero de Ruberh et illa de Ferna duabus. Illi autem qui refugium in cimiterio 10 de Bradefeld habent ad seruitium ueniant uel ad matrem ecclesiam uel ad capellam de Machna que satis propinqua est. Die sancte Pasche et diebus Rogationum et die Ascensionis, ⟨T, fo. 15 v⟩ Pentecostes, Natalis Domini et in Capite ieiunii, Dominica Palmarum et tribus proximis diebus ante Pascha, et in omnibus festiuitatibus sancte Marie et in solemnitate Omnium Sanctorum ad matrem ecclesiam sancte Marie de 15 Bodeham parochiani communiter ad seruitium ueniant. Consuetudines uero similiter quas ipsa mater ecclesia habere solet antiquitus communiter faciant et teneant.

Donationes huiusmodi sunt. Nicholaus de Machna dedit ecclesie sancte Marie de Bodeham unum ferdellum terre, dimidium apud Machna et dimidium apud 20 Risbergh, et medietatem omnium rerum quas possidet apud Machne, et totam post obitum fratris sui Roberti clerici uel si idem Robertus se ad religionem dederit; dedit etiam tertiam partem portionis sue cum obierit totius substantie que sibi contigerit; preterea communionem pasture sue et de Machna et de Risbergh. Hec ipse Nicholaus affidauit in manu mea coram Radulfo priore de Brecch(onia) et 25 parochianis de Bodeham.

Ceteri uero de cimiterio de Machna dederunt de unoquoque ferdello duas acras. Robertus quidem de sancto Albino qui Rueberch tenet in parochia de Bodeham dedit totam decimam suam de Rueberch et dimidium ibi ferdellum terre cum bosculo quodam et prato et communionem pasture et unam mansuram. Henricus 30 uero de Ferna dedit dimidium ferdellum cum mansura et communionem pasture tam in bosco quam in plano. ⟨T, fo. 16⟩ Illi de Bradefeld unum ferdellum dederunt cum quatuor mansuris et communionem pasture. Quia igitur necessitate cogente hec quatuor cimiteria feci in parochia ecclesie sancte Marie de Bodeham rogatu prioris et fratrum de Brecch(onia) quorum ipsa ecclesia est, concedo et hoc similiter 35 presenti scripto confirmo ut capelle eorum libere sint et quiete ab omni temporali consuetudine.

**290** 1–9 Sciant. . .duabus *om.* S   2–3 sancte *and* rogatu Nicholai. . .Brecon' *om.* T; *supplied from Tanner MS 342, fo. 171 v, an extract ending at this point. Tanner, however, reads* Nicholai prioris. *Since the donor was called Nicholas and the prior Ralph (see below), it seems clear that some words have fallen out*   6 fuit [ . . . ] *some words seem to have fallen out*   11 sancti TS   23 Risgh (?) S   36 consuedine T

**291**

[1148–55] Confirmation to Brecon priory of the grant by Walter del Mans and his wife Agnes of the church of Humber (Herefs) with its appurtenances.

The grant was confirmed by Roger earl of Hereford (*Cart. Brecon*, XIV, 149): his death in 1155 gives a *terminus* for nos. 290–1. Cf. *Taxatio*, p. 159.

Gilebertus Dei gratia Herefordensis episcopus omnibus sancte matris ecclesie filiis, salutem ⟨fo. 266v⟩ in Domino.

Nouerit uniuersitas uestra nos concessisse et confirmasse ecclesiam de Humbre priori et monachis sancti Iohannis de Brech(onia), quam Walterus del Mans et uxor eius Agnes coram nobis in perpetuam elemosinam cum omnibus pertinentiis suis 5 supradictis monachis ecclesie sancti Iohannis de Brech(onia) dederunt; et ne id quod pie et caritatis intuitu gestum est tempore procedente alicuius malignitate in irritum reuocetur, dictam donationem sigilli nostri appositione muniuimus.

**292**

[1148–55] Confirmation to Brecon priory of grant[1] by Roger earl of Hereford, of mills at and above Burghill (Herefs), with appurtenances, to settle a claim between the monks of Brecon and the canons of Llanthony (?) on the church of Burghill.

Vniuersis sancte matris ecclesie filiis G(ilebertus) Herefordensis episcopus, salutem et benedictionem.

Notum sit omnibus presentibus et futuris Rogerum comitem Hereford(ie) concessisse ecclesie sancti Iohannis de Brech(onia) molendinum de Burchull et molendinum quod superius est, cum terris et consuetudinibus omnibus que ad illa 5 pertinent, ita libere et quiete in perpetuum possidenda quemadmodum ille in dominio tenuit et antecessores sui: et hoc propter calumpniam deponendam que erat inter monachos de Brecch(onia) et canonicos Lant(onie) de ecclesia de Burchull; et quia hoc audiuimus et uidimus[2] hoc presenti scripto nostro confirmamus et episcopali auctoritate testificamur.                                                                                                    10

291 Bodl. MS Carte 108, fo. 266 (eighteenth-century transcript of Brecon charters; noted as on fo. 54 of lost cart. in Hutton's transcript in BM Harl. MS 6976, fo. 6; also note in Bodl. Tanner MS 342, fo. 171v). *Printed: Cart. Brecon*, XIV, 21.
292 Bodl. MS Carte 108, fo. 266v (eighteenth-century transcript of Brecon charters); note of in Tanner MS 342, fo. 171v (from lost cartulary: see no. 290). *Printed: Cart. Brecon*, XIV, 21.
8 Lant(onie)] Sant' *MS*

---

[1] *Cart. Brecon*, XIV, 150.
[2] Cf. I Joh. i. 1.

**293**

[17 July 1157] Notification by Bishops Richard of London, Rotrou of Évreux, Robert of Bath, William of Norwich, Hilary of Chichester, Gilbert of Hereford and Robert of Lincoln, judges delegate of Pope Adrian IV, that Silvester, abbot of St Augustine's abbey, Canterbury, has made his profession to Archbishop Theobald.

The famous dispute on the exemption of St Augustine's lasted from the late eleventh century until 1397; from the late twelfth century on, the abbey was usually victorious. See Knowles in *Downside Review*, L (1932), 401 ff., esp. 410; E. John in *Bull. of the John Rylands Library*, XXXIX (1956–7), 390–415; and for the documents on which the abbey based their case, W. Levison, *England and the Continent in the eighth century* (Oxford, 1946), Appendix I.

Vniuersis sancte ecclesie filiis et fidelibus Ricardus Lundoniensis, Rotrocus Ebroicensis, Robertus Bathoniensis, Willelmus Norwicensis, Hilarius Cicestrensis, Gill(ebertus) Herefordensis, Robertus Lincolniensis episcopi salutem.

Rerum gestarum memoria prouide litteris committitur ne tractu temporis ea que
5 semel recte terminata sunt, iteratis refragationibus perturbentur. Inde est quod uniuersitati uestre presentis scripti attestatione notum facimus quod controuersia temporibus nostris nata que inter uenerabilem patrem nostrum Theob(aldum) Cantuariensis ecclesie archiepiscopum et Siluestrum abbatem monasterii sancti Augustini Cant(uariensis) super facienda sibi professione ab eodem abbate uersaba-
10 tur, iuxta mandatum domini pape Adriani sub presentia nostra hoc modo terminata est. Dederat enim ipsi abbati prenominatus papa in mandatis precipiendo quatenus infra triginta dies post susceptionem litterarum suarum omni appellatione et occasione remota eam eidem archiepiscopo faceret sicut aliquem abbatum illius monasterii alicui archiepiscoporum Cantuariensium fecisse constabat. Sed quia
15 abbas diffitebatur sibi constare predecessores suos hanc professionem fecisse, licet hoc in regno publice innotuisset, religiosi uiri tactis sacrosanctis euangeliis iurauere se uidisse et audisse Hugonem eiusdem Siluestri decessorem memoratam professionem Willelmo pie recordationis Cantuariensi archiepiscopo more debito sine contradictione fecisse. Ad hec etiam uidimus scedulas in quibus professiones multo-
20 rum abbatum ipsius monasterii manifeste nobis scripte apparuerunt. Facta itaque fide abbati et his qui aderant, predecessorum suorum secutus uestigia, professionem in hec uerba fecit et crucis signo compleuit atque muniuit. 'Ego Siluester abbas ecclesie sanctorum apostolorum Petri et Pauli et beati Augustini primi Anglorum

---

**293** *Original* (16½ in. × 14⅘ in.): Canterbury Cathedral, Chapter Archives, Chartae Antiquae, A 51, and duplicate, A 49; also in the chronicle of Gervase of Canterbury.[1] (We print the text of A 51). *Printed: Acta Chichester*, no. 21; Gervase, I, 164–5. Seals of four of seven bishops survive, including Gilbert's (red wax on yellow silk cords). *Endorsements:* Professio Siluestri abbatis sancti Augustini Cant' Theobaldo archiepiscopo facta ad preceptum Adriani pape. Inseratur post ii bullam.

---

[1] Gervase adds the following: 'Facta est hec professio apud Northamtoniam, anno gratie MCLVII, Henrici regis secundi anno tertio, mense Iulio xvito kal. Augusti, presentibus episcopis octo, abbatibus xii, ipso quoque rege Henrico et quampluribus aliis tam de transmarinis quam de partibus Anglicanis.'

archiepiscopi promitto sancte Dorobernensi ecclesie et tibi reuerende pater Theob(alde), eiusdem ecclesie archiepiscope, tuisque successoribus canonicam per omnia 25 obedientiam.' Ex his igitur intelleximus quod nulla de cetero inter ipsorum successores de facienda professione contradictio debeat instaurari.

**294**

[1161–3] Settlement, as judge delegate of Pope Alexander (III), of the case between John, clerk, and Reginald of Pagham on the church of Crediton (?) (Devon): each took half the church.

On the outbreak of the papal schism in 1159, Henry II forbade appeals to Rome until he had decided which was the true Pope. It is most unlikely that Gilbert would have acted as a judge delegate for Alexander III before the decision was taken c. November 1160.[1] This letter may therefore be dated 1161–3.

Dilectis sibi in Domino uniuersis sancte matris ecclesie filiis frater G(ilebertus) Herefordensis ecclesie minister, salutem que nunc est et quam speramus a Domino.

Que litis inquietudine quandoque turbata sunt, ipsius sopito fomite denuo reuocantur ad pacem. Que nimirum inter aliquos reformata, ne facile quibusdam emergentibus causis euanescat, ut pactis legitimis firmanda est sic et excipienda 5 scripto, et in perpetuam sui soliditatem litterarum memoria testificanda pariter est et roboranda. Noscat itaque uestra discretio causam que inter Iohannem clericum et Reginaldum de Pagaham super ecclesia de Credintun' diu agitata est, que etiam a patre nostro domno papa Alexandro delegata est ut ipsam diligenter audiremus, et rationibus partium hinc inde diligenter auditis et cognitis, ipsam remoto appel- 10 lationis obstaculo mediante iustitia decideremus, in hunc tandem modum conquieuisse. Nam cum Iohannes adducta testium copia iamdictam ecclesiam in integrum sibi restitui postulasset, Reginaldus esse sciens ambigua fata causarum, anticipando iudicium integram medietatem iamdicte ecclesie Iohanni per omnia concessit, sicque cum eo transigendo liti finem imposuit. Elegit enim Iohannes 15 oblatam sibi ecclesie portionem potius in pace suscipere quam testes suos probationibus et iuramentis honerare. Tactis igitur euangeliis utrimque iuratum est ut neuter alterum sua de cetero portione fraudet, sed uterque alteri ius suum integrum illibatumque conseruet—sane aliquo ipsorum altero tamen superstite decedente, iure suo sibi in partis alterius recuperatione saluo per omnia permanente. Quod 20 quia coram nobis actum est, nos ad finem pacis cuncta redigi cupientes approbauimus et transactioni in hunc modum inite assensum prebuimus, ipsam ut in perpetuum conualescat, presenti scripto et sigilli nostri appositione testificando confirmauimus.

**294** G, no. 129; B, fo. 141 v.
13 fata] fc'a B    20 recuperatore B

---

[1] *JS Epp.* I, 263 ff.; cf. Saltman, pp. 45 ff., 543.

**295**

[December 1152] Report to Pope Eugenius III on the case between Henry and the monks of Ely, as papal judge delegate. Gilbert had been acting on a mandate to make the monks restore to Henry whatever he could prove had been taken from him after the restitution of the manor of Stetchworth to him. The first issue was the date of the restitution: the monks said it had been made by Bishop Nigel of Ely *c.* 12 May (1150), Henry claimed it had been made by the archbishop of Canterbury and the bishop of Chichester in mid Lent (1150). Henry failed to establish his point, and before judgement could be given on the other issue, renewed his appeal to the Pope.

The chronology of this complex case has been discussed most recently by Dr E. O. Blake in *Liber Eliensis*, pp. 405–7; the documents are all printed there, pp. 344 ff. What follows summarizes Dr Blake's conclusions. Henry was a clerk, son of William the Breton, archdeacon of Ely; he possessed a charter from Bishop Hervey to William, granting the manor of Stetchworth (Cambs). Some time before 1150 Henry visited Rome and had his right to Stetchworth acknowledged. The monks could have challenged this on the ground that Bishop Hervey's alienation was illegal—and Stetchworth seems to have been reclaimed by Bishop Nigel *c.* 1133–5 on this ground. Instead they challenged the authenticity of the charter. Henry went to Rome again and on his return was acquitted before Archbishop Theobald and Bishop Hilary of Chichester of forgery (mid Lent 1150); on the basis of this Bishop Nigel formally restored the manor of Stetchworth to Henry. This was the restoration acknowledged by the monks, while Henry evidently claimed that his acquittal was in effect a restoration, and thus that he had been restored about seven or eight weeks earlier than the monks admitted. But the issue of right was still not settled, and after various démarches Canterbury and Chichester, again appointed delegates, heard the case once more, including Henry's claim for damages since possession had not been restored. This time the monks appealed, and Eugenius III delegated the case to Gilbert, instructing him to settle first the question of damages, then, if the monks wished ('si...agere uoluerint', *Liber Eliensis*, pp. 352–3), to settle the question of right. No. 295 describes the pleading before Gilbert, which took place at Northampton on 18 Nov. (1152) and was carried on in London on 7 Dec., but suspended by Henry's appeal. Henry failed to prosecute his appeal, and on 28 Sept. 1153 Pope Anastasius IV settled the case in favour of the monks: he also issued a mandate to Theobald and Gilbert to put them in possession, and if Henry did not reopen proceedings within a year to adjudge the right to the monks (*Liber Eliensis*, pp. 358–61). The year elapsed, and in no. 296 Gilbert executed the papal decision (in or after Sept. 1154). At some subsequent date he issued a mandate to Henry and a group of his associates to abandon possession of the manor, which they had invaded, on pain of anathema (no. 297).

Patri suo uenerabili et domno summo pontifici Eugenio frater Gilebertus Herefordensis ecclesie minister, pie salutantis affectum et humiliter obsequentis officium.

In causa H(enrici) et monachorum Elyensium, que nobis a munificentia uestra delegata est, acta apud nos sullimitati uestre, pater, presenti scripto notificamus.

**295** Liber Eliensis, iii, 108: Ely, Dean and Chapter, MS, fos. 166v–169 (F); Trinity College, Cambridge, O. 2. 1, fos. 159v–161 (E); Bodl. Laud Misc. 647, fos. 96–7 (Ob); BM Cotton Titus A. i, fos. 44–46v (Cart. Ely) (G). *Printed:* ed. Holtzmann, *PUE,* II, no. 74; ed. E. O. Blake, *Liber Eliensis,* pp. 355–8 (whose text of nos. 295–7 is here reprinted, with minor adaptations to conform with this edition, and with the omission of variants between the manuscripts).
4 sullimitati *Holtzmann*; sullimitatis *MSS*

Litteris uestris nequaquam Henrici sed sola monachorum presentatione susceptis 5
iuxta formam mandati partes euocauimus, opportunum ut sperabamus locum
Warewic, tempus uero IX kalendas Octobris designantes. Quibus suam ipso die in
eodem loco presentiam exhibentibus, quia necessitate prepedita adesse nequiuimus,
[...] in eis significato die ipsis VII idus Octobris apud Sanctum Albanum, locum
ipsis scilicet aditu facilem, nobis uero remotum, constituimus. Vbi enim ipso die eis 10
audientiam prebituri sedissemus, Henricus se nimis festinata utraque citatione
nostra grauatum esse et ob hoc ad agendum minus paratum uenisse ait. Vnde, ne
preter rem nos contentio longa protraheret de loco et tempore, utriusque partis
arbitrio cessimus et, quia locum statui Norðhamtunam, tempus uero octau(as)
beati Martini, utrimque postulatum est. Ipso die nominato iam loco sedimus et 15
ipsis se exhibentibus hoc modo in cause cognitionem processimus: littere uestre in
presentia lecte sunt hoc in mandato complectentes, ut quicquid H(enricus) ab
hominibus monachorum uel ab aliis suggestione ipsorum post factam sibi eius de
qua agitur uille restitutionem legitime probare posset sibi fuisse ablatum, ei
faceremus cum integritate restitui.[1] Quibus perlectis ab Henrico in hunc modum 20
actitatum est: 'cum trecentas libras argenti iuste possem petere, ut tamen modestius
agam, ducentas michi libras huius auctoritate mandati peto restitui, quia post factam
michi restitutionem tantum michi ablatum esse horum uiginti testium assertione
probare paratus sum'. Producti uero uiginti testes tantum dampni illatum sibi
fuisse, ut in sequentibus dicetur, asserebant. Ad hec monachi: 'Restitutio, a qua 25
pendet ablatorum tibi repetitio, per manum dompni Elyensis episcopi tibi facta est
quarto die circa festiuitatem sancti Pancratii emensis iam duobus annis et paucis
mensibus. Possessio autem, de qua agitur, paucarum uirium est, ita ut a nimia eius
ualentia centum esse solidorum tu ipse in presentia domni pape expresseris. Vnde te
iniustum petitorem tempus breue tenuisque possessio manifestant.' Ad hec Henri- 30
cus: 'Tempore quidem, quo dicitis, michi per manum dompni Elyensis episcopi
restitutio facta est, sed et longe ante hoc, media scilicet quadragesima, auctoritate
domni Cantuariensis archiepiscopi et dompni Cicestrensis episcopi eadem michi
uilla restituta est, unde non solum post ultimam, sed et post primam restitutionem
ablata michi peto restitui.' Sciscitantibus uero nobis ab Henrico, quantum dampni 35
medio tempore incurrerit, ipsum medii temporis dampnum in quinquaginta
libras, testibus hoc assentientibus, estimauit. Exinde monachi: 'Domnus papa in
litteris suis eam tantum restitutionem, que tibi in presentia domni Cantuariensis
archiepiscopi et dompni Cicestrensis episcopi non si qua ab eis facta est exprimit;
que quia illa est, quam tibi in eorum presentia dompnus Elyensis episcopus fecit, 40
huius auctoritate rescripti nulla nisi post hanc restitutionem ablata restitui tibi recte
petis.' Ad hec Henricus: 'Domnus papa in litteris suis, etsi iudicem instruendo in
prelocutione restitutionem certam exprimat, mandatum tamen subnectendo nullam

---

**295** 8–9 nequiuimus [...] *Some words, referring to a letter of excuse, seem to be missing*
28 Possessio autem *Holtzmann*; possessionum *MSS*    30 petitorem *nos*; petitionem *MSS*
40 que *MSS*; sed *Holtzmann*

---

[1] *quicquid...restitui* echoes Eugenius III's mandate (*Liber Eliensis*, pp. 352 f.).

exprimit. Vnde quia mandati clausula nullam excludit, ablata et post eam, quam
45 dico restitutionem, michi restitui precipit. Item: quo iure potuit et debuit domnus
papa precipere, ut michi ablata post hanc restitutionem redderentur, eodem iure
precipere potuit et debuit, ut michi et post eam quam dico restitutionem ablata
redderentur. Vnde si horum petitio excluditur, procul dubio a dompni pape
sententia longe receditur.' Ad hec monachi: 'Cum domnus papa in prelocutione
50 exprimat, propter uniformem litterarum consequentiam expressio eadem et circa
mandati clausula⟨m⟩ attendenda est; habet enim auctoritas, ut uerbum semel positum, etsi in oratione non iteretur, frequenter tamen in sequentibus intelligatur. Vnde
cum precedens expressio sequenti quoque mandato annectenda sit, tibi iamdicta
quinquaginta librarum petitio denegatur.' Instantibus itaque monachis, ut secundum
55 eos circa articulum hunc pronuntiaremus, tum quia fauorabiliores sunt rei quam
actores[1] tumque fauorabilis est ecclesia, quam in tante summe petitione grauari
dicebant, nos tamen attendentes H(enrici) querimoniis restitutionis preceptum
indultum esse et, quod ob alicuius fauorem indultum est, ad eius lesionem retor-
quendum non esse, mandati uestri clausulam in nullo coartantes Henrico etiam
60 predictarum quinquaginta librarum petitionem, si eas et post factam sibi restitutionem ablatas sibi probare posset, scripti uestri auctoritate concessimus. Ad hoc
monachi: 'Adhuc te, Henrice, ab harum quinquaginta librarum petitione repellimus, quia restitutionem quam dicis numquam tibi factam fuisse plane [ . . . ] dicimus.'
Cum uero Henricus in huius rei euictionem uiginti testes produceret, data eis
65 audientia omnes ordine in hunc modum non addentes aut dementes aut mutantes
aliquid testificati sunt: 'Ego testificor, quia post factam domno meo H(enrico) in
media quadragesima restitutionem uille de Steuechewrde iam annis duobus
preteritis et aliquot huius anni mensibus uilla illa ducentis libris deterior facta est
consilio et facto monachorum Elyensium et hominum suorum.' Inquirentibus uero
70 nobis, quomodo in media quadragesima Henrico restitutionem factam fuisse
nouerint, responderunt: 'Equidem si per archiepiscopum aut per aliquem iudicem
restitutus fuit, nescimus. Vnum uero scimus, quoniam eo tempore in uillam ipsam
se contulit et per domnum Cantuariensem archiepiscopum et domnum Cicestrensem episcopum restitutum esse nobis facile persuasit.' Ad hec monachi: 'Omnes
75 testes tuos, H(enrice), repellimus, primo quia cuiusdam restitutionis tibi facte se
testes exhibuerunt et postmodum, an eadem unquam tibi facta fuerit, se prorsus
ignorare iam confessi sunt; secundo quia licet serui non sint, eius tamen sunt
conditionis, que proxima est seruituti, ascripti scilicet glebe, qui cum gleba uendi
possunt et dari et tibi in tantum subditi, ut in quodcumque uolueris possint ea qua
80 ipsis prees potestate compelli; tertio ob qualitatem uerborum et testimonii, quorum
tanta identitas est, ut nec ad sillabam differant, ut instructi magis et subornati ad
testificandum quam ueritatis conscii stare uideantur; quarto quia cum dampni tibi
illati testes sint nec tibi pecunia numerata sublata sit, dampnum ipsum per certas

**295** 59 coartantes *Holtzmann*; choortantes *MSS* (cohortantes G)    63 plane [ . . . ] *some words*
*seem to be missing*    78 ascripti *Holtzmann*; asscripta(o) *MSS*    82 quia *Holtzmann*; qui *MSS*

---

[1] Cf. *Digest*, 50, 17, 125.

species non distingunt, ut certam rei de qua agitur habere scientiam intelligantur; quinto quia, cum per nos et homines nostros dampnum tibi illatum asserunt, nullos 85 tamen hominum nostrorum nominibus suis aut certis aliquibus designant indiciis. Quos si designarent, eorum utique circa obiecta innocentiam probaremus. Godar‑ dum uero, quem solum nominant, tempore illati dampni nobis in nullo subiectum fuisse probare parati sumus.' Ad hec Henricus: 'Testes meos repelli propter hec obiecta non conuenit, cum licet non distinguant dampna per species nec datores 90 dampni designent ex nomine, iuxta formam tamen, litteris domni pape expressam, plane testificantur.' Attendens uero Henricus testes suos circa restitutionem, quam maxime querebamus, uacillare quam plurimum, se id, in quo ipsi deficiebant, testimonio dompni Cantuariensis archiepiscopi et dompni Cicestrensis episcopi data sibi die probaturum promisit. Vnde ne obscuritatem ueritas pateretur et 95 iustitiam H(enrici), si qua erat, sententia preceps obrueret, diem sibi octauas beati Andree Lundonie, quo dompni legati et suffraganeorum suorum futurus erat conuentus,[1] graue sustinentibus monachis constituimus. Ipso uero die Lundonie sedentes adhibito nobis domno episcopo Lundoniensi nostri copiam fecimus et, quia Henricus eorum, quos premiserat, neminem exhibebat, per dompnum 100 Lundoniensem episcopum et per personas alias a domno legato, quid super sepe‑ dicta restitutione fateretur, inquisiuimus. Qui negotii penes se gesti non immemor Henrico restitutionem quam dicebat se nunquam fecisse respondit. Deficiente itaque circa hunc articulum Henrico, monachos a sepedicta quinquaginta librarum petitione absoluimus, quas post factam Henrico restitutionem sibi non fuisse 105 ablatas H(enrici) dictis et ratione cognouimus. Monachi⟨s⟩ uero de petitione reliqui, centum scilicet librarum,[2] sibi sententiam dici postulantibus, cum ad pronuntiandum quod sentiebamus operam sapientum consilio preberemus, H(enricus) non expectans sententiam, ad audientiam uestram diem kalendas Augusti nominans appellauit. Monachi uero se in longum protrahi attendentes, 110 audientiam uestram ad 'Quasimodo geniti' appellantes, iniuncte nobis imposuere [. . .] Incolumitatem uestram ecclesie sue diu profuturam in longa tempora conseruet omnipotens Deus.

## 296

[Late 1154] Execution of the decision by Pope Anastasius (IV) on the case between Henry and the monks of Ely on the manor of Stetchworth (Cambs) in favour of the monks.

**295** 100 premiserat *MSS*; promiserat *Holtzmann (perhaps rightly)*   112 longo *MSS*; '*intended for* longa?' *Blake*
**296** Liber Eliensis, iii, 111. MSS as no. 295: F, fo. 170v; E, fo. 162v; Ob, fos. 97v–98; G, fo. 47v; Cambridge University Library, Ely Diocesan Records, Liber M (M), fo. 87. *Printed*: ed. Blake, *Liber Eliensis*, p. 361 (whose text is here reprinted with most of the variants omitted).

---

[1] This is the only known evidence of what seems to have been a provincial council held by Archbishop Theobald in London in December 1152 (cf. *Handbook*, 2nd ed. p. 550).
[2] Henry's claim was for £200, and he assessed the damage between March and May as £50. It is not clear why this figure is £100 not £150.

Dilectis sibi in Domino uniuersis sancte matris ecclesie filiis frater Gilebertus Herfordensis ecclesie minister, gaudia pacis et salutis.

Diffinitionem cause que inter monachos Elyenses et clericum Henricum nomine super manerio de Steuechewrða diu agitata est, et postmodum a bone memorie 5 Anastasio papa terminata, uestre presenti scripto intimare discretioni curauimus, ut antique litis germina ueritatis attestatione prorsus eradicemus. Contenta itaque lite inter predictos monachos et iamdictum clericum, cum post multas appellationes et appellationum prosecutiones in multorum presentia iudicum suis usi sufficienter allegationibus causam pro libito uentillassent, omnibus per rescriptum predicto pape 10 Anastasio declaratis, causa in hunc modum ab ipso decisa est. Monachos in possessionem iamdicti manerii inducendos esse decreuit, et nisi infra annum predictus Henricus cautionem sistendi parendique iudicio super eandem causam prestaret, idem manerium monachis et ipsorum ecclesie in perpetuum confirmandum esse adiudicauit, huiusque ab ipso sic date sententie dompnum Teodbaldum Cantuarien- 15 sem archiepiscopum et nos executores constituit. Apostolico itaque parentes mandato, ipsos in possessionem induximus, et quia elapso iam anno nichil a parte Henrici super sibi designata cautione audiuimus, predictum manerium Elyensi ecclesie in perpetuum apostolica auctoritate confirmamus, et ut ipsi manerium ipsum ab omni reclamatione Henrici et successorum eius quietum habeant eadem 20 auctoritate precipimus.

## 297

[After September 1154] Mandate to Henry and others who had invaded the manor of Stetchworth (Cambs), to leave it on pain of anathema.

Gilebertus Dei gratia Herfordensis episcopus Henrico clerico salutem.

Sicut meminisse potes cum in presentia nostra aduersus fratres nostros monachos Elyenses ex mandato domni pape super manerio de Steuechewrð stares, appellatione ad domnum papam interposita iudicium subterfugisti. Quoniam autem apellationem 5 tuam non es prosecutus, te a possessione predicti manerii auctoritate et mandato domni pape remouemus, et monachos Elyenses in possessionem eandem inducimus. Quod si mandatis nostris temperare renueris te anathematis sententia innodandum noueris. Vobis autem, Radulfe et Rogere et Willelme de Halstede, qui Henrici auctoritate eandem possessionem ingressi estis, apostolica denuntiamus auctoritate 10 ut absque dilatione ab eadem possessione recedatis. Quod si non feceritis, eadem anathematis sententia innodabimini, et ab ea nunquam nisi domni pape auctoritate absoluemini. Val(ete).

**296** 8 usi M; usu *ceteri*
**297** Liber Eliensis, iii, 112. MSS as no. 295: F, fos. 170v–171; E, fo. 162v; Ob, fo. 98; G, fo. 47v; M, fo. 87r–v. *Printed:* ed. Blake, *Liber Eliensis*, pp. 361–2 (whose text is here reprinted, omitting the apparatus).

## 298

[1148–63] Confirmation to Evesham abbey of grants by Hugh son of Roger and his wife Margaret of a cell dedicated to St John the Baptist at Southstone Rock (in Stanford-on-Teme, Worcs)[1] and by Payne de Noyers[2] of the island of *Serpeham* (unidentified) to the same cell; together with an indulgence to benefactors of the cell.

There is no evidence that this cell ever had any conventual life.

Gilebertus Dei gratia Herefordensis episcopus dilectis sibi in Christo uniuersis Hereford(ensis) ecclesie filiis, salutem et in Domino benedictionem.

Notum facimus tam presentibus quam posteris quod Hugo filius Rogeri per petitionem uxoris sue Marg(arete) et assensum, in terra sua de iure et patrimonio eius- dem domine locum quendam qui Sulstan dicitur, ad honorem Dei et reuerentiam 5 beati Iohannis Baptiste fundauit, et carrucatam terre liberam et quietam ab omni seruitio et exactione et subiectione eidem loco concessit, et ipsum locum et bene- ficia illi assignata beato Ecguuino et monachis Eoueshamensibus donauit. Preterea Paganus de Nuers petitione nostra et consilio insulam quandam que dicitur Ser- peh(am) eidem loco concessit. Vt autem omnia beneficia prefato loco concessa rata 10 et inconcussa in perpetuum maneant ipsa eidem loco presenti scripto et sigilli nostri attestatione confirmamus. Omnibus autem eiusdem loci benefactoribus benedic- tionem nostram concedimus. Eis uero qui ob amorem Dei et peccatorum suorum remissionem ibidem in festo sancti Iohannis Baptiste conuenerint et locum de beneficiis suis et elemosinis auxerint, de diuina clementia confisi, beneficiorum et 15 orationum que fiunt in Hereford(ensi) ecclesia participes constituimus, et de pena sibi iniuncta quindecim dies relaxamus. Postremo inhibemus ex parte Dei et nostra ne quis aduersus predictum locum Deo dicatum aliquid aduersi moliatur. Quod si presumpserit maledictionem nostram et Dei indignationem incurrat. Valete.

## 299

[1148–61] Settlement, as judge delegate of Archbishop Theobald, of the case between the abbot of Eynsham abbey and Alan, clerk, of Slaughter (Glos), on the tithes of Naunton (Glos)[3] in favour of Eynsham abbey; Alan is to farm them for his life for a pension of three shillings.

Before 1161 if the archbishop is presumed to be still alive.

**298** BM Cotton MS Vespasian B. xxiv, fo. 17 v (Ev); Harl. 3763, fo. 87 v (Eh) (Carts. Evesham).
3 posteris] futuris Eh    4 Mag. Ev    8 illa Eh    8 Egwino Eh    8 Euesh' Eh    14–15 Eh
*omits* Baptiste *and* et elemosinis    16 fiunt] fuerint Ev    18 quis] aliquis Eh    19 nostram et
Dei indignationem Ev; Dei et nostram Eh
**299** Oxford, Christ Church, Dean and Chapter MS 341, Cart. Eynsham, fo. 22 v. *Printed: Cart. Eynsham*, I, no. 45.

---

[1] See *PN Worcs.* pp. 79–80; in *Chron. Evesham*, p. 75, Payne's isle is spelt 'Serpham'.
[2] Unidentified: for the families of Noyers, see Loyd, *Origins*, p. 74.
[3] See H. E. Salter in *Cart. Eynsham*, I, 62, 63 n., 75 n., 204 n.

Dilectis sibi in Domino uniuersis sancte matris ecclesie filiis Gillebertus Herefordensis ecclesie minister, salutem in Christo.

Nouerit dilectio uestra delegatam nobis a domno et patre nostro Theobaldo
Cant(uariensi) archiepiscopo causam inter abbatem Egneshamie et Alanum
5 clericum de Sloctres super decimis dominii de Newenton', quod est de feodo
Rogerii de Oili, sub hoc tandem transactionis fine in presentia nostra apud Wigor-
n(iam) fuisse terminatam. Memoratus Alanus in iam dictis decimis ius monasterii
et conuentus Egnesham(ie) publiçe recognoscens easdem decimas sub annua
pensione trium solidorum ab abbate et conuentu in posterum tenendas suscepit, ad
10 monasterium Egnesham(ie) ipso decedente cum omni integritate deuoluendas.
Quod quia in irritum nolumus aut in dubium de cetero posse reuocari, presenti
scripto uniuersitati uestre significare et sigilli nostri auctoritate confirmare curauimus. His testibus: Radulfo de Saucei, Willelmo de Sceldeslega, Reginaldo de
Cudinton', Rogero de Cornwelle, Eilrico presbitero de Rollendrith, Hugone
15 Crollebacun, Waltero de Hard(e)pirer', Hugone clerico et multis aliis.

**300**

[*c.* 1148] Gilbert testifies that when he was abbot of Gloucester, Roger son of Hugh Parvus
settled a dispute about a virgate near Quedgeley (Glos) by granting a virgate of 64 acres in
Brookthorpe (Glos) to the abbey, to be held directly of the earl (of Hereford), with the
earl's consent. For this Gloucester cancelled Roger's debt to the abbey and paid 7 marks.

It is difficult to date most of the acts relating to Gloucester abbey with any precision.
No. 300 refers back to his abbacy in a way and on an issue, which suggest that he had
recently ceased to be abbot; if it can be assumed that the earl of Hereford was alive, it cannot
be later than 1155—and the casual references to 'de comite...tenendam', 'comite Herefordensi...assensum prebente', etc., not only suggest this, but would be strange between
1155 and 1200, when there was no earl of Hereford. The reference to his predecessor and the
'refugium pauperum' in no. 301 both suggest an early date, preferably in Stephen's reign.
The endowment of Kilpeck priory (founded 1134) in no. 302 refers to Earl Roger by name,
and so cannot be later than 1155; Maurice the sheriff, in addition, had been superseded by
then.[1] No. 303 establishes a monk of Gloucester as 'prior' of Bromfield (Salop), and was no
doubt approximately contemporary with the foundation of Bromfield, as a dependency of
Gloucester, in 1155.[2]
Nos. 304 and 305 are the only documents of the bishop, apart from no. 303, in which
Gilbert is given his surname 'Foliot'; their protocols are closely similar in other ways too.
Since one is dated in synod and the other in chapter, they were presumably not exactly con-
temporary, but it is likely that their originals were drawn up by a single scribe, and that they

300 PRO Chancery Records, C 150, Cart. Gloucester, fo. 10v. *Printed: Cart. Gloucester*, I,
176–7.

---

[1] Hugh of Kilpeck's charter (BM Add. Charter 19,588), which has two of the same witnesses
and may well have been drawn up on the same occasion, is also witnessed by Gilbert the
precentor of Hereford and Walter archdeacon (of Shropshire)—these suggest a date *c.* 1150–5.
Maurice was sheriff again in 1159–60, but by then the earl was dead.
[2] *Cart. Gloucester*, I, 19–20.

were not far apart in date. No. 305 contains the only known reference to a 'W.' dean of Hereford in this period. This would be suspicious, but for the fact that no less than five copies of this document survive. It is possible that some of these are copies of copies, but in no case can this be proved, and the exemplification at least ought to have been made from the original. There can, indeed, be no reasonable doubt that the dean bore the initial 'W.' in the original. If this was correct, an unknown dean W. must have held office between 1158, when Dean Ralph was still alive, and 1163, by which date Dean Geoffrey was well installed.[1] A date much later than c. 1158 for no. 304 seems improbable, since nos. 305–7 seem to be later than it; we therefore assign to nos. 304–5 the tentative date c. 1158.

In no. 306 the grants of nos. 304–5 are confirmed, and the abbot is empowered to install vicars in the churches of Cowarne (Herefs) and Taynton (Glos); 306 is presumably later than 304–5, although this cannot be regarded as certain, and no. 306 makes no mention of the sacrist or his office. In no. 304 the sacrist is exempted from tithe in Rodley and *Hyda*, apart from an old pension of two shillings to the church of Yarkhill. In no. 308, which is a confirmation of the endowments of the sacrist's office considerably fuller than 304, and seems to confirm and presume nos. 304–7, there is a reference to the abbey's tithe in *Hid'*, which it receives according to a transaction confirmed in a charter which is evidently no. 307. Comparison of these passages in 304 and 308 suggests that no. 307 was granted after 304 and before, perhaps shortly before, 308; once again, this cannot be regarded as certain, but the reference to the pension in no. 308 would be far more logical than that in no. 304 if 307 were already in existence. For these reasons we date 306–8 (presumably in that order) later than 304, c. 1158–63. No. 309 cannot be closely dated.

Gilbertus Dei gratia Herfordensis episcopus dilectis sibi fratribus uniuersis sancte matris ecclesie filiis in Domino, salutem et gratiam.

Quoniam Gloucestr(ie) ecclesie nobis aliquamdiu cura et sollicitudo commissa est, que ad eiusdem ecclesie utilitatem nobiscum uel a nobis acta sunt, interposito scripto memorie tradimus, ut si qua de hiis forte ut assolet emerserit aliquando 5 controuersia, rei geste ueritas, ex hiis que scripta sunt, elucescat; inter cetera igitur et hoc nominatim duximus exprimendum. Hugo Paruus quamdam uirgatam terre iuxta Quedesleyam, olim de predicta ecclesia annua decem solidorum pensione tenendam, susceperat. Cui⟨us⟩ rei ueritatem cum diligentius inquisissemus, ipsum a tempore predecessorum nostrorum usque ad nos annis iam pluribus, predictum 10 debitum minime persoluisse cognouimus. Quia uero ad heredem cum suo onere paterna transit hereditas, aduersus Rogerum Paruum eiusdem Hugonis heredem et filium actionem non solum ob patris debitum sed et ob suum—eo quod et ipse predictos decem solidos iam aliquot annis non persoluisset—instituimus. Quibusdam uero personis suam in hoc operam adhibentibus, lis proposita non iudicio sed 15 transactione et amicabili compositione in hunc modum decisa est. Rogerus predictam tenuram confessus et debitum, ut a lite proposita discederemus, quamdam uirgatam terre sexaginta quatuor acrarum in manerio suo de Brocthrop, ecclesie Gloucestr(ie) non de ipso tenendam sed ab eius tenura et feodo comitis, liberam semper habendam concessit. Nos uero consensu capituli nostri a predicti debiti 20 petitione conquieuimus, et uirgatam terre quam de ecclesia nostra eo usque

---

[1] See *GF*, p. 267; it is possible, but unlikely, that there were two deans called Ralph, and that W. belongs to the early 1150's.

tenuerat a tenura ecclesie liberam de comite inposterum tenendam concessimus et in stabilem transactionis huius auctoritatem assensum comitis impetrauimus. ⟨fo. 11⟩ Predicta uero transactio ne lucrosa nimis foret nobis et onerosa Rogero, 25 septem ei marcas argenti dedimus. Ita harum prestatione quam et debiti pristini acceptilatione, predicte etiam uirgate cessione, comite Hereford(ensi) in hoc assensum prebente, uirgatam de Broctrop in possessionem ecclesiasticam et beati Petri tuitionem suscepimus. Hoc quia in hunc modum processisse in ueritate cognouimus, presenti scripto et sigilli nostri impressione testificamur.

### 301

[? *c.* 1148] Notification that Gilbert has made a cemetery in Upleadon (Glos)[1] as a refuge for the poor, and that Upleadon church is to remain a chapel to its mother church; he has confirmed this in the dedication of the church, and also what his predecessor, Bishop Robert, did with the chapel and cemetery at Preston (Glos).

G(ilebertus) Dei gratia Herefordensis episcopus omnibus sancte ecclesie fidelibus salutem.

Notum uobis fieri uolumus quod ad salutem animarum et ad refugium pauperum in uilla de Ledene, necessitate ingruente, cimiterium fecimus: hoc addentes, ut 5 ecclesia eiusdem ⟨fo. 104v⟩ uille sue matri ecclesie tamquam capella respondeat, nec aliam quam capella consuetudinem faciat. Et hoc in prefate ecclesie dedicatione confirmauimus, et presenti scripto illud idem confirmauimus. Volumus etiam et firmiter precipimus ut quod Robertus felicis memorie predecessor noster de capella et cimiterio Preston' confirmauit, ratum et stabile omnibus habeatur.

### 302

[1148–55] Confirmation to Gloucester abbey, at the instance of Roger earl of Hereford and Hugh of Kilpeck, of Kilpeck priory and its endowments: the church of St David[2] and the chapel of St Mary in Kilpeck, with appurtenances, and Hugh's domain chapels and domain tithes, including the tithes of *Ferna* (? The Vern in Bodenham),[3] *Fenna* (? Venn's Green), Broadward (in Leominster), Hopton (? Herefs), Taynton (Glos), Bledisloe (in Awre, Glos), an annual pension of twenty shillings from the church of Baysham (Herefs) and

---

301 PRO Chancery Records, C 150, Cart. Gloucester, fo. 104. *Printed: Cart. Gloucester*, I, 375–6.
302 Gloucester Cathedral Library, Reg. A, fo. 72v.

---

[1] Cf. *PN Glos.* III, 189 (rather than Lydney, *ibid.* p. 257, since Upleadon was in Gloucester's possession and Lydney must almost certainly have had its own parish church before this). Preston is presumably the Preston in the same hundred as Upleadon (*ibid.* p. 184: Botloe Hundred).
[2] This was the parish church, which is still famous for its twelfth-century sculptures; the chapel of St Mary was in the castle, to whose remains the parish church is adjacent; the priory lay at a distance. Both churches had been granted in 1134 (*Cart. Gloucester*, I, 16; *Historical Monuments Comm.: Hereford*, I, 156–9).
[3] Cf. no. 290. For the place-names see also *Taxatio*, pp. 158–61.

one mark from St Nicholas, Hereford; also a general confirmation of tithes, pensions and churches in the diocese. An exchange between the abbot and Roger Walensis of Kilpeck of lands in Dewchurch (Herefs) and (?) Murcott[1] is also confirmed.

Gilbertus Dei gratia Herefordensis episcopus et eiusdem loci capitulum dilectis sibi in Domino sancte matris ecclesie filiis, salutem, gratiam, et benedictionem.

Que communi capituli nostri consensu in nostra presentia gesta sunt, placuit eorundem consilio in scriptum redigi ne quod pietatis intuitu ad honorem Dei et ecclesie utilitatem gestum est, possit in posterum aut lapsu temporis aut sinistra 5 aliquorum uoluntate conuelli. Nos presentibus domino Rogero comite Hereford(ie) et domino Hugone de Kylpec et aliis nonnullis ad eorum instantiam piam et deuotam ⟨fo. 73⟩ diuina pietate et pro animarum nostrarum salute, episcopali auctoritate et communi capituli nostri assensu et uoluntate, concedimus inperpetuum et confirmamus domino abbati et conuentui Glouc(estrie) in puram et 10 perpetuam elemosinam prioratum de Kylpec cum omnibus pertinentiis suis, et ecclesiam sancti Dauid cum capella beate Marie de Kylpec et cum omnibus terris, pratis et decimis, redditibus, libertatibus et consuetudinibus, et omnibus bonis suis; insuper et omnes capellas dominicas predicti Hugonis cum omnibus earum oblationibus et obuentionibus; et omnes decimas tam maiores quam minores tam 15 de assartis quam de aliis, de omnibus terris dominicis eiusdem Hugonis, uidelicet de Ferna, de Fenna, de Bradeford', de Hopton', de Teinton, de Blitheslowe; similiter et annuam pensionem uiginti solidorum de ecclesia de Bayesham, et unam marcam annuam de ecclesia sancti Nicholai de Herefordia; et omnes decimas, pensiones et ecclesias predicto abbati et conuentui in diocesi nostra a patronis earum in elemo- 20 sinam collatas aut concessas inperpetuum concedimus possidendas et habendas. Ratum et gratum habetur quicquid quilibet fidelium eisdem de bonis suis pro animarum suarum salute contulerit aut conferre uoluerit. Confirmamus etiam permutationem quarundam terrarum de Dewischirche et de Morchote coram nobis factam inter dominum abbatem et conuentum Glouc(estrie) et Rogerum 25 Walensem de Kylpec ut inperpetuum permaneat sicut in scriptis continetur inter eos confectis. Que itaque in hunc modum sunt gesta et a nobis sicut predictum est concessa et confirmata, ne futuri seculi cupiditate uel malitia ullo modo mutari possint aut a predictis uiris religiosis ullatenus extorqueri, presens scriptum sigilli nostri appositione et capituli nostri testimonio et sigilli ecclesie nostre inpressione 30 communiuimus. Ego autem Rogerus comes omnia predicta rata habeo et sigilli mei attestatione confirmo. Si quis uero deinceps hanc confirmationem nostram presumpserit impedire maledictionem Dei patris omnipotentis et beate Marie et omnium sanctorum se sciat incursurum, donec predictis abbati et conuentui satisfaceret competenter. Hanc sententiam dedit dominus Gilbertus Hereford(ensis) 35 episcopus pulsantibus campanis et candelis accensis in ecclesia cathedrali Hereford(ie) ad instantiam predicti Rogeri comitis et domini Hugonis de Kylpec et aliorum multorum nobilium uirorum. Hiis testibus Bader(one) de Monem', Roberto de Watteuyll', Mauricio uicecomite, Radulpho Auenel, Willelmo de

---

[1] ? in Minsterworth (Glos): *PN Glos.* III, 163.

40 Miner' (?), Oliuer' de la Mare, ⟨fo. 73 v⟩ Rogero de Burchull', Waltero Walens(i), Waltero de Fraxino, Hugone de Scudimor', Alano fratre predicti Hugonis de Kylpec, et aliis.

### 303

[*c.* 1155] Institution of Robert of Haseley, monk of Gloucester abbey, as rector and prior of Bromfield (Salop); Bromfield church is to retain its privileges as a royal chapel[1] and be exempt from episcopal jurisdiction.

Sciant omnes ad quos presens scriptum peruenerit quod ego Gilbertus Folioth Herefordensis ecclesie humilis minister de precepto et uoluntate domni Henrici bone memorie[2] regis Anglorum domnum Robertum de Haseleya monachum Gloucestr(ie) plene in personam et priorem constitui in ecclesia sancte Marie de 5 Brumfeld' cum omnibus capellis et omnibus libertatibus ad dictam ecclesiam spectantibus. Et quia memorata ecclesia propria dominica capella domni regis est, uult domnus rex et precepit ut ipsa sua plena gaudeat libertate sicut cetere consimiles capelle que sunt in Anglia. Nec permittit domnus rex me posse habere aliquam iurisdictionem in sepefatum priorem uel in aliquem ipsius successorem; set 10 nec procurationem nisi tantum de gratia prioris, si casu me contingat per illum locum transire. Et quia per malitias hominum poterint idem prior et homines sui aliquando molestari et terra sua depredari ⟨et⟩ necesse habebit ad auxilium ecclesie recurrere, ideo precipio districte ut ordinarii qui sub me sunt tales malefactores compescant. Vt autem ista omni posteritati relinquantur et illibata permaneant 15 presenti carte sigillum meum feci apponi. Teste tota sancta sinodo mea.

### 304

[*c.* 1158] Institution of Samson, sacrist of Gloucester, to the church of St Lawrence, Taynton (Glos), and appropriation of the church to his department, at the presentation and request of Matilda de Wattevile, lady of Taynton, and with the consent of Alured, chaplain, former rector, who will continue to hold the church and pay the sacrist an annual pension of ten marks. Gilbert has also confirmed to the sacrist one virgate in Taynton granted by Matilda to the church of St Lawrence in free alms; also the oratory on the land of Hugh the forester— when it is vacant the sacrist can dispose of it, so long as he keeps a chaplain there.

Omnibus ad quod presens pagina peruenerit, G(ilebertus) Foliot Herefordensis episcopus cum toto capitulo Herefordensi salutem.

   Cum Matilda de Watteuile domina de Teintona cum amicis suis multum instabat ad hoc ut ecclesiam sancti Laurentii eiusdem uille ex sua donatione apropriaremus

---

**303** Hereford, Diocesan Registry, Reg. Swinfield, fo. 152 (153). *Printed: Reg. Swinfield*, p. 426; translation in A. L. Moir, *Bromfield Priory and Church in Shropshire* (Chester, 1947), pp. 44–5. 13 distincte *MS*   14 omni...relinquantur] omnia posteritati mee linquant *MS* **304** Gloucester Cathedral Library, Reg. B, p. 20 (Matilda's charter is also on p. 20).

---

[1] See *GF*, pp. 84 n., 223.
[2] Surprising in reference to a reigning king, and possibly a later addition; but for a parallel, see *Misc. D. M. Stenton*, p. 49 n. 4.

ecclesie beati Petri Gloucestr(ie) ad luminaria et ornamenta in illo monasterio 5
inuenienda, et illud facere distulimus donec Aluredus capellanus et persona prefate
ecclesie de sua propria uoluntate personatum suum quoad illam ecclesiam totaliter
in manus nostras resignasset, ad suam instantiam et ad iugem interpellationem dicte
matrone Sampsonem sacristam Glouc(estrie) nomine abbatis et conuentus de dicta
ecclesia inpersonauimus, saluo sufficienti uictu dicti Aluredi in memorata ecclesia 10
ministrantis; et percipiet dictus sacrista de dicto Aluredo nomine personatus decem
marcas annuas, quinque ad Pascha et quinque ad festum sancti Michaelis, donec
prefata ecclesia plene uacauerit. Concedimus etiam et confirmamus auctoritate
Herefordensis ecclesie dicto sacriste unam uirgatam terre in uilla de ⟨p. 21⟩ Tentona
quam sepefata Matilda ecclesie beati Laurentii in puram et perpetuam elemosinam 15
donauit, et sit ista terra quieta ab omni decimatione omni tempore. Concedimus
etiam et confirmamus sepefato sacriste oratorium quod situm est in terra Hugonis
forestarii; cum igitur ut dictum est plene uacauerit dicta ecclesia, faciat idem sacrista
inde quod uoluerit, saluo tamen sufficienti uictu et honesto unius capellani. Et quia
uolumus quod hec nostra collatio dicto monasterio concessa et ad tales usus 20
deputata ut dictum est in ante iugiter perseueret, hanc cartam nostram sigillis nostris
appositis ita roborauimus. Teste capitulo nostro.

### 305

[*c.* 1158] Confirmation of grant by Bernard of Neufmarché[1] to Gloucester abbey of Much
Cowarne church (Herefs), and appropriation to sacrist's department, together with confirmation of other rights and privileges.

Omnibus fidelibus ecclesie G(ilebertus) Folyot Herefordensis episcopus, W.[*sic*][2]
decanus cum toto capitulo Herfordensi, salutem in Domino.

Noueritis nos, episcopali dignitate et auctoritate Herfordensis ecclesie, ex dono
nobilis uiri Bernardi de Nouo Mercato et ad instantiam multorum nobilium,
dilectos filios nostros in Christo abbatem et conuentum beati Petri Glouc(estrie) in 5
ecclesia sante Marie de Coura inpersonasse atque plenum personatum eisdem
concessisse, ad luminaria et ornamenta dicte ecclesie beati Petri inuenienda per
manum sacriste qui pro tempore fuerit, ita quod idem sacrista de prefata ecclesia de
Coura nomine personatus quindecim marcas annuas percipiet donec dicta ecclesia

---

**304** 6 Aluedrus *MS* (*and so passim; called Aluredus in his own charter, also on p. 20*)   10 uictu]
*MS adds* et honesto, *cancelled*
**305** Gloucester Cathedral Library, Seals and Deeds, viii, 1 (copy in exemplification of period
1275–87) (Sd); PRO Chancery Records, C 150, Cart. Gloucester, fo. 49r–v (Ga), and unfoliated,
no. 917 (Gb); Hereford Diocesan Registry, Reg. Cantelupe (1275–82), fo. 17a v (on inserted
slip after fo. 17) (K); Gloucester Cathedral, Reg. B, p. 57 (Gl) (spelling as Sd; select variants
only of other manuscripts). *Printed: Cart. Gloucester,* I, 252–3; III, 6; *Reg. Cantilupe,* pp. 49–50.
1 Omnibus] Gl *adds* Christi

---

[1]  Bernard of Neufmarché had been lord of Brecon; he was father-in-law to Milo of Gloucester,
Gilbert's cousin (see *GF,* p. 37). Bernard seems to have died in the 1120's (on him see Lloyd,
II, 436 ff.). On Much Cowarne, cf. *Taxatio,* p. 160.
[2]  See note to no. 300, Appendix I and *GF,* p. 267.

10 uacauerit. Qua uacante, licebit prefato sacriste illam ingredi et pacifice possidere
absque alicuius impedimento, dummodo capellanus siue uicarius ibidem ministrans
sufficientem atque honestam habeat sustentationem ad ualentiam decem marcarum,
et totum residuum conuertatur in usus proprios dicti sacriste secundum quod
melius disposuerit. Concedimus etiam eidem ut quietus sit ab omni decimatione de
15 manerio suo de Rodele, similiter et de Hyda, preter duos solidos annuos ecclesie de
Yarchulle ex antiquo persoluendos. Volumus etiam et concedimus ut abbas Glou-
c(estrie) quietus sit ab omni nostra synodo et qualibet procuratione spectante ad
episcopum Herefordensem ratione ecclesiarum habitarum in episcopatu Herfordensi. Et hoc facimus propter feruorem honeste religionis quam florere
20 nouimus et non sine fructu in monasterio Gloucestrensi; ex decreto itaque totius
synodi nostre in ecclesia Herfordensi sollempniter celebrate pupplice excommuni-
cauimus omnes qui aliquo tempore contra istam nostram ordinationem atque
confirmationem dictis monachis concessam ueniunt uel uenire presumpserint;
unde et hanc cartam nostram sigillis nostris ita communiuimus, presenti et teste
25 tota nostra synodo Herfordensi.

## 306

[c. 1158–63] Appropriation to Gloucester abbey of the churches of Cowarne (Herefs) and
Taynton (Glos), etc. (cf. nos. 304–5).

Notum sit tam presenti etati quam future posteritati, quod ego Gilbertus Dei
gratia Herefordensis episcopus concedo ecclesie sancti Petri Glouc(estrie) plenum
personatum ecclesie beate Marie de Coura et in ecclesia beati Laurentii de Teyntona,
cum capella et terris et decimis et omnibus pertinentiis, et unam uirgatam terre
5 quam Matild(is) de Teyntona ecclesie beati Laurentii pro anima sua et pro animabus
antecessorum in perpetuam elemosinam donauit. Concedo etiam abbati de Glou-
c(estria) ut in predictis ecclesiis pro uoluntate sua uicarios mittat, et si ei legittime
non seruierint, sub conscientia episcopi amoueat. Hoc quia ratum et inconuulsum
manere uolo, presenti scripto et sigilli mei attestatione confirmo.

## 307

[c. 1158–63] Settlement of the dispute between Hugh, clerk, of Yarkhill (Herefs)[1] and
Patrick sacrist of Gloucester abbey on the tithe of *Hida*.

G(ilebertus) Herefordensis Dei gratia episcopus dilectis sibi in Christo uniuersis
eiusdem ecclesie parochianis et filiis, salutem, gratiam et benedictionem.
Nouerit dilectio uestra controuersiam que inter Hugonem clericum de Ser-
chelle [*sic*] et Patricium sacristam Glouc(estrie) super decima de Hida diu agitata

**305** 15 Rudel' Gb    15 Hida Gl    16 Yarkhulle Gl; Yarhulle K; Parchulle Ga    19 fecimus
Ga    23 ueniant Sd
**306** PRO Chancery Records, C 150, Cart. Gloucester, no. 916. *Printed: Cart. Gloucester*, III, 5.
**307** Gloucester Cathedral, Reg. B, p. 55.

[1] Cf. no. 308: the form in the manuscript is impossible, and one should probably read *Gerchelle*.

est, in presentia nostra hoc tandem fine conquieuisse, ut Patricius ei annis singulis ii 5
solidos et unam sumam frumenti prebeat, et decimam suam in pace possideat;
quod quia ex utraque parte concessum est et nos eidem transactioni assensum
dedimus, ne quod actum est denuo reuocetur in dubium, nos idipsum et scripto
mandauimus et sigilli nostri appositione testificari curauimus. Valete. Hiis testibus:
Waltero archidiacono, magistro Waltero, Gileberto m(onach)o, Rogero clerico, 10
Hugone clerico, Lodewico.

## 308

[*c.* 1158–63] General confirmation to the sacrist's department of Gloucester abbey of churches
and tithes, etc., including confirmation of nos. 305–7, and of tithes and other property and
rights in Bache (Herefs), Rodley (Glos), Sutridge, the Forest of Dean (Glos) and all others
in the diocese of Hereford.

Vniuersis sancte matris ecclesie filiis ad quos presens scriptum peruenerit Gilebertus
Dei gratia Herefordensis episcopus, salutem, gratiam et benedictionem.

Notum fieri uolumus tam presenti etati quam future posteritati, nos diuine
pietatis intuitu et communi capituli Hereford(ensis) assensu, concessisse et episcopali
auctoritate confirmasse Deo et sancto Petro Glouc(estrie) et abbati et monachis 5
ibidem Deo seruientibus, ad luminaria et ornamenta ecclesie sue annuum censum
quinque marcarum de ecclesia beate Marie de Coura, et unam hidam terre cum
pertinentiis suis que appellatur Bache, et totam decimam de dominio suo de Hid',
secundum transactionem que facta est coram nobis inter Patricium sacristam et
Hugonem clericum de Gerchull', quam et carta nostra et sigilli nostri appositione 10
roborauimus; et duas marcas annuas de ecclesia sancti Laurentii de Teynton', et
unam uirgatam terre in eadem uilla cum pertinentiis suis. Concessimus etiam et
confirmauimus eisdem abbati et monachis in usus ecclesie eorum predictos duas
garbas decime totius dominii sui in Rudele quas ab antiquo possederunt, et omnes
decimas de assartis nemoris sui de Sudrugge, et decimam totius uenationis quam 15
capi contigerit, uel ab ipso rege uel a ministris suis, in predicto nemore et in tota ·
foresta de Dene sicut eam de dono et confirmatione reg(um) Anglie dudum habuerunt, et totam piscariam de Rudele et passagium et molendinum cum decimis
eorum; preterea omnes redditus, decimas et ecclesias in diocesi nostra a patronis
earum eis in elemosinam collatas, et possessiones alias et consuetudines quas 20
hactenus habuerunt, diuina eis pietate in perpetuum concedimus, et eas tam
presenti scripto quam sigilli nostri testimonio auctoritate episcopali confirmamus.

**307** 7 transactionem *MS*
**308** Gloucester Cathedral, Reg. B, p. 75.

**309**

[1148–63] Grant to Gloucester abbey of a villein, William son of Robert, his vine-dresser of Ledbury.

⟨Gilebertus⟩ Dei gratia Herefordensis episcopus omnibus fidelibus suis tam clericis quam laicis salutem.

Sciatis nos dedisse Deo et ecclesie sancti Petri de Glouc(estria) quemdam natiuum nostrum Willelmum scilicet filium Roberti uinitoris nostri de Ledebur(ia). Quod
5 quia nolumus in irritum posse reuocari, presenti scripto et testificari libuit et confirmare.

**310**

[c. 1150–63] Grant to Grenta son of Leofwin, with the assent of Adam son of Roger, of the land which Roger son of Grenta, Grenta's uncle, held in Linley (Salop, near Lydbury), at a graduated rent, and for castle-guard at Lydbury by one serjeant for forty days per annum.

This is followed in the Haughmond cartulary by quitclaims of the property to Haugh-mond abbey by Grenta of Middleton and his widow (fo. 136 v).

Notum sit omnibus tam presentibus quam futuris quod ego Gilbertus Hereforden-sis Dei gratia episcopus dedi et concessi Grente filio Leuewini concessu et assensu Ade filii Rogeri terram de Linlega quam ⟨Rogerus⟩ filius Grente tenuit tota ⟨u⟩ita ⟨sua, ita⟩ integre in bosco et plano et pratis et pascuis et aquis et molendinis et in
5 omnibus aliis rebus sicut eam plenius et melius tenuit Rogerus filius Grente auun-culus eius; tenendam de me et successoribus meis in feudo et hereditate, ita quod in duobus primis annis post receptionem terre tenebit illam quietam ab omni seruitio, tertio uero anno dabit dimidiam marcam, q⟨u⟩arto anno et annuatim deinceps dabit marcam unam singulis etiam annis ad summonitionem meam uel successorum
10 meorum. Inueniet iamdictus Grenta unum seruientem in custodia castelli de Lidebir' cum suis expensis per quadraginta dies. Hiis testibus: Petro archidiacono, Ricardo filio cancellarii, Waltero archidiacono, etc.

**311**

[c. 1150–63, probably early] Confirmation to Master Ranulf son of Erchemer, canon of Hereford, of his father's land in Hereford (?), at *Cocedeh*' and a garden at Barton, which he himself held from Bishop Richard's time (1121–7), and a messuage in addition, in return for homage and suit of court.

**309** PRO Chancery Records, C 150, Cart. Gloucester, fo. 112. *Printed: Cart. Gloucester*, II, 4.
1 ⟨Gilebertus⟩] E. *MS. That the author of the grant was Gilbert is proved from the list of donations* (op. cit. 1, 97)
**310** Shrewsbury Borough Library, Cart. Haughmond, fo. 136. *Printed:* Eyton, *Antiquities of Shropshire*, XI, 208 (abbreviated).
**311** *Original* (3 in. × 11½ in.): Hereford Cathedral, Dean and Chapter Muniments, no. 1360. *Printed:* Capes, pp. 11–12. Fragments of seal in bag. *Endorsed:* Heref'.

G(ilebertus) Dei gratia Herefordensis episcopus omnibus episcopis in ecclesia Herefordensi canonice substituendis, ceterisque eiusdem ecclesie tam prelatis quam subditis in Christo salutem.

Nouerint tam posteri quam moderni me concessisse et reddidisse in feudo et iure hereditario magistro Rannulfo canonico meo terram quam pater suus Erchemerus 5 Hereford(ie) tenuit, in qua diu domicilium habuit et ipse Ranulfus post eum a tempore uenerabilis Ricardi episcopi, predecessoris mei, cum pertinentiis suis, uidelicet agro qui est apud Cocedeh' et orto quodam apud Berthonam. Pro predictis hominagium eius recepi; pro seruicio autem debet ter in anno conuenienter submonitus placitis meis interesse Herefordie et successorum meorum. Preterea 10 dedi ei in augmentum masuram quamdam que prope predictum domicilium erat, de me et successoribus meis simili modo et predicto seruicio tenendam. His testibus: Waltero archidiacono, magistro Hugone de Clifort, Gisleberto capellano.

## 312

[c. 1155] Enfeoffment of William Folet with land in Hereford bought of Robert de Chandos,[1] two mills in the River Wye, land at Luntley (Herefs), Hereford and Barton (Herefs) (details given), etc., in return for acting as the bishop's cupbearer at great festivals at the bishop's expense and for suit of court.

'Henrico fratre comitis' suggests a date not much later than 1155;[2] the precentor and treasurer a date not before c. 1155.

Notum sit tam presentibus quam futuris quod Gilebertus Herefordensis Dei gratia episcopus consilio et consensu capituli mei concessi et dedi Willelmo Folet et heredibus eius ad tenendum de me et ⟨fo. 121 v⟩ successoribus meis in feudum et hereditatem totam terram quam emi in Hereford(ia) de Roberto de Chandos, et quam ipse ecclesie mee pro decem marcis inperpetuum habendam concessit; duo 5 etiam molendina in Vieua cum omnibus hiis que ad ea pertinent; et terram illam in Luttelea quam habuit Ranulfus cementarius; terram etiam illam quam habuit Alardus de Dodeham in burgo de Hereford(ia) et foris in Bertuna mea excepta tenura Siwardi de la Hulla et Teobaldi monetarii. Hanc tenuram consilio et consensu capituli mei concessi ei in feudum et hereditatem in perpetuum habendam 10 libere et quiete: et hoc quidem seruitio, ut in magnis solempnitatibus michi in cypho meo sumptu quidem meo seruiat et ad placita mea cum liberis hominibus meis cum summonitus fuerit, ueniat. Hanc uero donationem quia firmam et ratam permanere uolo, presenti scripto et sigilli mei et sigilli capituli mei attestatione confirmo. Hiis testibus: Petro archidiacono Heref(ordensi), Waltero archi- 15

312 Oxford, Bodl. MS Rawlinson B. 329, fo. 121 (Cart. Hereford).

---

[1] On this family, see Loyd, *Origins*, pp. 26–7. This Robert was presumably son of Roger (see *Monasticon*, VI, 1092–3) and so grandson, not son, of Robert de Chandos I, founder of Goldcliff priory.

[2] I.e. not long after his brother's death; but Henry survived until 1165 (Walker in *Camden Miscellany*, XXII, 9), so that a later date is by no means impossible.

diacono Salop', Reg(inaldo) cantore, Iuone thesaurario, Hugone Foliot, Radulfo de Ledeb(eria), magistro Gaufrido de Clifford, Ricardo Foliot et Rogero canonicis Herefordensibus, Gileberto capellano et Hugone clerico episcopi, Willelmo presbitero de Estenouera, Aluredo presbitero de Longaduna, Radulfo presbitero de
20 Bosebur(ia), Aluredo et Roberto uicariis de Ledebur(ia); militibus autem Willelmo de Chesney, Henrico fratre comitis, Radulfo de Verdun, Roberto Foliot et Rogero fratre eius, Rogero Foliot et Serlone fratre eius, et Radulfo Foliot nepote episcopi, Roberto de Abbatot et Osberto nepote eius, Willelmo Puher et Rogero de Mortuna, Willelmo de Mefflituna (?), Willelmo de Alkrug', Baldewino de Dunintona,
25 Ranulfo Britone de Mortuna; mancipiis episcopi Roberto de Breyles, Roberto dispensatore, Roberto pincerna, Reginaldo camerario; pueris autem Radulfo Foliot, Willelmo Foliot, Willelmo Banast(re) et Rogero fratre eius.

### 313

[*c.* 1155–*c.* 1158] Settlement of the dispute between Hereford cathedral and the Chandos family on the land called *Wariduna*, which Robert de Chandos has surrendered to the cathedral to increase, with its tithes, the prebend of David the priest (i.e. the prebend of Moreton).

Gilebertus Dei gratia Herefordensis episcopus dilectis sibi in Domino uniuersis Herefordensis ecclesie parochianis et filiis, salutem, gratiam et benedictionem. Vestre presenti scripto notum facimus discretioni controuersiam illam que antiquitus inter Herefordensem ecclesiam et antecessores Roberti de Candos super
5 quadam terra que Wariduna nominatur diu actitata est, hoc tandem fine conquieuisse. Robertus de Candos in presentia nostra, assidente nobiscum capitulo nostro Hereford(ie), ius ipsius ecclesie recognouit et iam dictam terram in augmentum prebende illius quam Dauid sacerdos tenet super altare beate Dei genetricis et sancti Ethilberti reddidit, factaque de ipsius decimis cum persona de
10 Walintona perpetua pace sicut carta ipsius testatur, eam una cum decimis liberam et quietam predicte prebende imperpetuum habendam dedit. Quod ita in presentia nostra actum, quia ei ratum et inconuulsum manere uolumus, presenti carta et sigilli nostri appositione testificamur et episcopali auctoritate confirmamus. Hiis testibus: Radulfo decano Hereford', Reginaldo cantore, Petro archidiacono, Iuone
15 thesaurario, magistro Rannulfo, magistro Willelmo de Salesbur(ia), magistro Dauid, Waltero capellano, et Hereberto clerico Roberti de Candos; Rogero et Symone de Candos, Hugone forestario, Willelmo filio Willelmi et Rogero fratre eius, Rogero de Lurneye, Ricardo Talebot, Philippo Alis et de Halimot de Walint(ona) Rein(aldo) et Stephano, Hugone et alteri [*sic*] Rein(aldo), Roberto et
20 Nicholao et aliis.

**312** 17 Gaufrido / Ricardo] Gaufridus / Ric's *MS*   21 Chetney *MS*
**313** Oxford, Bodl. MS Rawlinson B. 329, fos. 11 (Rc), 160 (Rd).
1 Gilbertus Rc   3 discretionem controuersionem Rc   4 Chandos Rd (*and so throughout*)
10 Walintuna Rc   10 sicut] sic Rc   15 Salesbury Rc; Sarr'bir' Rd   16 Candos] Rd *ends here with* et aliis.

## 314

[1148–63][1] Settlement of the case between Herbert canon of Hereford and William chaplain of Archbishop Theobald on the church of Inkberrow (Worcs): the church and the chapel of St Lawrence are recognized as a part of Herbert's prebend, but William is made vicar for life in exchange for a pension of 30 shillings.

Dilectis sibi in Domino uniuersis sancte matris ecclesie filiis frater G(ilebertus) Herefordensis ecclesie minister, in Christo dillectionem et salutem ⟨fo. 38⟩ perpetuam.

    Consensu contrahentium inita pacta stabile tunc demum robur accipiunt, cum eorum quorum hec firmare potest auctoritas excipiuntur litteris et firmantur 5 sigillis. Inde est quod conuentionem inter Herebertum canonicum nostrum et Gwillelmum capellanum domni T(heobaldi) Cant(uariensis) archiepiscopi habitam super ecclesia de Hinteberga scripto commendare curauimus, ut in hoc quod inter eos interposita fide compromissum est, obligatum utrumque alteri etiam scripto rem gestam fideliter interpretante teneamus. Herebertus ei in quandam partem 10 prebende sue ecclesiam scilicet de Hinteberga cum capella sancti Laurentii et aliis omnibus ad eandem ecclesiam pertinentibus iam dicto Villelmo in perpetua uicaria et elemosina annua xxx solidorum pensione tenendam habendamque concessit, et eum in nostra et capituli nostri presentia inuestiuit. Quia uero canonico de prebenda sua ultra diem functionis sue disponere de iure non licet, ego et tota 15 capituli nostri plenitudo, conuentionem eandem in totam iam dicti Willelmi uitam extendimus, hoc unanimi consensu concedentes et statuentes, ut si Willelmus *Hereberto superstes extiterit, ei qui Hereberto in prebenda eadem fuerit substitutus, in eandem et non ampliorem si id forte uoluerit summam teneatur, sed iam dictam pensionem soluendo, nostra et capituli nostri auctoritate securitate plenissima 20 potiatur. Post diem uero Gwillelmi libera sit facultas canonico nostro (quicumque tunc fuerit) super eadem ecclesia disponendo, ut eam uel ipse teneat, uel cui uoluerit ampliori pensione concedat. Quod quia firmum inconuulsumque ⟨permaneret⟩ discernimus, ego et capitulum nostrum presenti scripto et sigillorum nostrorum appositione firmamus. Testibus. . .                 25

## 315

[1158–63] Notification of the grant by Robert de Chandos to Hereford cathedral of the church of St Margaret, Wellington (Herefs), as a prebend.

**314** G, no. 122; B, fo. 37 v.
10 ei in] *sic* B. ?*omit*
18 *Heberto B    19 ampliorem] B *adds* si isi, *cancelled*    23 ⟨permaneret⟩ *om.* B
**315** Oxford, Bodl. MS Rawlinson B. 329, fo. 10v, 160v (Rc1, Rc2); Hereford, Diocesan Registry, Reg. Swinfield (1283–1316), fo. 21(17)v (Qa); *also in inspeximus by Bishop Hugh Foliot:* Hereford Cathedral, Dean and Chapter Muniments no. 2777 (original) (Hi); *copy in* Hereford Diocesan Registry, Reg. Swinfield, fo. 21(17)v (Qb). *Text based on Rc2; select variants of other MSS only. Printed:* Capes, p. 17; *Reg. Swinfield,* pp. 55, 55–6.

[1] Probably before 1161, since Theobald is referred to as if alive.

Gilebertus Dei gratia episcopus Herefordensis omnibus sancte matris ecclesie filiis salutem.

Notum sit uobis omnibus Robertum de Candos concessisse et dedisse ecclesiam beate Margarete de Walinton' in prebendam ecclesie beate Marie et beati Ethelberti
5 de Hereford(ia) in perpetuum. Inde est quod uolumus eam esse liberam et quietam ab omnibus episcopalibus consuetudinibus et auxiliis sicut ceteras prebendas. Quod quia ratum et inconuulsum manere uolumus presenti scripto et sigilli nostri attestatione confirmamus. Hiis testibus: Nicholao episcopo de Landaf', Gaufrido decano Hereford(ie), archidiaconis Petro et Waltero Foliot, Reginaldo cantore, Iuone
10 thesaurario, cum toto Herefordensi capitulo.

## 316

[c. 1163] Robert de Chandos is reminded that the rector of Wellington has common pasture for horses and oxen with Robert's and fuel and fencing from Robert's woodland (cf. nos. 313, 315).

For the date, see *CHJ*, VIII, 20.

G(ilebertus) Dei gratia Herefordensis episcopus R(oberto) de Candos salutem.

Sciatis quod in presentia nostra in capitulo recognitum est quod persona ecclesie de Welint' debet habere equis et bobus suis communia pascua cum equis et bobus dominii uestri, et in communibus pascuis et in defensis uestris et de nemore uestro
5 foco et clausture sine superfluitate necessaria. Vnde mandamus uobis et precipimus quatinus permittatis ecclesie libere uti iure suo, scientes quod nos neque possumus neque uolumus pati ut ius ecclesie minuatur uel ledatur in aliquo. Valete.

## 317

[c. 1150–5] Grant to St Guthlac's priory, Hereford (dep. of Gloucester abbey), of a meadow which was part of Walter of Bromyard's prebend, and land adjacent which was Walter's, for an annual rent of one mark.

Dated by the archdeacon of Shropshire and Earl Roger.

⟨N⟩otum sit omnibus quod ego Gilbertus Dei gratia Herefordensis episcopus assensu totius capituli eiusdem ecclesie concessi monasterio beatorum apostolorum Petri et Pauli et sancti Guthlaci Hereford(ie) et monachis ibidem Deo seruientibus,

315 1 ep. Her. RcQaQb; Her. ep. Hi    1 filiis] fidelibus Rc2    1–2 filiis salutem] filiis ad quos presens scriptum peruenerit salutem in Domino HiQb (*this is the address to the inspeximus itself, from which it was probably copied*)    3 Chandos Hi; Chaundos Qa; Chaundes Qb
6 sicuti Rc2    10 capitulo Herefordensi Rc
316 *Original* (6 in. × 2 in.): Hereford, Dean and Chapter Muniments, no. 1385; *copy* in Bodl. MS Rawlinson B. 329, fo. 14. *Printed:* Capes, p. 18. Strip for seal (simple queue) cut off short. *Endorsed:* Exortatoria super detentis (?) a domino (fourteenth century). Script' (fifteenth century).
317 Oxford, Balliol College, MS 271 (Cart. St Guthlac's Hereford), fos. 97 (X), and 103 v (Y), 104 v (Z). (Spelling as Z.)
2–3 beatorum apostolorum / et monachis ibidem Deo seruientibus *in* X *only*

pratum illud quod fuit de prebenda Walteri de Bromgzart et terram que fuit eiusdem Walteri predicto prato adiacentem, annua pensione unius marce argenti 5 inperpetuum tenend(a). Quod ut ratum maneat, presenti scripto et sigilli mei attestatione confirmo his testibus: Rogero comite, Radulfo decano, Gilberto cantore, Petro archidiacono Hereford(ensi), Waltero archidiacono Salop', Waltero de Bromgzart, Gaufrido de Cliff(ord), Ambrosio, Rogero clerico, et multis aliis.

## 318

[1148–55] Confirmatory clause by Gilbert to Ralph de Baskerville's confirmation of the grant of his father, Roger de Baskerville, to St Peter's Gloucester, on assuming the monastic habit there, of the land which Ralph Balee, Edwin Trunchepeni (?) and Ailnod son of Nod held.

Witnesses: Ralph dean of the church of Hereford, Peter archdeacon, Gilbert cantor (precentor), Walter treasurer, master Hugh de Clifford, master Ranulph, Ilbert dapifer and William constable.

Quam uero ego Gilbertus Herefordensis Dei gratia episcopus hanc donationem in presentia mea et predictorum testium et aliorum plurimorum factam, ratam et inconuulsam inperpetuum manere uolui [*sic*]; illam tam episcopali autoritate quam presentis carte inscriptione et sigilli mei attestatione confirmamus.

## 319

[1148–*c.* 1155] Confirmatory clause by Gilbert to grant by Aubrey de Loges, widow and nun, with the consent of her son Gerin de Loges, to St Guthlac's priory, Hereford, of half her land at *Lude* (prob. Lyde, Herefs) (being her dower) in alms, on condition that she and a daughter—until she is given in marriage—may have food and clothing, etc., as long as she lives. After her death prayers are to be said for her as for a monk, and Gerin her son is to receive thirty shillings annually and the right to take the habit of religion. For this the monks paid six marks.

Witnesses: Ralph dean, Gilbert cantor (precentor), Peter archdeacon, Hugh de Clifford, Walter de Bro(myard), William chaplain, Henry son of Wiger, Hervey de Muchegros, Milo his son, Hugh Travers, Roger de Burches, Nicholas de Mag(hena), Odo de Bereford [*sic*].

Hanc uero donationem in presentia capituli Herefordensis ecclesie et predictorum testium solempniter factam, ego Gilbertus eiusdem ecclesie Dei gratia minister et episcopus presenti inscripsione et sigilli mei attestatione confirmo etc.

**317** 4 Bromgezart X    6 ratum] B *adds* et inconcussum; X *adds* et inconcussum in omne tempus    6 mei] nostri Y    7 his testibus Z; et subscriptis testibus corroboro XY; Y *omits the witnesses*    8 Hereford(ensi)] X *ends here with* et aliis
**318** Oxford, Balliol College, MS 271, fo. 101.
**319** Oxford, Balliol College, MS 271, fo. 65.

**320**

[c. 1150–? c. 1155][1] Confirmation to St Guthlac's priory, Hereford, of the grant by Philip Alis of the church and advowson of Sutton (presumably Herefs).

⟨G⟩ilbertus Dei gratia Herefordensis episcopus clero et populo in episcopatu Hereford(ensi) constituto salutem ⟨et⟩ gratiam.

Notum uobis facimus quod Ph(ilippu)s Alis pro amore Dei et salute anime sue et antecessorum, dominium et aduocationem ecclesie de Suttona monachis sancti
5 Petri et sancti Guthlaci Hereford(ie) dedit [et] in perpetuam elemosinam concessit cum terris et decimis et omnibus iuste pertinentibus. Quod quia assensu nostro et permissione factum est presenti scripto et sigilli nostri attestatione confirmamus [...], subscriptis testibus: Waltero archidiacono, Hugone de Clifford', magistro Randulfo, canonicis Hereford(ensibus), Galfrido, Gilberto, Iuone, Rogero clericis
10 episcopi; Willelmo Folet, Willelmo Pouher, Gerin de Loges, et aliis multis.

**321**

[1148–63, probably early] Confirmation of Bishop Robert's foundation of St Guthlac's priory (1143)[2] and of the churches and chapels, etc., of the priory: the churches of St Cuthbert, Holme Lacy, St Giles, Edvin,[3] Acornbury (? or Avenbury), Ocle Pychard, St Peter, Mordiford (Herefs), *Lordford'*, the chapel of *Britwaldestreu*, the church of St Ouen, Hereford, the chapels of Felton,[4] Little Cowarne, Dormington (Herefs), Load (? Somerset), Little Sutton, Maund and Marden (Herefs).

Gilebertus Dei gratia Herefordensis episcopus dilectis sibi in Domino uniuersis eiusdem ecclesie parrochianis et filiis, salutem, gratiam et benedictionem.

Quod a predecessore nostro bone memorie domno Roberto episcopo ad honorem Dei et ecclesie sancte decorem pariter et utilitatem salubriter actum est et statutum,
5 nos eius immitati uestigia, ea que nobis a Deo concessa est auctoritate concedimus et confirmamus. Quoniam itaque iam dictus predecessor noster ecclesiam beati Petri in foro Hereford(ie) sitam et ecclesiam sancti Gutlaci intra castelli Hereford(ie) ambitum fundatam, in corpus unum redigere et unam beatorum apostolorum Petri et Pauli et sancti Gutlaci Heref(ordie) ex iam dictarum ecclesiarum posses-
10 sionibus constituere et in loco religioni aptissimo extra ciuitatem edificare, et in ea monacorum conuentum instaurare decreuit; nos hoc ipsum ratum habentes

320 Oxford, Balliol College, MS 271, fo. 88 v.
321 G, no. 125; B, fo. 38 v; Oxford, Balliol College, MS 271, fo. 103 (X) (the text of B is incomplete; that of X mutilated; select variants of X only, so far as B goes).
1 in] a B    3 Roberto] R. B    9 Heref(ordie) *om.* B    9 exclesiarum B

---

[1] If, as seems likely, Ivo the clerk is to be identified with Ivo the treasurer (*GF*, p. 268).
[2] See *CS*, p. 264 n.
[3] Neither Edvin has a church now dedicated to St Giles.
[4] For Holme Lacy, Ocle, St Ouen, Hereford and Felton cf. *Taxatio*, pp. 158, 160; for Dormington, *Herefs. DB*, p. 91.

annuimus et iamdicte ecclesie beatorum apostolorum Petri et Pauli et sancti Gutlaci omnes possessiones et dignitates et libertates a iam dictis duabus ecclesiis retroactis temporibus habitas, et sibi a iam dicto predecessore nostro confirmatas concedimus, et presenti scripto et sigilli nostri atestatione, ut imperpetuum sibi 15 firme permaneant confirmamus. In his uero hec propriis duximus exprimenda uocabulis: *ecclesiam sancti Guthberti de Hamma et ecclesiam sancti Egidii de Yeddefen et ecclesiam de Agnebur' et ecclesiam de Acla et ecclesiam sancti Petri de Mordford' et capellam de Lordford' et capellam de Britwaldestreu et ecclesiam sancti Audoeni de Heref(ordia) et capellam de Feltona et capellam de parua Coura 20 et capellam de Dormitona et capellam de Ladeo et capellam de parua Suttona et capellam de Maghene et ecclesiam de Mawr puden' (?); que omnia predicte iam ecclesie et fratribus in ea Domino seruientibus episcopali auctoritate concedimus et donationem nostram presenti scripto communimus; et ualete.

## 322

[1148–63] Settlement of the case between the priory of St Guthlac's, Hereford, and Ernisius the priest on the church of Edvin: Ernisius has surrendered any right he had for a consideration of three marks.

Gilbertus Dei gratia Herefordensis episcopus clero et populo in episcopatu Hereford(ensi) constituto, salutem et gratiam.

Nouerit dilectio uestra quod omnis controuersia que inter monachos Hereford(ie) et Ernisium presbiterum super ecclesia de Yedeuenna orta fuerat in hunc modum imperpetuum conquieuit. Predictus quidem Ernisius a lite recessit et totum ius quod 5 in prefata ecclesia habuerat in manu nostra refutauit, hac condicione, quod monachi infra biennium a die compositionis tres marcas ei persoluerint hiis terminis: natiuitate Domini dimidiam marcam, natiuitate sancti Iohannis Baptiste dimidiam marcam, in festo sancti Michaelis dimidiam marcam; in secundo uero anno eisdem terminis. Quod quia in presentia nostra et fratrum nostrorum actum est, scripto 10 nostro et sigilli inpressione testificamur.

## 323

[1148–63] Confirmation to St Guthlac's priory, Hereford, of John of Marden's grant on his deathbed of two-thirds of the tithes of his domain in *Lorteport*.

⟨G⟩ilbertus Herefordensis Dei gratia episcopus uniuersis Hereford(ensis) ecclesie filiis, salutem et benedictionem.

Nostra interest memoria comendare ea que ad honorem Dei et tranquillitatem

321 15 in presenti scripto (*for* et *read* in) X    16 firma permaneat B; firma permaneant confirmamus X    17 uocabulis] B *ends here*    17 *ecclesie X    17 *or* Guthlaci (*but the church is dedicated to St Cuthbert*)    22 ? *for* Mawrwarden (*Marden is recorded as* Maurdine *and* Magewardin)
322 Oxford, Balliol College, MS 271, fo. 53 (marked 'uacat' in margin).
8–10 *In the MS the order is confused: the six words* natiuitate . . . marcam *come after* eisdem terminis
323 Oxford, Balliol College, MS 271, fo. 69.
3 tranquillionem *MS*

religionis acta esse cognoscimus, ut si qua in posterum rerum gestarum dubitatio
5 emerserit scripti nostri testimonio ueritas luce clarius omnibus innotescat. Quod
itaque a Iohanne de Maurdina in extremis posito cum Hereford(ensi) ecclesia actum
est sic se habet: predictus siquidem Iohannes duas partes decime dominii sui de
Lorteport, concedente fratre suo qui eandem decimam ante tenuerat, sine omni
reclamatione monachis Hereford(ie) in perpetuam elemosinam concessit. Quod
10 quia ratum et inconuulsum manere uolumus presenti scripto et sigilli nostri
attestatione confirmamus. Valete.

## 324

[1148–63] Notification of Adam de Port's grant to St Guthlac's priory, Hereford, in free
alms of all his land in Rushock (presumably Herefs) and common in other lands, with the
consent of the abbot and convent of Vaucelles (in Crevecœur, Cist.: Cottineau, II, 3301–2).

⟨G⟩ilbertus Dei gratia Herefordensis episcopus uniuersis sancte matris ecclesie
filiis perpetuam in Domino [salute]m.
Quod iuste et diuino intuitu ad decorem domus Dei locis religiosis pia [fide]lium
deuotio contulerit, prouida solicitudine conseruandum est et testium auctoritate et
5 car[tarum] munimine transcurrendum; peruersorum autem malitia sedet in insidiis
et bene gesta in[mut]are uel Deo militantium requiem perturbare gaudet et
enititur (?). Huius conditionis ⟨fo. 83⟩ non immemores, quod in presentia nostra
et totius sinodi Hereford(ie) ad honorem Dei et ecclesie [uti]litatem fieri uidimus,
presenti scripto tam presentis etatis quam future posteritatis memori[e] commen-
10 dare curauimus, ne temporis interstitio in religionis detrimentum rei bene geste
mem[o]ria effluat uel uaccillet. Adam de Port pro salute anime sue et pro animabus
patris et matris sue et antecessorum suorum tantam (?) terram suam de Russoc in
nemore et plano sicut sibi a proauis iure hereditario competebat, liberam et
quietam ab omni humana exactione et terreno seruitio, ecclesie beati Petri et sancti
15 Guthlaci Hereford(ie) et monachis ibidem Deo seruientibus donauit et in perpetuam elemosinam concessit; adiecit etiam communitatem ceterarum terrarum
suarum in forestis, siluis, aquis et pascuis ad omnes usus suos cum omni quietudine
et libera consuetudine; predictam etiam terram tanquam possessionem ecclesiasticam
deinceps in usus monachorum gladio spirituali tuendam nobis contradidit. Huic
20 donationi assensum prebuit abbas Valcellensis monasterii et totum eiusdem loci
capitulum. Nos itaque de deuotione predicti Ade gratias agentes, quod pietatis
intuitu et Deo auctore concessit ratum habemus et prefatam donationem scripto
nostro cum sigilli appositione episcopali autoritate confirmamus etc.

324 Oxford, Balliol College, MS 271, fo. 82v.
5 transcurrnt' MS    15–16 imperpetuam MS

**325**

[1148–55 or 1159–60] Notification of the release[1] by Robert son of Jordan to St Guthlac's priory, Hereford, of two acres in their area of jurisdiction and a virgate which he held of the monks' fee in Holme Lacy (Herefs) for an annual rent of four shillings (?); for this Prior Robert paid thirty-two shillings.

Dated by the first witness (see no. 300 and n.).

G(ilebertus) Dei gratia Herefordensis episcopus dilectis sibi in Domino uniuersis sancte Herefordensis ecclesie parochianis et filiis, salutem, gratiam et benedictionem.

Nouerit dilectio uestra Robertum filium Iord(ani) in presentia nostra concessisse Deo et monasterio beati Petri et sancti Guthlaci Heref(ordie) et monachis ibidem Deo seruientibus duas acras de terra que in curia eorum sunt et unam uirgatam 5 terre quam predictus Robertus tenebat de feudo ipsorum monachorum in uilla de Hamma libere uel annua quatuor (?) solidorum pensione; et ut h⟨u⟩ius concessionis firma et inconcussa permaneret deuotio, dompnus Robertus predicti monasterii prior dedit eidem Roberto caritatis intuitu triginta duos solidos. Hiis testibus: Mauricio uicecomite Heref(ordescire), Willelmo presbitero, magistro Galfrido et 10 Rogero clericis episcopi.

**326**

[c. 1155–c. 1158] Settlement of the case between Master Godfrey and Ernald his uncle on the church of Holdgate (Salop) (?):[2] Godfrey is to be rector, Ernald vicar, and Ernald is to pay Godfrey an annual pension of ½ mark.

MS B ascribes this to a bishop of London; but it is clear from the witnesses that it belongs to Gilbert's time as bishop of Hereford. On the date, cf. no. 312.

⟨Gilebertus⟩ Dei gratia ⟨Herefordensis⟩ episcopus dilectis sibi in Domino uniuersis sancte matris ⟨Herefordensis⟩ ecclesie filiis, salutem, gratiam et benedictionem.

Prouidendum nobis est ne coram nobis decise controuersie iterum reuiuiscant in litem. Nouerit itaque dilectio uestra causam que inter magistrum Godefridum et Ernaldum patruum eius super ecclesia de Castello diutius agitata est, hoc tandem 5 fine conquieuisse. Ernaldus in iam dicta ecclesia nepotis sui ius recognoscens, illam in manu nostra per textum deposuit, quam nos Godefrido similiter per textum

**325** Oxford, Balliol College, MS 271, fo. 103 v.
5 terra] *MS adds* mea.
**326** G, no. 186; B, fo. 183.
1 ⟨Gilebertus⟩ *om.* B     1–2 ⟨Herefordensis⟩ / ⟨Herefordensis⟩] London' / Londonihen' B
(*see above: even as corrected the heading is odd; perhaps either* matris *or* Herefordensis *should be omitted.*)     3 reuiuifacant (?) B *partly corrected* (reuiuificant *is a possible reading, but makes no sense*)

---

[1] Since the two acres were in the monks' *curia* and the virgate in their fee in Holme, they were clearly buying a tenant out: presumably both pieces of property lay in Holme, but the two acres may have been in Hereford or elsewhere.

[2] Holdgate—*castellum Hologoti*—seems the most likely identification; Richard's Castle (Herefs) and Bishop's Castle (Salop) are not impossible.

restituentes, ipsum in ea personam constituimus. Deinde petitione Godefridi, Ernaldum in eadem ecclesia uicarium suscepimus, hac interueniente pactione, ut
10 Ernaldus iam dictam ecclesiam quamdiu superstes fuerit teneat, sub annua pensione dimidie marce Godefrido ab ipso ipsius ecclesie nomine annuatim soluende, ita ut medietas debite pensionis in media Quadragesima, altera uero medietas in festo sancti Michaelis, soluatur. Quod quia pleno utriusque partis consensu sub nostra ⟨fo. 183 v⟩ gestum est presentia, et iuramenti religione utrimque firmatum, ne in
15 dubium de cetero uel in irritum possit reuocari, presenti scripto uniuersitati uestre rerum gestarum seriem significare et utrique quod suum est sigilli nostri auctoritate confirmare curauimus. His testibus: Radulfo decano, Petro archidiacono, Galtero archidiacono, magistro Rannulfo, Henrico fratre comitis, Iuone thesaurario, Radulfo de Ledeb(eria), magistro Galfrido de Cliford', magistro Galtero de
20 Ardep', Rogero de Burkell', Rogero filio Mauricii, Radulfo scriptore.

### 327

[c. 1148] Settlement of the dispute between Hereford cathedral and Lanthony priory (Glos):[1] the priory is to retain the possessions granted by Bishop Robert de Bethune; Hereford cathedral is to receive an annual pension of sixty shillings, and to have ½ hide in Barton (Herefs) restored to it.

Dilectis sibi in Christo fratribus uniuersis sancte ecclesie filiis, frater Gilebertus Herefordensis ecclesie minister, totumque Hereford(ensis) ecclesie capitulum, salutem in Domino.

Tam presenti etati quam post nos future posteritati presenti scripto notificamus,
5 controuersiam quam aduersus Lanthon(iensem) ecclesiam hucusque habuimus, omni litis fomite consopito in hunc modum conquieuisse. Lanthon(iensis) ecclesia ecclesie nostre annis amodo singulis sexaginta solidos prestitura est, ex quibus triginta in festiuitate beati Æthelberti, triginta in festiuitate sancti Michaelis absque frustratoria uel dilatoria mora persoluentur; dimidiam etiam hydam terre ad
10 Bertonam nostram pertinentem nobis amodo quiete possidendam restituunt. Nos uero unanimi consensu et uoluntate predicte Lanthon(iensis) ecclesie possessiones omnes quas eis bone memorie domnus Robertus episcopus concesserat prout eis donate sunt, et tam scripto eius quam priuilegiis apostolicis confirmate, quamdiu a predicta non resiliet conditione, possidendas et absque omni reclamatione inper-
15 petuum habendas concedimus. Quod quia ratum et inconcussum manere decernimus, tam presenti scripto quam sigilli episcopalis et sigilli ecclesie nostre attestatione confirmamus.

326 13 plena B    18 thesaru' B
327 PRO, Chancery Masters' Exhibits, C 115/A 1 (unfoliated), section vi, no. 39 (Cart. Lanthony).

---

[1] Llanthony (sic) was originally founded in Monmouthshire. In 1136 it established a colony at Gloucester, which became for the rest of the century in effect the senior partner in a double house. For this dispute, see above, no. 80: it was presumably settled early in Gilbert's episcopate.

## 328

[1148–63] Confirmation of the grant by Ralph son of Ernald (cf. no. 329) of ten acres in free alms in Prestbury (Glos)[1] to Lanthony priory.

G(ilebertus) Dei gratia episcopus Herefordensis omnibus sancte ecclesie fidelibus salutem.

Notum sit omnibus uobis quod Radulfus filius Ernaldi dedit ecclesie Lanthon(ie) in Prestebur' decem acras terre in perpetuam elemosinam liberas et quietas ab omnimodo seruitio: quod ego concedo et episcopali auctoritate confirmo eidem 5 ecclesie perpetuo eas in eadem libertate tenendas.

## 329

[c. 1150–63] Confirmation of the agreement between Ralph son of Ernald (cf. no. 328) and Lanthony priory: Ralph has granted half a virgate and an arm of land to the priory in free alms for which Ralph answers for service to Hereford cathedral and the bishop; and the priory will provide food and clothing for Ralph's mother while she lives.

Gillebertus Herefordensis Dei gratia episcopus omnibus hominibus suis tam clericis quam laicis salutem.

Notum uobis facimus nos concessisse et ratam habuisse conuentionem que facta est inter canonicos Lanthon(ie) et Radulfum filium Arnaldi. Conuentio autem huiusmodi est: quod Radulfus concessit predictis canonicis dimidiam uirgatam 5 terre cum brachia quadam que eidem appendere solet, in perpetuam elemosinam et ab omni seruitio quietam et liberam; ita quod Radulfus ecclesie Hereford(ensi) et nobis de seruitio respondeat; canonici autem matri ipsius Radulfi in uita sua in uestitu et uictu prouideant. Et quoniam conuentionem hanc in omne tempus posteritatis ratam et inconuulsam manere ⟨A9, fo. 113 v⟩ uolumus etc. Testibus: 10 Waltero archidiacono Solopesir(e), Radulfo de Wycherch', et aliis.

## 330

[1151–7] Notification, addressed to John bishop of Worcester, of the grant of Ralph the Butler to Lanthony priory of land reclaimed from the wood of Oakle St (?) (Glos), made in Gilbert's presence when he dedicated the church there.

The dates are those of Bishop John.

Venerabili domno fratrique karissimo I(ohanni) Wygorn(iensi) Dei gratia episcopo, frater G(ilebertus) Herefordensis ecclesie minister, salutem in Domino.

328 PRO, Chancery Masters' Exhibits, C 115/A9, fo. 113; A1, section vi, no. 15.
329 PRO, Chancery Masters' Exhibits, C 115/A9, fo. 113; A1, section vi, no. 16.
7 quod *om.* A1    11 et aliis *om.* A9
330 PRO, Chancery Masters' Exhibits, C 115/A9, fo. 113 v; A1, section vi, no. 18. Text of A9 given.

---

[1] Cf. *Monasticon*, VI, 140.

Que ad honorem Dei et utilitatem proficiunt ecclesie ob hoc memorie tradi necesse est, ut quod agitur ratum maneat et lites inposterum penitus conquiescant.
5 Ob hoc uestre diligentie presenti scripto notificamus quod Radulfus pincerna in presentia nostra, cum eius ecclesiam in silua de Acheleya dedicaremus, terram quam de eadem silua erutam fratribus de Lanthon(ia) iam ante concesserat adeo ab omni seruitute liberauit, ut ipsi Radulfo per eundem fundum amodo uiam aut semitam, iter aut actum nisi predictorum fratrum consensu habere non liceat. Quod quia in
10 nostra presentia sub multorum testimonio actum est, presenti scripto notificamus, rogantes ut concessam dicte ecclesie libertatem diligentia uestra corroboret et auctoritas sancta stabiliat.

## 331

[Probably 1148–9] General confirmation to Lire abbey (Normandy) of the churches of Much Marcle, Linton, Wilton, Dewsall (Herefs), Tenbury (Worcs), Fownhope, Eardisland(?), Leadon (?) (Herefs), and Tidenham (Glos)—and testification that the church of Tidenham was adjudicated to them in the bishop's court against the men of Earl Gilbert (de Clare)[1] and the chapel of Albrighton (Salop) against the monks of Monmouth (dep. of St-Florent, Saumur) in general synod.

See note 1. On the English possessions of Lire, see C. Guéry, *Hist. de l'abbaye de Lyre* (Évreux, 1917), pp. 157 ff.; *Taxatio*, pp. 158–61.

Notum sit tam presentibus quam futuris quod ego Gilibertus Herefordensis Dei gratia episcopus concedo donno abbati de Lire et monachis omnes ecclesias et omnia ecclesiastica beneficia que in nostro episcopatu habent; inter que hec propriis duximus exprimenda uocabulis: ecclesiam de Marchelai et ecclesiam de Lintun' et
5 illam de Wilton' et ecclesiam de Fonte Dauid et illam de Tameteberia et ecclesiam de Hopa et illam de Leena et ecclesiam de Ledeneia et illam de Tedeham. Que omnia quia firma et rata esse uolumus pagine presentis inscriptione nostrique simul attestatione sigilli communimus. Testificamur etiam quod cum homines comitis Giliberti aduersus predictos monachos de donatione ecclesie de Tehedam [*sic*] litem
10 mouissent, die statuta predicti monachi nobis presentiam suam exhibentes, copia

330 6 *?* eis (*so* A1)   10–11 presenti...libertatem *om.* A1
331 Dom Lenoir MSS (in possession of M. le Comte de Malthou, Semilly, Manche), vol. XXIII, p. 484 (no. 83; eighteenth-century transcript of thirteenth-century Cart. Lire, 'parmi les mss. de la bibliothèque du collège des Jésuites de Paris') (Li); Bodl. MS Dugdale 11 (6501), fo. 66 v (seventeenth-century transcript 'ex uetusto chartulario Lirensis cenobii tempore Iohannis Angl' regis exarato (ut uidetur)'; *Monasticon ut inf.* adds 'penes Andream du Chesne 1640, n. 3') (Du) (text taken from a microfilm of Li, Archives Départementales de l'Eure, Évreux, IM: 2 (RI) and IM: 5 (R23), another in Archives Nationales, 104 MI 23; D is abbreviated, and only significant variants are given). *Abstract* in Archives Dép. de l'Eure. H 590, fo. 325 (Inventaire général des chartes...de Lire, 1739, vol. IV). *Printed: Monasticon*, VI, 1093.
1 Gilbertus Du   4 Merchelai Du   8 communimus] Du *ends here*

---

[1] Either the earl of Hertford (died 1151–3) or, more probably, his uncle the earl of Pembroke (died 1148–9), since Tidenham is not far from Chepstow, the caput of the honour of the earls of Pembroke. On these earls, see *CP*, x, 348 ff.

idoneorum testium donationem prefate ecclesie sibi iudicio optinuerunt. Capella etiam de Eilbrituna cum monachi de Monemua de ea eis litem mouerent in generali synodo eis adiudicata est. His testibus: magistro Hugone de Clifford', et Waltero de Bromyeard, et Hugone Foliot, et Haro(l)do et Ture [*sic*], Bernardo de Hopa, et Wimund de Linton', et Willelmo de Merchelay, et Adam decano de Roos et 15 Adam de Wiltona, et Gilberto de Suttum', et tota generali sinodo.

## 332

[1148–55] Charter of Roger earl of Hereford (1143–55), granting to Monmouth priory (dep. St-Florent, Saumur) the church of St Andrew of Awre (Glos) (cf. no. 333)— already granted by Robert son of Hugh, the earl's tenant, who had reclaimed it from the river Severn—and the land of *Haiward* in free alms, with a road giving access, with confirmation, and appropriation, by Gilbert. (Only the confirmation is printed).

Cf. S. Harris in *Journ. Hist. Soc. of the Church in Wales*, III (1953), 13.

... Hanc siquidem donationem in manu Gilleberti episcopi Herefordensis per aureum anulum posui, rogans quod dederam episcopali auctoritate muniri; et nichilominus scripto meo et sigillo apposito confirmaui, subiungens testes qui affuerunt, presentes, uidentes et audientes: Gillebertus episcopus Herefordensis, Rodbertus prior Mon(emud), Galfridus de Spiniauc, et Radulfus clericus; Badero 5 de Mun(emud) et uxor eius Roheis, et Mauricius de Heref(ordia).

Pretaxatam hanc donationem ab illustri comite Herefordensi R(ogero) factam ecclesie sancte Marie de Mon(emuda), ego Gillebertus Herefordensis Dei gratia episcopus episcopali auctoritate confirmo et corroboro: adiciens non solum presentationem clerici, que et laicis in ecclesiarum donatione conceditur, sed etiam 10 personatum predicte ecclesie de Aura, post mortem Hugonis clerici nunc eiusdem ecclesie persone, ad predictam ecclesiam pertinere. Terram preterea que dicitur Haiward quam ipse comes R(ogerus) a possessione laica in ecclesiasticam in presentia nostra transferens, ecclesie de Mon(emuda) concessit, nos de manu ipsius suscepimus et predicte ecclesie, tam presenti scripto quam sigilli nostri 15 attestatione, confirmamus. Quod qui presumptione temeraria cassare temptauerit, diuino ipsum examini relinquimus; sua uero predicte ecclesie iura conseruantibus, una cum fratrum in ea Domino seruientium oratione, nos quoque benedictionis nostre participationem annuimus. Amen.

**331** 16 toto Li
**332** *Original or contemporary copy* (see p. 27 n.): Archives dép. Maine-et-Loire, H 3710, no. 8 (8¼ in. × 5¼ in.); *copies: ibid.* H 3713, fo. 126r–v (Liber Albus of St-Florent, Saumur); fragment in Paris, Bibl. Nat. nouv. acquis. lat. 1930, fo. 140v–141 (Cart. St-Florent—nineteenth-century copy in Arch. dép. Maine-et-Loire H 3712); H 3711 (charter roll), no. 10. (No significant variants.) No seal, but original is cut at foot. *Printed: Bibliothèque de l'École des Chartes*, XL (1879), 183–5 (ed. P. Marchegay); *calendared: CDF*, no. 1143; *Inventaire sommaire...: Maine et Loire...*, Series H, II, ed. M. Sache, p. 473, cf. 474, 502. *Endorsed*: De Monemuda (twelfth century).
12 person[...] predictam *original*

**333**

[1148–55] Confirmation of the grant by Roger earl of Hereford (1143–55) of the church of St Andrew of Awre (Glos) to Monmouth priory (cf. no. 332) and appropriation of the church after the death of Hugh the priest.

Notum sit tam presentibus quam futuris quod ego Gislebertus Herefordensis Dei gratia episcopus concedo monachis de Munemuia dominium ecclesie sancti Andree de Aura cum appendiciis suis, quod Rogerus comes Heref(ordensis) eis donauit; et post decessum Hugonis presbiteri, qui eiusdem ecclesie persona est, personatum qui
5 ad me spectat eis concedo, saluo iure Hugonis in uita sua per omnia et saluis episcopalibus et sinodalibus. Et ut hec donatio firma et inconuulsa in perpetuum maneat, presenti scripto et sigilli mei attestatione ipsam confirmo. Huius etiam donationis sunt testes: Radulfus Herefordensis ecclesie decanus, et Petrus archidiaconus, et Ernulfus prior sancti Gud⟨l⟩aci, et Robertus prior supradicte Monemue,[1]
10 et Ricardus de Vestbiria, Galfridus de Cliffordia, et Walterus de Cluna, et Hugo de Caples, Gilebertus de Valford, et Walterus del Fredne. Si quis autem hanc confirmationem cassare attemptauerit, diuino eum relinquo iudicio.

CIROGRAFVM

**334**

[c. 1150–4] Notification that Walter del Mans and Agnes his wife have granted to Leominster priory (dep. of Reading abbey) thevirgate and meadow in *Purtlint(ona ?)* which William son of Symer holds for an annual rent of 4s., and 12d. rent from the mill which Hugh the miller son of Edwin holds. With the consent of Edward abbot of Reading, and at the request of the monks of Leominster, Gilbert has consecrated a cemetery for Walter and his wife at their chapel at Humber (Herefs), for one body only—the rest to be buried at Leominster as heretofore.

Abbot Edward died in 1154.

Gilebertus Dei gratia Herefordensis episcopus omnibus fidelibus parrochie sue, salutem et benedictionem.

Notum uobis esse uolumus quod Walterus del Mans et uxor eius Anneis dederunt in presentia nostra beato Petro et monachis de Leoministria in elemosinam

**333** Archives dép. Maine-et-Loire, H 3713 (Liber Albus of St-Florent, Saumur), fo. 125v (Fa); H 3711 (charter roll), no. 11 (Fr: select variants only). *Printed: Bibliothèque de l'École des Chartes*, XL (1879), 185; *calendared: CDF*, no. 1144; *Inventaire sommaire* (as no. 332), p. 473, cf. 474.
5 saluis] saluus Fa    9 Gudaci Fa; Cudaci Fr    10 H'ug' Fa; *missing in* Fr    13 CIROGRAFVM *in* Fr *only*
**334** BM Egerton MS 3031, fo. 56 (N); Cotton Domitian A. iii, fo. 61v (59v) (L) (Carts. Reading and Leominster).
1 Herf'N    2 et benedictionem *om.* L    3 Ennais L

[1] He occurs with his mother, Margaret, and stepfather, Hugh son of Richard, in *CDF*, nos. 1146, 1148 (c. 1151–7), and is probably the R. of no. 149. Prior Geoffrey occurs c. 1140 in *CDF*, no. 1139.

perpetuam quandam uirgatam terre in Purtlint(ona?) cum prato quam Willelmus 5
filius Symer tenet pro quatuor solidis per annum, duobus ad festum apostolorum
Petri et Pauli et duobus ad festum sancti Michaelis, et preter hoc duodecim denarios
de redditu molendini quod tenet Hugo molendinarius filius Edwini ad festum
sancti Michaelis. Ego autem G(ilebertus) episcopus Herefordensis concessu
Edwardi abbatis Rading(ensis) et rogatu monachorum de Leom(inistria) con- 10
secraui quoddam cimiterium eidem Waltero et uxori eius ad capellam eorum de
Humbro ea conditione ut sepulto ibi unius solummodo defuncti corpore, cetera
corpora cum diuisionibus defunctorum omnia ad Leom(inistriam) sicut solebant
antiquitus deferantur. Huius rei testes sunt ex parte monachorum: Walterus Foliot
archidiaconus Salopesb', Hugo nepos episcopi, W(alterus) de Clun' capellanus 15
episcopi, Adam de Eya decanus Leom(inistrie), G. capellanus de Humbre, Ail-
bricht uicarius eius, P(etrus) de Mapp(enora), R. frater eius, Herew' filius Alwardi,
Hugo de Leomin(istria), Walclinus dapifer; ex parte Walterii: Matheus filius eius,
W. nepos eius, et multi alii.

### 335

[1148-63 (possibly before 1154)] Notification of the consecration of a cemetery at Hampton
(Herefs)[1] at the request of Robert of Hampton as a sanctuary for his men; and of an agreement
between the monks of Leominster and Robert by which he gave the tithe of his own and his
men's land, 30 acres of arable, and an annual rent of $\frac{1}{2}$ mark which he had unjustly detained.
The agreement was confirmed by Elias de *Ponte*, burgess of Hereford, who held the land on
lease (or mortgage) at that time and promised to pay the rent.

The consecration of sanctuaries suggests that nos. 335-6 were written in the reign of
Stephen.

Gilebertus Dei gratia episcopus Herfordensis uniuersis sancte matris ecclesie filiis,
salutem et benedictionem.

Notum sit omnibus uobis quod ego rogatu Roberti de Hamtona et assensu
monachorum de Leomin(istria) consecraui quoddam cimiterium apud Hamt(onam)
ad refugium hominum Roberti. Robertus autem dedit in presentia nostra monachis 5
in elemosinam perpetuam omnem decimam dominii sui et hominum suorum in
feodo suo de Hamtona cum triginta acris terre; ⟨N, fo. 55 v⟩ preterea dimidiam
marcam argenti quam debebat annuatim Robertus ab antiquo ecclesie de Leoministria et iniuste aliquando detinuerat redditurum se sine intermissione et ab
herede suo reddendam promisit. Hanc conuentionem inter monachos et Robertum 10
audiuit et concessit Helyas de Ponte, burgensis de Hereford(ia), qui terram illam de
Roberto in uadium tunc temporis possidebat et eandem dimidiam marcam argenti

334  5 de Portlinton' L    5-6 tenet W. filius Simer L    8, 10 Eadwini / Eadwardi L    9 Herf' N
10 monachorum de N; fratrum L    11 W. L    13 omnia *om.* N    14 deferantur] L *ends
here with* t(estibus) etc.
335  BM Egerton MS 3031, fo. 55 (N); Cotton Domitian A. iii, fo. 62 (60) (L).
1-2 Gilebertus...benedictionem] G. Dei gratia etc. L    3 Rodberti de Hamtun' L (L *always
calls him* Rodbertus *or* R.)    9 retinuerat L    11 Herford' N

[1] Probably Hampton Wafer (*ex inf.* B. R. Kemp).

annuatim pro Roberto redditurum se monachis pollicitus est. Hanc donationem decime et terre et solutionem dimidie marce argenti fecerunt Robertus et Helyas
15 monachis per textum in manu nostra apud Leoministriam, presentibus et audientibus his testibus: Waltero Foliot archidiacono de Salopesb(eria), Waltero de Clune capellano episcopi, Hugone nepote episcopi, et multis aliis.

### 336

[1148–63 (possibly before 1154)] Notification that he has consecrated a cemetery at Risbury (Herefs) as a sanctuary for the men of Leominster priory and of Nicholas of Maund; and that Nicholas has given the priory the full tithe of the land of his men and two acres from each virgate, twelve acres from his own domain, half the tithe of the domain in his lifetime and the whole after his death.

Gilebertus Dei gratia Herefordensis episcopus omnibus parrochie sue fidelibus, salutem et benedictionem.

Sciant presentes et futuri quod ego G(ilebertus) episcopus Herefordensis consecraui quoddam cimiterium apud Riseburiam in terra monachorum de Leomin(is-
5 tria) ad refugium hominum ipsorum et hominum Nicholai de Magen'. Quod quia petitione Nicholai et assensu monachorum ad communem utilitatem factum est, dedit Nicholaus in presentia nostra monachis in perpetuum de terra hominum suorum plenariam decimam et duas acras terre de ⟨N, fo. 56⟩ singulis uirgatis, de dominio uero suo duodecim acras, et dimidiam suam decimam in uita sua, post
10 mortem autem totam. Hec uadiauit Nicholaus et homines eius in manu nostra et in manu monachorum se perhenniter seruaturos. Ipse uero Nicholaus cartam hanc coram omnibus ⟨L, fo. 59v⟩ lectam super altare beati Petri Leoministrie propria manu posuit et super textum iurauit. Huius rei testes sunt: Walterus Foliot archidiaconus Salopesb', Hugo nepos episcopi, et multi alii.

### 337

[1148–63] Notification of the consecration of a cemetery for the abbot of Reading at Hampton (Mappenore, Herefs); Peter of Mapenore has granted Leominster church (i.e. priory) the chapel within the cemetery, forty acres and the tithe of his domain and his men's land (cf. no. 335).

G(ilebertus) Dei gratia Herefordensis episcopus dilectis sibi in Christo uniuersis sancte matris ecclesie filiis, salutem et benedictionem.

Ex mandato et uoluntate domni abbatis Rading(ensis) cimiterium apud Hamtonam consecrauimus. Dominus autem loci Petrus de Mappenoura pro Deo et
5 salute anime sue et antecessorum suorum capellam infra predictum cimiterium

**335** 16 testibus] L *ends here with* etc.
**336** BM Egerton MS 3031, fo. 55v (N); Cotton Domitian A. iii, fo. 61 (59) (L).
1, 3 Herford' / Herf' N   4 Risebir' L   7 nostra *om.* N   10 Hoc L   13 sunt] L *ends here with* etc.
**337** BM Egerton MS 3031, fo. 55v (N); Cotton Domitian A. iii, fo. 62 (60) (L).
1 G(ilebertus)] Hil' N   1 Herf' N   2 et benedictionem *om.* L   4 Mappenoure L

sitam et quadraginta acras terre sue et omnem decimationem dominii sui et hominum suorum cum omni iure parrochiali matrici ecclesie de Leoministr(ia) in presentia nostra concessit. Quod ut ratum et inconuulsum in perpetuum maneat presenti scripto et sigilli nostri attestatione confirmamus.

## 338

[1148-55] Notification that Roger earl of Hereford (1143-55) has granted to Reading abbey the hamlet of Broadward (near Leominster, Herefs), which he obtained from Hugh of Kilpeck by exchange for Kingstone (Herefs), to which Robert Brito surrendered his claim.[1]

Gilebertus Dei gratia episcopus Herefordensis ecclesie omnibus fidelibus sancte ecclesie tam presentibus quam futuris, salutem et benedictionem.

Sciatis omnes quod Rogerus comes Hereford(ensis) pro salute ⟨Nb, fo. 121⟩ anime sue et omnium antecessorum suorum dedit Deo et ecclesie sancte Marie de Rading' et monachis ibidem Deo seruientibus uillulam de Bradeford' cum omnibus per- 5 tinentiis suis in perpetuam elemosinam. Quam uillulam predictus comes escam- biauit de Hugone de Kilpec et dedit ei in escambium pro ea uillam que uocatur Kingestuna quam acquietauit de Rodberto Britone et in capitulo Hereford(ensi) in presentia nostra et totius capituli saisiuit Hugonem de Kingestuna. Hugo uero comitem de Bradeford comes proinde saisiuit monachos de Rading' de Bradeford 10 per unum textum. Huius donationis isti sunt testes: ego G(ilebertus) episcopus Herfordensis cum toto capitulo nostro, Baderun de Munemue, Walterus de Clifford, et multi alii.

## 339

[Probably c. 1163] Grant of an indulgence to Reading abbey.

Gilbert granted two identical indulgences to Reading abbey, one as bishop of Hereford, one as bishop of London: no. 430. Since the original of no. 339 still survives, we may be confident that both were in fact issued. The fact that they are verbally identical suggests (though it does not prove) that they were issued about the same time, and it may well be that no. 339 was issued just before, 430 just after his translation to London. No. 430 was one of a group of indulgences probably issued about the time of the dedication of the abbey in 1164, or possibly in preparation for it somewhat earlier: on these see *Acta Chichester*, no. 45 and

338 BM Egerton MS 3031, fo. 55 (N); Cotton Vespasian E. xxv, fo. 66v (Na); Harl. 1708, fo. 120v (Nb) (select variants only of Na and Nb).
1 Gilbertus Na   1, 3, 8 Herfordensis (etc.) N   8 Roberto Na   11 textum] NaNb *end here* (Nb *adds* T(estibus))
339 *Original* (6½ in. × 4 in.): BM Add. Charter 19,587. Seal (red wax), repaired (simple queue). *Endorsed:* Gileb' Hereford' de absolutione penitentium in festo sancti I. xx dies (thirteenth century). *Copy* in BM Egerton MS 3031, fo. 58r-v. Variants of no. 430 (Egerton MS 3031, fo. 58) are noted. *Abstract* in J. B. Hurry, *Reading Abbey* (London, 1901), p. 163.

[1] The charters of Earl Roger and Hugh of Kilpeck are in MS Egerton 3031, fo. 45v; to both Gilbert is witness. For Broadward see *Herefs. DB*, p. 105.

note. It is, however, possible that no. 339 was originally issued in connexion with the presentation of a hand of St James to the abbey in 1156 (BM Cotton MS Domit. A. iii, fo. 31v (29v)).

Dilectis sibi in Domino uniuersis sancte matris ecclesie filiis frater G(ilebertus) Herefordensis ecclesie minister, salutem et dilectionem in Christo.

Dignitatis apostolice quanta sit eminentia uestram scimus karissimi prudentiam non latere, quibus magno Domini munere collatum est ut cum uite merita loca-
5 buntur, super sedes celestes cum ipso sedeant et iudiciariam nacti potestatem que sint unicuique remuneranda decernant. De quorum collegio magnus ille Iacobus est frater Iohannis apostoli, qui post passionem Domini ab Herode captus et ipsius gladio percussus primus in apostolorum numero meruit coronari. Cuius reliquias honorandas quia fratres Rading' summo fouent et uenerantur obsequio, fraterni-
10 tatem uestram pie commonemus in Domino ut in sollempnitate eiusdem apostoli ob ipsius reuerentiam ad iamdictam ecclesiam qua ipsius habentur reliquie deuo-tione debita conueniatis, ut uobis eius intercessione a Domino peccatorum ueniam et gratiam obtineatis. Omnibus uero qui ad eandem solempnitatem conuenerint uel ecclesiam ipsam infra eiusdem solempnitatis octabas uisitauerint et honorem
15 apostolo debitum orationibus et oblationibus sacris impenderint, nos de Domini misericordia et beati apostoli confisi meritis de iniuncta sibi penitentia uiginti dies relaxamus. Valete.

## 340

[1148–63][1] Grant of an indulgence to Leominster priory.

G. Dei gratia Herefordensis episcopus etc.

Notum sit omnibus quod monasterium Leom(inistrie) longis tribulationibus et multis aduersitatibus ita attenuatum est quod ad sustentationem eorum qui ibidem Deo deseruiunt uix sufficiat. Vnde omnibus qui ad predictum in festo beatorum
5 apostolorum Petri et Pauli ob amorem Dei et sanctorum reuerentiam conuenerint et aliquod beneficium contulerint, benedictionem nostram et societatem omnium bonorum Heref(ordensis) ecclesie concedimus, et de meritis eorum confisi ⟨fo. 72v⟩ hiis qui in criminali sunt quadraginta dies aliis uero uiginti de penitentia eis iniuncta relaxamus.

339 2 Herefordensis] Londoniensis 430    4 merita] munera 430    10 eiusdem] ipsius 430
17 relaxamus] 430 *adds* eosque beneficiorum spiritualium Londoniensis ecclesie, cui Deo auctore presidemus, participes constituimus in perpetuum
340 BM Cotton MS Domitian A. iii, fo. 74 (72).
2 sit] est *MS*

---

[1] The manuscript rubric reads 'Gileb.' Hereford.'' It is, however, possible that this is an act of Bishop William de Vere (1186–98).

## 341

[1148–63] Settlement in Gilbert's presence of the dispute between Leominster priory and Serlo priest of Kinnersley (Herefs) on the chapel of *Ewda* and the tithes pertaining to it: Serlo admits that it is not attached of right to his church, and in exchange is given care of it for his life for a pension of five shillings per annum.

Sciant presentes et futuri quod altercatio que inter ecclesiam de Leoministria et Serlonem presbiterum de Kinardesleg' extitit super capella de Ewda et decimis ad eam pertinentibus, presidente uenerabili disertoque uiro domno Gisleberto Herefordensi episcopo eiusdemque ecclesie assistente clero, serie tali discretionis uentilabro discussa huiusmodi exitum sortita est. Predictus etenim presbiter in contionis 5 medio positus sponte coram domno episcopo cleroque uenerando predictam capellam illius ecclesie cui preerat non esse iuris ore proprio professus est, eamque ab omni calumpnia liberam ecclesie de cuius territorio dinoscitur esse concessit, insuper et ius quod ecclesie sue prius uendicauerat—uel potius usurpauerat— abnegando deleuit. His igitur ordine tali peractis domno episcopo mediante 10 suppliciterque intercedente, clericis et laicis acclamantibus, ex permissione ecclesie Leoministrie eidem Serloni predicte capelle cura et ministratio delegata est quamdiu hac uita fruitur; ita sane quod annuatim ecclesie de Leom(inistria) persoluat quinque solidos in festiuitate beatorum apostolorum Petri et Pauli. Cum autem predictus Serlo ex hac uita migrauerit capella predicta cum decimis transeat in 15 proprios usus monachorum de Leoministria, ut tradant eam cui uoluerint uel si magis uoluerint ipsi in manu sua eam retineant. Huius conuencionis testes sunt etc.

## 342

[1154–63] Settlement of the case between Reading abbey and Gilbert of Hampton on the tithes of Hampton,[1] which had in the past belonged to the church of Leominster but were detained in time of war by Gilbert: the abbot of Reading proved in chapter at Hereford that full parochial rights belonged to Leominster (cf. no. 335).

'Tempore werre' implies that the anarchy is in the past.

Gilebertus Dei gratia Herfordensis episcopus dilectis sibi in Christo filiis clero et populo in episcopatu Herford(ensi) constitutis, salutem, gratiam et benedictionem.

Ad commissum nobis a Deo spectat officium emergentes in parrochia nostra lites dirimere et unicuique ⟨fo. 56v⟩ prout scimus et possumus ius suum[2] reseruare. Inde est quod discretioni uestre notificamus litem que fuit inter abbatem de Rading' et Gilebertum de Hamton' super decimis ipsius Hamt(one), quas ex 5

341 BM Egerton MS 3031, fo. 56 (N); Cotton Domitian A. iii, fo. 61v (59v) (L).
1 de *om.* L    2 Kinardesleg'] Chinardesl' L    2 Eiwda L    3 domno *om.* N    3–4 G. Herf' N    11 et (*inserted*) suppliciter L    11 cleris N    13 quod] ut L    13 de *om.* L 16 proprios *om.* N    16 de *om.* L    17 Huius...etc. L; his testibus N
342 BM Egerton MS 3031, fo. 56.

---

[1] 'Ricardi' in Hope-under-Dinmore (*ex inf.* B. R. Kemp).
[2] Cf. *GF*, p. 64.

antiquo iure ecclesie Leom(inistrie) pertinentes memoratus Gilebertus tempore werre uiolenter detinuit, predicta ecclesia Leomin(istrie) ius suum semper reclamante, hoc tandem fine conquieuisse. Abbas Rading' in presentia nostra et capituli
10 nostri Herf(ordie) iuramento sufficienti clericorum probauit et laicorum totum parrochiale ius predicte Hamt(one) uiuorum et mortuorum ad ecclesiam Leomin(istrie) pertinere et sic adiudicatam sibi inuestituram simul et possessionem accepit. Hoc in presentia nostra et capituli nostri ita terminatum ne posteris deueniat in dubium presenti scripto et sigilli nostri attestatione testificamur pariter
15 et confirmamus.

## 343

[1158–61] Confirmation to Reading abbey of what Bishop Richard (1121–7) confirmed to Abbot Hugh (the first abbot) of Reading: the church of St Peter, Leominster, and all the *parrochia* subject to it: Broadward (near Leominster), Ach, Monkland (?),[1] Dilwyn (both), Luntley (in Dilwyn), Kinnersley, Woonton, Sarnesfield (both), Titley, Hope-under-Dinmore, Wharton (in Leominster), Newton, Gater Top (both in Hope-under-Dinmore), Stoke Prior, Hatfield (both), Risbury, Humber, Edvin Ralph, Butterley, Broadfield (in Bodenham), Hampton Mappenore and 'Ricardi' ((?) in Hope-under-Dinmore), Ford (in Humber), Hennor, Eaton (near Leominster), Hampton Wafer (?) Stockton (in Kimbolton), Ashton (probably in Eye), Brimfield, Upton (in Brimfield), Middleton on the Hill (in Kimbolton), Drayton (?) (in Brimfield), Hamnish (in Kimbolton), the Whyle (in Pudleston), Pudleston, Brockmanton (in Pudleston), Ford (? in Pudleston), Luston (in Eye), Eye, and Croft (Herefs).

Roger became abbot of Reading in 1158; the charter was confirmed by Archbishop Theobald in the period 1158–61 (Saltman, no. 216). Bishop Richard's grant (*Monasticon*, IV, 56) is dated 1123. From these documents may be reconstructed the *parrochia* of the ancient minster church of Leominster, the minster of *Leon*, as that district of Herefs was known in early times; cf. *Taxatio*, pp. 159–60; *Herefs. DB*, pp. 9 ff., 84–9 and *passim*; *Monasticon*, IV, 58–60; *PN Herefs*. (ed. A. T. Bannister, Cambridge, 1916), *passim*. For Eye, Luston and Croft, Domit. A. iii, fo. 103v (100v).

Gilebertus Dei gratia Herefordensis episcopus dilectis sibi in Domino uniuersis sancte matris Herefordensis ecclesie filiis, salutem, gratiam et benedictionem.
Predecessoris nostri bone memorie Ricardi Herefordensis quondam episcopi uestigiis adherentes que ecclesie Radingensi et eius abbati primo domino Hugoni
5 ipse concessit et confirmauit nos quoque eidem ecclesie et eius abbati domino Rogero concedimus et confirmamus, scilicet ecclesiam sancti Petri de Leoministria cum omni ad ipsam pertinente parrochia, scilicet de Bradeford' et de Ach et de Leena et de Diliga prima et secunda que ambe magis proxime sunt Leomenistrie et

342 8 predicte ecclesie *MS*
343 BM Egerton MS 3031, fo. 55 (N); Cotton Domitian A. iii, fo. 60v (58v) (L).
1 Gislebertus L    1, 2, 3 Herfordensis N

---

[1] *Lenhale* in Theobald's confirmation: Saltman, p. 439; this suggests Lyonshall, but Leominster seems to have had an interest in the church of Monkland, not Lyonshall (*Taxatio*, p. 159).

de Luntelega et de Kinardeslega et de Winnetuna et de utraque Sernesfelda et de Titelega, de Hopa quoque *et Wauertuna et Niwetuna et de Gatredehopa, de 10 Stokes quoque et de utraque Hethfeld' et de Risebiria et Humbra et Gedesfenna et Buterlega et Bradefelda et utraque Hamtuna et Forda et Hanoura et Eatuna et Heentuna, de Stoctuna quoque ⟨L, fo. 59⟩ et Esscetuna et Bremesfelda et Vptuna et Miclatuna et Dreituna et Hamenesce et Wihale et Putlesduna et Brocmannetuna et Forda, de Lustuna quoque et Eya et Croftuna. Hec antiqui et auctentici uiri in 15 presentia prefati episcopi sicut in carta ipsius continetur attestati sunt ad parrochiam Leomin(istrie) pertinere. Que pariter omnia et nos Radingensi ecclesie confirmamus, salua iusticia quam unicuique seruare debemus.

## 344

[? c. 1150–c. 1158] Confirmation to Shrewsbury abbey of tithes granted for the building of the abbey church (founded c. 1083–90): all the tithes of Cold Weston, domain tithes of Henley, and two-thirds of the domain tithes of Stottesdon, Walkerslow, Newton (both near Stottesdon), Sibdon Carwood and Yockleton (Salop).[1]

A puzzling document, because the protocol, with the phrase *diuina miseratione*, suggests a date in the late twelfth century or later—i.e. of Bishop William de Vere (1186–98). But the witnesses belong to the period c. 1150–78 (archdeacon Walter, confirmed by David de Aqua), and the charter was inspected by Dean Ralph (died c. 1158), whose inspeximus was witnessed by Masters Geoffrey, Simon, and David, two of whom were probably also witnesses to this charter. We therefore feel bound to assume that it is a genuine act of Gilbert's, and the protocol must be either a scribal error or a chance anticipation of the later form.

Omnibus sancte matris ecclesie filiis ad quos presens scriptum peruenerit G(ilebertus) diuina miseratione Herefordensis episcopus, eternam in Domino salutem.

Vniuersitati uestre significamus nos dilectis filiis abbati et conuentui Salop(esberie) concessisse et confirmasse omnes decimas in diocesi nostra a bonis uiris ad constructionem ecclesie sue eis collatas: uidelicet decimas totius uille de Westone et 5 decimas dominii de Henneleg' et duas partes decimarum dominii de Stotdesdon' et duas partes decimarum dominii de Walkeslawe et duas partes decimarum dominii de Neuton' et duas partes decimarum dominii ⟨p. 297⟩ de Sibeton' et duas partes decimarum dominii de Iokethull' tam maiores quam minutas. Has igitur prefatas decimas predicte ecclesie collatas presenti scripto et sigilli nostri testimonio con- 10 firmamus. Hiis testibus: Waltero archidiacono, Dauid de Aqua, magistro Nicholao, magistro Edwardo, magistro Galfrido canonicis Hereford', et aliis quampluribus.

343 9–17 Chinardesl' / Titelleg' / Butt'leg' / Heanoura / Eatona / Heentona / Stochtun' / Bremefeld' / Whiale / Brocmanetun' / Heya / Crofta / Leomen' L   10 *et] L *adds* de 17 et nos omnia L
344 Aberystwyth, National Library of Wales, MS 7851D (ex Phillips 3516) (Cart. Shrewsbury), pp. 296–7; second copy in inspeximus by Dean Ralph and the Chapter on p. 297. Transcript of this (eighteenth century) in BM Add. 30311, fos. 270v–271. (Inspeximus gives as witnesses 'magistro Galfrido, magistro Symone, magistro Dauid canonicis Hereford' et aliis quampluribus'; otherwise variants trivial, e.g. Sibbetun', Iokethul'.)

---

[1] Cf. Eyton, *Salop*, I, 67–9, 101; IV, 153, 163, 171; XI, 268; VII, 51.

## 345

[1161–2] Judgement as judge delegate with Godfrey archdeacon of Worcester in the case between the canons of St Mary's Warwick (collegiate) and Prior Ralph and the canons of St Sepulchre's Warwick (canons of Holy Sepulchre), about parochial rights and a pension of 30*d*. On the evidence of six priests and six laymen the parochial rights were adjudged to St Mary's, and the pension likewise on the evidence of four priests and three laymen (cf. nos. 346–7).

The mandate of Alexander III (*PUE*, I, no. 84) is dated 3 August, i.e. 1160 or 1161, the confirmation of the decision (*op. cit.* no. 90) 23 (?) August (1162). It is unlikely that Alexander would have issued such a mandate before his recognition at the end of 1160, and so the case probably belongs to the years 1161–2, and this decision to the very end of 1161 or, more probably, to the first half of 1162.

Dilectis sibi in Domino uniuersis sancte matris ecclesie filiis frater Gillebertus Herefordensis ecclesie minister, a rege cui militant glorie assequi donatiuum.

Quod apostolica per nos auctoritate term⟨i⟩natum est, notitie communi mandare curauimus, ut diu protractam controuersiam ne denuo suscitetur in litem, presentis
5 scripti testimonio, iuuante Domino prorsus euacuemus. Accepto namque super hoc domni pape mandato, ut causam, que inter canonicos ecclesie beate Marie et Omnium Sanctorum et Radulfum priorem et canonicos sancti Sepulchri de Warewich' uertebatur, ego et domnus Godefridus Wigorn⟨iensis⟩ archidiaconus appellatione remota decideremus; ⟨fo. 18v⟩ ad hoc die statuto conuenimus et
10 coram nobis in hunc modum memorata iam causa deducta est. Conquesti sunt canonici beate Marie et Omnium Sanctorum magnam parochie sue partem sibi a iamdicto priore sancti Sepulcri et fratribus eius uiolenter auferri et annuam triginta denariorum pensionem sibi ab ecclesia sancti Sepulcri iamdiu debitam iniuste sibi iam aliquamdiu detineri, cumque hec duo intenderent manifestam utriusque
15 probationem et scriptis et testibus offerebant, prior uero dilatorias quasdam pretendens exceptiones et diu protelatam rem in tempus adhuc differre desiderans, nil prorsus rationis allegabat, quo uel partem illam parochie ad ecclesiam suam de iure pertinere, uel se iam memoratos triginta denarios iuste detinere ostenderet. Nos itaque quos ad ipsius cause decisionem apostolica urgebat auctoritas, atten-
20 dentes actori probationem de iure incumbere et oportere eum raciones habere quibus quod intendit uerum esse insinuet,[1] canonicis sancte Marie probationem eorum que intendebant, adiudicauimus. Sex itaque sacerdotum et sex laicorum iuramento probatum est, partem illam parochie quam uendicabant iamdicti cano-nici ad ecclesiam suam pertinere; et quatuor sacerdotum triumque laicorum iura-
25 mento item probatum est memoratos triginta denarios ecclesie sue ex antiqua pactione fuisse debitos, et per manum priorum sancti Sepulcri Almeri, Antonii, Radulfi ecclesie sue in solempnitate Omnium Sanctorum fuisse solutos—quorum utique iuramenti fidem faciebat e facili carta domni Simonis dudum Wigorn⟨iensis⟩

345 PRO Exchequer Records, K.R. Misc. Books, E 164/22, fo. 18 (Cart. Warwick).
19 dicisionem *MS*   19 auctoritate *MS*   21 probationum *MS*

---

[1] Cf. no. 96.

episcopi sigillo impressa, parochiam hanc ad ecclesiam sancte Marie et Omnium Sanctorum pertinere testificans, et hanc pactionem iam dicte pensionis triginta 30 denariorum annuatim soluendorum inter iam dictas ecclesias interuenisse et firmatam fuisse commemorans. Hiis itaque moti rationibus predictis canonicis beate Marie et Omnium Sanctorum et parochiam quam uendicabant et pensionem predictam ⟨fo. 19⟩ quam repetebant apostolica auctoritate adiudicauimus, et eos per textum euangelii super quod iuratum est, his que sibi competere probauerant, ego 35 et domnus Godfridus archidiaconus Wigorn(iensis) inuestiuimus, statuentes et apostolica auctoritate precipientes, ut eis decetero memorati triginta denarii persoluantur et ab omnibus quos ecclesia sancti Sepulcri iniuste ut nunc patet usurpauerat, parochialia sibi ad plenum iura reddantur; saluo tamen apostolico priuilegio quo ecclesie sancti Sepulcri fratrum suorum et conuersorum et familie 40 sue sepultura conceditur. Quorum occasione uerborum ne de cetero iam dictarum ecclesiarum iura turbentur, scriptum hoc apostolicum in presentia nostra benigne interpretatum est, et in ipsam interpretationem ex utraque parte concensum [sic], ut fratrum nomine canonici ipsi sancti Sepulcri, nomine conuersorum qui de seculo fugientes proprium habere iam desinunt et eorum magisterio se committunt, 45 nomine familie qui de ipsius mensa sunt larem alium non habentes, intelligantur. Valere uos optamus in Domino.

## 346

[c. 1162] Notification that when the decision in no. 345 was made, the canons of St Mary's Warwick granted the portion of the parish in question to Ralph, prior of St Sepulchre's Warwick, personally, so long as he lives and is prior, for an annual pension of ten shillings.

The confirmation of this by Archdeacon Godfrey follows in the cartulary (fo. 20).

Dilectis sibi in Domino uniuersis sancte matris ecclesie filiis frater Gillebertus Herefordensis ecclesie minister, in Christo dilectionem et salutem perpetuam.

Prona est presens etas in malum et que nascuntur e facili difficulter iurgia con-quiescunt. Vnde et pium duximus esse et ad conseruandam pacem ecclesiarum de Warewich' ualde necessarium, ut quod inter canonicos ecclesie sancte Marie et 5 Omnium Sanctorum et Radulfum priorem sancti Sepulcri de Warewich' sub nostra conscientia gestum est, scripture testimonio in publicam notitiam euocemus. Nouerit itaque dilectio uestra memoratos canonicos nostro et aliorum plurium interuentu illam portionem sue parochie quam eis ego et G(odefridus) Wigorn(ien-sis) archidiaconus apostolica adiudicauimus auctoritate, predicto priori sancti 10 Sepulcri Radulfo concessisse, persone uidelicet non ecclesie sancti Sepulcri, annua pensione decem solidorum quoad ipse uiueret et in officio prioris ibi ministraret possidendam. Vnde ne pretextu beneficii ipso priori personaliter indulti, ecclesia postmodum sancti Sepulcri aliquid sibi iuris in hoc usurpare presumat, quod gestum est in euum, quod gestum est modum, uniuersitati uestre significare et sigilli nostri 15 testimonio roborare curauimus. Valete.

346 PRO Exchequer Records, K.R. Misc. Books, E 164/22, fo. 19v.
15 modum] ? modo

## 347

[1162–3] Instruction to Godfrey archdeacon of Worcester, to instruct the rural dean to see that the terms of nos. 345–6 are fulfilled.

G(ilebertus) Dei gratia Herefordensis episcopus uenerabili fratri et amico G(ode-frido) Wigorn(iensi) archidiacono salutem.

Mandauimus uobis quatinus canonicos de Warewich' pactis cum Radulfo priore initis stare compelleretis; et si quid acceperant de parochia quam sibi adiudicauimus, 5 postquam eam Radulfo priori in uita sua annua decem solidorum pensione tenendam in presentia nostra concesserunt, hoc sibi restitui faceretis. Canonici uero eidem restitutioni parati sunt, concedentes ut tredecim denarii quos se de eadem parochia habuisse fatentur—de summa decem solidorum quos sibi prior debet—de-du⟨fo. 20v⟩cantur, uel si prior eos amplius habuisse probauerit, sibi que probata 10 fuerint compensentur. Genus enim solutionis optimum est compensatio—id est debiti inuicem contributio[1]—et qui debet optime soluit, cum debitori suo quantum ab eo exigitur de summa sibi debita remittit. Vnde uobis mandamus quatinus ad hoc directo decano uestro rem ipsam in parochia ipsa coram parrochianis ipsis circa hos fines mandati stare faciatis. Valete.

## 348

[1148–63, probably early] Confirmation to Ralph prior of Worcester and his successors of Bishop Robert's grant of the rectory of Lindridge (Worcs).[2]

The reference to his predecessor and the form suggest an early date.

Notum sit tam presenti etati quam future posteritati quod ego Gilbertus Herefor-densis ecclesie Dei gratia episcopus dompno Radulfo priori Wigorn(iensis) ecclesie et successoribus suis in perpetuum substituendis personatum ecclesie de Lindrugge, quem ei predecessor meus bone memorie dompnus Robertus episcopus concessit 5 scriptoque suo confirmauit, ipse quoque concedo; et ut hoc ratum inconuulsumque permaneat, presenti scripto et sigilli mei attestatione confirmo.

## 349

[c. 1148] Notification that one Benedict, made by judgement of Bishop Robert's court to swear his innocence, supported by seven priests, of his brother's murder, has fulfilled the sentence.

Evidently soon after Bishop Robert's death.

Dilectis sibi in Christo fratribus uniuersis sancte matris ecclesie filiis frater G(ileber-tus) H(erefordensis) ecclesie dictus episcopus, salutem et dilectionem in Domino.

**347** PRO Exchequer Records, K.R. Misc. Books, E 164/22, fo. 20.
**348** Worcester Cathedral, Dean and Chapter, Reg. A4 ('Reg. I'), fo. xxvii.
**349** G, no. 89; B, fo. 21.

---

[1] Cf. *Digest*, 16, 2, 1.                    [2] Cf. *VCH Worcs.* III, 448–9.

Caritati uestre presenti scripto notificamus nos certo religiosarum personarum cognouisse testimonio, presentium latorem Benedictum coram justitia[1] predecessoris nostri bone memorie R(oberti) episcopi septima sacerdotum manu iurasse 5 fratrem suum, de cuius morte suspectus fuerat, machinatione sua aut consensu, aut uoluntate, nunquam mortem incurrisse. Qui ut plene super hoc facto ostenderet innocentiam suam in presentia nostra multis nobiscum assidentibus, in hunc etiam modum iurauit. 'Parentes mei qui de morte fratris mei suspecti hactenus sunt habiti, mortem ipsi non intulerunt. Nemo etiam mei causa mortem ipsi machinatus 10 est, sic me Deus adiuuet ⟨B, fo. 21 v⟩ et hec sancta.' Quod iuramentum duodecim ilico sacerdotes in hunc modum confirmauerunt. 'Benedictum hunc super hac re uerum iurasse nobis certum est, sic nos Deus adiuuet et hec sancta.' Quod cum in presentia nostra sic actum est, ne solita deinceps innoscentia ipsius prematur infamia, quod uidimus, hoc testamur, et rem gestam presenti uobis scripto et sigilli nostri 15 inpressione declaramus. Valete.

**349** 3 reliosarum B

---

[1] I.e. court, an unusual use of the word.

# VII

## CHARTERS OF GILBERT FOLIOT AS
## BISHOP OF LONDON
### 1163–1187

### Nos. 350–476

## 350

[1163–c. 1180] Notification that R. of Ardleigh (Essex) has resigned the church of Ardleigh, and that G. de *Sur'* has been instituted as rector, on the presentation of the patron, in his place.

G(ilebertus) Dei gratia L(undoniensis) episcopus dilectis sibi in Domino archi-diaconis, decanis, et omnibus qui in episcopatu Lund(oniensi) consistunt ecclesiarum prelatis, salutem, gratiam et benedictionem.

Nouerit dilectio uestra quod R. clericus de Ardel' ecclesiam de Ardel' in manus nostras tam spontanee quam absolute resignauit, seque quod nichil in ea iuris 5 ulterius esset repetiturus, interposita iuramenti religione obligauit. Quam nos petitione quidem et presentatione aduocati, dilecto nostro G. de Sur' cum omni integritate sua perpetuo habendam et canonice possidendam concessimus, ipsumque in ea personam debita solempnitate constituimus. Quod quia in dubium nolumus aut in irritum de cetero posse reuocari, presenti scripto uniuersitati uestre id 10 notificare et episcopali auctoritate confirmare curauimus. His testibus [ . . . ]

## 351

[1175¹–80 (c. 1179)] Settlement of the dispute between Abbess Matilda and the convent of Barking (Essex, Benedictine nuns) and R., archdeacon of Avranches, rector of Buttsbury (Essex), on the church of St Edmund of Ingatestone and parochial rights in Ingatestone and Hanley Hall (in Ingatestone,² Essex): these are adjudged to Barking abbey, and William son of Walkelin is instituted as rector of Ingatestone on the petition of the convent for an annual pension of two wax candles of 4 lb.

G(ilebertus) Dei gratia Londoniensis episcopus omnibus sancte matris ecclesie filiis per episcopatum Londoniensem constitutis, salutem, gratiam et benedictionem.

Prouidendum nobis est ne controuersie coram nobis decise iterum reuiuiscant in litem. Proinde uolumus ad omnium peruenire notitiam quod cum inter dilectam ac uenerabilem filiam nostram Matildem abbatissam de Berking' et eiusdem loci 5 conuentum ex una parte et ecclesiam de Potuluesperie et R. Abricensem archi-diaconum personam ecclesie de Potuluespirie ex altera parte, super ecclesia sancti Eadmundi de Ging' et super iure parrochiali decimarum et parrochianorum de

350 G, no. 231; B, fo. 194.
351 *Original:* Chelmsford, Essex Record Office, D/DP T1/692. Seal (natural wax, repaired with red). *Endorsed:* Gynges (fifteenth century), Hanley (sixteenth century). Scriptum de ij cereis iiij librarum ponderis de ecclesia de Botulfespirie [*sic*] annuatim soluendis super magnum altare de Berkyng' die sancte Ethelburge etc. (fifteenth century).

---

¹ Matilda, daughter of Henry II, was appointed abbess between 1175 and 1179 (*Cal. Charter Rolls*, v, 286: between the election of John of Oxford to Norwich in Nov. 1175 and the death of Richard de Lucy in July 1179—or rather his retirement earlier that year: Delisle, *Recueil*, Introd. pp. 434–6). She was still abbess in 1198 (Feet of Fines, *PRS*, xxiii, 97), but had been succeeded by 1202 (*VCH Essex*, ii, 120).
² Cf. *VCH Essex*, ii, 120.

Ging' et de Hanleia, in presentia nostra controuersia diu uerteretur, post multas
10 tandem hinc inde altercationes utraque parte presente legittime facta est nobis fides,
quod prelibata ecclesia sancti Eadmundi de Ging' cum iure parrochiali omnium
decimarum et omnium parrochianorum de Ging' et de Hanleia ad memoratam
abbatissam de Berching' et eiusdem loci conuentum de iure spectabat, et quod
iamdictus R. Abricensis archidiaconus nomine ecclesie sue de Potuluespirie eam
15 illicite detinebat occupatam; nos igitur causa cognitionaliter examinata et partibus
comminus constitutis sepedictam ecclesiam sancti Eadmundi de Ging' cum iure
parrochiali omnium decimarum et omnium parrochianorum de Ging' et de
Hanleia liberam perpetuo et penitus absolutam ab omni parrochiali subiectione
ecclesie de Potuluesperie sepedictis abbatisse et conuentui de Berching' adiudicaui-
20 mus, ipsamque eis cum omnibus pertinentiis suis in terris, in decimis, in oblationibus
et obuentionibus siue quibuscunque rebus aliis ad ipsam pertinentibus iam siue
postmodum peruenturis, in pace et quiete, libere et pacifice, perpetuis temporibus
possidendam auctoritate pontificali assignauimus. Quod quia perpetuum et firmum
stabilitatis uolumus in posterum robur habere, presentis scripti patrocinio et sigilli
25 nostri appositione confirmare curauimus. Preterea sciendum est nos ad petitionem
et presentationem prelibate M(atildis) abbatisse de Berching' et eiusdem loci
conuentus, postquam antefata ecclesia de Ging' ipsis fuit a nobis adiudicata, concessisse et dedisse eam Willelmo filio Walkelini cum omnibus pertinentiis suis in
terris, in decimis, in oblationibus et obuentionibus, ipsumque in ea debita sollemp-
30 nitate constituisse personam, sub annua pensione duorum cereorum quatuor
librarum cere super maius altare monasterii Berchingensis in festo sancte Athelburge
uirginis singulis annis soluendorum. Testibus hiis: Nicholao archidiacono London(ie),
Radulfo de Diceto archidiacono Middelsexie, magistro Henrico de Norhamton',
magistro Ricardo de Storteford', magistro Radulfo de Altaripa, Gileberto Foliot,
35 Radulfo de Chiltun, Ricardo de Saresbir(ia), Waltero elemosinario, Lodewico
clericis.

### 352

[1163-c. 1180] Grant of an indulgence in support of the appeal for funds for the hospital at
Berkhamstead (Herts) (?).[1]

G(ilebertus) Dei gratia L(undoniensis) episcopus dilectis sibi in Domino uniuersis
eiusdem ecclesie parrochianis et filiis, salutem, gratiam et benedictionem.

Latores hii presentium nuntii sunt infirmorum de Berc'am',[1] qui per ipsos suam
uobis ostendentes inopiam, deuote supplicant ut ob Dei reuerentiam sibi subuenia-
5 tis, et de his que uobis diuina contulit misericordia ad eorum subleuandam inediam

---

352 G, no. 236; B, fo. 199v.

[1] The interpretation of *Berc'am'* is uncertain: there were various hospitals in Berkhamstead,
none hitherto known to be as old as the twelfth century (see KH, p. 254; *VCH Herts.* IV,
458–9), though St John the Baptist's, for lepers, founded before 1213, seems quite a likely
candidate. A possible alternative would be Berden (Essex).

beneficium aliquod prout uobis Dominus inspirauerit impertiatis. Quorum precibus nos quoque preces adicimus, rogantes et exhortantes in Domino ut corda uestra Christi pauperibus aperiatis, et dum potestis et uobis uita superstes est, Deum in membris suis honorando, illud ad memoriam reuocetis, quod suis in fine dicturus est: 'quod uni ex minimis meis qui in me credunt fecistis, michi fecistis';[1] et hoc 10 pre oculis habendo et opere complendo, quod hic pauperibus Christi ob eius reuerentiam erogaueritis, in futura uita in centuplum recipiatis. Qui uero nostris acquiescendo monitis eis in aliquo ad uite pro Christo sustentationem subuenerint, de eius confisi misericordia de iniuncta sibi penitentia decem dies relaxamus.

## 353

[1163–c. 1180] Grant of an indulgence in support of the appeal for the restoration of the church in Bishop's Stortford castle (Herts).[2]

G(ilebertus) Dei gratia Lundoniensis ecclesie minister dilectis sibi in Domino uniuersis eiusdem ecclesie parrochianis et filiis, salutem, gratiam et benedictionem.

Est apud nos in castello de Storteford locus reuerende uenustatis, locus olim sanctuario Dei et diuinis deputatus obsequiis, quem etiam nunc post ruinas, ob ea que ibi crebro apparuisse dicuntur sanctitatis indicia, fidelis populus cum multa 5 ueneratur et reueretur deuotione. Nos igitur ob amorem Dei et sacri loci reuerentiam in statum pristinum rem reformare et basilicam ibidem Deo reedificare disponentes, propositum pii laboris caritati uestre denuntiamus, optantes ut et uos pii nobiscum operis adiutores, debitique fructus et digne mercedis simul participes efficiamus. Hinc est quod uestram oramus et exhortamur in Domino dilectionem, 10 quatinus pietatis intuitu sancto operi huic opem et operam inpendatis, et ut ad complementum incepta perueniant, ad reparandam domum Domini qui omnia contulit, aliqua de bonis uestris conferatis, scituris his qui nostris in hoc monitis adquiescunt, quod orationum et beneficiorum sancte Lund(oniensis) eclesie eos specialiter constituimus esse participes. Penitentibus autem et peccata confessis, qui 15 in opus hoc ad honorem Dei aliquid karitatiue impertierint, de iniuncta sibi satisfactione misericorditer uiginti dies relaxamus.

## 354

[1163–87] Note of confirmation attached to the charter of foundation, by William Doo, of the hospital of *Sedeburghbrok*—Brooke St in South Weald.[3] William Doo gave the field on which the hospital was built, land 'Edwyni Regis', one oak per annum, woodland pasture for the hospital's beasts, especially for their pigs, tithe of his cornfield at the barn door at

353 G, no. 224; B, fo. 41.
4 scanctuario B
354 London, Guildhall Library, MS 9531/2, fo. 153 v (Reg. Simon of Sudbury). *Printed: Reg. Sudbury*, I, 210–11.

---

[1] Matt. xxv. 40.
[2] This castle was one of the bishop's palaces throughout the Middle Ages.
[3] Cf. *PN Essex*, p. 136.

Ockendon (Essex), tithe of cumin from his rent save for the land of his knights, tithe of pieces of meat in his kitchen and tithe of geese, tithe of the herbs of his garden—cabbages, leeks and onions *scalimiorum*; for the souls of all his family and of Earl Geoffrey (de Mandeville, earl of Essex, 1156–66) and his wife Rosia. Witnesses: Richard de le Rochele, Catellina his (evidently the founder's) wife, his sons Thomas, Reginald, William, clerk, Henry and Ralph Doo, Geoffrey de Gerpewelle, Hugh Doo, Roger his brother, Turruld de Halleford, William son of Richard, Nicholas Vascelin, David son of Geoffrey, William son of Geoffrey, John son of Geoffrey, Geoffrey Chelleworthe, Hugh Chelleworthe, Turold Chelleworthe, Ralph Chelleworthe, Richard Gernet, Algar de Piree, William de Tye, Peter de Lippewell, Richard de Stifford, Richard son of Blacsun, Alfric son of Sired, Reginald his brother, Litic son (? Leticia daughter) of Alward, 'et cum hiis omnes iuuenes et senes totius uille Hochidonie (Ockendon) et pluribus aliis'.

If Earl Geoffrey de Mandeville II (whose wife's name makes the identification tolerably certain) was alive, this could be dated 1163–6; but these clauses are treacherous evidence (see *EYC*, IV, pp. xxvii ff.).

Ego G(ilebertus) Londoniensis Dei gratia episcopus hanc donationem concedo et ratam habeo et sigilli mei attestatione confirmo. Hiis testibus: magistro Henrico, Roberto de Clifford', Ricardo de Sar(esberia), et multis aliis.

## 355

[1163–80] Notification to Abbot Hugh and the convent of Bury St Edmunds that Reginald of *Cotona*, clerk, has sworn to abide by the terms of his agreement with the abbey on the church of *Cotona*.

Abbot Hugh died in 1180.[1]

G(ilebertus) Dei gratia Lundoniensis episcopus uenerabili fratri et amico H(ugoni) sancti Edmundi abbati et conuentui salutem.

Que in nostra geruntur presentia tali uolumus firmitate roborari, ne prudentius ordinata aliqua malignantium peruersitate possint conuelli. Vnde uestre innotesci-
5 mus uniuersitati, nos sub multorum presentia Reginaldo clerico de Cotona instrumentum autenticum exposuisse, quo inter uos pactio super ecclesia de Cotona continetur inserta. Requirentes igitur coram omnibus ab eodem R(eginaldo) si que scripta fuerant omnibus prebuisset assensum, accepimus ab eius responso sccundum instrumenti tenorem sibi omnia complacuisse. Et ad cautelam habundantem iusiu-
10 randum, tactis sacrosanctis euuangeliis, eodem hoc petente suscepimus, quod bona fide secundum quod conuenerat et scripto fuerat insertum, inuiolabiliter obseruaret. Ne hoc igitur tam solempniter actum in dubium reuocetur in posterum, presentis scripti attestatione et sigilli nostri appositione communimus. His testibus [...]

355 G, no. 259; B, fo. 195. *See Plate III.*

---

[1] Formerly prior of Westminster, abbot of Bury, 1157–80, died 14 or 15 Nov. (*Memorials of St Edmund's*, ed. T. Arnold, RS, III, 6; I, 214–15; cf. *PR 27 Henry II*, p. 93; *Monasticon*, III, 155). It does not seem possible to decide which of the many Cotons, Cottons, etc., was in question: Cotton (Suffolk) is possible, but no connexion with Bury seems to be known.

## 356

[c. 1181-7] Confirmation and appropriation of the church of Felsted (Essex) to the nuns of La Sainte-Trinité, Caen (Normandy).[1]

Gilbertus Dei gratia Londunensis episcopus omnibus sancte matris ecclesie filiis ad quos presens scriptum peruenerit, salutem, gratiam et benedictionem.

Ex officio nobis iniuncto rebus ecclesiasticis que nostre iurisdictionis sunt et precipue locis religiosis imposterum prouidere, et hiis que canonice eis collata sunt ut in suo iure consistant, omnimodam tenemur sollicitudinem adhibere. Vnde nos 5 antiquum ius quod dilecte filie nostre sanctimoniales sancte Trinitatis de Cadomo in ecclesia de Felsted ab antecessorum nostrorum habuere temporibus plenius attendentes, prefatam ecclesiam eisdem monialibus cum omnibus ad eam pertinentibus confirmauimus, ⟨et⟩ ut ipsius ecclesie bona in proprios usus conuertant benigne concessimus, saluo tamen in omnibus iure Londunensis ecclesie et saluo duorum 10 capellanorum seruitio qui eidem ecclesie annuatim deseruient ad custum dictarum abbatisse et conuentus. Quod igitur a nobis sollempniter actum est ne de cetero possit ⟨in⟩ irritum reuocari presenti scripto et sigilli nostri appositione communire curauimus. Hiis testibus: Roberto Folet, Radulfo de Chilton', Gilleberto Banastre canonicis, Roberto, Waltero, Dauid capellanis, Magistro Waltero de Witten', 15 Iohanne de Witeng', Iohanne Storcestr', Radulfo de Warlemunt', Willelmo de Felested, Baldewino, Gaudefrido paruo, et multis aliis.

## 357

[1163-87][2] Settlement as papal judge delegate of the case between St Augustine's abbey, Canterbury, and Helton son of Richard on the tithes of Arnolton (in Eastling, Kent): Helton is adjudged to be a parishioner of the church of Faversham (Kent) and he concedes his tithes and sixteen acres in Sceldrichesham to the church.

⟨G⟩ilebertus Dei gratia Lundoniensis episcopus dilectis sibi in Domino uniuersis sancte matris ecclesie filiis salutem.

Suscepto mandato apostolico ut causam que inter monachos sancti Augustini Cantuarie et Heltonum filium Ricardi super decimationibus dominii de Ernoldintone et appendiciorum eius uertebatur audiremus, et eam remoto appellationis 5 obstaculo mediante iustitia decideremus, partes illico ⟨Pa, fo. 259⟩ ante nostram

356 London, PRO Transcripts, 31/8/140^B Pt. 3, fo. 205 (nineteenth-century transcript from a roll in private hands which cannot now be traced). *Abstract: CDF*, no. 433.
3 uobis *MS*  11 iustum *MS*  13 appensione *MS*  15 Dauide *MS*
357 BM Cotton MS Claudius D. x, fos. 254v (old 258v) (Pa) and 255 (259) (Pb) (Red Book of St Augustine's, Canterbury); *heading without text* in Cotton MS Julius D. ii, fo. 97v.
1 ⟨G⟩ilbertus Pb  4 dominii *om.* Pa

---

[1] Cf. P. Morant, *Hist. . . . of Essex*, II (London, 1768), 416-17.
[2] Probably early, since the charter of Helton (or Helta) referred to may be dated 1148-50 (*Reg. St Augustine's Canterbury*, ed. G. J. Turner and H. E. Salter, II, London, 1924, pp. 507-8), and Helton occurs in 1130 (D. C. Douglas, *Domesday Monachorum*, London, 1944, p. 37 n. 11).

presentiam euocauimus et eis diem competentem Lundon(ie) constituimus, quibus se nobis exhibentibus iam dicti monachi instrumenta autentica, testium etiam ydoneorum copiam producebant, quibus se iam dictas decimationes iuste possedisse,

10 et per prefatum militem iniuste et absque ordine iudiciario spoliatos fuisse constanter asseuerabant. Miles uero horum que aduersus eum dicebantur nichil infitians, se parochianum esse ecclesie de Fauersham, seque etiam iam dictas decimationes prefate ecclesie cum sexdecim acris de dominio suo de Sceldrichesham concessisse et ea sibi carta sua confirmasse asserebat. Nos igitur probationem eorum

15 suscipientes iam dictis monachis memoratarum decimationum possessionem adiudicauimus, et ne in posterum cuiusquam machinatione uel uersutia turbari possit, presentis scripti testimonio et sigilli nostri appositione ea qua in hoc negotio functi sumus auctoritate communire et confirmare curauimus. Valete.

### 358

[1176¹–80 (*c.* 1179)] Settlement of the case between Abbot Roger and the convent of St Augustine, Canterbury, and S. priest on the church of St Peter, Sandwich (Kent), in favour of the abbey.

Gilebertus Dei gratia Londoniensis episcopus uniuersis sancte matris ecclesie filiis ad quos presentes littere peruenerint, salutem in Domino.

Scripture suffragio non inmerito memorie commendantur per que litium finis exprimitur ne denuo suscitentur. Inde est quod uniuersitati uestre presenti scripto

5 curauimus intimare, causam que uertebatur inter uenerabilem fratrem nostrum R(ogerum) abbatem sancti Augustini Cantuarie eiusdemque loci conuentum et S. presbiterum super ecclesia sancti Petri de Sandwico, nobis a summo pontifice appellatione remota delegatam, hunc in nostra presentia terminum fuisse sortitam. Euocatus siquidem ad nostram presentiam S. presbiter, et tandem post multas

10 coactiones apparens, audito quod aduersus ipsum proponebatur, prefatam scilicet ecclesiam ad ius sancti Augustini esse pertinentem et eam ab ipso per multum tempus uiolenter fuisse detentam, post dubias quasdam responsiones, cum certius respondere iuberetur, tandem hiis que sibi obiciebantur assensit, et sepedictam ecclesiam ad prefatum abbatem pertinere, et oleum et crisma ab ecclesia sancti

15 Augustini recipere et semper recepisse recognouit. Nos itaque habito cum uiris prudentibus consilio, tum ex rationibus quas ex parte monachorum intelleximus tum ex aduerse partis confessione, iam dictam ecclesiam autoritate qua fungebamur apostolica et nostra, prefato S. presbitero abiudicauimus et eam uenerabili fratri nostro R(ogero) abbati sancti Augustini Cantuarie, qui causam agebat, et monachis

357  8 etiam *om.* Pa    9 iuste] quandoque Pb    10 spoliatum Pb    10–11 constanter *om.* Pb
12 Faueresham Pb    13–14 de dominio...concessisse Pa; concessisse de dominio suo de
Scheldrichesham Pb    16 ne] Pb *adds* sibi
358  BM Cotton MS Claudius D. x, fo. 182 (old 184). *Printed: Monasticon*, I, 143.
3 commendatur *MS*    13 assentit *MS*

¹ The accession of Abbot Roger (Biog. Index). Alexander III's confirmation is in Thomas of Elmham, *Historia*, pp. 434–5.

suis adiudicauimus. Vt igitur hec nostra sententia firma stet et in posterum per- 20
maneat inconuulsa presentis eam inscriptione pagine confirmauimus et nostri
pariter appositione sigilli roborauimus. Hiis testibus: S(imone) abbate sancti
Albani, Waltero abbate Colecestrie, Nicholao archidiacono Lund(oniensi),
magistro Ricardo de Stortef(ordia), Henrico thesaurario, magistro Radulfo de
Altaripa, Ricardo de Salesb(eria), Radulfo de Chiltone clericis nostris, magistro 25
Hosberto, magistro Mauritio, et multis aliis.

## 359

[1169–73] General confirmation to Colchester abbey of its churches, pensions, tithes and
possessions in the diocese of London: Brightlingsea, Weeley, Ardleigh, East Donyland,
Greenstead, Saint-Leonard-at-the-Hythe (Colchester) (?) (Essex), Newsells (in Barkway,
Herts), and a pension from Thornington (Essex); two-thirds of the tithes of Walter de
Haia in Dickley (in Mistley) and Mersea (Essex), and all the tithes of Roger de Vilers in
*Suthefleet* ('Surfleet' in St Osyth);[1] the chapel in Colchester castle and the chapel of St
Helen (Colchester); one-third of the church of St Peter, Colchester; the church of St Giles,
Colchester; two-thirds of the domain tithes of Boyton (?) and Takeley (Essex); the tithes of
*Aedgareslawe* (? Abbotsbury in Barley, Herts) (with specified exceptions); two-thirds of
the tithes of Pitsea, the whole domain tithe of Horndon, two-thirds of the tithes of Layer
(Breton)[2] and certain tithes in the other Layers (Essex); tithes of pannage, orchards and mills
on the estates of Eudo *dapifer* (the abbey's founder); the church of St Mary, Woolchurch
(Newchurch), and the chapel of St Stephen, Walbrook (London); the church of St John,
Pitsea (Essex); and all the privileges granted by King Henry (II?)[3] and Bishops Maurice and
Richard (de Belmeis I).[4]

The witnesses suggest that the charter was granted in the royal *curia*, possibly that of the
young king. The archdeacon of Bath is therefore almost certainly Thomas 'Agnellus'
archdeacon of Wells, who entered office *c.* 1169; and we may be sure that this charter is later
than Richard Foliot's return from Bologna in or after 1169. In 1173 the archdeacon of Poitiers
was elected bishop of Winchester and the archdeacon of Salisbury (i.e. Wilts) bishop of
Bath.

Gilebertus Dei gratia Lundoniensis episcopus omnibus sancte matris ecclesie filiis
ad quorum notitiam presens scriptum peruenerit salutem.

Quoniam presentis etatis malitiam ad nocendum bonis pronam conspicimus esse et
paratam, necesse est ut ecclesiis et ecclesiasticis personis et maxime uiris religiosis
iura sua integra seruare curemus et illibata. Hinc est quod dilectorum filiorum 5

---

**358** 25 Chitone *MS*
**359** Colchester Borough Library, Cart. Colchester, pp. 52–3 (copy for Morant, BM Stowe
MS 841, fo. 8 r–v; noted in Stowe 837, fo. 11). *Printed: Cart. Colchester*, I, 86–8.

---

[1] *PN Essex*, p. 349, cf. Morant, *Colchester*, p. 142 (and for Newsells and Mistley cf. *PN Essex*,
p. 343; *PN Herts.* p. 173).
[2] For *Aedgareslawe* see *VCH Herts.* IV, 37–8; for Layer Breton, Morant, I, 409.
[3] *Cart. Colchester*, I, 14 ff., 19 ff. etc. (one cannot be sure how many of Henry II's charters are
referred to).
[4] *Op. cit.* I, 81–3 (Richard).

nostrorum monachorum ecclesie sancti Iohannis Baptiste et precursoris Domini de Colecestr(ia) honestatis famam et religionis attendentes fragrantiam, ut eorum quieti in futuro cura prouideamus pastorali, possessiones sibi a fidelibus pie collatas tam in ecclesiis quam in ecclesiasticis beneficiis episcopali auctoritate confirmamus:
10 inprimis ecclesiam de Brithlingesya in eorum fundo sitam, et in eadem ecclesia annuum canonem sexaginta solidorum sibi solito more statutis terminis percipiendorum, et de dominio duas partes decimarum; ecclesiam de Wilege et ex eadem ecclesia annuum canonem decem solidorum, et de dominio duas partes decimarum; ecclesiam de Ardleg' et eius ecclesie omnes prouentus, salua honesta sustentatione
15 uicarii in eadem ecclesia ministrantis; ecclesiam de Estdoniland' et ex eadem ecclesia annuum canonem dimidie marce et de dominio duas partes decimarum; ecclesiam de Grenstede et ex eadem ecclesia annuum canonem quinque solidorum et de dominio omnes decimas; ecclesiam de Hea et ex eadem ecclesia annuum canonem quinque solidorum; ecclesiam de Nieweseles cum omnibus eius pertinentiis; et de
20 ecclesia de Turitun' annuum canonem trium solidorum; preterea duas partes decimarum Walteri de Haia in Dikeleya, et duas partes decimarum eiusdem Walteri in Mereseya et omnes decimas de Suthefleet Rogeri de Vilers; capellam etiam intra castellum de Colecestr(ia) cum omnibus pertinentiis; capellam sancte Helene cum pertinentiis; tertiam partem ecclesie sancti Petri intra muros Colecestr(ie); ecclesiam
25 sancti Egidii totam in eorum cimiterio fundatam; de Boitun' duas partes decimarum dominii; de Thakeleg' duas partes decimarum dominii; de Aedgareslawe omnes decimas preter tres trauas frumenti et tres trauas auene et preter unum purcellum et unum agnum que debentur more solito ecclesie parochiali; duas partes decimarum de Piches(eya) et totam decimam dominii de Hornud(ona) Euerardi; et duas partes
30 decimarum de Legra et quasdam decimas quas habent in aliis duabus Legris; preterea totam decimam pasnagii porcorum Eudonis dapiferi et uirgultorum et molendinorum eiusdem Eudonis; ecclesiam sancte Marie de Niewecherche, cum omnibus pertinentiis; capellam etiam sancti Stephani martyris super Walebroche; sed et omnes possessiones suas in episcopatu Lundoniensi constitutas. Confirmamus etiam eidem
35 sancte ecclesie sancti Iohannis ecclesiam de Piches(eya) in eorundam fundo sitam; leges etiam et consuetudines tam ab illustri rege Anglorum H(enrico) quam a bone memorie et M(auricio) et Ricardo predecessoribus nostris quondam Lundoniensis ecclesie episcopis eidem sancte ecclesie Baptiste et precursoris Domini indultas nichilominus confirmamus et episcopali auctoritate inperpetuum communimus.
40 Hiis testibus: Ricardo archidiacono Pictau(ensi), Iohanne decano Sar(esberiensi), Reginaldo archidiacono Sar(esberiensi), Thoma archidiacono Baton(iensi), Ricardo archidiacono Colecestr(ensi), magistro Nicholao canonico, magistro Henrico de Norhanton', magistro Iohanne Hierteshorn, Ricardo, Waltero capellanis.

**359** 19 *Or* Neeweseles   31 pagnagii parcorum *MS*   32 Niewech'eche *MS*   36 etiam etiam *MS*

**360**

[*c.* 1179–80] Settlement by Gilbert and Simon, abbot of St Albans,[1] as papal judges delegate, of the case between Colchester abbey and Higham priory (in Lillechurch, Kent, Benedictine nuns) on the church of Lillechurch. The monks surrendered all claim in exchange for the grant of land worth 30*s.* per annum, on condition that if the nuns helped them to possession of the piece of land called *Blunteshale* the monks would return the other land.

Gillebertus Dei gratia Lundoniensis episcopus et S⟨ymon⟩ eadem gratia abbas sancti Albani omnibus sancte matris ecclesie filiis, ad quos presentes littere peruenerint, salutem in Domino.

Caritatis opus esse dinoscitur inter religiosas precipue domos suscitatas lites extinguere, et ne peruersis malignantium fomentis semel extincte quouis possint 5 modo denuo suscitari diligentius procurare. Inde est quod ad communem omnium uestrum uolumus deuenire notitiam controuersiam que de mandato apostolico coram nobis inter abbatem et monachos sancti Iohannis Colecestr⟨ie⟩ et sanctimoniales de Lillecherche super ecclesia ipsa de Lillecherche uertebatur, hoc tandem fine in nostra presentia utriusque partis pari uoluntate et assensu conquieuisse. 10 Prefati siquidem abbas et monachi ius omne quod in prefata sibi uendicabant ecclesia spontanee resignauerunt et a lite quam intendebant penitus recesserunt. Memorate uero moniales ipsis monachis terram quandam ad prefatam pertinentem ecclesiam triginta solidorum per annum inperpetuum libere et quiete ab omni seruitio possidendam concesserunt, ita quidem quod si terra quedam que Bluntes- 15 hale dicitur ad eosdem monachos per ipsas moniales aut earum specialiter fauore per domnos aut per amicos suos quolibet modo sub ea libertate, sub qua prefata terra in Lillechirche eis concessa est, deuoluta fuerit, ipsam quam receperunt terram sepedictis sanctimonialibus restituent, et prenominatam terram de Blunteshale in commutationem eius accipient. Et ut hec transactio firma stet et inperpetuum 20 ualitura permaneat inter partes, conuenit ut monachi a sanctimonialibus, sanctimoniales uero a monachis autentica capitulorum suorum instrumenta super hac compositione confecta recipiant; et nos eam auctoritate domni pape et nostre pagine presentis inscriptione confirmauimus et sigillorum nostrorum attestatione corroborare curauimus. Hiis testibus: Ricardo archidiacono Colecestr⟨ie⟩, Roberto 25 archidiacono Essex⟨ie⟩, magistro Radulfo de Altaripa *magistro ⟨p. 260⟩ scolarum Lund⟨onie⟩, magistro Dauid, magistro Ricardo de Storteford, Gilleberto Foliot canonicis sancti Pauli, magistro Osberto de sancto Albano, Rogero de Wigornia, Ricardo de Salesberi, Radulfo de Ciltonia, Waltero elemosinario, Ricardo Banastre, Iohanne Swite⟨n⟩ge, magistro Roberto de Kent, magistro Heraclio, Beniamin 30 clerico, Osberto senescallo, Willelmo de Lillechirche, et multis aliis.

**360** Colchester Borough Library, Cart. Colchester, p. 259. *Printed: Cart. Colchester*, II, 526–7. 23 nostra *MS*     26 *magistro / magistro *MS*     29 Waltero] *MS adds* de

---

[1] Prior of St Albans, abbot 1167–83 (*Gesta abb. S. Albani, RS,* I, 183–4, 194 and n.; confirmed by ann. Horsham, Trinity Coll., Cambridge, MS R. 14. 9, fo. 10v); he was blessed on 21 May 1167 by Gilbert Foliot (*Gesta abb. loc. cit.* gives Sunday after Ascension, 13 kal. June; it was actually 12 kal. June—this Sunday never fell on the 20th between 1162 and 1173).

**361**

[1163–87, perhaps *c.* 1181–7] Appropriation to Colchester abbey of the church of Barkway (Herts), saving the support of a priest to serve the church—Martin, clerk, is to be vicar so long as he lives and remains a secular.

Barkway is not included in no. 359, so this should probably, but not certainly, be dated later than 1169. If Ralph of Chilton and Gilbert Banastre were canons, it must be later than *c.* 1181. Cf. *VCH Herts.* IV, 35.

Gilebertus Dei gratia Londoniensis episcopus omnibus sancte matris ecclesie filiis ad quos presens scriptum peruenerit, salutem et benedictionem.

Cum iniuncta nobis cura pastorali gregem prouidente superna clementia nobis commissum maximeque castris dominicis militantem protegere teneamur atque
5 fouere, iustitie censemus esse consonum ut in uiris religiosis quam in nobis minus esse conspicimus foueamus religionem. Hinc est quod seruorum Dei ⟨p. 52⟩ monachorum sancti Iohannis Baptiste Colecestr⟨ie⟩ religionem perspicuam attendentes, et eiusdem domus hospitalitatem que passim patet omnibus petentibus, uel necessitatem patientibus, pie considerantes, eorumque relligiositati pietatis
10 studio condescendentes, ad ipsorum sustentationem, ad hospitum susceptionem, ad pauperum etiam et peregrinorum recreationem, sancte relligionis et diuine pietatis intuitu ecclesiam de Bercqueia cum suis pertinentiis eisdem Dei ministris in propriis usibus concedimus habendam, et auctoritate pontificali ad eadem pietatis opera confirmamus possidendam; salua tamen uicaria Martini clerici nostri quamdiu
15 sub habitu uixerit seculari; salua etiam rationabili sustentatione sacerdotis in predicta ecclesia ministrantis, qui nobis et nostris successoribus de spiritualibus, monachis respondeat de temporalibus, que etiam sustentatio de prouentibus altaris eidem sacerdoti non annua sed perpetua erit assignanda. Quod quia ratum et in-conuulsum manere uolumus id pagine presentis inscriptione et sigilli nostri im-
20 pressione roborare curauimus. Hiis testibus: Radulfo de Chilton', G⟨ileberto⟩ Banast⟨r⟩e, Ricardo de Saresbir', Ricardo Banast⟨r⟩e, Radulfo cantore, Iohanne Hwiteng, Ricardo Folioth, Alano de Berking' decano, Osberto senescallo, Galfrido Escollant, Ricardo filio constabularii, Baldewino, Rogero camerario, Iohanne, Symone, Willelmo clericis, Willelmo marescallo, et aliis multis.

**362**

[*c.* 1181–7] Confirmation of the grant by Ailward, king's chamberlain,[1] to Colchester abbey of the domain tithes of Chalvedon,[2] except the tithes of one marsh, which Ailward has assigned to Benfleet church (Essex).

Gilebertus Dei gratia Londoniensis episcopus omnibus sancte matris ecclesie filiis ad quos hee littere peruenerint, salutem in Domino.

**361** Colchester Borough Library, Cart. Colchester, p. 51. *Printed: Cart. Colchester*, I, 83–4.
**362** Colchester Borough Library, Cart. Colchester, p. 51. *Printed: Cart. Colchester*, I, 83.

[1] See Eyton, *Itinerary*, index *s.v.* Camerarii.
[2] Great Chalvedon Hall in Pitsea (*PN Essex*, p. 167).

Ad communem omnium uestrum uolumus deuenire notitiam cartam dilecti filii nostri Ailuuardi domni regis camerarii nobis fuisse presentatam, ex cuius tenore perpendimus iam dictum A(iluuardum) pro sua suorumque salute concessisse Deo 5 et ecclesie sancti Iohannis Baptiste Col(ecestrie) et monachis ibidem Deo famulantibus, in liberam et perpetuam elemosinam, quicquid decimari debet in dominio suo de Chaluedon' preter decimam unius marisci quam ecclesie de Beanflet idem A(iluuardus) assignauit. Quam nos concessionem ratam habemus et acceptam, et ut 10 firma memorate ecclesie et predictis monachis perpetuo permaneat, ea qua fungimur auctoritate concedimus et pagine presentis inscriptione et nostri pariter appositione sigilli confirmamus. Testibus: Radulfo de Chilth(ona) canonico ecclesie beati Pauli, Waltero filio Walteri, Radulfo cantore, Iohanne Witing', Stephano Walensi, Gilleberto, magistro Pagano clericis, Roberto Par(age?), et aliis multis.

## 363

[1163–c. 1180] Grant of an indulgence in support of the Hospital of St Mary Magdalene, Colchester (dep. Colchester abbey, founded c. 1100).

Infirmorum apud Colec(estriam) diuturna egritudine laborantium egestati condolentes, dilectam nobis in Domino benignitatem uestram rogamus et attentius exhortamur in Domino, quatinus amore Dei et pietatis intuitu nuntios et procuratores eorum cum ad uos declinauerint ob animarum uestrarum remedium benigne recipiatis, et eorum paupertatem de elemosinarum uestrarum largitione, prout 5 uobis Deus inspirauerit subleuetis. Omnibus uero qui de peccatis suis confessi fuerint, et eis manum misericordie in aliquo impenderint, de Domini confisi misericordia de iniuncta sibi penitentia uiginti dies relaxamus, et orationum et beneficiorum ecclesie nostre participes esse concedimus.

## 364

Grant (doubtfully attributed to Gilbert Foliot) of an indulgence to those visiting the church of St Mary, Colne (Essex: i.e. Earl's Colne priory) on the Feast of the Annunciation.

If the reading of the manuscript is correct, this would seem to be an act of Gilbert of Hastings, bishop of Lisbon (1147–66), who is known to have visited England in 1150, and was very likely a member of the East Anglian family of Hastings (*De expugnatione Lyxbonensi*, ed. C. W. David, New York, 1936, pp. 178–81, esp. 178–80 n.; cf. B. Dodwell in *Misc. D. M. Stenton*, pp. 155–6). On the other hand, the reading of the manuscript is not clear, and it is possible that this was either an act of Gilbert Foliot, or of Gilbert the Universal, bishop of London 1128–34.

Ego Gillebertus Dei gratia Lisbonensis (?) episcopus omnibus sancte fidelibus ecclesie salutem.

**362** 10 eam *MS*

**363** G, no. 327; B, fo. 200 (marked 'uacat').

**364** Chelmsford, Essex Record Office, D/DPr. 149, Cart. Colne (deposited by Colne Priory Estate Archives; facsimile in BM Facs. 472), fo. 11. *Printed: Cart. Colne*, no. 27.
1 Lisbonensis *? sic MS* (? Lund' *in heading*)

Notum sit deuotioni omnium fidelium me condonasse omnibus ad ecclesiam sancte Marie de Colum uenientibus in die Annuntiationis eiusdem Virginis uno 5 quoque anno uiginti dies de penitentia peccatorum suorum, de quibus confessi fuerint.

## 365

[*c.* 1181–3, ? *c.* 1181] Settlement of the case between Prior Hugh[1] and the convent of Earl's Colne (Essex) and Alexander, rector of Aythorpe Roding (Essex),[2] on certain tithes, in favour of Colne priory.

G(illebertus) Dei gratia Lundoniensis episcopus omnibus sancte matris ecclesie filiis ad quos hee littere peruenerint, salutem in Domino.

Ad omnium uestrum uolumus deuenire notitiam, causam que uertebatur inter dilectum filium nostrum H(ugonem) priorem et monachos de Colun et A(lexand- 5 rum) personam ecclesie de Roinges super possessione quarundam decimarum et super uiolentia quadam priori et monachis—ut dicebatur—ab Alexandro illata hoc modo conquieuisse. Memoratus A(lexander) in nostra et multorum prudentum et discretorum uirorum presentia constitutus et a nobis diligenter requisitus utrum ecclesia de Colun predictas decimationes possederit, coram nobis confessus est 10 prescriptam ecclesiam de Colun dictas decimationes, quibus se per Alexandrum spoliatos uiolenter fuisse monachi proposuerunt, per multos annos inconcusse possedisse et eas in pace tenuisse. Repromisit etiam dictus A(lexander) firmiter quod occasione possessionis, quam ut dicebatur a monachis nactus est uiolenter, nullam eis uel ecclesie sue in posterum controuersiam mouebit aut aliquas eis exinde lites 15 suscitare studebit. Hec quidem gesta sunt ut utriusque ius ecclesie et de Colun et de Roinges conseruetur illesum, et nulla eis occasione predicta lesio generetur uel detrimentum. Nos itaque rebus sic coram nobis gestis, sepedictis priori et monachis possessionem decimationum que causa litis extiterant episcopali auctoritate cum integritate restituimus, et statu pristino in integrum reformato has utrique parti 20 literas in testimonium indulsimus. Testibus: Gilleberto archidiacono Middelsex(ie), Radulfo archidiacono Colocestr(ie), magistro Hugone a Lundon(ia), magistro Ricardo a Storteford', Ricardo de Saresbir', Radulfo a Chilthon', Iohanne Witeng, et multis aliis.

**365** Chelmsford, Essex Record Office, Cart. Colne (also BM Facs. 472), fo. 7 (the first two sentences, to *conquieuisse*, are repeated on fo. 8). Printed: *Cart. Colne*, no. 17 (and no. 20).

---

[1] He occurs before Jan. 1174; this is the latest known occurrence; he had been succeeded by 1185–6 (*Monasticon*, IV, 101; *Chron. Abingdon*, II, 243).

[2] Cf. *PN Essex*, p. 491. *Cart. Colne*, pp. 20, 64 and n., 90.

**366**

[1163–c. 1180] Grant of an indulgence in support of the building appeal for Combwell priory (Kent, Augustinian).[1]

G(ilebertus) Dei gratia Lundoniensis episcopus dilectis sibi in Domino uniuersis eiusdem ecclesie parrochianis et filiis, salutem, gratiam et benedictionem.

Quo magis, dilectissimi, inter caritatis opera lucet elemosinarum largitio, eo propensius earum erogationi insistere uos exortamur in Domino. Si enim opera misericordie in huius seculi peregrinatione seminatis, multiplicato fructu uitam 5 eternam metetis in celo. Vnde rogamus ⟨et⟩ monemus uos attentius, quatinus inopie fratrum de Cu⟨m⟩wella, qui pro defectis facultatibus ecclesiam sue religioni congruam construere non possunt, compatiamini, et pia ducti compassione, eis optata subsidia eternorum intuitu prebeatis, ut uestris adiuti suffragiis, oratorio sibi constructo feruentissime legi mandatorum Dei[2] inherere possint. Nos uero his qui 10 de suis facultatibus eidem loco quicquam largiti fuerint, de Dei misericordia confisi, de eorum penitentia decem dies relaxamus, et bonorum omnium que in nostra fiunt ecclesia, adiuuante Domino, eos participes constituimus. Valete.

**367**

[1163–c. 1180] Appropriation of Great Saling church (Essex) to Little Dunmow priory (Essex, Augustinian) on the presentation of Baldwin Wystard and Hugh his heir.

Baldwin's grant and Hugh's confirmation are in BM Harl. MS 662, fo. 36. Cf. Morant, II, 412.

Gilbertus Dei gratia Londoniensis episcopus omnibus sancte matris ecclesie filiis ad quos presens scriptum peruenerit, salutem in Domino.

Ad communem omnium presenti uolumus scripto deuenire notitiam nos diuine pietatis intuitu, ecclesiam de Salyng cum omnibus ad eam pertinentibus ad petitionem et presentationem Ba⟨l⟩dwini Wystard' et heredis sui Hugonis eiusdem 5 ecclesie aduocatorum monasterio beate Marie de Dunmow et canonicis ibidem Deo iugiter famulantibus in perpetuam et liberam elemosinam concessisse, ipsosque canonicos in eiusdem ecclesie personatum suscepisse. Quod quia de cetero firmitatis robur uolumus obtinere, presentis id scripti patrocinio confirmamus et sigilli nostri pariter appositione communimus. Hiis testibus: Ricardo archidiacono Colcest(rie), 10 etc.

**366** G, no. 229; B, fo. 193.
6 monemus rogamus, *marked for transposition* B
**367** London, Guildhall Library, MS 9531/6 (Reg. Robert Gilbert, 1436–48), fo. 180v.

---

[1] Or possibly Canwell priory (Staffs, Benedictine), founded before 1149.
[2] Cf. Bar. iv. 1; Eph. ii. 15.

**368**

[1167–80, probably after 1169] General confirmation to Little Dunmow priory: of its holdings, tithes, etc., in Little Dunmow, two-thirds of the domain tithes of Henham, Cold Norton (Essex) and Sturston (Norfolk), the domain tithes of Paslow Hall, and of Ernald le Blake in Barnston, tithe of Paglesham (Essex) (cf. *VN*, pp. 481–4) with the assart of *Lewyneswod'* and *Acho* and the turbary of *Esteya* as confirmed in charters of Robert son of Richard and Walter his son.

Gilbertus Dei gratia Londoniensis episcopus dilecto filio Hugoni decano totique London(iensis) ecclesie capitulo et personis omnibus in episcopatu London(iensi) constitutis, salutem, gratiam et benedictionem.

    Cartam uenerabilis patris nostri bone memorie Teobaldi Cant(uariensis) dudum
5 archiepiscopi et sedis apostolice legati, cartas uero uenerabilium predecessorum nostrorum Mauritii, Ricardi quondam London(iensis) ecclesie pontificum diligenter inspeximus; et eorum sicuti uestigia possessiones omnes et dignitates ipsorum auctoritate ecclesie de Dunmawe et canonicis ibidem Deo seruientibus concessas et confirmatas, nos quoque eidem ecclesie ea que nobis a Domino concessa est
10 auctoritate concessimus, et tam pagine presentis inscriptione quam sigilli nostri appositione confirmare curauimus. Que ut in communem notitiam annotatione certa deducantur, suis duximus exprimenda nominibus: teneuras scilicet omnes et decimas et libertates et alia dona et incrementa in terris et hominibus, pratis et pascuis, in bosco et plano, in decima prati et pannagii et molendinorum et communi
15 pastura uille de Dunmawe; duas etiam partes decime dominii de Henham et duas partes decime dominii *de Nortun' et duas partes decime dominii de Stereston' et decimam dominii de Passefeld et decimam de terra Arnaldi le Blake in Berneston' et decimam de Pakelesham cum assarta de Lewyneswod' et de Acho et turbariam de Esteya sicut in cartis Roberti filii Ricardi et Walteri filii eius eidem ecclesie confir-
20 mata sunt, nos in patrimonium et patrocinium ecclesie suscipimus et hec eis omnia episcopali auctoritate confirmamus. Hiis testibus: Roberto archidiacono Essex(ie), magistro Ricardo de Storteford', etc.

**369**

[1163–87] Confirmation to Eye priory (Suffolk, dep. of Bernay abbey) of the grant by Robert Malet, the founder, of the tithe of his domain in Wakes Colne (Essex: see *PN Essex*, pp. 382–3).

    It is possible that this is an act of Bishop Gilbert the Universal (1128–34).

**368** BM Harl. MS 662, fo. 8v (Cart. Dunmow) (Gl); London, Guildhall Library, MS 9531b (Reg. Gilbert), fo. 180v (fifteenth-century copy of inspeximus of 1243: select variants given) (Gr).
1 Gilbertus] G. Gl    4–5 Cartam...legati *om*. Gr    5 uero *om*. Gr    8,15 Dunmawe / Dunmow Gr    12 nominibus] Gl *adds* tenuras et [*after correction*]    15–16 Henham...dominii *de om*. Gr
16–19 Nortan' / Passeffeld / Bermeston' / Paklesham / Lewinesud' / Assho / Estheya Gr    16 et duas...Stereston' *om*. Gr    17 Arnaldi le Blake *om*. Gl    22 magistro Ricardo de Storteford' *om*. Gr
**369** Chelmsford, Essex Record Office, D/DBy Q 19 (deposited by Audley End Estate Archives), fo. 26 (Cart. Eye); *copy* in BM Add. MS 8177, fo. 109.

G(ilebertus) Dei gratia Londoniensis episcopus omnibus sancte ecclesie fidelibus, salutem et Dei benedictionem.

Nouerit uniuersitas uestra nos concessisse et auctoritate episcopali confirmasse Deo et ecclesie sancti Petri de Eya et monachis ibidem Deo seruientibus totam decimam de dominio Colum Malet quam Robertus Malet eorum fundator eis dedit 5 in episcopatu Londoniensi. Et in huius rei testimonium dedimus eis hoc scriptum sigillo nostro roboratum. Valete in Domino sempiterne.

## 370

[*c.* 1180–1] Settlement, as papal judge delegate, of the case between the Knights Hospitallers, the abbot of Eynsham (Oxon, Benedictine) and the prior of Dunstable (Beds, Augustinian) on the church of Marston (Oxon); half the church is recognized to belong to Dunstable priory; the other half is surrendered by Eynsham abbey to the Hospitallers in exchange for an annual rent of 1 mark in Oxford.

Vniuersis sancte matris ecclesie filiis G(ilebertus) Dei gratia Lundoniensis episcopus, salutem in Domino.

Vniuersitati uestre notificamus, causam que inter fratres Ierosolimitani Hospitalis et abbatem de Egnesham et priorem de Dunstapl' super ecclesia de Merston' uertebatur, a domno papa nobis delegatam in presentia nostra amicabili composi- 5 tione in parte hoc modo conquieuisse. Partibus siquidem in presentia nostra die sibi prefixa constitutis, cum iam dictus abbas et prior de Dunstapl' prefate ecclesie pro equis partibus se assererent possessores, seque iam ⟨fo. 23⟩ dictis fratribus obicerent aduersarios, post multas partium allegationes iamdictus abbas medietatem ecclesie prenominate in manus nostras libere et absolute resignauit, ipsis fratribus assignan- 10 dam et concedendam. Nos itaque auctoritate apostolica in iam dictam medietatem sepedictos fratres suscepimus, eosque in ea, debita cum sollempnitate, instituimus. Predicti uero fratres ipsi abbati et ecclesie de Egnesham ⟨redditum⟩ unius marce in Oxeneford(ia) perpetuo iure et libere et inconcusse tenendum dederunt et con- cesserunt, hac quidem adiecta conditione; si prior de Dunestapl' aduersus sepedictos 15 fratres supramemoratam medietatem petierit, et si in causa optinuerit, ecclesia de Egnesham prefatum unius marce redditum non amittet. Hoc etiam in conuentione adiectum est, quod si sepedictus abbas de Egnesham redditum illum per potentiam alicuius aut aliqua ui maiore amiserit, predicti fratres de Hospitali alibi tantundem redditus et dabunt et concedent. Hanc conuentionem, quia ratam et inconuulsam 20 perpetuo manere uolumus, presenti scripto et sigilli nostri attestatione confirmare et communire decreuimus. Testibus: Roberto episcopo Herefordensi, Radulfo archidiacono Colecestrie, magistro Ricardo de Storteford, magistro Henrico de Norhamton', magistro Nicholao de Leuechenor',[1] Rogero de Wigornia, Ricardo Banastr(e), Iohanne Wite⟨n⟩ge, Bartholomeo nepote abbatis.     25

370 Oxford, Christ Church, MS 341, Cart. Eynsham, fo. 22 v. *Printed: Cart. Eynsham,* I, 64, no. 47.
13 redditum *Salter; MS omits*

---

[1] He occurs as vice-archdeacon of Oxford *c.* 1185 (Cheney, *English Bishops' Chanceries,* p. 144).

**371**

[1163–87, probably early] Testification that when Gilbert was abbot of Gloucester, it was established that Robert Gernun had granted the churches of Wraysbury (or Wyrardsbury) and Langley (Bucks) to Gloucester abbey, and the grant had been confirmed by Henry I;[1] the bishop of Lincoln had instituted vicars at the presentation of the abbot and convent. Robert Gernun's honour passed to William de Muntfichet and then to his son Gilbert, whose guardian and uncle, Earl Gilbert (de Clare), tried to oust the abbey and institute Payne, clerk, of London, in Stephen's reign, when Gilbert was abbot. But in the synod of David, archdeacon of Buckingham, at Aylesbury, the abbot proved his right, with the aid of Bernard, bishop of St Davids, and other witnesses.

Dilectis sibi in Domino uniuersis sancte ecclesie filiis frater G(ilebertus) Londoniensis ecclesie minister, salutem que nunc est et quam speramus a Domino.

Elabuntur tempora et in obliuionem multa pertrahunt, que nisi scriptis excipiantur ad memoriam non facile reducuntur. Inde est quod uniuersitati uestre presenti 5 notifico, me, dum curam Glouc(estrensis) ecclesie permittente Domino administrarem, in inquirendis et requirendis eius possessionibus ex officii suscepti debito debitam sollicitudinem adhibuisse, et tam ex cartarum quarundam inspectione quam totius etiam conuentus Glouc(estrie) aliarumque personarum quamplurium attestatione manifeste cognouisse Robertum Gernun, dum uillam de Wirecesbur(ia) et 10 uillam de Lauerkestok' pleno iure et integro dominio possideret, priusquam honor ille qui dudum fuit Roberti Gernun ad Willelmum de Muntfichet patrem ⟨fo. 173 v⟩ Gilberti de Muntfichet deuolutus esset, ecclesias iam dictarum uillarum Wirecesbir(ie) scilicet et Lauerkestok' ecclesie beati Petri de Gloucestr(ia) concessisse, et regem H(enricum) primum hanc eius donationem sub multa nobilium regni sui 15 attestatione carta sua et sigillo corroborasse. Attendens itaque et multorum attestatione cognoscens ecclesiam Glouc(estrie) cui tunc preeram memoratas ecclesias a tempore regis H(enrici) usque ad tempus regis Stephani, quo pax regni turbata est, possedisse, domnum etiam Lincoln(iensem) ad abbatis et conuentus Glouc(estrie) presentationem uicarios in eis instituisse, ipsos etiam ab hiis ad arbitrium suum 20 pensiones annuas suscepisse; cum occasione cladis bellice commisse michi ecclesie possessio in ecclesiis iam dictis turbata fuisset per Gilbertum comitem, iam dicti Gileberti auunculum, qui tunc eius preerat patrimonio illi tutelam exhibens, qui ecclesias iam dictas auctoritate sua in quendam London(iensem) clericum Paganum nomine contulerat, ad dominum Lincoln(iensem) aduersus iam dictum comitem et 25 memoratum Paganum querelam detuli, commisse michi ecclesie iustitiam postulans exhiberi. Cuius auctoritate apud Eilesbur(iam) per Dauid archidiaconum de

371 PRO Chancery Records, C 150, Cart. Gloucester, fo. 173. *Printed: Cart. Gloucester*, II, 168–9.

---

[1] *Regesta Regum Anglo-Normannorum*, II, ed. C. Johnson and H. A. Cronne (Oxford, 1956), no. 1041 (cf. *CS*, p. 271 n.). Henry I's charter is suspicious in its present form, but if it is true that the bishop of St Davids gave witness to the authenticity of the transaction its reliability receives some confirmation, since he is said in *Regesta* no. 1041 to have witnessed Robert Gernun's gift as Bernard the Chaplain. On this case, see *GF*, pp. 221–2. For the place-names cf. *PN Bucks*. pp. 241 n., 244–5; *Taxatio*, p. 33.

Bukingham synodo pupplice conuocata, statuto michi die instructus affui, que supra sunt memorata proposui, bone memorie Bernardi dudum Meneuensis episcopi multarumque ipsius synodi personarum munitus testimonio, memoratas ecclesias synodali iudicio reportaui. In quas cum Gloucestrensis ecclesie nomine 30 agens episcopali auctoritate inductus fuerim, ipsa easdem in eo recuperauit obsequio et episcopali auctoritate per me et successorem meum usque in presens tempus optinuit. Cui in iam dictis ecclesiis cum totum collatum⟨fuisset(?)⟩ et quod potestas laica et quod episcopalis dignitas conferre potest, iustum uideri potest ecclesias iam dictas sibi in pace dimitti, et possessionem eius querelis iuuenis longe post nati 35 non debere conuelli. Valeatis.

## 372

[1164–79] Testification addressed to Roger bishop of Worcester (1164–79) that Gilbert had inspected the charter of Bishop Simon and recalled the settlement of the case between Gloucester abbey and Lanthony priory when he was abbot of Gloucester. It had been established that the abbey had parochial rights in Gloucester castle[1] and that the castellans and their households—including Roger de Pîtres and his brother Durand—had normally been buried there, even though Roger's son Walter of Gloucester had become a canon in the diocese of St Davids and been buried there (i.e. at Llanthony); and the canons of Llanthony had admitted that they had no right of burial, but as a special act of favour they had been allowed to bury Earl Milo in their priory.

Venerabili domno fratrique karissimo, R(ogero) Wygorn(iensi) Dei gratia episcopo frater G(ilebertus) Londoniensis ecclesie minister, salutem et felices ad uota successus.

Cartam predecessoris uestri patrisque nostri uenerande memorie S(imonis) Wygorn(iensis) dudum episcopi, que sigillo ipsius impressa apud fratres nostros 5 Glouc(estrie) monachos habetur, inspeximus et controuersiam ipsam que inter ipsos et canonicos Lantonie de corpore domni Milonis comitis Hereford(ie), cum humandum esset in presentia ipsius, exorta est et biduo actitata, in hunc modum partis utriusque assensu terminatam fuisse cognouimus. Monachi siquidem se fundum ipsum in quo castellum Glouc(estrie) nunc situm est ante ipsius castelli 10 constructionem possedisse, seque ibidem ortum habuisse et capellanum suum hominibus suis ibidem domicilia habentibus per eos iura parochialia ministrasse, et ipsorum corpora penes se sepulture tradidisse multis hoc attestantibus asserebant, adicientes se licet fundum ipsum commutauerint, ius tamen parochiale quod in ipso habuerant nulli umquam cessisse, sed se ius ipsum et ante et post castelli 15 fundationem usque tunc continue possedisse, asserentes Rogerum de Pistres cui post adquisitionem Anglie custodia castri Gloucestrie ⟨fo. 94 v⟩ primo commissa est, et totam eius familiam post ipsum—etiam Durandum de Pistres fratrem eius qui eidem custodie prefuit, et ipsius familiam totam—sepulturam penes se ut parochianos suos habuisse; filium[2] uero et familiam Walteri de Glouc(estria) qui 20

372 Gloucester Cathedral, Reg. A, fo. 94. *Printed: Cart. Gloucester*, I, pp. lxxvi–lxxvii.

---

[1] Cf. *CS*, p. 276.   [2] This son seems otherwise unknown.

successit eis, quique in episcopatu Meneuensi habitum suscepit canonici et ibi
sepultus est, et post hos quamplures ex familia successoris sui Milonis comitis penes
se repositos quieuisse; seque in hunc modum ius sepeliendi eos qui intra castri
ambitum decedebant continuasse sibi usu et antiquitate, quam firmum suis oportet
25 stare radicibus, asserebant. Que cum productis testibus probare parati essent lis hoc
tandem fine quieuit. Canonici corpus comitis de quo erat contentio nil sibi iuris
uendicantes in ipso, monachis liberum et quietum dimiserunt, monachi uero precibus
eorum quorum in carta domni Wygorn(iensis) predecessoris uestri fit mentio,
corpus ipsum in ecclesia de Lanton⟨i⟩a in quam allatum fuerat sepulture tradi
30 concesserunt, hac tamen condicione quod canonici ipsi domnum Rogerum filium
comitis et uxorem eius et heredes eorum omnes et quibus castelli de Glouc(estria)
foret commissa custodia, qui intra castri ipsius ambitum uite finem clauderent,
ecclesie beati Petri ad sepeliendos liberos et quietos absque omni reclamatione,
concesserunt; hoc quidem confirmand(o) memoratus S(imon) Wygorn(iensis)
35 tunc episcopus, Rogerum comitem filium Milonis comitis manu accipiens nobisque
tradens qui tunc Glouc(estrie) preeramus ecclesie, ipsum et successores eius ecclesie
sancti Petri atitulauit et in ea sepeliendos et humandos episcopali auctoritate
constituit. Quia uero hiis agendis interfuimus et hec in hunc modum processisse
pro certo nouimus, ea presenti scripto fraternitati uestre notificamus, quam recte
40 semper incedere et a uia non declinare iustitie preoptamus. Valeat in Domino,
karissime.

### 373

[1163–87 (? 1179)] Testification that Ralph archdeacon of Llandaff, and chaplains who serve
the church of St Cadoc of Llancarfan, are bound to pay Gloucester abbey an annual pension
of sixty shillings.

Gloucester abbey acquired the old *clas* church of St Cadoc from Robert FitzHamon
*c*. 1100, but failed entirely to oust the family which had been in possession—of which Archdeacon Ralph was doubtless a member.[1] He seems to have been dead by 1179.

Dilectis sibi in Domino uniuersis sancte matris ecclesie filiis ad quos iste littere
peruenerint, frater G(ilebertus) Londoniensis ecclesie minister, salutem in Christo.

**372** 34 quidem] quod *MS* (? *for* ad (confirmandum))
**373** PRO, Chancery Records, C 150, Cart. Gloucester, fo. 114 v. *Printed: Cart. Gloucester*, II,
11–12; *calendared:* Conway Davies, II, 665.

[1] Cf. Conway Davies, II, 506 ff.; Brooke in *SEBC*, pp. 223 ff.; *CS*, pp. 276 f., 283 ff. *Cart.
Gloucester*, II, 11–14, shows us three archdeacons concerned in the church of Llancarfan in the
time of Bishop Nicholas, Ralph, William and Urban. Dr Conway Davies, II, 522–3, suggests
that they were archdeacons in that order, and points out that another Urban was archdeacon
at the opening of Nicholas's episcopate. But it cannot be proved that William succeeded
Ralph, and it is even possible that there were two archdeacons concurrently (as apparently in
the late eleventh century; cf. *CS*, pp. 287–8). Ralph was archdeacon before 1161, acted as
royal clerk in the period 1169–71, and was alive after 1174; if (as seems likely) William and
Urban succeeded him, he must have been dead by 1179, for Urban was archdeacon by then,
and survived the bishop (Conway Davies, *loc. cit.*; *Cart. Gloucester*, II, 11–14; *JS Epp.* I, 98 n.).

Sicut ex recognitione et confessione Radulfi archidiaconi Land(auensis), sicut etiam ex litteris eius signatis accepimus, ecclesiam sancti Cadoci de Lancaruan de abbate et conuentu Glouc(estrie), interueniente auctoritate dyocesani e⟨fo. 115⟩pi- 5 copi, sub hoc tenore habendam ipse suscepit, quod si sexaginta solidos memoratis fratribus annuatim statutis terminis uel infra octauum ab eis diem non reddiderit, cadat a iure et possessione ipsius ecclesie, ita ut neque apellationis obstaculum neque reclamatio neque contradictio per ipsum uel per alium facta ei debeat suffragari, quominus monachi statim auctoritate sua, inconsulto episcopo et ministris eius, 10 eamdem adeant et ingrediantur ecclesiam, et tamquam suam et tamquam uacantem cum pertinentiis suis omnibus libere et quiete possideant. Capellanos etiam post-modum in eadem ecclesia ministraturos predicto abbati et monachis iurare faciet, quod si a predicta solutione cessauerit, reddita mox eis claue ipsius ecclesie, ipsisque in ea sine impedimento receptis, absoluti ab obligatione qua illi tenebantur astricti, 15 non per eum de cetero sed per monachos—si monachi uoluerint—inibi ministra-bunt, si minus penitus decessuri. Quod quia pleno partium hinc inde assensu, iuratoria quoque cautione a Radulfo prestita firmatum est et auctoritate diocesani episcopi comprobatum, nos quoque ne in dubium de cetero id queat reuocari, presenti scripto uobis notificare, et sigilli nostri attestatione coram uniuersitate 20 uestra testificari curauimus. Hiis testibus [. . .].

## 374

[11 June 1180][1] Settlement as papal judge delegate of the case between St Botolph's priory, Colchester (Augustinian), and the priory of St-Léonard-le-Noblat (near Limoges, Haute Vienne)[2] on the church of St Leonard, Great Bricett (i.e. St-Léonard's dependency, Great Bricett priory, Suffolk); St-Léonard's right was established and St Botolph's was paid three marks for expenses.

Cf. Dickinson, p. 121 and n.

G(ilebertus) Dei gratia Londoniensis episcopus omnibus sancte matris eclesie filiis ad quos presentes littere peruenerint, salutem in Domino.

Sicut opus est karitatis inter religiosorum precipue fratrum loca pacem reformare, ita pium esse dinoscitur reformatam perpetua stabilitate communire. Quod quia scripture suffragio efficacius effici posse credimus, uniuersitati uestre presentium 5 litterarum attestatione significare curauimus, causam que uertebatur inter dilectos filios nostros canonicos regulares sancti Botulfi Colecestrie et canonicos Nobilia-

---

**374** *Originals* (3): King's College, Cambridge, Muniment Room, B 17–19 (Ka, Kb, Kc) (size: B 17, 10¼ in. × 14½ in.; B 18, 10¼ in. × 8½ in.; B 19, 10¼ in. × 9 in.) (spelling as Kb). B 17 has fragments of seal (natural wax); B 18 seal tag only; B 19 has most of its seal (natural wax). *Endorsed*: B 17: de sancto Botulfo (fourteenth century); B 18: de sancto Butulfo Colcest' (fifteenth century); B 19: de sancto Botulfo (fourteenth century), compositio inter priorem de Bryset et abbatem de sancto Butulfo Co⟨l⟩cest' (fifteenth century).

---

[1] The reading *idus* shows that the date should not be read as 13 June (*idibus*) 1183, and this is confirmed by the fact that Robert Mantel witnesses as sheriff of Essex.
[2] See Cottineau, coll. 2764–5.

censis ecclesie super ecclesia sancti Leonardi de Bresete nobis a summo pontifice apellatione remota delegatam, hoc tandem fine in nostra presentia utriusque partis
10 in hoc concurrente assensu conquieuisse. Partibus siquidem in nostra presentia ad diem sibi peremptorie prefixum constitutis, et multis hinc inde rationibus propositis et allegationibus auditis et testibus productis, iuratis et sufficienter examinatis, cartis quoque quas Nobiliacenses canonici in sue partis assertionem produxerant perlectis, cum iam usque ad diffinitiuam peruentum esset sententiam, postquam
15 partes aliquandiu inter se de pace tractauerant, G(odefridus) prior et canonici sancti Botulfi amicorum suorum consilio, malentes ab actione quam instituerant spontanea uoluntate recedere quam iudicialis euentum calculi—qui plerumque solet esse dubius—expectare, omni iuri quod habuerunt, immo iuri si quod habuerunt in prelibata ecclesia sancti Leonardi de Bresete in manus nostras resignauerunt et
20 refutauerunt; et predictus Godefridus prior sancti Botulfi, qui per litteras conuentus sui ratihabitionis in causa illa ad agendum et componendum procurator confirmatus fuerat, et alii qui cum ipso ibidem in causa steterunt canonici, nomine suo et conuentus se nullam in perpetuum eclesie Nobiliacensi moturos super memorata ecclesia de Bresete controuersiam, propositis terribilibus quattuor euangeliorum
25 scripturis iuramentum corporaliter prestiterunt. Prior uero Nobiliacensis ecclesie, Castus nomine, pretextu expensarum quas ecclesia sua huius occasione litis fecerat, se nichil umquam ab ecclesia sancti Botulfi exacturum, et insuper se predictis canonicis sancti Botulfi tres marcas argenti daturum in reconpensationem expensarum quas ipsi in lite fecerant, similiter nomine suo et conuentus cum quibusdam
30 fratribus suis qui ibidem presentes aderant iuramenti cautionem exposuit. Nos itaque prefatos canonicos Nobiliacensis ecclesie ab impetitione canonicorum sancti Botulfi super prelibata ecclesia sancti Leonardi summi pontificis et nostra auctoritate penitus absoluentes, hanc inter ipsos celebratam compositionem ratam habuimus, et ne quorumlibet malignantium calliditate uel protractioris interiectu temporis
35 possit infringi, presentis eam inscriptione pagine et sigilli nostri pariter appositione confirmauimus. Facta est autem hec transactio apud Copford in ecclesia, anno ab incarnatione Domini MCLXXX, iii idus Iunii. His testibus: Henrico thesaurario Lond(oniensis) ecclesie, magistro Radulfo de Altaripa magistro scolarum London(ie), G(ileberto) Foliot canonico sancti Pauli, Ricardo de Sareb(eria), Radulfo
40 precentore, Iohanne Witenge, magistro Nicholao, Alano et Thoma decanis, magistro Samuele, magistro Iohanne de Stoches, magistro Godefrido, Roberto Mantel uicecomite Essex(ie), Radulfo filio Brieni, Alexandro et Andrea de Bresete clericis, et multis aliis.

**374** 8 Briesset' Ka    14 sententiam peruentum esset Ka    19 Brisset' Ka    20–1 sui conuentus Ka    22 causa *om.* Ka    24 ecclesia ecclesia de Brisset' Ka    28 sancti Botulfi canonicis Ka 33 compositionem celebratam Ka    35 nostri sigilli Ka    36 Copeford Ka    39 Salesberia Ka    40 Witenge] clerico Ka    40 et *om.* Ka    41 Stokes Ka    42 Essex(ie) *om.* Ka    42 Briennii Ka    42–3 clericis de Brisset' Ka

**375**

[1173–4] Notification to the bishop elect and chapter of Hereford of the settlement of the case between Roger prior of Great Malvern (Worcs, dep. Westminster abbey) and Roger priest of Lyonshall (Herefs), on the church of Lyonshall,[1] in which Gilbert acted as papal judge delegate. The right of Great Malvern priory was acknowledged, but Roger the priest and his vicar Walter priest of *Daubo* were given life tenure in exchange for annual pensions of half a mark and one mark respectively.

The bishop elect addressed was presumably Robert Foliot (1173–4): Robert de Melun was hardly bishop elect for long enough for such a case to have matured before his consecration.[2]

Gilebertus Dei gratia Lundoniensis episcopus dilectis in Domino sibi Roberto eadem gratia Hereford(ensi) electo totique eiusdem ecclesie capitulo salutem.

Que ad pacem ecclesie stabiliendam seu tutius muniendam pertinere dinoscimus iis diligentius assensum dare et ut in ⟨fo. 149⟩ perpetuum ualitura permaneant, hec scriptis et munimentis aliis roborare caritate id procul dubio suggerente debemus. 5 Eapropter fraternitati uestre presenti scripto notificamus, causam que inter uenerabilem fratrem nostrum Rogerum priorem Maluernie et Rogerum sacerdotem de Lenhal' super ecclesiam de Lenhal' diu uentilata est et ob uarios euentus rerum protracta plurimum, super qua mandatum apostolicum accepimus ut ei aut finem amicabili compositione imponeremus, aut ipsam auditis utrimque partibus 10 canonico fine decideremus, in presentia nostra hoc tandem ⟨modo⟩ conquieuisse et finem paci congruum accepisse. Predictus siquidem Rogerus de Lenhal' ius ecclesie de Maluernia in sepedicta ecclesia de Lenhal' recognoscens, ipsam in manu nostra resignauit, et priorem ⟨et⟩ ecclesiam de Maluernia per manum nostram apostolica auctoritate eadem inuestiri concessit. Quo debita sollempnitate peracto, prior totius 15 capituli sui assensu eandem ecclesiam ipsi Rogero per manum nostram apostolica interueniente auctoritate annua dimidie marce pensione in Pascha soluenda tota uita sua tenendam concessit; hoc etiam in caritatis augmentum totius capituli sui conniuentia annuens, ut cum predictus Rogerus aut uita decesserit aut se ad frugem melioris uite transtulerit, Walterus presbiter de Daubo qui in eadem ecclesia nomine 20 Rogeri aliquandiu ministrauit, in eadem nomine prioris et ecclesie de Maluernia ministret, et usque uel decesserit uel seculari uite renuntiauerit annua marce unius pensione in Pascha persoluende annuatim perpetuus in ea uicarius perseueret. Nominato uero Waltero uel obeunte uel se ad religionis habitum transferente, ecclesia de Lenhal' cum omni integritate sua Maluernensis ecclesie bonis accrescat, 25

375 G, no. 210; B, fo. 148v.
11 ⟨modo⟩ B omits: *a word is obviously missing, and of the two alternatives,* modo *and* fine, fine *seems unlikely on account of the repetition* finem *immediately following* 14 ⟨et⟩ *om.* B

---

[1] Cf. *Taxatio*, p. 159. *Daubo* seems corrupt.
[2] This would only be possible if Gilbert had been appointed delegate before his translation. Under later rules the delegacy would automatically have passed to his successor at Hereford: we cannot be absolutely sure that this would have happened in 1163, but in any case 1173–4 is the more probable date.

ipsamque Maluernensis ecclesia de cetero plene possideat. Quod quia saluo iure Hereford(ensis) ecclesie ratum inconuulsumque manere decernimus, scripti presentis annotatione et sigilli nostri appositione confirmamus. Hiis testibus: Roberto de Broi, Mauricio de Sabricteswrd', Rogero de Hereford(ia), Ricardo de
30 Saresber(ia), Lodowico, Waltero elemosinario, magistro Willelmo de Bernes, Hugone capellano de Hedam, ⟨fo. 149v⟩ Samsone clerico prioris, Reginaldo camerario, Waltero Foliot, Ricardo Brudle, Iocelino, Alano.

## 376

[1163-80 (*c.* 1179)] Notification that Richard (Foliot) archdeacon of Colchester has been instituted vicar of the church of Beaumont (Essex: cf. *VN*, p. 348) by Prior William and the convent of Hatfield Broad Oak, in exchange for a pension of three marks (i.e. Hatfield Regis, Essex, dep. St-Melaine, Rennes).

G(ilbertus) Dei gratia Lundoniensis episcopus omnibus personis ecclesiarum que in archidiaconatu Colecestrie consistunt, salutem, gratiam et benedictionem.

Vniuersitati uestre presenti scripto notificamus, nos presentatione Willelmi prioris de Hethfeld et conuentus sui conniuentia, Ricardo archidiacono Colecestrie
5 ecclesiam de Bellomonte cum omnibus ad eam pertinentibus concessisse, ipsumque in eam perpetuum uicarium, salua predictis priori et monacis de Hethfeld annua trium marcarum pensione, instituisse. Et quia concessionem hanc predicto archidiacono ab ipsis monacis factam in detrimentum ecclesie de Hethfeld redundare nolumus, sepedictis monacis concedimus ut postquam prenominatum archidia-
10 conum contigerit in fata concedere, liceat eis de ecclesia de Bellomonte pro uoluntate sua libere disponere. Nos igitur quia conuentionem hanc firmam et inconuulsam manere uolumus, eam scripti presentis attestatione et sigilli nostri appositione testificari pariter et confirmare curauimus. His testibus: Gilleberto Foliot, magistro Radulfo de Altaripa, Rogero filio Mauritii, Radulfo de Chiltona,
15 Hugone capellano de Heddeh', Gaufrido capellano de Hethfeld, Willelmo Foliot senescallo, Reginaldo camerario, Waltero Foliot, Roberto de Baut (?), Willelmo Morin, et aliis multis.

## 377

[1163-*c.* 1180] Settlement as papal judge delegate of the case between R. of Warwick and W., clerk, on the church of Hatton (? Middlesex). R. is to hold the church for life in exchange for an annual pension of one mark to W.; the survivor is to have full right.

Dilectis sibi in Domino uniuersis sancte matris ecclesie filiis frater G(ilebertus) L(ondoniensis) ecclesie minister, salutem, gratiam et benedictionem.

375 26 Maluernense B    28-31 Hiis testibus...Hedam (*i.e. foot of folio*) *crossed out in* B
376 *Original:* BM Add. Charter 28,332 (size 6¼ in. × 5 in.). *Facsimile: Facsimiles of...Charters in the British Museum,* 1 (ed. G. F. Warner and H. J. Ellis, London, 1903), no. 58. Slit for seal tag. *Endorsed:* Beaumond et Horflete (?) in episcopatu London' (fourteenth century).
377 G, no. 192; B, fo. 194.

Que sententiali finita sunt calculo, aut amicabili sopita pactione, ne iterum rediuiua suscitentur in iurgia nos pacis amatores decet attentius prouidere. Eapropter controuersia super ecclesia de Hattona inter R. de Warewic et W. clericum diu 5 agitata et ad de ea cognoscendum apostolica auctoritate nobis delegata, quo tandem fine quieuerit utriusque partis mutuo in id concurrente uoto, scripto commendare dignum duximus. R. itaque ecclesiam de Hattona quam prius petierat tenere debet quamdiu uixerit, soluendo pretaxato W. marcam argenti annuam infra octabas sancti Micaelis, prenominate ecclesie iure integro utrolibet eorum decedente 10 superstiti reseruato. Hanc pactionem uterque se bona fide obseruaturum interposita sacramenti religione promisit. Hoc autem tam solempniter actum ut firmitatem in posterum optineat, presentis scripti testificatione confirmamus, et sigilli nostri appositione communimus. His testibus [...]

## 378

[1163–87: *c.* 1177] Testification that when Gilbert was bishop of Hereford, Gilbert de Lacy and his successor Robert had owed service of two knights for the manor of Holme Lacy (Herefs).[1]

This case was settled between Bishop Robert Foliot and Hugh de Lacy in 1177, on the eve of the latter's departure for Ireland.[2]

G(ilebertus) Dei gratia Lundonensis episcopus uniuersis fidelibus ad quos littere iste peruenerint, salutem in Christo.

Peruenit ad nos quod quidam malitiose conantur in dubium deuocare quo et quanto seruitio Hugo de Laci pro manerio de Hamma episcopo Hereford(ensi) debeat respondere. Vnde ne Herefordensis ecclesia pro defectu testimonii nostri 5 aliquod sustineat iuris sui dispendium, quod super hoc longo usu didicimus, quodque recenti adhuc memoria certum tenemus, in scriptum redigere et scripture testimonio commendare curauimus. Nouerint ergo presentes et posteri quod tempore quo nos in Herefordensi ecclesia curam gessimus episcopalem cum res exigebat ut regi in militibus seruiretur, a Gilleberto de Lacy et postmodum a 10 successore et herede ipsius Roberto pro manerio de Hamma seruitium duorum militum plenarie et sine contradictione recepimus. Hoc presenti scripto publice protestamur et nostri attestatione sigilli declaramus. Valete.

378 Hereford Diocesan Registry, Reg. Swinfield, fo. 177v (179v); Bodl. Rawlinson MS B 329, fo. 149v (Rc) (select variants of Rc only). *Printed: Reg. Swinfield,* p. 477.
4 Lacy Rc    7 teneamus Rc    10 Lascy Rc    13 Valete *om.* Rc

---

[1] On this see H. M. Colvin in *Essays in History presented to Rose Graham,* ed. V. Ruffer and A. J. Taylor (Oxford, 1950), pp. 15–40.
[2] Colvin, art. cit. 20 ff., 36–7; for Hugh, see Eyton, *Salop,* v, 253–6: he died in Ireland in 1185. On Gilbert and Robert see above, nos. 93–6.

**379**

[1184] Settlement of the dispute between Thomas abbot of Gloucester and William prior of St Guthlac's Hereford and Ralph son of John of London on the domain tithes and a virgate of land in Mansell Lacy (?)[1] (Herefs), granted to the monks by Walter de Lacy: every rector presented by Ralph or his heirs to the church of Mansell Lacy (?) shall pay an annual pension of twenty shillings to the abbot of Gloucester and the monks of St Guthlac's.

G(ilebertus) Dei gratia Londoniensis ecclesie minister omnibus sancte matris ecclesie filiis ad quos hee littere peruenerint, salutem in Domino.

Ad communem omnium uestrum uolumus peruenire notitiam, conuentionem quandam factam fuisse coram nobis inter Thomam abbatem Glouec(estrie) et
5 Willelmum priorem et conuentum sancti Petri Heref(ordie) et Radulfum filium Iohannis de London(ia) super decimis dominii et de quadam uirgata terre in Mumwell', quas idem monachi habent de donatione Walteri de Lacy: uidelicet quod quecumque persona instituta fuerit in ecclesia de Mumwell' ad presentationem memorati Radulfi uel heredum suorum, singulis annis uiginti solidos exsoluet
10 abbati Glouec(estrie) et monachis Hereford(ie) ad duos terminos pro predictis decimis de dominio et de uirgata terre. Hec autem conuentio celebrata est apud London(iam) anno dominice incarnationis MCLXXXIIII in nostra et multorum presentia; quam quia firmam et inconcussam manere uolumus, nostri scripti testimonio et nostri pariter appositione sigilli roboramus. Hiis testibus: Nicholao
15 London(iensi) archidiacono, magistro Henrico de Norhamton', Roberto de Clifford', Radulfo de Chilt(on), Rogero filio Reigemeri alderemanno, Radulfo uinetario, et aliis.

**380**

[c. 1181–7] Confirmation of the grant of the church of Feltham (Middlesex) to the hospital of St Giles in the Fields, Holborn, by Hawise, countess of Roumare (Lincoln).[2]

G(ilebertus) Dei gratia Londoniensis episcopus omnibus sancte matris ecclesie filiis, salutem in Domino.

Ad uniuersitatis uestre notitiam presenti scripto uolumus deuenire, cartam nobilis femine Hadewise quondam comitisse de Rumare nobis presentatam fuisse,
5 ex cuius testimonio eandem comitissam infirmis sancti Egidii extra London(iam)

**379** Oxford, Balliol College, MS 271, fos. 96 (X) and 97 (Y) (clearly representing two originals).
1 ecclesie minister X; episcopus Y    2 hee] presentes Y    3 deuenire Y    4 Glouc' Y
7 Mumell' Y    11 decimis] Y adds et    11 et et X    12 incarnationis dominice Y    15 Norhampton' Y    16 Chilt(on)] Clifft' Y    16–17 Rogero...aliis X; canonicis sancti Pauli, Waltero filio Walteri, Thoma Bretone, Radulfo cantore, Roberto Foliot, et aliis Y
**380** BM Harl. MS. 4015, fos. 157 (Za) and 211 v (Zb) (Cart. St Giles in the Fields, London: select variants of Zb only).

---

[1] But cf. *Taxatio*, p. 159: St Guthlac's held the church of Mansell Gamage.
[2] Sister of Baldwin, first earl of Devon, wife of William de Roumare, earl of Lincoln, who died before 1161 (see *CP*, VII, 667–70, esp. pp. 669 f.).

in puram et perpetuam elemosinam pro sua suorumque salute ecclesiam de Feltham cum uniuersis pertinentiis suis ad predictorum exhibitionem infirmorum manifeste perpendimus contulisse. Vnde nos prefate comitisse deuotionem ac pie desiderium uoluntatis attendentes eandemque factam approbantes donationem, ipsam ut decuit ratam habuimus, et ut eadem nominatis infirmis perpetuo inuiolata permaneat, eam 10 presentis pagine conscriptione et sigilli nostri ab ipsa dependentis munimine confirmare curauimus et communire. Hiis testibus: Ricardo de Storteford magistro scolarum London(ie), Radulfo *de Chilton', Gilleberto Ban(astre), Ricardo de Saresbir', Ricardo Ban(astre), Radulfo cantore, Iohanne Witenge, Ricardo Foliot clericis nostris, et pluribus aliis. 15

## 381

[c. 1169-1180] Confirmation of grants to Horkesley priory (Essex: Cluniac, dep. Thetford): by Robert, son of Robert, of half the church of Boxted (Essex) with appurtenances and the tithe of corn used by his household (cf. *VN*, p. 347 and no. 401); by Robert, son of Godebold, of the church of St Peter, Horkesley (i.e. the priory church), and appurtenances, the church of Asheldham (Essex) with appurtenances, and tithes of the marsh of Foulness (Essex) and of *Lingu'*, of ..., and of Fordham (Essex).[1]

The witnesses are very similar to those of no. 360 (c. 1179-80).

Gillebertus Dei gratia Lundoniensis episcopus archidiaconis, decanis et omnibus ecclesiarum personis per episcopatum Lund(oniensem) constitutis, salutem, gratiam et benedictionem.

Vniuersitati uestre notificamus nos donatione et presentatione Roberti filii Roberti concessisse et confirmasse ecclesie sancti Petri de Horkesleie et monachis 5 ibidem Deo seruientibus totam medietatem ecclesie de Boncsted' (?) cum omnibus pertinentiis suis et decimam panis frumenti de domo sua, scilicet militum et armigerorum ubicumque sit in Anglia, siue in castellis, siue extra ad sustentationem eorundem monachorum in perpetuum. Preterea confirmauimus predictis monachis omnes donationes quas Robertus filius Godeboldi ad [sustentationem] eiusdem loci 10 eis fecit et [d]edit, scilicet ecclesiam sancti Petri de Horch(esleia) cum omnibus pertinentiis suis, ubi monachos Clun(iacenses) posuit ad seruiendum [Deo] in perpetuum, et ecclesiam Essildesh(am) cum omnibus pertinentiis suis et decimam de [marisco] de Fulenesse et de Lingu' et decimam de [...] et decimam de Ford-

380 7 exebucionem Za    7-8 contulisse manifeste perpendimus Zb    9 accedentes Za    9 facturam Zb    12 Sterdeford Zb    13 *de om. Za    13 Ban(astre)] Lan Za    14 cantore] Cante Za; Cantree Zb    14 Filiot Za; Iliot Zb
381 *Original*: Oxford, Bodl. Essex Charter a. 2 (size 6¾ in. × 5 in.) (partly illegible through damp, etc.). Tag for seal. *Endorsed*: Gilebertus episcopus (twelfth century). *Printed*: Monasticon, v, 157, no. II (from original, then *penes* A. Woode, Merton College).
10 [sustentationem] *So in the charter of Robert son of Godebold (Monasticon, loc. cit.).*    12-14 [Deo] ...[marisco] *So Dugdale (confirmation by Robert son of Philip, ibid., includes* totam decimam de marisco meo in Fulenesse).    14 Lingued *Dugdale*

[1] For Asheldham and Fordham see Morant, I, 368; II, 228. The missing name may be *Foleton* (or *Fultona*, unidentified: *Monasticon*, v, 156-7).

15 h(am) sicut carta Ricardi predecessoris nostri eis testatur. Et ut hec nostra concessio et confirmatio rata et firma in posterum permaneat presentis pagine conscriptione et sigilli nostri appositione roborare curauimus. Hiis testibus: Ricardo archidiacono Colec(estrie), Roberto archidiacono Essex(ie), magistro Ricardo de Stortef(ord), Ricardo de Sales(beria), Rogero de Wigornia, magistro Radulfo
20 cantore, Waltero elemosinario, magistro Eraclio, Beniamin clerico, et multis aliis.

### 382

[1163–73] Confirmation of the grants to the Knights Hospitallers of the churches of Standon (Herts), Kingsbury (Middlesex) (?) and Chaureth (in Broxted, Essex) and their appurtenances.[1]

Robert archdeacon of Oxford was elected bishop of Hereford in 1173.

Gilebertus Dei gracia Londoniensis episcopus dilectis sibi in Domino archidiaconis, decanis et omnibus qui in epischopatu Lo⟨n⟩d⟨onie⟩nsi consistunt ecclesiarum prelatis, salutem, gratiam et benedicionem.
Officii nostri nos ammonet et hortatur auctoritas ut beneficia que in nostra
5 diocesi fidelium deuotio pauperibus Christi in caritate contulit aut collatura est in posterum, ipsis confirmare et perpetua stabilitate communire curemus. Proinde ecclesiam de Standuna cum pertinentiis suis, et ecclesiam de Chingesberia cum suis itidem pertinentiis et ecclesiam de Chauria cum omnibus ad ipsam pertinentibus, quas earundem fundatores et aduocati ecclesiarum, sicut ex autenticis eorum scriptis
10 agnouimus, Deo et sancto Iohanni et fratribus Hospitalis Ierusalem pro sua et suorum salute in perpetuam destinarunt elemosinam, concessa nobis a Domino episcopali auctoritate, memoratis fratribus Hospitalis concedimus, et sub huius scripti testimonio in perpetuum confirmamus. His testibus: Hugone decano sancti Pauli, Roberto archidiacono Oxenefordie, Ricardo archidiacono Colecestrie,
15 magistro Nicholao, magistro Waltero, Willelmo de Norhala canonicis sancti Pauli; Willelmo de Piro, Henrico pictore, Roberto Huscharl', Roberto de Fuleham, Alfredo Bechet, Willelmo de Ver,[2] et ceteris. Valete.

### 383

[1163–72] Appropriation of the church of Harefield (Middlesex) to the Knights Hospitallers, in the person of Brother Richard Turcus, the prior of the English province, on the presenta-

**382** G, no. 226; B, fos. 164 (B1) and 166 (B2) (spelling as B1).
1–2 Lundon'/Lund' B2    7 Standune B2    13–17 B2 omits Hugone...Valete. In B1 Hugone decano, Pauli...Oxene- are partly erased
**383** G, no. 185; B, fo. 172v; BM MS Cotton Nero E. vi, fo. 84v (Kn) (Cart. Knights Hospitallers) (spelling as B).

---

[1] Cf. *VCH Herts.* III, 362 ff.; Morant, II, 449. *Cal. Papal Regs.* I, 63 confirms 'Chingesbiri' church to *St Albans* in 1219.

[2] Probably not William de Vere, canon of St Paul's and St Osyth, later bishop of Hereford (*GF*, p. 284), because he witnesses among the laymen.

tion of Geoffrey son of Baldwin and Beatrice de Bollers, his mother, and the resignation of Robert,[1] priest, the rector (see no. 384).

〈G〉ilebertus Dei gratia Lundoniensis episcopus omnibus sancte matris ecclesie filiis salutem.

Vniuersitati uestre notum esse uolumus quod Galfridus filius Baldewini et mater eius Beatrix de Bollers, ut ex cartis ipsorum perspeximus et ex eorundem uiua uoce probauimus, concesserunt et dederunt Deo et fratribus Hospitalis Ierusalem aduoca- 5 tionem ecclesie de Herefeld' cum omnibus pertinentiis suis in perpetuam elemosinam, nobisque presentauerunt fratrem Ricardum Turcum in Anglia priorem, ut per eum de personatu prefate ecclesie predictum Hospitale quantum ad ius episcopale pertinet inuestiremus. Cum igitur in eis que necessariis pauperum usibus destinantur promptum deceat et hilarem adesse consensum, nos eiusdem Hospitalis 10 religionem presertim et necessitatem attendentes, dictam concessionem grate suscepimus facileque probauimus, et cum Robertus presbiter, tunc temporis eiusdem ecclesie persona, liberam eam in manus nostras sponte refutasset, mox eandem prenominato Ricardo priori tradidimus et per 〈B, fo. 173〉 eum Hospitali suo personatum eiusdem concessimus. Quod quia ratum et indubitabile deinceps 15 manere uolumus presenti scripto et sigilli nostri testimonio confirmamus. Hiis testibus: Nicholao archidiacono Londoniensi, Ricardo archidiacono Colocestr(ie), magistro Nicholao, magistro Ricardo, magistro Gilberto, Willelmo de Beamis canonicis sancti Pauli, magistro Henrico de Northamton, Fulcone, Rogero, Roberto de Clifford', Ricardo de Sar(esbiria), Iohanne clerico, Germano.      20

## 384

[1163–72] Institution of Richard priest as perpetual vicar of Harefield for a pension of ten shillings to the Knights Hospitallers (see no. 383).

Gilbertus Dei gratia Londoniensis episcopus omnibus sancte matris ecclesie filiis salutem.

Vniuersitati uestre notum esse uolumus, quod Ricardus presbiter qui se gerebat personam ecclesie de Herefeld' eandem ecclesiam in manus nostras sponte refutauit. Ad cuius etiam petitionem et dominorum fundi presentationem mox de eadem 5 Hospitale Ierusalem per Ricardum Turchum tunc in Anglia priorem inuestiuimus et inpersonauimus, eiusdem deinceps prioris et fratrum ipsius rogatu ac presentatione prenominatum Ricardum presbiterum eiusdem ecclesie perpetuum uicarium constituimus, ut eam cum omnibus suis pertinentiis quamdiu uixerit teneat et possideat, reddendo inde Hospitali singulis annis decem solidos et consuetudines 10

383 1 Gilbertus Kn   1 London' Kn   4 ipsorum] eorum Kn   7 Turchum Kn   10 concessum Kn   12 Robertus] R. B   13–14 B omits eandem prenominato   16–20 B omits presenti... Germano
384 BM Cotton MS Nero E. vi, fo. 85.

---

[1] Perhaps for Richard: see no. 384. Beatrice de Bollers was second wife of Baldwin de Bollers, on whom see J. Bain in Genealogist, New Series, III, 195; cf. Eyton, Salop, XI, 121; Round, Geoffrey de Mandeville, p. 53 n. On Harefield, cf. VCH Middlesex, III, 253.

episcopales omnes faciendo. Quod quia uolumus ratum et indubitabile permanere presentium litterarum et sigilli nostri testimonio confirmamus. Hiis testibus: Nicholao archidiacono Lond(oniensi), Ricardo archidiacono Colocest(rie), magistro Nicholao, magistro Ricardo, magistro Gilberto, Willelmo de Beamis
15 canonicis sancti Pauli, Henrico, Roberto, Ricardo, Hugone, Lodowico clericis episcopi, Iohanne clerico, Germano.

## 385

[1163–74] Confirmation of the grant by Walter son of Robert[1] of the churches of Burnham and Woodham Walter (Essex) to the Knights Hospitallers.

The manuscript attributes this to Bishop Robert (cf. no. 387): the witnesses prove it to be Bishop Gilbert's.

⟨Gile⟩bertus Dei gratia Londoniensis episcopus dilectis in Domino filiis archidiaconis, decanis et omnibus alii⟨s⟩ qui in episcopatu London(iensi) consistunt ecclesiarum prelatis, salutem, gratiam et benedictionem. Perlatas ad nos uiri nobilis et dilecti filii nostri Walteri filii Roberti cartas ipsius
5 inpressas sigillo conspeximus, quibus se ecclesiam de Burneham cum omnibus pertinentiis suis et ecclesiam de Wudeham cum omnibus que ad eandem pertinent, Deo et sancto Iohanni Baptiste et sancto Hospitali Ierusalem, fratribusque eidem Hospitali seruientibus pro salute sua et heredum et omnium parentum suorum in perpetuam elemosinam concessisse testatur. Quam nimirum donationem, tum quia
10 dantis saluti plurimum ut credimus profutura est, tum quia fratrum predictorum in quos collata est donatio ad omnes qui [...] adeundum sepulcrum Dominicum maris et terrarum se periculis exponunt karitas late diffusa est, approbauimus. Et ut firmum robur optineat et eorum saluti ob quos facta est in perpetuum ualitura proficiat, nos easdem ecclesias iam dictis fratribus Hospitalis Ierusalem, ea que nobis
15 a Domino concessa est auctoritate, ipsos in eas personas constituendo concessimus, et ut saluo iure London(iensis) ecclesie perpetuum in eisdem personatum optineant, ipsas eis tam scripti presentis atestatione quam sigilli nostri appositione confirmauimus. Hiis testibus: Radulfo archidiacono Midelsex', Henrico Banastre, magistro Henrico de Norhamton', Gilberto Foliot, Rogero filio Mauritii, Radulfo
20 de Chiltona, Ricardo de Saresbir(ia), et multis aliis.

## 386

[1163–c. 1180] Grant of an indulgence in support of an appeal for the Hospital (of St John) at Jerusalem (i.e. the Knights Hospitallers), for which a fraternity (of subscribers) is being formed.

385 BM Cotton MS Nero E. vi, fo. 124v.
1 Robertus MS    15 ipsius MS
386 G, no. 237; B, fo. 199v.

---

[1] See Delisle, *Recueil*, Introd. p. 467: if identified correctly, he was a member of the house of Clare and a royal justice. Cf. no. 449. On the churches cf. *VN*, pp. 343, 482; Morant, I, 340.

G(ilebertus) Dei gratia Lundoniensis episcopus dilectis sibi in Domino archidiaconis, decanis, et omnibus in Lundon(iensi) diocesi constitutis ecclesiarum prelatis, salutem, gratiam et benedictionem.

In luce lucerna opus non est,[1] et cum quid sui per se natura clarescit, id testibus aut testimoniis euincere citra necessitatem est. Quanta siquidem caritatis studia, 5 quanta suffragia pietatis, quanta denique totius humanitatis obsequia peregrinis pauperibus Christi et omnibus necessitatem patientibus inpendat sanctum xenodochium Ierusolimitanum, sancta scilicet domus Hospitalis, ipsis iam olim rerum indiciis orbi innotuit, ut non iam nostro super hoc testimonio sed peruulgate magis ueritati fides debeatur. Qui nimirum locus uenerabilis ob meritorum insignia, 10 nonnullis meruit a regno simul et sacerdotio priuilegiis insigniri. Nos igitur patrum et prelatorum nostrorum uestigia debita ueneratione subsequentes, latores presentium nuntios et procuratores illius religiose domus, cum testimonio litterarum nostrarum destinamus ad uos, et quanta possumus deuotione commendamus ad gratiam, orantes et exortantes in Domino et in remissionem uobis iniungentes 15 delictorum quatinus cum ad uos ob colligendas fidelium elemosinas eos declinare contigerit, ipsos pii ministros operis pietatis intuitu benigne recipiatis, ope et opera misericorditer promoueatis, et iuxta commonitionem domni pape et indulta sibi priuilegia, debitam in omnibus reuerentiam exibeatis. Subiectos quoque uestros eorum fraternitatem suscipere, susceptamque ad finem usque fideliter obseruare, 20 sedulo commonere satagatis, scientes quoniam non possunt fructus non esse participes qui bonorum se operum exhibent adiutores. Omnes autem qui contemplatione Dei et pauperum Christi fraternitati huic se addixerint, eamque annua ut moris est obseruatione ⟨fo. 200⟩ compleuerint, orationum et omnium beneficiorum commisse nobis a Deo ecclesie participes et statuimus. Parrochianis uero 25 nostris quibus precipue debitores existimus, penitentibus uidelicet et peccata confessis, qui hanc societatem debita deuotione seruauerint, si in septem aut eo amplius annorum penitentia fuerint constituti, quadraginta, si minus, uiginti de iniuncta sibi satisfactione dies misericorditer relaxamus.

## 387

[1180–c. 1181] Confirmation of the grant of the church of Thurrock (Essex)[2] by William, earl of Ferrers (Derby), and appropriation to the Knights Hospitallers, saving a vicarage of five marks per annum.

The manuscript (both copies) attributes this to Bishop Richard (cf. no. 385); but the presence of Richard Foliot, archdeacon, and Richard of Stortford, apparently not yet Master of the Schools or archdeacon, seems to enforce a date not later than c. 1181—Dean Ralph gives it a *terminus a quo* of 1180. This is, however, the only charter of Gilbert to which Peter

386 3 prelatis,] B *adds* et   5 euiscere (?) B   18 sibi] B *inserts* penitentia, *expunct.*   25 et] *sic* B, *perhaps for* etiam; *or a word may be missing before* et
387 BM Cotton MS Nero E. vi, fos. 124 (Kn) and 204 (Ko).

[1] Cf. Apoc. xxii. 5.
[2] Probably West Thurrock; cf. *PN Essex*, pp. 130–1.

of Waltham (a frequent witness to those of his successor, Richard FitzNeal) was witness; it is a little surprising that Gilbert's confirmation of Thurrock (no. 388) should have been issued after this appropriation; and if the witness list is corrupt, the charter could be dated 1189–92, and attributed to Bishop Richard.

Gilebertus (?) Dei gratia Londoniensis episcopus archidiaconis, decanis et omnibus ecclesiarum prelatis in diocesi London(iensi) constitutis tam presentibus quam futuris, salutem, gratiam et benedictionem.

Nouerit uniuersitas uestra quod nos inspecta carta dilecti filii nostri Willelmi
5 comitis de Ferariis in eius serie conprehendimus, ipsum pro sua suorumque salute ecclesiam uille sue de Thurrok cum omnibus pertinentiis eius, quantum ad laicam donationem spectabit, fratribus sancte domus Hospitalis Ierusalem in perpetuam elemosinam concessisse. Nos itaque predicti comitis concessionem gratam habentes, considerantes quoque quam laudabiliter et deuote ipsi fratres Hospitalis Ierusalem
10 operibus pietatis sedule intendant, predictam ecclesiam de Thurrok predictis fratribus Hospitalis Ierusalem pontificali auctoritate concedimus, et ipsos eiusdem ecclesie cum omnibus pertinentiis suis perpetuos [sic] personas instituimus, concedentes quod ipsi omnes fructus et obuentiones ipsius ecclesie in usus suos habeant inperpetuum; salua uicaria ad ualentiam quinque marcarum argenti per annum,
15 quam ipsi fratres assignabunt uicariis qui ministrabunt in eadem ecclesia et nobis et officialibus nostris in spiritualibus consuetudinibus respondebunt, et London(iensis) ecclesie dignitate. Et ut hec concessio nostra rata et stabilis sit in perpetuum, eam presenti scripto et sigilli nostri appositione curauimus confirmare. Hiis testibus: Radulfo decano beati Pauli, Ricardo Foliot archidiacono, Henrico Banast(re)
20 thesaurario, magistro Henrico de Norhamt(ona), magistro Hugone de London(ia), magistro Osberto de Camera, magistro Ricardo de Storteford', magistro Petro de Waltham, et multis aliis.

## 388

[c. 1181] Confirmation of the grant by William, earl of Ferrers (Derby), of the churches of Thurrock and Stebbing (Essex) to Ralph de Diva, prior of the English province, and the Knights Hospitallers.

The grant of Stebbing church is dated 1181 (MS cit. fo. 218).

Gillebertus Dei gratia Londoniensis episcopus omnibus, etc.

Ad uniuersitatis uestre uolumus deuenire notitiam, cartas nobilis uiri Willelmi comitis de Fer(ariis) per dilectum filium nostrum Radulfum de Diua, priorem fratrum Hospitalis Ierusalem in Anglia, nobis fuisse presentatas, ex quarum inspec-
5 tione manifeste cognouimus memoratum comitem de Ferar', diuine pietatis intuitu et pro sua suorumque salute Deo et beate Marie, sancto Iohanni Baptiste, et fratribus Hospitalis Ierusalem in Anglia, ecclesias de Turrok et de Stebbyng cum omnibus ad eas pertinentibus, simul cum omni iure quod in eis habuerat in puram et

387 1 Ricardus KnKo    11 Ierusalemit' Kn    14 agenti Kn    16 spe'alibus Kn
388 BM Cotton MS Nero E. vi, fo. 218.

perpetuam elemosinam contulisse. Cuius nos attendentes deuotionem et factam donationem approbantes, supradictas ecclesias de Turrok' et Stebbyng' cum omni 10 integritate iuris quod in eis prescriptus comes habuerat, sicut ipsius carte testantur, supradictis fratribus Hospitalis Ierusalem auctoritate qua fungimur episcopali concedimus. Et ut hec eis facta donatio inperpetuum robur optineat, litterarum nostrarum testimonio, sigilli nostri munimine ipsis eam confirmauimus. Hiis testibus: Ricardo magistro scolarum London(ie), etc. 15

## 389

[*c.* 1186 (1186–7)] Appropriation of the church of Little Maplestead (Essex) to the Knights Hospitallers on the presentation of William son of Aldelin and the resignation of the rector, Ivo, clerk.

This confirms a charter dated 17 March 1186, at London.

G(ilebertus) Dei gratia Londoniensis episcopus omnibus sancte matris ecclesie filiis per episcopatum London(iensem) constitutis, in Domino salutem.

Ea que geruntur a nobis ad hoc scripture beneficio commendantur, ne longiori tractu temporis aliquatinus memorie subducantur. Hinc est quod ad uniuersitatis uestre notitiam presenti uolumus deuenire scripto, Iuonem clericum, qui ecclesie 5 de parua Mapeltrested' personatu gaudebat, iuri quod in eadem habebat publice coram nobis spontanee renuntiasse, nosque ⟨ad (?)⟩ petitionem et presentationem nobilis uiri Willelmi filii Aldelini dilectis filiis nostris priori et fratribus Hospitalis Ierusalemit(ani) ecclesiam ipsam, cum omnibus ad eam pertinentibus, concessisse et perpetuo dedisse, ipsosque eiusdem personas ecclesie pontificali auctoritate, saluis 10 nobis et officialibus nostris debitis inde consuetudinibus et seruitiis, solempniter constituisse. Quod quia perpetue firmitatis robur in posterum optinere desideramus pagina presenti et nostri atestatione sigilli confirmauimus. Testibus: Rogero de Wigorn(ia), Roberto Folet, Radulfo de Chilton' canonicis, magistro Waltero de Wutton' [*sic*], Iohanne Witteng', Thoma Britton(e), et multis aliis. 15

## 390

[1163–*c.* 1180] Grant of an indulgence in support of the appeal for the abbey of St Mary in the Valley of Josaphat, Jerusalem.[1]

G(ilebertus) Dei gratia Lundoniensis episcopus dilectis sibi in Domino archidiaconis, decanis, presbiteris et omnibus eiusdem ecclesie parrochianis et filiis, salutem et omnis gratie plenitudinem.

Cum loca sanctorum omnium, in quibus eorundem reliquie sancta fidelium

---

**389** BM Cotton MS Nero E. vi, fo. 305.
14 canonico *MS*
**390** G, no. 235; B, fo. 199.

---

[1] A Benedictine house, founded *c.* 1100; the community left Jerusalem in 1187, and was later established in Sicily. Cf. U. Berlière in *Revue Bénédictine*, XVII (1900), 425–7; *Chartes de Terre Sainte provenant de l'abbaye de N.-D. de Josaphat*, ed. H.-F. Delaborde (Paris, 1880).

5 deuotione reposite beatam prestolantur octauam, uenerari, sublimari, et piis
bonorum largitionibus reuerenter ampliari oporteat, nulli dubium relinquitur
illum precipue locum, qui in uallis Iosaphat medio inter montem Syon et montem
Oliueti sepulture beate matris Domini donatus est, et ad humanitatis eius obsequium
ab eterno prouisus, summe deuotionis eius obsequiis debere celebriter excoli, et ob
10 eius memoriam que manibus angelorum inde in celum corporaliter etiam, ut
credimus, euecta est modis omnibus honorari. Agatis itaque dilectissimi, monitis
salutaribus acquiescite, et nuntios beate matris Domini, uelud ab eius latere directos,
iocunda mente suscipite, et de eorum gaudentes aduentu de his que uobis a Domino
collata sunt—ut hylares decet datores—in eorum manus confidenter reponite quod
15 per eos beate matri Domini digne mittatis, quo eius sepulturam exhornetis et locum
quem preuidit sibi filius eius Dominus Iesus ut ad se inde ascenderet, collatis
beneficiis, infidelium repellendo rabiem defendatis. Hiis uero qui nostris acquiescentes monitis in causam hanc aliquid de suo contulerint, de beate matris Domini
confisi patrocinio, si in penitentia septem uel amplius annorum sunt, uiginti dies
20 relaxamus, si pauciori tenentur numero, dies decem remittimus. Valete in Christo.

## 391

[1170-2, probably 1171-2] Settlement of the case between the abbey of St-Léonard (see
no. 374) and Lewes priory (Sussex, Cluniac) on the churches of Steeple and Stansgate
(Essex, i.e. Stansgate priory, dep. of Lewes) and appurtenances, and 1½ hides and 10 acres in
Tillingham (Essex) and the tithe of Smithfield (? Middlesex), in the presence of King Henry II,
Roger archbishop of York and other bishops: St-Léonard has renounced its claim in
exchange for 30 marks and an annual pension of 1 mark to be paid by the monks of Stansgate.

Robert became archdeacon of Essex in 1167; Geoffrey archdeacon of Canterbury and
Richard archdeacon of Poitiers bishops elect of Ely and Winchester in 1173. The witnesses
strongly suggest that the case was heard in England, which narrows the dates to those of
Henry II's visits in 1170 and 1171-2; Master David was out of the country most of the period
c. 1166-71, archdeacons Richard and Robert c. 1167-9. June 1170, the time of the coronation
of the young King Henry, is possible; but David was probably then in Italy. The reference
to the older Henry as 'secundi' confirms that the document was drawn up after the coronation of Henry 'tertius' in June 1170.

G(ilebertus) Dei gratia Lundoniensis episcopus dilectis sibi in Domino uniuersis
sancte matris ecclesie filiis, salutem, gratiam et benedictionem.
Vniuersitati uestre presenti scripto notificamus controuersiam que inter ecclesiam
beati Leonardi de Nobiliaco et ecclesiam sancti Pancratii de Lewes, super ecclesia de
5 Stieple et omnibus eius pertinentiis, et ecclesia beate Marie Magdalene de Stanasgata

390 5 sublimare B
391 Originals: Cambridge, King's College, Muniment Room, B15 (size 6 in. × 7¼ in.) (Kd);
PRO Exchequer Records, T.R., Anc. Deeds (E40), A 14395 (size 7¾ in. × 5 in.) (Pr) (both in
the same hand). Spelling as Pr. (Kd) Fragment of seal (natural wax) on tag. Endorsed: Stanesgate
(early fourteenth century). (Pr) Tag for seal. Endorsed: Colc' (early fourteenth century).
Confirmacio Lond' episcopi de conconcordia [sic] inter priorem de Lewes et priorem de
Nobiliaco (early thirteenth century). See pp. 23 ff.; Plate II.

et omnibus que ad eam pertinent, hyda etiam et dimidia et decem acris in Tillinge-
ham et decima de Smedefeld', diu agitata est, in presentia domni nostri illustris
Anglorum regis H(enrici) secundi et domni Eborac(ensis) archiepiscopi Rogeri et
episcoporum quamplurium et nostra, hoc tandem modo sopitam, utriusque partis
assensu conquieuisse. Modus uero inter eos habite transactionis hic est: memorata 10
siquidem ecclesia sancti Leonardi a lite quam aduersus ecclesiam de Lewes institue-
rat, omnino recessit, et iuri—si quod in iam dictis ecclesiis et earum pertinentiis, et
his que supra nominata sunt, habuerat—in perpetuum renuntiauit; acceptis uidelicet
ab ecclesia de Lewes triginta marcis argenti et annuo unius marce redditu, per manum
monacorum de Stanasgata in Pascha et festo sancti Michaelis sibi in perpetuum 15
exoluendo. Quod ne temporis elapsu reuocetur in dubium, ob stabiliendam iamdictarum ecclesiarum pacem, scripto commendare curauimus; et ut ratum et inconuulsum permaneat, episcopali autoritate confirmamus. His testibus: domno
nostro rege H(enrico), Eborac(ensi) archiepiscopo Rogero, Saresbir(iensi) episcopo
Iocelino, Willelmo comite de Arundel, Hamelino comite de Warenn', Willelmo 20
comite Essex(ie), Ricardo de Luci, Laurentio abbate Westmon(asterii), Willelmo
abbate Rading', Gaufrido archidiacono Cant(uariensi), Ricardo archidiacono
Pictau(ensi), Nicolao, Radulfo, Ricardo, Roberto archidiaconis Lundon(iensibus),
magistro Dauid, magistro Henrico, magistro Gilleberto, magistro Hugone,
Roberto de Clifford' canonicis sancti Pauli, Radulfo filio Brientii, et aliis multis.   25

## 392

[1170–80, probably 1171–6] Settlement of the case between Lewes priory and Richard, clerk,
on the church of Reed (Herts): the church is appropriated to the priory on the presentation
of Henry de Scalariis and Hugh his son, and Richard instituted as perpetual vicar for an
annual pension of two shillings to the priory.

The *terminus a quo* is established by Stephen prior of Holy Trinity, Aldgate (1170–97), but
Master David was probably not in England in 1170–1; if Richard of Stortford was not yet a
canon, this must be before 1176.

⟨Gilebertus⟩ Dei gratia Londoniensis episcopus archidiaconis, decanis et omnibus
ecclesiarum prelatis per episcopatum Lundon(iensem) constitutis, salutem, gratiam
et benedictionem.

Notum sit uniuersitati uestre controuersiam que inter monachos Lewenses et
Ricardum clericum super ecclesia de Ritth' uertebatur, hoc tandem fine in nostra et 5
capituli nostri Lund(onie) presentia conquieuisse. Predictus siquidem Ricardus in
nostra et capituli nostri presentia iuri quod in eadem ecclesia de Ritth' habere
uidebatur plene renuntiauit, et eandem ecclesiam in manu nostra refutauit. Nos
itaque assensum in hoc prebentibus Henrico de Scalariis et Hugone filio eius,
eiusdem ecclesie aduocatis, eandem ecclesiam prenominatis monachis in perpetuam 10

391  13 nominata] memorata Kd   18 His *om.* Kd   19–20 Rogero Eboracensi archiepiscopo,
Iocelino Sar(esberiensi) episcopo Kd   24 Kd *places Hugh before Gilbert*   25 canonicis sancti
Pauli Pr; Roberto Huscarl' Kd   25 Kd *omits* et aliis multis
392  BM Cotton MS Vespasian F. xv, fo. 310 (Cart. Lewes). *Abstract in* Cart. Lewes, II, 126.

elemosinam concessimus et eos in prenominata ecclesia personas constituimus; et eorundem petitione et presentatione sepedictum clericum ad perpetuam eiusdem ecclesie uicariam sub annua duorum solidorum pensione sepedictis monachis persoluendorum suscepimus. Quod quia firmum et inconuulsum manere uolumus,

15 presenti scripto et sigilli nostri appositione confirmare curauimus. Hiis testibus: Nicholao, Radulfo archidiaconis London(iensibus), magistro Dauid, magistro Radulfo, Ricardo Ruffo et Ricardo fratre eius, Willelmo de Belmeys, Stephano priore de sancta Trinitate, magistro Ricardo de Storteford', Rogero filio Mauritii, ⟨fo. 310v⟩ Radulfo decano de Wadduna, Galfrido capellano, etc.

## 393

[1163–80] Settlement as papal judge delegate of the case between Lewes priory and Master Osbert of Bray on the church of High Bray (Devon): the priory's right was recognized, Master Ralph de Hauterive instituted as rector for a pension of 1 lb. of incense or 6d., and Master Osbert as perpetual vicar for a pension of 1 bezant to the rector, and after his death to the priory or its assigns.

G(ilebertus) Dei gratia Lundoniensis episcopus uniuersis sancte matris ecclesie filiis ad quos presentes littere peruenerint, salutem in Domino.

Vtiliter satis et necessarie prouisum est ut ea scripture suffragio memorie commendentur per que litigandi tolli possit occasio, et inter fratres habita perpetua pace

5 gaudere ualeat amicabilis compositio. Inde est quod uniuersitati uestre presenti scripto significare curauimus, causam que uertebatur inter monachos Lewenses et magistrum Osbertum de Brai super ecclesia eiusdem uille, nobis a summo pontifice appellatione remota delegatam, hoc tandem fine in nostra presentia utriusque partis in hoc concurrente assensu, post quamplures hinc inde auditas allegationes con-

10 quieuisse. Prefatus siquidem Osbertus ius quod prefati monachi sibi in eadem ecclesia uendicabant, eosdem in ipsa habere in iure recognouit, et ut ecclesiam ipsam cum omnibus ad eam pertinentibus magistro Radulfo de Altaripa de eis sub unius libre incensi uel sex denariorum pensione tenendam concederent, assensum spontanee prebuit. Iam dicti uero monachi et sepedictus R(adulfus) in hoc consenserunt,

15 ut memoratus Osbertus quamdiu uixerit eandem ecclesiam sub unius bisantii annua pensione in festo Purificationis beate Marie nomine ecclesie persoluendi de ipso R(adulfo) teneat; et si eodem Osberto superstite iam dictum R(adulfum) contigerit in fata concedere, in tantundem monachis ipsis uel cui pensionem ipsam assignare uoluerint sine maiori exactione respondeat. Adiecerunt etiam quod prememoratum

20 Osbertum sicut clericum eorum manutenere, et iterum sibi patrocinium sicut fideli suo debeant impendere. Nos igitur ea qua fungebamur auctoritate prefata ecclesia monachis de Lewes restituta, ad presentationem eorum magistrum R(adulfum) in ecclesia de Brai sub predicta pensione unius libre incensi uel sex denariorum de ipsis monachis tenenda suscepimus, et postmodum ad petitionem et presentationem

**393** *Original*: PRO Exchequer Records, T.R., Anc. Deeds (E 40), A 13876 (size 5¾ in. × 7¼ in.). Slit for seal tag. *Endorsed*: Confirmatio facta super ecclesia de Brai per testimonium G. episcopi London' etc. (early fourteenth century) ix. De ecclesia de Bray (fifteenth–sixteenth century).

monachorum ipsorum et prelibati R(adulfi) memoratum Osbertum in eadem 25
ecclesia perpetuum uicarium sub annua pensione unius bisantii predicto R(adulfo)
nomine ecclesie persoluenda, uel ipsis monachis si eundem R(adulfum) priusquam
Osbertum mori contingat, constituimus; et quo firma debeant in posterum hec
omnia et immutabilia permanere, memorati R(adulfus) et Osbertus hanc se compositionem fideliter obseruaturos, tactis sacrosanctis euangeliis iuramenti cautionem 30
exposuerunt; et nos eadem auctoritate summi pontificis et nostra presentis pagine
inscriptione et nostri pariter sigilli appositione confirmauimus. His testibus:
magistro Nicholao Lundon(iensis) ecclesie archidiacono, Radulfo de Disceto
Lundon(iensis) ecclesie archidiacono, magistro Dauid, magistro Henrico de
Norhamt(ona), magistro Ricardo de Storteford, Gileberto Foliot canonicis sancti 35
Pauli, Ricardo de Sarebir(ia), Radulfo de Cilton', Milone Folet, Alwardo le
Mercier, et multis aliis.

## 394

[1163-80] General confirmation to Lewes priory, confirming the grants by Robert of Essex
of the dependency of Prittlewell, by Ralph son of Brian of the dependency of Stansgate, by
Ranulf de Warenne of the church of Little Canfield,[1] 1 virgate and various tithes, and by a
certain Breton and his successor Richard, knight, of more tithe and land there, by the same
Ranulf of the tithe of Great Easton and of tithe in Yeldham, by Simon de Flamvill' of the
tithe of Epping, by the earl de Warenne of the tithe of *Pacheo*,[2] Patching, High Roding,
1 virgate and domain tithes (all in Essex), by Ranulf de Warenne of land in *Aselcroft*, by
Geoffrey Bainard of the church of Ashdon (Essex) and its appurtenances, forty-two acres of
arable, ten acres of woodland and three of meadow (cf. no. 395), and by Hugh de Scalariis of
the churches of Wyddial and Reed (Herts)[3] with appurtenances.

G(ilebertus) Dei gratia Lundoniensis ecclesie episcopus omnibus fidelibus per
Lund(oniensem) episcopatum constitutis, salutem, gratiam et benedictionem.

Nostri officii est ea que uenerabilibus locis fidelium deuotione collata noscuntur
episcopali auctoritate confirmare, et personas religiosas diligenti sollicitudine con-
fouere. Inde est quod ecclesias, decimas, terrasque in nostra diocesi sitas, que pietatis 5
intuitu monasterio sancti Pancratii de Lewes et monachis ibidem Deo seruientibus
collate sunt, et quas in presenti possident, confirmamus et sigilli nostri auctoritate
communimus. Inter que nominatim hec duximus exprimenda: ex donatione Rodberti de Essexa, cellam de Pritelwella cum accessionibus suis; ex donatione
Radulfi filio Briennii, cellam de Stanesgate cum pertinentiis suis; ex donatione 10
Ranulfi de War(enna), ecclesiam de Canefeld' et unam uirgatam terre, et totam
decimam de dominio et decimam feni, decimam quoque Ricardi militis, quam

---

**394** *Original:* PRO Exchequer Records, T.R., Anc. Deeds (E 40), A 13879 (size 12¼ in. × 5 in.).
Slit for seal tag. *Endorsed:* G. Lund' episcopi (twelfth century). H' exhibit' fuit 2 idus Iulii
cum...Meleford (?) (late thirteenth or fourteenth century).

---

[1] Cf. Morant, I, 464; *HKF*, III, 374 (and 371 ff. for Easton and Yeldham).
[2] ? Peyton Hall in Manuden (*ibid.* III, 371; *PN Essex*, p. 552).
[3] See *VCH Herts.* IV, 118; III, 253.

dedit quidam Brito qui terram tenuit ante Ricardum et postea ipse Ricardus, qui
duas acras adiecit cum pertinentiis suis; et decimam de Eston' quam dedit idem
15 Ranulfus, decimam de Gelham quam dedit predictus Ranulfus de terra quam tenuit
Godwinus; decimam de Epinges quam dedit Simon de Flamuill'; decimam de
Pacheo, decimam de Paching', ecclesiam de Roinges, et unam uirgatam terre, et
decimam de dominio in omnibus de dono comitis de War(enna); terram de
Aselcroft quam dedit Ranulfus de War(enna); ecclesiam de Essind(une) cum terris
20 et decimis ad eam pertinentibus, de dono Gaufridi Bainnardi, et duo et quadraginta
acras terre et decem acras nemoris quas idem Gaufridus postea adiecit, et tres acras
prati; ecclesiam etiam de Widdehala, et illam de Ruth cum pertinentiis suis, de dono
Hugonis de Scalariis. Ne igitur cuiquam liceat predictos fratres monachos sancti
Pancratii de Lewes temerariis uexationibus fatigare, neque bona eorum neque
25 possessiones ulla temeritate turbare, firmissime prohibemus et modis omnibus
inhibemus et sub interminatione anathematis interdicimus. Quisquis uero idem
Christi patrimonium conseruare et amplificare studuerit, Dominus conseruet eum
et beatum faciat in terra, multiplicans ei bona temporalia et eterna. Amen. Huius
nostre confirmationis testes sunt: dominus Radulfus archidiaconus de Midlessexa,
30 Ricardus Foliot archidiaconus de Colecestria, Iohannes de Tilleberia, Rogerius de
Hereford(ia), frater Rodbertus de Broi, Lodowicus de Landon', Ricardus de
Salesberia, Rogerus Camberleng', Radulfus dispensator, et multi alii.

## 395

[1163–c. 1180][1] Notification that the prior and monks of Lewes priory have presented
Master Robert of Kent to the rectory of Ashdon (Essex) for an annual pension of a hundred
shillings for the church and tithes, and for forty-two acres of arable, ten of woodland and
three of meadow in Ashdon, later granted to the monks by Geoffrey Bainard; saving the
right of Walter, vicar, for life.

The earliest surviving text of this charter is an early thirteenth-century copy looking
superficially like an original, with a fold at the foot and slits for a seal tag.[2] This suggests that
it was intended to pass as an original; and the fact that it comes from Lewes priory at this
sort of date makes forgery a definite possibility. On the other hand it has the formulas of a
genuine act, and the witness list seems certainly to belong to an act of Gilbert. Furthermore,
it is sewn together with three other related documents, all apparently genuine, which tend
to confirm its authenticity, since they make it very doubtful whether there could have been
a motive for forgery. They are: (i) a grant of Ashdon church to the priory by G. de

395 (? *Thirteenth-century copy*): PRO Exchequer Records, T.R., Anc. Deeds (E 40), A 13877
(ii) (size 6½ in. × 2¾ in.); *Cartulary copy* in BM Cotton MS Vespasian F. xv, fo. 175 v (Cart.
Lewes) ('xvj' in margin) (variants not given). *Abstract* in *Cart. Lewes*, iii, no. 58. Slit for seal
tag. *Endorsed*: Gileb' London' de Essendune xvj (early thirteenth century).

---

[1] The witnesses are very similar to those of no. 394. Roger of Worcester is presumably a clerk,
which gives a *terminus* of c. 1181.
[2] Dr Patricia Barnes tells us that it looks as if the tag was there until comparatively recently:
'the foot of the document is cleaner and there is a cleaner patch where the strip would have
been'.

Essend' (i.e. confirmation: 1202–12); (iii: ii is Gilbert's charter) Confirmation by Pope Celestine of Gilbert Foliot's grant of Ashdon church, 25 April 1196 (*PUE*, I, no. 330); (iv) Confirmation of G.F.'s confirmation by Bishop William of London, 3 March 1219. These seem to relate, not to no. 395, but to no. 394, in which the grant of Ashdon church is duly confirmed; and if the monks had been in any difficulty they would presumably have produced a straightforward confirmation from Gilbert rather than the indirect testimony of no. 395 to their rights. Nor can one see, with no. 394 and no. iii above (even if (i) and (iv) are later than the writing of no. 395), how the monks could be in difficulties. No. 395 is essentially an ephemeral document, and unless it was made to cover some dispute about the pension due from the church, it seems much more probable that it is a tolerably accurate copy of (perhaps) a damaged original than that it is a forgery.

G(ilebertus) Dei gratia Londoniensis episcopus omnibus sancte matris ecclesie filiis, salutem eternam in Domino.

Ad uniuersitatis uestre notitiam uolumus peruenire quod nos ad petitionem et presentationem dilectorum nostrorum prioris et monachorum de Lewes magistrum Robertum de Cantia ad personatum ecclesie de Essendune, cuius patronatus ad 5 eosdem monachos pertinere dinoscitur, admisimus, sub annua pensione centum solidorum prefatis priori et monachis soluendorum, tum nomine ecclesie cum terris et decimis ad eam pertinentibus, tum pro quadraginta duabus acris terre et decem acris nemoris et tribus acris prati eisdem monachis in eadem uilla a Gaufredo Bainardo postea collatis, saluo iure Walterii ibidem ministrantis quoad uixerit. 10 Hiis testibus: Roberto Foliot, Rogero Wigorniensi, Gileberto Banastre, Thoma Briton(e), Johanne Wyteng', Lodowico clerico, Radulfo cantore, Zakaria scriptore, Roberto de Broy, Ricardo de Salesbiria, Rogero Camberlano, Rogero de Hereford(ia), Johanne de Tylibiria, Radulfo dispensatore, et multis aliis.

## 396

[1163–73] Settlement as papal judge delegate[1] of the case between Richard (of Ilchester) archdeacon of Poitiers and Alexander, clerk, on the church of Great Milton (Oxon), which pertains to Richard's prebend in Lincoln cathedral (i.e. the prebend of Milton Ecclesia): Alexander agreed to hold the church for a pension of fifteen marks per annum to Richard.

The archdeacon was elected bishop of Winchester in 1173.

G(ilebertus) Dei gratia L(undoniensis) episcopus dilectis sibi in Domino fratribus uniuersis sancte matris ecclesie filiis, salutem, gratiam et benedictionem.

Lites amicabili fine sopitas tunc demum plene constat extingui cum pactiones ob pacem inter partes inite et utrimque concesse, eorum quorum id de iure firmat auctoritas excipiuntur litteris et sigillis robora⟨n⟩tur appositis. Vnde transactionem 5 inter uenerabilem fratrem nostrum R(icardum) Pic(tauensem) archidiaconum et

395 12 Lolowico *original; spelt* Lodowico *in cart.*
396 G, no. 187; B, fo. 186.

---

[1] Gilbert evidently had a mandate from the Pope to settle the case, and it appears that Alexander also had a mandate that he be restored to possession (under the common canonical procedure he had no doubt entered an *exceptio spolii*); but the order of events and the relation between the mandates is not clear.

A(lexandrum) clericum de super ecclesia de Mideltona coram nobis initam et utrimque concessam, notitie communi presenti scripto delegare curauimus, ut rediuiue litis in posterum occasionem ⟨fo. 186v⟩ inter eos omnem penitus ampute-
10 mus. Alex(ander) itaque, qui ad possessionem ecclesie de Midelt(ona) recuperan-dam auctoritate litterarum domni pape possessorium intendebat, intentionem hanc coram nobis omittens, ecclesiam ipsam de Midelt(ona), que ad prebendam uenera-bilis fratris nostri iam dicti archidiaconi quam in ecclesia Lincoln(iensi) habere dinoscitur indubitate pertinet, eius se de cetero nomine quindecim marcarum
15 pensione ipsi archidiacono, quamdiu prenominate prebende canonicus extiterit, annuatim soluenda et suscipere et tenere consensit; in presentia nostra tactis iurans euuangeliis se nunquam de cetero ipsi archidiacono, dum eiusdem erit prebende canonicus, super ipsam ecclesiam de Midelt(ona) litem aut fatigationem aut inquietudinem omnino moturum, et se pactionem super memorata iam pensione
20 ei et legittime et fideliter obseruaturum; iure tamen si quod ad petendam uel repetendam ipsam [...] possidere desierit, et ipsum superesse contigerit. Quod quia in nostra et in capituli nostri presentia sic gestum est, nos cui a domno papa eiusdem cause fuerat delegata cognitio et ratum habuimus, et pagine presentis inscriptione et sigilli nostri attestatione roborare curauimus.

### 396 a

[1163–87] Grant to Ralph, clerk, son of Elfsi, his man, of Stepney of all the (arable) land his father held, together with one quarter of the meadow of *Sunewincshamme* pertaining to it, and 2½ acres of assart on the west and south of the house Gilbert also granted to Ralph, for an annual rent of 9s. 1d.

G(ilebertus) Dei gratia Lundoniensis episcopus omnibus hominibus suis Francis et Anglis, salutem, gratiam et benedictionem.

Vniuersitati uestre presenti scripto notificamus nos dedisse et concessisse Radulfo clerico filio Elfsi homini nostro de Stibbeia totam terram que fuit patris sui, simul
5 et quartam partem prati de Sunewincshamme, quod ad eandem terram pertinet, necnon et duas acras terre et dimidiam de proprestura que sunt ab occidentali et meridionali parte domus sue quam eidem Radulfo similiter pro seruicio suo dedi-mus et concessimus, tenendas et habendas sibi et heredibus suis de nobis et succes-soribus nostris bene et in pace et honorabiliter, in uiis, in semitis, in pascuis, in
10 pratis, in boscho et plano, pro nouem solidis et uno denario ad quattuor terminos

396 7 Mideltn' B    21 ipsam [...] *Some words are missing here. The point of the sentence is that Alexander had two claims, a possessory and a proprietary or petitory (iure...si quod ad petendam ...). The possessory claim has been disposed of; and the missing words must have dealt with Alex-ander's proprietary right (if any), and cleared up what should happen if the archdeacon ceased to be in possession while Alexander was still alive—[si archidiaconus] possidere desierit, et ipsum [sc. Alexandrum] superesse contigerit*    21 et om. B; *there is an* et *in the margin, which presumably belongs here*
396 a *Copy in original inspeximus and confirmation by Bishop Richard FitzNeal (1189–98), St Paul's Cathedral archives, A27/146 (the inspeximus is witnessed by Alard archdeacon of London and so may be dated 1196–8).*

anni pro omni seruicio persoluendis: ad Natale uidelicet Domini uiginti septem denariis et totidem ad Pascha, totidem ad festum sancti Iohannis Baptiste, et uiginti octo denariis ad festum sancti Michaelis. Predictus etiam Radulfus et heredes sui terram hanc erga domnum regem pro dimidia hyda terre defendent. Et quoniam donationem et concessionem nostram firmam decetero et stabilem predicto 15 Radulfo et suis heredibus sicut dictum est esse uolumus, ipsam presenti carta nostra et sigillo confirmamus.

## 397

[1163–c. 1180] Grant to William the cook, for his service and 1 lb. of pepper per annum, of the land at Fulham (Middlesex) round the church, lying between the bishop's copse and the public road to the Thames.

Notum sit tam presentibus quam futuris quod ego Gilebertus Lundoniensis episcopus dedi Willelmo coco seruienti meo, pro seruitio suo, totam illam terram de antiquo managio apud Fuleham que iacet circa ecclesiam, sicut illa diuisa est per fossatam, hinc a uirgulto episcopi, inde a uia puplica que descen⟨fo. 166⟩dit in Tamisiam. Hanc autem dedi illi tenendam de me et successoribus meis libere et 5 hereditabiliter, pro una libra piperis annuatim ad festum sancti Michaelis exinde soluenda. Quod quia firmum et inconuulsum manere uolo, presenti scripto et sigilli mei attestatione confirmo. His testibus [ ... ]

## 398

[1163–87] Notification that Nicholas, chaplain, has been instituted as vicar of St Mary Magdalene, Milk Street (London), on the presentation of Bartholomew (doubtless the rector) and the chapter of St Paul's, on the same terms as his predecessor William, namely an annual pension to the chapter of two shillings.

Nicholas, nephew of the archdeacon, suggests a fairly late date, and so the Richard Foliot who witnesses was probably Richard Foliot II—if, however, he is the same as the archdeacon of Colchester, this could be dated 1163-7.

G(ilebertus) Dei gratia Lundoniensis episcopus omnibus sancte matris ecclesie filiis ad quos littere presentes peruenerint, salutem, gratiam et benedictionem.

Ad omnium uestrum uolumus peruenire notitiam, nos ad petitionem et presentationem Bartholomei et capituli canonicorum sancti Pauli Lundon(ie) Nicho-

397 G, no. 296; B, fo. 165 v.
398 *Original*: St Paul's Cathedral archives, A 17/1273[1] (size 6½ in. × 4¼ in.); *copy* in MS W.D. 1 (Liber A), fo. 22 b[2] (variants not given). *Printed*: Gibbs, no. 215; abstract in *Rep.* p. 18 b. Seal (red wax) on tag. *Endorsed*: super ecclesia beate Marie Magdalene Lond' et institutione uicarii eiusdem. Melcstret (thirteenth century).

[1] Probably in the same hand as A 37/1142 (charter of Canon William de Belmeis addressed to Gilbert).

[2] It is normal, as here, to refer to the Liber A by the more conspicuous medieval foliation; as this numbers the openings not the folios (so that folios 1 v and 2 r are both marked II), we have distinguished the sides as 'a' and 'b'; cf. Gibbs, p. xl.

5 laum capellanum in ecclesia sancte Marie Magdalene in Melcstred' uicarium
perpetuum suscepisse, ita scilicet quod Bartholomeus predictus soluet de prefata
ecclesia capitulo sancti Pauli annuam pensionem duorum solidorum per manum
memorati Nicholai, sicut ante consueuit per manum Willelmi eiusdem ecclesie
uicarii. Predictus itaque Nicholaus coram nobis et capitulo et Bartholomeo de
10 eadem ecclesia tactis sacrosanctis euangeliis fidelitatem iurauit. Igitur ne quod a
nobis sollempniter actum est de cetero reuocetur in dubium, uel contra ius canonicorum quod habent in eadem ecclesia aliquid statuatur in posterum, nos illud
auctoritate nostra roboramus, et presentis scripti patrocinio cum sigilli nostri
appositione communimus. His testibus: Ricardo de Saresb(iria), Ricardo Banastre,
15 Ricardo Foliot, Iohanne Witheng, Dauid capellano, Nicholao capellano, Nicholao
nepote archidiaconi Lund(oniensis), Radulfo Britone, Baldewino clerico filio
Roberti sacriste, et multis aliis.

## 399

[1163–80] Settlement of the case between the chapter of St Paul's and the convent of Strat-
ford-at-Bow (Middlesex, Benedictine nuns) on the church of Islington (Middlesex): Dean
Hugh and the chapter were recognized as rectors, and then he presented and the bishop
instituted the nuns to the church (evidently as 'vicar') for an annual pension of one mark; the
nuns are to find a chaplain to serve the church.

Sciant omnes quod controuersia que inter capitulum canonicorum sancti Pauli et
conuentum sanctimon⟨i⟩alium de Strafford' super ecclesia de Isoldona, in presentia
domni et patris nostri Gilberti Londoniensis episcopi secundi mota et aliquantulum
agitata est, eiusdem episcopi auctoritate et assensu hoc pacis fine quieuit. Suscepit
5 siquidem Hugo decanus loco capituli sui inuestituram et personatum predicte
ecclesie de manu domni episcopi qui ad eiusdem capituli petitionem et presentationem in eandem ecclesiam ut ipsam de canonicis teneant predictas moniales
introduxit, que inde reddent annuatim capitulo canonicorum unam marcam ad
duos terminos, in die scilicet proxima post festum sancti Leonardi dimidiam
10 marcam, et in octabis Pentecostes alteram dimidiam marcam. Predicte etiam
sanctimoniales libere presentabunt episcopo uel eius archidiacono capellanum qui
per eas ministrabit in eadem ecclesia. Et ut hec et cetera.

## 400

[1170–80] Settlement of the case between the chapter of St Paul's and Holy Trinity priory,
Aldgate, on the church of St Edmund the King (London). The bishop instituted Dean Hugh

**399** St Paul's Cathedral archives, MS W.D. 1 (Liber A), fo. 6a. *Printed:* Gibbs, no. 66.
5 inuesturam *MS*
**400** *Original:* St Paul's Cathedral archives, A 8/970 (CIROGRAPHIVM at head, upside down);
*copies* in BM Harl .6956, fos. 140v–141 (seventeenth-century transcript from original); BM
Lansdowne MS 448, fo. 8 (Cart. Holy Trinity, Aldgate) (presumably from another original, but
with trivial variants only, not given here). Tags for two seals (fragment of second, apparently
Holy Trinity priory's). *Endorsed:* Super (?) ecclesia S. Edm(undi) in London' (?) inter cap.
S. Pauli et cap. S. Trinitatis (twelfth[–thirteenth] century). o + 39. *Abstract* in *Rep.* p. 8a.

as rector on the chapter's behalf, and Prior Stephen (1170–97) as perpetual vicar on the priory's; the latter will pay a pension of twelve pence so long as Jocelin, priest, serves the church, and after he ceases to do so will fix a pension to be divided between priory and chapter.

*VN*, p. 329, shows the chapter and priory as joint patrons in 1254.

Sciant presentes et futuri quod controuersia que inter capitulum canonicorum sancti Pauli et conuentum fratrum sancte Trinitatis Lond(onie) super ecclesia sancti Edmundi, in presentia domni et patris G(ileberti) Londoniensis episcopi secundi mota et aliquatenus actitata est, eiusdem episcopi assensu hoc pacis fine quieuit. Hugo siquidem decanus uice capituli sui inuestituram et personatum predicte 5 ecclesie de manu domni episcopi suscepit, et domnus episcopus ad eiusdem capituli petitionem et presentationem perpetuam eiusdem ecclesie uicariam fratrum sancte Trinitatis conuentui tradidit, Stephano eorundem priore ipsam cum animarum cura suscipiente. Idem autem conuentus reddet inde annuatim capitulo canonicorum sancti Pauli in festo sancte Cecilie duodecim denarios quamdiu Gocelinus presbiter 10 eam tenuerit, postquam uero illam tenere desierit predictus conuentus clericum ibi canonice ponet, et certam pensionem inde reddendam prout melius poterit, ad communem sui et canonicorum sancti Pauli utilitatem sine omni dolo assignabit, sicque deinceps antedictus conuentus soluet annuatim canonicis sancti Pauli nomine illius ecclesie medietatem pensionis assignate et utrisque crescet equaliter uel 15 decrescet pensio secundum casus qui euenire poterunt. Soluetur autem hec medietas ad duos secundum quod inter eos tunc conueniet terminos. Vt autem tota huius conuentionis series memoriter teneatur et perpetuo firma permaneat, ipsa et scripto est commendata et sigillorum suorum testimonio communita, et firmissimo insuper sigilli domni episcopi robore est confirmata. 20

## 401

[*c.* 1179–*c.* 1180] Appropriation to Colchester abbey, on the presentation of Hugh son of Everard of Boxted (Essex), of half the church of Boxted (preserved in the archives of St Paul's, since the chapter subsequently took over the abbey's rights in the church: see Gibbs, nos. 98–101). Cf. no. 381 and *VN*, p. 347.

G(ilebertus) Dei gratia Lundoniensis episcopus uniuersis sancte matris ecclesie filiis ad quos presentes littere peruenerint, salutem in Domino.

Litteras dilecti filii nostri Hugonis filii Euerardi de Bocstede nobis directas inspeximus, ex quarum inspectione ipsum Hugonem Deo et monasterio sancti Iohannis de Colecestria et monachis ibidem Deo famulantibus ius patronatus quod 5 in medietate ecclesie de Bocstede habuerat, in perpetuam et liberam elemosinam

**401** *Original:* St Paul's Cathedral archives, A 40/1436 (size 6¼ in. × 5 in.); *copies* in W.D. 1 (Liber A), fo. 8 b (variants not given); BM Harl. 6956, fo. 25 v (seventeenth-century transcript of original). *Printed:* Gibbs, no. 92; Newcourt, II, 78; *abstract* in *Rep.* p. 40 b. Fragment of seal (natural wax, stained brown) on tag. *Endorsed:* G. Lond' episcopus de ecclesia de Boxsted' (twelfth[–thirteenth] century) d. xii (*bis*) (thirteenth century).
1 sancte sancte *original*

pro salute sua et suorum concessisse cognouimus: cuius nos autentico scripto fidem
habentes, ipsiusque erga Deum piam deuotionem attendentes, eius donationem
ratam habuimus, et domnum abbatem Colecestrie Gwalterum in his que ad ipsam
10 spectant medietatem ea que nobis a Domino concessa est auctoritate personam
constituimus. Et quia peruerse malignantium calliditates de die in diem suscipiunt
incrementum, et quod plerique deuoto inceperunt animo, eos ad id instigante
maligno frequenter ad deteriora uertere nituntur propositum, ne nostra quoquo
modo possit de cetero irritari donatio, pastorali cura prouidere curauimus, et ut
15 firmitatis robur optineat eam pagine presentis inscriptione, et sigilli nostri appositione, confirmauimus. His testibus: Ricardo Foliot archidiacono Colec(estrie),
magistro Radulfo de Altaripa magistro scolarum Lundon(ie), Gileberto Foliot,
Rogero de Wigornia, Ricardo de Sarebir(ia), Radulfo de Ciltona, Ricardo Banastre,
Waltero elemosinario, Iohanne clerico, magistro Reimundo, magistro Mauritio,
20 Beniamin clerico, Osberto senescallo abbatis.

## 402

[Probably 1174–80] Institution of Fulcher, priest, as perpetual vicar of the church of St
Pancras for an annual pension of 1 bezant or 2 shillings on the presentation of William de
Belmeis canon of St Paul's (prebendary of St Pancras).[1]

Since this was confirmed by Archbishop Richard (1174–84: see Gibbs, p. 123) it is probably
not earlier than 1174.

G(ilebertus) Dei gratia Lundoniensis episcopus omnibus sancte matris ecclesie filiis
ad quos presentes littere peruenerint, salutem in Domino.

Nouimus Willelmum de Beumeis ecclesie nostre canonicum dilecto nobis in
Domino Fulcherio presbitero ecclesiam Sancti Pancratii in perpetuam uicariam sub
5 annua pensione unius bisantii uel duorum solidorum Anglicane monete concessisse
et ipsum F(ulcherium) onera ecclesie debita in se suscepisse. Nos itaque prefate
concessioni episcopalis auctoritatis robur addentes memoratam uicariam in iam
dicta ecclesia sancti Pancratii sicut in carta ipsius Willelmi continetur expressa, ipsi
F(ulcherio) concessimus et ipsum sub predicta pensione sepefato W(illelmo) uel
10 successoribus suis persoluenda, in eadem ecclesia debita cum sollempnitate perpetuum uicarium constituimus. Quod ne de cetero et cetera. Hiis testibus et cetcra.

**402** St Paul's Cathedral archives, MS W.D. 1 (Liber A), fo. 16a. *Printed:* Gibbs, no. 158.

---

[1] Fulcher is presented (or his presentation confirmed) by the dean and chapter in a charter
printed by C. H. Hunter Blair in *Archaeologia Aeliana*, 4th Series, VII (1930), 82: for other
documents see *ibid.* pp. 81–3; Gibbs, nos. 159–60; Cheney, *English Bishops' Chanceries*, p. 156;
below, no. 403. It seems likely that the appropriation of St Pancras was in prospect when this
charter was made, and that the dean and chapter's charter was drawn up to secure the rights
of Fulcher, the sitting vicar; and that no. 403, in which no mention is made of Fulcher, was
composed after the latter's death or resignation.

**403**

[1183] Appropriation of the church of St Pancras to the chapter of St Paul's on the petition of William de Belmeis, prebendary of St Pancras.

G(ilebertus) Dei gratia Lundoniensis episcopus omnibus sancte matris ecclesie filiis ad quos hee littere peruenerint, salutem in Domino.

Ex commissi nobis cura regiminis tenemur astricti, ut si quas ecclesie nostre pia deuotione possessiones contulerimus, seu subiecta nobis plebs ob suam suorumque salutem erogauerint beneficia, litterarum ea monimentis excipiamus; et ne tractu 5 temporis future posteritati ueniant in dubium, auctoritate qua permittente Deo fungimur, sollicita studeamus diligentia roborare. Proinde ad communem omnium uestrum uolumus deuenire notitiam, nos dilectis filiis nostris decano et canonicis ecclesie beati Pauli ecclesiam sancti Pancratii cum omnibus ad eam pertinentibus, in terris, in hominibus, in decimis et obuentionibus, que ecclesia in territorio 10 prebende Willelmi de Belmeis extra muros London(ie) sita est et fundata, memo-rato Willelmo postulante quam plurimum et in hoc prebente assensum, in liberam et perpetuam elemosinam contulisse, ipsosque in ea personas sollempniter instituisse. Quam quidem donationem pia deuotione celebratam quia firmam et futuris duraturam temporibus manere desideramus, pagine presentis inscriptione con- 15 firmamus, et ne ualeat a quoquam infirmari de cetero, sigilli nostri appositione roboramus. Facta est autem hec nostra donatio in capitulo sancti Pauli, anno dominice incarnationis millesimo centesimo octogesimo tertio. Testibus: Radulfo de Diceto decano sancti Pauli, Nicholao archidiacono Lundon(ie), Willelmo archidiacono Gloucest(rie), Parisio Rofensi archidiacono, magistro Ricardo 20 magistro scolarum Lundon(ie), magistro Radulfo theologo, magistro Nicholao filio Clementis, Roberto de Clifford, magistro Hugone a Lundon(ia), magistro Henrico de Norhamt(onia), Ricardo iuniore, Radulfo de Chilton', Gilleberto Banastre canonicis, Ricardo de Sares(biria), Ricardo Banastre, Radulfo cantore, Iohanne Witenge clericis, Roberto de Fuleham, Riginaldo camerario et multis aliis. 25

**404**

[1183–4] Institution of Master Walter of Witney, the bishop's clerk, to the church of St Leonard Shoreditch (Middlesex) on the king's presentation, after it had been established in the *curia regis* that the presentation lay with the king not with Holy Trinity priory, Aldgate.

Dated by the first witness.

403 *Original:* St Paul's Cathedral archives, A37/1143 (size 7¼ in. × 7¾ in.); *copies* in MS W.D. 1 (Liber A), fo. 6b, and BM Harl. MS 6956, fo. 84 (abbreviated, from the lost Liber B, fo. 34) (variants not given). Fragment of seal (green wax) attached to tag. *Endorsed:* G. Lond' episcopus secundus de ecclesia sancti Pancratii concessa et confirmata capitulo sancti Pauli (thirteenth century). III. *Printed:* Gibbs, no. 72; *abstract in Rep.* p. 38b.

404 *Original:* St Paul's Cathedral archives, A40/1424 (size 6¾ in. × 3½ in.); *copy* in MS W.D. 1 (Liber A), fo. 5b (variants not given). *Printed:* Gibbs, no. 57; *abstract in Rep.* p. 40b. Fragment of seal (natural wax) on tag. *Endorsed:* confirmatio ecclesie de Sores' (*c.* 1300). 0 + xlvito.

G(ilebertus) Dei gratia Londoniensis episcopus omnibus sancte matris ecclesie filiis per episcopatum London(iensem) constitutis, salutem, gratiam et benedictionem.

Frequens est ut elabatur a memoria quod a presentibus agitur, nisi litterarum apicibus ad posteritatis notitiam commendetur. Proinde uniuersitati uestre presenti 5 scripto notificamus, nos ecclesiam sancti Leonardi de Soresdic' quam contra canonicos sancte Trinitatis London(ie), ad domni regis pertinere donationem in curia sua publice ostensum est, et plenarie comprobatum, presentatione domni regis, magistro Waltero de Witten(eia) clerico nostro dedisse et concessisse, ipsumque in ea personam solempniter constituisse. Quod quia firmum et stabile in 10 posterum esse uolumus, pagina presenti et nostri appositione sigilli confirmamus. Testibus his: Galtero de Constanciis episcopo Lincoln(iensi), Ricardo Elyensi archidiacono domni regis thesaurario, Radulfo archidiacono Hereford(ie) domni regis sigillario, Radulfo de Diceto decano sancti Pauli, Ricardo Brit(one), Gaufrido filio Petri, Amaurico dispensario, Ailwardo camerario, Roberto Folet, Radulfo de 15 Chilt(ona), Gilleberto Ban(astre) canonicis sancti Pauli, Waltero filio Walteri, Iohanne Witeng, Thoma Britone, Roberto Foliot clericis.

## 405

[*c.* 1181–7] Grant to the canons of St Paul's of an annual rent of sixpence (details given) for leave for the bishop and his tenants to have an aqueduct over chapter land outside Bishopsgate.

G(ilebertus) Dei gratia Londoniensis episcopus omnibus sancte matris ecclesie filiis ad quos hee littere peruenerint, salutem in Domino.

Vniuersitati uestre presenti scripto notificamus, nos concessisse dilectis filiis nostris canonicis ecclesie beati Pauli sex denarios annuatim ad duos terminos 5 soluendos, in Pascha uidelicet tres denarios, et in festo sancti Michaelis totidem; qui sex denarii de terris his exoluentur, pro aqueductu quem nobis et hominibus nostris habendum concesserunt per terram suam que proxima est extra barram que est extra portam nostram que uocatur Bissupesgate, uidelicet de terra Haldeni unum denarium, de terra Seamani Belle duos denarios, de terra Siwardi filii Willelmi 10 unum denarium, de terra Estrild' et Edricii unum denarium, de terra Eilredi tannarii unum denarium. Quem nimirum aqueductum homines nostri quando opus fuerit mundabunt et reparabunt expensis suis et seruabunt, ne iam dicti canonici in terris suis uel in redditibus aliquod omnino dampnum sentiant uel detrimentum. Volumus etiam et concedimus ut quicumque domum habuerit et 15 tenuerit per quam aqueductus cursum suum facit, memoratos sex denarios annuatim dictis terminis pro ipso aqueductu percipiat. Quod quia firmum et stabile manere desideramus, pagine presentis inscriptione et sigilli nostri munimine con-

**405** *Original:* St Paul's Cathedral archives, A24/834 (size 6¼ in. × 5 in.); *copy* in MS W.D. 1 (Liber A), fo. 6a (variants not given). *Printed:* Gibbs, no. 65; *abstract* in *Rep.* p. 25 b. Fragment of seal (natural wax) on tag. *Endorsed:* de sex denariis soluendis ecclesie sancti Pauli Lond' pro aqueductu hospitalis de Bissopesgate (thirteenth century). 178 C.
10 Edricii] *or* Editui (?)

firmamus. Testibus: Radulfo decano London(iensis) ecclesie, Nicholao archidiacono, Ricardo magistro scolarum London(ie), magistro Hugone de London(ia),
magistro Henrico de Norh(amtonia), Hugone de Racon' [*sic*], Willelmo de 20
Belm(eis), Radulfo de Chilthon' canonicis, Willelmo Foliot senescallo, Roberto de
Fuleham.

## 406

[1183-7] Institution of Alexander, clerk,[1] as perpetual vicar of the church of St Pancras
(London) in return for a pension of ½ mark on the presentation of Dean Ralph de Diceto and
the chapter of St Paul's. (After no. 403.)

G(ilebertus) Dei gratia Lundoniensis episcopus omnibus sancte matris ecclesie filiis
ad quos hee littere peruenerint, salutem in Domino.

Ad uniuersitatis uestre uolumus deuenire notitiam dilectum filium nostrum
Radulfum de Diceto decanum ecclesie sancti Pauli Lundon(ie) et eiusdem ecclesie
capitulum Alexandro clerico ecclesiam sancti Pancratii cum omnibus ad eam 5
pertinentibus, sub annua dimidie marce pensione ipsis ad Pascha soluenda, in perpetuam elemosinam concessisse et dedisse. Quod nos ratum habentes et acceptum,
auctoritate qua fungimur episcopali memorate ecclesie sancti Pancratii perpetuam
uicariam cum omnibus ad eandem ecclesiam pertinentibus sub predicta pensione
iamdicto Alexandro concessimus. Et ut concessio ei facta firmitate gaudeat in pos- 10
terum, eam pagine presentis inscriptione et sigilli nostri appositione confirmauimus.
Testibus: Radulfo de Chilton' canonico sancti Pauli, Radulfo de Verini, Thoma
Britone, Iohanne Witenc, Roberto Foliot clericis, Iohanne, Alexandro de sancto
Clemente, Reginaldo camerario, Alexandro de Camera, et multis aliis.

## 407

[*c.* 1181-7] Confirmation of the grant and assignment by Dean Ralph de Diceto of his houses
and chapel in the forecourt of the cathedral to the office of dean (and establishment of a
pittance on Ralph's anniversary).[2]

G(ilebertus) Dei gratia Londoniensis episcopus omnibus sancte matris ecclesie filiis
ad quos hee littere peruenerint, salutem in Domino.

**406** *Original:* St Paul's Cathedral archives, A 40/1454; *copy* in MS W.D. 1 (Liber A), fo. 6b
(variants not given). *Printed:* Gibbs, no. 71. Tag for seal. *Endorsed:* de ecclesia sancti
Pancratii (thirteenth–fourteenth century).
**407** *Original:* St Paul's Cathedral archives, A78/3015; *copies* in MS W.D. 1 (Liber A), fo. 57b
(two versions, one a copy of A78/3015, the other, Wd, from a lost original; significant
variants of Wd given). *Abstract* in *Rep.* p. 58b. Tag for seal. *Endorsed:* de domibus decani in
atrio... (fourteenth–fifteenth century).

---

[1] Alexander of Norfolk: see Gibbs, no. 70 and note, where, however, he is called rector,
apparently because the grantor, John of St Lawrence, William de Belmeis' successor in the
prebend of St Pancras, did not accept his predecessor's grants (cf. no. 403). For other documents concerning this case, see Cheney, *English Bishops' Chanceries*, p. 156 and n.
[2] This is recorded in text Wd only: see note to line 16.

Que pie deuotionis intuitu in perpetuum memoriale Dei conferuntur ecclesiis, ea iustum est firmitate gaudere et ne ualeant in posterum mutari, tutum est litterarum
5 apicibus communiri. Dilectus filius noster Radulfus de Diceto decanus ecclesie beati Pauli ad honorem Dei et patroni sui beati Pauli domos suas in atrio iamdicte ecclesie fundatas utensilibus suis et ornamentis munitas, et capellam suam cum libris et ornamentis suis omnibus concessione nostra et auctoritate decanatui assignando contulit et donauit, et ut concessionem suam ratam haberemus et firmam, precum
10 instantia postulauit. Cuius nos deuotioni approbantes, eius postulationibus annuimus, et donationem suam ratam habentes et acceptam ea qua fungimur auctoritate ipsam confirmamus. Nos etiam factum suum felici inchoatum proposito ad perfectum uolentes perducere et decanis succedentibus perpetuo prouidere, terram in qua iamdicte domus et capella site sunt, decanatui in perpetuum assignauimus; et ut
15 omnis decanorum memorate ecclesie successio eas sicut suprascriptum est possideat, benigne concessimus; et ne gesta nostra tam a nobis quam a supradicto decano concessa tractu temporis deuocari possint in irritum, ea scripti nostri patrocinio et sigilli nostri inpressione communire curauimus. Testibus: Gilleberto archidiacono Middelsex', Roberto archidiacono Essex', magistro Hugone a Lundon(iis), Rogero
20 a Wygorn(ia), Roberto Folet, Gilleberto Banastre, Radulfo de Chilton'.

## 408

[1186–7] Grant to the dean and chapter of St Paul's of the church of St Nicholas (in the Fishmarket, London), on the resignation of G(ilbert) Banastre, for the celebration of the anniversary of Gilbert's death.

Gilebertus Dei gratia Lundoniensis episcopus omnibus sancte matris ecclesie filiis ad quos hee littere peruenerint, salutem in Domino.

Cum ecclesiis uel locis diuinis mancipatis obsequiis possessiones siue beneficia a Deo deuotis fidelibus in eius honorem et laudem in perpetuum permansura con-
5 feruntur, ea tutum et iustum est litterarum monimentis excipi, et ne tractu temporis future posteritati uenire possint in dubium, maiorum debent auctoritate et diligentia roborari. Proinde ad communem omnium uestrum uolumus deuenire notitiam, dilectum filium nostrum G. Banastre personam ecclesie sancti Nicholai, que de donatione nostra esse dinoscitur in Lund(onia), ecclesiam memoratam cum iure
10 personatus quod in ea habuerat in manus nostras spontanea uoluntate resignasse,

**407** 15 possideat] Wd *adds* ita quod ibi habitet    16 concessimus;] Wd *adds* singuli etiam decani annuatim decem solidos in die anniuersarii memorati Radulfi decani per manum camerarii nomine predicti tenementi soluent ad pitanciam, et hoc se fideliter obseruaturos coram capitulo in sua institutione cauebunt.
**408** *Original*: St Paul's Cathedral archives, A 21/1576 (size 7 in. × 6 in.); *copies* in MS W.D. 1 (Liber A), fo. 6 a–b; BM Harl. MS 6956, fos. 36 (seventeenth-century transcript from original) and 83 v (from the lost Liber B, fo. 24) (variants not given). *Printed*: Gibbs, no. 67; Newcourt, I, 508 (incomplete); *abstract* in *Rep.* p. 22 b. Fragment of seal (green wax) on tag. *Endorsed*: Gilebertus Lond' episcopus de ecclesia sancti Nicholai in pisc(aria) data capitulo ad anniuersarium suum faciendum (thirteenth century) de ecclesia sancti Nicholai...ad obitum Gilberti Foliot (fourteenth century).

nosque diuine pietatis intuitu et pro salute anime nostre, ecclesie beati Pauli et dilectis filiis nostris decano et capitulo eiusdem loci Deo ibidem famulantibus, supradictam ecclesiam sancti Nicholai cum omni integritate sua in liberam et perpetuam elemosinam contulisse, ipsamque et omnes obuentiones ex ea proueni- entes ad anniuersarium depositionis nostre diem celebrandum in perpetuum, 15 predictis decano et capitulo assignasse. Quam quidem donationem pia celebratam deuotione, quia firmam et futuris manere temporibus desideramus duraturam, ipsam pagine presentis inscriptione confirmamus, et ne ualeat a quoquam in poste- rum infirmari, sigilli nostri appositione roboramus. His testibus: Roberto archi- diacono Essex', Henrico thesaurario ecclesie beati Pauli, Roberto Folet, Radulfo de 20 Chilton', magistro Waltero de Witen(eia) canonicis, Iohanne Witeng, Radulfo cantore, Gileberto Foliot, Henrico Foliot, Roberto Foliot clericis episcopi, Regi- naldo camerario, Roberto Parage, Roberto Trauers, Alexandro de Camera seruienti- bus, et aliis quampluribus.

## 409

[1186–7] Grant to Richard of Lichfield, serjeant, for his service, of one virgate with appur- tenances in Ealing (Middlesex) which was Alfwin of Ealing's, for an annual rent of five shillings and for three bezants *gersuma* (entry fine).

G(ilebertus) Dei gratia Lundoniensis episcopus omnibus hominibus suis Francis et Anglis, salutem, gratiam et benedictionem.

Ad omnium uestrum uolumus deuenire noticiam nos dedisse et concessisse Ricardo de Lichefeld seruienti nostro pro seruitio suo unam uirgatam terre in Ylling' que fuit Alfwini de Yllinges, cum omnibus ad ipsam uirgatam pertinenti- 5 bus, liberam et quietam ab omni seruitio et consuetudine, tenendam et habendam sibi et heredibus suis de nobis et successoribus nostris pro quinque solidis nobis ad quatuor terminos annuatim inde soluendis: predictus uero Ricardus iamdictam uirgatam ad regis geldum de tribus denariis per annum adquietabit. Et pro hac donatione et concessione dedit nobis nominatus Ricardus tres bisantios de gersuma. 10 Quod quia sibi firmum et stabile uolumus permanere, presentis carte inscriptione et sigilli nostri appositione roboramus. His testibus: Roberto archidiacono Essexie, Roberto Folet, Gileberto Banastre, magistro Waltero de Witteneia canonicis beati Pauli, Iohanne Witeng', Stefano Walense, magistro Radulfo cantore, Henrico Foliot, Gileberto Foliot clericis nostris, Willelmo de Punfret senescallo, Reg(inaldo) 15 dispensario, Rodberto Parage pincerna, Alexandro de Kamera, Turstano forestario, Andrea de Fuleham, Gileberto de Ylling' capellano, Willelmo de Westilling', Willelmo filio Osberti, Geruasio de Brenford, Willelmo Purcel, Alexandro de Hida hominibus nostris, et multis aliis.

**409** *Original:* St Paul's Cathedral archives, A 30/431 (size 6¾ in. × 3¾ in.). *Abstract: Rep.* p. 33a. Tag for seal. *Endorsed:* De i uirgata terre data apud Ylling' per Gilbertum episcopum (? four- teenth century) concessa Richardo de Lychefeld' et heredibus suis pro v solidis per annum soluendis [. . .] (? fifteenth century).

**410**

[2 Dec. 1178] Settlement in the presence of Gilbert and of Robert (Foliot) bishop of Hereford of the case brought by Walter of Bulmer, clerk, and associates against Master Ralph de Hauterive, on the churches of Bulmer and Brundon (Essex; cf. *VN*, p. 354), with the assent of Ralph de Diceto archdeacon of Middlesex, Gilbert of Yeldham rural dean (of Hedingham deanery), John Lemanant, knight and patron of Brundon, and the parties. Master Ralph and his successors as rectors of Brundon will pay an annual pension of two shillings to the church of Bulmer, and the parish boundaries are defined (details given).

G(ilebertus) Dei gratia Lundoniensis episcopus omnibus sancte matris ecclesie filiis ad quos presentes littere peruenerint, salutem in Domino.

Odiosas querelantium lites efficaciter uidetur secludere, qui autenticis litterarum monimentis modum quo fuerint semel extincte procurat excipere. Inde est quod
5 uniuersitati uestre presenti scripto curauimus intimare, controuersiam que uertebatur inter ecclesias de Bulemere et de Brandune motam magistro Radulfo de Altaripa a Waltero de Bulemere clerico et complicibus suis, omnium eorum clericorum qui in prefata ecclesia de Bulemere aliquid sibi iuris uendicabant, uidelicet dilecti filii nostri Radulfi de Disceto Lundon(iensis) ecclesie archidiaconi, Gileberti
10 etiam de Geldham decani, et prefati Walteri necnon et Iohannis Lemanant militis predicte ecclesie de Brandune patroni, et memorati Radulfi de Altaripa eiusdem persone communi uoluntate et in hoc concurrente assensu hoc tandem fine in nostra presentia assidente nobis uenerabili fratre nostro Roberto Herefordensi episcopo conquieuisse. Prenominate siquidem ecclesie de Brandune persona de eadem nomine
15 ecclesie singulis annis ecclesie de Bulemere duos solidos sterlingorum—unam medietatem infra octabas Pasche, reliquam infra octabas beati Michaelis—persoluet, saluo iure aduocationis sepedicte ecclesie de Brandune prefato Iohanni militi et eius heredibus, ut scilicet persona decedente, liceat ipsis libere et sine contradictione clericorum ecclesie de Bulemere, ad iamdictam ecclesiam de Brandune personam
20 idoneam diocesiano episcopo presentare, que post suam institutionem de persoluenda predicta pensione duorum solidorum ecclesie de Bulemere, sicut prefatus Radulfus iam prestitit fidelitatem, prestare debebit. Supra quam pensionem ecclesie de Bulemere uel eius personis ab ipsa ecclesia de Brandune uel eius personis nichil umquam exigere licebit. In hac etiam compositione ita inter eosdem conuentum
25 est, quod terre illius que est de feudo Iohannis Lemanant, et ab opposito domorum ecclesie de Brandune uersus occidentem, ex altera parte uie, eidem uie proxima iacet, ius parochiale tam in hominibus quam in decimis et ceteris omnibus cum ipsa terra, ecclesie de Brandune sine aliqua questione sibi ab ecclesia de Bulemere uel eius personis mouenda in perpetuum remanebit. Sed econtra de terra Hugonis de
30 Ponte, licet sit de feudo prefati Iohannis uel de terra Willclmi de Chantelu que sub nemore iacet, nullum ius parochiale sibi de cetero uendicabit. De hac uero compositione firmiter et inuiolabiliter obseruanda, prefati archidiaconus et decanus,

**410** *Original:* PRO Duchy of Lancaster Records, Anc. Deeds (DL 27), LS 89 (size 5½in. × 7½in.).
*Printed: Ancient Charters,* ed. J. H. Round (PRS), no. 46. Seal (green wax) on tag. *Endorsed:*
Brandone (thirteenth–fourteenth century).

Walterus etiam et magister Radulfus fidei religionem interposuerunt, et nos ut in posterum firma sit et inuiolata permaneat, presentis eam pagine inscriptione confirmauimus, et nostri pariter appositione sigilli roborauimus. Facta est autem 35 Lundon(ie) apud sanctum Paulum, anno ab incarnatione Domini MCLXXVIII quarto nonas Decembris. His testibus: Roberto Herefordensi episcopo, Hugone decano sancti Pauli, Richardo archidiacono Colecestr(ie), magistro Henrico de Norhamt(onia), magistro Ricardo de Storteford, Gileberto Foliot canonicis sancti Pauli, Radulfo Foliot Herefordensis ecclesie canonico, Rogero filio Mauritii, 40 Ricardo de Sarebir(ia), Radulfo de Ciltona, Milone Folet clericis nostris; Roberto senescallo domni Herefordensis, Waltero scriptore, Dauid sacerdote, Fabiano clerico, Radulfo de Binham, Ricardo Maleshwre.

### 411

[*c.* 1179–*c.* 1180] Settlement of the case between Master Ralph de Hauterive, Master of the Schools of London, and G. de St Ouen, knight, on the chapel of *Botenecca*,[1] of which G. claimed the advowson, and which Ralph claimed pertained to him as rector of Burstead (Essex). Ralph is to hold the chapel for life.

G(ilebertus) Dei gratia Lundoniensis episcopus omnibus sancte matris ecclesie filiis ad quos presentes littere peruenerint, salutem in Domino.

Que ad litium propellendas iniurias et stabilienda bona pacis aguntur, memorie non inmerito tenacius debent inprimi, et quo robur optineant in futurum, scripti cuiuslibet auctoritate fulciri. Inde est quod uniuersitati uestre presentium litterarum 5 testimonio curauimus intimare, controuersiam que uertebatur inter magistrum Radulfum de Altaripa, magistrum scolarum Lundon(ie), et G. de sancto Audoeno militem super capella de Botenecca, quam prefatus R(adulfus) ad ecclesiam suam de Burgested' iure parochiali omnimodis asseruit pertinere, et in qua econtra memoratus G. ius se dicebat aduocationis habere debere; hoc tandem fine in nostra 10 presentia conquieuisse. Sepedictus siquidem Radulfus uoluntate, assensu et beneplacito prefati G. militis capellam ipsam toto uite sue tempore quiete tenebit et libere, et tam oblationes quam obuentiones, et cetera ad prefatam capellam pertinentia, sine molestia aliqua ipsius militis uel heredum suorum uel hominum ipsius, debebit absque omni contradictione percipere. Est autem hec compositio 15 celebrata, saluo in omnibus iure ipsius militis et heredum suorum quod in eadem capella debebunt habere, et sine aliqua ecclesie de Burgestede in iure suo diminutione, saluo etiam debito ipsi capelle seruitio, quod idem magister Radulfus prestari faciet, qui emolumentum quod exinde poterit prouenire recipiet. Et ne huius facti memoriam protractioris temporis diurnitas debeat abholere, pagine presentis id 20

**411** *Original:* PRO Exchequer Records, K.R., Eccl. Documents, E135/19/48 (size 6 in. × 4 in.). Tag for seal. *Endorsed:* Capella de Bodenek' (thirteenth–fourteenth century).
17 *or* debebant

---

[1] Cf. Morant, I, 199–200, showing the holding of the St Ouen family in 'Le White-hall and Bodnecks' in Little Burstead in 1301; the bishop of London is and was the patron—hence, no doubt, the presence of Gilbert's nephew as rector.

annotatum inscriptione dependentis ab ea sigilli nostri testimonio curauimus
roborare. His testibus: Waltero filio Roberti, Rogero de Wigorn(ia), Ricardo de
Saresbir(ia), magistro Radulfo precentore, Waltero elemosinario, Ricardo Banastr',
Iohanne Witenc, Theodbaldo Paste, Odone de Burneham, Iohanne [...], Willelmo
25 preposito Hundredi.

### 412

[1163–74] General confirmation to Holy Trinity priory, Aldgate, London (Augustinian):
of the church of Layston with the chapel at Alswick Hall in Layston (Herts)[1] and the
churches of Broomfield, Black Notley (Essex),[2] St Botolph by Aldgate (London), Tottenham
(Middlesex) and Walthamstow (Essex) and appurtenances.

G(ilebertus) Dei gratia Lundoniensis episcopus archidiaconis, personis et uniuersis
sancte matris ecclesie filiis per episcopatum Lundon(iensem) constitutis, salutem,
gratiam et benedictionem.

    Quoniam ea que uiris religiosis per diocesim nostram tempore nostro canonice
5 conferuntur nostra debent auctoritate muniri, fraternitati uestre significamus quia
dilectis filiis nostris priori et canonicis ecclesie sancte Trinitatis Lundonie, episcopali
auctoritate qua fungimur, concedimus et confirmamus ecclesias et ecclesiastica
beneficia que inpresentiarum per episcopatum nostrum dinoscuntur possidere.
Inter que dignum duximus hec propriis exprimere uocabulis: scilicet ecclesiam de
10 Loefstaneschirche cum capella de Alsieswiche et cum aliis pertinentiis suis, et
ecclesiam de Brumfeld cum omnibus que ad eandem ecclesiam pertinent, ecclesiam
de Nutelege cum terris et decimis et omnibus aliis ad eandem ecclesiam pertinentibus; ecclesiam sancti Botulfi cum omnibus pertinentiis suis, ecclesiam etiam de
Totteham et ecclesiam de Wlcumestoewe cum omnibus que ad easdem pertinere
15 cognoscuntur ecclesias. Vt autem hec omnia firmiter et inconuulse possideant,
scripti presentis attestatione et sigilli nostri appositione hec ipsa—salua in omnibus
episcopo Lundoniensi debita subiectione—roborare curauimus. Testibus: Iohanne
de Hospitali, magistro Ricardo de Storteford', Ricardo de Saresbur(ia), Rogero filio
Mauritii, Henrico Banastr', Ludowico, Waltero elemosinario, Radulfo de Chiltona
20 clericis episcopi, Roberto decano de Walde.

### 413

[1163–c. 1180] Grant of an indulgence in support of the appeal of Brothers Adam, G., and G.
for funds for St Bartholomew's Hospital (Smithfield), London (cf. no. 414).

**412** *Original:* PRO Exchequer Records, T.R., Anc. Deeds (E40), A 10845 (size 8 in. × 4½ in.).
*Abstract* in *Cal. Ancient Deeds*, v, 55. Slit for seal tag. *Endorsed:* Gilleb' episcopus de omnibus
ecclesiis nostris nominatim que sunt in episcopatu Lond' (twelfth century) secunda confirmatio
episcoporum de pluribus locis. liii (fourteenth century).
13 sancti Botulfi *written over an erasure*
**413** G, no. 234; B, fo. 197v.

[1] Cf. *PN Herts.* p. 181.        [2] Cf. Morant, II, 125.

G(ilebertus) Dei gratia Lundoniensis episcopus dilectis sibi in Domino uniuersis eiusdem ecclesie parrochianis et filiis, salutem, gratiam et benedictionem.

Vestram spero, karissimi, non latere prudentiam, quam sit utilis multorumque necessaria comodis hospitalis illa domus que prope ecclesiam beati Bartholomei Lundon(ie) constructa est, in qua misericordie deseruitur operibus, et pauperum 5 Christi necessitas assidue multo studio multaque diligentia subleuatur. Que cum actis retro temporibus studiis huiusmodi uigilanter intenderit, ad presens tamen Domino gratiam ministrante solito clarius enitescit, ⟨fo. 198⟩ et studio bonorum fratrum Ade uidelicet, G. et G., qui se nuper eiusdem domus pro Christo manci-pauerunt et subdiderunt obsequiis, uberius solito pietatis opera omnibus ad eam 10 diuertentibus exhibendo, odoris boni fraglantiam iamiam plenius ex se circum-quaque diffundit. Hii nimirum cum iam sibi mundi gloria plurimum arrideret, et rerum temporalium affluentia satis responderet ad uotum, totum quod sibi uel iure patrimonii a parentibus obuenerat uel quod laboribus anxiis terra marique per-quisierant pro Christo relinquentes, id ipsum in usus pauperum Christi contulerunt, 15 et ut holocaustum acceptabile Domino plenius exhiberent, post sua seipsos eorun-dem obsequiis humillime deuouerunt. Qui cibum esurientibus, potum sitientibus, nudis operimenta, fatigatis tecti lectique requiem, uberem egrotis misericordiam sollicite subministrantes, laboris et obsequii sui mercedem sperant et exspectant a Domino, ipsam utique quam repromisit ipse diligentibus se. Quorum conuersa- 20 tionem et opera quia Domino placere non ambigimus, uniuersitati uestre preces affectuose porrigimus, ut domum illam in qua Domino iugiter obsequuntur, affectuosius diligatis, et elemosinas uestras per manus illorum in commune bonum pauperum Christi fideliter erogandas, sibi uel his quos destinauerint ad uos fidentis-sime committatis. Omnibus uero qui de suis facultatibus eidem domui ad opera 25 misericordie sustentanda quicquam inspirante Domino largiti fuerint, de Domini misericordia confisi, de iniuncta sibi penitentia uiginti dies relaxamus, et orationum et bonorum que tam in nostra quam sua fiunt ecclesia, participes in hoc fiduciam subministrante Domino constituimus. Valete.

## 414

[1163–c. 1180] Grant of an indulgence in support of St Bartholomew's Hospital (Smith-field), London (as no. 413).

Nonnullis innotuisse credimus quanto foueantur solacio pauperes Christi diuertentes ad hospitale iuxta sanctum Bartholomeum in Lundon(ia), et quantis egeat domus illa que tot milibus singu[lis] diebus est necessaria, et solacium ministrat uniuersis. Huius ergo tam religiose domus intuitu uniuersitatem uestram hortamur attentius rog[an]tes et obsecrantes in Domino et in remissionem uobis [in]iungentes delic- 5 torum, quatinus latores presentium nuntios et procuratores illius uenerabilis loci benigne inter uos ad seminandum Dei uerb[um] recipiatis, et fratribus qui ibidem sunt diuinis mancipati obsequiis per uos et per commissos uobis populos beneficiis

---

**414** G, no. 323; B, fo. 198 (*the margin is cut away with the loss of a few letters*).
8 beneficia B

et elemosinarum larg[it]ione misericorditer subueniatis. Nos quoque de diuina
10 confisi misericordia omnibus qui pro a[more] ⟨fo. 198 v⟩ Dei aliquod illi domui
beneficium contulerint omnium orationum et beneficiorum Lundoniensis ecclesie
concedimus participationem. Valete.

## 415

[c. 1181–7] Confirmation of the grant by William of Theydon, with the assent of Robert
his brother and heir, to St Bartholomew's Hospital of the church of Little Wakering (Essex).

G(ilebertus) Dei gratia Londoniensis episcopus omnibus sancte matris ecclesie filiis,
salutem in Domino.

Ad uniuersitatis uestre uolumus deuenire notitiam nos ex tenore carte dilecti filii
nostri Willelmi de Taidena aduocati ecclesie de parua Wakeringa nobis presentate
5 et exhibite cognouisse, ipsum Willelmum dedisse et concessisse diuine caritatis intuitu
Deo et sancte Marie et hospitali sancti Bartholomei de London(ia) et fratribus
eiusdem loci ecclesiam de parua Wakeringia cum omnibus ad eam pertinentibus, in
puram et perpetuam elemosinam, de assensu et concessione et uoluntate Roberti de
Taidena fratris predicti Willelmi et eiusdem heredis, cuius etiam super hoc cartam
10 inspeximus. Has igitur concessiones nos ratas habemus et acceptas, et ut firmitate
gaudere possint imposterum, eas pagine presentis inscriptione et sigilli nostri
appositione confirmauimus. Testibus: magistro Henrico de North(amtonia),
Radulfo de Chilton', Gilberto Ban(astre) canonicis sancti Pauli, Willelmo de
Carnamuilla, Thoma Brithowe, Ricardo de Sare(beria), Iohanne Witeng', Radulfo
15 cantore clericis; Reginaldo filio Ricardi, Henrico filio Alwyni, Reginaldo camerario,
Reginaldo dispensario, Roberto pincerna, et multis aliis.

## 416

[c. 1182–6] Settlement by Gilbert, Ralph (de Diceto) dean of St Paul's and Nicholas archdeacon of London, as delegates of Pope Lucius (III) (1181–5), of the case between Prior Alan
and the brothers of St Bartholomew's Hospital and Peter of Wakering on the church of
Little Wakering (Essex). Since Peter never answered their summons, possession is adjudged
to the prior and canons.

The case lasted at least a year after Lucius's delegation.

G(ilebertus) Dei gratia Londoniensis episcopus et Radulfus decanus et Nicholaus
archidiaconus London(ienses) omnibus sancte matris ecclesie filiis, in Domino
salutem.

**415** London, St Bartholomew's Hospital Muniments, Cok's Cartulary, fo. 530v (430v)
(picture of bishop in margin; on fo. 531 v confirmation by donor's brother Robert with very
similar witnesses). *Printed:* Norman Moore, I, 198 n.
**416** *Original:* London, St Bartholomew's Hospital Muniments, no. 1318 (size 6¼ in. × 3¾ in.);
*copy* in Cok's Cart., fo. 532 (432). *Printed:* Norman Moore, I, 147 n. (with facsimile opposite).
Three seals: I. missing; 2. Gilbert Foliot's (brown wax); 3. rounded oval, head facing right,
surrounded by double line of inscription (Archdeacon Nicholas's). Outer ring: TIBI.S...ETV.
CELAS (?)...IV (?)...; inner ring: N[ ]DIAC. *Endorsed:* De ecclesia de Wakerinke (twelfth–
thirteenth century) xiiij (fourteenth–fifteenth century).

Vniuersitati uestre presenti scripto duximus intimandum, quod cum cause cognitio que inter dilectos nostros Alanum priorem et fratres sancti Bartholomei 5 et Petrum de Wakering' super ecclesiam de Waker(ing) uertitur, nobis a summo pontifice domno papa Lucio audienda et fini debito contradenda commissa fuisset; nos domni pape mandatum effectui mancipare uolentes, predictum P(etrum) semel, secundo, demum etiam edicto peremptorio citare curauimus; set cum nec per se nec per responsalem sufficientem coram nobis aliquatenus compareret, 10 prefatum priorem et fratres in possessionem ipsius ecclesie causa rei seruande decreuimus inmittendos, donec idem P(etrus) se nobis exhibens possessionem suam, prestita cautione, iudicio sisti recuperare mereretur. Elapso uero anno cum memoratus P(etrus) nec per se nec per alium sui nobis copiam exhiberet, habito super hoc cum uiris discretis consilio, sepedictum priorem et fratres ueros iamdicte ecclesie 15 possessores constituendos decreuimus, et eos auctoritate qua fungebamur, salua eidem P(etro) questione proprietatis, in corporalem predicte ecclesie possessionem induci fecimus. Bene ualete.

## 417

[1175–c. 1181] Confirmation of the agreement between Richer precentor of Rouen, canon of St Paul's, and the brothers of St Bartholomew's Hospital on that portion of land which William of Ely had held and had granted to the Hospital for an annual pension of twenty-six shillings. Richer granted it to them, except for the land held by Richard mercer of London, to be held of himself for the same pension.

Notum sit tam presentibus quam futuris quod ego Gillebertus Lundoniensis De⟨i⟩ gratia episcopus g⟨r⟩atam habeo conuentionem que habita est inter dilectum filium nostrum Richerium precentorem Rothomagensem ⟨at⟩que canonicum ecclesie sancti Pauli et fratres hospitalis sancti Bartholomei Lundon(ie) super terra prebende ipsius Richerii, super ea scilicet ipsius terre portione quam Willelmus de 5 Heli diu tenuerat, quamque fratribus ipsius hospitalis sub annua uiginti sex solidorum pensione tenenda⟨m⟩ concesserat; hanc siquidem terram prenominatus Willelmus in manu nostra refutauit et iuri si quod umquam in ea habuerat plene renuntiauit; tandem itaque terram totam, excepta ea portione quam Ricardus mercerius London(ie) habuit, iamdictus Richerius prefatis fratribus hospitalis sancti 10 Bartholomei de se in capite tenendam concessit annua uiginti et sex solidorum pensione, qui sibi quatuor terminis, in Natale scilicet Domini et in Pascha et in Natale sancti Iohannis Baptiste et in festo sancti Michaelis, soluentur. Hanc itaque conuencionem ratam habeo et ut predicti fratres et eorum successores iamdictam terram in pace teneant quamdiu pensionem supramemoratam ipsi Richerio et 15 successoribus eius legittime persoluerint, ea que nobis a Domino concessa est auctoritate et sigilli mei appositione confirmo. Saneque hoc commemorandum

417 London, St Bartholomew's Hospital Muniments, Cok's Cartulary, fo. 475 (374). *Printed:* Norman Moore, I, 199 n. (*omitting* hanc siquidem...pensione defendent *and reading for* 'Willelmus de Heli diu' 'Willelmus de Heli domini regis thesararius'). 7 sequidem *MS* 9 tandem] laudem *MS* 15 supramemora' *MS*

existimo quod sepedicti fratres cum terra quam susceperunt onus in se omne
suscipient et terram ipsam uersus regem et officiales eius et alios quosque salua
20 Richerio supramemorata pensione defendent. Hiis testibus: Roberto archidiacono
Essex(ie), magistro Henrico de Norhamt(onia), magistro Hugone de London(ia),
Ricardo Ruffo, Roberto de Clifford', Gilleberto Foliot, Willelmo de Heli, Michaele
de Valecin(is), Roberto de Fuleham, Gocelino piscatore, Henrico filio Ricardi,
magistro Ricardo de Storteford'.


## 418

[1163–*c.* 1180] Grants of indulgences in support of R., who is collecting money for the
repair of London Bridge and the bridge and causeway at Stratford (Middlesex).

We have here the texts of two separate indulgences on the same model.

Dilectis sibi in Domino uniuersis sancte matris ecclesie filiis frater G(ilebertus)
Lundoniensis ecclesie minister, salutem, gratiam et benedictionem.

Que donantur Domino, carissimi, donanti nequaquam pereunt, sed ei a quo
donata sunt in perpetuum utique reseruantur. Inde est quod caritatem uestram
5 commonemus in Domino, quatinus latori presentium R., qui ob amorem Dei et
salutem anime sue ad reficiendum pontem de Lund(onia) operam prebet, de
facultatibus uestris prout uobis Dominus inspirauerit aliquod auxilium conferatis,
ut a Deo ob ipsum collata die illa in centuplum recipiatis. ⟨B2, fo. 193v⟩ Omnibus
autem qui ei ad predictum opus perficiendum aliquod beneficium prestiterint,
10 orationum et beneficiorum ecclesie nostre partem concedimus, et insuper de Domini
confisi misericordia confessis de penitentia sua uiginti dies relaxamus. Valete.


## 419

[1163–*c.* 1180] Grant of an indulgence to those helping to support Nicholas, a converted
Jew.

Salutem et gaudere semper in Domino.

Licet omnibus quos fidei catholice commendat religio benefacere debitores
sumus, hiis tamen propensius intendere pietas hortatur, qui Iudeorum spreta
perfidia, sacra ⟨fo. 196v⟩ baptismatis unda renati, Iesu Christi fidem nudi plus
5 eligunt quam ut caducam habentes opulentiam occidentem legis literam sectari
uelint. Et ne rectitudinis zelum in bone uoluntatis uoto cotidiane necessitatis turbet
instantia, eo sollertius ⟨est?⟩ prouidendum, quo timetur iustius, ne in neophitis
eruditionis noue planta marcescat citius, quam in manentem caritatis radicem
solidetur. Vnde uestram in Christo dilecti exhortamur caritatem, ut in latorem
10 presentium ad fidem Christi Lundon(ie) nouiter conuersum occulos misericordie et
pietatis uiscera benignius intendatis, quatinus fraterne caritatis in eum exhibita
deuotio, eum tam nouellum adhuc ad suscepte gratie summam fortius augeat, et ad

**418** G, nos. 183, 188; B, fos. 164 (B1) *and* 193 (B2) (*spelling as* B1).
6 de Lundonia] et calcedam de Stretford' B2    11 Valete] B2 *adds* in Christo
**419** G, no. 309; B, fo. 196.

idem alios inuitet. Nos autem hiis qui remunerationis eterne intuitu, huic Nicol(ao) aliquam de facultatibus suis portionem ad releuandam eius tenuitatem dederi⟨n⟩t, de Dei misericordia et apostolorum Petri et Pauli intercessione confisi, de iniuncta 15 sibi penitentia uiginti dies relaxamus, et orationum et beneficiorum que in nostra fiunt ecclesia, participes constituimus. Valete in Christo.

## 420

[1173–7] Settlement by Gilbert and Bartholomew bishop of Exeter, as papal judges delegate, of the case between Abbot Adam and the canons of Missenden abbey (Bucks, Augustinian) and Ingelram of the Lee (nr Great Missenden, Bucks) about land at the Lee: Ingelram will hold it for life, or so long as he remains a layman, of the abbey, to which it reverts on his death, and will provide food and clothing for two canons living there with him. His wife will have no access to it save to the chapel.

Adam became abbot of Missenden in or after 1173; William of Northolt archdeacon of Gloucester in 1177. This curious transaction seems to establish, or regularize, a sort of hermitage at the Lee for Ingelram and the canons.

(Gile)bertus Londoniensis et Bartholomeus Exon(iensis) Dei gratia dicti episcopi omnibus fidelibus ad quos presens scriptura peruenerit salutem. Ne ea que semel recte finita sunt iteratis perturbationibus ualeant instaurari notum facimus uniuersitati uestre quod causa que super terra de la Leie uertebatur inter dilectos in Christo fratres nostros Adam abbatem et canonicos de Messend(ene) et 5 Ingelramum de la Leie, quam domnus papa nobis delegauit fine debito terminandam, in hunc modum coram nobis sopita est. Predicti abbas et canonici concedunt Ingelramo terram de la Leie de qua controuersia fuit cum pertinentiis suis, tenendam de eis liberam et quietam ab omni exactione et consuetudine et omni seruitio ad eos pertinente; ita quidem quod predictus I(ngelramus) duobus canonicis cum eo 10 ibidem semper morantibus necessaria in uictu et uestitu inueniet sufficienter et honeste. Illam autem terram tenebit Ingelramus quamdiu in seculari habitu uixerit, et post decessum eius sine omni contradictione reuertetur ad dominium abbatie de Messendene. Vxor uero prefati I(ngelrami) nullam ibi habebit residentiam nec frequentationem neque ullum accessum nisi ad capellam sicut cetere 15 honeste mulieres. Hanc autem conuentionem fide media firmauit Ingelramus se sine fraude et malo dolo obseruaturum; et memoratus abbas econtra ex parte sua et conuentus idem firmauit in uerbo Domini. Et ut hec conuentio rata et inconcussa permaneat, nos qui iudices eramus delegati eam presentis scripti munimine fecimus roborari. Hiis testibus: Hereberto de Northhampton' et Ricardo Barre Luxouiensi 20 archidiaconis, Willelmo de Norhale, magistro Henrico Pium, Helia clerico, Helia de Scaccario, Nigello de Berton', Dauid de Ailesberia, Roberto de Broc, Rogero de Messend(ene).

420 BM Harl. MS 3688, fo. 59 (Cart. Missenden). *Printed: Cart. Missenden*, I, no. 247.
1 Libertus *MS (no. 'Lij' in margin: the rubricator seems to have mistaken number for initial)*

**420a**

[1167–74] Inspeximus of confirmation by Bishop Richard (de Belmeis II) of the grant of the church of Purleigh (Essex) to Monks Horton priory (Kent, Cluniac, dep. of Lewes) by Robert de Vere, Adelina his wife, and Henry of Essex.

Henry of Essex, royal constable, held the Montfort manor in Purleigh 'between 1152 and his trial for treason in 1163'.[1] Robert de Vere was presumably his predecessor. This manor was the most substantial holding in Purleigh; the tithes of the other large holding appear to have passed somewhat earlier into the hands of the nuns of Wix priory.[2]

Omnibus Christi fidelibus presentes literas uisuris uel audituris Gilibertus Dei gratia Londoniensis episcopus, salutem in Domino.

Noueritis nos inspexisse cartam bone memorie Ricardi predecessoris nostri in hec uerba: Ricardus Dei gratia Londoniensis episcopus Radulpho decano et capitulo
5 sancti Pauli London⟨ie⟩ salutem. Ad episcopalem curam pertinet ea que religiosis uiris et Domino seruientibus conferuntur donatione principum seu ceterorum fidelium pastorali prouisione confirmare. Inde est quod ecclesiam de Purlai cum omnibus pertinentiis et accessionibus suis a Roberto de Ver et Adeluda uxore eius, sed et Henrico de Essexia, monachis de Horton' in perpetuam elemosinam donatam,
10 sicut ipsorum carte testantur, auctoritate episcopali confirmamus et presentis scripti pagina communimus; adicientes quod quicumque donationem nostram uel confirmationem peruertere aut impugnare attemptauerint diuina ultione feriantur. Nos quoque quod ab eo rationabiliter gestum est ratum habentes, idem quantum in nobis est intuitu diuino damus et concedimus ac sigilli nostri appositione corro-
15 boramus, saluis etiam nobis et successoribus nostris episcopalibus consuetudinibus. Hiis testibus: magistro Roberto archidiacono Essex⟨ie⟩, Ricardo de Storteford⟨ia⟩, Henrico Bane⟨st⟩r', Radulpho de Chiltinton' episcopi clericis, Willelmo Foliot senescallo, Iohanne de Suministr', et multis aliis.

**420b**

[? c. 1167–74] Grant to the monks of Monks Horton priory of an annual pension of twelve marks from the church of Purleigh.

This is unlikely to be earlier than, and may be approximately contemporary with, no. 420a; there is a striking similarity in diplomatic form.[3] The pension is noted in *VN*, p. 342.

Vniuersis Christi fidelibus ad quos presens scriptum peruenerit Gilbertus Dei gratia Londoniensis episcopus, salutem in Domino.

420a BM MS Stowe 935, fo. 24 (Cart. Monks Horton priory).
9 Henricus *MS*    17 Foliot *MS*
420b BM MS Stowe 935, fo. 24 (inspeximus of Bishop Richard FitzNeal, 1190–6).

[1] B. Dodwell in *Misc. D. M. Stenton*, p. 155; see pp. 147, 150, 154 ff. for the history of Purleigh.
[2] *Misc. D. M. Stenton*, pp. 156 f., 48 ff. Robert de Vere, son of Bernard de Vere, lord of Haughley, etc., was husband of Adelina or Alice, daughter of Hugh de Montfort, and so presumably acquired his right to the Montfort manor in Purleigh (see *CP*, x, Appendix J, pp. 111–12). Henry of Essex's confirmation is ed. J. R. Scott in *Archaeologia Cantiana*, x (1876), 273.
[3] In Gilbert's acta the 'adicientes' clause only occurs here and in the charter quoted in no. 420a.

Ad uniuersorum notitiam uolumus peruenire nos concessisse et dedisse Deo et beate Marie et sancto Iohanni apostolo et euangeliste de Horton' et sancto Pancratio et monachis sancti Pancratii apud Horton' Deo seruientibus et seruituris imper- 5 petuum annuam pensionem duodecim marcarum de ecclesia de Purle nostre diocesis. Quare uolumus et episcopali auctoritate precipimus ut prefati monachi dictam pensionem duodecim marcarum de prenominata ecclesia libere et incon- cusse et quiete imperpetuum percipiant, saluis etiam nobis et successoribus nostris episcopalibus consuetudinibus. Vt autem hec concessionis et donationis nostre 10 pagina ⟨firma (?)⟩ et inconcussa perseueret, eam et sigilli nostri appositione et testium subscriptione communimus, adicientes quod quicumque concessionem uel donationem nostram peruertere aut impugnare temptauerint diuina ultione feriantur.

## 420 c

[1163–80] Settlement as papal judge delegate of a dispute between Master John of Cornwall[1] rector of Sandon, and G. prior of Monks Horton, on the tithes of assarts in Purleigh; the tithes are to pertain to Sandon church, which is to pay an annual pension of four marks to the priory (details of the tithes are given).

Gillebertus Dei gratia Londoniensis episcopus omnibus sancte matris ecclesie filiis ad quos hee litere peruenerint, salutem in Domino.

Ad communem omnium uestrum uolumus deuenire notitiam causam a summo pontifice nobis delegatam que uertebatur inter magistrum Iohannem Cornubiensem et G. priorem de Horton' super quibusdam decimis de assartis de Purleia quas 5 iamdictus Iohannes ad ecclesiam suam de Sandona pertinere dicebat, amicabili inter memoratas ⟨fo. 25⟩ personas et ecclesias de Sandona et Purleia interueniente transactione in hunc modum in nostra conquieuisse presentia: uidelicet quod memorata ecclesia de Sandona subscriptas decimationes quas supradictus I(ohannes) nomine ecclesie sue de Sandona petebat perpetuo possidebit reddendo nomine 10 predictarum decimarum ecclesie de Purleia quatuor solidos annuatim ad duos terminos, in Natiuitate sancti Johannis Baptiste duos solidos, in Natiuitate Domini duos solidos. Decimationes uero super quibus coram nobis transactum est sunt hee: decima decem acrarum de terra quam Radulphus Tristran tenuit; item de terra Willelmi filii Watgar de decem acris; item de terra Watgar de decem acris; item de 15 terra Lamberti de tribus acris; de terra Estrilde de una acra; de terra Willelmi parcarii de duabus acris; de terra Iohannis fabri de decem acris; de terra Ricardi de Stanre de octo acris; de terra Siwardi de Stanre de quinque acris de ueteri assarto et de quinque de nouo. Preterea si quid nouum fuerit assartum de bosco de Purleia post factam coram nobis hanc transactionem, sepedicta ecclesia de Purleia omnes 20

**420 c** BM Stowe 935, fo. 24 v.

---

[1] Presumably to be identified with the Oxford theologian, later archdeacon of Worcester (c. 1197–1199/1200), on whom see E. Rathbone in *Recherches de théologie ancienne et médiévale*, XVII (1950), 46–60.

decimaciones de assarto illo prouenientes libere et sine contradictione percipiet, ita quod ecclesia de Sandona nichil in eis iuris poterit uendicare. Nos igitur cupientes omnimodis ut transactio hec auctoritate summi pontificis celebrata perpetue firmitatis robur optineat eam pagine presentis inscripsione roborauimus, et nostri
25 pariter appositione sigilli duximus communire. Testibus: magistro Ricardo de Stort(efordia), magistro Hugone de London(ia), magistro Henrico de Norf', Radulfo de Chilth(onia), Phelippo de sancta B⟨r⟩igida,[1] Ricardo de Sar(esberia), Radulfo cantore, Iohanne Wyting' capellano, et multis aliis.

**421**

[1163-87, probably before 1184] Settlement, as papal judge delegate, of the case between Reginald, clerk, de *Campo florido*, and William, clerk, and the abbot of Montebourg on the church of Powerstock (Dorset), in favour of the abbot and William.

This decision was kept in the muniments of Salisbury cathedral because Powerstock church was granted to the cathedral by the abbot in the early thirteenth century (*Reg. St Osmund*, 1, 224-5). The bishop's initial may already have been difficult to read when the cartulary copies were taken;[2] but the handwriting of the original and the seal establish that it was an act of Gilbert's. This would in any case be probable from the style, and internal evidence shows that the charter belongs to the second half of the twelfth century, a decade or two after the grant of Powerstock to Montebourg in 1157,[3] but probably before the death of Bishop Jocelin of Salisbury in 1184.[4]

**420c** 22 uendicari *MS* 26 *sic, ?* Norh'.
**421** *Original:* Salisbury Cathedral, Dean and Chapter Muniments, 1/1/6 (C. 144) (size 7 in. × 4¼ in.), defaced by damp. Passages in square brackets are illegible on the original, and have been filled in from the cartulary copies (minor variants not noted). *Copies:* Salisbury Cathedral, Dean and Chapter Muniments, Liber Evidentiarum C, pp. 131-2 (thirteenth century); Salisbury, Diocesan Registry, Liber Evidentiarum B, fo. xlir-v; Liber Ruber, fo. 34r-v (fourteenth century). *Printed:* Sarum Charters, pp. 31-2. Seal (natural wax). *Endorsed:* De Portsche ecclesiam [*sic*] (thirteenth century).

---

[1] Possibly an addition to the list of bishop's clerks in *GF*, pp. 289-91.
[2] The initial is not rubricated in Liber B or Liber C, but in Liber C the guide letter 'H' is written in the margin; the initial in Liber Ruber is 'R', but since this occurs between two other Rs which appear to be rubricator's guesses, this may be a guess and throw no light on the state of the original at the time. On the original there is a seventeenth-century endorsement which describes the document correctly as 'pacificacio...facta per G. episcopum London'. Thus the absence of a correct initial in any of the cartularies may only be due to a scribal slip in Liber C or its source: minor agreements between the cartularies against the original suggest that the other versions are copies from a cartulary very similar to Liber C. The original is in the same hand as no. 426 (see p. 27 n.).
[3] *Sarum Charters*, pp. 26-9.
[4] A distinction seems to be drawn between Roger, 'late' bishop, and the bishop of Salisbury who instructed archdeacon Adelelm to try the case. One presumes that the latter was still alive. Since Adelelm had been succeeded by 1173 (*Sarum Charters*, p. 38, cf. 43), the bishop is evidently Jocelin. This does not amount to proof, but the circumstances of the case make a date early in Gilbert's episcopate probable in any event.

[G. Dei gratia] Londoniensis [episcopus] dilectis [sibi in Domino] uniuersis sancte matris ecclesie filiis ad quos presentes litere peruenerint, salutem que nunc est et quam speramus a Domino.

[Que] ad [ecclesiarum utilitatem et earum] perpetuam tranquillitatem stabilita [sunt, h]is assensum prebere, et ut in perpetuum ualitura permaneant, hec scriptis et 5 munimentis [aliis] rob[orare, caritate] id proculdubio suggerente, [debe]mus. Eapropter uniuersitati uestre presenti scripto notificamus causam que uertebatur inter Reginaldum [cler]icum de Campo [Florido et abbatem] de Munteburgo et Willelmum clericum iamdicti abbatis super ecclesia de Powestoc', nobis a domno papa delegatam, [hoc tandem] modo conquieuisse. [Partibus siquidem] statuta 10 [sibi die] in nostra presentia constitutis, iamdictus Reginaldus se memoratam ecclesiam de Powestoc' [pre]sentatione Roberti de Arundell' [eiusdem] quondam ecclesie aduocati, per manum bone memorie Rogeri quondam Saresbir(iensis) episcopi canonice adeptum, ipsam [diu]tius possedisse, [et] ⟨ex (?)⟩ ea se post-modum uiolenter eiectum fuisse constanter asseuerabat, postulans ut eorum que 15 dicebat probationem admitteremus, et ipsi [prefate] possessionem ecclesie iuxta mandatum domni pape restitui faceremus. Iamdicti uero abbatis procuratores, quos ad hoc ad nos direxerat, et prefatus Willelmus clericus qui presens aderat, peremp-toriam sibi incontinenti exceptionem opponentes, iniuste sibi super prenominata ecclesia de Powestoc' a iamdicto Reginaldo moueri contro[uersiam] asserebant, 20 [pro]ponentes quod cum Eilmero eiusdem quondam ecclesie persone super [hac] eadem ecclesia in presentia Alelmi Dorseten(sis) archidiaconi, ex mandato domni Saresbiriensis episcopi, iam pridem mota fuisset controuersia, idem Reginaldus iuri si quid unquam in eadem ecclesia habuerat, in ipsius archidiaconi et totius capituli presentia, sponte renuntiauit, et se nunquam super ecclesia hac moturum con- 25 trouersiam fidei interpositione firmauit. Nobis itaque super hiis que ab eis dice-bantur, tam scripto ipsius archidiaconi quam uiua uoce testium omni exceptione maiorum fide sufficienter facta, memoratum abbatem de Munteburgo et sepedic-tum Willelmum a iamdicti Reginaldi petitione, auctoritate domni pape qua in hoc functi sumus negotio, absoluimus, et eidem Reginaldo super eiusdem ecclesie 30 repetitione silentium perpetuum imposuimus. Reginaldus uero ea que super refutatione a se facta dicebantur ad memoriam reuocans procedens in medium liti huic in perpetuum sponte renunciauit, et se nunquam decetero monachis de Munteburgo, uel Willelmo clerico uel successoribus eius, super ecclesia de Powe-stoc' moturum controuersiam tactis sacrosanctis euangeliis firmissime repromisit. 35 Ne igitur quod actum est in dubium aut in irritum reuocari possit in posterum, id ipsum presentis scripti testimonio et sigilli nostri appositione communire, et ea qua in hoc functi sumus negotio auctoritate confirmare curauimus.

### 422

[1163–73] Confirmation of the grant by King Henry II to the prior and convent of St Bernard Montjoux of the church of Hornchurch (Essex).[1]

Laurence abbot of Westminster died in 1173. This confirms *Oxford Charters*, no. 35.

G(ilebertus) Dei gratia Lundoniensis episcopus dilectis sibi in Domino archidiaconis, decanis et uniuersis earum que in Lundon(iensi) episcopatu si[t]e sunt ecclesiarum prelatis, salutem, gratiam et benedictionem.

Nouer[it] dilectio uestra nos per presentationem domni nostri regis Anglorum
5 Henrici dedisse et in perpetuam elemosin[am] concessisse priori et conuentui ecclesie sancti Bernardi de Monte Iouis [ecclesi]am de Haueringis cum omnibus pertinentiis suis. Quod quia in dubium [nol]umus aut in irritum de cetero posse reuocari, uniuersitati uestre presen[ti] scripto id notificare et sigilli nostri anne[x]atione confirmare curauimus. His testibus: Laurentio abbate Westmon(asterii),
10 Nicholao archidiacono Lundon(ie), Gilleberto, Waltero [ . . . ]

### 423

[1163–c. 1180] Appeal for funds for Delapré abbey, Northampton (Cluniac nuns).

G(ilebertus) Dei gratia Lundoniensis episcopus dilectis sibi in Domino archidiaconis, decanis, clericis per episcopatum Lundoniensem constitutis, salutem, gratiam et benedictionem.

Que in usus pauperum misericorditer inpenduntur donantibus non pereunt,
5 immo ad eterne retributionis gloriam conseruantur, et temporalium pia largitio uitam eternam operatur. Vnde nos de salutis uestre profectu solliciti, propensius caritatem uestram exhortamur in Domino, quatinus piis operationibus prouidere indulgeatis ut de bonis uobis permittente Deo concessis, dum tempus habetis, dum licet, eternitatis fructum mereamini. Nos itaque ancillarum Christi Deo et beatis-
10 sime Marie de Norhamt(onia) iugiter seruientium egestati compatientes, rogamus, monemus et uos exortamur in Domino ut cum ad uos uenerint suam proponentes miseriam, eas benignius suscipiatis, et de facultatum uestrarum copia earum releuetis inopiam, ut bonorum que tam in nostra quam sua fiunt ecclesia, auctore Domino sitis participes. Valete.

### 424

[1163–c. 1180] Grant of an indulgence in support of the appeal for funds for St Leonard's Hospital, Northampton.

**422** *Original:* Oxford, New College archives, Hornchurch deeds, no. 399 (much rubbed; letters in square brackets supplied from copy); *copy* in New College cartulary (seventeenth century). *Calendared:* H. F. Westlake, *Hornchurch Charters*, no. 399. Strip for seal, *simple queue*.
**423** G, no. 230; B, fo. 193.
**424** G, no. 305; B, fo. 195v.

---

[1] Cf. *PN Essex*, p. 112.

G(ilebertus) Dei gratia Lundoniensis episcopus dilectis sibi in Domino clericis et laicis per episcopatum Lundon(iensem) constitutis, salutem, gratiam et benedictionem.

Pium est fratres karissimi operibus misericordie ad propositum caritatis sic properare stadium ut tempore messionis eterne salutis optate brauium compre- 5 hendamus, sic dum uiuitur seminare, ut multiplicato fructu expectate iocunditatis stolam excipiamus. Vnde uos attentius exhortamur in Domino, quatinus promisse remunerationis fiducia, cura propensiori piis actibus indulgeatis, inter quos elemosinarum lucet largitio que peccatorum ⟨fo. 196⟩ delet offensam, que dilectionis Dei et proximi nobis lumen infundit. Cum itaque leprosi sancti Leonardi de 10 Norhamt(onia) non solum corporis intolerabili torqueantur cruciatu, uerum extrema laborare dinoscuntur inedia, pro eis uniuersitati uestre supplicare pietatis affectio nos impellit, quatinus per hunc latorem presentium eorum nuntium, de facultatibus uestris aliquam portionem ad eos mittentes, eorum releuetis miseriam, et quod propriis non possunt uestris impendiis adiuti, quod ad miserabilem uictum 15 sufficiat per uos habere se gaudeant. Nos uero de Dei confisi misericordia hiis qui saltem modicum iam dictis fratribus erogauerint, uiginti dies relaxamus, et bonorum omnium que in nostra fiunt ecclesia participes constituimus. Valete in Christo.

## 425

[1163–74] Announcement that he has settled the case between William, bishop, and the monks of Norwich and Herbert, clerk, de *Marisco*.

Bishop William died in 1174.

Dilectis sibi in Domino uniuersis sancte matris ecclesie filiis frater G(ilebertus) L(ondoniensis) ecclesie minister, salutem, gratiam et benedictionem.

Controuersias amicabili pactione sopitas firmitatis tunc demum robur perpetuum accipere constat, cum eorum quorum hec firmare potest auctoritas, et literis consignantur et appositis muniuntur sigillis. Vnde transsactionem inter uenerabilem 5 fratrem nostrum W(illelmum) Norwic(ensem) episcopum una cum eiusdem loci monachis et Herbertum clericum de Marisco super questione muri et aliis querelis inter eos habitis, presenti scripto in lucem redigere curauimus, ut rediuiue litis in posterum iniqua penitus auferatur occasio. Herbertus itaque, nobis ad super eadem lite cognoscendum ex mandato domni pape residentibus, producto in medium 10 autenti⟨fo. 194⟩co domni Norwic(ensis) episcopi instrumento tactis sacrosanctis ewangeliis fiurauit se omnia que concepta fuerant instrumento, bona fide etiam inuiolabiliter obseruaturum, seque omnibus querelis inter eum et predictas personas hactenus habitis renuntiare uiua uoce proposuit. Nos itaque id exigente iuris ordine tam domnum episcopum quam monachos a iam dicti H(erberti) petitione penitus 15 absoluimus. His testibus[ . . . ]

**425** G, no. 191; B, fo. 193 v.

### 426

[summer–autumn 1174] Mandate to Philip vice-archdeacon of Oxford to put Osney abbey (Oxon, Augustinian) in possession of the church of St Mary Magdalene (Oxford), since Gilbert, as papal judge delegate, has decided that they were ejected by force by the canons of St Frideswide's (Oxford, Augustinian priory).

See no. 427.

G(ilebertus) Dei gratia Lundoniensis episcopus Philippo uicearchidiacono Oxen(e-fordie) salutem.

A domno papa mandatum suscepimus, ut de causa que inter abbatem et fratres de Osen(eia) et priorem et canonicos sancte Frideswide diu agitata est, super ecclesia
5 sancte Marie Magdalene que extra portam Oxen(efordie) sita est, ueritatem diligenter inquireremus, et si constaret nobis iam dictos fratres de Osen(eia) a possessione memorate ecclesie sancte Marie Magdalene fuisse uiolenter eiectos, ipsis omni occasione et appellatione remota eiusdem ecclesie possessionem restitueremus, et causam postmodum audiendo, eam mediante iustitia decideremus. Huius auctori-
10 tate mandati, statuto die partes euocauimus, et ipsis coram nobis positis, et eorundem rationibus hinc inde plenius auditis, supradictos fratres de Osen(eia) a possessione memorate ecclesie per uiolentiam eiectos fuisse idoneorum testium sufficienti probatione cognouimus; et apostolici mandati formam sequentes, ipsis eiusdem ecclesie possessionem adiudicauimus. Quia uero quod in causa a iudice delegato
15 statuitur, id per ordinarium iudicem effectui recte mancipatur, mandamus uobis et apostolica auctoritate iniungimus, quatinus sepedictos fratres de Osen(eia) in corporalem eiusdem ecclesie possessionem auctoritate apostolica inducatis. Et si quis uobis in hoc resistere aut aliquatenus impedire presumpserit, uos in eum, omni occasione et appellatione postposita, ecclesiasticam exercere iustitiam non differatis,
20 et ecclesiam ipsam a diuinis cessare faciatis. Valete.

### 427

[1176] Settlement by Gilbert and Roger bishop of Worcester of the case between the canons of Osney and of St Frideswide's, Oxford, on the church of St Mary Magdalene, Oxford. In Roger's absence, Gilbert had decided at London (in the summer or autumn of 1174) that Osney had been forcibly ejected from possession; after a long delay, and a further appeal by

426 *Original:* Bodl. MS Christ Church Charter 626 (size 6¾ in. × 3¼ in.); *copy* in BM Cotton MS Vitellius E. xv, fo. 14 (Cart. Osney: variants not given). *Printed:* Cart. *Oseney*, II, 224–5. Seal (natural wax, varnished brown). *Endorsed:* Littere G. Lond' episcopi de ecclesia sancte Marie Magdalene (twelfth century) e.i.ij. (twelfth century) 13.
427 BM Cotton MS Vitellius, E. xv, fos. 14v–15v (V) (damaged in the Cotton fire and so defective). H. E. Salter also used the original, formerly in the Christ Church, Oxford, archives, which cannot now be found. This was mutilated, and it is not now possible to decide precisely how much of Salter's text was derived from the original. Our text is based on the Cotton MS; additions in square brackets are from Salter; words bracketed by him as conjectural and departures from his readings are given here in italics. (We have had much kind help from the authorities in Christ Church and the Bodleian Library in pursuit of the lost original.) *Printed:* Cart. *Oseney*, II, 219–23 and 217–18. The bulls are in *PUE*, III, nos. 213, 234, 79.

both parties, the two delegates acting on a second mandate from Pope Alexander III had confirmed the earlier decision of Pope Eugenius III, which the canons of St Frideswide's claimed was forged, that the canons of Osney had the church by right; and they decided that St Frideswide's should pay Osney four marks for loss of income when Osney was not in possession.

The reference to the dean, now elect of Chichester,[1] proves that the first mandate of Alexander III, dated Anagni, 12 April, was issued in 1174 (see Biog. Index, *s.n.* Chichester). This was followed by the settlement of the issue of possession; then came a delay of about a year and a new appeal to the Pope. Alexander's second mandate (Anagni, 12 April)[2] can be dated to 1176—the Pope's confirmation of the final decision of the judges delegate was issued on 4 March 1177. This decision was presumably made in the second half of 1176 (see Morey, pp. 56 ff.; *Cart. Oseney*, II, 215).

Gilebertus Dei gratia Lundoniensis et Rogerus eadem gratia Wigorniensis episcopi omnibus fidelibus et sancte matris ecclesie filiis, salutem quam promisit Deus diligentibus se.

Cognoscat pro ueritate religionis uestre discretio, ad quos presens pagina peruenerit, nos accepisse mandatum domni pape Alexandri tertii de causa que 5 uertebatur inter canonicos Osen(eie) et canonicos sancte Frideswide super ecclesia sancte Marie Magdalene in hunc tenorem:

'Alexander episcopus seruus seruorum Dei uenerabilibus fratribus G(ileberto) Lundoniensi et R(ogero) Wigorniensi episcopis, salutem et apostolicam benedictionem. Ex parte abbatis et fratrum de Osen(eia) nostris est auribus intimatum, 10 quod cum inter ipsos ac priorem et canonicos sancte Frideswide in presentia pie ac recolende memorie patris et [ante]cessoris nostri Eugenii pape super ecclesia sancte Ma[rie] Magdalene que est sita extra portam Oxenefordie [controuersia] uerteret[ur], tandem fuit ordine iudici[ario termi]nata et sententia scripti apostolici muni[mine] roborata. Postmodum uero cum idem fratres essent [in prefate] ecclesie posses- 15 sionem inducti consequenter, per [*Hugonem* de] Pluchenei militem uiolentia eis illata [*de eadem fueru*]nt ecclesia spoliati, cumque super uiolentia [ipsa] ad uenerabilem fratrem nostrum B(artolomeum) Exoniensem episcopum [et dilectum fili]um I(ohannem) tunc decanum Cicestrensem, nunc dictum [electum *episcopum*, littere] a nobis essent impetrate et causa coram eis [agitaretur,] superueniens unus de 20 canonicis sancte Fri[deswide] asseruit predictam ecclesiam ad ius ecclesie sancte [Frideswide] pertinere, et prohibens ne iudices in causa proce[derent, in nost]ram audientiam appellauit. Iudices litteras predicti prede⟨ce⟩ssoris nostri quibus to[ta lis de sepedicta] ecclesia decisa uidebatur, consideran[tes insuper perfect]issimas probationes tam de proprieta[te *quam de leg*]itima possessione predictorum fratrum 25 [*exhibitas esse et iuste eos*]dem fratres de milite fuisse conquestos, [appellationem predictorum] canonicorum quasi super re iam iudi[cata frustrato]riam omnino censentes, fratribus [de Oseneia possessi]onem adiudicarunt et ipsos per ar[chi]diaconum loci i]llius in corporalem possessionem miserunt. [*Sed* cum] prior de

**427** 4 pagina presens *Salter*   15 essent *om. Salter*   16 *?* Bluchenei V   17 fuerunt *Holtzmann*; fuissent *Salter*   23 Iudices *om. Salter*   28 adiudicauerunt *Salter*

---

[1] If the reading is correct.

[2] It is odd, however, that that both mandates have the same date, and this may be an error.

30 Osen(eia) et aliqui de fratribus suis cum [ipso ibidem mor]arentur, superuenientes
canoni[ci sancte Frideswide c]um mul[titudine arma]torum [eos ex eadem *ecclesia*
eiecerunt. Sepedictos *ergo fratres compatientes et uolentes omnia* que contra iuris
ordinem sunt ad religionis statum reuocare et suam iustit]iam conseruare, fraternitati uestre per apostolica scripta precipiendo mandamus, quatinus conuocatis
35 partibus et rationibus hinc inde plenius auditis et cognitis, si noueritis sepedictos
fratres de Osen(eia) a possessione fuisse uiolenter eiectos, ipsis omni occasione et
appellatione remota possessionem restitui faciatis, et tunc causam audiatis et eam
remoto appellationis obstaculo mediante iustitia terminetis, ita quidem quod si
uobis constiterit prelibatos fratres de Osen(eia) coram prenominato predecessore
40 nostro prefatam ecclesiam, nulla de proprietate questione reseruata, per iudicium
optinuisse, prelibatis canonicis sancte Frideswide tam de proprietate quam de
possessione auctoritate nostra silentium imponatis, et ecclesiam ipsam fratribus de
Osen(eia) in pace faciatis et quiete dimitti. Ceterum si uterque uestrum interesse
non poterit, alter nichilominus que predicta sunt ⟨diligentius⟩ exequatur. Dat'
45 Anagn(ie) II Idus Aprilis.'
    Prefixa quidem partibus die et illis in mea Londoniensis presentia constitutis, cum
dilectus frater noster Wigorn(iensis) absentiam suam necessariam excusaret et nobis
litteras suas ratihabitionis destinaret, post multa causarum merita hinc inde allegata,
uisum fuit michi et de consilio prudentium, tum pro qualitate facti tum ex con-
50 sentanea canonum apostolicique mandati uoluntate, testes super uiolentia facta
canonicis de Osen(eia) esse admittendos. Quibus igitur admissis et iura[tis], deinde
diligenter examinatis, motus ex [e…] assertione concordi et fama sue oppinion[i
con]sentanea, predictis canonicis de Os[eneia posses]sionem commemorate ecclesie
adiudic[aui, de qua] iam constabat probatorum uirorum attest[atione il]los fuisse
55 uiolenter eiectos a canon[icis sancte] Frideswide. Cumque de proprietate procedere
[uellem] et de aliis articulis cause, prorogatum [est nego]tium fere per annum et
demum utraque pars ad [au]dientiam apostolicam appellauit, et post multa
temporum interualla canonici Oseneie litteras predicti pape s[ecundo tulerunt nobis
in huiusmodi] formam:
60   ⟨V, fo. 15⟩ 'A[lexander episcopus seruus seruorum Dei dilect]is [fratribus
*Gileberto Lundoniensi et Rogero Wigorniensi episcopis salutem et*] apostolicam [*benedictionem. Accepta querela abbatis et* ca]nonicorum [*de Oseneia quod* prior sancte
Frideswide eos ab ecclesia sancte Marie Magdalene *contra sentent*]iam beate recordationis patris et predecessoris nostri Eugenii pape per canonicos suos ui et armata
65 manu eiecisset, et clerici eorundem canonicorum uulnerati fuissent, fraternitati
uestre, si bene meminimus, per scripta nostra mandauimus quod si constaret
predictos canonicos de Osen(eia) a prelibata ecclesia uiolenter fuisse eiectos, eam
ipsis restitui faceretis; demum uero de proprietate cognoscentes, si constare posset
controuersiam que inter predictos canonicos super eadem ecclesia uertebatur a
70 prefato predecessore nostro fuisse decisam, ita quod nichil questionis esset reseruatum, canonicis sancte Frideswide tam de proprietate quam de possessione, appella-

---

**427** 40 per iudicium *om. Salter*   42 possessione] Salter *adds* perpetuum   44 diligentius Salter;
*om.* V   46 Londoniensi Salter   52 exe[que] Salter   62 Accepta *Holtzmann*; Cum ex Salter

tione remota, perpetuum silentium imponeretis, et clericos et laicos quos constaret
uiolentiam intulisse uel inferri fecisse denuntiaretis excommunicatos. Cumque
probata uiolentia canonici de Osen(eia) restituti fuissent et uos de proprietate
uelletis cognoscere, predictus prior licet appellatio inhibita fuerit ad nostram 75
audientiam appellauit, kalendas Nouembris nuper preteritas diem sue appellationi
prefigens. Canonici autem multis expensis grauati et attendentes quod uos aliis
occupati diem uelletis differre, in uocem appellationis proruperunt; et ipsis nuntium
suum destinantibus prior nec uenit nec aliquem pro se responsalem transmisit. Nos
igitur uolentes laboribus et dispendiis predictorum canonicorum pro nostri officii 80
debito prouidere, fraternitati uestre per apostolica scripta precipiendo mandamus et
mandando precipimus, quatinus si uobis constiterit per litteras prefati predecessoris
nostri supramemoratam [*appellatio*]nem ita fuisse decisam, quod nichil questionis
fuisset reseruatum, priori et canonicis sancte Frideswide super memorata ecclesia
tam de proprietate quam de possessione, omni occasione et appellatione remota, 85
perpetuum silentium imponatis, non impedientibus [appellati]onibus factis, non
obstantibus litteris ueritate [*tacit*]a impetratis. Preterea fructus a tempore illate
uiolentie perceptos eisdem canonicis restitui faciatis, et clericos et [laicos quos]
tantam uim intu[*lisse uobis constiterit*] remoto ap[pellationis obstaculo excommuni-
catos] denuntietis, do[nec passis iniuriam congrue satisfaciant, et cum litteris 90
uestris [ . . . *adierint limina* apostolica. *Quod si uterque uestrum*] his exequendis interesse
non poterit, alter ea nichilominus exequatur, maiori in eorum executione diligentia
et cura adhibita, quam primum studueritis adhibere; quia si secus egeritis, graue
nobis esset et molestum ac negligentiam et tepiditatem uestram cogeremur dure
punire. Dat' Anagn(ie) II idus Aprilis.'                                               95

   Conuocatis ergo partibus et illis in mea iterum Lundoniensis presentia ad diem
constitutis apud London(iam), prior sancte Frideswide litteras bone memorie
R(oberti) Dei gratia quondam Herefordensis episcopi ad domnum papam Eugenium super diffinitione huius cause olim destinatas, quarum infra in litteris predicti
pape fit mentio, falsas dixit et illas exhiberi postulans appellauit. Postea uero, ut 100
alius dies eis prefigeretur, appellationi facte ipse et canonici sui [re]nuntiauerunt,
prefixusque est eis dies peremptorius a[pud] Oxen[efordiam.] Carta autem felicis
memorie pape Eu[genii] talis est:
   'Eugenius episcopus seruus seruorum Dei dilecto filio Wigod[o] priori sancte
Marie de Oseneia, salutem et apostolicam [benedictionem]. Sicut officii nostri 105
consideratione astringimur ea, [que in] controuersiam deducuntur, rationabili fine
d[ecidere,] ita nimirum ordo rationis expostulat [que rationa]biliter fuerint decisa
firmare, et ne in [dubium] recidiuo litigio deducantur, sedis [apostolice] munimine
stabilire. Ideoque, dilecte [in Domino] fili, controuersiam que super ecclesiis sancti
Georgii et sancte Marie Magdalene inter te et filium nostrum Robertum [priorem] 110
sancte Frideswide agitabatur, nostro iudicio [termi]natam in scripti seriem decreui-

---

**427** 80 igitur *om. Salter*    87 [*tacit*]a] *Cf. Salter's note ad loc.*    95 Anag' *Salter*    96 Lundoniensi
*Salter*    104 Eugenius] *This bull of Eugenius III is also in Corpus Christi College, Oxford (in Bodl.),
MS 137, fo. 89v (Corp.: twelfth-century copy), whose text includes all the words in brackets, except
where noted. Salter refers to Bodl. Oseney Charter 493, but this is a different bull of Eugenius III*

mus redig[endam;] et ne prolatam a nobis super ea se[ntentiam in am]biguitatem
posteritas secutura de[ducat eam] auctoritate huius pagine sta[tuimus munien]dam.
Iamdictus siquidem prior ideo sibi [ius in ecclesia] sancti Georgii uendicabat quo-
115 niam W[alterus, archidiaconus] quondam Oxenef(ordie) et ecclesie prefate
[canonicus, postquam] ecclesia sancti Georgii per patronos i[psius et uenerabilem]
fratrem Robertum Lincolniensem ep[iscopum fuit ecclesie] tue commissa, in parte
prebend[e sue sub ecclesie nomine edificium] quoddam [erexit quod idem prior]
ecclesie sue per ipsum a[rchidiaconum dicebat fuisse colla]tum; super ecclesia uero
120 [sancte Marie Magdalene ideo controuersiam tibi mouebat, quoniam bone
memorie Robertum quondam Herefordensem episcopum, qui causam que super
eadem ecclesia inter ipsum priorem et ecclesiam sancti Georgii ⟨fo. 15 v⟩ olim
noscitur agitata susceperat terminandam, eam non ex integro definisse, sed aliquid
questionis in ea reseruasse dicebat. Nos autem rationibus utriusque partis diligentius
125 auditis et cognitis, quoniam prescriptus archidiaconus, sicut ex scriptis uenerabilium
fratrum nostrorum Tiedbaldi Cantuariensis archiepiscopi et apostolice sedis legati et
antefati Lincolniensis episcopi euidenter innotuit, contra prohibitionem eorum
ipsum edificium non tam religiose quam inuide inuentus est construxisse, et
quoniam archidiaconi sine coniuentia suorum episcoporum ecclesiam alicui con-
130 cedere de canonum censura non possunt, predictum edificium et quicquid perinde
iuris prenominatus prior in ecclesia sancti Georgii requirebat ei abiudicauimus, [et]
te ab illius impetitione de cetero fore censuimus absolutum. Super ecclesia uero
sancte Marie Magdalene quoniam [pre]scriptus Herefordensis episcopus, sicut ex
litteris eius manifeste [ap]paruit, nichil questionis inuentus est in causa quam ut
135 [predictu]m est decidendam susceperat reseruasse, atque [cum] sepefatus prior
litteras in dubium reuocaret, [tu] eas ueras duobus idoneis testibus iuramen[tum
pre]stantibus approbasti, te ab illius impetitione [absolu]imus, et sententiam sepedicti episcopi auctori[tate sed]is apostolice confirmauimus. Si quis igitur hanc
[diffi]nitionis nostre paginam sciens contra eam [temere] uenire temptauerit,
140 indignationem omnipoten[tis Dei et] beatorum Petri et Pauli apostolorum eius se
no[uerit incu]rsurum. Dat' Sign(ie), VIII idus Februarii.'

[Cum nos ergo] die prefixo de causa cognituri, partibus presentibus ambo, [in
iudicio] sederemus, assidentibus nobis abbate Gloe[cestrie et a]bbate de Egenesham
aliisque uiris dis[cretis, prior sancte] Frideswide et canonici sui iterum [postulaue-
145 runt littera]s commemoratas exhiberi, asse[rentes quod ex]hibitas falsas accusarent.
Sed [cum hoc prior] prefate ecclesie sibi fieri postu[lauit, contra he]c canonici
Osen(eie) allegabant [litteras illas ad papam] Eugenium olim destinatas [esse et ad
exh]ibitionem se non teneri, nec opus [esse quod exhibere]ntur, cum contra eas olim
questione fal[si mota in prese]ntia predicti pape uere sunt probate, [sicut predicte
150 littere eiusdem pape manifeste testabantur. Restitutionem fieri neg]abant, quoniam
ipsi iuste [et iudicio sedis] apostolice possidebant [...mand]atum domni pape ad
nos [...allegata sibi et rursum in iudicium uocari. Nos igitur his et aliis cause

427 115 quondam Oxenef. archid. *Corp.*    118 quoddam erexit *Corp.*; quod clam sub...V
120 tibi controuersiam *Corp.*    124 Nos] His V    126 Teodbaldi *Corp.*    135 sepefatus *om.*
*Salter*    142 ambo presentibus *Salter*

meritis] quampluribus ex utraque parte litigantium auditis et appensis, possessionis restitutionem predicto priori et canonicis suis negantes, quam iudicio amiserant, et questionem falsi semel et precipue per summum pontificem sopitam decernentes 155 non admitti, iuxta formam nobis prescriptam et secundum tenorem litterarum pape Eugenii, prenominato priori et canonicis sancte Frideswide tam de proprietate quam de possessione sepedicte ecclesie, scilicet sancte Marie Magdalene, perpetuum silentium auctoritate apostolica qua fungebamur imposuimus, et illos nomine fructuum a tempore uiolentie perceptorum in quattuor marcas, habita taxatione 160 moderata, predictis canonicis Osen(eie) condempnauimus.

Restitutioni autem facte prefatis canonicis interfuerunt uiri magne auctoritatis et opinione preclari, uidelicet: Hugo de Maren' decanus ecclesie beati Pauli Lond(oniensis), Henricus thesaurarius eiusdem ecclesie, Radulfus de Disci, Robertus Banest(re), Ricardus Foliot archidiaconi, magister Hugo, magister Ricardus, 165 magister Radulfus, magister Dauid, magister Henricus, Ricardus [de] Belmeis, Willelmus de Belmeis canonici prefate ecclesie, magister Ricardus *de Storteford, magister Radulfus de Altaripa, magister Rogerus, Ricardus de Saleberi et quamplures alii. Sententie uero diffinitiue tam de proprietate quam de possessione apud Oxeneford(iam) late affuerunt uiri auctoritate graues, abbas uidelicet Gloecestrie et 170 abbas de Hegenesh(am), magister Ricardus de Storteford', Ricardus de Salesberi, Radulfus de Altaripa, magister Siluester, magister Sanson et alii quamplures.

## 428

[1163–c. 1180] Grant of an indulgence in support of the building appeal for Prittlewell priory (Essex, Cluniac, dep. of Lewes).

⟨G⟩ilebertus Dei gratia Lundoniensis ⟨fo. 172 v⟩ episcopus dilectis sibi in Domino uniuersis sancte Lund(oniensis) ecclesie parrochianis et filiis, salutem, gratiam et benedictionem.

Cogit nos caritatis affectio pro indigentia fratrum de Pritew(ella) uniuersitati uestre suplicare, qui nimirum inchoatam ecclesie sue fabricam suis non sufficiunt 5 impendiis consummare, nisi deuotio fidelium uotis eorum misericorditer subueniat. Proinde latores presentium nuntios et procuratores paupertatis sue sub nostrarum testimonio litterarum uobis commendamus ad gratiam, orantes et exortantes in Domino et in remissionem uobis iniungentes delictorum, quatinus eos pro communi fratrum necessitate pie laborantes propter Deum benigne suscipiatis, et de 10 collatis uobis a Domino facultatibus ad extruendam predicte fabricam ecclesie elemosinas et beneficia uestra misericorditer impendatis, ut domum Domini in terris edificando, permansura uobis edificia preparetis in celo. Clericis uero presbiteris et personis ecclesiarum per nostram constitutis parrochiam specialiter supplicamus, ut illis suscipiendis, exhibendis et honorandis sollicitius intendant, et ad 15 comissas sibi plebes deuota eos exortatione commendent, scituris omnibus qui eos hospitio seu beneficio quolibet honorauerint, quod eos orationum et beneficiorum

427 154 predicto *om. Salter*    163–4 Lond(oniensis) *om. Salter*    167 Belmeis...*de *om. Salter*
428 G, no. 228; B, fo. 172.

sancte Lundon(iensis) ecclesie constituimus fore participes. Penitentibus etiam et peccata confessis sub nostro scilicet constitutis sacerdotio quia maiori indigent
20 remedio, maiorem adicimus misericordiam, et si in septem annorum uel supra penitentia fuerint uiginti, si minus, decem, de iniuncta sibi satisfactione dies relaxamus.

**429**

[1163-78] Settlement, as papal judge delegate, of the case between William abbot of Ramsey (1161-77/8),[1] and Godfrey, priest, on the church of Burnham Deepdale (Norfolk). Godfrey had been presented by Walter de Grisiomonte, knight, who confessed that Ramsey abbey had the advowson; this was also confessed by Godfrey, and the case was decided in Ramsey's favour.

G(ilebertus) Dei gratia Lundoniensis episcopus omnibus ad quos presens carta peruenerit salutem.

Vniuersitati uestre notum fieri uolumus quod causam que uertebatur inter domnum Willelmum abbatem de Rameseia et Godefridum presbiterum super
5 ecclesia de Depedala a domno papa nobis delegatam, mediante concordia hoc modo terminauimus. Partibus in presentia nostra constitutis, miles quidam Walterus de Grisiomonte, quem dictus presbiter sue presentationis laudauit auctorem, publice cognouit quod ius patronatus illius ecclesie ad Rameseense monasterium pertineret; et si quid iuris ad eum uel ad fundum eius super ea re pertinebat, in manu nostra
10 resignauit et Rameseiensi monasterio concessit, fide data promittens quod nunquam de cetero per se uel per alium aduersus eos super hoc querelam moueret. Quo facto prenominatus presbiter procedens in medium publice confessus est quod personatum illius ecclesie per iniustam presentationem fuisset adeptus, et eandem in manu nostra liberam spontanea uoluntate resignauit. Nos igitur ius Rameseiensis monas-
15 terii ex confessione partium plenius cognoscentes, tam ius aduocationis quam ipsam ecclesiam, quantum ad nos pertinebat, apostolica freti auctoritate, domno abbati et per eum Rameseiensi monasterio assignauimus perpetuo possidendam et presenti scripto confirmauimus. Hoc autem factum est Lundon(ie) apud sanctum Paulum, sub presentia nostra et meliorum capituli nostri, et sub his testibus: Radulfo de Dici
20 et Ricardo Folioth archidiaconis, magistro Hugone et magistro Henrico canonicis

**429** *Original*: PRO Exchequer Records, T.R., Anc. Deeds (E40), A 11176 (size 7¼ in. × 4½ in.); *copies* in BM Add. Roll 39,668, no. 6; Bodl. MS Rawlinson B. 333, fo. 51; PRO Exchequer Records, K.R., Misc. Books, E 164/28, fo. clxvi (variants not given). *Printed*: *Cart. Ramsey*, II, 192-3; *Chron. Ramsey*, pp. 309-10; *abstract* in *Calendar of Ancient Deeds*, V, 105. Small fragment of seal (green wax) on tag. *Endorsed*: Carta G. episcopi Lond' de causa que uertebatur inter Willelmum abbatem de Rames' et Godefridum capellanum de Depedal' super ecclesia de Depedal' (thirteenth-fourteenth century).

[1] William Anglicus, monk of Cluny, prior of St-Martin-des-Champs, abbot of Ramsey, 1161-77, when he was elected abbot of Cluny; but he did not leave Ramsey, it seems, till 1178; he died on 7 Jan. 1180 (*Chron. Ramsey*, p. 341; Torigny, pp. 210, 287-9; *HF*, XII, 316, 447; Diceto, I, 424; Ann. Wint. in *Ann. Mon.* II, 61; *PR 7 Henry II*, p. 11; *26 Henry II*, p. 38).

nostris, Iohanne et Alexandro monachis, decano de Holmo, Ruelando, Petro de Brancest(ria), Hugone arch' de Bramc(estria), Ada presbitero de Burnaam, Willelmo de Deped(ala), et aliis multis.

## 430

[c. 1163-4] A reissue of no. 339 (q.v. for variants).

## 431

[1163-c. 1180] Notification that Roger of Stifford (Essex) had abandoned his case against his lord Gilbert Malet, royal *dapifer*, on the advowson of Stifford (Essex), by confessing that he had surrendered the advowson to Gilbert long before.

Doubtless earlier than no. 432, or (more probably) part of the same transaction. Gilbert Malet gave the church of Stifford to Rochester cathedral priory (*Reg. Roffense*, p. 118), and his grant was confirmed by Henry II in or after 1174 (*op. cit.* pp. 45-6). Hence the presence of nos. 431-2 among the Rochester muniments: cf. nos. 433-5.

Gilebertus Dei gratia Londoniensis episcopus uniuersis sancte matris ecclesie filiis, salutem, gratiam et benedictionem.

Tutum est litterarum monimentis excipere ea que aliter possent in posterum controuersiam suscitare. Veniens siquidem in presentiam nostram Rogerus de Stiford ius patronatus ecclesie eiusdem uille quod ad se pertinere de iure multis 5 retro temporibus asserebat in manu domni sui Gileberti Malet domni regis dapiferi, magnis nobis uiris assidentibus resignauit, seque eidem Gileberto de prauo consilio super hoc controuersiam mouisse proposuit. Quod petitionibus partis utriusque ne super eadem re denuo lis posset ⟨fo. 147v⟩ oriri testificari curauimus, et litteris a sigillo nostro dependentibus que coram nobis gesta sunt euidenter expressimus. 10 Hiis testibus et cetera.

## 432

[1163-c. 1180] Institution of Ralph son of Roger of Stifford, clerk, as rector of Stifford, on the presentation of Gilbert Malet.

G(ilebertus) Dei gratia Lundoniensis episcopus omnibus sancte matris ecclesie filiis per episcopatum Lundon(iensem) constitutis, salutem, gratiam et benedictionem.

Ad uniuersitatis uestre uolumus deuenire notitiam nos petitione et presentatione Gilleberti Malet, ecclesie de Stifford' aduocati, eandem ecclesiam de Stifford' Radulfo filio Rogeri de Stifford' clerico dedisse et concessisse, ipsumque in eadem 5 debita cum solempnitate personam constituisse. Quam donationem et concessionem

**431** BM Cotton MS Domitian A. x, fo. 147 (old 148) (reg. Rochester).
**432** *Original*: London, St Paul's Cathedral archives, A28/284 (size 6¼ in. × 2½ in.); *copies* in BM Harl. MS 6956, fo. 28 (seventeenth-century transcript from original), Cotton Domitian A. x, fo. 147v (old 148v) (reg. Rochester) (variants not given). *Abstract* in *Rep.* p. 32a. Tag for seal. *Endorsed*: de ecclesia de Stifford'. iiij. (twelfth[-thirteenth] century).

nostram quia de cetero inconuulsam manere uolumus, ipsam et scripto presenti et nostri appositione sigilli communimus pariter et confirmamus. Testibus his: Radulfo de Chilton', Gilleberto Ban(astre), Waltero filio Walteri, Thoma Briton(e),
10 Ricardo de Saresbir(ia), Radulfo cantore clericis, Reg(inaldo) camerario, Roberto Parag', et aliis pluribus.

## 433

[? *c.* 1186] Appropriation of the church of Stifford to Rochester cathedral priory on the presentation of Gilbert Malet after the resignation of Ralph of Stifford (see no. 432).

Evidently some years later than no. 432, and possibly about the same time as no. 435.

Gilebertus Dei gratia Londoniensis episcopus uniuersis sancte matris ecclesie filiis ad quos hee littere peruenerint, salutem in Domino.

Que nostra dilectissimi ad honorem Dei et ecclesiarum comodum geruntur presentia, scripture non inmerito debemus committere beneficio, et ut firmitatis 5 robur optineant in posterum et posteritati nequaquam ueniant in dubium, concessa nobis auctoritate tenemur diligen⟨fo. 148⟩tiori cura prouidere. Hinc est quod ad communem omnium uestrum scripti presentis testimonio uolumus deuenire notitiam Radulfum de Stiford clericum, cui quondam ecclesiam ipsius uille ad presentationem nobilis uiri Gileberti Malet eiusdem ecclesie aduocati concessimus, 10 coram nobis et multis aliis uiris honestis et discretis constitutum, iuri quod in memorata habuerat ecclesia spontanee et absolute renuntiasse, et eandem ecclesiam in manu nostra resignasse; quam nos ecclesiam cum omnibus ad eam pertinentibus presentatione iam dicti Gileberti Malet dilectis nobis in Christo priori et monachis Roffensibus qua fungimur auctoritate contulimus, ipsosque cum debita solempni-15 tate in ea personas instituimus. Et ut ea⟨m⟩ perpetuo gaudeant carte nostre muni-mine confirmauimus. Teste Nicholao archidiacono London(ie), et multis aliis.

## 434

[? *c.* 1186] As no. 433, but noting that Ralph of Stifford is now vicar for life and that the priory will be responsible for episcopal and other dues after his death or resignation.

Gilebertus Dei gratia Londoniensis episcopus omnibus sancte matris ecclesie filiis ad quos hee littere peruenerint, salutem in Domino.

Ad uniuersitatis uestre uolumus deuenire notitiam nos ad presentationem dilecti nostri Gileberti Malet quem ius patronatus ecclesie de Stiford de iure contingit, 5 priori et monachis Roffensibus memoratam ecclesiam de Stiford cum omnibus ad eam pertinentibus concessisse, ipsosque in eadem personas cum solempnitate debita constituisse; et quoniam Roffensem ecclesiam et in ea famulantes Domino ratione multiplici diligere tenemur, et eorum commodis attentius prouidere, eis duximus indulgendum ut post obitum Radulfi de Stiford clerici qui eam nomine uicarii de

432 7 cetero] *original adds* et, *erased*
433 BM Cotton MS Domitian A. x, fo. 147v (old 148v).
434 BM Cotton MS Domitian A. x, fo. 148v (old 149v).

ipsis tenet, uel postquam ipse eam aliquomodo possidere desierit, monachi ipsam 10
ecclesiam habeant et teneant et fructus et obuentiones ad ipsam proue⟨fo. 149⟩-
nientes in usus proprios conuertant et nobis et officialibus nostris pro ea
respondeant et debitas consuetudines nichilominus exoluant. Vnde ne que gesta
sunt rationabiliter tractu temporis infirmari possint aut in irritum deuocari, ea
pagine presentis inscriptione confirmamus et nostri pariter appositione sigilli 15
communimus. Hiis testibus: Nicholao Lond(oniensi) ⟨archidiacono⟩ [...].

## 435

[1186] Report to Pope Urban (III, 1185[1]–7) that on the resignation of Ralph of Stifford, and
on the presentation of Gilbert Malet, Gilbert had appropriated the church of Stifford to
Rochester cathedral priory. The claim of John of Blackmore, canon, against the priory, is
based only on evidence that he acted as farmer and received tithes, etc.; in his twenty-three
years as bishop (i.e. 1163–c. 1185–6) Gilbert has never heard that he was instituted or given
just possession of the church.

Patri suo et domno summo Dei gratia pontifici Vrbano frater Gilebertus eadem
gratia Londoniensis ecclesie minister, salutem et debitum prompta deuotione
famulatum.

Celsitudini uestre, pater sancte, duximus intimandum, quod cum dilectus in
Christo filius Radulfus clericus de Stifford', quem in ecclesia de Stifford' petitione 5
et presentatione militis cuiusdam illius ecclesie patroni Gileberti Malet personam
constitueramus, eandem ecclesiam spontanea uoluntate in manus nostras absolute
resignasset, idem ad nos miles accedens priorem Roffensis ecclesie ad eandem nobis
uacantem ecclesiam presentauit, asserens se eidem priori et conuentui Roffensi
eandem ecclesiam ut patronum diuino intuitu concessisse, unde concessionem suam 10
auctoritate episcopali instanter a nobis petiit confirmari et prefatum priorem et
⟨Da, fo. 149v⟩ conuentum ad eandem ecclesiam admitti. Communicato igitur
super hoc prudentium uirorum consilio prefatam militis concessionem gratam
habuimus et acceptam, et prefatos priorem et conuentum Roffensem in preme-
morata ecclesia solenniter instituentes concessionem sibi factam et eorum institu- 15
tionem scripti nostri autentici conscriptione roborauimus. Procedente uero tempore
ad aures nostras peruenit canonicum quendam Iohannem de Blakemora in nostra
diocesi constitutum predicto priori et conuentui de Roffa super sepedicta ecclesia de
Stifford' controuersiam mouere ipsosque occasione cuiusdam possessionis, quam se
nactum fuisse proponebat, ad audientiam quorundam iudicum a celsitudine uestra 20
delegatorum traxisse. Cum autem tam a nobis quam coram ipsis iudicibus sepius

**434** 16 Nocholao Lond' *MS*
**435** BM Cotton Domitian A. x, fos. 207 (208) (Db) and 149 (old 150) (Da). (Select variants of
Da only. Db seems to be a twelfth-century copy sewn on to the end of the cart.) *Printed: PUE,*
II, no. 239.
5 Stiford' Da (*and so throughout*)   8 resignasset Da; resignasse Db   17, 18 Blacamora / Rofa
Da   19 ipsisque *MSS*   21 ipsis *om*. Da

[1] Elected 25 November 1185; so this letter cannot be earlier than 1186.

esset requisitus, an possessionem prefate ecclesie quam petebat auctoritate episcopali aut officialium eius et consensu patroni obtinuisset, nec auctoritatem episcopi nec consensum patroni pro se uoluit allegare nec possessionem ut canonice adeptam 25 ⟨Db, fo. 207v⟩ repetere, set nude et simplici quorundam laicorum assertioni adherens, qui eum tempore quo prefate ecclesie firmarius extitit, fructus et decimas ad eandem ecclesiam pertinen⟨Da, fo. 150⟩tes percepisse affirmant, eorum abutens simplicitate et ipsam ad assertionem quasi prius optente possessionis malitiose detorquens, possessionem prefate ecclesie seu canonica sit siue non mandati 30 uestri optentu sibi postulabat assignari. Nouerit igitur uestra serenitas nos permittente Domino in regimine Londoniensis ecclesie uiginti trium annorum perseuerasse curriculis, nec aliquo unquam nobis patuit indicio prefatum Iohannem in pretaxata ecclesia canonicam institutionem aut iustam possessionem per aliquem nactum fuisse, cuius auctoritate possessionem ecclesie iuste potuisset optinere. 35 Huius autem rei ueritatis seriem sullimitati uestre significamus, ne per eius suppressionem discretionem uestram malitiose circumueniri permittamus. Paternitatem uestram custodiat omnipotens Dominus per longa tempora incolumem, pater sancte.

## 436

[1173-*c.* 1180] Institution of Herbert prior of the Hospital of St James, i.e. of Le Mont-aux-Malades, Rouen,[1] to the church of Vange (Essex) on the presentation of Cecily Talbot, and appropriation of the church to the Hospital. Cf. *VN*, p. 339.

The reference to the charter of St Thomas suggests a date later than his canonization in 1173.

[...] Quia piis desideriis pronum adhibere debemus assensum, uniuersitati uestre presenti scripto notificamus, nos ex concessione nobilis femine Cecilie uidelicet Talebot ecclesiam de Feenges, que in eius patrimonio sita est, ecclesie beati Iacobi supra montem Rothomagi et fratribus et infirmis in eadem commanentibus et 5 iugem Domino famulatum exhibentibus, ea qua permittente Domino fungimur auctoritate, in perpetuam elemosinam concessisse, et uenerabilem fratrem nostrum Herbertum ipsius ecclesie sancti Iacobi priorem in ea personam, ipsius eiusdem ecclesie sancti Iacobi nomine, debita solempnitate constituisse. Quod ne deinceps reuocari possit in dubium aut aliqua forte machinatione conuelli, presenti scripto 10 confirmamus et sigilli nostri appositione corroboramus, et quia funiculus triplex non facile rumpitur[2] donationem hanc primo iam dicte Cecilie, deinde nostra, postmodum sancti Thome dudum Cant(uariensis) archiepiscopi carta firmatam, in perpetuum ualituram Domino iuuante confidimus. His testibus [...]

**436** G, no. 326; B, fo. 199.
10 finiculus B.

---

[1] An Augustinian priory, founded as a leper hospital before 1135: see *Revue Mabillon*, XI (1921), 72.
[2] Cf. Eccl. iv. 12.

**437**

[1163–*c.* 1180] Confirmation to the monks of Cluny and the prior and convent of Rumilly-le-Comte (Pas-de-Calais, France) of the churches of Stanford Rivers, High Ongar, High (?)[1] and Little Laver, Coggeshall, Great Tey,[1] and Langenhoe (Essex), with appurtenances, granted to them by Count Eustace (III, of Boulogne, their founder).

Cf. *JS Epp.* I, nos. 2–4.

Gilebertus Dei gratia ⟨Londoniensis⟩ epischopus dilectis sibi in Domino uniuersis eiusdem ecclesie parrochianis et filiis, salutem, gratiam et benedictionem. ⟨fo. 164v⟩

Qui Domino deuotius obsequuntur, digne ab ipsius fidelibus in petitionibus suis iustis exaudiuntur. Inde est quod uniuersitati uestre presenti scripto notificamus, nos dilectis fratribus monachis scilicet Clunniaci et nominatim priori de Rumuli et 5 ipsius loci conuentui omnes ecclesias et ecclesiastica beneficia concessisse, que sibi a comite Eustachio donata et concessa sunt, et ipsius carta quam inspeximus confirmata, et ab ipsis multis iam ante annorum curriculis quiete et inconcusse possessa. In his uero hec propriis duximus exprimenda uocabulis: ecclesiam de Stanford et ecclesiam de Angra, ecclesiam de Lahaphara et Lagaphar' parua, ecclesiam de 10 Cogeshala, ecclesiam de Orteia, ecclesiam de Langahou, et quicquid ad eas pertinet in capellis, in terris et decimis, uiddelicet de porcis, de agnis, de lana, de caseis, de uitulis, de pullis equorum, de pasnagio, de feno et lino. Has iam dictas ecclesias cum omnibus ad ipsas pertinentibus iam dictis fratribus concedimus et episcopali autoritate confirmamus, et hanc donationem nostram sigilli nostri attestatione 15 corroboramus. Testibus Rica⟨r⟩do archidiacono...

**438**

[Shortly after 1163] Confirmation of the privilege granted by Bishop Richard (de Belmeis II) to Saffron Walden priory (Essex, Benedictine) that anyone who wishes may be buried there.

The witnesses suggest an early date and a confirmation of this kind would normally be given early in the episcopate.

Gillebertus Dei gratia Lundoniensis episcopus dilectis sibi in Domino omnibus sancte Lundon(iensis) ecclesie parochianis et filiis, salutem, gratiam et benedictionem.

Ex inspectione autentici scripti predecessoris nostri bone memorie Ricardi Lundoniensis quondam episcopi, intelleximus ipsum omnibus sancte Lund(onien- 5 sis) ecclesie parochianis et filiis—liberis tamen hominibus—concessisse ut quicumque eorum clericus uel laicus monasterii sancti Iacobi de Waleden' et fratrum iugem

---

**437** G, no. 227; B, fo. 164.
1 ⟨Londoniensis⟩ *om.* B    8 currucul' B    16 archidiacono] B *adds* de Col', *erased*
**438** BM Harl. MS 3697, fo. 38 (Cart. Saffron Walden).

---

[1] But they do not appear to have held the advowsons of High Laver or Great Tey: *VCH Essex*, IV, 93; Morant, II, 208; for the other churches cf. *VCH Essex*, IV, 216, 182, 100 (the identification of *Great* Tey seems established, since it was Count Eustace's in 1086; Morant, II, 205; *VCH Essex*, I, 465).

ibidem Deo famulatum exhibentium fraternitatem expetierit, uel apud eos locum sepulture sue habere uoluerit, liberam dandi se uel corpus suum cum concessis sibi
10 a Domino facultatibus illuc transferendi habeat potestatem; salua tamen in omnibus ecclesie cuius parochianus extitit et ipsius ecclesie persone debita consuetudine et dignitate. Hanc itaque concessionem et factam a iam dicto predecessore nostro permissionem, quia memorate ecclesie de Waleden' et ipsius ecclesie fratribus firmam et inconuulsam manere uolumus, ipsam eis presenti scripto et sigilli nostri
15 appositione confirmamus. Hiis testibus: magistro Ricardo de Stortef(ord), Roberto de Clifford, Rogero filio Mauritii, Ricardo de Sar(esberia), Luudouico, Radulfo de Chilton', Milone Folet, Waltero elemosinario, magistro Radulfo cantore.

## 439

[1163-72, ? 1169-72] General confirmation to Saffron Walden priory: of the churches of Saffron Walden, Great Chishall, Heydon, Great Waltham, High Easter (Essex), Enfield, Edmonton, South Mimms, Northolt (Middlesex), Thorley, Gilston (Herts), with their appurtenances.[1]

Richard Foliot archdeacon of Colchester was out of the country *c.* 1167-9, and may not have become archdeacon long before his departure; if the reading 'Hugone elemosinario' is correct, however, this charter may be very early in Gilbert's episcopate.

Gilbertus Dei gratia Londoniensis episcopus dilectis sibi in Domino archidiaconis, decanis et omnibus qui in episcopatu Lundon(iensi) consistunt ecclesiarum prelatis, salutem, gratiam et benedictionem. Suscepti nos cura commonet et compellit officii ut beneficia que ecclesiis et
5 ecclesiasticis ⟨Sa, fo. 38 v⟩ personis in nostra dyocesi religiosa contulit fidelium deuotio aut collatura est in posterum, in specialem Dei et sancte ecclesie protectionem suscipere, eisque pro quorum gubernatione et sustentatione pie concessa sunt perpetua stabilitate comunire debeamus. Proinde ecclesias de Waledena, de Chishella, de Haidena, de Waltham, de Estra, de Eieneffeld', de Eadelmetona, de
10 Mimmes, de Norhala, de Torleia, de Edelhestuna, cum capellis, terris et decimis et aliis quibuscumque pertinentiis que ad eas uel in presenti pertinent uel in futuro canonice pertinebunt, quas quidem monasterio sancti Iacobi de Waledena et monachis ibidem Deo seruientibus earundem fundatores et aduocati ecclesiarum, sicut ex autenticis eorum scriptis cognouimus, in perpetuam destinarunt ele-
15 mosinam, ipsis episcopali concedimus et confirmamus autoritate. Quod quia in

**438** 13 nemo rate *MS*    14 presentis scripti *MS*    17 Falet' *MS*
**439** BM Harl. MS 3697, fos. 38 (Sa) and 39 (Sb); cf. also no. 440 (Sc). Sb adds Monken Hadleigh to the list of churches: see n. 1.
9 et de Haydena Sb    9 Hienefeld' Sb; Enefeld Sc    9 Hedelmetona Sb; Edelmetona Sc
10 Mymmes / Thorleia Sc    10 Eedelhestuna Sb, *and adds* de Hadlega; Eedelestuna Sc (*for additions, see no. 440*)    11 futura Sa    15 ipsis] Sc *adds* monachis

[1] One text adds Monken Hadleigh, whose hermitage was among the founder's gifts (*Cal. Charter Rolls*, I, 337); but there is no other evidence of a church so early. For the other places, cf. *VN*, pp. 357-62; Morant, II, 89, 548, 602, 607-8; *VCH Middlesex*, I, 19; *VCH Herts*. III, 323.

dubium nolumus aut in irritum de cetero posse reuocari, uniuersitati uestre presenti scripto id notificare nostrique testimonio sigilli corroborare curauimus. Hiis testibus: Ricardo archidiacono Colocestr(ie), magistro Waltero de Hardeperier, Waltero Map, Ricardo de Saresbir(ia), Roberto *de Clifford', Hugone, Lodowico clericis episcopi, Philippo decano de Wyches, Roberto de Audeberia, Gilleberto de 20 Metcing', Mauricio de Sabricteswrd, Willelmo capellano de Storteford, Godardo capellano de Waledena.

## 440

[c. 1181–3] Reissue of no. 439, adding the churches of Ainsworth (now Chartwell in Arkesden),[1] Arkesden, Lindsell and Elsenham (Essex).

For Ainsworth see no. 444, for Arkesden no. 446, Lindsell, no. 445, Elsenham, no. 442. The witnesses of no. 446 are very similar, and the charters may be contemporary.

*Identical with no. 439 (q.v. for variants) save for the addition of...* de Eineswrda, de Aarkesdena, de Lindesele, de Elsenham... *and the witness list:* Hiis testibus: Radulfo decano ecclesie sancti Pauli, Gilberto archidiacono Middelsex', Radulfo archidiacono Colec(estrie), Roberto archidiacono Essex(ie), magistro Ricardo de Stort(efordia) magistro scolarum, Roberto de Clifford, Rogero de Wigorn(ia), 5 Ricardo de Saresbir(ia), Radulfo de Chilthon(a), Ricardo Banastr(e), Radulfo cantore, Iohanne Witeng, Waltero elemosinario, Michaele de Burnes, Reginaldo camerario, et multis aliis.

## 441

[1180–3] Grant of free possession to Saffron Walden priory after the death of the present vicars, and to increase the pensions, of their appropriated churches of Great Chishall, Heydon, High Easter, Elsenham (Essex), South Mimms (Middlesex), Thorley (Herts), Northolt (Middlesex) and the chapel of Ainsworth in Arkesden (Essex).

The significance of 'libere possidendas' is not clear, but presumably the monks thought that their vicars had excessively good terms, and there may well have been some disputes between the monks and new vicars on their appointment.

Gilbertus Dei gratia Lundoniensis episcopus omnibus sancte matris ecclesie filiis ad quos hee litere peruenerint, salutem in Domino.

Religiosorum non inmerito sunt promouenda uota uirorum, presertim cum necessitas ipsorum postulationis existit occasio, et ut exaudiri debeant suadet pia consona rationi deuotio. Inde est quod dilectorum filiorum nostrorum prioris et 5 fratrum ecclesie sancti Iacobi de Waled(ena) necessitatem considerantes, et in

**439** 18 testibus] *For Sc's witness list, see no.* 440  19 *de om.* Sa  19 Hugone] Sb *adds* elemosinario  19 Ludowico Sb  20 de Wyches *om.* Sb  20 Gilberto Sa
**440** BM Harl. MS 3697, fo. 39 (*note:* Exhibitum est apud Stort'. j.).
**441** BM Harl. MS 3697, fo. 38.

[1] *PN Essex*, p. 517.

ecclesiis quibusdam de nostra dyocesi precipuam portionem sustentationis sue deputatam esse attendentes, piis misericordie stimulis agitati et eorundem commoti querimoniis et precibus, ecclesias de Chishell', et de Haidena, de Estra, de Elsenham,
10 de Mimmes, de Torleia, de Norhale, et capellam de Eineswrda, cum terris et decimis et omnibus suis pertinentiis in quibus personatum habere dinoscuntur, post uicariorum qui easdem possident decessum ipsis libere possidendas concessimus, et de augenda pensione in quantum pot⟨u⟩erint, saluis nobis et successoribus nostris et officialibus debitis de eisdem ecclesiis consuetudinibus, liberam sibi facultatem in-
15 dulsimus. Quod quia firmum et inconuulsum manere uolumus pagine presentis id inscriptione et sigilli nostri appositione communiuimus. Testibus: Radulfo archi-diacono Colec⟨estrie⟩, Rogero de Wygorn⟨ia⟩, Ricardo de Saresbir⟨ia⟩, Radulfo de Chilton⟨a⟩, Ricardo Banastr', Radulfo cantore, Iohanne Wyteng, Waltero ele-mosinario, Reginaldo camerario, Rogero hostiario, et aliis.

### 442

[1174–80] Grant in alms to Saffron Walden priory of the church of Elsenham, on the presentation of Beatrice de Say and petition of William de Mandeville earl of Essex (1166–89).

Gilbertus Dei gratia Londoniensis episcopus R⟨icardo⟩ archidiacono Colecestrie et omnium ecclesiarum personis que per archidiaconatum Colecestrie constitute sunt, salutem, gratiam et benedictionem.

Nouerit uniuersitas uestra nos presentatione Beatricis de Sai necnon consensu et
5 petitione dilecti filii nostri Willelmi de Mandeuilla comitis Essexie, dedisse et concessisse priori et conuentui de Waledena ecclesiam de Elsenham cum omnibus ad eam pertinentibus in elemosinam libere habendam, quiete tenendam, perpetuo possidendam. Quod quia ratum et inconuulsum manere uolumus, presentis pagine inscriptione, necnon et sigilli nostri appositione corroborare pariter et confirmare
10 curauimus. Hiis testibus: Hugone decano sancti Pauli, Ricardo archidiacono Colocest⟨rie⟩, Henrico thesaurario, magistro Ricardo de Storteford', Gileberto Foliot, Iohanne de Marenni sancti Pauli canonicis, Rogero filio Mauritii, magistro Radulfo de Altaripa, Ricardo de Sarebir⟨ia⟩, Radulfo de Chilton⟨a⟩, Milone Folet, Ricardo Agulun, Galfrido persona ecclesie de Henham, Martino persona ecclesie de
15 Lutlebir⟨ia⟩, Reginaldo camerario, Gileberto hostiario, et aliis quampluribus.

**441** 16 communuimus (?) MS
**442** BM Harl. MS 3697, fo. 38 v.
2 omnium] *sic? for* omnibus

**443**

[*c.* 1174–80] Confirmation of the grant by Prior Reginald[1] and the convent of Saffron Walden to John, clerk, of Elsenham, for life (evidently as vicar), of the church of Elsenham for an annual pension of ten shillings.

Presumably later than no. 442.

Gilbertus Dei gracia Londoniensis episcopus Ricardo archidiacono Colocestr(ie) et omnibus ecclesiarum que in eodem archidiaconatu consistunt personis, salutem, gratiam et benedictionem.

Vniuersitati uestre presenti scripto notificamus nos inspecta carta dilecti filii nostri Reginaldi prioris de Walden et totius ecclesie sue conuentus, qua se Iohanni 5 clerico de Elsenham ecclesiam ipsius uille toto uite sue tempore, annua decem solidorum pensione ecclesie sue de Walden soluenda tenendam, testificantur ⟨(?) concessisse⟩, concessionem suam ratam habere. Et ne in posterum aliqua possit calliditate debilitari, ipsam tam pagine presentis inscriptione quam sigilli nostri appositione ea qua fungimur autoritate episcopali confirmamus. Hiis testibus: 10 magistro Radulpho de Altaripa, Rogero filio Mauritii, Ricardo de Saresbir(ia), Radulfo de Chiltona, Waltero elemosinario clericis episcopi, Waltero decano de Claueryng, Thoma decano de Sanford, Gaufrido clerico de Hennham, Nicholao de Hautuilla persona ecclesie de Thakeleie.

**444**

[*c.* 1170–80] Appropriation to Saffron Walden priory of the chapel of Ainsworth in Arkesden, on the presentation of William Guet.

Gilbertus Dei gratia Lundoniensis episcopus dilecto filio Ricardo archidiacono Colec(estrie) ⟨et⟩ omnibus ecclesiarum personis per archidiaconatum Colec(estrie) constitutis, salutem, gratiam et benedictionem.

Nouerit uniuersitas uestra nos presentatione Willelmi Guet dilectis filiis nostris priori et fratribus de Waledena capellam de Eineswrda cum omnibus ad eam 5

**443** BM Harl. MS 3697, fo. 45.
10 confirmare *MS* (*for text cf. no. 444; but possibly* confirmare curauimus)
**444** BM Harl. MS 3697, fo. 38 v (*note*: dupplic'). William Guet's grant is on fo. 132.
2 ⟨et⟩ *om. MS*

[1] Master Reginald, formerly clerk ('vice-chancellor') to King Stephen, monk, prior and abbot of Reading (see Biog. Index), second prior and first abbot of Saffron Walden: prior, *c.* Jan. 1166–90, first abbot from 1 August 1190–1203/4, died 5 Feb. (*Chron. Walden*, XLV, 149, 150–1; XLVI, 164–5, 220). There are various difficulties in these dates. Reginald's predecessor died 12 Dec. 1164; there was a vacancy of 1 year, 1 month and 2 days. If correct, this makes Reginald succeed about 14 Jan. 1166; he was prior 26 years, 6 months and a few days and abbot 9 years, 6 months and a few days, which would make him become abbot July–Aug. 1192 and die Jan.–Feb. 1202. But the statement that he became abbot in August 1190 is confirmed by the day of the week—it was a Wednesday; and the Pope addressed him as abbot on 6 Jan. 1191 (*PUE*, I, no. 268, cf. 277). It seems, therefore, that the dates are more reliable than the regnal periods in the chronicle). His obit is given as 3 Feb. in BM Cotton Vesp. E. v, fo. 12.

pertinentibus concessisse, ipsosque in eadem capella debita cum solempnitate personas constituisse. Quod quia in dubium uel in irritum uenire nolumus, idipsum presenti scripto et sigilli nostri appositione ea qua fungimur autoritate episcopali confirmamus. Testibus: Ricardo archidiacono Colec(estrie), Roberto archidiacono
10 Essex', magistro Iohanne de Tillebir(ia), magistro Roberto de Stort(eford), Henrico thesaurario, Rogero filio Mauritii, Ludowico, Radulfo de Chiltona, Waltero elemosinario, et multis aliis.

### 445

[c. 1179–80] Appropriation to Prior R(eginald) and Saffron Walden priory of the church of Lindsell, on the presentation of Ralph Pirot, after the resignation of Master Henry Pirot.

This was confirmed, with a specific reference to the bishop of London's charter, on 16 April 1180 by the Pope (PUE, I, no. 179). Cf. Morant, II, 446; HKF, III, 155 ff. (for the Pirots).

Gilbertus Dei gratia Lundoniensis episcopus uniuersis ecclesiarum prelatis per episcopatum Lond(oniensem) constitutis, salutem, gratiam et benedictionem.
Vniuersitati uestre presenti scripto notificamus magistrum Henricum Pirot in presentia nostra constitutum iuri quod in ecclesia de Lindesele ⟨habuerat⟩ sub multorum
5 testimonio renuntiasse, ipsamque ecclesiam in manus nostras uoluntate spontanea refutasse. Nos uero petitione et presentatione nobilis uiri Radulfi Pirot, quem ius patronatus in iamdicta ecclesia contingere dinoscitur, ipsam ecclesiam monasterio beati Iacobi de Waledena et R(eginaldo) priori et conuentui eiusdem loci, magistro Henrico presente et ad id assensum prebente, concessimus et R(eginaldum) priorem
10 ea qua fungimur autoritate episcopali personam iamdicte ecclesie debita cum solemnitate, saluo iure nobis et successoribus et officialibus nostris debito, constituimus. Quod ne de cetero in dubium uel in irritum reuocetur, presenti id scripto et sigilli nostri appositione confirmare curauimus. Hiis testibus: Ricardo archidiacono Colec(estrie), magistro Radulpho de Altaripa magistro scolarum Lun-
15 don(ie), Rogero de Wigorn(ia), Ricardo de Saresbir(ia), Ricardo Banastr(e), Waltero elemosinario, Radulfo cantore, Iohanne Witeng, Philippo de Wigorn(ia), Reginaldo Folet, et multis aliis.

### 446

[c. 1181–3] Appropriation to Prior R(eginald) and Saffron Walden priory of the church of Arkesden, on the presentation of William son of Arnulf and Eudo of Arkesden, on condition of providing a suitable chaplain to serve it.

Gilbertus Dei gracia Lundoniensis episcopus omnibus sancte matris ecclesie filiis ad quos presentes litcre peruenerint, salutem in Domino.
Piam deuotionem dilectorum filiorum nostrorum Willelmi filii Ernulphi et

444 10 Roberto sic
445 BM Harl. MS 3697, fo. 39.
446 BM Harl. MS 3697, fo. 38v (Note: Exh' arch'.v.—Supplic'.). Eudo's charter is on fo. 132v, and a confirmation of no. 446 by Archbishop Richard on fo. 42.

Eudonis de Arkesdena ad debitum uolentes effectum perducere, ecclesiam de
Arkysden(a) cum omnibus ad eam pertinentibus, ipsorum petitione et presentatione, 5
monasterio sancti Iacobi de Waledena et monachis ibidem Domino dignum
prebentibus obsequium diuine pietatis intuitu concessimus, et karissimum nobis in
Christo filium R(eginaldum) ipsorum priorem nomine uniuersitatis ad personatum
prefate ecclesie recipimus, statuentes ut eandem ecclesiam de cetero libere teneant
et in pace possideant, ita quidem quod per ydoneum capellanum memorate 10
ecclesie de Arkesden' digne deseruiant, et tam nobis quam substituendis episcopis et
officialibus nostris omnibus de debitis nobis de eadem ecclesia consuetudinibus sine
aliqua contradictione respondeant. Quod quia uolumus in perpetua retineri
memoria, presentis id inscriptione pagine uniuersitati uestre notum facimus et
sigilli nostri pariter appositione confirmamus. Hiis testibus: Radulfo de Diceto 15
decano ecclesie sancti Pauli, Ricardo de Stort(eford) magistro scolarum, magistro
Hugone, Rogero de Wigorn(ia) canonicis sancti Pauli, Ricardo de Saresbir(ia),
Radulfo de ⟨? Chiltona⟩, Radulfo cantore, Waltero elemosinario, Ricardo
Banastr(e), Iohanne Vityng clericis, Reginaldo camerario, Michaele de Turneham,
et multis aliis.                                                                                      20

## 447

[1163–87] Grant of an indulgence in support of the building appeal for Saffron Walden
priory.

Gilebertus Dei gratia Lundoniensis episcopus dilectis sibi in Domino uniuersitati
eiusdem ecclesie parochianis et filiis, salutem, gratiam et benedictionem.

   Ad nostri curam spectat officii ut uniuersitatem uestram crebro commoneamus
et diligenter exhortemur in Domino, ut ipsum pre oculis habentes et que ⟨et⟩
quanta pro uobis pertulerit ad memoriam reuocantes, personas religiosas iugem illi 5
famulatum exhibentes et loca sanctis eius misteriis dedicata uenerantes, ipsum in
seruis suis honoretis, et ipsi domicilia in terris construendo uel constructa iam
uestris sumptibus sustentando, uobis in celestibus habitacula in eternum permansura
preparetis. Ecclesia siquidem de Waledena que ibidem in memoriam beati Iacobi
solicita ⟨cura (?)⟩ monachorum ibi Deo seruientium ut plantatio nouella consurgit, 10
ope Christi fidelium et amicorum beati Iacobi plurimum indiget ut inceptum opus
ad honorem Dei et sancti sui apostoli ipsorum auxilio fine tandem possit optato
consummari. Omnibus itaque qui ad eiusdem monasterii constructionem ob Dei et
apostoli sui reuerentiam aliquid caritatiue contulerint, de Dei confisi misericordia,
si in septem uel annorum amplius penitentia sunt, uiginti quinque dies, hiis uero qui 15
minus onerati sunt, dies decem relaxamus, et orationum ecclesie nostre participes
constituimus. Valete.

**446** 4–5 ad. . .Arkysden(a) *added in margin*     18 ⟨? Chiltona⟩ *A space left in MS*
**447** BM Harl. MS 3697, fo. 38.     4 exhortamur *MS*

**448**

[? 1163–*c.* 1180] Grant of an indulgence to those contributing to the repair of the church of St Ivo (presumably St Ives, Hunts).

Que donantur Domino karissimi donanti nequa[quam des]unt, sed iuxta uocem Domini ei a quo donata sunt amplissime remuneranda conseruantur, 'mensuram bonam et confertam et coagitat[am] et supereffluentem conferent in sinum uestrum'.[1] Nos itaque de salutis uestre profectu sollic[iti ca]ritatem uestram commonemus
5 in Domino, quatinus [ad repar]ationem ecclesie beati Yuonis, et ad ref[icien-dum] eiusdem uille pontem et calcedam, ubi dis[iunctus] admodum est com-meantium transsitus, de [facul]tatibus uestris aliquod auxilium conferatis et D[eum in] sanctis suis honorando diuinam uobis g[ratiam] et peccatorum ueniam acquiratis. Omnibus uero [qui ad pre]taxatum opus aliquid ob Deum hortat[i] contulerint, de
10 Domini confisi misericordia de in[iuncta] sibi penitentia decem dies relaxa[mus, et] bonorum omnium que in nostra fiunt ecclesia [et orati]onum participes constitui-mus. Valete.

**449**

[1163–*c.* 1180] Confirmation to St Neots priory (Hunts, Benedictine, dep. of Bec) of the grant by Walter son of Robert[2] of the advowsons of Wimbish (Essex) and St Andrew (Holborn), London (see *VN*, p. 360).

G(ilebertus) Dei gratia Lundoniensis episcopus dilectis sibi in Domino archidiaconis, decanis et omnibus ecclesiarum personis per episcopatum Lundon(iensem) con-stitutis, salutem, gratiam et benedictionem.

Que religiosis locis diuine contemplationis intuitu collata sunt, episcopali iustum
5 est auctoritate firmari, ne ualeant in posterum rerum facili mobilitate conuelli. Inde est quod auctenticum instrumentum illustris uiri Walteri filii Roberti sequentes, quo ecclesie sancti Neoti et monachis ibi Deo seruientibus ius dominii et aduoca-tionis quod habuerat in ecclesia de ⟨fo. 197⟩ Wimbis et in ecclesia sancti Andree infra muros Lund(onie) confirmat, nos quoque id ipsum eisdem concedimus, et ut
10 sibi de cetero firmum et inconuulsum permaneat, episcopali eis auctoritate et sigilli nostri attestatione corroboramus. Valete.

**448** G, no. 314; B, fo. 197 (*the margin is cut away, and the end of most of the lines lost*).
7 auxlium B
**449** G, no. 233; B, fo. 196v.
7 dñinii B

---

[1] Luc. vi. 38.        [2] See no. 385.

**450**

[1163–74] Confirmation of the agreement between Abbot A(bel) and the convent of St Osyth (Essex, Augustinian) and G(odfrey) treasurer of St Paul's on the church of Southminster (Essex).[1]

Although there is no heading, this was clearly issued by a bishop of London, and since Godfrey was treasurer from *c.* 1162–3 until *c.* 1170–4 there is no doubt that it is Gilbert's.

A charter of Henry III refers to the confirmation by Gilbert of an agreement between the chapter of St Paul's and St Osyth on Southminster 'et de Merlanda et Alesthorne...in cartis predicti Gilberti'.[2]

Que ad honorem Dei et utilitatem sancte geruntur ecclesie iustum est firma con-sistere, et suis radicibus inconuulsa permanere. Inde est quod conuentionem inter A(bel) abbatem sancte Osythe et eiusdem ecclesie conuentum et G(odefridum) Lundoniensis ecclesie tesaurarium super ecclesia de Simin' habitam, nos quia Deo placitam et ecclesie sancte comodam attendimus, sicut cirographo inter eos con- 5 scripto et sigillis eorum utrimque firmato concepta est approbamus, et concessa nobis a Deo auctoritate roboratam, ut in posterum inconuulsa permaneat, sigilli nostri attestatione firmamus.

**451**

[*c.* 1181–7] Confirmation of the agreement between the abbey of Saint-Valéry-sur-Somme and Robert de *Baut'* and Beatrice his wife and his heirs about the mill-pool at Birchanger (Essex) and the road leading to the mill and the meadow beside the pool.

G(ilebertus) Dei gratia Lundoniensis episcopus omnibus hominibus suis Francis et Anglis, salutem, gratiam et benedictionem.

Ad uniuersitatis uestre uolumus deuenire notitiam quod nos conuentionem inter ecclesiam sancti Walerici et Robertum de Baut' et heredes suos ac Beatricem uxorem eius factam, de stagno uidelicet molendini de Birichangr' et de uia que 5 ducit ad ipsum molendinum per feudum prefati Roberti, necnon et de pratulo quodam quod nominato stagno adiacet, sicut scriptum inter eos factum super hoc plene testatur, concedimus, eamque ratam habentes ipsam ne de cetero queat infirmari, pagina presenti et nostri pariter appositione sigilli confirmamus. His testibus: Gilleb(ertus) Middelsex(e), Radulfo Colecestr(ie) archidiaconis, Ricardo 10 de Storteford' magistro scolarum Lund(onie), Radulfo de Chilton(a), Gilleb(erto) Ban(astre) canonicis, Willelmo Foliot senescallo, Reginaldo camerario, Reginaldo Foliot, Willelmo Morin, et aliis multis.

450 G, no. 312; B, fo. 197.
451 *Original:* Oxford, New College, Birchanger Deeds, no. 49. Fragment of seal on tag. *Endorsed:* G. episcopus London' de composicione de Birchangre (fourteenth century).

---

[1] Southminster was appropriated to the treasurership in 1162–3; though the form 'Simin'' seems corrupt, the identification is almost certain (cf. Gibbs, nos. 47, 192–3, 231; *Monasticon*, VI, 310). Abel was prior of St Osyth until *c.* 1160, when it was raised into an abbey; he was abbot from *c.* 1160 until his death in 1184 (*JS Epp.* I, 120 n.; his predecessor, Fulk, occurs in 1127, and probably in 1139–40, Saltman, p. 385).

[2] *Monasticon*, VI, 310. Either the present charter is a fragment, or one or more are lost.

## 452

[1173–c. 1180] Grant of an indulgence in support of the building appeal of the Hospital of St Thomas of Canterbury, Southwark.

Presumably later than the canonization of St Thomas in 1173, but not much later, since it occurs (twice) in manuscript B. It is the earliest document known for St Thomas's.

Gilebertus Dei gratia Lundoniensis episcopus dilectis sibi in Domino uniuersis sancte Lund(oniensis) ecclesie parrochianis et filiis, salutem, gratiam et benedictionem.

Particeps mercedis efficitur quicumque se bonorum operum adiutorem exhibet,
5 nec irremuneratum relinquitur, quod in pietatis usus fuerit intuitu pauperum erogatum, dicente Domino 'quod uni ex minimis meis fecistis michi fecistis'.[1] Inde est quod uniuersitatem uestram monemus attentius et rogamus, et in peccatorum uestrorum remissionem iniungimus, quatinus ad construendum xenodochium quod in honore Dei et beati Thome martiris Lundon(ie) apud Sudwerc' ad pauperum et
10 infirmorum susceptionem pariter et sustentationem de nouo est inchoatum, amore Dei et pietatis intuitu manum auxilii misericorditer porrigatis, et ad pauperum refectionem pariter et sustentationem de concessis uobis a Domino facultatibus impertientes, Deum ob collatam sibi in menbris suis gratiam remuneratorem et uite uobis eterne largitorem habeatis, et orationum et beneficiorum que ⟨B1, fo. 151⟩
15 in iamdicto fient xenodochio participes uos constituatis. Omnibus uero qui ad predictum pietatis opus manum auxilii porrexerint, et eiusdem loci pauperibus uel in modico subuenerint, de Domini confisi misericordia uiginti dies relaxamus de iniuncta sibi penitentia et orationum et beneficiorum que in nostra fient ecclesia eos participes esse concedimus.

## 453

[1163–c. 1180] Settlement, as papal judge delegate, of the case between Stoke-by-Clare priory (Suffolk, Benedictine, dep. of Bec) and Benedict of Reepham, William of Haveringland, Gervase of Norwich, clerks, and Roger de Gisnai on the church of St Clement, Norwich, and certain tithes. The priory abandoned its claim to the church in exchange for two-thirds of the tithes of Roger's domain in *Witewelle*, Haveringland[2] (Norfolk) and Norwich, which the clerks are to hold of the monks for a pension of twenty shillings per annum. After the departure of the second successor (i.e. the death of the third tenant) the tithes are not to be alienated from the monastery by Roger or anyone else.

Gilbertus Dei gracia Lundoniensis episcopus omnibus sancte matris ecclesie filiis ad quos hee litere peruenerint nostre, salutem in Domino.

452 G, no. 225; *MB Epp.* 803; B, fos. 150v (B1) *and* 200 (B2) (*marked* 'uacat') (*spelling as* B1).
1–3 Dilebertus B1; B2 *omits* Gilebertus…benedictionem     4 exhibet adiutorem B2
9 Sutwerc B2     10 inchoatum est B2     14 benefactorum B1     16 uel *om.* B2     17–18 uiginti de iniuncta sibi penitentia dies relaxamus B2; B1 *omits* uiginti
453 BM Cotton MS Appendix xxi, fo. 58v (Cart. Stoke-by-Clare).

---

[1] Matt. xxv. 40.     [2] Cf. *VN*, p. 369.

Nouerit uniuersitas uestra causam que uertebatur inter monachos de Stokes et Benedictum de Refham et Willelmum de Haueringeland' et Geru(asium) de Norwic' clericos et Rogerum de Gisnai super ecclesia sancti Clementis in Norwic' 5 et quibusdam decimis, nobis a summo pontifice delegatam, partium in hoc concurrente assensu hoc tandem fine post plurimas auditas hinc inde allegationes in nostra presentia conqui(e)uisse. Monachi siquidem de Stok' ab actione quam super ecclesia sancti Clementis intendebant resedentes, penitus se ultra in ipsa nichil uendicaturos firmiter promiserunt. Prefatus uero Rogerus duas partes decimarum 10 totius dominii sui quod habuit in Witewelle et in Haueringelonde et in Norwic', assensu et uoluntate predictorum clericorum, tamquam ad ecclesiam de Stokes pertinentes, in manus nostras resignauit, et nos ipsa apostolica auctoritate memoratis monachis restituimus. Quas ipsi monachi iam dictis clericis de eis tenendas sub annua uiginti solidorum pensione coram nobis concesserunt, ita quidem quod 15 liberum erit unicuique prescriptorum clericorum conpetentem sibi portionem sepe dictarum decimarum alii cui uoluerit ecclesiastice persone, monachis tamen et prefato milite in hoc prebentibus assensum, assignare, sub ea qua et ipse tenebat pensione tota uita sua tenendam. Post secundi uero successoris discessum nec prefato militi nec cuilibet alii prescriptas decimas alias quam ad monasterium de Stokes transferre, 20 uel ab ipso quolibet modo alienare licebit. Hanc autem conuentionem fidei in hoc interueniente (fo. 59) religione, se fideliter obseruaturam pars utraque promisit. Et nos ne de cetero possit in dubium uel in irritum reuocari presentis eam pagine inscriptione confirmauimus, et nostri pariter appositione sigilli roborauimus. Hiis testibus: Ricardo archidiacono Colcestrie, magistro Hugone de Lund(onia), et aliis. 25

## 454

[1163–80] Confirmation to Stoke-by-Clare priory of the church of Steeple Bumpstead (Essex) and appropriation of the church to the priory (cf. *VN*, p. 355).

Gilbertus Dei gratia Londoniensis episcopus archidiaconis, decanis, et ecclesiarum que in eodem episcopatu constitute sunt personis omnibus, salutem, gratiam et benedictionem.

Vniuersitati uestre presenti scripto notificamus nos instrumenta prioris et monachorum de Stok' inspexisse, que ecclesiam de Bumestede monasterio de Stok' ab eiusdem ecclesie aduocatis donatam et predecessorum nostrorum auctori- 5 tate concessam fuisse commemorant et testantur. Vnde quia iustum est ut suis stet antiquitas inconuulsa radicibus, et que a predecessoribus nostris recte (fo. 57) statuta sunt iustum est ut obseruemus, uobis in commune notum facimus nos eandem donationem ratam habuisse, ipsamque ut predicto monasterio firma permaneat pagine presentis inscriptione et sigilli nostri attestatione corroborasse. 10 Concedimus itaque quod predictus prior de Stokes et fratres in eodem monasterio deuotionis sue Domino prestantes obsequium, memoratam ecclesiam de Bunstede

---

**453** 7 post] postquam *MS*   9 resedentes] *sic, for* recedentes   18 prebente assensu *MS*
24 nostrum *MS*
**454** BM Cotton MS Appendix xxi, fo. 56v.

cum omnibus ad eam pertinentibus possideant, et obuentiones eius in usus proprios
15 honeste conuertant, sic quidem ut sacerdos qui in eadem ministrabit de ipsa necessaria sibi iusta archidiaconi nostri taxatione percipiat, et ecclesia ipsa ecclesie beati
Pauli et eius officialibus canonicam in omnibus obedientiam semper exhibeat. Huius
nostre concessionis testes hii sunt: Radulfus de Dici, et Ricardus Fol(iot) archi-
d(iaconi) Lundon(ienses), et multi alii.

## 455

[1163–87] Confirmation to Stoke-by-Clare priory of the grant by Geoffrey son of Baldwin
of two-thirds of his domain tithes in Little Sampford (Essex)[1] and Harefield (Middlesex).

Probably before no. 456 (1173–80).

Gilbertus Dei gracia Londoniensis episcopus dilectis in Domino filiis archidiaconis,
decanis, et omnibus ecclesiarum personis per episcopatum Londonie constitutis,
salutem, gratiam et benedictionem.

Ad uniuersitatis uestre notitiam peruenire uolumus nos cartam Galfridi filii
5 Baldewini inspexisse, ex cuius tenore manifeste perpendimus ipsum concessisse et
confirmasse dilectis filiis nostris monachis de Stokes duas partes decimationum
totius dominii sui, de terris et de boscis et de omnibus aliis rebus unde decima debet
dari, tam minutarum quam maiorum, de Samford et de Herrefeld in liberam et
puram elemosinam perpetuo possidendas. Nos autem eandem concessionem, sicut
10 memoratis monachis a predicto G(alfrido) facta est, ratam habentes, gratam et
acceptam, supramemoratas decimas eisdem habendas et iure perpetuo possidendas,
auctoritate qua presidemus episcopali concedimus et presentis scripti patrocinio
commun⟨i⟩u⟨i⟩mus. Hiis testibus: Radulfo archidiacono, Dauid capellano, et
aliis.

## 456

[1173–80] Appropriation to Stoke-by-Clare priory of Thaxted church (Essex) on the
presentation of Earl Richard de Clare (earl of Hertford), and general confirmation of the
churches of Great Bardfield, Ashen, Little Yeldham, Pebmarsh, Toppesfield, Steeple
Bumpstead, Foxearth and Stambourne (Essex), of two-thirds of the tithes of Geoffrey son
of Baldwin in Little Sampford (Essex) and Harefield (Middlesex: cf. no. 455), of Lambert
and of Robert son of Richard in Steeple Bumpstead, of Richard son of Simon in Hempstead (Essex), of Fulk de Blandac in Stambourne, of Gilbert Willde, Robert Buzcal and
Margaret in Toppesfield, of half the tithes of Solomon in Tilbury-iuxta-Clare, of two-thirds
of the tithes of Richard de Nazanda in Wickham (? Bishops), the tithe of Walter de Langetot
in Belchamp Otten (next Ashen), of Hilger in Ashen, of two-thirds of the tithes of Hamo
*Peccatus* in Gestingthorpe, of the tithe of Adam son of Warin in Binsley (lost village in

455 BM Cotton MS Appendix xxi, fo. 56.
9 elemosimam *MS*    10 memorati *MS*
456 BM Cotton MS Appendix xxi, fo. 57.

---

[1] Cf. *Taxatio*, p. 22b.

Bulmer: *PN Essex*, p. 418), of two-thirds of the tithes of William son of Ralph in Finching-field, of Peter, William and William Hurand in Halstead, of Walter son of Humphrey in *Barewe* (? Barrow Hall in Little Wakering: *PN Essex*, p. 204), of Roger of St German in Naylinghurst Farm (in Braintree; *PN Essex*, p. 417), of Reginald de Codeham in *Muchelheia*, of Peter in Belchamp (? Otten), of Roger in Pentlow (Essex), and of various holdings: in Birdbrook by grant of Geoffrey de Blauenni, in (? Steeple) Bumpstead of Gilbert de Baillol and Walter son of Humphrey, in Hempstead of Robert de Watteville, Pitley Farm (in Great Bardfield: *PN Essex*, p. 505) of Gilbert de Dammartin, in Bardfield of Ailward the forester, Godfrey the butler and Gilbert son of Robert, in Stambourne of Fulk de Blandac and Baldwin son of Serlo, in Birdbrook of Hamo *Peccatus* (Peche), in *Vuittine* (?) of Solomon, in Henny of Adam son of Warin, in Stambourne of Aubrey (Albereda), in Ridge-well of the wife of Ralph son of Sired, in Ashen of Ilger, of a meadow by the monks' garden of William de Pirenho, and of a meadow and the tithe of hay of William de Musterol in Claret Hall (in Ashen: *PN Essex*, p. 407).

Earl Richard succeeded in 1173; his charter is on fos. 26v–27. For the place-names, cf. *VN*, pp. 353–4; *Valor*, III, 469; *Taxatio*, p. 18b; Morant, II, 274, 334, 344, 355, 521, 525, 528.

Gilbertus Dei gratia Lundoniensis episcopus dilectis sibi in Domino archidiaconis, decanis, et omnibus ecclesiarum prelatis per episcopatum Lundoniarum constitutis, salutem, gratiam et benedictionem.

Que inspirante Domino ecclesie Dei largitione fidelium ob animarum suarum salutem in locis iurisdictioni nostre suppositis pia deuotione conferuntur, hec con- 5 cedere et ea que nobis a Domino concessa est auctoritate imperiosa caritatis lege confirmare constrin⟨fo. 57v⟩gimur. Eapropter uniuersitati uestre mandamus et presenti scripto notificamus, nos presentatione dilecti filii nostri uiri nobilis Ricardi comitis de Clara priori et fratribus de Stokes ecclesiam de Taxtede cum omnibus ad eam pertinentibus concessisse, nosque ipsos in eadem ecclesia debita cum solempni- 10 tate personas constituisse. Ecclesias etiam et beneficia ecclesiastica que in eos largitione fidelium collocata fuisse et ab hiis tempore predecessorum nostrorum inconcusse possessa fuisse cognouimus, eis concessimus; inter que suis hec duximus exprimenda uocabulis: ecclesiam de Berdefeld cum omnibus pertinentiis suis, ecclesiam de Essa cum omnibus pertinentiis suis, ecclesiam de Geldam cum omnibus 15 pertinentiis ⟨suis⟩, ecclesiam de Pebenersc cum omnibus pertinentiis suis, ecclesiam de Topesfeldia cum omnibus pertinentiis suis, ecclesiam de Bumstede cum omnibus pertinentiis suis, ecclesiam de Foxherde cum omnibus pertinentiis suis, ecclesiam de Stamburna cum omnibus pertinentiis suis; duas etiam partes decimationis Galfridi filii Baldewini in Samfordia, duas etiam partes decimationis eiusdem Ga⟨l⟩fridi 20 filii Baldewini in Herrefeldia, duas etiam partes decimationis Lamberti in Bunstede, et duas partes decimationis Roberti filii Ricardi in eadem uilla, et duas partes decimationis Ricardi filii Symonis in Hamstede, et duas partes decimationis Ful-conis de Blandac in Stamburnia, et duas partes decimationis Gilberti Willde in Topesfeldia, et duas partes decimationis Roberti Buzcal in eadem uilla, et duas partes 25 decimationis Margarete in eadem uilla, et dimidiam decimationis Salomonis in Tillebiri, et duas partes decimationis Ricardi de Nazanda in Wicham, et decimam Walteri de Langatot in Bello campo, et totam decimam Hilgeri in Essa, et duas

partes decimationis Hamonis Peccati in Gestingetorp, et totam decimam dominii
30 Ade filii Warini in Bunsleia(?), et duas partes decimationis Willelmi filii Radulfi in
Finchingefeld, et duas partes decimationis Petri in Halstede, et duas partes decimationis Willelmi in eadem uilla, et duas partes decimationis Willelmi Hurand in
eadem uilla, et duas partes decimationis Walteri filii Humfr(idi) in Barewe, et duas
partes decimationis Rogeri de sancto Germano in Neilingeherst, et duas partes
35 decimationis Rainaldi de Codeham in Muchelheia, et duas partes decimationis
Petri ⟨fo. 58⟩ in Belcham, et duas partes decimationis terre Rogeri in Pentelawe,
terram etiam et pratum ex dono Galfridi de Blauenni in Bridebroc, terram etiam ex
dono Gilberti de Baillol in Bunstede, terram etiam ex dono Walteri filii Humfr(idi)
in eadem uilla, terram etiam ex dono Roberti de Wateuilla in Hamstede, et terram
40 et mansuram de Piteleiheg' cum pertinentiis suis ex dono Gilberti de Dammartin, et
terram ex dono Ailwardi forestarii in Berdefeld, terram etiam ex dono Godefridi
pincerne in eadem uilla, et terram ex dono Gilberti filii Roberti in eadem uilla, et
terram ex dono Fulconis de Blandac in Stamburne, terram etiam ex dono Baldewini filii Serlonis in eadem uilla, et terram et pratum ex dono Hamonis Peccati in
45 Bridebroc, et terram ex dono Salomonis in Vuittine, et terram ex dono Ade filii
Warini in Heneia, et terram Alberede in Stamburna, et terram ex dono uxoris
Radulfi filii Siredi in Redeswelle, et terram ex dono Ilgeri in Essa, pratum etiam de
dono Willelmi de Pirenho iuxta ortum monachorum, et pratum ex dono Willelmi
de Must(er)ol in Claretta, et totam decimationem feni eiusdem Willelmi in eadem
50 uilla. Que quia eis pietatis intuitu largitione fidelium concessa sunt nos quoque eis
concedimus, et ut ea sibi quieta et inconuulsa permaneant ea presentis scripti
testimonio et sigilli nostri appositione ea que nobis a Domino concessa est auctoritate confirmamus. Hiis testibus: Radulfo de Disc(i) archidiacono, Ricardo archidiacono Colcest(rie), Roberto archidiacono Essex(ie), et aliis.

**457**

[c. 1179–80] Institution of Alexander, chaplain, as perpetual vicar of the church of Toppesfield, on the presentation of Prior N(icholas) and the monks of Stoke-by-Clare, with conditions, including a pension of four marks per annum.

Gilbertus Dei gracia Lundoniensis episcopus omnibus sancte matris ecclesie filiis ad
quos presentes littere peruenerint, salutem, gratiam et benedictionem.

Ad communem omnium uolumus deuenire notitiam nos ad petitionem et
presentationem N(icholai) prioris et fratrum de Stok' Alexandro capellano per-
5 petuam in ecclesia de Thopesfeld uicariam concessisse, ipsumque in eadem sub
annua quatuor marcharum pensione iam dictis priori et fratribus ad statutos inter
eos terminos soluenda perpetuum uicarium constituisse; ita quidem quod supradictus Alexander nobis et successoribus nostris et officialibus debitas nobis pro
eadem consuetudines exsoluet, et debitam per omnia exhibebit obedientie reueren-

**456** 45 Salomononis *MS*    50 intuiti *MS*
**457** BM Cotton MS Appendix xxi, fo. 52.
2 presens *MS*

tiam. Quam nimirum concessionem sibi factam et nostram institutionem quia 10 firmam et inconuulsam manere uolumus, presentis eam scripti patrocinio et sigilli nostri munimine corroborare curauimus. Testibus: Ricardo archidiacono Colcestrie, magistro Radulfo de Altaripa sancti Pauli cancellario, et aliis.

## 458

[*c.* 1181–7] Confirmation of the grant to Stoke-by-Clare priory of the church of Stambourne by Robert de Greinvill', knight.

Gilbertus Dei gratia Londoniensis episcopus omnibus sancte matris ecclesie filiis ad quos hee litere peruenerint, salutem in Domino.

Ad uniuersitatis uestre uolumus deuenire notitiam nos cartam dilecti filii nostri Roberti de Greinuill' militis inspexisse, ex cuius tenore concepimus ipsum Robertum pro salute sua et patris et matris et antecessorum suorum dilectis filiis monachis 5 Beccensibus, apud Stok' Deo famulantibus, ecclesiam de Stamburnia cum omnibus pertinentiis suis in puram et perpetuam elemosinam concessisse. Cuius nos deuotionem approbantes concessionem suam ratam habuimus, et memoratam ecclesiam de Stamburn' cum omnibus ad eam pertinentibus supradictis monachis auctoritate pontificali contulimus. Et ut ea perpetuo gaudeant ipsam eis literarum nostrarum 10 inscriptione et sigilli nostri appositione confirmauimus. Testibus: G(ileberto) archidiacono Midd(elsexe), Ricardo magistro scolarum London(ie), et aliis.

## 459

[1163–*c.* 1180] Grant of an indulgence in support of an appeal by the Knights Templars.

G(ilebertus) Dei gratia Lundoniensis episcopus dilectis sibi in Domino uniuersis ecclesie beati Pauli parrochianis et filiis, salutem, gratiam et benedictionem.

Clamat ad uos, karissimi, sancta ciuitas illa Ierusalem, in qua uos a morte perpetua Dominus noster Iesus Christus sua morte liberauit. Clamat ad uos sepulcrum Domini, locus ille sanctissimus a quo Dominus Iesus die tertia morte superata resurgens, 5 ⟨fo. 40⟩ nos in fide et spe resurrectionis et salutis eterne confirmauit. Clamant ad uos sancta loca illa omnia que iam dudum Dominus presentia sua corporali frequentans, nos ab infidelitatis errore reuocando, ea signis et uirtutibus mirabiliter illustrauit. Hec fidelium Christi labore magnifica a paganorum iam diu potestate liberata et eruta, in eorundem manus et potestatem iterato recidere perhorrescunt. Plorant 10 loca sancta principum suorum lamentabilem casum, quorum aliis gladio cesis, aliis in seruitutem deductis, terra illa sancta propugnatore iam carens, tanquam preda infidelibus et inimicis crucis Christi[1] nisi cito manum Dominus apposuerit exposita

458 BM Cotton MS Appendix xxi, fo. 56.
459 G, no. 239; B, fo. 39v.
8 reuocandos B

---

[1] Cf. Phil. iii. 18. It is possible that the lack of a defender indicates that this letter was written after the death of one of the kings of Jerusalem—either Baldwin III in 1163 or Amalric in 1174—possible, but not perhaps very likely. The disasters of 1187 occurred after Gilbert's

est. Onus istud sustinent fratres nostri karissimi et milites Templi, qui ob locorum
15 sanctorum et in his manentium fidelium Christianorum defensionem omnibus se
periculis exponere, mortem etiam ipsam pro Christo et fratrum salute subire parati
sunt. Quibus ad reppellendam multitudinem illam infinitam quantis opus sit,
discretio uestra non ignorat. Vnde pietati uestre tota supplicat orientalis ecclesia, ut
qui sibi presentia corporali subuenire non potestis, facta sibi rerum uestrarum
20 largitione per manum defensorum suorum militum scilicet Templi subueniatis, et
iminentia sibi pericula fraterne karitatis ope subueniatis. Hortatur in hoc karitatem
uestram domnus papa, hortamur et nos in Christo karissimi, omnibus qui eorundem fraternitatem susceperint et eis annuatim et in fine suo quod sibi Dominus
inspirauerit, prece et ammonitione nostra contulerint, orationum ecclesie nostre
25 suffragia concedentes, et de iniuncta sibi penitentia dum in eadem fraternitate
permanserint, quadraginta dies annis singulis concessa nobis a Domino potestate
relaxantes. Valere uos optamus in Domino, karissimi.

## 460

[1163-4, probably late 1163] Instruction to Godfrey archdeacon of Worcester to fulfil the
papal mandate (*PUE*, II, no. 100) for the restoration to St Mary's Warwick of the fruits
adjudicated against St Sepulchre's priory, Warwick, in no. 345.

Gilbert was acting as vicar of the diocese of Worcester (1161-4) on a mandate dated
3 August 1163.

G(ilebertus) Dei gratia Londoniensis episcopus uenerabili fratri et amico karissimo
G(odefrido) Gwigorn(iensi) archidiacono salutem.

Compellimur ex mandato domni pape quod ad nos de nouo emissum est, cuius
uobis copiam latores presentium exhibebunt, ut canonicis ecclesie sancte Marie de
5 Warewich fructus, quos ipsis in causa aduersus canonicos sancti Sepulcri adiudicauimus remota apellatione, restitui faciamus. Qua in re uices nostras uestre fraternitati
committimus, rogantes quatinus commune negotium suscipere et memoratis
canonicis sancte Marie de Warewich' adiudicatorum sibi fructuum restitutionem
iuxta formam apostolici mandati plene et pacifice facere satagatis. Valete.

## 461

[*c.* 1179-80] Confirmation of the grant to R(eginald) bishop of Bath, and Wells cathedral,
of the advowson of Shalford (Essex), by Hamo son of Geoffrey and his heir Robert, as

459 20 *A marginal note in* B [. . .]am (? eam) foueatis *may indicate that we should read* eam foueatis
*for* subueniatis *or add* et eam foueatis
460 PRO Exchequer Records, K.R., Misc. Books, E 164/22, fo. 21 v (Cart. St Mary's, Warwick).
461 Wells Cathedral, Dean and Chapter Muniments, Liber Albus I, fos. 47 v and 49 (thirteenth
century) (Wa); Liber Albus II, fo. 400 v (Wb), also, from a different original, fo. 371 (Wc)
(fifteenth century). Text and spelling as Wb (significant variants of Wa, a less complete copy
of the same original as Wb, and Wc, are noted). *Abstract: HMC, Wells,* I, 56.

death; and the deaths of Baldwin IV and V in 1185-6 are almost certainly too late for MS B.
But as in no case was there a vacancy of any length, it seems much more likely that this
passage has a general application to the plight of the kingdom in its later years.

endowment for a perpetual prebend in Wells cathedral. The bishop of Bath is to control and dispose of the prebend, and the canon who holds it is to pay customary dues to the bishops of London and their officials.

G(ilebertus) Dei gratia Lundoniensis episcopus omnibus sancte matris ecclesie filiis ad quos presentes littere peruenerint, salutem in Domino.

Que ecclesiis Dei diuino conferuntur intuitu iustum est firma consistere et ne possint tractu temporis aliqua peruersitate mutari, pontificali debent auctoritate confirmari. Hinc est quod ad omnium uestrum uolumus notitiam peruenire nos 5 concessionem a nobili uiro Hamone filio Gaufridi et herede suo post ipsum uenerabili fratri nostro Reginaldo Bathoniensi episcopo et ecclesie sancti Andree de Well' factam super aduocatione ecclesie de Scaldeford', quam predicti Hamo et Robertus pia deuotione prefate Wellensi ecclesie perpetuam prebendam fieri concesserunt, ratam habere; et ut concessio nostris facta temporibus debita possit firmitate 10 gaudere, iam dicto facto nos auctoritatis nostre munimen, prout decet, adhibere. Pium itaque predictorum Hamonis et heredis sui desiderium approbantes, supradictam ecclesiam de Scaldeford' cum omnibus pertinentiis suis libere et quiete Wellensi ecclesie in prebendam concedimus, et ut in perpetuum ecclesie Wellensis prebenda consistat assignamus, ita quod Bathoniensis episcopus de ea sicut de aliis 15 prebendis ordinet et disponat et eiusdem prebende canonicus debitas nobis et successoribus nostris et officialibus consuetudines ad modum aliarum nostre diocesis ecclesiarum exoluat. Quam nimirum concessionem nostram et donationem quia firmam et inconuulsam manere uolumus, eam presentis scripti patrocinio et sigilli nostri munimine confirmamus. Hiis testibus: Radulfo de Diceto archidiacono 20 Middelsex(e), Ricardo archidiacono Colec(estrie), Roberto archidiacono Essexie, magistro Radulfo de Altaripa magistro scolarum London(ie), Rogero Wigorn(iensi), Ricardo de Saresbir(ia), Radulfo de Chilton(a), Radulfo cantore, Waltero elemosinario, Iohanne Witeng', et quampluribus aliis.

## 462

[1163–c. 1181, probably early] General confirmation to Westminster abbey of the churches of St Martin-in-the-Fields with a pension of 20s., St Clement Eastcheap with a pension of 5s., St Dunstan-in-the-East with a pension of 16s., St Bride with a pension of 1 mark, St Martin, Ludgate, with a pension of 15s., St Alban, Wood St, with a pension of 1 mark, St Agnes within Aldersgate with a pension of 7s., St Clement, Candlewick St, with a pension of 32d., St James, Garlickhithe, with a pension of 20s., St Lawrence Pountney with a pension of 20s., St Matthew, Friday St, with a pension of 10s. and land adjacent worth 14s. rent,

**461** 4 Wc *places* possint *after* aliqua    6 nobili] uenerabili Wc    6 et] Wc *adds* Roberto    7 Reginaldo Wc; R. WaWb    8 homo Wb    12 et] Wc *adds* Roberti    16 prebendis] Wc *adds* Wellensibus    20–4 Radulfo...aliis] Wa *om. witnesses*; Wc *reads* Ricardo arch. Colec., Rad. arch. Middlesex(e), Henrico thesaurario, Radulfo de Altaripa magistro scolarum, magistro Dauid, magistro Hugone de Lund(onia), magistro Ricardo de Storteford', Ricardo de Saresbir(ia), Radulfo de Chilton(a)    22 Altabipa Wb
**462** Westminster Abbey Muniment Room, Domesday Cartulary, fo. 627 (W); BM Cotton MS Faustina A. iii, fos. 253v–254 (U) (Carts. Westminster abbey) (spelling as W).

St Margaret, New Fish St, with a pension of 10s., half the church of St Magnus Martyr with a pension of 1 mark (all in London), the churches of North Ockendon with a pension of 20s., Kelvedon with a pension of 100s.,[1] Feering (Essex) with a pension of 20s., Sawbridgeworth (Herts)—pertaining to their sacrist's office—with a pension of £15, Hendon (Middlesex) with a pension of 2 marks, the chapel of Little Tey with a pension of ½ mark, tithes of White Roding (Essex) pertaining to the precentor's office.

Gilbertus Dei gratia Londoniensis episcopus omnibus Christi fidelibus ad quorum notitiam littere iste peruenerint, eternam in Domino salutem.

Que locis religiosis et in eisdem deuotum Deo famulatum exhibentibus collata sunt beneficia, dignum est imperpetuum illesa conseruari et ne aliquando qualibet
5 machinantium calliditate ualeant immutari, ea pontificali confirmari decet auctoritate. Quocirca religionem monachorum domus Westm(onasterii) et publice famam assertionis attendentes ipsorumque in quantum possumus de iure indempnitatibus speciali affectione prospicere cupientes, quasdam ecclesias suas nostre iurisdictionis ipsis auctoritate qua presumus expressis nominibus duximus confirmandas: eccle-
10 siam uidelicet sancti Martini de la Cherringe cum pensione uiginti solidorum; ecclesiam sancti Clementis prope Templum, cum pensione quinque solidorum; ecclesiam sancti Dunstani cum pensione sexdecim solidorum; ecclesiam sancte Brigide cum pensione marce unius; ecclesiam sancti Martini de Ludgate cum pensione quindecim solidorum; ecclesiam sancti Albani cum pensione marce unius;
15 ecclesiam sancte Agnetis cum pensione septem solidorum; ecclesiam sancti Clementis in Kande⟨l⟩wykistret cum pensione triginta duorum denariorum; ecclesiam sancti Jacobi in uiniteria cum pensione uiginti solidorum; ecclesiam sancti Laurentii apud pontem cum pensione uiginti solidorum; ecclesiam sancti Mathei cum pensione decem solidorum et terram que iuxta eam est et ad eam pertinet que reddit
20 quatuordecim solidos; ecclesiam sancte Margarete prope pontem cum pensione decem solidorum; medietatem ecclesie sancti Magni martiris prope pontem cum pensione marce unius; ecclesiam de Wokendon' cum pensione uiginti solidorum; ecclesiam de Kenleuedene cum pensione centum solidorum; ecclesiam de Feringes cum pensione uiginti solidorum; ecclesiam de Sabrichteswurth' ad sacristiam eorum
25 pertinentem cum pensione quindecim librarum; ecclesiam de Hendon' cum pensione duarum marcarum; capellam de Theye cum pensione dimidie marce; decimas de Roing' ad officium cantoris pertinentes. Hec igitur ut perpetua stabilitate gaudeant presentis pagine inscriptione et sigilli nostri testimonio roboramus. Hiis testibus: magistro Ricardo de Storteford', magistro Rogero de Wyrecestre, magis-
30 tro Sampsone, G(ileberto) Banastre, Nicholao cantore, Radulfo de London(ia), Ricardo de Saresb(eria), Ricardo de Berking', et multis aliis.

**462** 16 Kandelwikestrete U    17 uinetria U    19 reddet W    21 medietatem ecclesie U; ecclesiam W    22–7 *For place-names* U *reads* Wokendune / Kelleueden' / Fering' / Sabricheswrthe / Teye / Roynges    28 presenti W    29 testibus] F *ends here with* etc. (*om. witnesses*)

---

[1] Cf. *VN*, pp. 335, 344. For the London churches, cf. *VN*, pp. 326–33, 359; for St Alban, Wood St, *Valor*, I, 414. For Little Tey, Morant, I, 204.

## 463

[1163–87, probably early] Settlement of the case between himself and Westminster abbey on the jurisdiction of Kilburn priory (in Hampstead, Middlesex, Benedictine nuns, dep. of Westminster abbey), and acknowledgement that the priory is subject to the abbey *in spiritualibus* and exempt from the bishop's jurisdiction.

The nature of the case and the formulas suggest an early date, and it is not impossible that this is an act of Bishop Gilbert the Universal (1128–34).

Omnibus sancte matris ecclesie filiis ad quos presens scriptum peruenerit Gilebertus Dei gratia Londoniensis episcopus salutem.

Nouerit uniuersitas uestra quod cum inter nos et abbatem Westm(onasterii) et conuentum questio uerteretur super subiectione et iurisdictione celle de Keleborne cum suis pertinentiis, attendentes eandem cellam a fundatione sua cum pertinentiis 5 suis dicto abbati et conuentui Westm(onasterii) pertinere, concedimus et presenti carta nostra confirmamus eidem abbati et successoribus suis inperpetuum iurisdictionem et subiectionem in spirit⟨u⟩alibus predicte celle cum suis pertinentiis: ita quod memorata cella cum pertinentiis suis a iurisdictione et subiectione Lund(oniensis) ecclesie inperpetuum penitus sit exempta; et quod abbas Westm(onasterii) 10 et conuentus et successores eorum omnem habeant potestatem ordinandi et disponendi per se et procuratores suos quod eidem celle uiderint expedire, absque ulla contradictione Lund(oniensis) ecclesie inperpetuum. Et ⟨fo. 637⟩ ut hec nostra concessio et confirmatio firma sit et stabilis, presens scriptum sigilli nostri appositione roborauimus. Ad maiorem uero securitatem sigillum capituli nostri de 15 assensu ipsius fecimus apponi.

## 464

[1175–9, probably 1175–7] Confirmation of the foundation of the hospital of St Lawrence, *Bordwadestone* (Boston House in Brentford, Middlesex),[1] with church and cemetery attached, by Ralph Brito, for the salvation of King Henry II and his children and of his lord Richard de Lucy and of himself and his family, with the consent of William of Northolt rector of the parish church of Hanwell, and of Walter abbot of Westminster (1175–90), with definition of the rights of the parish church.

Richard de Lucy appears to be alive: he died in 1179; if after 1177, William of Northolt would probably (but not certainly) be given the title archdeacon of Gloucester.

Vniuersis sancte matris ecclesie filiis frater G(ilebertus) Londoniensis ecclesie minister, salutem in Domino.

Que ad pacem geruntur ecclesie literarum monimentis excipere tutum est, ut si pro lapsu temporum eorum que gesta sunt contigerit aliquando uacillare memo-

---

**463** Westminster Abbey Muniment Room, Domesday Cartulary, fo. 636 v (W); BM Cotton MS Faustina A. iii, fo. 239 r–v (U) (spelling as W).
4 Kileburn' U    12 expedire *om.* W
**464** Westminster Abbey Muniment Room, Domesday Cartulary, fo. 131.

---

[1] Cf. *PN Middlesex*, p. 32.

5 riam, concepti super hiis instrumenti inscriptione reuocentur ad notitiam. Inde est quod in communem omnium deducimus hoc scripto notitiam Radulfum Brit(o-nem) deuotum beati Pauli et sancte London(iensis) ecclesie parrochianum, ob Dei et beate Virginis Marie et omnium sanctorum reuerentiam, ob illustris etiam regis Angl(o-rum) H(enrici) et liberorum eius salutem, nichilominus et ob salutem domni sui 10 Ricardi de Luci in cuius seruitiis educatus est et promotus, et iuuante Domino bonis temporalibus ampliatus, ob suam etiam et uxoris sue N. et liberorum suorum salutem, in uilla sua que dicitur Bordwadestone domum hospitalem que tredecim infirmorum in habitationem sufficiat, una cum hiis competentibus officinis, edifi-casse, et ei de redditibus suis quos in locis diuersis habet, quantum procurationi 15 iamdictorum fratrum et seruientium suorum honeste sufficere possit, assignasse. Huic uero domui contiguam in honore beati Laurentii martiris erexit et confirmauit ecclesiam, et cimiterium in quo iamdictorum ⟨fo. 131v⟩ infirmorum et clericorum et seruientium suorum corpora sepeliantur instantia continuate precis impetrauit. Quia uero intra terminos parochialium ecclesiarum que iamdiu dedicate et epis-20 copali auctoritate limitate sunt oratorium erigi uel cimiterium dedicari absque assensu persone matricis ecclesie, cui infra fines ipsos ius parochiale plene competit, canonicum non est, presenti hac testificatione notum cuntis facimus Willelmum de Norhalle ecclesie beate Marie de Hanewelle personam intra cuius fines parochiales uilla de Bordwatest(one) tota consistit, consensu domni Walteri uenerabilis 25 abbatis de Westm(onasterio) et conuentus sui edificationi iamdicte ecclesie beati Laurentii et dedicationi cimiterii ipsius assensum in hunc modum prebuisse: ut annue decimationes totius bladi quod in uilla de Bordwatest(one) singulis annis excrescet, memorate ecclesie de Hanewelle integre persoluantur, et corpora omnium hominum de Bordwatest(one) cum diuisis suis ad eandem ecclesiam sepelienda 30 deferantur; cetere uero obuentiones omnes ad ius parochiale pertinentes predicte erunt ecclesie beati Laurentii, que in usus eiusdem ecclesie et iamdictorum fratrum eius consilio cui fuerit eiusdem ecclesie cura commissa disponentur; capellanum uero eidem ecclesie beati Laurentii deseruientem infirmi suis sumptibus absque onere matricis ecclesie plene in omnibus exhibebunt. His etiam ad recognoscen-35 d(am) dignitatem matricis ecclesie de Hanewelle et istud adiectum est et utrimque concessum, ut omnes parochiani de Bordwatest(one) exceptis infirmis et eorum seruientibus ad Natale Domini et ad Pascha et ad Pentecosten et in Natiuitate beate Virginis Marie ecclesiam de Hanewelle adeant et eam ut matricem ecclesiam suam honorent. Ecclesia uero de Bordwatest(one) in festiuitate beati Laurentii martiris in 40 cuius honore edificata est, in oblatione cerei unius duarum librarum cere ecclesiam beate Marie de Hanewelle recognoscet. Hec quia coram nobis acta sunt et omnium ad quos res spectat assensu firmata, nos quoque ea que nobis a Domino concessa est auctoritate firmauimus, et ut in perpetuum firma et inconcussa permaneant, tam pagine presentis inscriptione quam sigilli nostri attestatione roborare curauimus.

**464** 6 notitiarum MS   12 Rodwadestone MS (Bord- *in rubric and below*)   28 memorate memorate MS   29 eandem] laudem MS   32–4 capellanum...exhibebunt *an addition in MS: noted for insertion before* cui fuerit eiusdem (MS eidem); *but the sense demands the order given in text* 41 Marie Marie MS

Hiis testibus: Waltero abbate Colecestrie, abbate de Stratford', Ricardo archi- 45
diacono Colecestrie, R(oberto) archidiacono Essex(ie), Henrico tezaurario,
magistro Hugo⟨ne de⟩ Lund(onia), magistro Dauid, magistro R(icardo) de
S⟨t⟩ort(eford), G(ileberto) Foliot canonicis sancti Pauli.

### 465

[1175–c. 1180] Settlement as papal judge delegate of the case between Walter abbot of
Westminster (1175–90) and Ran(d)ulf, clerk, of Feering (Essex), alleged to have become a
canon regular at Missenden abbey, and so to have lost his right to the church of Feering, in
favour of the abbot, and institution of Master Maurice, abbot's clerk, as vicar.

G(ilebertus) Dei gratia Londoniensis episcopus omnibus sancte matris ecclesie filiis
ad quos presentes littere peruenerint, salutem in Domino.

Ad uniuersitatis uestre uolumus deuenire notitiam, nos a sede apostolica mandatum suscepisse, ut Randulfum clericum de Feringes quem dilectus filius noster
Walterus abbas Westm(onasterii) in manibus abbatis de Messend(ena) seculo 5
abrenuntiasse et in eius ecclesia religionis habitum assumpsisse asseuerauerat,
moneremus diligentius et commissa nobis auctoritate compelleremus, ecclesiam de
Fering' ad abbatem Westmonasterii pertinentem quam idem R(andulfus) iniuste
presumpsit detinere, predicto abbati Westm(onasterii) restituere, uel in nostra
presentia remota apellatione iustitie plenitudinem exhibere. Nos igitur iniuncta 10
nobis ad debitum uolentes effectum perducere, partes scitari fecimus, quibus coram
nobis positis, post multas hinc inde allegationes communicato prudentum
uirorum consilio, prememoratam ecclesiam de Fering' sepedicto Randulfo auctoritate nobis a summo pontifice commissa, sollempniter abiudicauimus, eamque
predicto abbati Westm(onasterii) plene restitui fecimus. His itaque debita cum 15
sollempnitate transactis nos petitione et assensu eiusdem abbatis Westm(onasterii)
eandem ecclesiam magistro Mauritio clerico domni abbatis, nomine ipsius abbatis
possidendam et de ipso tenendam concessimus, et ut hec firmitatis robur optineant
in posterum, pagine presentis inscriptione et sigilli nostri appositione confirmare
curauimus. Testibus: magistro Dauid, magistro Henrico de Norhamt(ona), 20
magistro Radulfo de Altaripa, Radulfo de Chilt(ona), R(adulfo) cantore, Waltero
elemosinario, Laurentio Vacca, Osberto de Feldste, G. aurifabro, Roberto de
Bureswell', Ricardo Aguill(um), Iohanne clerico, et multis aliis.

**464** 48 canonicus MS
**465** *Original:* Westminster Abbey Muniments, no. 1045 (size 5½ in. × 5¼ in.); *copies* in Domesday
Cartulary, fos. 262v–263, BM Cotton MS Faustina A. iii, fo. 245 (variants not given). Tag for
seal. *Endorsed:* Carta Londoniensis episcopi super abiudicatione facta ab eo (twelfth century). de
resignatione ecclesie de Fering' et restitutione per episcopum Lond' (thirteenth century). xj.

### 466

[1175–c. 1180] As no. 465, with additional details: that Ranulf was a brother of Pope Adrian IV, that his son N. pledged the fee he holds of the abbot of St Albans not to lay claim to the church.

G(ilebertus) Dei gratia Londoniensis episcopus omnibus sancte matris ecclesie filiis ad quos hee littere peruenerint, salutem in Domino.

Quia rerum gestarum series nisi litterarum excipiantur apicibus processu temporis ab humana facile poterunt excidere memoria, scripto commode committuntur
5 et provide, ut finita semel negotia pace debita conquiescant et iniuste calumpniantibus penitus excludatur litigandi aditus et facultas. Hac igitur ratione finem cause que inter dilectum nostrum W(alterum) abbatem Westmonasterii et Ranulfum clericum de Feringes nobis a summo pontifice delegata uertebatur, pagine beneficio duximus committendum, ut quod in ea domni pape gessimus auctoritate cunctis
10 fieret liquidum, et peruersa machinantibus denuo litem super ea suscitandi adimeremus regressum. A sede siquidem apostolica mandatum suscepimus ut memoratum R(anulfum) clericum, quem supradictus abbas in manibus abbatis de Messenden' seculo abrenuntiasse et in eius ecclesia religionis habitum assumpsisse asseuerauerat, moneremus diligentius et commissa nobis auctoritate compelleremus ecclesiam de
15 Fering' ad abbatem Westm(onasterii) pertinentem, quam idem R(anulfus) iniuste presumpsit et illicite detinere, sepedicto abbati restituere, uel in nostra presentia remota appelatione iustitie sibi plenitudinem exhibere. Nos igitur iniuncta nobis ad debitum uolentes effectum perducere, partes scitari fecimus, quibus coram nobis comparentibus sepenominatus R(anulfus)—frater quondam bone memorie pape
20 Adriani—post multas hinc inde lites et allegationes iuri quod in ecclesia de Fering' habuerat et habere se dicebat in nostra et multorum presentia renuntiauit, et ecclesiam ipsam tam spontanee quam absolute in manus nostras refutauit, et quod eandem nec per se nec per alium de cetero repeteret, nec in ea iuris aliquid uendicaret, iuramento corporaliter prestito firmiter repromisit. Ipsius etiam R(anulfi)
25 filius N. nomine simile prestitit sacramentum, et preterea se in hac re pro patre suo fideiussorem constituit, et ne temere pater suus uel ipse contra iuramentum suum uenire presumerent totum feodum quod idem N. de abbate Sancti Albani tenet pignori obligauit. Hiis ucro gestis solempniter nos supradictam ecclesiam de Fering' abbati Westmon(asterii) restituimus et magistro Mauritio domni abbatis
30 clerico eam de ipso tenendam, R(anulfo) in hoc assensum prebente, concessimus et ut hec firmitatis robur optineant in posterum, pagine presentis inscriptione et nostri pariter sigilli appositione confirmare curauimus et communire. Testibus: magistro Dauid, magistro Henrico de Norhamton', magistro Radulfo de Altaripa, Radulfo

---

**466** *Original:* Westminster Abbey Muniments, no. 1044 (size 7 in. × 7¼ in.); *copy* in Domesday Cartulary, fo. 262v (variants not given). Tag for seal. *Endorsed:* Testimonium episcopi Londoniensis super abiuratione facta a Ranulfo ecclesie de Feringes (twelfth century). *Original reproduced* in *New Palaeographical Society,* First Series, II, Plate 98b.
8 delegate *orig.*

de Chilton(a), Radulfo cantore, Waltero elemosinario, Laurentio uacca, Oseberto de Felst(ed), G. aurifabro, Roberto de Bureswelle, Ricardo Agillu(m), Johanne 35 clerico, et multis aliis.

## 467

[1175–87] Settlement as papal judge delegate of the case between Abbot Walter (1175–90) and the convent of Westminster and Master Alexander vice-archdeacon and canon of Lincoln and Henry and Haket, clerks, on the churches of Doddington and Thorp (Lincs): Alexander and the clerks surrendered their claim, Master Nicholas was instituted on the presentation of the abbot and convent, and Nicholas granted half the churches to Alexander and Robert Code, the other half to Haket, to hold for annual pensions of fifty shillings from each half, with arrangements for succession.

G(ilebertus) Dei gratia Lundoniensis episcopus omnibus sancte matris ecclesie filiis ad quos presentes litere peruenerint, salutem in Domino.

Ad uniuersitatis uestre uolumus deuenire notitiam, causam que inter uenerabilem abbatem W(alterum) et conuentum Westm(onasterii) et magistrum Alexandrum uicearchidiaconum, Lincoln(iensis) ecclesie canonicum, et Henricum et Haketum 5 clericos super ecclesiis de Dodinton' et de Torp uertebatur, quam a domno papa nobis conmissam iudicio uel concordia terminandam susceperamus, ⟨fo. 501v⟩ partibus coram nobis assistentibus, post multas ipsarum allegationes hoc tandem fine conquieuisse. Predicti siquidem magister A(lexander) et Henricus et Haketus ecclesias de Dodinton' et de Torp in manus nostras refutauerunt et iuri si quid in eis 10 habuerant, spontanea uoluntate renuntiauerunt. Nos igitur ad petitionem memorati abbatis et conuentus Westm(onasterii) magistro Nicholao clerico suo supradictas ecclesias de Dod(inton) et Torp cum omnibus ad eas pertinentibus concessimus, ipsumque in eisdem ecclesiis auctoritate apostolica, ea qua debuimus sollempnitate, personam instituimus; Nicholaus uero assensu et auctoritate memorati abbatis et 15 conuentus earundem ecclesiarum medietatem supradicto A(lexandro) et Roberto Code, et alteram ipsarum ecclesiarum medietatem Haketo clerico toto uite sue tempore de se tenendam, concessit; ita saltem quod magister A(lexander) et R(obertus) Code supramemorato Nicholao annuos quinquaginta solidos et Haketus similiter quinquaginta solidos annuatim ei nomine ecclesiarum ad statutos inter eos 20 terminos persoluent. Et si prescripti A(lexander) et R(obertus) quoquomodo ab ipsis ecclesiis prius quam Haketus recesserint, eorum pars Haketo cedet; et si Haketus ab eis quoquomodo recesserit, ipsius pars memoratis A(lexandro) et R(oberto) cedet, salua sepedicto N(icholao) integra centum solidorum pensione; et si eundem Nicholaum in fata decedere uel uitam mutare, uel alio modo ab eisdem 25 recedere contigerit, suprascripti A(lexander) et R(obertus) et H(aketus) prenomina- tam centum solidorum pensionem ecclesie et conuentui Westm(onasterii), uel ei quem abbas et conuentus ad eam percipiendam assignauerint, integre persoluent. Hanc autem pensionem magistro N(icholao) quoad uixerit et ecclesie Westm(onas-

467 Westminster Abbey Muniment Room, Domesday Cartulary, fo. 501.
9 Haketus] Hab' MS

30 terii) uel ei quem abbas post Nicholai decessum assignauerit se fideliter soluturos, et
conuentionem inter eos factam firmiter obseruaturos, sepenominati A(lexander) et
R(obertus) et Haketus sacramento corporaliter prestito in nostra et multorum
presentia repromiserunt. Nos itaque que taliter acta sunt ne denuo super eis lites
suscitentur et iurgia, ut posteritati liqueant, in scriptum redegimus, et ut de cetero
35 firmitatis robur optineant, pagine presentis inscriptione et sigilli nostri appositione
apostolica qua in causa hac functi sumus auctoritate communiuimus. Valete.

## 468

[c. 1181 (1180)–1187] Institution of Henry of Bayeux as rector of Greenford and Hanwell
(Middlesex) on the presentation of Abbot Walter and the monks of Westminster abbey.

G(ilebertus) Dei gratia Londoniensis episcopus uniuersis sancte matris ecclesie filiis
per episcopatum London(iensem) constitutis, eternam in Domino salutem.

Elabenti hominum memorie prudenter satis et apte prospicitur, cum quod a
modernis agitur ne in posterum irritetur, litterarum beneficio commendatur. Inde
5 est quod ad communem omnium uestrum uolumus deuenire notitiam, nos ex
consensu dilectorum filiorum nostrorum W(alteri) abbatis et fratrum Westm(onasterii) dilecto filio nostro Henrico Baiocensi ecclesias de Greneforde et de Hanewelle
cum omnibus ad eas pertinentibus perpetuo concessisse, ipsumque in eisdem debita
cum sollempnitate personam instituisse. Hanc autem institutionem nostram ne de
10 cetero ualeat irritari presentis pagine testimonio et sigilli nostri appositione decreuimus communire. Testibus hiis: Gileberto archidiacono Middelsex(e), Rogero de
Wygorn(ia), Roberto Folet, Radulfo de Chilton' canonicis sancti Pauli, magistro
Waltero de Witten(eia), Iohanne Wyteng, Thoma Briton(e), Lodowico, Radulfo
precentore, Roberto Foliot, Stephano Walense, Zacharia, et multis aliis.

## 469

[1163–c. 1180] Institution of H., clerk, as rector of Wickham Bishops, with its chapel, the
church of Langford (Essex).[1]

Certainly an act of a bishop of London, and so presumably Gilbert's.

Vniuersitati uestre presenti scripto notifico me ecclesiam de Wicham cum capella
sua, ecclesia uidelicet de Langeford', ceterisque omnibus ad eam pertinentibus H.
clerico in elemosinam concessisse, ipsumque in eisdem ecclesiis personam ea que
nobis a Deo concessa est auctoritate constituisse. Quod ne reuocari possit in
5 dubium, pagine presentis inscriptione et sigilli mei appositione testificari pariter et
confirmare curaui.

468 Westminster Abbey Muniment Room, Domesday Cartulary, fo. 131 (W); BM Cotton
MS Faustina A. iii, fos. 245 v–246 (U).
4 airritetur W     11 U *ends here with* Hiis testibus
469 G, no. 325; B, fo. 198 v.

---

[1] Cf. *PN Essex*, pp. 313, 304; *VN*, p. 345.

**470**

[1163–87] Settlement as papal judge delegate of the case between Henry, priest, of Huns-
worth, and Ralph prior of Worcester (1146/7–1189), on the church of Bromwich (Warwicks)—Nicholas, royal chaplain, acting as Henry's proctor. The prior granted Nicholas the
church for life for an annual pension of five shillings, and Nicholas accepted Hugh, priest,
who had served the church as the prior's nominee, as vicar for an annual pension of one mark.

Dilectis sibi in Domino uniuersis sancte matris ecclesie filiis frater Gilebertus
Lundoniensis ecclesie minister, salutem in Christo.

Nouerit karitas uestra quod cum causam inter Henricum presbiterum de
Huneswordʼ et Radulfum priorem ecclesie Wigorn(ensis) super ecclesia de
Bromwichʼ ex delegatione domni pape cognoscendam terminandamque suscepisse- 5
mus, idem Henricus, eo quod pro etatis imbecillitate suis non satis commode poterat
superesse negotiis, dilectum nostrum Nicholaum domni regis capellanum sibi in
eadem causa ad agendum siue transigendum procuratorem instituit, suamque in
iudicio personam sub nostra simul et aduerse partis presentia confirmauit. Eo igitur
procurante negotium, cum res ob uarias causas in longum fuisset protracta, cumque 10
ad ipsius examen ambo aduersus priorem Henricus scilicet et Nicholaus forte
conuenissent, memorata controuersia hoc tandem transactionis fine conquieuit.
Domnus siquidem prior iamdictam ecclesiam de Bromwichʼ cum omni integritate
sua Nicholao quoad uiueret habendam et nomine Wigornensis ecclesie de se suisque
successoribus tenendam concessit, sub annua pensione quinque solidorum ad Pascha 15
soluendorum. Nicholaus uero Hugonem sacerdotem qui in eadem ecclesia nomine
prioris ante ministrauerat, accepta ab eo fidelitate, in uicariam eiusdem ecclesie sub
annua pensione unius marce dimidie ad Pascha et dimidie in kalendis Augusti
persoluenda, quamdiu fideliter seruierit admisit, et sub hoc tenore presente et
assensum prebente domno litis Henrico ab instituta prorsus lite recessit; eo etiam 20
pactis adiecto quod nunquam in uita Nicholai aut ipse Nicholaus aut Henricus
procurabit quominus sepedicta ecclesia de Bromwichʼ ad ecclesiam Wigorn(ensem),
ipso Nicholao decedente, in eo quo erat statu quando transactum est, reuertatur, ita
scilicet ut nullum ecclesie Wigorn(ensi) uel ecclesie de Huneswordʼ ex hac transactione preiudicium generetur. Quod quia pleno partium assensu comprobatum et 25
fide hinc inde prestita in manu nostra prorsus confirmatum est, ne in dubium possit
aut in irritum de cetero reuocari, presenti scripto uniuersitati uestre notificare et ea
qua fungimur auctoritate confirmare curauimus.

**470** Worcester Cathedral, Dean and Chapter Muniments, A4 ('Reg. Iʼ), fo. xxvi (Cart.
Worcester Cathedral priory).

**471**

[1163–c. 1180] Certificate that the bearer, N., has been ordained priest.

G(ilebertus) Dei gratia Lundoniensis episcopus dilectis sibi in Domino uniuersis sancte matris ecclesie filiis ad quos littere iste peruenerint, salutem in Christo.

Nouerit dilectio uestra latorem presentium N. diuina benedictione et nostre manus impositione ad sacerdotii gradum esse promotum. Quod quia in dubium
5 ⟨fo. 164⟩ nolumus posse reuocari, presenti scripto uniuersitati uestre id notificare curauimus, uestram orantes et exortantes in Domino dilectionem, quatinus pro amore Dei et reuerentia ordinis sui, ipsum in executione officii sui benigne recipiatis, et debitum illi honorem propter Deum exhibeatis. Valete.

**472**

[1163–c. 1180] Letters dimissory for R., ordained priest by R. (Robert or Richard), bishop of London.

G(ilebertus) Dei gratia Lundoniensis episcopus dilectis sibi in Domino uniuersis sancte matris ecclesie filiis, salutem in Domino.

Notum uestre facimus caritati latorem presentium R. a predecessore nostro bone memorie R. Lundoniensi quondam episcopo ad gradum sacerdotii promotum, in
5 ipso episcopatu diu ministrasse et prout sacerdotali congruit officio digne conuersatum fuisse. Quem cum in partes exteras trahat ad presens oborta necessitas, has sibi dimissorias ordinationis et honestatis sue, date etiam sibi a nobis dicedendi licentie testes concessimus; dilecte nobis in Domino beniuolentie uestre preces affectuose porrigentes, quatinus ob diuini reuerentiam ordinis ipsum in quo locorum
10 uenerit inter uos in caritate suscipiatis, et honorem quem Domini ministris exhibere iustum est sibi misericorditer impendatis. Valere uos optamus in Domino.

**473**

[1163–c. 1180] Notification that T., clerk, has renounced his case against the bishop of Norwich.

G(ilebertus) Dei gratia Lundoniensis episcopus uniuersis ecclesie filiis, salutem, gratiam et benedictionem.

Que semel rite finita sunt, ne rediuiua suscitentur in iurgia propensiori cura prospicere conuenit, in his presertim que fidei firmat religio, ne illa cita usurpatione
5 conuellantur. Vnde uestre innotescimus uniuersitati T. clericum querele, quam coram nobis aduersus uenerabilem fratrem nostrum Norwic(ensem) episcopum

---

**471** G, no. 182; B, fo. 163 v (*in left-hand margin of* B, *evidently referring to this letter* (*partly cut away*): dilectio inuocata [u]estra latorem [pres]entium N. [ordin]atus (*sic*) ordi[ni prom]ouisse ...dubium).
**472** G, no. 189; B, fo. 193 v.
7 sue sue B
**473** G, no. 190; B, fo. 193 v.
4 illi B

super uiolentia [...] iam secundo instituere destinauerant, in capitulo Lundon(ie) nobis ad super eadem causa cognoscendum residentibus, in multorum presentia renuntiasse, et fide interposita id se in perpetuum obseruaturum firmasse. Quod ut in posterum liquidum fiat presentis scripti patrocinio et sigilli nostri appositione 10 communimus. Valete.

## 474

[1163–c. 1180] Grant of an indulgence in support of the appeal by the monks or canons of an unidentified house[1] for the rebuilding of their church, destroyed by fire.

G(ilebertus) Dei gratia Lundoniensis episcopus omnibus sancte matris ecclesie ministris, necnon et uniuersis Christiane professionis in sua diocesi commorantibus ad quos litere iste peruenerint, compassionis habundare uisceribus.

Capiat in nobis,[2] fratres karissimi, ewangelice doctrine frequens et cotidiana ammonitio, qua instruimur et informamur opis indigentibus manum misericordie 5 alacriter porrigere, et oppressorum necessitatibus celeri remedio occurrendo subuenire. Scriptum namque est, 'alter alterius onera portate, et sic adimplebimus legem Christi'; et iterum, 'hilarem datorem diligit Deus'; et alibi, 'date et dabitur uobis'; et iterum, 'caritas operit multitudinem peccatorum'; et alibi, 'caritas nunquam excidit'.[3] Nos igitur ecclesie sancte uirginis N. et fratribus in Christi 10 seruitio ibidem commorantibus alacriter succurrentes, unusquisque iuxta facultatis sue mensuram imminentis paupertatis aggrauationem misericorditer supportemus, et ad reedificationem ecclesie ignis incendio uastate, aliquid de beneficiis nobis a Deo collatis cum cordis hilaritate largiamur. Omnibus autem qui ad prefatum opus misericordie ea deuotionis intentione qua oportet manum auxiliatricem porrexe- 15 rint, de Domini gratia et meritis tante uirginis confisi, duodecim dies de penitentia sua relaxamus, et bonorum omnium que in nostra fiunt ecclesia, adiuuante Domino eos participes constituimus.

## 475

[? 1163–c. 1180] Confirmation of the agreement between M. and A.

Stylistically characteristic of Gilbert's charters.

Pastoralis officii nos ammonet auctoritas singulari cura prospicere, ne lites coram nobis transactione sopitas in iurgia suscitet litigantium peruersitas, et quod utiliter

---

**473** 7 uiolentia] *Some words giving the grounds of the dispute and explaining the construction of* destinauerant *are clearly missing at this point* 9 et se B
**474** G, no. 232; B, fo. 195. *See Plate III.*
**475** G, no. 306; B, fo. 196.

---

[1] The name is reduced to a formula; but if the formula is close to the original, one may observe that not many houses were designated by the name of a Virgin alone, and conjecture that the house was St Osyth (Essex, Augustinian).
[2] Cf. Jo. viii. 37.
[3] Galat. vi. 2; II Cor. ix. 7; Luc. vi. 38; I Pet. iv. 8; I Cor. xiii. 8.

est ordinatum iterato reuocetur in dubium. Vt igitur plenum robur optineat compositio inter M. et A. mutuo consensu inita, nos eam literis mandare decreui-
5 mus, que in presentia nostra tandem hoc fine conquieuit. Nos itaque hanc conuentionem non solum iniuncta nobis auctoritate approbamus, uerum etiam sigilli nostri appositione communimus, fraternitatem uestram rogantes attentius, ut et uestrum in hiis assensum prebeatis et auctoritatem.

## 476

[? 1163–*c.* 1180] Letter in support of the appeal for the church of St N.

There is no proof that this is Gilbert's, though it is likely enough.

Qui ad celestem patriam peruenire desiderant, opus est ut misericordie operibus diligenter intendant, et de facultatibus sibi a Deo collatis pauperibus et precipue piis locis ignis incendio uastatis elemosinas largiantur. Vnde nos de salutis uestre profectu ut iustum est solliciti, uniuersitatem uestram rogamus, monemus et exhorta-
5 mur in Domino, quatinus operationi ecclesie sancti N. aliquod auxilium conferatis, ut tam per hec quam per alia bona que in hac uita feceritis ad gaudia eterna feliciter pertingere ualeatis. Valete.

476 G, no. 307; B, fo. 196.
1 celestiam B   2 diligenter] B *adds* insistant, *cancelled*

# APPENDICES

# APPENDIX I

The dates of all the letters and of many of the charters are explained in notes at their heads. In many cases, however, one note covers a group of letters or charters (e.g. nos. 38–41, 49–57, 300–9); often no explanation is given when the dates are simply those of one of Gilbert's periods of office (e.g. 1139–48 as abbot of Gloucester); sometimes the date of a person or event is noted in brackets in the opening summary and no further explanation given.

A high proportion of the charters are dated by members of the chapters of Hereford and London, and to save repetition the dates based on these are laid out below: the page references are to *GF*, Appendix IV, where the evidence for these dates is given.

+ means in or after; − in or before.

| | |
|---|---|
| *1139–48* | Gilbert Foliot, abbot of Gloucester |
| *1148–63* | bishop of Hereford |
| +*c.* 1150 | Walter Foliot, archdeacon of Shropshire (p. 268) |
| −*c.* 1155 | Gilbert, precentor; Walter and Reginald, treasurers of Hereford (pp. 267–8) |
| +*c.* 1155 | Reginald, precentor; Ivo, treasurer of Hereford (pp. 267–8) |
| −*c.* 1158 | Ralph, dean of Hereford (p. 267) |
| *c.* 1158 | W., dean of Hereford (p. 267) |
| +1158 | Geoffrey, dean of Hereford (p. 267) |
| *1163–87* | bishop of London |
| +1163/7 | Richard Foliot, archdeacon of Colchester (p. 273) |
| −1167 | Richard Rufus, archdeacon of Essex (p. 272) |
| +1167 | Robert Banastre, archdeacon of Essex; probably +1169, because at Bologna *c.* 1167–9 (p. 272, cf. 48–9) |
| *c.* 1167–71 | Master David in Italy (p. 277 and ref.; note to no. 191) |
| +*c.* 1170 | Henry Banastre, treasurer of St Paul's (p. 275) |
| −1172 | Robert of Clifford, clerk (p. 285) |
| −1174 | Godfrey, treasurer of St Paul's; Henry Banastre, clerk or canon (p. 275) |
| +1174 | Richard of Stortford, canon (p. 280) |
| +1175 | Richer de Andelys, precentor of Rouen (p. 282) |
| −1176 | Richard of Stortford, clerk (p. 280) |
| −1177 | William of Northolt, canon, *not* archdeacon of Gloucester (p. 284) |
| −*c.* 1179 (1180) | Ralph de Hauterive, clerk (pp. 275–6) |
| *c.* 1179–*c.* 1180 | Ralph de Hauterive, Master of the Schools (pp. 275–6) |
| −1180 | Hugh de Marigny, dean of St Paul's; Ralph de Diceto, archdeacon of Middlesex (p. 271) |
| +1180 | Ralph de Diceto, dean of St Paul's; Ralph de Hauterive, archdeacon of Colchester; Roger of Worcester, canon (pp. 271, 274, 276) |
| −*c.* 1180 | Richard Foliot, archdeacon of Colchester (pp. 273–4)—also, completion of MS B (above, p. 8) |

1180–*c.* 1181(?)  Richard Foliot, archdeacon of Middlesex (pp. 273–4)

−*c.* 1181  Roger of Worcester, clerk; Gilbert Foliot I, canon; Richard of Stortford, clerk or canon (pp. 276, 273)

+*c.* 1181 (1180)  Gilbert Foliot, archdeacon of Middlesex; Richard of Stortford, Master of the Schools; Ralph of Chilton, canon; Robert Folet, canon (pp. 273, 276, 286–7)

−1183 (*c.* 1181)  Ralph of Chilton, clerk; Richard of Stortford, canon; Gilbert Banastre, clerk (pp. 286, 276, 279)

+1186  Walter of Witney, canon (p. 288)

# APPENDIX II

Since the dates of many of Gilbert's letters depend on Theobald's travels, and on his changes in title, it seems convenient to lay out the known facts here.

*c. Christmas 1143.* Theobald set off for Rome, returning *c.* summer 1144—he took part in the consecration of St-Denis on 11 June 1144 (Saltman, pp. 20–1).

*5 May 1145.* Pope Eugenius III granted primacy to Theobald (*PUE*, II, no. 43, cf. no. 52; St Bernard, *Ep.* 238).

*May 1147.* Theobald, accompanied by Gilbert, visited Eugenius III in Paris (they were certainly there on 25 May) (Saltman, pp. 23–4). Gilbert's presence is proved by nos. 69–70.[1]

*March 1148.* After consecrating bishops at Canterbury under Stephen's eye on 14 March (for the date, W. Stubbs, *Registrum Sacrum Anglicanum*, p. 46; *Trans. St Paul's Ecclesiological Soc.* VII, 169), Theobald escaped to Rheims, with very few attendants, including Gilbert, where he attended the council (21 March to mid April) (cf. Gervase, I, 134 f.; JS *HP*, P, pp. 7–8; C, pp. 6–7; *MB*, III, 356; VI, 57). After a brief return, he left England again *c.* June, and in July was at Arras with Gilbert (no. 78); on 5 September he consecrated Gilbert at St-Omer (*GF*, p. 97); he returned to England *c.* October, presumably with Gilbert, who was certainly with him in December in London (*Trans. St Paul's Ecclesiological Soc.* VII, 169; cf. Gervase, I, 135 ff.; *HP*, P, p. 49; C, p. 49; Saltman, pp. 26 ff.).

*Early 1150.* Eugenius III granted the legateship to Theobald (*GF*, p. 92 n.; Saltman, pp. 30–1). This was confirmed by Anastasius IV and Adrian IV (*PUE*, II, no. 84). Although Adrian IV addressed him as legate *before* his confirmation (*ibid.* no. 83), and it is doubtful whether the doctrine that a legateship lapsed with the Pope's death was fully established at this time,[2] it

---

[1] Theobald made four visits to the continent while Gilbert was abbot (if one counts those of 1148 as two; it is possible, though improbable, that there were others of which we have no record). It can be shown that Gilbert accompanied him on three, but not on all four of these. Nos. 24–5 contain a refusal (or two refusals) to accompany the archbishop; the note to no. 24 points out that this can most naturally be dated 1143, and nos. 372 and 26 seem to show that Gilbert was in fact in England at the end of 1143 and between then and spring 1144. No. 57 shows that Gilbert was toying with the idea of a visit to the papal Curia (if correctly dated) in the summer of 1146; no. 56 shows that he agreed to accompany the archbishop on some journey about the same time; cf. also no. 61. Nos. 69–70 show that Gilbert was present with the archbishop some time before the council of Rheims of March 1148. It is in fact clear that Gilbert accompanied Theobald on his visit in 1147, which fits perfectly all these indications. No. 64 asserts Gilbert's intention of going to the council, evidently of Rheims; and that he was there is implied in nos. 74 ff. No. 78 and records of his consecration (*GF*, p. 97) show that Gilbert was with the archbishop again in the summer of 1148. In the notes to some of these letters the results of this inquiry are assumed: it will be seen, however, that without any special assumptions it can be shown to be highly probable that Gilbert was not with the archbishop on his first visit, but accompanied him both in 1147 and in 1148; in the latter year, after the archbishop's abortive return to England in the late spring, Gilbert returned to the continent with him: see above.

[2] Thus Henry of Blois held legatine councils on 10 and *c.* 30 Nov. 1143, although he can hardly have been ignorant of the death of Innocent II on 24 Sept. (cf. Thorne, p. 1804, cited Voss, *Heinrich von Blois*, p. 48 and n.; cf. JS *HP*, P, p. lv). But he surrendered the title, at least, when it became clear that Celestine II was not going to renew it.

may be assumed that Theobald was either technically not legate, or would not have regarded himself as such, between the death of Adrian IV in September 1159 and the acceptance of Alexander III in England late in 1160.[1]

In Theobald's acta, he used the titles archbishop, archbishop and primate, archbishop, primate of all England and legate, and archbishop, primate of the English (*Anglorum primas*) and legate. Professor Saltman showed that in general this order is chronological, but he argued that he sometimes failed to use the title legate after 1150. In *Journ. of Theological Studies*, New Series, VIII (1957), 189–90 n., C. N. L. Brooke has suggested that this failure was sometimes, perhaps nearly always, due to the circumstances of 1159–60; although Dr Mayr-Harting (*Acta Chichester*, no. 36 n.) has shown that there is evidence that Theobald called himself legate while Alexander III was Pope. In any event, the vast majority of Theobald's acta follow these rules:

> Archbishop alone: 1139–45[2]
> Archbishop and primate: 1145–50, 1159–60
> Archbishop, primate and legate: 1150–9, 1160–1[3]

In view of the efforts involved in achieving these titles, and Gilbert's interest in these efforts, one would expect to find Gilbert's use of them in addressing Theobald in his letters fairly precise—though the circumstances of the age and of the letters' transmission[4] would not lead one to expect that the addresses would be an infallible guide to the dates of the letters. These expectations are fulfilled. Nos. 24–5, 33 (all probably before May 1145) are addressed to the archbishop; nos. 47, 51–2, 56, 58, 61, 79 (all 1145–50) to archbishop and primate of all England; nos. 94, 96, 111 (1150 and later) to archbishop, primate of the English (*Anglorum primati*) and legate. Four of the period 1148–50 are (wrongly) addressed to archbishop alone.[5] This leaves no. 4, addressed to the archbishop alone, and so probably, though not certainly, 1139–45; nos. 65–6, addressed to archbishop and primate of all England, and so probably 1145–8.

[1] *JS Epp.* 121–30 show how warily Theobald trod in this situation. It is curious that there are three bulls of Alexander III for Bardney abbey apparently of January 1160 (*PUE*, I, nos. 76–8); but these may have been solicited before the situation in England was understood. Otherwise the run of bulls does not begin until October–November, by which time the position was becoming clarified, although the formal acceptance by Henry II did not come till November.

[2] I.e. before the grant of primacy (whose significance was not noted by Professor Saltman). Cf. no. 48; Osbert de Clare, *Ep.* 32; *GF*, p. 91. This rule is only broken by no. 76 (archbishop alone, 1148: but see below, n. 5); nos. 5, 168, 188 have the primatial title early, but none can be proved earlier than the grant.

[3] The change of primacy title ('totius Anglie primas' to 'Anglorum primas') cannot be precisely dated. But it seems likely that Theobald or his clerks took to the latter as they became aware that the Pope did not intend the primacy to give him authority over York (cf. *GF*, p. 91). In Saltman, no. 221, and possibly 110, 232–3, the legatine title appears prematurely.

[4] There are sufficient errors in Gilbert's titles to make it hazardous to lay too much stress on the precise addresses. But there is sufficient uniformity to set a pattern, if not a rule.

[5] Nos. 89, 91–2, 123. It is just possible that Gilbert was deliberately omitting the title after Theobald's attempt to establish authority over York had been rebuffed at Rheims (JS *HP*, P, pp. 5–6; C, p. 5).

# APPENDIX III

(Adapted from *EHR*, LXIII (1948), 523–6)

We know little of the history of Cerne during the twelfth century and the Foliot letters give us a fairly complete picture, tantalizing as it sometimes is in its omissions, of a stormy episode which reached its conclusion with the Council of Rheims in 1148. A disreputable abbot named William Scottus or Scotus had encouraged a serious state of laxity in the community which led to his deposition by Bishop Jocelin of Salisbury some months before June 1145 (no. 38, 1144–5). The monks of Cerne then elected Gilbert Foliot's own prior of Gloucester, Bernard, and sent a deputation to secure the abbot's consent. Permission was given and Foliot wrote to Bishop Jocelin to obtain the latter's agreement to the choice of Bernard. Meanwhile a papal legate, Imar, bishop of Tusculum, had reached England and the prior and monks of Cerne met the legate to obtain papal confirmation. The election was confirmed and Imar ordered the reluctant Bernard to assume office (cf. no. 53). This was the 'plantatio prima' which Imar established in England and must therefore have been made at the outset of his visit (nos. 39, 41).

Bernard was met in solemn procession by the Cerne community and installed (see no. 53). The abbatial blessing should have followed at the hands of the diocesan, Jocelin of Salisbury, but the latter made it conditional on payments to which Bernard, a reformer of scrupulous nature, was unable to agree. Dismayed by the state of his community and the simoniacal demands of the bishop he expressed his anxieties in a letter to Foliot which elicited a generous promise of help, and advised reference of the difficulty over the blessing to Cardinal Imar (no. 39, early 1145). Foliot agreed to write himself to the legate on Bernard's behalf. He also wrote to Bishop Jocelin asking him to respect Bernard's scruples and perform the blessing; a refusal would lead to an appeal (no. 40, 1145, before 10 June). The appeal was entered and Imar sent Foliot an order for forwarding to the bishop instructing him to perform the blessing. This letter was acknowledged by Foliot who asked Imar to write again to the bishop and apologized for not having fulfilled the legate's wish for a meeting (no. 41, 1145, before 10 June).[1]

The meeting was at length arranged and Foliot wrote to Bernard urging him to join their conference on the following Sunday at Winchester (no. 46, 1145, before 10 June). It took place on 10 June 1145, the date fixed by Imar for the appeal of the

---

[1] Foliot informs the legate of the trouble which had begun at Cerne 'post discessum uestrum'. This most likely refers to his departure from the west country to London where he met many of the bishops; see *PUE*, II, no. 45. The meeting referred to in no. 53 may imply that Imar landed in the west of England; he may have decided to visit first the districts held for the empress, who was perhaps reckoned more favourable to the Church than Stephen.

prior of Ewenny against Uhtred, bishop of Llandaff.[1] The meeting was successful and Bishop Jocelin was evidently forced to confer the blessing on Bernard (cf. no. 53), but almost immediately a revolt broke out at Cerne against the new abbot and Foliot wrote to the prior and community urging support for Bernard; a monk named Adelardus had left Cerne for Canterbury, and was probably *en route* for Rome to appeal to the Pope (no. 49, after 10 June 1145–6).

This appeal to the Cerne community failed, the situation deteriorated, and the ex-abbot returned to drive Bernard out (cf. no. 51). Foliot appealed next to Archbishop Theobald who sent orders for the ex-abbot's ejection which were forwarded to the bishop of Salisbury and by him ignored (no. 50, after 10 June 1145–6). In a further letter to the archbishop complaining of Jocelin's inaction Foliot advised recourse to the earl of Gloucester (no. 51, after 10 June 1145–6). The advice was followed but the monk of Cerne who set out for Gloucester was attacked by the followers of the ex-abbot, pulled from his horse and gravely injured, and Foliot therefore returned to the charge with Theobald, stressing the latest contempt for his authority and suggesting suitable reprisals on those responsible (no. 52, 1145–6).[2] Evidently the primate ordered *inter alia* the transfer of the rebellious monks to another monastery (cf. no. 55), but his authority was unable to prevail and at length Bernard decided on an appeal to the Pope. Four letters of Foliot, written most probably in the summer of 1146 (cf. the reference to Michaelmas in no. 56), deal with this appeal: the first, to Eugenius III, contains a statement of the case (no. 53), the second enlists the support of Bishop Robert of Hereford (no. 54), a third to the bishop of Salisbury encloses letters to him from the archbishop written prior to the appeal and states Bernard's terms for a settlement (no. 55), the fourth to the archbishop announces the appeal and asks for protection of Bernard's property during his absence (no. 56; see Appendix II).

Eugenius III committed the appeal for hearing in England to four bishops, of whom the bishop of Exeter was one (nos. 63, 62). Foliot therefore wrote to the bishop urging him to be at Bath on the appointed date, 1 June 1147 (no. 62, before that date). A decision was given favourable to Bernard but he was unable to secure restitution. Meanwhile some of the Cerne monks, presumably returning from the Curia, had secured the support of Nivard, brother of St Bernard of Clairvaux, and he had enlisted the aid of the empress. She now wrote to Foliot requesting better treatment for the monks of Cerne and received a reply announcing the papal decision, the judgement of the four judges delegate, and his own decision to uphold it (no. 63, early 1148). Surprising as it may seem the abbot of Cerne's troubles were not yet over, and the final letter of the series advises him, since he had failed to establish himself, to attend the coming Council of Rheims and obtain permission

---

[1] Cf. no. 45. The Ewenny case was to be heard 'ad *Domine in tua misericordia*', i.e. on the first Sunday after Pentecost. In both no. 45 and no. 46 Foliot states that he himself will be present *uita comite* which suggests that the two letters refer to the same occasion.

[2] We may probably read into the phrase in no. 52 'cumque toto orbe Britannico lateque patentibus insulis occidentis, ecclesia uestra Dei uestro se parere glorietur imperio' a reference to the primacy recently bestowed on Theobald by Eugenius III (5 May 1145): see Appendix II.

from the Pope to resign (no. 64, before March 1148). Bernard retired and was ultimately to find a safe harbour as abbot of Burton.[1]

The Cerne letters give an interesting glimpse of the history of a lesser Benedictine house during Stephen's reign and of a state of things fortunately not typical of monasticism during that period. They reveal that an obscure community could defy the united efforts of bishops, primate, and Pope, rejecting in the end an abbot who had been confirmed in office by a papal legate, duly blessed by his diocesan, and upheld by formal verdict of papal judges delegate. No doubt the disturbed political conditions of England at the time may be in some degree held responsible.

[1] Ann. Burton *s.a.* 1160 (*Ann. Mon.* I, 187): 'Bernardus abbas venit, monachus Glovernie, quondam abbas de Cerne, unde recessit propter magnas eiusdem domus exordinationes.' Cf. Biog. Index *s.n.* Cerne; *GF*, p. 81.

# APPENDIX IV

In no. 72 Gilbert testified to St Bernard that Kingswood abbey had been founded (in 1139 as we know from other evidence)[1] by William of Berkeley and William abbot of Tintern, with the assent of the empress and Milo of Gloucester; that it had been a daughter house of Tintern. But it is evident that it had been claimed or suggested that Tintern had abandoned its rights as mother house. On this Gilbert refuses to pronounce—wisely, it would seem, since the dispute on Kingswood's relationship to Tintern, of which Gilbert's letter is the earliest evidence, was not settled till over forty years later.

The records of the Cistercian general chapter reveal that a case between Kingswood and Tintern was raised and deputed to the abbots of L'Aumône and Quarr in 1192, and settled, in favour of Tintern, in 1193.[2] This must clearly be associated with a narrative of the history of Kingswood, printed by Dugdale,[3] which was evidently the abbot of Tintern's deposition for this case. A covering letter describes its author as E. abbot of Tintern and is addressed to William abbot of Cîteaux. The only E. abbot of Tintern of the late twelfth century known was Eudo, formerly abbot of Kingswood (c. 1180–8), who was promoted to Tintern in 1188; and so William of Cîteaux must be Abbot William II, 1184–92.[4] Thus the narrative can be dated 1188–92. Since its author tells us that the case had been raised at general chapter in his absence, we may with some confidence associate it with the entry in the chapter records and date it to 1192.

---

[1] L. Janauschek, *Originum Cisterciensium, tomus* I (Vienna, 1877), p. 58: 7 Sept. 1139.

[2] *Statuta...Ordinis Cisterciensis,* ed. J.-M. Canivez, I, 153, 170–1: Tintern's superiority over Kingswood was confirmed. It is a little curious that the dispute was between Tintern and Kingswood, not between Kingswood and Waverley, as Abbot Eudo indicates. Presumably the formal procedure was that Kingswood claimed independence of Tintern, and Eudo was concerned to emphasize that Waverley was responsible. In any case a dispute between Tintern and Kingswood must have involved the rights of the mother house, and this detail hardly serves to throw doubt on the identification of the entries in the chapter records with the dispute revealed in the Kingswood documents.

[3] *Monasticon,* V, 425–6 (1st ed. I, 811–12). The cartulary from which this was taken has disappeared (see Davis, *Cartularies,* no. 513). A few original charters survive: see *HMC, 5th Report,* App. pp. 333 ff.; *Trans. Bristol and Gloucs. Arch. Soc.* XXII (1899), 179–256. For Kingswood abbey in general, see E. S. Lindley in *ibid.* LXXIII (1954), 115 ff.; LXXIV (1955), 36 ff.; LXXV (1956), 73 ff.

[4] Ann. Waverley, *Ann. Mon.* II, 245 (previously abbot of Kingswood), cf. 242; *Gallia Christiana,* IV, 986 ff. The covering letter was written by William abbot of Quarr and the abbot of Woburn (not named), and a difficulty is raised by the fact that the abbot of Quarr in the 1190's was apparently called Walter (*Cart. Sandford,* II, 207, probably after 1194; *Devon Fines,* I, no. 29, 1199) and was succeeded by William, who resigned in 1205 (William of Newburgh, ed. Howlett, *Chrons. of the Reigns of Stephen, etc.,* RS, II, 508). But we do not know that Walter was abbot as early as 1192; William was a common name; and confusion of the names William and Walter was in any case easy.

The story it tells is as follows. William of Berkeley gave Kingswood to Tintern to found there a Cistercian abbey; this was confirmed by the Empress Matilda.[1] In the course of time the monks of Kingswood bought Hazleton (near Kemble) from John of St John, who had obtained it from King Stephen during the anarchy ('tempore hostilitatis'). It had been part of the fee of Reginald of St-Valéry, and with the restoration of peace he received it back, turned the monks off and did them much damage. Subsequently Reginald found himself compelled, by way of penance, to found a monastery of the order of Cîteaux. This he accomplished by summoning the monks from Kingswood to Hazleton, and settling them there. It transpired that the water supply at Hazleton was inadequate, and Reginald shifted the abbey a few miles south-west to property he held at Tetbury. Meanwhile Roger of Berkeley III, cousin, overlord and successor in the foundership to William of Berkeley, had objected to the removal of the monks from his property. He accepted the loss, however, on condition that one monk should remain at Kingswood to say mass for him and his family in perpetuity. Subsequently, on the demand of the abbot of Cîteaux,[2] he agreed that this mass should be said at Tetbury.

'Omnibus...hiis ita se habentibus', a chapter was held at Kirkstead, at which Philip abbot of L'Aumône, the mother house of Tintern and Waverley, Henry abbot of Waverley and Payne abbot of Tetbury were present, to decide a controversy between the abbots of L'Aumône and Waverley.[3] Part of the agreement was to settle monks of Waverley at Kingswood, and to this Payne agreed, being 'simplex et nullius astuciae'. Neither Tintern nor the monks of Tetbury accepted the arrangement, and somewhat later, at a meeting at Kingswood, the monks from Waverley were forced to withdraw. By now the community at Tetbury had decided that their site was too cramped, and arranged to return to Kingswood. Bernard of St Valéry, their present patron, bought forty acres from Roger of Berkeley III at 'Mireforde', adjacent to the old site of the monastery, and there the monks were established, the new monastery being called Kingswood.[4] For twenty-

---

[1] Her charter is printed in *Monasticon*, v, 426 (no. III). On the Berkeley family, see H. Barkly in *Trans. Bristol and Gloucs. Arch. Soc.* VIII (1883–4), 193–223. Thomas, first abbot, had been prior of Tintern (Ann. Waverley, *Ann. Mon.* II, 228).

[2] G. in *Monasticon*, v, 426–7 (no. VI), i.e. G(ozuin), 1151–5 (or, just possibly, G(ilbert), 1163–7).

[3] This was evidently the occasion of John of Salisbury's *Ep.* 106 (and see *JS Epp.* I, Appendix IV, and esp. p. 262 n. 1 on the abbot of L'Aumône), in which Archbishop Theobald admonished the abbots of Waverley's daughter houses to obey Waverley and not agree to the schism being encouraged by Philip abbot of L'Aumône. It may well be that Waverley's settlement at Kingswood was the solution to her problem of schismatic monks. But it is clear from Gilbert Foliot's letter that this was not, as Eudo evidently wished to imply, the beginning of Waverley's direct influence over Kingswood (this holds, even though Waverley is not mentioned by name in Gilbert's letter). Eudo goes on to say that the arrangement was repudiated 'et super ea diu litigatum etiam in praesenti capitulo'; it is not clear whether he regarded this as part of his own case or a separate, though obviously connected, issue.

[4] See charters of Bernard and Roger IV, *Monasticon*, v, 426–7, nos. IV, VII. Eudo says that Roger IV (still alive) witnessed the arrangement at Kingswood when the Waverley monks were withdrawn; Eudo calls him *fundator*, although his father must still have been alive at this time. The version of Bernard's charter in *HMC*, v, 337, has Simon bishop of Worcester

eight years or more, says the abbot of Tintern, we held her as a daughter in peace and subject to no claim, until in the last general chapter, when I was not present nor anyone who could speak for me, the abbot of Waverley produced charters (evidently purporting to show that Kingswood was subject to his house), and the abbot of L'Aumône, with the connivance of the chapter, has handed Kingswood abbey over to him.

This narrative is no doubt broadly speaking correct; but its chronology needs some revision, and Eudo was evidently disingenuous (or misinformed) on the early history of Waverley's claim. Kingswood was indeed founded by William of Berkeley as a daughter of Tintern, as Gilbert's letter proves, and William was in due course succeeded by Roger as patron. John of St John seems to have been enfeoffed with the St Valéry lands *c.* 1143–4, and to have died in September 1150.[1] The first move to Hazleton probably took place *c.* 1149–50, not, as Eudo says, after 1154.[2] The arrangement between Berkeley and Reginald of St Valéry presumably took place in the mid fifties—in the era of Roger of Berkeley's eclipse (after 1153–4); and it had certainly been accomplished before the meeting at Kirkstead, which can be dated 1157–61. Reginald of St Valéry died in 1166–7, Roger of Berkeley III *c.* 1170; so one would expect an arrangement between Roger and Reginald's successor, Bernard of St Valéry, to be dated 1166–*c.* 1170, and this may well be the true date of the final establishment of Kingswood. But Eudo implies that this had taken place twenty-eight years or more before he was writing, i.e. not later than 1164. Either he or a scribe or editor has mistaken the period, or the move took place in Reginald's lifetime.[3]

The purpose of Eudo's narrative was to establish that Tintern's rights as mother house of Kingswood were and always had been unambiguous. By 1192 the rights of a Cistercian mother house were clearly defined, and it used to be thought that

among the witnesses; since Simon died in 1150, this deceived Dr Rose Graham (*VCH Glos.* II 100) into telescoping the whole story into the years 1148–9. This is manifestly impossible, and since Bernard only inherited in 1166–7 (see below), and his charter refers to King Henry and Queen Eleanor (i.e. is later than 1154), there is evidently a mistake in the witness list—possibly for Simon *archdeacon* of Worcester (1167–89).

[1] Roger of Berkeley III appears as patron in a charter dated 10 March 1148 (just possibly for 1149), by which date William was presumably dead (*Monasticon*, v, 427, no. x). On John of St John and Reginald of St Valéry, see H. E. Salter, *Facsimiles of Early Charters in Oxford Muniment Rooms* (Oxford, 1929), notes to nos. 46, 80. These dates are not perhaps quite certain, but minor adjustments in them would not affect the main lines of our reconstruction. It is, however, clear that the story of these men's fiefs was more complex than Eudo realized. We are very grateful to Mr R. H. C. Davis for advice on this and other aspects of this appendix.

[2] Before John's death, probably in 1150 (see above); but Roger of Berkeley's charter (1148) and another of Henry II before he became king (of 1149) strongly suggest that the monks were still at Kingswood then. There is, however, the difficulty that there is reason to suppose, as sometimes happened with Cistercian houses on the move, that the community continued to be known as Kingswood abbey even on its travels (cf. *PR 8 Henry II*, p. 14).

[3] It is possible that Bernard acted while his father was still alive. There is evidence of his doing so in Normandy even in the 1140's or early 1150's (*CDF*, nos. 1057–8), and he may have taken over effective control while his father was in the Holy Land in 1157–60 (if he was: see note to no. 174).

this had been so since Stephen Harding first drafted the *Carta Caritatis*, before Waverley, Tintern or Kingswood were founded. It is now known that this was not the case,[1] and some of the obscurities of the issue between Tintern and Waverley may have been due to constitutional ambiguity. Thus Waverley, Kingswood's aunt, seems in the 1140's to have tried to override Tintern's rights, and L'Aumône, Waverley's parent, to have overridden Waverley's in the 1150's. But in each situation there may well have been a simpler, more personal reason. The abbot of L'Aumône was probably of an interfering character. Kingswood was Tintern's only daughter before 1200, and Tintern may herself have been a poor, struggling community in the 1140's,[2] inclined to defer to the abbot of Waverley, head of a growing family and accustomed to manage other houses. And the affair was no doubt complicated by the intimacy of the leading characters involved in this story. Eudo abbot of Tintern, the narrator, had been abbot of Kingswood; Henry abbot of Waverley, a leading figure in earlier years, had been abbot of Tintern—possibly already at the time of Gilbert's letter, certainly in the 1150's—before becoming abbot of Waverley (after 1157–82).[3] It is clear that Abbot Eudo used the complex story of Kingswood's relations with her lay patrons to hide an equally complex story—of which, in fairness, he may only have been partly aware—of her relations with her Cistercian forebears. It seems clear from Gilbert's letter that the dispute between Tintern and Waverley as to which should exercise the rights of mother house over Kingswood had arisen already in the 1140's, before any of the translations or schisms which complicated the later development of the issue.

[1] For the literature of the controversies on the early Cistercian documents, see D. Knowles, *Great Historical Enterprises* (London, 1963), pp. 197 ff.
[2] Her poverty was later noted by the author of the *Vita Wulfrici* (ed. M. Bell, pp. 74–5).
[3] *JS Epp.* I, 263 and n.; Ann. Waverley, *Ann. Mon.* II, 242.

# APPENDIX V

The following list is not the result of comprehensive inquiry, but gives such references to lost charters as we have noted.

## Hereford

(1) Grant of an indulgence of forty days in connexion with the dedication of the church of Coddington (Herefs). Note in document describing dedication of three altars in the church by Bishop Hugh Foliot in 1231 'ut didicimus secundum opinionem quorundam eadem ecclesia dedicata fuit a bone memorie Gilberto Foliot Herefordensi episcopo, cum quadraginta dierum relaxatione'—so that there may have been no written record of the indulgence. *Reg. Caroli Bothe*, p. 199 (checked by Hereford Diocesan Registry, Reg. Booth (etc.)) (1516–39), fo. 139v).

(2) Charter (subject unknown) for Dore Abbey (notes in BM Cotton Julius MS C. vii, fo. 252; Harl. 5804, fo. 258).

(3) ? Grant of land in *Herlingeham* (Orlham in Ledbury, Herefs) to Robert Lambert. Charters of Gilbert Foliot and Robert Foliot are referred to in Bishop William's (1189–98) settlement of the suit between William of Burghill and William the chamberlain on the land; the latter's case was that Bishop Robert Foliot had granted it to him after Robert Lambert's death; the former produced letters of H(ubert Walter) archbishop and justiciar (held both offices 1193–8), and witnesses. The former won (in the shire court), and after consulting charters of G.F. (whose terms can only be conjectured) and R.F., the bishop confirmed him in his tenure. Hereford Cathedral Muniments, no. 1363, printed by D. Walker in *Misc. D. M. Stenton*, pp. 266–7; cf. 257–8.

## London

(4) ? Decision as judge delegate on the tithes of Runcton, known from the agreement on the case of a pension from the church of Mundham (Sussex) and certain tithes between Jocelin, canon of Chichester, who held the church in the name of the monks of Boxgrove, and the abbey of Troarn. The disputes had gone before Jocelin, bishop of Salisbury (d. 1184), and R(ichard), archdeacon (presumably of Wiltshire, i.e. not before 1173); previously some tithes had been disputed before Bartholomew, bishop of Exeter (d. 1184), and Baldwin, abbot of Forde (i.e. before 1180); and the tithes of Runcton (Sussex) before G. F. William of St John, lord and patron of Mundham, intervened and made peace: the monks of Troarn renounced their claim and the monks of Boxgrove granted them the tithe of corn at Runcton and tithes of two hides in addition after Master Jocelin's death. It is not clear if Gilbert had issued any decision. *Cart. Boxgrove*, no. 61 (p. 51); *Cart. Bruton*, no. 339 (omitting reference to Gilbert), *Acta Chichester*, no. 60 (15 Jan. 1179, ? for 1180).

(5) Decision in the case between the prior and canons of Holy Trinity, Aldgate, and Robert 'philosophus' on the parish of Smithfield: Robert claimed that it had been taken from his church of St Peter in the Tower when he was attending Henry II at the siege of Toulouse (1159); but it was decided that the parish adhered to the canons' church of St Botolph by Aldgate. The surviving documents are a statement by the prior and canons and a charter of Nicholas archdeacon of London; no charter of Gilbert may ever have existed. But the

case was ventilated 'sepius coram archidiacono Nicholao...et aliquando coram Gilberto episcopo' and settled in 1166: 'et hoc factum est septimo idus Maii apud Westmonasterium, in capella infirmorum die illo quo placitum fuit inter comitem Albericum et uxorem eius quando appellauit apud papam' (cf. above, no. 187) when Robert 'renuntiauit petitioni sue predicte in manum domni G. episcopi...'. Cart. Holy Trinity, Aldgate, Glasgow Univ. Library, Hunterian MS U. 2. 6 (215), fo. 172.

(6) *Littera testimonialis* (terms uncertain) relating to the affairs of Holy Trinity priory, Aldgate, known only from note in *Historia* in Glasgow University Library, Hunterian MS U. 2. 6, fo. 5v (printed Hearne, William of Newburgh, III, 705–7): '(1167) et extitit ista domus sine priore per duos annos xxxijas septimanas et j diem. Omnia ergo que fiebant per sigillum commune illis diebus fiebant sub nomine prioris Ed'i, cum nullus talis creatus extiterat, ut patet per litteram testimonialem Gylberti Lond' episcopi scriptam in Quanta (*sic*) cum littera B. folio xco' (*Quanta* is the normal term in this cart. for the priory registers; 'ut...xco' is an addition in MS). See Biog. Index *s.v.* London for the problems raised by this curious passage.

(7) Institution of Thomas, clerk, son of Andrew, to the church of Radwinter (Essex: Radewintr') on the presentation of Jordan, chamberlain of Richard de Lucy. Confirmed by Bishop Richard (witnessed by Master Alard as canon of St Paul's, and so 1190–6). PRO E 40/13,828.

(8 and 9) Letters of G.F. for the prior of Saffron Walden, c. 1165, and on tithes of a chapel in Pleshey (Essex), c. 1180, are referred to in the *Liber de fundatione* of Saffron Walden priory (later abbey) (*Chron. Walden*, in *Essex Review*, XLV (1936), 150, 228; on MSS see Davis, *Cartularies*, no. 985).

(10) Grant of the church of *Westhamma* (presumably West Ham, Essex) to the monks of Stratford Langthorn (Essex, Cist.) with the assent of Gilbert of Muntfichet, referred to in confirmation by Baldwin, archbishop of Canterbury, primate and legate (1185–7). BM Harl. Charter 43. G. 26.

(11) Confirmation of the grant of the Church of All Hallows the Great, London ('que dicitur Semmanesir') (cf. *VN*, p. 333) to Tewkesbury Abbey. *Monasticon*, II, 71, from BM Cotton MS Cleop. A. vii, fo. 76.

(12) Charter to the nuns of Wix priory (Essex), referred to in confirmation by Archbishop Richard (1177–82). Ed. C. N. L. Brooke in *Misc. D. M. Stenton*, pp. 59–60 (the genuineness of this document is defended *ibid.* pp. 51–2), from PRO E 40/5269.

(13) Grant (presumably confirmation) to the monks of Bec of the church of Dunton (Waylett, Essex), referred to in confirmation by Bishop Richard (1189–98; witnessed by Master Peter of Waltham, not yet archdeacon, and so c. 1189). *The Manuscripts of St George's Chapel, Windsor Castle*, ed. J. N. Dalton (Windsor, 1957), p. 47 (XI. G. 5). (Cf. *Select Documents of the English lands of the abbey of Bec*, ed. M. Chibnall, Camden 3rd Series, LXXIII, 1951, pp. 14–15.)

ADDENDUM. After the final proof of this book had been passed, it was brought to our notice by the kindness of Dr B. R. Kemp that a charter to Wix priory (presumably no. 12 above) survives in an Inspeximus of 1310 in Cambridge, Christ's College Muniments, Manorbier A: it confirms the grant of Wormingford Church to the nuns by Walter (*sic*) of Windsor, and may be dated c. 1170–9. We hope to publish the full text elsewhere shortly.

# APPENDIX VI

**1**

From a letter to a friend; from the style probably Gilbert's.

Iocunditas michi et exultatio exuberat quotiens obsequio fame uos bene ualere et uigere cognosco. Et enim solempne michi est uos ut domnum colere, uos amplecti, uestramque promotionem et sospitatem inter meos assignare successus. Inde est ut michi ad plenitudinem gaudii cedant que circa uos prospera sunt, ad cumulum uero uos esse incolumem. Mendacii arguar si frustra postulatis a me quod possit et expediat amico erogari. Interim rogo ut ad me uestra transferatur pagina qua misterium uestre uoluntatis et salutis agnoscam.

**2**

Heading of a letter to (or possibly from) the bishop of Hereford.

Lund' Hereford'. Amantes se diligere, et optantibus sibi bona, bene uelle.
    Cum michi sepenumero...

**3–4**

Pious preambles for a letter to a friend (3) and a charter (4).[1]

[3] Moris esse solet amantium ut rei dilecte mentionem nunquam audire fastidiant, quin potius ex ipsa confabulandi frequentia humanus affectus circa rem quam diligit amplius inardescat.

[4] Que ad honorem Dei et utilitatem sancte ecclesie in usus pauperum deuotione fidelium conlata sunt eis nequaquam cuiusquam temeritate sunt auferenda sed eis potius obseruanda sunt et augenda.

**5**

A legal comment.[2]

In Codice legitur: Quod si quis dixerit imperatorem perfidum, atrocem, ⟨iniu⟩stum, uel quid simile profuderit, si ex leuitate processerit, contempnendus (lubricum enim lingue ad penam facile trahendum non est); si ex insania, furoris uiniue rabie, miseratione dignum; si ab iniuria, ad nos transmittendum. Ideo ex personis hominum pensemus dictum tale debere puniri, inpunitumue relinqui.

1 G, no. 289; B, fo. 111.
2 B, fo. 111v (*not in* G).
3–4 G, no. 294; B, fo. 144.
5 G, *wrongly printed as part of no. 197*; B, fo. 188.

---

[1] Cf. nos. 330, 450.        [2] *Code*, 9, 7, 1, pr. and 1, very freely rendered.

**6**

The pious sentiment to conclude an address.

Inter mundi huius uarietates illuc dirigere mentis intuitum ubi nullum est uarietatis periculum.

**7**

Preamble of a letter of thanks.

Quicquid in hoc mundo constat esse felicius et in futuro prestantius, sincere postulatio uoluntatis effectu debet persequente compleri, ut deuotionis sinceritas laudabiliter enitescat et res postulata uires indubitanter assumat. Quocirca excellentie uestre gratias et gratiarum actiones...

**8**

Expression of friendship.

Quantum mei cordis affectus de uestra dilectione delectetur, nec uox nec scribentis calamus potest intimare. Tamen ut multa paucis concludam, scitote me pro posse meo uestre semper uoluntati esse obnoxium. Hoc utique uestra probabit dilectio cum aliquid a me fieri optauerit.

**9–15**

The pious preamble of a charter or legal decision: five pious sentiments from addresses or the like; and the preamble to a legal decision.

[9] Quoniam generatio transsit et generatio aduenit, et quod a transeuntibus geritur a succedentibus nisi certis indiciis elucescat ratum non tenetur, utile duximus rerum gestarum series literarum testimonio et sigilli impressione confirmare. Sciant ergo uniuersi...

[10] Infortunio pauperum amicorum, affectu pietatis condescendere.

[11] Sacro proposito firmiter adherere.

[12] Perfectam dilectionem cum debita subiectione.

[13] Magis sperare in Domino quam in homine.

[14] Apud Deum adoptari in filium.

[15] Satagendum nobis est et procurandum sollicite ne lites in nostra decise presentia, ulla possint iterum occasione in controuersiam denuo suscitari.

6 G, *wrongly attached to no. 299*; B, fo. 189 v.
7 G, *printed as part of no. 214*; B, fo. 192.
8 G, *printed as part of no. 214*; B, fo. 192.
9–15 G, no. 303; B, fo. 195 v.

## 16

The sealing clause for a composition.

Et ut conuentio hec inter eos illesa conseruetur, eam presenti scripto et sigilli nostri appositione confirmamus.

## 17

A sentence from a letter.

Nouerit dilectio uestra karissime me in omnibus uestro gratanter paratum seruitio, et si i[d] forte immineret, sponsioni respon[surum de]uota operis exhibitio.

## 18

Fragment of a petition.

De benignitate uestra simul et dilectio[ne] paternitati uestre pro latore presentium N. pre[ces hu]miles et deuotas porrigimus, impense ro[gantes] ut eum amore Dei et ob reuerentiam beati [     ] nostre si placet precis intuitu benigne s[uscipiatis et] clementer exaudiatis. Quicquid autem in ocul[is uestris] gratie et benignitatis inuenerit nobis indultum...

## 19–22

Fragments from letters, one answering a petition, two petitions, and the fourth a commination against someone (apparently a layman) who had seized tithes belonging to the church of Fulham.

[19] Salutem et pronum deuote fidelitatis obsequium.

Vetus est et antiquum 'qui fidenter diligit loquitur confidenter', nec de eius affectu hesitare quis potest cuius sincera dilectio omnem suspicionis fecem eliminat. Inde est quia preces uestras negare non possumus, presertim ubi nos uincit instantia, et magna intercedit auctoritas et dilectio.

[20] De uestra domne confisus liberalitate obnixe uestre supplico paternitati, quatinus ut uobis in omnibus ex deuoto deuotior existam, ad ecclesie uestre beneficium aliquod uestra me uocare dignetur excellentia, quod uobis honestum sit dare et michi a uestra suscipere largitate.[1]

---

16 G, no. 310; B, fo. 196v.
17 G, no. 315; B, fo. 197.
2 exhibitio] *presumably for* exhibitione
18 G, no. 316; B, fo. 197 (*some words cut away with the margin*).
3 beati [     ] *The saint's name is lost*
19 G, no. 318; B, fo. 197v.
20 G, no. 319; B, fo. 197v.

---

[1] This was evidently from (or a formula for) an appeal to Gilbert for a benefice, not written by him.

[21] Quod aliquid a bonitate uestra postulare presumo, non precedentium confidentia meritorum sed uestre benignitatis facit intuitus.

[22] Grauiter ut audio delinquis qui manus tuas ad decimas ecclesie que ad solum ius diuinum pertinent manum mittere non formidas. Vnde tibi mando et super Christianitatem tuam iniungo quatinus decimas ad ecclesiam de Fuleham pertinentes sibi sine dilatione rest⟨it⟩ui facias, ne si eas iniuste detinueris, iram ex hoc Dei incurras et sententiam in te quam mereris excipias.

## 23

From a letter enjoining charity to the poor.

Cum singule uirtutes karissimi acceptentur in conspectu Dei nulla magis Deo placere legitur quam elemosina. Scriptum namque est: 'date elemosinam' dicit Dominus, 'et omnia munda sunt uobis'.[1] Qui[cum]que igitur Deo placere desiderat, ex beneficiis sibi diuinitus collatis pauperibus erogare alienis necessitatibus subuenire intendat, ut a Domino ob ipsis collata die illa in centuplum recip[ere] ₅ ualeat.[2] Vnde quia ex iniuncto nobis officio uestri curam gerimus, uestram studiosius fraternitatem commonemus quatinus ut et elemosina uestra pluribus in [ex]emplum boni operis pateat attendatis.

## 24

From a petition.

Gloria et honore in perpetuum coronari.

Latorem presentium filium uestrum B., honeste quod ad conscientiam nostram conuersatum apud nos, caritati uestre commendamus atentius, preces in hoc deuote porrigentes, ut eum tanquam deuotum filium cum gratia suscipiatis, et nostre petitionis intuitu de cariore cariorem habeatis, ut nos ex hoc et dilectionis et ₅ amplioris gratie debitores habeatis.

## 25

The preamble to a composition.

Tutum, fratres, reputamus et utile literarum monumentis excipere, que paci inter personas ecclesiasticas reformande, id firmius in posterum conseruande certum fuerit expedire, ne que conniuentia iudicum et assensu partium transsactione uel amicali compositione ad pacem redacta fuerint, a memoria tractu temporis euanescere aut in litem rediuiuam iterato contingat exurgere. Hinc ⟨est⟩ quod ₅ controuersia...

21 G, no. 320; B, fo. 197v.
22 G, no. 321; B, fo. 197v. 1–2 manus|manum *sic* B
23 G, no. 322; B, fo. 198 (*the margin cut with the loss of a few letters*).
24 G, no. 324; B, fo. 198v.
2 contientiam B
25 G, no. 328; B, fo. 200.
6 controuersia...] Hinc controuersia B, *with* quod *added*

---

[1] Luc. xi. 41.                    [2] Cf. Matt. xix. 29.

# APPENDIX VII

Nos. 1–3 are anonymous letters (or parts of letters) in R and Va, with insufficient indication that they are Gilbert's to be included above. No. 4 purports to be an agreement in which he was involved as abbot of Gloucester, but is probably spurious, at least in its present form. No. 5 is the only unprinted document in MS B.

## 1

Extract from a letter of denunciation.

This has been added at the foot of a leaf in R containing nos. 22, 5. It appears to be a letter demanding punishment, perhaps from a bishop ('patrem'), and is similar in tone to Gilbert's denunciations of the crimes of the anarchy to Robert de Bethune and Simon of Worcester (nos. 2, 5, etc.). It may be an extract from a similar letter, the rest of which is now lost; or from some quite alien source, added here on account of its appropriateness to some of Gilbert's early letters.

De turpitudinibus eius quibus terra sordet et facte sunt omnibus in parabolam supersedeo polluere labia mea, et uestras aures. Nullus perpetua dignior inclusione, nichil eius perpetuo silentio iustius. Hoc autem est quod amicum et patrem cupimus esse admonitum ut hec ipsa ultio que facienda est eo zelo quo facienda est fiat,
5 quatinus non solum presens facinus multatum esse uideatur, sed etiam a simili temeritate audiens omnis malignitas compescatur.

## 2

[? *c.* 1172–3] To the Pope.

A report of the case between Master William, clerk and *medicus* of the English king, and Laurence clerk of *Hotun'* on the church of *Hotun'*, which had been delegated to the author by letter 'domnorum cardinalium'. Laurence had been adjudged the church by the bishop of Durham and the abbot of Vaudey acting as papal judges delegate; William claimed that this was done when he was abroad on royal business and had not received a summons. Laurence appealed to the Pope.

The reference to the cardinals seems most likely to be to Albert and Theoduin, who came to Normandy and England in 1171–3 to settle the affairs of the English Church after Becket's murder (Tillmann, pp. 68–72); it seems probable that they delegated this case in the months following the settlement at Avranches in 1172. The author was presumably an English bishop who was using Master David, in whose Register the letter survives, as his representative at the Curia, and this points to Gilbert, Roger of Worcester or Bartholomew of Exeter; but there seems no clear indication which of the three is the most likely.

1 R, fo. 206, *added at foot (with 'B'' in the margin)*.
2 Va, fo. 148; Liverani, pp. 582–3.

Domno pape.

Lator presentium magister Willelmus, clericus et medicus illustris domni regis Anglorum, domnorum cardinalium litteras ad nos detulit, quibus nobis in mandatis dederunt, ut super possessione ecclesie de Hotun', a qua se iniuste per Laurentium clericum de Hotun' querebatur deiectum, plenam ei iustitiam exhiberemus. 5 Allegauit itaque in presentia nostra constitutus, dum ob publicas regni causas ac deuota regie necessitatis obsequia longe ageret in partibus transmarinis, se iamdicte ecclesie possessione contra omnem iuris ordinem destitutum, uelut qui a nemine in iudicio defensus fuit, uelut ad quem nulla omnino citatio peruenit. Super hac absentia sua reipublice causa, et quod in possessione nominate prius ecclesie fuerit 10 cum causa reipublice ceperit abesse, nichilominus et infra annum reuersus, de lite suscipienda cautionem sepius obtulerit, sufficiens et idoneum plurium honestorum uirorum testimonium produxit; sed et aliorum instrumentorum eandem possessionis causam instruentium plurimam nobis copiam exhibuit. Omnem etiam nobis optulit cautionem quod, restituta sibi possessione, coram iudicibus prius a sanctitate 15 uestra delegatis, a quibus fuerat expoliatus, uel incontinenti coram nobis uel coram aliis quibuscumque, quos ipsemet Laurentius eligeret, litem super principali negotio subiret: nichilominus ex habundanti et super aliis causis, si quas aduersus ipsum supranominatus Laurentius habuerit, ei sine tergiuersatione responderet. Laurentius uero litteras quasdam uenerabilium fratrum nostrorum Dunelmensis 20 episcopi et abbatis de Valle Dei exhibuit, quibus nobis significarunt quod eum in ecclesie supradicte possessionem miserant. Hec autem missio, utrum de iuris ordine uel contra iuris ordinem processerit, ex earundem litterarum inspectione, quarum transcriptum uobis dirigimus, uestra discretio paucis et de facili aduertere poterit; huic enim cognitioni partes nostras non accomodauimus. Illis siquidem litteris 25 exhibitis, in uocem appellationis sine temporis prefinitione incontinenti ad audientiam uestram erupit. Magister Willelmus nichilominus institit, et de lite suscipienda cautionem offerens, possessionis restitutionem sibi fieri postulauit. Interpositam appellationem multis de causis frustatoriam et iniquam, immo nullo modo admittendam docuit, cum in causa momentanee possessionis ex ciuilis iuris constitu- 30 tione[1] appellatio inueniatur inhibita—que quidem constitutio postea nec iure legum nec canonum legitur retractata. Huic tamen appellationi, siue fuerit equa siue iniqua, ob sedis apostolice reuerentiam deferentes, in negotio nobis ab eorum celsitudine commisso, nequaquam ulterius processimus.

## 3

A petition for preferment or endowment for Master N.

The presence of this letter in Master David's Register makes Gilbert a possible candidate for authorship; and Master N. could be the young scion of the London chapter, Master Nicholas, who occurs in other letters in the Register. But there are no positive indications, and the initial may be a cipher, for any name.

**3** Va, fo. 151 v; Liverani, pp. 621–2; *MB Epp.* 388.

---

[1] *Code*, 7, 69, 1.

Inuitant me aliqui quandoque ad opus michi meticulosum, et quod haut umquam nisi cum timore et pudore aggredior. Postulant namque nonnulli plerumque preces nostras ad uos, qui quod sibi merita denegant, intercessorum patrocinio facilius optinere confidunt. Verum quanto paratior est uenia de presumptione, tanto maior
5 debet esse moderatio in postulatione, ne si forte semel obstruatur aditus gratie, erubescat uterque et qui petiit pro repulsa, et pro quo petiit pro fallacia. Precamur itaque et obnixe rogamus quatenus magistrum N. uirum uobis pernecessarium ob amorem nostrum benignius suscipere, et propter necessitates nostras citius dimittere dignemini. Pro N. nostro rogare non audeo, uerumtamen ut paupertatem eius et
10 terre sue multimodam insufficientiam pietas uestra respicere dignetur, deuotissime exoro. Ait quidam sapiens: 'Quia utilius hauritur puteus ad usum quam exhauritur ad defectum.'[1]

## 4

[29 September 1146] Agreement (probably spurious) between the abbot and community of Gloucester and Robert Harding: Robert received the manor of Tregoff (Glam) with the land of Pennon and all other lands and rents pertaining to the manor, and the church of Llancarfan and its appurtenances and tithes for five years, for £80; to be restored to the abbot and monks if they repay the money sooner.[2]

The purported original is written in a hand of the late twelfth or early thirteenth century, and makes William earl of Gloucester nearly a year before his father's death. It is possible that it is a somewhat corrupted copy of a genuine mortgage taken out by Gilbert with the Bristol citizen Robert FitzHarding who subsequently became lord of Berkeley. But these holdings were in dispute at this time between the abbey and the old family of Llancarfan (see nos. 70–1; *CS*, pp. 276 ff.; Conway Davies, II, 506–37); and it seems rather improbable that Gloucester had sufficient hold on them to use them as security for a loan. It may be that the document represents a genuine transaction, which has been not quite correctly represented, either by inadvertence, or by deliberate alteration on account of the running dispute with the Llancarfan family. It is less likely that it was entirely fabricated, since a forger would hardly have invented what might have been regarded in the twelfth century as a usurious transaction (see note 2).

Sciant presentes et futuri quod hec est conuentio facta inter abbatem et conuentum sancti Petri Glouc(estrie) et dominum Robertum Harding anno incarnationis

3 8 cititius Va
4 *Original (or pretended original)*: PRO, Chancery Records, C 150/2; *copy ibid.* C 150, fo. 162. *Endorsed*: Rob. filius Harding (? twelfth century); De Treigof' (thirteenth century); Non indiget registrari (fourteenth/fifteenth century); . . .ija de laic' t' (thirteenth century). *Printed*: *Cart. Gloucester*, II, 139.

---

[1] Not identified.
[2] The clause which allows for Robert to render a fair account of his takings was no doubt intended to prevent the transaction from looking like a mortgage, in which the lender received the rent, and which was therefore regarded as usurious (see 'Glanvill', *De legibus*, ed. G. D. G. Hall, NMT, p. 124). But it seems clear, and implied in 'dummodo fuerit michi. . .satisfactum', that Robert was in fact to receive interest, and the transaction would seem on the borderline of respectability. This does not make the transaction itself surprising, though it is perhaps remarkable that it should have been made in full shire court, but it does make it somewhat unlikely that it is a total fabrication.

dominice millesimo centesimo xlvi in festo beati Michaelis, quod ego Robertus
Harding recepi manerium de Tregof in Glamorgan cum terra de Pennum et cum
aliis terris et redditibus omnibus ad dictum manerium pertinentibus et eclesiam de 5
Lancaruan cum domibus et curtilagiis et decimis ad dictam eclesiam spectantibus de
dictis abbate et monachis usque ad terminum quinquennii sequentis pro quater
uiginti libris argenteis; ita quod si memoratus abbas possit uel uelit dictam pecuniam
michi uel uxori mee uel heredibus meis ante prefatum terminum persoluere,
computato rationabiliter commodo rerum receptarum ex parte mea, dummodo 10
fuerit michi uel meis satisfactum, ego uel heredes mei absque omni difficultate
dictum manerium de Tregof et prefatam eclesiam cum omnibus prenominatis
dictis abbati et conuentui restituemus. Huius conuentionis testes sunt: domnus
Willelmus comes Glouc(estrie), et totus comitatus de Kairdif.

CYROGRAPHVM


5

[1170] Terms of inquiry for the Inquest of Sheriffs.

This remarkable document is preserved only in MSS B and D, in both of which it follows
the *capitula* of 1166 (see p. xlix); apart from being a royal injunction not much later than the
*capitula*, it seems to bear little relation to its present context; but no doubt the last clause
explains Gilbert's special interest. It has never before been printed; it does not, however, add
materially to our knowledge of the Inquest, on which see J. H. Round in *Commune of
London*, pp. 125–36; *Red Book of the Exchequer*, I, pp. cclxvii–cclxxxiv; there can be no doubt
that it refers to this.[1]

[i] Dicetis super sacramentum uestrum quid uicecomites uel bailiui eorum ceperunt
quoquomodo de singulis hundr(edis), singulis uillatis, singulis hominibus postquam
domnus rex transfretauit. [ii] Dicetis quot et quas terras uicecomites uel bailiui
eorum emerint uel inuadiauerint. [iii] Dicetis quid et quantum uicecomites uel
bailiui eorum dederint iustic(iis) errantibus. [iv] Dicetis quid actum sit catallis 5
fugitiuorum, qui propter asisam de Clarendun' fugerunt. [v] Dicetis si aliquis fuit
retatus et postea premio relaxatus ⟨fo. 89v⟩ et reuersus. [vi] Dicetis quid datum
sit ad filiam regis maritandam et cui traditum sit. [vii] Dicetis si uicecomites uel
bailiui eorum, uel domni uillarum aliquam pacem fecerint uel faciant cum hominibus grauatis, ne querimonia coram rege uel iustic(iis) ueniret. [viii] Dicetis de 10

5 B, fo. 89; D, fos. 87v–88.
3 domnus *om.* B    3 quas D; quos B

---

[1] It follows closely the terms of inquiry printed by Stubbs in *Select Charters...* (9th edn, ed.
H. W. C. Davis, Oxford, 1913), pp. 175–8; but whereas that is in the form of instructions to
the commissioners, this gives instructions to those giving evidence at the inquest. Cc. i–xiv of
this document correspond to nos. i & iii, ii, v(?), vi (pt. 1), vi (pt. 2), vii, x, xi, xiii, xiv,
iv, viii, —(cf. x), xii. This document is naturally the shorter of the two; this is not the place,
however, for a detailed investigation of the differences, which would be instructive. Of the
clauses in the longer document, nos. ix, xv alone are wholly omitted, since they were not in
the form of questions.

admerciatis si quis relaxatus fuerit et per quem. [ix] Dicetis si aliquis est qui homagium non fecerit domno regi uel filio suo. [x] Dicetis de dominiis domni regis, si sic sunt ut rex precepit antequam rex transfretauit. [xi] Dicetis de his qui habent aliquam bailiam de rege in custodia, siue de archiepiscopatu, siue de
15 episcopatibus, siue de abatiis, uel de aliqua eschaeta, quid ipsi uel bailiui eorum ceperint, uel quid in bailia illa adquisierint. [xii] Dicetis quid forestarii uel bailiui eorum ceperint de forestis domni regis et si aliquem relaxauerint qui retatus fuerit de foresta. [xiii] Dicetis quid domni uillarum uel seneschalli eorum ceperint preter rectam consuetudinem. [xiv] Dicetis quid et quantum archidiaconi uel
20 decani ceperint iniuste et sine iudicio.

5 13 sic] ? facte D    14 archidiac' *MSS* (archiepiscopatu, *Select Charters*, p. 176)    15 aliqua *om.* B

# APPENDIX VIII

## DECRETALS AND OTHER PAPAL MANDATES ADDRESSED
## TO GILBERT FOLIOT

In compiling the following list we have had invaluable help from the late Professor W. Holtzmann. It is intended only as a skeleton catalogue of legal mandates and decretals addressed to Gilbert, or to a bishop of London unnamed who can with reasonable probability be identified with Gilbert.[1] Other letters (notably *MB Epp.* 18, 26, 37, 81, 93, 106, 157, 178, 627, 700, 702, 721, 756) are not included, nor decretals and mandates addressed to all the bishops of the province of Canterbury, etc. It is not possible to give full grounds for the identifications here; but it is normally reasonable to assume that a bishop of London addressed by Alexander III was Gilbert Foliot, since his predecessor was sinking into his last illness by the time Alexander was recognized as Pope in England. A bishop of London addressed by Lucius III (1181–5) must be Gilbert Foliot. Slightly more arbitrary is our assumption that a bishop of Hereford addressed by Alexander III was Robert of Melun or Robert Foliot—but only 2½ years intervened between the recognition of Alexander in England and Gilbert's translation to London. There are, however, a number of cases in which the addresses vary (as so commonly) in the decretal collections. In this list we have accepted Holtzmann's conclusions, which can only be fully justified when his great edition of early decretals is published. Thus JL 14,142 is addressed to the bishops of London and Coventry in the *Collectiones Tanner, Sangermanensis* and *Abrincensis*, to Worcester and Coventry (correctly) in all other early collections; this case had been delegated to Gilbert formerly. JL 13,998 is addressed to London in a group of systematic collections including the *Appendix Concilii Lateranensis*, XVI, 10; earlier collections, including *Alcobacensis I, Bridlington* and *Claudiana*, address it to the bishop of Exeter, probably rightly. C. 10 of the Council of Westminster appears in some collections as a decretal addressed to the bishop of London (see *Traditio*, XIII (1957), 478). The bishop of London also occasionally appears in addresses to JL 13,821 (to Canterbury and suffragans), 13,869 (to Durham), 13,995 (to Llandaff) and 14,350 (to York). JL 14,007–8 illustrate a very easy source of confusion: they were in fact addressed to Lund.

On the decretal collections see especially Holtzmann, in *Nachrichten von der Akademie der Wissenschaften in Göttingen*, phil.-hist. Klasse, 1945–8, pp. 15–36; S. Kuttner in *Traditio*, VI (1948), 345–51 and supplements in later numbers of *Traditio*; C. Duggan, *Twelfth-Century Decretal Collections* (London, 1963).

[1] We give references normally to collections of the 'English', 'Bridlington' and 'Worcester' groups (see Duggan, ch. IV), and to non-English primitive collections where relevant. When decretals were copied in later systematic collections this is noted; though the number of these is somewhat arbitrary, since, e.g., the *Appendix Concilii Lateranensis* or the *Bambergensis* and other members of their families are counted as distinct collections, whereas the *Compilationes* only count for one each.

*Hereford*

(1) *Causam que*, Eugenius III to Gilbert. *PUE*, II, no. 71; *Liber Eliensis*, pp. 352–3; JL 9,591. Cf. no. 295.

(2 and 3) *Causam que*, Alexander III to Gilbert and G(odfrey) archdeacon of Worcester. *PUE*, I, nos. 84,90. Cf. no. 345.

(4) *Ex iniuncto*, Anastasius IV to Theobald archbishop of Canterbury, and Gilbert. *PUE*, II, no. 80; *Liber Eliensis*, pp. 358–9; JL 9,745. Cf. no. 295 n.

(5) *Ex litteris karissimi*: no. 141 above.

*London*

(6) *Accepimus querelam*, Alexander III 'Lundoniensi et Exoniensi episcopis', on the case between T. clerk and G. priest on the church of Bungay (Suffolk). This is one of a group of decretals (the others are addressed to Exeter and Worcester, and one also to the abbot of Bury) dealing with a long case between Thomas, clerk of Hugh Bigod, earl of Norfolk, and Guimar, priest, *c.* 1174–6. (*Collectio Floriacensis* (St Florian Stiftsbibliothek, MS III. 5, fos. 173–83), no. 171: the others in the case are nos. 168–72).

(7) *Accepta querela*: see no. 427, pp. 464–5.

(8) *Ad audientiam*, Alexander III 'G. Londoniensi episcopo'. JL 14,223; Giles, no. 362 (only in the *Belverensis*). 1163–81.

(9) *Ad aures nostras*, Alexander III 'Lundoniensi episcopo'. JL 13,992, 14,181, 13,996, 13,990. Complete texts in *Collectiones Dertusensis* (see Holtzmann in *ZRG, Kan. Abt.* XVI (1927), 39–77), no. 41; *Eberbacensis* (see *idem, ZRG, Kan. Abt.* XVII (1928), 548–55), xiv, 1; *Aureaevallensis* (see *idem, ZRG, Kan. Abt.* XVI (1927), 77–109), no. 45; *Floriacensis*, no. 159; *Wigorniensis* (see H.-E. Lohmann, *ZRG, Kan. Abt.* XXII (1933), 36–187), iii, 12; *Claustroneoburgensis* (see F. Schönsteiner in *Jahrbuch des Stiftes Klosterneuburg*, II (1909), 1–154), nos. 125–7; (partial in) *Cheltenhamensis* (BM Egerton MS 2819, fos. 11–102v), ii, 15, fos. 28v–29; *Cottoniana* (BM Cotton MS Vitellius E. xiii, fos. 204–88), vi, 89, fo. 274r–v; partial texts in numerous systematic collections. 1163–81.

(10) *Causam que inter*, Alexander III to Gilbert. *PUE*, III, no. 237; *Cart. Oseney*, II, 226. 1177.

(11) *Causam que inter*, Alexander III 'Lundoniensi episcopo'. Only in *Coll. Wigorniensis*, ii, 34. *c.* 1175 (R(obert), abbot elect of Malmesbury).

(12) *Causam que inter*, Alexander III 'Londoniensi et Wintoniensi episcopis'. JL 14,002; *Coll. Roffensis* (see Duggan, pp. 173–84), no. 60; *Dunelmensis* (Durham Cathedral Library, MS C. III. 1, fos. 5–18), iii, 63; *Regalis* (BM Royal MS 15 B. iv, fos. 107v–18v), no. 151, fo. 118; *Bridlingtonensis* (Oxford, Bodl. MS 357, fos. 80–133v), no. 143 (142, Holtzmann), fo. 121r–v; *Wigorniensis*, vii, 9; *Claustroneoburgensis*, no. 200; *Cheltenhamensis*, ix, 66, fo. 50v; *Cottoniana*, ii, 71,fo. 223; *Peterhusensis* (Cambridge, Peterhouse,—deposited in Univ. Library—fly-leaves to MSS 114, 193, 203, 180), i, 81 (MS 114, final quire, fo. '17' (1) v); also six systematic collections; *Extra*, iv, 17, 7. The names are preserved in *Roffensis* (which gives an abbreviated text) and show that it is an earlier decretal in the same suit as JL 13,932 (cf. Morey, pp. 68–70). 1174–81.

(13) *Conquestionem abbatis*, Alexander III 'Londoniensi et Wygorniensi episcopis'. JL 12,787; *Reg. Malmesbury*, I, 374. 1177.

(14) *Constitutus in presentia*, Alexander III '...Lundoniensi episcopo et...priori de Kineldewod'' (Kenilworth) (so *Alcobacensis I*). *Coll. Alcobacensis I* (Lisbon MS Alcob. 144 (314), fos. 1v–39v), no. 72; *Wigorniensis*, vii, 67; *Brugensis* (see E. Friedberg, *Die Canonessammlungen*, pp. 136–70), xlv, 7. 1163–81.

(15) *Cum discretionem*, Alexander III 'G. Lundoniensi episcopo'. Only in *Parisiensis I* (see Friedberg, *op. cit.* pp. 45–63), no. 33 (p. 54). 1165–70.

(16) *Cum ecclesia*, Alexander III 'Londoniensi et Cicestrensi episcopis'. *PUE*, III, no. 302. Prob. 1163–81.

(17) *Cum Hugo de Diva*, Alexander III, 'G. (so *Cantuariensis* only) Londoniensi episcopo'. *Coll. Cantuariensis* (see Duggan, pp. 162–71), iii, 18; *Dunelmensis*, ii, 10; *Fontanensis* (Bodl. Laud Misc. 527, fos. 24–45 v), i, 29, fo. 28; *Regalis*, no. 84, fo. 113 r–v; *Wigorniensis*, vi, 4; *Claustroneoburgensis*, no. 191; *Cheltenhamensis*, xv, 17, fo. 80 v; *Cottoniana*, iii, 31, fo. 230 r–v; *Peterhusensis*, ii, 19, 3 (MS 193, unfoliated (fo. 2 v)); also three systematic collections. 1163–81.

(18) *Cum sicut ex*, Alexander III 'Londoniensi et Wygorniensi episcopis'. JL 12,780; *Reg. Malmesbury*, I, 370. 1177.

(19) *Cum tibi sit*, Alexander III 'Londoniensi episcopo' (occasionally 'Hereford''). JL 13,991; *Coll. Cusana* (Cues Hospitalbibliothek MS 229, fos. 67–123), no. 200; *Cantuariensis*, i, 21; *Roffensis*, no. 39; *Fontanensis*, ii, 53, fo. 39 v; *Bridlingtonensis*, no. 102 (101, Holtzmann), fo. 108 v; *Claudiana* (BM Cotton MS Claudius A. iv, fos. 189–216), no. 88, fo. 203; *Wigorniensis*, vi, 3; *Claustroneoburgensis*, no. 190; *Cheltenhamensis*, xv, 16, fo. 80 v; *Cottoniana*, iii, 52, fo. 235; *Peterhusensis*, ii, 28 (MS 193, fo. (5)); and ten systematic collections. 1163–81.

(20) *Cum teneamur*, Alexander III 'Londoniensi episcopo'. JL 13,994; *Coll. Cusana*, no. 28; *Claudiana*, no. 195, fo. 214 ('Ravennati archiepiscopo'!); *Cheltenhamensis*, xviii, 27, fo. 95; *Cottoniana*, vi, 74, fo. 272; also in eleven systematic collections and *Extra*, iii, 5, 6. Prob. 1173–6 (*Cusana* gives date: 'Anagnie, ii kal. Maii').

(21) *Dilecti filii*, Alexander III to Gilbert and G(odfrey) archdeacon of Worcester. *PUE*, I, no. 100. 1163.

(22) *Ex conquestione*, Alexander III 'Londoniensi episcopo et...abbati de Eversham' (*sic*). JL 12,777; *Reg. Malmesbury*, I, 373–4. 1177.

(23) *Ex litteris uenerabilis fratris*, Alexander III to Gilbert (name in full in *Claudiana*) and S(imon) (so *ibid.* and *Bridlingtonensis*), abbot of St Albans. *Coll. Alcobacensis I*, 58; *Bridlingtonensis*, no. 93, fos. 106 v–107; *Claudiana*, no. 77, fo. 199 v; *Wigorniensis*, vii, 64; *Cheltenhamensis*, vi, 11, fo. 34 v; *Cottoniana*, iii, 60, fo. 236; *Peterhusensis*, ii, 23, 2 (MS 193, fo. (3 v)); *Dunelmensis*, iv, 97; also six systematic collections. 1167–9.

(24) *Ex parte abbatis*, Alexander III to Gilbert and Roger bishop of Worcester. See no. 427, pp. 463–4. 1174.

(25) *Ex parte Adeline*, Alexander III 'Londoniensi episcopo'. *Coll. Cottoniana*, iv, 55, fo. 249 v; *Peterhusensis*, iii, 56 (MS 180, first quire, fo. '45'). On the case of Adelina, who had entered Cheshunt abbey pregnant, with a 'dowry'; either she is to be received or the money restored. 1163–81.

(26) *Ex parte conuentus*, Lucius III to Gilbert and Benedict abbot of Peterborough. *PUE*, II, no. 221. 1182.

(27) *In beati Petri*, Alexander III to Archbishop Thomas and Gilbert. JL 11,839; Giles, no. 345 (only in the *Belverensis*). 1170.

(28) *Mandamus fraternitati uestre*: Alexander III G. Londoniensi et R. Wigorniensi episcopis.
Mandamus fraternitati uestre atque precipimus, quatinus non obstantibus litteris posterius impetratis, nisi ibi contineatur expressum, quod causam ipsam uestro iudicio subtraxerimus, partes ante presentiam uestram conuocetis et eidem cause iuxta tenorem priorum litterarum appellatione remota finem imponatis. (*Coll. Alcobacensis I*, no. 117; *Claudiana*, no. 19, fo. 191; *Parisiensis I*, no. 35; text as first two, with following variants: Alexander *Cl.*, Inde *Alc.*; *Cl.* om. G....R.; subtraxerimus *Cl.*, subtraximus *Alc.*). 1164–79.

(29) *Nobilis mulier*, Alexander III to Gilbert. Above, no. 164.

(30) *Nos attendentes*, Alexander III 'Londoniensi et Wintoniensi episcopis'. JL 13,106; Diceto, I, 427–8. 1178.

(31) *Peruenit ad nos*, Alexander III 'G. Lundoniensi et R. Wigorniensi episcopis'. JL 13,160; *Coll. Cusana*, no. 43; *Cantuariensis*, i, 54; *Roffensis*, no. 53; *Regalis*, no. 56, fo. 111; *Bridling-tonensis*, no. 19, fo. 84v; *Cheltenhamensis*, viii, 10, fo. 42; *Cottoniana*, iii, 75, fo. 239v; *Peterhusensis*, ii, 46, 2 (MS 203, final quire, fo. (1 v)); and ten systematic collections. 1164–79.

(32) *Querelam abbatis*, Alexander III 'Londoniensi episcopo et...abbati de Eversham (sic)'. JL 12,776; *Reg. Malmesbury*, I, 372–3. 1177.

(33) *Querelam R. canonici*, Alexander III 'Lundoniensi et Wigorniensi episcopis'. JL 14,001; *Coll. Regalis*, no. 94, fo. 114; *Claudiana*, no. 178, fo. 212v; *Cheltenhamensis*, xiv, 2, fo. 73; eleven systematic collections and *Extra*, ii, 24, 10. 1164–79.

(34) *Referente dilecto filio*, Alexander III to Gilbert and John, bishop of Chichester. JL 13,309; Thomas of Elmham, *Historia*, p. 436 (cf. *PUE*, I, p. 73). 1179.

(35) *Referente magistro N.*, Alexander III 'Lundoniensi et Wigorniensi episcopis'. JL 14,000; *Coll. Bridlingtonensis*, no. 165 (164, Holtzmann), fo. 126v; *Cottoniana*, iv, 19, fo. 244; *Peterhusensis*, iii, 7 (MS 203, final quire, fo. (4r–v)); and eight systematic collections. 1164–79.

(36) *Regularis discipline*, Alexander III 'Londoniensi et Saresbyriensi episcopis'. *PUE*, III, no. 254; *Cart. Thame*, II, no. 206. 1163–79.

(37) *Relatum est*, Alexander III 'Londoniensi et Wigorniensi episcopis'. JL 12,401; *Reg. Malmesbury*, I, 371–2. 1174.

(38) *Relatum est*, Alexander III 'Londoniensi episcopo'. JL 13,997; *Coll. Wigorniensis*, ii, 24; *Claustroneoburgensis*, no. 114, 1; *Cheltenhamensis*, x, 13, fos. 61v–62; *Cottoniana*, iv, 39, fo. 247v; *Peterhusensis*, iii, 43 (MS 180, first quire, fo. '43'(3)); four systematic collections and *Extra*, iii, 50, 7. 1163–81.

(39) *Religiosis locis*, Urban III 'episcopo et...aliis ecclesiarum prelatis per episcopatum Londoniensem'. *PUE*, I, no. 235. 1186.

(40) *Significatum est*, Alexander III to Gilbert and R. archdeacon. JL 14,222; Giles, no. 361 (only in the *Belverensis*). 1163–81.

(41) *Significatum est*, Alexander III 'Lundoniensi et Wigorniensi episcopis'. *Coll. Roffensis*, no. 120; *Dunelmensis*, iii, 67; *Wigorniensis*, vii, 7; *Claustroneoburgensis*, no. 198; *Chelten-hamensis*, xvi, 2, fo. 81v; *Cottoniana*, v, 70, fo. 263; and four systematic collections. 1164–79.

(42) *Si Stephanus*, Alexander III 'Londoniensi episcopo'. JL 13,993; *Coll. Claudiana*, no. 179, fo. 212v; *Cheltenhamensis*, xiv, 3, fo. 73r–v; and ten systematic collections (the conclusion of a decretal; the rest not known). 1163–81.

(43) *Suggestum est auribus*, Alexander III to Gilbert. JL 13,827; Thomas of Elmham, pp. 434–5 (see no. 358). 1176–81.

(44) *Vniuersalis ecclesie*, Alexander III to Gilbert. JL 14,267; Giles, no. 360, from *Coll. Belverensis* (with full heading); also *Coll. Alcobacensis I*, no. 121; *Parisiensis I*, no. 34; *Aureaeval-lensis*, no. 36; *Berolinensis* (see J. Juncker in *ZRG, Kan. Abt.* XIII (1924), 284–426), no. 41; *Floria-censis*, no. 91; *Cusana*, no. 12; *Cantuariensis*, i, 15; *Roffensis*, no. 92; *Regalis*, no. 13, fo. 108; *Bridlingtonensis*, no. 35, fo. 93r–v; *Claudiana*, no. 39, fo. 195r–v; *Cheltenhamensis*, xvii, 12, fo. 88; *Cottoniana*, vi, 5, fo. 264 ('Herefordensi'); also eleven systematic collections (in some collections opens 'Accepimus quod'). 1171–81.

(45) *Veniens ad apostolice sedis clementiam*, Alexander III 'Londonensi et Cicestrensi episcopis'. About a complaint by Master James that he has been ejected from the vicarage of 'Asbernat'' (? Ashburton, Devon) by Bartholomew, bishop of Exeter (1161–84), to which he had been instituted by Bishop R(obert), on the ground that he had received it by heredi-

tary succession after his father. James claimed that another parson had intervened and that he had been instituted 'ante decreti promulgationem';[1] also that he had been despoiled after appeal. The delegates are instructed to restore anything taken after appeal and then hear and decide the case on the vicarage. *Coll. Bridlingtonensis*, no. 94, fo. 107r–v; *Claudiana*, no. 78, fos. 199v–200. Probably 1163–9 (since the circumstances suggest a date early in Bartholomew's time, and so the bishop of Chichester is more likely to be Hilary, died 1169, than John, consecrated 1174).

(46) *Veniens ad apostolice sedis clementiam*, Walter cardinal bishop of Albano to Gilbert and the decanal chapter of Rochford (Essex). Giles, no. 442 (in *Belverensis* only).

*Addendum.* Dr C. Duggan has pointed out to us that no. 38 also occurs in the *Coll. Trinitatis*, ii, 24 (Trinity College, Cambridge, MS R. 14. 9, fo. 82: see Duggan in *Traditio*, XVII (1961), 517).

---

[1] This presumably refers to *II Lateran*, c. 16 (*Decretum*, C. 8, q. 1, c. 7; cf. *JS Epp.* 6) of 1139—although this only repeated earlier canons, and hereditary succession had been forbidden in English councils in 1102, 1125 and 1138 (see *Councils and Synods*, I, forthcoming). It is to be observed that the Pope makes no observation on James's defence of his institution.

# BIOGRAPHICAL INDEX

We give here a few notes on persons who figure prominently, or to whom there are scattered references, in the letters, and particularly to bishops, abbots and archdeacons, who are arranged (as are earls, etc.) under their titles. It was originally intended to make this Index more elaborate (hence the references, not all fulfilled, in *JS Epp.* 1: see p. lxiv); but now that the new edition of Le Neve's *Fasti* (ed. under the auspices of the Institute of Historical Research) and *Heads of English Monastic Houses before 1215* (ed. D. Knowles, C. N. L. Brooke and V. London) are in active preparation, it seemed reasonable to restrict the scope of this Index. Notes on Gilbert Foliot's clerks, etc., and on men who held dignities or prebends at Hereford or St Paul's in his time, are collected in *GF*, Appendix IV. Persons referred to in only one letter or group of letters are not usually included here, but given a brief note in the context in which they occur. Dates of bishops are as in *Handbook* (2nd edn).

BADERON OF MONMOUTH, lord of Monmouth, son of William son of Baderon, and so great-nephew of Wihenoc, the Breton founder of this lordship (*CDF*, no. 1142, etc.; Round in *Studies in Peerage and Family History*, pp. 120 ff.). *CDF*, no. 1138, may suggest that Baderon was not born in 1101–2; he had certainly succeeded by 1144 (*CDF*, no. 1142). He was still alive in 1170, dead by 1176 (*Sir Christopher Hatton's Book of Seals*, ed. L. C. Loyd and D. M. Stenton, p. 138). His wife, Rose, was daughter of Gilbert FitzRichard de Clare (Round, *Feudal England*, facing p. 473).

BATH, BISHOP OF, ROBERT, 1136–66 (died 31 Aug.); previously monk of Lewes. R. H. C. Davis in *EHR*, LXXVII (1962), 209–32, argues cogently that he was author of the *Gesta Stephani*, and also points out that there seems no available evidence that he was (as often stated) prior of Winchester. For his career at Bath and Wells, see J. Armitage Robinson, *Somerset Historical Essays*, pp. 55 ff.

— REGINALD FITZJOCELIN, son of the bishop of Salisbury (*q.v.*), born in Lombardy, arch-deacon in the Salisbury diocese (prob. of Wiltshire) by 1161 and clerk of Thomas Becket; later deserted the archbishop (see nos. 206–8). El. bishop of Bath late April 1173, consec. 23 June 1174; el. archbishop of Canterbury 27 Nov. 1191, died 26 Dec. 1191. See *GF*, p. 56 and n.; *EC*, p. 19; J. A. Robinson, *op. cit.*, esp. pp. 106 ff.

BAYEUX, BISHOP OF, HENRY DE BEAUMONT: dean of Salisbury, *c.* 1155–65; el. bishop of Bayeux, 1165; died 1205. As dean, succeeded Robert, *q.v.* under Exeter, succeeded by John of Oxford, see under Norwich; see also Torigny, p. 225; *MB Epp.* 112; *EYC*, II, no. 1120 (occurs ? 1162–5). Torigny, p. 225, gives his election under 1165; he was referred to as bishop in late summer 1165 (*MB Epp.* 115, cf. 112–13). A document in the *cartulaire noire* of Bayeux cathedral (*Antiquus cartularius ec. Baioc.*, ed. V. Bourrienne, I, 62 ff.) shows that the see was vacant in 1164 (April, also September, see *ibid.* p. 154); a curiously garbled account of this in the *Gallia Christiana* (XI, 364) has misled later writers into thinking that Henry was already el. in 1164. He died in 1205 (Ann. Caen, *HF*, XVIII, 349) on 18 Nov., according to *Gallia Christiana*, XI, 364–6. On him see S. E. Gleason, *An Ecclesiastical Barony of the Middle Ages* (Cambridge, Mass., 1936), pp. 31–5.

BORDESLEY, ABBOTS OF, HAMO I AND II (?): 1138–c. 1155 (?), c. 1155–66 or later (occurs in *Cart. Trentham*, p. 316, with Hervey sheriff of Staffs. Delisle, *Recueil*, I, nos. XLVII, LI, suggest a vacancy c. 1155–8); *Cart. Stoneleigh*, pp. 15, 149, seem to show that there were two Hamos, but suggest that the second was abbot by c. 1153. Their successor, William, resigned in 1188 (Ann. Waverley, *Ann. Mon.* II, 245).

BRIAN FITZCOUNT, son of Count Alan IV, Fergant, of Brittany (*Anglo-Saxon Chron.*, E, *s.a.* 1127), possibly illegitimate; brought up in court of Henry I and married to Matilda of Wallingford, and so lord of the honour of Wallingford. From 1139 a staunch supporter of the empress (see no. 26); last heard of in 1153, when Duke Henry relieved him when besieged for the third time by Stephen. On his family, see *EYC*, IV, ch. II; on him, Round in *DNB*.

CANTERBURY, ARCHBISHOP OF, THEOBALD: abbot of Bec, el. 1136, blessed 1137; archbishop, el. 24 Dec. 1138, consec. 8 Jan. 1139, died 18 April 1161. See *GF*, pp. 88 ff.; above, Appendix II; Saltman, *passim*; *JS Epp.* I; and, for his dates as abbot of Bec, and of death, see *Vita Lanfranci* in *PL*, CL, 733–4; Torigny, pp. 130, 133, 135.

— THOMAS BECKET: royal chancellor and archdeacon of Canterbury, 1154/5–62; archbishop of Canterbury, el. 23 May, consec. 3 June 1162; died 29 Dec. 1170. As archdeacon, succeeded Roger, see under York. The facts of his career are still most conveniently collected in J. C. Robertson, *Becket, archbishop of Canterbury* (London, 1859), based mainly on materials now in *MB*. For recent studies, see Knowles, *Historian and Character*, ch. 6, and *EC*.

— RICHARD: monk of Christ Church, Canterbury, chaplain of Theobald, prior of Dover, 1157–73, el. archbishop, 3 June 1173, consec. 7 April 1174, died 16 Feb. 1184. On him see *DNB*; H. Mayr-Harting in *Journ. Eccl. Hist.* XVI (1965), 39–53; no. 220 and notes; for early career, Saltman, pp. 310, 542–3.

— BALDWIN: clerk of Bishop Robert II of Exeter, archdeacon of Totnes, c. 1161–70, monk of Forde, abbot of Forde before 1175–80; consec. bishop of Worcester 10 Aug. 1180, postulated archbishop of Canterbury December 1184, died 19 or 20 Nov. 1190. On him see *DNB*; Morey, pp. 105–9, 120–1; C. Holdsworth in *Trans. Royal Hist. Soc.* 5th series, XI (1961), 125; Duggan, pp. 110–15; Stubbs in *Epistolae Cantuarienses*, pp. xxxiii ff. and *passim*.

CANTERBURY, ST AUGUSTINE'S, ABBOT OF, SILVESTER: previously prior of St Augustine's, elected 1151, died 5 Aug. 1161 (William Thorne, ed. Twysden, pp. 1810–15).

— CLAREMBALD (intruded): 1162/3–74 (Thorne, pp. 1815–19; cf. Gervase, I, 173; *PR 20 Henry II*, p. 1, *21 Henry II*, p. 221, showing a vacancy mid 1174 to 1175).

— ROGER: monk of Christ Church, Canterbury, el. abbot, 9 Oct. 1175, died 20/21 Oct. 1212 (Gervase, I, 256; Thorne, pp. 1819–64). For the disputes about these abbots and their blessing and profession to the archbishop, see JS *HP* (P), pp. li–lii, and articles of D. Knowles and E. John cited on p. 356.

CERNE, ABBOT OF, WILLIAM SCOTUS: monk of Caen, abbot 1114–44/5, deposed (*Anglo-Saxon Chron.*, H, *s.a.* 1114; for his deposition, Bernard's tenure, and William's reinstatement, see Appendix III).

— BERNARD: prior of Gloucester, abbot 1145–8, resigned and returned to Gloucester; later, abbot of Burton (1160–75 according to Ann. Burton, *Ann. Mon.* I, 187; but the annals are not trustworthy, and seem on the whole to be running a year late in this period. Gregory of Caerwent (Cotton MS Vesp. A. v, fo. 199v), gives the dates 1160–73. But there is some confirmation that Bernard died in 1174 in the obits in *Monasticon*, III, 47–8, which give his death as Tuesday, 29 Jan.: this date was a Tuesday in 1174. But these obits are late and unreliable).

— WILLIAM SCOTUS, resumed *c.* 1148, died *c.* 1158 (his successor's appointment is noted under 1158 in Torigny, p. 198).

CHESTER OR COVENTRY, BISHOP OF, ROGER DE CLINTON: nephew of Geoffrey de Clinton; archdeacon of Bucks, nominated October, consec. 22 Dec. 1129, died 16 April 1148 (cf. Orderic, IV, 429; John of Worcester, p. 29; Henry of Huntingdon, p. 303).

— WALTER DURDENT: prior of Christ Church, Canterbury, *c.* 1143–1149 (Gervase, I, 141; cf. *JS Epp.* I, 250 n.); consec. 2 Oct. 1149, died 7 Dec. 1159 (*JS Epp.* I, 266 n.).

— RICHARD PECHE: son of Bishop Robert Peche, archdeacon of Coventry, consec. before 18 April 1161, res. 1182, died 6 Oct. 1182. See Diceto, I, 305. He was very likely appointed archdeacon by his father, but first occurs 1135–47 (*Reg. Lichfield*, no. 169).

CHICHESTER, BISHOP OF, HILARY: clerk of Henry of Blois bishop of Winchester, dean of Christ Church, Twynham (Hants), advocate at the papal Curia; nominated bishop 1146, consec. 3 Aug. 1147, died *c.* 13 July 1169. On him see Knowles, *EC*, pp. 24–7, etc.; H. Mayr-Harting in *EHR*, LXXVIII (1963), 209–24, and *The Bishops of Chichester, 1075–1207* (Chichester, 1963), pp. 7–12.

— JOHN OF 'GREENFORD': dean of Chichester and canon of St Paul's (see *GF*, p. 282), el. late April 1173, consec. 6 Oct. 1174, died 26 April 1180. See Mayr-Harting, *The Bishops of Chichester*, pp. 12–14.

CIRENCESTER, ABBOT OF, ANDREW: ?*c.* 1147–76, died 27 Dec. (*Gesta Henrici*, I, 136; for the year, see also Ann. Tewkesbury and Worcester, *Ann. Mon.* I, 51; IV, 383). His predecessor, Serlo, occurs in a bull of 11 Feb. 1147, and Andrew is said to have succeeded in that year (*PUE*, III, no. 61; Browne Willis, *Mitred...Abbeys*, I, 61; Serlo's obit is 3 kal. Feb. in Leland, *Itinerary*, ed. L. T. Smith, I, 265–6).

— ADAM: 1177–*c.* 1183 (Ann. Tewkesbury, *Ann. Mon.* I, 52–3).

CLUNY, ABBOT OF, PETER THE VENERABLE: son of Maurice de Montboissier, monk of Soucilange, prior of Domaine, abbot of Cluny, el. Oct. 1122, died 25 Dec. 1156 (with a brief interval in 1125–6, when his predecessor, Pons, was restored). See *Vita*, Martène and Durand, *Amplissima Collectio*, VI, 1187–1202; J. Leclercq, *Pierre le Vénérable* (Saint-Wandrille, 1946); *Dict. de théologie catholique*, XII, 2065–81; *Petrus Venerabilis*, ed. G. Constable and J. Kritzeck (Rome, 1956); G. Constable's edition of his *Letters*, forthcoming.

— HUGH: 1157–61, deposed (actually left in 1163). On Hugh and Stephen, see no. 147 and n.

— STEPHEN BURGENSIS: el. 1161, established 1163, died 12 Aug. 1173 (*HF*, XII, 316; Torigny, p. 258; cf. p. 213; *Obit. Sens*, I, i, 450, 526). Previously abbot of Saint-Michel-l'Ecluse, and occurs as such in (?) 1154 (*HF*, XII, 325, 440, 453).

DURHAM, BISHOP OF, WILLIAM OF SAINTE-BARBE: dean of York, *c.* 1135–43, el. bishop 14 March, consec. 20 June 1143, died *c.* 13 Nov. 1152. See C. T. Clay in *Yorks Arch. Journal*, XXXIV (1938–9), 364–5.

— HUGH DU PUISET: nephew of King Stephen, treasurer of York, 1143(?)–53, el. 22 Jan., consec. 20 Dec. 1153, died 3 March 1195. See G. V. Scammell, *Hugh du Puiset, bishop of Durham* (Cambridge, 1956); Clay in *Yorks Arch. Journal*, XXXV (1940), 10–11.

— MASTER BARTHOLOMEW: archdeacon of Exeter, 1155–61, consec. after 18 April 1161, died 14 Dec. 1184 (Morey, *passim*; for dates, pp. 5 ff., 43, 117–18; Howden, II, 289; Exeter MS 3518, fo. 58v, has 14 Dec. 1184).

GLOUCESTER, ABBOT OF, GILBERT FOLIOT: 1139–48. See *GF*, pp. 78–9, 96–7, and ch. v *passim*.

— HAMELIN: subprior of Gloucester, abbot 1148–79, died 10 March (*Cart. Gloucester*, I, 19, 22; Ann. Winchcombe, *Misc. D. M. Stenton*, pp. 129, 137).

— THOMAS CARBONEL: prior of St Guthlac's Hereford (*q.v.*), abbot 1179 (enthroned 17 Sept.)–1205, died 21 July (*Cart. Gloucester*, I, 22–3; Ann. Winchcombe, *op. cit.* p. 137).

GLOUCESTER, EARLS OF, ROBERT: illegitimate son of Henry I, born *c.* 1090, earl 1122, died 31 Oct. 1147 (*CP*, V, 683–6, XI, Appendix D, p. 106). He married Mabel, daughter of Robert FitzHamon. See *GF*, pp. 115–17, 142–3, etc.

— WILLIAM, son of Robert, earl 1147–83, died 23 Nov. (*CP*, V, 687–9). He married Hawise, daughter of Robert, earl of Leicester.

HEREFORD, BISHOP OF, ROBERT DE BETHUNE: prior of Llanthony (occurs ?*c.* 1123, *Ancient Charters*, no. 11), consec. bishop 28 June 1131, died 16 April 1148. See *GF*, pp. 21 ff., etc.; *Vita* in *Anglia Sacra*, II, 293–321 (a new edition has been prepared as an Oxford B.Litt. thesis by Miss B. J. Parkinson); for dates *ibid.* II, 304–5, 307, 314 ff., esp. 319; Ann. Winchcombe, in *Misc. D. M. Stenton*, p. 126. Torigny, p. 121, calls him a Fleming. For bishops' obits see obituary cited in *GF*, p. 33 n.

— GILBERT FOLIOT: 1148–63. See *GF*, pp. 96–9.

— ROBERT DE MELUN: English by origin, eminent scholar, taught at Paris and Melun, consec. 22 Dec. 1163, died 27 Feb. 1167. On him see *Dict. de théologie catholique*, XIII, 2751–3.

— ROBERT FOLIOT: protégé of Bishops Alexander and Robert de Chesney, canon of Lincoln and Hereford, archdeacon of Oxford 1151–73/4, el. bishop of Hereford late April 1173, consec. 6 Oct. 1174, died 9 May 1186. See *DNB*; *GF*, pp. 44 f., etc.; *JS Epp.* (ed. Giles), no. 317; below, *s.v.* Oxford; early references are in *Cart. Thame*, II, 104; *Cart. Missenden*, I, 78; *Danelaw Charters*, p. 213. He was a clerk of Archbishop Thomas in 1163, but did not follow him into exile in 1164 (*Cart. Ramsey*, II, 197; *Chron. Ramsey*, p. 306; *MB*, III, 524).

HEREFORD, EARL OF, MILO OF GLOUCESTER: son of Walter of Gloucester, succeeded father *c.* 1126, royal constable, joined empress 1139, earl 25 July 1141, died 24 Dec. 1143. Related to Gilbert Foliot: see *GF*, pp. 35 ff.; on Milo see also D. Walker in *Trans. Bristol and Glos. Archaeol. Soc.* LXXVII (1958–9), 66 ff.; *CP*, VI, 451–4; *Handbook*, p. 431 and n. Married Sybil, daughter of Bernard of Neufmarché.

— ROGER: son of Milo, earl 1143–55; became a monk of Gloucester and died in 1155. See Walker in *op. cit.* LXXIX (1960–1), 174 ff.; *CP*, VI, 454–6; R. H. C. Davis in *Misc. D. M. Stenton*, pp. 139 ff.; *GF*, pp. 36–7. Founder of Flaxley abbey (Glos, Cist.); married Cecily, daughter and heiress of Payne FitzJohn, sheriff of Herefordshire and Salop.

HEREFORD, ST GUTHLAC'S PRIORY, PRIOR OF, WARIN: occurs 1143–8 (no. 21). St Guthlac's was formed in 1143 (p. 55 n. 3 and references) by amalgamation of the churches of St Guthlac and St Peter. A John, prior of St Peter's, occurs 1131–7 (Harl. MS 6976, fo. 14v); and it is possible that St Peter's was conventual. But it is more probable that it was then a mere cell, and that the formation of conventual life, and the appointment of Warin, followed the foundation of St Guthlac's in 1143.

— ERNULF: occurs 1148–52, 1148–55 (Balliol MS 271, fos. 34v–35, 79v; no. 333).

— ROBERT: occurs 1148–55 or 1159–60 (no. 325).

— OSBERN: occurs 1168, 2 Oct. 1172 (Balliol MS 271, fos. 16, 107v).

— THOMAS CARBONEL: promoted abbot of Gloucester in 1179 (q.v.).

— WILLIAM: occurs 1184 (no. 379).

LEICESTER, EARL OF, ROBERT II: born 1104, earl 1119, chief justiciar (with Richard de Lucy) c. 1155, died 5 April 1168. Twin brother of Waleran, count of Meulan and earl of Worcester (1104–66). Married Amice, daughter of Ralph, seigneur of Gaël and of Montfort (Brittany), who had previously been betrothed to Richard, illegitimate son of Henry I, lost in White Ship in 1120. Amice survived her husband and is said to have entered the convent at Nuneaton. See CP, VII, 527–30; L. Fox in EHR, LIV (1939), 385–402; and on Waleran, CP, VII, 737 ff.; and G. H. White in Trans. Royal Hist. Soc. 4th series, XIII (1930), 51 ff., XVII (1934), 19 ff.

LINCOLN, ARCHDEACON OF, ROBERT 'IUNIOR': before 1145–71 (?), died 15 Jan. (cf. Giraldi Cambrensis Opera, VII, 154). On these archdeacons, see K. Major in Reg. Lincoln, VII, 202–5. Miss Major points out that it cannot be proved that all the references to Robert were to a single man, and that Richard d'Ameri may have held the archdeaconry for a time; but he was certainly archdeacon of Stow, and in our view probably only of Stow. PR 16 Henry II, p. 147, may indicate that he died in 1170, but 'mortuus est' is a later addition. Robert was custodian of the see 1166/7–70/1 (PR 13 Henry II, pp. 57–8; 16 Henry II, p. 152).

— GEOFFREY, SON OF HENRY II: archdeacon, 1171–3, bishop elect of Lincoln, 1173–82; royal chancellor 1181/2–9; archbishop of York, el. 1189, consec. 1191, died 1212. See GF, p. 283; Delisle, Recueil, Introd. pp. 103 ff.

LINCOLN, BISHOP OF, ALEXANDER: nephew of Roger, bishop of Salisbury, archdeacon in the Salisbury diocese (? Salisbury: occurs 1121), nominated bishop April, consec. 22 July 1123, died c. 20 Feb. 1148 (Reg. Regum Anglo-Normannorum, II, no. 1301; John of Worcester, ed. Weaver, p. 17; Henry of Huntingdon, p. 245; DNB).

— ROBERT DE CHESNEY: uncle of Gilbert Foliot (GF, p. 33 and n.), archdeacon of Leicester c. 1135–48, el. bishop 13 Dec., consec. 19 Dec. 1148, died prob. 27 Dec. 1166. On his family see Cart. Eynsham, I, 411 ff.; GF, pp. 33 ff. As archdeacon he succeeded Walter, who died 26 April (Giraldus Cambrensis, Opera, VII, 157), perhaps in 1135 (Henry of Huntingdon, pp. 297, 319, 297–8 n.; cf. Reg. Lincoln, II, no. 553). For his election, etc., see nos. 80–1 and references. PR 13 Henry II, pp. 57–8, shows that he died c. Christmas 1166, and this explains why the chroniclers are divided between 1166 and 1167 for the year (1166: Ann. Tewkesbury, Worcester, Winchester, Ann. Mon. I, 49, IV, 381, II, 59; 1167— i.e. prob. on or after Christmas Day 1166—William of Newburgh, Chrons. of the reigns of Stephen, etc. I, 154 (cf. 117 n. 3), Ann. Oseney, Wikes, Ann. Mon. IV, 33; the two latter give a vacancy of 16 or 17 years before the consec. of Walter of Coutances on 3 July 1183; the Magna Vita of St Hugh (ed. D. L. Douie and H. Farmer, NMT, 1961–2), I, 93, makes it 15 years. Torigny (p. 229) shows that he died before Lent 1167. Diceto (I, 329) makes him die 7 kal. Feb. 1167; Howden (I, 269) 6 id. Jan. It is highly probable that the latter is a scribal error for 6 kal. Jan., which is the date in the twelfth-century Lincoln obituary (Giraldi Cambrensis Opera, VII, 164; cf. p. 36 n.). The latter makes 27 Dec. 1166 the most probable date. The report of his death in MB Epp. 254 of early Nov. 1166 (certainly before 18 Nov.) must have been exaggerated. On him see Knowles, EC, pp. 15–16.

— GEOFFREY (elect): see under archdeacons.

LLANDAFF, BISHOP OF, URBAN: 1107–34 (on him, see *SEBC*, pp. 218 ff.; Conway Davies, I, 148 ff.; II, 515 ff.).

—UHTRED: apparently archdeacon of Llandaff (*ibid.* II, 519; occurs 1126), bishop 1140–8, died 1 Feb. (so Ann. Winchcombe, in *Misc. D. M. Stenton*, p. 129. *Handbook*, 1st ed. p. 198 n., and Conway Davies, II, 637, suggest divergent evidence in other sources, but T. Jones's translations of the *Brut y Tywysogyon* (Peniarth MS, Cardiff, 1952, p. 56; *Red Book of Hergest*, 1955, p. 131) show that the original read '1148'; Uhtred was certainly alive late in 1147, when nos. 70–1 were addressed to him, and dead by March 1148 (see below)).

— NICHOLAS: monk of Gloucester, consec. bishop 14 March 1148, died 6 July 1183 (on him see Conway Davies, II, 521–2; but the view that he was *sacrist* of Gloucester rests on Giles's reading in no. 13. For the date of his consecration see *ibid.* II, 645; C. E. Woodruff in *Trans. St Paul's Ecclesiol. Soc.* VII (1911–15), 169; 14 March 1148 was a Sunday).

LONDON, BISHOP OF, ROBERT DE SIGILLO: royal clerk, keeper of the seal from 1133, became monk at Reading, appointed bishop, June 1141, by the empress, died 29 Sept. 1150 (*Reg. Regum Anglo-Normannorum*, II, p. x; H. W. C. Davis in *Essays...presented to R. L. Poole*, pp. 181–2 (cf. Florence of Worcester, II, 131); Hexham, p. 309. Hexham, p. 324, gives 1151 for his death, but the years have been altered, wrongly, in the MS, and one should read 1150 with *UGQ*, p. 82 (and Gervase, I, 142—but his witness is confused). The earliest St Paul's obituary, MS W.D. 12, fo. 14, gives 29 Sept. as the day; a later one gives 28th). Cf. Brooke in *Hist. of St Paul's*, pp. 27–8.

— RICHARD DE BELMEIS II: nephew of Richard de Belmeis I (bishop 1108–27), archdeacon of Middlesex before 1127; temporarily supplanted, but reinstated 1138, el. 1152, consec. 28 Sept. 1152, died 4 May 1162. On him and his family (he was related to Gilbert Foliot), see *GF*, pp. 43, 202 ff.; *CHJ*, x, ii (1951), 125 f.; Stubbs, introd. to Diceto, and Diceto, I, 250 ff.; Eyton, *Salop*, VIII, 212 ff.; above, nos. 99–103, 109, 139–40 and notes to no. 99.

— GILBERT FOLIOT: 1163–87 (see *GF*, pp. 99–103).

LONDON, HOLY TRINITY PRIORY, ALDGATE, PRIOR OF, RALPH: previously subprior, el. 17 Jan. 1147, died 14 Oct. 1167. These dates and those of Prior Stephen are supplied by the *Historia* in Cart. Holy Trinity, Hunterian MS (Glasgow University Library) U. 2. 6, fo. 5r–v (printed by T. Hearne in his edition of William of Newburgh, III, 705–7). According to this, Ralph's death was followed by a vacancy of 2 years, 32 weeks, 1 day, when the priory's affairs passed under the name of a fictitious Prior Edward or Edmund (see Appendix v, no. 5). Whatever the meaning of this rigmarole, the *Historia* seems to have overlooked the tenure of one or two short-lived priors, Osbern (?) and William.

— ? MASTER OSBERN: previously prior of Cirencester, occurs as such 1167–8 (*Cart. Oseney*, v, 27); elected prior 1167–8 (no. 187), but there is no evidence that he actually moved to London.

— WILLIAM: occurs 1169 (*MB Epp.* 527). But the evidence for him consists of a single letter, only surviving in MS D. It is possible that Osbern and William were never fully accepted as priors, and/or that William did not exist. It is more likely that the author of the *Historia* misunderstood the records of his house.

— STEPHEN: el. 17 May 1170, deposed 2 May 1197, died 14 Aug. 1198.

MALVERN, GREAT, PRIOR OF, ? RICHARD: see no. 28: if the reading of MS H is correct the prior in 1144–8 was Richard. His predecessor seems to have been Walcher, the scientist, who died 1 Oct. 1135 (J. Nott, *Some of the Antiquities of 'Moche Malverne'*, p. 28).

— ROGER MALEBRAUNCHE: occurs 1159, *c.* 1158–69 (*Monasticon*, III, 455; Nott, *op. cit.* pp. 40–1); became abbot of Burton in 1177 (*Gesta Henrici*, I, 180: *c.* 1 July; Ann. Burton, *Ann. Mon.* I, 187, gives 1178, but several of its dates seem slightly wrong—see *Cerne*. The late and unreliable list of abbots in *Monasticon*, III, 48, gives his predecessor's obit as Friday, 17 Nov. 1177; for what it is worth, 17 Nov. was Friday in 1176. But the annals also give 1177 for this. The annals and list of abbots agree that Roger died in 1182, but the details in the latter fit no year between 1181 and 1183).

— WALTER: *c.* 1177–*c.* 1216 (see no. 239 and notes).

NEVERS, BISHOP OF, BERNARD DE ST-SAULGE: 1159–76, died 9 or 15 Jan. (Ann. Nevers, *MGH, Scriptores*, XIII, 88–91; obit. Sens, *Obituaires de la province de Sens*, III, 464; cf. *Gallia Christiana*, XII, 639–40).

NORFOLK, EARL OF, HUGH BIGOD: born ? *c.* 1095, earl Dec. 1140 or Jan. 1141, died shortly before 9 March 1177. See nos. 159–61 and notes; *CP*, IX, 579–86.

NORWICH, BISHOP OF, WILLIAM DE TURBA: prior of Norwich, el., consec. 1146, died 16 Jan. 1174 (Knowles, *EC*, pp. 31–3; Saltman, pp. 102–3, for el.; *Reg. Norwich*, pp. 70, 76, 82).

— JOHN OF OXFORD: son of Henry of Oxford (sheriff: *Cart. Oseney*, II, 80), royal clerk, rector of St Mary and (?) St Peter-in-the-East, Oxford, dean of Salisbury 1165–75 (see Salisbury), el. 26 Nov. 1175, consec. 14 Dec., died 2 June 1200. See Delisle, *Recueil*, Introd. pp. 397–8; Knowles, *EC*, pp. 111–12; *Cart. Oseney*, I, 242, 306; *Reg. Norwich*, pp. 76, 82.

OXFORD, ARCHDEACON OF, WALTER: occurs 1111–12, died 1151 (*Chron. Abingdon*, II, 120; H. E. Salter in *EHR*, XXXIV (1919), 384). Associate of Geoffrey of Monmouth (referred to in preface of *Hist. Regum Britanniae*).

— ROBERT FOLIOT (see Hereford): 1151–73 (for date of appointment, see Salter, *loc. cit.*).

OXFORD, EARL OF, AUBREY DE VERE: son of Aubrey de Vere, Master Chamberlain; born *c.* 1110, count of Guînes, 1140/1, earl of 'Cambridge' 1142 (but took title Oxford), supported Stephen except in 1142–3; died 1191. Married (1) Beatrice, heiress of Guînes, in or before 1139; marriage dissolved; (2) in or before 1152, Euphemia, daughter of William de Canteleu; died 1153/4; (3) Agnes, daughter of Henry of Essex—see nos. 162–4 and notes. His brother, Geoffrey de Vere, was lord of Clun (Salop), sheriff of Suffolk (temp. Stephen) and Salop (1167–70); he married as his second wife Isabel, daughter of Elias de Say, lord of Clun (see no. 117). See *CP*, X, 199–207 and App. J, p. 113.

POITIERS, BISHOP OF, JOHN OF CANTERBURY, OR AUX BELLESMAINS: born at Canterbury, clerk of Archbishop Theobald, treasurer of York 1153/4–62 (also canon of St Paul's, see *GF*, p. 286), bishop of Poitiers 1162–82, archbishop of Lyons 1182–93; resigned to be monk of Clairvaux, died *c.* 1204. See C. T. Clay in *Yorks Arch. Journ.* XXXV (1940–3), 11–19; P. Pouzet, *L'Anglais Jean dit Bellesmains...* (Lyon, 1927); *JS Epp.* I, pp. xxvii, xxviii and nn.; Saltman, p. 214.

RALPH OF WORCESTER, landlord in Worcs and Glos under Stephen and Henry II (see esp. *Cart. Winchcombe*, I, 65; also Round, *Geoffrey de Mandeville*, p. 53 and n.).

READING, ABBOT OF, EDWARD: prob. 1136–c. 1154: el. 1136, occurs 1145 (*UGQ*, p. 11; Saltman, p. 450).

— REGINALD (RAINALD): 1154–8; resigned, later pr. and abb. Saffron Walden (see p. 477 and n.; *Flores Historiarum*, II, 72, 75; Ann. Reading, *EHR*, XXXVII (1922), 400).

— ROGER: 1158–65, died 20 Jan. (Ann. Reading *ut supra*, 400–1; *Flores Historiarum*, II, 75; Ann. Winchester, *Ann. Mon.* II, 58; obit, fo. 11 v).

— WILLIAM THE TEMPLAR: abbot 1165–73; archbishop of Bordeaux, consec. 25 Feb. 1173, died (?) 15 Sept. 1187 (Delisle, *Recueil*, Introd. p. 474; Ann. Reading, *ut supra*, p. 401; *Flores Historiarum*, II, 84; *HF*, XII, 443; *Gallia Christiana*, II, 818–19).

ROGER DE PORT, lord of Kington (Herefs) and Mapledurwell (Hants), son of Adam de Port, founder of Andwell priory (Hants) and sheriff of Herefs. Adam was alive 1130, but probably died soon after; Roger occurs in 1143; he became a monk at Andwell before his death. His retirement took place well before Theobald's confirmation to Andwell priory (Saltman, pp. 236–7, prob. 1150–4), since it confirms grants by his son and successor, Adam II. Married Sybil d'Aubigny. On the Ports, see J. H. Round in *Genealogist*, New Series, XVI (1900), 1–13; XVIII (1902), 137–9; additional information in *PR 31 Henry I*, pp. 14, 18, 123 (Adam alive 1130); *Cart. Gloucester*, III, 257; Winchester College Muniment Room, Andwell Drawer, nos. 5–6, 8–11, 15, esp. no. 9; *Cart. Wardon*, no. 276.

ROUEN, ARCHBISHOP OF, ROTROU: son of Henry, earl of Warwick, archdeacon of Rouen (Orderic, V, 119), bishop of Évreux 1139–65, archbishop of Rouen 1165–83, died late November. See Delisle, *Recueil*, Introd. pp. 454–6; and for his dates, Orderic, V, 119, 163; Torigny, pp. 139 (*s.a.* 1140), 225, 308; Torigny, ed. Delisle, II, 228, 124 ('1182'); *HF*, XVIII, 336 and n., 348 (1183); *Gesta Henrici II*, I, 308 (1183). His obit is 24 Nov. in obituary of St-Victor (*Obituaires de la province de Sens*, I, i, 602); 25 Nov. in obit. Évreux and Mont-St-Michel; 26 Nov. in obit. Rouen; 28 Nov. in obit. Jumièges (*HF*, XXIII, 465, 581, 369, 422; but in the last he is placed together with Archbishop Geoffrey, and the decision probably lies between 25 and 26 Nov.).

ST DAVIDS, BISHOP OF, BERNARD: royal clerk, chaplain of Queen Matilda, consec. bishop 19 Sept. 1115, died 22 April 1148. On him see Conway Davies, I, 114 ff. and *passim*; Brooke in *SEBC*, pp. 215–18, and, for his death, p. 218 n.

— DAVID FITZGERALD: uncle of Gerald of Wales, archdeacon of Cardigan, consec. bishop 19 Dec. 1148, died 8 May 1176. On him see Conway Davies, I, 268–84; cf. *Giraldi Cambrensis Opera*, III, 50, 154–5; Woodruff in *Trans. St Paul's Ecclesiol. Soc.* VII (1911–15), 169.

SALISBURY, BISHOP OF, JOCELIN DE BOHUN: nephew of Engelger de Bohun, archdeacon of Winchester under Henry of Blois (occurs 1139–42, *CDF*, no. 157; cf. Hexham, p. 302; predecessor occurs 1126–9, prob. 1128–9, *Anglia Sacra*, I, 279); bishop 1142–84, resigned, died 18 Nov. 1184. On him see Knowles, *EC*, pp. 17–22, 157 and *passim*; *GF*, pp. 55–6.

SALISBURY, DEAN OF, AZO: before 1139–1145/8. For the succession of deans, see K. Edwards in *VCH Wilts*, III, 207–8; on Azo, also J. Fowler in *Notes and Queries for Somerset and Dorset*, XXIII (1942), 319–20. He may have been the Azo who was previously archdeacon (of Wilts?), brother of Roger of Ramsbury, archdeacon of Wilts (?) after Azo—for these and other possibilities see Brooke in *CHJ*, XII (1956), 16 n.; it is also possible that Roger of Ramsbury should be identified with Roger le Poer, royal chancellor 1135–9, son of Bishop

Roger of Salisbury and Matilda *of Ramsbury*—Orderic, v, 120. This would presumably make Azo a son of Bishop Roger, which cannot be proved, but is far from unlikely.

— ROBERT, occurs 1148; bishop of Exeter in 1155 (*q.v.*).

— HENRY DE BEAUMONT: *c.* 1155–64, bishop of Bayeux (*q.v.*).

— JOHN OF OXFORD: 1165–75, bishop of Norwich (*q.v.*). On both these, see Edwards, *loc. cit.*, and above under Bayeux.

TEWKESBURY, ABBOT OF, ROGER: 1137–61 (Ann. Tewkesbury, *Ann. Mon.* I, 46, 49—called Robert under 1161, but this seems to be a slip for Roger, who was still abbot on 13 Dec. 1157, *Cart. Gloucester*, II, 106).

— FROMUND: 1162–78 (Ann. Tewkesbury, *Ann. Mon.* I, 49, 52). For the troubles leading to his election, see nos. 135–7.

WESTMINSTER, ABBOT OF, GERVASE OF BLOIS: son of King Stephen, blessed as abbot 18 Dec. 1138 (possibly el. 1137), deposed in or about 1157. On the dates of these abbots see *Flete*, pp. 142–4; cf. P. Chaplais in *Misc. D. M. Stenton*, p. 90 n. On Gervase, see Chaplais, *ibid.* pp. 90 ff.; Richardson and Sayles, pp. 413 ff.

— MASTER LAURENCE: *c.* 1158–73 (cf. *PR 19 Henry II*, p. 184, *21 Henry II*, p. 79, for this vacancy). Previously monk of St Albans; died 10 April (Trinity Coll., Cambridge, MS O. 9. 25, fo. 137v).

— WALTER: 1175–90, died 27 Sept. Previously prior of Winchester.

WILLIAM DE BEAUCHAMP, son of Walter de Beauchamp, succeeded 1133, supported Stephen and succeeded Milo of Gloucester as constable, but joined empress in 1141; sheriff of Worcs to 1169 or 1170. On him see H. W. C. Davis in *Essays...presented to R. L. Poole*, pp. 169 ff.; Round, *Geoffrey de Mandeville*, esp. pp. 313–15.

WILLIAM DE CHESNEY, brother of the bishop of Lincoln and Gilbert Foliot's uncle, leading supporter of Stephen in midlands; probably died *c.* 1164–70. See H. E. Salter in *Cart. Eynsham*, I, 415–18; *GF*, pp. 33–4.

WINCHESTER, BISHOP OF, HENRY OF BLOIS: son of Stephen, count of Blois and Chartres, and Adela, daughter of William I, brother of King Stephen (see *GF*, p. 78 and n.). Monk of Cluny, abbot of Glastonbury 1126–71, bishop of Winchester, nominated 4 Oct., consec. 17 Nov. 1129, died 8 Aug. 1171. Knowles, *EC*, pp. 34 ff.; *Monastic Order*, pp. 287–93; L. Voss, *Heinrich von Blois* (Berlin, 1932).

— RICHARD OF ILCHESTER (or 'Tokeliuus'): related to Gilbert Foliot, clerk of Robert earl of Gloucester before 1147 (*GF*, p. 38), protégé of Becket (*MB*, III, 120), royal clerk by 1159 (Lambeth MS 241, fo. 59v), archdeacon of Poitiers from 1162/3, el. bishop late April 1173, consec. 6 Oct. 1174, died 22 Dec. 1188. See *DNB*; Delisle, *Recueil*, Introd. pp. 431–4; C. Duggan in *Trans. Royal Hist. Soc.*, 5th series, XVI (1966), 1–21.

WORCESTER, ARCHDEACON OF, WILLIAM CUMIN: clerk of Bishop Geoffrey Rufus of Durham, chancellor of King David of Scotland, tried to seize bishopric of Durham after his uncle's death in 1141, condemned, excommunicated by the Pope, and removed from his benefices at the Council of London *c.* 14 March 1143 (Hexham, pp. 309, 313–14; Laurence of Durham, ed. J. Raine, Surtees Soc. LXX (1870), pp. 7–8, etc.; *PUE*, II, nos. 29–31; cf. notes to *Councils and Synods*, I, forthcoming). The benefices included the archdeaconry of Worcester (Hexham, p. 314), which William had probably held since his predecessor's death in 1125 (John of Worcester, p. 19). He was reconciled in 1144, and slowly recovered some of his benefices. He was clerk to Archbishop Theobald (occurs 1146–7, Saltman, pp. 538, 370, cf. p. 170) and Henry II, both before and after his accession (Delisle, *Recueil*, Introd. pp. 475–6 and I, nos. lix\*, lxiii\*, cxxxiv; Z. N. and C. N. L. Brooke in *EHR*, LXI (1946), 85 n. He last occurs as royal clerk in 1156; the W.C. noted by Delisle in 1167–9 from *PR 14–16 Henry II* was probably a layman). This helps to explain the revival of his fortunes—partial restoration of benefices by 1152 (*PUE*, II, nos. 72–3; cf. Saltman, pp. 144–6); further restoration in 1156–7, which evidently included his archdeaconry (*JS Epp.* I, 47 and n., 48, 151–2), for he appears as archdeacon in 1157 (Saltman, pp. 501–2). Presumably the arrangement was that he should hold it for life, and his successor be restored after his death. Godfrey had been restored by 1161–2 (no. 345). It seems highly likely that *JS Epp.* I, no. 98, which refers to 'the transaction of Godfrey and William', is concerned with the disposal of some of Cumin's other benefices; it has been dated 1158–60, but it refers to the wishes of the Pope, who must presumably be Adrian IV, and so was probably written in 1158–9. It therefore seems probable that William Cumin died *c.* 1158–9.

— MASTER GODFREY: 1144 (see nos. 33–4; occurs 1151–7, *Cart. Gloucester*, I, 263)–1156/7; restored *c.* 1158–9, died 1167 (see above; Ann. Tewkesbury and Worcester, *Ann. Mon.* I, 50, IV, 382).

WORCESTER, BISHOP OF, SIMON: chaplain and chancellor of Queen Adela (William of Malmesbury, *Gesta Pontificum*, RS, p. 290; John of Worcester, pp. 18–19), el. before 29 March, consec. 24 May 1125, died prob. 20 March 1150 (but see *GF*, p. 92 n.).

— MASTER JOHN OF PAGHAM: clerk of Archbishop Theobald, consec. 4 March 1151, died 31 March 1157 (cf. Poole, *Studies in Chronology and History*, pp. 271–2; on him see Saltman, pp. 116–17, 215).

— MASTER ALFRED: enthroned 13 April 1158, died 1160, 31 July. Previously royal clerk (Saltman, pp. 127–8; Delisle, *Recueil*, Introd. p. 354; *JS Epp*, I, 151 n.; cf. Ann. Winchcombe in *Misc. D. M. Stenton*, p. 131); possibly also clerk of the bishop of Bath and canon of Wells (*Cart. Bath*, I, 62, 64; *Cart. Bruton*, nos. 52, 54).

— ROGER OF GLOUCESTER: son of Robert, earl of Gloucester, el. March 1163, consec. 23 Aug. 1164, died 9 Aug. 1179 (buried at Marmoutier: T. D. Hardy, *Catalogue of Materials*, II, 416). On him see Oxford B.Litt. thesis by M. G. Hall (Mrs Cheney) (1940); Knowles, *EC*, pp. 22–3; *DNB*.

— BALDWIN: 1180–4 (see Canterbury).

— WILLIAM OF NORTHOLT: 1186–90 (see *GF*, p. 284).

WORCESTER, PRIOR OF, DAVID: el. 1143, deposed 1145 (Ann. Winchcombe, in *Misc. D. M. Stenton*, p. 129 n.; cf. *Cart. Gloucester*, I, p. lxxvi; no. 47 n.).

— OSBERN: 1145–*c.* 1146 (see above and no. 47; evidently Ralph succeeded between 26 Jan. 1146 and 27 Jan. 1147, because 26 Jan. 1148 (i.e. in this case from context 1149) fell in his third year: Worcester, Dean and Chapter Reg. A4, fos. x v–xi).

— RALPH: 1146/7–1189 (see above; Ann. Worcester, *Ann. Mon.* IV, 386).

YORK, ARCHBISHOP OF, ST WILLIAM FITZHERBERT: treasurer of York, 1108/14–1143, el. archbishop Jan. 1141, consec. 26 Sept. 1143, deposed 1147, restored Oct. 1153, died 8 June 1154. See Knowles, *Historian and Character*, chapter 5; Clay in *Yorks Arch. Journal*, XXXV (1940), 8–11.

— HENRY MURDAC: clerk, ?canon of York, monk of Clairvaux, abbot of Vauclair 1134/5–44, of Fountains 1144–7 (retained superiority over Fountains till his death), el. archbishop July 1147, consec. by the Pope 7 December, died 14 Oct. 1153. On him see Knowles, *Historian and Character*, pp. 88–91; Clay in *Yorks Arch. Journal*, XXXVIII (1952), 16 f.; Hexham, pp. 317–18.

— ST WILLIAM (restored, see above).

— ROGER OF PONT L'ÉVÊQUE; clerk of Archbishop Theobald, archdeacon of Canterbury 1148–54 (succeeded Walter, consec. bishop of Rochester 14 Mar. 1148; Roger occurs 26 Jan. 1149: see Saltman, pp. 215, 103–4, 546, and 122–3 on Roger's election to York); consec. 10 Oct. 1154, died 26 Nov. 1181.

# ADDENDA AND CORRIGENDA TO
# 'GILBERT FOLIOT AND HIS LETTERS'

No note is made here of minor misprints, or of cases in which further information is given in commentaries to the letters.

282  Henry of Northampton occ. before 1174 (*Rep.* p. 24a–b, dated by Godfrey the treasurer).

284  Walter de Belmeis occ. 1152–*c.* 1154 (*Cart. Clerkenwell*, no. 162).

286  John Witing occ. 1 March 1223 (Harl. MS 6956, fos. 24v–25).

289  Henry Foliot, omit reference to no. 359.

291  Thomas Bartholde: the MS of no. 415 reads Brithowe, i.e. Brito.

# INDEX OF MANUSCRIPTS

The numbers refer to *letters and charters* for which the manuscript provides a text, except for those in *italics*, which refer to *pages of the Introduction*. Documents in Appendices VI, VII (but not V, VIII) are included. Printed books, or chronicles for which individual MSS are not specified, are not included: for these see pp. *17, 19 f.*, and nos. 138, 155, 166–7, 293.

Aberystwyth, National Library of Wales, MS 7851 D (Cart. Shrewsbury): 344

Cambridge, Corpus Christi College, MS 123: 167; 295 (Co): *18–19, 29*; 155, 167–9, 171, 181, 198, 200–1, 203

—— King's College Muniments, B 15 (Kd): 391; B 17–19 (Ka, Kb, Kc): 374

—— Trinity College, MS O. 2. 1 (E): 295–7

—— Trinity Hall, MS 24 (O): *19, 30*; 155, 167–9, 171, 198, 200

—— University Library, Ely Diocesan Muniments, Liber M (M): 296–7

Canterbury Cathedral, Chapter Archives, Cartae Antiquae, A 49, A 51: 293; C 115, C 117: 289

Chelmsford, Essex Record Office, D/DBy Q 19: 369; D/DPr. 149 (Cart. Colne): 364–5; D/DP T 1/692: 351

Colchester Borough Library, Cart. Colchester: 359–62

Ely, Dean and Chapter, MS of *Liber Eliensis* (F): 295–7

Glasgow University Library, Hunterian U. 2. 6 (215): note to 162

Gloucester Cathedral Library, Reg. A: 302, 372; Reg. B (Gl): 286–8, 304–5, 307–8; Seals and Documents, viii, 1 (Sd): 305

Hereford Cathedral, Dean and Chapter Muniments, no. 1385: 316; no. 1360: 311; no. 2777 (Hi): 315

—— Cathedral Library, MS P. i. 15 (H): *xxxv–vi, 2, 8, 10–13, 29*; 1–2, 5–7, 14, 22–8, 32, 38–9, 48

——Diocesan Registry, Reg. Cantelupe (K): 305; Reg. Swinfield (Qa, Qb): 303, 315, 378

London, British Museum

Add. Charter 19, 587: 339; 28, 332: 376

Add. MS 8177 (copy of Cart. Eye): 369

Arundel MS 219 (Ar): *19, 30*; 168–9, 181, 198, 200–1, 203

Cotton MS Appendix xxi (Cart. Stoke-by-Clare): 453–8; Claudius B. ii (C), *10, 18–22 passim, 29*; 155, 166–71, 181, 197–8, 200–1, 203; Claudius D. x (Red Book of St Augustine's, Canterbury) (Pa, Pb): 357–8; Cleopatra E. i: 289; Domitian A. iii (Cart. Leominster) (L): 334–7, 340–1, 343; Domitian A. x (Cart. Rochester) (Da, Db): 431–5; Faustina A. iii (Cart. Westminster) (U): 462–3, 465, 468; Julius D. ii (Cart. St Augustine's): 357; Nero E. vi (Kn, Ko) (Cart. Hospitallers): 383–5, 387–9; Titus A. i (Cart. Ely) (G): 295–7; Vespasian B. xxiv (Cart. Evesham) (Ev): 298; Vespasian E. xxv (Cart. Reading) (Na): 338; Vespasian F. xv (Cart. Lewes): 392, 395; Vitellius E. xv (Cart. Osney): 426–7

Egerton MS 3031 (Cart. Reading) (N): 334–9, 341–3, 430

Harleian MS 215 (Ha): *18, 30*; 165; 662 (Cart. Dunmow) (Gh): 368; 1708 (Cart. Reading) (Nb): 338; 3688 (Cart. Missenden): 420; 3697 (Cart. Saffron Walden) (Sa, Sb, Sc): 438–47; 3763 (Cart. Evesham) (Eh): 298; 4015 (Cart. St Giles in the Fields, London) (Za, Zb): 380; 6956 (Hutton's transcripts): 400–1, 403, 408, 432; 6976 (the same) (T): 290–1

# DATES OF LETTERS AND CHARTERS

The numbers refer to *letters and charters*, not to pages. Months and days have been ignored. Dateable items in Appendix VII are included; documents undateable (including nos. 273–83) are omitted.

1139–43: 3
Probably 1139–45: 4
1139–48: 5–11, 13, 285–8
?1139–48: 12
1140: 1–2
1140–8: 14–16
1142–8: 17–19
c. 1142–8: 20
1143: 22–5
1143–4: 26
1143–5: 33
1143–8: 21
1144: 284
1144–5: 31, 38
c. 1144–5: 32
1144–6: 27
1144–8: 28
?1144–8: 29–30
1145: 34–5, 39–48
1145–6: 49–52
1145–7 (?1145): 36–7
Probably 1145–8: 65–6
?1145–8: 67
1146: 53–6, Appendix VII, 4
Probably 1146: 61
? 1146: 57–60
? 1146–8: 68
1147: 62, 69–71
1147–8: 63
c. 1147–8: 72–3
1148: 64, 74–81, 289
c. 1148: 300, 327, 349
? c. 1148: 301
Probably 1148–9: 331
Probably 1148–50: 92
1148–53: 82–6
1148–54 (?): 290
Probably 1148–54: 87–8
1148–55: 291–2, 302, 318, 332–3, 338
1148–c. 1155: 319
1148–55 or 1159–60: 325
1148–61: 299
Probably 1148–50 or 1162–3: 123
1148–63: 114–21, 298, 309, 314, 321–4, 328, 335–6 (possibly before 1154), 337, 340–1, 348
? 1148–63: 122
1149–50: 89
Probably 1149–50: 90 (1148–60), 124

c. 1149–50: 91
1150: 93–6
1150–3: 97–8
c. 1150–4: 334
c. 1150–5: 317
c. 1150–? c. 1155: 320
? c. 1150–c. 1158: 344
1150–9: 110
1150–61: 111
c. 1150–63: 310–11, 329
1151–7: 330
1151–63: 124
1152: 99–100, 295
1153: 101–6, 108
c. 1153 or later: 107
1153–61: 112
c. 1153–61: 113
1154: 109, 296–7
1154–63: 125, 342
c. 1155: 303, 312
1155–7: 128–30
c. 1155–c. 1158: 313, 326
1156: 127
1157: 293
1157–8 (or 1161–3): 131
c. 1158: 304–5
1158–61: 343
1158–63: 315
c. 1158–63: 306–8
1160: 132–3
c. 1160–3: 126
1161: 134
1161–2: 135–6, 345
c. 1161–2: 139
1161–3: 138, 294
1162: 137
c. 1162: 346
1162–3: 140, 347
1163: 141–6
c. 1163: 147, 152 (or 1160), 316
Probably c. 1163: 150 (1163–9), 339
? 1163: 151 (1163–5)
1163 or shortly after: 149, 438
1163–4: 148, 460 (probably 1163)
c. 1163–4: 430
1163–6: 172–3
1163–7: 174
1163–8: 194–5, 196 (? 1165–8)
1163–72: 383–4, 439 (? 1169–72)

1163–73: 229–31, 382, 396, 422
1163–74: 233, 385, 412, 425, 450
1163–76: 236
1163–77: 237
1163–78: 429
1163–79: 241
Probably 1163–c. 1179: 245
1163–80: 244, 355, 376 (1163–c. 1179), 393–4, 399, 420c, 454
1163–c. 1180: 253, 255–9, 261–7, 350, 352–3, 363, 366–7, 377, 386, 390, 395, 397, 413–14, 418–19, 423–4, 428, 431–2, 437, 449, 453, 459, 469, 471–4
? 1163–c. 1180: 268, 448, 475–6
1163–5 or 1174–81: 246
1163–81: 247–50
1163–c. 1181: 462
1163–83: 252
1163–87: 270, 354, 357, 361 (perhaps c. 1181–7), ? 364, 369, 371, 373 (? 1179), 396a, 398, 421 (probably before 1184), 447, 455, 463, 470
1164: 153
1164–79: 242–3, 372
1165: 154–60
Probably 1165–7: 175
? 1165–7: 176
1165–73: 232
1165–c. 1180: 254
1166: 161–2, 165–70
1166–7: 171
1166–72: 163
1166–73: 179
1166–70 or 1174–c. 1180: 260
1167: 180–3
Probably 1167: 177 (1166–70), 178 (1166–73)
1167–8: 184–7
c. 1167–8: 188–9
1167–74: 420a
? c. 1167–74: 420b
1167–80 (probably after 1168): 368
1168: 193
c. 1168: 190
1168–9: 191–2
c. 1168–9: 197
1169: 198–210
1169–73: 359
c. 1169–80: 381

547

35-2

1170: 211, 214, Appendix VII, 5
? 1170: 212, 213 (1169–70), 215–16
1170–2, probably 1171–2: 391
1170–80: 392 (probably 1171–6), 400
c. 1170–80: 444
1171: 217–18
? 1171–2: 219
1172: 164
? c. 1172–3: Appendix VII, 2
1173: 220–2
1173–4: 223–5, 375
Probably 1173–4: 227
1173–7: 420
1173–80: 456
1173–c. 1180: 436, 452
1174: 226, 426
c. 1174: 228
1174–80: 442

Probably 1174–80: 402
c. 1174–80: 443
Probably 1174–81: 251
1174–86: 272
1175: 234–5
1175–9 (probably 1175–7): 464
1175–80 (c. 1179): 351
1175–c. 1180: 465–6
1175–c. 1181: 417
1175–87: 467
1176: 427
1176–80 (c. 1179): 358
? 1177: 238
c. 1177: 239, 378 (1163–87)
1178: 410
c. 1178–87: 271
Probably 1179: 240
c. 1179–80: 360, 445, 457, 461
c. 1179–c. 1180: 401, 411

1180: 374
1180–c. 1181: 387
c. 1180–1: 370
1180–3: 441
c. 1181: 388
c. 1181–3: 365 (? c. 1181), 440, 446
c. 1181–7: 356, 362, 380, 405, 407, 415, 451, 458, 468 (1180–7)
c. 1182–6: 416
1183: 403
1183–4: 404
1183–7: 406
1184: 379
1186: 269, 435
c. 1186 (1186–7): 389
? c. 1186: 433–4
1186–7: 408–9

# INDEX OF QUOTATIONS AND ALLUSIONS

The references are to *pages* of this book

## A. BIBLICAL

## B. LEGAL

## C. CLASSICAL, PATRISTIC AND MEDIEVAL

(see also GF, pp. 17 f.)

# GENERAL INDEX

*Numbers in this index refer to* pages. The following abbreviations are used: abb. = abbess, abbey, abbot; abp. = archbishop; archd. = archdeacon; bp. = bishop; can. = canon; card. = cardinal; chanc. = chancellor; clk. = clerk (of bp., chapter or parish);[1] d. = dean; H. = Hereford; k. = king; L. = London (St Paul's); m. = monk; pr. = prior, priory; prec. = precentor; treas. = treasurer.

Office-holders are indexed under their names. Cross-references are given for bps., abbs., etc.; but not for cans., H. and L., who are listed in *GF*, Appendix IV.

Page-references alone are given for entries in both text and notes on the same page.

---

[1] And not only Gilbert Foliot's clks., as in the index of *GF*: for a list of these, see *GF*, pp. 288–91; cf. above, p. 543.

Cave, Sir Thomas, 6, 12 n.
Celestine II, Pope (1143–4), 57–8, 60, 66, 505; III (1191–8), 437, as Cardinal Jacinctus, l, 324 n.
cemeteries, 131, 133–4, 386–8
Cenomannenses, *see* Maine
Cerealia, 278–9
Cerisy, abb. of, *see* Martin
Cerne abb. (Dorset), 1, 7, 76–9, 82–93, 97–9, 507–9; abbs. of, *see* Bernard, Scotus; ms. of, *see* A(d)elardus, John; pr. of, 507–9 *and see* R.
Chaldeans, 115
Chandos family, 373 n.
chapel, royal, 368
chapter, decanal, 190
Charité-sur-Loire, La, pr., 177–8; m. of, *see* Adam; pr., *see* Humbald, Moraunt, Rainald
Charlston (Sussex), 200–1
Chartres, count of, *see* Stephen
Chaumont (near Gisors), 289
Chelleworthe, Geoffrey, Hugh, Ralph and Turold, 404
Chenedin, 49
Cheney, C. R., 29 n.
Chepstow (Mon) (Strigueil), 50, 384 n.
Chertsey abb. (Surrey), abb. of, *see* Hugh
Cheshunt abb. (Herts), 527
Chester and Coventry, bps. of, 38–9, 172–3, 325–6, 525, *and see* Durdent, Gerard la Pucelle, Peche, Roger de Clinton; diocese of, 172–3
Chesterfield, Thomas, 172 n.
Chichester (Sussex), bp. of, 325–6, 527, *acta* of, 1 n., *and see* Hilary, John of Greenford; cathedral, 200 n.; can., *see* Jocelin; d., *see* John of Greenford; diocese, 38–9, 292 ff.
Chilton (Berks), 326 n.
Chilton Foliat (Wilts), 326–7
chirograph, 386, 523
Chishall, Great (Essex), 474–6
Christ Church (Twynham, Hants), d. of, *see* Hilary
Christina of Markyate, 216 n.
Cicero, 171
Cirencester abb. (Glos), 260; abbs., *see* Adam, Andrew, Serlo; can., *see* A.; pr., *see* Osbern
Cîteaux abb., Cistercian order, 146–9; abbs. of, *see* Gilbert, Gozuin, Harding, William
Clairvaux abb., 270; abb. of, *see* Bernard; ms. of, *see* John of Canterbury, Murdac
Clare family, 428
Clarembald, abb. St Augustine, Canterbury, 531
Clarendon (Wilts), assize of, 523; Council of, and Constitutions, 11 n., 212 n., 233–4, 239, 240 n.; decree supplementary to, l
Clermont, 203
Clifford family, 347 n.
Clun (Salop), 157, 537
Cluny abb., Cluniacs, 41, 65, 119 n., 192–3, 473; abbs., *see* Hugh, Peter the Venerable, Pons, Stephen, William (abb. and m.); m., *see* Henry de Sully; pr., *see* Foliot

Coates (Glos), 135 n.
*Cocedeh'*, 372–3
Coddington (Herefs), 514
Code, Robert, 495
Coggeshall (Essex), 473
Colchester (Essex), abb., 407–11, 441–2, *and see* Walter; archds. of, *see* Foliot, Ralph de Hauterive; archdeaconry, 150; castle, 407–8; churches in, 407–8; hospital of St Mary Magdalene, 411; St Botolph's pr., 419–20, *and see* Godfrey
*collectiones*, decretal collections, 8, 9, 11 n., 525–9; *and see* Belvoir
Colne, Earls', pr. (Essex), 411–12
Colne, Wakes (Essex), 414–15
Combermere abb. (Ches), and abb., 152–3; *see also* Geoffrey, William
Combwell pr. (Kent), 413
Copford (Essex), 420
coronation, 191, *and see* Henry 'III'
Cotentin, 161
*Cotona*, 404
Councils, 40, 67, *and see* London, Oxford, Pavia, Rheims, Tours, Westminster
courts, ecclesiastical, cases in (not on appeal to the Pope): on jurisdiction over clerks, criminous clerks, etc., 195–6, 268–9, 396–7; debt, 158; parish churches and rights, 80–1, 104–5, 108–9, 125–6, 152–3, 159, 190–1, 302–3, 372, 379, 381–2, 391–2, 401–2, 416–18, 432–4, 440–1, 448–9, 469; marriage law, 309–10; monastic jurisdiction and discipline, 83–4, 106–7, 491; tithes, 391, 412, 424, 432–3; unknown grounds, 54–5, 95–6, 461; *and see* appeals, judges delegate
Coventry, archd. of, *see* Peche; bps. of, *see* Chester; cathedral pr., 172–3; pr. of, *see* Laurence
Cowarne, Little (Herefs), 378–9; Much, 365, 369–71
Crassus, 329
Crediton (Devon), 357
Croft (?) (Herefs), 392–3
Crollebacun, Hugh, 364
Crusades, 111, 241 n., 247 n.
Cumin, William, archd. Worcester, 72–3, 539–40
*Cundel* (?), 349

Damascus, 34
Dathan, 236
*Daubo*, 421
David, 34, 89
David I, k. Scotland, 72, 83–4, 539–40
David, archd. Bucks, 156 n., 416–17
David, Master, can. H., 374
David, chaplain, 405, 440, 484
David, m. Evesham, 124
David, priest, 449
David, pr. Worcester, 540
David, son of Geoffrey, 404
David de Aqua, can. H., 374, 393